shakespearean criticism

"Thou art a Monument without a tomb,
And art alive still while thy Book doth
live
And we have wits to read and praise to
give."

*Ben Jonson, from the preface
to the First Folio, 1623.*

Mr. WILLIAM SHAKESPEARES

COMEDIES, HISTORIES, & TRAGEDIES.

Published according to the True Originall Copies.

Martin Droeshout sculpsit London.

LONDON

Printed by Isaac Iaggard, and Ed. Blount. 1623.

Frontispiece to the First Folio (1623). By permission of the Folger Shakespeare Library.

ISSN 0883-9123

Volume 45

shakespearean criticism

Excerpts from the Criticism of
William Shakespeare's Plays and Poetry,
from the First Published Appraisals
to Current Evaluations

Michelle Lee
Editor

Kathy D. Darrow
Assistant Editor

The Gale Group

DETROIT • SAN FRANCISCO • LONDON • BOSTON • WOODBRIDGE, CT

STAFF

Michelle Lee, *Editor*
Kathy D. Darrow, *Assistant Editor*

Janet Witalec, *Managing Editor*

Maria Franklin, *Interim Permissions Manager*
Kimberly F. Smilay, *Permissions Specialist*
Kelly A. Quin, *Permissions Associate*
Sandy Gore, *Permissions Assistant*

Victoria B. Cariappa, *Research Manager*
Tamara C. Nott, Tracie A. Richardson, *Research Associates*
Patricia T. Ballard, Corrine Stocker, *Research Assistants*

Randy Bassett, *Image Database Supervisor*
Robert Duncan, Michael Logusz, *Imaging Specialists*
Pamela A. Reed, *Imaging Coordinator*

This book is printed on acid-free paper that meets the minimum requirements of American National Standard for Information Sciences—Permanence Paper for Printed Library Materials, ANSI Z39.48-1984.

Library of Congress Catalog Card Number 86-645085
ISBN 0-7876-2421-7
ISSN 0883-9123

Printed in the United States of America
Published simultaneously in the United Kingdom
by The Gale Group International Limited
(An affiliated company of The Gale Group)
10 9 8 7 6 5 4 3 2 1

The Gale Group

Contents

Preface

*S*hakespearean Criticism (SC) provides students, educators, theatergoers, and other interested readers with valuable insight into Shakespeare's drama and poetry. A multiplicity of viewpoints documenting the critical reaction of scholars and commentators from the seventeenth century to the present day derives from the hundreds of periodicals and books excerpted for the series. Students and teachers at all levels of study will benefit from *SC*, whether they seek information for class discussions and written assignments, new perspectives on traditional issues, or the most noteworthy analyses of Shakespeare's artistry.

Scope of the Series

Volumes 1 through 10 of the series present a unique historical overview of the critical response to each Shakespearean work, representing a broad range of interpretations. Volumes 11 through 26 recount the performance history of Shakespeare's plays on the stage and screen through eyewitness reviews and retrospective evaluations of individual productions, comparisons of major interpretations, and discussions of staging issues.

Beginning with Volume 27 in the series, *SC* focuses on criticism published after 1960, with a view to providing the reader with the most significant modern critical approaches. Each volume is ordered around a theme that is central to the study of Shakespeare, such as politics, religion, or sexuality. The topic entry that introduces the volume is comprised of general essays that discuss this theme with reference to all of Shakespeare's works. Following the topic entry are several entries devoted to individual works. Volume 45 is devoted to the topic of dreams in Shakespeare's works, and provides commentary on that topic as well as the plays *A Midsummer Night's Dream, The Tempest,* and *The Winter's Tale.*

SC also compiles an annual volume of the most noteworthy essays published on Shakespeare during the previous year. The essays, reprinted in their entirety, have been recommended to Gale by an international panel of distinguished scholars. The most recent volume, *SC Yearbook 1997,* Volume 42 in the series, was published in October 1998.

Organization of the Book

Each entry consists of the following elements: an introduction, critical essays, and an annotated bibliography of further reading.

- The **Introduction** outlines modern interpretations of individual Shakespearean topics, plays, and poems.

- The **Criticism** for each entry consists of essays that are arranged both thematically and chronologically. This provides an overview of the major areas of concern in the analysis of Shakespeare's works, as well as a useful perspective on changes in critical evaluation over recent decades. Footnotes that appear with previously published pieces of criticism are reprinted at the end of each essay or excerpt. In the case of excerpted criticism, only those footnotes that pertain to the excerpted text are included.

- All of the individual essays are preceded by **Explanatory Notes** as an additional aid to students using *SC.* The explanatory notes summarize the criticism that follows.

- A complete **Bibliographical Citation** providing publication information precedes each piece of criticism.

- Each volume includes such **Illustrations** as reproductions of images from the Shakespearean period, paintings and sketches of eighteenth- and nineteenth-century performers, photographs of modern productions, and stills from film adaptations.

- The annotated bibliography of **Further Reading** appearing at the end of each entry suggests additional sources of study for the reader. Explanatory notes summarize each essay or book listed here.

- Each volume of *SC* provides the following indices:

  Cumulative Character Index: Identifies the principal characters of discussion in the criticism of each play and non-dramatic poem.
  Cumulative Critic Index: Identifies each critic that has appeared in *SC*.
  Cumulative Topic Index: Identifies the principal topics in the criticism and stage history of each work. The topics are arranged alphabetically, by topic.
  Cumulative Topic Index, by Play: Identifies the principal topics in the criticism and stage history of each work. The topics are arranged alphabetically, by play.

Citing *Shakespearean Criticism*

Students who quote directly from any volume in the Literature Criticism Series in written assignments may use the following general forms to footnote reprinted criticism. The first example pertains to material drawn from periodicals, the second to material reprinted from books.

[1]Gordon Ross Smith, "Shakespeare's *Henry V*: Another Part of the Critical Forest," in *Journal of the History of Ideas,* XXXVII, No. 1 (January-March 1976), 3-26; excerpted and reprinted in *Shakespearean Criticism,* Vol. 30, ed. Marie Lazzari (Detroit: Gale Research, 1996), pp. 262-73.

[2]Katherine Eisaman Maus, *Inwardness and Theater in the English Renaissance* (The University of Chicago Press, 1995); excerpted and reprinted in *Shakespearean Criticism,* Vol. 33, ed. Dana Ramel Barnes and Marie Lazzari, (Detroit: Gale Research, 1997), pp. 112-17.

Suggestions Are Welcome

The editors encourage comments and suggestions from readers on any aspect of the *SC* series. In response to various recommendations, several features have been added to *SC* since the series began, including the topic index and the sample bibliographic citations noted above. Readers are cordially invited to write, call, or fax the editors: *Shakespearean Criticism,* Gale Research, 27500 Drake Rd., Farmington Hills, MI 48331-3535. Call toll-free at 1-800-347-GALE or fax to 1-248-699-8049.

Acknowledgments

The editors wish to thank the copyright holders of the excerpted criticism included in this volume and the permissions managers of many book and magazine publishing companies for assisting us in securing reproduction rights. We are also grateful to the staffs of the Detroit Public Library, the Library of Congress, the University of Detroit Mercy Library, Wayne State University Purdy/Kresge Library Complex, and the University of Michigan Libraries for making their resources available to us. Following is a list of the copyright holders who have granted us permission to reproduce material in this volume of *SC*. Every effort has been made to trace copyright, but if omissions have been made, please let us know.

List of Plays and Poems Covered in *SC*

Volumes 1-10 present a critical overview of each play, including criticism from the seventeenth century to the present.
Beginning with Volume 11, the series focuses on the history of Shakespeare's plays on the stage and in important films.
The Yearbooks reprint the most important critical pieces of the year as suggested by an advisory board of Shakespearean scholars.
Beginning with Volume 27, each volume is organized around a theme and focuses on criticism published after 1960.

Volume 1
The Comedy of Errors
Hamlet
Henry IV, Parts 1 and 2
Timon of Athens
Twelfth Night

Volume 2
Henry VIII
King Lear
Love's Labour's Lost
Measure for Measure
Pericles

Volume 3
Henry VI, Parts 1, 2, and 3
Macbeth
A Midsummer Night's Dream
Troilus and Cressida

Volume 4
Cymbeline
The Merchant of Venice
Othello
Titus Andronicus

Volume 5
As You Like It
Henry V
The Merry Wives of Windsor
Romeo and Juliet

Volume 6
Antony and Cleopatra
Richard II
The Two Gentlemen of Verona

Volume 7
All's Well That Ends Well
Julius Caesar
The Winter's Tale

Volume 8
Much Ado about Nothing
Richard III
The Tempest

Volume 9
Coriolanus
King John
The Taming of the Shrew
The Two Noble Kinsmen

Volume 10
The Phoenix and Turtle
The Rape of Lucrece
Sonnets
Venus and Adonis

Volume 11
King Lear
Othello
Romeo and Juliet

Volume 12
The Merchant of Venice
A Midsummer Night's Dream
The Taming of the Shrew
The Two Gentlemen of Verona

Volume 13
1989 Yearbook

Volume 14
Henry IV, Parts 1 and 2
Henry V
Richard III

Volume 15
Cymbeline
Pericles
The Tempest
The Winter's Tale

Volume 16
1990 Yearbook

Volume 17
Antony and Cleopatra
Coriolanus
Julius Caesar
Titus Andronicus

Volume 18
The Merry Wives of Windsor
Much Ado about Nothing
Troilus and Cressida

Volume 19
1991 Yearbook

Volume 20
Macbeth
Timon of Athens

Volume 21
Hamlet

Volume 22
1992 Yearbook

Volume 23
As You Like It
Love's Labour's Lost
Measure for Measure

Volume 24
Henry VI, Parts 1, 2, and 3
Henry VIII
King John
Richard II

Volume 25
1993 Yearbook

Volume 26
All's Well That Ends Well
The Comedy of Errors
Twelfth Night

Volume 27
Shakespeare and Classical Civilization
Antony and Cleopatra
Timon of Athens
Titus Andronicus
Troilus and Cressida

Volume 28
1994 Yearbook

Dreams in Shakespeare

INTRODUCTION

To a degree, Shakespeare's varied and extensive use of dreams in his plays reflects the widespread currency of the motif on the English Renaissance stage—where it was a common feature, originating in the theater of classical antiquity. Yet, Shakespeare is also credited with imaginatively expanding and shaping the dramatic representation of dreams. The romances particularly have earned the attention of critics intrigued by their unique settings in dream-like worlds of fantasy, for example, in the bucolic forest of *The Winter's Tale*, Prospero's magical island in *The Tempest*, and the illusory, faerie world of *A Midsummer Night's Dream*. In addition, Shakespeare has made significant use of dreams throughout his oeuvre, in many instances evoking the classical conception of the dream as a medium of supernatural powers or as a premonition of future events. This approach is a common feature in the early histories, notably *Henry VI* in which the Cardinal of Winchester experiences a dream that prefigures the Duke of Gloucester's death. Similarly, Shakespeare employs dreams and foreboding omens in *Richard III*. Dreams also figure prominently in the tragedies. In *Romeo and Juliet* Romeo dreams of his own death only to imagine that Juliet has arrived, and with a kiss brought him back to life. *Macbeth*, *Hamlet*, and *King Lear* also offer dreams and visions that take on ominous, preternatural overtones as they herald the approach of ghosts, witchcraft, or madness.

Modern criticism of dreams in Shakespearean drama has tended to focus on psychoanalysis. Appropriately, several critics have observed the importance of Shakespeare's works as raw material for later, Freudian theories on the significance of dreams in human psychology. Among them, Frankie Rubinstein (1986) has located Shakespeare's dramatization of dreams as precursors of Sigmund Freud's "dream-material." Kay Stockholder (1987) has examined the unconscious blending of violence and sexuality in Shakespeare's tragedy *Macbeth*, uncovering the deep-seated and perverse motivations in the half-waking dreams of the play's title character. Further explorations of dreams in various plays have unearthed considerable material for psychoanalytic critics. Among them, Terrence N. Tice (1990) has commented on the implications of Calphurnia's dream portending the murder of Caesar in *Julius Caesar*, which Tice sees as a device for conveying the psychological state of depression to the viewing audience. Joseph Westlund (1993), meanwhile, has focused on Posthumus's dream in *Cymbeline* as a manifestation of his search for psychological integration.

Other critical avenues on the subject of dreams have included readings of particular plays as the dream-narratives of individual characters. Thus, Kay Stockholder (1991) has interpreted *The Merchant of Venice* as if its plot were the dream of Portia's dead father, using this unique perspective to discover the sources of the play's obsessive themes of wealth and desire. Likewise, Simon O. Lesser (1976) has discussed *Macbeth* as a play driven by the unconscious dreams and fantasies of its protagonist as they are brought to bloody fruition. The negative consequences of a blurred distinction between dream-fantasy and reality are the subject of Marjorie Garber's (1974) influential study *Dream in Shakespeare*. In it Garber surveys Shakespearean tragedy from *Richard III* to *Antony and Cleopatra*, uncovering the importance of dreams as the representations of internal landscapes in the early histories and the tragedies *Hamlet*, *Macbeth* and *King Lear*, and as symbolic—rather than psychological or naturalistic—manifestations in the later plays.

OVERVIEWS: DREAMS AND PSYCHOANALYSIS

Frankie Rubinstein (essay date 1986)

SOURCE: "Shakespeare's Dream-Stuff: A Forerunner of Freud's 'Dream Material,'" in *American Imago,* Vol. 43, No. 4, Winter, 1986, pp. 335-55.

[*In the following essay, Rubinstein explores the dream language and imagery of Shakespeare's dramas and the relation of these to Freudian psychoanalysis.*]

> "We are such stuff / As dreams are made on, and our little life / Is rounded with a sleep."
>
> *The Tempest,* IV.i

> "Sleep, thou hast been a grandsire, and begot / A father to me; and thou hast created / A mother . . . Gone! they went hence as soon as they were born; / And so I am awake . . . and find nothing. 'Tis still a dream, or else such stuff as madmen / Tongue and brain not; either both or nothing; / Or senseless speaking, or a speaking such / As sense cannot untie. Be what it is / The action of my life is like it . . ."
>
> *Cymbeline,* V.iv[1]

What Freud calls the "material" of dreams, Shakespeare had earlier called the "stuff," knowing that many in his audience would recognize in this word his frequent double entendre on coital stuffing and the stuff of semen and brothel occupants. They would know these puns from many plays; for example, *Timon of Athens,* where Apemantus's father "in spite put stuff / To some she beggar and compounded" him; *Pericles,* where the Bawd describes her brothel wenches as "the stuff we have"; *Much Ado About Nothing,* where Beatrice who complains she is "stuffed" and "cannot smell," meaning only that she has a cold, nonetheless has her chastity jestingly challenged by Margaret, who responds, "A maid, and stuffed!"; and *Cymbeline,* where the diseased "hired tomboys" with whom Iachimo accuses Posthumus of fornicating, are called "boyl'd stuff," a pun on their being the boiled stuff of a stew, a word Shakespeare used for both a vessel for boiling and also a brothel, like the very "stew" that, a few lines later, Iachimo is accused of having come from. There is also the implication that they have boils and are candidates for the sweating tubs of boiling water that were used to treat venereal disease; and there may be a hint of sexual deviance (since Iachimo has a "beastly mind") in that the "boyl'd stuff" may be boyl'd boys; TOMBOYS,[2] by which Shakespeare meant masculine girls or effeminate boys. In using a word that has a potential for bawdy, like "stuff," Shakespeare can establish a certain distance of ironic detachment from a however thoughtful character speaking however earnestly, as in the above quotations from *The Tempest* and *Cymbeline.*

Freud's pioneering contribution to contemporary studies that utilize psychoanalytic concepts for interpreting Shakespeare was enormous. He revealed certain larger dramatic themes and fleshed out certain characters, as Shakespeare had understood them or had unconsciously recognized them to be, as in his seminal concept that *Macbeth* is only secondarily a study of overweening political ambition and that the play's unbridled violence stems from its being primarily a drama of father-son relations and the curse of barrenness.[3] And his perceptions and theories have been enriched, as well as redefined and revised, by the detailed verbal analyses in contemporary psychoanalytical criticism.[4]

In *King Lear* and *The Merchant of Venice,* Freud saw the presentation of an old mythological and folk dilemma, that of man's necessity to choose among three women, the choice devolving on the third, whom he likens to the third spinner of man's Fate, Atropos, the inevitable, or death.[5] Crucial to an understanding of the choice in both plays is the specific quality shared by the chosen: dumbness. Cordelia, whose voice was "ever soft, / Gentle, and low," will "Love, and be silent"; and Portia, hidden in the third casket (where the casket, an old symbol for the essential *part* of woman comes to represent woman herself), says of herself that "a maiden hath no tongue but thought." Portia, whose eyes once gave "speechless messages" to Bassanio, is not "contained" or concealed in caskets of clamorous gold or silver, but in silent lead, now chosen by him because its "paleness [alternate reading: plainness] moves me more than eloquence."[6] In dreams, Freud explains, "dumbness" familiarly represents death, as do "concealment" and "striking pallor"; and such are their meanings here.

These Freudian significations can be detected in other of Shakespeare's plays, as in *A Midsummer Night's Dream,* in Thisbe's comic plaint, "Speak, speak. Quite dumb! Dead, dead?"; and most telling in *Henry IV, Part 2,* when Suffolk says, "Gloucester is dead," and Carlyle responds, "I did dream tonight / The duke was dumb." Paleness, too, is often linked to death: "death's pale flag" (*Romeo and Juliet*); "pale-dead eyes" (*Henry V*). In *Pericles,* the trio of dumbness, paleness, and death are linked: "['martyrs'] tell thee, with speechless tongues and semblance pale . . . with dead cheeks." And in *A Midsummer Night's Dream,* in the comic vein, it is "The Sisters Three . . . With hands as pale as milk" who "shore / With shears his thread of silk" when Death claimed Pyramus. Many of Shakespeare's audience, knowing well their Bible, may even have heard in these metaphors echoes of the "pale horse" whose rider is Death (Revelation 6:5).

On the lead casket lies a message from Portia's dead father: "Who chooseth me must give and hazard all he hath." In the sixteenth century gambling game of hazard (and this choosing among the three caskets is certainly a gambling game), the hazard (Arab, *al zār,* the die) was the die, singular form of "dice" (Shakespeare quibbles on "the hazard of the die," *Richard III*). Portia's "picture" was contained in lead, a frequent Shakespearean symbol for death, its instrument and final home; for example, all the "leaden" swords, shot, daggers; the "leaden mace of murderous slumber"; the corpse that might "burst his lead and rise from death"; and in *The Merchant of Venice,* the surmise that it is not possible "lead contains her . . . it were too gross / To rib her cerecloth in the obscure grave."

Freud explained that the symbolism in plays, like that in dreams, often seems to lack literal applicability to the immediate story line because of inversion, a tendency of the mind to replace an element with its exact opposite. Thus, of the last scene of *King Lear,* in the English war camp, when Lear enters with the dead Cordelia in his arms, Freud tells us:

> Cordelia is Death. If we reverse the situation it becomes intelligible and familiar to us. She is the Deathgoddess who, like the Valkyrie in German mythology, carries away the dead hero from the battlefield. Eternal wisdom, clothed in the primaeval myth, bids the old man renounce love, choose death and make friends with the necessity of dying.[7]

In interpreting *The Merchant of Venice,* Freud again used inversion or "reaction-formation" to explain why the third casket, the lead one, is Portia, the fairest woman. Rebelling against his subjection to the inevitability of death (the third Fate), man constructed derivative myths wherein the chosen Goddess of Love takes the place of the unavoidable Goddess of Death, a not difficult substitution since this replacement by the wish-opposite derives from the ancient identity of the Greek Aphrodite, goddess of love and beauty, who was once also goddess of death and the underworld. (In Hinduism, Nataraj, the dancing god with four arms, carrying a drum, is he who both creates and destroys the universe.)

Knowing that dreams show a "preference for combining contrasts into a unity or for representing them as one and the same thing,"[8] let us look a little closer at the allegory of the three caskets. In addition to all the other clues that Portia illicitly gives Bassanio—who at one point says, "my torturer / Doth teach me answers for deliverance!"—she tells him she would detain him "Before you venture for me." Venture, which literally means hazard, risk oneself, is almost an open directive to Bassanio to go with the lead casket that requires him to "give and hazard all," the one he recognizes "threatenest." Portia says, "I am lock'd in one" of the caskets, and "I stand for sacrifice." Her musicians conclude with a little song that toys with the contradictions in "fancy dies / In the cradle where it lies"—disguise: death and birth, caskets and cradles; and Bassanio, who had asked "Promise me life" and been told "Live thou I live," opts for lead or death. And under it all flows the current of a religious metaphor, the choice of a *death* that leads to *life:* "sacrifice" and "deliverance"; a "new-crowned monarch" and a "bridegroom": the "Lord Bassanio."

In dreams, inversion functions to further wish fulfillment. Shakespeare recognized that dreams tell us what we wish to hear: "Thus have I had thee as a dream doth flatter— / In sleep a king, but waking no such matter" (Sonnet 87). In his study of the sonnets, Joseph Pequigney argues that this flattering "matter" or dream material is libidinal: the sonneteers has "had" a lover who "gav'st" his self but ultimately proved too dear for "possessing"—three words that signify carnal possession.[9] I would add that MATTER is a Shakespearean pun on the penis and semen.[10] Since Pequigney argues that Shakespeare's sonnets describe his love for both a man and a woman, it may be worth nothing here that Freud commented on the frequency with which inversion occurs in dreams that derive from repressed homosexual impulses.

Elizabethan writers recognized the contrariness of dreams, a proverbial view as old as *The Golden Ass of Apuleius:*

> the visions of the night do often chance contrary: and indeed to dream of weeping, beating, and killing

is a token of good luck . . . whereas contrary, to dream of laughing, filling the belly with good cheer, or dalliance of love, is a sign of sadness of heart, sickness of body, or other displeasure.[11]

Shakespeare's fellow playwright John Lyly tells us in *Mother Bombie:* "they that in the morning sleep or dream of eating, Are in danger of sickness or of beating." Similarly, Shakespeare writes in *Much Ado About Nothing:* "I have heard my daughter say she hath often dreamt of unhappiness and wak'd herself with laughing"; and in *Julius Caesar,* before the mob "Tear [Cinna] to pieces," the victimized poet says, "I dreamt tonight that I did feast with Caesar / And things unluckily charge my fantasy."

Shakespeare's plays are full of incongruities, equivocations, verbal antitheses, contradictions, oxymorons; the shifts in person, sudden reversals and contradictory moods within a single poem, clashing elements in a single scene that are typical of the Elizabethan style.[12] According to Patrick Cruttwell, seventeenth century writers developed this new "psychological impressionism" to convey their awareness of the ever incongruous states of the human being; hence John Donne's "contraryes meet in one" in his "Holy Sonnets" and Shakespeare's "compounds strange" in Sonnet 76. He maintains the futility of trying to decide which of any two opposing attitudes, such as levity or seriousness, is the intent of a poetic phrase or line, since only by recognizing the fusing of both elements within one metaphor can we grasp the entirety, the full meaning that is beyond the scope of either separately.

Freud likewise speaks of arrangements of words that permit the expression of more than one dream thought, it being the very nature of a word to be the junction of a multiplicity of ideas, to possess an inherent, a "predestined" ambiguity. The particular words taken up into dream content are chosen, he says, because they are nodal points, the meeting place of several trains of thought and because they are of manifold significance.

A quotation from *King Lear* (IV.vi) may serve to illustrate the similarity between the productions of dream-work and Shakespeare's puns that function consistently, coherently and simultaneously on two or more levels, his metaphors whose dramatic service is not at all impeded by but, in fact, derives from their ambiguity. I have chosen the seemingly simple lines, "I will die bravely, like a smug bridegroom. What! I will be jovial. Come, come, I am a king" for several reasons: (1) they contain (as Edgar says of Lear's madness) "matter and impertinency mixed! Reason in madness"; (2) Cruttwell described the first half as having a "queer tightrope affect almost beyond analysis, with bawdy on one side and heartbreaking pathos on the other";[13] and (3) my own conviction that Shakespeare's bawdry usually has specific relevance and particular meaning for the play in which it occurs.

Freud's caveat about interpreting the symbolism that disguises repressed sexual material, namely, that like Chinese script, its correct meaning can be provided only by context, applies as well to any attempt to understand Shakespeare's sexual metaphors. So we shall examine Lear's sentence in its immediate context; the context of the entire play, where similar wordclusters appear; other of Shakespeare's plays in which the same elements occur and where repetitive patterns of association emerge; and, finally, how the word or phrase was used by Shakespeare's contemporaries and in the several languages and literatures that he, like so many of the poets and playwrights of his day, had an acquaintance with or knowledge of.

Earlier, Lear had come to terms with his failure as a king and evinced a sympathy of sorts for the downtrodden, but he still did not accept personal responsibility for his ills, still saw himself as "more sinned against than sinning." Self-pitying to the end, Lear says, "I am mightily abused. I should e'en die with pity, / To see another thus" (IV.vii). Blame for his own evil doing he lays at the doors of "fortune's blows" and his daughters, who "Have . . . done [him] wrong" though "cause, they have not." Lear conveniently forgets the emotional games he has played with his daughters, and the obvious favoritism he displayed toward Cordelia: "I loved her most"; and he is blind to the hate this engenders in the two older girls. He remains an egotist, bitterly cynical and at war with all sexuality. "Adultery" he accepts as the way of the world: "Let copulation thrive" in man, since it is natural to all other creatures—and besides, "I lack soldiers!" Sexually biased, he reviles women, whose genitals revulse him: "nor the soil'd horse goes to't [lechery] / With a more riotous appetite . . . Beneath ["the girdle"] . . . There's hell [the vagina]; there's darkness, there's the sulphurous pit [vagina] / Burning, scalding, stench, consumption."[14] The stench is such that he needs an "ounce of civet [perfume derived from a cat's anal glands] . . . to sweeten my imagination" and needs to "wipe" his hand, for "it smells of mortality." Lear concludes this section saying he is ready to "kill, kill, kill, kill, kill, kill."

Shakespeare exploits the conventional Elizabethan word play on dying as meaning the end of life and the orgasm: Lear is ready for either death. Let us for a moment entertain the possibility that Lear, who had railed against the "simular man of virtue / That art incestuous," harbored (and perhaps even acted out) incestuous feelings for his daughters. Their hatred, then, may have the "cause" he refuses to acknowledge, and it becomes salient that his excessive emphasis on killing is directed specifically toward his "sons-in-law," two of whom are quite loyal to him. In the other plays where the word "incest(uous)" occurs, it has direct bearing on a relationship within the play; in *Hamlet,* the five times it is used, it denotes his mother's incestuous marriage with an ex-brother-in-law and may well be a projection of the other union Hamlet unconsciously desired; in *Pericles,* it denotes the achieved incest of a father and his daughter; in *Measure for Measure,* it is used metaphorically for the degree and kind of love between a brother and sister: "Wilt thou be made a man out of my vice? / Is't not a kind of incest for a brother to take life / From his own sister's shame?" Her questions refer to Claudio's taking, i.e. rescuing his own life at the expense of her submitting to an adulterous act. However, Shakespeare pointedly does not say rescue or save but "take," a word he repeatedly used to mean copulate with. And in the erotic context of incest and her brother's being *made* a *man* out of her *vice* (which is not only sin, but also a Shakespearean pun on the pudendum and closed thighs), one realizes that her "shame," too, has overtones of her privy members—the Biblical and sixteenth century usage.[15] But even saving life can be a sexually symbolic concept according to Freud: "Under the laws governing the expression of unconscious thoughts, the meaning of rescuing may vary" depending on whose fantasy it is. If a man's, it can mean "making a child," if a woman's, "giving birth" to it.[16] Since in each of these other examples, the word "incest" has specific pertinence for some aspect of the play, is *King Lear,* then, the only play in which incest is gratuitously, as it were, dragged in—and by the main character.[17]

To kill, like to die, was a sexually charged phrase, as it is to the present in the sentiment that women kill men with their sexual demands, that expending semen weakens man, that men kill women with the weapon of their phallus ("You slay me") and so on.[18] In "Venus and Adonis," the passion-driven Venus tells Adonis, "O thou didst kill me; kill me once again." And when her rival, the boar, "the loving swine / Sheathed unaware the tusk in [Adonis's] soft groin," she says, "Had I been tooth'd like him, I must confess / With kissing him I should have killed him first." And in *Othello,* the anguished Moor madly alternates killing and loving: Kissing her, he says, "Be thus when thou art dead, and I will kill thee, / And love thee after" (V.ii). His last words in the play are, "I kiss'd thee ere I kill'd thee; no way but this; / Killing myself, to die upon a kiss." One of the most explicit identifications of killing and coitus is in John Donne's "An Anatomie of the World":

> For that first marriage was our funerall; One woman at one blow, then kill'd us all, And, singly, one by one, they kill us now. We doe delightfully our selves allow To that consumption; and profusely blinde, Wee kill ourselves to propagate our kinde.

Lear embellishes this concept with the particular addition that he will die "bravely," that is, with masculine valour in the feats of the marital bed and courage in deeds leading up to a death bed—bravely or with bravery, a word that connoted wedding finery and also mere show or bravado. The ambiguity continues in Lear's use of 'smug,' meaning trim and gay but also complacent. Both the moods of bravado and complacency fit his character.

In the wider context of the play, the words in this line stand revealed as nodal points and as over-determined.[19] Whereas here Lear speaks of himself in a seemingly positive tone as the "bridegroom," "jovial," and a "king," a very similar constellation of these three elements had established a contrary mood in an earlier scene in which his daughters, current possessors of his wealth and power, figuratively emasculated him. Thus Kent wonders why the king had "come with so small a train." And Lear says Goneril has deprived him of "half my train," and can not believe that Regan would "cut off my train . . . scant my sizes / And in conclusion to oppose the bolt / Against my coming in."

In these capsule comments, we find five sexually suggestive terms that are recurrent Shakespearean puns: a TRAIN is literally a tail or tail feathers, hence a pun on man's tail or penis; SIZE, from French *taille,* evokes tail/tale, one of the most common public-anal puns;[20] CONCLUSION signified coitus as far back as Chaucer, and in *Othello* Iago described lechery thus: "They met so near with their lips that their breaths embraced together . . . [then] hard at hand comes the master and main exercise, the incorporate conclusion;"[21] BOLT, meaning any stout pin with a head and also to discharge, is a pun on the penis and ejaculation; and "come" was a standard Elizabethan word for sexual emission.

The emasculation imagery continues when Goneril and Regan decide they will leave him "not one follower." "What need one?" They say that Lear's "injuries"—these physical deprivations, when they "cut off" his "men" (manhood)—must be his "schoolmaster," a phrase conveying his reduction from the state of virile manhood to the impotence of childhood.[22] Lear will be deprived of his "train" or tail; his "size" or *taille* will be "scanted"—made short, insufficient or lacking—as in Freud's report of a dream in which a tailor caught a wolf by his tail and pulled it off, which Freud said was undeniably an allusion to the castration complex.[23] Not even *one* of his followers, those "men of . . . rarest parts" (I.iv), the rare/rear parts that make up his train, will be left—not one symbol of power or potency.[24]

But Lear defies their treatment, saying he will not "bear it tamely . . . let not women's weapons, water-drops, / Stain my man's cheeks!" They can not TAME him (literally, cut, carve out, prune), make him less wild, with its connotations of sexual ardor. He will not be effeminized and "bear it," Shakespeare's customary phrase for the female role, in which bearing refers to the coital position and child-bearing. The Fool had been wise: "fathers that bear bags / Shall see their children kind"; fathers should retain their power, bear only two things: money bags and the bag of their scrotum.[25]

Since in some dreams a general reversal takes place, so that the male organ is represented by the female and vice versa, Freud recommended caution in interpreting bisexual symbols. Shakespeare's metaphors require equal alertness. Lear will not use women's weapons or water-drops; he will use man's "weapon"—for Freud and Shakespeare a phallic symbol.[26] Because of its context, Lear's metaphor suggests dream language, where bodily secretions such as tears, mucus, urine and semen are interchanged, the "indifferent" one replacing the significant one, such as semen.[27] Waterdrops, by they tears, urine, or semen, will not stain—a word Shakespeare uses for sexual defilement and uncleanliness—Lear's cheeks, a common displacement for the buttocks, in dreams and in seventeenth century literature.[28] Lear's preoccupation was always with his manhood, maleness;[29] and these are specifically his "man's" cheeks.

Lear's metaphor could be innocent; but on a deeper level, it could also reveal his desire to dispel the image of impotence. He will not permit those "unnatural hags," his daughters, to make him also unnatural, to stain his cheeks with tears; he will not wet his cheeks/ buttocks by urinating like a woman or in futile ejaculation. In a parallel scene of the emasculation of the old and once powerful Gloucester, Regan turned to her husband who had "set his foot on the eye" (Freudian symbol for penis) of Lear's close friend and said, "One side will mock another; the other too" (a one, two quibble having genital implications), after which they threw the "eyeless" (displacement for castration) Gloucester out of doors, just as they had shut their doors on Lear.[30]

Threatened thus, Lear remembers his third daughter, Cordelia, whom he felt had also denied him love and married "the hot-blooded France," another king, not himself. Staying with his two castrating daughters is as hateful to him as if he had to kneel to France and "beg to keep *base* life *afoot*" (Folio: a foot)—beg to keep his life (sexuality) a FOOT, common pun on French *foutre,* to coit (cf. similar pattern in *3 Henry IV: "A foutre* for . . . worldlings *base!"* Italics added). He would rather be a "slave and sumpter / To this detested groom," he says, pointing to Oswald, the DETESTED/ de-teste-d, expressing his fear of an encroaching threat of kinship with his daughter's servant, whom he had earlier called "slave" and "beggar," the same terms with which he now describes himself. Since a sumpter is a beast of burden or a porter, it seems that one way or another, Lear fears he must bear, be effeminized.[31] Nevertheless, for reasons we shall soon see, this always vengeful man (who a few lines later plans "revenges") says his daughters need not fear he will tell "tales to high-judging Jove" of their wanting to cut off his tail or train.

As we peel away the layers of his thoughts and discover that the "hot-blooded France that . . . took" Cordelia (and took her sexually) is ever on his mind, then the appropriateness of the French puns is even more apparent.

Three crucial elements from Act II, "groom," "king," and "Jove," the superior judge of all men, reappear, again clustered, in the line from Act IV that we originally set out to analyze. Now Lear is all three, groom, king, and jovial (i.e. merry and Jove-like). This king who is going to die, to marry death, the third of the Fates, his chosen third daughter Cordelia whom he carries in his arms at the play's end, still thinks of himself as a brave and lusty bridegroom. This is the same Lear who, when the play began, had wanted to know which of his daughters "doth love us most." As Freud said, though old, though dying, he is not "willing to renounce the love of women" and insists on being told how much he is loved.[32] When speaking of Cordelia's suitors, there may be ambiguity in Lear's saying, "The princes, France and Burgundy, / Great rivals in our youngest daughter's love, / Long in our court have made their amorous sojourn." True, they were rivals to each other, but is Lear not also expressing his own part in the rivalry for Cordelia's love: their *amorous* presence seemed "long" to him in his "court" (court = French for short), a quibble on their virility and his lack of it. When he addressed Burgundy, "who with this king / Hath rivall'd for our daughter," presumably he looked toward France, but *this king* is also himself. He was certainly furious with the reprimand to him implicit in Cordelia's question, "Why have my sisters husbands, if they say / They love you all?" and with her promising to give "Half my love" to her husband: "I shall never marry like my sisters, / To love my father all."

It is this truth that precipitates his dismissing Cordelia with the revealing phrase, "I loved her most, and thought to set my rest / On her kind nursery." Annotations usually say this refers to a card game and means I stand pat or I stake my all. That gloss, however, ignores several emotive phrases. First, let us consider that Shakespeare and his contemporaries made puns on "rest" as sexual repose, with the penis in its desired place of rest.[33] Second, in the context of the emotional argument on degrees and kinds of love, Lear's hope to set his rest on Cordelia's "kind nursery" brings to mind Shakespeare's habitual associations of a nursery with a breeding place, a womb: "nurse and breeder" (*The Two Gentlemen of Verona*), "This nurse, this teeming womb" (*Richard II*)—consistent with the "child-changed" Lear's saying (IV.vii) Cordelia "must bear with" him. Third, there is Shakespeare's frequent use of "kind" in its sixteenth century meaning of sex, as in "the deed of

kind" (*The Merchant of Venice*) or "to be after kind," to seek sex (*As You Like It*). Lear himself told of a man who "hotly lust'st to use" a whore "in that kind / For which [he] whipp'st her" (II.vi). He also spoke of his daughter Regan as "kind and comfortable," as having eyes that "Do comfort," as knowing "The offices of nature," and not being one "to oppose the bolt / Against my coming in." Comfortable is another of Shakespeare's sexually charged phrases; for example, Portia asks Brutus is she only to "comfort your bed" (*Julius Caesar*) and Juliet's new husband will "Ascend her chamber . . . and comfort her" (*Romeo and Juliet*). Certainly, at least in his unconscious, Lear substitutes his daughters for the wife he does not have.

When Lear compares himself to Jove, another king, does Shakespeare not mean the archetypal "lusty Jove" of *Much Ado About Nothing,* his "multipotent Jove" of *Troilus and Cressida?* This is how Lear wishes to see himself. Now we understand why he need not tell tales about his daughters to "high-judging Jove." *He* is that king of heaven; *he* will be Jovial; *he* will pass judgment on his daughters—as he has always done, as he did when the play opened and again in his simulated arraignment and trial of them (III.vi).

This man who sees himself as a smug bridegroom had just finished reviling women's sexuality: "Down from the waist they are Centaurs," a comparison to their being the half-men, half-horses known as symbols of sexual bestiality; and a pun on their physiological CENTERS, Elizabethan word for the vulva, called the "centrique part" by poet John Donne and the "Garden's Centre" by poet Charles Cotton. In this attack he gave unconscious expression to a sexual aspect of himself. King Lear is Jove, heaven's archadulterer and sometimes bestial lover, as in *The Merry Wives of Windsor,* where Jove "wast a bull for Europa" and committed "a beastly fault" seducing her in the form of a bull, and then a "foul fault in the semblance of a fowl," seducing Leda in the form of a swan.

A line of thought in *Pericles* may be pertinent to our understanding the dynamics of King Lear. By alluding to Jove's incestuous history, a cautious Pericles conveys to King Antiochus his knowledge of the king's incestuous relationship with his own daughter: "Kings are earth's gods; in vice their law's their will; / and if Jove stray, who dares say Jove doth ill." The mad Lear also feels impervious to censure: "They cannot touch me for coining: I am the king himself." Coining was often used figuratively, "esp. in a bad sense 1561" (OED); and Shakespeare has several puns on coining or stamping children, as in *Measure for Measure,* II.iv: "these filthy vices . . . [to] coin heaven's image / In stamps that are forbid," that is, to beget children illicitly.

Here then, in those two deceptively simple lines of Lear's is material quite similar in function to "dream-material," subjected to compression and displacement, and requiring for its understanding an approach akin to dream analysis. A vital difference, however, is that the productions of the dream-work were *"not made with the intention of being understood,"*[34] whereas Shakespeare's productions were. Of course, just as the dreamer often utilizes verbal wit for the purpose of disguise, and the political writer resorts to Aesopian language to outwit his censor, so Shakespeare may have at times intended that his wit be fully understood only by an inner circle.[35] Freud had asked himself whether many of the symbols representing sexual material might not have permanently established meanings like "short-hand" signs; and it is interesting to note how many of the substitutions he identified had been used several centuries earlier by Shakespeare as sexual puns and metaphors.

That the symbolism used by Shakespeare, Joyce, and others, consciously and unconsciously, is very often the same with which we disguise our dream thoughts may be a partial explanation of the resistance it arouses, the reluctance to probe critically beneath the surface of what is apparent, the resentment toward the disclosure of multi-layered meanings, as if what is remote must be sinister. Hence the question to what extent a Shakespearean pun or metaphor is a *conscious* literary device is raised most often and assumes a particular urgency when it is a specifically sexual one, the implication being that if it is unconscious, then it is irrelevant, can be dismissed and not heard.

However, bawdry (too frequently omitted in texts and productions) can be expunged only by doing violence to the vitality of the plays.[36] Unfortunately, Shakespeare's amazing word-play is not always recognized as being verbally *and* conceptually related to the serious elements of the play, but on the contrary often meets resistance akin to that put up by the dreamer who says that the particular stuff of dreams has no meaning and can be adequately explained as deriving from an attack of indigestion or the inchoate remains of the last conscious thoughts of the day.

This bias against attributing meaning is exemplified in a comment made by literary critic A. P. Riemer, who, of Shakespeare's comedies, has written, "exegesis they resist":

> Comedy is sport; to go beyond that statement is to risk perverting the essentially meaningless nature of these plays . . . The function of the profundities and significances contained in them is almost always abstract and "aesthetic". . . .[37]

Riemer relies on a quote from *A Midsummer Night's Dream:* "Man is but an ass if he go about to expound this dream," following which he says that "Critics have not taken . . . sufficient heed of Bottom's warn-

ing." But certainly the critical attempt to find meaning in the apparently meaningless is attempted by analysts who see that the "warning" was delivered by *Bottom,* who calls himself and is called by others an "ass"—whereas his dream is the creation of Shakespeare, who is not one.

In a section on "Absurd Dreams," Freud observed that the presence of the ridiculous in some dreams was the chief ammunition of the opponents of dream interpretation. But, he explained, it is just where the dream seems most absurd that it may have its profoundest meaning: "In every epoch of history those who have had something to say but could not say it without peril have eagerly assumed a fool's cap."[38] To illustrate that it is only with an aim that the dream-work produces anything ridiculous, Freud cited an absurd dream whose purpose was to show that this is a "topsy-turvy" world where society is "crazy" and those who do not care for a thing get it while those who deserve it do not.[39]

In this, Freud could not have been talking more to the point of *A Midsummer Night's Dream,* which develops the folly of aspects of love (including "too high to be enthralled to low") and the irresponsibility of lovers who flee offered love and seek those whom they conquer by force, those who are forbidden to them, or those who reject them. And one integral element of the play is the topsy-turvy dream of the lowly artisan who agrees to *"under*take" a part in a small play where he, *"Nick Bottom"*[40] is *"set down"* for Pyramus" (italics added). During the preparations in the wood, where Bottom expected to "rehearse most obscenely and courageously" he is "changed" and "translated" and falls asleep a few feet from four foolish lovers who are having equally confused dreams. And there "Bully Bottom," whose "chief humour" was to play "a tyrant"—but who settled for a role he describes as that of a "poor knight"—has a midsummer night's / knight's dream in which he may wear an ass's head and eat an ass's food, but a queen, the wife of a tyrant who instigated her adultery, becomes "enamour'd" of him! Only when the shamed woman agrees to give up a beloved child to her bullying husband is she released by him from her dream bondage. Then Bottom, who in real life is lucky to earn "sixpence a day," awakens from his dream of luxury and mismated love with a woman too high to be enthralled to lowly Bottom. And though he says it is "past the wit of man" to understand his dream, still he would like to sing it at "the latter end of a play" in which he is an actor.

This is not meant to suggest that Shakespeare realized symbolic dream language served to disguise repressed sexual material. Nevertheless, it is interesting how many times he does directly link dreams to sexuality: in *Cymbeline,* he alludes to the unlikelihood that Diana, goddess of chastity, "had hot dreams"; in *The Merry Wives of Windsor,* Ford dreams of his wife's infidelity in terms of a "hole made in [his] best coat"; in *Henry VIII,* a constant woman is defined as "One that ne'er dreamed a joy beyond his [her husband's] pleasure"— pleasure being a favorite euphemism for sexual joy;[41] in *Othello,* there is the open eroticism of Cassio's alleged dream of sexual intercourse with Desdemona, as recounted by his male bed-companion Iago, in which Cassio laid his leg over Iago's thigh and did "kiss me hard"; and in *Coriolanus,* there is the homoeroticism of Coriolanus's entry into the house of Aufidius, whose enraptured heart then "dances"[42] more "Than when I first my wedded mistress saw / Bestride my threshold"; and, Aufidius continues, "I have nightly since / Dreamt of encounters ["love-bout": Partridge; "amatory meeting, Shaks.": *OED*] 'twixt thyself and me; We have been down together in my sleep / Unbuckling helms, fisting each other's throats"; and so on.

Modern scholars agree that the Elizabethans heard words in ways that we do not and that many of Shakespeare's double entendres are overlooked by modern audiences. What can be counter-productive is to stress the dichotomy "between 'unconscious' and 'conscious' meaning . . . What we really experience instead of either of these extremes is a range of different ways of being aware."[43] And even in those cases where Shakespeare's word-play was not conscious or was a habitual verbal association, as through consonance or assonance, we, his audience, also have "unconscious minds."[44]

One cannot emphasize too strongly the need to give full weight to each of Shakespeare's words, asking why the line is so and not otherwise. Shakespeare's creative material was, after all, not paint or clay or the musical note, but the color, form and sound of "Words, words, words," "wild and whirling words," "hard words," and "Words of so sweet breath composed / As made the things more rich" (*Hamlet*). On them he relied for the conveyance of his creative impulse; they were his material and his stuff.

Notes

[1] Each of these reflections that life is (like) a dream, brief, its meaning eluding us, followed a masque that spoke of love, the marriage blessing and increase: "the womb" and "nature [that] Moulded the stuff so fair." They draw on familiar Shakespearean symbols: beginning with the sleep in the womb, life is "rounded" ("round-wombed," *King Lear*), comes full circle, with the final sleep—and perhaps rebirth—in another womb, the grave ("The earth that's nature's mother is her tomb; / What is her burying grave that is her womb," *Romeo and Juliet*). Sleep, that "rounded," "begot" and "created," began life in another sense also, for it meant then, as now, lie with in sexual intercourse: the eroticism of "two branches . . . whose circling shadows kings have sought to sleep in" (*Titus Andronicus*) is meant to connote not only Lavinia's arms but her legs

("my legs like loaden branches," *Henry VIII*) with their circling (pudendal) shadows. For other examples that circle = vulva, see Eric Partridge, *Shakespeare's Bawdy* (London: Routledge, Kegan Paul, 1968) and E. A. M. Colman, *The Dramatic Use of Bawdy in Shakespeare* (London: Longman, 1974). Hereafter, these books will be cited respectively as Partridge and Colman.

[2] Words that are printed in capital letters are discussed fully in Frankie Rubinstein, *A Dictionary of Shakespeare's Sexual Puns and Their Significance* (London: Macmillan, 1984), hereafter cited as Rubinstein.

[3] Sigmund Freud, "Some Character-Types Met with in Psycho-Analytic Work," in St. Ed. 14, p. 321. I would add that the child-parent motif—"Mac," a Gaelic prefix = son (of)—starts with Macbeth, "*wayward* son" of the "*weird* [O.E. wyrd = fate] sisters" (italics added); and culminates in the childless, "unmann'd" Macbeth's ultimate impotence against another fateful son, Macduff, "from his mother's womb / Untimely ripp'd."

[4] For example, Murray M. Schwartz and Coppélia Kahn, eds., *Representing Shakespeare: New Psychoanalytic Essays* (Baltimore: Johns Hopkins University Press, 1980); and Marianne Novy, *Love's Argument: Gender Relations in Shakespeare* (Chapel Hill: University of North Carolina Press, 1984).

[5] Freud, "The Theme of Three Caskets," St. Ed. 12, pp. 291-301. See Shakespeare's comic employment of the Fates in *2 Henry IV*: "Untwine the Sisters Three! Come Atropos, I say!"

[6] "Pale as lead" was a familiar simile, as in "The King and the Beggar," a ballad cited in two of Shakespeare's plays. However, "plainness" has the conceivable advantage of punning on the plainsong that "moves" (also a musical term) Bassanio (with its flagrant rhymes on lead and references to birth) to realize that the plain (can = belly: Partridge) lead casket is the *plein* (French for full) casket, the belly or womb that "contains" / "contained" Portia, or that Portia contains (by the process of inversion in dreams and wit). See Freud, *The Interpretation of Dreams,* St. Ed. 4, p. 154: German *Büchse* = box and a vulgarism for the female genitals.

[7] Freud, "The Theme of Three Caskets," St. Ed. 12, p. 301.

[8] Freud, "The Antithetical Meaning of Primal Words," St. Ed. 11, p. 155.

[9] Joseph Pequigney, *Such Is My Love* (Chicago: University of Chicago Press, 1985), pp. 1, 46, 47.

[10] For example, *The Two Gentlemen of Verona*: "how stands the matter with them?"—"Marry, thus; when it stands well with him, it stands well with her."

[11] *The Golden Ass of Apuleius,* trs. W. Adlington (New York: The Modern Library, 1928), pp. 94-5.

[12] Patrick Cruttwell, *The Shakespearean Moment* (New York: Random House, 1960), Chapter 2.

[13] *Ibid.,* p. 51.

[14] John Florio, *A World of Words* (Ann Arbor: University of Michigan, Microfilms, n.d.): *fossa,* a pit, woman's pleasure pit. Hereafter cited as Florio. See Rubinstein, s.v. Pit; and Partridge, s.v. Hell: a symbol for the vagina, as in Boccaccio's story of "putting the devil in hell" (*Tales of Decameron,* Day 3, Tale 10). The "burning" of venereal disease (*Oxford English Dictionary,* hereafter cited as *OED*) is also suggested in Sonnet 144, where the vaginal "hell" will "fire" the man in it. "Consumption" (as in the Donne quote, p. 343) means sexual absorption—by woman's con/cunt. See Stephen Booth, *Shakespeare's Sonnets* (New Haven: Yale University Press, 1977), p. 231, on the "potential for suggesting "vulva" . . . that Shakespeare was ready to hear in any word containing con, or cun, or a similiar sound"; also Helge Kökeritz, *Shakespeare's Pronunciation* (New Haven: Yale University Press, 1966), s.v. Con. Hereafter cited as Kökeritz.

[15] *OED* defines shame as the privy members, quoting Isaiah 47: 2 . . . 3. Cf. Randall Cotgrave, *A Dictionarie of the French and English Tongues* (Columbia: University of South Carolina Press, 1950) s.v. *vergongne,* shame and the privy parts. Hereafter cited as Cotgrave. Shakespeare used "to take" in the sense of to admit the male sexually; of the male, to possess carnally (Colman, Partridge). See Partridge: Make, Man.

[16] Freud, "A Special Type of Choice of Object Made by Men," St. Ed. 11, p. 174.

[17] See Meredith Skura in Schwartz and Kahn, *op. cit.,* p. 205, for the significance of the "hinted" threats of incest between Leontes and his rediscovered daughter (*The Winter's Tale*) and in Prospero's jealousy of a potential son-in-law (*The Tempest*) and Cloten's desire to wed his step-sister (*Cymbeline*).

[18] Madelon Gohlke, in Schwartz and Kahn, *ibid.,* pp. 172-182, gives important expression to a feminist psychoanalytic interpretation of "sexual intercourse" as "a kind of murder."

[19] David Willibern, in Schwartz and Kahn, *ibid.,* p. 245, states that "Shakespeare's overdetermined language typically includes bawdy meanings," as in Cordelia's "nothing" (no *thing* or phallus) and the "ubiquitous anxieties in the play concerning bodily injury or losses, such as Gloucester's eyes, Lear's 'cut-off' train of soldiers . . . Lear himself as nothing ('an O without a figure')."

[20] Partridge; and Colman, s.v. Tale: "speake to her, a woman has ever a hole open to receive a man's tale" (1640).

[21] Thomas W. Ross, *Chaucer's Bawdy* (New York: E. P. Dutton, 1972), s.v. Conclusioun. Hereafter cited as Ross. Note the innuendo in *hard* at *hand,* a phallic symbol to Freud and a pun on the penis to Shakespeare (Kökeritz, p. 59).

[22] Joel Fineman, in Schwartz and Kahn, *op. cit.,* p. 100, speaks of the "viperish sexuality" of Lear's daughters, two of Shakespeare's "horrible women" whose males are "correspondingly emasculated, infantilized, almost (and the language of the plays bears this out) feminized by their relationship" to these women.

[23] Freud, "The Occurrence in Dreams of Material from Fairy Tales," St. Ed. 12, p. 285.

[24] Rear/RARE were spelling doublets, hence subject to quibbles as in *A Midsummer Night's Dream,* where *Bottom* says he could play an actor's part "rarely"; and relates his "rare" vision of having been an *ass.*

[25] Cf. *The Winter's Tale:* "No barricado for a belly; know't; It will let in and out the enemy with bag and baggage." Partridge: bag = scrotum; baggage = penis or scrotum. See Frued, *The Interpretation of Dreams,* St. Ed. 5, p. 358: "luggage often turns out to be an unmistakable symbol of the dreamer's own genitals."

[26] Freud, *ibid.,* pp. 354, 356. *Romeo and Juliet:* "Draw thy tool . . ."—"my naked weapon is out."

[27] Freud, *ibid.,* p. 359. Shakespeare and his contemporaries also interchanged these elements: milking, masturbating and urinating produced comparable ejaculations. Ben Jonson, *The Alchemist:* "For she must milk his epididimis [a duct of the testicle]." John Wilmot, "The Disappointed:" "May'st thou ne'er piss that did'st refuse to spend [emit semen]." In *All's Well That Ends Well,* Parolles, who sat in the stocks all night, "weeps like a wench that had shed her milk; he had confessed himself"—a condensed picture of a man who had poured out at every orifice: his eyes, his mouth; had probably wet himself and may have ejaculated, for he is as wet as the wench whose milk was, not spilt—the expected word—but SHED, literally to ejaculate semen or cast seed out of a receptacle. She reminds one of a similar wench in *The Tempest:* "as leaky as an unstanched wench."

[28] Freud, *op. cit.,* p. 387: cheeks (German *Backen*) are a dream symbol for the buttocks (*Hinterbacken,* back-cheeks). See Dekker and Webster, *Northward Hoe:* "If I catch master pricklouse ramping so high again . . . I'll make him know how to kiss your blind cheeks sooner"; *A Midsummer Night's Dream,* in which Bot-

tom (a "tender ass") has "yellow cowslip cheeks"—YELLOW (the color of ordure) as cowslip, Old English cu-slyppe, cow-dung.

[29] As early as I. 1, behavior the others call mad, Lear calls his "power," "nature," and "potency made good." By I.iv, he defines his rejection in terms of emasculation: he is "ashamed" his daughters can "shake my manhood thus . . . Thou shalt find / That I'll resume the shape which thou dost think / I have cast off for ever." In the context of weakened "manhood"—Latin *virilitas,* common euphemism for the male organ, usually occurring "in contexts in which castration is at issue" (J. N. Adams, *The Latin Sexual Vocabulary* [Baltimore: Johns Hopkins University Press, 1982], pp. 69-70)—SHAKE assumes its sixteenth century coital implications, and Lear's cast off SHAPE takes on its meaning of male as well as female sex organs (*OED,* s.v. shape; Ross, s.v. shap). See Partridge and Ross, s.v. Man(ly), for link to copulatory service. Also see Gohlke, *op. cit.,* p. 231: for Lear "tears threaten not only the dreaded perception of himself as feminine, and hence weak, but also the breakdown of his psychic order."

[30] Freud, "The Uncanny," St. Ed. 17, p. 231: a "substitutive relation between the eye and the male member" exists in dreams, myths and fantasies. In blinding himself, Oedipus was "carrying out a mitigated form of the punishment of castration."

[31] For these euphemisms and frequent word associations, see (a) Colman and Partridge, s.v. Foot, Foutre; (b) Thomas Nashe's erotic poem "The Choice of Valentines," with its pun on sexual satisfaction, her "content"/cunt and his "life"/penis: "O not so fast! my revished mistress cries, / Lest my content that on thy life relies, / Be brought too soon"; and (c) the "barren detested" vale where "nothing breeds" (*Titus Andronicus,* II.iii).

[32] Freud, "The Three Caskets," St. Ed. 12, p. 301.

[33] A lance in rest was in position for the charge. Thomas Dekker, *The Comedy of Old Fortunatus:* "set your heart at rest, for I have set up my rest . . . to get a young king or two . . . of you." He set up his rest to beget a child, as in *Romeo and Juliet,* IV.v: "Sleep for a week; for the next night . . . County Paris hath set up his rest / That you shall rest but little."

[34] Freud, *The Interpretation of Dreams,* St. Ed. 5, p. 341.

[35] Philip Edwards writes in *Sir Walter Raleigh* (London: Longman, Green, 1953), p. 52, that many courtly poets of Shakespeare's age wrote only for their own circles, which "provided an attentive audience with sensibility" like their own; and many of Shakespeare's plays were written for performance before the sophisticated audiences in The Inns of Court, the house of some nobleman, or the royal court.

[36] A persuasive argument against literary abridgement is that of Isaac Disraeli, *Amenities of Literature* (New York: W. J. Middleton, 1874), edited by his famous son Benjamin Disraeli: "Great writers admit of no abridgment. If you do not follow the writer through all the ramifications of his ideas . . . you can receive only interrupted impressions, and retain but an imperfect and mutilated image of his genius."

[37] A. P. Riemer, *Antic Fables* (New York: St. Martin's Press, 1980), pp. 223, 228.

[38] Freud, *op. cit.,* p. 444.

[39] Freud, *ibid.,* p. 435.

[40] Nick = breach and slit (vulva): Colman s.v. Nick, and Kökeritz, pp. 72, 131, 133.

[41] Partridge, s.v. Pleasure: "Th'incestuous pleasure of his bed," *Hamlet,* II.iii.

[42] Dance is an old euphemism for fornicate; see "the olde daunce" (Ross, s.v. Daunce); and Thomas Dekker, *The Honest Whore, Part 1:* the bawd "guard'st the dore / Whiles couples go dauncing."

[43] Skura, *op. cit.,* pp. 203-204.

[44] M. M. Mahood, *Shakespeare's Wordplay* (London: Metheun, 1979), p. 17.

Terrence N. Tice (essay date 1990)

SOURCE: "Calphurnia's Dream and Communication with the Audience in Shakespeare's *Julius Caesar,*" in *Shakespeare Yearbook,* Vol. 1, Spring, 1990, pp. 37-49.

[*In the following essay, Tice comments on the importance of Calphurnia's dream in* Julius Caesar, *especially as it is used to communicate the psychological state of depression to the viewing audience.*]

Shakespeare's 1599 play *The Tragedy of Julius Caesar,* though a mere year away from *Hamlet,* is only a bridge to the more deeply existential later plays; and, as such, it has won less thoroughgoing attention among recent critical scholars.[1] Yet, as Harold Bloom has recently stated, it is "a very satisfying play, as a play, and is universally regarded as a work of considerable aesthetic dignity."[2] Moreover, this drama bearing the name of the historical figure most often mentioned by Shakespeare, and about whose life circumstances the playwright showed sustained interest, continues to move audiences profoundly. Certainly it evokes strong feelings of recognition and concern during any time marked by high anxiety about the public's future, by revelations of self-justifying evil connivance among powerful men in whom the public has placed its trust, and by ambitious, prideful, incautious decisions on the part of leaders. These conditions would appear to be even more pronounced and worrisome for present-day audiences than for Shakespeare's own. Thus the play bears a special capacity to connect with contemporary moods encompassing failure, loss, hurt, or impending disaster.

I wish to use some remarks on the dream of Caesar's wife, Calphurnia, a dream portending his murder, in order ultimately to suggest an underlying depressive theme in the work and, along the way, to indicate where both merits and limits in psychoanalytic contributions to interpreting literature may be found. The focus is placed on communication of affect-laden awarenesses to the audience—first by the writer, then by subsequent directors and actors. Sometimes, I believe, this occurs by extraordinarily subtle means, even in a reputedly "simple" drama like *Julius Caesar;* often the awareness is absorbed unconsciously by the audience, and occasionally it appears to be purveyed unconsciously by the author or later surrogates.

Analysis of Dream Material in Shakespeare

Calphurnia's dream itself has attracted very little notice in the literature. The chief reasons are probably that its function as a portent has been thought to be self-evident—sufficient in itself—and that psychoanalytic interpretations of Shakespeare have tended to focus on Shakespeare and his characters rather than on other material that is to me more fully and legitimately analyzable: notably, relations between events in the plays and expectable audience responses. The latter I take to be an important, more nearly supportable function of such interpretation, which has often tended, without real warrant, to import schema normally suitable only for an extended analysis of a living person.[3] I have selected Calphurnia's dream precisely because extremely little is told of her, so that the interpreter must look almost exclusively at its actual manifest content and at plausible associations within the play as a whole.

Over the past three decades and more, three books have purported to emphasize dreams and visionary content in Shakespeare, and a search for articles has yielded only bits and pieces (e.g., Camden and Rubenstein). Only one, by Marjorie Garber, has dealt with dream in *Julius Caesar,* of necessity referring to Calphurnia's dream, though John Arthos also alludes to the dream and many others mention it in passing. Arthos winsomely interprets a poem and four plays, including

Calphurnia tells Caesar of her dream in Act II, Scene iii of Julius Caesar.

Julius Caesar, as conveying "metaphysical matters"—"the sense of realms of being across the threshold of the waking sight" (13, 9). Kay Stockholder cleverly offers a psychoanalytically informed interpretation of the plays, but not specifically treating *Julius Caesar,* as "dream works." In doing this she attempts to show "ways in which the most private passions depicted in Shakespeare's figures are shaped by and expressed in the most public conventions and ideological conflicts" (x).

Garber's 1974 chapter "Dream and Interpretation: *Julius Caesar*" aptly expounds the following thesis: "The play is full of omens and portents, augury and dream, and almost without exception these omens are misinterpreted. Calpurnia's [*sic*] dream, the dream of Cinna the poet, the advice of the augurers, all suggest one course of action and produce its opposite" (see, perhaps most conveniently, in Bloom 43).[4] Her statement is not quite accurate, in that such material, as she herself indicates, is used accurately to foretell disaster and its aftermath and in that the material itself does not "produce" the opposing actions, but *reactions to the material,* both deliberate (Decius Brutus) and unconsidered (Caesar), do.

The theme of misinterpretation is important nonetheless, though to my mind the varied, numerous interactions between interpretation and event are what loom large throughout; the chief transactions of play and audience follow. As Garber herself contends: "More and more it becomes evident [in the play] that signs and dreams are morally neutral elements, incapable of effect without interpretation. By structuring his play around them, Shakespeare invites us to scrutinize the men who read the signs—to witness the tragedy of misconstruction" (Bloom 47). As she points out, this is "the last of his plays to use dreams and omens primarily as devices of plot" (Bloom 52), whereas in the later plays the movement is to dream as a universalizing, transcendent state of mind, which ultimately serves powerfully in metamorphosis of the self through imaginative effort. Thus it is of value to see exactly how Shakespeare carries out this earlier use.

Calphurnia's Dream

By the second scene of Act Two, plans, omens, and portents of Caesar's impending death have already built up to a high pitch, but so far his household has not been touched by them. As the scene opens Caesar reports:

> Nor heaven nor earth have been at peace to-
> night:
> Thrice hath Calphurnia in her sleep cried out,
> "Help, ho! They murther Caesar!"
>
> (2.2.1-3)

Calphurnia enters, and in pleading for him to stay home speaks of signs that should deter him; he at first resists, then relents. She says to him:

> Caesar, I never stood on ceremonies,
> Yet now they fright me. There is one within,
> Besides the things that we have heard and seen,
> Recounts most horrid sights seen by the watch.
> A lioness hath whelped in the streets,
> And graves have yawn'd and yielded up their
> dead;
> Fierce fiery warriors fight upon the clouds
> In ranks and squadrons and right form of war,
> Which drizzled blood upon the Capitol;
> The noise of battle hurtled in the air,
> Horses did neigh, and dying men did groan,
> And ghosts did shriek and squeal about the
> streets.[5]
> O Caesar, these things are beyond all use,
> And I do fear them.
>
> . . . . .
>
> When beggars die, there are no comets seen;
> The heavens themselves blaze forth the death
> of princes.
>
> (2.2.13-26, 30-1)

Then comes a discussion with Decius Brutus, wherein Caesar lays out the dream Calphurnia has related to him, but Decius offers a flattering counterinterpretation and Caesar decides to go forth to the Capitol after all. This is the dream itself, as Caesar gives it:

> She dreamt to-night she saw my statue,
> Which like a fountain with an hundred spouts
> Did run pure blood; and many lusty Romans
> Came smiling, and did bathe their hands in it.
> And these does she apply for warnings and
> portents
> And evils imminent; and on her knee
> Hath begg'd that I will stay at home to-day.
>
> (2.2.76-82)

Such is the dream and its setting in the play, which embellishes greatly on the report by Plutarch though following his outline of events: the sleep-talking and a dream, both portending Caesar's death, Caesar's fear and indecision, his consulting augurers, and Decius' fateful influence. In Plutarch she was simply reported to have "dreamed Caesar was slain and that she had him in her arms" and, regarding a pinnacle that the Senate had placed on the top of Caesar's house, that "she saw it broken down." Decius there advises Caesar to make only a brief appearance to salute the Senate "and return again when Calpurnia should have better dreams." The rest, including the recital of signs, is all masterfully Shakespeare's.

Interpretation of Calphurnia and her Dream

Calphurnia, Cato's daughter, was Caesar's fourth wife, probably younger than Caesar, who was then fifty-six. She had borne no child, and Caesar's only legitimate child, Julia, whom he had given to the great Pompey in marriage, had died. All that we learn of her earlier in the play, however, is that Caesar has humiliated her by asking Antonius to "touch" her in the Lupercalian race (to strike her with white leather thongs carried by the naked runners, explains Plutarch), in order to rid her of her "sterile curse," as was the custom (1.2). This is the same occasion wherein Caesar thrice refuses the laurel crown that the runner Antonius would place on his head, to indicate his kingly status. Brutus reports that Caesar is angry and "Calphurnia's cheek is pale" (1.2.183).

Apart from Zelda Teplitz's unpublished paper presented at the 1972 annual meeting of the American Psychoanalytic Association, Garber's 1974 chapter employs Calphurnia's dream more fully than any study I have encountered (see in Bloom 48-51). This is what she does. She regards the dream as a crux of the play; it is a portent, among others, of unnatural events, "an apocalypse of sorts, the last judgment of Rome." Calphurnia has been established as an accurate and lyrical prophetess. As is the case in other Shakespearean dreams, hers makes the dead man into a statue, and she views the spouting of blood as death. The ambiguity in her dream enables the irony that Decius' interpretation, "that from you great Rome shall suck / Reviving blood," is "as true in its way as Calpurnia's." Its significance lies not only in its functional role of furthering the action but also in that it "symbolically foreshadows events to come, supporting the theme of 'all amiss interpreted' which is central to the play's meaning." However, Garber finds the later scene of Cinna the poet, who also has a portentous dream, "the most symbolically instructive of the whole play," for he has the premonition but chooses to disregard it, and when he goes out he meets a bad end simply through a playing with his name (like Caesar, the private and public name). Thereby "the whole myth of the play is concisely expressed."

In contrast, I do not believe that this highly complex play can be reduced to a single myth, though Garber's reading of the scenes involving Calphurnia and Cinna seems entirely accurate and helpful short of that claim. Although a great many associations to Calphurnia's dream and to the other signs she indicates can be made throughout the play, alongside those by Casca, Cinna, and others, I shall restrict myself to a few additional features of special importance.

First, partly through her earlier, 1958 work on sleep-talking, Teplitz was able to discern what hidden hostility the barren Calphurnia might have felt toward Caesar, who sports aspirations to supremely royal status, wishes for a blood heir, and has humiliated her publicly. That is, her active sleep-talking would replace more passive fears regarding hostile, murderous impulses toward her husband. In possible support, one might add that Plutarch, though he does not mention Calphurnia among the noble women to be touched, tells of Calphurnia's dreaming that she held the slain Caesar "in her arms" (perhaps at once wife, mother, and fantasied murderer?). This detail Shakespeare omits, but it could well have influenced him. The possible feature is plausible, given the action of the play, but it is only weakly supportable.

Second, it would also be relevant to expand on the following: on the association Shakespeare (but not Plutarch) has her give of a lioness reported to have "whelped in the streets," one of the "horrid sights seen by the watch"; on the lion Casca describes as glaring at him on the Capitol, where Caesar would be murdered, but passing by without harming him (in Shakespeare's day lions were a tourist attraction at the Tower of London, an edifice it was said Julius Caesar had bestowed); and on Caesar's symbolic description of himself as a twin lion "littered in one day" with danger yet danger's master. These and the numerous other interlocking images of augury and fury to be found in the play intensify the sense of frightening danger that

often accompanies murderous or ambitious feelings. So do the conflicts that Caesar experiences over his decision to go to the Capitol. Decius the flatterer—similar to those who served the childless, aging Queen Elizabeth, who was in 1599 over sixty-five years old—tries to smooth it all over with a "vision fair and fortunate" of the living king from whom Rome shall draw revitalizing substance. Caesar had been sufficiently affected by his wife's dream and the servant's report from the augurers to think that he would play it safe and stay home. Were it not for his regard for Decius, he could scarcely have admitted this to him as the occasion for his decision. However, Caesar claims to make the decision, either way, as an expression of his own sovereign will. Thus he blunders into disaster just as those closest to him (Decius, Brutus, perhaps Calphurnia as well) secretly or openly desire him to. Of such human frailties—his and theirs—is tragedy made.

Third, strictly speaking, Decius' interpretation of the dream denies and obscures the bloody criminal result of Caesar's decision, both for him and for his assassins. Decius largely fails to perceive the revengeful quality of Caesar's ensuing immortality. Robed in flattery, Decius' interpretation accentuates the problems that Caesar's immense ambition, popularity, and pretentiousness are seen to create for virtually everyone in the dream: Caesar's conspiring rivals, his wife, his alarmed friends, and later on even Cinna the poet, the innocent bystander. Were the play's structure not so wonderfully complicated—every image and relationship that emerges creating ripple effects throughout the remaining scenes—it might even be appropriate to suggest that Decius' interpretation bespeaks the earlier conspiracy scenes and that Calphurnia's interpretation foreshadows the scenes that follow. However, it does not appear that Shakespeare really prepares us for the literally mortifying ironic immortality of Caesar's spirit by either interpretation: for the agonizing outburst of short-lived triumph and sudden revenge, or for the ghostly, inexorable presence of Caesar even beyond the play's end. Calphurnia's dream and her attendant anxieties have such a powerful effect precisely because they reveal the terribly confused, uncertain consequences of letting Caesar have his way—consequences nonetheless so intractable that even his wished-for death cannot halt their influence.

Fourth, unquestionably Shakespeare used Calphurnia's dream and its interpretations to deepen the integration of the play. The second scene of Act Two is especially well placed for that effect. However, he used other structural devices as well: (1) an unparalleled close description of vitality (the exciting, never gruesome or disgusting talk of blood; fire; eating, drinking, waking from sleep, the brother of death; spirit effort; even the details of peoples' clothing and faces)—of vitality versus disorder, sickness, and infirmity;[6] (2) cold-blooded resolve versus sympathizing tears; (3) the favorite Elizabethan conflict of immortal spirituality, nobility, and reason with unruly passion and the attendant consequences of self-deception and misjudgment; (4) a continuous mixture of mythic savagery and ceremony, of emplacement and displacement; (5) the long shadow of Pompey, himself never present but constantly alluded to; (6) men's proud, twisted construing of events versus the surprising, promiscuous determination of destiny by the events themselves; (7) a series of exciting, explosive encounters; (8) the cumulative contrasts between public and private life, between stoic invulnerability and the outbreak of emotion, between willful detachment and forced involvement, as well as the monstrous exploitation of friendship for imagined honor or glory; (9) the redistribution of the dominating personalities and their conflicts from act to act; (10) the orations of Brutus and Antony; and (11) the continuing dread disturbances of the night. All but a couple of these devices are spread throughout the play, eliciting a direct emotive response from the audience. It is striking to notice how raw and elemental, how full of what Freud called *primary process* most of this material is, as is true in the dream. In this sense, there is a distinct dream quality about most of the play, so that Calphurnia's actual dream fits right in place.

Fifth, I have already referred to the theme of blood, which also serves as a powerful connection between Calphurnia's discourse and the rest of the play—not least to the self-bloodletting of Portia, the wife of that other powerful man, Brutus, whose presence dominates much of the play. In his 1951 study *The Imperial Theme* G. Wilson Knight makes much of the blood imagery and of this general connection (45-51). As he points out, the loss of Caesar's blood is a costly business, the loss of a noble, vital, spiritual force. In the end, however, Caesar bleeds to death, but his spirit lives on to haunt and inspire. More is to be said about this blood. For one thing, David Shelley Berkeley has surveyed the characteristics and means of diminishing high, noble, superior blood in Shakespeare's work and in other related English literature. "Shakespeare's plays suggest with few exceptions," he summarizes, "that the poet especially desiderated the potentialities inherent in the bright red, hot, thin, fast-flowing, sweet-tasting blood of divinely sanctioned kings, and rated every departure from this blood, by the extent of its divergence, as a diminution in human quality" (14). Likewise, in his plays no gentle person is ever said to smell (52). Berkeley comments further:

> Julius Caesar in Shakespeare's play, although not a king because of Rome's republican traditions, is physiologically fit to occupy this exalted place because, although old enough to be Brutus' father and therefore supposedly possessed of little blood, he bleeds so much at his stabbing that the conspirators bathe their hands in his blood . . ."up to the elbows." Moreover, Calphurnia's dream of Caesar's statue,

> "Which like a fountain with a hundred spouts / Did run pure blood, and many lusty Romans / Came smiling and did bathe their hands in it" . . . , implies by its strong emphasis on abundant, flowing blood, rendered even more prominent by Decius' interpretation, that Caesar is physiologically legitimate (and therefore naturally legitimate) to be king or ruler of Rome. The conspirators are ill advised to tamper with the primate of nature. (87)

Another sign of high blood, Berkeley notes, is the ability to experience heartbreak, like Lear:

> In *Julius Caesar,* Antony tells the mob that Caesar, who had lost much blood from his several wounds in the Forum, yet possessed enough blood to "burst his mighty heart" (3.2.186) if grief at the sight of Brutus among his murderers had not overcome him. The implications is that Caesar's age is no bar or hindrance to his being worthy of being ruler of Rome, crown or no crown, because he has the cachet of being able to experience heartbreak in the autumn of his life. (88-9)

This information from Berkeley's study is the kind that enables accurate reconstruction and an understanding of what an original audience was likely to have in mind. Less successful in this respect, though highly suggestive nonetheless, is Gail Kern Paster's attempt to equate the then-supposed demeaning, grotesque, unstoppable menstrual flow and lactation with Caesar's blood and thus his planned feminization and diminution as a person. These characteristics of the blood could possibly be listed among the many determinants of meaning by play's end. They by no means comprise all, or, by all evidence, even set the main point. The blood in this play is variously feminine and masculine, ordinary and regal; above all, it is exciting, vital, plenteous in its outflow toward death and life, and even ritually redeeming. All these latter qualities, save the very last, Shakespeare has the anxious Calphurnia announce.

Finally, we must ask why Calphurnia, a woman, should serve these functions? Juliet Dusinberre emphasizes that despite Shakespeare's inherited skepticism about women in view of his society's notion of women as a separate, inferior species, he took the best of the Calvinistic Puritanism of his time and tended to see them as equal with men. Thus, for him both men and women express "an infinite variety of union between opposing influences" (308). In this perspective, she reports, he was at one with the general trend in drama within the 1590-1625 period, "feminist in sympathy" and treating women as individuals (5). Juliet Cook, in seeming agreement, emphasizes the striking "independence" of Shakespeare's women and (for his time) the unmatched variety of roles he gave them. In the historical plays they have "very subordinate roles," however; and in the Roman plays, drawing from Plutarch, Shakespeare makes all of them relatively insignificant and powerless compared to the men—in short, they are typical Roman wives (all but Volumnia). Calphurnia and Portia are "classic vignettes of the Roman wife," though in Calphurnia Shakespeare emphasizes women's "intuition and even foreknowledge of events" (64-5). In a study of gender in Shakespeare's writings, Linda Bamber adds still another feature: "In the comedies Shakespeare seems if not a feminist then at least a man who takes the woman's part. Often the women in the comedies are more brilliant than the men, more aware of themselves and their world, saner, livelier, more gay. In the tragedies, however, Shakespeare creates such nightmare female figures as Goneril, Regan, Lady Macbeth, and Volumnia" (2). R. S. White points to other female characters as "innocent victims." Understandably missing from each contrasting treatment of female figures is the middling but focal figure of Calphurnia.

Perhaps the most secure answer to our question—why Calphurnia, a woman, serves these functions—is threefold. (1) Plutarch has her there. (2) Shakespeare had been developing an interest, as Caesar is made to do, though less trustingly, in the intuitive aspect of things, represented in his mind especially by women. (3) The audience was sufficiently varied and open to sympathetic portrayals of women's contributions for him to make at least this slight venture. All these statements are, in any case, quite true. In *Julius Caesar,* moreover, neither Calphurnia nor Portia is a nightmarish figure, but as wives of powerful men they are indeed set in the midst of nightmarish events.

The major thrust of this play, dealing as it does with the conflicting mortality/immortality of Caesar, is patently a deliberate design of its author, enriched not by one but by many unconscious meanings. These often ambiguous meanings the action of the play partly nudges into consciousness. These meanings, along with what remains unconscious but is nonetheless communicated, become the audience's possession however they may have arisen for Shakespeare, however Shakespeare may have imagined them to arise for his characters, or however they may have emerged for the historical figures themselves.

As a philosopher greatly interested in the arts and in educative impacts of aesthetic means, I feel that the major contribution that psychoanalytically oriented criticism can make to the interpretation of art is to focus not so much on the artist or on the artist's characters as on the ground for vital communication between artist and audience.[7] As with an actual psychoanalysis, one wants to keep as close to the current derivatives of the more deeply lodged material of experience as possible. One must hover over the material listening for unconscious themes, not jumping too quickly to an ad hoc interpretation of symbols and actions. One must expect the material to be multiply determined, thus subject to several layers or facets of interpretation. Thus, interpretation can arise variously and afresh with each new generation because the grounds of communication, continuously opened up though also limited by the actual material of the art work, are ever shifting with changes in experience.

In closing, I should like to point out something else that, to my knowledge, no interpreter has yet indicated in psychoanalytic terms. I refer to the overwhelming depressive, sometimes alternatively manic mood that pervades most of this play—precisely in all the details that Edith Jacobson brilliantly outlines in her 1971 papers on moods and depression. According to Jacobson, a depressive mood necessarily involves aggressive conflict. This becomes amalgamated with an experience of loss or failure or the like and may persist through various narcissistic identifications. Moods tend to flood ego functioning. They are a "barometer of the ego state," displaying detachment from specific object cathexes and effecting blanket appraisals of self and object representations (notably alternating dependence on an idealized love-object and pseudo-independence of superego functioning). They may express themselves in words and actions as well as in affects. Now in a more general sense, as Charles Brenner has more recently indicated, the more depressive and the more anxious side of our affects are temporally two sides of the same coin, the one tending to point back and the other to point forward; furthermore, the two qualities of affect as they emerge within a mind in conflict may be closely associated and are probably never wholly isolated from each other.

It is this general feature of the affective quality in *our* experience that enables us as audience to apprehend representations of depression and anxiety in art, not only their occasional existence as moods. In *Julius Caesar* we see the characters under a cloud of depression interspersed with elation. As the pivotal second scene of Act Two opens, Shakespeare has Caesar himself depict the all-encompassing mood by crying: "Nor heaven nor earth have been at peace to-night." Caesar himself does not seem to experience much of a sense of failure or loss or hurt or disaster, though the aggressive, strutting, expansive qualities of his conflicts are obvious enough, but we the audience are made to feel this both through the other characters and through the very setting of Shakespeare's play. What is communicated above all, as has been only partly indicated in the themes outlined in this essay, is a set of moods and their underlying, largely hidden conflicts.

Notes

[1] The occasion for an early version of this essay was a paper on Calphurnia's dream by Zelda Teplitz, a psychoanalyst and devoted Shakespeare scholar, at the American Psychoanalytic Association annual meeting

in New York, December 1, 1972. I was then a candidate at the Michigan Psychoanalytic Institute and offered some extended comments. To my knowledge, her paper remains unpublished. I am grateful for the stimulus of her work, though I must take responsibility for my own, rather different, ideas. As a philosopher-historian who works especially with educators and planners, my critical interest in the possibilities and limits of psychoanalytic interpretation has continued to grow in the intervening years. This essay is intended to serve as a brief indicator of what I have learned. In immediately practical terms, I hope that the findings presented here may be of particular help to secondary school teachers, since *Julius Caesar* is in the curriculum of almost every high school in America, as frequently elsewhere, and does contain elements of special appeal to adolescents.

2 Harold Bloom, *William Shakespeare's* Julius Caesar, 1. Bloom here collects nine of the best among studies on the play from 1969 to 1985. In 1951 Harold C. Goddard had already depicted the play as Shakespeare's "bridge" to the later tragedies, explaining this in these terms: "From *Julius Caesar* on, his greater characters and greater plays are touched with the dream-light and dream-darkness of something that as certainly transcends the merely human as do the prophets and sibyls of Michelangelo" (308). Of unusual breadth among earlier psychoanalytic essays treating of the play is a 1966 study by Andrew Wilkinson in which he pays comparatively greater notice to Calphurnia than usual but not so much in psychoanalytic terms.

3 In his 1966 *Psychoanalysis and Shakespeare* and later works Norman N. Holland has taken a position close to mine, except that he prefers to use psychoanalysis on our own reactions as readers or audience. I believe that it can also serve purposes of historical reconstruction and in detail, subject both to rigorous canons of evidence and to provisos, recently emphasized by Marjorie Garber, having to do with the "uncanny," multi-determined, in-varying-degrees-lost origins of authorship. Also compare Holland's *The Shakespearean Imagination,* wherein Chapter 8 is on *Julius Caesar.*

4 For convenience, page references are to Garber's chapter included in Bloom, as probably the more accessible source. Her entire work, however, is of one piece and is an outstanding account of the changing nature and function of dreams in Shakespeare's writings.

5 Compare these lines from *Hamlet,* a year later: "In the most high and palmy state of Rome, / A little ere the mightiest Julius fell, / The graves stood tenantless, and the sheeted dead / Did squeak and gibber in the Roman streets" (1.1.113-6).

6 G. Wilson Knight, who had a great eye for metaphoric detail, notes that "nearly everyone in the play is ill" (40).

7 For example, though not resorting to psychoanalytic tools, Phyllis Rackin offers a substantial analysis of "The Role of the Audience in Shakespeare's *Richard II,*" *Shakespeare Quarterly* 36 (1985): 262-81.

Works Cited

Arthos, John. *Shakespeare's Use of Dream and Vision.* Totowa, N.J.: Rowman and Littlefield, 1977.

Bamber, Linda. *Comic Women, Tragic Men: A Study of Gender and Genre in Shakespeare.* Stanford: Stanford UP, 1982.

Berkeley, David Shelley. *Blood Will Tell in Shakespeare's Plays.* Graduate Studies, No. 28. Lubbock: Texas Tech University, 1984.

Bloom, Harold, ed. *William Shakespeare's* Julius Caesar. New York: Chelsea House, 1988.

Brenner, Charles. *The Mind in Conflict.* New York: International Universities P, 1982.

Camden, Carroll, Jr. "Shakespeare on Sleep and Dreams." *Rice Institute Pamphlet* 23 (1936): 106-33.

Cook, Judith. *Women in Shakespeare.* London: Harrap, 1980.

Dusinberre, Juliet. *Shakespeare and the Nature of Women.* London: Macmillan, 1975.

Garber, Marjorie B. *Dream in Shakespeare: From Metaphor to Metamorphosis.* New Haven: Yale UP, 1974.

———. *Shakespeare's Ghost Writers: Literature as Uncanny Causality.* London: Methuen, 1987.

Goddard, Harold C. *The Meaning of Shakespeare.* Chicago: U of Chicago P, 1951.

Green, David C. Julius Caesar *and Its Source.* Salzburg: Institut für Anglistik und Amerikanistik, Universität Salzburg, 1979.

Holland, Norman N. *Psychoanalysis and Shakespeare.* New York: McGraw-Hill, 1966.

———. *The Shakespearean Imagination.* New York: Macmillan, 1964.

Jacobson, Edith. *Depression: Comparative Studies of Normal, Neurotic, and Psychotic Conditions.* New York: International Universities P, 1971.

Knight, G. Wilson. *The Imperial Theme: Further Interpretations of Shakespeare's Tragedies Including the Roman Plays.* London: Methuen, 1951.

Paster, Gail Kern. "'In the spirit of men there is no blood': Blood as Trope of Gender in *Julius Caesar.*" *Shakespeare Quarterly* 40 (1989): 284-98.

Rubinstein, Frankie. "Shakespeare's Dream-Stuff: A Forerunner of Freud's 'Dream Material'." *American Imago: A Psychoanalytic Journal for Culture, Science, and the Arts* 43 (1986): 335-55. [The subject matter is similar to that in the author's book, *A Dictionary of Shakespeare's Sexual Puns and Their Significance* (London: Macmillan, 1984), not on dreams in the plays.]

Shakespeare, William. *Julius Caesar,* The Arden Edition, 6th edn., ed. T. S. Dorsch. London: Methuen, 1955. [Compare this volume in *The Oxford Shakespeare:* Julius Caesar, ed. Arthur Humphreys (Oxford: Oxford UP, 1984).]

Stockholder, Kay. *Dream Works: Lovers and Families in Shakespeare's Plays.* Toronto: U of Toronto P, 1987.

Teplitz, Zelda. "The Ego and Motility in Sleepwalking." *Journal of the American Psychoanalytic Association* 6 (1958): 95-110.

White, R. S. *Innocent Victims: Poetic Injustice in Shakespearean Tragedy.* Rev. edn. London: Athlone P, 1983.

Wilkinson, Andrew M. "A Psychological Approach to Julius Caesar." *Review of English Literature* 7 (1966): 66-78. [Rpt. in Melvin D. Faber, *The Design Within: Psychoanalytic Approaches to Shakespeare* (New York: Science House, 1970), 63-78.]

Kay Stockholder (essay date 1991)

SOURCE: "Dreaming of Death: Love and Money in *The Merchant of Venice,*" in *The Dream and the Text: Essays on Literature and Language,* edited by Carol Schreier Rupprecht, State University of New York Press, 1993, pp. 133-56.

[*In the following essay, originally written in 1991, Stockholder reads* The Merchant of Venice *as the dream of Portia's dead father in order to unravel the play's psychological and social concerns with wealth and sexual desire.*]

Psychoanalytic criticism over the years has generated a refined understanding of the ways literature renders the complex, dynamic organization of human emotion. However, there are two persistent grounds on which most forms of psychoanalytic literary practice have been censured. The first is that they detach literary portrayals of human complexities from the social and political institutions, conscious values, and cognitive systems in which literature embeds them. In concentrating on a presumed latent content, psychoanalytic criticism tends to ignore the interaction between the unconscious emotions and ideas, those that would derive from the past of persons like those represented, and the present world they are depicted as confronting. By limiting meaningfulness to unconscious motivations, this critical approach depreciates representations of social reality, consciousness, and cognition. The second charge against psychoanalytic criticism is that it fails to account for the formal characteristics and aesthetic dimensions of literature. This omission generates criticism that reduces literature to authorial biography, or to characters' case histories; to projecting screens for its audiences' predilections, or to sets of rhetorical manipulations of its readers.[1]

The mode of criticism that this chapter will bring to bear on *The Merchant of Venice* includes these otherwise excluded dimensions by taking the protagonist as the dreamer of his play.[2] To regard the entire configuration of the drama as the protagonist's dream renders significant all that he confronts as external to himself, and reads the genre form itself as expressive of the dreamer's habitual stance towards his or her emotional life. He is analogous not to us dreaming, but rather to the figure in our dreams that we identify as ourselves when we awaken. As well, the play's conclusion reveals the desire implicit in its beginning, and provides thereby the psychological concomitant to the sense of inevitability that contributes to the aesthetic force of fiction. The play's formal properties, the discourse in which the story is articulated, express the modes by which the protagonist mediates between the demands of unacknowledged desires that shape what he confronts as an external world, and his consciously espoused values. This approach makes appropriate some Lacanian and semiotic vocabulary, that is, to trace the ways in which various aspects of the text, including what one normally thinks of as characters, function as a chain of interlocking signifiers. However, unlike Lacanian approaches it centers the work in subjective human experience. Seeing each component as a signifier that collects the affect of multiple signifieds allows one to trace the changing ways in which aspects of works that are generally the focus of psychoanalytic study are linked to, or signify, the dominant ideas that constitute the social and cultural nexus of the worlds that produce them. The entire work becomes a picture of the protagonist's strategy of signification as he negotiates between the demands of unconscious drives, his conscious value systems, and what he experiences as his external worlds. The work becomes a chain of the protagonist's associations that reveals the way his self-experience is interconnected to the structure of signification that constitutes his culture (Silverman 1983). Therefore, to regard the play as the protagonist's dream keeps us closer to and takes more account of the play's surface than does a conventional psychoanalytic account. It addresses the formal patterns of action without losing sight of an experiencing human conscious-ness within them. By attending to the relationships between conscious and unconscious states, rather than regarding the products of consciousness as clues to what they conceal, one can ascertain some possible emotional correlates of lives shaped within a historical reality other than one's own.

While in principle one can regard any figure as the protagonist of the play, to choose a figure at the pe-riphery of the action is to read the play as the dream of one who defines himself as observer rather than as participant in her or his world. In tragic or serious literature things fall into place more simply by choos-ing a figure who is at the play's emotional center, so that the choice of whom to regard as protagonist is relatively straightforward. It is, however, the nature of comedy to obscure its emotional center, and to substi-tute plot for feeling in a way that renders comedy, viewed in this way, as revelatory of more deeply re-pressed material than is tragedy. That is, while watch-ing a tragedy we are more engaged in the action as it affects the central characters than for its own sake, while the reverse is so for comedy. Therefore, in com-edy one often more deftly penetrates the play's emo-tional center by attending to whomever or whatever functions as the moving force of the plot, however obscure the figure may seem, rather than by focusing on the most emotionally heightened figure. In *The Merchant of Venice,* the central focus of this chapter, all the action stems from Portia's dead father. He ar-ranges his daughter's marriage, and sets in motion all that flows from it. Therefore I will regard this shadowy figure as the dreamer of the play.

This choice is more heuristic than substantive. That is, one could select any of the characters, Shylock, Anto-nio, Portia, Bassanio, or even Lorenzo. Ultimately one would be telling the same story from different perspec-tives; for each figure the others would signify repudi-ated aspects of his or her emotional configuration. For example, if one chose Portia as dreamer, the dead but still influential father would reveal her ambivalence about the paternal authority that she contests in assum-ing power over the other male figures. Her psychologi-cal drama would be the mirror image of her father's, whose ambivalence about male authority is manifested in his retreat from it and in his substitution of Portia for himself (see note 11, p. 154). However, designat-ing the Father as dreamer draws one in more imme-diately to the male psychodynamic that generates the play and choosing him rather than one of the other male figures highlights the significance of the plot line that derives from his initial retreat. All the action flows from his move to control his daughter's mar-riage and the transmission of his wealth.

Therefore to think about the play as the Father's dream relates the central concerns with wealth and money,

which shape the figures and actions he defines as ex-ternal and separate from himself, to the psychological significance of the emotionally heightened aspects that more readily suggest psychodynamic meanings. To bring Portia's father from the obscurity of his grave is to locate in a subject what otherwise appear as textual gaps and breaks, and to read them as links in a semiotic chain that is bounded within the single text. In this way one can penetrate most efficaciously what one might call the play's social psychology, or its political unconscious, in relationship to the more usual con-cerns of psychoanalytic criticism.

To foreground this occulted figure casts light on oth-erwise obscure links between this play and others, some of which I will indicate in the process of the argument that follows. As the attributes of characters combine and recombine into a variety of figures in other plays, Shakespeare adopts different strategies to harmonize the conflicts that in his world inhere in romantic mar-riage. These links suggest that the concern with money that is so obvious in this play has submerged impor-tance in other plays by Shakespeare, and that the con-flicting ideologies of this play were not resolved, but rather were submerged in his later work. However, to move in this way from a textual to an intertextual frame, and to relate the experience of one protagonist to that of another, one clearly must consider Shake-speare to be the dreamer, and the various protagonists as avatars of one who casts himself as an invisible observer to his own vast dream.

To think about Shakespeare as the dreamer does not imply that the plays, like dreams, took shape without conscious intention and craft. Rather, to do so assumes that in addition to conscious decisions about what kind of play to write and what ideas it was to incorporate, an intuitive sense of what was fitting guided Shake-speare in making the myriad of choices from the ways his world made it possible for him to accomplish his goals.[3] Such intuitive choices, ranging from the largest components, such as genre, convention, and dramatis personae, to the smallest details of language, draw on the psychic forces that shape dreams out of the con-tents of our waking lives. In order to elucidate these links between personal psychology and public ideol-ogy, the last part of this chapter will place in their historical context the interrelated concerns with mar-riage and money that emerge from this study.

Considering Portia's father as the dreamer renders *The Merchant of Venice* like a dream of one for whom only such a radically self-denying strategy as dying could provide a compromise between contradictory ideas and desires. His having dreamt himself dead suggests self-hatred and condemnation so intense that he cannot live with himself. Having thus avoided the challenge to become conscious of his psychic drama, he idealizes himself as a beneficent magical power reaching into the world from beyond the grave. He reveals Portia's centrality to the conflicted emotions from which he retreated by the central role he assigns her. His desires pull in two contrary directions. On the one hand, his desire that she join him in the grave to which he has retreated appears in the world-weariness of her opening words, "By my troth, Nerissa, my little body is aweary of this great world" (I.ii.1-2). She makes a more oblique but more trenchant connection between death and marriage, or death and sexuality, when she says that she would "rather be married to a death's-head with a bone in his mouth" than to her suitors. This grotesque image adds a sexual dimension to Portia's world-weariness, which indicates that the Father has initiated, but not completed, a version of a love-death romance such as is suggested when Lear wants to "crawl towards death" while living with Cordelia, and is explicit in *Pericles* between Antiochus and his daughter. The Father's concentration on Portia's marriage reveals not only his denied incestuous desires; the fact that his sexuality is expressed through incest connotes his association of sexuality in general with the debasement of family affection, violation, evil, and death. This last association is made through his own dream death, as well as in the risk of death incurred by those who seek Portia's hand.[4] This aspect of his mentality remains submerged, but it is the opposite side to the idealization of Portia, who, once married, becomes the Father's surrogate magical agent to preside over Belmont, which functions as a Neoplatonic alternative to the commercial Venice.

While Portia's language manifests the Father's pull on her, his revulsion from his own desires forces a compromise formation in which he substitutes for his forbidden erotic desires control over her marriage choice and the disposition of his wealth. The tension between these contrary pulls appears in Portia's lament that she "may neither choose whom I would nor refuse whom I dislike; so is the will of a living daughter curbed by the will of a dead father" (I.ii.25-7).[5] The Father justifies his hold on her by defining himself as a benign magus whose power will serve her interests when Nerissa says that only one "who you shall rightly love" (I.i.36) will choose the right casket. By thus idealizing himself as a benign magical force, as Prospero more overtly does later, the Father achieves a sleight-of-hand reconciliation between his craving for control, which functions as a devious expression of and substitute for sexual desire, and a romantic conception of marriage. That is, Portia's father cannot forgo his paternal dominion, which is energized by his denied sexual desire; but he cannot assert it explicitly because his ideology of marriage incorporates romantic love. He exonerates himself by defining his control as a magical emanation from the grave that serves not only Portia's best interests, but also her desires. By these means the Father achieves a trickster's reconciliation of the usually mutually exclusive desires both to control his daughter's will and have her marry for love.

However, marriage based on romantic love conflicts not only with the Father's erotic claims; it conflicts as well with the function of marriage as a means of ensuring the transmission of wealth. The pivotal place of wealth in the Father's psyche first appears when Nerissa rebukes Portia for failing to appreciate the abundance of her fortunes (II.i.4-5). It is inscribed more deeply in the casket device that inaugurates the play's major action. Here the Father expresses both his espoused ideal of romantic marriage uncontaminated by material concerns and his sense of the danger of such contamination. The underlying equation of love and money appears in the elaborate denial of the casket device, which associates Portia with valueless lead and gold with "carrion death." In this configuration the Father radically separates love and marriage from money and wealth, but reveals the hidden links by associating Portia with the golden fleece. On the one hand that image presages Portia's function as representative of spiritual gold, but the denied material desires condition the plot in which Portia is a material golden fleece for Bassanio. Bassanio's need for money in order to achieve status and wealth and Antonio's presumed indifference to the money he has acquired from commerce (that is, from buying cheap and selling dear) show the opposed levels of material concerns sliding into and representing each other. The sleight of hand by which the Father reconciles the competing claims of romance and the transmission of inheritance reveals not only his erotically charged concentration on controlling his wealth, but also the self-hatred occasioned by desires that would destroy his self-image should he espouse them. The only compromise he has found for these convoluted desires has been to retreat into death while designing a fairy-tale world to perpetuate images of himself that defend him from self-hatred and self-condemnation.

As we will see later, the Father's psychological dilemma has its roots in the consequences of a romantic ideology of marriage. While marriage was conceived primarily as a financial arrangement between families, a father of daughters was required to part with some of his wealth for their dowries, but he could substitute for forbidden erotic desires an intense connection to a daughter through controlling her will. If a daughter is to marry for love, then her father loses the compensatory satisfaction of control. As Cordelia later puts it, not only will she give her husband half her heart; her love rather than only her father's choice will determine the destination of the dowry. Portia's father, however, has not only accepted romantic marriage, but spiritualized it. Having rendered it symbolic of transcendent, as opposed to material, gold, he must drive his material concerns into his unconscious where they join the guilt and shame associated with forbidden incestuous desires. Having thus fused love and wealth, the Father becomes an aristocratic version of Shylock's confusion of daughters with ducats.[6]

The emotional strife between desires and the values that render them guilty shapes the two paternal surrogates into which he splits himself, Antonio and Shylock, each of whom becomes the other's alter ego. The self-image generated by his denied desires generates Shylock, the Jew denied by society. His possessiveness of Portia appears as Shylock's of Jessica, while his shame for conflating Portia with wealth appears in Shylock's explicit equation of the two—"My daughter, my ducats." In caricaturing Shylock's ugliness and grasping possessiveness, the Father portrays his repressed self-image and the concomitant self-loathing that forced him to repudiate his desires. Though the Father foregrounds Shylock's hatred of Antonio and his love of money, it is Jessica's elopement with Lorenzo that triggers the climactic action. The play obscures whether it was in jest only that Shylock made the bond with Antonio, but it is certainly only after Jessica's marriage that the jest turns to earnest. The linked sexual and monetary components of Shylock's claim on Jessica also appear when Shylock laments that she has stolen her mother's jewels, in effect stealing the dowry that the court later forces him to give her. This configuration reveals the Father's fears that unless he retains extraordinary powers, his daughter's free choice of a husband will wrest his wealth from him and debase his family.

In a self-splitting more radical than that of King Lear, who victimizes Cordelia while victimizing himself to Goneril and Regan, in the despised Shylock the Father embodies his fierce possessiveness of both daughters and ducats, and in the melancholy Antonio he expresses his grief and drift toward death. This is the emotional consequence of having repressed both his erotic and monetary passions. He also embodies in Antonio a short-circuited quest for a homoerotic alternative to his embattled heterosexuality. However, he associates homoeroticism with a depletion of life energies that is expressed in the loss of money. Antonio betrays the same associations of love with wealth that are expressed in the casket motif. Just as the motif betrays the equation of love with money that it is intended to conceal, so do Antonio's answers to his fellow merchants when they ask why he is melancholy. To their suggestion that he is melancholy because he cannot cool his soup or go to church without bringing to mind the rocks upon which the winds might drive his ships, Antonio denies that all his wealth is at hazard. He denies as well their suggestion that he grieves for Bassanio's imminent departure. But the action belies both denials, for were all his wealth not at hazard he would have been able to meet the bond that he would not in the first place have had to make. And were he not grieving for Bassanio, he would not cast himself as competitor with Portia for Bassanio's love, as he does in the trial scene when he uses his predicament as a means by which to draw Bassanio away from Portia.[7] He explicitly contrasts his self-sacrificing love to Portia's when

he tells Bassanio to, "Say how I lov'd you, speak me fair in death; / And, when the tale is told, bid her be the judge / Whether Bassanio had not once a love" (IV.i.276-78). As well, when he urges Bassanio to part with Portia's ring, he demands that Balthazar's "deserving, and my love withal / Be valu'd gainst your wife's commandment" (IV.i.454-55).

The action in which Antonio's coffers are drained by Bassanio's pecuniary needs associates the Father's homoerotic move with loss of wealth, which is in turn associated with the loss of the life's blood that will drain from Antonio should Shylock cut his pound of flesh. The two are further linked by the image in which Bassanio tells Portia that "I freely told you all the wealth I had / Ran in my veins" (III.ii.255-56).[8] In Antonio's melancholy, then, the Father expresses the emotional consequence of having repressed both forms of erotic satisfaction, along with the desire for money that signifies them both. Antonio's apparently unmotivated self-denigration as a "tainted wether of the flock" surrounds his figure with an aura of self-loathing and death that reveal him as an emanation from the Father's grave.

But the intensity of hatred between the wolfish Shylock and his natural prey, the flock's tainted wether, Antonio, is so great that it raises the possibility of another and darker level of homosexuality than appears in the gentle relationship between Antonio and Bassanio. As we have seen, in Shylock the Father manifests the repressed conflation of incestuous desire and ruthless greed and consequent self-loathing that bars his access to heterosexual love. Shylock's remoteness from his own figure, both socially and in the topography of his dream, manifests his underlying vision of himself as a social outcast. Having marginalized Shylock in this way, he also expresses through the intensity of the mutual hatred of Shylock and Antonio, out of which they forge their "bond," his most deeply buried homosexual eroticism. In turn, homosexuality is also associated with Shylock's open display of the greed and possessiveness for which the Father despises himself. This complex of feeling appears in the configuration created by Bassanio, Antonio, and Shylock, in which he rejects as debasing and disgusting his unconscious desire for his socially outcast alter ego, and masks it with his attachment to the more socially acceptable Bassanio. In the figure of Bassanio he asserts his rights to membership in the aristocratic world in which generosity and insouciance about the money upon which its display depends is a necessary symbol of rank and status (Stone 1967). Representing in Antonio the frustration and self-hatred that surfaces in consciousness only as melancholy and ennui, he forges a compromise between frustrated desire and fear by moving towards a nightmare version of sexual fulfillment. In Shylock's refusal to accept reified money in lieu of Antonio's literal flesh, the Father desublimates his desire, and in the culminating scene in which Antonio bares his breast to Shylock's knife, he reveals his terror of and desire for an enactment that will simultaneously punish and gratify his guilty desires. Furthermore, by casting Antonio as Shylock's victim with Bassanio as audience he has additional gratification of seeing Bassanio feel guilt for taking his daughter and with her his wealth, while, through Antonio, simultaneously enjoying being the object both of his horrified and loving gaze and of Shylock's terrible intimacy. He assuages his guilt through Shylock's punishment, and through Antonio gets the masochistic reward of being victimized, as well as the delight of being the object of Portia's compassionate concern. In this way the Father's dream exemplifies Freud's depiction of the way the superego taps the resources of the id.[9]

The strategy of splitting enables the Father to keep both his surrogates in the land of the living, but the inadequacy of the compromise appears in the fact that both Shylock and Antonio are in the end comforted only by the wealth, without which they would, in Antonio's words, "view with hollow eye and wrinkled brow / An age of poverty" (IV.i.271-72), an odd conclusion to a play that thematically opposes Venetian reified value to Belmont's spiritual gold. Shylock has only enough money to survive in his bitter humiliation, and the Father generates no fourth female to sweep Antonio into the comedic celebration of multiple marriages. To the end he remains an isolated and melancholy figure. These hidden links between the hero and the villain, two figures who are on the surface so radically opposed, reveal that the Jew is not as alien as the Father would like him to be. The failure to resolve the conflicts that generate the play appears as well in Shylock's unsettling comparison of his rights to Antonio's flesh to the Venetian rights over their purchased slaves. The ambivalence about the commerce that characterizes Venice and that her laws are designed to protect also generates sympathy for Shylock. The underlying sense that Antonio and Shylock are twin births, that Shylock functions as scapegoat for the love of money upon which Venice is founded and Belmont is dependent, wells up in Shylock's assertion of his humanity and justifies his vengefulness.[10] It also reflects the Father's ultimate unwillingness completely to forgo his unacknowledged desires, as well as his underlying rage at having been forced to repress them.

The Father's ambivalence about the ideology in terms of which he conceives his cure fractures the light that plays around Portia and problematizes the play's emotional impact. In order both to inherit her father's mantle and to remain a desirable sexual object, she must demonstrate feminine submissiveness, first to her father's will and then to Bassanio. However, her submission of herself and her estate must be token only; she must be heir to her father's power in order to cure in Venice her father's ills. The virtue that is to be therapeutic or redemptive is compassion, as it is in Desdemona, Cor-

delia, and Miranda, though they are denied Portia's shaping power. Portia shows her compassion first in her eagerness to rescue Antonio, and later in pleading for mercy that is "as the gentle rain from heaven." However, compassion and mercy are private and quiet virtues; to heal a sick world and the Father from whom that world has issued, these virtues must be wedded to the more active and difficult public virtue of justice. Therefore, while protecting the feminine image by having Portia don male disguise, the Father ascribes to her the wisdom and power by which he defines himself, as well as the trickster mentality that allows him to give the illusion of reconciling the conflicting demands of justice and mercy. But justice is a harsh virtue, one easily confused with cruelty. The cunning Portia inherits from him empowers her compassion, but it also entails a capacity for cruelty that threatens to tarnish her image as advocate of mercy and agent of harmony. This capacity also relates her to Shylock in a way that threatens to merge her image into his in ways dangerous to the entire configuration. Furthermore, since she punishes Shylock for his greed and cruelty, and he functions as a stand-in for repudiated aspects of the father, her punishment of Shylock fulfills the Father's fearful desire for the punishment he thinks justice demands. The Father's misgivings about the only compromise formation he has been able to generate are expressed in the precarious comedy of the trial scene when Bassanio and Shylock in turn celebrate Portia as "a Daniel come to judgment."

Portia's money also links her to Shylock. Shylock's gold allows Bassanio to win Portia and endangers Antonio, while Portia's money is the necessary, though not sufficient, condition for her activity. The final action links the two more closely, when, without explaining the source of her knowledge, Portia informs Antonio that his ships are returned and his wealth secure. This odd circumstance reveals the complicity of the idealized Neoplatonic Belmont with the commercialized Venice to which it is posited as a spiritual alternative. The polarized images of society are represented by polarized images of Portia as at once compassionate and cruel. The split in woman's image is not fully realized here, since both sides inhere in the same figure.[11] In *King Lear* the split is more radical; Cordelia, who will not give love for money, symbolizes a transcendent idealization of traditional order, while Goneril and Regan's greed, and the wealth and status to which Edmund aspires through them, demonize the actuality. Since sexuality is associated with the evil sisters, male heterosexual desires come to signify desire for every kind of violation, all of which are in turn signified by incest. As we will see later, incest taboos concern the transmission of wealth as do other marital prohibitions.

All of these motifs are inextricably knotted into the pound of flesh around which the action turns. In Freudian terms it is an overdetermined dream element; in

Lacanian terms it is a floating signifier hungry for signifieds, which in turn function as signifiers for it. Its most obvious signified is the money for which it is substituted, but money, as we have seen, has been equated with both Portia and Jessica. Therefore, the passion for money is fueled by the desire for woman's body, Portia's "little body," that it also represents. Shylock's desire for it then expresses the Father's denied desire for both money and his daughter, equated with each other. The Father has also associated money with the relation between Antonio and Bassanio. Antonio's denied desires for Bassanio being signified by the money which enables him both to send him to Portia and to call him back. Shylock's refusal to accept money as a substitute for Antonio's flesh expresses the ambivalent homoeroticism with which the Father has tinged Antonio's figure. The fears that render the homosexual element elusive between Antonio and Bassanio appear in the ferocious hatred between Shylock and Antonio. Antonio's willingness to sacrifice his pound of flesh for Bassanio and Shylock's desire for it associate homosexuality with castration. In turn, castration signifies death when Portia exposes Shylock's murderous intent. In the death to which Antonio is so ready to go, the Father expresses both his self-punitive impulses and the desire to kill in Antonio the idealized self-image (generously indifferent to money and unpossessive in love) that renders guilty his desires both for money and for his daughter. At its most general level the pound of flesh represents the reified values of Shylock's Venice, whose laws are designed to protect Antonio's commerce. These values the Father contrasts to those of Neoplatonic Belmont, which express his self-idealization. But the father's dream shows self-condemnation and self-idealization to be two sides of a single coin: the self-aggrandizement by which the Father defends himself against his desires amplifies their power to defile what he defines as sacred.

In the union of Bassanio and Portia, the father envisions releasing Portia from the orbit of his desire into the arms of a younger version of himself, so finding vicarious compensation for his loss. However, his vexation about passing Portia on to another man remains apparent in the thinness of Bassanio's characterization, as well as in the postponement of the nuptial celebration beyond the limits of the text. Not only is the wedding night disrupted by Antonio's letter, but the consummation of their marriage retreats into infinite futurity when the last act substitutes for a conventional romantic reunion a more playful version of the court scene in which Bassanio replaces Shylock as Portia's victim, and is punished for dividing his allegiance between her and Antonio. In Portia's privileged knowledge of her identity, by which she reconciles the dilemma she has devised for Bassanio, the Father repeats, in a lighter vein, the earlier configuration in which his magic reconciled otherwise incompatible values. However, the improbability that defines romantic comedy expresses the father's awareness that the conflicts that generated the configuration are still in place, that he has substituted daydream fantasy for genuine dream resolution of conflicts. The incommensurateness of the conclusion to the magnitude of Shylock's figure reveals the Father's dissatisfaction with his own strategy. Shylock's resistance to containment within the comic frame reveals the pressure of the Father's desires toward fuller actualization, a pressure that appears as well in the exclusion of both Shylock and Antonio from the domestic resolution.

That these conflicts remained unresolved appears in the fact that the sleight of hand by which Portia's father generates an illusory resolution of competing value systems most fully characterizes Prospero, who even more trickily contrives to leave his daughter free to choose according to his will, and then celebrates his cleverness in having stage-managed her rebellion. Whereas Portia's father withdraws into death, Prospero withdraws into his study; whereas Portia's father bathes his world in a quasi-magical aura, Prospero emerges from his study with explicitly magical powers on which he bases the superiority that shapes his self-definition. Like his dramatic progenitors, he has only a daughter through whom to control the destiny of his lineage. Sexual passions remain linked to money, for the ideal commonwealth to issue from Ferdinand and Miranda's union is contrasted to the ordinary world in which Sebastian, Antonio, and Stephano anticipate making commercial capital out of Caliban. Caliban represents the unruly sexuality that renders him at once a lump of deformed flesh and a marketplace commodity.

The persistent, if attenuated, ways in which monetary concerns are woven into later plays suggest that Shakespeare, no more than Portia's father, could not remove the taint of money from his imagination of redeeming love and ideal authority. In various ways in different plays he tried to envision a generative heterosexual love that would inseminate a just kingdom with redeeming nurturing compassion, but he could not prevent grotesque images of cruelty and greed from attaching to the active side of multidimensional female figures. Having only daughters to inherit the considerable fortune he acquired in the process of writing and staging plays that deplored the erosion of the traditional hierarchy by the tide of commerce and related ambitions, Shakespeare himself might well have been overwhelmed by the self-loathing and world-weariness he depicts in characters from his royal merchant to his triumphant magician.

. . . . .

The momentous psychological importance I have found related to money may seem to contradict a Freudian conception in which the primacy of sexual concerns derives from their infantile sources. But as Freud often reminds his readers, the unconscious knows no time. In his topographical model of the unconscious, temporal precedence does not endow events with more affective power than later accretions to which affect may be transferred, and a literary use of the dream model is necessarily concerned with the dynamic interplay of factors within the textual time frame rather than with conceptual origins. Furthermore, though modern sensibilities may be slow to perceive money and wealth as the locus of severe psychological tension, the picture changes when one allows the plays to give emotional resonance to the relationships that existed in their own time between money, wealth, and marriage. Further to widen the frame of reference in this way, to attach signifieds from the time in general to signifying figures within the plays, is to regard Portia's father and his creator as persons experiencing and shaping the age's conflict-ridden nexus of marriage, money, and traditional wealth and status.

In a general way Georg Simmel facilitates an understanding of the pychological stresses in the Renaissance. He argues that the significance of money is that it "expresses the relativity of objects of demand through which they become economic values" (Simmel 1978, 130). Such a fear that the money nexus erodes a social system that authorizes itself on the basis of absolute value is classically expressed by Gaunt in Shakespeare's *Richard II* when he accuses Richard of becoming "England's landlord, not her king." Gaunt's accusation resonates more deeply in view of Simmel's statement that,

> The powerful character of money . . . appears at its most noticeable, at the least at its most uncanny, wherever the money economy is not yet completely established and accepted, and where money displays its compelling power in relations that are structurally antagonistic (p. 244).

He adds that the "utilization of such a mysterious and dangerous power as capital necessarily appeared as immoral, as criminal misuse" (p. 244). Lawrence Stone's study of complex interrelations between traditional wealth and the rising tide of commerce shows the relevance of this general comment to sixteenth-century England. Stone discusses the sleight of hand necessary to bring new blood into a hereditary aristocracy, and particularly the ways in which the sale of titles by James I inflated the honours of the established orders (Stone 1967, 54). Though he says that Elizabeth was parsimonious in creating new titles, in her reign the busy market in land sales enriched a large group of people who became contenders to entry into noble ranks in the next reign (p. 76). At the same time that wealth, accumulated in commerce, might through marriage provide entrée into the ranks of the elite, membership in that elite still entailed scorn for the money that had both provided access to elite status, and that remained indispensable for maintaining the display of generosity

and grandeur that "served as symbolic justifications of rank and status" (p. 266). The consequences of this dilemma can be seen in the configuration of *King Lear*, in which an idealized version of traditional wealth is represented by Cordelia, the "unprized precious maid," while greed for the luxury on which status depends is represented by Goneril and Regan, whose gorgeous clothing scarcely keeps them warm.

The situation Stone describes is one in which persons of trditional welath, like Portia's father, might well despise themselves for coveting money. On the one hand they required money to maintain a display that signified their status, while that same status required of them their indifference to the money upon which it depended. Money was clearly important: for the landed aristocrats it was the despised conduit that underwrote their status; for the aspiring it promised access both to status and privileges they both despised and envied; and lacking money entailed the social death envisioned by Antonio and Shylock or experienced by such "poor naked wretches" as Poor Tom. But money can be acquired by any clever trickster, by the worthy and the unworthy alike, and when land is for sale money can buy it, along with the honors associated with its ownership, and the hands of noble heiresses. Furthermore, the confusion of status and money went in two directions and threatened to erode the distinctions among the social orders as the aristocracy participated in commercial enterprise. Stone observes that it was the noblemen "still traditionalist in their views . . . and not social groups more deeply affected by the spirit of capitalism, who provided the economy with just that element of risk money without which it could not have moved ahead" (p. 182). He does not discuss the psychological conflicts possible between absolutist values and financial activities, but the situation he envisions is consistent with the weary psychology of bad conscience I have attributed to Shakespeare's characters and, more hypothetically, to Shakespeare.

Some more intimate dimensions of these economic issues are brought into focus in complementary ways by the work of Georges Duby and Jack Goody. Duby describes the conflict in twelfth-century France between the knights and the priests, or between what he calls the lay model of marriage and the clerical model that gradually gained ascendancy. The knights were engaged in a struggle to build up the wealth that would establish their families as honourable, and straight-forwardly looked upon marriage as a means of doing so. In the situation Duby describes, one son only was allowed to contract a legal marriage and to have legitimate offspring. Wives who did not produce offspring were easily discarded, for knights and princes, as well as kings, paid little heed to church regulations. In his discussion of the importance the aristocracy placed on controlling their family lines so that their honor would be inherited by their progeny, Duby comments on the difficulty facing a man who had no sons. The solitary heiress was a "target for matrimonial intrigue" among the disinherited younger sons in constant search for wealthy wives (Duby 1977, 110, 145). In this world a father of daughters might well wish he had magic at his disposal, but would feel no guilt at using whatever means he deemed expedient.

However, two factors combined to bring pressure upon what Duby calls the lay model of marriage. First, the younger sons who could not marry within the system pursued wealthy married women, often trying to abduct them. These marauding young men, who valued adventure and daring exploit and who justified their amours in the name of love, formed, Duby argues, the social base from which arose the ideology and literature of courtly love (Duby 1978, 14). Second, between the thirteenth and sixteenth centuries the Church struggled to establish its authority over marriages. Condemning sexual pleasure, certainly outside of marriage and even within it, the Church defined marriage as instituted by God in order to ensure propagation. It

> emphasized the union of two hearts in marriage and postulated that its validity rested more on the betrothal (*desponsatio*) than on the wedding, and especially on the consent (*consensus*) of the two individuals concerned. (Duby 1978, 17)

An unintended, and ironic, consequence of the Church's success was to encourage love matches at the expense of arranged marriages, for it was by defining marriage as a sacrament performed by consenting partners that the Church gained ascendancy over the knights (Duby 1978, 17). As the priests became more powerful, they added "certain acts of benediction and exorcism to all the solemn rites, whose climax they imperceptibly shifted from the house to the entrance gate of the Church, and eventually to its interior" (Duby 1978, 19). In the process of rendering marriage sacred in this way, the Church increased its power to define legitimate marriage. It condemned remarriage, even by widowers, as well as the practice of repudiating wives who failed to produce progeny; it undermined paternal authority over marriage by requiring the children's consent. It opposed "closed marriage," often involving marriage between first cousins, by which great families consolidated their fortunes, and asserted its authority simultaneously extending the range of prohibited relationships and inculcating a deep horror of incest.

Duby emphasizes the long struggle between these competing conceptions of marriage as the Church gradually shaped men's consciences. In the midst of such conflict a man could maintain his authority over the will of his children, as well as his rights to put aside a wife who produced no sons, but he would do so with increasingly conflicted feelings. A man who had only daughters might well encounter internal as well as

external opposition in the pursuit of a new wife to give him a male heir; at the same time as his control over the destination of his wealth through his daughter would be constrained both by the increasingly wide definition of incest, and by pressure to give some measure of attention to her preferences. By the time one gets to sixteenth-century England, these developments have merged. The Church's success in redefining marriage as inclusive of love, which carried over into Protestant England, made it possible for the Church to gather in the romantic ideals spawned by courtly love. Furthermore, as Spenser's work makes clear, this combination of romantic ideals and the Christian ideal of married chastity was further spiritualized by being merged with the Neoplatonic tradition that had developed through the Florentine Platonists. One can see in the progress of Shakespeare's plays, from *The Merchant of Venice* to the late romances, the enormous significance of marriage as the center of spiritual value for both the participants and the society at large. However, the economic aspects of marriage were subject to the same tensions and ambivalence that Stone describes in the economic aspects of status. That is, marriage was at once a sacrament and the means by which great families controlled the transmission of wealth. It was a means of acquiring money necessary to maintain or to acquire status, and an ideal consummation of spiritualized romantic love. In this circumstance, in which the social realities are at cross-purposes both with the ideology of love and marriage and the strong emotions that ideology fuels, the bad conscience of Portia's father is comprehensible, as well as the desire to have recourse to magic to resolve otherwise intractable conflicts.

A further dimension to this murky mixture of love and money is suggested by Jack Goody. He argues that the Church served its own interests in its efforts to Christianize marriage. Its advocacy of mutual affection as the basis of marriage lifted clerical above secular authority. As well, it benefited materially from its success in preventing second marriages, for in the failure of progeny it often was the beneficiary of a dying line. Its efforts to inspire a horror of incest and to broaden its definition were also in its own interests. By complicating and enlarging prohibited degrees of kinship, it interfered with the claims of extended kin over land donated to the Church by a kinsman seeking his soul's salvation (Goody 1983, 153). As well, by acquiring power of judgment over whether a proposed or contracted marriage lay within interdicted degrees of relationship, it also secured the power to grant, and to set the price for, exceptions. Goody concludes,

> For the Church to grow and survive it had to accumulate property, which meant acquiring control over the way it was passed on from one generation to the next. Since the distribution of property between generations is related to patterns of marriage and the

legitimization of children, the Church had to gain authority over these so that it could influence the strategies of heirship. (p. 221)

Goody's analysis of the intermingled pecuniary and spiritual motivations behind the Church's strictures on marriage not only supports the argument that as marriage took on the aura of the sacred, the material interests of the parents could be driven underground and rendered guilty by the increasingly powerful clerical definitions. It also follows that those caught in the bad conscience engendered by competing value systems would be aware, in dim or acute ways, that their consciences were being manipulated in the interests of the Church's struggle for power and wealth. Portia's father is like a person who has internalized both value systems and at the same time resents being forced to suffer the consequent bad conscience and its related agonies. Neither Duby nor Goody explores the psychology engendered by these conflicting value systems, but the issues I have discussed in *The Merchant of Venice* and their links to later plays give evidence that both value systems were internalized sufficiently to survive into Protestant England and to torment the consciences of Protestant Englishmen.[12]

. . . . .

The assumption of this chapter has been that there are two ways by which Shakespeare drew his psychological landscapes from an inner life shaped by the contradictions inherent in his time. That is, his unique childhood experience within his particular family was conditioned by the social institutions and values governing families at the time, and as he grew his modes of dealing with his personal life were both limited and shaped by the social and cultural milicu he confronted. His way of being an artist was conditioned by the nature of the theater, the dramatic conventions, and literary traditions he inherited. All of these elements became part of the fabric of his plays. It follows from this that the kaleidoscopic recombinations of characteristics into different dramatis personae confronting their various worlds represent strategies to resolve or come to terms with conflicts that have both personal and social dimensions.[13] Approaching literature in the way that I put forward here provides an efficient way to penetrate that which is historically distant, and to capitalize both on what makes us different from those who lived at other times and places, and on what makes us similar to them. Though there must be continuities in human experience in order for us to appreciate and respond to the products of distant times and places, the ways in which people experience common or fundamental human desires must differ in relation to different social realities. Though the dreams of people in Elizabethan England would in some respects resemble those of people living now, in other respects they would differ. Both then and now one's dreams might express resentment of authority, but an Elizabethan person's expression of that resentment would be imbued with the dense emotional matrix of the family upon which political structures were modeled. Such a person might dream of killing the king, or of killing his or her superior in the local hierarchy, but he could not dream of a president failing to win an election. That we have such an option has more psychological significance than one might suppose. Our abstract and depersonalized conception of authority renders objections to and resentment of it less guilty, because less charged with infantile emotion. Both our modern dream of unseating the president, and the older dream of killing the king, may have their roots in animosity towards one's father, but in the modern context that animosity itself involves less psychological stress because the world provides more legitimate outlets for it. There is no way to prove it, but one might well suppose that contemporary dreams reflect our relatively positive attitude towards ourselves as freely aspiring individuals, or even as potential rebels, and show less intense conflict around these issues than those of our forebears. We may dream of losing or stealing or accumulating money, and money in our dreams may express our conflicted attitude towards giving and receiving love. But money in our dreams is unlikely to carry shame so intense as to augment the infantile conflicts that initiated the dream, as it does for Portia's father, and possibly for Shakespeare, who enriched himself and advanced his status by writing plays that condemned undue social aspirations and the mercantile values that nurtured them.

To ordinary ways of thinking there can be no two realms as remote from each other as the values that are inscribed in our political and cultural institutions, and the deeply private images we recall when we awaken from our sleep. But to trace in literature the connections between them brings home to us what postmodern theory calls the social construction of reality. To approach the plays as the dreams of their protagonists is to unite a historical understanding of experience with the emotional immediacy of dreams. In this way the polarity between traditional humanist criticism and deconstruction softens, and the question of meaning is differently framed. What a work means has to do with what the structure, array of characters, language, etc., means to the protagonist, just as a dream's meaning has to do with what the various elements of the dream signify for the dreamer. A fiction, then, is like a dream that contains within itself all associations necessary for its unraveling, and the method of interpretation I have applied to *The Merchant of Venice* does not differ greatly from the way one might think about one's own dreams, if one thinks about them as including the associations to the dream report one has generated later. Without having associations from a dreaming person one would not know how his or her dreams related to the reality of his or her life, but one would know something about the dreamer's self-definition and strategies for dealing with other people. With associations, particularly in connection with the day's residue that occasioned the dream, one starts to know something about the ways in which the actual circumstances of the dreamer's present life signify, for the dreamer, the emotional forms of the past. One starts to know something about the dreamer's structure of signification, just as one comes to know that of a literary character. It is true that most psychoanalytic approaches to dreams deemphasize the manifest content, the aspect of the dream that is usually more present-oriented and more immediately related to the day's residue, in order to concentrate on the latent, or past, content. That is, analysts tend to be interested in early causal traumas, rather than in the linkages that can be traced between past and present forms, or the way in which one's experience of past forms is shaped by the particularities, both personal and cultural, of the present. But in principle, Freud's dream theory does not preclude such an approach, and there is considerable interest and perhaps gain to be had from the angle of vision towards one's life circumstance such a way of thinking engenders.

Finally, a word on the difference between art and dream. I do not want to give the impression that they are the same in my view. They differ not only because, as I have said, literary work incorporates and integrates the author's conscious values into the unconscious or dream dimensions of the creative process. They differ also in that an art work offers itself for judgment by standards that have nothing to do with the process of its creation or its creator. The nature of those standards constitutes a subject beyond the scope of this chapter. However, this chapter does involve the belief that the age-old intuition, expressed first in our culture by Plato, that art and dream have something to do with each other is based on a psychological reality. That psychological reality has to do not only with the process by which artists draw on their unconscious drives to advance their conscious purposes in the specific ways I believe I have demonstrated; it also has to do with the reception of the work. Immersion in a work of art combines in a unique way the unmediated experience that we have while we dream with the conscious, cognitive and esthetic values that we bring to it and judge it by. Therefore to both experience and to reflect upon an art work may be thought of as training us in self-reflection and perhaps increasing our awareness of the devious ways by which we channel, for good or ill, our inward being into the outward world.

Notes

[1] There are two exceptions: Jameson clearly attends to political and social dimensions of literary work, but denigrates the personal realm, which he regards as epiphenomenal. Holland (1968) attends to formal aspects of literature, regarding them as defense strategies which simultaneously conceal and reveal the work's core fantasy. Though my theory overlaps with Holland's in important ways, his conception of the formal is less inclusive than mine, which, by eliminating the latent/manifest distinction, renders all aspects equally expressive of the compromise between competing desires and fears.

[2] For a full explanation of and rationale for this mode of criticism see Stockholder, pp. 3-25.

[3] As will become clear in the course of this argument, I do not agree with the perspective on Shakespeare's relation to his time favored by most new-historicist critics such as Greenblatt, Cartelli, and Meller. While it may be true, as Cartelli says (25n), that an orthodox Shakespeare was created rather than discovered by Tillyard's school, it is just as likely that a subversive Shakespeare is created, rather than discovered, by the new-historicists.

[4] The close parallels between this scene and the one in *Pericles* in which the suitors risk their lives on a correct guess suggest that the death's heads that adorn the chamber in the later play, and the overt incest of Antigonus and his daughter, make explicit what here hovers in the interstices.

[5] Freud in "The Theme of the Three Caskets" discusses Portia as a figure representing death for Shakespeare but seeing the play from my perspective renders Freud's insight more specific and relates it to the rest of the play. The father associates Portia with death because it is only in death that he can allow himself to imagine having her.

[6] A related approach to the intertwined themes of love and money is taken by Engle, who argues that the theological terms in which economic issues are articulated "also define a system of exchange or conversion which works to the advantage of . . . those who, by religion or social situation, are placed to take advantage of exchange patterns" (Engle 1986, 21). Engle, however, sees no problem generated by the disparate value systems. A view closer to my own is held by Shell who says that "the beautiful marriage bond is not far removed from the ugly bond that made it possible in the first place" (Shell 1979, 91).

[7] Engle also believes that Antonio lies here (Engle 1986, 22). He sees Antonio's sadness as a "market-linked phenomenon" (p. 28), and he associates his self-sacrificing stance with homosexuality (p. 24).

[8] Whigham equates Bassanio with Shylock as a fellow social climber (Whigham 1979, 102). However, Bassanio's equation of wealth with family blood, as well as the father's apparent approval of him, makes it more plausible to think of him as an impecunious aristo-

cratic younger son. The merchant's love of Bassanio, then, makes him, rather than Bassanio, vulnerable to the charge of social climbing. See below for the significance of this attribution.

[9] In "The Ego and the Id," Freud's discussion of the ways in which the superego taps the repressed desires of the id and merges them with the guilt that occasioned their repression seems particularly apt for this play (Freud 1987, 394-50). As well, in the configuration of Bassanio, Shylock, and Antonio, the father nicely confirms Freud's observation that "in mild cases of homosexuality" the identification with an esteemed figure "is a substitute for an affectionate object-choice," which in turn has substituted for erotically imbued hostility and aggression among siblings (p. 377).

[10] The links between Shylock and the Venetian world, and Shylock's role as scapegoat, have been seen in various ways. See Engle, Shell, Whigham, Meller, Cartelli, Sharp, and Girard.

[11] To regard Portia as the dreamer would be to see her as one who tries to mediate between maintaining a self-image that conforms to the conventional demands for femininity and repressing rage at men who would control and possess her. Her rage would also contain an erotic component that mirrors her father's association of sex with incest and death.

[12] Stone argues that the English clergy's emphasis on sacred marriage functioned similarly as a way to ensure social control (Stone 1977, 144), and Goody argues that despite the reduction of prohibited degrees in 1540, the Reformation had little impact on the English forms of marriage until the mid-seventeenth century (Goody 1983, 152). The persistence of the tensions from these earlier times into a Protestant England where marriage increasingly took on the sanctity that had once inhered in Catholic sacraments, suggested by Barber, is evident in the literature. Whatever gulf existed between literature and social practices, the mental sets that created literary characters formed part of the social ferment. Stone ignores this complexity in his assumption that literary renderings of romantic love had no bearing on people's management of their lives (Stone 1977, 181).

[13] I would not, however, claim that one can construct an author's biography from his or her work. We can never know from writings the exact balance and proportion that constitute a lived self, and it should be kept in mind that the simplest person is vastly more complicated than any literary figure.

References

Barber, C. L. "The Family in Shakespeare's Development: Tragedy and Sacredness." In *Representing Shakespeare: New Psychoanalytic Essays,* edited by Murray M. Schwartz and Coppélia Kahn. Baltimore: Johns Hopkins University Press, 1980, 188-202.

Cartelli, Thomas. "Ideology and Subversion in the Shakespearean Set Speech." *ELH* (Spring 1986): 1-25.

Duby, Georg. *The Chivalrous Society.* Translated by Cynthia Postan, London: Edward Arnold, 1977, 110, 145.

————. *Medieval Marriage. Two Models from Twelfth-Century France.* Translated by Elborg Forster. Baltimore: Johns Hopkins University Press, 1978.

Engel, Lars. "'Thrift is Blessing': Exchange and Explanation in *The Merchant of Venice.*" *Shakespeare Quarterly* 37 (1986): 20-37.

Freud, Sigmund. "The Theme of the Three Caskets," (*Collected Papers,* vol. IV).

————. *Jokes and Their Relation to the Unconscious* (SE vol. VIII, 1905).

————. *Character and Anal Eroticism, Collected Papers* vol. II, 45-50.

————. *On Metapsychology: Theory of Psychoanalysis* (vol. II, Pelican Freud Library, 1987) 350-408.

Girard, René. "'To Entrap the Wisest': a Reading of *The Merchant of Venice.*" In *Literature and Society,* edited by Edward Said. Baltimore: Johns Hopkins University Press, 1980, 100-19.

Goody, Jack. *The Development of the Family and Marriage in Europe.* Cambridge: Cambridge University Press, 1983, 153.

Greenblatt, Stephen. *Renaissance Self-Fashioning: From More to Shakespeare.* Chicago: University of Chicago Press, 1980.

Holland, Norman. *Dynamics of Literary Response.* New York: Oxford University Press, 1968.

Hyman, Lawrence W. "The Rival Lovers of *The Merchant of Venice,*" *Shakespeare Quarterly* 21 (1970): 109-16.

Jameson, Fredric. *The Political Unconscious.* New York: Cornell University Press, 1981.

Lacan, Jacques. *Écrits.* Translated by Alan Sheridan. New York: Norton, 1977.

Meller, Horst. "A Pound of Flesh and the Economics of Christian Grace: Shakespeare's *Merchant of Venice.*"

In *Essays on Shakespeare,* edited by T. R. Sharma. Meerut, India: Shalabh Book House, 1986, 150-174.

Sharp, Ronald. "Gift Exchange and the Economy of Spirit in *The Merchant of Venice,*" *Modern Philology* 83 (1986): 250-65.

Shell, Marc. "'The Wether and the Ewe': Verbal Usury in *The Merchant of Venice.*" *Kenyon Review* (Fall 1979): 65-93.

Silverman, Kaja. *The Subject of Semiotics.* New York: Oxford University Press, 1983.

Simmel, Georg. *The Philosophy of Money.* Translated by Tom Bottomore and David Frisby. London: Routledge & Kegan Paul, 1978.

Stockholder, Kay. *Dream Works: Lovers and Families in Shakespeare's Plays.* Toronto: University of Toronto Press, 1987.

Stone, Lawrence. *The Crisis of the Aristocracy: 1558-1641.* London: Oxford University Press, 1967.

————. *The Family, Sex and Marriage in England: 1500-1800.* London: Weidenfeld and Nicolson, 1977.

Whigham, Frank. "Ideology and Class Conduct in *The Merchant of Venice.*" *Renaissance Drama* (1979): 93-115.

DREAMS AND IMAGINATION

Marjorie B. Garber (essay date 1974)

SOURCE: "A Dagger of the Mind: Dream and 'Conscience' in the Tragedies," in *Dream in Shakespeare: From Metaphor to Metamorphosis,* Yale University Press, 1974, pp. 88-138.

[*In the following excerpt, Garber analyzes the blurring of dream and reality in the tragedies* Hamlet *and* Antony and Cleopatra.]

> *Conscience is but a word that cowards use.*
> *Richard III* V.iii.310

> *Thus conscience does make cowards of us all.*
> *Hamlet* III.i.83

Richard III . . . is Shakespeare's first truly psychological play. The long, self-revelatory soliloquies, the apparitions, and the narrated dreams all create a reality both inside and outside Richard, wedding the subjective condition of consciousness to the objective condi-

tions of London and Bosworth Field. The word "conscience" echoes repeatedly throughout the play: Margaret rails at Richard "the worm of conscience still begnaw thy soul" (I.iii.221); one of Clarence's murderers, though he acknowledges "certain dregs of conscience" (I.iv.122-23) in himself, concludes that conscience is a thing he'll "not meddle with," since it "makes a man a coward" (136-37). Richard himself, badly shaken by the parade of apparitions at Bosworth Field, for a moment concedes that

> My conscience hath a thousand several
>   tongues,
> And every tongue brings in a several tale,
> And every tale condemns me for a villain.
> [V.iii.194-96]

But the play is really a systematic rejection of conscience, the tragic record of a failed self-knowledge. Richard's last defiant assertion, that "conscience is but a word that cowards use," is a denial of that interior reality, a desperate attempt to obliterate from mind all the reflective events of the play. We have been preparing for this rejection since the play's first moments: the refusal by Clarence to heed the warning of his own dream, Hastings's disregard of omen, the apparent emptiness of Margaret's curse—all of these are failed recognitions, moments when the realm of self-conscious awareness tries and fails to assert its primacy. It is appropriate that all of these moments are part of that complex of supernatural occurrences, omens, ghosts, and warnings, which we have come to associate with the world of dream. The dream world is able to exercise a controlling power beyond that of any of the play's characters, although none of them acknowledge its sovereignty. The undervaluing of conscience becomes, for the play as a whole, a sign of a larger misunderstanding. For, like those of *A Midsummer Night's Dream,* the characters of *Richard III* are affected by the subconscious and the dream state without ever fully realizing it. We see the play largely through Richard's persona, as a simultaneous portrait of his history and his soul; but he himself refuses to accept the correlation of the two spheres, and his final flaw is lack of self-knowledge.

"Conscience" in *Richard III* is predominantly a moral term, having its modern meaning of "sense of duty" or "remorse." When Richard associates conscience with cowardice, he is talking about feelings of guilt and responsibility, essentially societal values internalized into a moral system. But "conscience" in Shakespeare's time also carried the primary meaning of "consciousness." Hamlet's "conscience does make cowards of us all" is a tacit recognition of the primacy of "consciousness" in the human spirit; "conscience" in his phrase contains both of its root meanings and yet goes beyond them, to express the essential condition of man. To Richard, only cowards capitulate to conscience; by the time of *Hamlet,* though Richard's meaning is retained, "conscience" in the sense of "consciousness" has reversed the terms; and cowardice, if one equates it with a sensitivity to the subjectiveness of human experience, is finally the condition which draws us all together. That man should be in this state, confronting rather than avoiding the problem of his own consciousness, is a prelude to the tragic experience. And in the great tragedies from *Hamlet* to *Antony and Cleopatra* Shakespeare develops the theme of consciousness to a point where the world of one man's imagination, the psychological dream state, takes over the landscape and the characters of the drama.

The relationship between subjective and objective experience, the thing thought and the thing done, is a constant concern in Shakespeare's plays from the earliest histories to the last romances. Of all the plays, *Hamlet* perhaps best illustrates the problem of subjectifying experience, the reduction of "what happens" to "what is thought," the temporary, often playful, yet always significant exchange of the fictive for the "real." This is a reversal we have considered at some length in relation to *A Midsummer Night's Dream;* in *Hamlet* the means of exchange is subtly different, because it has its root in Hamlet's own conscience. Dream here, as in the other great tragedies of the middle period, is most nearly equivalent to consciousness, the world subjectively glimpsed through the lens of imagination. At one pole this encompasses all that is terrifying, irrational, inexplicable: the ghost of old Hamlet, the *Macbeth* witches, the storm on the heath in *King Lear.* At the other, equally true, are the redemptive moments, grounded in common experience uncommonly viewed: Cleopatra's dream vision of Antony, the awakening of Lear. Literal, encapsulated dreams of the sort of Clarence's dream have almost entirely disappeared: the only traditionally "told" dream in all these plays is the supposed dream of Cassio, and significantly it is not really a dream at all, but rather a fiction crafted and controlled by Iago. This replacement of the episodic dream by the dream state is a dramaturgical advance, permitting a steady flow of plot and language without the interruption of artificially impacted flashbacks or recapitulations. At the same time, however, refinement in dramatic construction is paralleled by refinement in thematic development, as the dream state more and more encompasses the entire world of the play. The theme of consciousness, which unites the inner world of private vision with the outer world of visible reality, deliberately blurs distinctions between the factually "real" and the purportedly "imagined," so that the audience, as much as the protagonist, is forced to make wholly subjective choices among equally possible truths.

The familiar supernatural background of shaded omen and sign is established for *Hamlet* by the remarkable opening scene. The time is midnight, midway between dusk and dawn, and the night so dark that the sentries cannot see. That they tensely mistake one another for intruders is our first symbolic indication of a danger which lurks within Denmark, rather than without. Almost immediately the subject of the ghost is introduced, together with the crucial question "Is it real?"

> *Marcellus:* What, has this thing appeared
>   again tonight?
> *Barnardo:* I have seen nothing.
> *Marcellus:* Horatio says 'tis but our fantasy,
> And will not let belief take hold of him
> Touching this dreaded sight twice seen of us;
> Therefore I have entreated him along
> With us to watch the minutes of this night,
> That, if again this apparition come,
> He may approve our eyes and speak to it.
> *Horatio:*   Tush, tush, 'twill not appear.
>   [I.i.21-30]

The terrifying vagueness of "this thing" immediately intensifies the mood of mystery: the ghost is unclassifiable uncontrollable, and therefore frightening. Barnardo replies with the factual "I have seen nothing," which is meant to convey the fact that the ghost has not yet appeared. Yet our experience of the word "nothing" and its potential for ambiguity should alert us here; behind Barnardo's assertion is the covert meaning "I have seen a ghost; I have seen something made of 'nothing.'" Barnardo, of course, does not intend this meaning; the poet's adroit manipulation of language preserves verisimilitude on the literal level while permitting the audience a glimpse of deeper symbolic significance. It is a pattern we have seen before, and it here once more reinforces the important fact that dream goes beyond reason into the subjective realm of poetry. Having lightly but unmistakably established this theme, the scene moves away from it with superb economy. Horatio, rational man in his most attractive guise, is also present on the ramparts, and Marcellus makes it clear that he finds the idea of the ghost incredible. According to him it is "fantasy," meaning not creation but delusion, a phantom vision induced by an atmosphere of terror. For a moment we are drawn to agree with him, as we are meant to; the reassuring finality of "tush, tush" is a prosaic and welcome assertion of the boundary between the actual and the fantastic. But the well-bred control which is later to caution against considering "too curiously" is almost immediately demonstrated as the limited gift it is, as the appearance of the ghost on the platform abruptly negates all Horatio's scholarly assumptions.

Each of these independent figures represents an aspect of the mind of Hamlet; it is part of Shakespeare's astonishing craftsmanship that he should be able to present characters and settings simultaneously as subjective interior perceptions and objective exterior realities. In its treatment of the dream state *Hamlet* may therefore be viewed as an internal landscape projected by the protagonist, a shadowy world inhabited by figures inseparable from the "conscience" of Hamlet himself. Thus the ghost can be interpreted both as superego and as old Hamlet, guardian of ancient values; Horatio, both as Freudian censor and ʔs the wise and temperate scholar from Wittenberg. Laertes and Fortinbras also appear in the play as alter egos for Hamlet—Laertes a skilled fencer and fiery champion of Ophelia, Fortinbras a "most royal" prince—and Hamlet's progress toward self-knowledge in the play depends in large part upon his readiness to recognize these identities within himself.

The metaphorical equivalency of interior and exterior worlds is set forth with great clarity in an early exchange between Hamlet the father and Hamlet the son. Fading from the battlements, the ghost enjoins at the last, "Remember me" (I.v.91), and Hamlet cries

> Remember thee?
> Ay, thou poor ghost, whiles memory holds a
>   seat
> In this distracted globe.
>
> [I.v.95-97]

Clearly, the phrase "distracted globe" here carries a primary meaning of "confused mind"; metaphorically, Hamlet pledges to remember as long as he has a memory, which is to say, as long as he lives. But the literal meaning of "globe" is also appropriate here, since the world of the play is likewise "distracted" by the murder of the king, all the personae of the kingdom blighted in language and action; the madness Hamlet assumes when he puts on his "antic disposition" (I.v.172) is a madness already present in the state of Denmark. Moreover, the "distracted globe" may well carry a third relevant meaning, since the theater in which the play's Elizabethan audience "held a seat" was also called the Globe. Hamlet's pledge thus takes on the added meaning "as long as the play is remembered or performed," a sense enriched further by the traditional belief that Shakespeare himself appeared in the original production in the role of the ghost: not only will old Hamlet be remembered, but so too, through him, will the playwright and the play. The mysterious world of theatrical illusion of course becomes itself a principal subject for the play as a whole, and it is a "distracted" world in part because of the difficulty of distinguishing actor from audience. Claudius thinks of himself as merely a spectator watching a play in the "Mousetrap" scene (III.ii); he is not aware that he is at the same time a character in a larger play of Hamlet's devising, or that he and Gertrude are soon to be revealed as an actual "player king" and "player queen." Polonius, considering that "more audience than a mother" (III.iii.31) should hear Hamlet's conversation with the queen, conceals himself behind the arras in her chamber; he is tragically transformed into an actor when his shouts for help provoke Hamlet to stab him blindly through

the curtain. Everywhere reality has become elusive, as we have already seen in Horatio's confident rejection of the supernatural and the immediately subsequent entrance of the ghost. Just as boundaries between Norway and Denmark, youth and age, life and death seem to be constantly shifting in this play, so too do boundaries between reality and illusion. "My father, methinks I see my father," exclaims Hamlet to a startled Horatio. "Where, my lord?" "In my mind's eye, Horatio." "My lord, I think I saw him yesternight" (I.ii.184-85, 189). This sudden transition from conventional recollection to supernatural vision, especially when voiced by the supremely rational Horatio, is a leap into the world of illusion.

Hamlet himself is of course perfectly capable of distinguishing in basic terms between the actual and the dreamlike or fictive. The challenge of the ambiguity comes in his conscious refusal to sort these aspects of experience according to conventional classification. There is something electric in the emotion which seizes him when confronted, suddenly, with the denizens of the imagination. It is important to keep in mind that in *Hamlet* the ghost and the players are parallel entities, compounded of fact and fiction, reason and something beyond reason. In *Richard III* the characters of dream were ghosts, apparitions, omens which impinged upon the passive consciousness of Richard and of Clarence; in *A Midsummer Night's Dream* the dream world was inhabited by creative and fertile sprites whose presence was inseparable from concepts of play and imagination. In *Hamlet,* fittingly, the two senses come together, fused by the imagination of Hamlet himself, now in the condition of Everyman, the man of "conscience" or consciousness. Thus there is a strange but unmistakable triumph in his reply to Horatio, as the ghost cries in the cellarage:

> *Horatio:* O day and night, but this is
>   wondrous strange!
> *Hamlet:*   And therefore as a stranger give it
>   welcome.
> There are more things in heaven and earth,
>   Horatio,
> Than are dreamt of in your philosophy.
>
> [I.v.164-67]

Horatio's exclamation is an admission that the appearance of the ghost violates his canons of experience. We would expect this to be more or less the same for Hamlet, as it has been for the other members of the watch. But the effect of the apparition on Hamlet is in fact one of liberation rather than of amazement. In part this is because the reality of the ghost is validated by his own imagination. "Touching this vision here, / It is an honest ghost" (137-38), he assures the frightened watchmen. Its message, in fact, has apparently been subconsciously suggested to him before the actual apparition—"O my prophetic soul!" (40), he cries out at news of the usurpation, in a phrase at once wonderfully expressive and remarkably condensed. The foreboding of prophecy, which in the earlier plays required the extensive narration of monitory dream, is here magically contained in a moment.

Hamlet's exchange with Horatio is made even more significant, however, by the addition of the element of wordplay. "And therefore as a stranger give it welcome," he urges. He alludes in part to the courtesy proverbially accorded to visitors from foreign parts, a category in which he affects, somewhat whimsically, to include the ghost. Horatio is thus urged to accept the presence of the apparition without question, extending his cautiously delimited concept of the logical and the real. But at the same time the resonant word "stranger" in folklore denotes "something foreboding the arrival of an unexpected visitor," in effect an omen or sign. The ghost is an apocalyptic forecast of a later revelation. As such it represents the rich and proper sphere of dream, implicitly contrasted by Hamlet with the conventional things "dream of," or envisioned, in Horatio's study. The puns and double meanings here are of great importance, as they will be throughout the play. Hamlet, an inveterate punster and wit whose caustic, ribald humor resembles that of Mercutio, repeatedly attempts to control his environment and indeed the entire external world through the manipulation of language. In doing so he asserts the primacy of the imagination, the dream state of creation in which "words, words, words" are greater than and different from the mere "matter" they contain.

His starting point, of course, has been the message of the ghost, a message itself delivered in a tone strikingly different from that of the surrounding drama. The ghost of old Hamlet has within the play a dual reality: as an apparition he is really more closely related to the omens and oracles of earlier plays than to spirits of imagination, and he appears only to give his fateful report, reappearing once to Hamlet to "whet [his] almost blunted purpose." (III.iv.112) He is a "real" illusion in the sense in that he can be seen, not only by Hamlet, but by Horatio and the sentries. Yet the queen will see "nothing at all" (III.iv.133) when he appears in her closet; though the audience, once more included in Hamlet's interior consciousness, can both see and hear him. The ghost is in fact an intuition or perception in the mind of Hamlet at the same time that he is corporeally distinct from him, and a willingness to accept this seeming paradox is essential to an understanding of the dynamics of dreaming throughout the play.

A revenge figure descended not only from Elizabethan and Senecan models but also from Patroclus of the *Iliad,* old Hamlet comes, like his Homeric predecessor, to press his dilatory champion to action in an epic world. His associations with the epic are manifold: he is dressed in "complete steel" (I.iv.52), and his mode

of warfare is the single combat in which he defeated old Fortinbras; both costume and martial demeanor contrast as sharply as possible with the luxurious furnishings of the Claudian court and its twin weapons, the rapier and the "painted word." His language, too, is epic in style: "List, list, o list," he intones, (I.v.22); "Of life, of crown, of queen at once dispatched" (75); "unhouseled, disappointed, unaneled" (77); "O, horrible! O, horrible! Most horrible!" (80); and finally, "Adieu, adieu, adieu" (91). We have heard these portentous triplets before, in "The most lamentable comedy, and most cruel death of Pyramus and Thisby," where Shakespeare was clearly burlesquing the language of early tragedy in a play obviously intended by its actors to rival the best of the genre: "Thou wall, O wall, O sweet and lovely wall" (*MND* V.i.176); "O grim-looked night! O night with hue so black! / O night, which ever art when day is not!" (170-71); "And farewell, friends. / Thus Thisby ends. / Adieu, adieu, adieu" (344-46). The voice of the ghost in *Hamlet,* of course, sounds quite a different note; his incitement to revenge is a plea for Hamlet to return to an Old Testament world as well as to a world of epic values and heroic wrath. But with the murder of the king and the ascension of the political Claudius such a return is rendered impossible, as it will be after the death of Hector in *Troilus and Cressida* or the defeat of Antony in *Antony and Cleopatra*—both, like old Hamlet, epic heroes anachronistic in a modern world.

Yet the voice of epic is close to the voice of myth, and the tale of horror the ghost comes to tell has the spare authority of myth and the symbolic form of dream. Significantly, it is a tale of a sleep and a visitor to sleep; equally significantly, it is a tale which has been misconstrued and which requires a new interpretation.

> 'Tis given out that, sleeping in my orchard,
> A serpent stung me. So the whole ear of Denmark
> Is by a forged process of my death
> Rankly abused. But know, thou noble youth,
> The serpent that did sting thy father's life
> Now wears his crown. . . .
>
>   . . . Sleeping within my orchard,
> My custom always of the afternoon,
> Upon my secure hour thy uncle stole
> With juice of cursed hebona in a vial,
> And in the porches of my ears did pour
> The leperous distillment. . . .
>
>   [I.v.35-40; 59-64]

This is an Edenic myth of corrupted innocence, the invasion of a medieval *hortus conclusus.* In the ghost's interpretation, the metaphorical "serpent" is replaced by the specific "thy uncle," Claudius, the literal invader of the peaceful orchard The version of his death widely accepted in Denmark is unmasked as a fiction which hides the truth through metaphor: "The serpent that did sting thy father's life / Now wears his crown." The tale is important because it interprets the dream which deludes Denmark; its images will recur repeatedly throughout the play and dominate its plot and imagery, constantly reminding us—as well as Hamlet—that old Hamlet was killed in a *garden,* by a human *serpent,* who poured *poison* in his *ears.* "'A poisons him i' th' garden for his estate" (III.ii.265), as Hamlet will gloss the play-within-the-play.

The garden or orchard assumes the character of a despoiled Eden of the purer past, a garden of attempted innocence which is literally associated with its biblical antecedents by the gravedigger's punning joke about "Adam's profession" (V.i.31), now shared by "gard'ners, ditchers, and grave-makers" (30). It is a garden in which Gertrude's marriage to Claudius "takes off the rose / From the fair forehead of an innocent love, / And sets a blister there" (III.iv.43-45), bringing together the themes of garden and poison. Ophelia calls Hamlet "th'expectancy and rose of the fair state" (III.i.153); she herself, addressed as a "rose of May" (IV.v.158) by Laertes, sings mad songs which are all too apt in their scattering of telltale flowers, and her watery death, "When down her weedy trophies and herself / Fell in the weeping brook" (IV.vii.174-75), seems to translate into action the language of Hamlet's first bitter soliloquy on self-slaughter: "Fie on't, ah, fie, 'tis an unweeded garden / That grows to seed" (I.ii.135-36).

The "serpents" who infiltrate this garden are many: not only Claudius, but also his willing instruments, the insinuating Rosencrantz and Guildenstern, whom Hamlet vows he will trust "as I will adders fanged" (III.iv.204). The poison administered by such "serpents" is that which is rotten in the state of Denmark: the ulcers beneath the skin, cosmeticked over with lies, the contagion that spreads unwholesomely through the night, and above all the poisonous language of deceit and pretense which is everywhere in the play poured into unsuspecting ears. There is, too, the "certain convocation of politic worms" (IV.iii.20) to whom Hamlet consigns the body of Polonius, and the all-conquering Lady Worm, a special and victorious serpent who abides as the genius loci of that ultimate garden, the graveyard.

The ears of the ghost's tale are also omnipresent in *Hamlet:* in the advices of fathers to sons which occupy so much of the first act; in the "ear of Denmark" which is abused by the false account of the king's death; in the constant practice of eavesdropping: Claudius and Polonius behind the arras listening to Hamlet and Ophelia; Polonius again concealed, this time in the queen's chamber; Claudius sending for Rosencrantz and Guildenstern to eavesdrop on Hamlet's plans; Polonius dispatching Reynaldo to ascertain "by indirections" Laertes' reputation in France. Words enter like daggers into Gertrude's ears; Hamlet seeks to know if the king will "hear this piece of work" (III.ii.46-47) as he prepares the play; and the ghost himself, who has initiated the theme, enjoins his son to "List, list, O list."

Indeed there is a sense in which, by the very act of telling his tale, old Hamlet pours poison into the ear of young Hamlet, inflaming him to agony, soul-searching, and revenge, so that the "antic disposition" and the protective cloak of "words, words, words" become for him a temporary but necessary means of escape from the sudden burden of fact and responsibility for action. Thus we find in *Hamlet* the same triple pattern we have elsewhere observed, from exterior "real" world to interior psychological landscape and back—in *A Midsummer Night's Dream,* the journey from court to country to court. Here it emerges as a journey into the world of art, play, and fiction, whose own proper personae are the players—players who almost seem to materialize out of his own sudden awareness that the world about him is replete with posture and pretense. Hamlet's journey is a journey into the mental territory of the irrational, and the later "real" voyage to England, where the gravedigger will jest that all men are "as mad as he" (V.i.154), becomes its metaphorical counterpart.

The interior landscape is deftly described by Hamlet himself in a deceptively playful dialogue with Rosencrantz and Guildenstern on the subject of his "bad dreams," (II.ii.243-70), a dialogue which ends with the defiant assertion, "I cannot reason." The entire scene is highly reminiscent of Mercutio's dry disquisition on Queen Mab, contained within a verbal pattern closely analogous to dream logic. But unlike the amiable linguistic duel of Romeo and Mercutio, this contest of wits is a mask for pointed accusation and revelation. There is a heady recklessness in Hamlet's tone, for he is playing with his schoolmates as skillfully as he later intercepts their attempt to "play upon" him. He is wise enough to recognize the limitations of rationality in a world in which fear and death play major roles. His delight in badinage sharpened by double meaning is especially keen when the recipients of his verbal thrusts—Rosencrantz, Guildenstern, Polonius, Osric—perceive only the deceptive surface. In his remarks to Rosencrantz and Guildenstern, the form with which he is playing is *argumentum,* or syllogistic reasoning, a favorite university game and one well suited to the occasion. His final abjuration, "I cannot reason," rejects not only the triviality of the *argumentum* but also the self-interest, policy, and cold-blooded "reasoning" of these "indifferent children of the earth" (230). For Hamlet himself is far from indifferent. In an attempt to discover meaning and moral values in a world without them, he places the boundaries of that world metaphorically within himself. Thus he argues that the world is a "prison" (255) not because of the "ambition" suggested by the ambitious Rosencrantz, but rather because he has "bad dreams." He is confined not by physical boundaries, but instead by boundaries which are psychological, part of the realm of imagination. His "bad dreams" are a clear reversal of outer and inner worlds, for the "dreams" are not dreams at all, but rather intimations of the truth behind real events in Denmark. Unprotected by a "nutshell" to insulate him against the pain of sensibility, he moves forward into an area of willed subjectivism, in which "dream" becomes a term synonymous with his own vision. "I cannot reason" thus announces his readiness to abandon logic for emotion. Verbally, at least, he embraces the irrational, preferring Guildenstern's disparaging "dream," and Polonius's "madness," to a world in which logic has replaced human values.

We have noticed that the world of Denmark contains at least three distinct, if related, kinds of illusion: the apparently real illusion of the ghost, verified by the evidence of Hamlet's eyes and ears; the patently false illusion which is the common language of pretense in Claudius's court; and the deliberately fictive illusion of the players, whose world is the world of creative imagination, and whose materials are the same materials as those of the larger play, *Hamlet,* which contains them. In choosing the world of the creative irrational, the players' world, Hamlet attempts to penetrate the atmosphere of "seeming" which so vexes the court. The instinctive desire to play a part, to escape from the prison of unyielding reality into the interior world of dream and illusion, is a fundamental aspect of his character, and nowhere is it more clearly shown than in his sincere affection for "the tragedians of the city" (II.ii.336). The players' stock-in-trade is this very business of illusion, and it is clear that he feels far more comfortable in their world than in his own. When they are announced, Hamlet once more assumes that strange gaiety which informs his other moments of "playing." Yet he remains mindful of his own limitations; while urging the first player to recite a half-remembered speech, he is suddenly struck by the contrast with his own reaction to actual events. As in *Richard III,* the soliloquy here becomes the instrument of his own psychological revelation; it is yet another indication of the unity of physical and psychological worlds in Hamlet's persona that we hear his thoughts as if they were spoken aloud:

> Is it not monstrous that this player here,
> But in a fiction, in a dream of passion,
> Could force his soul so to his own conceit
> That from her working all his visage wanned,
> Tears in his eyes, distraction in his aspect,
> A broken voice, and his whole function
>   suiting
> With forms to his conceit?
>
> [II.ii.556-62]

"Dream" is here explicitly equated with "fiction," and also with the poetical terms "forms" and "conceit."

Hamlet is appalled that the player can evince more emotion in a fictive circumstance than he himself in a real one. But once more the implication is of the strangely extended power of dream and creative imagination over reality. The players' element is dream; Hamlet for a moment covets both the element and the response. Later in the same speech he will deprecate himself further, drawing the parallel directly:

> Yet I,
> A dull and muddy-mettled rascal, peak
> Like John-a-dreams, unpregnant of my cause,
> And can say nothing.
>
> [572-75]

The short line is a pivot turning the subject from the player to Hamlet himself. Where dream in the player's world was a powerful creative tool, dream in Hamlet's bitter estimate of himself is the nonproductive daydream of the village idler, concomitant of inaction. Yet we might observe that the self of whom Hamlet speaks has ceased in part to exist some thirty lines before, at the point when he determined to become not only an actor but also a playwright and director. In conceiving the plan to play "The Mousetrap" before the king, he has begun to exchange the unprofitable musings of John-a-dreams for "dreams of passion" which will provoke passion itself. His self-castigation is once again couched in terms of utterance: he "can say nothing." Yet when he asks for "The Mousetrap," he calls for speech in its most carefully crafted form; and with the insertion of "some dozen or sixteen lines" of his own he speaks through the play, transforming it into a new and private artifact of his own. "Nothing," as always, is a clue to ambiguity here. But what is most significant is that Hamlet has chosen poetry, the realm of the imagination, as the most congenial instrument here; he, too, will "by indirections find directions out" (II.i.66), controlling the world of dream for a moment to make it reveal a hidden truth in the realm of reality.

In all of these instances, concepts of truth and reality have become subjective quantities, controlled and defined by Hamlet's consciousness. It is often remarked that the entire play is full of questions, verbal and thematic, which are never satisfactorily resolved, and which seem to exist for the sake of the question rather than in the hope of any answer. Maynard Mack, in his classic essay "The World of *Hamlet,*"[1] points out that "Hamlet's world is pre-eminently in the interrogative mood," and that this is an aspect of a prevailing mood of "mysteriousness" throughout the play. Indeed it is this very atmosphere of mystery which is most hospitable to the world of dream. Dreaming for Hamlet becomes a kind of private and individual myth-making, in which we are included through the vehicle of the play, but which remains a closed system of coordinated symbols and images all related to one fulcrum: "conscience," the moral and spiritual dilemma of man.

This central question of conscience and its relation to the dream state is explicitly introduced in the great soliloquy which marks the play's midpoint, the "To be or not to be" speech of act III, scene i. As in so many cases we have examined, the position of the speech is of extreme importance; for a moment Hamlet stands suspended between the real and the illusory, the returning and the going o'er. His is a position very like that described by Keats in a letter to J. H. Reynolds (3 May 1818)—a letter which itself takes the form of a modern dream vision. In it Keats recalls

> that tremendous (effect) of sharpening one's vision into the heart and nature of Man—of convincing one's nerves that the world is full of Misery and Heartbreak, Pain, Sickness and oppression—whereby this Chamber of Maiden Thought becomes gradually darken'd and at the same time on all sides of it many doors are set open—but all dark—all leading to dark passages—We see not the ballance of good and evil. We are in a Mist. *We* are now in that state—We feel the "burden of the Mystery."[2]

The "burden of the Mystery" is exactly what grips Hamlet at this moment; he will accuse Rosencrantz and Guildenstern of wanting to pluck out its heart. He, too, "see[s] not the ballance of good and evil," for his view of life, like his view of reality, is rendered wholly subjective by the workings of his mind. Yet even in the extremity of moral crisis he plays with verbal images, drawing out a long conceit to make it yield a cryptological solution. The image he chooses, significantly, is once more the central metaphor of sleep and dream.

> To die, to sleep—
> To sleep—perchance to dream; ay, there's the rub,
> For in that sleep of death what dreams may come
> When we have shuffled off this mortal coil
> Must give us pause. There's the respect
> That makes calamity of so long life:
> For who would bear the whips and scorns of time,
> Th' oppressor's wrong, the proud man's contumely,
> The pangs of despised love, the law's delay,
> The insolence of office, and the spurns,
> That patient merit of th' unworthy takes,
> When he himself might his quietus make
> With a bare bodkin? Who would fardels bear,
> To grunt and sweat under a weary life,
> But that the dread of something after death,
> The undiscovered country, from whose bourn
> No traveler returns, puzzles the will,
> And makes us rather bear those ills we have,
> Than fly to others that we know not of?
> Thus conscience does make cowards of us all,
> And thus the native hue of resolution

> Is sicklied o'er with the pale cast of thought,
> And enterprises of great pitch and moment,
> With this regard their currents turn awry,
> And lose the name of action.
>   [III.i.64-88]

Even here both language and meaning suggest that the "undiscovered country" of dream is more real to him than his immediate surroundings. The magic of sleep is here made metaphorically equivalent to death, so that "to dream" means to take part in some life after death. It is striking that to him "what dreams may come" are more real and more terrifying than the physical fact of dying, just as the world of playing is more real than the world of fact. Yet there is a curious academicism here, a verbal detachment in the midst of this Mercutian catalogue of wrongs. In this speech Hamlet speaks as the philosopher of Everyman, articulating the crucial questions of the human spirit. For all its solitude, it is a formal and public utterance in which the fears and discouragements of all mankind are brought forward and examined. Denmark is a prison; so is all the world. Even the "dreams" of the afterlife are frightening and limiting images, the ultimate case of the embodied irrational. What Hamlet speaks in these lines is a manifesto of the human condition, a subjectivism so far advanced that he identifies with all men rather than with his individual conscience. He is well on his way to the graveyard scene, where the dust of Alexander may be discovered stopping a bunghole.

What happens to Hamlet—and it is a paradigm, in part, for what will happen in each of the tragedies—is that out of his subjectivity grows acceptance and consequent strength. His victory lies in the fact that at last he is able to perceive both the world of dream and the world of reality, the inner world of conscience and the outer world of event. It is this comprehension upon which the drama depends. Hamlet's triumph is an equivocal one, compact of sorrow and resignation, but grounded in an increased self-knowledge. For there comes to him at the last a species of revelation—as Brutus says of himself, his state, "like to a little kingdom, suffers then / The nature of an insurrection" (*Julius Caesar* II.i.68-69). Most appositely, the revelation comes in the graveyard scene, when Hamlet's confrontations with the world of dream and the supernatural have expanded from the individual (the ghost) to the collective (the human condition) and so to the spiritual or eternal. The eternity of the graveyard is the ultimate leveler, in which Lady Worm claims indifferently the homage of lord and jester. Once more the tone of Hamlet's serious wit may remind us of Mercutio, as he catalogues the residents of the place: politician, courtier, lawyer, jester—again, all aspects of his own complex role. The gravedigger is his final and most telling counterpart, succeeding the ghost and the first player as a repository of values against which he consciously measures himself.

Yet the gravedigger's language differs sharply and significantly from the sonorous epic triplets of the ghost and the mimetic rhetoric of the player; his is no voice of fiction or illusion, but rather one of uncompromising fact, and he speaks a determinedly literal language of spades, shrouds, and skulls. The Hamlet whom he addresses, much altered by his confrontation with the world of dream, is an apt pupil whose psychological landscape may now be identified with the churchyard in which he finds himself; he is at last prepared to accept the literal realities of human frailty and the mortal condition. That he comprehends the lesson of the gravedigger's determined literalism is made plain by his approving aside to Horatio:

How absolute the knave is! We must speak by
    the card, or equivocation will undo us.

[V.i.137-38]

The state of equivocation, or ambiguity, has been his own dominant characteristic for much of the play and is of course central to the processes of dream. But in act V the "absoluteness" of the churchyard enforces a rejection of metaphor, euphemism, and verbal disguise; Yorick's skull is literally "chapfall'n" (192) as well as figuratively so. The apparently reductive and often disconcertingly comic literalism of the gravedigger's language, like that of the equally literal and equally comic clown in *Antony and Cleopatra,* carries with it an insistence on viewing things as they are. Civilizing fictions are stripped away and seen from the perspective of eternity: "let her paint an inch thick, to this favor she must come" (193-94), just as Claudius's "painted word" will be belied by his deeds.

Hamlet's return to the "real" world, the world literally of things, is made possible by his experience of "equivocation" in language and action—of doubt, fear, misunderstanding, subjectivism, and deliberate ambiguity and pretense. At the play's close he is able to reenter the political world of action because he has made this private journey through the transforming world of dream. And just as a chapfallen skull is remembered because it "had a tongue in it and could sing once" (75-76), so the world of the mortal and "real" is immortalized in the world of art. Thus Hamlet's dying request to Horatio,

Absent thee from felicity awhile,
And in this harsh world draw thy breath in
    pain
To tell my story

[V.ii.349-51]

is in a political sense an instruction to inform Fortinbras and the English ambassador of the true state of affairs in Denmark. In another, equally valid sense, however, it is an injunction to perform the play, to tell *The Tragedy of Hamlet, Prince of Denmark.* We have seen parallel resolutions to recount in *Romeo and Juliet* and *A Midsummer Night's Dream,* and we will see them again in *Othello, King Lear,* and *Antony and Cleopatra.* The play as an artifact—"my story"—becomes in each case a surrogate and an example, precluding the necessity for a literal repetition of human tragedy. As life becomes history and history becomes "story," both the audience in the theater and that on the stage—in Hamlet's phrase, "mutes or audience of this act" (337)—are offered a new opportunity for self-knowledge; just as Claudius and Gertrude were the play Hamlet watched, while they themselves watched a play, so we as audience watch ourselves in *Hamlet.* By viewing the world of Hamlet's interior imagination as dramatically and symbolically equivalent to the exterior political world of Denmark, and the personae of the play as aspects of his consciousness, Shakespeare explores a new dimension of the nature of dream; by further resolving those worlds into a self-conscious fiction, he hints once more at the inseparability of dream from what we loosely call "reality" and suggests that redemption can be approached, and perhaps achieved, by transmutation into art. . . .

In the later tragedies . . . Shakespeare moves . . . toward a new treatment of dream: a transitional stage in which symbols greater than the facts themselves overtake and dominate the world of the play. It is a movement from the particular toward the universal, from the story of one man to the story of all. W. B. Yeats, in an essay called "Emotion of Multitude," perceptively suggests that "there cannot be great art without the little limited life of the fable, which is always the better the simpler it is, and the rich, far-wandering, many-imaged life of the half-seen world beyond it."[6] This second "life," that of the "half-seen world" beyond the fable, is dream as we have described it. Yet Yeats's two kinds of artistic life can hardly be separated; as he says elsewhere in the same essay, they copy one another "much as a shadow upon the wall copies one's body in the firelight."[7] It is the merging of these two lives, the growing unity of dream and fable, that takes place in the last plays. And in the last of the "great tragedies," *Antony and Cleopatra,* this unity is in part achieved by the continued growth of subjectivity, the eradication of the boundaries between seeming and being in the consciousness of the protagonists.

It has frequently been pointed out that *Antony and Cleopatra* is not a tragedy of the same type as [*Hamlet, Macbeth, Othello,* and *King Lear*]. The most popular alternative designation has been "Roman play," a category which includes *Julius Caesar* and *Coriolanus* as well as *Antony and Cleopatra* and which seems to stress a classical as opposed to a Christian framework. With equal validity, perhaps, we may regard it as the last and greatest of the chronicle plays. For our purposes we may accept a mixture of categories without strain, since we are predominantly concerned with a chronological development, and observe that *Antony* partakes at once of tragedy, chronicle, "Roman play," "problem play," and even, to a certain extent, comedy. This mixture of modes is in fact exactly what we should expect of Shakespeare at this time: it is just this bold synthesis of major tropes which makes the play so vast, a many-colored tapestry of titanic actions and gorgeous language. Shakespeare is at the top of his powers here, and the broad canvas of *Antony and Cleopatra* gives him scope to incorporate much of what he has previously learned.

Perhaps the most obvious and yet important change from the sequence of *Hamlet, Macbeth, Othello,* and *King Lear* is that this play's title links *two* characters, in the pattern of *Romeo and Juliet* and *Troilus and Cressida.* Our attention is thereby drawn to the linking "and," the connection between the two, rather than to either specific consciousness without the other. We are not concerned only with love, even with the titanic love of Antony and Cleopatra, which in its imagery as well as in its oscillation from Rome to Egypt bids fair to encompass the world. Instead we may perhaps conjecture that the entity "Antony-and-Cleopatra" in itself has meaning—essentially, that these two majestic figures, towering over the play which bears their names, are aspects of a single conscience, a single—and outmoded—way of looking at the world. Theirs is an ancient world of heroic values, not unlike that of old Hamlet, or, indeed, of Hector. They are, we might say, older than the thrones upon which they sit; their view of the world, and the extent to which it is controllable and manipulable by their own private actions, is a view which must give way to the practical, colorless reason and "high order" of Octavius Caesar. "Conscience" connotes awareness of self, and of all characters in Shakespeare perhaps none are more intrinsically self-aware than Antony and Cleopatra. "The nobleness of life / Is to do thus;" says Antony,

> When such a mutual pair
> And such a twain can do't, in which I bind,
> On pain of punishment, the world to weet
> We stand up peerless.
>
> [I.i.38-40]

The fact that there are two of them means, in dramatic terms, that they are more often than not characterizing one another; even more significantly, characterizations of them are extremely alike. "She makes hungry / Where most she satisfies," (II.ii.239-40) says Enobarbus, Antony's closest companion, of Cleopatra; and Cleopatra in her great dream vision of Antony says of his bounty, "an autumn 'twas / That grew the more by reaping" (V.ii.87-88). Their relationship to the world of dream as we have described it is an extremely close one: they, like Othello, are votaries of dream, believers in prophecy and the supernatural. Antony's exchange with the soothsayer is paralleled by the augurers in Cleopatra's retinue. Dreaming is looked upon by the practical Romans as superstitious delusion: "he dreams," scoffs Pompey, dismissing a false report (II.i.19). The dichotomy we have previously observed, between the scoffers who try to control dream and the believers who are controlled by it, is softened here because of the concentration on character, or what we have been calling "conscience." Antony's encounter with the soothsayer is a good example, because it simultaneously sets a thematic tone and gives us a rapid insight into Antony's overwhelming strengths and weaknesses.

The soothsayer appears at a pivotal moment in Antony's thought. We have met him before at Cleopatra's palace, where in the play's second scene he performed the oracular dramatic function of forecasting in riddle the course of the drama, predicting to Cleopatra's attendants that they will outlive their mistress. Characteristically, the attendants misinterpret this as an omen of long life; yet it is literally true in another sense, since they will die within a few moments of one another and, indeed, within moments of their mistress. In this first encounter the soothsayer is thus parallel to the soothsayer of *Julius Caesar* or to the earlier monitory dreams. "In Nature's infinite book of secrecy," he says, "A little I can read" (I.ii.10-11); and the fact that it is "Nature's book" will assume a growing thematic importance as the play proceeds. His second appearance, however, is markedly different in tone. We have by now accepted the official place of soothsayers and augurers in the Egyptian court as a major distinguishing factor between the worlds of Egypt and Rome. When the soothsayer appears again, however, he is in Rome; and this subtly but completely alters the comfortable climate of belief. Antony has just accepted the hand of Octavia in a political marriage calculated to bring peace between him and Caesar. With her goodnight to him the soothsayer enters and is catechized by Antony on the prospects of the future.

> *Antony:* Now sirrah: you do wish yourself in Egypt?
> *Soothsayer:* Would I had never come from thence, nor you thither.
> *Antony:* If you can, your reason?
> *Soothsayer:* I see it in my motion, have it not in my tongue, but yet hie you to Egypt again.
> *Antony:* Whose fortunes shall rise higher, say to me, Caesar's, or mine?
> *Soothsayer:* Caesar's.
> Therefore, O Antony, stay not by his side.
> Thy daemon, that thy spirit which keeps thee, is
> Noble, courageous, high, unmatchable,
> Where Caesar's is not. But near him thy angel
> Becomes afeard, as being o'erpow'red: therefore
> Make space enough between you.
>
> [II.iii.10-22]

Plainly, this is in part an internal monologue. . . . The soothsayer has a corporeal existence and even a dramatic history in the play; he is not imaginary within the play's terms. But the voice of warning we hear through him is Antony's own voice, projecting a brooding internal premonition of disaster. The soothsayer, like the witches, is here simultaneously an internal and an external character. Maynard Mack, in "The Jacobean Shakespeare," points out that when the soothsayer says, "I see it in my motion," he means "intuitively," and that this is also true of Antony. Mack acutely calls this prediction a "visual surrogate for Antony's own personal intuition."[8] As such it follows the patterns of many similar supernatural or irrational happenings we have already noted in the tragedies: to put it in its simplest form, the personae and the loci of the drama are themselves consistently surrogate, or complementary, to the operations of conscience in the main characters themselves. We should also note the incorporation of an older theatrical device—the good and bad angels, familiar from the moralities and *Doctor Faustus*—into the soothsayer's language of metaphor. Once more the irrational is, so to speak, domesticated, made plausible. When later we hear that the "god Hercules, whom Antony loved" (IV.iii.15) leaves him, the effect is the same: a set of character traits—courage, boldness, integrity—have been concretized into a character with a name, though that character's appearance, like that of the "daemon" above, is entirely allusive in the drama itself.

We have touched upon the fact that Antony and Cleopatra are associated with old heroic values which their world can no longer support. In its tacit relationship to myth-making, this tendency is clearly related to the concept of the dream state. Nowhere is the confrontation between this world of heroic gesture and the real, tactical, and unromantic political present made more evident than in Antony's desire to meet Caesar in single combat. He has lost the battle of Actium, and, desperate to regain his honor, he sends a challenge back to Rome for Caesar to meet him "sword against sword, / Ourselves alone" (III.xiii.27-28). The mode of the challenge recalls the world of old Hamlet, who "the ambitious Norway combated" (*Ham.* I.i.61), and that of Hector, who seeks to settle the seven years' Trojan conflict by meeting singly with a champion of the Greeks. Both in *Hamlet* and in *Troilus and Cressida* these heroic moments are relics of a past age; old Hamlet falls victim to the wily and politic Claudius, and, despite the dreams of his wife and the warnings of Cassandra, Hector is slaughtered by the terrifyingly modern-seeming Myrmidons of Achilles. Antony's challenge is no less doomed to failure. Enobarbus murmurs aside on hearing it:

> Yes, like enough: high-battled Caesar will
> Unstate his happiness and be staged to
>   th'show

Against a sworder! I see men's judgments are
A parcel of their fortunes, and things outward
Do draw the inward quality after them
To suffer all alike. That he should dream,
Knowing all measures, the full Caesar will
Answer his emptiness! Caesar, thou has
    subdued
His judgment too.

                                    [III.xiii.29-37]

Enobarbus is another of those interpreter figures we have found so frequently in the tragedies, who perceives and reports the facts uncolored by imagination. He knows that Antony's behavior is wholly unrealistic; that, unlike Hector, he will not even receive the satisfaction of an affirmative reply. For Antony's mind dwells with the heroism of an earlier age. "Things outward / Do draw the inward quality after them"—this is precisely the movement toward subjectivity we have been recording. Fittingly Enobarbus calls it "dream," and although for him, as for so many, this means "delusion," it is a strength in Antony as well as a mortal weakness. His "judgment," that omnipresent marked boundary of reason, is perhaps his least reliable attribute.

However, it is not for his judgment that we seek to admire Antony, but rather for his superb imagination, which turns all things to dream. His imagination is incommensurate with the exigencies of reality, and what is real to Antony is properly dream to Enobarbus. Yet Antony's self-awareness, his conscience, is by and large adequate to apprehend these shifting realities. His remarkable capacity lies in a kind of negative capability, what in the Antony of *Julius Caesar* was a strong impulse toward chaos; he is not afraid of metamorphosis. Consider his self-analysis to an only partially comprehending Eros, after the second defeat of his forces:

> *Antony:*   Sometime we see a cloud that's
>   dragonish,
> A vapor sometime like a bear or lion,
> A towered citadel, a pendant rock
> A forkèd mountain, or blue promontory
> With trees upon't that nod unto the world
> And mock our eyes with air. Thou hast seen
>   these signs:
> They are black vesper's pageants.
> *Eros:*   Ay, my lord.
> *Antony:*   That which is now a horse, even
>   with a thought
> The rack dislimns, and makes it indistinct
> As water is in water.
> *Eros:*   It does, my lord.
> *Antony:*   My good knave Eros, now thy
>   captain is
> Even such a body: here I am Antony,
> Yet cannot hold this visible shape, my knave.
>   [IV.xiv.2-14]

Antony's metaphor is clearly related to Hamlet's teasing of Polonius, as well as to Theseus's speech on "airy nothing" and imagination. The play metaphor ("black vesper's pageants") suggests the fictive quality of the visual metamorphosis he is describing; the effect is once more that of a reversal of categories, the "air" here as in *A Midsummer Night's Dream* a mockery of reality, which imitates and simulates the real objects of nature. The apparitions of tree and horse shift under the scrutiny of the imagination "even with a thought"—a temporal notation which recalls Lysander's "short as any dream." Antony is acutely aware of his own role-playing existence; the "real" Antony is as indistinguishable from the many momentary shapes as the "real" cloud from rock or dragon. He looks upon himself as a quicksilver entity in a real world—as protean as Puck, but burdened with the mortal substance of Hamlet. He is torn between conflicting sets of values, neither of which he can wholly embrace, and both of which are by this point largely corrupt. When, only moments later, he receives the false message of Cleopatra's death, his personal pattern of reversal becomes complete. Reduced to a sense of total subjectivity in the cloud passage above, he is now moved to action once more, but an action which is still conditioned by the dream of an older age. Convinced by this crowning illusion—that Cleopatra is dead—he makes it come true by killing himself in response. His method of suicide, the ancient Roman custom of running on his sword, is like the earlier impulse to single combat, a heroic gesture which belongs to another time. For Antony's personal dream is a kind of myth-making, the translation of the mortal to the immortal. It is what T. S. Eliot has called "the point of intersection of the timeless with time." And the defeat of time, as we have seen, is a major achievement of the world of dream.

Antony's death comes at the close of act IV, and the whole of the fifth act is therefore Cleopatra's. Cleopatra's sense of self is very acute; she is a constant manipulator of illusion and reality, herself the embodiment of the irrational, the ultimate exception to all rules:

> she makes hungry
> Where most she satisfies; for vilest things
> Become themselves in her, that the holy priests
> Bless her when she is riggish.
> [II.ii.239-42]

She, too, shows an intuitive understanding of the workings of dream, the degree to which reality is only a partial truth. When the clown brings her the "pretty worm of Nilus" in a basket, he warns her not to touch it, "for his biting is immortal" (V.ii.246-47). The malapropism, "immortal" for "mortal," is precisely the impulse we have been tracing in both Antony and Cleopatra; as in so many similar cases, subjective truth comes to the audience in the guise of error, and the clown speaks better than he knows.

Cleopatra's choice of a death is the heroic alternative to a demeaning captivity, a captivity which she particularizes for her attendants by means of the play image:

> The quick comedians
> Extemporally will stage us, and present
> Our Alexandrian revels: Antony
> Shall be brought drunken forth, and I shall see
> Some squeaking Cleopatra boy my greatness
> I' th' posture of a whore.
> [V.ii.216-21]

The image is that of a downward metamorphosis, a rude translation back from the splendid world of Egypt to the shallow imitations of the stage. A version of the play-within-the-play incorporated into natural allusive speech, Cleopatra's verbal picture is a mirror of what has actually been happening upon the stage, but a mirror with a basic distortion. In a sense the reversal is reversed. Sigurd Burckhardt, in *Shakespearean Meanings,* puts the matter clearly: "What happens here is that we are compelled, against common sense and the everyday certitudes about truth and falsehood, to accept illusion *as* illusion, trickery *as* trickery, and in this acceptance find truth."[9]

But while *dramatic* reality is boldly exposed for itself, magically without destroying the spell of the play, there is another kind of reality which is deliberately undercut. If there is a truth about Cleopatra, it lies in the "serpent of old Nile" and not in the squeaking boy. For Cleopatra, like Antony, projects what is in a sense a myth of herself, which is incompatible with political fact and yet transcends it. She is too large for the world which tries to contain her. And *Antony and Cleopatra,* like the chronicle plays of the second *Henriad* with which it has so much in common, is compelled to suggest the impossibility of a coexistence between dream and "reason" in its limiting sense of "order." "The air," says Enobarbus

> but for vacancy,
> Had gone to gaze on Cleopatra too,
> And made a gap in nature.
> [II.ii.218-20]

The air would have—if it could have. But it could not. Order in nature must be maintained. The "airy nothings" of Theseus, the "air . . . thin air" of Prospero and even the "piece of tender air" of Posthumus's riddle must give place in this play to natural law, just as the dream world of Antony and Cleopatra themselves is forced to give way to civil law. Reality, as exemplified by the coming of the sober order of Caesar, is in itself a significant limitation. And yet Cleopatra, conscious of so much, is conscious of this too. In her last magnificent dream vision of Antony she confronts the problem of art and nature, vision and reality; her answer, which is both a tortured and a transcendent one, is our direct and proper portal into the dream world of the romances.

Dolabella is Cleopatra's confidant here, as Eros and Enobarbus have been Antony's; significantly, a great deal of the play's character analysis is verbalized through the device of a major character speaking to a subordinate. It is a more sophisticated dramatic device than that of soliloquy, and in effect it externalizes the interior dialogues of earlier protagonists with t hemselves. As concrete evidence we may note the comparative simplicity of syntax, as compared, for instance, with an extreme example like Hamlet's "rogue and peasant slave" soliloquy, which contains eleven rhetorical questions, nine exclamations, and twelve sentences in direct discourse. By contrast Cleopatra, though her words are mostly for her own ears, is fairly straightforward.

> *Cleopatra:* You laugh when boys or women tell their dreams,
> Is't not your trick?
> *Dolabella:* I understand not, madam.
> *Cleopatra:* I dreamt there was an Emperor Antony.
> O, such another sleep, that I might see
> But such another man.
> *Dolabella:* If it might please ye—
> *Cleopatra:* His face was as the heav'ns, and therein stuck
> A sun and moon, which kept their course and lighted
> The little O, th' earth.
> *Dolabella:* Most sovereign creature—
> *Cleopatra:* His legs bestrid the ocean: his reared arm
> Crested the world: his voice was propertied
> As all the tunèd spheres, and that to friends;
> But when he meant to quail and shake the orb,
> He was as rattling thunder. For his bounty,
> There was no winter in 't: an autumn 'twas
> That grew the more by reaping. His delights
> Were dolphinlike, they showed his back above
> The element they lived in. In his livery
> Walked crowns and crownets: realms and islands were
> As plates dropped from his pocket.
> *Dolabella:* Cleopatra—
> *Cleopatra:* Think you there was or might be such a man
> As this I dreamt of?
> *Dolabella:* Gentle madam, no.
> *Cleopatra:* You lie, up to the hearing of the gods.
> But if there be nor ever were one such,
> It's past the size of dreaming; nature wants stuff
> To vie strange forms with fancy, yet t' imagine

> An Antony were nature's piece 'gainst fancy,
> Condemning shadows quite.
>
> [V.ii.74-100]

Cleopatra's dream is a waking dream, but it is a true one—true, at least, within her own "conscience" and communicating itself to us. She acknowledges the generally low reputation of dream among the forthright Romans; "boys or women" are the dreamers there. Her description of Antony, however, is no weakling's delusion, but rather virtually a theogony in little. In her eyes he becomes a figure like Mars or Thor—related indeed to the Julius Caesar of Cassius's disgruntled description, who "doth bestride the world like a colossus." When we look closer, however, we can notice that a great deal of her description is actually natural imagery: the "sun and moon" in his eyes, his anger like "rattling thunder," his generosity of spirit a constant harvest, with "no winter in't." He is a relative of Adam Kadmon, the sum of the world's inheritance rather than a beneficiary. "Realms and islands were / As plates dropped from his pocket." The structural principle of this description is of considerable interest, for it is actually the reverse of what we have been calling "internal landscape." Where in *King Lear,* for example, the heath mirrored an aspect of Lear's state of soul, here Antony's soul is the subject, and the world of nature the applied metaphor. This is the creative function of dream again, the dream work producing a verbal artifact. The literal man is indeed, as Dolabella gently implies, not wholly recognizable here; but the dream has an independent verisimilitude of its own. It is the last and greatest production of Cleopatra's conscience. Derek Traversi has remarked, apropos of this subject, that "Cleopatra is living in a world which is the projection of her own feelings. That world, while it lasts, is splendidly valid, vital in its projection; only death, which is the end of vitality, can prevent her awakening from it."[10] The connection we have been striving to demonstrate between conscience and dream is here made manifest.

Even the pacing of this remarkable scene is nothing short of brilliant; just at the point when Dolabella's exasperation begins to communicate itself to us, in the middle of a breath-taking virtuosity of creative description, Cleopatra finely turns the dialogue back to her listener for a moment, before drawing the lesson of her own vision. She is dreamer and augurer in one, expounder and interpreter, and her hyperbole is so instinct with vitality and conviction that she carries us with her through an extraordinary train of reasoning: if there had ever been anyone like the dream—Antony she has described—and there has been and is from the moment she describes him—he would be "past the size of dreaming," since the process of dream itself is not capable of such a creation. Things of nature are not as wonderful as things created by the fancy, she continues; yet to imagine an Antony—

as she has, and as Shakespeare has—gives nature for once a creature more extraordinary than those of fancy, defeating the fictive, the "shadows," by means of the real. The circle is complete, the exchange of the dream for the reality translated back into a new form of reality which includes and transcends "shadows." At this level of the imagination the two categories at last flow into one another unimpeded. We have had a hint of the same transcendence in Enobarbus's earlier description of Cleopatra, "O'erpicturing that Venus where we see / The fancy outwork nature" (II.ii.202-03). And it is most fitting that in their ultimate enshrinement they should be again equal, as they have been throughout.

The new concept of nature here beginning to make its appearance is one which includes both dream and reality. It is characteristic of the language of *Antony and Cleopatra,* and indeed of all the tragedies, that Cleopatra should state the concept in terms of argument: "Nature's piece 'gainst fancy." To Perdita and Polixenes it will become "great creating Nature," incorporating without strain the one pole into the other. For in the romances a renewed and expanded nature will in a sense become equivalent to the world of dream, a temporary but transcendent stage of regenerative awareness; the "art" which "itself is Nature" will encompass for a significant moment the antinomies of illusion and reality.

Notes

[1] *Yale Review,* 41 (1952), 502-23.

[2] *The Selected Letters of John Keats,* ed. Lionel Trilling (Garden City, N.Y.: Doubleday, 1951), p. 99.

[6] In *Ideas of Good and Evil* (New York: Macmillan, 1903), p. 341.

[7] Ibid., p. 340.

[8] In *Jacobean Theater,* Stratford-upon Avon Studies, No. 1 (New York: St. Martin's Press, 1960), p. 27.

[9] "The King's Language" (Princeton: Princeton University Press, 1968), pp. 281-82.

[10] *An Approach to Shakespeare,* 2d ed. (Garden City, N.Y.: Doubleday, 1956), p. 258.

Joan Ozark Holmer (essay date 1996)

SOURCE: "'Begot of Nothing?': Dreams and Imagination in *Romeo and Juliet,*" in *Classical, Renaissance, and Postmodernist Acts of the Imagination: Essays Commemorating O. B. Hardison, Jr.,* edited by Arthur F. Kinney, Associated University Presses, 1996, pp. 195-210.

[In the following essay, Holmer examines Romeo and Juliet, *investigating Shakespeare's imaginative transmutation of Thomas Nashe's ideas on dreams and dreaming in the play.]*

Critics have seen the witty Mercutio's Queen Mab speech as his most imaginative flight in *Romeo and Juliet.* But the extent to which Shakespeare himself is imaginative in his fusion of dream lore and a diminutive demon has not been fully understood. The idea of small fairies does not originate with Shakespeare. They appear in old folklore traditions, recorded in the late Middle Ages by authors such as Giraldis Cambrensis and Gervase of Tilbury, and particularly in Welsh lore; John Lyly often is credited with being the first to introduce into Elizabethan drama the small fairies, who would be aptly played by the smaller of his boy actors.[1] Lyly's language, however, reveals that his small fairies in *Endimion* are not meant to be imagined as extremely diminutive, but rather as childlike in their stature because he calls them "fair babies."[2] Shakespeare breaks new dramatic ground in *A Midsummer Night's Dream* and *Romeo and Juliet* when he combines the subject of mortals' dreams with small fairies (Titania and Oberon, who can assume mortal size) and with very diminutive fairies (in *Dream* the courtly attendants who can wear coats of bats' wings and in *Romeo* the agate-stone-sized Queen Mab).

This originality of Shakespeare's coupling of fairy and dream has been overlooked. In *An Encyclopedia of Fairies* Katherine A. Briggs presents comprehensive information about fairies, but there is no entry for dreams as a subject directly related to fairies.[3] Indeed, Shakespeare's description of Queen Mab as "the fairies' midwife" (1.4.54)[4]—the fairy whose role it is to bring to life the dreams of sleeping mortals—should surprise us. The idea of a fairy playing midwife to humans reverses the popular idea, recorded by Briggs, of mortal women who act as midwives to fairy mothers in the delivery, not of dreams, but of fairy offspring.[5] Is Shakespeare's demon-dream association "begot of nothing but vain fantasy" (1.4.98)?

I suggest that Shakespeare's stylistic habit of borrowing and transforming material found in other literary sources applies as well in this situation. The source I propose for considering Shakespeare's imaginative transformations is also markedly original in presenting the first literary association of extremely diminutive spirits and their causative roles in the dreams we mortals have: Thomas Nashe's *The Terrors of the Night, or a Discourse of Apparitions* (1594).[6] In his work Nashe greatly develops much of the earlier work on demonology done for his *Pierce Pennilesse* (1592),[7] but his two most substantive additions are diminution and dream lore as he spoofingly expatiates on his wide-ranging single "theame . . . the terrors of the Night" (1:360). Just as Robin Goodfellow in *A Mid-*

summer Night's Dream provides his audience with the option to think they "have but slumbered" and "this weak and idle theme, / No more yielding but a dream" (5.1.403-6), so also Nashe with a puckish gesture of self-depreciation dismisses his work as "but a dream": "& to say the troth, all this whole Tractate is but a dreame, for my wits are not halfe awaked in it" (1:360-61).

To begin, dreams and the Romeo-Mercutio exchange about dreams are Shakespeare's innovative additions to the acknowledged source for his play, Arthur Brooke's poem, *The Tragicall Historye of Romeus and Juliet* (1562).[8] Despite extensive critical discussion of the possible influences on Mercutio and his Queen Mab speech on dreams and despite a growing awareness of Nashe's influence on Shakespeare,[9] it is surprising that Nashe's *The Terrors of the Night,* with its satirically spirited use of diminutive demonology and dreams, has been overlooked as a possible source for Shakespeare's paradoxical use of dream and his characterization of Mercutio as a dream-mocker and Romeo as a dream-believer. Mercutio's very debunking of dreams, those "children of an idle brain, / Begot of nothing but vain fantasy" (1.4.98-99), closely apes Nashe's own dismissal of dreams as "fragments of idle imaginations" (1:355) or "ridiculous idle childish invention" (1:356) of "the phantasie" (1:354). When Romeo interrupts Mercutio's supportive spoof on dreams, "Peace, peace, Mercutio, peace! / Thou talk'st of *nothing*" (1.4.95-96; my italics), he echoes Nashe's denouement: "But this is *nothing* (you will obiect) to our journeys ende of apparitions" (1:377). And Romeo's conclusion regarding his belief about his dream, that "with this night's revels" (1.4.109) begins some dire consequence, changes the mood but recalls that phrase from Nashe's conclusion: "my muse inspyres me to put out my candle and goe to bed: and yet I wyll not neyther, till, after all these *nights reuells,* I haue solemnly bid you good night . . . and sleep quietly without affrightment and annoyance" (1:384; my italics).

Perhaps one reason that might help explain the oversight of Nashe's possible influence is the impoverished reputation of *The Terrors of the Night.* Ronald B. McKerrow concluded about Nashe's piece, "It is a slight production . . . a hasty piece of work . . . and on the whole of very little importance either as regards Nashe's biography or the history of letters in his time" (5:23). McKerrow's dismissal rests chiefly on his view that Nashe's work is very unoriginal: "a mere stringing together of matter taken from elsewhere"; most of it "might well have been gathered by miscellaneous reading" (4:107). But as Donald J. McGinn rightly observes, McKerrow "admits being unable to identify any of these sources."[10] Especially for Nashe's dream lore McKerrow can cite no particular source.[11] Even Briggs dismisses Nashe's work: "He has, however, nothing to add to our knowledge

except a remark on the small size of spirits, which makes them even smaller than Drayton's fairies."[12]

G. R. Hibbard revises this negative appraisal. Although he does not suggest any connection between Shakespeare's *Romeo* and Nashe's *Terrors,* he praises Nashe's work—its spirit and style—in terms suggestive for recalling Mercutio's spirit and style in his Queen Mab speech:

> This combination of over-wrought description on the one hand, and mocking skepticism on the other, is the outstanding characteristic of the whole pamphlet and the real unifying factor in it, for *The Terrors of the Night* is essentially a *jeu d'esprit* . . . one of the most sophisticated prose-works of the age . . . too sophisticated for Nashe's contemporaries; only one edition of it appeared during his lifetime. . . . It seems to me, further, that *The Terrors of the Night,* although it had no influence on anything written after it, does have its place in the history of letters in Nashe's time. . . . It is one of the first, if not the first, prose works in English that exists for no other end than to give pleasure a discriminating reader can find in a . . . display of stylistic ingenuity that carries with it the impress of a personality. . . . In essence, *The Terrors of the Night* is a piece of literary clowning, and good clowning in writing, no less than in the theatre or the circus, is neither a common nor a contemptible thing.[13]

Shakespeare is precisely the sophisticated audience, the "discriminating reader," on whom Nashe's "literary clowning" was not lost. Shakespeare reshapes it to develop Mercutio's character as a mirthful scoffer, not unlike Tom Nashe himself, and to craft the tenor, tone, and function of his Queen Mab "improvisation."[14]

Shakespeare uses much of Nashe's dream lore, but he also recasts what he borrows, chiefly through the cultivation of paradox, personalization, and tragic irony, all elements conspicuously absent from Nashe's work. His adaptive borrowing from Nashe covers a wide range: tone (chiefly Mercutio's satirical stance on credulity); text and context (the opposition between serious belief and comic nonbelief regarding spirits and dreams as species of nightly "terrors"); and language (the lexicon used to describe these terrors and how they are interrelated). Even the tonal framework for Nashe's work, which shifts from a serious and religious tone (1:345-48) to witty spoofing (1:349-84) and back again to a graver concluding tone of admonition (1:384-86), might have provided Shakespeare with a hint for comic-tragic juxtaposition, a hint that Shakespeare improves upon throughout his scene by interplaying these opposing moods between melancholic Romeo and mirthful Mercutio.

Within this context the purpose for the Romeo-Mercutio exchange on dreams reveals itself. Romeo clearly believes in the truth of dreams, and because his love melancholy has been the butt of Mercutio's humor from the beginning of this scene, Mercutio probably anticipates some ominous announcement when Romeo implies why they show "no wit" in going to this mask, "I dreamt a dream tonight" (1.4.50). Mercutio attempts to deflect Romeo's gravity, "And so did I" (1.4.50), to which the polite Romeo falls pat, "Well, what was yours?" (1.4.51). Mercutio's rejoinder concisely expresses his attitude "that dreamers often lie" (1.4.51), which Romeo refutes in a clever pun, "In bed asleep, while they do dream things true" (1.4.52). Mercutio's Queen Mab speech is a loquaciously witty rejoinder, even a *jeu d'esprit,* wherein he tries to laugh Romeo out of his lover's melancholy and restore him to his "sociable" (2.4.73) self by debunking Romeo's belief in dreams as cleverly as he can. Mercutio's sportive wit that seeks to uplift Romeo's downcast spirit informs all his previous rejoinders in this scene—"You are a lover, borrow Cupid's wings. / And soar with them above a common bound" (1.4.17-18)—because Mercutio, eager to go to the Capulet feast, seeks to draw Romeo from "the mire, / Or (save your reverence) love, wherein [Romeo] stickest / Up to the ears" (1.4.41-43).

Mercutio's wittily skeptical attitude toward dreams and Queen Mab, who delivers these fancies, parallels Nashe's treatment of dreams and diminutive spirits in both language and thought as Nashe seeks to counsel his reader about nightly terrors, even to the point of providing a good-night prescription for how to avoid bad dreams. In his pamphlet Nashe's shift from a serious to a comic tone begins with his introduction of tiny spirits who inhabit the four elements, as well as humans whose humors correspond to those four elements and indeed inhabit everything in our world, and who are so diminutive as to be almost microscopic: "In *Westminister* Hall a man can scarce breath for them; for in euery corner they houer as thick as moates in the sunne" (1:349). Mercutio's extremely diminutive depiction of Mab as "in shape no bigger than an agate-stone / On the forefinger of an alderman" (1.4.55-56) is a very similar, if more elaborate, version of Nashe's description of men who "haue ordinarily carried a familiar or a spirite in a ring in stead of a sparke of a diamond" (1:350). Shakespeare's use of "an alderman" as the "spritely" ring bearer seems to be his specification of Nashe's general "man" likely to be found in Westminster Hall.[15]

But far more telling than these verbal parallels is Shakespeare's debt to Nashe for the idea and imagery that lie behind Shakespeare's imaginative depiction of his Mab as the fairies' midwife. Hibbard implies that Nashe merely juxtaposes spirits and dreams because Nashe "rambles on" so that "ultimately spirits lead to melancholy and melancholy back to dreams."[16] But Nashe actually forges the causative relation between

the tiniest of spirits and dreams; he uses language of birthing to define the causal relationship in which diminutive, elemental spirits use melancholy to "engender" dreams in mortals: "the spirits of earth and water have predominance in the night; for they feeding on foggie-brained melancholly, engender thereof many vncouth terrible monsters . . . engendereth many mishapen objects in our imaginations . . . many fearfull visions . . . [and] herein specially consisteth our senses defect and abuse . . . [that] by some misdiet or misgouernment being distempered . . . [they] deliuer vp nothing but lyes and fables" (1:353-54). Friar Lawrence echoes this concern about distemperature when he sees young Romeo up too early, suggesting such behavior "argues a distempered head," a Romeo "uproused with some distemp'rature" (2.3.32-40) or imbalance of humors. Mercutio's view, however, that dreamers "lie" (1.4.51) is more satirically dismissive and parallels Nashe's quip: "What heede then is there to be had of dreames, that are no more but the confused giddie action of our braines, made drunke with the innundation of humours?" (1:370). For Mercutio's sporting with fairy and dream, Shakespeare enhances Nashe's causal relationship by personalizing the diminutive earthly spirits into one chief figure who is both "queen" and "quean," who is specifically named as "Mab," and whose function is to be the fairies' "midwife" in the delivering of mortals' dreams.

Nashe interrelates tiny spirits (chiefly earthly ones, whose identifying element of earth corresponds in Renaissance psychology to the humor of melancholy), mortals' melancholy, and dreams in order to mock dreams as "ridiculous idle childish invention" (1:356), "trifling childish" (1:371), "toyish fantasies" (1:373), "froth of the fancie" (1:355), "an after feast made of the fragments of idle imaginations" (1:355), and "but the Eccho of our conceipts in the day" (1:356). Nashe rambles but manages to sum up concisely: "When all is said, melancholy is the *mother of dreames,* and of all terrours of the night whatsoeuer" (1:357; my italics). Shakespeare cultivates Nashe's generalized use of "childish" by personifying dreams as "children of an idle brain, / Begot of nothing but vain fantasy" (1.4.98-99). But Shakespeare probably derives his "midwife" image from Nashe's "mother of dreams" and his linguistic emphasis on "engendering" for how spirits use melancholy to create dreams.

Various sources have been suggested for Mercutio's descriptions of different dreamers and their appropriate dreams (1.4.70-88n). Shakespeare's depiction of Mab as a midwife who delivers dreams that are dreamers' wish-fulfillments finds an analogue in Nashe's far less succinct but similarly satiric and decorous presentation of the elemental natures of spirits and their corresponding inhabitation of like-minded mortals who live, and who, it is implied, dream accordingly. For example, "terrestriall spirits" ally with soldiers and "confirme them in their furie & congeale their mindes with a bloodie resolution" (1:352). Spirits of the air are "all show and no substance, deluders of our imagination," and "they vnder-hand instruct women" in how "to sticke their gums round with Comfets when they haue not a tooth left in their heads to help them chide withall" (1:353). Nashe's violent soldiers and comfit-comforted women are not far from Mercutio's throat-cutting soldier and his ladies whose eating of sweet-meats (or "kissing-comfits") cannot cover up their blistered lips and "tainted" breaths (1.4.75-76). This descriptive matter immediately precedes Nashe's explanation of how spirits engender dreams (1:353). But Shakespeare also refashions Nashe's hints into his own imaginative dreamscape by appropriate amplification, and he attributes all power specifically to Queen Mab's role, deftly versified, in the delivery of appropriate dreams, such as the lovers' dreams of love, the ladies' dreams of kisses, and the soldier's dreams of violence.

Although Romeo dismisses Mercutio's words, "Thou talk'st of nothing" (1.4.96), and Mercutio concurs, "True, I talk of dreams, / Which are the children of an idle brain, / Begot of nothing but vain fantasy" (1.4.96-98), their exchange is not for naught within the context of the play. Fundamental to their exchange is the opposition between two views of dream that frame their dialogue: Mercutio's belief that dreams are lies or fantasies and Romeo's belief that dreamers "dream things true" (1.4.52). Nashe's general attitude toward his subject as trivial and his view of dreams as delusions, ensconced in a variety of popular superstitions (1:361-62), parallels Mercutio's dismissal of Romeo's apparent belief in the truth of dreams as prophetic. Some of Nashe's remarks are quite pertinent for Shakespeare's treatment of dream in his play; he imitates Nashe and improves Nashe's associations chiefly through tragic effect heightened by irony and paradox. In Nashe's attack on excessive credulity, he debunks some popular superstitions concerning dreams—for example, the belief that a happy dream foreshadows misfortune and a sad dream good luck (1:362). Nashe develops his double-pronged view of dreams as caused immediately by melancholy and ultimately by night-dominant spirits when he adds his cautionary emphasis on the danger of emotional extremes that induce "most of our melancholy dreames and visions" (1:377). Romeo's susceptibility to dreams correlates with his temperamental imbalance due to excessive extremes of grief and joy, inviting our sympathy for his plight. The danger of excess is a philosophical idea that Friar Lawrence expounds, chiefly in proverbial terms (2.6.9-15).

Romeo has two dreams that resemble Nashe's dream psychology. His first dream probably is caused at least partially by his too-much-changed emotional state that his father so fears: "Black and portentous must this humour prove, / Unless good counsel may the cause remove" (1.1.132-33). Romeo's persistent suffering of

love melancholy is Shakespeare's significant change of Brooke's handling of Romeus's decision to attend the Capulet feast. Brooke's Romeus responds positively and immediately to his friend's advice that he forswear his unrequited love and seek another love; his healing process is well underway before he goes to the Capulet feast (ll. 141-50). Although Shakespeare's Romeo may appear fickle to us and even to Friar Lawrence, who persists in seeing him as but a "young waverer" (2.3.89), Romeo does intend at least, unlike the far more fickle Romeus, to remain true to Rosaline until experience itself, the vision of Juliet, thwarts his faithful intention. Shakespeare's change here effectively keynotes one of his recurrent themes, that experience often changes intention, and in many ways *Romeo and Juliet* gains tragic poignancy through the persistent pattern of good intentions that run amuck. In Romeo's unhealthy state of love melancholy his dream of ill portent could be interpreted as being engendered by his continued grief over Rosaline's rejection of him. Nashe commonsensically observes that when "a solitarie man [lies] in his bed" (1:376), he tends to think over his recent experiences. If his experiences have been sad, then he feels overwhelmed by misfortune. Given the popular superstition that dreams prove contrary, "that euery thing must bee interpreted backward . . . good being the character of bad, and bad of good" (1:361), an idea that Romeo seems not to know, his sad dream of "untimely death" that begins "with this night's revels" (1.4.109-11) should foreshadow good luck. And in one respect it does. That very "blessed, blessed night" (2.2.139) Romeo doffs his inky cloak of melancholy to wrap himself in the joy of Juliet's love, despite his fear that this might be "but a dream / Too flattering-sweet to be substantial" (2.2.141).

On the other hand, Shakespeare invests his use of dream with more paradox than Nashe because the same dream can be interpreted as false and as true. This same seemingly blessed night does begin, for various reasons, the cycle of time that will ultimately cost much more than just the "vile forfeit" (1.4.111) of his life. Although Nashe argues against "the certainety of Dreames" (1:371) and focuses on the folly of "anticke suppositions" (1:378), he does not completely deny the prophetic power of all dreams, especially of those heaven-sent "vnfallible dreames" foretelling the deaths of the saints and martyrs of the Primitive Church (1:372), or even some of the historical "visions" that were "sent from heaven to foreshew" the rise and fall of "Monarchies" (1:361), the usual stuff of tragic drama so foreign to Shakespeare's new matter here, the rise and fall of young lovers. And Nashe closes with "the strange tale" of an English gentleman's "miraculous waking visions," which are left to the reader's judgment to decide whether they be "of true melancholy or true apparition" (1:378). But Nashe believes that fearful dreams provoke much more terror than the reality they foreshadow: "the feare of anie expected euill, is worse than the euill it selfe"

(1:376). Romeo's dream proves an exception to this general truth when the audience finally sees the stage as a graveyard, littered with dead bodies—Romeo, Juliet, Paris, and Tybalt—and knows of the deaths of Mercutio and Lady Montague, with Lady Capulet's death imminent. Although Romeo, like Hamlet (2.2.256), is susceptible to bad dreams because he is melancholic enough to refer to his life as "a despised life" (1.4.110), his "terror of the night" proves no idle apparition by the play's end.

Nashe makes a point of focusing exclusively on the time of night for his "terrors," and Shakespeare adapts this setting of night, the time when dreams usually occur, to suit the genre of the play he is writing. In the romantic comedy, *A Midsummer Night's Dream,* night becomes the time when friendly fairies help to resolve the waking nightmares of mortals. But Shakespeare's use of night in *Romeo and Juliet* is more complicated and parallels his paradoxical presentation of dream. Nashe strikes the expectant tragic chord regarding night: "When anie Poet would describe a horrible Tragicall Tragicall accident; to adde the more probabilitie & credence vnto it, he dismally beginneth to tell, how it was dark night when it was done, and cheerfull day-light had quite abandoned the firmament. Hence, it is, that sinne generally throughout the scripture is called the workes of darknesse; for neuer is the diuell so busie as then, and then he thinkes he may aswel vn-discouered walke abroad, as homicides and outlawes" (1:386). But in the benighted world of Verona's hate-ful feud, night contrarily becomes the lovers' friend so that Juliet's knight can come to her safely, and "civil Night," their "sober-suited matron," can teach them how "to lose a winning match / Played for a pair of stainless maidenhoods" (3.2.10-13). "Love-performing Night" (3.2.5) is love's traditional element. On the other hand, the joyful nights of their first meeting and mari-tal consummation change to the contrary when Romeo returns in the night, once again as a torchbearer (5.3.25, 283), this time, however, going not to life's celebratory feast with his fears submitted to the guidance of a higher power (1.4.11-12, 35-38), but rather journeying passionately in a spirit of defiance to death's feast to be feasted upon:

> . . . then I defy you, stars! . . .
> Thou detestable maw, thou womb of death,
> Gorged with the dearest morsel of the earth,
> Thus I enforce thy rotten jaws to open,
> And in despite I'll cram thee with more food.
> (5.1.24, 45-48)

When Romeo first saw Juliet, he found her beauty bril-liant: "O she doth teach the torches to burn bright!" (1.5.43). Likewise in death her beauty makes the vault "a feasting presence full of light" (5.3.85-86). Romeo's own mood, "a light'ning before death" (5.3.90), may recall for the audience, through memorial wordplay,

Juliet's premonitory warning about the "lightning" nature of their love (2.2.117-24).

Shakespeare adds Romeo's dark dream, which, like the opening choric Prologue, signals the genre of trag-edy within the predominately comic context of the first two acts. Brooke warns that Romeus would have re-mained happier if he had never forsworn his first love (ll. 151-54), but he presents no dream of ominous pre-monition. With the Mercutio-Romeo exchange over dreams, Shakespeare heightens dramatic tension for the audience's hopes and fears, and he also elevates the sense of mystery involved in human tragedy and the problem of epistemology. Whence comes Romeo's dream? If heaven-sent, then no mere delusion, or as Nashe might say, it is "true melancholy or true appa-rition" (1:378). Romeo links his mysteriously fatal dream to "some consequence yet hanging in the stars," and this imagery reflects the "star-crossed" motif of the Prologue and anticipates "a greater power" (5.3.153), a punitive "heaven" that kills with love (5.3.153, 293), to which Friar Lawrence and Prince Escalus submit. Romeo resolves to journey onward by committing his direction to a higher power (1.4.112): "But He that hath the steerage of my course / Direct my sail!" (1.4.111-12). Likewise Nashe, in his discourse on night-ly terrors, comforts the reader by indicating that "look-ing to heauen for succor" (1:346) is the only way to fight the blinding power of darkness.[17] Nashe illus-trates this idea with the true story that partially moti-vated him to write his treatise, the story of a sick English country gentleman who had various visions that took the form of temptations (1:379). The gentleman, whose physical eye could not determine whether the seduc-tive apparition was an angel or fiend, relied on his "strong faith" in God "to defie & with-stand all his iugling temptations" (1:380).

Although Romeo has no waking visions, Juliet does have one, the germ of which is in Brooke's poem, while the superstition regarding such a vision is re-corded by Nashe. The articulation of this palpable vision is Shakespeare's own, however, and he uses it for negative premonition that begs to be construed correctly by the audience as it vacillates painfully be-tween fear and hope for the lovers. Juliet's soliloquy as she deliberates whether she should or can take the sleeping potion, with all its attendant dangers, cli-maxes with a vision that so fires her imagination that she resolves to drink immediately. Like Romeo, Juliet is now suffering from deep melancholy, and her fe-verish state also makes her susceptible to such appa-ritions. Juliet's waking vision might prompt some members of an Elizabethan audience to fear for her life. Nashe mentions one popular superstition that "none haue such palpable dreams or visions, but die presently after" (1.383). In Brooke's poem the pro-vocative part of Juliet's vision is the vivid reseeing by "the force of her ymagining . . . / The carkas of

Tybalt, / . . . in his blood embrewde" (11. 2378-82), which in turn spawns her fear of "a thousand bodies dead" (1. 2393) around her; before she can lose her nerve, she frantically drinks the potion.

But Shakespeare goes beyond Brooke by having his Juliet drink to save her beloved from Tybalt's hate. She thinks she "see[s]" (4.3.54) the rancorous ghost of Tybalt carrying the feud beyond the grave in order to revenge himself on "Romeo that did spit his body / Upon a rapier's point" (4.3.56-57). This specific recollection of their duel ironically anticipates the next deadly duel. Juliet's palpable vision proves paradoxically true and false, and as Nashe might gloss it, Juliet's vision is born of her own fears and her overwrought psychological state. It is not dead Tybalt but live Paris who seeks Romeo when he misconstrues Romeo's intention—"Can vengeance be pursued further than death?" (5.3.55)—and who pays with his life for his misguided but well-meant interference. However, as a gentleman Romeo honorably seeks both Paris's and Tybalt's forgiveness (5.3.101).[18] Tybalt does not seek Romeo's life; Romeo seeks his own. One principle of dreams in Nashe, which Shakespeare only partially acknowledges, concerns the role of personal responsibility in the shaping of one's fortunes and one's dreams: "of the ouerswelling superabundance of ioy and greefe, wee frame our selues most of our melancholy dreames and visions. . . . Euerie one shapes hys owne fortune as he lists. . . . Euerie one shapes his owne feares and fancies as he list" (1:377). In his desperate torment Romeo unwisely reasons: "O, what more favour can I do thee [Tybalt] / Then with that hand that cut thy youth in twain / To sunder his that was thine enemy" (5.3.98-100). But there is no friendly hand present this time to stay his own.

Romeo's second dream, this time with the contents specifically relayed to the audience, also fulfills Shakespeare's paradoxical perspective and complements the dramatic structure, where "all things change them to the contrary" (1.4.90), from "ordained festival" to "black funeral" (4.5.84-85). Romeo's dream, unlike his first one, is joyful so that despite his concern again about "the flattering truth of sleep," his dream uplifts him "with cheerful thoughts" that "some joyful news [is] at hand" (5.1.1-11). Given the popular superstition described by Nashe, this dream should foreshadow misfortune. Nashe warns: "He that dreams merily is like a boy new breetcht, who leapes and daunceth for joy his pain is past: but long that joy stays not with him, for presently after his master the day, seeing him so iocund and pleasant, comes and dooes as much for him againe, whereby his hell is renued" (1:356). Right on cue Balthasar enters with the tragic news of Juliet's death that initiates Romeo's defiance of the stars. Because Balthasar is described in the stage direction of the first quarto as "booted,"[19] he has apparently left Verona in such great haste,

once he saw Juliet laid low, that he must not have gone to Friar Lawrence to obtain the promised correspondence of "every good hap" that the Friar and Romeo had agreed would be carried between them by Balthasar (3.3.169-71).

To underscore the paradoxical significance of Romeo's dream, Shakespeare changes the role of Romeo's servant in the sources by having Friar Lawrence prudently assign him the function of letter-bearer and go-between.[20] Romeo asks Balthasar for such letters twice, once before and surprisingly once after he hears Balthasar's tragic news. But Balthasar, curiously, never explains his hasty departure from Verona. The audience might expect Romeo's first inquiry, but his second intelligent one, "Hast thou no letters to me from the Friar?" (5.1.31), intensifies the tragic tension because the audience knows Friar Lawrence sent "with speed" the important letters to Romeo by means of a fellow friar (4.1.122-24); the friar could not risk waiting for Balthasar's return to Verona once he and Juliet had decided on their desperate plan with the potion, intended to achieve Romeo's secret rescue of Juliet for their sojourn together in Mantua (4.1.105-17). But the plague unexpectedly delays Friar John, and Lord Capulet's joyful resolve to hasten the intended wedding day from Thursday to Wednesday, the very next morning, also complicates this desperately hopeful plan.[21] On his way to Friar Lawrence, Balthasar sees the funeral and returns swiftly instead to Romeo. Had Balthasar consulted Friar Lawrence as originally planned, he would have returned with the good news that would rightly interpret the meaning of Romeo's joyful dream.

In Romeo's dream the life and death positions of Juliet and himself appear to be reversed from what ultimately will happen, but Nashe reminds us that the nature of dreams is chaotic and "a Dreame is nothing els but the Eccho of our conceipts in the day" (1:356). However, despite apparent contradiction, Romeo's happy dream would prove true if he had not resolved upon suicide when he received Balthasar's unwittingly false news. Juliet would have revived the spirits of "a dead man" (5.1.7; 5.3.87), such as he describes himself when he is without her, and she would breathe "such life with kisses in [his] lips" (5.1.8) that he would triumph like "an emperor" in his sweet possession of love (5.1.10-11). Shakespeare's puns make Romeo's expectations and Balthasar's news all the more painful for the knowing audience: "Nothing can be ill if she be well" (5.1.17), and she is well in fact because Balthasar, speaking more truly than he knows, reminds us that her body only "sleeps in Capels' monument" (5.1.18). Instead, Romeo's "misadventure" (5.1.29) as "a desp'rate man" (5.3.59) leaves Juliet to find him literally dead. Her kisses cannot restore him to physical life, but if "some poison yet doth hang on" Romeo's lips, her kiss or "restorative" will enable her to die and lie with

Romeo (5.3.165-66). "Thy lips are warm" (5.1.167) may be the most tragic utterance in the play as Juliet realizes how close has been the *hamartia* of tragedy. Because the audience has just witnessed the deadly duel between Romeo and Paris, Balthasar's lines on his dream might seem superfluous:

> As I did sleep under this yew tree here,
> I dreamt my master and another fought,
> And that my master slew him.
>
> (5.3.137-39)

Nashe explains that noises that a dreamer subconsciously hears can inspire a dream: "one Eccho borrowes of another: so our dreames (the Ecchoes of the day) borrow of anie noyse we heare in the night" (1:356). But that does not explain Shakespeare's choice of the yew tree, which for Elizabethans could symbolize death. As John Gerard's *Herball* clarifies, the yew tree is common in many countries, including Italy and England, but it "is of a venemous qualitie, and against mans nature . . . and that if any do sleepe under the shadow thereof, it causeth sicknes, and oftentimes death."[22] While not prophetic, Balthasar's dream is nontheless true. He is probably inspired by the noise of the duel between Paris and Romeo to dream things true; his master did indeed fight and slay another. Thus Shakespeare allows for the truth, as well as the delusion, of what may or may not be an illusion.

If we grant any of these arguments, then we should also grant that Shakespeare's imaginative power of unifying into a more complex whole that which he finds separate or scattered in his source materials helps to demonstrate that he is very much an artist of Renaissance temperament. His ingenious use of sources favors the Renaissance ideal of "imitatio," whereby the combination of old material with new is expressed in an original manner. According to Renaissance critical theory regarding the operation of the poetic imagination, the imagination's transforming or "feigning" power is guided by reason to create art: the poetic feigning of images is described in the sixteenth century as a process of severing and joining things real to form things imagined.[23] As O. B. Hardison argues, "Shakespeare seems to have known what he was doing," deriving his "sense of artistry . . . from the experience of writing plays."[24] Romeo and Juliet, Hardison reminds us, are "among the most poignantly charming characters [Shakespeare] ever created."[25] And they are so attractive partly in relation to their dramatic world, which derives partly and complexly from Shakespeare's strikingly original use of Nashe. For the intricately unified world of his play, Shakespeare imaginatively transmutes and integrates various ideas, images, and intentions from Nashe's work on demons and dreams. Shakespeare's range of invention broadens our more limited sense of "source" because he

mines the literary convention of "sources" in such unconventional ways. In dramatizing the story of Romeo and Juliet as only he can, Shakespeare's imaginative art takes us "past the size of dreaming" (*Ant* 5.2.97) so that when we leave the theater and wake from the suspension of our disbelief in the imaginative act we have just experienced, like Caliban, we wake only to cry "to dream again" (*Tem* 3.2.143).

Notes

[1] See Katherine A. Briggs, *The Fairies in Tradition and Literature* (London: Routledge & Kegan Paul, 1967), 6-7; *The Anatomy of Puck* (London: Routledge & Kegan Paul, 1959), 18, 44, 56-70; *An Encyclopedia of Fairies* (New York: Pantheon Books, 1976), 120-21, 275, 295, 368-69. See also Harold F. Brooks, ed., *A Midsummer Night's Dream*, Arden Shakespeare (London: Methuen, 1979), lxxii and n.; R. A. Foakes, ed., *A Midsummer Night's Dream*, New Cambridge Shakespeare (Cambridge: Cambridge University Press, 1984), 6-7.

[2] See John Lyly, *Endimion*, in *The Dramatic Works of John Lyly*, ed. R. Warwick Bond (Oxford: Clarendon Press, 1967), 3:4.3.166; cf. 4.3.132. See also Lyly's *Gallathea* 3.2.5-7, where no specific size is indicated. Lyly does not directly connect fairies and dreams, nor does he use extreme diminution or the detailed and fanciful description that appears in both Shakespeare's *Dream* and *Romeo*.

[3] Briggs praises *Dream* as "our greatest fairy poem," especially its "shining unity of so many different materials." See Briggs, *Puck*, 44; cf. 45-50. But curiously overlooked is the new connection between fairy and dream in *Dream* and even more directly in *Romeo*. In her *Encyclopedia* Briggs hypothetically attempts to connect diminutive fairies from medieval tradition with a sleeper's dreams, based on the fairies' connection with the dead (not the living) and the idea of the sleeper's soul as a tiny creature whose extracorporeal "adventures are the sleeper's dreams" (98-99). This hypothesis does not relate to Shakespeare's presentation of diminutive fairy and dream in either *Dream* or *Romeo*. For different interpretations of dream in *Romeo and Juliet*, see Warren D. Smith, "Romeo's Final Dream," *MLR* 62 (1967): 579-83, and Marjorie B. Garber, *Dream in Shakespeare: From Metaphor to Metamorphosis* (New Haven and London: Yale University Press, 1974), 35-47.

[4] All quotations are from *Romeo and Juliet*, ed. G. Blakemore Evans, New Cambridge Shakespeare (Cambridge: Cambridge University Press, 1984). Quotations from other plays are from The Riverside Shakespeare, ed. Evans.

[5] See Briggs, *Encyclopedia*, 296-98.

[6] See Nashe, *The Works of Thomas Nashe,* ed. Ronald B. McKerrow, 5 vols. (1904-10; reprint, Oxford: Basil Blackwell, 1958), 1:339-86. References to volume and page are cited parenthetically.

[7] See ibid., 1:227-39.

[8] All references to Brooke's poem are documented parenthetically in my text and refer to Geoffrey Bullough, *Narrative and Dramatic Sources of Shakespeare* (London: Routledge and Kegan Paul, 1957), 1:284-363.

[9] For critical commentary on Mercutio's Queen Mab speech, see H. H. Furness, ed., *Romeo and Juliet,* Variorum Shakespeare (Philadelphia: J. B. Lippincott, 1899), 61-67; Brian Gibbons, ed., *Romeo and Juliet,* Arden Shakespeare (London: Methuen, 1980), 67: 1.4.53-54n; Evans, 21-22, 1.4.53-54n. 199 and note on 1.4.53; Joseph A. Porter, *Shakespeare's Mercutio: His History and Drama* (Chapel Hill: University of North Carolina Press, 1988), 104-5, 121, 124, 156, 245, n. 5 and passim. For arguments discussing Nashe's influence on Shakespeare, see Evans, 3-6; Kenneth Muir, *The Sources of Shakespeare's Plays* (London: Methuen, 1977), 9, 93, 67, 75.

[10] See McGinn, *Thomas Nashe* (Boston: Twayne Publishers, 1981), 63.

[11] It seems likely that Nashe's dream lore would draw on some popular traditions; he himself dismisses other authors on dreams, such as Artemidorus, Synesius, and Cardan, whom he has not had "the plodding patience to reade" (1:361). Reginald Scot, whose *Discoverie of Witchcraft* Nashe admits he has read (1:351), is cited by McKerrow for mentioning the proverb in England that dreams prove contrary. See McKerrow, 4:204. 32n. But even if we could identify all the popular traditions behind Nashe's lore, not just this particular one, we can not underestimate Nashe's collection of all these theories and his combination of them with the subject of diminutive spirits, dreams, and melancholy, as well as the sportive tone that characterizes Shakespeare's Mercutio.

[12] Briggs, *Puck,* 23. But Briggs does suggest that Nashe's playful granting of a spirit to all things, including mustard, may provide a hint for Shakespeare's naming of "Mustardseed" (23).

[13] See Hibbard, *Thomas Nashe: A Critical Introduction* (Cambridge: Harvard University Press, 1962), 12, 115, 117, and 118.

[14] Regarding the inspiration of Nashe for Shakespeare's characterization of Mercutio, see my essay "Nashe as 'Monarch of Witt' and Shakespeare's *Romeo and Juliet,"* *Texas Studies in Literature and Language* 37 (1995): 314-43.

[15] Evans cites verbal borrowings from Nashe (4, 169, 173, 203).

[16] Hibbard, *Nashe,* 114-15.

[17] Cf. Nashe's *Pierce Pennilesse* regarding the power of prayer as the only sure way to prevail against evil spirits (1:238-39).

[18] For gentlemanly behavior in the honorable duello, see my essays "Shakespeare's Duello Rhetoric and Ethic: Saviolo Versus Segar," *ELN* 31 (1993): 10-22, and "'Draw, if you be men': Saviolo's Significance for *Romeo and Juliet,"* *Shakespeare Quarterly* 45 (1994): 163-89.

[19] For the servant's hasty departure in the sources, see Brooke: "(Alas) too soone, with heavy newes he hyed away in post" (1, 2532); see Painter: Pietro "incontinently tooke poste horse." For Painter, see William Painter, trans., *The Palace of Pleasure,* ed. Joseph Jacobs (1890; reprint, New York: Dover Publications, 1966), 115.

[20] In Brooke (1, 2529) and in Painter (114), it is Romeo who originates the idea to have this man (Peter/Pietro) be a spy for him in Verona and to do his father, Lord Montague, service.

[21] See Evans, 4.2.23n, p. 203. Shakespeare contracts time (that is, he moves up the wedding date) and adds details to heighten tragic timing, eliciting more sympathy from well-intentioned characters caught in time's juggernaut. Friar Lawrence, for example, takes precious time to write again to Romeo to communicate "these accidents" (5.2.26-30), given Friar John's mishap, even though Juliet will awaken "within these three hours" (5.2.25). The Friar arrives before she awakens, but a "full half an hour" (5.3.130) after Romeo has entered the vault.

[22] See Gerard, *The Herball or Generall Historie of Plantes* (London: John Norton, 1597), 1188. Cf. Shakespeare's other references to the fatal yew: *Tit* 2.3.207; *R2* 3.2.117; *TN* 2.4.55; and *Mac* 4.1.27.

[23] For Renaissance critical theory, see William Rossky, "Imagination in the English Renaissance: Psychology and Poetic," *Studies in the Renaissance* 5 (1958): 49-73, esp. 58-59. Cf. also, Sir Philip Sidney, *A Defence of Poetry,* ed. J. H. Van Dorsten (Oxford: Oxford University Press, 1966), 24, 32, 36; John Milton, *Paradise Lost,* ed. Merritt Y. Hughes (New York: Odyssey Press, 1962), 5. 100-21.

[24] Hardison, "Shakespearean Tragedy: The Mind in Search of the World," *The Upstart Crow* 6 (1986): 80.

[25] Ibid., 79.

DREAMS AND VIOLENCE: *MACBETH*

Simon O. Lesser (essay date 1976)

SOURCE: "*Macbeth*: Drama and Dream," in *Literary Criticism and Psychology,* edited by Joseph P. Strelka, The Pennsylvania State University Press, 1976, pp. 150-73.

[*In the following essay, Lesser argues that* Macbeth *is to a great degree written in "the language of the unconscious," and interprets the play as a dramatization of "its protagonist's dreams, fantasies, and thoughts."*]

With the exception of *Hamlet,* and perhaps *King Lear,* more may have been written about *Macbeth* than any other play, yet some of the most significant aspects of the drama have gone unremarked—or noted too casually to provoke curiosity and analysis. Consider the many loose ends and apparent inconsistencies in the play, for example. Lady Macbeth speaks of having "given suck," but Macbeth has no son and no further reference is made to his wife's child, or children. Although Macbeth sees apparitions even before the murder of Duncan and, in general, seems unsure of his course and plagued by guilt, it is his strong-willed wife who breaks down first; though it is he who feels that "all great Neptune's ocean" cannot wash Duncan's blood from his hand and balks at returning the daggers, it is his wife who returns them and belittles the deed. It is she who futilely tries, while walking in her sleep, to rid her hands of the smell of blood. Or consider all that is made of the fact that Banquo has a son who may become king and father to a line of kings. For a time Macbeth regards Banquo and Fleance as the obstacles to the content he expected to feel as king and he steeps himself more deeply in blood to have them killed. Though Fleance escapes and the prospect that Banquo's descendants will rule is visualized during Macbeth's second visit to the weird sisters, nothing further is made of this plot thread. It is Duncan's older son, Malcolm, who is to be crowned king as the tragedy ends.

Even among the critics who show some awareness of *Macbeth*'s defects, few conclude that the play is badly flawed. This is a more remarkable tribute to the play than it may seem, for, as I shall try to show, some of its strengths have also gone unremarked. Shakespeare does such a superb job of storytelling in *Macbeth* that we read it in an almost trancelike state and refuse to be distracted by this or that apparent flaw. To be sure, this is true to some extent of all of Shakespeare's plays and for that matter all competently written imaginative literature. Fiction is usually read with a willing suspension of disbelief, or to put Coleridge's insight into the

language of our century, with a suspension of the vigilance normally exercised by the ego. But it is inadequate to regard Shakespeare's achievement in *Macbeth* as merely quantitative. Here as in some other cases a quantitative difference becomes qualitative—and of decisive importance. In most instances the extent and number of the departures from realism which occur in *Macbeth* would cause a reader to withdraw the trust he has provisionally granted the drama and to begin to read it detachedly and critically. Shakespeare does not permit this to happen. He induces a regression so deep that we read *Macbeth* as though it were an account of a dream.

More accurately, it is an account of a *series* of dreams, fantasies, and thoughts—a chain of mental speculations, mostly of the "What if . . . ?" kind. "What will happen if my valor comes to the attention of Duncan?" "What if he rewards me by making me one of the most powerful men in the land?" "What if he were to die and by some series of events I become king?"

It is remarkable that *Macbeth* can provide this sense of being privy to its hero's most secret thoughts and dreams, for drama is the most objective of all genres and may seem to have no devices save soliloquies and asides, which are somewhat awkward for taking a reader inside the mind, where thoughts and dreams are born. Shakespeare not only surmounts this difficulty with ease; he simultaneously accomplishes something which some might say is impossible in a drama; he tells his story largely from what today would be called the point of view of one of its characters. Macbeth's dreams are the basic subject of the play, and we see those dreams taking shape not only when he is on stage but often even when he is not. In scenes in which Macbeth plays a part, other characters—to say nothing of witches and apparitions—often talk and act as if they were enactments of Macbeth's dream-and-thought-fabric. More amazingly, when Macbeth is not physically present, other characters sometimes behave as if they were acting out his dreams. *Macbeth* may seem to be written in the same fashion as the other tragedies, but a close look reveals that it is not. Whole scenes, or crucial parts of scenes, are dramatized, not objectively (as they are, for example, in *Hamlet, King Lear,* and *Othello*) but *as Macbeth would imagine them.* Present or absent, he dominates almost the entire action. *Macbeth* is developed by what might be called, anachronistically, an objectified stream-of-consciousness technique.

Another important difference between *Macbeth* and Shakespeare's other plays, a formal one, is still less likely to be noted. To an astonishing extent *Macbeth* is written in the language of our dreams and daydreams, in what Freud calls the language of primary process thinking.[1] This is appropriate, but I am not sure it was deliberate. It would be my guess that Shakespeare let things well up from the unconscious to an exceptional degree while writing *Macbeth,* and that—allowing for the cuts, interpolations and loose ends, discontinuities and other changes believed to have been made by others—this is the main factor responsible for blemishes.

Whatever the genetic explanation may be, extensive use of primary process thinking in *Macbeth* contributes to an achievement of the highest order. It gives the play an organic quality it might otherwise lack. It lulls us into a state of relaxation in which we not only brush off inconsistencies, many of which, we sense, are only apparent or unimportant, but also understand the play much better and more easily than we would if we were more alert. It is largely responsible for our reading the play subliminally as a tissue of Macbeth's dreams, fantasies, and thoughts as well as an objective drama—this without becoming aware of the many violations of objectivity. Finally, it is responsible for the fact that we feel no need to choose between these two ways of apprehending the play. The shift back and forth between them is unconscious and effortless because the two ways of viewing the material of the play reinforce and enrich one another. At points the objective confirmation of some dream or desire is synergistic in its effect.

The claim that almost every scene of *Macbeth* can be experienced as a dream and an event dramatized, not objectively but from the hero's point of view, can be illustrated by glancing at the first three scenes. These fall into a pattern of increasing complexity. Other scenes will also be discussed, but the consideration of the opening three should show how almost any scene of the play can be understood simultaneously as dream and as event.

Perhaps Macbeth's second encounter with the weird sisters (IV. iii) is the scene which can most obviously be read as a dream. Until the appearance of Lennox at the end, the only characters besides Macbeth are witches, who are easy to see as embodiments of Macbeth's thoughts, and apparitions, whose claim to existential reality is more tenuous still. The fact that Macbeth does not even have to voice his questions to the apparitions confirms the impression that he has evoked them into being, and other characteristics of the scene help to establish its dreamlike quality.

Only a little less obviously, the first scene of the play is also a dream of Macbeth's, or a fragment of a dream: the witches are planning a meeting with him. What they will propose—that is, the exact nature of the desires stirring in Macbeth—is undefined; but the fact that the proposals are projected onto witches shows that they are felt to be evil. The "Fair is foul, and foul is fair" motif applies, not to those desires, but to Macbeth's battles, which are not only lost and won, but have evil as well as good effects.

It is not easy for a modern reader also to perceive the scene as objective. However, most Jacobean spectators evidently did not have this difficulty. They found it relatively easy to accept the existence of witches, perceived as embodiments of the evil in the world. As a corollary to this, they apparently found it no more difficult than the Greeks to think that such spirits would be concerned with mankind and individual people. The three witches in *Macbeth* are clearly concerned with the play's hero: this one touch suggests that the play is not wholly objective but often developed from Macbeth's point of view. Modern readers too, I believe—if not at the beginning at any rate by the time they are under the spell of the play— provisionally accept the existence of the witches as incarnations and agents of evil. This does not interfere with their perception of them as externalizations of the evil gestating in Macbeth.

The second scene is more easily read as objective; indeed, readers are seldom aware of having understood it in any other way. Unconsciously, the scene is read as a classic wish-fulfilling dream. Evidently Macbeth's desire to have his valor praised by everyone, and recognized and rewarded by the King, involves no conflict or self-reproach. In his dream, his exceptional bravery is not only brought to the attention of the King but singled out for special praise by the Captain. Duncan asks a question which couples his generals, but his only other interruption of the Captain's account is to praise Macbeth. And the scene ends happily, as a wishful dream should, with Duncan dispatching Ross to inform Macbeth that he has been named thane of Cawdor—and praising him once again.

The very factors which make the scene so satisfying to read as a dream tilt the scene so far in Macbeth's favor that, if we were not already in a quasi-trance-like state, we would be dissatisfied with it. Evidently Banquo is also an able and courageous general. If we were more alert, the desire for both justice and formal symmetry would make us feel that he should be accorded more praise and that there should be some indication that he too will be rewarded. (So far as we are informed, he never is.)

Scene iii reads equally well as dream or as objective but actually Macbeth-dominated dramatization. The most obvious basis for apprehending the scene as a dream is the reappearance of the witches. This together with Macbeth's immediate reference to "foul and fair" may make us think of the scene as a continuation of the dream begun in scene i. Subliminally, we may also be struck by the close correspondence between the material in this scene and what Macbeth would be thinking at this very time.

We know that he is walking to see his sovereign and if, as I believe, we are by now inside his mind, we know that one of the things he is thinking about is how he will be rewarded for his valor and his victories. We even know what Macbeth has dreamed but perhaps momentarily forgotten, that one of his rewards has been decided upon. And we have no doubt that it is Macbeth's dream which is unfolding. The first part of the scene tells us that it is Mecbeth the witches are awaiting. When he and Banquo appear, Banquo addresses them at length, but it is Macbeth they respond to. Not only the substance of what they say but the incantatory way they express themselves show that it is Macbeth they are thinking of—or projections of his thoughts.

Even Banquo may be part of Macbeth's dream fabric. If Macbeth were walking alone to see his sovereign and speculating about how he is to be rewarded, it would be natural for him to think of his fellow general. Banquo is a rival claimant for the recognition and honors for which Macbeth longs. Moreover, Macbeth fears Banquo. One of his fears is alluded to in the scene: Banquo has a son who may someday rule Scotland; Macbeth has no son. The second fear is not mentioned until III.i, an example of the extent to which the play follows primary process logic. (In other instances explanation also follows thought or act—or is not given at all.)

Much of I.iii revolves around two prophecies the witches make to Macbeth: they call him thane of Cawdor (this may be no more than an announcement), and promise him he will be king "hereafter." We may assume that both statements express wishes of Macbeth. No explanation of either wish is offered, and I will postpone discussion of speculations about the motives afforded by the play. What should be noted without delay is that the scene can also be read as a dramatization of actual events; though here, perhaps to a greater extent than in scene ii, the occurrences are presented as Macbeth would imagine them. This is obviously true up to line 50. Banquo, beginning with his second speech, acquires substantiality. He alerts us to Macbeth's reactions to what the witches tell him, as he does later to Macbeth's reactions to what he learns from Ross and Angus. Banquo also induces the witches to notice him and prophecy to him. The prediction is interesting to Macbeth and Banquo, who does not hesitate to warn Macbeth of the dangers latent in the prophecy that Macbeth will become king. Each general confirms the prediction made to the other, as though neither can quite believe what he has heard.

With the entrance of Ross and Angus the scene acquires additional substantiality. Here also, however, developments are dramatized from Macbeth's point of view and/or the focus is on him. The news the emissaries bring (I.iii.89-107) is all too obviously presented as Macbeth would imagine it. Although Banquo is present he is given neither praise nor a share in the King's bounty; indeed, he is utterly ignored. A critically alert reader would realize that this part of the scene would be embarrassing to all four participants. But being so completely under the spell of the play, the reader does not engage in reality testing. Shakespeare further protects the material by displacing our attention from the news Ross and Angus bring to its connection with the prophecies of the witches.

This scene illustrates Shakespeare's ability to induce the reader to slip back and forth between the two ways of apprehending the play. The first fifty lines of the scene are probably understood as being predominantly a part of Macbeth's dream-thought-fabric and, as mentioned, the Second Witch's speech, "All hail, Macbeth! Hail to Thee, Thane of Cawdor!"[2] is apprehended as an expression of his wish. In contrast, the King's emissaries seem to be real visitors from a real world. Ross's news that Duncan has actually named Macbeth Thane of Cawdor is such a startling coincidence that even Banquo is profoundly affected by it. To Macbeth the news is like a sign from fate. It seems to validate—and legitimatize—his most secret dreams, the whole pattern of desire of which becoming Thane of Cawdor is a part. It casts shadows beyond itself, appearing to sanction even the wish to become king. Macbeth's first words after Angus explains the fate of the previous thane tells us it has had this magical significance for him: "Glamis, and Thane of Cawdor: / The greatest is [to follow]."

The coincidence may make a modern reader think of a similar incident in a great nineteenth-century work of fiction—the apparently chance discovery by Raskolnikov that at precisely seven o'clock the next evening Lisaveta will be absent from her sister's apartment—a discovery that makes him feel he must go through with a murder which up to that point has seemed dreamlike and unreal. Shakespeare uses another conjunction of this sort in the very next scene of *Macbeth*. Duncan's decision to visit Inverness is interpreted by both Macbeth and Lady Macbeth as a sign that they should proceed with the terrible act they are contemplating. However, whereas it is a clear "go" signal to Lady Macbeth, it simultaneously imposes another constraint on her husband—and reminds him of all the other arguments telling him to abstain from the unjustified murder. But this attempt to strengthen his defenses is ineffectual. What he wants appears within easy reach and his scruples are overcome, or lost sight of, in a matter of minutes.

Shakespeare's double vision of almost every scene of *Macbeth* may have been inadvertent. Since he had two potential male heroes, he probably felt a need to emphasize Macbeth so that Banquo would simply be a foil to him, not a rival claimant for our interest. The emphasis was also necessary to induce audience identification with Macbeth.

The half-"real," half-dreamlike world Shakespeare conjures up in *Macbeth* is so enthralling that we feel no disposition to choose between alternatives, to decide on a single attitude toward the play, which would break its spell. It is helpful of course that Macbeth dominates both ways of perceiving the story, so that the gap between them is not great. Each kind of reality, or unreality, that of dreams, that of the actual, comes to suffuse the other. Thus we are not even taken aback when, in IV.i, Macbeth asks Lennox, "Saw you the weird sisters?" But we could wonder how Lennox even knows what Macbeth is talking about.

The deep suspension of disbelief with which we read helps to explain our refusal to pay much attention to other slips, gaps, inconsistencies, and the presentation of material in apparently illogical sequence. We do not question the primary process language and we tend to be uncritical even in thinking about the play after reading or viewing it. To accept I.iii as realistic would involve provisional belief either in witches or in the rare psychological occurrence of *folie à deux*. Few readers, or critics, seem troubled by such considerations.

The only casualties of our uncritical reading of the play are parts of it which do not admit of double vision and whose single strand of reference takes us away from Macbeth for what seems a considerable time. Parts of scenes which seem wholly objective—for example, II. iii up to the appearance of Macbeth—do not suffer, for they are swiftly traversed. Nor do objective, highly dramatic scenes which introduce appealing characters; the scene at Macduff's castle (IV.ii) will serve as an example. It is only when a scene is objective and takes us away from Macbeth for an extended period that our interest tends to flag. The scene in which Malcolm tests Macduff's loyalty (IV.iii) is perhaps the only good example. We may explain our dissatisfaction on some other basis, such as lack of realism, but its chief source, I believe, is our impatience to return to Macbeth.

Since *Macbeth* appears to have been written in a state of regression, it is not surprising that there are delayed explanations and numerous omissions. In particular, little attention is paid to motivation, even in Macbeth's case, despite the fact that we are often inside his mind. We are never told, for example, why Macbeth dreams of being named thane of Cawdor. Nor are we told why Macbeth wanted to be king. Some of the immediate determinants of the desire are fairly easy to surmise. From dreaming of being rewarded by the King to dreaming of becoming king is but a short and pleasant step. The skill and courage Macbeth displayed in the battles, which in a sense begin the tragedy, influence him in a more direct way. They may make him think of himself, probably with warrant, as preeminent on the fields of battle. Why not then preeminent during peacetime also? Almost certainly, Macbeth's victories bolster his sense of his own worth, make him feel that his countrymen in general will now esteem him more. This in turn makes the idea of higher station seem a realistic possibility. In a sense the criminal dreams which undo Macbeth are born of success. But as we shall see, that is not their ultimate source.

It is important to note that this first intimation that Macbeth will become king arouses fear rather than satisfaction. There could be no better evidence that the idea of murdering Duncan is already gestating in his mind. A little later he does face the need for this murder—only to be overcome by such fears that he falls into a trance in which he becomes oblivious to the presence of Banquo, Ross, and Angus. He shies away from the idea of killing Duncan with the wish that chance will crown him, but it seems that neither the reader nor Macbeth has any faith in this solution. Before his crime is named, Macbeth begins to suffer from guilt. The Crown is not golden even in anticipation, but mottled and tarnished.

The most strenuous objection to the way of reading *Macbeth* being developed here will come, I suspect, from those who believe that Lady Macbeth is a stronger character than her husband and maintain that she dominates him and the action of the early part of the play. Of course, she is not a stronger character or she would not collapse completely before her husband—and for that matter the play would not be called *Macbeth*. The failure to understand the nature of the interaction between Macbeth and his wife must stem in part from failure to read the work with sufficient care or to recall all we sensed as we read, in part from ignorance of ourselves and human nature generally—or temporary lack of access to what we know.

If we read the play carefully and have some experience of life and knowledge of ourself, it seems to me we can hardly fail to perceive that, far from Lady Macbeth dominating her husband, Macbeth skillfully enlists and uses his wife's help. In I.iv Macbeth encounters an apparently new obstacle to his desire with far less fear and ambivalence than he showed in the preceding scene. At the same time, before we so much as meet Lady Macbeth, he diagnoses the weakness in himself which may make it impossible for him to attain his desire:

> The Prince of Cumberland! That is a step
> On which I must fall down, or else o'erleap,
> For in my way it lies. Stars, hide your fires;
> Let not light see my black and deep desires:
> The eye wink at the hand; yet let that be
> Which the eye fears, when it is done, to see.
> (I.iv.48-53)

What Macbeth is hoping for is some way of outwitting conscience—or to use the language of twentieth-century depth psychology, the superego. His attempt to secure his wife's help is the most ingenious of the devices he employs, and her goading and participation reduce his guilt to the point where he can go through with the murder. Still, he is just barely able to do so; and after the first murder his efforts to circumvent or mollify his conscience are still less successful. To be sure, his superego does not stop him from murdering Duncan or others, but it does prevent him from deriving any satisfaction from the murders. Even this formulation is inadequate: as we have seen, Macbeth is tormented by guilt and anxiety before the murder of Duncan—even before the crime has assumed definite shape in his mind. At the time he plans the murder of Banquo and Fleance, he deliberately tries to harden himself in order to be impervious to the stings of conscience. Although he does in fact become harder and his sensibility dulls, this stratagem is no more successful than the others. He is guilt-ridden when he reluctantly enters the combat with Macduff which ends with his death. He goes to his grave without having achieved any satisfaction or even respite from self-reproach from his career of crime. Each murder augments his guilt, increases his self-condemnation, deepens his depression, and intensifies his fear of, and even desire for, punishment.

The fact that Macbeth has a severe superego must be stressed in order to correctly understand the play. Macduff and his other enemies talk of him as a devil, but they do not know him from the inside, as we do. Shakespeare does not want us to accept their judgment without important qualifications. I have no wish to extenuate, much less excuse, Macbeth's crimes, but he is a murderer of the Brutus or Raskolnikov kind, not the Richard III kind. The killing of the grooms perhaps excepted, he is never able to murder cold-bloodedly. He is never able to deceive himself by justifying his crimes.

Despite his inability to distort reality, it seems that his ego is crippled in some respects. It behaves like the ego of a person suffering from an obsession or compulsion. Otto Fenichel writes: "In all psychoneuroses the control of the ego has become relatively insufficient. . . . In compulsions and obsessions, the fact that the ego governs motility is not changed, but the ego does not feel free in using this governing power. It has to use it according to a strange command of a more powerful agency, contradicting its judgment. It is compelled to do or think, or to omit certain things; otherwise it feels menaced by terrible threats."[3] The hypothesis that Macbeth's ego is impaired in some such way as this helps to explain the anomaly of a man with a conscience like his being able to murder. The hypothesis also explains the feeling the play gives that the agonizing inner struggle Macbeth undergoes is between id and superego, with practically no mediation by the ego. As a result of its weakness, he is victimized by both of the opposed and never reconciled parts of his psyche: he yields to his impulses but is lashed before, during, and after each surrender.

Macbeth realizes that he must do everything he can to deceive his conscience, and, immediately after expressing the vain wish to be blind to his own acts, he writes to his wife. Although sequence is not always a reliable guide in *Macbeth,* it does occasionally help in establishing causal connections. One does not have to examine Macbeth's letter searchingly to see that one of its aims is to induce his wife to persuade him to murder Duncan. If she persuades him, Macbeth believes he can claim that the idea comes from outside and he can deny his own responsibility. The ending of the letter is seductive in tone. It tries to recruit his wife not simply as a helper but as an accomplice in crime, and twice offers her an incentive for giving him her support. "This have I thought good to deliver thee, my dearest partner of greatness, that thou mightst not lose the dues of rejoicing, by being ignorant of what greatness is promised thee. Lay it to thy heart, and farewell" (I.v.11-15).

Macbeth wants to create the illusion that external forces are impelling him onward. The attempt to secure his wife's involvement is of a piece not only with his later use of hirelings to commit his crimes; it squares also with his tendency to externalize temptations, wishes, and fears in the forms of witches and apparitions.

The mechanism Macbeth hopes to take advantage of in enlisting the help of his wife must be older than marriage—as old as continuing close relationships of any kind between two people: a person communicates something to a confidant in order to provoke an anticipated and desired response.[4] Often a person wants encouragement to do something which he wants to do but which arouses so much conflict that it cannot be done without outside support—or support which appears to come from outside. Alternatively, help may be desired in resisting a course of action which is tempting, but which is perceived to be wrong and/or likely to lead to trouble.

Macbeth's situation and procedure fall into a common pattern. His desire to be king is so overpowering that he is *almost* willing to kill Duncan to attain his goal, though he recognizes he has no justification for such an act. He acquaints his masculine, aggressive, not overlyscrupulous wife with his dilemma on the assumption that she knows him well enough to identify his dominant wish and to give him just the kind of encouragement and active assistance he needs to gain it. (He is right about this, though it seems to me that Lady Macbeth never recognizes the basis of her husband's hesitancy as clearly as his speeches permit us to recognize it.) Whether his reasoning is conscious or, as is more likely, unconscious, Macbeth must feel that the letter is an important step in doing what he senses to be necessary—overcoming the inner resistances which keep him from killing Duncan. Meanwhile, the very act of sharing his tempting but frightening dream with his wife may somewhat reduce his guilt feelings.

Once aroused Lady Macbeth does such a vigorous job of persuasion we may forget that it was her husband who enlisted her support. The intensity of her desire that he become king may be a surprise to him and to Lady Macbeth herself. In the great invocation in I.v, which begins, "Come, you spirits / that tend on mortal thoughts, unsex me here . . ." she appears to be summoning strength from reserves never before tapped. There can be no questioning of Lady Macbeth's wifely devotion. She mobilizes all her strength to play the role she feels she must play to bring happiness to her husband and herself.

It is necessary to ask why Macbeth should want to kill Duncan, whom he cannot find fault with as man or king and who has been particularly gracious and generous toward him. Neither Macbeth nor, interestingly, Lady Macbeth ever makes an attempt to extenuate, much less justify, the murder. But if we did not feel that there was an adequate explanation for what Macbeth does, we would not have a high opinion of the tragedy.

Perhaps Macbeth is actuated by unconscious hostility. Some psychoanalytic interpretations of the drama have been based on this hypothesis: Macbeth is seen as a bad son acting out some unextirpated hatred for the father upon a surrogate. But apart from the fact that Macbeth at no point seems to be a son figure, unless the murder of Duncan itself admits of no alternative explanation, there is no trace of such hatred, either before or after the crime. When at the end of the superb after-the-murder scene with Lady Macbeth, he exclaims to the unknown person knocking at the gate, "Wake Duncan with thy knocking! I would thou couldst!" we have no doubt that he means it. There is more reason to suspect his public comment on Duncan's death in the next scene (II.iii.93-98), since he is here trying to make himself one with the others lamenting the murder, but I believe that, ironically, the occasion provides a welcome opportunity to say something he deeply feels; and his prognosis of his own situation is uncannily accurate.

What circumstances, what motive or motives, could drive a man like this to kill when there is no excuse for killing? As we have seen, it was success which crystallized and gave urgency to the desire to be king; and rewards stemming from success, such as being named thane of Cawdor and being visited by Duncan, seemed like signs from fate that he should act to attain his desire. But Lady Macbeth's reaction to her husband's letter—her lack of surprise as much as what she says—indicates that unrest and amorphous ambition antedate the action of the play.

Those feelings were born of failure, not success. Macbeth went through with an act for which he knew himself unqualified and killed a man he loved because he

was an unhappy, discontented, even desperate man, who found life sterile and empty. And because he was desperate, he nurtured the absurd, groundless hope that being king would somehow change everything. When the play begins, Macbeth is already a thane of Scotland and a renowned general; but he is also middle-aged, childless, friendless, and loveless. Moreover, though an intelligent man, he is without any interests which might make his life seem meaningful.

The claim that Macbeth is loveless seems to be contradicted by his closeness to his wife during the early part of the play, but it is possible, even likely, that their partnership in crime brought them closer together than they had been for a long time, or perhaps ever before. The crime offered the vaguely defined but alluring promise of curing their discontents, of making their lives more fulfilling. During the planning of the murder of Duncan, as G. Wilson Knight points out, they are "in evil with" one another, just as Antony and Cleopatra are in love with one another. Even during this period of closeness, however, though Lady Macbeth is loyal and devoted to her husband and each of them is dependent to some extent on the other, there is no indication of passionate love, past or present, on either side. It is possible that Macbeth has had no children by his wife because he is impotent. His complaint about the "barren scepter" (III.i.62) the weird sisters have put in his grasp may include this second meaning. There are more definite indications that his marriage, like so many middle-aged marriages, has deteriorated into a kind of business partnership. Perhaps it had never been more than that.

If these speculations are correct, Macbeth is susceptible to the dream of becoming king because for a long time before the play opens he had been oppressed by a discontent so profound that he felt almost any change would be for the better. Perhaps Macbeth's willingness to court death was born of desperation, of a feeling that matters might as well be either better or worse. He fights Macduff with the same fury at the end of the play when he is not only desperate but hopeless. Interestingly, two of the murderers Macbeth enlists to kill Banquo and Fleance, the First Murderer in particular, express the very psychology I am describing as they accept their assignment:

> And I another
> So weary with disasters, tugged with fortune,
> That I would set [risk] my life on any chance,
> To mend it or be rid on't.
>
> (III.i.111-14)

Later there is firmer evidence that Macbeth was impelled to his first crime by discontent. He reminds his wife that the purpose of killing Duncan had been to gain their peace, but the statement, the most explicit the play offers, is embedded in a speech of such eloquence

("We have scorched the snake, not killed it . . .") that, bewitched by its beauty, we may not take in the plain sense of much that is said:

> better be with the dead,
> Whom we, to gain our peace, have sent to peace,
> Than on the torture of the mind to lie
> In restless ecstasy [frenzy].
>
> (III.ii.19-22)

The placement of the revelatory phrase, "to gain our peace," may also keep it from attracting the attention it deserves.

Just before Macbeth's entrance, his wife had soliloquized: "Nought's had, all's spent, / Where our desire is got without content." This too suggests that the hope for something like peace, a feeling of satisfaction and well-being, gave birth to the desire of Macbeth and his lady to become king and queen.

The still more famous "She should have died hereafter" passage (V.v.17-28) also may be evidence of this motive. The passage is usually viewed as a set piece, with no important relationship to the play as a whole, but I believe that the feelings of the emptiness, sterility, and meaninglessness of life it expresses are feelings Macbeth was trying to combat from the very beginning. To be sure, now that his wife is dead and the mistakenness of his course is becoming more apparent with each new development, the feelings are being reexperienced with greater poignancy.

Even with goading from his wife, Macbeth proceeds with the murder of Duncan only with great difficulty. With the hysteric's facility for converting thoughts and feelings into somatic or external terms, he conjures up a dagger, and a little later sees it covered with gouts of blood. Not only these hallucinations, but various things he says show that he is already tormented by guilt: yet his crime is still "but fantastical." In I.iii, once he began sensing what he would have to do to become king, he took refuge in wishful thinking:

> If chance will have me King, why, chance may crown me,
> Without my stir.

Although he now realizes that this is a vain hope, he has not otherwise made much progress. He is still hoping that the "sure and firm-set earth"—and by this I think he means the gods and destiny, not simply the human beings at Inverness—will remain ignorant of his deeds. Revelatory also is the phrase, "I go, and it is done." He glides over, is unwilling to visualize, the murder itself.

What he tells his wife in II.ii makes it clear that during or immediately after the murder—here as elsewhere

time indications are uncertain—his guilt deepened further. Even more significant is the way his unconscious desire to be caught and punished discloses itself in the very execution of his crime: he has forgotten to smear the grooms with blood and to leave their daggers near them, and he has brought the daggers to his own chamber. Now he is so overwhelmed by guilt that he cannot return them and bloody the grooms. It is Lady Macbeth who undertakes these repugnant errands. His speeches when he hears the knocking confirm the intensity of his guilt: he is continuing his self-punishment and clearly plans to punish himself further.

Macbeth again receives desperately needed help from his wife after the murder of Banquo. But after killing Duncan, Macbeth never again *asks* for her help. It is important to observe what causes this turnabout. His own inner feeling is the primary factor. He had unjustifiably hoped that his wife's help would enable him not only to go through with a wanton murder, but to kill his King-benefactor-cousin-guest with little or no guilt. Instead he is flooded with guilt. His disappointment may make him realize that he has been unrealistic in his expectations and that his wife cannot give him the escape from self-reproach he had hoped for. After III.iv, he no longer gives her his full confidence, and the reader feels that some of his endearments are perfunctory. He thinks of her less and less thereafter. Once it is committed, the crime that was to bring them together and make their marriage more fulfilling isolates them further.

The banquet scene (III.iv), the last scene in which Macbeth speaks with his wife, or imagines himself doing so, may also be understood as a dream. Indeed, if we had not by this point abandoned reality testing we could scarcely accept it in any other way. It is hard to explain how the banquet guests could fail to note Macbeth's conversation with the First Murderer, harder still to explain how they could avoid overhearing the exchange between Macbeth and his wife, whose second speech to him (61-69) makes it plain that he is the murderer of Duncan.

We do not see Lady Macbeth again until the sleepwalking scene (V.i), and that is the last time we see her. In V.iii, the doctor gives Macbeth a report of her illness, and in the final speech of the play we learn that she may have killed herself. The sleepwalking scene does not seem to be part of Macbeth's dream fabric, but rather something which took place after he became so immersed in his anxieties that he seldom thought of his wife. It is possible, however, that, preoccupied as he was, he had become aware of his wife's disturbed and depressed state of mind and even of her sleepwalking. In that case Macbeth could have dreamt the sleepwalking scene to deal with the anxiety he felt about others learning of his wife's condition and, what was more frightening still, learning of his crimes from what she said and did while in a somnambulistic state.

Although Macbeth has become separated from his wife, it seems to me that his responses to the news of her illness and the news of her death both show that he feels deep sympathy for her. His response to the account of the "thick-coming fancies / That keep her from her rest" is rich in feeling. It is obvious here (V.iii.39-54) and in the speech he makes when he learns of her death that some of the regret he expresses is for himself. He is in fact confusing his wife's situation and his own. Nothing could show more clearly that the tie with her is still not severed. To be sure, the second speech seems dry and impersonal, but its tone is a defense against feeling. Although Macbeth is controlled and detached, what he says expresses regret, and self-reproach, for such separation as has occurred between him and his wife, for the futility and meaninglessness of their crimes and their lives, and for her suffering and disappointment no less than for his own.

Certain parts of the group of scenes we have been considering—the Porter's soliloquy and exchange with Macduff and Lennox, and the exchange between Ross and the unnamed Old Man—do not seem to be products of Macbeth's mind. They lack resonance in consequence. Here and throughout the play the most intense scenes seem to be both parts of Macbeth's thought fabric and accounts of events. Their intensity derives in large part from the fact that they are apprehended in both ways.

Although Macbeth renounces the idea of using his wife a second time to deceive his superego, he tries to achieve the same end by different means. He never ceases to hope that, should he have to kill, he can find some way of doing so without being crushed by guilt.

In the final speech of the conversation with his wife which follows the planning of the murder of Banquo and Fleance, he invokes "seeling night" to "scarf up the tender eye of pitiful day." I think he is also expressing the wish that *he* may be blindfolded. Although the ambiguous "bond" he wants night to "cancel and tear to pieces" almost certainly refers to the prophecy that Banquo's sons will someday rule Scotland, it may also refer to *his* bond to his fellow general and to mankind.

Indirectly and obscurely Macbeth is expressing the old wish that he can be blind to his own acts and he reverts to it once more in III.iv.140-41. Nevertheless, it seems unlikely that he still has any real faith in this possibility. As we know, however, he has employed three murderers to get rid of Banquo and Fleance, and he appears to hope, in this way, to reduce or eliminate his own feeling of responsibility. He tries to prove his innocence to the Ghost of Banquo by claiming that he had not killed him. But the very fact that he conjures up the Ghost, whether in a hallucination or a dream, shows how ineffectual this new stratagem is in evading guilt.

In III.ii and again, more sharply, in III.iv, he expresses the wish that by deliberately hardening himself, by immersing himself more deeply in evil, he can make himself impervious to guilt:

> My strange and self-abuse
> Is the initiate fear that wants hard use.
> We are yet but young in deed.
>
> (III.iv.143-45)

At the time Macbeth makes this speech he is evidently already contemplating the murder of Macduff. By this point he has coarsened a great deal, and he coarsens further before our eyes in IV.i as a result of the rage and fear he feels when he learns that Macduff has fled to England. He again employs murderers, this time to do away with Macduff's family. But the combined effects of these mechanisms for hoodwinking the superego or becoming indifferent to its reproaches is nil. Whatever his actions may suggest, he never achieves cold-bloodedness and indifference to conscience. We learn this from Macbeth's first comment to Macduff on the battlefield before Dunsinane:

> Of all men else I have avoided thee.
> But get thee back! My soul is too much
>   charged
> With blood of thine already.
>
> (V.viii.5-7)

Although against his will, Macbeth is a moral man to the very end of the tragedy, and this is his real problem: the source of his efforts to deceive conscience and keep himself in ignorance of his own deeds. Those efforts are foredoomed to failure. He is unable to keep any aspect of his behavior from awareness; he is compelled to perceive not merely his acts, but their wrongness and their consequences. From the time he subterraneously reaches the decision that murder is not too high a price to pay for being king (in the play seen as an action), his situation is probably hopeless. Certainly it is hopeless from the moment when, against the dictates of his own mind and heart, he goes through with the crime. He commits a murder for which he knows there is no excuse, and his punishment, whether "actual" or imagined, is Dantesque: he becomes a murderer.

His situation is irremediable and he knows it. The scorpions which have taken possession of his mind are an integral part of his punishment: he is plagued incessantly by self-reproach and the feeling that, to achieve a sense of security, he must murder again and again. The death he finally achieves is a release as much as a punishment. Two speeches in V.iii, 19-29 ("Seyton!—I am sick at heart . . .") and 39-45 ("Cure her of that . . ."), corroborate what the very toneless-ness of the "She should have died hereafter" speech tells us more subtly: for some time he has been ready to welcome death.

Macbeth's feeling that he must do away with Banquo and Fleance may easily be perceived as another part of his dream fabric. His rivalry with Banquo and fear of him can be sensed in I.iii and is of course expressed explicitly in III.i. His fear of Banquo's descendants is unmistakable even in the earlier of these scenes and is heavily emphasized in lines 57-72 of the later scene. In dreams no less than in real life, even if he finally succeeded in killing Duncan and Banquo, he would continue to worry about the prophecy that Banquo's descendants would eventually rule Scotland.

Act IV, scene i, can be read like an account of an actual dream. Shakespeare had to be deeply inside the mind of Macbeth to write the scene; in addition to flowing like a dream and dealing with the worries which preoccupy Macbeth at this point, the scene expresses them in the logic and images Macbeth would fall into. If Macduff is not a friend, then he is an enemy. Thus the apparition of the Armed Head, which expresses his fear of Macduff.

We might suppose that at this point the dreamwork would attempt to provide reassurance against the warning. If so, the attempt is unsuccessful. It is ominous to begin with that Macbeth conjures up a Bloody Child. We know that as early as I.iii he feared the Crowned Child he is soon to see. The Bloody Child extends this fear to a still-to-be-born or just-born child; it must seem to Macbeth that he must fear all children, even those not yet conceived. At the same time the Bloody Child represents the retributive fears he has as a result of the murder of Banquo and the attempt to murder Fleance; and, equally, of the consequences of the "strange things" taking shape in his mind which crystallize at the end of the scene—the decision to kill Macduff's wife and children.

Nor do the words of the Bloody Child succeed in reassuring Macbeth. The way its promise is phrased— "none of woman born / shall harm Macbeth"—seems calculated to allow for loopholes. As we read, we notice this, if at all, only subliminally, but Macbeth's response shows clearly that his fear has not been quieted:

> Then live, Macduff: what need I fear of
>   thee?
> But yet I'll make assurance double sure,
> And take a bond of fate. Thou shalt not live;
> That I may tell pale-hearted fear it lies,
> And sleep in spite of thunder.
>   (IV.i.82-86)

The image of "a Child Crowned, with a tree in his hand" condenses Macbeth's deepest and most terrifying fears. From the beginning the realization that some other man's child would succeed him has galled him, making him aware of his childlessness and perhaps his impotence, and it has intensified his guilt by making

his crimes seem selfish and futile. The tree the Child has in its hand is a fertility symbol, contrasting with Macbeth's "barren scepter." Inevitably, the apparition calls to mind the promise the witches have made to Banquo. He asks the apparition about this just before it disappears; and it paves the way for the heartbreaking image of the eight kings and Banquo—the "family tree" which the weird sisters show him immediately afterward. In an only slightly hidden way the apparition also voices Macbeth's growing fear of "conspirers." At some level he realizes that he is creating the coalition of forces which will ultimately destroy him.

We may become consciously aware of the hedged nature of the promise that Macbeth shall not be vanquished until "Great Birnam Wood to high Dunsinane Hill / Shall come against him." It is not until the play is analyzed that we are likely to realize how natural it is that Macbeth, a general used to sizing up terrain and developing strategies of attack and defense, should have thought of the trick which later occurs to Malcolm. The connection between the tree the child carries and fertility gives another implication to the moving wood, which later exposes the futility of Macbeth's hopes and leads to his death. Shakespeare wants us to feel that a sterile and death-oriented man like Macbeth cannot prevail for long against life-affirming forces.

Just as the news Ross and Angus brought after Macbeth's first encounter with the witches seems to confirm his hopes and justify the terrible act he is considering, so Lennox's news that Macduff has fled to England confirms his fears and is seized as an excuse to proceed with murders more wanton and useless still. I have had to scant the artistry of *Macbeth*. The formal symmetry of I.iii and IV.i is another example of how pervasive it is. The artistry is all the more remarkable if, as I suspect, *Macbeth* was written while Shakespeare was in a distraught state.

To a greater extent than any other drama I know, *Macbeth* is "written" in the language of what Freud calls primary process thinking, the language of the unconscious. This would perhaps be more apparent if the play were less concerned than it is with Macbeth's anxieties and fears. Primary process thinking is usually under the sway of the pleasure principle; its common function is to provide the hallucinatory gratification of desires. But there are anxiety dreams and fantasies as well as wish-fulfilling ones. Even when Macbeth seems preoccupied with his anxieties, numerous characteristics of primary process thinking are clearly in evidence.

If Shakespeare were less of an artist, gross content elements would make us aware of the extent to which primary process thinking prevails in *Macbeth*. Readers not only accept, but quickly begin to take for granted the strange world the play conjures up. In this world the prophecies of supernatural creatures and apparitions often correctly foreshadow and even seem to bring about events. Prophecies hinge upon such things as a wood moving or a person being invulnerable to someone born of a Caesarian operation, but not to someone born in the ordinary way. Our credulity is explained in part by our intuitive ability to understand primary process language—in particular, to perceive the subjective meaning of something apparently objective.

Other things besides unrealistic story elements suggest the extent to which *Macbeth* is written in the language of the unconscious. Like our fantasies and dreams the play is a rebus in which cause often follows effect and explanation often follows act. Equally significant is the almost complete disregard of time. Psychoanalysis has taught us that the idea of time does not exist in the unconscious. Similarly, in *Macbeth* there are practically no clues to the passage of time, though this plays an important part in the Holinshed account upon which Shakespeare drew. Not only have we no idea of how long a period of time the play covers; we seldom have a sure idea of how much time elapses between any two scenes. Such references to time as appear are often vague or careless. In the banquet scene Macbeth refers to charnel houses and graves sending "Those that we bury back," but in fact when he speaks there would not have been time to bury Banquo.

Perhaps more significant still is the extent to which a tendency to picture everything manifests itself in *Macbeth*. Wishes, fears, means, and guilt feelings (the bloody dagger, the Ghost of Banquo) are externalized, often personified, shown, and/or voiced. Figures of speech abound, pour out in such profusion that more than one metaphor seems mixed, more than one speech incoherent. As Cleanth Brooks shows, however, the images and symbols which run through the play are (like many of our dreams) better organized than they appear to be.[5] Moreover, the more we penetrate the surface of the play, the more unified and understandable they become.

As we have seen, *Macbeth* can be read as a tissue of its protagonist's dreams, fantasies, and thoughts. Even when viewed as a dramatization of events, those events are often shown as they would be imagined by Macbeth: to some extent nearly every scene reflects his wishes or fears. Thus there is really little difference between the two ways of apprehending the play, and we feel no disposition to choose between them. Moreover, the play is written to an exceptional extent in the language of our dreams and fantasies. Although *Macbeth* has rivals in our century, for example, *Six Characters in Search of an Author,* it may remain the most subjective play ever written. We read it in a state of relaxation, in much the way we read fairy stories in childhood. However it is apprehended, we accept it primarily, I believe, as a dramatization of psychic reality.

Still, Shakespeare brings off the miracle of persuading us provisionally to accept *Macbeth* as an account of "real" events. A priori, nothing seems more improbable than the idea that a man with such an unrelenting conscience as Macbeth's would embark on a career of crime. Yet Shakespeare makes a play based upon such apparently irreconcilable plot elements believable. However understood, *Macbeth* is among other things one of the world's greatest cautionary tales. Even a person of probity and strong conscience might *dream* of committing an unjustified murder to obtain something desperately desired. Moreover, even such a person might find it impossible to relinquish the dream. Against his will he might find himself returning to it night and day, embellishing it, visualizing ways and means, imagining this or that vicissitude and contingency until, to his horror, a whole series of crimes had been thought through from beginning to end. As Shakespeare has shown, however, what would be upper-most in the mind of such a person is not the crimes or their rewards but the punishment to be endured. Again and again the dreamer would in effect be telling himself, "Only evil and suffering would come of this." The result, if not the purpose, of the dream-thought-fabric would be to pare down the temptation and emphasize its consequences, so that the feared impulse could be controlled. In most cases only the dreamer would profit from this, but when the dream fabric is embodied in a work of art readers and spectators share in the benefits.

Considered as a dramatization of actual occurrences, *Macbeth* is probably a still more effective cautionary tale. When events seem less contingent and more real, tragedy has its maximum impact on us-though the events are experienced vicariously. The vicarious gratification of impulses, which plague us no less than Macbeth, would make them less urgent and hence more amenable to control, especially if the gratification was apparently real. The emphasis, or overemphasis, on punishment would remind us of the terrible price the gratification entails and hence provide a constraint against yielding to desire.

It is of the utmost importance that Macbeth's first crime, which is the one that fathers all the others, is the murder of his sovereign, who is important in his own right and is the symbol of order in the state. Moreover, it is a murder he knows to be unjustified. No crime could better symbolize what might be called the sacred crimes, the violations of the primeval taboos upon which civilization rests. Nor could any crime better illustrate the strength and tenacity of our anarchistic desires. Many of those desires and the tendency to put the satisfaction of the desires above everything else go back to childhood, but neither the desires nor this tendency is ever completely relinquished; they may still be troublesome when we are grown-up. In our minds and hearts we have all experienced the temptation to which Macbeth was subjected, or temptations analogous to it, and at one time or another we have yielded to them, in thought if not in deed. The fact that *Macbeth* has this reference to a wide range of our most primitive desires and conflicts helps to explain its unshakable hold on the imagination of mankind.

Notes

[1] Primary process thinking is largely in the service of the id, secondary process thinking in the service of the ego. It is easiest to understand the first mode of thinking by comparing it with the second, the kind of thinking dominant most of the time in maturity. Secondary process thinking is "ordinary, conscious thinking." It is "primarily verbal" and it follows "the usual laws of syntax and logic."

In contrast, primary process thinking "is characteristic of those years of childhood when the ego is still immature." This helps to explain its characteristics. Since it is initially the mode of thought of the preverbal child, it makes relatively little use of verbal representation, often substituting "visual or other sense impressions" for words. It shows no concern with time and makes no use of "negatives, conditionals and other qualifying conjunctions." It permits opposites to replace one another and mutually contradictory ideas to "coexist peacefully." It makes frequent use of "representation by allusion or analogy . . ." and may employ "a part of an object, memory or idea . . . to stand for the whole, or vice versa. . . ." In addition to dominating our dreams and fantasies, primary process thinking plays a considerable though subordinate role in the thinking of adult life-in jokes and slang, for example, and also in such a highly esteemed activity as the creation of poetry. I have here mainly relied upon and often paraphrased Charles Brenner, *An Elementary Textbook of Psychoanalysis* (Garden City, N.Y.: Anchor Books, 1955). The quotations are also from this valuable book, pp. 52-55.

[2] This and all other quotations from *Macbeth* are from the Signet Classic edition, ed. Sylvan Barnet (New York: New American Library, 1963).

[3] *The Psychoanalytic Theory of Neurosis* (New York: Norton, 1945), p. 268.

[4] For a wonderful example of this mechanism in contemporary fiction, see *To the Lighthouse,* "The Window," Ch. 7—the account of the way Mrs. Ramsey musters her energies to provide the sympathy and reassurance she senses her husband needs.

[5] "The Naked Babe and the Cloak of Manliness," in *The Well Wrought Urn* (New York: Reynal and Hitchcock, 1947).

Kay Stockholder (essay date 1987)

SOURCE: "*Macbeth*: A Dream of Love," in *American Imago,* Vol. 44, No. 2, Summer, 1987, pp. 85-105.

[*In the following essay, Stockholder discusses the dream-like mingling of sexuality and violence in* Macbeth.]

Plato in the *Republic* reflected uneasily that even a good man might dream that he slept with his mother, and Freud tried to reassure the audience to his *Introductory Lectures to Psycho-Analysis* when he reminded them that there was someone in the real world actually doing the horrible things of which they merely dreamed.[1] The combination of the involuntary nature of our dreams and their emotional power can remain a source of worry even though most of us exempt from moral judgment the expressions of desires in the willess realm of dreaming. However, any action that ensues from a state of mind that seems on the borderline between waking and dreaming, any engulfing or compulsive emotion, raises troublesome questions about whether desires as well as actions are subject to moral judgment.

In literature a similar kind of question appears in the gulf between an aesthetic and moral apprehension, between the impulse to savour the formal beauty in which any kind of experience is rendered, and the impulse to come to literature, as Sydney suggested was appropriate, for delightful teaching. That there might be some kind of gulf between these two aspects of literature is implied by Freud and developed by Norman Holland, who in the *Dynamics of Literary Response*[2] argued that the moral aspect of literature, by sublimating the core phantasy, allows us secretly to indulge, much as we do in dreaming, otherwise forbidden desire. The parallel dichotomies between dreaming and waking experience and between the aesthetic and moral aspects of art suggest that the dream level of art is not as easily integrated into the cognitive and rational aspects as Anton Ehrenzweig and other theorists suggest.[3] Rather, it suggests that art contains an inherent internal conflict of a kind that Stephen Greenblatt saw in an historical context.[4] It suggests that the moral aspect of art may be at odds with an amoral aesthetic apprehension in a way similar to traditional conflicts in religion between mystics and churchmen, or in love relations between romance and marriage. In all of these, the sense of oneself as a moral agent and some sense of a self-authenticating and unchosen immediacy, must live with each other, and may not be able to live without each other, but remain in uneasy tension. Life itself, in the gulf between dreaming and waking states, presents us with the most polarized version of this dichotomy, and even Plato, who by casting out the artists sought to preserve his republic from this kind of discord, recognized that he couldn't do away with dreams.

In art this tension between a moral and an appreciative mode appears in the polarity between the narrative content and the formal structuring of it. That is, the formal properties of art, those devices of structure and rhetoric that give a work a sense of internal coherence, a sense that the end is contained in and therefore flows inevitably from the beginning, generates an aesthetic stasis that counters the moral or ideological component that by definition assumes that things might have been otherwise. A work that makes this internal struggle particularly visible is *Macbeth*. It does so because it simultaneously maintains strongly moral concerns, and is also amongst the most dream-like of works.

Of Shakespeare's plays *Macbeth* is one of the most morally straightforward in that its condemnation of the evils of regicide and untoward ambition is unambivalent. But it is also one of the most puzzling, not only because of the preternatural events, but also because the dense poetry is generated by the protagonists as they themselves invoke the standards by which their actions are condemned. As a consequence the play's moral forces even as it is evoked, tends to be absorbed into the desire-laden atmosphere, producing a world so pervaded by compelling emotion that the protagonists seem to have little control over the forces that move them. This quality not only renders the action dream-like, as others have noted.[5] It coalesces with the formal ordering to challenge the moral ordering that it also incorporates. In dreams all detail of action, of the landscape with which the dreamer is surrounded, all that he encounters in his dream, expresses his emotional dynamic rather than the logic of ordinary causality. In *Macbeth* the language in which the protagonists anticipate their crime rises from and echoes in the language of other figures, both those that are dream-like and those that are naturalistic. As a consequence these figures, while to a greater or lesser degree maintaining a sense of independent identity, also function as aspects of the protagonists' inner landscape. They become images writ large, part of what one critic has called a "subtextual wave."[6] They merge with other images, as well as with the dense network of forebodings and foreshadowings, that resonate from one voice to another throughout the text. In this way the text adumbrates the dream-likeness of the protagonists' experience—Macbeth's encounter with the witches which leaves him feeling that "nothing is but what is not,"[7] his hallucinations, and Lady Macbeth's sleep-walking. The fluidity with which images of evil transform into action and characters, and actions and characters in turn generate images, creates patterns that highlight the sense of aesthetic inevitability. This strong sense of inevitability, that things could not be other than they are, becomes a metaphorical expression of the dream-like sense of external event being shaped by the protagonists' desires that have eluded their consciousness and will. The force of the desire from which events arise is at once so compelling to the

Macbeth and Lady Macbeth hold each other as the witches look on.

protagonists and so inimical, not only to others' well-being, but any ordinary conception of their own, that it both arouses and negates a moral response.

In *Macbeth* the desire that moves the text is peculiarly intense because it is also that which defines the love between its protagonists, and the play is rendered more dream-like because the story of their love, which is not the overt subject of the play, structures the text. In dreams we do not expect the structuring principle, the force of desire and fear that generates the dream and is, as it were, its theme, to be visible, precisely because the dream is designed, as Freud tells us, to conceal that which it is designed to express. Similarly, *Macbeth* places in the centre of our vision a morally forceful story of untoward ambition, regicide, tyranny and the slaughter of children. But the text is structured by and its unique aura generated by the relation between Macbeth and his wife, who become like dream figures who encounter in the surrounding world representations of seemingly self-authenticating desires they do not experience directly. The combination of collusive intimacy and their violent action suggests people who are bound together by a perverse love, one that joins erotic passion to aggression and terror rather than to tenderness. The sexual overtones of the language surrounding the murder therefore express the lovers' erotically perverse passions. As in dreams, the accompanying fear and terror signify the distance between their desires and those that generate ordinary well being. That distance defines their love within an alternate reality, as dreams can seem to challenge the reality of our waking lives.

Since *Macbeth* is not a dream, but a play, and therefore must include what would be the latent content of dream within itself, one can more easily than in dreams reach into the shadows of the text and draw the figures into the centre of intellectual focus. As soon as one turns attention away from the play's moral and political issues, which obscure the love relation, it becomes clear that Macbeth and Lady Macbeth are the most intimate of Shakespeare's lovers. They intuit each other's deepest feelings, are known to each other, and have a common enterprise. They fully rely on each other, and, most importantly, in sharing the same figural language they contribute equally to the range of images that characterizes the play. They collude both in murdering Duncan, and in generating the images of guilty eroticism that characterize the text. Their collusion in murdering Duncan is so fine-tuned that neither is more responsible than the other. As a consequence, the murder rises from their relationship rather than from the character of either of them, neither of whom alone is portrayed as capable of it. As a single person's deed expresses the character of the person, or as a single character is defined by his or her actions and language, so the action that arises from a relationship characterizes that relationship. The action of the play, the planning, execution and consequences of the murder become extended images expressive of the emotions the protagonists generate in each other. The overt subject matter, while carrying its own import, also functions as a metaphorical expression of the emotional dynamic which constitutes the protagonists' relationship. That relationship generates the dream-like aura even while, and because, it remains in our peripheral vision rather than at the center of our attention. Ehrenzweig makes a similar argument about painting when he says that the shapes perceived subliminally in the background detail lend meaningfulness to the foregrounded figures.[8]

The play's dream-like inevitability and the love between Macbeth and Lady Macbeth intersect in the figures of the witches who most clearly situate the play on the borders between dream and waking, between the realm of the ethical and that of compulsive. In so far as they are seen by Banquo as well as Macbeth, they are part of Macbeth's waking world, but their supernatural attributes blend them into a dream realm. Since we see before Macbeth does what later fuses to his dream-like state of mind, the witches become part of the textual metaphor that expresses Macbeth's unconscious desire. The desire which they represent, however, is not primarily for the crown with which they tempt him, not only, as J.I.M. Stewart argues, for the murderous vision that enraptures him.[9] It is precisely for the fusion of violence and femininity represented by the witches. The fear that accompanies Macbeth's desire is expressed in their ugliness, while the force of his unknown desire is expressed in the aura of supernatural force that defines them. The attributes and images that the witches share with Lady Macbeth and their role in instigating the murder that he and his wife will together perform, render them textual expressions of Macbeth's unconscious associations with his wife. As they are of indeterminate sex, bearded women, so Lady Macbeth acts with traditionally masculine initiative and calls upon them, as 'fateful ministers' to unsex her; as we encounter them planning to seduce Macbeth into his crime, so we encounter Lady Macbeth planning to steady his will; as they arise from a barren heath, so Lady Macbeth's barrenness, flowing in the text from her denial of feminine tenderness, renders fruitless Macbeth's crown and sceptre, and radiates to the country at large, changing it from "our mother" to "our grave." Therefore, it is as though Macbeth in encountering the witches on the heath encounters attributes that he unconsciously associates with his wife. A further link between the witches and Lady Macbeth is suggested by Dennis Biggins who argues that traditionally witches are associated with lust, perverse sexuality and female dominance.[10] This sexual association appears in the text through the sequence of scenes in which the witches' plan to meet Macbeth is followed by the depiction of battle in which Macbeth appears as "Bellona's bridegroom." These images of frighteningly seductive women amidst the violence of battle form the atmosphere from which Lady Macbeth emerges when she appears reading Macbeth's letter. The letter comes out of a textual vacuum, but realistically can only have been written as Macbeth's first act toward fulfilling the dark desires stirred in him by the witches' prophecies. He seems to assume that his wife will continue what the witches began. By so speedily informing her of the events he both defines his project as jointly hers, and expresses his knowledge of her powers to advance it.

The trenchant brevity of his letter to Lady Macbeth suggests the intimacy that is more formally expressed in its close, "This have I thought good to deliver thee, my dearest partner of greatness, that thou mightst not lose the dues of rejoicing by being ignorant of what greatness is promis'd thee" (I. v. 9-12). She instantly intuits Macbeth's excited fear, and assumes, like Macbeth, that they will not rely on circumstances to fulfill the witches' prophecy. As Macbeth immediately envisioned Duncan's murder, rather than himself enthroned, so she will 'catch the nearest way.' The accord of her mind to his suggests that in writing to her he relied on her resolve to steady his. This dramatized mutuality is supported textually by the echo of his words in hers.

He said,

> Stars, hide your fires;
> Let not light see my black and deep desires;
> The eye wink at the hand; yet let that be
> Which the eye fears, when it is done, to see.
>
> (I, iv, 51-54)

She says,

> Come, thick Night,
> And pall thee in the dunnest smoke of hell,
> That my keen knife seen not the wound it
>   makes,
> Nor Heaven peep through the blanket of the
>   dark,
> To cry 'Hold, hold!'
>
> (I, v, 51-54).

When the action in which she functions, as he anticipated, to help him "wrongly win" that which he would
not "play false" to attain, arises from this rich texture
of dream-like images, it is as though they share their
dream as well as their waking lives.

Her response demonstrates that his estimate of her character is as accurate as is hers of his. Their mutual
knowledge and, even more, their acknowledgments that
they are known to the other, along with their joint
enterprise, give their relation an intimacy and power
that propels them into their fearsome phantasies. She
assumes in his character precisely the vacillation he
has already demonstrated, and she adds substance to
Macbeth's "horrible imaginings" when she anticipates
Duncan's fatal entrance under her battlements. She also
draws the images of violence first encountered on the
battlefield into familial and sexual realms when she says,

> Come, you spirits
> That tend on mortal thoughts, unsex me here,
> And fill me from the crown to the toe top-full
> Of direst cruelty! Make thick my blood,
> Stop up th'access and passage to remorse,
> That no compunctious visitings of nature
> Shake my fell purpose, nor keep peace
>   between
> Th' effect and it! Come to my woman's
>   breasts,
> And take my milk for gall, you murth'ring
>   ministers,
> Wherever in your sightless substances
> You wait on nature's mischief!
>
> (I. v. 41-51)

Lady Macbeth opposes her normal sexuality to violence in asking, as Jenifoy La Belle argues, to be rid
of her femaleness.[11] But a new and perverse sexuality
reappears when she wants herself filled "from the
crown to the toe with direst cruelty," for that image
gives to violence the body's sensuality. Her reference
to her woman's breasts merges the image of female
sexuality into those of nurturing, but in fear of her
own tender nature, as she is of Macbeth's being "too
full of the milk o' human kindness," she perverts that
image by envisioning 'murth'ring ministers' sucking
her milk, now turned to gall. In concluding her anticipation of the murder with the image of the blanketed
darkness that is like Macbeth's image, she adds a
sexual resonance to her denial of familial and sensuous tenderness.

In the aura of that perverse sexuality she greets Macbeth, feeling 'the future is in the instant,' in the same
way Macbeth felt that "nothing is but what is not."
That instant contains for Lady Macbeth the generative
power that she denied in the previous passage. The
"night's great business" will give birth to 'sovereign
sway and masterdom,' to power, rather than to a sucking infant. Macbeth enters into his wife's unspoken
thought and defines their love within it when he responds, "My dearest love, / Duncan comes here tonight" (I. v. 59-60). The intense and intuitive mutual
understanding that informs their terse exchange drains
of impact Macbeth's vacillating demure, "We will speak
further" (I. v. 72). The rhythm by which each excites
the other to the point of action structures the scenes
that lead to the murder. The first movement occurred
in Macbeth's sending the letter, Lady Macbeth's response, and his collusive reaction to her. The second
begins when Macbeth, momentarily free of the rush of
desire, enters a Hamlet-like meditation on the 'bank
and shoal of time' between life and death. He appreciates the unusual array of ordinary pleasures of life—
domestic ease, honour, paternal affection from his
king—and fears the consequences that he intuits will
follow upon violating the obligations that he can so
pleasurably fulfill. Opposed to both fear of reprisal
and pleasure in doing that which forestalls it is only
the sheer rush of incomprehensible desire. As though
intuiting the nature of that desire, Macbeth imagines
the retributive forces in the image of a child, a "naked
new-born babe / Striding the blast." (I. vii.22-3). That
image, taken textually, joins related images of babies
and of barrenness to be discussed shortly. Taken as
indicative of Macbeth's character, it suggests his intuition that his desire violates not only his obligations as
Duncan's kinsman, subject and host, but also strikes at
the core of the fertility embedded in love, sexuality,
and family. His mind for the moment on ordinary pleasures and free of perverse desire, he is left only with
"vaulting ambition" which without the spur of desire,
"o'er leaps itself / And falls to the other side." Previously Macbeth came, as though called, after Lady
Macbeth's soliloquy. Now she comes, as though called,
to do in fact what both she and Macbeth anticipated
she would. By chastising "with the valor of [her] tongue
/ All that impedes [him] from the golden round" (I. v.
28-9), she functions to bring his enraptured vision,

initially so separate from his ordinary reality and daily life into "Time and the hour [that] runs through the roughest day" (I. iii. 152). In writing the letter he took the first step toward integrating his phantasy to his reality. She overcomes the impeding pity, associated by Macbeth with fertility in his image of the "new born babe," by equating it to cowardice and by equating the murder to his sense of manliness:[12]

> What beast was't then,
> That made you break this enterprise to me?
> When you durst do it then you were a man;
> And, to be more than what you were, you
>   would
> Be so much more the man. Nor time, nor
>   place,
> Did then adhere, and yet you would make
>   both:
> They have made themselves, and that their
>   fitness now
> Does unmake you. I have given suck, and
>   know
> How tender 'tis to love the babe that milks
>   me—
> I would, while it was smiling in my face,
> Have pluck'd my nipple from his boneless
>   gums,
> And dash'd the brains out, had I so sworn
> As you have done to this.
>
>   (I. vii. 46-58)

In imagistically killing her infant, she exposes the intuition that underlay Macbeth's earlier image of the babe striding the blast. She assumes that their love which will be consummated in the murder represents some alternate reality, intrinsically opposed to fertility, family, and society, all represented in the image of children. In arguing that Macbeth's pledge to her is more binding than the pledge of a mother's love to a child, given the strong analogy generated throughout the play between the kingdom and a family, she makes an encompassing scale of creaturely accord that extends from sucking infants to social harmony, and opposes to it the love between herself and Macbeth. Lady Macbeth defines their love in enmity towards kind and country, tenderness and children. Her images, which resonate in the same ranges that his previously did, far from repelling him, bring him to the point where he can join the desire that was first expressed in the horrifying images of the witches to his own "act and valour" (I. vii. 40).

Narratively the murder is a consequence of the action preceding it, but textually it is a kind of vortex that collects and transforms all of the emotional forces that constitute the play. The text has defined Macbeth's and Lady Macbeth's love in their plans to murder Duncan, and it renders their sexual consummation in the murder.

That the murder represents their sexual relationship appears in many ways. It appears in the rhythm by which they excite each other to the "sticking place," as well as in those images that associate the murder with their dark privacy when Macbeth asks that light not see his "black and deep desires." Lady Macbeth deepens the image when she imagines the knife wound made beneath "the blanket of the dark." These images collect into Duncan's unseen, and therefore doubly private, bedroom, and, as Berry argues, Macbeth adds phallic force to the sexual suggestiveness in saying that he will "bend up / Each corporal agent to this horrible feat" (I. vii. 79-80).[13] The hallucinatory dagger that points him towards Duncan indicates a state of mind mid-way between dreaming and waking when it fuses with the one he carries in his hand. In that fused state of consciousness Macbeth makes explicit the previously subtle associations between sexuality and violence when he says,

> Now o'er the one half world
> Nature seems dead, and wicked dreams abuse
> The curtain'd sleep: Witchcraft celebrates
> Pale Heccat's off'rings; and wither'd Murther,
> Alarum'd by his sentinel, the wolf,
> Whose howl's his watch, thus with his
>   stealthy pace,
> With Tarquin's ravishing strides, towards his
>   design
> Moves like a ghost.
>
>   (II. i. 49-56)

Having identified himself with "wither'd Murther," celebrated by witchcraft, the "stealthy pace" with which he approaches Duncan's bed suddenly becomes that of Tarquin about to rape Lucrece. It is not only that the murder carries sexual force, as others have argued.[14] The fused image of murder and of rape completes the sexuality between Macbeth and Lady Macbeth that was implied when Macbeth on the battlefield was referred to as "Bellona's bridegroom." After calling Macbeth, as he emerges from the room, "My husband" (I. ii. 14), Lady Macbeth participates in the murder that consummates their love as well as their joint enterprise in entering the bedroom that Macbeth has just left. There she smears with Duncan's blood the swinish grooms, and returns to declare to Macbeth that "My hands are of your color" (II. ii. 61).

The knocking at the Porter's gate that breaks in upon the couple's intense privacy intensifies their intimacy and the Porter's speech adds to the sexual suggestiveness of the previous scene. Having associated himself with the murder by calling himself the porter of hellgate, the Porter enumerates the social forms of equivocating trickery and treachery. This comic version of the witches' "Fair is foul and foul is fair," echoed in myriad ways in the text, foreshadows the social chaos that will radiate from and express the hell of perverse sexuality within the castle. The Porter's jokes on the morally equivocal are associated later to the diabolic witches by Macbeth when he blames his impending defeat on "the equivocation of the fiend / That lies like truth" (V. v. 43-4). The Porter links that moral equivocation to sexuality when he says that in provoking desire but inhibiting performance, drink "may be said to be an equivocator with lechery: it makes him, and it mars him; it sets him on, and it takes him off; it persuades him, and disheartens him; makes him stand to, and not stand to; in conclusion, equivocates him in a sleep, and, giving him the lie, leaves him" (II. iii. 30-37). Earlier Lady Macbeth, when Macbeth's will wavered, asked, "Was the hope drunk / Wherein you dress'd yourself?" (I. vii. 35-6). Like the Porter, she associates drunkenness with being unable to "be the same in thine own act and valor / As thou art in desire" (I. vii. 40-1). A few lines later she plans to ply Duncan's chamberlains with "wine and wassail." With little justice (especially since it later appears that she has also drugged their drink) but much imagistic force, she then talks of the "swinish sleep" of the "spongy officers." The image of the swinish and drunken chamberlains acquires sexual overtones when the Porter associates drunkeness with impotence. The cluster of images adds a sexual dimension to Lady Macbeth's contempt of what she sees as Macbeth's unmanly vacillation. The cluster associates the peaceful sleep that Macbeth foregoes with the drunken grooms who "mock[ing] their charge with snores" (II. ii. 6-7) are the object of Lady Macbeth's contempt. Therefore her eagerness to "chastise with the valor of [her] tongue / All that impedes [him] from the golden round" (I. v. 28-9) intimates her scorn for and impatience with swinish impotence. That impotence she so scorns is also associated with Duncan through the image of Duncan in the bedroom surrounded by the sleeping grooms, who later also are gilded with his golden blood. But the character of Duncan, who promised to plant [Macbeth] and labour to make him full of growing,' embodies the images of soft nurturing that she despises in Macbeth and represses in herself in order to excite him to manly action. Manliness in both its social and sexual aspects is realized in murder, while quiet sleep, nurture, and hierarchical harmony are associated with sexual and social impotence. The text therefore leaves no middle-ground between impotence and the "restless ecstasy" of erotic violence for ordinary, loving, sexuality. The porter scene, not only extends the theme of equivocation from the witches into the social fabric of the play's world;[15] its portentous grotesquerie reaches into the deepest psychological recesses of the text in the way Freud described jokes revealing what earnestness conceals.

The violence within which Macbeth and Lady Macbeth consummate their sexuality generates both the story of their barren love and the images of children that pervade the text. The witches' barren heath and Macbeth's barren sceptre are born of, or express, the violent love

they lead to, while the normal fruition of love, children and parenthood, become textual representatives of the protagonists' own outraged feelings that will constitute their nemesis.[16] In the text the opposition between their barren love and a fertile world appears first in the contrast between the castle, guarded by the croaking raven, in which they consummate their love, and the images of birds in their "pendant bed and procreant cradle" observed by Duncan and Banquo as they approach it. Before the murder Macbeth saw "pity" as an avenging babe; after the murder an image of children represents the equivocating witches when a "bloody child" assures him that he cannot be killed by man "of woman born," and a crowned child tells him that he will live till Birnam wood comes to Dunsinane. That tenderness as such has become his enemy appears when the first act that flows from his resolve to let the "firstlings of his heart . . . be / The firstlings of his hand" (IV. i. 146-7), is to kill Lady Macduff and her children, though their murder cannot succeed in assuaging the terrible fears that afflict his nights. In doing so Macbeth generates Macduff's outraged parenthood which coalesces with the images of avenging children and the more general images of Macbeth's loss of creature comforts—sleep, communal eating, communal membership. Instead of joining the festive table, Macbeth 'sups full of horrors' at the witches' cauldron; instead of having children, images of them represent inimical fates, and instead of experiencing the tenderness of parenthood, Macbeth is fated to be killed by one who represents those feelings he and his wife have denied. In all these ways Macbeth will confront in the plot as a whole, and in what he takes to be a real world, the extended images of their internal state that earlier characterized his rich imagination, while Lady Macbeth, whose role it was to affirm the primary reality of the external world, will confront its equivalent in the overtly nightmare realm she has now entered. They will change places in the course of the action, but the polarities will remain unchanged.

The erotic violence central to Macbeth's and Lady Macbeth's relationship radiates in widening circles to the most public ranges of their lives. The images that express Macbeth's and Lady Macbeth's isolation from ordinary pleasure echo in the words that describe the country over which they rule. Wanting relief from their nocturnal agonies, Macbeth determines that they "shall no longer eat in fear and sleep / In the affliction of these terrible dreams / That shake us nightly" (III. ii. 17-19); and Lennox says that Macduff seeks help in England so that they may "Give to our tables meat, sleep to our nights; / Free from our feasts and banquets bloody knives" (III. vi. 33-5). The violent images that surrounded the sexualized murder also describe the body-politic when Lennox adds, "I think our country sinks beneath the yoke; / It weeps, it bleeds, and each new day a gash / Is added to her wounds" (IV. iii. 39-41). When Ross responds, "Alas, poor country, / Almost afraid to know itself! It cannot / Be call'd our mother, but our grave" (IV. iii. 164-6), the commonwealth becomes an image of Lady Macbeth's violation of her maternity. The language spreads from the heart of their relationship to the periphery, the textual level metaphorically expressing the emotional dynamics of their violent eroticism.

Once the images of their eroticism have emerged from the blanketed darkness, neither can confront the image of themselves they see in the other, and the force that bound them begins to separate them. As his inner turmoil is transformed into images of his country's anguish, Macbeth gradually redefines himself in relation to Lady Macbeth. The collusive intimacy between them fades almost immediately after Duncan's murder, for Macbeth begins to espouse her definition of him as an unthinking man of action, and to redefine her in a more conventionally feminine role, while she becomes more tentative in relation to him. The altered relationship appears in Macbeth's secrecy about his plan to murder Banquo, and in Lady Macbeth's secrecy about her inner state. She says, echoing Macbeth's earlier lines,

> Nought's had, all's spent,
> Where our desire is got without content.
> Tis safer to be that which we destroy
> Than by destruction dwell in doubtful joy.
>
>   (III. ii. 4-7)

But she denies her anguish by dismissing his when Macbeth envies Duncan who sleeps well "after life's fitful fever" (III. ii. 24), and he revels in his secret plans to murder Banquo when he tells her to let her "remembrancer apply to Banquo." Each withdraws from the other as they now make their faces "vizards to [their] hearts" (III. ii. 30, 35) not, as previously, to secrete themselves from the outside world, but rather to remain hidden from each other. Macbeth indirectly approaches his plan, saying "O! full of scorpions is my mind, dear wife! / Thou know'st that Banquo, and his Fleance, lives." When she responds, "But in them Nature's copy's not eterne" (III. ii. 36-9), he secretly obtains her validation of his unspoken plan. She addresses him as "gentle, my lord," and he her as "love," but in calling her "dearest chuck" (III. ii. 28, 30, 46), and withholding knowledge from her, he denies the equality that was assumed when she asked, "What cannot you and I perform upon the unguarded Duncan?" (I. vii. 69-70). Macbeth thus reestablishes the conventional protectiveness of a man towards a woman.[17]

Having covertly gained her consent, Macbeth proves that he fulfills her standards of manliness by arranging Banquo's death alone. But the eroticized violence, the sexual version of the witches' fair-foulness and foul-fairness, remains in the language with which he anticipates Banquo's death:

> Ere the bat hath flown
> His cloister'd flight: ere to black Heccat's
>   summons
> The shard-borne beetle with his drowsy hums
> Hath rung Night's yawning peal, there shall be
>   done
> A deed of dreadful note.
>
>   (III. ii. 40-4)

"Heccat's summons," "drowsy hums," and "night's yawning peal" suggest the dark ease of seductive sleep that overwhelms and cancels the moral horror that is the overt content. He continues to savour the images in which he couches the contemplated murder when he says, "Light thickens, and the crow / Makes wing to th' rooky wood. / Good things of day begin to droop and drowse, / Whiles night's black agents to their preys do rouse" (III. ii. 49-52). Enjoying Lady Macbeth's silent "marvel," Macbeth anticipates the murder with a kind of swoon into an auto-erotic violence that excludes her. The process of the lovers' separation, begun after the first murder, is completed after the second. The banquet at which no food is consumed not only represents the dissolution of social accord, but also the accord between Macbeth and his wife. Banquo's ghost, unlike the airborne dagger which Macbeth recognized as unreal, is a full hallucination. It is Macbeth's last revel in the aura of desire before the fearful delights of nightmare retreat, and Macbeth begins to see the world his dream has generated in harsh day light.

Macbeth's horror at Banquo's ghost expresses his attitude toward his own compelling desires. Since he cannot acknowledge the desires that have generated the image, he cannot look upon it. His consciousness approaches what the play of images has already inscribed in the text when he says,

> Blood hath been shed ere now, i' th' olden
>   time,
> Ere humane statute purg'd the gentle weal;
> Ay, and since too, murthers have been
>   perform'd
> Too terrible for the ear. The times has been,
> That, when the brains were out, the man
>   would die,
> And there an end. But now they rise again,
> With twenty mortal murthers on their crowns,
> And push us from our stools. This is more
>   strange
> Than such a murther is.
>
>   (III. iv. 75-83)

Macbeth here approaches a recognition that the horror that fills his world does not arise from the act of regicide, but rather from his imagination of it. With this recognition the gestation begun beneath the blanket of the dark completes itself in a perverse birth. From his imagination, Macbeth is reborn in Lady Macbeth's image of manliness when he says, "Augures and understood relations" have "By maggot-pies, and choughs and rooks brought forth / The secret'st man of blood" (III. iv. 122-5). This new Macbeth will, by enacting the "strange things [he] has in head before . . . they are scann'd (III. iv. 139-40), create his world in the image of his previous inner life, while Lady Macbeth succumbs to the "thick night" she had invoked and yields to the those "thick-coming" fancies that previously defined him. Banquo's image not only encapsulates Macbeth's past; it also foreshadows his future. Macbeth says of it, "Thy bones are marrowless, thy blood is cold; / Thou hast no speculation in those eyes / Which thou dost glare with" (III. iv. 94-6). Macbeth's sense of life's meaningfullness lay in the confused passion of his relationship to Lady Macbeth; therefore in having excluded her from his consciousness he also denied his own inwardness, and so finds himself "fallen into the seare, the yellow leaf" (V. iii. 22). The underlying bond with her remains visible on the plot level when he prepares for his final battle outside the castle, while inside the castle she vainly washes her hands. His fear of meeting death and his concerns for her become a single issue when he simultaneously addresses the Doctor and Seyton. He intertwines directions for the battle with the language appropriate to his despair of curing the "thick-coming fancies" and the memory of a "rooted sorrow" that constitute both her disease and his past:

> Come, put mine armor on. Give me my staff.
> Seyton, send out.—Doctor, the thanes fly from
>   me.—
> Come, sir, dispatch.—If thou couldst, doctor,
>   cast
> The water of my land, find her disease,
> And purge it to a sound and pristine health,
> I would applaud thee to the very echo,
> That should applaud again.—Pull't off, say.—
> What rhubarb, cyme, or what purgative drug
> Would scour these English hence?
>
>   (V. iii. 48-56)

Apart from Lady Macbeth he is bereft of the rich if horrifying meaningfulness that was contained in their relationship. Having become the man of action she wanted him to be, and repudiated the imagination he shared with her, he can respond to her death with only ashen emptiness:

> She should have died hereafter;
> There would have been a time for such a
>   word.
> To-morrow, and to-morrow and to-morrow,
> Creeps in this petty pace from day to day,
> To the last syllable of recorded time;
> And all our yesterdays have lighted fools
> The way to dusty death. Out, out, brief
>   candle!

> Life's but a walking shadow, a poor player
> That struts and frets his hour upon the
>   stage,
> And then is heard no more. It is a tale
> Told by an idiot, full of sound and fury,
> Signifying nothing.
>
>   (V. v. 17-28)

Since Macbeth is preoccupied both with reassuring himself that he is invulnerable to death in battle, he refuses to recognize the mortality that her death implies. As well, he dismisses the reminder of the nightmare realm he bequeathed to her when he says "She should have died hereafter." To avoid the impact of her death in the present, his mind moves first to the future, and then to the past. But having emptied the present of significance, the future stretches ahead, "Tomorrow, and to-morrow, and to-morrow," partaking of the present emptiness and "petty pace." He can take no joy in the prospect of escaping death in the coming battle, or of everlasting life, when all recorded time is made up of the insignificant syllables of meaningless action. On the phrase "creeps in this petty pace" his mind swings from the future to the past, suggesting an association between the image of creeping at a petty pace and the earlier images of children. Like the future, the past also has been drained of meaningfullness, rendering illusory the desire that lit all those "yesterdays" from infancy, or from the play's beginning, to the present. Now they lead only to the "dusty death" he projects onto the future. Therefore he wants life's candle out, the light by which he can read the meaning of Lady Macbeth's death. Not wanting to read it, he sees life itself as a "walking shadow," an image that expresses his sense of himself as a bloodless husk, emptied of desire. The image of the moving shadow suggests one of the stage, but since the candle has been blown out, it is a darkened stage, a scene like Duncan's bedroom that Macbeth both wants and fears to see. Earlier the staged sounds of the clamour at the Porter's gate replaced the images of Duncan's gore, so now Macbeth in his mind's ear hears in the darkness the player who "struts and frets" upon the "bloody stage" his world has become. Rather than seeing an image of Duncan's bloody bedroom coloured by his own desires and revulsion, guilt and rage, he takes a further and final means to distance himself from that vision. He transforms the image of the stage to the less immediate one of a tale, but denies what the tale might reveal by attributing it to an enlarged and grotesque version of a child—an idiot—and so eradicates the meaning of his past, present, and future. But thereby hangs another tale of the process by which Macbeth, in fearing to confront the significance of Lady Macbeth's death, transforms his life into a tale "signifying nothing."[18]

The textual excitement fades after Lady Macbeth's death, allowing the moral level greater ascendancy as the play nears its close. Macduff, characterized by his grief and outrage for the loss of children, fittingly defeats the intrinsically barren Macbeth and ends a brutal tyranny that has rendered Scotland a barren wasteland. At the end of the play Macbeth and Lady Macbeth die separately. Macbeth's head is on a pole, and Lady Macbeth lies within the castle. The text, however, subtly links them when Malcolm in the play's closing speech evokes them as "this dead butcher and his fiend-like queen" (V. ix. 35).

Macbeth is not the first of Shakespeare's plays that yokes sexuality to violence. The vision of heterosexuality that is implicit in *Macbeth* and that is expressed in the world that emanates from these lovers, I believe develops from the violence, both passive and active, that more subtly led Othello and Desdemona to consummate their love in death. Their love for each other, in that it creates a world apart from ordinary obligations and reality, is like that between Romeo and Juliet, as well as like that between Macbeth and Lady Macbeth, but the idyllic romance of the earlier play was opposed to a violent external world which destroyed it. That same violence seeped into the love of Hamlet and Ophelia, Desdemona and Othello, to render them, in different modes, self-destructive. In the sequence that begins with *Romeo and Juliet,* one sees violence and aggression first as the frame that surrounds two idealized young lovers who are seen brought to their tragic end as a consequence of forces external to them. In *Othello* the violent forces are defined initially as external, with only faint echoes in the language of the characters, but they slowly invade and define the lovers. The process completes itself in *Macbeth* in which the violence explicitly characterizes the lovers, and, as fears and desires shape dreams, extends from them to define their world and to shape the text that contains them.

Notes

[1] *The Republic of Plato,* tr. Francis MacDonald Cornford (Oxford, 1941), p. 296. Sigmund Freud, *Introductory Lectures on Psychoanalysis,* tr., James Strachey (New York, Penguin, 1974), p. 179.

[2] Norman Holland, *Dynamics of Literary Response* (New York: Oxford, 1968), p. 314.

[3] For some discussions of the relation between art and either dream or primary process thought see Ernst Kris, *Psychoanalytic Explorations in Art* (New York: Schocken, 1952), Anton Ehrenzweig, *The Hidden Order of Art* (London, 1967), pp. 256-79, Arthur L. Marotti, 'Countertransference, the Communication Process and the Dimension of Psychoanalytic Criticism," *Critical Inquiry* 4 (1978) 471-89, and Alan Roland 'Imagery and the Self in Artistic Creativity

and Psychoanalytic Literary Criticism,' *The Psychoanalytic Review,* 68 (Fall, 1981), pp. 409-20.

[4] Stephen Greenblatt, Renaissance Self-Fashioning (Chicago: Univ. of Chicago Press, 1980), pp. 253-54.

[5] See particularly Simon O. Lesser in '*Macbeth:* Drama and Dream,' *Literary Criticism and Psychology,* ed., Joseph P. Strelka (University Park: Pennsylvania State Univ. Press, 1976), pp. 150-73.

[6] Ralph Berry in *Shakespearean Structures* (London: Macmillan, 1981) in a precise and careful way argues for a 'subtextual wave' (90) of associations and for what he calls 'chameleon words' (91) that weave sexual puns into other levels of the play. See also a related argument by Harry Berger, Jr., in 'Text Against Performance in Shakespeare: The Example of *Macbeth,*' *The Power of Form in the English Renaissance,* ed., Stephen Greenblatt (Norman, Oklahoma: Pilgrim Books, 1982) pp. 49-81, who says that the textual reading of the play undermines the impact of a stage performance by revealing the way in which the 'good' thanes are involved in the 'scapegoating' of women (74).

[7] All quotations are taken from the Yale edition, ed., Eugene M. Waith (London, Oxford Univ. Press, 1954).

[8] Ehrenzweig, pp. 32-46.

[9] J. I. M. Stewart in *Character and Motive in Shakespeare* (London: Longmans, Greene, 1949) observes that it was the 'crime and not the crown that compels Macbeth' (93).

[10] Dennis Biggins in 'Sexuality, Witchcraft and Violence in *Macbeth,*' *Shakespeare Studies,* 8 (1976), pp. 255-77, points out that traditionally witches were presumed to be lustful, sexually perverse and sexually dominant. See also Vesny Wagner, '*Macbeth:* 'Fair is Foul and Foul is Fair,' *American Imago,* 25 (1968), pp. 242-57,.

[11] Jenifoy La Belle in "A strange infirmity,' Lady Macbeth's Amenorrhea," *Shakespeare Quarterly,* 31 (1980), 381-86, argues from contemporary medical terminology, that Lady Macbeth invokes infernal powers literally to stop her menstruction, the sign of her sex as well as of her fertility, and later experiences the physiological and emotional consequences of her request having been granted (384). She relates that to the blood images which then substitute for the natural flow. Her argument that literal amenorrhea grounds Lady Macbeth's images, gives additional force to my argument that the murder functions as a sexual act.

[12] For the relation of destructiveness to vulnerability see Joan M. Byles, '*Macbeth:* Imagery of Destruction,'

American Imago, 39 (1982), pp. 149-64, and Coppélia Kahn, *Man's Estate* (Berkeley: Univ. of California Press, 1980), p. 145.

[13] Berry, p. 92.

[14] See Richard Wheeler in *Shakespeare's Development and the Problem Comedies* (Berkeley: Univ. of California Press, 1981), p.145, Biggins also perceives the sexualized violence of the play in seeing the murder as a kind of rape and Berry says that the Tarquin image joined to the idea of murder creates a phallic murder that is at 'this play's heart of darkness' (92). See also Muriel Bradbrook, *Aspects of Dramatic Form in the English and Irish Renaissance: The Collected Papers of Muriel Bradbrook* (Brighton, Sussex: Harvester Press, 1983) and Madelon Gohlke who in "I wooed thee with my sword'; Shakespeare's Tragic Paradigms," *The Woman's Part:* Feminist Criticism of Shakespeare, eds., Carolyn R. Lenz, Gayle Greene and Carol Thomas Neely (Urbana: Univ. of Illinois Press, 1980): pp. 150-70, relates this play to *Othello* with the observation that in both murder is a loving act, and love a murdering one (156).

[15] See Kenneth Muir, Introduction to the Arden edition of the play (London: Methuen, 1951), (xxiii-xxix).

[16] For other views on the significance of images of children see Ludwig Jekels in 'The Riddle of Shakespeare's Macbeth,' *The Design Within,* (243), Cleanth Brooks, 'The Naked Babe in the Cloak of Manliness,' *The Well Wrought Urn* (London: Dobson Books, 1968), pp. 17-39, and Marjorie Garber in *Coming of Age in Shakespeare* (London: Methuen, 1981), 153-4.

[17] For discussions of the ways in which the relative dominance of Macbeth and Lady Macbeth have been related to contemporary feminist issues see D. S. Kastan in 'Shakespeare and the Way of Womenkind,' *Daedalus,* 11 (1982), pp. 115-30, Joan Larsen Klein, "Lady Macbeth; 'Infirm of Purpose,'" *The Woman's Part:* pp. 240-55, see also Carolyn Asp, "'Be Bloody, Bold and Resolute': Tragic Action and Sexual Stereotyping in *Macbeth,"* *Studies in Philology,* 78 (1981), 153-69, and D. W. Harding in 'Women's Fantasy of Manhood: A Shakespearean Theme,' *Shakespeare Quarterly,* 20 (1969) 245-53.

[18] Holland gives a penetrating reading of the core phantasy of this speech as though it were an independent poem (106-14). Where he sees a primal scene phantasy, I see developments from and references to the previous action. The coherence between his reading and mine substantiates my view that imagery and sequence of action in the text substitutes for what would constitute unconscious motivations from the past of a person like Macbeth.

POSTHUMUS'S DREAM: *CYMBELINE*

D. E. Landry (essay date 1982)

SOURCE: "Dreams as History: The Strange Unity of *Cymbeline,*" in *Shakespeare Quarterly,* Vol. 33, No. 1, Spring, 1982, pp. 68-79.

[*In the following essay, Landry examines the thematic link between dreams and the historical unity of* Cymbeline.]

Cymbeline is most remarkably a play about dreams, about the various and often inexplicable functions of the unconscious mind. It is also a romance, a history play, and a tragicomic pastoral. Naturally, critics have found it difficult to interpret the play in any unified way, difficult to assign it any governing structure. Most are still in tacit agreement with Johnson, who deplored its "incongruity" and "unresisting imbecility"; even critics who claim some fondness for its oddities tend to explore particular aspects, leaving the unwieldy bulk of the threefold plot largely unexplained.[1] Frank Kermode and Northrop Frye, respectively, have come closer to pinning down the play's peculiar tone by calling it "experimental,"[2] and "academic," with a "technical interest in dramatic structure."[3]

In *Cymbeline,* Shakespeare is indeed experimenting, but experimenting most resonantly, I think, with the underlying significance of certain natural cycles and their dramaturgical counterparts, with the processes of sleep as a perpetual "ape of death" (Iachimo's phrase; II.ii.31),[4] waking as a symbolic rebirth, dream as a ritualized purgation. The main dreamers, Posthumus and Imogen, are also the characters with the strongest focus. They are, moreover, the agents of the erotic plot through which the plots of familial and national affection can be salvaged and resolved.[5] By a series of analogies, the experience of Posthumus and Imogen comes to represent that of the whole community of Cymbeline's kingdom.

I

The play's structural complexities imply an equation: dreams, which contain in however concealed a fashion the facts of personal history, are to one's identity as a nation's past, recovered through legend and chronicle-history, is to its sense of itself *as* a nation, a true community. *Cymbeline* is at once the most local and historical of the romances, the only one explicitly grounded in events from Britain's past, and as transcendently primitive as any, with considerable interest in the ritualistic, largely unconscious roots of the drama. In *Cymbeline,* however, the primitivism or archaic interest of the themes of dreams and chronicle-history is treated with wit and sophistication. The apparent naiveté of the folk-tale plot is constantly undermined by self-consciously theatrical artifice. The panegyrical quality of the chronicles—especially as interpreted under the Tudors with an eye toward legitimating royal authority by aligning it with the national interest[6]—is gently deflated. The play closes with Cymbeline, the King himself, commenting a little wryly on the expeditious nature of the peace just negotiated between Britain and Rome: ". . . Never was a war did cease, / Ere bloody hands were wash'd, with such a peace" (V.v.482-83). It is just this tone of naive wonder undermined ever so quietly but insistently by archness and self-control that distinguishes Shakespeare's last plays in general, and *Cymbeline,* as a peculiar blend of romance and history play, in particular.

Romances are traditionally concerned with the recovery and reconstitution of identity. Quite a bit has been written about the unusual status of Posthumus as a hero.[7] His absence from the stage is indeed more noticeable than his presence. And yet, at the same time, his experience functions as the only facsimile of developing character we are offered in the play. Not only Posthumus but the entire court and, by analogy, all of Britain undergo a kind of purgation through dream or dreamlike experience. The purgation is dreamlike in that it acts as a working out or incorporation of potentially disruptive elements, which Freud describes as the basis of the dream-work; the pattern or structure of the dream itself incorporates these usually erotic impulses by permitting them to be expressed, however covertly or metaphorically, in the dream's action.[8] The play suffers a certain break in consciousness followed by a descent to a demonic realm when Posthumus retreats from the action. In romance, the demonic or night world to which the self descends is the domain of tyrannous circumstances, filled with images of displacement of the self: a world of doublings, disguises, misnamings, and mistaken identities, the conventions both of romantic or tragicomic drama and of dreams.

It is as if Posthumus' physical absence were somehow paralleled by Imogen's absence of mind. Though repudiated unfairly as an adulteress, as Posthumus' wife Imogen remains in Shakespearean conception his lawful helpmate, his other and better self, and, most significantly, his "soul" (V.v.263) in her mind and ours. Throughout the pastoral scenes which follow near Milford Haven her masculine disguise further identifies her with the absent Posthumus. As Fidele she comes to embody Posthumus' own capacity for virtue in the same way that Cloten, as a parodic double, enacts his tendencies toward vice.[9] The pastoral setting, with its magical and ironic overtones,[10] is an ideal distancing device, and it reinforces in these scenes the sense of a kind of dream action. Both Fidele and Cloten become figures of displacement for the embattled psyche of

Posthumus and allow bestial and erotic instincts to surface in a distanced, and therefore acceptable, way. Posthumus' absence from the stage does not preclude his growth as a hero, because we are given instead a psychomachic enactment of his development through the adventures of Imogen, Cloten, and the royal brothers. The relation these scenes bear to Posthumus' moments of crisis and insight—neatly following his disappearance and preceding his return—suggests, I think, at least a subliminal sense of Posthumus himself offstage, dreaming the pastoral action. His very exile to Italy is a kind of sleep, an abatement of his ordinary powers of action and discourse. As the Queen puts it:

> His fortunes all lie speechless, and his name
> Is at last gasp.
>
>   (I.v.52-53)

But the dreaming itself resolves the various dilemmas of the court and of his tenuous hold on identity. When Cornelius predicts the effect of the drug Imogen takes in Belarius' cave, his words are appropriate for the effect produced by the pastoral sequence as a whole:

> . . . but there is
> No danger in what show of death it makes,
> More than the locking up the spirits a time,
> To be more fresh, reviving.
>
>   (I.v.39-42)

We may think first of the explicit patterning of Posthumus' fifth-act dream in the jail, when imprisonment and impending execution lead directly to revelation and new hope. But the pattern is implicit also in Imogen's "show of death" and revival, followed by Posthumus' change of heart.

Frye has commented upon the "extraordinary blindness"[11] of the play's characters, calling attention particularly to Imogen's speech to Pisanio as she prepares to depart on her journey—in psychic terms, her descent—to the wilds of Wales:

> I see before me, man. Nor here, nor here,
> Nor what ensues, but have a fog in them
> That I cannot look through. Away, I prithee;
> Do as I bid thee. There's no more to say;
> Accessible is none but Milford way.
>
>   (III.ii.77-81)

There is a sense of encroaching murkiness, of blurred horizons, of the contraction of vision. Only a journey to Milford, a sacred or enchanted place since Posthumus is supposed to be there, will serve to restore the natural order; it is time for the quest. And that quest requires that Imogen prepare for "the gap" that she "shall make in time" (III.ii.61-62)—a phrase suggestive of a lapse of ordinary consciousness—by wearing "a mind dark" as her fortune is (III.iv.142-43) as well as a boyish disguise. By assuming a false identity as Fidele, she literally becomes the truth of Posthumus' psychic experience. As Pisanio says, with the insouciance characteristic of the many speakers of dramatic ironies in the play, by vanishing as herself she will "tread a course / Pretty and full of view" which will bring her, in Lucius' service, close enough to Posthumus to receive accurate news of him:

> . . . yea, happily, near
> The residence of Posthumus; so nigh, at least,
> That though his actions were not visible, yet
> Report should render him hourly to your ear
> As truly as he moves.
>
> (III.iv.146-50)

Indeed, his actions, his change of heart, will not be made visible, but her actions will signify in the minds of the audience the emergence and eventual triumph of his native virtue. The method is one of visual enactment of a subtext never made verbally explicit, another strategy perhaps originally derived from dreams.

A psychomachia becomes inevitable, then, with the arrival of Cloten, whose thinly noble veneer and underlying rashness and brutal sexuality parody Posthumus' much-touted virtue. For we are given reason to believe that Posthumus' reputation, which has been much "extended" since the first scene of the play when the First Gentleman sings his praises unequivocally, is, in fact, much overblown. His eagerness to imagine Iachimo coupling with Imogen makes us highly suspicious of his not only unchivalrous but entirely cold-blooded protests that she "oft" restrained him of his "lawful pleasure" (II.v.9-10). These are his parting words to the audience before his disappearance, and they usher in the pastoral sequence. By the time we see Cloten in Posthumus' clothes, we know that Posthumus too has feet of clay and more than a little of Cloten's brutish instinct. Guiderius' beheading of Cloten neatly gelds the rashness of Posthumus. When Cloten and Imogen are laid to rest side by side, the audience sees a concise literalization of a rather unwieldy metaphor: Posthumus' psychomachic drama is resolved with Imogen/Fidele waking live and therefore triumphant. In one formulation, with Cloten's death the old Adam is laid to rest. Appropriately enough, the audience is prepared early in the play (however ironically) for Cloten to serve as a ritual sacrifice. As the First Lord cautions him after Cloten has bullied the departing Posthumus: "Sir, I would advise you to shift a shirt; the violence of action hath made you reek as a sacrifice" (I.ii.1-3). In the light of what happens "Milford way," especially with the various changings of garments, Cloten's reply acquires a deeper significance: "If my shirt were bloody, then to shift it." However nonchalant the presentation, the suggestion is clear: Cloten is more than simply a bully, buffoon, or ironic double, though he is something of all three. He is from our first sight of him a marked man,

and he serves, as in a quieter way his mother does, as a scapegoat for the purging of the whole community.

Of course, it has been necessary for Imogen as well to undergo a ritualized death for Posthumus' sake. But, phoenix-like, having been deemed by Iachimo "the Arabian bird" (I.vi.17), she also undergoes a ritual of rebirth. In this she is not unlike Hero in *Much Ado About Nothing,* for each manages by so doing to bring her lover to his senses. In her identification with Posthumus, Imogen assumes the status not only of a receptacle of displaced psychic energies, but of a sacrificial offering. As Freud notes in his essay "The Theme of the Three Caskets,"[12] in folktale a feigned or implied death will often serve as the penance through which a rebirth can be achieved. He cites the Grimm story of "The Six Swans" in which a sister frees her enchanted brothers by remaining dumb for a number of years. Her enforced silence represents a ritualized death on their behalf. Similarly, Imogen is reduced by fatigue, fasting, and a peculiar sapping of inner strength which seems to derive from the Milford landscape, as Cloten also experiences it.[13] Her familiar "tune" (V.v.238) is forced into abeyance first by physical helplessness and then by the drug's suspension of consciousness. Interestingly, just as Cloten is allied with sacrificial notions from Act I on, early in the play Cymbeline consigns Imogen to a ritualized ordeal:

> Nay, let her languish
> A drop of blood a day and, being aged,
> Die of this folly.
>
> (I.i.156-58)

And she herself reiterates the theme, begging Pisanio to carry out Posthumus' command that she may in dying "pang" Posthumus' memory, a proper penance for his rashness:

> Prithee dispatch.
> The lamb entreats the butcher.
>
> (III.iv.94-95)

The suggestiveness of the play's vaporous atmosphere and many allusions to unconscious lapsings becomes evident when one realizes that Shakespeare explicitly casts her ordeal in the form of dream.

Waking next to Cloten, she recalls the sense of dislocation and haziness which marks her setting out for Milford and, indeed, seems indigenous to the place. She is unable to distinguish between dream and reality and imagines that her association with Belarius/Morgan and, more ironically, with her as-yet-undiscovered brothers must have been a dream:

> . . . I hope I dream;
> For so I thought I was a cave-keeper,
> And cook to honest creatures. But 'tis not so;

'Twas but a bolt of nothing, shot at nothing,
Which the brain makes of fumes. . . .

(IV.ii.298-302)

Shakespeare then makes a characteristic leap, so that
we become aware of the entire pastoral sequence as a
kind of dream:

The dream's here still. Even when I wake it is
Without me, as within me; not imagin'd, felt.

(IV.ii.307-8)

The setting itself, featuring Belarius' cave which "instructs" his royal charges in a proper reverence for the natural world and "bows" them "to a morning's office" (III.iii.3-4), becomes a landscape charged with meaning. The pastoral generally provides safely distanced, naturalized outlets for martial and erotic conflicts—the *paragone*, the singing competition, the hunt as sport. As I have suggested, Cloten's pursuit of Imogen both purges and makes apparent in a displaced fashion Posthumus' residual brutish instincts. And I detect a certain suppressed eroticism in the relations between Imogen and her brothers which is diffused, I think, into the landscape in their hunting talk and in the sense of consummation of the natural cycle contained in their burial obsequies.[14] In their eyes Fidele is quite literally returned to rest in homely earth. Her waking to the grotesque possibility the pastoral idyll has concealed at once violates its conventions and reaffirms them; for it is merely Cloten, the distinctly unpastoral scapegoat, who has been destroyed.

Shakespeare's rather puzzling use of anachronism, which has long perplexed critics, may also be linked with the play's dream-like texture: plain-spoken Roman soldiers and Machiavellian intriguers just up from Renaissance Italian courts are perfectly free to mingle and skirmish in dreams with Celtic mountaineers. The analogous juxtaposition of these respective representatives of the three plots suggests something more than dream-logic, but I shall take up this matter in a moment.

When Posthumus returns to the stage at the beginning of Act V, it is apparent that he is as changed a man as if he too had witnessed or undergone Imogen's ordeal. In the logic of the double- or triple-plot, he has in effect undergone such an ordeal within himself. The demonic drama of the pastoral sequence of Acts III and IV has laid to rest those disturbances of character which had sundered him from wife and "soul," from his own best self. And that self is finally inseparable from the greater social harmony. His alienation has been both signified and compounded by banishment from his native soil. Dramatically, the pastoral sequence prepares him, and us, for a visitation by the past in the dream of the parents and brothers he, born literally posthumously, has never known:

Post. [Waking] Sleep, thou hast been a
grandsire and begot
A father to me; and thou hast created
A mother and two brothers. But, O scorn,
Gone! They went hence so soon as they were
born.

(V.iv.123-26)

Still under the dream's spell, he falls into couplets like the ghosts. But though they have vanished, a token has been left behind—the riddle which prophesies Posthumus' eventual good fortune as part of Britain's newly found prosperity in peace. Less tangibly, the dream's legacy is a legitimation, through the recovery of origins, of his full identity as Posthumus Leonatus, a warrior-patriot, now strong in the defense of peace. The curious thing is that the more he comes to know himself, the more he ceases to matter as a character at all and comes instead to embody the psychic experience of the play as a whole. He whose reputation has been so hyperbolically "extended" becomes in fact symbolically dilated to encompass both the realms of dream and waking, of alienation and identity. The strangeness of Posthumus as a hero may be more easily accounted for if we remember that the nature of "identity," as it functions within comic, or tragicomic, structure, is always twofold. The singular sense of identity comes close to our conventional notion of the word; its larger sense requires that the social tyranny with which the play begins be dismantled and the community more harmoniously rebuilt. Posthumus' experience is, I think, both profoundly individual and social, at once peculiar to him—the recovery, through dream, of his personal history—and, by analogy, comparable with a larger movement—the recognition of a growing sense of national identity through the dramatization of national history, with its politic blend of fact and legend, reportage and myth.

Because his potential for virtue was always present, merely waiting to be purged of its darker impulses, in the course of the play Posthumus is changed, and yet not changed. He experiences a dilation of being in at least two senses. The pastoral action—itself a dream displaced and enacted—functions as an incorporation of the unconscious, without some acknowledgment of which a complete and seamless identity is impossible, and as a preparation for his actual dream, in which his personal history is returned to him. In a larger sense, Posthumus' being is dilated through the pressure of such incorporation to signify, by analogy, the experience of the play as a whole, its pattern of purgation and reintegration of consciousness in communal and national terms.

II

Empson describes the phenomenon of the "identification of one person with the whole moral, social, and at last physical order" as a device fundamental to the structure of the double-plot.[15] In its capacity for complex sympathy, says Empson, the Elizabethan imagination was for some reason quite at home with both a great deal of dramatic ambiguity and the double-plot's "vague suggestiveness."[16] In contrast to most modern critics, *Cymbeline*'s first audiences would have perceived not only the connection between Posthumus' experience and that of the other characters, but the analogies yoking the three plots as well. The doctrine of analogy as it applies to history, both personal and national, seems to have been firmly implanted in their minds. They were, after all, not so very far from the tradition of medieval exegesis, which in the reading of church history encouraged a particular sensitivity to a layering of analogous relationships. Indeed, one could characterize the structure of feeling at work in *Cymbeline* as a kind of dialectical relation between the one and the many. On one hand, the play's deepest experience is distilled into the psyche of Posthumus; on the other, the audience is made aware of certain forces compelling the action on several levels, so that the last act especially bears witness to an overriding order, a sense of unity in multiplicity.

Critics who complain of the play's lack of unity seem to have trouble most often with the historical elements, particularly the Roman/British pact, with its accompanying aura of anachronism. Some of the sense of illogicality and dislocation can, as I have suggested, be attributed to play's dream-like texture. But I also think that the abrupt yoking of the issues of personal, familial, and communal or national reunification heightens the audience's awareness of the correspondences between them. Each plot becomes a metaphor for the other two; we are shown the destinies of man, family, and the larger community under the same reassuring management. In what Kermode wryly calls the "twenty-four-fold denouement"[17] of Act V, scene v, implied relationships become visible, a movement characteristic of the play's controlling pictorial or spatial technique. Just as Posthumus' divided psyche is spatially realized in Cloten and Imogen side by side, the unity of the narrative strands upheld by various characters is made manifest on the stage. Clusters form and are forcibly joined: Posthumus-Iachimo-Imogen; Imogen-the brothers-Cymbeline; Cymbeline-the brothers-Lucius. These groups correspond to the erotic, familial, and national plots, respectively. As Granville-Barker takes pains to emphasize, the wondrous impact of the recognitions can only be achieved through the cooperation of all the actors in a sustained panoply of characterization.[18]

The obvious question, then, is what precisely constitutes the compelling force yoking individual natures with their larger contexts? The play has its share of references to an unseen power, all of them, I think, deliberately murky. Jupiter's utterance of the doctrine

of *felix culpa*—"whom best I love I cross"—is delivered in a self-consciously theatrical context, to the rumble of thundering machinery and the chime of strained and stagey rhymes:

> No more, you petty spirits of region low,
> Offend our hearing; hush! How dare you
>   ghosts
> Accuse the Thunderer whose bolt, you know,
> Sky-planted, batters all rebelling coasts?
>
>   . . . . .
>
> Be not with mortal accidents opprest:
> No care of yours it is; to make my gift,
> The more delay'd, delighted. . . .
>
>   (V.iv.93-102)

To which the ghosts of Posthumus' family respond with exaggerated awe:

> *Sici.* He came in thunder; his celestial breath
>   Was sulphurous to smell; the holy eagle
>   Stoop'd, as to foot us. His ascension is
>   More sweet than our blest fields. . . .
> *All.*   Thanks, Jupiter!
>
>   (V.iv.114-19)

The explicit artifice of the spectacle renders Jupiter's pronouncement formally *de rigueur,* and therefore commonplace—a requirement of the tragicomic structure rather than a satisfying answer to the powerful suggestion offered by one of Cymbeline's lords:

> The want is but to put those pow'rs in motion
> That long to move.
>
>   (IV.iii.31-32)

Here, of course, Frye and others speak of Christian providence, of the play as a religious allegory, though Frye maintains that the signs are implicit and point beyond the play to the greatest known event of Cymbeline's time, the birth of Christ. Certainly the play is imbued with a sense of impending catastrophe followed by ameliorating circumstance, always beyond the characters' control. A certain amount of helplessness seems a rare virtue. In the case of Imogen, physical reduction and the surrendering of consciousness yield the salvation of her husband, her marriage, her family circle, her country, and, by implication if the Christian allusions are taken into account, the collective soul of the community. Similarly, the jailed Posthumus submits his will to the powers that be and receives the sight of his dead forebears and Jupiter himself as absolution, while Cymbeline capitulates to the Roman demand for tribute that peace may reign. A religious allegorist might specify Christian humility as a covering answer. But I hesitate to invoke a Christian interpretation too emphatically; the play seems to me to be deliberately infused with pre-Christian, primitive elements. From Guiderius' designation of a Celtic burial, head eastward, for Fidele, to the Soothsayer's panegyric to "radiant Cymbeline" (V.v.473), there seems, to be sure, a double vision, but the emphasis is earthly. The play itself, in fact, makes sacred the local habitations and names of this world.

In his persuasive discussion of the historical groundings of the play, Emrys Jones argues for an implicit unity exactly where many critics have found fault—in the play's historical dimension. Jones refers to both the contemporary, topical significance of certain aspects of the play and to Shakespeare's reliance upon his audience's possessing a strong sense of national history. The topical references surface mainly in relation to Cymbeline as a figure of the peace-making king, an obeisance to James I. This homage-to-patron also yields such dramaturgical features as the masque-like theophany, since James was fond of masques. Jones also pins the main flaw of the dramatic design to the Cymbeline/James analogy in an interesting way, attributing certain inconsistencies of character to Shakespeare's various strategies for avoiding giving offense. While I am not persuaded that the play is as logically flawed as Jones suggests, I would agree that a proper understanding of its intricacies depends to a great extent upon a recognition of its use of history.

Jone's most penetrating comments concern the significance of the history which shrouds Milford Haven: its importance as the landing-place of the Earl of Richmond, soon to be Henry VII, and thus its function as a cradle for the Tudor-Stuart line of which James was the latest embodiment. Certainly, Shakespeare goes to some lengths to give Milford a peculiar resonance, so that it becomes a magical and sacred place; its irresistible drawing power is especially evident in relation to Imogen. I think that Shakespeare uses this strategy for dramaturgical as well as political reasons. But let us look first at what Jones says about the place as conceived in strictly historical terms. He quotes G. Wilson Knight and proceeds from there:

> 'She is, one feels, magnetized to this, enchanted, spot. . . .' She is indeed 'magnetized' to Milford Haven. Without knowing it, she is helping to fulfill a 'prophecy'. But the compelling force is ultimately nothing other than the facts of history:

> > the Earl of Richmond
> > Is with a mighty power landed at Milford.[19]

The analogies the play makes between the logic of events of chronicle-history and the logic of dreams point up the disorder and illogic of unreconstructed historical facts, and the essentially fictive structure the historian, like the dramatist, must impose to give shape to his narrative. It is not that the sanctity of national his-

tory is being deliberately undermined, but that Shakespeare makes us aware that history *is* constructed, that both our personal and national myths must of necessity scaffold truth with an artificial, purposive design. By heightening theatrical artifice throughout the play, Shakespeare makes us aware of the instrumental use we make of history to further present ends. In the case of Milford Haven, the play confers lasting significance on a particular time and place in history and makes obeisance to James as a peacemaker, but we are aware all the while of the dramatic illusion, of the necessity of incorporating politic facts into the play's design. Again, the closing lines of the play encapsulate this tension and redound upon all that has gone before:

> *Cym.* . . . . Set we forward; let
> A Roman and a British ensign wave
> Friendly together. So through Lud's Town
>   march;
> And in the temple of great Jupiter
> Our peace we'll ratify; seal it with feasts.
> Set on there! Never was a war did cease,
> Ere bloody hands were wash'd, with such a
>   peace.
>
> (V.v.477-83)

The celebration of the Tudor ascendancy we find in Shakespeare's histories is framed in *Cymbeline* with irony designed to deflate the panegyrical and demystify the larger political use of national history, but not to demolish it. It is an irony which flirts with but refuses to embrace outright satire.

Milford Haven *is* sanctified and made memorable, and *Cymbeline* is unique among Shakespeare's romances in its historical particularity and its hallowing of a specific, real place. Instead of a flight or withdrawal to an imaginary island, we are made to see the English landscape as magically charged. Milford Haven is "blessed" (III.ii.58); the very topography conspires in a British victory when Belarius, Guiderius, and Arviragus, fighting in their narrow lane, are "Accommodated by the place" (V.iii.32). We are also, by analogy, made to feel reverence for the kingdom as a spiritual community, whether explicitly Christian or not. That there is something transcendent in the movement of the play from incipient tragedy through purgation to "the harmony of this peace" (V.v.465) can hardly be denied. But the kingdom is specifically Britain, the body politic of Shakespeare's "scept'red isle," at peace with the aggressor, Rome, after having maintained an impressive defense. For all our interest in the psychic identities of Posthumus and Imogen, the "radiant" Cymbeline, King of Britaine, as the Folio title stresses, is the center about whom all others are meant to move. Interestingly, Imogen too is firmly attached to the nation, as a mother of succeeding generations of Britons; her saving grace is not, though the two are very close in Renaissance thought, the magical integrity of virginity, but rather Milton's "Sun-clad power of Chastity."[20] She draws her strength from her marital *fidelity*, her sacred social union. T.S. Eliot is perhaps striving for a similar conjunction of time-hallowed place and the recapturing of our collective ancestral history when "East Coker" he recalls:

> The association of man and woman
> In daunsinge, signifying matrimonie—
> A dignified and commodious sacrament.
> Two and two, necessarye, coniunction,
> Holding eache other by the hand or the arm
> Whiche betokeneth concorde. . . .[21]

The erotic plot, anchored as it is in the dreams of Posthumus and Imogen, becomes both necessary to and emblematic of a greater social harmony.

Perhaps the play's concern with this connection between private and social experience may help account for its strange tone, its mixture of archness and affecting simplicity. As Freud defines them, wit and dreams share a common parentage in the unconscious; the most important difference lies in their "social behavior." Freud holds the dream to be "a perfectly asocial psychic product," which not only finds it "unnecessary" to be intelligible, but "must even guard against being understood" since it can only exist in disguised form. Wit, on the other hand, Freud considers "the most social of all those psychic functions whose aim is to gain pleasure." Wit requires an audience.[22] In *Cymbeline* Shakespeare conveys much of the experience of dreams and some of their wonder within a sophisticated dramatic vehicle, aware of its own artifice.

As Granville-Barker recognized, in Imogen's waking next to Cloten and in the final recognition scene especially, the audience is both sympathetically engaged and ironically distanced. The grotesque irony of the former scene is replaced in the latter by the potentially "farcical associations,"[23] in Kermode's phrase, of so many revelations so neatly contrived. In both cases, the core of the narrative moves us; it is the palpable presence of the master dramatist pulling both affective and witty strings which holds us apart. Within the conventions of the tragicomic double plot, heroic and pastoral or comic episodes reflect and redound upon one another, but remain distinct. But *Cymbeline*'s complexity of tone derives from a deliberate confounding of the two.

While it sounds paradoxical, in this respect *Cymbeline* is a peculiarly medieval play. The sacred and the profane exist side by side, and to some degree merge in their essential effect. The grotesque and the farcical help give the transcendent an earthly location. At the same time, they allow the controlled intrusion of unconscious impulses, an acknowledgment of man's kin-

ship with the beasts, and at once direct the mind upward toward reverence. I am reminded of Hugh of St. Victor's belief that

> The ugly is still more beautiful than beauty itself. . . .
> Beauty encourages us to linger. The ugly does not
> permit us to rest; it forces us to depart, to transcent
> it. . . .[24]

This is the impulse which underlies those medieval grotesques carved into Miserere seats. And Shakespeare captures it to some extent in the the union of sympathy and ironical amusement he manages to evoke in *Cymbeline*. The play's rarefied atmosphere of wittiness infused with the insouciance of dreams, its impression of artlessness artfully executed, is not only a sophisticated exploration of tragicomic form, but an unusually primitive dramaturgical experience. Beside *The Winter's Tale* or *The Tempest, Cymbeline* provides relatively few verbal clues to its underlying meaning; its effects are mainly visual, its affectiveness a concatenation of texture and atmosphere. There is an implicit silence in the play, suggested by those quietenings down which occur as the various characters fall asleep. And these lapsings, these cessations of consciousness which yet contain the deepest truth of that consciousness, suggest the silence which signifies that state of complete identity in which the perils and restorative rituals of the romance are no longer necessary.

Cymbeline's greatest interest lies, I think, in the suggestiveness of its bold peculiarities. As Granville-Barker described the play:

> . . . One turns to it from *Othello,* or *King Lear,* or
> *Antony and Cleopatra,* as one turns from a masterly
> painting to, say, a fine piece of tapestry, from
> commanding beauty to more recondite charm.[25]

This rather specialized charm is probably what Shaw had in mind when he ventured to suggest that the proper setting for a modern production of *Cymbeline* was not the London stage, but a village schoolroom.[26] There, unself-consciously, the drama would be played with the degrees of ardor and artlessness natural to it, and to a nation's sense of itself when it fancies it has recently come of age. The smallish stature of the actors would adumbrate their faint absurdity as heroes without bringing down charges of unpatriotic license, and we as the audience could remain complacently detached, congratulating ourselves on our greater historical sophistication.

Notes

[1] Richard Levin, in his study of the various kinds of unity achieved in Renaissance multiple-plot drama, merely alludes to *Cymbeline* in a footnote with the comment that, while certain parallels exist between the

rash condemnations Cymbeline and Posthumus bestow on Belarius and Imogen, "little is done with the relation of the two areas"; *The Multiple Plot in English Renaissance Drama* (Chicago: Univ. of Chicago Press, 1971), p. 167. In his psychoanalytic reading, Murray M. Schwartz attempts to link the play's concern with "sexual and familial" integrity with "British self-esteem," but he never develops the connections, concentrating instead on the psychoanalytic "meaning" of individual characters and incidents; see "Between Fantasy and Imagination: a Psychological Exploration of *Cymbeline*," in *Psychoanalysis and Literary Process*, ed. Frederick Crews (Cambridge, Mass.: Winthrop, 1970), pp. 219-83. In her subtler psychoanalytic reading, Meredith Skura links certain "unconscious" elements in the play with its themes of familial and personal identity, but she stops short of transforming these categories into the political ones of nation and community: "*Cymbeline* has been called a history play, but it is a history play of the individual too, and it shows that what we are now comes out of what we *were*"; "Interpreting Posthumus' Dream from Above and Below: Families, Psychoanalysts, and Literary Critics," in *Representing Shakespeare: New Psychoanalytic Essays*, ed. Murray M. Schwartz and Coppélia Kahn (Baltimore: Johns Hopkins Univ. Press, 1980), p. 213. I am most indebted to Arthur Kirsch's application of dream theory to the play in his *Shakespeare and the Experience of Love* (Cambridge: Cambridge Univ. Press, 1981), pp. 144-73. Although he and I come to many similar conclusions, different emphases lead us to different valuations of the play's political import.

[2] In generic exasperation, Frank Kermode has christened the play an "'historical-pastoral' tragi-comical romance"; he agrees with those who sense behind the odd combination of naiveté of plot and virtuosity of dramatic technique "an effect almost of irony," a sense that the dramatist is "somehow playing with the play"; *The Final Plays* (London: Longmans, Green and Co., 1963), pp. 29, 22.

[3] Northrop Frye, *A Natural Perspective* (New York: Columbia Univ. Press, 1965), p. 70.

[4] The text used for all quotations from and references to Shakespeare's writings is that of *The Complete Works*, ed. Peter Alexander (London and Glasgow: Collins, 1951).

[5] In Howard Felperin's formulation, each of the three plots may be subsumed to some extent under the heading "erotic plot": "The genius presiding over Elizabethan dramatic romance is ultimately Eros, or an Eros figure, who embodies the principle of love in either its narrower sense of sexual union or in its wider ones of family solidarity and social harmony or in its widest Christian one of 'the love that moves the sun and the other stars,' as Dante put it at the end of *The Divine*

Comedy"; see *Shakespearean Romance* (Princeton: Princeton Univ. Press, 1972), p. 21. While applauding his notion of analogous relations among the three levels of affection, I prefer to reserve the term "erotic plot" for the relations between Posthumus and Imogen.

[6] I am grateful to G. M. MacLean for introducing me to crucial changes in British historiographical models. For a distillation of current scholarship on the subject and an up-to-date bibliography, see his unpublished Ph.D. dissertation, "Time's Witness: English Historical Poetry, 1600-1660" (University of Virginia, 1981), pp. 11, 100, 253, 267. See F. J. Levy's study, *Tudor Historical Thought* (San Marino, Cal.: Huntington Library, 1967) for a general discussion of changes in contemporary historiography and interpretation.

[7] See, for example, Homer Swander's "*Cymbeline*: Religious Idea and Dramatic Design," in *Pacific Coast Studies in Shakespeare*, ed. Waldo F. McNeir and Thelma N. Greenfield (Eugene: University of Oregon Books, 1966), pp. 248-62, and his "*Cymbeline* and the 'Blameless Hero,'" *ELH*, 31 (1964), 259-70, and Joan Hartwig's *Shakespeare's Tragicomic Vision* (Baton Rouge: LSU Press, 1972), pp. 61-103.

[8] Sigmund Freud, *The Interpretation of Dreams*, trans. James Strachey (New York: Avon, 1965), pp. 544-46.

[9] Schwartz sees Iachimo as another vice-like double for Posthumus, but one whose sexual proclivities run to looking rather than "tasting," pp. 227-31; I find him much closer than Cloten to the conventional vice—a less demonic Iago, scaled to fit a tragicomic rather than a tragic design.

[10] William Empson, *Some Versions of Pastoral* (New York: New Directions, 1974), p. 29.

[11] Frye, *A Natural Perspective*, p. 67.

[12] Freud, *The Complete Psychological Works*, trans. James Strachey (London: Hogarth Press, 1958), XII, 296.

[13] Cloten enters the environs of Belarius' cave with the words: "I cannot find those runagates. That villain / Hath mocked me. I am faint" (IV.ii.62-63).

[14] Schwartz overreads the relations between Imogen and her brothers by suggesting that "Their unconscious recognition of familial bonds affirms defenses against the play's incestuous anxieties," p. 258.

[15] Empson, pp. 42-43.

[16] Empson, p. 65.

[17] Kermode, p. 28.

[18] Harley Granville-Barker, *Prefaces to Shakespeare* (Princeton: Princeton Univ. Press, 1946), I, 490.

[19] Emrys Jones, "Stuart *Cymbeline*," *Essays in Criticism,* 11 (1961), 99.

[20] John Milton, *Comus, Complete Poems and Major Prose,* ed. Merritt Y. Hughes (Indianapolis: Odyssey Press, 1957), p. 108.

[21] T.S. Eliot, *Four Quartets,* from *Collected Poems* (London: Faber and Faber, 1974), p. 197.

[22] Freud, "Wit and Its Relation to the Unconscious, *The Basic Writings,* ed. A.A. Brill (New York: Modern Library, 1938), 760-61.

[23] Kermode, p. 29.

[24] Edgar De Bruyne, *The Esthetics of the Middle Ages,* trans. Eileen B. Hennessy (New York: Frederick Ungar, 1969), p. 61.

[25] Granville-Barker, p. 543.

[26] G.B. Shaw, *Shaw on Shakespeare,* ed. Edwin Wilson (London: Cassell, 1961), p. 39.

Joseph Westlund (essay date 1993)

SOURCE: "Self and Self-validation in a Stage Character: A Shakespearean Use of Dream," in *The Dream and the Text: Essays on Literature and Language,* edited by Carol Schreier Rupprecht, State University of New York Press, 1993, pp. 200-16.

[*In the following essay, Westlund studies the psychological changes precipitated by Posthumus's dream in* Cymbeline.]

Near the end of Shakespeare's *Cymbeline* the play's central character, Posthumus, has a dream that critics and directors often treat as exterior—as a vision of Jupiter—rather than as the depiction of an interior event.[1] Nevertheless, the appearance of Jupiter and the ghosts of Posthumus's family is the theatrical representation of an interior event within the character who lies sleeping before us on the stage. As such, the dream allows us to speculate about how Shakespeare conceives of the function of dreaming and how he prepares Posthumus and the audience for the imminent happy reunion with Imogen. Posthumus's dream offers an irresistible attraction to anyone attempting to figure out the motivation of this elusive character.

The dream is especially intriguing to psychoanalytic critics, among whom Meredith Skura offers the best and most extensive account.[2] My interpretation differs from hers in large part because my perspective is that of "self psychology," an extensive revision of Freudian theory proposed by the psychoanalyst Heinz Kohut (1913-1981). Kohut offers an unusually effective approach to analyzing dreams in real life—and by extension in literature. One of my aims in this essay is to demonstrate the value of the shift in psychoanalytic assumptions which Kohut and other psychoanalysts propose under the term "self psychology." To put the innovation very briefly, such proponents emphasize the "self" as the central organizing and stabilizing principle of the personality, (as different from Freudian emphasis upon conflict among various agencies such as the id/ego/superego, conflict arising from sexual and aggressive drives and culminating in the Oedipus complex).

Kohut's psychology shares with other twentieth-century systems of psychology certain implicit value judgments; for instance, it is better to be autonomous than dependent. Kohut emphasizes the centrality of self-esteem even more than other psychoanalytic theorists do; he often refers to it as "healthy narcissism" so as to stress the value of basic rudimentary self-love. To claim that self-love is essential for an individual may grate upon some Renaissance scholars who feel that in Shakespeare's world one has to lose one's self, and one's self-esteem, to find oneself. The alternative view of self such scholars offer is roughly that of Christianity which de-emphasizes autonomy and the independent individual in favor of dependence upon, and merger with, God. Nevertheless, Christianity, and in particular Protestantism, lays extraordinary demands upon the individual to whom it delegates sole responsibility for personal salvation. It is dangerous to assume that we know for certain what the range of possibilities was for a Renaissance, much less a Shakespearean, conceptualization.

Kohut's theory illuminates an important aspect of Shakespeare. Shakespeare's works are among the very first to contribute to our contemporary perception of the vital role of a sense of self. Shakespeare at once creates and depends upon a heightened awareness of individuality, autonomy and self-fashioning. By scrutinizing the dream of Posthumus we gain further insight into the vicissitudes of the individual as conceptualized during the Renaissance. In Posthumus's roles as heroic soldier, trusting spouse, and repentant murderer he seems unable to perceive himself as a coherent center of initiative persisting over time. In this shaky sense of self he has much in common with Hamlet. Posthumus is also similar to Gloucester's younger son Edgar in *King Lear,* Edgar's antic creation of several roles and disguises strikes some interpreters as a prelude to his self-integration—or, to others, seems a sign of his self-fragmentation.

My interpretation of Posthumus's dream builds upon Skura's excellent account. She points out that Posthumus, unlike other heroes and heroines in the romances, does not find his family members literally alive; instead he recreates them in his dreams. To find himself as a husband, Skura argues, Posthumus must find himself as a son—as part of the family he lacked because his mother died giving birth to him after the death of his brothers and the more recent death of his father. "Posthumus's trouble at the beginning of the play is that he does not know who he is—and this is partly because he does not know who his family is" (Skura 1980, 208). The King, Cymbeline, takes him in and Cymbeline's own family provides the first substitute for the one Posthumus misses. However, Posthumus violates his proper place in this surrogate family when he elopes with Cymbeline's daughter, the princess Imogen. When Posthumus joins a second foster family (Imogen's long-lost brothers and the lord who abducted them), "he takes his proper place: brave, but not overbearing; accepting his position as a nameless third son, subduing his own ends to those of the little family" (Skura 1980, 209). Skura argues that in this manner Posthumus mends a flaw in his character: the overpossessiveness, derived from Cymbeline's family, which led to his destructive marriage:

> Posthumus's achievement as a husband and a son is crowned by this vision of his family [in the dream]. Dead though they are, they appear physically on stage, breaking into the current action and revealing their implicit presence all along. They appear just when Posthumus finds himself, and the dream is a perfect climax to his story. (p. 210)

Skura concludes that "after his dream, nothing has changed except his state of mind: Posthumus has simply recognized his past and therefore recognized himself" (p. 212).

I want to modify this account by challenging some of its assumptions about dreams and the nature of the change in Posthumus.[3] As far as I can see he has not achieved much success as a husband or a son by the point he has the dream; indeed, he is self-destructive and explicitly suicidal when he falls asleep. Nor is it clear exactly how his state of mind alters; that "he recognizes his past and therefore recognizes himself" suggests some sort of "working through," but I am not certain that such a process can be imagined to occur here.

Skura sees Posthumus as a coherent, autonomous character. This view strikes me as improbable. For instance, he rarely interacts with other characters as if they were entities outside himself; he does not treat them as autonomous "objects" distinct from himself as a "subject." Instead, he continually treats them as what Kohut terms "selfobjects"; that is, Posthumus merges with others and treats them as if they were part of himself. Thus, to me his sense of self is more primitive and

incoherent than most interpreters assume; he is less firm in his sense of the boundaries between himself and others. This trait suggests that Posthumus behaves in a way similar to that of real-life persons who were arrested at an early developmental stage; for instance, it suggests a reason why instinctual conflict is not central to his characterization. Skura also concentrates upon matters other than instinctual conflict. Despite his apparently adult behavior during much of the play, Posthumus also exhibits, in my opinion, a chaotic and rather infantile side.

Posthumus's State of Mind Before the Dream

For members of the audience the effect of the dream depends upon what we imagine to be Posthumus's "state of mind" before he falls asleep. This is particularly important given Kohut's insistence upon the need to clarify both the specific and the general *vulnerabilities* of the dreamer having the dream, for he argues that the dream arises from and unconsciously addresses such vulnerabilities.

My view of Posthumus's state of mind before the dream differs from Skura's in several important ways. When Posthumus reappears at the start of the final act he repents having had Imogen murdered (5.1.1-29); nevertheless, I argue that he repents in an antic and radically ambivalent manner. He shifts from his Roman dress into that of a "Briton peasant" (5.1.29-33), and silently vanquishes Iachimo (5.2. stage direction). Then Posthumus reenters "and seconds the Britons"—that is, Belarius and the two princes. In doing so, he saves the king and Britain in a battle scene long on action but short on dialogue (5.2.14-17). Nevertheless, each of the three other defenders speaks, if only, like the two princes, to share a line such as "Stand, stand, and fight!" (5.2.13). Posthumus says nothing during the scene; he simply reenters, fights, and leaves at the same time as the three other heroes leave.

That the text allows us to feel an air of disengagement in Posthumus may be unimportant, for we can assume that he is a compelling physical presence during the scene. Still, that he says nothing forms a pattern. That he reenters once the battle has begun and remains silent during the scene conveys an air of detachment on his part, which the following scene intensifies. Right after the defeat of the Romans there follows a scene in which Posthumus describes the battle to a taciturn cowardly Lord (5.3). At first glance, it seems difficult to guess why Shakespeare put this scene here; we in the audience have just witnessed the battle through our own eyes—and have never before seen the Lord nor will we see him again. As a result, critics often dispute the authorship of the scene. They also grow puzzled about what Posthumus means to say here (see Nosworthy, the New Arden Edition, pp. 148-49).

I suggest that, like the dream itself, this scene is designed to offer a glimpse of Posthumus's inner world. By hearing his own version of the battle, we can reexperience it from his own subjective viewpoint. From this viewpoint, from his own perspective, his deed loses much of its power to validate him as a worthy man. He disavows his heroic role even while he describes the battle on the narrow bridge. Instead of describing his own efforts and success—or simply assuming them with quiet modesty—Posthumus becomes almost overwhelmed with rage. His anger is apparently directed at the coward, but it has an indeterminate, archaic quality: the rage seems far out of proportion to the fact that the Lord was one of the men who fled. Why should Posthumus work himself up to such a state over a coward when the battle was victorious? More to the point, why should Shakespeare want to present Posthumus as beside himself with rage at a moment when we might expect to see the hero attending to other more pressing matters (such as consolidating his gains, or proceeding to repentance)?

Since the audience already knows Posthumus is valiant and the battle won, the scene's effect is to alert us to his overwhelming anger, his vulnerability, and his tendency to be self-defeating. The scene reinforces our sense that the three traits are linked in Posthumus, for we see them flare up elsewhere. For instance, the issue of Imogen's chastity kindles all three responses—as does Iachimo's challenge, apparent success, and the result of this success. Posthumus seems unable to *experience* himself in any positive behavior: as beloved husband, as national hero, as repentant sinner. Instead, he falls prey to fits of bedeviled rage.[4]

In growing angry he silently, ominously, deletes himself from the list of heroes who saved the day. He tells the Lord that there was "an ancient soldier" (Belarius) who "with two striplings" (the Princes) fought off the Romans:

> These three,
> Three thousand confident, in act as many,—
> For three performers are the file when all
> The rest do nothing. . . .
>
> (5.3.28-31)

Since Posthumus was also engaged in the fight, there were four soldiers who defended the bridge, not three. Why does he fail to mention himself? Perhaps he simply intends to be modest (although he might have mentioned some unknown warrior who assisted the others). It seems more likely, however—given Posthumus's excessive and unfocused anger at this point—that Posthumus omits himself because of his sense of disengagement and worthlessness. This interpretation gains support from the fact that once Posthumus has driven the Lord away, he shifts his anger to himself and contemplates suicide.

Many viewers join Meredith Skura in expecting that some healing benefit must result from Posthumus's valor. His heroic deeds offer Shakespeare an excellent reason why Posthumus has an auspicious dream and why he is worthy of reunion with Imogen. However, the text here and in the dream suggests that Posthumus *disavows* his heroism: it apparently means nothing to him for he cannot own it as his. So, too, he gives no sign that he feels at one with Belarius and the young princes (who, Skura suggests, aid in the healing process which culminates in the dream [Skura 1980, 209]). Instead, the scene with the Lord heightens the discrepancy between how we expect Posthumus to react and how he actually views himself.

Posthumus's estrangement from the three Britons and from himself as British hero is underscored in symbolic terms. Once more he changes his clothes. Again, this is not modesty or self-abnegation, for he draws attention to himself by his anger and self-contempt. Since the British are now triumphant, he decides he will no longer be one of them: "No more a Briton, I have resumed again / The part I came in" (5.3.75-76). He assiduously takes on the costume of the vulnerable. First, he dressed as a Briton when the Romans were marching against them; now he changes into Roman garb as soon as the Romans are vanquished. The manner in which he changes clothes, like his disavowal of his heroism, heightens the audience's sense of his self-defeat and desolation; he looks defeated, he sounds defeated, and he focuses on such failings at the very moment he has helped achieve victory.

Posthumus's despair must stem in large part from losing Imogen, but it is more diffuse and global than we might expect from such a loss. For instance, he seems unable to focus upon his loss of Imogen so that he might properly mourn her. He apparently can conceive of no way out of his plight—at least not in waking life.

Even his words of repentance in jail seem forced and rather unconvincing. Many critics assume that he repents, but he tends to confuse the issue in his oblique and tortured rumination. For instance, he addresses himself by saying:

> My conscience, thou art fetter'd
> More than my shanks and wrists: you good
>   gods, give me
> The penitent instrument to pick that bolt,
> Then free for ever. Is't enough I am sorry?
> So children temporal fathers do appease;
> Gods are more full of mercy.
>
> (5.4.8-13)

It is not clear to me how the "penitent instrument" death can free his conscience. Death might make conscience irrelevant since God's judgment would prevail; but in this lower world only repentance can assuage conscience. Critics note that he employs traditional language in distinguishing the three parts of repentance (Nosworthy, the New Arden Edition, pp. 155-56). Nevertheless, he undermines his attempts at penitence by his doggedly ambivalent tone. He seems defensive or even truculent when he asks of the gods "Is't enough I am sorry?" Does he mean to praise the gods for their degree of mercy, or to blame them for being less merciful than temporal fathers? When he addresses the gods again, he asks them to take his life:

> For Imogen's dear life take mine, and though
> 'Tis not so dear, yet 'tis a life; you coin'd it.
>   (5.4.22-23)

His attitude verges on being accusatory. The gods allow all that happens to happen, and thus allowed Iachimo to seduce Imogen; still, Posthumus is also to blame, although he avoids saying so here and in his long soliloquy at the outset of the final act (5.1.1-33). Posthumus resists facing the fact that he is responsible for his deed; without this vital first step, any forms of repentance can mean but little. He devotes much of his energy to accusing the gods of unfairness. He asks that they take his life although it is "light" and not worth much. This characteristic self-devaluation also carries with it an implicit denigration of the gods. He adds the idea that since the gods made him they really ought to accept his life—light though it be. Such baroque and confused reasoning undermines his attempt at repentance. If the gods are meant to be at all like the Christian God, they are not likely to see his soliloquy as an effective step toward repentance.

Self-validation in the Dream

Posthumus now falls asleep on stage. He is in jail, having provoked imprisonment by those whom he had just saved from the Romans. He seems to be at a nadir of self-fragmentation and self-defeat rather than a climax of healing. Critics sometimes assume that he is saved by a vision of Jupiter, by an arbitrary external power. Anything is possible as soon as a deity enters; one might even argue for an analogy to the mysterious workings of Christian grace. Still, it seems more likely that we are meant to see the dream as a dream, and to conceive of it as signaling some positive change from within his own nature and characterization.

For a moment, let me stand back and generalize about his "state of mind" as it is represented to us at the moment the dream begins. He has much in common with real-life persons whom Kohut describes in terms of a "vertical split" of character disorders (as distinct from the "horizontal split" of repression within a unified self which Freudians use to describe neurotics). Posthumus vacillates between two poles: a grandiose self, and an empty or deprived self. His grandiosity manifests itself in presuming to test Imogen, to assume

her guilt, and to have her murdered. One might choose other terms than "grandiose" to describe his attitude (such as hubristic, sinful, cruel), but the term is useful in that it refers to a trait which Posthumus reveals in other significant areas of his behavior.

Posthumus also reveals an empty self in direct contrast to the grandiose self: profoundly deprived, he gives the impression of being unable to fulfill his needs by his own deeds. This emptiness manifests itself in his depression and also in his inability to *own* anything as his—whether heroic deeds or wicked ones.

That he is so vulnerable suggests his dream can profitably be interpreted as a "self-state dream." Kohut argues that such a dream differs from the traditional formulation of dreams by psychoanalysts. From a Freudian perspective dreams are assumed to deal with hidden instinctual wishes (mainly sexual and aggressive), with conflict, and with attempted solutions of conflict. For a Kohutian perspective, self-state dreams respond to a crisis in which the sense of self-coherence begins to fragment. Kohut suggests that our scrutiny of the manifest content of self-state dreams can "allow us to recognize that the healthy sectors of the patient's psyche are reacting with anxiety to a disturbing change in the condition of the self—manic overstimulation or a serious depressive drop in self-esteem—or to the threat of the dissolution of the self" (Kohut 1977, 109).[5]

Skura makes some roughly similar assumptions in her deemphasis of conflict and drives, and in her emphasis on Posthumus's need for his lost family. Where we differ is in my focus upon Posthumus's vacillation between grandiosity and emptiness, and in my sense of his extreme vulnerability at the time of the dream. What he needs, and what he creates in his dream, is not simply a family to recognize but a family (and a deity) who mirror his worth and sustain him.

Let me shift more decisively into Posthumus's own perspective on the dream. In doing so I follow one of Kohut's ill-understood but revolutionary clinical precepts: I emphasize the *subjective* nature of the dreamer's dream, rather than look at it objectively—as most interpreters do without being aware of their stance.[6] Kohut refers to such attempts as "empathy" and they from the basis of both the data and the theory of self psychology. At first glance, empathy seems a mild and sentimental attitude; the term often draws scorn from those who miss his point, or find his advice difficult to follow. Kohut insists that the analyst can understand only through experiencing within himself or herself what the other person is feeling. He stresses this move not because of a wish to be supportive (although such a move can be valuable). Instead, Kohut uses the concept of "empathy" to confront the inevitable bias of the interpreter who will inevitably distort the reality of the other since it differs from his or her own reality. Because of his awareness of this inevitable bias, Kohut insists upon the need to try not to look at others from the outside with preconceived theories of what the person "must really be feeling."

All theory limits what one can perceive, and this includes psychoanalytic theory. Since theory is unavoidably limiting—and often just plain wrong—and since every person is intensely different and individual, Kohut asks that the interpreter try to set aside assumptions about what goes on in the emotional life of others. Instead, the interpreter should attempt to feel in himself or herself, by a kind of vicarious introspection, what the other person feels. In a clinical setting this is an attempt on the analyst's part to put himself or herself into the patient's shoes, rather than to try to be an external observer of events taking place in an isolated entity out there in what is sometimes referred to as an intrapsychic apparatus.

Following the method Kohut articulates, we need to put ourselves in Posthumus's shoes if we wish to understand his dream. We need to attend to his vulnerability at this point in the play, and set aside the assumption that he must have derived benefit from his heroism in battle—or from his attempts at repentance. Similarly, we need to attend to what *he* finds significant, not just what we find significant or think that he finds or should find significant.

The dream validates Posthumus in ways which we as outsiders could barely conceive possible. It should come as a surprise that by dreaming he gives himself what he has never before been able to give himself. What he creates is not a family out there—as autonomous entities from whom he has more or less successfully differentiated himself. Nor, I think, is it so important that he recognizes them. What is crucial is that they recognize *him* and validate his sense of worth. As a dreamer Posthumus focuses upon his family's and his deity's nurturing relation to himself. We might expect other familiar figures such as Imogen to appear in his dream, but only his family and Jupiter do so. Members of the audience might very well have expected him to dream about his wife, for his last waking words were "O Imogen, / I'll speak to thee in silence" (5.4.28-29). That he does not dream about her is another sign that we are in the presence of a selfstate dream. Posthumus's dream seems to have little to do with such matters as instinctual conflict, guilt, resistance, or possible solutions of conflict. Indeed, his dream seems to ignore his relation to others as objects outside himself—say, to his estranged and murdered wife. The implication is that his sense of self is not cohesive enough to allow for this.

Posthumus dreams not of a murdered wife, nor of an Imogen who was (in wish fulfillment) saved from being murdered. Nor does he "resist" dreaming about her at the manifest level only to do so on the latent level—as psychoanalytic interpreters might suspect. He dreams instead about what most concerns him: not having lost Imogen but being in the presence of an admiring family and deity. He dreams of selfobjects who function as part of himself, literally, for he creates them out of whole cloth. He never has seen them (except, perhaps, for his brothers); thus he cannot technically recognize them in their existence outside his imagination. My point may at first seem pedantic; that it does might well remind us of the need to perceive the dream from his own perspective. We need to look at his dream from the inside, rather than from the point of view of our own preconceived ideas of what must be important. His family and Jupiter serve as selfobjects created by his own sense of need for them. They have no traits other than what he needs to find in them: absolute and convincing support.

Imogen cannot very well enter in his dream, for she would either be disturbing as a reminder of his all-but-disavowed guilt, or intrusive as a reminder of her own (apparent) guilt for adultery. Perhaps we can spot an allusion to her in the shape of his mother, who enters with his father as part of a united couple: enter Sicilius Leonatus "attired like a warrior, leading in his hand an ancient Matron (his wife, and mother to Posthumus)" (5.4.29 stage direction). Posthumus's dream thus seems to hint at his identifying with his father and wishing for his own wife. If we are right to discover Imogen in this wish fulfillment about a united couple, it is appropriate that she should appear in the guise of an all-supportive figure with no traits of her own—such as she would have as his murdered wife—but only as a selfobject to validate his sense of worth.

In his dream, Posthumus creates a deity whose role is similarly restricted. Jupiter comes across as little more than a supportive self-object, as a god who does not seem particularly godlike. For instance, Jupiter states: "No more, you petty spirits of region low / Offend our hearing: hush! How dare you ghosts / Accuse the thunderer" (5.4.93-95). Still, the "hush!"—although peculiar diction for a thunderer—precisely conveys the nourishing, parental tone Posthumus needs from all his dream figures. So, too, Jupiter's explanation sounds rather offhanded even for divine planning: "Whom best I love I cross; to make my gift / The more delay'd delighted" (5.4.101-02). Nevertheless, Jupiter speaks directly to Posthumus's need at this point: not a need for a plausible account of anything in particular but for paternal validation. Perhaps "avuncular" is a better term, for "paternal" has connotations of stern accountability. What Posthumus needs is not confrontation, or forgiveness, or even the sort of stunning theophany which Wilson Knight conjures up in his interpretation of the vision. What Posthumus needs and what he gives himself, in his dream, is comforting reassurance.

All of Posthumus's dream figures speak in ways which offer narcissistic enrichment. They exemplify confirmation of the self, for they demand it for themselves as well as extend it to him. When speaking about his son, Sicilius Leonatus emphasizes that both Posthumus and he are worthy: "Great nature, like his ancestry, moulded the stuff so fair, / That he deserved the praise o' the' world, as great Sicilius' heir" (5.4.48-51). Similarly, the ghosts take care when complaining that they do not undermine Jupiter's dignity; while they chasten him, they also bolster his self-esteem by addressing him as "Jupiter, thou king of gods" (5.4.77). They force him to validate Posthumus as the only way of saving face. In this dream, the dreamer allows no one, much less himself, to suffer a loss of self-esteem.

In such ways the dream serves a benign purpose. Nevertheless, it also reveals troublesome aspects of the dreamer's inner state. The healthy aspects are bound up with the unhealthy ones, as they would be in a real-life dream of someone in Posthumus's position. The dream partakes of that trait in Posthumus which I refer to as his grandiosity. Many dreams in reality and in fiction are full of magical thinking, but Posthumus's dream exceeds the usual: he imagines that ghosts arise from the dead to minister to his needs, and Jupiter descends with a divine plan for his special denefit. In conceiving of such narcissistic support, the dreamer perpetuates his archaic wish to discover validation from *outside* himself rather than from within himself through his own actions. In a word, he still conceives of himself in a merged state rather than as an autonomous individual who can and must fend for himself.

The dream implies that Posthumus's state of mind has changed for the better in that he can conjure up narcissistic supplies. Still, he remains both grandiose and needy; he remains in the state Kohut describes in terms of the "vertical split." For instance, Posthumus has no active role in the events of the dream. He conceives of others who nurture him, but aside from this he does nothing to fulfill his needs. He performs no deeds. His family, not Posthumus, calls upon Jupiter to save him. Since he uses his family as selfobjects he thereby indirectly puts himself into the dream; the figures he imagines in dreaming the dream function, to a great degree, as aspects of himself. Still, it is striking that he should be so absent in his own right from the dream. Perhaps we never think of this while watching the play since he lies before us while the dream goes on around him. Still, in his use of self-objects Posthumus creates others who do for him what he might be expected to do in his own right were he not so dependent upon them—upon others whom he can experience only as extensions of himself.

The Extent of Posthumus's Change

Kohut's premises are worth invoking at this point in the discussion of the dream. One is to try to put one-self in the dreamer's shoes rather than look at the dream "objectively." Another, to try to find signs of a healthy sector rather than dwell solely upon pathological aspects. As in so much of Kohut's work, these aims may seem obvious and easy to attain. They are not. A psychiatrist who was in training with Kohut, and thus armed with the best intentions, attests to the difficulty of following these simple maxims; he soon reverted to the habit of looking at a patient's dreams from his own perspective—not the dreamer's—and confronted the dreamer with signs of pathology rather than discover healthy aspects peering out from under them.[7]

By searching for signs of the healthy aspect, the interpreter discovers—and thereby confirms—a vital and often disavowed aspect of the dreamer's inner reality. The healthy part is one which has been submerged by pathological parts. The latter are precisely those most accessible to the observer and thus most often, unhelpfully, emphasized by the observer—and by the person himself or herself. The germ of a true but undeveloped self lies arrested in development and hidden within the predominant and more obvious false self.

Posthumus's dream owes much of its poignancy to the glimpse of the healthy sector in him which it allows. The ghosts and Jupiter continually attest to his worth, but other factors even more forcefully indicate a healthy sector hidden within his despairing and self-defeating nature. First, he can *conceive* of such validation at a low point in his career. And second, he can *experience* this benign nurturance as his own and use it, rather than disavow it as he does virtually all his waking experiences.[8]

Dreamers conceive of and make their own dreams. This vital principle can easily be lost even to the most ardent dream interpreters unless we keep reminding ourselves about dreaming's intensely subjective nature. The healthy sector of Posthumus's dream appears, first, in his advance from a position of neediness. When awake he seems unable to get what he wants, but in dreaming he creates it from within himself: he obtains self-confirmation by creating an idealized family and deity. He says immediately upon awakening:

Sleep, thou hast been a grandsire, and begot
A father to me: and thou hast created
A mother, and two brothers; O scorn!
Gone! they went hence so soon as they were
  born:
And so I am awake.

(5.4.123-25)

Characteristically, Posthumus assigns the process of creation to "Sleep" rather than to his own generative and creative capacities. Nevertheless, even Posthumus's deference to grandsire Sleep can be thought of as part of his persistent effort to create for himself a family whose every move is attuned to his needs.

The second principal indication of a healthy sector lies in his being able to experience and use his dream, instead of treating it as though it happened to someone else or as though it were worthy of contempt. Unlike his disengagement from his heroic deed against the Romans, his response to his dream is to own it: he acknowledges and incorporates what the dream gave him into his sense of himself. He owns his need for what his grandsire sleep begot for him, however temporary and however strange. Then he turns to the book with the riddle, and attests to its value even though he cannot be sure what it is:

> 'Tis still a dream: or else such stuff as
>   madmen
> Tongue, and brain not: either both, or nothing,
> Or senseless speaking, or a speaking such
> As sense cannot untie. Be what it is,
> The action of my life is like it, which
> I'll keep, if but for sympathy.
>
> (5.4.146-51)

He identifies the riddle with the dream, and with life, as a tangible reminder. And he vows to keep the riddle, the dream, and his life. He cherishes them as significant parts of his experience, rather than disavowing them as irrelevant or insufficient—as would be so easy for him and so typical of him. Posthumus attaches explicit positive value to his dream and links it to his life whatever it may mean: "Be what it is, / The action of my life is like it."[9]

That Posthumus values the dream and riddle as his own signals a benevolent change of mind. Upon awakening from a dream in which others cherish him and his worth, he himself now begins to have a sense of self-esteem. That he should do so strikes me as the first sign of a more viable Posthumus than the one we have seen earlier.

Before the dream occurs, Posthumus is presented as a character who does not seem to have a sense of living his own experiences. He rarely conceives of himself as an autonomous agent in any of his roles: heroic soldier, trusting spouse, repentant murderer. In terms of self psychology, his disavowal suggests an inability to identify with his own experiencing self. He gives the impression that someone else lives his life, as in a way is quite true: one part of him is grandiose and lives in a fantasy world imperfectly attuned to reality. The other part of him—the part who lives in outside reality—seems unable to feel, or experience, or gain much from that life.

Because of the two split-off parts of himself, grandiose or empty, Posthumus appears incapable of giving himself anything or doing anything for himself. He cannot even experience anything as his own. The grandiose self is merged with an archaic other, as for example it is when he tests Imogen. Or the empty self gets nothing it wants since it has surrendered volition to the grandiose self. We have seen this surrender in his scene with the Lord: Posthumus disavows his truly heroic deeds in the battle against the Romans, and instead contrives fantasies of freeing himself from his guilty conscience by suicide.

In dreaming, however, Posthumus gives the impression of having established contact with his split-off empty self; he seems to have connected himself to the kernel of his otherwise disavowed true self. When he creates validating figures he indicates that he can draw upon narcissistic supplies from *within* himself. I stress the significance of this accomplishment as coming from within the dreamer. We in the audience see the dramatization of a dream, which means that we see a stage on which the family and Jupiter may seem to exist outside Posthumus. Still, insofar as the stage dream is the dramatization or the outward realization of an inner psychological event, the dream figures are not external but internal. The character Posthumus—not Shakespeare—peoples his dream with validating figures at a moment when he is empty, depressed, and suicidal, and in doing so gives himself what he needs.

In conclusion, I think that Posthumus reveals contradictory aspects of himself in *Cymbeline:* a self-defeating and near-tragic aspect tinged with grandiosity and neediness, and an aspect which suggests that a healthy kernel of self-esteem can quicken to life when he reunites with Imogen. He begins to seem capable of integrating into his sense of himself aspects to which his family and Jupiter attest: that he is of central importance, that he is brave, noble, and lovable.

The dream serves not so much as a sign of a changed state of mind as the harbinger of such a change. From now to the end of *Cymbeline* when he becomes reconciled to the King and to Imogen, Posthumus tentatively begins to validate his own worth rather than simply conceive of it as being affirmed—or, invalidated—by figures outside himself. Like the regeneration of other protagonists of Shakespeare's romances—Pericles, Leontes, and Prospero—Posthumus's regeneration is more tentative and thus, I think, more poignant than critics have for a long time allowed.

Notes

[1] Posthumus himself comments upon what he has witnessed as a dream: "Poor wretches, that depend / On greatness' favour, dream as I have done, / Wake, and find nothing. But, alas, I swerve: / Many dream not to find, neither deserve, / And yet are steep'd in favours; so am I, / That have this golden chance [the book he

finds on his breast when awaking]"; he concludes that "'Tis still a dream: or else such stuff as madmen / Tongue, and brain not" (5.4.127-31, 147-48). Throughout I quote from the New Arden edition of *Cymbeline,* edited by J. M. Nosworthy (1955; reprint London: Methuen, 1979). Nor does Posthumus see what has transpired as a vision brought about by Jupiter; he fails to mention the spectacular appearance of the deity and refers instead to the agency of sleep: "Sleep, thou hast been a grandsire, and begot / A father to me: and . . . / A mother, and two brothers" (5.4.123-25).

G. Wilson Knight demonstrates the Shakespearean nature of the episode despite the doubts of those who find it irrelevant and thus suspect (Knight [1947] 1966. However, Knight treats the dream as a vision or theophany—despite Posthumus's remarks just quoted. J. M. Nosworthy follows Knight in seeing the episode as a vision. Nosworthy states that "in making him [Jupiter] literally the *deus ex machina* Shakespeare flies in the face of Aristotelian doctrine, but necessity is above precept" since one cannot suppose that the rapid change of fortune at the end is brought about by human agency. I argue that the psychological implications of the dream convey a sense of human agency at work here. (Nosworthy [1955] 1979, xxxiii-xxxvii)

² "Interpreting Posthumus' Dream from Above and Below: Families, Psychoanalysts, and Literary Critics" (Schwartz and Kahn, 1980, 203-16). Her account for the most part follows Freudian precepts. Also see Arthur Kirsch, *Shakespeare and the Experience of Love* (Cambridge: Cambridge University Press, 1981); he interprets the dream in explicitly Freudian ways and concludes that "the recovery of a childhood literally lost . . . enables him [Posthumus] to reintegrate himself as a man and reunite with Imogen" (p. 167).

³ Can a character be said to posses a state of mind? Many people readily assume that Posthumus does, so lifelike is his representation and so pressing is our need to imagine that characters reflect ourselves. This psychological need is especially pressing when a play is staged and an actor bodies forth the representation. I also raise for a moment the question of whether viewers—or characters—can be thought to possess a unified self of the sort which colors such assumptions. My interpretation of Posthumus and of his dream discovers a divided nature in terms of Kohut's "vertical split," but I still postulate that such unity is inherent in the unfolding of the self when not arrested in its development.

For a long time critics have assumed that the romance genre (in which most place *Cymbeline*) is the polar opposite of "realism" (psychological or otherwise). Posthumus's dream is not the locus of the unreal or of the surreal, for it seems clearly to reveal human agency.

⁴ On this see Heinz Kohut. Kohut argues that because of the excess of anger beyond what the situation would seem to provoke, "such bedevilment indicates that the aggression was mobilized in the service of an archaic grandiose self and that it is deployed within the framework of an archaic perception of reality" (Kohut 1978, 643).

I think that Posthumus's behavior here is of a piece with his behavior elsewhere. He does not simply "disown" his pride in his heroic behavior as some Renaissance heroes do. Modesty or Christian self-abnegation differ from Posthumus's anger. Instead of being modest or self-abnegating, Posthumus draws extraordinary attention to himself, his presumed failures, and those of others.

⁵ For a more extended account of this technique, see James L. Fosshage, "Dream Interpretation Revisited," *Frontiers in Self Psychology,* ed. Arnold Goldberg, Vol. 3 of *Progress in Self Psychology* (Hillsdale, N. J.: Atlantic Press, 1988), 161-75.

⁶ For a lucid account of this controversial view, see Paul H. Ornstein and Anna Ornstein, "Clinical Understanding and Explaining: The Empathic Vantage Point," *Progress in Self Psychology,* ed. Arnold Goldberg (New York: Guilford Press, 1985), Vol. 1, 43-61.

⁷ See Jule P. Miller, "How Kohut Actually Worked," *Progress in Self Psychology,* Vol. 1, 22-29.

⁸ Fosshage argues that "dreaming mentation not only serves to maintain organization, but contributes to the development of new organizations, a crucially important dream function that has remained unrecognized with the classical model" (Fosshage 1988, 164).

⁹ Director Elijah Moshinsky chose this speech as the core quotation of the play for a production that is especially attuned to the play's psychological implications. Moshinsky emphasizes the centrality of this passage: "'This is a most astonishing line . . . Shakespeare is saying the confusion of the play is like life: it's bizarre and emotionally penetrating and psychologically intense. And very lifelike.'" See Henry Fenwick 1983, p. 26.

References

Fenwick, Henry. "The Production." In the BBC Television Edition of *Cymbeline.* New York: Mayflower Books, 1983.

Fosshage, James L. "Dream Interpretation Revisited." In *Frontiers in Self Psychology,* edited by Arnold Goldberg. Vol. 3, *Progress in Self Psychology.* Hillsdale, N.J.: Atlantic Press, 1988.

Kirsch, Arthur. *Shakespeare and the Experience of Love.* Cambridge: Cambridge University Press, 1981.

Knight, G. Wilson. "The Vision of Jupiter." In *The Crown of Life.* 1947. Reprint. New York: Barnes and Noble, 1966.

Kohut, Heinz. "Thoughts on Narcissism and Narcissistic Rage." In *The Search for the Self: Selected Writings of Heinz Kohut: 1950-1978,* edited by Paul H. Ornstein. Vol. 2. New York: International Universities Press, 1978.

————. *The Restoration of the Self.* Madison, Conn.: International Universities Press, 1977.

Nosworthy, J. M. Introduction to *Cymbeline,* by William Shakespeare. 1955. Reprint. London: Methuen, 1979.

Ornstein, Paul H. and Anna Ornstein. "Clinical Understanding and Explaining: The Empathic Vantage Point." In *Progress in Self Psychology,* edited by Arnold Goldberg. Vol. 1. New York: Guilford Press, 1985.

Skura, Meredith. "Interpreting Posthumus's Dream from Above and Below: Families, Psychoanalysts and Literary Critics." In *Representing Shakespeare: New Psychoanalytic Essays,* edited by Murray M. Schwartz and Coppélia Kahn. Baltimore: Johns Hopkins University Press, 1980.

FURTHER READING

Arthos, John. *Shakespeare's Use of Dream and Vision.* Totowa, N. J.: Rowman and Littlefield, 1977, 208 p.

    Extensive study of dreams and apparitions in Shakespeare's dramas and poetry.

Cook, Eleanor. "'Methought' as Dream Formula in Shakespeare, Milton, Wordsworth, Keats and Others." *English Language Notes* XXXII, No. 4 (June 1995): 34-46.

    Examines Shakespeare's influential use of the word "methought" as a prelude to the recitation of a dream.

Garber, Marjorie B. "Dream and Plot: *Richard III.*" In *Dream in Shakespeare: From Metaphor to Metamorphosis,* pp. 15-26. New Haven: Yale University Press, 1974.

    Comments on Richard's prophetic dream in *Richard III.*

James, L. L. "The Dramatic Effects of the Play-Within-a-Play in Shakespeare's *Hamlet* and Marlowe's *Dr. Faustus.*" *Litteraria* 5, No. 9 (1995): 17-31.

    Explores Hamlet's metaphysical statement, "I could be bounded in a nutshell and count myself a king of infinite space—were it not that I have bad dreams" as indicative of a crisis of knowledge analogous to that of the title character of Christopher Marlowe's *Faustus.*

Presson, Robert K. "Two Types of Dreams in the Elizabethan Drama, and their Heritage: Somnium Animale and the Prick-of-Conscience." *Studies in English Literature 1500-1900* VII, No. 2 (Spring 1967): 239-56.

    Recounts the presentation of dreams resulting from "discomforts of the body" or from suppressed anxieties in the works of Shakespeare and others.

Skura, Meredith. "Interpreting Posthumus' Dream from Above and Below: Families, Psychoanalysts, and Literary Critics." In *Representing Shakespeare: New Psychoanalytic Essays*, edited by Murray M. Schwartz and Coppélia Kahn, pp. 203-16. Baltimore, Md.: The Johns Hopkins University Press, 1980.

    Investigates the psychological importance of family in Shakespeare's *Cymbeline,* emphasizing the climactic revelation of this theme in Posthumus's dream.

Smith, Warren D. "Romeo's Final Dream." *Modern Language Review* 62, No. 4 (October 1967): 579-83.

    Interprets Romeo's final dream in *Romeo and Juliet*—in which Juliet finds Romeo dead then kisses and revives him—as symbolically true.

Stockholder, Kay. "'So Many Fathoms Deep': Love and Death in *Hamlet.* In *Dream Works: Lovers and Families in Shakespeare's Plays*, pp. 40-64. Toronto: University of Toronto Press, 1987.

    Discusses how Hamlet commingles his dreams of sex and death and turns them into realities.

A Midsummer Night's Dream

For further information on the critical and stage history of *A Midsummer Night's Dream*, see *SC*, Volumes 3, 12, and 29.

INTRODUCTION

The role of dreams in *A Midsummer Night's Dream* is of primary interest to critics who wish to uncover the relationships between dreams and the reality of the play's world, as well as between dreams and the reality of Shakespeare's world. Not surprisingly, some critics approach the play from a psychological perspective in order to dissect such connections. Jan Lawson Hinley (1987) examines the role of dreams in the play from such a standpoint and asserts that Shakespeare uses dreams as a way to illuminate the psychological foundation of the sexual anxieties of the four lovers. For example, Hinley maintains that Hermia's dream of the snake attacking her while Lysander stands by, watching, demonstrates Hermia's fears of male sexuality and betrayal and also reflects her anxiety regarding the social pressures in Athens. Similarly, Hinley goes on, the "triple dream of Bottom, Titania, and Oberon" reinforces the sense of tension that appears to be inherent in creating and maintaining a sexual and romantic love relationship. Hinley concludes that the struggle of the lovers to secure a balance between their sexual desires and the requirements of society is brought to an end when stable relationships are established and condoned within a "benevolent patriarchal society." Peter Holland (1994), like Hinley, advances a psychological approach to dreams in the play. Holland begins by stating his belief that dreams in the play are better understood from a Jungian viewpoint, in that the play, as a dream, reveals more than it conceals. Holland states that Oberon and Puck create a situation in which the characters in the play, as well as the audience, are able to see the play as a "true dream experience," not simply something *like* a dream. In exploring the historical context of this transformative power of the dream, Holland explains how Shakespeare's audiences may have regarded dreams as a source of "true understanding." In conclusion, Holland observes that Oberon relates dreams to visions, that Puck advises the audience that it has seen visions, and that Bottom views his experience as a vision. Holland stresses that if as audience members "we have responded to the play fully" then we will share Bottom's assessment, and should therefore regard the play not as trivial but as the "revelation of another reality." Just as Holland observes the significance of visions, Marjorie B. Garber (1974) notes that in the play, visions are contrasted with dreams, and are regarded as correctly interpreted and valued dreams. Garber maintains that the view of dreams presented in *A Midsummer Night's Dream* is a "redemptive" one which "arises in part from a new emphasis upon transformation as a creative act." Furthermore, Garber contends that the dream state, as a transforming and creative process, orders the events of the play. The contrast between sleep and wakefulness, between reality and illusion, between reason and imagination, and between the realms of Theseus and Oberon, are all "structurally related to portrayal of the dream state," Garber explains. Similarly, Garber notices other structural analogs, including the relationship between metaphor and the dream state. Garber closes her essay by emphasizing that in this play, dreams have the power to reveal insight and truth, and to "interpret and transform" reality.

OVERVIEWS

Louis Montrose (essay date 1996)

SOURCE: "Stories of the Night," in *The Purpose of Playing: Shakespeare and the Cultural Politics of the Elizabethan Theatre,* The University of Chicago Press, 1996, pp. 124-50.

[*In the following essay, Montrose examines the mythological subtext of* A Midsummer Night's Dream, *claiming that Hippolyta's presence at the play's opening invokes Amazonian mythology, which Montrose describes as the "embodiment of a collective, masculine anxiety about women's power to dominate, create, and destroy men."*]

The opposed domestic emphases of Brooks and Olson—the former, romantic and companionate; the latter, authoritarian and hierarchical—abstract and oversimplify what may be construed as potentially complementary or contradictory elements in the dramatic process whereby *A Midsummer Night's Dream* figures the social relationship between the sexes in courtship, marriage, and parenthood. Among the cultural materials employed in the construction of the gender system that is figured in *A Midsummer Night's Dream,* those of classical myth are perhaps the most conspicuous. The play dramatizes or alludes to numerous episodes of classical mythology that were already coded by a venerable tradition of moral allegorization, and its treatment of such mythographic traditions is, like the traditions themselves, far from unequivocal. In this chapter, I want to focus upon the mythological subtext of *A Midsummer Night's Dream* and upon its articulation with the gendered discourses of human physiology and domestic economy.

I

The beginning of *A Midsummer Night's Dream* coincides with the end of a struggle in which Theseus has been victorious over the Amazon warrior:

Hippolyta, I woo'd thee with my sword,
And won thy love doing thee injuries;
But I will wed thee in another key,
With pomp, with triumph, and with revelling.
(1.1.16-19)

Descriptions of the Amazons or allusions to them are ubiquitous across the range of Elizabethan writing and performance genres. For example, all of the essentials are present in popular form in William Painter's "Novel of the Amazones," which opens the second book of *The Palace of Pleasure* (1575). Here we read that the Amazons "were most excellent warriors"; that "they murdred certaine of their husbands" at the beginning of their gynecocracy; and that,

if they brought forth daughters, they norished and trayned them up in armes, and other manlik exercises.
. . . If they were delivered of males, they sent them to their fathers, and if by chaunce they kept any backe, they murdred them, or else brake their armes and legs in sutch wise as they had no power to beare weapons, and served for nothynge but to spin, twist, and doe other feminine labour.[19]

Amazonian mythology seems symbolically to embody and to control a collective (masculine) anxiety about women's power not only to dominate or to repudiate men but also to create and destroy them. It is an ironic acknowledgment by an androcentric culture of the degree to which men are in fact dependent upon women: upon mothers and nurses, for their own birth and nurture; upon chaste mistresses and wives, both for the validation of their manhood and for the birth and legitimacy of their offspring.

Shakespeare engages his wedding play in a dialectic with this mythological formation. The Amazons have been defeated shortly before the play begins, and nuptial rites are to be celebrated when it ends. *A Midsummer Night's Dream* focuses upon different crucial transitions in the masculine and feminine life cycles of early modern English society: The fairy plot focuses upon taking "a little changeling boy" from the

relatively androgynous or feminized state of infancy into the more decisively gendered state of youth, from the world of mothers and nurses into the world of fathers and masters. In *The Book named The Governor,* Sir Thomas Elyot advised, "after that a [boy] child is come to seven years of age, I hold it expedient that he be taken from the company of women" and assigned "a tutor, which should be an ancient and worshipful man." As Stephen Orgel has recently pointed out, *à propos* of *The Winter's Tale,*

Elizabethan children of both sexes were dressed in skirts until the age of seven or so; the 'breeching' of boys was the formal move out of the common gender of childhood, which was both female in appearance and largely controlled by women, and into the world of men. This event was traditionally the occasion for a significant family ceremony.[20]

Shakespeare's Athenian plot focuses upon conducting a young gentlewoman from the state of maidenhood to the state of matrimony, upon conveying her from her father's house to her husband's. This, too, of course, was a transition marked by significant ritual and ceremonial events—namely, betrothal, wedding, and the bedding of the bride. The pairing of the four Athenian lovers is made possible by the magical powers of Oberon and made lawful by the political authority of Theseus. Each of these rulers is preoccupied with the fulfillment of his own desires in the possession or repossession of a wife. It is only *after* Hippolyta has been mastered by Theseus that marriage may seal them "in everlasting bond of fellowship" (1.1.85). And it is only *after* "proud Titania" has been degraded by "jealous Oberon" (2.1.60, 61), has "in mild terms begg'd" (4.1.57) his patience, and has readily yielded the changeling boy to him, that they may be "new in amity" (4.1.86).

The unfolding action of *A Midsummer Night's Dream*—its diachronic structure—eventually restores the inverted Amazonian system of gender and nurture to a patriarchal norm. But the initial plans for Theseus's triumph are immediately interrupted by news of yet another unruly female. Egeus wishes to confront his daughter Hermia with two alternatives: absolute obedience to the paternal will, or death. Theseus intervenes with a third alternative: If she refuses to marry whom her father chooses, Hermia must submit,

Either to die the death or to abjure
Forever the society of men.

. . . . .

For aye to be in shady cloister mew'd,
Chanting faint hymns to the cold, fruitless
moon.
Thrice blessed they that master so their blood

To undergo such maiden pilgrimage;
But earthlier happy is the rose distill'd
Than that which, withering on the virgin thorn,
Grows, lives, and dies, in single blessedness.
                                    (1.1.65-66, 71-78)

Theseus's rhetoric concisely stages a Reformation debate on the relative virtues of virginity and marriage. He concedes praise to the former, as being exemplary of self-mastery, but nevertheless concludes that the latter more fully satisfies the imperatives of earthly existence. He implies that maidenhood is a phase in the life-cycle of a woman who is destined for married chastity and motherhood; that, when it persists as a permanent state, "single blessedness" is reduced to mere sterility.

Theseus expands Hermia's options, but only in order to clarify her constraints. In the process of tempering the father's domestic tyranny, the Duke affirms his own interests and authority. He represents the life of a vestal as a punishment, and it is one that fits the nature of Hermia's crime. The maiden is surrounded by her father, her lovers, and her lord; and each of these men claims a kind of property in her—in her body, her fantasy, her will. Yet Hermia dares to suggest that she has a claim to property in herself: She refuses to "yield [her] virgin patent up / Unto his lordship whose unwished yoke / [Her] soul consents not to give sovereignty" (1.1.80-82). Like Portia or Rosalind, Hermia wishes the limited privilege of giving herself. Theseus appropriates the sources of Hermia's fragile power, her ability to master her blood and to deny men access to her body. He usurps the power of virginity by imposing upon Hermia his own power to deny her the use of her body. If she will not submit to its use by her father and by Demetrius, she must "abjure forever the society of men," and "live a barren sister all [her] life" (1.1.65-66, 72). Her own words suggest that the female body is a supreme form of property; a locus for the contestation of authority; the site of a struggle between man and woman, and between man and man. Although displaced into the thoroughly anachronistic setting of Theseus's Athenian court, Hermia's predicament activates the vexed and contested status of Elizabethan women as conscious and willing subjects and as objects of patriarchal sovereignty. The self-possession of single blessedness is a form of resistance against which are opposed the dominant domestic values of Shakespeare's culture and the very form of his comedy.[21]

The conflict between Egeus and Hermia and its mediation by Theseus constitute a paradigm case for Northrop Frye's influential theory of Shakespearean comic form. According to Frye, a Shakespearean comedy

> normally begins with an anticomic society, a social organization blocking and opposed to the comic drive, which the action of the comedy evades or overcomes. It often takes the form of a harsh or

irrational law, like . . . the law disposing of rebellious daughters in *A Midsummer Night's Dream*. . . . Most of these irrational laws are preoccupied with trying to regulate the sexual drive, and so work counter to the wishes of the hero and heroine, which form the main impetus of the comic action.

> (*A Natural Perspective,* 73-74)

Frye's account of Shakespearean comic action emphasizes intergenerational tension at the expense of those other forms of social and familial tension from which it is only artificially separable. The interaction of personae in the fictive societies of Shakespearean drama, like the interaction of persons in the society of Shakespeare's England, is structured by a complex interplay among culture-specific categories, not only of age and gender but also of kinship and social rank. The ideologically unstable Elizabethan gender system articulated in Shakespeare's plays is structured both in terms of *difference*—as opposition, and as complementariness; and in terms of *hierarchy*—as superiority/inferiority, and as domination/subordination.

In Shakespearean comedy, as in Shakespearean drama generally, (gentle)women are represented variously as volitional and reasonable agents, as objects of masculine desire or anxiety, and as victims of masculine aggression or slander. Frye unequivocally identifies the heroines' interests with those of the heroes. Nevertheless, the "drive toward a festive conclusion" (*Natural Perspective,* 75) that liberates and unites comic heroes and comic heroines also binds together generations of men through the giving of daughters, confers the responsibilities and privileges of manhood upon callow youths, and subordinates wives to the authority of their husbands. Women's wit may be acknowledged and accommodated in the new domestic economy that has been prepared for, or established by, the end of the comic action; however, the plays' imagined societies show little if any sign of genuine structural transformation. According to Frye, "the main impetus" of Shakespearean comic action is the defeat of attempts "to regulate the sexual drive." (Unlike more recent studies of the poetics of desire in Shakespearean drama, *A Natural Perspective* conceives of the Shakespearean erotic as exclusively heterosexual and as gender-neutral.) I would suggest a pattern different from and more equivocal than that proposed by Frye: In *A Midsummer Night's Dream,* as in other Shakespearean comedies, the *main* impetus is to regulate the concupiscible passions through the social institution of marriage, thus fabricating an accommodation between law and desire, between reason and appetite; however, a subliminal or oblique counter-impetus, of varying strength, frames these acts of regulation and accommodation as tentative, partial, or flawed.

In devising Hermia's punishment, Theseus appropriates and parodies the very condition that the Amazons sought to enjoy. They rejected marriages with men and alliances with patriarchal societies because, as one sixteenth-century writer put it, they esteemed "that Matrimonie was not a meane of libertie but of thraldome."[22] The separatism of the Amazons is a repudiation of men's claims to have property in women. But if Amazonian myth figures the inversionary claims of matriarchy, sorority, and female autonomy, it also figures the repudiation of those claims in the recuperative act of Amazonomachy. At the opening of *The Two Noble Kinsmen,* in a scene generally ascribed to Shakespeare, one of the suppliant queens addresses the about-to-be-wedded Hippolyta as

> Most dreaded Amazonian, that hast slain
> The scythe-tusk'd boar; that with thy arm, as
> strong
> As it is white, wast near to make the male
> To thy sex captive, but that this thy lord,
> Born to uphold creation in that honor
> First Nature styl'd it in, shrunk thee into
> The bound thou was't o'erflowing, at once
> subduing
> Thy force and thy affection.

> (*TNK,* 1.1.78-85)

The passage registers Hippolyta's imposing combination of physical beauty and physical strength as something wonderful but also as something unnatural and dangerous, and requiring masculine control. The judgment that the Amazon is monstrous and that Theseus is a champion of the natural order is given (ironically) greater credence when it is pronounced by a queen. Here, as at the beginning of *A Midsummer Night's Dream,* what seems to interest Shakespeare (and, perhaps, Fletcher) about Theseus's participation in the Amazonomachy is that it leads to his marriage with his captive. In the story of Theseus and Hippolyta, Amazonomachy and marriage coincide, reaffirming the Amazons' reputed estimation "that Matrimonie was not a meane of libertie but of thraldome."

Elsewhere in *A Midsummer Night's Dream,* Shakespeare displaces the myth of Amazonomachy into the vicissitudes of courtship. Heterosexual desire disrupts the innocent pleasures of Hermia's girlhood: "What graces in my love do dwell, / That he hath turn'd a heaven unto a hell!" (1.1.206-07). Hermia's farewell to Helena is also a farewell to their girlhood friendship, a delicate repudiation of youthful homophilia:

> And in the wood, where often you and I
> Upon faint primrose beds were wont to lie,
> Emptying our bosoms of their counsel
> sweet,
> There my Lysander and myself shall meet;
> And thence from Athens turn away our eyes,
> To seek new friends, and stranger companies.

> (1.1.214-19)

Helena is sworn to secrecy by the lovers; nevertheless, before this scene ends, in order to further her own desire, she has determined to betray her sweet bedfellow's secret to Demetrius. Before dawn comes at last to the forest, the "counsel" shared by Hermia and Helena, their "sisters' vows . . . school-days' friendship, childhood innocence" (3.2.198, 199, 202), have all been torn asunder, to be replaced at the end of the play by the primary demands and loyalties of wedlock.

On the other hand, the hostilities between the two male youths have, before dawn, dissolved into "gentle concord" (4.1.142). From the beginning of the play, the relationship between Lysander and Demetrius has been based upon aggressive rivalry for the same object of desire—first for Hermia, and then for Helena. Each youth must despise his current mistress in order to adore her successor; and a change in the affections of one provokes a change in the affections of the other. R. W. Dent has pointed out that the young women do not fluctuate in their desires for their young men, and that the ending ratifies their constant if inexplicable preferences.[23] It should be added, however, that the maidens remain constant to the objects of their desire at the cost of inconstancy to each other. On the other hand, Lysander and Demetrius are flagrantly inconstant to Hermia and Helena but the pattern of their romantic inconstancies stabilizes a relationship of rivalry between them. The romantic resolution engineered by Oberon and approved by Theseus transforms the nature of their mutual constancy from rivalry to friendship by contriving that each male will accept "his own" female. In Puck's jaunty and crude formulation:

> And the country proverb known,
> That every man should take his own,
> In your waking shall be shown:
>   Jack shall have Jill,
>   Nought shall go ill:
> The man shall have his mare again, and all
> shall be well.

> (3.2.458-63)

In *A Midsummer Night's Dream,* as in *As You Like It,* the dramatic process that forges the marital couplings simultaneously weakens the bonds of sisterhood and strengthens the bonds of brotherhood.[24]

II

In the play's opening scene, Egeus claims that he may do with Hermia as he chooses because she is his property: "As she is mine, I may dispose of her" (1.1.42). This claim is based upon a stunningly simple thesis: She is his because he has made her. Charging that Lysander has "stol'n the impression" (1.1.32) of Hermia's fantasy, Egeus effectively absolves his daughter from responsibility for her affections because he cannot acknowledge her capacity for volition. If she does not—cannot—obey him, then she should be destroyed. Borrowing Egeus' own imprinting metaphor, Theseus explains to Hermia the ontogenetic principle underlying her father's vehemence:

> To you your father should be as a god:
> One that compos'd your beauties, yea, and one
> To whom you are but as a form in wax
> By him imprinted, and within his power
> To leave the figure or disfigure it.
>
> (1.1.47-51)

Theseus represents paternity as a cultural act, an art: The father is a demiurge or *Homo faber* who composes, in-forms, imprints himself upon, what is merely inchoate matter. Conspicuously excluded from Shakespeare's play is the relationship between mother and daughter—the kinship bond through which Amazonian society reproduces itself.[25] The mother's part is wholly excluded from this account of the making of a daughter. Hermia and Helena have no mothers; they have only fathers.[26] The central women characters of Shakespeare's comedies are not mothers but mothers-to-be, maidens who are passing from fathers to husbands in a world made and governed by men. Here, the proprietary claims of patriarchy are taken to their logical extreme, and the female subject is wholly denied the capacity to have property in herself.[27]

In effect, Theseus's lecture on the shaping of a daughter is a fantasy of male parthenogenesis. Titania's votaress is the only biological mother in *A Midsummer Night's Dream*. But she is an absent presence who must be evoked from Titania's memory because she has died in giving birth to a son. Assuming that they do not maim or kill their sons, the Amazons are only too glad to give them away to their fathers. In Shakespeare's play, however, Oberon's paternal dominance must be directed against Titania's maternal possessiveness:

> For Oberon is passing fell and wrath,
> Because that she as her attendant hath
> A lovely boy, stol'n from an Indian king—
> She never had so sweet a changeling;
> And jealous Oberon would have the child
> Knight of his train to trace the forest wild;
> But she perforce withholds the loved boy,
> Crowns him with flowers, and makes him all
>   her joy.
>
> (2.1.20-27)

In his *De Pueris,* Erasmus approves of the mothers of infants, who "swaddle their children and bandage their heads, and keep a watchful eye on their eating and drinking, bathing and exercising"; however, he excoriates those who would prolong infancy into later childhood: "What kind of maternal feeling is it that induces some women to keep their children clinging to their skirts until they are six years old and to treat them as imbeciles?"[28] A boy's transition from the woman-centered world of his early childhood to the man-centered world of his youth is given a kind of phylogenetic sanction by myths recounting a cultural transition from matriarchy to patriarchy.[29] Such a mythic charter is represented at the very threshhold of *A Midsummer Night's Dream:* Oberon attempts to take the boy from what Puck suggests is an indulgent and infantilizing mother, and this attempt is sanctioned by Theseus's defeat of the Amazons, a matriarchate that maims and effeminizes its male offspring. Oberon will make a man of the boy by subjecting him to service as his "henchman" and "Knight of his train," thus exposing him to the challenges of "the forest wild." Yet, "jealous" Oberon is not only Titania's rival for the child but also the child's rival for Titania: Making the boy "all her joy," "proud" Titania withholds herself from her husband; she has "forsworn his bed and company" (2.1.62-63). Oberon's preoccupation is to gain possession not only of the boy but also of the woman's desire and obedience; he must master his own dependency upon his wife.[30]

In his pioneering essay on "the double standard" in regard to sexual conduct, Keith Thomas notes that the importance of legitimate heirs to Englishmen of the property-owning classes has frequently been cited to explain and justify the emphasis on wifely chastity. However, he concludes that the property issues involved include not only "the property of legitimate heirs, but the property of men in women." Virginity before and chastity during marriage have been regarded as of paramount importance in women because "the absolute property of the woman's chastity was vested not in the woman herself but in her parents or her husband."[31] This perspective on the persistence of "the double standard" in English law and custom helps to focus more sharply the gendered thematics of power and possession that characterize both of the conflict-generating plots in *A Midsummer Night's Dream,* those contesting the statuses of Hermia and the changeling. Thus, the conflict between the King and Queen of Faeries, like those between Egeus and Hermia and between Theseus and Hippolyta, revolves around issues of authority and autonomy, around claims to have property in others and in oneself, as these claims are generated in relations between husbands and wives, parents and children.

Titania has her own explanation for her fixation upon the changeling:

> His mother was a votress of my order
> And in the spiced Indian air, by night,
> Full often hath she gossip'd by my side;
> And sat with me on Neptune's yellow sands,
> Marking th'embarked traders on the flood:
> When we have laugh'd to see the sails
>   conceive
> And grow big-bellied with the wanton wind,

Which she, with pretty and with swimming
  gait
Following (her womb then rich with my young
  squire),
Would imitate, and sail upon the land
To fetch me trifles, and return again
As from a voyage rich with merchandise.
But she, being mortal, of that boy did die,
And for her sake do I rear up her boy;
And for her sake I will not part with him.

(2.1.123-37)

Titania's attachment to the changeling boy embodies her attachment to the memory of his mother. As is later the case with Bottom, Titania both dotes upon and dominates the child; her bond to the child's mother attenuates his imprisonment to the womb: "And for her sake I will not part with him." What Oberon accomplishes by substituting Bottom for the boy is to break Titania's solemn vow. As in the case of the Amazons, or of Hermia and Helena, here again the play enacts a masculine disruption of an intimate bond between women—first by the boy, and then by the man. It is as if, in order to be freed and enfranchised from the prison of the womb, the male child must kill his mother: "She, being mortal, of that boy did die." Titania's words suggest that mother and son are potentially mortal to each other. Thus, embedded within the changeling plot are transformations of the collective masculine fantasies of powerful and dangerous motherhood that are figured in Amazonian myth. The matricidal male infant has a reciprocal relationship to the infanticidal Amazon. Elizabethan family life was characterized by a high incidence of spontaneous and induced abortion and of infant mortality, and a pervasive perception that pregnancy and parturition were life-threatening to the mother. Material conditions of existence such as these are given imaginative articulation in Shakespeare's play as an inherently dangerous relationship between mother and son.[32]

Titania represents her bond to her votaress as one that is rooted in an experience of female fertility. The women "have laugh'd to see the sails conceive / And grow big-bellied with the wanton wind"; and the votaress has parodied such false pregnancies by sailing to fetch trifles, at the same time that she herself bears a treasure within her womb. The riches of the maternal womb and those of the merchant venturer provide the dramatic poet's rich with with matter for similitudes. Yet, in part because of the gendered perspective of the similitude's fictive speaker, the passage not only gives priority to the woman's (fatal) generativity but also gives voice to women's proprietary relationship to their own bodies and to the products of their maternal labor. In this sense, the passage provides a lyrical counterstatement to the paternal and patriarchal claims upon Hermia. Specifically, the notion of maternity implied in Titania's speech counterpoints the notion of paternity formulated by Theseus in the opening scene. In

Theseus's description, neither biological nor social mother—neither *genetrix* nor *mater*—plays a role in the making of a daughter; in Titania's description, neither *genitor* nor *pater* plays a role in the making of a son. The father's daughter is shaped from without; the mother's son comes from within her body: Titania dwells upon the physical bond between mother and child, as manifested in pregnancy and parturition. Like an infant of the Elizabethan upper classes, however, the changeling is nurtured not by his natural mother but by a surrogate. Here it is worth remembering that in early modern social practice, men were rarely present during labor and birth; and that the work of midwives and wetnurses, and the custom of female visitations during the period of lying-in, strongly reinforced the sense of childbirth as a collectively and exclusively feminine modality of experience. As Adrian Wilson has characterized it, "the social space of the birth . . . was a collective female space, constituted on the one hand by the presence of gossips and midwife, and on the other hand by the absence of men."[33] By emphasizing her own role as a foster mother to the offspring of the votary who "gossip'd by [her] side," Titania links the biological and social aspects of parenthood together within a wholly maternal world, a world in which the relationship between women has displaced the relationship between wife and husband.

In *A Midsummer Night's Dream,* the mother is represented as a vessel, as a container for her son; she is not his maker. Lemnius' *Secret Miracles of Nature,* a sixteenth-century treatise translated in 1658, demystifies the lyrical similitude for maternal fecundity that Shakespeare gives to Titania. Lemnius attacks such a conception of conception, one that teaches women that

> Mothers afford very little to the generation of the child, but onely are at the trouble to carry it . . . as if the womb were hired by men, as Merchants Ships are to be straited by them; and to discharge their burden . . . women grow luke-warm, and lose all humane affections towards their children.[34]

In contrast to such a representation of maternity, the implication of Theseus's description of paternity is that the male is the only begetter; a daughter is merely a token of her father's potency. Such an implication reverses the putative Amazonian practice, in which women use men merely for their own reproduction. Taken together, the speeches of Theseus and Titania may be said to formulate in poetic discourse, a proposition about the genesis of gender and power: Men make women and make themselves through the medium of women.[35]

Despite the exclusion of a paternal role from Titania's speech, the embryological notions represented in *A Midsummer Night's Dream* have a recognizably Aristotelian coloring. In the Aristotelian tradition, the actively in-forming *sperma* of the male is the efficient cause of generation, and the passively receptive *catamenia* of the female is the material cause of generation.[36] Whereas Aristotle emphasizes two distinct sexes, Galenic anatomy and physiology emphasize what Thomas Laqueur calls a "one-sex" model: There is a homology between the genital organs of man and woman, the latter being an inverted and internalized version of the former. Accordingly, both sexes contribute their "seed" to conception, and both have to experience orgasm and ejaculation in order for conception to take place.[37] However, when Angus McLaren writes that, in Galenic medicine, "both sexes were presented as contributing *equally* in conception" (*Reproductive Rituals,* 17; emphasis added), he may give the wrong impression that this implies an egalitarian sex/gender system. It would be more accurate to say that, in Galenic theory, males and females contribute to conception according to their homologous but inherently unequal abilities: The Galenic "one-sex" model is based upon the norm of male anatomy and physiology; the female is an imperfect version of the male, unable to realize the *telos* of masculinity due to a lack of vital heat in her constitution. The act of generation brings man and woman into a relationship that is both complementary and hierarchical. Thus, there exists a homology between ideologies of sexual and domestic relations: genitor is to genetrix as husband is to wife.

According to *The Problemes of Aristotle,* a popular Elizabethan medical guide that continued to be revised and reissued well into the nineteenth century,

> The seede [i.e., of the man] is the efficient beginning of the childe, as the builder is the efficient cause of the house, and therefore is not the materiall cause of the childe. . . . The seedes [i.e., both male and female] are shut and kept in the wombe: but the seede of the man doth dispose and prepare the seed of the woman to receive the forme, perfection, or soule, the which being done, it is converted into humiditie, and is fumed and breathed out by the pores of the matrix, which is manifest, bicause onely the flowers [i.e., the menses] of the woman are the materiall cause of the yoong one.[38]

Incorporating Galenic elements into its fundamentally Aristotelian perspective, this text registers some confusion about the nature of the inseminating power and about its attribution to the woman as well as to the man. Although the contributions of both man and woman are necessary, the female seed is nevertheless materially inferior to that of the male. The notion of woman as an unperfected, an inadequate, version of man extends to the analogy of semen and menses: "The seede . . . is white in man by reason of his great heate, and because it is digested better. . . . The seede of a woman is red . . . because the flowers is corrupt, undigested blood" (*Problemes of Aristotle,* E3r). Although Laqueur insists upon a sharp theoretical distinction

between a "one-sex" and a "two-sex" model, in practice such distinctions may have been neither clear nor absolute to most men and women in early modern England. A widely read medical text like *The Problemes of Aristotle* suggests the existence of a syncretic and sometimes internally contradictory popular discourse, both written and oral, extending beyond the confines of a learned discourse that was based almost exclusively upon the Galenic corpus.

What most people today tend to think of as the "facts of life" have been established on the basis of observations and hypotheses made relatively recently in human history, since the development of microbiology that began in Europe in the late seventeenth century.[39] Whatever unexamined assumptions and hidden agendas motivate and skew the quest for "objective truth" in modern scientific research, few would dispute that present-day knowledge of anatomy and physiology is not merely different from but also quantitatively and qualitatively superior to that possessed by Shakespeare's contemporaries. In Elizabethan England, it seems to have been widely held that seminal and menstrual fluids are relevant to generation, and that people have a natural father as well as a natural mother. Nevertheless, the configuration and articulation of such beliefs, and their epistemological foundations, differed— sometimes, radically—from our own. Biological maternity has always been a readily observable material datum, a natural and universal fact—yet one, nevertheless, that is subject to widely varying, culture-specific representation, experience, and understanding. Outside the modern laboratory, however, biological paternity has everywhere remained a cultural construct for which ocular proof is unavailable.

This consequence of biological asymmetry calls forth an explanatory—and compensatory—cultural asymmetry in many traditional embryological theories, both learned and popular: Paternity is procreative, the formal and/or efficient cause of generation; maternity is nurturant, the material cause of generation. The quasi-Aristotelian procreative propositions of *A Midsummer Night's Dream* work against some of those Galenic propositions that were dominant in the learned tradition of Shakespeare's culture, propositions that are represented or implied elsewhere in his plays.[40] *A Midsummer Night's Dream* articulates a relatively extreme— but, nevertheless, not wholly anomalous—perspective on the Elizabethan system of gender and sex. Whatever the particular and subjective occasion of its invention by the playwright, this culturally inscribed phallocentric rhetoric overcompensates for the observable natural fact that men do indeed come from the bodies of women. Furthermore, it overcompensates for the cultural fact that consanguineal and affinal ties between men were established through their mutual but differential relationships to women, who were variously positioned as mothers, wives, or daughters.

Whether in folk medicine or in philosophy, notions of maternity have a persistent natural or material bias, while notions of paternity have a persistent social or spiritual bias. And such notions are articulated within a belief-system in which nature is subordinated to civility, and matter is subordinated to spirit. Thomas Hobbes avers that, "in the condition of meer Nature, where there are no Matrimoniall lawes, it cannot be known who is the Father, unless it be declared by the Mother: and therefore the right of Dominion over the Child dependeth on her will" (*Leviathan,* 254). Traditional sex/gender systems impose law upon mere nature in order to secure a conceptual space for paternity. However, the legitimation of paternity as a general principle does not guarantee the establishment of specific and individual paternity, the physiological link between a particular man and child. This bond has always been highly tenuous—at least, until very recent advances in forensic genetics. The role of *genetrix* is selfevident but the role of *genitor* is not. As Launcelot Gobbo puts it, in *The Merchant of Venice,* "it is a wise father that knows his own child" (2.2.76-77).

A cynical quip attributed to Sir Henry Wotton summarizes the modalities in which a man's relationship to matrimony and paternity might be realized: "Next to no wife and children, your own wife and children are best pastime; another's wife and your children worse; your wife and another's children worst."[41] Man's worst condition is to be made a cuckold by his wife and the unwitting provider for another man's offspring; less bad, to make another man a cuckold by begetting one's own bastards upon his adulterous spouse; better, to be secure in the chasteness of one's spousal relationship and the legitimacy of one's offspring; but, best of all, to be a bachelor and thus invulnerable to the degrading temptations of the flesh and to the threat of contaminated blood lines, one's own and others'. In Shakespearean drama, the uncertain linkage of father and child is frequently a focus of anxious concern, whether the motive is to validate paternity or to call it into question. For example, Lear tells Regan that if she were not glad to see him, "I would divorce me from thy mother's tomb, / Sepulchring an adult'ress" (*King Lear,* 2.4.131-32). And Leontes exclaims, upon first meeting Florizel, "Your mother was most true to wedlock, Prince, / For she did print your royal father off, / Conceiving you" (*Winter's Tale,* 5.1.124-26). In the former speech, a father who is vulnerable to perceived acts of "filial ingratitude" invokes his previously unacknowledged wife precisely when he wishes to repudiate his female child. In the latter speech, a husband who is subject to cuckoldry anxieties rejoices in the ocular proof of paternity; he celebrates wifely chastity as the instrument of masculine self-reproduction. *A Midsummer Night's Dream* dramatizes a set of claims that are repeated in various registers—and not without challenge—throughout the Shakespearean canon: claims for a spiritual kinship among men that

is unmediated by women; for the procreative powers of men; and for the autogeny of men.

III

While Shakespeare's plays reproduce such legitimating structures, they also produce challenges to their legitimacy. Within the course of a given dramatic action, representatives of opposition and difference are usually defeated, banished, converted, or otherwise apparently contained by the play's ideologically dominant forces and forms. Nevertheless, in its very representation of alternatives and resistances, the play articulates and disseminates fragments of those socially active heterodox discourses that the politically dominant discourse seeks, with only limited success, to appropriate, repudiate, or suppress. The play may try to impose symbolic closure upon the heterodoxy to which it also gives voice, but that closure can be neither total nor final. And such ideological instability or permeability in the drama may be a consequence not only of its performance but also of its inscription. It is obvious that theatrical productions and critical readings originating from beyond the cultural time and place of the text's own origin may work against the grain to achieve radically heterodox meanings and effects. But it may also be the case that the appropriative potential of such subsequent acts of interpretation is enabled by Elizabethan cultural variations and contradictions that have been sedimented in the text of the play at its originary moment of production.

I want to turn now to some of those instances in which *A Midsummer Night's Dream* produces challenges to its own legitimating structures, a focus to which I shall return at greater length in chapter 11. At the close of the play, Oberon's epithalamium represents procreation as the union of man and woman and marriage as a relationship of mutual affection:

> To the best bride-bed will we,
> Which by us shall blessed be;
> And the issue there create
> Ever shall be fortunate.
> So shall all the couples three
> Ever true in loving be.
>
> (5.1.389-94)

This benign and communal vision is predicated upon the play's prior reaffirmation of the father's role in generation and the husband's authority over the wife. Nevertheless, although *A Midsummer Night's Dream* reaffirms essential elements of a patriarchal ideology, it continues to call that reaffirmation into question, thus intermittently undermining its own comic propositions. The all-too-human struggle between the fairy king and queen—the play's already married couple—provides an ironic prognosis for the new marriages. As personified in Shakespeare's fairies, the divinely ordained imperatives of Nature call attention to themselves as the humanly constructed imperatives of culture; Shakespeare's naturalization and legitimation of the domestic economy deconstructs itself. Oberon assures himself that, by the end of the play, "all things shall be peace" (3.2.377). But the continuance of the newlyweds' loves and the good fortune of their issue are by no means assured. As soon as the lovers have gone off to bed, the rustic and sylvan Puck appears within the confines of the ducal court; he remains a central presence there until the end of the play, and then speaks the epilogue. Now, at the close of the wedding day and while the marriages are being consummated, Puck begins to evoke an uncomic world of labor, fear, pain, and death (5.1.357-76): "The hungry lion roars"; "the heavy ploughman snores, / All with weary task fordone"; "the screech-owl . . . / Puts the wretch that lies in woe / In remembrance of a shroud" (357, 359-60, 362-64). Puck's invocation of night alludes to the heritage of the Fall and the burden of Eve's transgression—a grim prelude that gives some urgency to Oberon's blessing of the bridal beds (389-400). The dangers are immanent and the peace is most fragile.

The play ends upon the threshhold of another generational cycle, in which the procreation of new children will also create new mothers and new fathers. This ending contains within it the potential for renewal of the forms of strife exhibited at the opening of the play. The promised end of romantic comedy is not only undermined by dramatic ironies but is also contaminated by a kind of intertextual irony. I do not mean to imply that such ironies necessarily registered in the minds of most members of Shakespeare's audience, nor that it was the playwright's intention that they should. Rather, I am trying to (re)construct an intertextual field of representations, resonances, and pressures that constitutes an ideological matrix from which—and against which—Shakespeare shaped the mythopoeia of *A Midsummer Night's Dream*. The mythology of Theseus is well supplied with examples of terror, lust, and jealousy; and these are prominently recounted and censured by Plutarch in his *Life of Theseus* and in his subsequent comparison of Theseus with Romulus. Shakespeare uses Plutarch as his major source of Theseus lore but does so selectively, for the most part down-playing those events "not sorting with a nuptial ceremony" (5.1.55) nor with a comedy. At their first entrance, Oberon accuses Titania of abetting (or actually compelling) Theseus's abuses—an accusation she dismisses as "the forgeries of jealousy" (81):

> Didst not thou lead him through the
>   glimmering night
> From Perigouna, whom he ravished;
> And make him with fair Aegles break his
>   faith,
> With Ariadne and Antiopa?
>
> (2.1.77-80)

This is perhaps the play's only explicit reference to Theseus's checkered past.[42] However, as Harold Brooks's Arden edition has convincingly demonstrated, the text of *A Midsummer Night's Dream* is permeated by echoes, not only of Plutarch's parallel lives of Theseus and Romulus but also of Seneca's *Hippolitus* and his *Medea*—by an archaeological record of the texts that shaped the poet's fantasy as he was shaping his play.[43] Thus, sedimented within the verbal texture of *A Midsummer Night's Dream* are traces of those forms of sexual and familial violence that the ethos of romantic comedy seeks to neutralize or to evade: acts of bestiality and incest, of parricide, uxoricide, filicide, and suicide. In the mythological record, such sexual fears and urges erupt into cycles of violent desire that stretch from Pasiphaë's consummated taurophilia to Phaedra's frustrated lust for her stepson.[44] It is precisely this lurid mythological subtext of unchecked, violent, and polymorphous desire that the play text's dominant discourse seeks to contain.

Shakespeare's play actually calls attention to its own mechanisms of mythological suppression, however, by an ironic metadramatic gesture: Theseus demands "some delight" with which to "beguile / The lazy time" (5.1.40-41) before the bedding of the brides. The list of available entertainments includes "The battle with the Centaurs, to be sung / By an Athenian eunuch to the harp," as well as "The riot of the tipsy Bacchanals, / Tearing the Thracian singer in their rage" (5.1.44-45, 48-49). Theseus rejects both on the grounds that they are already too familiar. These brief scenarios encompass the extremes of reciprocal violence between the sexes. The first offering narrates a wedding that degenerates into rape and warfare; the singer and his subject—emasculated Athenian and phallic Centaur—are two antithetical kinds of male monster. In the second offering, what was often regarded as the natural inclination of women toward irrational behavior is manifested in the Maenads' terrible rage against Orpheus. The tearing apart and decapitation of the misogynistic Ur-poet at once displaces and vivifies the Athenian singer's castration. It also evokes the fate of Hippolytus, the misogynistic offspring of Theseus and Hippolyta: Hippolytus' body was torn apart upon the rocks when his horses bolted at the instigation of his father, who had been deceived by Phaedra's charge that her stepson had attempted to rape her.

The seductive and destructive powers of women figure centrally in Theseus's career; and his habitual victimization of women, the chronicle of his own rapes and disastrous marriages, is a discourse of anxious misogyny that persists as an echo within Shakespeare's text, despite its having been variously muted or transformed. In Seneca, as in Plutarch, the mother of Hippolytus is named Antiopa. Shakespeare's deliberate choice of the alternative, Hippolyta (an apparent back-formation from the name of her son) obviously evokes the future

Hippolytus. A profoundly ironic context is thus provided for the royal wedding, for Oberon's intention to bless "the best bride-bed," and for his prognosis that "the issue there create / Ever shall be fortunate." (In a related example of intertextual irony, by choosing the name of Theseus's father, Egeus, for the Athenian patriarch whose will is overborne by the Duke, Shakespeare effects a displacement within his comedy of Theseus's negligent parricide.) Seneca's Hippolytus emphasizes Theseus's abuse of women; Phaedra's invective gives voice to his victims. At this point in his sordid career, Theseus has forsaken (or, perhaps, killed) Antiopa/Hippolyta and married Phaedra. Hippolytus, as Phaedra's nutrix reminds him, is the only living son of the Amazons (Seneca, *Hippolytus*, 577). It is by his very misogyny—his scorn of marriage, and his self-dedication to virginity, hunting, and the cult of Diana—that Hippolytus proves himself to be his mother's son; he is "genus Amazonium" (*Hippolytus*, 231). Oberon's blessing of the marriage bed of Theseus and Hippolyta evokes precisely that which it seeks to suppress: the cycle of sexual and familial desire, fear, violence, and betrayal that will begin again at the very engendering of Hippolytus, whose fate is already written in his name.

In *The Palace of Pleasure,* Painter recounts the battle between the Amazons, led by Menalippe and Hippolyta (both sisters of Queen Antiopa), and the Greeks, led by Hercules and Theseus. Hercules returned Menalippe to Antiopa in exchange for the queen's armor, "but Theseus for no offer that she coulde make, woulde he deliver Hippolyta, with whom he was so farre in love, that he carried her home with him, and afterward toke her to wyfe, of whom hee had a sonne called Hipolitus" (163). Plutarch reports that Antiopa (conflated with Hippolyta in Shakespeare's play) was not conquered in personal combat but was captured by Theseus with "deceit and stealth" (55). Hippolyta is divorced from her sisters and from the society of Amazons as a consequence of Theseus's possessive passion—the deceitful, violent, and insatiable lust that North's Plutarch suggestively calls his "womannishenes" (116). To term masculine concupiscence "womannishenes" implies that a man who continually lusts after women is behaving like a woman; he has become enslaved to his passions. Indeed, "womannishenes" suggests that masculine heterosexual desire is itself, in its essence, effeminizing; that concupiscence weakens and degrades manly virtue. Ironically, the very opening of *A Midsummer Night's Dream* finds Hippolyta counseling restraint and patience to Theseus, who restlessly longs for his wedding night (1.1.1-11). Shortly thereafter, we are introduced to Oberon, who is jealous and vengeful because his wife has "forsaken his bed and company," and has made the changeling "all her joy." Sir Thomas Elyot's counsel regarding the education of boys, partially quoted above, is impelled by a fear of incipient womanishness:

After that a child is come to seven years of age . . . he [should] be taken from the company of women . . . for though there be no peril of offence in that tender and innocent age, yet in some children nature is more prone to vice than to virtue, and in the tender wits be sparks of voluptuosity which, nourished by any occasion or object, increase in time to so terrible a fire that therewith all virtue and reason is consumed. Wherefore, to eschew that danger, the most sure counsel is to withdraw him from all company of women, and to assign him to a tutor, which should be an ancient and worshipful man. (*The Book named The Governor*, 19)

It is fear of the consequences of womanishness, too, that makes Wotton consider "no wife and children" to be a man's best option. The term "womannishenes" suggests that there exists within the Elizabethan ideology of gender, a complementary and compensatory relationship between attitudes of uxoriousness and misogyny.

Notes

[19] William Painter, *The Palace of Pleasure* (1575), ed. Joseph Jacobs, 3 vols. (1890; rpt., New York: Dover Books, 1966), 2:159-61. Page citations are to volume 2 of this edition. For a sense of the ubiquity of Amazonian representations in Elizabethan culture, see the valuable survey by Celeste Turner Wright, "The Amazons in Elizabethan Literature," *Studies in Philology* 37 (1940), 433-56.

[20] See Sir Thomas Elyot, *The Book named The Governor,* ed. S. E. Lehmberg (London: Dent, 1962), 19; Stephen Orgel, "Nobody's Perfect: Or, Why Did the English Stage Take Boys for Women?" *South Atlantic Quarterly* 88 (1989), 7-29; quotation from 10-11. Also see Patricia Crawford, "The Construction and Experience of Maternity in Seventeenth-Century England," in *Women as Mothers in Pre-Industrial England: Essays in Memory of Dorothy McLaren,* ed. Valerie Fildes (London and New York: Routledge, 1990), 3-38, esp. 12-13: "Contemporaries usually judged that a mother was responsible for the care of children under the age of 7. . . . In the upper levels of society, maternal education for boys was confined to their earlier years. After about the age of 7, boys from the gentry were usually entrusted to the care of a schoolmaster or tutor. . . . Although mothers were responsible for the education of daughters, they were subject to paternal authority."

[21] Linda T. Fitz, "'What Says the Married Woman?': Marriage Theory and Feminism in the English Renaissance," *Mosaic,* 13:2 (Winter 1980), 1-22, suggests that "the English Renaissance institutionalized, where it did not invent, the restrictive marriage-oriented attitude toward women that feminists have been struggling against ever since. . . . The insistent demand for the right— nay, obligation—of women to be happily married arose as much in reaction against women's intractable pur-

suit of independence as it did in reaction against Catholic ascetic philosophy" (11, 18). And Amy Louise Erickson, *Women and Property in Early Modern England,* points out that, "In spite of legal, demographic, economic and social shifts, an underlying continuity ties the women of 1550 and earlier to the women of 1750 and later. Men's perceived need to restrict women legally within marriage is as constant as their need to persuade women to think in terms of marriage as the natural female state" (232).

Despite the dominance and desirability of marriage as a social expectation and norm, the work of social historians and historical demographers suggests that significant numbers of Elizabethan women—and men— never married, chiefly because they were unable to accumulate the material resources necessary to establish a household.

[22] André Thevet, *The newefounde Worlde,* trans. T. Hacket (London, 1568), 102r.

[23] Robert W. Dent, "Imagination in *A Midsummer Night's Dream,*" *Shakespeare Quarterly* 15 (1964), 115-29; see 116. On the permutations of desire among the lovers of *MND,* see René Girard, "Myth and Ritual in Shakespeare: *A Midsummer Night's Dream,*" in *Textual Strategies,* ed. Josué V. Harari (Ithaca: Cornell University Press, 1979), 189-212. On the relationship of Hermia and Helena, see the discussion in James L. Calderwood, *Shakespearean Metadrama* (Minneapolis: University of Minnesota Press, 1971), 126.

[24] For a detailed analysis, see my essay, "'The Place of a Brother' in *As You Like It.*"

[25] In this connection, see Hobbes's interesting remarks in his discussion "Of Dominion Paternall, and Despoticall" (*Leviathan,* pt. 2, ch. 20): Hobbes construes the parent-child relationship as the condition of dominion or sovereignty by generation, with the proviso that this dominion is not established through mere procreation but rather by contract. Hobbes reasons that, because "there be always two that are equally Parents: the Dominion therefore over the Child, should belong equally to both"; however, this "is impossible; for no man can obey two Masters." Hobbes notes that "in Common-wealths, this controversie is decided by the Civill Law: and for the most part, (but not alwayes) the sentence is in favour of the Father; because for the most part Common-wealths have been erected by the Fathers, not by the Mothers of families." However, in the (hypothetical) state of "meer Nature, either the Parents between themselves dispose of the dominion over the Child by Contract; or do not dispose thereof at all. . . . We find in History that the *Amazons* Contracted with the Men of the neighboring Countries, to whom they had recourse for issue, that the issue Male should be sent back, but the Female remain with themselves: so that the dominion of the Females was in the Mother." See Thomas Hobbes, *Leviathan* (1651), ed. C. B. Macpherson (Harmondsworth, Middlesex: Penguin Books, 1968), 253-54.

[26] I first emphasized this point in "Shaping Fantasies" (1983). Now see Mary Beth Rose, "Where Are the Mothers in Shakespeare? Options for Gender Representation in the English Renaissance," *Shakespeare Quarterly* 42 (1991), 291-314. In her meticulous study, Rose sketches a range of attitudes toward, and representations of, motherhood in Elizabethan-Jacobean England; she concludes that Shakespearean maternal representations are almost exclusively of the most traditional and conservative sort. In this construction, motherhood, "lagging behind the altering definitions of other family roles . . . remains most resolutely limited to the private realm, inscribed entirely in terms of early love and nurture. As a result, motherhood in this formulation can be dramatized only as dangerous or as peripheral to adult, public life" (313). For an excellent overview of the early modern representation and practice of motherhood, based primarily on diaries, letters, and guidebooks, see Crawford, "The Construction and Experience of Maternity in Seventeenth-Century England"; and, for a powerful psychoanalytic reading of the problematic representation of motherhood in Shakespeare's later plays, see Janet Adelman, *Suffocating Mothers: Fantasies of Maternal Origin in Shakespeare's Plays, "Hamlet" to "The Tempest"* (New York and London: Routledge, 1992).

[27] This may be an extreme form of the proprietary fantasy of patriarchy but it is nevertheless securely grounded in the gender ideology and customary and legal practices of early modern England. See, for example, the observations of Amy Louise Erickson:

> Many men would have liked to regard women as property in and of themselves; but while married women's legal disabilities put them in the same category as idiots, convicted criminals and infants, they were never legally classed with chattels. Nonetheless, there are ways in which women were treated as a form of property. The specious theory of the "unity" of husband and wife, and the constant threat of legal incapacitation; the association of a woman's marriage portion with her sexual honour; the view of rape as a form of theft, not from the victim but from her husband or male relatives; the prosecution of adultery only in cases where the woman was married; and the implications of even a practice as apparently innocuous as losing one's name upon marriage—all of these smack of men's ownership of women. Certainly in the seventeenth century a number of women (and a very few men) protested that women were treated little better than slaves.
>
> (*Women and Property in Early Modern England,* 232-33)

[28] *De pueris statim ac liberaliter instituendis declamatio* ("A Declamation on the Subject of Early Liberal Education for Children"), trans. Beert C. Verstraete, in *Collected Works of Erasmus*, vol. 26 (Literary and Educational Writings, vol. 4), ed. J. K. Sowards (Toronto: University of Toronto Press, 1985), 295-346; quotations from 300, 309.

[29] See Joan Bamberger, "The Myth of Matriarchy: Why Men Rule in Primitive Society," in *Woman, Culture and Society*, ed. Michelle Zimbalist Rosaldo and Louise Lamphere (Stanford: Stanford University Press, 1974), 262-80, esp. 266, 277.

[30] Some of the play's (masculine) critics have approved of Oberon's actions as undertaken in the best interests of a growing boy and a neurotic mother. Two of the play's most rewarding critics must be included among them: see Barber, *Shakespeare's Festive Comedy*, 119-62, esp. 137; Calderwood, *Shakespearean Metadrama*, 120-48, esp. 125.

[31] Keith Thomas, "The Double Standard" (1959), rpt., with revisions, in *Ideas in Cultural Perspective*, ed. Philip P. Wiener and Aaron Noland (New Brunswick, New Jersey: Rutgers University Press, 1962), 446-67; quotations from 461, 464. Thomas quotes Juan Luis Vives's influential Tudor treatise, *The Instruction of a Christen Woman*, to the effect that "A woman hath no power of her own body, but her husband; thou dost the more wrong to give away that thing which is another body's without the owner's licence" (trans. R. Hyrde [1541], 66r).

[32] For evidence regarding infant mortality, see R. S. Schofield and E. A. Wrigley, "Infant and Child Mortality in the Late Tudor and Early Stuart Period," in *Health, Medicine and Mortality in the Sixteenth Century*, ed. Charles Webster (Cambridge: Cambridge University Press, 1979), 61-95; on spontaneous and induced abortion, and fears of pregnancy, see Linda A. Pollock, "Embarking on a Rough Passage: The Experience of Pregnancy in Early-Modern Society," in *Women as Mothers in Pre-Industrial England*, 39-67; also, Crawford, "The Construction and Experience of Maternity in Seventeenth-Century England," *ibid.*, 21-23.

[33] Adrian Wilson, "The Ceremony of Childbirth and Its Interpretation," in *Women as Mothers in Pre-Industrial England*, 68-107; quotation from 73. Also see Crawford, "The construction and experience of maternity in seventeenth-century England," *ibid.*, 21, 25-29.

[34] L. Lemnius, *The Secret Miracles of Nature* (London, 1658), 23; quoted in Crawford, "The Construction and Experience of Maternity in Seventeenth-Century England," 7.

[35] In *Love's Labour's Lost*, such an assertion seems to be implied in Berowne's ostensible paean to the ladies of France: "Or for men's sake, the authors of these women, / Or for women's sake, by whom we men are men" (*LLL*, 4.3.355-56).

[36] On classical embryological theory, I have found the following useful: F. J. Cole, *Early Theories of Sexual Generation* (Oxford: Clarendon Press, 1930); Joseph Needham, *A History of Embryology*, 2nd ed., rev. (New York: Abelard-Schuman, 1959); Maryanne Cline Horowitz, "Aristotle and Woman," *Journal of the History of Biology* 9 (1976), 183-213; Thomas Laqueur, *Making Sex: Body and Gender from the Greeks to Freud* (Cambridge, Mass.: Harvard University Press, 1990), and also his earlier essay, "Orgasm, Generation, and the Politics of Reproductive Biology," *Representations* 14 (Spring 1986), 1-41.

[37] On theories of sexuality and conception in early modern English culture, see Audrey Eccles, *Obstetrics and Gynaecology in Tudor and Stuart England* (Kent, Ohio: Kent State University Press, 1982); and Angus McLaren, *Reproductive Rituals: The Perception of Fertility in England from the Sixteenth to the Nineteenth Century* (London: Methuen, 1984). Also see Laqueur, *Making Sex*.

[38] *The Problemes of Aristotle, with other Philosophers and Phisitions* (London, 1597), E3v-E4r.

[39] The following discussion is indebted to J. A. Barnes, "Genetrix: Genitor:: Nature: Culture?" in *The Character of Kinship*, ed. Jack Goody (Cambridge: Cambridge University Press, 1973), 61-73.

[40] For a reading of Shakespearean comedy and Elizabethan theatrical crossdressing that is based upon Galenic theories of sexuality and is much influenced by the perspective of Laqueur, see "Fiction and Friction," in Stephen Greenblatt, *Shakespearean Negotiations*, 66-93. As I have already suggested, I believe that the Elizabethan discourse of sexuality and generation was wider and significantly more heterogeneous than Greenblatt's provocative essay implies.

[41] Logan Pearsall Smith, *The Life and Letters of Sir Henry Wotton*, 2:490.

[42] Compare Plutarch, "The Life of Theseus," in *The Lives of the Noble Grecians and Romanes*, trans. Thomas North (1579) from Amyot's French trans., 6 vols., The Tudor Translations (1895; rpt., New York: AMS Press, 1967):

> The Poet telleth that the Amazones made warres with Theseus to revenge the injurie he dyd to their Queene Antiopa, refusing her, to marye with Phaedra. . . . We finde many other reportes touching the mariages

of Theseus, whose beginnings had no great good honest ground, neither fell out their endes very fortunate: and yet for all that they have made no tragedies of them, neither have they bene played in the Theaters. For we reade that he tooke away Anaxo the Troezenian, and after that he had killed Sinnis and Cercyon, he tooke their daughters preforce: and that he dyd also marye Peribaea, the mother of Ajax, and afterwards Pherebaea, and Ioppa the daughter of Iphicles. And they blame him much also, for that he so lightly forsooke his wife Ariadne, for the love of Aegles the daughter of Panopaeus. . . . Lastly, he tooke awaye Hellen: which ravishement filled all the Realme of Attica with warres, and finally was the very occasion that forced him to forsake his countrye, and brought him at the length to his ende. (1:58-59)

[43] For a review and analysis of the play's sources and analogues, see Brooks's edition, lviii-lxxxviii; 129-53; and the notes throughout the text. D'Orsay W. Pearson, "'Vnkinde' Theseus: A Study in Renaissance Mythography," *English Literary Renaissance* 4 (1974), 276-98, provides an informative survey of Theseus's "classical, medieval, and Renaissance image as an unnatural, perfidious, and unfaithful lover and father" (276). Olson characterizes the traditional Theseus as uneqivocally embodying "the reasonable man and the ideal ruler of both his lower nature and his subjects" ("*A Midsummer Night's Dream* and the Meaning of Court Marriage," 101), thus oversimplifying both the tradition and the play.

[44] Many details in the texts of Plutarch and Seneca that have not been considered previously as "sources" for Shakespeare's play are nevertheless relevant to problems of gender, generation, filiation, and licit desire, which seem to me to be central to *MND.* Here I can do no more than enumerate a few of these details. The following discussion cites Shakespeare's classical sources from the following editions: Plutarch, *The Lives of the Noble Grecians and Romanes,* trans. Sir Thomas North (1579), Tudor Translations, cited by page numbers in volume 1; Seneca, *Tragedies,* trans. F. J. Miller, Loeb Classical Library, 2 vols. (London: Heinemann, 1960-61), cited by line numbers in the Latin texts.

In his *Lives,* Plutarch relates that Theseus was "begotten by stealth, and out of lawfull matrimony" (30); that, "of his father's side," he was descended from the "Autocthones, as much to say, as borne of them selves" (30); that, having been abandoned by Theseus on Cyprus, the pregnant Ariadne "dyed . . . in labour, and could never be delivered" (48); that, because the negligently joyful Theseus forgot to change his sail as a sign of success upon his return from Crete, his father Egeus, "being out of all hope evermore to see his sonne againe, tooke such a griefe at his harte, that he threw him selfe headlong from the top of a clyffe, and killed him selfe" (49). In Seneca's *Hippolytus,* Hippolytus reminds Phaedra that she has come from the same womb

that bore the Minotaur, and that she is even worse than her mother, Pasiphaë (688-93). At the end of the play, Theseus's burden is to refashion his dead son from the "disiecta . . . membra" of his torn body (1256-70). Now a filicide, as well as a parricide and uxoricide, Theseus has perverted and destroyed his own house (1166).

DREAMS

Marjorie B. Garber (essay date 1974)

SOURCE: "Spirits of Another Sort: *A Midsummer Night's Dream,*" in *Dream in Shakespeare: From Metaphor to Metamorphosis,* Yale University Press, 1974, pp. 59-87.

[*In the following essay, Garber studies the role of dreams in* A Midsummer Night's Dream, *arguing that dreams are a source of creative insight and have the power to transform reality. The creative, transforming process of dreams, Garber states, is not only the subject of the play, but the force which guides the play's action.*]

> *If we shadows have offended*
> *Think but this, and all is mended:*
> *That you have but slumb'red here,*
> *While these visions did appear.*
> *And this weak and idle theme,*
> *No more yielding but a dream.*
>
> V.i.422-27

Puck's closing address to the audience is characteristic of the tone of *A Midsummer Night's Dream;* it seems to trivialize what it obliquely praises. All the key words of dream are here, as they have been from the play's title and opening lines: "shadows," "slumb'red," "visions," and "dream" itself. Puck is making an important analogy between the play and the dream state—an analogy we have encountered before in Shakespeare, but which is here for the first time fully explored. For *A Midsummer Night's Dream* is a play consciously concerned with dreaming; it reverses the categories of reality and illusion, sleeping and waking, art and nature, to touch upon the central theme of the dream which is truer than reality.

Puck offers the traditional apologia at the play's end; if the audience is dissatisfied, it may choose to regard the play as only a "dream" or trifle and not a real experience at all. The players, as Theseus has already suggested, are only "shadows" (V.i.212); the play, in short, is potentially reducible to a "weak and idle theme" of no significance. Yet everything which has gone before points in precisely the opposite direction: sleep in *A Midsummer Night's Dream* is the gateway, not to folly, but to revelation and reordering; the "visions" gained are, as Bottom says, "most rare" (IV.i.208), and the "shadows" substantial. Puck's purposeful ambiguity dwells yet again on a lesson learned by character after character within the play: that reason is impoverished without imagination, and that we must accept the dimension of dream in our lives. Without this acknowledgment, there can be no real self-knowledge.

The fundamental reversal or inversion of conventional categories which is a structuring principle of this play is familiar to us in part from the framing device of *The Taming of the Shrew*. The Athenian lovers flee to the wood and fall asleep, entering as they do so the charmed circle of dream. When Puck comes upon them and anoints their eyes, the world of the supernatural at once takes over the stage, controlling their lives in a way they cannot guess at, but must accept, "apprehending" "more than cool reason ever comprehends." In the great dream of the forest experience and the smaller dreams within it, we might say paradoxically that their eyes are opened; this is the fundamental significance of the key word "vision," which appears several times in the play, offsetting the deliberately disparaging use of "dream" to mean something insignificant, momentary. "Swift as a shadow, short as any dream" (I.i.144), says Lysander in the first scene, describing what he takes to be the inevitable tragedy of romantic love, and Hermia replies that they must have patience, "As due to love as thoughts and dreams and sighs" (154), where dreams are once again the customary furniture of passion, illusory and conventional.

By contrast "vision," as it is introduced into the play, is a code word for the dream understood, the dream correctly valued. Often the user does not know that he knows; this is another of the play's thematic patterns, supporting the elevation of the irrational above the merely rational. As a device it is related to a character type always present in Shakespeare, but more highly refined in the later plays, that of the wise fool. Thus Bottom, awakening, is immediately and intuitively impressed with the significance of his "dream," which we of course recognize as not a dream at all, but rather a literal reality within the play.

> I have had a most rare
> vision. I have had a dream, past the wit of
> man to say what dream it was.
>
> [IV.i.205-07]

Similarly Oberon, to conceal the truth of events, instructs Puck to straighten out the mismatched lovers by crushing a magic herb into Lysander's eye, "and make his eyeballs roll with wonted sight" (III.ii.369). When the lovers wake, then,

> all this derision
> Shall seem a dream and fruitless vision.
>
> [370-71]

The "vision" has been true, but he will make it appear to have been "fruitless," illusory, with the submerged Eden pun in "fruit" underscoring one of the play's principal mythic themes. Again, Titania, roused from her sleep, cries out

> My Oberon, what visions have I seen!
> Methought I was enamored of an ass.
>
> [IV.i.77-78]

Her "visions," like the others, were "play" reality, and not dream or illusion. Moreover, the mental concept of "vision" in her phrase is picked up again in the more literal and physical reference in the next line (80) to his face or the way he looks. The association with images of sight, literal and metaphorical, is thematically significant. Early on, Helena suggests that "Love looks not with the eyes, but with the mind" (I.i.234):

> Things base and vile, holding no quantity,
> Love can transpose to form and dignity.
>
> [232-33]

She does not, of course, comprehend the larger implications of this doctrine; yet this is what the mind of Titania in the dream state does to the loathsome visage of Bottom, and the mind of the bewitched Demetrius to the formerly despised Helena. It is this transposition or transformation which is the special prerogative of the dream state and the center of interest of the whole of *A Midsummer Night's Dream*. Dream is truer than reality because it has this transforming power; it is part of the fertile, unbounded world of the imagination.

Standing in opposition to this world, which exists only within the wood, is the practical everyday world of Athens, in which reason and law hold sway. Interestingly, reason is a limiting rather than a liberating force for Shakespeare, close to Blake's "bound or outward circumference of energy," and this is particularly true in *A Midsummer Night's Dream*. Theseus attempts to impose a "reasonable" solution upon the lovers without regard for passion or imagination, with the result that no one's happiness is taken into account. Lysander, his eyes anointed in error by Puck so that he swears his devotion to Helena, given "reason" as the excuse for his change of heart:

> The will of man is by his reason swayed
> And reason says you are the worthier maid.
> Things growing are not ripe until their season:
> So I, being young, till now ripe not to reason.
> And touching now the point of human skill,
> Reason becomes the marshal to my will,
> And leads me to your eyes, where I o'erlook
> Love's stories, written in love's richest book.
>
> [II.ii.115-22]

It is characteristic of *A Midsummer Night's Dream* that Lysander should produce this speech at a point when his actions are completely supernaturally or subconsciously controlled, without the slightest hint of either reason or will. Delusion is the prelude to illusion. Likewise it is fitting that the oracular Bottom, unknowingly transformed into a monster, should observe placidly to Titania that "reason and love keep little company together nowadays" (III.i.142-43). Reason has no place in the dream state, which possesses an innate logic of its own; and when characters attempt to employ it, they frustrate their own ends. Thus the lovers, awakened in act IV by the arrival of Theseus's hunting party, are bemused by what has taken place:

> *Demetrius:* These things seem small and
> undistinguishable,
> Like far-off mountains turnèd into clouds.
> *Hermia:* Methinks I see these things with
> parted eye,
> When everything seems double.
> *Helena:*   So methinks:
> And I have found Demetrius like a jewel,
> Mine own, and not mine own.
> *Demetrius:*   Are you sure
> That we are awake? It seems to me
> That yet we sleep, we dream.
>   [IV.i.188-95]

Although they reap the benefit of the night's dreams, they do not fully apprehend them. Significantly the images they choose to describe their experiences are those of ambiguous and incomplete vision: "parted eye," "far-off mountains turnèd into clouds." The memory of the dream is itself obscuring, because as the mind tries to rationalize what has occurred, it inevitably distorts. The instinct of the mind is to set boundaries, while the process of dream blurs and obliterates those boundaries. Demetrius's hypothesis—"that yet we sleep, we dream"—is literally incorrect, but there is another sense in which these dreamers are not, and will not be, awakened. We as audience are made aware of the primacy of the dream state, but the lovers, the means of our enlightenment, remain themselves unenlightened.

The pattern of the play is thus in part controlled and ordered by a series of vital contrasts: the opposition of the sleeping and waking states; the interchange of reality and illusion, reason and imagination; the disparate spheres of influence of Theseus and Oberon. All of these are structurally related to portrayal of the dream state; while the lovers sleep, the world of dream and illusion inhabited by the fairies dominates the stage. For the world over which Oberon presides, peopled by Puck and Titania, by Peaseblossom and Mustardseed, is itself a dramatic metaphor for the dream world of the subconscious and the irrational. "Spirits" are moods and energies as well as sprites, and the fruitful ambiguity of the word may stand as a sign of the multiplic-

ity of the world they inhabit. As was the case with Queen Mab, and will be again with Ariel, the diminutive fairies of Shakespearean fantasy are elemental indwellers of the imagination, quicksilver manipulators of dream. The simultaneity of dream world and spirit world is central to an understanding of the special magic of *A Midsummer Night's Dream.*

There is, of course, a traditional literary basis for the dream world, which extends back to the French and Middle English dream visions of the fourteenth century. Throughout *A Midsummer Night's Dream* formal reminders of this tradition appear, often characteristically transformed into sophisticated commentaries on the received forms. Particularly prominent among these motifs are those of the god of love, the enchanted garden, the journeying lovers and the May morning, all present in whole or in part in the play. Of these the most important for our purpose is the traditional figure of the god of love, who acts as intermediary between the lover and the beloved. This role is taken in *A Midsummer Night's Dream* by Oberon, the fairy king, whose intent it is to bring together the right pairs of lovers in the forest. Essentially he appropriates to himself the role of stage manager, a role we have seen utilized by the lord in *The Shrew* for the purpose of controlling Christopher Sly's "dream," and one which will attain its greatest prominence in the later and richer dream management of Prospero and Autolycus.

Oberon's stage-managing falls somewhere between the relatively mechanistic deception of the *Shrew* lord and the apocalyptic hegemony of Prospero. His intentions are in the main benevolent; when he tells Puck to bring "death-counterfeiting sleep" (III.ii.364) to the lovers, so that what has occurred may appear to them "a dream and fruitless vision," he is attempting to redress an inadvertent error by his mischievous and unreliable messenger. The relation of sleep to death, which will be strongly emphasized in *The Tempest,* is here deliberately underplayed; Oberon, though he is a god of sorts, is not trafficking in resurrection. Shakespeare has made him a kind of tongue-in-cheek fairy king, a little pettish, something of a buffoon. But like so many characters in this play, Oberon speaks fairer than he knows; what to him are independent and pragmatic actions, the putting to sleep of the lovers and of Titania, have a much more far-reaching thematic significance for the play as a whole. It is no accident that he regards the events of the night as "accidents" (IV.i.69), which can be made to seem to all "but as the fierce vexation of a dream" (70). He undervalues dream and mechanizes "translation," and he, like the lovers, is an accidental rather than a controlling instrument of the doctrine of creative dream.

As the play's god of love, Oberon is structurally complemented by Peter Quince, who casts and manages the "most lamentable comedy" of Pyramus and Thisby;

and both are deliberately made parallel to Theseus, Duke and arbiter of Athens, so that the cognate worlds of reason, art, and imagination are juxtaposed through plot. It is notable that all three authorities manage with more zeal than skill; Theseus appears to appropriate the role of the reasonable adjudicator, but in fact he fails to analyze the situation of the lovers properly and later is persuaded to reverse his earlier ruling. The events of the "dream" have altered his sense of reality, just as they have ours. The dream vision situation, in which the lover is thwarted by jealousy, idleness, and false appearances and is both helped and hindered by the god of love, is here simultaneously echoed and commented upon.

If Oberon may be usefully compared to the much more complex figure of Prospero, there is also a sense in which Puck looks forward to Ariel. Puck is a more deliberately earthbound figure, a local British spirit not unlike Mercutio's Queen Mab. He emerges from a world of regional superstition and old wives' tales. "I jest to Oberon and make him smile," he tells us,

> When I a fat and bean-fed horse beguile,
> Neighing in likeness of filly foal:
> And sometimes lurk I in a gossip's bowl,
> In very likeness of a roasted crab;
> And when she drinks, against her lips I bob
> And on her withered dewlap pour the ale.
> The wisest aunt, telling the saddest tale,
> Sometime for three-foot stool mistaketh me;
> Then slip I from her bum, down topples she,
> And "tailor" cries, and falls into a cough;
> And then the whole quire hold their hips and
>   laugh,
> And waxen in their mirth, and neeze and
>   swear
> A merrier hour was never wasted there.
>   [II.i.44-57]

This is the same theme of transformation we have observed before, and to which we shall want to return at greater length. Puck is a quicksilver figure, capable of lightning transformations and astonishing impersonations; he is a true denizen of dream. Yet he lacks the sublimity of Ariel, the moral and spiritual grace. He is mischievous, and he makes mistakes. When he leads the mechanicals astray, frightening them with the apparition of the transformed Bottom, he so reverses their ideas about perception and comprehension that he places them in the midst of nightmare:

> Their sense thus weak, lost with their fears
>   thus strong,
> Made senseless things begin to do them
>   wrong;
> For briers and thorns at their apparel snatch;
> Some sleeves, some hats, from yielders all
>   things catch.

> I led them on in this distracted fear,
> And left sweet Pyramus translated there:
> When in that moment, so it came to pass,
> Titania waked, and straightway loved an ass
>   [III.ii.27-34]

Likewise, when commanded by Oberon to keep Lysander and Demetrius safe from harm, he impersonates first one, then the other, in a frantic round robin that leads them both to abandon the chase for sleep. But there is a significant difference between Puck's coltishness, even on a supernatural level, and the more apocalyptic and controlled transformations of Ariel. The unholy triumvirate of Stephano, Trinculo, and Caliban poses a much more profound threat to art and humanity as represented by Prospero than does anything in *A Midsummer Night's Dream*. Prospero is severely distressed when, in the middle of the pageant of fertility, he remembers the existence of the plot against his rule; and Ariel's treatment of the rebels, though in many ways formally related to Puck's horseplay with the lovers and mechanicals, sounds a far deeper note which takes cognizance of tragedy:

>   I beat my tabor;
> At which like unbacked colts they pricked
>   their ears,
> Advanced their eyelids, lifted up their noses
> As they smelt music. So I charmed their ears
> That calf-like they my lowing followed
>   through
> Toothed briers, sharp furzes, pricking goss,
>   and thorns
> Which ent'red their frail shins. At last I left
>   them
> I' th' filthy mantled pool beyond your cell,
> There dancing up to th' chins, that the foul
>   lake
> O'erstunk their feet.
>   [*Tmp.* IV.i.175-84]

This is a profoundly moral landscape, the projected vision of the internal state of a soul. It is a dimension which, with the less ambitious and more playful Puck, Shakespeare is careful to leave unexplored.

But the problem of the nature of the spirit world extends beyond Puck, even beyond Oberon. These are not apparitions, such as we found in *Richard III* and in *Julius Caesar,* nor are they creatures clearly contained within the fancy, as was the case with Mercutio's Queen Mab. They partake in part of the spirit of genius loci, especially in the account of Puck as a hobgoblin and in the names given to Peaseblossom, Cobweb, and Mustardseed—all, in Theseus's phrase, precisely "airy nothing" given "a local habitation and a name." But the fairies are predominantly inhabitants of an in-between world, neither wholly fictive nor wholly explainable in natural or even psychological terms. An important dialogue between Puck and Oberon touches usefully on this in-between state, a state which, like dream vision, takes place in half-light; between sleeping and waking.

> *Puck:* My fairy lord, this must be done with
>   haste,
> For night's swift dragons cut the clouds full
>   fast,
> And yonder shines Aurora's harbinger;
> At whose approach, ghosts, wand'ring here
>   and there,
> Troop home to churchyards: damnèd spirits
>   all,
> That in crossways and floods have burial,
> Already to their wormy beds are gone.
> For fear lest day should look their shames
>   upon,
> They willfully themselves exile from light,
> And must for aye consort with black-browed
>   night.
> *Oberon:* But we are spirits of another sort.
> I with the Morning's love have oft made
>   sport;
> And, like a forester, the groves may tread,
> Even till the eastern gate, all fiery-red,
> Opening on Neptune with fair blessèd beams,
> Turns into yellow gold his salt green streams.
> But, notwithstanding, haste; make no delay.
> We may effect this business yet ere day.
>
> [III.ii.378-95]

"But we are spirits of another sort"—Oberon's reminder charts a distinction without which we can hardly comprehend the importance of dream in the play. All the spirits of which Puck makes mention, ghosts and damned spirits immured in dusty churchyards, are the creatures of a superstitious super naturalism, allied to witchcraft and fear. Not only the ghost of Caesar, but also old Hamlet and the *Macbeth* witches are inhabitants of this realm. We may usefully call them night or evening spirits, because they were thought to roam only in darkness; hence Horatio recounts the Christmastime phenomenon when "the bird of dawning singeth all night long" and no spirit dares to stir abroad. But they are evening spirits in another way as well, spirits which recall and recollect what has gone before, shadows whose substance is past. As such they stand in marked contrast to Oberon's "spirits of another sort"— morning spirits, or spirits of dawning. It is perhaps not too fanciful to compare such spirits with the impulse to creation, working in the half-light of the subconscious, shadows in place of and in some ways greater than the substance they portend.

This redemptive view of dream and its creatures arises in part from a new emphasis upon transformation as a creative act. We have seen that somatic dreams function through the use of transformations, described by

Freud as displacements and condensations, by means of which the underlying meaning is bound into an apparently fictive plot. This process is clearly analogous in many ways to that of conscious fiction-making in literature; words like "symbol," "image," and "meaning" are common analytic terms for both the psychoanalyst and the literary critic, and the patterns of interpretation they employ each involve, at some stage, a search for subconscious and associative meanings which have been transformed or translated into the finished artifact, poem or dream. Our word "translate" overlaps both categories; when Peter Quince exclaims, "Bless thee, Bottom! Bless thee! Thou art translated" (III.i.117-18), he is describing the appearance of Bottom in an ass's head as a kind of awful change. The spectator knows, however, that Bottom is metaphorically an ass, a fool or buffoon. His "translation" is therefore in other terms a kind of identity, bringing the hidden to the surface through a literal symbol, the ass's head. The stage event has become a metaphor.[1] This is, as we have said, the special provenance of the dream world, that it presents the imagined as actual and that it does so by means of transformation.

In *A Midsummer Night's Dream* this transforming creative process becomes the subject as well as the technique of the play. The structural paradigm of transformation is the overall movement from court to wood and back, the transition from childhood and innocence to experience and adulthood. This is the fundamental Shakespearean pattern of growth and renewal, and it is anticipated in this play by the transformation which has already taken place in the lives of Theseus and Hippolyta. Theseus, the warrior and abductor, who "wooed [Hippolyta] with his sword" (I.i.16), is now the governor of a city, the guardian of the Athenian law, who will wed her "in another key" (18); Hippolyta, the warlike Amazon, erstwhile forest companion of Hercules and Cadmus (IV.i.113-19), is to be his wife in Athens. As the play opens these changes have already taken place, and they provide a frame or prologue for the works of transformation yet to come. Theseus now appears as the ostensible embodiment of civilized reason. Yet the choice he offers to Hermia between an unwelcome marriage and life in a nunnery is more like tyranny than reason or justice, and either alternative would run counter to the concept so often stressed in this play—that fertility is an important component of a creative and harmonious order. Throughout the play, and even at its close, Theseus stands as the apostle of reason against imagination, and therefore as a kind of limit to the transforming world of dream.

Not only the court-wood-court structure, but also the very nature of the landscape itself, form part of this spatial pattern of natural and supernatural transformation. We have touched upon the question of the landscape of the mind, the correlation between psychological and geographical description. This phenomenon might well be called "visionary landscape," because it is a projection of the subconscious state of mind upon the external state of terrain and climate—what Wallace Stevens was in his poetry to call "weathers." Early in the play we learn from Titania that her quarrel with Oberon has in fact brought about such a change; what was formerly a fairy place, *locus amoenus,* is now all disordered, its rivers overflowing their banks, its corn rotten before it is ripe, its cattle dead or dying.

> And thorough this distemperature we see
> The seasons alter: hoary-headed frosts
> Fall in the fresh lap of the crimson rose,
> And on old Hiems' thin and icy crown
> An odorous chaplet of sweet summer buds
> Is, as in mockery, set. The spring, the
>   summer,
> The childing autumn, angry winter, change
> Their wonted liveries; and the mazèd world,
> By their increase, now knows not which is
>   which.
> And this same progeny of evils comes
> From our debate, from our dissension;
> We are their parents and original.
>   [II.i.106-17]

This is a strangely solemn note for a comedy. Suggestions of the fall from paradise are unmistakable, yet the ostensible cause (possession of the Indian page boy) seems insufficient. Here we are directly confronted with the terrifying and inexplicable world of the irrational unconscious. What was once perfect, regular, and orderly is now out of all proportion. Even the place of ritual joy-making and fertility rites, the "nine men's morris," is now "filled up with mud" (98). The overwhelming impression is that of sterility, and this is important because it is the opposite of fruitful creation and change. Everywhere in the plays of Shakespeare the progression of the seasons is taken as a significant figure for the just and orderly progression of life; in the most season-oriented of all the plays, *The Winter's Tale,* Leontes greets the disguised Perdita as "Welcome hither, / As is the spring to th' earth" (*WT* V.i.151-52). Titania is describing the world of *A Midsummer Night's Dream,* and it is a world which greatly needs this seasonal change. In a sense the Athenian wood is at this point a parodic version of Eden, a timeless but paradoxically disordered realm which seeks a fortunate fall into knowledge.

This pattern of fall and redemption is clearly a valuable mythic analogue within the play. Both the Bible and the dream vision tradition classically present the image of a timeless garden, invaded and despoiled by a snake or its human counterpart. In Shakespeare's plays the same motif appears many times indirectly, as for example in the death of King Hamlet in the orchard, but it is nowhere so clearly and directly set forth as in *A Midsummer Night's Dream.* The innocent or unfallen version of the image is that of Titania as pictured by Oberon:

> I know a bank where the wild thyme blows,
> Where oxlips and the nodding violet grows,
> Quite overcanopied with luscious woodbine,
> With sweet musk roses, and with eglantine.
> There sleeps Titania sometime of the night,
> Lulled in these flowers with dances and
>   delight;
> And there the snake throws her enameled
>   skin,
> Weed wide enough to wrap a fairy in.
>   [II.i.249-56]

Here we have a harmonious composition, suggestively Edenlike: the garden, the flowers, the unsuspecting lady, significantly asleep, and the amiable snake, herself engaged in benevolent natural transformation. Yet Oberon is describing this retreat in order that Puck may go there with the transforming love juice, to "make her full of hateful fantasies" (258). Thus Titania's apparently secure world is actually in the process of a fall—a fortunate fall, as it turns out, since the fantasy experience in the wood helps to reunite her with Oberon and to restore order to the fairy world.

An equivalent structure can be perceived in Hermia's dream, the only literal dream in the play. Highly evocative, full of fruitful associations, the dream—in which Hermia is attacked by a serpent, while Lysander sits by "smiling at his cruel prey" (II.ii.150)—is especially susceptible to the kind of dream analysis we have been attempting. The snake, long a representative of violation and betrayal in scripture and in emblem books, is also a familiar Freudian image for male sexuality, and sexual fears are clearly in Hermia's mind: "gentle friend, for love and courtesy," she says before they sleep, "Lie further off, in human modesty" (II.ii.56-57). At the same time her dream is monitory and predictive, describing in metaphorical terms the estrangement which is actually taking place. Puck has anointed Lysander's eyes, and his love has been transferred from Hermia to Helena. The snake image is vivid and literal within the dream, just as the ass's head was literal in the dream world of the enchanted Bottom. Interestingly, however, when Hermia awakes, into a world which is now for her fallen, she begins to use the same image in a figurative, allusive way. Demetrius, whom she suspects of doing away with Lysander, is a "worm," an "adder," a "serpent":

>   with doubler tongue
> Than thine, thou serpent, never adder stung.
>   [III.ii.72-73]

Where she was controlled by the snake image while dreaming, she here controls it with her conscious mind.

We may note the difference in technique between the conscious and unconscious formulations. A protective distortion operates in the dream; by means of what Freud calls "displacement," Hermia separates Lysander, the beloved, from the serpent with whom she instinctively identifies him. The serpent eats at her heart, as does her love for the perfidious Lysander; and Lysander himself is made merely a passive onlooker. She reproaches him for smiling, but she does not take the further step of blaming him directly for her unhappy condition. The splitting of the menacing figure into two, Lysander and the snake, may thus be considered as a compensatory action on the part of the subconscious. By contrast Hermia feels no such compunctions about accusing the despised Demetrius. She is able to use the snake image as a direct metaphor. The imputation of the "double tongue" is clearly the culmination of her outburst, and this is appropriate, because the question of duplicity and its near relative, ambiguity, is central to the concerns of the play.

Duplicity in Demetrius's case is really a matter of lack of self-knowledge; Berowne's maxim that we "lose our oaths to find ourselves" is again apposite here. Hermia, however, like so many others in this play, is afraid of ambiguity and double meanings and equates them with guile. Fiction to her is a species of deceit. Hers is a regressive attitude, antithetical to the potentialities of dream, which is itself ambiguous and contains many things in one. The activities of condensation and displacement, essential elements in the dream work, are based upon the concept of multiplicity of meaning. In fact, this positive pluralism is at the heart of the whole question of dream, as we began to perceive in our examination of "truth" and "fiction" in *The Taming of the Shrew*. The exchange of shadow and substance, illusion and reality, is implicit in the dream state, and it is the very impatience of the Athenians with such an exchange which renders them insensible for a while to the play's subtlest discoveries. Hermia's experience in the woods, however, is a first step toward a heightened awareness, a necessary incident in the pursuit of self-knowledge. Both specifically Edenic moments in the play thus utilize a fundamentally comic form: the fortunate fall leads ultimately to reintegration, and the apparently innocent unfallen state is seen to be fraught with danger and concomitant with an interior disorder. Experience and change are clearly necessary if the persons of the play are to progress toward a fuller understanding of themselves.

Change itself is essentially an aspect of creativity in the realm of time; from the opening lines of the play it is evident that time, too, is in a state of fallenness or disorder which requires reparation.

> *Theseus:* Four happy days bring in
> Another moon; but O, methinks, how slow
> This old moon wanes! . . .

> *Hippolyta:* Four days will quickly steep
> themselves in night,
> Four nights will quickly dream away the time.
>
> [I.i.2-4,7-8]

Hippolyta uses "dream" here to mean "make to seem unreal." She is suggesting an illusion, the compression of an objective span, "four days and nights," into a subjective experience, "short as any dream." This imaginative compression is achieved in part through the "reality" of theatrical time, the fictive "four days" presented in two hours on the stage. "This palpable-gross play hath well-beguiled / The heavy gait of night," (V.i.366-67) says Theseus at the close of the "Pyramus and Thisby" play, underscoring the point, as the lovers depart for their nuptial beds. With the wedding night comes the promise of fertility, the reunion of Oberon and Titania and the consequent restoration of fertility and change to the landscape. Puck's last speech is appropriately concerned with progeny, since here at the play's close the fertility theme intersects with the theme of creativity and imagination.

Seasonal and temporal change are thus for *A Midsummer Night's Dream* active agents of transformation. With the initial premise "our quarrel has caused a disruption in the seasons" we are abruptly ushered into a world in which dream logic takes precedence over reality. Moreover, this impression is heightened when the proper personae of the wood appear. For one of the essential properties which is shared by Puck and Oberon is the ability to change shape at will—to present the illusion of something they are not. In a long jubilant passage we have already examined. Puck reports his successive metamorphoses from "filly foal" to "roasted crab" and then to "three-foot stool" (II.i.44-57). Setting out to bait the Athenian lovers, he boasts

> Sometime a horse I'll be, sometime a hound,
> A hog, a headless bear, sometime a fire;
> And neigh, and bark, and grunt, and roar, and
> burn,
> Like horse, hound, hog, bear, fire, at every
> turn.
>
> [III.i.107-10]

Similarly Oberon is taxed by Titania for his impersonation of a love-struck shepherd:

>   I know
> When thou hast stolen away from fairy land
> And in the shape of Corin sat all day,
> Playing on pipes of corn, and versing love
> To amorous Phillida.
>
> [II.i.64-68]

Puck's antics seem largely drawn from the native folkloric tradition, though they may owe something as well to the figure of Proteus; Oberon's more explicitly pastoral posturing recalls Jove, another king of gods, and hints at a classical parallel. These associations help to place the play in a larger imaginative context, to give it dimension and depth by suggesting a body of tradition. But in all cases these allusions are subsidiary to the central purpose, which is to develop and refine the growing sense of a dream world whose essence is change.

Physical transformations of this type are of necessity metaphorical in the language of the Athenian lovers: Helena at one time calls herself a "spaniel" (II.i.203), and at another laments "I am as ugly as a bear" (II.ii.94). Oberon, because of his fairy powers, is able to transmute the metaphor into literal reality at will, sending Puck for the flower whose juice will bewitch Titania's eyes:

> What thou seest when thou dost wake,
> Do it for thy true love take;
> Love and languish for his sake.
> Be it ounce, or cat, or bear,
> Pard, or boar with bristled hair,
> In thy eye that shall appear
> When thou wak'st, it is thy dear.
> Wake when some vile thing is near.
>
> [II.ii.27-34]

This is the literal enactment of Helena's homily on blind Cupid, which was only meant as a figure: "Love looks not with the eye but with the mind." The effect is a devastating parody of romantic love, not unlike Mercutio's relentless baiting of Romeo. Women "dote" beyond all control—"How I dote on thee!" exclaims Titania to Bottom (IV.i.46)—and "dote" is throughout Shakespeare's plays a sign word for shallow, meaningless affection; men are literally turned into asses by romantic folly. Further, these literal transformations are echoed and answered by the behavior of the Athenian lovers, since it is a fundamental structural principle of the play that the creatures of the dream world enact literally what is undergone figuratively or metaphorically by the citizens of the court. The result is a kind of visual punning, with the metaphors physically present on the stage, as we have seen in the case of Bottom. At the same time, moreover, this process is a dramatic counterpart of the workings of the dream state, in which ideas and concepts are conveyed as visual symbols.

Metaphor, then, is a condition structurally analogous to the dream state. Moreover, in *A Midsummer Night's Dream,* the spectator's eye is continually directed to the act of metaphormaking, the visible exchange of literal for figurative and fictive. The whole play is almost a tour de force in this regard, and its sustaining creativity is developed, at least in terms of felt energy, as a crucial counterpart to the literal comedic values of fertility and marriage. Almost inevitably, then, the play begins to take on meanings which are at once direct and reflexive. The act of artistic creation, so clearly a conscious parallel to the subconscious activities of memory and imagination, is now brought before our eyes directly in a series of fictional artifacts: a sampler, a ballad, and a play. The availability of art as an ultimate form of transformation, a palpable marriage of dream and reason, emerges as a logical extension of the recognized dream state. Thus Helena, distraught and offended, reminds her childhood playmate of their earlier contentment together:

> We, Hermia, like two artificial gods,
> Have with our needles created both one
> 　flower,
> Both on one sampler, sitting on one cushion,
> Both warbling of one song, both in one key.
>
> [III.ii.203-06]

She pictures them as twin creators, "artificial gods," that is, gods of artifice, although the other meaning of "artificial" is also present in a muted and fallen way. As an image this anticipates the later and more resounding recollection of Polixenes, "We were, fair queen, / Two lads that thought there was no more behind / But such a day tomorrow as today, / And to be boy eternal" (*WT* I.ii.62-65). "Artificial" is thus darkly predictive, but the memory itself remains joyous. The girls are singing, an act with creative associations, as they perform the godlike act of creating flowers, transforming nature into art. The incident itself is lightly stressed within the play, a momentary glimpse rather than a vivid occurrence. As a memory, however, it retains a certain understated power, anticipating the more direct creative moments to come.

A more central incident for the play as a whole, and one crucial to the question of art as transformation, is the recapitulation of "Bottom's Dream." Significantly, as we have noted, the "dream" is of course not a dream at all; as was the case with Christopher Sly and others, the dreamer thinks he is awakening when he is actually moving from one kind of real experience to another. Bottom is the quintessential naïve percipient, and his approach to his "dream" is unfettered by reason:

> 　　　　　　I have had a most rare
> vision. I have had a dream, past the wit of man to
> say what dream it was. Man is but an ass, if he go
> about to expound this dream. Methought I was—
> there is no man can tell what. Methought I was—
> and methought I had—but man is but a patched
> fool if he will offer to say what methought I had.
> The eye of man hath not heard, the ear of man hath
> not seen, man's hand is not able to taste, his tongue
> to conceive, nor his heart to report, what my dream
> was. I will get Peter Quince to write a ballet of this
> dream. It shall be called "Bottom's Dream," because
> it hath no bottom; and I will sing it in the latter end
> of a play, before the duke. Peradventure to make it
> the more gracious, I shall sing it at her death.
>
> [IV.i.205-19]

Daniel Evans, Howard Crossley, and Desmond Barrit as Thisby, Wall, and Pyramus in Act V, Scene i of the Royal Shakespeare Company's 1994 production of A Midsummer Night's Dream.

His text is well chosen; the passage from Saint Paul he quotes in scrambled form[2] is not only a sign of his ignorance but also, and more importantly, of his radical wisdom. Paul is expounding the doctrine of the spirit in its primacy over the letter—an important crux for metaphorical expression itself and one which has a bearing upon the symbolic medium of dream. "God," he says, "hath chosen the foolish things of the world to confound the wise; and God hath chosen the weak things of the world to confound the things which are mighty" (I Cor. 1:27). The allusion is more meaningful to author and audience than it is to Bottom; though he would doubtless acknowledge himself one of the "foolish things of the world," he is not taking the context of his quotation into account—he is intent merely upon utilizing an orthodox expression of wonder. In part, the biblical quotation is thus a learned joke at Bottom's expense. But we have learned by now that this kind of joke is almost always superseded in *A Midsummer Night's Dream* by a greater joke upon the learned perceiver. Bottom's multiple confusion—"the eye of man hath not heard, the ear of man hath not seen, man's hand is not able to taste, his tongue to conceive,

nor his hand to report"—is a synesthetic mixture highly characteristic of dream sensation. The inversion of "eye" and "ear" is a structural parody of the Pauline original; that "tongue" should "conceive," however, is both more profound and more relevant to the interests of the play. In each of these phrases Bottom unconsciously warns us that the senses are untrustworthy; at the same time, his malapropisms are related to the important theme of transformation. He remains himself unaware of these further implications; like the others in the play, he sees and says more than he consciously knows, and like them he is fundamentally a determined realist. But his words speak to us with a special significance; like the porter in *Macbeth,* and the clown in *Antony and Cleopatra,* he unknowingly hits upon the central themes of the play. Despite his intellectual and cultural limitations, his inadvertent role as the wise fool and his willingness to suspend disbelief in the world of dream place him closer to the top than to the bottom of an evaluative scale. This is the same handy-dandy with which we are becoming familiar; what Sidney called with disapprobation "mingling Kinges and Clownes"[3] has a supreme logic of its own in the world of dream.

Language as well as scriptural allusion seems to have a transforming energy of its own within "Bottom's Dream." The pun on "Duke" and "gracious," for example, is doubtless hidden from Bottom himself, following the pattern of a more or less oracular diction, truer than it is conscious of being. The obvious irony of "man is but an ass," and the fleeting invocation of the "patched fool," a figure which throughout Shakespeare's plays is representative of the imaginative capability of mankind, hint at deeper meanings than Bottom can rationally perceive. But perhaps the clearest evidence of the creative impulse to transformation is present on the level of art, in Bottom's avowed desire to have Peter Quince "write a ballet of this dream." The writing—and perhaps the performing—of the ballad is conceived as a kind of verification, the manufacturing of a palpable artifact from the material of a transient experience. In Bottom's eyes to "expound" the dream is a fruitless and foolhardy task; what can be done instead is to transform it into an independent, unchanging work of art. The choice of "ballad" again emphasizes the enormous difference between the intellectual and cultural assumptions of Bottom and the author and audience, while the unerring movement from spiritual transformation through dream to *ekphrasis,* transformation into art, mirrors the informing structural design of the play as a whole.

The ballad of "Bottom's Dream" is of course never performed for the Duke. Instead the play's two audiences—the court of Theseus and ourselves—are privileged to witness an even more gloriously flawed artifact, "the most lamentable comedy, and most cruel death of Pyramus and Thisby," which in its parodic form summarizes and unites the themes of transformation in art, in nature, and in language. In part a failed transformation, a transformation out of control which keeps on transforming, the "Pyramus and Thisby" play is ultimately nothing less than a countermyth for the whole of *A Midsummer Night's Dream,* setting out the larger play's terms in a new and revealing light. In the body of the playlet, the audience sees before it a transformed vision of the events of the play. For "Pyramus and Thisby," while comic in performance, is unrelievedly tragic in conception. In it we see the spectacle of a father who harshly opposes the marriage of his daughter, just as was the case with Egeus and Hermia. But here the result is not reconciliation, but tragic death for the lovers. Similarly the menacing forest of the playlet, which contains the fatal lion, stands as a tragic alternative to the amiable world of the Athenian wood, where animal shapes are mischievous but benevolent, and natural spirits are agents of amelioration rather than of harm. Misconceptions and misinterpretations dominate both situations—the delusion of crossed loves among the Athenians is balanced by Pyramus's mistaken belief in the death of Thisby—but in the cathartic world of art the outcome is death, not marriage. The play-within-a-play thus absorbs and disarms the tragic alternative, the events which did not happen. Art becomes a way of containing and triumphing over unbearable reality.

Here, too, language has its part in demarcating patterns of transformation. The prologue, spoken by Peter Quince, is an accurate forecast of what will take place throughout the play-within-a-play.

> Consider, then, we come but in despite.
>   We do not come, as minding to content you,
> Our true intent is. All for your delight,
>   We are not here.
>   [V.i.112-15]

"Like a tangled chain; nothing impaired, but all disordered" (V.i.125-26) is Theseus's opinion of this performance. The clear intention of the text is amusingly and totally reversed by the delivery of the speaker. "Nothing impaired, but all disordered," is in fact the prevailing condition of the world of *A Midsummer Night's Dream*—a fruitful disordering in a comic realm which leads to a renewed understanding. Its articulation here in a most literal way, through the collision of a rationally intended text and a passionate Peter Quince caught up in his role as actor, makes plain the kinship of unreason and imagination while hinting at their real dangers.

Characteristically, Bottom is vividly aware of the dangers of imagination and illusion, while at the same time he is attracted by them. He is eager, for example, to protect the court audience against untoward effects of illusion. Thus his first thought at the rehearsal of the mechanicals is that "Pyramus must draw a sword to kill himself; which the ladies cannot abide" (III.i.9-11). His answer, again characteristic, is to extend his own part:

> I have a device to make all well.
> Write me a prologue, and let the prologue seem to say, we will do no harm with our swords, and that Pyramus is not killed indeed; and, for the more better assurance, tell them that I Pyramus am not Pyramus, but Bottom the weaver. This will put them out of fear.
>
>   [III.i.15-21]

This is comic in part because the play as we perceive it is hardly realistic enough to contain the dangers he fears for it. But what is most telling about Bottom's plan here is his emphasis upon the literal truth: "Pyramus is not killed indeed"; "I Pyramus am not Pyramus, but Bottom the weaver." He sees the principal fiction of the "Pyramus and Thisby" play as somehow dangerous and misleading. By seeking to destroy or control the illusion, he demonstrates his faith in its power, together with his own limited understanding of that power. The same is true in the case of the lion's part:

"To bring in—God shield us!—a lion among ladies, is a most dreadful thing" (III.i.29-30). Snug the joiner is therefore instructed to reassure the audience:

> If you think I come hither as a lion,
> it were pity of my life. No, I am no such
>   thing. I am a man as other men are.
>
>   [41-43]

"And there indeed," says Bottom, "let him name his name, and tell them plainly, he is Snug the joiner" (44-45). Part of the humor, as is usual with a play-within-a-play, comes from the doubling of the illusion: in trying to strip off artifice ("not Pyramus, but Bottom the weaver"; "tell them plainly, he is Snug the joiner") the speaker substitutes something equally artificial, since "Bottom" and "Snug" are fictions as surely as are Pyramus and the lion. But the limits of illusion for Bottom are not the same as those for the spectator. Distanced by our vision of the whole play, we can see that nothing is but what is not; Bottom is and is not Pyramus the mythical lover, just as he possesses and does not possess an ass's head, and has seemed to Titania both an "angel" (III.i.128) and a monster. The equality of all roles in a fictive world is vividly clear, just as in dreams a "composite person"[4] may simultaneously represent father, teacher, and lover. But to Bottom the artifice of imagination is more literal and more threatening. Insulated by laughter, the spectator can view the doomed lovers and the lurking lion without a sense of tragic identity. To Bottom, for whom they are not comic at all, the imitation and the tragedy are dangerously persuasive. The prologue serves as a deliberate breaking of the frame, paralleled by illusion-shattering asides from Wall, Moon, and Pyramus in the body of the play. In the analogy of dream, these are manifest content and latent thoughts at once, and their clear purpose is to warn against the dangers of the irrational: for the world of art, the lion in the fictional forest; for the subconscious imagination, the equally frightening serpent of Hermia's dream.

But if illusion and the imagination are not without their dangers, they are nonetheless, in the terms of this play, preferable to their radical opposite, "cool reason," in Theseus's phrase. We have already observed the follies of Lysander when he claims to be acting on the promptings of "reason," and considered the wisdom of Bottom's conclusions about reason and love. *A Midsummer Night's Dream* is throughout a celebration of the irrationality of love, not a criticism of the failure of reason. The indistinguishable Athenian lovers and their changeable passions are emblems, not of love's disorderliness, but of its creative power, more akin to the logic of dream than to that of waking reason. Yet it is part of the play's design that none of the Athenians, including even Theseus and Hippolyta, should fully comprehend the lessons of the dream state. It might be said of them that they have had the experience and

missed the meaning—missed it in part because of the preoccupation with reason and the rational which dominates the civilized world of Athens. Puck's highly suggestive closing words, with which we began this examination of *A Midsummer Night's Dream,* are thus fittingly juxtaposed to Theseus's great speech on imagination, a speech so frequently considered out of context that it is rivaled only by Polonius's "This above all, to thine own self be true," for distorted interpretation within the Shakespearean canon.

Theseus's position as a rational lawgiver has been somewhat impugned by the tyrannous sentence he imposes upon Hermia, an exercise of "cool reason" without imagination or generosity which calls into question his own understanding of love. By the end of the play he has amended these rigorous views; he approves the love matches of the Athenians and is generously inclined toward the performers of "Pyramus and Thisby." His fundamental ideas about the relative values of reason and imagination, however, remain largely unchanged, and stand in sharp contrast to the doctrine of dream and the dream state as articulated by events in the interior world.

> *Hippolyta:* 'Tis strange, my Theseus, that
>   these lovers speak of.
> *Theseus:* More strange than true. I never may
>   believe
> These antique fables, nor these fairy toys.
> Lovers and madmen have such seething
>   brains,
> Such shaping fantasies, that apprehend
> More than cool reason ever comprehends.
> The lunatic, the lover, and the poet
> Are of imagination all compact.
> One sees more devils than vast hell can
>   hold,
> That is the madman. The lover, all as frantic,
> Sees Helen's beauty in a brow of Egypt.
> The poet's eye, in a fine frenzy rolling,
> Doth glance from heaven to earth, from earth
>   to heaven;
> And as imagination bodies forth
> The forms of things unknown, the poet's pen
> Turns them to shapes, and gives to airy
>   nothing
> A local habitation and a name.
>
>   [V.i.1-17]

In these lines words like "fantasies" and "fables" are clearly deprecatory, as indeed is "fairy"; fictions and the world of the supernatural, because not "true," become suspect and of little value. Imagination itself is equated with madness and with the irrational—qualities which, in this play of "midsummer madness," have demonstrated enormous energies and the ability to bring about self-knowledge through transformed vision. The triad of lunatic, lover, and poet is meant to demean the roles of poet and lover and comes oddly from a Theseus who has won Hippolyta by the sword. Yet in this association Theseus, like Bottom before him, speaks truer than he knows and defines the very creative and imaginative unities toward which all of *A Midsummer Night's Dream* has been striving. The image of the poet's transforming power to make "shapes" of the "forms of things unknown" follows closely the processes of dream as we have seen them; the "airy nothing" which is the raw material of poetic vision is clearly related to the volatile "nothing" of other early plays. Though "nothing" may be pejorative to Theseus, from his stance of practical rationality, it is akin to Puck's "shadows" and imparts the same sense of transcendent wonder. "Airy nothing" is clearly an appropriate figure for the fairy folk who inhabit the Athenian wood. It is equally telling as a description of the subconscious dreams and conscious fictions which preoccupy the play's human characters. And, even more, it is an emblem of the spirit of creative gaiety which is so important to the festive world of *A Midsummer Night's Dream*. Theseus himself intends his words in a critical and instructive sense as a defense of reason. Yet with the ambiguity so characteristic of utterances throughout the play, he sets forth, as well, an unexampled praise of imagination.

Theseus would partition experience into the true and the false, the dream and the reality, much as did Christopher Sly in *The Taming of the Shrew:* "Or do I dream? Or have I dreamed till now?" But the transforming effect of the dream world upon the Athenian lovers has been to teach them to suspend disbelief in order to inhabit two worlds at once. "It seems to me / That yet we sleep, we dream" says Demetrius (IV.i.194-95) as the lovers follow Theseus out of the wood, and significantly, a moment later, "Why then we are awake. Let's follow him, / And by the way let us recount our dreams" (199-200). This final impulse to recount is a counterpart of the ballad projected by Bottom, a creative transformation turning experience and insight into a self-contained verbal form. Like the "winter's tale" and *The Winter's Tale,* a symbolic artifact within the play and the play itself as a symbolic artifact, the dreams in *A Midsummer Night's Dream* have attained an important reflexive function as emblems of the visionary experience. In Hippolyta's perceptive phrase, the lovers see now with "minds transfigured" (V.i.24)—the ultimate turning inward of the world of dream. Moreover, the impulse to recount and remember is merged with the impulse to return, so that the redemptive energies of the play come to rest at last in a harmonious moment of self-realization. At the last, as Puck alone remains upon the stage, the "shadows" of *A Midsummer Night's Dream* have become inexhaustibly evocative, "no more yielding but a dream," in a dramatic world where dreams are a reliable source of vision and heightened insight, consistently truer than the reality they seek to interpret and transform.

Notes

[1] It is interesting to note that Quintilian (*Institutio Oratione* VIII.2.6) equates *translatio,* "transfer," with the Greek figure Μεταφορά. See Ernst Robert Curtius, *European Literature and the Latin Middle Ages,* trans. Willard R. Trask (New York: Pantheon Books, 1952), p. 128.

[2] "Eye hath not seen, nor ear heard, neither have entered into the heart of man, the things which God hath prepared for them that love him" (I Cor. 2:9).

[3] *Defence of Poesie,* in *The Prose Works of Sir Phillip Sidney,* ed. Albert Feuillerat (Cambridge: Cambridge University Press, 1962), II, 39.

[4] See Freud, *Interpretation of Dreams,* pp. 297ff.

Jan Lawson Hinley (essay date 1987)

SOURCE: "Expounding the Dream: Shaping Fantasies in *A Midsummer Night's Dream,*" in *Psychoanalytic Approaches to Literature and Film,* edited by Maurice Charney and Joseph Reppen, Fairleigh Dickinson University Press, 1987, pp. 120-38.

[*In the following essay, Hinley contends that in* A Midsummer Night's Dream, *Shakespeare uses the "accepted illogic of the dream" as a means of examining the psychological basis of the lovers' sexual anxieties. Hinley concludes that in the end the lovers establish stable romantic relationships within the boundaries of patriarchal society.*]

The movement from sexual confusion and tentative bondings to sexual certainty and mutually desired and socially beneficial unions, particularly significant in Shakespearean "green world" comedies, is nowhere so clearly marked as in *A Midsummer Night's Dream*. There Shakespeare, moving from the structured Athenian world to the supernatural night world of the forest, is freed by the accepted illogic of the dream to explore the psychological roots of his characters' sexual conflicts.[1] Two dreams are at the center of *A Midsummer Night's Dream:* the quadruple dream of the four lovers and the triple dream of Bottom, Titania, and Oberon. By examining these dreams we can reach into Shakespeare's controlling "dream" of the tensions and difficulties seemingly inherent to the process of establishing and maintaining the bond of reciprocal sexual/romantic love. A third "dream," the play of Pyramus and Thisbe, rehearsed in the forest but presented before the court, presents in burlesque nightmare form the disastrous results of unmediated sexual tensions. Through these dreams individual sexual anxieties are released and transformed, and social harmony is reestablished.

The play begins in a determinedly male-oriented society. Theseus, the ruler of Athens, is in the process of celebrating his triumph, soon to be consummated in marriage, over the Amazon, Hippolyta. His words imply that his struggle, though difficult, is over, and that he is about to "lock" up his happiness by the marriage ceremony: "Hippolyta, I wooed thee with my sword, / And won thy love doing thee injuries; / But I will wed thee in another key, / With pomp, with triumph, and with reveling" (1.1.16-19).[2] The struggle between Theseus and Hippolyta was at least a direct conflict between male and female, but Egeus, Lysander, and Demetrius introduce two other conflicts that deny the woman involved any substantial role in deciding her fate. The first is the struggle between two rivals for the same woman, Hermia; the second is the insistence of Egeus, Hermia's father, that his fatherly prerogatives include the right to place Demetrius, his approved surrogate, in his daughter's bed. Egeus's determination to control his daughter's sexuality and Demetrius's tacit assumption that his masculine privileges include fickleness toward one woman and bullying sexual dominance over another, reinforced by the patriarchal structure of Athenian society, are supported by Theseus, the embodiment of the dominant male as ruler and lover.

Patriarchal attitudes thus block the lovers' efforts to work out reciprocal relationships: marriage is treated primarily as a matter of competition between younger males for the approval of a dominant older male. Demetrius, the most overtly problematic lover, can ignore Hermia's rejection by focusing on Lysander as its cause, and Egeus's approval is accepted by him as more significant than Hermia's right of choice. Correspondingly, this society also negates the selfhood of the young women of the play. In Athens Hermia is not an individual, but "as a form in was, / By him [her father] imprinted" (1.1.49-50), and Helena, having lost Demetrius's love, can think of no recourse but to lose her "self" as well, to be "translated" into the desired love object, Hermia.

Hermia and Lysander, followed by Helena and Demetrius, flee Athenian society. Their movement, to borrow some of the categories used by David Young (1966), is from waking to dream, from reason to imagination, from sanity to madness, from limitation to freedom, and from order to anarchy. It is also a movement from exercise of conscious choice to helplessness before the apparent caprice of unconscious fantasies. Their dream experiences in the forest clarify, through exaggeration, through role exchange, and through the irrationality of sexual hysteria, the psychological sources of their sexual anxieties. Though they share the dream the audience witnesses, their minds being "transfigured so together," the dream is different for each (5.1.24). Each dream enables the lover to "work through" internal blocks to mutual love. Once these blocks are overcome, Egeus's patriarchal authority is seen, properly, as secondary to the desires of the lovers, and the marriages can be celebrated.

Of the four lovers Hermia has received the most individual comment because she alone has an overt dream within the play. Her dream, a symbolic but "true" reflection of her experience, has been thoroughly analyzed by M. D. Faber (1972) and by Norman Holland (1980). Faber sees it as a reflection of Hermia's fear of sexual consummation of her love. She dreams that "a serpent eat my heart away," while Lysander "sat smiling at his cruel prey" (2.2.149-150). The phallic serpent (also a symbol of male inconstancy) is carefully disassociated by Hermia's dreaming mind from the "smiling Lysander," but as Faber points out, the dream reflects the anxieties aroused by Lysander's efforts to share a "bank" with Hermia; "One turf shall serve as pillow for us both, / One heart, one bed, two bosoms, and one troth" (2.2.41-42). As a defense mechanism used "to disguise something that is wished for" (Faber 1972, 182), the dream seems an appropriate response from a young virgin who finds herself alone in a wild forest, suddenly unprotected by the external forces of society from the power of those attractions that have led to the elopement.

Holland, in his richer reading of the dream, emphasizes Hermia's separation of Lysander into two aspects, the "sexual, hostile, intrusive being right on top of her" [the snake] and the "milder but also hostile man at some distance" (6). Holland sees Hermia caught between the fear that union with Lysander will be a "deadly possession that would prey upon and eat away her very being" and the fear that rejection of this union will lead to "another kind of cruelty through distance and indifference. . . ." (9).

Seen in a larger context, Hermia's fears are not merely irrational and sexual, but reflect anxieties entirely appropriate to Athenian social pressures. She is fleeing a father whose unreasoning opposition to Lysander, a man of rank and fortune equal or superior to those of Demetrius, suggests that Hermia is the object of her father's incestuous desires, desires he can appease by delivering her "virgin patent" to a man he can see as an extension of himself. To Lysander's scornful remark, "You have her father's love, Demetrius; . . do you marry him," Egeus affirms, "True, he hath my love, / And what is mine my love shall render him. / And she is mine, and all my right of her / I do estate unto Demetrius" (1.1.93-98). She is also fleeing a law that allows her only the choices of marriage to a man she hates, a lifetime of enforced chastity, or death. The openly threatening third male in the play, Demetrius, has betrayed her close friend and seeks to enforce his claims against her expressly stated objections. Her only recourse is to escape with Lysander, but this involves Hermia in a tremendous risk. She becomes utterly dependent on Lysander's "love and courtesy" (2.2.56).

Her underlying fears about the course she has chosen appear in the oath with which she seals her agreement to meet him in the forest:

> And by that fire which burned the Carthage
>   queen,
> When the false Troyan under sail was seen,
> By all the vows that ever men have broke,
> In number more than ever women spoke, . . .
>   (1.1.173-76)

A rueful regret for the tranquil existence she led before loving Lysander comes out in her words to Helena, "Before the time I did Lysander see, / Seemed Athens as a paradise to me. / O, then, what graces in my love do dwell, / That he hath turned a heaven unto a hell" (1.1.204-07). As her dream implies, Lysander is the serpent who has turned Hermia away from her state of Edenic presexual innocence. Her hopes for the future rest on a Lysander who is significantly different in his relationship with her from the other men in the play, a Lysander whose love does not "lie."

Hermia's nightmare, expressive of her fears of unleashed male sexuality and betrayal, finds almost immediate confirmation in the encompassing midsummer dream experience. Her fears of phallic aggressiveness are transferred to Demetrius, whom she accuses of having slain Lysander in his sleep. Demetrius becomes the "adder," the "serpent" with "double tongue," who has "stung" Lysander (3.2.71-73). Her fears of male betrayal are even more graphically realized when she is rejected by both the "inconstant" Demetrius and the trusted Lysander. The inexplicability of male desires, which so bewilders Helena and which forms the burden of her conversations with Hermia ("The more I hate, the more he follows me." "The more I love, the more he hateth me." [1.1.198-99]), is dramatically underlined for Hermia by Lysander's sudden hatred. Hermia's shaky reliance on her own "vision" of love, "I would my father looked but with mine eye" (1.1.56), abandons her as she enters the "dark night, that from the eye his function takes" (3.2.177) to discover insult and rejection. In lines which, though expressing his loathing for her, connect him with the serpent of her dreams, Lysander orders, "Vile thing, let loose, / Or I will shake thee from me like a serpent!" (3.2.261).

While Hermia undergoes the nightmare fall from desired to despised love object, Helena experiences the opposite movement. Her first-scene wish, to be "translated" to Hermia, to "catch" her "favor," her "voice," her "eye," her "tongue," is apparently granted, for both Demetrius and Lysander now swear to Helena the love they earlier swore to Hermia. Helena, not Hermia, becomes the object of their petulant male rivalry. But Helena's response to this is frantic disbelief and intense dismay. Demetrius's hatred, at first a devastating blow to her self-esteem, may now protect

her against the undependable idealizations of male romantic passion and the threat of sexual engagement feared by Hermia in her dream. Perhaps, even, the alacrity with which she informs Demetrius of the elopement plans reflects an unconscious preference for a continuation of the status quo. Seeing Hermia as the cause of Demetrius's sudden transfer of affection, Helena decides at once to tell him how he may prevent her rival's escape:

> For ere Demetrius looked on Hermia's eyne,
> He hailed down oaths that he was only mine;
> And when this hail some heat from Hermia
>   felt,
> So he dissolved, and show'rs of oaths did
>   melt.
> I will go tell him of fair Hermia's flight.
>   (1.1.242-46)

This betrayal insures that Demetrius will stay in pursuit of Hermia as Helena continues in pursuit of him. Her excuse for this apparently self-defeating gesture, that she means "to enrich my pain, / To have his sight thither and back again," indicates the masochistic delight she has begun to take in the self-abasement of unreciprocated love (1.1.250-51). Reflecting the psychology of love most common in the Renaissance, Helena, like the Petrarchan lover, transforms Demetrius's cruelty, something "base and vile," into "form and dignity" (1.1.232-33). His "justified" scorn of such an unworthy lover proves his worth by denying her own.

The fretful self-pity Helena expresses in Athens finds exaggerated release in the woods, and she wallows in the abjectness of her unloved state, making her sufferings an excuse for a cloying possessiveness:

> I am your spaniel; and, Demetrius,
> The more you beat me, I will fawn on you.
> Use me but as your spaniel, spurn me, strike
>   me,
> Neglect me, lose me; only give me leave,
> Unworthy as I am, to follow you.
> What worser place can I beg in your love—
> And yet a place of high respect with me—
> Than to be used as you use your dog.
>   (2.1.202-10)

In Athens her shattered self-esteem could take some comfort from the good opinions of society, "Through Athens I am thought as fair as she' (1.1.227), but in her "dream" Demetrius becomes "all the world. / Then how can it be said I am alone, / When all the world is here to look on me?" (2.1.224-26). His opinion is the only opinion. Self-abasement is expressed as a desire for self-annihilation, either through rape or murder, "I'll follow thee and make a heaven of hell, / To die upon the hand I love so well" (2.1.243-44).

By the time she encounters Lysander she has concluded that she is "as ugly as a bear," (2.2.94), and accepted Hermia's manifest superiority: "What wicked and dissembling glass of mine / Made me compare with Hermia's sphery eyne?" (2.2.98-99). Helena's exaggerated acceptance of her own worthlessness at least defends her ego from the pain of further rejection, and her abrupt change of status from all-despised to all-desired is a kind of psychic rug-pulling. Recoiling from the problematic sexual union with the unpredictable male, Helena seeks to renew the childhood innocence of an earlier oneness with Hermia:

> We, Hermia, like two artificial gods,
> Have with our needles created both one
>   flower,
> Both on one sampler, sitting on one cushion,
> Both warbling of one song, both in one key;
> As if our hands, our sides, voices, and
>   minds,
> Had been incorporate. So we grew together,
> Like to a double cherry, seeming parted,
> But yet a union in partition;
> Two lovely berries molded on one stem;
> So, with two seeming bodies, but one heart; . . .
>
> (3.2.203-12)

Having earlier desired to be transformed into Hermia in order to win Demetrius's love, Helena now wishes to merge with Hermia to avoid the impetuous onslaught of male desires.

Lysander's first love speech to Helena contained an image of visual penetration, "Transparent Helena! Nature shows art, / That through thy bosom makes me see thy heart" (2.2.104-5); Demetrius now finds her lips tempting, "those kissing cherries," and her hand, "this princess of pure white" (3.2.140, 144). In response, Helena fearfully withdraws hands, cherry lips, and heart into the self-contained image of two virgin sisters creating "both one flower." Hermia's rejection of this childhood female bond and her subsequent discovery that Lysander is now in love with Helena precipitate the two women into the state of sexual rivalry that heretofore characterized the two men. In their rivalry they seek tangible physical "reasons" for the switch of affections—short versus tall, brunette versus blonde— but this attempt to explain the distinctions perceived by Lysander and Demetrius degenerates into hysterical declarations that such distinctions do exist and can explain such bewildering masculine inconstancy.

Helena's idyllic memory of "school day friendship" gives way to "She was a vixen when she went to school; / And though she is but little, she is fierce," while she characterizes herself as "a right maid for my cowardice," and "simple" and "fond" (3.2.324-25, 302, 317). Helena works to assert an identity now independent of Hermia, while Hermia tries to hold onto the selfhood

and bond she fought to establish in Athens, "Am I not Hermia? Are not you Lysander? / I am as fair as I was erewhile" (3.2.273-74). Having turned from the artificial image of childhood sameness, Helena and Hermia seek as well to separate themselves from the image of woman as stereotyped, idealized, de-individualized sexual object for Lysander and Demetrius. They assert their particularity in the face of that aspect of male desire that responds not to the woman's reality but to the fantasies projected on her by the male ego which, "if it would but apprehend some joy, / It comprehends some bringer of that joy" (5.1.19-20).

This night encounter with passionate sexual love divorced from valid distinction is an encounter with the love symbolized by the potion placed in the lovers' eyes. Oberon's description of the genesis of the potion connects it with unleased priapic sexual energy, "A certain aim he [Cupid] took / At a fair vestal throned by the west, / And loosed his love shaft smartly from his bow, / As it should pierce a hundred thousand hearts" (2.1.157-60). The "quenching" of "young Cupid's fiery shaft" by the chaste moon serves only to deflect this energy elsewhere; "It fell upon a little western flower, / Before milk-white now purple with love's wound, . . ." (2.1.161, 66-67). In this account aggressive sexual energy, not its object, is important, a sexual energy that "wounds" and deflowers, that causes those who feel it to "madly dote" (2.1.171). This love is frightening because its discriminations keep no company with reason.

On the human level it is the two men who feel the force of this potion, for their immaturities in love reflect the competitive and self-centered nature of their desires. They denigrate the woman rejected by the rival and their desires increase in ratio to the increase of competition. The first scene of the play seems to distinguish between Demetrius, the "spotted and inconstant man," and Lysander, the true lover (1.1.110). But it also suggests their basic similarity, a sameness that engenders strong competition (Nevo 1980). "I am, my lord," Lysander asserts, "as well derived as he, / As well possessed; my love is more than his; / My fortunes every way as fairly ranked / (If not with vantage) as Demetrius'" (1.1.99-102). Demetrius's potion-inspired change from love of Hermia to love of Helena suggests that his love for Hermia originated in his unconscious attempts to mimic and outdo his rival/ double, Lysander. While in the spell-induced sleep he must hear, at least subliminally, Lysander's avowals of love for Helena, for he wakes, on cue, to protest at "Demetrius loves her, and he loves not you" (3.2.136).

In the following scene of confused love, Demetrius and Lysander reverse roles in a manner similar to Hermia and Helena: Demetrius becomes the preferred lover, Lysander the lover rejected by the desired woman and pursued by the despised. Lysander's responses in this case mimic Demetrius's earlier postures. Demetrius has threatened Helena with violence, "Or, if thou follow me, do not believe / But I shall do thee mischief in the wood" (2.1.236-37), and desired to remove his rival by murdering him, "I'd rather give his carcass to my hounds" (3.2.64). Lysander now insults Hermia, "Out, tawny Tartar, out! / Out loathed med'cine! O hated potion, hence!" (3.2.63-64), and wishes to destroy Demetrius, "O how fit a word / Is that vile name to perish on my sword" (2.2.106-7). Like Demetrius, he avoids facing sexual rejection from Helena by focusing on his rival as the only impediment: "Now follow, if thou dar'st, to try whose right / Of thine or mine, is most in Helena" (3.2.336-37).

Lysander is guilty of only one infidelity, and his lapse is usually attributed to Puck's carelessness. But he, like Hermia, is affected by the tensions Athenian society has created by opposing social and individual desires. He sees love as a brief and uncertain phenomenon, attacked by the hostile forces of nature and society, "war, death, or sickness" (1.1.142) and, in itself, unstable:

> Swift as a shadow, short as any dream,
> Brief as the lightning in the collied night,
> That, in a spleen, unfolds both heaven and
>   earth,
> And ere a man hath power to say, "Behold!"
> The jaws of darkness do devour it up:
> So quick bright things come to confusion.
>   (1.1.144-49)

In his attempt to flee with Hermia from society's hostile power he loses his way, and his desire to find solace with Hermia is rebuffed with, "Lie further off yet, do not lie so near" (2.2.44). His protestations of innocence are gently but firmly rejected, "Lie further off, . . . So far be distant" (2.2.57,60). It is at that moment that Puck anoints his eyes; he opens them to see not the surprisingly cold Hermia but the lovelorn and, as he thinks, sexually eager, Helena. His subsequent behavior revenges Hermia's slight and brings to a climax his own quasi-sibling rivalry with Demetrius.

The abortive fight in the woods becomes a substitute sexual consummation, where would-be murderous triumph over the competing male could prove the masculinity they have not achieved in heterosexual coupling. As they pursue each other with weapons "drawn and ready," the language, particularly Puck's, suggests the frustrated sexual desires that fuel their anger, "Up and down, up and down, / I will lead them up and down: . . ." "Speak! In some bush? Where dost thou hide thy head?" "And wilt not come? Come, recreant! Come, thou child! / I'll whip thee with a rod. He is defiled / That draws a sword on thee." "We'll try no manhood here." "Coward, why com'st thou not?" "Thou . . . dar'st not stand, . . ." (3.2.396-424).

The end of the scene finds all four lovers assembled on stage in a state of confused exhaustion. When they wake, they do not understand what has happened; hatred has been changed to "gentle concord," and the entangled chain of desires has been sorted out. Within the dream experience they entered a state of frightening release, of almost Dionysian excess. Through role exchange and the purging of excess, this nightmare/dream in the woods has managed to move all the lovers closer to the standard of mature reciprocal sexuality that Shakespeare treats as the necessary prerequisite for festive comedy marriage. Demetrius and Lysander have acted out both their male rivalry and their mixture of desire and hatred toward the women who have the power to frustrate passionate desires or the bad taste to demand fidelity once desire has vanished, to demand, in other words, that love be more than a mere function of appetite. Demetrius can now return to his original choice, Helena, the woman he apparently chose before competition with Lysander led him to claim Hermia. When awake he rejects his role as Egeus's surrogate and Lysander's competitor for the role of Helena's lover. His love for Hermia, "an idle gaud / Which in my childhood I did dote on." based on male competition rather than "natural taste," has been outgrown in the night's emblematic movement from adolescence to adulthood (4.1.170-71).

The women, as well, have been altered by the experiences of the night. Hermia's dream, symbolizing her precarious balance between the phallic devouring serpent-lover and the maliciously smiling detached-lover, is tilted in favor of an acceptance of the sexual union with Lysander as preferable to the loneliness of abandonment and rejection. Helena, whose self-abasement led toward degradation and loss of autonomous identity, reasserts herself in opposition to Hermia and to the tormenting male lovers. Rather than blame the blind "boy Cupid" for the disappointments of love, she accuses the two men of lack of "pity, grace, or manners"; accepts the undesirability of merger with Hermia; and attempts to leave, saying, "'Tis partly my own fault, . . ." (3.2.241, 243). Helena's newfound sense of self, receiving the daylight reinforcement of Demetrius's vows of love, permits her to give to Demetrius some of the autonomy she has gained. In words that reflect her uncertainty about the night, but that also grant Demetrius both mutuality and autonomy, she speaks of finding "Demetrius like a jewel, / Mine own, and not mine own" (4.1.192-93). Hermia's moves toward the necessary trust in the loved male, and Helena's reassertion of herself as Helena, neither Demetrius's spaniel nor Hermia's double, have prepared them for the daylight return to mature reciprocal love.

This concord among the lovers is also important in reconciling Lysander and Hermia to society. Theseus not only supports the new couplings, he shares his own wedding ceremony with the lovers. They are reintegrated into the now more flexible patriarchal society of Athens. Demetrius, still uncertain of this approval and of the events of the night, asks:

> Are you sure
> That we are awake? It seems to me
> That yet we sleep, we dream. Do not you think
> The duke was here, and bid us follow him?
>
> (4.1.193-96)

Hermia's response, her last words in the play, testify to the restoration of parental bonds, if not of parental tyranny, "Yea, and my father" (197).

The lovers' night in the woods, a "dream" reflection of their baffled and immature desires, receives in turn its own reflection, the mirror of "art," Ovid's tale of Pyramus and Thisbe as "disfigured" by Bottom and his crew. Critics have often pointed out how this play parallels the lovers' flight to the woods, but reverses the outcome so that irrational love leads to death rather than happiness. But this play also rehearses "most obscenely and courageously" (1.2.105), the societal blocking, tentative bondings, and superficial apprehensions experienced by the lovers. The basic source of these confusions is the wall, symbolic of the hostility of the fathers, which "did these lovers sunder" (5.1.132). The wall, whose "stones" are cursed by Pyramus, is played by the actor who was first assigned the role of Pyramus's father, Tom Snout the tinker (both names suggesting masculine sexual activity). Blocked by the wall, the lovers, though full of hyperbolic passion, can scarcely recognize each other:

> *Pyramus.* I see a voice: now will I to the
>   chink,
> To spy and I can hear my Thisbe's face
> *Thisbe.* My love thou art, my love I think.
>
> (5.1.192-94)

They associate themselves specifically with classical prototypes whose names are shared by two of the play's lovers, as Pyramus declares, "like Limander, am I trusty still," and Thisbe rejoins, "And I like Helen, till the Fates me kill," these lines seeming to glance at Lysander's proclaimed trustworthiness and Helena's masochistic devotion (5.1.196-97). The dismal outcome of the love is foreshadowed by the bungled vows, "Not Shafalus to Procrus was so true." "As Shafalus to Procrus, I to you" (5.1.198-99). Unfortunately, Cephalus accidentally killed his wife, Procris.

The thwarted sexual development and frustration of the lovers blocked by this recalcitrant wall is bawdily suggested by a hodgepodge of vaginal, phallic, and anal allusions (Goldstein 1973; Gui 1952-53). The wall suggests both the female and male sexual organs. The phrases "the crannied hole, or chink," "the cranny," "right and sinister,"; the stage direction, *Pyramus draws*

near the wall; and Pyramus's address to "Thou wall, O sweet and lovely wall, / Show me thy chink, . . ." all allude to the female genitalia aspects of the wall (5.1.158-77). Thisbe, for her part, is unintentionally scatological when declaiming, "My cherry lips have often kissed thy stones, / Thy stones with lime and hair knit up in thee," and "I kiss the wall's hole, not your lips at all" (5.1.190-91, 201).

The ill-fated elopement occurs at night, but a night presided over by a moon that seems to represent the absence of any female influence for this travestied patriarchal tragedy.[3] The role of moonshine is enacted by Starveling the tailor, who was originally cast for the role of Thisbe's mother, a tailor often being mocked as an effeminate man. Poor Starveling, who as the man in the moon appears with a lantern that represents the moon, a thorn bush, and a dog, is soundly ridiculed by his courtly audience, for his inept portrayal reduces to "moonshine" the female powers of nature represented by Titania. The moon's gender is further distorted by Demetrius, who suggests the "horned moon" is a cuckold, and by Pyramus, who confuses it with its masculine opposite by thanking it for its "sunny beams" (5.1.270). Under this "disfigured" moon, Thisbe encounters not her lover, Pyramus, but the lion, who frightens her from the appointed rendezvous. The lion, one of the "vile" things Oberon wished Titania to love, humorously represents the malevolent potential of patriarchal authority. Played by Snug, the joiner, it "joins" these lovers in death rather than in marriage, an echo of Egeus's earlier savagery. The lion's staining of the mantle with "bloody mouth" is misinterpreted by Pyramus, who, assuming "lion vile hath here deflow'red my dear," kills himself in grief (5.1.143, 290). Pyramus's death is comically described by Thisbe as a kind of castration:

> O Sisters Three,
>   Come, Come to me,
> With hands as pale as milk;
>   Lay them in gore,
> Since you have shore
> With shears his thread of silk.
>
> (5.1.335-40)

Like Pyramus, she kills herself with the phallic sword, deaths that playfully recall the sexually motivated sword play and suicidal hyperboles at the end of act 3.

This play is comic not only because it is so clumsy, but also because it carries one step further the sexual anxieties the lovers experience. In the main plot the four lovers struggle to find appropriate, self-enhancing outlets for their powerful though unfocused sexual desires and to bring their desires and the prescriptive demands of society into harmony. Male sexual dominance in the green world (embodied in Oberon) reinforces male social dominance in Athens (represented by Theseus), and the lovers arrive at stable love relationships within the framework of an orderly and, finally, benevolent patriarchal society. In the Pyramus and Thisbe play, however, anxiety about sexual roles intensifies into confusion about sexual gender. The four lovers' painful attempts to make meaningful distinctions about sexual objects is transformed into a ludicrous lack of gender distinctions. Snout (the wall) possesses hole, chink, and stones; the horned moon shines "sunny beams." Even the lion, a traditional symbol of lordly male dominance, is travestied—itself both male and female ("a lion fell, nor else no lion's dam"), it is a "fox for valor," "goose for discretion," and, far from deflowering Thisbe in "wildest rage," "mouses" her discarded mantle and flees (5.1.222, 230, 231, 221).

The ineptness of the actors not only undercuts hilariously the stereotyped masculine and feminine roles they play, but also mocks the gender distinctions these roles reflect. As Demetrius comments, "A mote will turn the balance, which Pyramus, which Thisbe, is the better; he for a man, God warr'nt us; she for a woman, God bless us!" (5.1.317-19). This palpable-gross play thus gains much of its explosive comic vitality by presenting an implicitly anarchic sexual world. Psychic health and sexual identity being interdependent, this loss of gender distinction is the true stuff of nightmare, the suppressed terror that edges the lovers' dream actions with violence and hysteria. The linked breakdown of sexual gender and social role in the play-within-the-play mocks and exaggerates the confusions experienced by the lovers. By its "merry and tragic" blurring of sexual distinctions it prepares us to celebrate the ordered sexuality of the traditional marriages at the play's end.

The most significant preparation for this affirmation, however, occurs in the dream at the center of *A Midsummer Night's Dream,* the dream of the union of Titania and Bottom. This dream, which parallels the lovers' experience in the wood, finds release for tensions felt at a deeper level than those transitory uncertainties characteristic of adolescent romantic passion. Infinitely suggestive, the dream has been alternately interpreted as comic, mystic, or grotesque; it mirrors the play as reflected in the metamorphic eye of the viewer.[4] At the bottom of the dream one sees the harried critic peering myopically out of the ass's head. The following reading is one attempt to respond to the multiple resonances of this elusively complex dream.

Part of this complexity is caused by the fact that the dream, usually called Bottom's dream, belongs to three characters. Like the dream of the lovers, which is a single dream for the audience but four impinging dreams for the lovers, this dream shifts meaning as its perspectives shift from Bottom to Titania to the voyeur and creator of the dream, Oberon. Behind these perspectives is Shakespeare, who like Oberon creates the dream and like Bottom turns it into art, who dreams the dream the audience enters.

Oberon's dream is a response to Titania's challenge to his patriarchal authority and an attempt to reestablish outraged male dominance. Their quarrel, as the "parents and original," has disordered the world of nature (2.1.117). The immediate cause of the quarrel, Titania's refusal to give Oberon the changeling Indian boy, serves as the symbol of an encompassing breakdown of the trust and reciprocity necessary to a mutually satisfying bond of love. Though Puck, who first recounts the argument, ascribes Oberon's rage to his desire to have the boy as a "knight of his train," the first exchange with Oberon furnishes Titania with an earlier source of hostility, Oberon's infidelity. Their opening exchange establishes Titania's denial to Oberon of her sexual favors and companionship and Oberon's angered attempt to make her resume her proper subordinate position:

> *Titania.* What, jealous Oberon! Fairy, skip
>   hence.
> I have forsworn his bed and company.
> *Oberon.* Tarry, rash wanton; am not I thy
>   lord?
> *Titania.* Then I must be thy lady: but I know
> When thou has stolen away from fairy land
> And in the shape of Corin sat all day,
> Playing on pipes of corn, and versing love
> To amorous Phillida. . . .
>
>   (2.1.61-68)

Oberon defends himself by accusing Titania of similar faults, but she rejects his accusations and gives a long description of the harmful results of their quarrels. Oberon's response is simply, "Do you amend it, then; it lies in you: / Why should Titania cross her Oberon? / I do but beg a little changeling boy, / To be my henchman" (2.1.118-21).

In reply, Titania details a picture of feminine companionship that excludes Oberon and that, more threateningly, seems to portray a female nuclear "family," Titania and her pregnant votaress, of joyous and fulfilled sexuality independent of the male:

> Her mother was a vot'ress of my order,
> And in the spiced Indian air, by night,
> Full often hath she gossiped by my side,
> And sat with me on Neptune's yellow sands,
> Marking the embarked traders on the flood;
> When we have laughed to see the sails
>   conceive
> And grow big-bellied with the wanton wind;
> Which she, with pretty and with swimming gait
> Following—her womb then rich with my
>   young squire—
> Would imitate, and sail upon the land, . . .
>   (2.1.123-32)

This female bond, intensified by the woman's death in childbirth, Titania now values more than her chafing marital bond with Oberon: "And for her sake do I rear up her boy, / And for her sake I will not part with him" (2.1.136-37). Titania's possession of the boy is a further defiance of male authority and denial of male paternal rights in that he was "stolen from an Indian king," the boy's father (2.1.22). This Indian boy Titania now makes "all her joy," and "jealous" Oberon insists that the boy is the price of their reconciliation (2.1.26). Titania's rebellious refusal to pay that price arouses Oberon's desire for vengeance, "Thou shalt not from this grove / Till I torment thee for this injury" (2.1.146-47).

This "torment," Oberon's revenge, is his dream. It is a dream of love reduced to animality, for it limits unleashed sexual energy to purely animal gratification. Oberon will use the magic potion to create another kind of conceiving than that of Titania's votaress, to make Titania "full of hateful fantasies" (2.1.258). Titania shall "pursue," with the "soul of love," "some vile thing," "lion, bear, or wolf, or bull," "meddling monkey," "busy ape," "ounce, or cat, or bear / pard, or boar with bristled hair" (2.1.180-82;2.2.30-31, 34). His imagination ranges over phallic, savage, or grotesque animals.

Jan Kott (1964) has, perhaps, responded most perceptively to the essential brutality and male wish-fulfillment of Oberon's dream, though he generalizes this view as the single perspective the dream represents: "The love scenes between Titania and the ass must seem at the same time real and unreal, fascinating and repulsive. They are to rouse rapture and disgust, terror and abhorrence. They should seem at the same time strange and fearful." He compares them to the "fearful visions of Bosch" an to the "animal eroticism" of Goya. "Titania has embraced the ass's head and traces his hairy hooves with her fingers. She is strikingly white. . . . The ass's hooves are entwining her more and more strongly. He has put his head on her breasts. The ass's head is heavy and hairy. . . . Titania has closed her eyes: she is dreaming about pure animality" (82-86).

But the dream of animality belongs only to Oberon. Hermia's dream, reflective of her fears of Lysander, is from another angle reflective of Oberon's malicious delight at Puck's message, "My mistress with a monster is in love." "This falls out better than I could devise," is Oberon's response—the smiling lover who watches the serpent at the breast of his beloved (3.2.6, 36). Oberon's cruelty is linked to his sense of loss. When setting out his plan to corrupt Titania's imagination with the magic potion, he describes his sleeping, no longer accessible wife in terms conveying the enchantment which that picture holds for him:

> I know a bank where the wild thyme blows,
> Where oxlips and the nodding violet grows,
> Quite overcanopied with luscious woodbine,

> With sweet musk roses, and with eglantine.
> There sleeps Titania sometime of the night,
> Lulled in these flowers with dances and
>   delight; . . .
>
> (2.1.249-54)

Excluded from this Edenic vision, Oberon will destroy it. He will replace the child in Titania's bower with a savage phallic extension of himself. The charms the fairies sing are vain attempts to protect their queen from desecration:

> You spotted snakes with double tongue,
>   Thorny hedgehogs, be not seen;
> Newts and blindworms, do no wrong,
>   Come not near our Fairy Queen.
>
> Philomele, with melody
> Sing in our sweet lullaby;
>
> . . . . .
>
> Weaving spiders, come not here;
>   Hence, you long-legged spinners, hence!
> Beetle black, approach not near;
>   Worm nor snail do no offense.
>
> (2.2.9-14, 20-23)

The double-tongued snake, recalling Hermia's fears of phallic intrusion and male inconstancy; the "thorny," hence dangerous, hedgehog; the slimy and repulsive newts and blindworms (all which later appear among the disgusting ingredients of *Macbeth's* witches' caldron); the creeping beetles and snails; and the ravished and mutilated Philomela, another victim of male lust and ego, are images of the designs of Oberon's jealous mind. They also anticipate in *The Winter's Tale* Leontes's spiders, nettles, tails of wasps, as Leontes's recoil from Hermoine's fulfilled maternal sexuality and his denial to her of both son and daughter recall and exaggerate Oberon's resentment. Even the spiders, the "long'legged spinners," represent the hateful fantasies Oberon will weave into Titania's dreams—"Wake when some vile thing is near" (2.1.34). Her waking is, of course, a waking into Oberon's dream. "Your actions," says Leontes, "are my dreams" (*WT,* 3.2.80), but Leontes has been overpowered by a sick dream that expresses itself as his reality, while Oberon deliberately uses his power to translate his fantasies into reality.

Oberon's dream, however, as it is given dreamlike enactment in Titania's experience, is lost to Oberon's control. Her love for Bottom is not savage and bestial, but nurturing and tender, capable of transforming the ignoble asshead Bottom into "an angel," "as wise . . . as beautiful," her "gentle joy" (3.1.128, 147). Though Titania's love for Bottom may strike the beholder as strange and comic, it is neither perverse nor animalistic: "And I will purge thy mortal grossness so, / That thou shalt like an airy spirit go" (3.1.159-60). It is transfigured from Oberon's fantasy of revenge into something touching, even charming, by the delicately straightforward erotic and maternal nature of her response. She tempts Bottom with toys, "jewels from the deep," music, and food, "apricocks and dewberries, / With purple grapes, green figs, and mulberries; / The honey bags . . . from the humblebees" (3.1.157, 166-68). Like a doting mother, she finds Bottom's every action precious and unique. Stroking his cheeks, winding roses in his head, kissing his "fair large ears," and twining him in her arms, Titania's love images the solicitous love union of mother and child, a grotesquely tender and erotic madonna and child.

Yet Titania herself, once awake, rejects her "visions" of loving an ass: "O how mine eyes do loath his visage now" (4.1.80). The potion-induced "vision" that Titania awakes to loath is the dream of sexually consummated maternal love. In her dream the place of the Indian boy ("But she perforce withholds the loved boy, / Crowns him with flowers, and makes him all her joy") has been taken by the child/animal Bottom ("For she his hairy temples then had rounded / With coronet of fresh and fragrant flowers") (2.1.27;4.1.53). Her dream has released the genital/sexual desires ordinarily diffused into the polymorphous sensuality not regarded as sexual in a mother's love—the suppressed perverse or incestuous component of maternal love latent in her earlier exclusive preoccupation with the child. This love, for all its tenderness, is smothering and possessive. It denies its object any other identity than that of the beloved: "Out of this wood do not desire to go. / Thou shalt remain here, whether thou wilt or no." "Tie up my love's tongue, bring him silently" (3.1.151-52, 200). Her love for Bottom is unnatural in part because it is "out of season." Bottom is not an infant, however childlike he seems, but Titania, in her doting love, refuses to recognize his true state as she refuses to relinquish the Indian boy to the masculine pursuits and male identity of Oberon, who "would have the child / Knight of his train to trace the forests wild" (2.1.25-26). In her anger with Oberon and attachment to her votaress, she would deny her "child" the autonomy that would separate him from infant dependency on the female and give him over to the male-dominated patriarchal world.

All the love, sexual and maternal, nurturing and erotic, rightfully divided between child and father, has been directed to the boy. Oberon's jealousy was not unfounded:

> Come, wait upon him; lead him to my bower.
>   The moon methinks looks with a wat'ry eye;
> And when she weeps weeps every little
>   flower,
>   Lamenting some enforced chastity.
>
>   (3.1.197-200)

> So doth the woodbine the sweet honeysuckle
> Gently entwist; the female ivy so
> Enrings the barky fingers of the elm.
> O how I love thee! How I dote on thee.
>
>   (4.1.45-48)

The sexual imagery of the last quotation is unavoidable. In medieval and Renaissance beast lore the ass was noted for its sexual potency and long, hard phallus. The monster that Titania loves is the child with the phallus. Her recoil, upon awakening, is in response not only to the actual situation (the assheaded man in her bed), but to the fantasy of an overextended maternal love this situation has embodied. Purged of this vision, she joins Oberon in calling for music, and the two "new in amity," will restore sexual harmony to the world of Athens (4.1.88).

Bottom shares Titania's dream from his own perspective, but unlike Titania, he does not reject it when he wakes. Richard Wheeler (1981) points perceptively to Bottom's dream as a recovery of "the protected environment of early childhood, a refusion of self and magically responsive world, of sensual and tender longings, . . ." (170). From the standpoint of the young child the exclusive union with the mother is desirable and necessary, forming the basis of all future ability to love. Bottom, before his transformation, is engaged in a play with sexual roles that exaggerates the uncertain role-switching of the lovers. Assigned the role of Pyramus, "a lover who kills himself, most gallant, for love," Bottom declares he had rather play "Ercles," his "chief humor" being "for a tyrant" (1.1.25, 29, 30). Denied this he is willing to hide his face, "speak in a monstrous little voice," and play the female, Thisbe (1.2.52-53). The lion's part, which bears a certain resemblance to the rant and power of Hercules, also draws him, "I will roar that I will do any man's heart good to hear me. I will roar that I will make the duke say, "Let him roar again, let him roar again" (1.2.71-72). But if his roars are too frightening, he will "roar you an 'twere any nightingale" (2.1.83). His attraction to all these roles suggests the metamorphic sexual identity of a child: lover, tyrant, woman, savage or gentle beast—all seem to Bottom within his range, though Quince, the director, declares he can "play no part but Pyramus; . . . a sweet-faced man, a proper man . . ." (1.2.84-85). Puck, however, gives Bottom a role that, with the creative logic of dreams, lets him play contradictory parts simultaneously—he is both lover and beast. In a fantasy related to the early longings of a child, he will become the lover of the mother and receive not only the readily available oral and tactile gratification, but the denied genital union as well. Though the dream is censored, for the audience if not for the impervious Bottom, even as it occurs—the child lover is unnatural and grotesque, half-human, half-animal—Bottom's childlike enjoyment of Titania's infatuation, which grows from dubious acceptance ("to say the truth, reason and love keep little company nowadays") to lordly command ("scratch my head, "bring me a honey bag") underlines the nurturing and positive nature of his experience (3.1.142; 4.8.7, 13). For the awakened Bottom, the dream was wonderful, a "most rare vision . . . a dream past the wit of man to say what dream it was" (4.1.205-7).

Bottom has the last word on the dream: "It shall be called 'Bottom's Dream,' because it hath no bottom; . . ." (4.1.215-16). But he cannot explain it: "Man is but an ass if he go about to expound this dream" (4.1.207-8). The dream belongs to that part of the self out of reach of the conscious, rational, interpreting mind. From that point of view the dream "hath no bottom," for it exists in a developmental phase before Bottom's discovery of himself, when the functions of the senses are mingled together in one blur of sensation, the eye hearing, the ear seeing, the hand tasting, the tongue conceiving. It is that vision of wholeness, that "feeling of an indissoluble bond, of being one with the external world as a whole," which Freud (1930, 12) notes as a form of mystic religious experience and connects with the "limitless narcissism" (15) of "An infant at the breast [that] does not as yet distinguish his ego from the external world as the source of sensations flowing in upon him," (13-14). This connection of the dream with religious experience is also suggested by the fact that Bottom, sensing the inappropriateness of rational discourse to "expound" his dream, emphasizes its inexpressibility by garbling St. Paul's assertions of man's inability to conceive of the glory of the final merging with God: "Eye hath not seen, nor ear heard, neither have entered into the heart of man the things which God hath prepared for them that love Him" (1 Cor. 2:9). It is the ballad of this dream that Bottom thinks to sing "to make it the more gracious," at Thisbe's death (4.1.219). This lost dream-vision of the perfect oneness of mother and child imaged in the intimacy of Titania and Bottom will become Pyramus's lament for his loss of the romantic love object through which the male lover hopes to recapture the earliest and most important source of love.

There seems a sense in which Titania's loving acceptance of the assheaded Bottom, their total entwinement in "the cradle of the Faerie Queen," supplies the metaphor of basic trust that enables the warring and uncertain lovers to arrive at mature sexuality. In his classic study of the first oral stage of infantile sexuality, Erikson (1963) comments, "One may say (somewhat mystically, to be sure) that in thus getting what is given, and in learning to get somebody to do for him what he wishes to have done, the baby also develops the necessary ego groundwork to get to be a giver. . . . Where this fails, the situation falls apart into a variety of attempts at controlling by duress or fantasy rather than by reciprocity" (76). This play is full of turmoil that reflects the characters' inabilities to reconcile love and

sexuality through the achievement of reciprocal, genital love. It is surely significant that Demetrius and Lysander both image the young women in terms of despised or desired food, food that nourishes or nauseates. The play also echoes with male efforts to control through duress, "I wooed thee with my sword," "As she is mine, I may dispose of her," "I shall do thee mischief in the wood," "I will shake thee from me like a serpent" (1.1.16; 1.1.42; 2.1.237; 3.2.261). And it contains at least one attempt, successful as it turns out, to control through fantasy. "Wake when some vile thing is near" (2.2.34).

Oberon's fantasy of erotic savagery has been recreated by Titania's maternal tenderness, and Oberon's jealous rage is cured: "Her dotage now I do begin to pity" (4.1.48). Having replaced his rival with a grotesque "twin" that he knows Titania, freed of the spell, will reject, Oberon has asserted his authority over both wife and child. But this exercise of masculine authority is saved from its initial brutality by Titania's capacity for transforming love. Titania's intended sexual debasement becomes, instead, Bottom's wonderful and comic glorification. This central dream thus reestablishes basic trust in part by demonstrating woman's ability to transform, through love, even the most ignoble object. And, in the play as a whole, man's need to trust is reassured by the woman's ability to love the instrument of her injury, by Hippolyta's ability to love her conqueror, by Hermia and Helena's abilities to overlook the infidelities and cruelties of Lysander and Demetrius, by Titania's capacity to accept as natural both the asininity of Bottom and the "lordship" of Oberon. To merit such love the men, on the other hand, must forgo both ego-oriented pretense of idealized worship and the societal reality of uncompromising masculine control to achieve a loving equality founded on respect, the kind of relationship perhaps suggested by the voice and counter-voice exchanges between Theseus and Hippolyta and the final "hand in hand" appearance of Titania and Oberon to bless the bride-beds.

The roles these lovers achieve at the play's end do not overthrow the old patriarchal hierarchies, but transform them. Thus the societies of both worlds are not altered but completed by the play's movement from the narcissistic and "injurious" love characteristic of courtship to the reciprocal and trusting love necessary for harmonious marriage. The psychological mechanisms of these transformations are the materials shadowed forth by the dreams. Both types of love are, perhaps, equally irrational, but the first has the irrationality of fear, the second of faith.

Notes

[1] Marjorie Garber (1974) in her study of Shakespeare's dramatic treatment of dreams, speaks of Shakespeare's using the dream for "the important dramatic function

of representing subjective events, like the workings of the imaginations and the activities of the subconscious. . . . " (p. ix). Ruth Nevo (1980) connects the magic potion with the therapeutic function of dreams: "It discovers, enlarging as in a distorting mirror, the shadowy wishes and fears of the mind, and by so doing enables the victims to enfranchize themselves from their obsessions: (106).

[2] All quotations are from *The Complete Signet Shakespeare.*

[3] George Sandys, in *Ovid's Metamorphosis: Englished, Mythologized, and Represented in Figures,* ed. Karl Hulley and Stanley Vandersall (Lincoln: University of Nebraska Press, 1970) moralized the tale as an indictment of tyrannical parents "who measure their childrens by their owne out-worn and deaded affections; in forcing them to serve their avarice or ambition in their fatall mariages (aptly therefore compared to the tyranny of Mezentius, who bound the living to the dead till they perished by the stench) more cruell therein to their owne, then either the malice of foes or fortune: . . ." (212).

[4] See C. L. Barber (1959, 154-57), Jan Kott (1964, 69-88), and Frank Kermode (1961, 214-20) for very different readings of this fascinating dream.

References

Barber, C. L. 1959. *Shakespeare's Festive Comedy: A Study of Dramatic Form in Relation to Social Custom.* Princeton: Princeton University Press.

Barnet, Sylvan, ed. 1972. *The Complete Signet Shakespeare.* New York: Harcourt Brace Jovanovich.

Erikson, Erik. 1963. *Childhood and Society.* New York: W. W. Norton.

Faber, M. D. 1972. "Hermia's Dream: Royal Road to *A Midsummer Night's Dream.*" *Literature and Psychology* 22:179-90.

Freud, Sigmund. 1930. *Civilization and Its Discontents.* Edited and translated by James Strachey. New York: W. W. Norton, 1962.

Garber, Marjorie. 1974. *Dream in Shakespeare: From Metaphor to Metamorphosis.* New Haven: Yale University Press.

Goldstein, Melvin. 1973. "Identity Crises in a Midsummer Nightmare: Comedy as Terror in Disguise." *Psychoanalytic Review* 60:169-204.

Gui, Weston A. 1952-53. "Bottom's Dream." *American Imago* 9:251-305.

Holland, Norman. 1980. "Hermia's Dream." In *Representing Shakespeare: New Psychoanalytic Essays,* edited by Murray M. Schwartz and Coppélia Kahn, 1-20. Baltimore: Johns Hopkins University Press.

Kermode, Frank. 1961. "The Mature Comedies." In *Early Shakespeare,* 3:214-20. London: Stratford-Upon-Avon Studies.

Kott, Jan. 1964. *Shakespeare Our Contemporary.* London: Methuen.

Nevo, Ruth. 1980. *Comic Transformations in Shakespeare.* London: Methuen.

Sandys, George. 1970. *Ovid's Metamorphosis: Englished, Mythologized, and Represented in Figures.* Edited by Karl Hulley and Stanley Vandersall. Lincoln: University of Nebraska Press.

Wheeler, Richard P. 1981. *Shakespeare's Development and the Problem Comedies: Turn and Counter-Turn.* Berkeley: University of California Press.

Young, David. 1966. *Something of Great Constancy: The Art of "A Midsummer Night's Dream."* New Haven: Yale University Press.

Peter Holland (essay date 1994)

SOURCE: An introduction to *William Shakespeare's A Midsummer Night's Dream,* written and edited by Peter Holland, Oxford at the Clarendon Press, 1994, pp. 1-21.

[*In the following essay, Holland reviews the history of dream analysis and discusses the Elizabethan conception of dreams and their meaning, concluding that the play may be taken not as a "false or trivial" dream, but as a "revelation of another reality."*]

Of all the commentators on Shakespeare, perhaps the oddest is Ulrich Bräker, a Swiss weaver, who in 1780 finished writing his thoughts on the plays under the title *A Few Words about William Shakespeare's Plays by a poor ignorant citizen of the world who had the good fortune to read him.* Bräker did not like much of *A Midsummer Night's Dream:*

> I don't want to run down your dream, but I just can't make it out. The whole tone of the piece doesn't appeal to me. If I ever dreamt of entering a community where affairs are conducted in this tone then I'd leap out of bed, I'll be bound, without even waking up! A certain Theseus, a certain Lysander, every fairy in fact, is busy spouting his own wooden verses. I don't know what fairies are like, and if I did, I'd make a point of not mixing with them—they'd be too quick for me.[1]

Only the workers appealed to this Swiss Bottom: 'The characters of the interlude in this dream—they're the ones for me!' (p. 29).

I doubt if there are many who would agree with Bräker. *A Midsummer Night's Dream* is probably the most performed of all Shakespeare's plays, not least because, in schools, it is so often the way children first encounter Shakespeare. It has always seemed to me a play peculiarly perfect, ideally compact and coherent in its form. At this early stage in his career, in *A Midsummer Night's Dream* as in *The Comedy of Errors,* Shakespeare's approach to comic form is to transmute the enormous range and divergent nature of the materials that lie behind the play into a surface of disarming simplicity.

Like the work of Freudian analysts of genuine dreams, critics considering *A Midsummer Night's Dream* find that the play has a 'manifest' level behind which lurks their own version of the 'latent dream'.[2] For Freudians, dreamers change their dreams as they remember them, this 'dream-work' transforming the latent dream through a process of distortion involving four techniques, identified as condensation, displacement, representation and symbolisation. The task of the critic should then be to uncover the dream-work that has made the 'real' subject of the play, its anxieties and repressions, acceptable.[3] The childlike world of the play is then, along such a line, part of its attempt to avoid the repressed conflict or to resolve it through the fantasy of fictitious solutions 'that are marked by infantile characteristics and are often contradictory among themselves'.[4]

For Jungians, this approach to decoding the secrets of a dream is mistaken. There is for Jung no latent dream since the manifest dream is not a disguise: 'dreams are a part of nature, which harbours no intention to deceive our eyes, but expresses something as best it can'.[5] Our problem, as spectators and critics, is then to learn how to read the dream. If we cannot understand the text, the fault lies in the reader, not the text, since 'the dream attempts to reveal rather than conceal'.[6]

But modern scientific analysis of dreams has moved from the psychoanalytic to the psycho-physiological, finding the source of dreams in neural activity. The most delightful surprise in such research turns out to be its emphasis on the pleasure of dreaming. Dreams can be seen as a form of entertainment and their function a form of relaxation. As Hobson argues: 'Why can't we accept the autocreative function of dreams as something given to us . . . for our own pleasure?'.[7]

This introduction will sometimes try to uncover the latent in *A Midsummer Night's Dream;* it will more often accept that the play reveals rather than conceals; and it will, I hope, always try to keep in the foreground the pleasure of watching or reading the play. The opening sections of the introduction set out a late sixteenth-

century context for dreams and dreaming. Since dreams, even dramatic ones like *A Midsummer Night's Dream,* are constructed out of odd scraps of different material, the next sections explore the play by setting out from the 'day-residue', the sources which fed this particular dream. . . .

Dreams

Dreams and Dreaming. Wittgenstein, worrying how to pinpoint his sense of disliking Shakespeare, tried comparing his work to dreams:

> Shakespeare and dreams. A dream is all wrong, absurd, composite, and yet at the same time it is completely right: put together in *this* strange way it makes an impression. Why? I don't know. And if Shakespeare is great, as he is said to be, then it must be possible to say of him: it's all wrong, things *aren't like that*—and yet at the same time it's quite right according to a law of its own . . . [Shakespeare] is completely unrealistic. (Like a dream.)[8]

There is no evidence to indicate whether Wittgenstein knew *A Midsummer Night's Dream* and yet this passage could in so many ways be an anxious paraphrase of the exchange between Theseus and Hippolyta at the opening to Act 5. Wittgenstein's description of a dream as 'all wrong, absurd' belongs firmly within the rationalist framework of Theseus's 'More strange than true' (5.1.2); his awareness that it can also be 'composite' and 'completely right' shares Hippolyta's understanding that, however strange it may be, it 'grows to something of great constancy' (5.1.26). Theseus wants it to 'be possible to say of' the events of the night in the wood that 'things *aren't like that*' but the night-world has, as the audience by this stage is well aware, laws of its own that he does not understand. Indeed, like a dream, which has its own internally consistent sense of realism, an awareness of reality that communicates itself to the dreamer, or that the dreamer creates in creating the dream, the play as a whole is both 'completely unrealistic' and yet 'at the same time . . . quite right'.

How true the play is, *how* far it can be described as 'quite right' I shall come back to frequently. But, however much *A Midsummer Night's Dream* is 'like a dream', it is not one.[9] It contains only one description of something that may unequivocally be taken to be a dream, one 'real' dream, Hermia's dream of the serpent:[10]

> Help me, Lysander, help me! Do thy best
> To pluck this crawling serpent from my breast!
> Ay me, for pity. What a dream was here?
> Lysander, look how I do quake with fear.
> Methought a serpent ate my heart away,
> And you sat smiling at his cruel prey.
>
> (2.2.151-6)

Everything else that is recounted by mortals or fairies as having been part of a dream is not a dream at all. The experiences have been turned into dream, experienced as if they were dream—but they were not. Titania, waking, tells Oberon 'what visions have I seen' but her 'love', the image she ascribes to her dream of an ass she had fallen in love with, lies rather solidly beside her (4.1.75, 77). The lovers return 'back to Athens' assuming that 'all this derision' that they experienced in the wood is perhaps, as Oberon promises, nothing more than 'a dream and fruitless vision' (3.2.370-1), though they worry about whether it is indeed fruitless. Bottom wakes having had what he without hesitation describes as 'a dream past the wit of a man to say what dream it was' (4.1.202-3). Robin even gives the whole audience the option of considering the entire play as a dream in his epilogue:

> If we shadows have offended,
> Think but this, and all is mended:
> That you have but slumbered here,
> While these visions did appear
>
> (5.1.414-7)

If we wish to dismiss the play, we can choose to treat it as a 'weak and idle theme, / No more yielding but a dream' (5.1.418-19). This is the final, largest-scale version of this recurrent device in the play, reducing vision to dream or reaccommodating an accurate perception of experienced reality into the more comfortable framework provided by dream.

Oberon and Robin make it possible for the other characters—and the audience—to see the play as a dream, not, that is, *like* a dream but as a dream itself, a true dream experience not a similitude. This extraordinary ability to transform experience into dream needs to be placed against an understanding of what dream was, where it came from and what it signified.

Oneiro-criticism, to give it its pedantic title, was a standard and important part of classical divination. Only one major account of early Graeco-Roman interpretation has survived: the *Oneirocritica* by Artemidorus of Daldis, written in the second century AD.[11] Artemidorus emphasizes throughout that dream-analysis must not only take into account what happens in the dream but also the name of the dreamer, his or her occupation, habits and attitudes. His method is non-superstitious and he scrupulously refuses to distinguish between dreams sent by the gods and dreams that are products of the dreamer or even to indicate whether dreams could be so divided.[12]

Artemidorus is, from the start, concerned to classify dreams, providing a system of significance within which all dreams may be easily placed.[13] The process of classifying a dream-experience, pigeon-holing it conveniently or troublingly, is central to the way that char-

acters in *A Midsummer Night's Dream* relate to their forms of dream and Artemidorus' system is fundamental to Western thinking about dreams until well after the date of Shakespeare's play. His basic distinction is between a predictive dream, which he terms *oneiros,* and a non-predictive one, termed *enhypnion.* The latter are simply 'anxiety-dreams and petitionary dreams' (1.6). There is for him nothing at all interesting in the fact that a lover may dream of the beloved, hungry people dream of food and thirsty people dream of drink. Such dreams, clearly generated by what will later be termed 'day-residue', are not for interpretation. These dreams, belonging with apparitions and phantasmata, lie outside his professional concerns. Dreams of the past and present are necessarily less interesting to his clients; they will also lie outside the concerns of most subsequent dream-analysis.

But if *enhypnion* dreams can be disregarded as insignificant or irrational fantasies, *oneiroi* matter enormously. These dreams or visions, occurring to people who are not anxious, are the stuff of his analysis, the raw material on which he can work, using his simple technique: 'the interpretation of dreams is nothing other than the juxtaposition of similarities' (2.25). Such proper dreams can be further subdivided into two groups: direct or theorematic and indirect or allegorical. Direct dreams show without metaphor what will occur: a dream of a shipwreck may indeed mean that the next day the dreamer will be shipwrecked. Allegorical dreams signify by replacement. A dream is, for Artemidorus, a claim by the mind; 'in a way it cries out to each of us', he writes, 'look at this and be attentive, for you must learn from me as best you can' (1.2).

His attempts to categorize dreams are full and inventive. Some features of a dream are treated as tightly defined within their range of meanings. Other dream-features may have multiple possibilities. A serpent such as appeared to Hermia could signify a king, because of its strength, or time, because of its length and skin-changing, or wealth, because it often guards treasure, or any of the gods who use it as a symbol of their sacredness. A serpent is not the same as a snake: snakes signify sickness or an enemy; if a man dreams that his wife has a pet snake which she keeps in her bosom it signifies that she is adulterous. Artemidorus even analyses the different meanings for watersnakes and blindworms.

At the same time he is concerned to emphasize that the same dream may have different meanings according to the circumstances of the dreamer. He gives examples of seven women who had the same dream, during pregnancy, of giving birth to a serpent. In each case the relationship between the serpent of the dream and the son varied. One child became a famous public speaker, because speakers share with serpents the advantages of forked tongues. One son became a priest because the serpent is a sacred animal and the dreamer was a priest's wife. A prostitute's son was wanton because a serpent is slippery. A bad woman's son was a thief and beheaded because serpents are beheaded when caught. A slave woman's son became a runaway slave because serpents do not follow a straight path. Artemidorus does offer a precise explanation for Hermia's dream; dreaming that a serpent is 'entwined about someone and binds him . . . foretells imprisonment' and 'portends death for the sick' (2.13).

There were sixteenth-century translations of Artemidorus into Latin, Italian, French and German. A fairly full English translation by Robin Wood—from the French translation of the Latin translation—was first published in 1606 as *The Judgement or Exposition of Dreams* and had reached its twenty-fourth edition by 1740.[14]

The major late-classical statement on dreams is by Macrobius, part of his enormous commentary on the dream of Scipio in Cicero's *De Re Publica* written around AD 400.[15] The popularity of Macrobius ensured that his dream-classifications became the basis of much early medieval dream-theory. Hence Chaucer includes a lengthy summary of the dream of Scipio in *The Parliament of Fowls* (ll. 29-112) and it is to Macrobius that Chauntecleer turns in 'The Nun's Priest's Tale' (ll. 3123-6).[16] Macrobius plainly derives his ideas from Artemidorus and translates his divisions and classifications into Latin. *Oneiros* dreams are broken down into three types: *somnium, visio* and *oraculum* (enigmatic, prophetic and oracular). These are for Macrobius, as for Artemidorus, the only significant kinds of dream. *Enhypnion* dreams are divided into *insomnium* and *visum* (nightmare and apparition); neither is prophetic.

But medieval writers were less concerned with a classificatory system for a Macrobian typology of dreams than with the means to decode those dreams that could be seen as visionary, oneiric or somnium dreams; the means to do it acquired greater sophistication. There were four types of medieval dreambooks: chancebooks often used with psalters, physiological dreambooks defining dreams as indications of physiological ailments, dream-lunars which (intriguingly for *A Midsummer Night's Dream,* a play recurrently and almost obsessively concerned with the moon) interpreted dreams differently according to the day of the lunar month and hence the phase of the moon, and alphabetical dreambooks.[17]

It is the last category that were most common, particularly the *Somnia Danielis,* the dreams of Daniel. Known in hundreds of different manuscripts from the ninth century to the fifteenth, the *Somnia Danielis,* an alphabetical list of dream topics, is 'a library of ancient dream topoi',[18] far more reliable as a guide to medieval use of dream topoi than Artemidorus whose work was

at that stage only available in Greek and Arabic. In different versions of the *Somnia,* Hermia's serpent most often indicated enemies, conquered or victorious according to what happened to the dream-serpent, though it could also indicate deception by a woman.[19] To dream of an ass usually signified hard work.[20]

What the long tradition of dream-theory suggests above all is that the indecipherability of dreams, the ambiguity of their sources, underlines the danger for the dreamer. As Steven Kruger comments,

> The dreamer stands in a precarious position . . . The realm of dreams, poised between truth and fiction, is also torn between good and evil; it provides a ground . . . in relation to which human beings must make complicated decisions—decisions with crucial implications for their moral lives.[21]

But the tradition also emphasized, particularly in late medieval theory, the extent to which dreams underline the humanity of the dreamer: 'The dream stands . . . in a quintessentially human position: between brute animals on the one hand and God and the angels on the other; between the mundane and divine, body and idea, deception and truth'.[22] Bottom and the other 'dreamers' are all the more human for having dreamed, Theseus, in his rejection of the dream-world, all the more limited.

Renaissance Dreams. English Renaissance texts on dreams, their causes or interpretations, are rarely original. They derive their classificatory systems and their analysis of causality from the kind of works I have already referred to, as well as such sources as Aristotle's brief studies of dream in the *Parva Naturalia* and Aquinas's distinction between inward and outward causes. The conventionality of Renaissance thinking on the subject provides the framework within which the experiences within *A Midsummer Night's Dream* and that of the whole play by the audience would have been understood. How the lovers understand their dream or the audience the play depend on reconciling the experience with the forms of dream with which Oberon (for the lovers) or Robin (for the audience) align the action.

Thomas Hill, in *The Most Pleasant Art of the Interpretation of Dreams* (1576), made perhaps the most coherent attempt in the period to provide an orthodox presentation of dream-science in English, deriving his work from Averroës, Aristotle, Artemidorus and Aquinas, filtered through Italian sources. For Hill, true dreams 'only happen to such, whose spirits are occupied with no irrational imaginations, nor overcharged with the burthen of meat or drinks, or superfluous humours, nor given to any other bodily pleasures' (sigs. [A] 2r-v). Any others are, as we would expect, 'vain dreams, no true signifiers of matters to come but rather showers of the present affections and desires of the body' (sig.

[A]2ᵛ). Hill provides four categories according to whether the causes are bodily or not and new or not; causes can be categorized as food, humours, anxieties and, the most important group, those 'which frame the superior cause come unto the soul' or are divinely caused (D7ʳ). But all natural dreams, inwardly caused, are generated by the soul; as Wood's Artemidorus states, 'a dream therefore is a motion or fiction of the soul in a diverse form' (p. 1). They are created through the operation of the imagination, one of the three internal senses of the sensitive part of the soul, on material provided by the other two internal senses (common sense and memory) or by the 'vegetative' soul, while the external senses are quiescent. The memory provides images derived from the events that immediately preceded falling asleep; the vegetative soul provides images from the state of the body during sleep, for example, cold, thirst, sexual desire.[23] Thomas Nashe, the most contemptuous of Renaissance commentators on dream-theories, puts it even more forcefully:

> A dream is nothing else but a bubbling scum or froth of the fancy, which the day hath left undigested; or an after-feast made of the fragments of idle imaginations . . . our thoughts intentively fixed all the daytime upon a mark we are to hit, are now and then overdrawn with such force, that they fly beyond the mark of the day into the confines of the night.[24]

Such dreams are unlikely to be true, or as Nashe puts it, 'there is no certainty in dreams',[25] since the soul is working without the active support of the external senses; as Vandercleeve suggests, in *The Wisdom of Doctor Dodypoll,* an anonymous play of 1600, 'these present our idle fantasies / With nothing true, but what our labouring souls / Without their active organs, falsely work' (D2ʳ). But, as Alphonso answers Vandercleeve, there is always the other category of dream:

> My lord, know you, there are two sorts of
>   dreams,
> One sort whereof are only physical,
> And such are they whereof your Lordship
>   speaks,
> The other hyper-physical: that is,
> Dreams sent from heaven, or from the wicked
>   fiends,
> Which nature doth not form of her own
>   power,
> But are extrinsicate, by marvel wrought,
> And such was mine.[26]

Wood's Artemidorus and Hill's accumulation of fragments of Renaissance theory are, as one would expect, full of curiosities, such as the belief that dreams dreamed 'in the hour of the full moon or change' will come true 'within 15 days after'.[27] But, however fascinating such a timetable may be for *A Midsummer Night's Dream,*

it seems less significant than, for instance, the confident assertion of that sense of true understanding that comes through the dream. As Hill puts it, 'And a man also doth more comprehend in his dream than waking in the day-time, because in a dream is more resolved than that in the day which is troubled through the doings of the outward sense' (B2ᵛ). Or, as Timothy Bright will later phrase it, 'in sleep our fantasy can perceive those truths which are denied to it when we are awake'.[28] All one then has to do is to recall the dream: Wood recognises that 'before the attempting to interpret he willeth that one should have perfect remembrance of the beginning, the middle, the end, and all the circumstances of his dream' (A6ᵛ). As Demetrius will say in Act 4 of *A Midsummer Night's Dream,* 'And by the way let us recount our dreams' (4.1.197). Similarly, Nashe's venom for dream-interpreters matters less than his sense of dreams as part of the curative function of sleep: 'You must give a wounded man leave to groan while he is in dressing: Dreaming is no other than groaning, while sleep our surgeon hath us in cure' (C2ʳ). But even Nashe carefully preserves the distinction between the impenetrability and untrustworthiness of dream, Artemidorus's *enhypnion* or Macrobius' *insomnium,* compared with the power of vision, *oneiros* or *somnium,* even while he is lambasting Artemidorus and others:

> Could any man set down certain rules of expounding of Dreams, and that their rules were general, holding in all as well as in some, I would begin a little to list to them, but commonly that which is portentive in a King is but a frivolous fancy in a beggar . . . Some will object unto me for the certainty of dreams, the dreams of *Cyrus, Cambyses, Pompey, Caesar, Darius and Alexander.* For those I answer that they were rather visions than dreams, extraordinarily sent from heaven to foreshow the translation of Monarchies. (D4ʳ)

Lodge, too, is reminded to prove that

>   spirits either good or bad,
> In forms, and certain apparitions clad,
> Can further force, or else infuse by right,
> Unfeigned dreams, to those that sleep by
>   night. (F1ʳ)

His reminder is Apollo, for, as Wood states, 'dreams and their interpretations seem particularly to agree and belong to poets, because that to their Apollo . . . is attributed and dedicated, not only the art of Poetry, but also the knowledge and interpretation of dreams' (A2ᵛ-A3ʳ), a more sympathetic insight into the poet's imagination than that offered by Theseus.

Not all dreams have such divine sources. Hermia's dream appears to have a straightforward and direct cause. When Hermia and Lysander prepare themselves for sleep, Lysander is determined to be as close to

Hermia as possible, while she, modestly and accurately, distrusts his intentions and wants to be sure he keeps his distance. Tired and lost though he may be, Lysander sees the opportunity of being alone with Hermia in the woods as too good to pass up. For all the elegant virtuosity of his reasoning (2.2.47-52) it is clear he has sex al fresco in mind and Hermia has to be fairly insistent in giving him the verbal equivalent of a goodnight peck on the cheek (2.2.62-7). Most Lysanders, however, manage to find in 'Here is my bed' (2.2.70) a certain begrudging indication of just how uncomfortable that spot of the stage is.

Eighteenth-century productions had difficulty with this part of the scene. Francis Gentleman, in 1774, marked the lines for omission, for, 'though founded in delicacy, they may raise warm ideas'.[29] The Morality of the moment was troubling: how could Lysander, a gentleman, be seen to be suggesting premarital sex and how could Hermia, a virtuous maid, understand what he had in mind? In the version David Garrick prepared with George Colman the Elder in 1763, the passage is substantially rewritten. Barely into his stride, Lysander's attempt at seduction is halted by Hermia's firm request and he offers to stand guard:

> My honor is the best security for thine.
> Repose thee, love; I'll watch thee thro' the
>   night,
> Nor harm shall reach thee—
> Sleep give thee all his rest.

Garrick's Robin has to produce some fairy music to 'throw this youth into a trance', a 'sweet enchanting harmony' that Lysander cannot resist. Shakespeare's awkward morality is rendered acceptable and a convenient opportunity for music found in the process, cultural adjustment combined with theatrical efficiency.

But such rewriting removes the primary source of the dream. It did not need Freud to identify the serpent of Hermia's dream as a phallic threat. Lysander has presented Hermia with the problem of his sexual desire, and her dream enacts her anxiety about it. At the same time the dream represents Hermia's careful disjunction of Lysander as phallic serpent from Lysander himself, who sits smiling and separate from the actions of his penis, thereby ensuring that the phallic threat from Lysander is dissociated from the 'person' Lysander to some extent. A Freudian reading of the dream would find in the object of the phallic attack, Hermia's breast and heart, a displacement from her vagina. Lysander, in this reading of the dream, is both passive and complicit, accepting, in effect, the sexual desire that Hermia has for him but that she has refused to acknowledge.[31] In Alexandru Darie's production for the Comedy Theatre of Bucharest (1991), it was only with great difficulty that Hermia kept her modesty and her clothes on, so strong was her desire for Lysander.

But Hermia offers her own explanation of the dream when she wakes. Accusing Demetrius of having murdered Lysander she turns him into a serpent:

> And hast thou killed him sleeping? O brave
>   touch!
> Could not a worm, an adder do so much?
> An adder did it, for with doubler tongue
> Than thine, thou serpent, never adder stung.
>   (3.2.70-3)

Demetrius has, in effect, eaten Hermia's heart out by killing her love Lysander. In her comparison with the adder and its double tongue, Demetrius' protestations of innocence, which she sees as lies, intensify his status as serpent. Rather than facing the problem of her repressed desire and Lysander's sexuality as represented by the dream, she displaces the fear *of* Lysander into fear *for* Lysander and fear *of* Demetrius. The dream is now somehow Demetrius' fault.

This is grotesquely and comically unfair to Demetrius for, if Hermia's dream has obvious cause in the events preceding sleeping, it is also oneiric in its warning of an event taking place as Hermia dreams: for Lysander, drugged by Robin, has transferred his affections from Hermia to Helena and is therefore the classic betrayer, smiling on another. Lysander is, of course, a passive actor in this change and his passivity in Hermia's dream seems to mimic this. The dream is then also an inner experience for Hermia reflecting the action that takes place during her sleep.

But this does not quite explain why Hermia should dream of a serpent. Where in effect does the dream come from? There seems to be something about the place where Hermia dreams that makes a dream about a serpent both likely and richly resonant. The bank where Titania sleeps has been defined by the fairies' lullaby as a place to be guarded against snakes: 'You spotted snakes with double tongue' (2.2.9). Oberon had already defined it as a place where 'the snake throws her enamelled skin' (2.1.255), defining this beneficial snake that is a source of fairy clothes ('Weed wide enough to wrap a fairy in', l. 256) as female. This useful female snake contrasts with the male snakes/ serpents elsewhere in the play. Lysander as the serpent of the dream and Demetrius as the serpent of Hermia's accusation belong with the spotted snakes of the lullaby.

Demetrius is accused by Hermia of having a 'doubler' tongue than an adder; he has also, in Act I, been accused by Lysander of being 'spotted and inconstant' (1.1.110) for changing from Helena to Hermia. The line links 'spotted' with inconstancy; the lullaby links 'spotted' with snakes. Hermia's dream turns Lysander into a serpent at the very moment that he is being 'spotted and inconstant'. The atmosphere around Titania's bank is full of links back to the world of

Theseus' court. It is a place full of suggestions sufficient to generate the precise terms of Hermia's dream.

The richness of this suggestiveness even allows the dream to transfer from one person to another. When Hermia does find Lysander again, now changed and spotted, she hangs on to him as he tries to shake her off: 'Hang off, thou cat, thou burr; vile thing, let loose, / Or I will shake thee from me like a serpent' (3.2.260-1). He has now turned her into a serpent entwined around him. Hermia has not had a chance to tell Lysander her dream; the dream seems to have caught him, entwined him into it. His first line here contains an odd and magical echo of Oberon, half-heard by a character who could not have heard it at all. Oberon's spell on Titania conjures up her possible objects of desire: 'Be it ounce, or cat, or bear, / Pard, or boar with bristled hair' (2.2.36-7). 'Or cat, or bear' has now become for Lysander 'thou cat, thou burr'. The echo is imprecise, as echoes are wont to be. The effect is of sounds and serpents inhabiting the place, the language and the minds of characters who stray near there.

Dramatic Dreams. Hermia's dream may, from this perspective, be a rich *oneiros* such as Artemidorus would have been proud to interpret, a dense enigma to be read across the whole play. But the whole play, of course, calls itself a dream. The fascination with dream as an overarching device, an embedding form for poetry is an immense and powerful tradition in English medieval poetry.[32] It may indeed be because the Chaucerian form of dream-vision was so overwhelmingly successful, so broad in its imaginative sweep and magnificent in its application of literary form to its concerns, that the device is comparatively rarely used in the Renaissance. Dream is, in any case, a mode no longer to be comfortably trusted. Thomas Churchyard's poem 'A Dream', in *Churchyard's Challenge* (1593), rehearses all the warnings about dreams as the product of 'the roving thoughts of idle braine', ending uncertainly,

> Well, be thy visions good or bad,
>   or swevens [dreams] of the night:
> Such idle freaks as fancy had,
>   now shall you hear aright.
>
> (p. 179)

before going on to give a serious dream-warning about death, vanity and the deceptiveness of the world.

Dream-poetry and dream-narrative seem, however, to have been of particular recurrent interest only to Robert Greene, in works like *A Quip for an Upstart Courtier* (1591), 'A Maiden's Dream' (1591), *Greene's Vision* [1592], 'A most rare and excellent dream' (in *The Phoenix Nest*, 1593), and, published after the date of *A Midsummer Night's Dream, Greene's Orpharion* (1599.[33]) At his best he considers the paradoxes of dream in terms worth considering alongside Shakespeare's play:

> Why art thou not (O dream) the same you
>   seem?
> Seeing thy visions our contentment brings;
> Or do we of their worthiness misdeem?
> To call them shadows that are real things?
> And falsely attribute their due to wakings?[34]

Dream-plays had always been a much less common device. Robin's offer to the audience to consider the whole play as something that has taken place while they have been asleep (5.1.414-19) had been made twice before in plays by John Lyly. For *Sapho and Phao* (1584), Lyly offered an apologetic prologue for performance at court, speaking directly to the Queen:

> Whatsoever we present, whether it be tedious (which we fear) or toyish (which we doubt), sweet or sour, absolute or imperfect, or whatsoever, in all humbleness we all, and I on knee for all, entreat, that your Highness imagine yourself to be in a deep dream, that staying the conclusion, in your rising your Majesty vouchsafe but to say, *And so you awaked.*[35]

Lyly's elaborate humility is an artful piece of modesty. While *Sapho and Phao* has some passages on dreams there is no need to consider the whole play as a dream, except as a means of excusing its weaknesses. The dramatic device is no more than a conventional ritual of excuse. In *The Woman in the Moon* (performed *c.*1591-3), Lyly uses the prologue to extend the notion of dream from an excuse for the experience of the play in performance to an excuse through a recognition of the play's origin:

> Our Poet slumbering in the Muses' laps,
> Hath seen a woman seated in the moon, . . .
> This, but the shadow of our Author's dream,
> Argues the substance to be near at hand: . . .
> If many faults escape her discourse,
> Remember all is but a Poet's dream.[36]

The entire play is now a product of the poet's dream "in *Phoebus*'s holy bower"[37] and the audience's tolerant response is to be the result. But Lyly does not combine the two ploys, treating the performance as a dream and recognizing the poet's work as the product of a dream.

The most intriguing version of a dream-play, not least because of its vexed relationship to Shakespeare, is the ending of *The Taming of A Shrew* (1594), the play that is somehow connected with Shakespeare's *The Taming of The Shrew.*[38] Shakespeare's Induction has Sly who has fallen drunkenly asleep found by a Lord who, for fun, has Sly carried off, transformed into a gentleman and made to sit and watch a play. At a point equivalent to Shakespeare's 5.1.102 *A Shrew*'s Sly falls asleep again. When the play performed for him is over, the Lord has Sly changed back into his own clothes and put back 'in the place where we did find him' (passage D, l. 4).

As in the experience of the mortals who enter the wood in *A Midsummer Night's Dream,* the play's events can be taken to be nothing more than a dream, in this case a dream of metamorphosis of social status that is subordinated in the play to the dream-play that is presented for Sly. Unlike Bottom, Sly is only too keenly aware of the person he was (is) outside this 'dream-experience': 'What, would you make me mad? Am not I Christopher Sly—old Sly's son of Burton Heath' (Induction 2.16-17). Only as the others insist does he convince himself that this state is true reality and his previous existence only a dream in its turn:

> Am I a lord, and have I such a lady?
> Or do I dream? Or have I dreamed till now?
> I do not sleep. I see, I hear, I speak.
> I smell sweet savours, and I feel soft things.
> Upon my life, I am a lord indeed,
> And not a tinker, nor Christopher Sly.
>   (Induction 2.67-72)

Sly, of course, much prefers this new reality and 'would be loath to fall into my dreams again' (Induction 2.123).

The Lord had assumed that the experience will be for a reawakened Sly nothing more than 'a flatt'ring dream or worthless fancy' (Induction 1.42). But, as Sly explains to the Tapster who wakes him up at the end of the play, this dream, 'The bravest dream . . . that ever thou / Heardest in thy life' (passage E, ll. 11-12), will have unexpected results:

> TAPSTER
> Ay, marry, but you had best get you home,
> For your wife will curse you for dreaming
>   here tonight.
> SLY
> Will she? I know now how to tame a shrew.
> I dreamt upon it all this night till now,
> And thou hast waked me out of the best
>   dream
> That ever I had in my life. But I'll to my
> Wife presently and tame her too,
> An if she anger me.
>   (passage E, ll. 14-21)

Sly's assumption that he can put the dream-play into effect against the unseen stereotype of the wife waiting for the drunken husband with the Elizabethan equivalent of the rolling-pin may be comic bravado. But in *A Midsummer Night's Dream* the question of what will be the consequence of the dream-play in the woods is far from simply comic. Where in *A Shrew* the events after awaking from the 'dream' occupy a brief epilogue scene, in *A Midsummer Night's Dream* there is

Paul Freeman as Oberon and Cameron Blakely as Puck in the Open Air Theatre's 1994 production of A Midsummer Night's Dream.

the whole of Act 5 to come. The reaccommodation of the people to the post-dream world is now not only comic but also complex and worrying.

We would expect that a play with the word 'dream' in its title would make fairly frequent use of the word. But Shakespeare seems to have been particularly interested in the word at this stage of his career: nearly a third of all Shakespeare's usages of the word 'dream' occur in only three plays, *Richard III, Romeo and Juliet* and *A Midsummer Night's Dream,* plays written close in time to each other.

In *Romeo and Juliet,* written, most probably, immediately before *A Midsummer Night's Dream,*[39] Shakespeare makes the matter of dreams Mercutio's and places it in the world of Queen Mab. Romeo, trying to quiet the wild exuberance of Mercutio's description of Mab, advises him 'Thou talk'st of nothing' (1.4.96) but Mercutio turns the nothing of dreams into its own fantasy:

> True. I talk of dreams,
> Which are the children of an idle brain,
> Begot of nothing but vain fantasy,
> Which is as thin of substance as the air,
> And more inconstant than the wind
>
> (ll. 96-100)

Dream, that nothing that is so powerfully something, may be mocked and belittled—throughout *A Midsummer Night's Dream* it often is—but it strikes back at those who mock it. Lysander defines true love as 'short as any dream' (1.1.144) but the play will make the true love of Lysander and Hermia endure much longer than a night of adventures in the wood. Hippolyta reassures Theseus that 'Four nights will quickly dream away the time' (1.1.8) before their wedding but the time will be dream in senses other and far richer than her lines suggest. Oberon may say of the lovers, 'When they next wake, all this derision / Shall seem a dream and fruitless vision' (3.2.370-1); yet his next line suggests that this dream is not a fruitless vision at all, since the result will be that 'back to Athens shall the lovers wend / With league whose date till death shall never end' (ll. 372-3), exactly the same contrast between the supposed empty brevity of the nothing of the dream and the enduring consequences that hover over Lysander's 'short as any dream'. Viewed in this light, Oberon's line suggests a different emphasis: it is not that the derision *is* a dream, but that it should *seem* so.

Oberon's line has combined dream and vision. If the lovers may find the experience a 'fruitless vision', for Bottom it was 'a most rare vision' (4.1.202). Even Robin advises the audience that it has seen 'visions' (5.1.417). The audience can choose to take them as trivial, 'No more yielding but a dream' (5.1.419), but, if we have responded to the play fully, we will share with Bottom the sense of vision, of something revealed from out there, from the world of fairy, not the false or trivial world of dream but a revelation of another reality. The obligation on the audience is to treat the play as a benevolent *oneiros*, a true prophetic dream. This dream is an attempt to resolve the great puzzle of dream-theory, the source of dreams, for this dream is not the product of the dreamer's imagination or the reformulation of the experiences of the day but a phenomenon generated by extra-human forces. Such dreams matter greatly. . . .

Notes

[1] Ulrich Bräker, *A Few Words about William Shakespeare's Plays,* ed. Derek Bowman (New York, 1979), p. 29.

[2] Among the many texts on modern dream-theory, I have found the following most helpful: Sigmund Freud, *The Interpretation of Dreams,* Penguin Freud Library, 4 (Harmondsworth, 1976); C. G. Jung, *Memories,* *Dreams, Reflections* (1963); James A. Hall, *Clinical Uses of Dreams* (New York, 1977); James L. Fosshage and Clemens A. Loew, *Dream Interpretation: A Comparative Study* (New York, 1978); David Foulkes, *A Grammar of Dreams* (Brighton, 1978); Charles Rycroft, *The Innocence of Dreams* (1979); Liam Hudson, *Night Life: The Interpretation of Dreams* (1985); J. Allan Hobson, *The Dreaming Brain* (New York, 1988).

[3] For a full-blown psychoanalytic reading see James L. Calderwood, *A Midsummer Night's Dream* (Hemel Hempstead, 1992).

[4] Angel Garma in Fosshage and Loew, p. 28.

[5] Jung, p. 185.

[6] Edward Whitmont, 'Foreword' to Hall, p. xv.

[7] Hobson, p. 297.

[8] L. Wittgenstein, *Culture and Value,* ed. G. H. von Wright, trans. P. Winch (Oxford, 1980), p. 83e.

[9] For approaches to the play in the context of dream see Marjorie B. Garber, *Dream in Shakespeare* (1974), pp. 59-87, and John Arthos, *Shakespeare's Use of Dream and Vision* (1977).

[10] For a discussion of different performances of Hermia's dream see H. R. Coursen, *Shakespearean Performance as Interpretation* (Newark, Del., 1992), pp. 74-84.

[11] Artemidorus, *The Interpretation of Dreams: Oneirocritica,* trans. R. J. White (Park Ridge, N. J., 1975): references are by chapter and section; see also S. R. F. Price, 'The Future of Dreams: From Freud to Artemidorus', *Past and Present,* 113 (1986), pp. 3-37.

[12] See Ruth Padel's review of White's ed. of Artemidorus, *TLS,* 23 April 1976, p. 494.

[13] See further A. H. M. Kessels, 'Ancient Systems of Dream-Classification', *Mnemosyne* (4th series), 22 (1969), pp. 389-424.

[14] Price, p. 32.

[15] See Macrobius, *Commentary on the Dream of Scipio,* trans. W. H. Stahl (New York, 1952). The *somnium Scipionis* itself was available in English translation in, e.g., Thomas Newton's translation of *Fowre Severall Treatises of M. Tullius Cicero* (1577).

[16] See also *The Book of the Duchess,* ll. 284-9; Alison Peden is however sceptical about the extent of the influence of Macrobius on Chaucer: see her 'Macrobius and Medieval Dream Literature', *Medium Aevum,* 54 (1985), pp. 59-73, esp. pp. 67-9.

[17] See Steven R. Fischer, 'Dreambooks and the Interpretation of Medieval Literary Dreams', *Archiv für Kulturgeschichte,* 65 (1983), pp. 1-20; his *The Dream in the Middle High German Epic* (Bern, 1978) and his edition of the *Somnia Danielis* as *The Complete Medieval Dreambook* (Bern, 1982); see also Lynn Thorndike, 'Ancient and Medieval Dreambooks' in her *A History of Magic and Experimental Science* (1923), vol. 2, pp. 290-302, and Jacques Le Goff, 'Dreams in the Culture and Collective Psychology of the Medieval World', in his *Time, Work and Culture in the Middle Ages,* trans. A. Goldhammer (Chicago, 1980), pp. 201-4.

[18] Fischer, 'Dreambooks', p. 7.

[19] Fischer, *Complete Medieval Dreambook,* pp. 134-5.

[20] Ibid., p. 27.

[21] Steven F. Kruger, *Dreaming in the Middle Ages* (Cambridge, 1992), pp. 52-3.

[22] Ibid., p. 82.

[23] Neatly summarised by Sears Jayne, 'The Dreaming of *The Shrew*', *SQ* 17 (1966), pp. 41-56, esp. pp. 43-4. See also Thomas Lodge's distinction between bodily and mental causes in 'To Master W. Bolton, Epistle 2', in *A Fig for Momus* (1595), sig. E4[r].

[24] Thomas Nashe, *The Terrors of the Night* (1594), sig. C3[v].

[25] Ibid., sig. F2[r].

[26] There are exceptions to this general theory, of course. See, e.g., Stephen Bateman's notion that 'the air is the cause of dreams' (S. Batcman, *Batman uppon Bartholome* (1582), sig. 2F5[r]) or Christopher Langton's straightforward approach, as befits the author of *An Introduction into Physicke* [1547]: 'A dream is nothing, but an imagination made in the sleep' (quoted by Carroll Camden, 'Shakespeare on Sleep and Dreams', *Rice Institute Pamphlets,* 23 (1936), p. 121).

[27] Hill, sig. E2[r].

[28] Quoted by Camden, p. 122.

[29] *Bell's Shakespeare* (1774), viii. 159.

[30] David Garrick, *The Plays,* ed. Harry W. Pedicord and Frederick L. Bergmann (Carbondale, Ill., 1980-2), iv. 199. I have corrected their 'reach the' to 'reach thee', the clear reading of the MS (Folger prompt-book MND 6).

[31] For Freudian readings of this dream see, among many, M. D. Faber, 'Hermia's Dream: Royal Road to *A Mid-*summer Night's Dream', *Literature and Psychology,* 22 (1972), pp. 179-90, and Norman N. Holland, 'Hermia's Dream', in Murray M. Schwartz and Coppélia Kahn, eds., *Representing Shakespeare* (1980), pp. 1-20.

[32] See for example A. C. Spearing's brilliant study, *Medieval Dream Poetry* (Cambridge, 1976); for Chaucer see B. A. Windeatt, *Chaucer's Dream Poetry: Sources and Analogues* (Cambridge, 1982) and Piero Boitani, 'Old Books Brought to Life in Dreams: the *Book of the Duchess,* the *House of Fame,* the *Parliament of Fowles*', in Piero Boitani and Jill Mann, eds., *The Cambridge Chaucer Companion* (Cambridge, 1986), pp. 39-57.

[33] *Greene's Orpharion* was entered in the Stationers' Register on 9 February 1590. Thomas H. McNeal, in 'Studies in the Greene Shakspere Relationship', *Shakespeare Association Bulletin,* 15 (1940), pp. 210-18, argued unconvincingly for Greene's poems as an object of Shakespeare's satire in Bottom's dream.

[34] 'A most rare, and excellent Dreame' in *The Phoenix Nest* (1593), p. 43 (ed. H. E. Rollins (Cambridge, Mass., 1931), p. 51).

[35] Lyly, *Works,* ii. 372.

[36] Lyly, *Works,* iii. 241, ll. 1-2, 12-13, 16-17.

[37] Ibid., l. 18; compare the bowers of Oberon and Titania (3.1.186, 3.2.6-7 and n., 4.1.60).

[38] The precise relationship of *A Shrew* and *The Shrew* is irrelevant here but I share Oxford's assumption that the additional Sly passages, present in *A Shrew* and not in *The Shrew,* could have existed in some form in a version of Shakespeare's text; certainly productions of Shakespeare's play have often very successfully incorporated the other Sly comments and particularly the ending. I use the text of the passages printed as Additional Passages to Oxford's text of *The Shrew.*

[39] See below, p. 110.

LOVE AND MARRIAGE

Jane K. Brown (essay date 1987)

SOURCE: "'Discordia concors': On the Order of *A Midsummer Night's Dream,*" in *Modern Language Quarterly,* Vol. 48, No. 1, March, 1987, pp. 20-41.

[In the following essay, Brown explores the relationship between the themes of imagination and love in A

Midsummer Night's Dream, and argues that the play is allegorical rather than mimetic in its emphasis on the importance of love as means of knowing a higher truth.]

A Midsummer Night's Dream is concerned with marriage, relations between the sexes, creativity and imagination, fancy, and love. The themes of love and imagination are so pervasive in the play that their relation has seemed almost too obvious to merit analysis. Recent readings have tended to focus either on the theme of love and marriage (sometimes "sexual politics") or on the theme of imagination, but not on the link between the two.[1] This essay will explore the connection between love and mental activity in the play and locate it in the popular Neoplatonist doctrine of love described by Edgar Wind.[2] Not only does this Neoplatonist "mystery" permeate *A Midsummer Night's Dream,* but it also organizes the play in terms of plot structure, cast, and imagery. Analyzing *A Midsummer Night's Dream* in this context leads to the conclusion that the play is fundamentally allegorical rather than mimetic. In other words, the play "bodies forth" ideas, and these ideas take primacy over character and plot as organizing principles. Thus, the play represents neither the views on sex and marriage nor the views on fancy held by Shakespeare and his contemporaries; instead, it presents the significance of love as a way of knowing higher truth. Because love becomes an analogue—indeed a metaphor—for what the play also calls fancy or imagination, *A Midsummer Night's Dream* ultimately is concerned with the nature and location of truth.

Occasional critics have recognized Neoplatonist thinking on the nature of love and art in the play and have even offered more extended readings in this vein.[3] But these studies suffer from two difficulties. First, even the main highways of Renaissance Neoplatonism are tortuous in the extreme; the better informed the Neoplatonist reading, the less accessible it is.[4] Second, because Neoplatonism has entered and reentered the tradition at so many different times and in so many different ways, it is a particularly ill-defined movement. Indeed, it is less a movement than a way of thinking. For these reasons, rather than examining specific Neoplatonist ideas or themes, or recognizing particular Neoplatonist myths and motifs (such as Orpheus, the wise fool, or Midas), I will outline more general Neoplatonist structures and patterns of thinking and identify where and how Shakespeare goes beyond the fashionable clichés of the period.

I will introduce the relevant structures by describing what Edgar Wind called the "mystery of love" in his discussion of Neoplatonist themes in Renaissance painting. Wind uses the term *mystery* to identify the "serious games" of Renaissance Neoplatonists, the paradoxical allegories that expressed profound religious truths to those initiated into their secrets. But the most paradoxical aspect of these secrets is that they were not really secrets; they were rather, as Wind implies in passing, widely known among Renaissance intellectuals.[5] Despite the lack of positive evidence that Shakespeare knew the work of either Ficino or Pico, the fact that these "esoteric mysteries" were widely known, their pervasiveness in the play, and the coherence of the interpretation to which they lead justify my approach.

For the Renaissance Neoplatonist, love is the force that mediates between the world and divinity, just as Plato had defined it in the *Symposium.* There Plato develops a theory of two kinds of love based on the two different myths of the birth of Aphrodite. The first is worldly love, Aphrodite Pandemos, daughter of Dione and Zeus. This love is sensual, vulgar. The other, higher or spiritual love is Aphrodite Urania, born from the foam that arose after the genitals of the castrated Uranus fell into the sea. By virtue of her birth, she is a mediator or connecting link between the sensual world embodied in the sea and the spiritual sphere, the divine spark of Uranus's semen. The two Venuses are not simply opposed, but the lower one is in fact an image or metaphor for the other: sensual love thus can be a steppingstone to a purer, spiritual love, which in turn can lead the votary to perception of the divine itself. Ficino and Pico elaborated this theory into complex systems that need not concern us here. Rather, my concern is the emphasis on the metaphoric aspect of sensual love. In the Renaissance, sensual love is not only a steppingstone to love of the divine, as in Plato, but can also represent spiritual love in the world: it can be its second face.

The Neoplatonist rarely stepped directly from lower to higher love, however; instead the movement toward transcendence proceeded through a rather fluid dialectic known as the *coincidentia oppositorum,* the harmony of opposites. Such harmonization—of sensual and spiritual love, of sensual love and chaste love, of world and spirit, of the all and the one—was the ideal in every respect for these thinkers, so that finally any one of these dichotomies could stand for all. By analogy, an enormous vocabulary of signs could represent the opposition and relation of the two kinds of love: sensual love versus absolute chastity, sensual love versus chaste married love, earthly Venus versus heavenly Venus, Venus versus Diana, the bow of Cupid versus the bow of Diana—to choose examples relevant only to *A Midsummer Night's Dream.* For Renaissance Neoplatonists, however, these pairings represent conjunctions as well as oppositions. The bow is ambiguous because it *is* the attribute of both Cupid and Diana; Venus-Diana figures abound in Renaissance iconography, and Diana herself, as the moon, embodies the conflicting attributes of chastity and lunacy.[6] Ultimately, both opposition and conjunction are signs of the same harmony of opposites in which higher truth was understood to be veiled.

A second, equally important aspect of the mystery of love is the epistemological dimension of the theory. Love is the force that enables man to transcend the world and perceive the divine One. In this context "perceive" means "enter into mystical unity with," for the One cannot be perceived through the senses, but only by submersion into it of the entire mind. Higher love is not sensual in the most literal terms; as Helena articulates, heedless of the higher significance of her words, "Love looks not with the eyes but with the mind; / And therefore is wing'd Cupid painted blind" (I.i.234-35).[7] Two important and quite different implications follow from this view of love. The first is that love is an epistemological mode; only the lover has access to the most profound truths of human existence. Thus a play that deals with love in the Neoplatonist sense is a play about knowledge and truth. The second implication is really the first turned inside out: because access to truth is through the metaphoric transformation of love from sensual to spiritual, any statement about knowledge or truth accessible to the senses is not itself truth, but only metaphor or distant image. Thus, the fact that *A Midsummer Night's Dream* is preoccupied with its own illusoriness can be read as a concern about its own truthfulness.

We may begin, as Shakespeare does, with Theseus and Hippolyta. In the first scene Theseus is impatient and Hippolyta patient regarding their approaching marriage: their attitudes immediately define the topic of the play as the opposition between sensual and chaste love. The repeated references to the moon, especially Hippolyta's "like to a silver bow / New bent in heaven" (I.i.9-10), invoke Diana as huntress, that is, the moon in its aspect of chastity. This opposition will be resolved in their marriage, for Hippolyta's chastity is not the absolute virginity of the nun, but the chastity of faithful married love. Similarly, this marriage represents the end of warfare between Athenians and Amazons, thus social as well as spiritual harmony. And harmony is the proper word here, for Theseus plans to wed Hippolyta "in another key" (18): after all the co fusions are sorted out, Hippolyta and Theseus will arrive to the musical discord of their hounds in Act IV, awaken the lovers with the music of their hunting horns, and thus resolve the love conflicts of the play in harmonious discord.

Yet it would be too simple to describe Hippolyta and Theseus as simply chaste and sensual love or higher and lower love uniting to realize an image of truth in marriage. In Act II, Titania describes Hippolyta to Oberon as "the bouncing Amazon, / Your buskin'd mistress, and your warrior love" (II.i.70-71), while dismissing parallel charges that she herself loves Theseus as "forgeries of jealousy" (81). The opposition is maintained, while the polarity, so to speak, is reversed. Similarly, in Act V, Hippolyta is now impatient for the change of the moon ("I am a-weary of this moon. Would that he would change!" [251-52]) and Theseus patient

("It appears, by his small light of discretion, that he is in the wane; but yet in courtesy, in all reason, we must stay the time" [253-55]). The issue is not constancy or development of character, nor is it how either feels about the wedding, but that the two between them maintain that state of harmonious discord to which the play gives the name *marriage.*[8]

The rest of the love plot elaborates the initial opposition between chaste and sensual love. The conflict between Hermia and her father is identified by the language of the scene as a conflict between fancy or imagination and law—a familiar enough conflict from Shakespeare's comedies of this period. Many recent readers have focused on Hermia's oppression by patriarchal power structures in and outside the play.[9] But the conflict is neither strictly intellectual nor strictly sexual; it is actually a variation—one of the many metaphors—of the pattern already established in the dialogue between Theseus and Hippolyta. Consider for a moment Hermia's actual alternatives. She is offered marriage to Demetrius, death, or eternal chastity. Although Egeus demands her death, Theseus and Hermia really consider only marriage to Demetrius or entering a cloister. It is clear to everyone in the scene—except Egeus and Demetrius, who are blinded by the language of law—that the second alternative is better: "Thrice blessed they that master so their blood" (I.i.74), says Theseus, unconsciously echoing Hippolyta's position from the first scene. The other alternative is "earthlier happy" (76), but "earthlier" must carry equal weight here with "happy." Theseus has identified Hermia's alternatives as the two loves of Plato. Indeed, were Hermia to marry Demetrius, whom she does not love, their relationship would be strictly physical; as a nun her love of the divinity would be strictly spiritual. As she puts it, her *soul* denies Demetrius's sovereignty (82). The law of Egeus and Demetrius is thus a social manifestation of the worldliness of sensual love, and fancy becomes a way of connecting physical and spiritual generation, of connecting carnal and spiritual knowledge. As the scene progresses, the Demetrius-nunnery opposition is substituted for the Demetrius-Lysander opposition; at the end of the scene, marriage to Lysander, or chaste married love, returns as the mediating possibility. But even the union of Hermia and Lysander couples oppositions, for to Lysander's distress, Hermia chastely insists that they sleep apart in the wood, since they are not yet married: like Hippolyta's, her chastity opposes the more sensual haste of her beloved.

The uneasy opposition between the two kinds of love also manifests itself in the relationship between the two pairs of young lovers. Often they seem indistinguishable from one another. Lysander and Demetrius have remarkably similar taste, for until the denouement both always love the same girl simultaneously. Nor is this surprising, since Hermia and Helena, "Like to a double cherry, seeming parted, / But yet an union in partition" (III.ii.209-10), are longtime friends and apparently distinguishable mainly in respect to height. Though for most of the play Hermia seems gentler and more serious than Helena, the confusions of III.ii show that under the right circumstances they can exchange roles. Yet the pairs of lovers are undeniably different from one another. If Lysander and Hermia sound rather like Romeo and Juliet, Demetrius especially speaks in a parody of that language.[10] Hermia and Lysander are associated with fancy and imagination, but Helena's language, when she first appears, is less fanciful than it is witty.[11] Thematically she reverses Hermia's insistence on the identity of sight and judgment. In the famous exchange between Hermia and Theseus, Hermia wishes her father looked at Lysander and Demetrius with her eyes, and Theseus responds that she must rather see with her father's judgment. Later Hermia cries out, "O hell, to choose love by another's eyes!" (I.i.140). For Hermia, vision and judgment coincide, and the end of the play validates her vision by according her her chosen lover. Helena, by contrast, insists upon the blindness of love: "Love looks not with the eyes but with the mind" (I.i.234). In the context of Neoplatonism, the phrase refers to the total spirituality of true love, which is love of God. But Helena—and this is her mistake—intends to castigate the total arbitrariness of sensual love; she divorces love entirely from judgment—"Nor hath Love's mind of any judgment taste" (236), she continues. Indeed, Helena loves Demetrius not with judgment, but like a spaniel (203). The thematics of animal love continues when Helena compares herself to a bear and a monster (II.ii.94, 97) and when Hermia rejects Demetrius as a dog (III.ii.65). Helena's love is not the higher, chaste love of Hermia (Demetrius's threats to her virginity daunt her not a whit) but the lower, sensual love—what the Italian humanists called *Venere bestiale*.

The adventures of Oberon and Titania embrace these oppositions between sensuality and chastity in the greatest complexity of all. The contest over the Afric boy is to some extent a contest for control rather than one between opposing kinds of love. Yet Titania and Oberon still express their positions using the vocabulary of love. Oberon is "jealous" (II.i.61), while Titania's love for the child is entirely disinterested, for she raises him as an act of generosity to her dead friend. If Titania's generosity seems higher, more "Platonic," than Oberon's jealousy, it is strange that Titania's description of the mother is a sensuous paean to nature's fecundity. And Titania's sensuous memory of the mother is immediately juxtaposed to Oberon's chaste memory of how Cupid's arrow *missed* the virgin of the West. Once again the polarity is reversed while the opposition between sensuality and chastity remains. The way the fairy rulers love in the play maintains the same complexity. Oberon incites Titania to love the ass-headed Bottom, literally to love a beast (as Helena, like a dog,

loves the beastly Demetrius). Yet the nature-*spirit* Titania responds to this love by tender care for the beloved and, more important, by patience and generosity to Oberon when he next demands the Afric boy (reported by Oberon, IV.i.57-61). Similarly, Oberon, who seems to degrade and mock his wife, is yet the most compassionate figure in the play.[12] He wants to rectify the relations among the mortals to restore *true* love; he takes pity first on Helena, before he has gained the boy, and then on Titania. Except for Hermia, who continues to worry about Lysander's safety even after he has abused and abandoned her (III.ii.447), only Oberon and Titania clearly rise above concern for self in their love. Such disinterested love is another version of Hermia's spiritual love. Thus, neither Oberon nor Titania is perfectly spiritual or perfectly chaste, for perfection is invisible to the Neoplatonist. Even spirits, if they are visible to human eyes, must combine the two modes of love within themselves: they must be natural (physical) as well as spiritual; they must be nature-spirits.

All of the couples in the play embody in different ways the harmony of opposed forms of love. Furthermore, they can be ordered according to where they fall on a scale between the two kinds of love. Oberon, the spirit king, and Titania occupy the highest, most spiritual position. They fall out over who is to bring up the Afric boy: the issue is a version of what the *Symposium* defines as the highest form of human love, the love between an older man and a youth, which manifests itself in the act of education. While Oberon and Titania's relationship maintains a constant opposition between passionate, physical love and spiritual love, their alternate acts of generosity and compassion represent the most spiritual, indeed most Christian versions of love in the play.

Next come Theseus and Hippolyta, highest representatives of the mortal realm, the success of whose marriage is to guarantee not only the order of their own previously less chaste lives, but also that of the world they rule. Theseus, who had been too self-involved to control the erring Demetrius, in the last act has seemingly infinite patience and kindliness for the bumbling mechanicals. The appearance of Hippolyta in hunting dress, surrounded by the musical discord of her hounds, is the closest the play approaches to a theophany: Hippolyta is the earthly image of that pure ideal to which we give the name Diana.

Hermia and Lysander are next in line: they remain faithful to one another in adversity and chaste in their wanderings in the forest. Lysander turns to Helena only under the influence of the juice of the purple flower, which is administered to him by mistake. The flower derives its power from Cupid's arrow, and its color, "Before milk-white, now purple with love's wound" (II.i.167), further associates it with lust and sensuality.

Lysander is healed to his "wonted sight" (III.ii.369) by the juice of another herb, perhaps the unstained flower, whose whiteness, closer in color to the silver bow of Diana, would signify chastity.

Toward the lower end of the scale come the less pure Helena and Demetrius. Demetrius is treated only with the purple flower, not at all with the other one: by himself he does not even achieve the level of the healthy, sensual love that animates the natural world of the play, as his initial unfaithfulness to Helena shows. The bottom of the scale is occupied not by the spaniel-like Helena, but by the literally bestial Bottom, whose name not only turns out to be very eloquent in its own right, but also calls attention to the hidden eloquence of another name, Oberon.

That Titania is Bottom's consort provides a doubly ironic closure. Titania appears at both the top and the bottom of the scale, as the consort of both Oberon and Bottom, as the embodiment of pure [step]motherly love and bestial sensuality. But in this duality she is the living image of the *discordia concors,* the unity of chaste and sensual love, the natural spirit, better known as the spirit of nature. The other irony arises from another literary allusion, for Bottom derives from *The Golden Ass* of Apuleius, which was considered a significant and specifically Platonist text in the Renaissance. There Lucius is freed from his ass's shape by the goddess Isis, who has appeared to him; the return to human form is associated with an epiphanic insight. Bottom's famous speech about his inarticulable dream (IV.i.204-19) parodies the standard Neoplatonist stance on epiphany—that God cannot be perceived by the senses or articulated in the language of the senses, but only in paradox.[13] Thus Bottom, in some sense, also moves to the top of the hierarchy to establish the Christian paradox that the bottom shall be top.

Such a hierarchy implies a static plot structure, for, with the exception of Bottom and Titania, the characters move about relatively little on this scale. The action consists not of their movements on the scale—not of their development—but rather of the revelation of their proper positions on it. Under the influence of Frye and the discoverers of medieval plot structures in the comedies, *A Midsummer Night's Dream* has been read, I believe, too much in terms of purification and conversion.[14] It is hard to talk about a purification of love or realignment of love and reason in the play when in fact the couples are scarcely realigned. In the initial conflict between Hermia and her father, the love-struck maiden turns out to be right: the father is not converted; he simply disappears from the play after he is overruled. Only one lover must have his sight permanently adjusted. The fact that Demetrius's vision is adjusted only by the purple flower indicates that his real problem is not impure or unreasonable love, but inability to love at all. The couples are not purified or

permanently transformed. Rather, the implicit nature of their relationships is revealed to us, the spectators; the forms of things unknown are "bodied forth" to us.

Yet what does it mean to call this play, which has been so successful as a ballet, "static"? It is hard to imagine a comedy with a surer progression from the disorder of the human and fairy realms, through a green world, to restored order in Act IV, when Theseus and Hippolyta, the highest earthly representatives of divine order, receive their reordered world from the hands of the nature-spirits. The play moves to order or harmony, but harmony in the plot—in the love relationships, for example—is not stable peace; it is, rather, the paradoxical *coincidentia oppositorum,* the *discordia concors* of the Neoplatonists. The play insists on this definition of order precisely at the moment when the lovers pass from the control of the spirit king back to that of the earthly king in Act IV. There Theseus appears with Hippolyta, she in hunting garb as an earthly Diana, and they discuss at length the music of their hounds. The discussion bears no connection to the explicit themes of the play (love and nature), but makes perfect sense in the implicit context with its repeated formulas for *discordia concors:*

> We will, fair queen, up to the mountain's top,
> And mark the *musical confusion*
> Of hounds and *echo in conjunction*
>
> . . . . .
>
>   for besides the groves,
> The skies, the fountains, every region near
> Seem *all one mutual cry.* I never heard
> So *musical a discord, such sweet thunder.*
>   (IV.i.109-18; my italics)

The movement in the passage to the past tense emphasizes the impermanence of this orderly disorder. All order, like all insight, must be constantly reestablished anew. It is equivalent to the order of the dance that has just celebrated the reunion of Oberon and Titania. To be sure, dancing is a symbol of order and harmony, but it is a dynamic symbol; just as in Sir John Davies's "Orchestra," concord is continuously reestablished in a series of mutual movements in which a single misstep would return the order of the dance to chaos. Because the harmony of the play's conclusion is a harmony of disorder, the true plot is not the progression from disorder to order, but the revelation of the order implicit in the disorder.

It is now possible to see that the play's hierarchy of lovers is implicit in the characters' names. It has always been obvious that the names of the mechanicals playfully suggest their various crafts, but the apparently conventional classical names of the lovers are equally suggestive. The names Hermia and Demetrius derive from Hermes and Demeter. During the Renaissance, both divinities were most important for their association with pagan mystery cults, Demeter with the famous mysteries at Eleusis, Hermes with Hermes Trismegistus, the variously supposed author, collector, or codifier of a great body of mystical, magical writings from whom our word *hermetic* derives. At the same time both divinities are fertility principles—Demeter is the earth mother, known in mythology as the giver of grain, visible in this capacity under her Latin name, Ceres, in Prospero's masque in *The Tempest;* Hermes is a phallic principle.[15] The names of these two lovers thus evoke the doubleness of love in the play, physical and generative on the one hand, spiritual and mystical on the other. Hermia is the most spiritual and Demetrius, the most physical, of the four young lovers; thus the similar names do not characterize them as individuals but articulate the themes the characters are made to embody. Similarly, the fact that Hermia's name derives from a male god and Demetrius's from a goddess both dissociates the individuality of character from the name and offers yet another example of the all-pervasive harmony of opposites in the play.

The names of these characters' partners also elaborate the dual nature of love. Lysander, a conventional name, etymologically means *liberator.* By convincing Hermia to run away with him, Lysander does in fact liberate her in the name of imagination from the tyranny of her father and the law. To the extent that this liberation sets imagination or fancy over the narrow legalism of Egeus and Demetrius, it shares in the higher, spiritual aspect of love. Yet as Hermia is well aware when she will not let Lysander sleep too close to her, too much liberation can degrade love to its strictly physical aspect; this danger is immediately afterward realized in the most literal way when Puck sprinkles the juice of the purple flower in Lysander's eyes and he falls in love with Helena. Similarly, Helena is the name of the woman who was both an inspiring beauty—"the face that launch'd a thousand ships"—and a demonic paramour who tempted great men to their doom. Indeed, Demetrius must be brought up to Helena's level, while Lysander seems to "fall" in his love for Helena and must be purified again by the juice of the other flower. Once again the names articulate thematic possibilities.

In mythological terms, Theseus and Hippolyta vary this pattern. Theseus was one of the great lascivious men of antiquity: Plutarch lists nine other wives or mistresses besides Hippolyta and suggests that his many rapes "dyd geve men occasion to suspect that his wommanishenes was rather to satisfie lust, then of any great love."[16] *A Midsummer Night's Dream* appropriately begins with Theseus's impatience to consummate his marriage. Like those of the other mortal lovers, the name Theseus implies a strong tendency to sensual love; like the others, it implies something higher as well. For myth and poetry know also of a tragic Theseus

whose virtue abhorred Phaedra's lust for Hippolytos; Plutarch knows also of a generous and noble Theseus who renounced his royal power to establish the Athenian commonwealth.[17] Thus in *A Midsummer Night's Dream* the same Theseus impatiently awaits the consummation of his own marriage yet tells Hermia that the unmarried state is "thrice blessed" (I.i.74). Hippolyta's patience in that first scene similarly emphasizes her fundamental mythological attribute, chastity. As queen of the Amazons she was by definition a votary of Diana, dedicated to the virgin goddess whose silver bow she mentions in her first speech, and whose hunting costume she dons in Act IV.[18] Shakespeare follows Plutarch in his preference for the name Hippolyta (over the name Antiope, which Plutarch mentions as an alternate name for the Amazon bride of Theseus), doubtless because the name itself means "looser of horses," and horses are a standard Platonist symbol for the passions. In the tragedy of Hippolytos and Phaedra, the main quality of Hippolytos is his chastity. Yet Amazons were hardly totally spiritual beings. They were renowned warriors, so renowned and effective that Plutarch doubts they were women.[19] For the Elizabethans they signified "a false usurpation of the duties of the male reason by the lower, female passions."[20] Thus, as an Amazon, Hippolyta is an ambiguous sign that points to both a lower, sensual love and a higher, spiritual one. Shakespeare emphasizes, it seems to me, Hippolyta's Diana-like aspects, yet there is enough of the Amazon in her for other critics to stress her role in power struggles between the sexes. Again, the play itself draws out the possibilities implicit in these names.

The names of the fairy rulers close this scheme neatly. Titania is an Ovidian epithet meaning daughter of the Titan; the name refers both to Circe (in Book 14) and to Diana (in Book 3) in the *Metamorphoses*. Titania-Diana appears in the Actaeon story, where the chastity and purity of the goddess are the central issues. By contrast, Titania-Circe appears as a lustful man chaser in Ovid, and through him, is characterized similarly throughout the Renaissance. The name is thus associated with the extremes of lust and purity, of physicality and spirituality; indeed, Titania consorts alternately with the semibestial Bottom and with Oberon, ruler of nature. The sources that Shakespeare drew on for Oberon show a similar doubleness. In the epic *Huon of Bordeaux,* the fairy king Oberon is a mischievous trickster, but Spenser associates both Huon and Oberon with Sir Guyon, his knight of temperance.[21] As I have suggested, the name Oberon puns on *over.* He is indeed the ruler over the others in *A Midsummer Night's Dream,* and his name speaks most clearly of all.

It is scarcely surprising that the manipulations of Oberon and Puck so freely disrupt whatever constancy of character Shakespeare allows his lovers, for the significance of the plot has nothing to do with what happens to particular characters or with how they grow and develop. Rather, the significance of the play is implicit in their names, and the plot reveals this significance through its symmetrical juxtapositions and rearrangements of figures to illuminate the order of love implicit in the dark wood of the world. This is the sense in which they play is allegorical rather than mimetic.

The imagery, too—I will consider eyes, tears, and mythological references—involves a process of revelation. Kermode has identified how the association of eyes and judgment begins as a playful figure of speech, then becomes literally important with the manipulations of Oberon and Puck (p. 210); but he overlooks the pattern that the association follows. At both the beginning and end of the play, vision and judgment are identical. But in the middle, they separate because supernatural powers intervene: this is the season for lunatics, lovers, and poets; it is also the time of "Dark night, that from the eye his function takes" (III.ii.177). In the woods the lovers are literally and figuratively blind. Literal blindness, Hermia tells us, sharpens the hearing (III.ii.178); figurative blindness, Helena has told us in Act I, sharpens the mind to perceive higher truth (I.i.234-35). In Act III there emerges a brief moment of reciprocity: human eyes stop looking and instead the stars, "eyes of light" (III.ii.188), shine down upon the lovers. When judgment is in abeyance, the mind is open to a higher radiance. Returning to the world in Act IV, we also return to vision as judgment, but we do so with our judgment enriched by that higher radiance that can sometimes shine in, by an implicit faculty of the eyes higher than judgment.

Tears work in a similar way. At the beginning of the play they appear in conventional witty formulations as the "tempest" of the eyes (Hermia, I.i.131; Bottom moving storms in the eyes of the audience, I.ii.27). At the end of the play the clowns raise tears of merriment (V.i.69). But in between there are tears, especially Helena's, of genuine sorrow (II.ii.92-93, III.ii.158). More important, tears are seen as a quality of the moon, which governs the action of the play: the moon governs floods (II.i.103) and beholds her visage "in the wat'ry glass" (I.i.210); the "chaste beams of the wat'ry moon" quench the fire of Cupid's arrow (II.i.162); and when the moon weeps, "weeps every little flower, / Lamenting some enforced chastity" (III.i.199-200). If tears designate the moon—the principle of heavenly love—then when Helena weeps she is indeed out of her usual witty worldly self. Finally, tears unite nature and the heavens at the moment Oberon begins to pity Titania:

> And that same dew which sometime on the
>   buds
> Was wont to swell like round and orient
>   pearls,
> Stood now within the pretty flouriets' eyes,
> Like tears that did their own disgrace bewail.
>
>   (IV.i.53-56)

If dewdrops are the tears of nature, man's tears allow him to participate in the generative transforming powers of nature. Once again this excursion into creativity occurs in the hiatus in the play; poets are indeed like lunatics (followers of the moon) and lovers. When we return to the play of the clowns and Philostrate's tears of merriment, this power is once again only implicit, but not forgotten.

Nowhere is this implicit higher harmony more important in the play than in the mythological references, for the opposition of the two kinds of love is also expressed through the opposition between Cupid and Diana. It appears first in the ambiguity of the bow: the moon is likened to a silver bow, the attribute of Diana, in the first exchange between Hippolyta and Theseus; later Hermia swears to Lysander by Cupid's strongest bow (I.i.169). The moon is indelibly associated with the chastity of Diana; nevertheless, so much emphasis is laid upon its mutability and its beneficent interaction with the world that it equally implies Diana's opposite, the generative power of the physical world. Cupid and Diana are more obviously opposed in the two flowers, on which the action turns. The purple flower originally receives its power when it is struck by Cupid's arrow. The arrow, though it is aimed at the fair vestal of the west, is quenched by "the chaste beams of the wat'ry moon" (II.i.162). When the resolution approaches, the fair vestal has become, in effect, the white companion flower that quenches the potency of the purple one. But not only Cupid opposes Diana; Venus does as well, for Hermia also swears by the doves of Venus (I.i.171). Venus returns in Act III as the morning star, the harbinger of dawn and of the final harmony. Whether Venus seems to be the morning star ("Aurora's harbinger" [III.ii.380], "yonder Venus in her glimmering sphere" [61]) or explicitly the goddess ("the Venus of the sky" [107]), the goddess is present in all these formulations, for the "Venus of the sky" is Venus Urania, the heavenly Venus, embodiment of the love that is the harmony of the cosmos. She is here not the opposite of Diana but the glorious synthesis of the opposing tendencies represented by Diana and by the lower, earthly Venus of the doves. It is in this part of the play that the eyes of the lovers light up into stars. This Venus embodies the true love of Renaissance Neoplatonists—love that embraces vulgar and heavenly love. Diana-Venus and Diana-Cupid are again aspects of one another, implicit in one another and, as moon and stars, in nature as well.[22]

Two aspects of these patterns of imagery are important. The first is that the moments of revelation of the higher, spiritual truth implicit in the image tend to come in the middle of the play. We are offered flashes of insight and then a return to more ordinary uses of the image at the end, just as we are taken from the fairy forest back to the more "real" court at the end of the play. We learned from the love stories that the "plot" of *A Midsummer Night's Dream* is really the revelation of implicit order in disorder, and the imagery shows the mechanism of that revelation: epiphanic moments (the "dreams" of the characters), whose radiance, internalized by the spectator, continues to illuminate the world long after the moment has passed. The second important aspect is the way figures and images, with seemingly endless capacity to substitute for one another, are woven in an elaborate web of analogy. This fluid and rich signifying capacity of the world is typical of the Neoplatonist mode, as is the temporal dynamic of the imagery. In the seemingly limitless ability of the world and love to signify more than what appears to the eye lies access to higher truth.

By the end of the fourth act, *A Midsummer Night's Dream* thus appears to have established its hierarchy of the Neoplatonist mystery of love and its typically Neoplatonist mode of communicating its higher truth. What remains for the rest of the play? Is the mechanicals' play to be understood as a burlesque of the Neoplatonist theme, as it clearly is of the love story at the level of plot? Or does it elaborate the Neoplatonist order of the play by extending it explicitly to the realm of poetics? Or does it go off in some new direction altogether? The difficulty, and the triumph, of the play is that all three of these alternatives seem to be the case.

It is not difficult to identify the burlesque elements in the clown plot. Just as the absurd traged reverses the only slightly less absurd comedy of the love plot, the famous results of the tragedy in Ovid (that the berries of the mulberry tree turn forever after from white to purple) reverse the hierarchy of the plain, presumably white flower over the purple one in the main plot. Bottom's report of his supposed vision in the wood parodies, as we have already seen, the Neoplatonist insistence on the ineffability of knowledge of higher truth. But the confusion of the senses that constitutes the humor of Bottom's speech ("The eye of man hath not heard, the ear of man hath not seen," etc. [IV.i.211-14]) pervades the entire play of the mechanicals: Pyramus sees a voice and tries to hear his Thisby's face (V.i.192-93); by the "sunny beams" of the moon he asks his eyes if they can see (V.i.272-79); he dies crying "Tongue, lose thy light" (V.i.304); and Lion offers the audience the choice of seeing the epilogue or of hearing a Bergomask dance (V.i.352-54). The themes of light and darkness, and seeing and judgment, so richly variable in the main plot, remain uniformly confused and absurb for the mechanicals. Similarly, Oberon renders the abstractions of the hierarchy of love concretely visible in the two flowers; when Puck renders Bottom's foolishness equally visible by giving him an ass's head, we seem to be once more in the realm of the burlesque.

Yet precisely this motif shows the ambiguity of the burlesque in this play. As we have already seen, in

Apuleius the theme of the fool turned into an ass had serious import for the Neoplatonists. Indeed, the fact that the clowns perform so badly—the essence of their burlesque—also has a positive function. The theory of love embodied in the play treats the lower sensual love as a metaphorical steppingstone to the higher love of the divine and thus to the experience of the divine. But the earthly lover who overlooks the metaphorical nature of sensual love and remains caught in it, who mistakes it for the only or the "real" love, is little better than a beast.[23] Similarly, the error of the ass Bottom is that he mistakes the literal level of the text for its significance. But so gross is this error that it paradoxically emphasizes the truth that Bottom overlooks—the metaphorical nature of the text. The clowns' play is so bad that no one could possibly mistake it for reality, for something known, and thus fail to see that it "bodies forth / The forms of things unknown" (V.i.14-15). The destruction of illusion in the play frees us from the illusion of the world and reminds us of its—and the text's—allegorical nature.[24] The text suggests that the improbable, dreamlike nature of the play, its disjointed plotting, and its lack of differentiated characters are its greatest strengths.

Nor must we overlook the mediating function of the clowns. Bottom becomes, willy-nilly, the instrument of mediation between Oberon and Titania.[25] Titania's love for Bottom evokes both Titania's generosity and Oberon's pity, what we have identified as the highest forms of love in the play, and the two actions about which the plot turns. Bottom's "election" to this role appears to be quite random; but, for a Neoplatonist, chance must of necessity rule in a world not illuminated by divine truth. In any case, it is not entirely by chance, for Bottom has already demonstrated an extraordinary willingness to play any role the world or Quince might have to offer. The fact that the occupations of the mechanicals all involve repair and/or joining together is surely significant; they are all by definition mediators. And of these occupations, the one that can serve as a metaphor for poetry is Bottom's—weaving. It is only appropriate, then, that their play should tie the knot of the marriages at the end of the play. Indeed, the play is another of these knots, for in terms of the thematics of *A Midsummer Night's Dream* both marriage and play constitute a harmony of opposites: marriage is a human metaphor, a union of male and female; the play is an aesthetic metaphor, the union of literal and figurative, physical reality and higher truth.[26] Theseus even asks, after reading the title of the play, "How shall we find the concord of this discord?" (V.i.60). The thematics of the clown plot thus extend the concord/discord theme to the realm of poetics, where the poles are not two kinds of love, but two kinds of reality; for the humor turns on the clowns' inability to separate the physical reality of their play from the "truth" it represents. But if love and play are equivalent, if true love is knowledge of truth, then *A Mid-*

summer Night's Dream is not most usefully thought of as a play about marriage. It is better thought of as a play about how we know.

The exchange between Theseus and Hippolyta on the strangeness of the lovers' story that immediately precedes the play within the play would appear to fit with this extension into the realm of poetics. Poetry in this play indeed "bodies forth / The forms of things unknown" and transfigures minds. But the very interest of Hippolyta and Theseus's exchange depends on the shimmering tension between reality and illusion that is central to the clown plot. Theseus and Hippolyta are, the first scene has told us, *the* Theseus and Hippolyta of Greek myth. Theseus reminds us again of this fact when he refers to his kinsman Hercules and his own conquest of Thebes (V.i.46-51). It is not a little curious, then, that Theseus is unwilling to believe these "antic fables" (V.i.3). It is even more curious when we note that Plutarch, Shakespeare's source, begins his biography of the hero by saying:

> . . . I would have wished that the fables of antiquity had been set out so in our writings, that we might yet have graced them with some appearance of historical narration. But if by chance in some places they range a little too boldly out of the bounds or limits of true appearance, and have no manner of conformity with any credibleness of matter, the readers in courtesy must needs hold me excused, accepting in good part that which may be written and reported of things so extremely old and ancient.[27]

Shakespeare's Theseus derives his power and centrality in this play precisely from his paradoxical union of the mythic with the rational. Puck reformulates Plutarch's apology in the epilogue, significantly transforming the stories of antiquity—antic fables—into dreams and visions, Neoplatonist vehicles of higher truth. Both Puck and Theseus refer in these passages to the love plot, not to the clown plot. Nevertheless, the strategic location of these passages as a frame to a play whose whole interest turns on the relation of reality to illusion identifies clearly enough the serious aspect of the clowning. The central issue in the play is the relation of reality to illusion, of reality to higher significance, and that significance is accessible only in the visionary dream of the play.

Yet if the play really proposes such a poetics, as it seems to do, why should Theseus, who rejects the madness of the visionary poet, emerge as the defender of the mechanicals? For Theseus insists, over the opposition of Philostrate and Hippolyta, that their play be performed, claiming that his own imagination will mend their defects. Such a poetics of complicity is surely typical of Shakespeare—one need only think of the prologues to *Henry V*—but it goes beyond Neoplatonism in significant ways. When Theseus concludes "Love, therefore, and tongue-tied simplicity / In least

speak most, to my capacity" (V.i.104-5), the inadequate expression of the actor would seem to be an imperfect, typically Neoplatonist metaphor for an ineffable truth; but when the imperfect metaphor must be supplemented from the imagination of the spectator, we have moved into a new realm. Neoplatonist higher truth is there, transcendent and ineffable though it may be, always ready to be apprehended in some moment of ecstasy and insight; it is apprehended in dreams and visions. But the willed imaginative act of the spectator is not a moment of revelation that transforms the spectator into a passive vessel of the truth. Were the spectator a frenzied poet, such might be the case. But Theseus, Hippolyta, Demetrius, and Lysander are not poets, and most certainly not while they are commenting on the play of the mechanicals. The imaginative aid Theseus brings to the play within the play is not higher insight, but human reason. The locus of its truth is not transcendent but in the human mind.

In one sense this doubling of the truth is typical of the pattern we have seen in the play. As there is a pure, spiritual love, there is also physical love, Diana *and* Cupid, healing flower *and* purple flower. Here is but another discord of which the play itself is the concord. This discord is resolved for the last time in Puck's epilogue:

> If we shadows have offended,
> Think but this, and all is mended,
> That you have but slumb'red here
> While these visions did appear.
>
> (V.i.423-26)

Whether these visions are understood to embody Neoplatonist truth or nothing at all, they nevertheless appear to a slumbering, passive audience, while Puck's call "Think but this" engages the active complicity about which Theseus spoke. This synthesis seems to me deliberately weak (the visionary moment is much stronger than the active, imaginative one) and therefore discordant. It is also weakened by its irony. Theseus has appeared as a rationalist whose point of view the play largely discredits. His "poetics" is synthesized here with that of the incompetent mechanicals by the trickster Puck. Yet as a trickster, liar, and mis-leader of souls in the dark, Puck is a dark reflection of Hermes, mystic synthesizer of the wisdom inherited by the Neoplatonists. The obvious playfulness emphasizes the real discord. It suggests that these two kinds of truth are not simply Plato's call for an expositor to interpret the visions that can come only to one who is out of his wits (*Timaeus* 72a). Theseus's imaginative supplementation far exceeds anything Plato says about interpretation in the *Timaeus:* there is no synthesis between these opposing truths except the play itself.[28]

Thus the doubleness of truth is, despite Puck's epilogue, more than Neoplatonist playfulness. It offers a way of describing what we often perceive vaguely as Shakespeare's universality. The play unambiguously locates truth both in the transcendent realm—in the mind of the Neoplatonist God—and simultaneously in the mind of the spectator. Such doubleness is astonishing but does occur in the work of Shakespeare's Spanish contemporaries. *Don Quixote* balances between a world in which the givens come from without (in part 1) and within the fiction (in part 2). Similarly, Lope de Vega is capable of leaving deliberately unclear at the end whether certain fundamental truths, on which the validity of an entire play depends, are grounded in anything more than the will of certain characters in the play and, ultimately, of the play's spectators.[29] In Cervantes and Lope de Vega the complicity of the spectator is a tantalizing game, an intriguing and entertaining twist; but in *A Midsummer Night's Dream,* it is neither a problem nor tantalizing, it is simply there. Truth is both transcendent and immanent in *A Midsummer Night's Dream* and because it is unproblematically everywhere, the play itself embodies a kind of universal order, the concord of all discord.

Notes

[1] On fancy and imagination see C. L. Barber, *Shakespeare's Festive Comedy: A Study of Dramatic Form and Its Relation to Social Custom* (Princeton: Princeton University Press, 1972), pp. 116-62; and Marjorie B. Garber, *Dream in Shakespeare: From Metaphor to Metamorphosis* (New Haven: Yale University Press, 1974), pp. 59-87. On marriage and sexual politics, see Paul A. Olson, "*A Midsummer Night's Dream* and the Meaning of Court Marriage," *ELH,* 24 (1957): 95-119; Louis Adrian Montrose, "'Shaping Fantasies': Figurations of Gender and Power in Elizabethan Culture," *Representations,* 1 (Spring 1983): 61-94; and Shirley Nelson Garner, "*A Midsummer Night's Dream:* 'Jack shall have Jill; / Nought shall go ill,'" *WS,* 9 (1981/82): 47-63.

[2] *Pagan Mysteries in the Renaissance,* rev. ed. (New York: W. W. Norton, 1968); on the centrality of love in the Neoplatonist mysteries, see p. 38. The description of this "mystery" below is a condensation of issues relevant to *A Midsummer Night's Dream* from Wind's discussions in the first chapters.

[3] Challenging discussions of the poetics of the play in the context of Renaissance Neoplatonism may be found in Richard Cody, *The Landscape of the Mind: Pastoralism and Platonic Theory in Tasso's "Aminta" and Shakespeare's Early Comedies* (Oxford: Clarendon Press, 1969), pp. 127-50; and in Jackson I. Cope, *The Theater and the Dream: From Metaphor to Form in Renaissance Drama* (Baltimore: Johns Hopkins University Press, 1973), pp. 219-25. Neoplatonist thematics in *A Midsummer Night's Dream* are also addressed in John Vyvyan, *Shakespeare and Platonic Beauty* (London: Chatto & Windus, 1961), pp. 77-91, and, briefly,

in Frank Kermode, *Shakespeare, Spenser, Donne: Renaissance Essays* (London: Routledge & Kegan Paul, 1971), pp. 207-9, and Howard Nemerov, "The Marriage of Theseus and Hippolyta," *KR,* 18 (1956): 633-41.

[4] The line of transmission to Shakespeare would be through Ficino's translations into Latin and Italian, with commentary, of Plato and Plotinus—possibly directly, certainly at least through the transmission of Castiglione and Spenser (Vyvyan, pp. 33-61); Cody also traces lines of transmission through Sidney, Montemayor, and Tasso, pp. 81-82. Cody communicates, *passim,* a good sense for the bewildering complexity of Ficino's thought, as does Michael J. B. Allen in *The Platonism of Marsilio Ficino: A Study of His "Phaedrus" Commentary, Its Sources and Genesis* (Berkeley: University of California Press, 1984).

[5] E.g., pp. 73-77, 97; Shakespearean wordplay on Neoplatonist phraseology is discussed on pp. 58 and 92. See also Cody: "To an audience familiar with Ovidian mythology and how the Platonists read it, the esoteric sense of the fairy plot [of *A Midsummer Night's Dream*] is quite as overt as its absurdity" (p. 136).

[6] On the ambiguity of the bow, see Wind, p. 78; on Venus-Diana and the unity of chastity and love, see pp. 77-79, 200. Compare also the extended discussion of the unity of the three graces (Beauty, Chastity, and Pleasure), pp. 73-75.

[7] All quotations of Shakespeare are taken from *The Riverside Shakespeare,* ed. G. Blakemore Evans (Boston: Houghton Mifflin, 1974). Wind points to the Neoplatonist significance of this line (p. 58).

[8] David Marshall, "Exchanging Visions: Reading *A Midsummer Night's Dream,*" *ELH,* 49 (1982): 543-75, justifiably criticizes the tradition of "Thesean" readings of the scene, but offers, as he admits, a "Hippolytan" one, pp. 549-52. My reading is instead dialectical. Cf. also Cody, p. 146.

[9] See Marshall, pp. 551-54; cf. also Montrose, pp. 61-94, and Garner, pp. 52-59.

[10] N.B. III.ii.137-44: "O Helen, goddess, nymph, perfect, divine!" etc., which is broad parody of Petrarchan language. Lysander uses this language briefly, while he is under the influence of the purple flower; Demetrius, however, remains under its influence until the end of the play.

[11] In her elaborate word play she is much closer to the language of *Love's Labor's Lost* than any of the others; it is she who introduces rhymed couplets into the play.

[12] Garner argues that Oberon humiliates Titania, citing only Titania's line "O, how mine eyes do loathe his

visage now!" (IV.i.79) in support, pp. 49-51. Nothing in the text warrants extending this loathing of Bottom's face into self-loathing.

[13] The specific object of the parody is 1 Corinthians 2: 9-13, an extremely Platonist moment in that text. See Kermode, pp. 208-9.

[14] Kermode, for example, reads the play as a purification of vision; Olson sees a triple structure of order, a "fall" into "unbridled passion," and a return to order (see especially p. 101).

[15] Recognized as such in *herm*aphrodite (see Wind, p. 200), and in the sacred marriage of the alchemists, in which the element mercury (Mercury = Hermes) was the male lover. In the Renaissance alchemy functioned as a debased form of Neoplatonism—applied mysticism, so to speak; see Wind, pp. 214-15. Cf. Wayne Shumaker, *The Occult Sciences in the Renaissance: A Study in Intellectual Patterns* (Berkeley: University of California Press, 1972), p. 196.

[16] Cited from Sir Thomas North's translation in Geoffrey Bullough, *Narrative and Dramatic Sources of Shakespeare,* 8 vols. (London: Routledge and Kegan Paul, 1957-75), 1: 388.

[17] Bullough, pp. 385, 388.

[18] Such a connection appears explicitly in William D'Avenant's *Salmacida Spolia,* where the queen appears as an Amazon and is connected to Diana and her purity (*The Dramatic Works of Sir William D'Avenant,* 5 vols. [Edinburgh and London, 1872], 2: 323-24).

[19] Bullough, p. 386.

[20] Olson, p. 102.

[21] *The Faerie Queene,* II.i.6. The chaplet from the fairy-king Auberon presented to Elizabeth under the name of Phoebe in "The Entertainment at Elvetham" (1591; in John Nichols's *Progresses and Public Processions of Queen Elizabeth,* 3 vols. [London, 1823], 3:100-121) also documents the accepted logic of connecting Oberon with chastity in the late sixteenth century.

[22] See Wind on Venus-Diana and on the intriguing possibility that the cult of Elizabeth as Diana was in fact also a cult of her as Venus, pp. 77-78.

[23] This is precisely the problem of Apuleius's Lucius, who lives his life as an ass until he transfers his love from women to the goddess Isis.

[24] Cf. Cope's contextualization of the dramaturgy of the mechanicals in the Renaissance controversy on the

significance of dreams, pp. 222-24, and Marshall's discussion of the play as being about figuring, p. 569.

[25] Cf. Cody on Bottom as Midas, read by the Neoplatonists as a version of the "wise fool," pp. 136-38.

[26] Cf. J. Dennis Huston's observation that the mechanicals, like the lovers, also flee to the woods in his excellent discussion of the mechanicals' plot as parody of the love plot in *Shakespeare's Comedies of Play* (New York: Columbia University Press, 1981), p. 108.

[27] North's translation, cited from *Shakespeare's Library,* ed. W. C. Hazlitt, 6 vols. (London, 1875), 1:8.

[28] For a different, more psychologically focused reading of the need for participatory imagination in this play, see James L. Calderwood, *Shakespearean Metadrama: The Argument of the Play in "Titus Andronicus," "Love's Labour's Lost," "Romeo and Juliet," "A Midsummer Night's Dream" and "Richard II"* (Minneapolis: University of Minnesota Press, 1971), pp. 135-38.

[29] In *El perro del hortelano,* for example, Teodoro wins the countess Diana because his valet tricks everyone into believing the hero to be a nobleman. In a fit of honesty Teodoro reveals that his parentage is in truth unknown, but the countess does not care, so long as the valet and the audience will keep the secret. Here the play ends.

Jeffrey Shulman (essay date 1987)

SOURCE: "Bottom is Up: The Role of Illusion in *A Midsummer Night's Dream,*" in *Essays in Arts and Sciences,* Vol. XVI, May, 1987, pp. 9-21.

[*In the following essay, Shulman studies the relationship between illusion, love, and art in* A Midsummer Night's Dream, *arguing that the "process of illusion" offers insight into both love and art, and that Shakespeare uses illusion to guide his characters to more mature perspectives about love and marriage.*]

Like Hermia, the student of *A Midsummer Night's Dream* needs to see "with parted eye" (IV.i.188)[1] for the *Dream* has a double focus. It is on the one hand about love and the relationship of the varieties of love experience to marriage; on the other hand, it is about art and the uses and abuses of artistic expression, and particularly the dramatic experience. The "concord of this discord" (V.i.60) lies in the concept of illusion, which, at least in the world of the *Dream,* is the common denominator of love and art. In both cases, the process of illusion is the vehicle of insight. In both cases, the process of illusion involves the surrendering of one way of seeing, of one identity, for a new and more mature perspective. That surrender of identity is a difficult though equally comic experience. The path to maturity is a woodland track fraught with the magical tumult of delusion, madness, blindness, and nonsense.

The volume of interpretation on the twin themes of love and art in the *Dream* is, to say the least, imposing. While this paper borrows from much past criticism,[2] I have tried to examine an aspect of the *Dream's* coherence which has received relatively little attention. In the context of the Dream, the problems of both true love and good art may be seen as problems of perception, of finding the focal distance between object and subject, between the mere literalism of strict objectivity—seeing only with the eyes—and the sheer madness of extreme subjectivity—seeing only with the mind. Proper lovers and artists see with what Sydney calls the "eyes of the mind."[3] This vision entails a meeting of subject and object in a creative perceptual act, synthesizing other and self, the literal and the imaginative (or, in Theseus' words, the faculties of comprehension and apprehension) and thus offers us a new and more complete reality. Shakespeare's *Dream* uses illusion to motivate, bewilder, and ultimately lead his lovers—and his readers—to a better understanding of this creative synthesis both in marriage and drama.

A Midsummer Night's Dream moves in two directions. It moves chronologically and, as it were, horizontally through the action of the drama. This movement employs the familiar comic patterns of Saturnalian release which Barber finds to be the mechanism of clarification in the "festive" plays of Shakespeare. Barber identifies the particular pattern of the *Dream* as "a release of shaping fantasy which brings clarification about the tricks of strong imagination":

> As in *Love's Labour's Lost* the folly of wit becomes the generalized comic subject in the course of an astonishing release of witty invention, so here in the course of a more inclusive release of imagination, the folly of fantasy becomes the general subject, echoed back and forth between the strains of the play's imitative counterpoint.[4]

The horizontal pattern of sexual clarification is tripartite: it involves the movement from a stage of youthful bonding preliminary to the action of the drama, through the literal or metaphoric battle of opposite sexes, to the eventual "conjuction [of] natural opposites"[5] in marriage. As we move from Athenian daylight to the moonlit woods, the poetic terms of the clarification movement change from the literal to the symbolic, but the process of clarification remains the same.

The *Dream* also moves vertically through a psychological hierarchy of love. As Andrew Weiner has noted, the four sets of lovers form a composite picture of the varieties of love experience:

> Through these four sets of characters and their interaction, Shakespeare anatomizes various facets of the relationships between men and woman (taking, for a moment, Oberon and Titania as man and woman) as they progress towards the state of husband and wife or struggle to remain husband and wife or fail to become husband and wife.[6]

Equally important is the fact that the eight lovers form a composite picture of the reasoning and imaginative faculties of the human psyche. The worlds of cool reason and heated fancy are links in a common chain; as we shall see, Theseus himself is inextricably tied to the fairy world he so disdains. Though Shakespeare does not intend a formal psychomachia, the *Dream* deals less with personality and motive than with states of mind. Perhaps I should add states of a *single* mind whose multiple perspectives are not the static stage properties of set characters but the natural propensities of the mind at different stages of human growth.

Moreover, Shakespeare has interrelated the top and bottom rungs of the psychological hierarchy—the courts of the real and fairy worlds—in his revelation of the amorous histories of the royal couples: Titania's attachment towards Theseus and Oberon's enchantment with Hippolyta. Besides framing and somewhat paralleling the mixed matches of the young lovers, this arrangement significantly presents the world of forest fancy as a force operative in, and perhaps subversive of, the royal reign of reason. The intricate and unsuspected tie between the rational and the imaginative spheres of the human psyche is given climactic expression in visual representation as the train of fairies, its peace again restored, sings and dances round the sleeping royal household in a prophetic vision of harmony and fruition.

Of course, these two structures overlap; they are in fact one structure, and their very simultaneity makes the dramatic point. In the world of the *Dream,* the clarification of attitudes towards love and marriage is realized only through a necessary psychological descent to the "folly of fantasy," to the magic of illusion. Perspective about love can be achieved only through illusion, through loss of perspective. In this play, love and reason keep little company. Most critics emphasize one aspect of the total structural design over the other and fail to see the fall into fantasy as the fortunate means of sexual clarification. Thus they either simplify the *Dream* as merely the folly of imaginative abuse or trouble themselves with Platonic allegories or Christian moralisms in looking at the meaning of the love design within the *Dream*. The assumption that the main action of this midsummer night is Shakespeare's wry comment on the irrationality of heady love has seemed self-evident to most critics. However, the influence of irrational love is, in fact, the force which conducts the lovers from their preliminary stages of love experience to the maturity of marriage. It is the illusive power of dotage which enables the lovers to escape the confines of self and past. To understand why illusion should play such a central role, it is first necessary to examine the hierarchy of the imagination against which we may evaluate the constancy of the lovers' "story of the night" (V.i.24).

I

Naturally enough, the forest world of irrational misadventure has attracted a considerable volume of critical effort intent on pinning down its exact nature. It has been seen as a world of Platonic norms, of Christian grace, of the Freudian subconscious, of elemental nature, of primitive folklore--the list has no end.[8] When Bottom tells us "Man is but an ass if he go about to expound this dream" (IV.i.203-4), to a certain extent, he is right; elusiveness is the nature of dream. However, if the critic can resist the imposition of his own forms, the fierce vexation of the midsummer night might yield more than weak and idle themes. In fact, objectifying experience by the imposition of preconceived form is precisely what characterizes the world of Theseus and Egeus. Egeus conceives of romantic love in terms of this process:

> Thou has by moonlight at her window sung
> With feigning voice verses of feigning love,
> And stol'n the impression of her fantasy.
>
> (I.i.30-2)

Theseus echoes Egeus' "aesthetic" in his conception of filial love:

> What say you, Hermia? Be advised, fair
>   maid.
> To you your father should be as a god,
> One that composed your beauties; yea, and
>   one
> To whom you are but as a form in wax,
> By him imprinted, and within his power
> To leave the figure, or disfigure it.
>
> (I.i.46-52)

They both see love and obedience as a stamping process, in which the love-object is made to conform to the will of the maker, in this case, to enforced marriage or enforced chastity. There is no illusion involved in this aesthetic of love; Theseus and Egeus want a literal change in Hermia.

Diametrically opposed to this extreme is the treatment of love as totally independent of the will of the perceiver and the literal reality of the love-object—a thoroughly subjective operation of the fantasy. This is the virtue of love-in-idleness, which "will make or man or woman madly dote / Upon the next live creature that it sees" (II.i.171-2). It is, of course, the extreme sub-

jectivity of Titania's response to this potion that makes even Bottom aware of the ludicrousness of enchantment: "Methinks, mistress, you should have little reason for that. And yet, to say the truth, reason and love keep little company nowadays" (III.i.129-31). In one sense, however, Titania's victimization by illusion is not so absurd. She is the denizen of a moonlit world where forms are not fixed, where objective reality is everywhere subject to constant change. The genial spirits of the forest, Oberon and Puck, are masters of illusion, both in transforming themselves and others. Oberon is director of Puck's performances; like Peter Quince, though, he has his difficulties controlling his actor once the spirit of illusion is freed. Titania herself is identified in Shakespeare's Ovidian sources (particularly, *Met.* III, 173) with Diana, goddess of the changing moon. As the many guises of Puck remind us, to describe the inhabitants of the fairy world as divine, human, vegetable, or mineral, is to delimit, not to define:

> I'll follow you; I'll lead you about a round
> Through bog, through bush, through brake,
>   through brier.
> Sometime a horse I'll be, sometime a hound,
>   A hog, a headless bear, sometime a fire;
> And neigh, and bark, and grunt, and roar, and
>   burn,
> Like horse, hound, hog, bear, fire, at every
>   turn.
>
> (III.i.96-101)

These are the symbols of illusion and illusion's power to alter reality.

Between the objective world of law and war and the subjective world of change and confusion exist the two sets of lovers. Theirs is a progress to a new view of love as a creative act of perception, neither grossly literal in its demands nor patently absurd in its subjective assertions. True love blends subject and object in a new union, a new identity. It is illusion, it is the elfish Puck, which confuses subject and object and, by doing so, makes us question who we are. The medium of Puck's power is love, and its effects are two-fold. It compels the women into a reversal of their customary roles, with both positive and negative results, and it also suggests to the men the indiscretion of love that looks only with the eyes.

II

It is in the women of the *Dream* that we most clearly find evidence of a preliminary stage of youthful association, in this case, same-sex bonding. Hippolyta is the former Amazonian queen. Helena is appalled when she assumes that Hermia has joined the confederacy of men; she calls forth the memory of a bygone corporate identity:

We, Hermia, like two artificial gods,
Have with our needles created both one
    flower,
Both on one sampler, sitting on one cushion,
Both warbling of one song, both in one key,
As if our hands, our sides, voices, and
    minds
Had been incorporate. So we grew together,
Like to a double cherry, seeming parted,
But yet an union in partition—
Two lovely berries moulded on one stem;
So, with two seeming bodies, but one heart;
Two of the first, like coats in heraldry,
Due but to one, and crowned with one crest.

                            (III.ii.203-214)

Not only does Titania recall the moment of feminine alliance, but the memory evokes a sense of the continuing responsibility of sisterhood:

    Set your heart at rest.
    The fairyland buys not the child of me.
    His mother was a vot'ress of my order,
    And in the spiced Indian air, by night,
    Full often hath she gossiped by my side;

              . . . . . .

    And for her sake do I rear up her boy;
    And for her sake I will not part with him.
                            (II.i.121-4, 136-7)

Barber sees in this passage "a glimpse of women who gossip alone, apart from men and feeling now no need of them, rejoicing in their own special part of life's power."[9] The effects of this sororal loyalty are well known, but it should always be kept in mind that the main action of the *Dream*—the lovers' adventures—is framed not only by marital ordering in the social world but by marital disorder in the underworld of psychic symbols. The connections between these worlds are intimate enough so as to make the movement to sexual clarification in society dependent upon the restoration of sexual harmony in the psychic order.

Oberon's semi-rhetorical query to his queen—"Am not I thy lord?" (II.i.63)—reinforces another consideration of particular importance to Shakespeare's women in this preliminary stage of the *Dream*'s sexual movement—the question of possession. Athenian law says that the unmarried woman belongs to the father. The law speaks through Egeus:

    Be it so she will not here before your Grace
    Consent to marry with Demetrius,
    I beg the ancient privilege of Athens:
    As she is mine, I may dispose of her.

And again:

    Scornful Lysander, true, he hath my love,
    And what is mine my love shall render him.
    And she is mine, and all my right of her
    I do estate unto Demetrius.
                            (I.i.39-42, 95-8)

Possession is, at least, a form of identification and definition. However, as the pattern of sexual clarification proceeds and we leave the world of father and law and struggle toward a new identity in marriage, we must leave behind our sense of who and what we are. This feeling of dispossession characterizes Hermia and Helena as they are alternately pursued and abandoned.

Obviously enough, the women are not helped in their confusion by the male characters, who are undergoing changes of their own. The youthful associations of the males are marked not by same-sex bonding but by a cavalier attitude of fickleness, unfaithfulness, even treachery towards the opposite sex. The legendary exploits of "Thesea crudelem"[10] are alluded to:

    Oberon
    How canst thou thus, for shame, Titania
    Glance at my credit with Hippolyta,
    Knowing I know thy love to Theseus?
    Didst thou not lead him through the
        glimmering night
    From Perigenia, whom he ravished?
    And make him with fair Aegles break his
        faith,
    With Ariadne, and Antiopa?
                            (II.i.74-80)

Oberon's past proclivities have set no model of princely decorum:

    Titania
    Then I must be thy lady; but I know
    When thou has stolen away from fairyland,
    And in the shape of Corin sat all day,
    Playing on pipes of corn, and versing love
    To amorous Phillida. Why art thou here,
    Come from the farthest steep of India,
    But that, forsooth, the bouncing Amazon,
    Your buskined mistress and your warrior love,
    To Theseus must be wedded, and you come
    To give their bed joy and prosperity?
                            (II.i.64-73)

And Demetrius shares the taint of the general censure:

    Lysander
    Demetrius, I'll avouch it to his head,
    Made love to Nedar's daughter, Helena,
    And won her soul; and she (sweet lady) dotes,
    Devoutly dotes, dotes in idolatry,
    Upon this spotted and inconstant man.
                            (I.i.106-10)

Only Lysander is unmarred by actions preliminary to the play, but his exemption is short-lived.

The males at this state are as far removed from hetero-sexual marriage as the women "rejoicing in their own special part of life's power." Their untrustworthiness itself must seem excuse enough for the perpetuation of sororal relations. Certainly, Hermia is aware of this obstacle to the course of true love when she swears "by all the vows that ever men have broke" (I.i.176). For the men at this stage, woman has become objec-tified, impersonalized—a something to have, to pos-sess, without fear of the investment of the self. Theseus, who has literally won Hippolyta with his sword, is unable to see Hermia other than as an object of her father or the law: "Be advised, fair maid. To you your father should be as a god." It is an exaggerated will-ingness to subjectify love experience, to invest the self in the love object, that characterizes the fumbling efforts of Lysander and Demetrius in their groping towards the union of subject and object in marriage. That same willingness, however, will ultimately in-sure their success.

Criticism of the *Dream* invariably treats the four lov-ers as common victims of love-sickness. While it is true that they are not differentiated as individuals, there are distinctions to be made. Most noticeably, the women are constant in their attachments; they are not the vic-tims of "fairy ointments." They sense very early in the play that love is not a mere question of objective ex-perience. Hermia wishes Egeus could see Lysander "with my eyes" (I.i.56), that is, from her subjective point of view, and Helena gives a fuller exposition of the same idea:

> Things base and vile, holding no quantity,
> Love can transpose to form and dignity,
> Love looks not with the eyes, but with the
>   mind,
> And therefore is winged Cupid painted blind.
> Nor hath Love's mind of any judgement
>   taste;
> Wings, and no eyes, figure unheedy haste.
>   (I.i.232-37)

This is why the physical differentiation of the males is so insignificant; we need to see them with the eyes of Helena and Hermia. Furthermore, the women are aware of the dangers involved in such subjectivity. Helena's words recall Hermia's "false Troyan" oath:

> And therefore is Love said to be a child,
> Because in choice he is so oft beguiled.
> As waggish boys in game themselves
>   forswear,
> So the boy Love is perjured everywhere.
> For ere Demetrius looked on Hermia's eyne,
> He hailed down oaths that he was only mine;

> And when this hail some heat from Hermia
>   felt,
> So he dissolved, and show'rs of oaths did
>   melt.
>   (I.i.238-45)

Hermia's dream of the serpent at her breast leaves her quaking with the fear of premonition.

Nevertheless, love comples the women to abandon the situations by which they were previously defined and to seek a new, more aggressive, more fully hu-man role. The power which motivates Hermia is not consciously understood; it carries the strength of a deeper conviction:

> I do entreat your Grace to pardon me.
> I know not by what power I am made bold,
> Nor how it may concern my modesty
> In such a presence here to plead my thoughts;
> But I beseech your Grace that I may know
> The worst that may befall me in this case
> If I refuse to wed Demetrius.
>
>   . . . . .
>
> So will I grow, so live, so die, my lord,
> Ere I will yield my virgin patent up
> Unto his lordship whose unwished yoke
> My soul consents not to give sovereignty.
>   (I.i.58-64, 79-82)

Though Helena wants to be used as Demetrius' spaniel, love's complexities put her in the position of pursuit:

> Run when you will. The story shall be
>   changed:
> Apollo flies and Daphne holds the chase,
> The dove pursues the griffon, the mild hind
> Makes speed to catch the tiger—bootless
>   speed,
> When cowardice pursues, and valor flies.
>   (II.i.230-4)

When they are faced with rejection, however, the women become the victims of their lovers' exaggerated sub-jectivity, despising and questioning their own identi-ties. This is Helena's situation from the start of the play:

> Sickness is catching. O, were favor so,
> Yours would I catch, fair Hermia, ere I go;
> My ear should catch your voice, my eye your
>   eye,
> My tongue should catch your tongue's sweet
>   melody.
> Were the world mine, Demetrius being hated,
> The rest I'd give to be to you translated.
>   (I.i.186-91)

It is the feeling of dispossession to which Hermia succumbs:

> O me, what news, my love?
> Am not I Hermia? Are not you Lysander?
> I am as fair now as I was erewhile.
> Since night you loved me; yet since night you
>   left me.
>
>   (III.ii.280-4)

This sense of loss of objective being is fortunately only the prelude to a union beyond self and possession—the union of true marriage.

Demetrius and Lysander, on the other hand, lose themselves in the excess subjectivity of love until they actually do lose themselves in "drooping fog as black as Acheron" (III.ii.374), until they are literally as well as figuratively blind. They never question the objective reality of their experience; their changes of affection never lead to self-doubt. The opposite physical differentiation of the women—blond and black, tall and short are equally beautiful—makes the males' conversions the more ridiculous, but that is lost on them. They are not alone in their oblivion, however, for none of the lovers is really certain of the nature of the transformations of the night. Demetrius echoes Hermia in his explanation of what appears to be unmotivated behavior:

> But, my good lord, I wot not by what
>   power
> (But by some power it is) my love to
>   Hermia,
> Melted as the snow, seems to me now
> As the remembrance of an idle gaud
> Which in my childhood I did dote upon;
> And all the faith, the virtue of my heart,
> The object and pleasure of mine eye,
> Is only Helena.
>
>   (IV.i.163-70)

What the lovers do realize upon awakening is that things look (and of course feel) differently:

> *Demetrius*
> These things seem small and
>   undistinguishable,
> Like far-off mountains turned into clouds.
>
> *Hermia*
> Methinks I see these things with parted
>   eye,
> When everything seems double.
>
> *Helena*
>   So methinks;
> And I have found Demetrius like a jewel,
> Mine own, and not mine own.

> *Demetrius*
>   Are you sure
> That we are awake? It seems to me
> That yet we sleep, we dream.
>
>   (IV.i.186-194)

The language of this confusion is significant. We have travelled from the world of daylight perception through the increasing blindness of the forest darkness. With the dawn, however, emerges a new way of seeing, something between literal eye-sight and subjective dream-sight. And with a new perspective comes a new love, a union sanctioned by both Oberon and Theseus, in which our partners are and are not our own—a "league whose date till death shall never end" (III.ii.373).

What the lovers do not know, we do. We know that the restoration of harmony in the fairy world has allowed the cycle of growth to continue—visually symbolized in the royal dance round the sleeping couples—and need not ask for rationality in last-minute changes of heart. Reminding us of the role of perceptual confusion and loss in this process in Bottom's verbally confused version of Corinthians: "The eye of man hath not heard, the ear of man hath not seen, man's hand is not able to taste, his tongue to conceive, not his heart to report what my dream was" (IV.i.208-211). His rendition of Scripture suggests that to the degree dream-magic makes us doubt our senses and sense of self, it partakes of mystery. There is another kind of magic in the play other than love—the illusory magic of art. The mechanicals' sub-plot, in fact, forms a kind of running commentary on the romantic antics of the lovers, and it is to this ironic critique that we turn for the last laugh.

III

Shakespeare embroiders his love story with metaphors of art as symbols of aspects of illusion, but he also juxtaposes it with the presentation of the analogous story of Pyramus and Thisbe by the mechanicals. As the love story suggests the usefulness of illusion in extending the boundaries of the self, so the playlet's failure to appeal to the "eyes of the mind" suggests the folly of exteme literalism on the one hand and extreme subjectivity on the other. In his excellent analysis of imaginative failure in the playlet, Robert W. Dent discusses the curious combination of these follies:

> Except for a few lines of actual rehearsal . . . , the whole rehearsal is concerned with how the mechanicals abuse their own imaginations by a failure to understand those of the audience. On the one hand they fear their audience will imagine what it sees is real, mistaking "shadows" for reality; on the other, they think the audience unable to imagine what it cannot see. Paradoxically, although they lack the understanding to think in such terms, they think their audience both over- and under-imaginative, and in both respects irrational.

Dent goes on to argue that proper illusion, the magic of Shakespeare's own play, insures the imaginative involvement of the audience by avoiding either extreme:

Significantly, Shakespeare opens the rehearsal scene as follows:

Bottom. Are we all met?
Quince. Pat, pat; and here's a marvail's convenient place for our rehearsal. This green plot shall be our stage, this hawthorne brake our tiring house . . .

The stage is a stage, not a green plot; the tiring house is a tiring house, not a hawthorne brake. The Lord Chamberlain's Men ask us to imagine a green plot and hawthorne brake; . . . The play perpetually makes such demands upon us, and even greater ones. . . . Most basic of all, it asks us to enter imaginatively into a world dominated by fairies, and to accept them as the ultimate source of disharmony and harmony, while at the same time not asking us to "believe" in them at all.[12]

This is certainly true, but there is more to it. Dent's thesis rests on his view of Shakespeare's "thematic distinction between the worlds of imagination and 'reality.'"[13] Fiction is, after all, only fiction. But if we look more closely at the rehearsal scene, it seems to involve a more complicated thematic distinction than Dent proposes. "The Lord Chamberlain's Men ask us to imagine a green plot and hawthorne brake. . . . " Yes, but they then ask us to go one step further: "This green plot shall be our stage, this hawthorne brake our tiring house" (III.i.3-5). We start with reality (a real stage), replace it with fantasy (a green plot and hawthorne brake), and then substitute a further fantasy (a stage) which exactly duplicates the reality. The formula of this metamorphosis is simple: illusion equals reality.

Yet Shakespeare is illusion's advocate in a far bolder way. The significance of the fifth act lies in the irony of the court audience's reaction to the playlet. As we watch these creations of fancy who, in their limited understanding, either condescend to fancy (Theseus) or fail to see its relevance (Lysander and Demetrius), even the faulty illusion of the playlet comes to embody more of the truth than its audience. *We* recognize in the "tragical mirth" (V.i.61) of the mechanicals' shadow Shakespeare's parody of the lovers' misadventures; *they* do not. Furthermore, the imaginative folly of the mechanicals transforms the tragic potential of the Pyramus and Thisbe story into a comic statement of reconciliation (the wall is down) and regeneration (Bottom is up). Barber's note places Bottom's resurrection in the perspective of Tudor popular comedy:

Perhaps when Bottom starts up, very much alive despite his emphatic death, to correct the Duke in the matter of the wall, his comic resurrection owes

something, directly or via the jig, to the folk play. When the St. George, or Fool, or whoever, starts up, alive again, after the miraculous cure, the reversal must have been played as a moment of comical triumph, an upset, more or less grotesque or absurd, no doubt, but still exhilarating—to come back alive is the ultimate turning of the tables on whatever is an enemy of life.[14]

From our perspective as Shakespeare's "real" audience, we know that the playlet's "tragical mirth" parallels the escape of the lovers from the potentially fatal rigor of the law and their regeneration in love through imaginative folly. Illusion replaces reality as Shakespeare works through shadow to reveal substance. The effect on the "real" audience is not lost; by the time of the fifth act, we are no longer permitted to watch this drama with the casual condescension of the Athenian court. We are no longer permitted, in other words, to ignore the role of illusion in life and life's artistic mirror. Shakespeare's *Dream* demonstrates the power of illusion to teach and to transform, and we ought not to forget that the play's final word belongs to Puck.

Notes

[1] All citations from *A Midsummer Night's Dream* in my text are to the Pelican Shakespeare edition of the play, ed. Madeleine Doran (Baltimore, 1962).

[2] I am particularly indebted to the following: Paul A. Olson, "*A Midsummer Night's Dream* and the Meaning of Court Marriage," *ELH,* 24 (1957), 95-116; R.W. Dent, "Imagination in *A Midsummer Night's Dream,*" *SQ,* 15 (1964), 115-129; Andrew D. Weiner, "'Multiformitie Uniforme': *A Midsummer Night's Dream,*" *ELH,* 38 (1971), 329-349; and C.L. Barber, *Shakespeare's Festive Comedy* (Princeton, 1959), pp. 119-162.

[3] *The Defense of Poesie,* in *The Prose Works of Sir Philip Sidney,* ed. Albert Feuillerat (Cambridge, 1963), III, 7.

[4] Barber, p. 124.

[5] R. A. Zimbardo, "Regeneration and Reconciliation in *A Midsummer Night's Dream,*" *Shakespeare Studies,* 6 (1970), p. 46.

[6] Weiner p. 344.

[7] Barber limits the play within the confines of "unshadowed gaiety" (p. 161) while Olson and Weiner tend, I think, to exaggerate its Platonic and Christian implications, respectively.

[8] Platonic and Christian interpretations have already been discussed. For a Freudian point of view, see

Melvin Goldstein, "Comedy as Terror in Disguise: Identity Crises in *A Midsummer Night's Dream*," *Psychoanalytic Review*, 60 (1973), 169-204. Zimbardo and Barber discuss the importance of the forces of elemental nature and primitive folklore, respectively.

[9] Barber, pp. 136-7.

[10] Ovid, *Ars Amatoria*, I, 531. See D'Orsay W. Pearson, "'Vnkinde' Theseus: A Study in Renaissance Mythography," *ELR*, 4 (1974), p. 297.

[11] Dent, p. 126

[12] Dent, p. 126

[13] Dent, p. 129. Cf. Barber p. 161-2.

[14] Barber, p. 154.

William T. Liston (essay date 1991)

SOURCE: "Paradoxical Chastity in *A Midsummer Night's Dream*," in *The University of Dayton Review*, Vol. 21, No. 2, Summer, 1991, pp. 153-60.

[*In the following essay, Liston claims that the Protestant idealization of marriage is a theme of* A Midsummer Night's Dream, *and that this theme is explored through the conflicting image of the moon as barren or fertile, for example, and through Oberon's restoration of Titania's sight as a signal of "the triumph of chastity over erotic love."*]

Chastity, said one of the early feminists more than a decade ago, is the only sexual perversion. Neither Shakespeare nor any of his contemporaries would have agreed with her. To the Elizabethans, according to Nancy Cotton Pearse, "Chastity . . . [was] a woman's only honor" (56). And whereas "In the Middle Ages lechery ran a poor and rather venial seventh in the lists of deadly sins," during the Elizabethan period it was second or third after pride." The extreme opposition of chastity and lechery in Elizabethan theory was an outgrowth . . . of the vigorous idealization of marriage" (59).

In *A Midsummer Night's Dream* lechery is hardly an issue, but Shakespeare establishes chastity as one of the major issues in the first scene, and certainly it is of central importance to the action in the forest scenes. And through the imagery of the play, chastity is insistently, and paradoxically, linked with the moon and with water. The paradox is that the moon, especially through its personifications as Diana, the goddess of chastity, is also the symbol of fertility (Brooks, Arden ed., cxxix-cxxx; all citations are to this edition). This paradoxical and ambiguous yoking of apparently opposed ideas within the symbol reflects, no doubt, an ambiguous attitude toward chastity and sexuality among the Elizabethans: and it strongly implies that chastity is not to be equated with virginity, though there is no doubt that that equation obtains often in Elizabethan—including Shakespearean—literature.

C. S. Lewis pointed out some years ago that "Celibacy and the praise of virginity are Catholic; the honour of the marriage bed is Puritan" (117). My point is not to assert that Shakespeare was a Puritan, but that chastity is not virginity, and that the Protestant "vigorous idealization of marriage" is one of the themes of *A Midsummer Night's Dream*. Certainly Puritanism was a middle-class movement; and certainly the values of the play, especially with respect to the four young lovers, are middle-class values. But Theseus and Hippolyta, and even Oberon and Titania, share the same values, as do the rude mechanicals ("You must say paragon. A paramour is, God bless us, a thing of naught" [4.2.13-14]).

In their opening exchange, Theseus and Hippolyta mention the moon explicitly three times and once by allusion ("pale companion," 1. 15). The moon in its movement is their measure of time. Further, in these references to the moon they establish metaphors that appear again and again in the play. Theseus likens it in its slow movement "to a step-dame or a dowager / Long withering out a young man's revenue" (an image of sterility and barrenness), and Hippolyta replies:

> Four days will quickly steep themselves in night;
> Four nights will quickly dream away the time;
> And then the moon, like to a silver bow
> New bent in heaven, shall behold the night
> Of our solemnities.
>
> (7-11)

There is an implicit sexual image in *steep* in her first line, the events that give the play its title are anticipated in the second line, and the silver bow, of course, anticipates the Cupid's bow of 2.1, whose "fiery shaft," missing its target, produced the magic love potion in the "little western flower" (155-74); and maybe, as Brooks states in his note to the line, the bent bow "is an archetype of fruitful union: the woman draws the man but follows him; together they protect the child."

A few moments later, when Hermia asks Theseus what penalty may befall her "If I refuse to wed Demetrius" according to her father's wish, Theseus replies:

> Either to die the death, or to abjure
> Forever the society of men.
>
> (65-66)

And death is preferable to the alternative:

> To live a barren sister all your life,
> Chanting faint hymns to the cold fruitless moon.

Thrice blessed they that master so their blood
To undergo such maiden pilgrimage;
But earthlier happy is the rose distill'd
Than that which, withering on the virgin thorn,
Grows, lives, and dies, in single blessedness.

(72-78)

The moon in this image is, as often in the play, barren; the blessed life of a virgin is unblessed. And on the contrary, the rose distill'd—the flower whose lively juice is used—is "earthlier happy." Again we have a paradox in "the virgin thorn," a phallic image applied to a female; and "withering" alludes to Theseus' earlier reference to his unmarried state. But most important, probably, is the phrase "earthlier happy." As in *Measure for Measure,* virginity is unnatural, a cold condition that denies human warmth and growth and therefore happiness. Before leaving, Theseus repeats, in equally forbidding terms, the fate to which Hermia is subject if she does not bow to her father's will: death.

Or on Diana's altar to protest,
For aye, austerity and single life.

(89-90)

A short while later, the moon takes on another aspect when Lysander reveals what he and Hermia intend:

Helen, to you our minds we will unfold:
Tomorrow night, when Phoebe doth behold
Her silver visage in the wat'ry glass
Decking with liquid pearl the bladed grass
(A time that lovers' flights doth still conceal).
Through Athens' gates have we devis'd to
    steal.

(208-13)

Here the moon, seen through lovers' eyes, takes on an entirely different aspect. "Wat'ry" and "liquid pearl" (swelling rotundity) imply life and fruitfulness, and the mere allusion to Phoebe's beholding "lovers' flights" and stealing implies at least connivance and probably blessing of their act by the moon goddess—as if it were a habitual act for lovers.

These images anticipate exactly our introduction to the forest scenes and fairy plot. In answer to Puck's "How now, spirit! Whither wander you?" the Fairy answers.

I do wander everywhere
Swifter than the moon's sphere;
And I serve the Fairy Queen,
To dew her orbs upon the green.

. . . . .

I must go seek some dew-drops here,
And hang a pearl in every cowslip's ear.

(2.1.1-15)

Estelle Kohler as Titania and Robert Lang as Bottom in Act IV, Scene i of the Open Air Theatre's 1994 production of A Midsummer Night's Dream.

Here we have the moon combined with rotundity in *sphere* and by extension in *orbs,* the same pregnant shape combined with water in the dew images, and the liquid *pearl* again.

With the entrance of Oberon and Titania, all these images swell to their fullest development. Before replying fully to Oberon's "Ill met by moonlight, proud Titania" (60), Titania tells the fairies that "I have forsworn his bed and company" (62), making explicit the disruption of natural, marital sexuality. Titania goes on to assert that their marital discord has engendered discord in nature:

Therefore the winds, piping to us in vain,
As in revenge have suck'd up from the sea
Contagious fogs; which, falling in the land,
Hath every pelting river made so proud
That they have overborne their continents.

(88-92)

Of these lines, Brooks notes that "Waters rising over their 'continents', the bounds which should contain them, are Shakespeare's recurrent image for anarchical insubordination." For several lines, Titania continues to list the perverted fecundity—the crops rotted by the floods, e.g.—and the resultant failure of human joy, until she asserts

> Therefore the moon, the governess of floods,
> Pale in her anger, washes all the air,
> That rheumatic diseases do abound.
>
> (103-05)

The seasons are disordered,

> And this same progeny of evils comes
> From our debate, from our dissension;
> We are their parents and original.
>
> (115-17)

The final image of the section emphatically asserts the generative power of the Fairy King and Fairy Queen gone awry; efficacious, but misused.

At this point, Theseus begs the changeling boy, and in denying Theseus the boy, Titania recalls the boy's mother in the last months before his birth. The images are all of water and rotundity, and what seems to be impregnating wind (Louis Montrose notes that "in Titania's description, neither *genitor* nor *pater* plays a role in the making of a son," as "neither biological nor social mother—neither *genetrix* nor *mater*—plays a role in the making of a daughter" in Theseus' assertion to Hermia that she was "imprinted" by her father at 1.1.47-51 [75]):

> His mother was a votress of my order;
> And in the spiced Indian air, by night,
> Full often hath she gossip'd by my side;
> And sat with me on Neptune's yellow sands,
> Marking th'embarked traders on the flood:
> When we have laugh'd to see the sails
>   conceive
> And grow big-bellied with the wanton wind;
> Which she, with pretty and with swimming
>   gait
> Following (her womb then rich with my young
>   squire),
> Would imitate, and sail upon the land
> To fetch me trifles, and return again
> As from a voyage rich with merchandise.
>
> (123-33)

But having denied Theseus the boy, Titania offers a measure of reconciliation:

> If you will patiently dance in our round,
> And see our moonlight revels, go with us.
>
> (140-41)

The dance is, as always, an image of harmony, and the *round* in the moonlight continues the image of pregnancy.

When Titania leaves, Oberon tells Puck of the time he saw,

> Flying between the cold moon and the earth,
> Cupid all arm'd: a certain aim he took
> At a fair vestal, throned by the west,
> And loos'd his love-shaft smartly from his bow
> As it should pierce a hundred thousand hearts.
> But I might see young Cupid's fiery shaft
> Quench'd in the chaste beams of the watery
>   moon;
> And the imperial votress passed on,
> In maiden meditation, fancy-free.
> Yet mark'd I where the bolt of Cupid fell:
> It fell upon a little western flower,
> Before milk-white, now purple with love's
>   wound:
> And maidens call it 'love-in-idleness'.
>
> (156-68)

Though these lines have received enormous quantities of comment, especially with respect to the possibility that the "fair vestal," the "imperial votress," refers to Queen Elizabeth, there seems to be no comment, at least to my knowledge, on one aspect of what happened to "Cupid's fiery shaft." The image of l. 162 suggests that the lovearrow was quench'd in flight, by watery beams of the watery moon, thereby losing its motive power; and it was this failure of power that caused the shaft to fall upon the "little western flower." But why should the "chaste beams" quench the shaft? (The image here, like many others in the play, is paradoxically sexual—the quenching of the love-shaft in something moist, and therefore endowed with fecundity.) The only answer, I think, is that the fair vestal had chosen her state freely, and the shaft aimed at her would have violated her own elected chastity—more specifically, virginity. This is essentially the view of Brooks in his Arden Introduction:

> The freely chosen virginity it [the myth of the imperial votaress] exalts is, moreover, in contrast with the virginity to be enforced, if Theseus' sentence stands, upon Hermia. To find place for a noble virginity in his marriage-play must have been deeply satisfying to Shakespeare's 'comprehensive soul'. (cxxxii)

The theme of elected chastity under pursuit is picked up immediately in another plot:

> *Enter* DEMETRIUS, HELENA *following him.*
>
> (187 s.d.)

In the topsy-turvy state of this pair of young lovers, Demetrius is in the position of the chaste vestal, at least with respect to the lover who is pursuing him.

When, in the following scene, the exhausted Hermia and Lysander appear, Hermia has little trouble in persuading him to "lie further off" with

> Such separation as may well be said
> Becomes a virtuous bachelor and a maid.
>
> (2.2.57-58)

Despite their running off from the constraints of Athens with respect to their particular marriage—that she accede to her father's will—their values are Athenian public values with respect to marriage and sexuality. And, in fact, there hardly seems to be an overt sexual dimension to their relationship: what interests them is a marriage fully in accord with all of the constraints of English society (and middle-class Protestantism) except for the lack of fatherly consent.

There follows the scene in which Bottom is translated into an ass, and it closes ambiguously. Having directed her attendants to lead Bottom to her bower, Titania then comments:

> The moon, methinks, looks with a watery eye,
> And when she weeps, weeps every little flower,
> Lamenting some enforced chastity.
> Tie up my love's tongue, bring him silently.
>
> (3.1.191-94)

What is it that the moon and the flowers lament? Most annotators gloss *enforced* as "violated" (Arden and Riverside, e.g.), but Bevington glosses as "forced, violated; or, possibly, constrained (since Titania at this moment is hardly concerned about chastity)." The first meaning is the more conventional—that the moon and flowers weep because of a rape, a deflowering; but the second meaning, according as it does with Titania's mood at the moment, also accords with Theseus' sentiments in Act 1: chastity is a lamentable penalty when imposed on a person who has not freely chosen it herself. Note also Brooks' "enforced" virginity in his comment on "the myth of the imperial votaress," cited above (155).

The final line here, Titania's direction to the fairies to enforce silence on Bottom, is full of ramifications. Many scholars in recent years have shown that *chastity* and *silence* were often synonyms in Elizabethan England. In *Chaste, Silent, and Obedient: English Books for Women, 1475-1640,* Suzanne W. Hull writes:

> The message in the title of this book—be chaste, silent, obedient—comes through time and time again in the women's literature. . . . Church rules (including St. Benedict's) include the message; philosophers repeat it:

> . . . let her kepe silence. For there is nothinge that doth so much commend, avaunce, set forthe, adourne, decke, trim, and garnish a maid, as silence.
> (Thomas Becon, *Worckes.* [London: 1560-64])

> Bibliographies, traditional tales, and prayers reinforce it:

> There is nothing that becommeth a maid better than sobernes, silence, shamefastnes, and chastitie, both of bodie & mind. For these things being once lost, she is no more a maid, but a strumpet in the sight of God. (Thomas Bentley *The Monument of Matrones.* [London: 1582]) (Hull 142)

What is the segue in Titania's thinking in her final two lines that makes her connect *chastity* and *silence?* Clearly, as Bevington states, she is not interested in chastity at the moment. Is it possible that a culturally indoctrinated woman instinctively associates the terms? Or, as is more likely, is it that Bottom's continued asinine talking will prevent her from accepting him as a lover? David Marshall equates the silence here with that in other scenes; for example, Hippolyta's silence in the opening scene that prompts Theseus' "What cheer, my love?" (122):

> Hippolyta is, I believe, tongue-tied, as if she were the serious reflection of Bottom at the moment when Titania comically ravishes him with the command to the fairies: "Tie up my lover's tongue, bring him silently." (94)

In an unequal love-match, the lesser must be silent.

If Bottom and Titania consummate their extra-marital love, they do so off stage. When we next see them, Bottom is about to go to sleep, and Titania will wind him in her arms as "the female ivy so / Enrings the barky fingers of the elm" (4.1.42-43). Certainly there are sexual overtones here; but these tones are much more present in Oberon's narration, a few lines later, of one of their love scenes (possibly this one) as he tells Puck that he "will undo / The hateful imperfection of her eyes" (61-62). He says that

> meeting her or late behind the wood
> Seeking sweet favours for this hateful fool,
> I did upbraid her and fall out with her:
> For she his hairy temples then had rounded
> With coronet of fresh and fragrant flowers;
> And that same dew, which sometime on the buds
> Was wont to swell like round and orient pearls,
> Stood now within the pretty flowerets' eyes
> Like tears, that did their own disgrace bewail.
>
> (47-55)

What is particularly interesting in this description is that we have, as often, the fecund images of dew swelling to pearlish rotundity, but now these pearls are like tears in the flowerets' eyes, signifying the abuse of fecundity in the abuse of chastity. When "she in mild terms begg'd" his patience and then gave him the changeling child (57-59), acceding to his will in all things, he was moved to forgive her earlier disobedience. We are moving back to the patriarchal system of values so prized by the conservative middle-classes of Elizabethan England.

In restoring Titania's proper sight a moment later with the power of "Dian's bud o'er Cupid's flower" (72), Oberon is clearly signifying the triumph of chastity over erotic love. This antidote (which Puck had applied to Lysander's eyes at Oberon's direction earlier [3.2.450-52]), Frank Kermode asserts, "by keeping men chaste keeps them sane" (218).

The more or less explicit statements concerning the chastity theme almost disappear after this point in the play. From this point on, statement is replaced by fulfillment—by the working out of the theme in action. For the young lovers, the chaste experiences they have undergone during their night in the forest prefigure something of great constancy in their marriages; the mature demeanor of both Theseus and Hippolyta implies the same for them.

Works Cited

Shakespeare, William. *A Midsummer Night's Dream.* Ed. Harold F. Brooks. New York: Methuen, 1979 (Arden).

Hull, Suzanne W. *Chaste, Silent, & Obedient: English Books for Women, 1475-1640.* San Marino: Huntington Library, 1982.

Kermode, Frank. "The Mature Comedies." *Early Shakespeare.* Ed. John Russell Brown and Bernard Harris. New York: Schocken, 1966, 211-27.

Lewis, C.S. "Tasso." *Studies in Medieval and Renaissance Literature.* Cambridge: Cambridge UP, 1966.

Marshall, David. "Exchanging Visions: Reading *A Midsummer Night's Dream.*" *William Shakespeare's "A Midsummer Night's Dream": Modern Critical Interpretations.* Ed. Harold Bloom. New York: Chelsea House, 1987, 87-115. Reprinted from *ELH* 49 (1982), 543-575.

Montrose, Louis Adrian. "*A Midsummer Night's Dream* and the Shaping Fantasies of Elizabethan Culture: Gender, Power, Form." *Rewriting the Renaissance: The Discourses of Sexual Difference in Early Modern Europe.* Ed. Margaret W. Ferguson, Maureen Quilligan, and Nancy J. Vickers. Chicago: U of Chicago P, 1986, 65-87.

Pearse, Nancy Cotton. *John Fletcher's Chastity Plays: Mirrors of Modesty.* Lewisburg: Bucknell UP, 1973.

BOTTOM

René Girard (essay date 1986)

SOURCE: "Bottom's One-Man Show," in *The Current in Criticism: Essays on the Present and Future of Literary Theory,* edited by Clayton Koelb and Virgil Lokke, Purdue University Press, 1986, pp. 99-122.

[*In the following essay, Girard maintains that Bottom's transformation, as well as the world of the fairies, are products of the mimetic process acting on the mechanicals and the four lovers. Girard explores in particular how Bottom's eagerness to take on so many theatrical roles contributes to his metamorphosis.*]

In *A Midsummer Night's Dream,* two groups of human beings spend the night in the wood. The first consists of four unhappy lovers who tear each other apart, the second of some local craftsmen who prepare a play for the celebration of Theseus's wedding.

Wretched as it is, their stage adaptation of *Pyramus and Thisby* remains beyond the capacities of these illiterate amateurs. But their passion for the theater is intense, especially in the case of Bottom, a born actor with an enormous appetite for impersonation.

At the craftsmen's first meeting—in act 1, scene 2—Quince, the director, distributes the various roles. Bottom gets asked first. He will play the leading man, Pyramus. He wishes it had been "a tyrant," but it is a lover and a lover will do. Bottom feigns indifference, but he is so eager to act, so excited by the prospect, that he will grab any role. Speaking compulsively, he announces that he will "move storms." Eager to stop this ranting, Quince turns to Flute and asks him to play Thisby.

Flute feels awkward at the thought of a woman's role. He tries to excuse himself on the ground that he has "a beard coming." Bottom begs Quince to let him have the role of Thisby. He will not give up playing Pyramus; yet he wants the other role as well, and immediately, even though he knows nothing of the story, he tries to show what he can do with it:

> And I may hide my face, let me play Thisby too. I'll speak in a monstrous little voice. "Thisne! Thisne! Ah, Pyramus, my love dear! thy Thisby dear, and lady dear!"[1]

Quince disagrees. He thinks that the hero and the heroine should be played by different actors:

"No, no, you must play Pyramus; and, Flute, you Thisby."

In order to avoid further trouble, Quince hurriedly proceeds to assign two more roles, Thisby's mother and Pyramus's father, with no interference from Bottom this time, but then comes the turn of the lion. The role goes to Snug, who complains that he is "slow of study" and requests "a written score." You may do it "extempore," Quince replies, "for it is nothing but roaring." To Bottom, this reluctance of the prospective lion is an irresistible temptation and, once again, he asks for the role:

> Let me play the lion too. I will roar, that I will do any man's heart good to hear me. I will roar, that I will make the Duke say, "Let him roar again; let him roar again."

The role leaves little room for interpretation, but Quince is so irritated that he challenges Bottom's understanding of it:

> An you should do it too terribly, you would fright the Duchess and the ladies, that they would shrike; and that were enough to hang us all.
>
> *All.* That would hang us, every mother's son.

The craftsmen hang on every word of their leader and then always mimic him in a chorus. In the face of unanimous opposition, Bottom makes a hasty retreat. He is too much of a mime not to give an audience what it requests:

> I grant you, friends, if you should fright the ladies out of their wits, they would have no more discretion but to hang us; but I will aggravate my voice so that I will roar you as gently as any sucking dove; I will roar you and 'twere any nightingale.

As long as Bottom gets his role, whatever the populace wants, the populace will get. But even if the lion, now, sounds like a nightingale, it must retain some features of the former beast or it would not be identifiable as such. Bottom is turning it, therefore, into a birdlike lion, a warring conflation of opposites, some kind of monster.

Too much mimetic adaptability is seen as unfavorable to the creative imagination. It would seem to stifle it, but beyond a certain threshold—which Bottom is crossing—the two tend to merge. With his most remarkable talent for changing anything into anything else, Bottom's handling of his various roles already resembles the process of mythological metamorphosis. Unlike Alberich of *The Ring,* Bottom has no need of magical contraptions such as the *Tarnhelm.* At the slightest signal from his public, he can transform himself, now into a ferocious dragon, now into the sweetest little nightingale.

An exasperated Quince repeats in no uncertain terms that Bottom will play no part but Pyramus. Next, the question arises of how the moon should be represented, and also the dreadful wall, the famous wall that cruelly separates the two lovers. The solution almost goes without saying. Let an actor impersonate the wall, let an actor impersonate the moon.

Bottom would love to be that moon, Bottom would love to be that wall. To play the beloved as well as the lover does not satisfy his appetite for acting; in addition, he wants to be the obstacle that stands between the two. He and his fellows can passionately embrace even those objects that seem to lie beyond the wildest dreams of impersonation, turning them into an infinite number of theatrical parts. All of these Bottom would like to keep for himself, and even the most insignificant ones he can relinquish only with the sense of a huge personal loss.

Try as he may, Quince will not find a role that does not suit Bottom's talent. *Mimesis* is running wild. Even the slightest hint, now—almost any gesture—can trigger new impersonations. The man reminds us of a suggestible subject in the hands of a clever hypnotist. The only difference is that he needs no hypnotist; he is gifted and mixed up enough to play both roles, the hypnotizer and the hypnotized. He enters into all conceivable and inconceivable roles with such passion that he is losing sight of his own personality.

The first scene with the craftsmen, as well as the first scene with the lovers, takes place in the city, whereas the second takes place in the woods. Each group seems to have some business out there, but the real business is the midsummer night madness.

We can see right away that, in the interval between act 1 and act 3, the bumpkins' excitement has not abated but increased. Bottom is the first to speak, as always, and he finds a way to compel the attention of Quince:

> *Bottom.* There are things in this comedy of Pyramus and Thisby that will never please. First, Pyramus must draw a sword to kill himself; which the ladies cannot abide. How answer you that?

Quince was the one, earlier, who conjured up the specter of the frightened ladies *à propos* of the lion. Bottom cleverly extends this concern to the suicide of Pyramus. He mimics the argument of Quince and wraps himself up in the mantle of the *metteur en scène.* The better to manipulate Quince, he surrenders once again to his hysterical penchant for mimicry and shows us that his talent for impersonation is not limited to theatrical roles. He undermines the authority of Quince by turning himself into a second Quince and a contagious example to everybody else. Quince cannot silence him, this time, without silencing himself.

> *Snout.* By'r lakin, a parlous fear.
>
> *Starveling.* I believe we must leave the killing out, when all is done.
>
> *Bottom.* Not a whit! I have a device to make all well. Write me a prologue, and let the prologue seem to say we will do no harm with our swords, and that Pyramus is not killed indeed; and for the more better assurance, tell them that I Pyramus am not Pyramus, but Bottom the weaver. This will put them out of fear.

Once again, of course, the only purpose of Bottom is to monopolize the stage. He wants to be the prologue and the epilogue and everything in between.

In his desire to prevent any confusion between a simulated death and a real one, Bottom wants the fictional Pyramus—himself—to emphasize his real identity; but he devises his prologue in such a way as to suggest the opposite of what he means.

The prologue should say: "My name is Bottom and I am merely pretending to be a certain Pyramus whose suicide is feigned"; but Bottom names Pyramus first, in the first person, saying in fact: "I Pyramus" as if it were his real identity and wishing, no doubt, that it were. And then, when his real name, Bottom, finally shows up, it is treated as an actor's part in the title page of a printed play; it is followed by a mention of the man's trade. The prologue says: "Bottom the weaver," which is the way the name appears in the listing of roles at the beginning of *A Midsummer Night's Dream*.

We are listening, we feel, to an actor named Pyramus who has to play a fictional weaver named Bottom, a modest role with which he is not very pleased. Inside the play, this belief is wrong but, from the spectators' standpoint, it makes good sense. We are actually watching a play that includes a fictional weaver named Bottom. It is quite possible that the actor might be named Pyramus.

Bottom contaminates us with his own madness; we share in the general dizziness, but so mildly that not even the most timid ladies can be frightened. It feels like a few bubbles of champagne on an empty stomach.

In order to describe what is going on here, the grayish jargon of "identity crises" and "split personalities" will not do. It may be appropriate to the static condition of the contemporary neurotic, patiently rehashing his various "problems" and the interminable "analysis" of the same, until death do them part. It is ridiculously inad-

equate here. Bottom's crisis is more tempestuous and *critical* than the neurotic's condition but, unlike that of the psychotic, it will leave no traces. It is temporary, and it will have a resolution. It is also collective. Bottom is only the supreme exemplification of what happens to all his companions.

This crisis is an attenuated or partly ritualized version of the mimetic crisis described in *Violence and the Sacred.*[2] All words, images and gesticulations intended by the craftsmen as a preventive against the imaginary panic of the ladies are really worsening symptoms of that crisis. As they exhibit their mimetic symptoms to one another, they also mimic them, bringing them to fever pitch. The entire scene describes a mimetic contagion of lost identity that affects Bottom most spectacularly but not him alone, as we soon shall see.

The "I Pyramus" is only a portent of things to come. It represents a transitional phase on the road to a collective hallucination similar to the climax of a primitive ritual, because all rituals are the more or less ritualized reenactment of the real crisis that precedes.

Shakespeare is aware that the theater is itself a form of ritual, and—like all rituals—it can go wrong, it can revert to the real mimetic crisis in which it originates. This is what happens with the craftsmen, but only to a certain extent. The comedy will not turn into a tragedy.

A few lines down we have another clue to the rapid disintegration of Bottom's normal handling of reality. Our old friend the lion once again serves as a catalyst. We can surmise that, between the two meetings, this lion has haunted the imagination of the mechanicals. Now even the quiet ones, Snout the tinker and Starveling the tailor, begin to evince panic.

> *Snout.* Will not the ladies be afeard of the lion?
>
> *Starveling.* I fear it, I promise you.
>
> *Bottom.* Masters, you ought to consider with your-[selves], to bring in (God shield us!) a lion among ladies, is a most dreadful thing; for there is not a more fearful wild-fowl than your lion living; and we ought to look to't.
>
> *Snout.* Therefore another prologue must tell he is not a lion.
>
> *Bottom.* Nay; you must name his name, and half his face must be seen through the lion's neck, and he himself must speak through, saying thus, or to the same defect: "Ladies," or "Fair ladies, I would wish you," or "I would request you," or "I would

entreat you, not to fear, not to tremble: my
life for yours. If you think I come hither as
a lion, it were pity of my life. No! I am no
such thing; I am a man as other men are";
and there indeed let him name his name,
and tell them plainly he is Snug the joiner.

Just as Bottom imitated Quince a little earlier, now
Snout imitates Bottom. His turn has come to emulate
Bottom and demand still one more reassuring prologue after the style of his hero. But Bottom does not
recognize the idea as his own when he hears it from
the mouth of someone else. Great artists do not like
to be copied. Just as he had been interrupted by
Quince, he now keeps interrupting Snout; he has a
brighter idea: a speech by the dumb beast himself. As
the actor will "name his name" and fasten himself
solidly to his real identity, "half his face must be seen
through the lion's neck."

The first metamorphosis of the lion was not scary
enough. Now we have a second one. A creature half-
man, half-beast is uncannier than a combination of beast
and beast, uncannier, *a fortiori,* than the honest-to-
goodness lion demanded by the original script. The
mere invention of this improved monster sends shivers
down the spine of the inventors.

This fragment of a human face surrounded by leonine
features looks strikingly like the sort of primitive mask
that Shakespeare had probably never seen but that his
genius invents almost *ex nihilo.* The playwright's sense
of timing is excellent. We have reached the moment
when the participants in an orgiastic ritual would put
on masks quite similar to the one imagined by Bottom: weird compositions of animal and human features. The inspiration is very much the same because
the experience is the same. Bottom and his friends
are going through the type of crisis after which rituals
are patterned.

Bottom's compulsive impresonations resemble the possessive trance as much as the resulting images resemble
primitive masks. The craftsmen live in a culture that
does not encourage such phenomena. But perhaps the
distant past was different. At one time, the midsummer
festival may have been a ritual similar to the orgiastic
rituals in ancient and primitive cultures.

Turn-of-the-century anthropologists such as Sir James
George Frazer thought that they were the first to redis-
cover that origin, but, two and three centuries ahead of
modern research, Shakespeare already thought along
similar if not identical lines. The midsummer festival
figures only in the title. The play itself contains one
single mention of "the rites of May," and that is all.
This inconsistent vagueness does not really matter. All
these festivals were similar; any one of them can provide the ritual framework in which the experience of

Bottom and the craftsmen can be fitted because they
were all generated by the type of mythical genesis that
Shakespeare describes.

The possessive trance may closely resemble playact-
ing, but it is an error simply to equate the one with the
other, as some researchers such as Michel Leiris have
been inclined to do. When genuine, the trance represents a degree of involvement so great that the impersonation becomes involuntary and cannot be stopped
at will. Correspondingly, it represents a high degree of
self-*dispossession,* higher, no doubt, than what normally happens in the Western theater.

It all happens to Bottom. Shakespeare seems to regard
the theater as a mild form of the trance, one that must
derive from the "real thing" originally and can revert to
it on occasion—with highly predisposed individuals such
as Bottom, or when the circumstances are favorable.

All our craftsmen tacitly assume that the weaker sex in
their audience—which really means the queen of the
Amazons and her attendants—will be extremely prone
to panic. Their principal reason for thinking so is that
they themselves are on the verge of a panic. It is normal for people in that condition to project it outside of
themselves. They detect a threat of imminent panic
somewhere in the vicinity and devise hasty measures
against it. As they try to implement these measures,
they make one another believe that the panic has already arrived, which indeed it has, as soon as everybody believes that it has. Their strategy is the one an
infinitely clever man would select if he had joined a
group of terrorists with the express intention of triggering a mass panic.

The solicitude for the ladies is a facade behind which
the craftsmen can unleash their imaginations and produce more and more horrifying monsters. As the craftsmen try to reassure the hypothetical fears of others,
they only succeed in scaring themselves out of their
wits, and *there is not the slightest difference between
their self-induced but nevertheless objectively real
panic,* which is a sociological event occurring in the
real world, *and the ritual pattern to which that panic
necessarily conforms,* because all ritual originates in
some event of this type.

A transitional product of Bottom's "seething brain,"
the humanlike lion belongs to a phase more advanced
than the birdlike lion of the previous phase; it corresponds to an intensification of the crisis, a greater loss
of "self-identity." But the final and climactic phase is
still to come.

In the second phase, we already have full-fledged monsters—creatures no longer "species-specific," as the
modern specialists would say (rather redundantly and
mimetically, being threatened themselves with un-

differentiation). But the craftsmen do not yet quite *believe* in the reality of their own creations.

Give them one more minute and they do. This is the only difference between the ass-headed Bottom and the shenanigans that precede this not-so-mysterious apparition. To all his friends, Bottom has become a real monster. And we are apprised of the fact in a manner so strikingly suited to the force of the hallucination that we are likely to miss the point entirely.

Shakespeare treats Bottom's amazing *translation* both as if it were "the real thing" and also as if it were a prank that Puck is playing on the bumpkins. But Puck is no one but the spirit of the entire midsummer night. And the progress of its spirit can be traced both in an irrational manner by following the evolution of Puck, which pleases the light-hearted and absent-minded spectators, and in the slightly less transparent manner of our analysis, which does not uncover anything that Shakespeare has not intentionally written into his text. The anthropological genius of the playwright displays itself openly from the beginning to the end of this magnificent text.

The apparition walks upon the stage. The imaginary products of Bottom's "seething brain" have been elevated to the status of "real" characters. This shift in the dramatic handling of the theme expresses the climax of the crisis with such power that it makes it invisible to the average spectator. Even the best critics have yet to understand what their author is really up to.

If the spectator has missed the manner in which the monstrous gradually insinuates itself among the near-hysterical craftsmen, he/she will take Puck, Oberon, Titania, and their cortege of fairies at face value, mistaking them for the heroes and heroines of one more subplot that is just as independent of the other two as these two are, or rather seem to be, of one another.

From the simultaneously structural and genetic standpoint of our "neo-mimetic" criticism, the "translation" of Bottom and the intervention of the "fairies" mark the culmination of the dynamic process triggered by the collective decision to perform a play. It is not a magical irruption, a sudden and inexplicable disturbance in a static situation of bucolic peace among people going peacefully about their business of acting, it is the climax of successive structural transformations that are related to one another in such a way that, ultimately, they must be regarded as a *continuous process*. This precedence of continuity over discontinuity is not a return to a pre-structural perspective.

Out of mimetic sympathy with Bottom, mixed with a good deal of exasperation, the craftsmen all cross the threshold of hallucination simultaneously in act 3, scene 1:

[*Enter* Puck, *and* Bottom *with an ass's head.*]
Bottom. "If I were fair, Thisby, I were only thine."
Quince. O monstrous! O strange! We are haunted.
Pray, masters, fly, masters! Help!
[*Exeunt* Quince, Snug, Flute, Snout, *and* Starveling.]

. . . . .

Quince. Bless thee, Bottom, bless thee! Thou art translated.

Quince is first to tip over the brink, and he takes everybody with him; or rather, everybody follows him into the abyss of unreason because everybody imitates him. Until then, Quince had seemed the most clear-headed of the lot; the asinine interruptions of Bottom must have undermined his strength. In a sense, he does not lose his mind: he finally sees with his own eyes the ass-headed monster that keeps persecuting him.

Half the face of an ass can be seen through Bottom's neck. The body remains mostly human, being that of a great lover, but it takes more than a mere Thisby to conquer this Pyramus. It takes the queen of the fairies whom, to a large extent, Bottom himself has become. She talks as wittily as a prologue, but he retains a curious predilection for hay, as well as the immobility of a brick wall, another well-known characteristic of the ass.

If we do not see the mimetic process behind the weird metamorphosis of Bottom, we will have to believe that *someone* rather than something is responsible, and we will have to reinvent Puck, or Robin Goodfellow, the hobgoblin of English folkore, or perhaps Oberon, Titania, etc. They can all be metaphors for the entire process because they all are the products of Bottom's "seething brain."

That is why they reproduce the antics of the craftsmen and of the lovers at their own supernatural level. And since Puck is supposed to plant only a cardboard ass-head upon the real head of Bottom, even the ladies and the critics that would be most offended by any degree of mimetic undifferentiation between violence and the sacred do not have to understand anything and therefore fear nothing.

The habitual reading is that the intervention of Puck and the intersection of the three plots depend on no rationally intelligible sequence. Shakespeare is "playing" in haphazard fashion. Puck provides a welcome break with the trivial realism of the craftsmen, a delightful diversion but no more. The important thing, today, is that the play should make no sense at all. The play must be as senseless as the lovers and the craftsmen imagine their experience to be. It must be the child of a capricious and unmotivated imagination. If we tried to make sense out of it, we would spoil the pleasure of the text.

The chaotic and the discontinuous are present at the dramatic level only, for the spectators who watch the play as naively as the craftsmen and the lovers experience it. There is another rationale for the various incidents that Shakespeare has deliberately inscribed into the play, but he has done so in such a fashion that only a certain type of attention will see it.

When Bottom turns into an ass and marries Titania, the panic that had been brewing for a while reaches ebullition. The same generative force produces the entire world of the fairies that earlier had produced the still-half-believed "translations" and conflations of various beings, the monstrous mixture of a lion and of a man, and the metamorphosis of the lion into a nightingale.

If Bottom could choose one theatrical role and stick to it, he would not lose his mind. One single impersonation would have enough stability and permanence to prevent the generation of monsters. The weaver becomes drunk on a kaleidoscope of impersonations that keeps revolving faster and faster.

He resembles these clowns whose act consists in changing suits so fast that they seem to be wearing the same suit all the time, but it is made up of many colors and shapes all jumbled together. Bottom ends up with a very strange costume, indeed. Maybe it is Joseph's "coat of many colors."

Bottom's roles are too different from each other to be arranged into a harmonious "synthesis," Hegelian or otherwise, and yet Bottom assumes them all almost simultaneously and with such passion each time that he commits himself totally to each one simultaneously.

Inside Bottom, as in the uterus of their mother, there are always a Jacob and an Esau fighting for supremacy, and many other twins as well. Bottom cannot fail to be torn apart, literally shredded by all these totalitarian claims upon his undivided attention. His is the *diasparagmos* of the actor, his mimetic passion.

Beyond a certain threshold, the feverish impersonations of Bottom impinge upon one another as the multiple images in a cinematic film and breed a whole host of monsters. Then the swirl becomes so dizzying that another threshold is reached, and Bottom himself becomes the monster, first in the eyes of his fellows, then in his own eyes as well, mimetically.

As new impersonations keep crowding in, the whole system becomes destabilized, then explodes into fragments that tend to reorganize in weird bits and pieces like a mosaic of broken glass. Bottom is "translated" into a sparkling jumble of fragments from his various roles, with a unifying preponderance of the original ass.

What is the relationship between the two subplots? Can the craftsmen have anything in common with the four mixed-up lovers? The first have gathered to perform a play, the others to love and hate one another. Does their Eros have an affinity for the frantic theatrical impersonations of a half-crazed Bottom?

It certainly does. In order to justify this assertion, I must summarize the argument of an earlier essay about the four lovers.[3]

With the help of Theseus, Hermia's father seeks to prevent his daughter from marrying Lysander. The boy and girl flee to the woods. On their heels comes Demetrius in hot pursuit of Hermia, whom he still loves even though she no longer loves him. On his heels comes Helena in hot pursuit of Demetrius, whom she ardently loves even though he has never loved her.

It seems that the first two lovers have a sound enough reason to flee their Athenian homes. Fleeing one's parents and other oppressive political forces is a comic prop so traditional that it is taken at face value. It is never examined, and yet this time the theme is deceptive in the sense that there is a more convincing cause for the troubles of the lovers. The parental figures are no more responsible for getting the frenzy started than the fairies, a little later, for making it worse.

Even in the case of Lysander and Hermia, "true love" needs no parental or supernatural interference to run into trouble. Shakespeare slyly informs us that, until Lysander appeared upon the scene, Hermia was happy enough to marry Demetrius. Her father's choice was her own choice.

This information is unnecessary to the plot, but it is highly suggestive of an instability among the four lovers that cannot be blamed on the older generation or even on the disruptive influence of the midsummer spirit.

Lysander may well be the original troublemaker. It would be wrong, however, to attach too much importance to him personally, or to anyone else for that matter. In this play, individuals as such do not matter. The traditional critics correctly observed their lack of personality and their interchangeability, but they mistakenly regarded it as a weakness of the play, as something unintended that Shakespeare would have remedied if he had been able to.

In reality, Shakespeare is in complete control of his literary effects, but his goal is the opposite of the only one these traditional critics could conceive, which was the creation of stable character differentiations. Shakespeare wants to show the pressure of fads and fashions inside a group of idle young aristocrats. It can become so intense that it extends to matters of the heart.

Shakespeare portrays what happens to adolescents who read too many romances and choose to live in a world of literary imitation. Taking fictional heroes as models predisposes them to real-life experiments with erotic mimicry, and the results can be simultaneously disastrous and comical. They become a "living theater."

Everybody feels compelled to choose what everybody else has already chosen. The two boys are never in love with the same girl for long, but at any given time they are both in love with the same girl—Hermia first, Helena later. Neither one can desire anything that the other one will not immediately desire as well. Even the girls are carried away in the end by the dominant desire—the one fashionable desire—and compelled to yield to the mimetic pressure of uniformity. This is the reason Helena, at the beginning, seems to desire Hermia even more than Demetrius. The reason is that Hermia is already desired by the two boys; she is the star of the entire show, and Helena feels irresistibly attracted by her success.

All characters do their falling in love according to the falling in love in the vicinity. They remind us of these modern consumers who already have everything and never experience a real need, therefore, but who cannot hear that a product is "popular" or see people standing in line to buy something without rushing themselves to join that line. The longer the line, the more valuable the prize seems at the end of it. But the line can dissolve as quickly as it will re-form behind something else. The queue that forms behind Hermia at the beginning will shift to Helena in the middle of the night for no reason whatever.

Let us listen to the first encounter of Helena and Hermia in act 1, scene 1:

> *Hermia.* God speed fair Helena! whither away?
>
> *Helena.* Call you me fair? That fair again unsay.
> Demetrius loves your fair, O happy fair!
> Your eyes are lodestars, and your tongue's sweet air
> More tuneable than lark to shepherd's ear
> When wheat is green, when hawthorn buds appear.
> Sickness is catching; O, were favor so,
> [Yours would] I catch, fair Hermia, ere I go;

> My ear should catch your voice, my eye your eye,
> My tongue should catch your tongue's sweet melody.
> Were the world mine, Demetrius being bated,
> The rest I'll give to be to you translated.

The homosexual flavor is undeniable. Shakespeare certainly wanted it there. For this, we cannot pin the blame or the merit—whichever term we choose—upon some authorial "unconscious." The only serious critical question is: why did the author do it? I doubt very much that he wanted to demonstrate the cleverness of Jacques Lacan, or even of Sigmund Freud. I also doubt that he wanted to promote an "alternative life-style." Shakespeare must have had a purpose of his own when he wrote these lines.

There is a passage in *Coriolanus* with an even more unmistakable homosexual flavor, but this time the two characters are male. *Vis-à-vis* Coriolanus, his sworn rival, Aufidius expresses sentiments similar to those of Helena for Hermia.

If you compare the two passages, you will see that the only common feature is the mimetic rivalry of two characters, male or female. The gender makes no difference at all. Quite as ardently as Helena, Aufidius desires something his rival possesses in great abundance, military glory. Aufidius wants the many victories of Coriolanus. Helena wants the many lovers of Hermia, her superior erotic glory. In front of Coriolanus, Aufidius feels like a failure. In front of Hermia, Helena feels like a failure.

A few lines after our passage, Helena is alone and, in a soliloquy, vents her bitterness against her rival. She claims that she is just as pretty as Hermia. Should we conclude that her mood has changed, or that she was a hypocrite in the previous scene? The answers are a little more complicated. Helena's worship of Hermia is more than a polite compliment. It is just as genuine as the hatred of a moment later. Aufidius also feels ambivalent towards Coriolanus.

The mimetic model is worshipped as a model and hated as a rival. The duality is inescapable; desire cannot mimic its friends without turning them into irritating obstacles, but the mimetic lover never seems to understand the self-generated process of his/her own frustration and keeps complaining that someone else is interfering with "true love."

To Helena, Hermia is perceived as a paragon of success, the true goddess of everything a normal girl may wish—elegance, wit, glamor, erotic triumphs . . . How can Hermia fail to be more interesting than either of the boys since she dominates both of them, at least for the time being . . .

The homosexual connotations must be acknowledged but must not blind our critical eyes to the context. Helena's fascination for Hermia is part of a larger story, the story of the mimetic rivalry. In an erotic triangle, the obsession can become so acute that the rival of the same sex tends to supersede the object of the other sex.

Demetrius, the object of Helena's desire, rates only half a line in this passage, which is not much compared to the eleven lines dedicated to Hermia. This type of inbalance gets worse and worse as the mimetic crisis intensifies and the obsession for the rival increases. Here again, the midsummer night is a description of a deepening crisis.

Beyond a certain threshold of intensity, the veritable object becomes the model. If we conclude that Helena has to *be* a homosexual in the same sense that she is a tall, blonde girl, or Hermia short and a brunette, we freeze solid a relationship that should be kept light and airy. We surrender our wits either to the current pedantry of sexuality or to the former puritanism. The two are equally disastrous for the understanding of what Shakespeare is talking about, which we would all understand intuitively if we were dealing with it in a real-life situation.

A Midsummer Night's Dream is much more like a real-life situation than people with their heads full of nihilistic critical theory will ever realize. The final predominance of the model means that the ultimate goal of mimetic desire is that model's "being." This ontological mirage is a must, of course, in a play that is a veritable encyclopedia on the subject, written by the greatest expert ever:

> Were the world mine, Demetrius being bated,
> The rest I'll give to be to you translated.

The last verse sums up and transcends the erotic poem that we quoted before, in the same sense that the metaphysical dimension sums up and transcends the more physical aspects of mimetic desire.

Those who desire mimetically are really trying to exchange their own despised being against the glorious being of their victorious model. Like Bottom, they seek a total metamorphosis, and ultimately their wish will be granted in the same paradoxical fashion.

How can Helena hope to reach her goal? How can she be *translated* to Hermia? Through imitation, of course: the exchange that follows makes it abundantly clear that the only technique of metaphysical desire is *mimesis:*

> O, teach me how you look, and with what art
> You sway the motion of Demetrius' heart.

We must take this language literally: "Teach me how to impersonate you" is what Helena is asking Hermia. We should not regard this effort at impersonation as a mere consequence of some preexisting desire. We should not regard it only as a cause, either. It is really a circular process in which Hermia's choice of Demetrius, before Lysander's arrival upon the scene, is both a cause and a consequence of Helena's own choice.

Helena would like to resemble her model in everything; she wants every feature of her body to be an exact replica of Hermia's. Her ultimate desire is to worship herself rather than Hermia, but the only conceivable method to achieve that goal seems to be to worship the more successful Hermia first and to become a perfect duplicate of the person she really wants to be.

This is what magazines and books about fashionable people are, in our world anyway. They are how-to books. This is a recurrent problem with self-worship. The would-be worshipper always ends up worshipping someone else.

When Helena's hour of success finally arrives, it is too late for her; she can no longer enjoy it. She has been buffeted too much during the midsummer night. She believes she is the victim of some kind of hoax. Her newly found lovers are as sincere as they always were, and yet she is right not to trust either one. Each new combination proves more unstable and short-lived than the previous one.

Everybody ends up equally frustrated. The final outcome is conflict, failure and despair for everybody. No desire is ever fulfilled, and no desire is ever reciprocated, because all desires are one and the same. In order to respond to one another, desires must be differentiated; identical desires will all converge on the same object and can only *cross* one another.

Why is the system of mimetic desire so unstable? Why must the long-suffering Helena finally exchange places with Hermia and become everybody's idol while Hermia now is universally loathed? The reason lies with the universal dependence on *imitation*. The unanimous mimetic convergence seems enormously convincing because it does, indeed, convince everybody. It seems destined to last forever, and yet it is anchored in a pure mimetic effect rather than in anything concrete and objective. It floats half an inch above the ground, and in one instant, the same wind of fashion will topple the idol that it had erected a few instants before.

Ultimately this universal snobbery of imitation constitutes a surrender to pure randomness. The dabbing of the "wrong eyes" with the magical potion is unnecessary as a method of accounting for the fickleness of the lovers, but, like all mythical themes, it half reveals the disquieting truth that it dissimulates. We choose to desire mimetically, but then mimetic desire chooses for us; it deprives us of all power to choose and discriminate. This is what the operation of the love juice suggests quite explicitly. It makes Titania as well as the young people fall in love *at random:*

> *Oberon.* Having once this juice,
> I'll watch Titania when she is asleep,
> And drop the liquor of it in her eyes;
> The next thing then she waking looks upon
> (Be it on lion, bear, or wolf, or bull,
> On meddling monkey, or on busy ape),
> She shall pursue it with the soul of love.

The name of the potion thus introduced in act 2, scene 1—*love-in-idleness*—is a satirical barb at the type of people portrayed in the play. Only youngsters with nothing to do, like the aristocrats of Shakespeare's time, or the entire well-to-do middle class in our day, can waste their time playing such self-destructive games as our four lovers.

The laws and patterns of mimetic desire govern the entire theater of Shakespeare, I believe, if only negatively, in such plays as *As You Like It* that do conform much more consistently than *A Midsummer Night's Dream* to the conventions of traditional romance. Much of the play runs completely counter to these laws, but in a spirit of caricaturally slavish obedience to the mystique of "true love" that really amounts to another form of satire, and therefore another assertion of mimetic desire.

Other plays of Shakespeare illustrate only certain aspects of mimetic desire, fragments of the entire crisis-and-resolution pattern. *A Midsummer Night's Dream* represents the whole dynamic cycle in a speeded-up version that can fit the time frame of a single night.

This is the same fundamental process as in the great tragedies. In their common desire to distinguish themselves from one another, the four lovers engage in a mutual imitation that brings about a warring confusion of everything and ultimately would result in violent murders, were it not for the "supernatural" intervention of Puck and Oberon.

The characters' interpretation of what happens is very much like that of the average spectator, totally blind to the logic of mimetic desire and open, therefore, to suggestions of scapegoating on the one hand and supernatural intervention on the other. The one and the other enable the victims of mimetic desire to not identify mimetic desire as the real culprit and to substitute someone or something else as an explanation.

Their view of the mimetic process is the very reverse of the truth. As all the characters become more and more alike in their undifferentiated frenzy, they perceive an immense difference between themselves and their models. As a result, they themselves feel more and more inferior, or beastly, and they perceive their models as more and more superior and divine. Between these two extremes, emptiness prevails and common humanity is on the way out. Physical violence enters the picture, and the four wander at the edge of the inhuman. Their language reflects the shift. When they speak of themselves they use images of animality and confuse their models with various supernatural figures and even gods.

As the night advances, these images become more insistent. During this last evolution, the four seem to lose control entirely; they feel dizzier and dizzier; their perception becomes blurred. They are moving closer to the trancelike condition of the participants in orgiastic rituals. Shakespeare is obviously writing his own playful reconstitution not so much of the rituals themselves as the type of hysterical mimetic conflicts that must lie behind them.

This is what we already observed in the case of the craftsmen. As the cauldron boils over, the lovers lose their ability to distinguish their overworked metaphors from real beasts and real divinities. Beyond a certain threshold, these metaphors assume a life of their own, but not an "independent" life in the sense of their being well separated from one another. The system is too unstable for that; the substitutions and recombinations are occurring too rapidly.

The youngsters start taking their beasts and their gods seriously at the point when they can no longer tell them apart. Gods and beasts are on the way to forming these weird assemblages that we call mythical monsters. As a result of the dismembering and disorderly *remembering* of normally differentiated creatures, with no regard for the original differentiation, all sorts of fantastic creatures appear.

We already know which ones actually appear. We are back with our old friends, the ass-headed Bottom, Puck, Oberon, Titania and all the fairies. The subplot of the four lovers constitutes a gradual genesis of the mythical metamorphoses that parallels the genesis in the subplot of the craftsmen.

This invasion of the four lovers' speech by animal images corresponds to the excessive preoccupation of Bottom and his companions with the lion and to the early metamorphoses of that terrible beast. In both subplots the images of infrahuman and superhuman creatures prepare the ground for a final metamorphosis that is the same in the two subplots.

After the four lovers wake up and leave the wood, they give Theseus and Hippolyta their own account of what happened during the night. This account is not given on the stage because it would be a repetition of everything that has occurred to both groups during the midsummer night. In other words, the four lovers end up "dreaming" more or less the same "dream" as Bottom and his friends. Even though the two groups are not aware of one another's presence in the woods, they both participate in the genesis of the same mythology, and that is why the fairies are supposed to interfere with both groups.

The craftsmen and the lovers take a not-so-different road to end up in exactly the same place. This comes as no surprise to us. We found, indeed, that the erotic desire of the lovers was no less mimetic than the impersonations of the actors. The tendency for the idolatrous *imitatio* to focus not on one adolescent permanently but on this one now, then on another, then on a third, constitutes the equivalent of Bottom's urge to play all the roles and turn *Pyramus and Thisby* into a one-man show.

In each case, it is the same *hybris,* the same desire to dominate everyone and everything, that ends up destroying the goal it tries to reach because it destroys the very order that makes domination significant. This is the demise of "degree" in Ulysses' speech in *Troilus and Cressida.* This is the essence of tragedy.

What Shakespeare sees better than the Greeks is the reason why *hybristic* pride is self-defeating at the individual level. Mimetic desire is a desire for self-centeredness that cannot be distinguished from mimetic "de-centering," from the desire to "be" the model. A more radical alienation cannot be conceived. It lies at the root of the subject and depends on no sexual, economic or other determinations—unlike all the partial alienations of Marxism, Freudism and other contemporary theories. The four lovers resemble Bottom in their desire for turning the group into a one-man show and their ultimate inability to do so.

We can understand why Shakespeare resorts to the same word to express what the lovers desire and what happens to Bottom in the middle of the rehearsal. The lovers desire to be *translated* to their models. When Bottom turns into the ass-headed monster, Quince says to him: "Bottom, thou art translated."

Translation expresses both the desire for the *being* of someone else, and the paradoxical "success" of that desire, the monstrous metamorphosis. In both subplots the metamorphosis is the reward or, rather, the punishment for this desire.

The two subplots are closely patterned on one another. In both instances, the first scene is a distribution of roles. In principle, each character is supposed to play a single role, but in each case, signs of instability and disintegration immediately appear.

In both instances, as the crisis worsens, we shift from the city of Athens to the wood nearby. This is what the young people in England were supposed to do on midsummer nights. The wilderness is the right place, ritually speaking, for the two escalations of mimetic frenzy and the commingling between human and supernatural beings, the temporary destruction of civilized differentiation.

In both instances we have the same two levels of interpretation that I distinguished *à propos* of the craftsmen: 1) the dramatic level takes the monsters and fairies at face value, regarding them either as a genuine apparition or as a gratuitous product of a purely *individual* imagination, which is what Theseus does in his great speech; 2) a "genetic" level sees these same monsters and fairies as the product of mimetic impersonation gone mad, mimetically affecting all the characters in the two subplots.

Everything is alike in both subplots. Shakespeare makes the whole scheme of mimetic desire obvious to the point of caricature, and then he channels it into a dramatic effect that disguises it, for the benefit of those—the immense majority—who would rather not acknowledge the existence of mimetic desire. As in the case of the actors, the mimetic behavior produces the very mythology that it needs to transfigure its own folly into the mischievousness of Puck.

The author must maintain the illusion that a "true" pairing of the quartet exists. There must be a "right" combination: the myth of "true love" demands it. If it does not have the permanence required, or if it cannot be found at all, we can always pin the blame on the "fairies," or, better still, on the Oedipal father represented by Egeus, or on the power of the state represented by Theseus. These are the only fairies in which a modern critic is allowed to believe, the Freudo-Marxist fairies.

The happy ending of a comedy is one of these conventions that must be respected. The author does not want to offend the possible censors in his audience, or the really pure at heart. Unlike our modern demystificators, even in his most daringly cynical plays, Shakespeare always allows for the possibility of innocence, as if there were no deep resentment in him, or as if it were somehow transcended.

The characters in the two subplots have no contact at all during the night. They come together only during the play within the play. The craftsmen are on stage and the lovers in the audience. It is traditional as a result to regard the two subplots as unrelated or loosely related. The comical antics of the craftsmen serve as an introduction to the play within the play, but their relevance to the work as a whole remains problematic.

The play is about monsters and has often been regarded as a trifle superficial, an elegant but somewhat empty fantasy, a mosaic of unrelated themes. The current fashion of incoherence and discontinuities has made this view more popular than ever, and yet it is completely false. But the formidable coherence of the play is of a sort that traditional criticism has never suspected.

With the blessing of its author, the play turns into a serious theory of its own mythological aspects, which most spectators and critics have always interpreted and will continue to interpret as a pure fantasy, arbitrarily superimposed on the more realistic aspects of the work. The force of the mythical metamorphosis ultimately stems from the craftsmen's and lovers' excessive taste for "translation," or for a type of "identification" that must be identified with *mimesis,* imitation, both because it is Shakespeare's view, and because it accounts for everything in the play. Shakespeare's own theory is the best theory of the play and of the anthropology behind it.

The proof that I have Shakespeare's blessing when I speak as I do is to be found in the smart reply of Hippolyta to the rather stodgy positivism of Theseus in act 5, scene 1, when he tells her what she should believe regarding the cause of the midsummer night. Like Polonius, Theseus does not say anything that is not true, and yet he understands nothing. Hippolyta understands everything. In my earlier article, I have quoted her in connection with the lovers only; I will quote her here once again more appropriately, in connection with the craftsmen as well:

> But all the story of the night told over,
> And all their minds transfigur'd so together,
> More witnesseth than fancy's images,
> And grows to something of great constancy;
> But howsoever, strange and admirable.

Shakespeare reveals the patterns of mimetic desire and their relationship to mythic creation so powerfully in the subplot of the four lovers that the case for its presence can be made on internal evidence only. No help is needed from the other subplot, the theatrical *mimesis* of Bottom and his friends.

But this help is always available, and a comparison of the points the two subplots have in common is enormously enlightening. Mimetic desire remains controversial, no doubt, but since Plato and the *Poetics* of Aristotle, *mimesis* has been the major concept of dramatic criticism. In the Renaissance, the mimetic interpretation was not simply the preferred interpretation, it was just about the only one.

In *A Midsummer Night's Dream,* the presence of *mimesis* as a Shakespearean theme is unquestionable. I assume, therefore, that my readers will have no difficulty agreeing with me on this point: the subplot of Bottom and his friends entails a perpetual and perfectly explicit reference to *mimesis.*

Mimesis is certainly part of the picture in the case of the craftsmen, but something else is needed to complete that picture. The aesthetic *mimesis* of the philosophers and the critics does not explain why the craftsmen decided to perform *Pyramus and Thisby:* They are not professional actors. They did not embark on their theatrical enterprise for aesthetic reasons primarily, or to make a living, or even out of a sense of obligation to the duke. To celebrate the wedding of Theseus, they might have come up with something better suited to their cultural shortcomings. Why did they choose to do a play?

The obvious answer is: personal ambition, narcissism, desire, mimetic desire. Since all the craftsmen show up every time they are summoned, since not one of them is ever missing, the same desire for impersonation must possess each and every one of them, including the most timid, the ones who stand at the other extreme of Bottom and act out the part of the reluctant actor. The reluctance of the reluctant actor means the same thing, ultimately, as the extreme eagerness of Bottom.

Bottom, we found, could never settle on any role, not even the leading one, the most flattering to his ego. His avidity was finally punished, or rewarded, by his metamorphosis into a monster.

Most people enjoy watching a play, but the more they enjoy it, the more they also enjoy being watched by others and therefore performing as actors. The craving for impersonation corresponds to a perfect fusion of *mimesis* and desire.

The desire for the theater consists not in imitating some specific model but in the undifferentiated avidity of Bottom that inevitably conflicts with the pretentions of Quince and the other actors, just as the desires of the four lovers must necessarily "cross" one another.

In the case of the lovers, the one component that is identified most easily is desire. The critic does not have to demonstrate that desire belongs in the picture. But here again, this is not the whole picture; something more is needed to account for the systematic and almost algebraic aspect of the lovers' antics.

If we have *mimesis* plus desire in the case of the craftsmen, we must have desire plus *mimesis* in the case of the lovers. The second component must be imitation or impersonation. The picture is reversed, but to Shakespeare, obviously, it is fundamentally the same picture.

If *mimesis* is really present in the case of the actors, the case for a *mimesis of desire* that would belong to Shakespeare's own conception of both subplots and of the entire play becomes inescapable. A mimesis of desire can always reverse itself into a desire for mimesis. The two subplots are *perfect* mirrors of one another, and together, they breed the fairies. This triunity is the unity of *A Midsummer Night's Dream.*

Unlike the ancient and modern students of imitation, unlike the Freudian students of desire, Shakespeare is not merely aware that imitation and desire cannot be divorced from each other; he realizes that, far from being the bland ingredient that the modern world sees in it, a source of sheepish gregariousness in society and of a platitudinous "realism" in the arts, *mimesis* (because of its admixture of desire) is an explosive combination. It constitutes the disruptive factor par excellence of human relations, the major reason for the fragility of even and especially the closest friendships and the most tender erotic relationships. The closer the friends, the more likely they are to imitate one another's desires and therefore to turn into enemies. This is Shakespeare's tragic as well as his comic insight par excellence, and it is undistinguishable from the fusion of mimesis and desire that he perpetually portrays.[4]

Notes

[1] William Shakespeare, *A Midsummer Night's Dream,* in *The Riverside Shakespeare,* ed. G. Blakemore Evans (Boston: Houghton Mifflin Company, 1974). All subsequent quotations in the text are taken from this same source.

[2] René Girard, *Violence and the Sacred* (Baltimore: Johns Hopkins University Press, 1978).

[3] "Myth and Ritual in Shakespeare: *A Midsummer Night's Dream,*" in *Textual Strategies,* ed. Josue Harari (Ithaca: Cornell University Press, 1979), 189-212.

[4] This essay should lead to a consideration of the play within the play. The theme is too rich, however, and too long for the present essay; it will be instead the subject of a separate essay, the third in a three-part study of *A Midsummer Night's Dream.* The author apologizes for his long delay in treating the fascinating encounter between the two types of mimetic actors.

Harold Bloom (essay date 1987)

SOURCE: An introduction to William Shakespeare's *A Midsummer Night's Dream,* written and edited by Harold Bloom, Chelsea House Publishers, 1987, pp. 1-5.

[*In the following essay, Bloom praises Bottom as the heart of the play, and as its most original figure. Bloom goes on to contrast Bottom's goodness, common sense, homeliness and humanity with Puck and his world, which threaten to "ravish reality away."*]

On the loftiest of the world's thrones we still are sitting only on our own Bottom

MONTAIGNE, "Of Experience"

I will get Peter Quince to write a ballet of this dream. It shall be call'd "Bottom's Dream," because it hath no bottom.

I

I wish Shakespeare had given us Peter Quince's ballet (ballad), but he may have been too wise to attempt the poem. *A Midsummer Night's Dream,* for me, is Puck and Bottom, and I prefer Bottom. Perhaps we reduce to Puckish individuals or Bottoms. Pucks are more charming, but Bottoms are rather more amiable. Shakespeare's Bottom is surpassingly amiable, and I agree with Northrop Frye that Bottom is the only mortal with experience of the visionary center of the play. As the possible lover (however briefly) of the Fairy Queen, Bottom remains a lasting reproach to our contemporary fashion of importing sacred violence, bestiality, and all manner of sexual antics into Shakespeare's most fragile of visionary dramas. For who could be more mild mannered, better natured, or sweetly humorous than the unfailingly gentle Bottom? Titania ends up despising him, but he is simply too good for her!

Bottom, when we first encounter him, is already a Malaprop, inaccurate at the circumference, as it were, but sound at the core, which is what his name means, the center of the skein upon which a weaver's wool is wound. And surely that is his function in the play; he is its core, and also he is the most original figure in *A Midsummer Night's Dream.* Self-assertive, silly, ignorant, he remains a personage of absolute good will, a kind of remote ancestor to Joyce's amiable Poldy. Transformed into an outward monstrosity by Puck, he yet retains his courage, kindness, and humor, and goes through his uncanny experience totally unchanged within. His initial dialogue with Titania is deliciously ironic, and he himself is in full control of the irony:

TITANIA: I pray thee, gentle mortal, sing again.
Mine ear is much enamored of thy note;
So is mine eye enthrallèd to thy shape;
And thy fair virtue's force (perforce) doth
    move me
On the first view to say, to swear, I love thee.
BOTTOM: Methinks, mistress, you should have
    little reason for that. And yet, to say the truth,
    reason and love keep little company together
    now-a-days. The more the pity   that some
    honest neighbors will not make them friends.
    Nay, I can gleek upon occasion.

TITANIA: Thou art as wise as thou art beautiful.
BOTTOM: Not so, neither; but if I had wit
    enough to get out of this wood, I have
    enough to serve mine own turn.

Knowing that he lacks both beauty and wisdom, Bottom is realistic enough to see that the faery queen is beautiful but not wise. Charmed by (and charming to) the elve foursome of Peaseblossom, Cobweb, Moth, and Mustardseed, Bottom makes us aware that they mean no more and no less to him than Titania does. Whether or not he has made love to Titania, a subject of some nasty debate among our critical contemporaries, seems to me quite irrelevant. What does matter is that he is sublimely unchanged, for worse or for better, when he wakes up from his bottomless dream:

> BOTTOM: [*Awaking.*] When my cue comes, call me, and I will answer. My next is, "Most fair Pyramus." Heigh-ho! Peter Quince! Flute the bellowsmender! Snout the tinker! Starveling! God's my life, stol'n hence, and left me asleep! I have had a most rare vision. I have had a dream, past the wit of man to say what dream it was. Man is but an ass, if he go about [t'] expound this dream. Methought I was—there is no man can tell what. Methought I was, and methought I had—but man is but [a patch'd] fool, if he will offer to say what methought I had. The eye of man hath not heard, the ear of man hath not seen, man's hand is not able to taste, his tongue to conceive, nor his heart to report, what my dream was. I will get Peter Quince to write a ballet of this dream. It shall be call'd "Bottom's Dream," because it hath no bottom; and I will sing it in the latter end of a play, before the Duke. Peradventure, to make it the more gracious, I shall sing it at her death.

Bottom's revision of 1 Corinthians 2:9-10 is the heart of the matter:

> Eye hath not seen, nor ear heard, neither have entered into the heart of man, the things which God hath prepared for them that love him.
>
> But God hath revealed them unto us by his Spirit.
> (ST. PAUL)

> The eye of man hath not heard, the ear of man hath not seen, man's hand is not able to taste, his tongue to conceive, nor his heart to report, what my dream was.
>
> (BOTTOM)

Bottom's scrambling of the senses refuses St. Paul's easy supernaturalism, with its dualistic split between flesh and spirit. Our prophet Bottom is a monist, and so his dream urges upon us a synesthetic reality, fusing flesh and spirit. That Bottom is one for whom God has prepared the things revealed by his Spirit is made wonderfully clear in the closing dialogue between the benign weaver and Theseus:

> BOTTOM: [*Starting up.*] No, I assure you, the wall is down that parted their fathers. Will it please you to see the epilogue, or to hear a Bergomask dance between two of our company?
>
> THESEUS: No epilogue, I pray you; for your play needs no excuse.

Only Bottom could assure us that the wall is down that parted all our fathers. The weaver's common sense and natural goodness bestow upon him an aesthetic dignity, homely and humane, that is the necessary counterpoise to the world of Puck that otherwise would ravish reality away in Shakespeare's visionary drama.

II

Puck, being the spirit of mischief, is both a hobgoblin and "sweet Puck," not so much by turns but all at once. *A Midsummer Night's Dream* is more Puck's play than Bottom's, I would reluctantly agree, even as *The Tempest* is more Ariel's drama than it is poor Caliban's. If Puck, rather than Oberon, were in charge, then Bottom never would resume human shape and the four young lovers would continue their misadventures forever. Most of what fascinates our contemporaries about *A Midsummer Night's Dream* belongs to Puck's vision rather than to Bottom's. Amidst so much of the Sublime, it is difficult to prefer any single passage, but I find most unforgettable Puck's penultimate chant:

> Now the hungry [lion] roars,
> And the wolf [behowls] the moon;
> Whilst the heavy ploughman snores,
> All with weary task foredone.
> Now the wasted brands do glow,
> Whilst the screech-owl, screeching loud,
> Puts the wretch that lies in woe
> In remembrance of a shroud.
> Now it is the time of night
> That the graves, all gaping wide,
> Every one lets forth his sprite,
> In the church-way paths to glide.
> And we fairies, that do run
> By the triple Hecat's team
> From the presence of the sun,
> Following darkness like a dream,
> Now are frolic. Not a mouse
> Shall disturb this hallowed house.
> I am sent with broom before,
> To sweep the dust behind the door.

Everything problematic about Puck is summed up there; a domestic, work-a-day spirit, yet always uncannily *between*, between men and women, faeries and humans, nobles and mechanicals, nature and art, space and time. Puck is a spirit cheerfully amoral, free because never in love, and always more amused even than amusing. The triple Hecate—heavenly moon maiden, earthly Artemis, and ruler of Hades—is more especially Puck's deity than she is the goddess worshipped by the other faeries. Hazlitt wisely contrasted Puck to Ariel by reminding us that "Ariel is a minister of retribution, who is touched with the sense of pity at the woes he inflicts," while Puck "laughs at those whom he misleads." Puck just does not care; he has nothing to gain and little to lose. Only Oberon could call him "gentle," but then Oberon could see Cupid flying between moon and earth, and Puck constitutionally could not. Puck says that things please him best "that befall preposterously," where I think the last word takes on the force of the later coming earlier and the earlier later. As a kind of flying metalepsis or trope of transumption, Puck is indeed what the rhetorician Puttenham called a far-fetcher.

The midsummer night's dream, Puck tells us in his final chant, is ours, since we "but slumb'red here, / While these visions did appear." What are we dreaming when we dream Puck? "Shadows" would be his reply, in a familiar Shakespearean trope, yet Puck is no more a shadow than Bottom is. Free of love, Puck becomes an agent of the irrational element in love, its tendency to over-value the object, as Freud grimly phrased it. A man or woman who incarnates Puck is sexually very dangerous, because he or she is endlessly mobile, invariably capable of transforming object-libido back into ego-libido again. Puckish freedom is overwhelmingly attractive, but the blow it strikes you will cause it no pain. Falling in love with a Puck is rather like turning life into the game of hockey.

Theseus, in the play's most famous speech, associates the lover with the poet and the lunatic in a perfectly Freudian conglomerate, since all forsake the reality principle, all assert the omnipotence of thought, and all thus yield themselves up to an ultimate narcissism. If Theseus is a Freudian, Bottom is not, but represents an older wisdom, the amiable sapience, mixed with silliness, of the all-too-natural man. Puck, quicksilver and uncaring, defines the limits of the human by being so far apart from the human.

How can one play contain both Bottom and Puck? Ariel and Caliban both care, though they care on different sides and in different modes. Puck has no human feelings, and so no human meaning; Bottom is one of the prime Shakespearean instances of how human meaning gets started, by a kind of immanent overflow, an ontological excess of being in excess of language. Only a dream, we might think, could contain both Bottom and Puck, but the play, however fantastic, is no fantasy, but an imitation that startles the reality principle and makes it tremble, rather like a guilty thing surprised.

Michael Schneider (essay date 1987)

SOURCE: "Bottom's Dream, the Lion's Roar, and Hostility of Class Difference in *A Midsummer Night's Dream,*" in *From the Bard to Broadway: The University of Florida Department of Classics Comparative Drama Conference Papers,* Vol. VII, edited by Karelisa V. Hartigan, University Press of America, 1987, pp. 191-212.

[*In the following essay, Schneider asserts that the issue of class tension and aggression is suggested in* A Midsummer Night's Dream *through the language of the working class characters (Bottom and his associates), and especially through the Bottom and Titania episode, whose source is "classical social satire."*]

As the name itself could hardly suggest more emphatically than it does, *A Midsummer Night's Dream* is a play that—on surface appearance anyway—has little to do with politics, let alone class conflict. Among Shakespeare's early comedies, *MND* is often seen as a precursor to the late romances, *A Winter's Tale* and *The Tempest*—an association which, at least traditionally, tends further to disassociate it from a socio-political reading. Shakespearean romance-comedy has been particularly amenable to twentieth-century critical work; Northrop Frye, as a notable instance, has elevated it to a privileged place. In *A Natural Perspective,* Frye's study of Shakespearean comedy and romance, Bottom's monologue in *MND* represents a definitive moment for the representation in language of the ineffable essence of dream (1965, 108-09):

> I have had a most rare vision. I have had a dream, past the wit of man to say what a dream it was: man is but an ass, if he go about to expound this dream. Methought I was—there is no man can tell what. Methought I was—and methought I had—but man is but a patched fool, if he will offer to say what methought I had. The eye of man hath not heard, the ear of man hath not seen, man's hand is not able to taste, his tongue to conceive, nor his heart to report, what my dream was. I will get Peter Quince to write a ballad of his dream: it shall be called Bottom's Dream, because it hath no bottom; and I will sing it in the latter end of a play, before the Duke: peradventure, to make it the more gracious, I shall sing it at her death.

> (IV i 203-16)

Frye draws from Freud to maintain that dream at its bottom, so to speak, as expressed in this speech, forms a point of contact with the unfathomable, the incommunicable powers and paradoxes of which are, for Frye, the vital source of literature. "It is quite consistent," writes Frye, arguing for a wisdom born of folly, "with the use of incredible events and the demand for an uncritical response in Skakespearean comedy that such oracular things should be said, or hinted at, by characters even simpler than we are" (Frye, 1965, 109).

Frye's notion that the play demands an uncritical response coincides with his structural analysis of *MND*, and comedy in general, and the concomitant notion of comic catharsis—raising of sympathy and ridicule on the way to a redemptive calm of mind.[1] *MND* begins by raising desire for the fulfillment of desire—the plight of Hermia and Lysander—then thwarts it—the sharp Athenian law—creating a dissonance which verges toward nightmare in the bewilderment of the four lovers in the forest, only to be rescued and perfectly resolved—through the *deus ex machina* of Oberon's magic flower. As Puck proclaims it: "Jack shall have Jill; / Nought shall go ill; / The man shall have his mare again, and all shall be well" (III ii 461-63). The last act revels celebrate the impending nuptial and powerfully evoke—especially in the context of May Day, with its echos of pagan festival—an uncritical sense of participation in the symbols of union both within the human and with the natural world. For Frye, it is a vision of transcendence, temporary but nonetheless realized, and Shakespearean romance-comedy for him represents comedy at the level of Christian myth: an enactment of redemption from the pain and chaos of the real (Frye, 1948, 171).

This reading of the play is not only Frye's; C.L. Barber's as well, arising as it does out of the anthropologically based work of the Cambridge school, is essentially congruent (Barber 119-62), and this way of reading, in broad terms, is implemented to a large degree in nearly all modern productions of the play. It is comedy, replete with happy ending and the wonderful comic effects of Bottom and Titania and the Pyramus and Thisby play. I would like in this paper to subvert and decenter this reading (and thereby enlarge possibilities for dramatic presentation) through a close reading that follows from the cultural-materialist approach of James Kavanagh, in particular, but also borrows heavily from Freud. As my reference to Marxist thought and Freud in the same sentence might suggest, my method is implied by Frederic Jameson's title: *The Political Unconscious.* I do not, however, presume to the structural-analytical rigor of Jamesonian theory and practice. To put it simply, if very reductively, much as a Freudian analyst studies dreams and slips of the tongue for signs of what is repressed or denied in the individual personality, one may see in the literary text signs of socio-political tension at the historical moment of production that the text—as part of its mediating function in culture—seeks to repress or deny.[2]

From the Marxist view of repression, what is almost always denied or understated or placed conveniently in the background of literary work, is class struggle. From this point of view, a romance-comedy, such as *MND*, which even by its title seems to deny the working day

world, becomes suspect. From the modern view, even a reading like Frye's, drawing as it does on Freud, marks romance-comedy as a form of wish-fulfillment dream, which if we read as Freudians signifies its opposite as—what has been termed—present absence. The oxymoronic seeming illogic of "present absence" is, in fact, a fundamental logic of wish-fulfillment and desire—a child dreams of eating a candy bar when in waking life there is no candy bar to eat. What we "want" is what we don't have, what is absent in reality but present in thought, imaged as the object of desire. Elizabethan England of the mid-1590s, when *MND* was written and first produced, was (as I will develop) an extremely trying time even within the context of normal Elizabethan life, and suggests a rough analogy to the considerably less severe 1930s American depression, a period that produced its own popular romance-comedy, "The Wizard of Oz," as an enactment of escape from the working-class life inscribed within it. With respect to *MND,* several phenomena of the text offer concrete support for reading class struggle as a present absence. The language of the working-class characters, Bottom and his rude-mechanical colleagues, is a repository of verbal play—Bottom's monologue is only one instance—which hints at meaning beyond what is expressed. The play also contains, in Titania's monologue, a direct reference to the contemporary economic turmoil. It is also pertinent to this analysis that the Bottom and Titania episode has its source in classical social satire, Apuleius' *Golden Ass.* Each of these "nodes of meaning" points, as if the text were an overdetermined dream, toward class conflict as latent content of the play.

Many readers of *MND* are struck by what seems to be a fairly blatant aristocratic smugness in the derogatory remarks of Theseus and his coterie and Bottom and his working-class colleagues in the last act, and this action provides the entry-point for my analysis. When Philostrate, Master of Revels for Theseus' grand wedding celebration, describes to Theseus the production of Pyramus and Thisby which Peter Quince and his fellow amateurs have prepared, he ridicules their "tedious, brief scene" and find its pretensions to serious tragedy to be unworthy of the Duke:

> And it is nothing, nothing in the world;
> Unless you can find sport in their intents,
> Extremely stretched and conned with cruel
>   pain, to do you service.
>
> (V i 78-81)[3]

Philostrate's scorn for the artisans—"hard-handed men," he calls them, "which never labored in their minds till now (72-73)"—reemphasizes the class demarcation already marked by Puck, who terms Quince and company "hempen homespuns" and "rude mechanicals." Philostrate also marks himself as a prig and pretentious poser; and even though his role is minor, he represents a type (along with Egeus) of the blocking character or *alazon* identified in Frye's analysis of comic structure (Frye, 1971, 172-73, 226-28). By urging Theseus not to see the mechanicals, he blocks the comic release which will be provided by their performance; and by insulting them, he draws antipathy on himself, at least from those elements of the audience sympathetically aligned with the mechanicals. Their clearly defined working-class status would tend by itself to arouse an identification response from many in a theater audience of the Elizabethan 1590s as well as now, and other factors also dispose us favorably toward them. By this stage of the play, they have entertained us three times. Their desire to appear before and please royalty seems ready-made to appeal to that part of each of us that wants to please our superiors (and thereby raise ourselves in social or economic status).[4] As the play's broad comic relief, they are its best fun, and Bottom is the star comic role (probably played in the earlier productions by the famous Will Kempe).

As it turns out, Philostrate correctly anticipates the response of Theseus, Hippolyta and their coterie of young friends (who are happily anticipating conjugal bliss) to the mechanicals' performance. They view it as laughably amateurish. Nevertheless, Theseus dismisses Philostrate's objections and insists on hearing the play.

> I will hear that play,
> For never anything can be amiss
> When simpleness and duty tender it.
>
> (V i 81-83)

On one hand, the text at this point seems to intend that we participate in Theseus' generous sentiments. He has rescued the comedy from Philostrate, which releases the tension set up by Philostrate's bad review of the Pyramus-Thisby play. Philostrate's aristocratic snobbery, furthermore, makes him a foil for Theseus, authorizing us to see Theseus as the "good" Duke, a benign aristocrat who represents the "nobility" of his class and a ruler who like a loving parent appreciates his subjects' earnest desire to please regardless of their professional competence. Many in Shakespeare's audience may have responded in this way, and such a reading coincides with E.M.W. Tillyard's argument that faith in an ordered, hierarchic pattern in the cosmos and in socio-political relations constituted the prevalent Elizabethan ideology. Theseus' immediately succeeding homily on aristocratic graciousness (V i 89-105) further encourages us to feel harmonious reconciliation of class difference, a reconciliation consistent with the traditional analysis of comic structure.

Recent Marxist criticism of Shakespeare, however, tends to complicate such an ideologically stable reading (Kavanagh, Tennenhouse). From a twentieth-century point-of-view, furthermore, it is hard (at least for this reader) not to be irritated by the patronizing, far-from-benign smugness of Theseus' exhortations to simplicity and duty. The resemblance to the last line of Blake's "The Chimney Sweeper," in which an incipient working-class consciousness appears by way of ironic understatement, is rather striking: "So if all do their duty, they need not fear harm." My experience of teaching Blake's poem has been that it will not disturb the "innocent" reader who wants or needs to read it as properly pious Christian humility in the face of suffering. It tends, in fact, to corroborate the belief of such a reader, at least until he or she learns more about the poverty of London slums and the mortality rate of chimney sweepers, and reads some of Blake's more openly satiric verse. Even then, the Christian reading may persist in a provocative dialectic with the ironic reading, in a way which interrogates the meaning of "duty" and "harm" and deepens the resonance of the poem. A similar interrogative unease regarding the patriarchal order is inscribed within *MND* and stands in a provocative counterpoise against it, so that the play speaks in a double discourse similar to Blake's poem. It is more subtle and complex, however, in *MND* because the underside of the double discourse, which represents class struggle as an issue struggling to assert itself as presence in the text, is more repressed, more effectively defended against in this text than in Blake.

In Theseus and his coterie, the play presents a small model of Elizabethan aristocratic society, the dominant ideology of which is asserted at the beginning, when Theseus characterizes his conquest of Hippolyta—"I wooed thee with my sword" (I i 16) (see Gohlke)—and also when Egeus invokes law to bind the arranged marriage of Hermia to Demetrius. In subversion of the patriarchy, which orders personal relations according to economic and political considerations, Hermia and Lysander invoke desire, their love for each other. But this "subversion," which instigates movement to an alternative domain, the "green world" as Frye terms it (1949, 169 et seq.), is reintegrated and contained within the final harmonius reordering represented by the wedding celebration. Ultimately, this "subversion" mounted by thwarted desire of young love doesn't seriously challenge dominant ideology as much as provide a context for its re-legitimization.[5] In Bottom and the mechanicals, however, the text constitutes a genuine ideological threat to the dominant order, and because the threat is real it must be (and is) carefully submerged. The text figures this threat in various ways, but most insistently in the concern about the roaring of the lion before the ladies. The mechanicals' dialogue reveals that this threat must be presented with "discretion" or their lives are at risk, a risk which they unanimously acknowledge in their first scene—"That would hang us, every mother's son's" (I ii 71)—and which they acknowledge several times more in later scenes (I ii 57-70; II i 25-41). When Snug the Joiner makes his appearance as lion before the court, he follows Bottom's careful instructions for his speech (III i 32-41) nearly to the letter: "For if I should as lion come in strife / Into this place, 'twere pity on my life" (V i 222-23).

These tensions between courtly decorum and uncon-strained expression enfigured by the lion's roar and the threat of being hanged repeat tensions which were inherent in the class differences of Elizabethan soci-ety,[6] and which were particularly heightened during the years 1594-96 when *A Midsummer Night's Dream* was first performed. Three wet summers in succession caused disastrous grain harvests which sent food prices skyrocketing and created inflation—with speculation and profit for some, grain merchants in particular, and disaster for many of the artisan class, whose buying power decreased drastically. The price of grain, as compared to wages has in England probably not been as high before or since (Clay, vl 299; Gregg, 206; Walter and Wrightson). It is this situation of dearth and depression which Titania describes during her first appearance in the play:

> Therefore the winds, piping to us in vain,
> As in revenge, have sucked up from the sea
> Contagious fogs; which falling in the land
> Hath every pelting river made so proud
> That they have overborne their continents.
> The ox hath therefore stretched his yoke in
> vain,
> The ploughman lost his sweat, and the green
> corn
> Hath rotted ere his youth attained a beard.
>   (II i 87-95)[7]

Titania's speech dwells upon the calamitous weather which had disturbed the accustomed order of nature, but there were also outbreaks of rioting during these years; and the potential for large-scale social disorder was generally perceived as serious,[8] as evidenced in particular by the enactment in 1597 of England's first Poor Law.[9] These stressed social conditions form an element of the background to the production of *MND* which cast light upon the mechanicals and their discre-tion before royalty. It suggests that consciousness of class difference and, in particular, lower class resent-ment toward the aristocratic and rich might well have been a significant factor in contemporary response to the mechanicals' "naive" buffoonery.

The text tends to support this supposition. For instance, although Philostrate, Theseus, Demetrius and Lysander see the mechanicals as simpleton fools and laugh con-descendingly at (not with) their antics, the mechanicals' dialogue reveals a certain degree of awareness about what they are doing and why. As Snug reveals at the end of Act IV, when Bottom has not yet arrived to join the others, they expect to be hand-somely rewarded for their effort, and they fear Bottom's absence will spoil their opportunity: "If our sport had gone forward," says

Snug, in disappointment, "We had all been made men" (IV ii 16). Flute predicts that Bottom, as their star performer, would have been awarded "sixpence a day" for life, which in 1595 was a considerable addition to the daily wages of a weaver and may have been enough to live on (Furness 198n.25). This goes far in provid-ing plausible motivation for the mechanicals to un-dertake the risk of offending nobility, particularly if it is understood as occurring under conditions of eco-nomic-social disorder considerably more dire than 1930s America. Flute's reference to Elizabethan units of currency, furthermore, would have had the imme-diate effect for the Elizabethan audience of locating the mechanicals' aspirations within contemporary eco-nomic conditions. The Athenian mythical setting, which provides a distancing from contemporary reality nec-essary to appreciate the fantasy-world love play, in effect falls away before Bottom and the mechanicals, whose needs and desires are grounded in basic eco-nomic reality.

It is apparent, furthermore, that the mechanicals *expect* to be laughed at when they perform. As Quince an-nounces at his first appearance, their play is a "most lamentable comedy" (I ii ll). Bottom considers their Pyramus-Thisby play to be "a sweet comedy" (IV ii 39). Yet Philostrate and Theseus seem to miss the point. Philostrate describes the play to Theseus as if he be-lieves it was intended to be tragical and that his "merry tears" and "passion of loud laughter" occur because "there is not one word apt, one player fitted" to its tragical pretensions (V i 61-70). As Theseus views the play, he follows Philostrate's lead and also speaks condescendingly, as if he believes the mechanicals are attempting serious tragedy: "This passion, and the death of a dear friend, would go near to make a man look sad" (V i 281-82). Neither Philostrate nor Theseus, nor others of the court party seem to realize they are watch-ing a burlesque which parodies tragic love; they in-stead seem to assume that "hard-handed men" are in-capable of acting with the depth of feeling appropriate to tragic love. In this respect, the text represents its aristocrats in accord with the hierarchic ideology which upholds their status; according to the dominant con-ception of ordered degree in nature and society, aris-tocrats are "better" than working-class artisans not because they are richer, but because they are inher-ently more refined specimens of humanity, closer to the angels, more capable, for instance, of a "noble" passion like tragic love.

At the same time, however, the text presents the mechani-cals as acting in subversion of this ideology. Their Pyramus-Thisby play parodies romantic love in a play in which the aristocratic characters are actuated solely by romantic love (see Young 186-87). The mechanicals, despite a certain degree of self-awareness granted to them by the text, are represented as naive and unaware before royalty. This is, of course, consistent with the

First Fairy (Julie Jupp), Moth (Oliver Darley), Cobweb (Angela Sims), Mustardseed (Carl Antony), and Peaseblossom (Caroline Fitzgerald), surround Titania (Estelle Kohler) and Bottom (Robert Lang) in Act IV, Scene i of the Open Air Theatre's 1994 production of A Midsummer Night's Dream.

behavior of an underclass.[10] Furthermore, as Freud has recognized, the mechanicals' comic effect before royalty (and before us)—and thus their chance at being "made men"—depends upon appearing naive, i.e., without *intention* to make fun of romantic love (763 et seq.). It is only at perceiving naive lack of intention, says Freud, that we may release the inner inhibition that allows us to laugh at our own folly. Bottom recognizes the advantages of obsequiousness when he offers to moderate the lion's roar: "I will roar you as gently as any sucking dove" (I ii 75)"; and the mechanicals' discretion in general is, in effect, a representation of the text's astute awareness of the line between satire and saturnalia, (30, 37, 57).[11] This line defined a limit even to such authorized misrule as May Day. While authorities tended to recognize that the license permitted by festival enhanced their authority, this license did not include ridicule of public figures or even representation that openly implicated contemporary public events.[12]

The apparent naivete of the mechanicals as they enact a burlesque parody of the indulgence of the leisure class is one way in which the text of *MND* discretely submerges its subversive tendency, and this discretion

points toward other interesting and less obvious textual discretions. There is within the language and action of the mechanicals considerable indication of the submerged aggression characteristic of class resentment. It is as if the text itself enacts an effort at repression or self-control that nevertheless, perversely and subversively, reveals itself in spite of itself. The repetitive word slips, for instance, that help to constitute—from the aristocrats' point of view—the naive laughableness of the mechanicals, form a consistent pattern; in every case, the word slips can be read as undercutting the sense that the mechanicals' play is offered in simplicity, duty, and loving obeisance. In rehearsal, Bottom tells Snug that his face should appear through his lion's neck and he should speak to the ladies "to the same defect" (III i 34). As Pyramus, Bottom speaks of "flowers of odious [instead of odorous] savors" (III i 73), and Quince says that Starveling should announce that he comes "to disfigure" moonshine (III i 52). The most remarkable instance of this subversive word-slippage, is the first part of Quince's prologue, which could hardly be more pointed in its double discourse. At each turn of phrase, class resentment and aggression undercut what appears on the surface as an obsequious desire to please:

If we offend, it is with our good will
  That you should think we come not to
  offend,
But with good will. To show our simple skill,
  That is the true beginning of our end.
Consider then, we come but in despite.
  We do not come, as minding to content you,
Our true intent is. All for your delight,
  We are not here. That you should here
  repent you,
The actors are at hand: and, by their show,
You shall know all, that you are like to know.
                    (V i 108-117)

If one thinks of the great chain of being as referent, Theseus' immediately succeeding comment on this prologue is especially apt: "His speech was like a tangled chain; nothing impaired, but all disordered" (V i 124-35).[13]

The text also couches its ideological threat in the form of submerged sexual aggression.[14] The lion's roar itself suggests sexual threat, especially since it engenders repeated concern for the ladies—"to bring in (God shield us) a lion among ladies is a most dreadful thing" (III i 27-28), says Bottom. Bottom also concerns himself about the effect of his sword, which as Pyramus he must draw to kill himself—"which the ladies cannot abide" (IV i 10). Bottom's concerns about his sword echo the patriarchal phallicness of Theseus' "I wooed thee with my sword" (I i 16).[15] With regard to phallic imagery, furthermore, it is notable that the mechanicals' rehearsal in the woods takes place "At the Duke's Oak" (I ii 98). It is on this plot of ground, or near it, that the text represents Bottom enacting, throught his night of love with Titania, what might be thought of as a male working-class fantasy of emasculating the patriarchy by cuckolding the king (in this case, the Duke).[16] Bottom's magical transformation to an ass's head not only provides a ludicrous visual effect, it also presents a powerful symbolic image of working-class ethos. The ass as "beast of burden" suggests subjugation to a master as well as strength and steady, humble persistence at the tasks necessary to survival, values which contrast sharply with the leisure and self-indulgence of the aristocrats in the play. Furthermore, as Jan Kott has argued, the ass— as beast commonly credited with having the longest, hardest phallus—represents animal sexual potency (Kott 220).[17] Titania's barely contained lust for Bottom, while he remains stolidly impervious to her charms (III i 124-86), plays out the fantasy of power. The subversiveness of this fantasy is well-submerged by its representation in symbolic imagery and its containment within a dramatic context of hilarious comedy. Nevertheless, even the comic effect of this scene has a subversive edge, to the extent that it arises from the representation of unrestrained lust in a "good" woman, especially one—who as the fairy queen—would be seen by some in the Elizabethan audience as a reference to Elizabeth herself.[18]

Though Shakespeare's text carries no explicit decoding of the ideological or sexual implications of the ass image, both are patently apparent in Apuleius' *The Golden Ass,* Shakespeare's probable source for Bottom's transformation and erotic adventure with Titania.[19] Apuleius' protagonist, Lucius, is accidentally transformed to an ass by his lover, and in one episode is visited by a rich noblewoman who, enamored of his sexual equipment, has paid for the chance to spend the night with him. Her attempts at seduction while Lucius is unmoved parallel Titania with Bottom, though the description in Apuleius is considerably more explicit. Through his travels as an ass, Lucius experiences slavery and other examples of man's cruelty to man in the ancient world, and *The Golden Ass* is frequently read as a satire on social and economic patterns of the time (Frye, 1965, 106-07; Lindsay 22). As a probable source and background to *MND,* it provides an intertextual basis for finding that the language and action of the text are informed by class struggle.[20]

Furthermore, though the ass image is more explicitly marked as a sexual-ideological signifier in Apuleius, Shakespeare's text signals the cuckolding implications of Bottom's night with Titania. Bottom's singing about the "plain-song cuckoo," "whose note many a man doth mark," and his sexual punning—to "give a bird the lie"—are the first lines he utters after Titania's "What angel wakes me from my flow'ry bed?" (II i 116-123), and it is unlikely than many in an Elizabethan audience would miss the bawdy import of these lines. In the same vein, Quince's wordslip—"paramour" for "paragon" (IV ii 11-12)—describing Bottom's "sweet voice," (when his absence threatens to ruin their chance to be "made men") goes quite to the point of explaining his lateness. As if for emphasis, it is repeated and clarified by Flute: "You must say 'paragon.' A paramour is (God bless us!) a thing of naught" (IV ii 13-14). Once tuned to this sexual word play which provides the immediate context for Bottom's transformation, it is also hard to ignore Flute's line, during the rehearsal in the woods, which is Bottom's cue to return on stage. Speaking as Thisbe, Flute says: "O—As true as truest horse, that yet would never tire" (III i 92). In its context, spoken by Flute as Thisby to Bottom as Pyramus, as he appears for the first time "with the ass-head,"—the line strongly suggests sexual endurance and would very likely have been played for this laugh, a laugh which brings the power fantasy resonances of Bottom's transformation more to the surface of the play than is at first apparent.

Bottom's night of love instigates the unraveling of the discord between Oberon and Titania, and is also the pivotal point at which the mainstream comic action of the four bewildered lovers clarifies. Puck's lines at the end of Act III, which institute harmony among the lovers, also introduce the Bottom and Titania post-coital scene (IV ii) with another play on animal eroticism:

"The man shall have his mare again, and all shall be well" (III ii 463). Other commentators have noted the centrality of the Bottom and Titania action and have conferred privileged status on Bottom as a grounded center within the play's various levels of action and irony (Barber 154; Frye, 1965, 108-09; Young 186-187). He is the sole mortal character who directly participates in the fairy world. Unlike the Athenian lover, and even his fellow mechanicals, he is not frightened or bewildered but remains self-possessed, even to the point of blithely shedding Titania's declaration of love. "Methinks, mistress, you should have little reason for that" (III i 129-130). He is, as a representative of working-class consciousness, free from the "what fools these mortals be" antics of the aristocrat lovers.

Bottom's aplomb and unperturbed self-esteem are also a focal point for the text's repetitions of the word "ass," which establish an ironic interplay between the idea of being an ass and calling someone else one.

> SNOUT O Bottom, thou art changed. What do I see on thee?
>
> BOTTOM What do you see? You see an ass-head of your own, do you?
>
> QUINCE Bless thee, Bottom, bless thee! Thou art translated.
>
> BOTTOM I see their knavery. This is to make an ass of me, to fright me, if they could. But I will will not stir from this place, do what they can. I will walk up and down here, and will sing, that they shall hear I am not afraid.
>
> (III i 104-111)

Bottom *has* been translated; his friends and the audience see his ass-ness, and yet he doesn't waver in his steadfast sense of self. With the possible exception of Puck, who is himself (as Oberon's servant) a fairy-world evocation of working-class status, Bottom would seem to represent the character most immune to self-aggrandizing pretensions. Even in the childish enthusiasm of his aspirations to play all the parts in Quince's play, Bottom seems only to want to fulfill a role for himself as star player that his fellows, his social peers, are quite willing to grant him. Certainly in the sense of freedom from romantic illusion, Bottom is among the mortals the least ass-like; and he asserts his non-assness most when he is, in the literal sense, most an ass. Thus, when Demetrius refers to the mechanicals as asses (V i 152) and later Theseus specifically to Bottom as an ass (V i 304), we should be skeptical about their perception. I have already outlined the inability of Theseus and his coterie to perceive the parodic effect of the Pyramus-Thisby play. Theseus is also represented in his lunatic, lover, poet speech as blind to the fairy activities which govern the action of the play (V i 2-22). It would seem, therefore, that in representing the aristocrat characters as quick to apply

the epithet "ass" to others, the play invites us to judge them as the more justly deserving of it themselves.[21]

To arrive at this class-conscious rendering of the text requires that one read through the polite surface to the aggressive gestures underneath. The text submerges and contains its class resentment behind a conventional comic structure which invites harmony and reconciliation of difference. In this way, the text, in effect, regulates itself before its audience. It seeks not to offend and in that very effort, in the careful awareness of limit, reveals its desire to transgress limit and to subvert order. This same gesture, an avowed desire to please which at the same time reveals underlying aggression, repeats in the relation which Puck's closing speech establishes between Shakespeare's play in performance and its audience:

> If we shadows have offended,
> Think but this, and all is mended—
> That you have but slumb'red here
> While these visions did appear.
>
> (V i 412-15)

This speech is a direct call for applause—"Give me your hands, if we be friends" (V i 426)—which echoes the mechanicals' desire to please and places the actors and playwright (in early performances at least) in the same economic and political relationship to their audience as Bottom and the mechanicals assume before Theseus' court. The first lines of Puck's speech ring clear echoes on Quince's prologue, and its double discourse is heard in the suggestion that the audience, if offended, should simply assume they have been sleeping.

Bottom's night with Titania, which heals the breach between her and Oberon, is directly linked, through Titania's Act II monologue, to redress of the economic chaos and disorder in mid-1590s, real-world England. "And this same progeny of evils," says Titania to Oberon, "comes / From our debate, from our dissension; / We are their parents and original" (II i 115-117). Bottom returns from his experience with a vague awareness of transforming vision, but retains only enough to know that the vision is beyond telling. "I have had a dream," says Bottom, "past the wit of man to say what a dream it was: man is but an ass, if he go about to expound this dream" (IV i 203-05). "Perhaps Bottom," says Frye, "with what Puck calls his own fool's eyes, has seen something in the heart of comedy that our wisdom does not see" (Frye, 1965, 109). On the other hand, however, perhaps Bottom has experienced something which his discretion, his concern for the ladies and for his own neck, does not permit him to share. Bottom's bergomask, which closes the mechanicals' performance, is a rustic dance arising from folk tradition that expresses the working-class spirit of festival, a momentary freedom which must inevitably submit to necessity, as announced by Theseus: "The iron tongue of midnight hath told twelve" (V i 352); but the roaring of the lion, the ideological threat of working-class resentment, is not quelled or reconciled by closure in this play. As Puck enters with his broom "To sweep the dust behind the door," he signals the prudent discretion and care for appearance which check the threat that lies as if behind the door of this text. His first words, describing the midnight dream world of "graves, all gaping wide" refer directly to the mechanicals' play: "Now the hungry lion roars" (V i 360).

In leaving this reading of *MND* with the lion roaring, my intention is not to valorize unreconciled hostility as an ideal of literary content; rather, I mean to crystallize with an image the notion that class hostility is an ever-present subtext of this play. I mean to suggest not that Shakespeare was a proto-Marxist so much as to de-value the notion, from Frye and elsewhere, that the "correct" response to Shakespearean comedy is uncritical participation in the symbols of union which the play invokes. Walter Benjamin has written that our cultural treasures "owe their existence not only to the efforts of the great minds who have created them, but also the anonymous toil of their contemporaries" (256-257). To aestheticize Shakespearean comedy as a moment of transcendence, a moment out of history, as Frye asks us to do, is in effect, I believe, a form of voyeurism that tends by its passivity to reproduce the oppressive social structures that defined Shakespeare's practice. Through an historical-critical awareness, such as this reading encourages, we may more responsibly participate in the hard-won moments of freedom from eco-nomic-necessity which our cultural treasures represent.

Notes

[1] Both C.L. Barber and Frye (1948) find Shakespearean comedy to be structured so as to effect a comic cathar-sis. Barber's terminology is "Through Release to Clari-fication" (Barber 6-10 et passim.)

[2] In using the word "text" as an active agent, I mean to signal that my argument regarding the representation in *MND* of class-issues at its historical moment does not depend upon the conscious intention of Shakespeare.

[3] Quotations and text references are to Shakespeare, *The Complete Works,* ed. Alfred Harbage (New York: Viking, 1969) 146-174.

[4] Elizabethan popular literature and drama frequently represented the artisan class as wanting to appear be-fore royalty and to imitate their manners and dress (Camp 99-148).

[5] Marriage for love was an emergent ideology (and practice) in its own right in Renaissance England (Wright 201-09; Stone 178-95). And the gratification of this desire within the context of harmonious closure tends

to validate (rather than to subvert) the authority struc-tures that impinged on an Elizabethan subject (Montrose 69-70; Kreiger 47-51).

[6] Elizabethan and Jacobean drama frequently repesented rivalry and hatred between the artisan and courtly classes (Camp 141 et seq.).

[7] Because this speech refers to weather conditions like those of 1594-96 in England, it is one of the primary pieces of internal evidence relied upon to date com-position of *MND*. Contemporary descriptions of this weather appear in Furness (Appendix 248-53).

[8] There were instances of prosecution for sedition aris-ing out of "rebellious" speeches made against the "cornmongers" and urging the poor to organize against the rich (Greenblatt 14-15; Emmison 64-65). Sermons preached during the period also reveal concern about unruly elements of society which threatened good or-der, and a lecture by a Dr. King at York in 1594 refers to these unruly elements as "lion's whelps" (Furness, Appendix, 251), a metaphor that happens to coincide intertextually with "the lion's roar" in the reading of *MND* which I am advancing here.

[9] The economic crunch also forced many rural poor to migrate into towns and cities, where strict vagrancy laws—which provided for ear-boring and hanging as penalties—were in effect and tended to be enforced with renewed stringency (Clay II 235-36, 240-41; Beier; Gregg 263-66).

[10] Alice Walker in *The Color Purple,* for instance, has depicted Southern blacks feigning ignorance and sub-mission before the dominant class as a way to get what they want. It is also demonstrated in the narratives of Frederic Douglass and in Latin American writing such as Manlio Argueta's novel *One Day of Life* (New York: Vintage, 1983).

[11] Barber's discussion of Talboys Dymoke and the Martin Marprelate controversy illustrate the operation of this line between satire and saturnalia.

[12] In addition to the sort of overt censorship to which Barber calls attention, the practice of Elizabethan the-ater was, of course, conditioned by implicit consider-ations inherent in the need to cultivate royal patronage and, at the same time, please a paying audience (see Kavanagh 149-51). This reading of *MND* is, in effect, an attempt to identify and elaborate the traces of this overt and covert censorship.

[13] It may be seen as consistent with the vanity and blindness to themselves of these aristocrats that Theseus, Lysander and Hippolyta dwell on Quince's "ignorant" punctuations and perceive no intended offense (V i 118-25). While I have no way to prove it, I strongly suspect that working-class aligned elements of an Eliza-

bethan audience would have been greatly entertained by this prologue and the aristocrats' response.

[14] Jan Kott's reading of this play focuses on its animal eroticism as a representation of social decadence, a reading I would amend principally by showing that Bottom and the mechanicals stand apart from the decadence and constitute an opposed, potentially corrective ideology.

[15] The text also hints in other ways that "sword" is to be heard with sexual connotations. Bottom, for instance, on parting from his fellows in the first act, says that when they meet again in the woods they "may rehearse most obscenely" (I ii 97). The word slip, once again, is more than merely comic. Furthermore, when Bottom proposes a prologue to amend the potential frightening effect of his sword, he casts his noun in the plural rather than singular number: "let the prologue seem to say we will do no harm with our swords" (III i 16-17).

[16] As Theseus' former lover, Titania represents a fairy world double of Hippolyta, the mortal soon-to-be duchess, a doubling which is often played in performance and which literalizes the cuckolding of Theseus impicit in Bottom's night with Titania.

[17] Though Kott does not document this assertion, it is well supported by a reading of Apuleius' *The Golden Ass,* the probable source. Lucius, the protagonist, observes that the "the only consoling part of this miserable transformation [to an ass] was the enormous increase in the size of a certain organ of mine" (Graves 71).

[18] Louis Montrose's discussion of Simon Forman's dream of intimacy with Queen Elizabeth further develops the political implications of this fantasy (Montrose, 62-65) which are, of course, heightened by the relation between Elizabeth's mystique of virginity and political power, the question of an heir.

[19] *The Golden Ass* was translated into Engish by William Aldington in 1566 (Muir 68).

[20] Apuleius functions in this play much like Montaigne's essay "Canibals" for *The Tempest,* i.e., as an intertextual support for reading political content as inscribed within the play.

[21] This is, at least, consistent with the Shakespeare who has his good captain Antonio in *Twelfth Night* saying "In nature there's no blemish but the mind;/ None can be called deformed but the unkind" (III iv 347-48).

References

C.L. Barber, *Shakespeare's Festive Comedy, A Study of Dramatic Form and its Relation to Social Custom* (Princeton: Princeton University Press, 1972)

A.L. Beier, "Vagrants and the Social Order in Elizabethan England," *Past and Present* LXIV (August 1974) 3-29.

Walter Benjamin, "Theses on the Philosophy of History," in *Illuminations,* trans. Harry Zohn (1968; rpt. New York: Schocken, 1969).

Charles W. Camp, *The Artisan in Elizabethan Literature* (New York: Columbia University Press, 1924).

C.G.A. Clay, *Economic Expansion and Social Change: England 1500-1700.* 2 vols. (Cambridge: Cambridge University Press, 1984).

F.G. Emmison, *Elizabethan Life: Disorder* (Chelmsford: Essex County Council, 1970).

Sigmund Freud, "Wit and Its Relation to the Unconscious," in *The Basic Writings of Sigmund Freud,* ed. A.A. Brill (New York: Random House, 1938).

Northrop Frye, "The Argument of Comedy," in *Modern Shakespeare Criticism, Essays on Style, Dramaturgy, and the Major Plays,* ed. Alvin B. Kernan (New York: Harcourt, Brace, 1970), 165-73, rpt. from *English Institute Essays 1948,* ed. D.A. Roberts (New York: Columbia University Press, 1949) 58-73.

N. Frye, *A Natural Perspective, The Development of Shakespearean Comedy and Romance* (New York: Columbia University Press, 1965).

N. Frye, *Anatomy of Criticism* (Princeton: Princeton University Press, 1971).

Horace Howard Furness, ed., New Variorum Edition of *MND* (Philadelphia; J.B. Lippincott, 1895).

Madelon Gohlke, "I wooed thee with my sword": Shakespeare's Tragic Paradigms," in *Representing Shakespeare, New Psychoanalystic Essays,* ed. Murray M. Schwartz and Coppelia Kahn (Baltimore: Johns Hopkins University Press, 1982). 170-187.

Apuleius, *The Golden Ass,* trans. Robert Graves (New York: Farrar, Straus, 1950).

Stephen Greenblatt, "Murdering Peasants: Status, Genre, and the Representation of Rebellion," *Representations,* 1983, 1-29.

Pauline Gregg, *Black Death to Industrial Revolution, A Social and Economic History of England* (London: Barnes and Noble, 1976).

The Political Unconsicious, Narrative as a Socially Symbolic Act (Ithaca: Cornell University Press, 1981).

James H. Kavanagh, "Shakespeare in Ideology," *Alternative Shakespeares,* ed. J. Drakakis (London and N.Y.: Metheun, 1985) 144-65.

Jan Kott, "Titania and the Ass's Head," in *Shakespeare, Our Contemporary* (New York: Doubleday, 1964) 207-28.

Elliot Kreiger, *A Marxist Study of Shakespeare's Comedies* New York: Barnes and Noble, 1979).

Jack Lindsay, "Introduction," Apuleius' *The Golden Ass* (Bloomington: Indiana University Press, 1967) 5-29.

Louis Adrian Montrose, "Shaping Fantasies. Figurations of Gender and Power in Elizabethan Culture," *Representations* I, 1983, 61-94.

Kenneth Muir, *The Sources of Shakespeare's Play* (New Haven: Yale University Press, 1978).

Lawrence Stone, *The Family, Sex and Marriage in England 1500-1800* (New York: Harper and Row, 1977). Leonard Tennenhouse, "Strategies of State and Political plays; *A Mid-summer Night's Dream, Henry IV, Henry V, Henry VIII," Political Shakespeare, New Essays in Cultural Materialism* (Ithaca and London: Cornell University Press, 1985) 109-28.

E.M.W. Tillyard, *The Elizabethan World Picture* (New York: Vintage, n.d.).

J. Walter and K. Wrightson, "Dearth and the social order," *Past and Present* LXXI (May 1976) 22-42.

Louis B. Wright, *Middle-Class Culture in Elizabethan England* (Ithaca: Cornell University Press, 1935).

David P. Young, "'A Midsummer Night's Dream': Structure" in *Modern Shakespeare Criticism, Essays on Style, Dramaturgy, and the Major Plays,* ed. Alvin B. Kernan (New York: Harcourt, Brace, 1979) 174-189.

LANGUAGE AND STRUCTURE

Jay L. Halio (essay date 1990)

SOURCE: "Nightingales That Roar: The Language of *A Midsummer Night's Dream,*" in *Traditions and Innovations: Essays on British Literature of the Middle Ages and the Renaissance,* edited by David G. Allen and Robert A. White, University of Delaware Press, 1990, pp. 137-49.

[*In the following essay, Halio maintains that the language of the play, in its darkness, complexity, and in the contradictions it contains suggests that, contrary to the apparently happy ending, "benevolent providence does not always or inevitably enter into human affairs to make things right."*]

In an essay called "On the Value of *Hamlet,*" Stephen Booth has shown how that play simultaneously frustrates and fulfills audience expectations and otherwise presents contradictions that belie or bedevil the attempts of many a reductionist critic to demonstrate a coherent thematic pattern in Shakespeare's masterpiece. Booth's commentary is particularly directed to the language and action of act 1 which, from the very outset, arouse in the audience a "sensation of being unexpectedly and very slightly out of step" with the drama that the players unfold. "In *Hamlet,*" Booth says, "the audience does not so much shift its focus as come to find its focus shifted."[1] The end result, though initially disturbing, is not finally so: "People see *Hamlet* and tolerate inconsistencies that it does not seem they could bear. . . . Truth is bigger than any one system for knowing it, and *Hamlet* is bigger than any of the frames of reference it inhabits. *Hamlet* allows us to comprehend—to hold on to—all of the contradictions it contains."[2]

The kind of linguistic and dramatic complexity that Booth describes, while preeminently demonstrable in *Hamlet,* is by no means limited to that play. It is far more prevalent than perhaps has been recognized, although several critics before and since Booth's essay have tried to show similar situations in other plays. David Bevington, for example, has shown how in *A Midsummer Night's Dream* the debate between Oberon and Puck in act 3, scene 2 "reflects a fundamental tension in the play between comic reassurance and the suggestion of something dark and threatening."[3] In "Titania and the Ass's Head" Jan Kott argued that *A Midsummer Night's Dream* is "the most erotic of Shakespeare's plays" and nowhere else is the eroticism "expressed so brutally."[4] Kott's focus is largely upon the animal imagery and erotic symbolism. The metaphors in Helena's speech to Demetrius in which she proclaims herself his "spaniel," his "dog" (2.1.203-10), Kott regards as "almost masochistic." Contrary to the romantic tradition, reinforced by Mendelssohn's music, the forest in *Dream* represents anything but a version of Arcadia, inhabited as it is by "devils and lamias, in which witches and sorceresses can easily find everything required for their practices."[5] Titania caressing the monster with the head of an ass is closer to the fearful visions of Hieronymous Bosch, in Kott's view, than to the gentler depictions of Chagall and countless other illustrators of Shakespeare's dream play.

Like Bevington, we need not go as far as Kott does. We need not imagine Titania's court consisting of toothless old men and shaking hags, "their mouths wet with saliva" as they, sniggering, "procure a monster for their mistress."[6] But there is a good deal more going on beneath the play's surface than many have been willing to notice, or have deliberately been persuaded (or lulled) into not noticing. This surely was the point, in part, of Peter Brook's 1970 production: to shake us out of complacency. In much of the poetry, indeed in some of the most celebrated passages, there is a repeated undercutting of the tenor by the vehicle Shakespeare chooses, or a subverting of the overall tone by the actual sense of the language employed. Although this point is related to Kott's, it is, I think, a more general one and characterizes similar phenomena in other plays.

As so often in Shakespearean drama, the first clues come early, in the very opening speeches. Theseus tells Hippolyta that their nuptial hour approaches and he is, like any bridegroom, impatient for the event. But the specific language suggests a crass motive and includes images that are otherwise scarcely flattering to his bride, who is, like Theseus, somewhat advanced in years:

> Four happy days bring in
> Another moon—but O, methinks how slow
> This old moon wanes! She lingers my desires,
> Like to a stepdame or a dowager
> Long withering out a young man's revenue.
>
> (1.1.2-6)[7]

Hippolyta's response, meant to be reassuring, yet includes the simile of a "silver bow / New-bent in heaven" that reminds Theseus in his turn how he wooed her with his sword and won her love by doing her injuries. He promises to wed her in "another key," but suggestions of discord have already been sounded, and many more will follow before Oberon's final benediction and Puck's epilogue—and their interesting peculiarities.

One such discord occurs immediately with the entrance of Egeus, Hermia, and her two suitors. It is a situation not unlike the opening scenes of *Othello,* and Egeus's complaints against Lysander are similar to Brabantio's accusations of the Moor: the young man has "bewitched" the old man's daughter with rhymes and presents, "messengers / Of strong prevailment in unhardened youth" (34-35). As the dialogue develops, however, it is clear that if any bewitching has so far occurred—some will certainly occur later—it has been Hermia who has enchanted the affections of both young men. Nevertheless, Egeus's determination to have his way, or his daughter's death, is more than a little disconcerting. It is Theseus—not Egeus—who recalls a third alternative that he makes sound, in this dramatic context, less attractive than a more orthodox view requires. Hermia, after all, can become a nun:

> Therefore, fair Hermia, question your desires,
> Know of your youth, examine well your
>   blood,

> Whether, if you yield not to your father's
>   choice,
> You can endure the livery of a nun,
> For aye to be in shady cloister mewed,
> To live a barren sister all your life,
> Chanting faint hymns to the cold fruitless
>   moon.
> Thrice-blessèd they that master so their
>   blood
> To undergo such maiden pilgrimage;
> But earthlier happy is the rose distilled
> Than that which, withering on the virgin
>   thorn,
> Grows, lives, and dies in single blessedness.
>
> (67-78)

Anachronisms apart, Theseus's description of a "thrice-blessèd" life is shall we admit, rather forbidding. The whole conception of devotion—filial, religious, amorous—is further subverted a few lines later when Lysander mentions Helena's love for Demetrius, who has jilted her:

> she, sweet lady, dotes
> Devoutly dotes, dotes in idolatry
> Upon this spotted and inconstant man.
>
> (108-10)

And, strangely enough, Theseus sets his own wedding day as the date on which Hermia must make her fateful decision:

> Take time to pause, and by the next new
>   moon—
> The sealing day between my love and me
> For everlasting bond of fellowship—
> Upon *that* day either prepare to die
> For disobedience to your father's will,
> Or else to wed Demetrius, as he would,
> Or on Diana's altar to protest
> For aye austerity and single life.
>
> (83-90; my italics)

Left with the three alternatives that Theseus enumerates, the lovers look for consolation from each other. Lysander tries to comfort Hermia with a disquisition upon the theme, "The course of true love never did run smooth." The stichomythia in which they then engage reveals only the most obvious way Lysander's words of "comfort" are undercut: "O cross! . . . O spite! . . . O hell!" begins each of Hermia's comments. She eventually allows herself to be persuaded by the lesson Lysander seems to be emphasizing—"Then let us teach our trial patience"—only to discover, contrary to his explicit assent, that this is not what he really has in mind at all. His "therefore" (156) leads in quite a different direction, wherever his earlier logic might have been pointing, as he presents to Hermia his plan to elope.

Hermia's ready agreement to the plan concludes with what is, again given the dramatic context, a most curious set of oaths. It begins conventionally enough, but then something happens to the conventions, or rather some oddly inappropriate ones intrude:

> I swear to thee by Cupid's strongest bow,
> By his best arrow with the golden head,
> By the simplicity of Venus' doves,
> By that which knitteth souls and prospers
>   loves,
> And by that fire which burned the Carthage
>   queen
> When the false Trojan under sail was seen,
> By all the vows that ever men have broke—
> In number more than ever women spoke,—
> In that same place thou hast appointed me
> Tomorrow truly will I meet with thee.
>
> (169-78)

Hermia may be merely teasing her lover, so sure she is of him, as Alexander Leggatt says, and the joking does no harm.[8] But teasing always contains a barb, and (not only in light of what comes later) the allusions to male infidelity are ominous, to say the least. In any event, the rhetoric of the first eight lines is neatly undercut by the final couplet, whose jingling and prosaic simplicity collapses the soaring quality of what precedes it. This may all be part of the comic effect intended, and Lysander's flat "Keep promise, love," while confirming the anticlimactic effect, at the same time suggests by its peremptoriness that he may be caught a little off balance by Hermia. But before we can ponder this exchange further, Helena enters with paradoxes of her own.

Consider her lines on love and the imagination. Although earlier she laments how Demetrius is misled in large part by Hermia's external beauty, here Helena complains of the transforming power of the imagination under the influence of love:

> Things base and vile, holding no quantity,
> Love can transpose to form and dignity.
> Love looks not with the eyes, but with the
>   mind,
> And therefore is winged Cupid painted blind.
> Nor hath love's mind of any judgement taste;
> Wings and no eyes figure unheedy haste.
> And therefore is love said to be a child
> Because in choice he is so oft beguiled.
>
> (232-39)

Throughout her speech Helena shows remarkable maturity of insight, except of course that all of her insight helps not a jot to correct her own love's folly. She errs as badly as Demetrius, by her own admission. Nor is she correct about visual susceptibility. As much of the central action of the play demonstrates, the eyes decid-

edly lead—or mislead—lovers. The capacity for transposing "things base and vile" to "form and dignity" is not in the imagination, or "mind," but in the fancy, which as she indicates is devoid of judgment. Shakespeare shows the relation between eyesight and fancy (or love) in a song from *The Merchant of Venice:*

> Tell me where is fancy bred,
> Or in the heart or in the head?
> How begot, how nourished?
>   Reply, reply.
> It is engendered in the eyes,
> With gazing fed; and fancy dies
> In the cradle where it lies.
>
> (3.2.63-69)

Later, in a speech notable for its dramatic irony, Lysander justifies his sudden passion for Helena by an appeal to his reason, which he claims has led his will, or desire (2.2.121-23). But like others in the Athenian forest, he is led by his eyes, influenced by Puck's misapplied herb juice, which has engendered his fancy. And it will be through his eyes also that his fancy, his infatuation for Helena, will die. Although the terms were often used interchangeably by Shakespeare and his contemporaries, the power of the imagination *could* be distinguished from the fancy, as some Elizabethans knew two centuries before Coleridge's *Biographia Literaria*. It is, moreover, this power, fancy (or phantasy), that Theseus unfortunately calls "imagination" in his famous fifth act speech, which connects the lunatic, the lover, and the poet.[9]

The frequent malapropisms of the rude mechanicals' dialogue also add to our growing sense of linguistic (and other) disorder. Here Bottom is the most notorious, because the most pretentious; but he is not the only one. Wanting the role of Lion, as well as the roles of Pyramus *and* Thisbe—and Ercles, too, if that "part to tear a cat in" could somehow be worked into the play—he pleads that he will use moderation in his roaring so as not to frighten the ladies in the audience:

> But I will aggravate my voice so that I will roar you
> as gently as any sucking dove. I will roar you an
> 'twere any nightingale.
>
> (1.2.76-78)

Peter Quince, the stalwart impresario, also gets tangled up in his language, not only in failing to stand upon his points in the Prologue, but earlier, speaking more accurately than he realizes, when he explains how moonlight can be provided for their play. As an alternative to leaving the casement window open, he suggests "one must come in with a bush of thorns and a lantern and say he comes to *disfigure* or to present the person of Moonshine" (3.1.53-55; my italics). When it is finally staged before the court, the *"most lamentable comedy . . . Pyramus and Thisbe"* will function on various levels of significance well prepared for by the kinds of linguistic subversion that appear elsewhere in the play.

The sense of disorder that characterizes much of *A Midsummer Night's Dream* is, in one way, explained by the conflict between Oberon and Titania. These adept lovers, when they meet in act 2, upbraid one another with accusations of jealousy, philandering, insubordination, and downright meanness. As a result of their quarrel, Titania complains that everything in nature has turned topsy-turvy (2.1.81-117). The vagaries of love have power, apparently, in these supernatural beings to make the seasons alter:

> . . . hoary-headed frosts
> Fall in the fresh lap of the crimson rose,
> And on old Hiems' thin and icy crown
> An odorous chaplet of sweet summer buds
> Is as in mockery set.
>
> (107-11)

But the disorder is conveyed in other, more subtle ways than in this image of old Hiems and his fragrant chaplet. Immediately after Oberon vows to "torment" his queen for her injurious behavior, he calls upon his "gentle" Puck. Again, as he describes hearing a mermaid on a dolphin's back "uttering such dulcet and harmonious breath / That the rude sea grew civil at her song," he notes that at the same time "certain stars shot madly from their spheres / To hear the sea-maid's music" (2.1.150-54). How can it happen both ways: the rude sea grows civil, but certain stars go mad in the firmament? The subsequent magnificent passage describing the "fair vestal throned by the west" concludes with the sad plight of the once milk-white flower, love-in-idleness, stained purple, which will provide Oberon with the magic he needs for his plot against Titania. The epitome of this kind of double-speak occurs in the famous passage where Oberon describes his plan in detail:

> I know a bank where the wild thyme blows,
> Where oxlips and the nodding violet grows,
> Quite overcanopied with luscious woodbine,
> With sweet muskroses and with eglantine.
> There sleeps Titania some time of the night,
> Lulled in these flowers with dances and
>   delight.
> And there the snake throws her enamelled
>   skin,
> Weed wide enough to wrap a fairy in.
> And with the juice of this I'll streak her eyes,
> And make her full of hateful fantasies.
>
> (2.1.249-58)

As Harold Brooks remarks, the lines are "famous for their melody, as well as for their imagery, which is no less lyrical."[10] The mellifluousness of the verse, the lulling rhythms of the end-stopped lines, but especially the beauty of the images combine to hide for the reader or spectator almost entirely the edge of Oberon's real malice. If the image of the snake is hardly an image here that repels, its appearance is at least problematical—whatever generic relation it may have to Hermia's dream of the crawling serpent on her breast after Lysander deserts her in the next scene. Jan Kott has noted a parallel in the fairies' lullaby in act 2 where the linguistic effect is reversed:

> You spotted snakes with double tongue,
>   Thorny hedgehogs, be not seen.
> Newts and blindworms, do no wrong,
>   Come not near our Fairy Queen.
> Philomel with melody
>   Sing in our sweet lullaby,
> Lulla, lulla, lullaby; lulla, lulla, lullaby.
>   Never harm
>   Nor spell nor charm
>   Come our lovely lady nigh.
>   So good night, with lullaby.
> Weaving spiders, come not here;
>   Hence, you longlegged spinners, hence!
> Beetles black, approach not near,
>   Worm nor snail, do no offence.
> Philomel with melody. . . .
>
> (2.2.9-24)

Despite its invocation to Philomel in the refrain, this is not the sort of lullaby to forecast or inspire pleasant dreams. But the harmonies of sound, especially enhanced by music (as in many lullabies), do everything—or almost everything—to hide from us the actual horrors. The same point can be illustrated where Titania explains her opposition to Oberon's demand for the changeling Indian boy:

> His mother was a votress of my order,
> And in the spicèd Indian air by night
> Full often hath she gossiped by my side,
> And sat with me on Neptune's yellow sands,
> Marking th'embarkèd traders on the flood,
> When we have laughed to see the sails
>   conceive
> And grow big-bellied with the wanton wind;
> Which she with pretty and with swimming gait
> Following—her womb then rich with my
>   young squire—
> Would imitate, and sail upon the land
> To fetch me trifles, and return again
> As from a voyage, rich with merchandise.
> And she, being mortal, of that boy did die,
> And for her sake do I rear up her boy;
> And for her sake I will not part with him.
>
> (2.1.123-37)

The beauty of the passage—"spiced Indian air," the imagery of conception, and the mocking gait of the pregnant young woman—bears the full emphasis, and the serious point of the speech—the mother's child-birth death, leaving her son an orphan—becomes almost anticlimactic, certainly less emphatic, though to Shakespeare's audience the dangers of childbirth were quite real.

Bottom's meeting with Titania also offers some surprising paradoxes. Can Oberon really mean to have himself cuckolded by an asinine country bumpkin? We may laugh, and are surely meant to do so, when Titania greets Bottom's rustic song: "What angel wakes me from my flowery bed?" (3.1.122). But Bottom goes on, providing some interesting clues to what actually is about to happen:

> The finch, the sparrow, and the lark,
>   The plainsong cuckoo grey,
> Whose note full many a man doth mark
>   And dares not answer "Nay"—
>
> for, indeed, who would set his wit to so foolish a
> bird? Who would give a bird the lie, though he cry
> "cuckoo" never so?
>
>   (123-129)

Cuckoos and cuckolds—need one remark?—traditionally have a strong association, which modern audiences may miss, but Shakespeare's would not. Oberon plans to punish Titania and succeeds—not without some cost to himself, however, which he may ignore or perhaps relish ("This falls out better than I could devise!" he says to Puck at 3.2.35). But Bottom's song and comment point to what the cost actually is.[11]

These linguistic and dramatic complexities and contradictions serve, as Stephen Booth has said about *Hamlet,* to keep us from simplistic reductions of experienced situations, specifically the play's mirrored experiences of reality, to say nothing of its own reality. As such, they force us out of, rather than into, an artificial prison that R. P. Blackmur has (in another connection) described as a tendency to set artistic unity as a chief criterion of excellence.[12] Coherence, existentially considered, is more, much more, than rhetorical cohesiveness, though to some extent that kind of coherence is also necessary. But however necessary, it is not a sufficient condition of great art, such as Shakespeare's. The point can be illustrated as well by examples from the great literature of music, such as the late Beethoven quartets. But (to remain with Shakespeare) let me expand the reference to other plays of the same period as *A Midsummer Night's Dream.*

In an essay on "Shakespeare and the Limits of Language," Anne Barton some years ago contrasted Richard II's verbal adeptness with Bolingbroke's political skill to show how, despite his manifold successes, Shakespeare did not allow language, the efficacy of

the word, an "unexamined triumph."[13] In the deposition scene, for example, Barton shows how it is the weak king who insists upon inventing a rite, creating a litany that will, through words, invest the transference of power with meaning. The speech she specifically cites uses the well metaphor as its controlling device:

> Here, cousin, seize the crown.
> On this side my hand, and on that side thine.
> Now is this golden crown like a deep well
> That owes two buckets, filling one another:
> The emptier ever dancing in the air,
> The other down, unseen, and full of water.
> That bucket down and full of tears am I,
> Drinking my griefs, whilst you mount up on
>   high.
>
>   (4.1.181-88)

As Barton says, Bolingbroke's submission is "oddly qualified"; he reaches out his hand, but verbally he will not cooperate; his blunt inquiry—"I thought you had been willing to resign"—tears through and destroys the validity of the metaphor.[14] Or does it? We can see Bolingbroke containing himself in patience while Richard goes through his ceremonies of self-debasement, for Bolingbroke fully understands the political might he now controls. Richard's wit is keener than Bolingbroke suspects, or lets on. The well metaphor, like much else in this scene, carries more than an acknowledgment of Richard's defeat and Bolingbroke's success. Richard, the heavier bucket, down and unseen, is also fuller, weightier; Bolingbroke, the high bucket, is also lighter, emptier, frolicking in the air as in a dance. The word, as Richard delivers it then, in this speech as in others, is hardly impotent. Its triumph is not an unqualified one, but neither is Bolingbroke's. Many of Shakespeare's plays make the same point.

In the last act of *The Merchant of Venice* the equations appear reversed. Some of the same verbal inconsistencies that analysis of *A Midsummer Night's Dream* revealed occur in the opening speeches between Lorenzo and Jessica, creating the initial tension that leads indirectly to the tensions created by the ring trick that Portia and Nerissa have played upon their husbands. Or are all of these tensions, as Jonathan Miller's production (with Laurence Olivier as Shylock) seemed to argue, actually the result, or aftermath, of those generated in the previous act, where Shylock learns the meaning of justice as taught him by Portia and Antonio and the rest?

Lorenzo and Jessica are sitting outside Portia's house in Belmont. Lorenzo speaks:

> The moon shines bright. In such a night as
>   this,
> When the sweet wind did gently kiss the trees

And they did make no noise, in such a night
Troilus methinks mounted the Troyan walls
And sighed his soul toward the Grecian tents,
Where Cressid lay that night.

                              (5.1.1-6)

The first three lines set both the scene and time and
prepare for the lovely passage fifty lines later that
begins, "How sweet the moonlight sleeps upon this
bank!" But here as later a discordant note slips in,
even as the mellifluousness of the lines, the soft allit-
erations and rhythm beguile the listener—the less attentive audience, at any rate—but not Jessica. She
follows Lorenzo's allusion to the tragedy of Troilus
and Cressida with:

                    In such a night
Did Thisbe fearfully o'ertrip the dew,
And saw the lion's shadow ere himself
And ran dismayed away.

                              (6-9)

And so on, back and forth, through Dido and Medea
until Lorenzo openly teases Jessica about stealing away
with him to Belmont, and she retorts in kind. Only the
entrance of a messenger apparently halts the contest;
but later, as they await Portia's return and Lorenzo
describes the music of the spheres, Jessica feels compelled to say: "I am never merry when I hear sweet
music" (69). And so on, again, throughout the scene
concords find discords, discords concord, in a seemingly unending series. Although the overall tone is
joyful and the teasing playful, Shakespeare does not
let us forget the more somber aspects of human relationships, which can and do intrude.

The same kind of linguistic and dramatic strategy is at
work in the final act of *A Midsummer Night's Dream.*
Philostrate's list of possible wedding entertainments is
an odd one, beginning as it does with "The battle with
the Centaurs, to be sung / By an Athenian eunuch to
the harp" (5.1.44-45). His fourth possibility brings us to

"A tedious brief scene of young Pyramus
And his love Thisbe; very tragical mirth."

                              (56-57)

Theseus's reaction summarizes ours:

Merry and tragical? Tedious and brief?
That is, hot ice and wondrous strange snow.
How shall we find the concord of this
    discord?

                              (58-60)

Philostrate's condescending reply to the question does
not probe deeply enough, of course: How indeed shall
we find the "concord of this discord"? Not, I submit,
by simply acquiescing in the general merriment of the
stage spectators while the playlet is in progress, beginning with the "tangled chain" of Quince's Prologue.
Even if we grant that the play was first performed at
an actual wedding celebration, with fun and laughter
very much in the spirit of the occasion, we cannot stop
there. However well things may turn out for Theseus
and Hippolyta, Lysander and Hermia, Demetrius and
Helena, Oberon and Titania, there is still one couple
whose fortunes do not end happily. Within the happy
framework of this celebration, the solemn notes of tragedy still intrude, all but obliterated by peals of mirth
that the simple rustics inspire, but nonetheless there.

Critics have been at some pains to show how Shakespeare "brilliantly reconciles opposites"[15] in his dream-
play. The usual reference is to the passages on Theseus's
hounds in act 4, scene 1, lines 109-26, specifically to
"So musical a discord, such sweet thunder" that their
baying offers. Not remarked often enough, perhaps, is
the providential role that characters like Oberon and
Theseus enact in bringing about the concord between
the jarring couples in the play. (Shakespeare as playwright is of course the relevant analogy here.) But my
purpose has been to show that the concords exist at
only one level, and that one not the most profound.
The thunder may be "sweet," but it is still thunder.
Oberson overmasters Titania, reduces her to tears, and
has his way finally. Theseus suavely ignores the law
Egeus and he himself have invoked in act 1 to enable
the young couples to be married, and Egeus (with
whatever silent, grudging acceptance) goes along: Theseus quite frankly tells him "I will overbear your will"
(4.1.178). Shakespeare is hardly as direct, but in effect
he overbears ours as well, lulling or beguiling us into
an acceptance of concord and amity, however achieved,
through the artistry of his verse and the adeptness of
his comic genius. But he has left sufficient pointers
(for those willing to recognize them) that this is artifice, after all; that a benevolent providence does not
always or inevitably enter into human affairs to make
things right. His most significant indication of that fact
is in the play-within-the-play, where no providential
solution to Pyramus and Thisbe's plight appears. The
"thunder" there may be nearly drowned out by laughter and jollity, but it still rumbles. And what the thunder says is *not* a message of concord or reconciliation
of opposing wills.

Of this situation Marjorie Garber has commented that
the play-within-the-play is "ultimately nothing less than
a countermyth for the whole of *A Midsummer Night's
Dream,* setting out the larger play's terms in a new and
revealing light."[16] If the playlet "absorbs and disarms"
the tragic alternative to the happy outcome that the
other couples have experienced, it is nevertheless present
to remind us of what we all know but usually prefer to
ignore or forget, especially on such occasions as this.
By framing the images of nightmare terrors in "an illusion within an illusion," as James Calderwood has

said, Shakespeare here dissolves their threat in laughter. But the laughter is generated, Calderwood continues, at least in part by the act of self-recognition that follows from the transformation of "subjective vagueness" into the "objective clarity" of dramatic form.[17]

As "the iron tongue of midnight" summons the couples to bed, with Theseus's anticipation of yet a fortnight of "nightly revels and new jollity," Puck steals in and reminds us that

> Now the hungry lion roars
>   And the wolf behowls the moon,
> Whilst the heavy plowman snores
>   All with weary task foredone.
>
> (5.1.361-64)

Not that the fairies' work is done, and Puck is "sent with broom before / To sweep the dust behind the door" (379-80). Perhaps that is the best image for Shakespeare's strategy in this play. As every housewife knows, sweeping the dust behind the door, or under the rug, may hide it for awhile, but does not get rid of it. In *A Midsummer Night's Dream* Shakespeare, like Puck, is busy with his broom, but we do not altogether lose sight of his, or the world's, dust.

Notes

[1] In *Reinterpretations of Elizabethan Drama,* ed. Norman Rabkin (New York: Columbia University Press, 1969), 143.

[2] Booth, "Value of *Hamlet,*" 175.

[3] "But We Are Spirits of Another Sort: The Dark Side of Love and Magic in *A Midsummer Night's Dream,*" *Medieval and Renaissance Studies* 7 (1975): 81.

[4] *Shakespeare Our Contemporary,* trans. Boleslaw Taborski (Garden City, N.Y.: Doubleday, 1964), 212.

[5] Ibid., 218.

[6] Ibid., 219.

[7] Quotations are from the New Penguin Shakespeare, ed. Stanley Wells (Harmondsworth, England: Penguin, 1967).

[8] *Shakespeare's Comedy of Love* (London: Methuen, 1974), 95. The New Arden editor, Harold Brooks, also refers to Hermia's "tender teasing."

[9] See David P. Young, *Something of Great Constancy* (New Haven: Yale University Press, 1964), 126-41. For an acute analysis of Helena's speech, cf. Ruth Nevo, *Comic Transformations in Shakespeare* (London: Methuen, 1980), 98-99.

[10] Introduction to *A Midsummer Night's Dream,* New Arden ed. (London: Methuen, 1979), cxxx. Cf. Leggatt, *Comedy of Love,* 96, on the experiences of the Athenian lovers in the forest: "Over and over, the violence of the ideas is lightened by jingling rhythm and rhyme."

[11] On the other hand, as Bevington notes, these gods "make a sport of inconstancy." Out of her love for Theseus, Titania has helped him to ravish Perigouna, break faith with Aegles and with others; while Oberon has made love with Aurora as well as, apparently, with Hippolyta. "This is the sort of mysterious affection," Bevington says, "that only a god could practice or understand." See "Spirits of Another Sort," 90.

[12] *Form and Value in Modern Poetry* (New York: Doubleday, 1957), 83. Cf. Stanley Wells's comments on the theme of concord in his introduction to *A Midsummer Night's Dream,* 31. He says that the baying of Theseus's hounds is "a symbol of the possibility of a unity that is not sameness, an agreement that can include disagreement." Cf. Young, *Great Constancy,* 86.

[13] In *Shakespeare Survey* 24 (Cambridge: Cambridge University Press, 1971), 20.

[14] Barton, "Limits of Language," 22.

[15] Wells, introd. to *A Midsummer Night's Dream,* 28. Cf. Leggatt, *Comedy of Love,* 114: "But the artistic vision itself, which draws these disparate experiences together, is also limited."

[16] *Dream in Shakespeare* (New Haven: Yale University Press, 1974), 81.

[17] "*A Midsummer Night's Dream:* The Illusion of Drama," *Modern Language Quarterly* 26 (1965): 522. Cf. Madeleine Doran, *Shakespeare's Dramatic Language* (Madison: University of Wisconsin Press, 1976), 16, on *Pyramus and Thisbe* as a suitable antimasque for the wedding ceremony.

Stuart M. Tave (essay date 1993)

SOURCE: "A League Without the Town: *A Midsummer Night's Dream,*" in *Lovers, Clowns, and Fairies: An Essay on Comedies,* The University of Chicago Press, 1993, pp. 1-25.

[*In the following essay, Tave examines the structure of* A Midsummer Night's Dream, *including the arrangement of the characters, the plot, and the language, and praises the play as "perfect in its detailed beauty and its practical workmanship."*]

A Midsummer Night's Dream is the perfect place to begin. Shaw the minor social scientist insisted that *A*

Doll's House, in its utilitarian way, will have done more useful work in the world, but Shaw the major artist knew that "'A Doll's House' will be as flat as ditch water when 'A Midsummer Night's Dream' will still be fresh as paint . . ." ("The Problem Play," 1895). Only a major artist would use such flat phrases with the instinct that here they were bluntly and exactly right. *A Midsummer Night's Dream* is not only perfect in its detailed beauty and its practical workmanship but it works everything out perfectly.

To begin with, there is the arrangement of characters: they are disposed in three groups and there is never a question of who belongs to which. One is the Athenian court circle, Duke Theseus and his bride, Queen Hippolyta, Hermia and Lysander, Helena and Demetrius: all beautiful; all so classically and medievally and attractively named; all upper-class, the ruling center of the best society; all so well-spoken in blank verse and couplets and so witty when the occasion offers; and, most importantly, all in love. Then there is the lower class, "a crew of patches," fools, clowns, "rude mechanicals," uncultured artisans who labor with their hands, who "work for bread," whose absurd names identify them by the limited tools or qualities of their several occupations: Quince the carpenter, Flute the bellows mender, Snout the tinker, Snug the joiner, Starveling the tailor, and "the shallowest thick-skin of that barren sort," that dull-witted lot, Bottom the weaver, whose name combines so pleasantly both the mechanical trade and the level of mind (III, ii, 9-10, 13). Their uneducated prose gives them away as soon as they open their mouths. They are great misusers of words, especially when, "Hard-handed men . . . Which never laboured in their minds till now" (V, i., 72-73), they try to play the "mimic" (III, ii, 19), to act out of their class, speak a finer speech, copy a higher art; and they get it all wrong, right down to the level of punctuation, masters of unintentional fallacies.

> We do not come as minding to content you,
> Our true intent is.
>
> (V, i, 113-14)

They are trying to imitate the manners of their betters to attract favorable attention to themselves and be rewarded accordingly. They can never elevate themselves, never change class, because they are such clowns. (In quarto and folio they are, by the convention of their roles, sometimes so identified—"Enter the Clownes"—and some of Bottom's speech prefixes are "Clowne" or variant spellings of that.) Finally there are, surprisingly enough, most remarkable creatures: with their names, both natural and romantically more than natural, Oberon and Titania, the Puck, Peaseblossom, Cobweb, Moth (Mote), Mustardseed; and with their powers, both overwhelming and delicate, of nature in the villagery and of romance. They are not subject to mortality, barely subject to time or space. Puck, swifter

than arrow from the Tartar's bow, can put a girdle round about the earth in forty minutes (III, ii, 100-01; II, i, 175-76). He is "that merry wanderer of the night" (II, i, 43); wandering is usually a lost state for mortals, not being able to locate themselves, as it is with mortals of this play whom he misleads in the night; but not so for Puck, merry because free of the limiting condition. They are, these space-commanding creatures of the night, invisible. Their speech can be supernaturally lyrical, with no effort, when the occasion is there. They have magical powers and can lead the unknowing mortals in any direction, knowing as they do, invisibly present, what the mortals are thinking and, capable as they are, of altering those minds instantly. These are fairies. The three groups cannot be mixed; they are separate orders of beings and there is never a possibility of a member of one set moving permanently into another. If the Queen of Fairies falls in love with the Bottom of clowns that's marvellously absurd, and part of the secure fun in seeing that is the knowledge that this mismatch cannot possibly last for long.

So there we are with lovers, clowns and fairies, a complete cast, all we need, all perfect in their functions. What do they do? The lovers chase in a dance, running after one another, changing partners and then returning to first positions, working out the pattern of their pairing until they have achieved their desire. Hermia and Lysander are in love with one another and Helena loves Demetrius, who is the only piece out of place by his insistence on Hermia. If he would only fall in love with Helena all would be well, and since we are told that he was indeed once in love with her he may very well switch again. In fact that is what happens, so the problem has been solved in its simplest and most obvious solution—but only in the most complicated way, not by the one sensible move but by a complete scrambling of the original situation, so that we have lost such order as we had to start with. All is worked out to a happy end as we expected, by a means we could not have anticipated.

Hermia has a problem because of her father, Egeus; he wants her to marry Demetrius and he has an authority to enforce his demand. By the ancient privilege of Athens as she is her father's he may dispose of her either to Demetrius or to her death, according to the law immediately provided, and Theseus enforces the law. Theseus explains it to her carefully. To a daughter her father should be as a god, composer of her beauties to whom she is a form in wax "within his power" to make or mar. There is not much to choose between the two young gentlemen except that her father chooses Demetrius. "I would my father looked but with my eyes," she suggests; but no, "Rather your eyes must with his judgement look." She won't give in. This rather naughty little girl (of "stubborn harshness," her father says, and later events do let us see that he has something of a point), knowing already that the punishment for her disobedience is death, but still checking out her options, asks Theseus what is the *worst* that may befall her in this case if she refuses Demetrius. Not a foolish question it turns out, because there is a fate perhaps worse than death in this kind of play, life-long virginity. Theseus cautions her sensibly to think if she is the kind of young woman who can suffer that; "question your desires," he says, "Know of your youth, examine well your blood," whether she can endure the alternative of the livery of a nun in a shady cloister,

> To live a barren sister all your life,
> Chanting faint hymns to the cold fruitless moon.

They are thrice blessed that can master so their blood but she would seem to be a girl with the warm blood for this earth, likely to be "earthlier happy" by becoming the rose distilled than by withering on the virgin thorn or in that cool ambiguity of "single blessedness." She has said she does not know "by what power" she is made bold where so much power is being brought to bear upon her, but she evidently has something stronger than the godlike power arrogated by her father and ratified by ancient law which will now be executed by his Grace the Duke. She is ready to live and die in the single life rather than yield her virgin patent, her privilege, to a lordship her soul consents not to give sovereignty. Sensible Theseus tells her to take time to pause over these awful alternatives of disobedience, until the next new moon when he and Hippolyta his love will marry (I, i, 38-90). It's good advice from an experienced ruler, less convincing as coming from a man impatiently in love, and time will not make any difference. We know quite well by what power she is made bold and love will not be defeated.

That is clear enough for us to see and to say, but what is she to do? Hermia and Lysander discuss the problem, in a gracefully pathetic and not immediately relevant catalogue of lovers' crosses, a stichomythic series that lets us know the degree and kind of concern we must feel. They are not intellectuals but they do know, and it is rather a comfort, that their plight is not peculiar. All Lysander could ever read, could ever hear by tale or history, is the old story: "The course of true love never did run smooth," as he reports to Hermia, in his lovely gift not for original thought but imperishable words. It is certainly a wise saw applicable to any stage of civilization, before or after, as the more talented young Dickens, picking up the very latest technology in smooth transportation, was able to remind us once again in *Pickwick,* Chapter 8, "Strongly illustrative of the position that the course of true love is not a Railway." But such journeys do arrive safely at their desired end if lovers can devise the means, or some power devises for them. Hermia is restrained by a law that keeps lovers apart, the law of the state, of fathers, death, sterility. It is, she knows from the perspicuous Lysander's lecture—they do enjoy playing on the big

stage—an "edict in destiny." In this immediate exemplar it is the law of Athens and he proposes that they run off to another place, where he will have another home with a more sympathetic widow aunt, "a dowager, / Of great revenue, and she hath no child. / . . . and respects me as her only son": just the sort of sentimental old lady who can handle this sort of difficulty and provide all good things. In that place "the sharp Athenian law / Cannot pursue us." The aunt's house is "remote seven leagues," so he proposes to meet Hermia "a league without the town" (I, i, 132-68). There they will begin their journey. They do meet and they do depart for that happy place where they will be free of frustrating law, where all problems will be solved and all loving desires fulfilled. But they don't have the boots for seven leagues. They do certainly find a place where other laws obtain, but it is not what they thought it would be and the laws are not what they could ever have anticipated or ever do understand; and their problems are both complicated and resolved by means more wonderful than anything they could have imagined. Young lovers have strong but limited imaginations. They will devise to steal through the gates of Athens, to meet in the wood,

> And thence from Athens turn away our eyes
> To seek new friends and stranger companies.
>   (218-19)

New and stranger the companies will be ("strange companions," say quarto and folio). Young lovers find themselves, at the beginning of the journey of their lives, in a dark wood where the straight way is lost, under the moon, in a dream. Something has happened to those eyes we have been hearing about. We will hear much about eyes, both here and in subsequent works.

Meanwhile the other and lesser class of mortals of Athens, those clowns, have their own desires and their own difficulties which they too have to work out before the next new moon, in mounting that play they want to create and enact before the Duke and the Duchess on the wedding day at night. "Is all our company here?" The play is the "most lamentable comedy" about Pyramus and Thisbe, a very good piece of work, we are assured, and a merry (I, ii, 1-11). We are already convinced that this is a problem they will never solve, so utterly incapable as they are, but so thick that they are not even aware of their impotence and we can enjoy without any need to worry about them. Their problem, as they see it at first, is simply to find a good place to rehearse and so Quince, author and producer-director, distributes parts and tells all to meet him tomorrow night in the wood, "a mile without the town," by moonlight. There they will rehearse, for if we meet in the city, he says, "we shall be dogged with company, and our devices known." Bottom agrees that there they will meet and "rehearse most obscenely and courageously. Take pains be perfect" (80-86). In their kind, the best in their kind, they are always perfect. It is not certain if Quince's mile and Lysander's league are the same and it doesn't make much difference because they never run into one another or know that the other is there; but the wood is certainly the same place and the "company" they find there is certainly the same, new and stranger than either looked for, and their devices are known. Both young lovers and clowns come under the spell of the fairies.

What do fairies do? They are clever and mischievous, and the first thing we hear of Puck is that he is "that shrewd and knavish sprite / Called Robin Goodfellow." He enjoys laughing and jesting, as both another fairy and he tell us, scares maidens, misleads night wanderers; he's a great mimic, beguiles a fat and bean-fed horse by neighing in the likeness of a filly foal, and we will later see him doing just that sort of thing with a man or two infatuated with a girl or two (and indeed the man shall have his mare again—certain distinctions are not important to him); he has more than mortal powers of mimicry, animating objects both natural and artificial, lurking in the very likeness of a roasted crab apple in an old-woman's ale to bob against her lips and make her spill it on herself, or setting up this old favorite, always good for a "loffe":

> The wisest aunt, telling the saddest tale,
> Sometimes for threefoot stool mistaketh me;
> Then slip I from her bum, down topples she . . .

Then the whole choir hold their hips and loffe, and swear a merrier hour was never wasted there (II, i, 32-57). But this village humor of pulling chairs out from under old women, robust as it is, isn't half as much fun as the more intimate, inside, revealing tricks he can play. The fairies streak the eyes of the young men. The mortals think they are being most reasonable when they are most mistaken. "The will of man is by his reason swayed, / And reason says you are the worthier maid" (II, ii, 121-22): that is the bright Lysander, under the spell, wooing the wrong maid. Puck, agent of the Fairy King, has a juice, the juice of the little western flower, and maidens call it "love-in-idleness," which changes vision, makes lovers blind, makes them madly dote upon the next live creature that they see (II, i, 166-72). Lysander goes to sleep saying to Hermia, "end life when I end loyalty!" and jumps up saying, "And run through fire I will for thy sweet sake! / Transparent Helena" (II, ii, 69, 109-10). That is one blind young lover.

Under the fairy spell the lovers change partners in a pretty, choreographed movement. Lysander and Demetrius had both been in love with Hermia in their *pas de trois* and poor Helena had been without a partner, chasing Demetrius; but now Lysander with his altered eyes runs to Helena, who still chases Demetrius, who still chases Hermia, who is now chasing the now faithless Lysander, all in a circle; then Demetrius is given

new eyes and both he and Lysander chase Helena in their *pas de trois* and poor Hermia is without a partner, chasing Lysander. One might think that Helena, who had been so unhappy when no one loved her, so unattractive as she thought herself, in her bad moments— "I am as ugly as a bear" (II, ii, 100)—would be delighted now when any man need only see her to love her; but she has never been so unhappy, certain that a cruel joke is being played on her by both the men and Hermia, her oldest and closest, only girl friend. Then the two young men grow hot in their claims to Helena and begin to chase one another in preparation for a fight. Hermia, totally confused by everyone's actions and never one to take things lying down (as we have seen, with an importunate father or an importunate lover), now grows hot with Helena, who she is certain has been the thief of love; and Hermia is eager to get her nails at that friend's eyes. All is in chaos with them, as mixed up couples and mixed up friends, and individually mixed to the point of loss of identity.

> O me, what news, my love
> Am not I Hermia? Are not you Lysander?
> (III, ii, 272-73)

And from that point, the lowest of their fortunes, all comes right, as Lysander returns to love and pair off with Hermia, and Demetrius is paired with helena; and that in fact was the pattern of their configuration before the play began, so the change of partners in the dance has been worked out with a lovely symmetry. The choreography seems to have been designed by an artful nature long before these particular lovers were led through its moves; and other young partners will perform it on other stages.

It has all come right because Puck, at Oberon's direction, has changed Lysander's vision once again so that he now sees clearly which girl he ought to love. The fairies have a double power. If Puck at his entrance tells us how he pulls out chairs from under old aunts, in his last appearance he sweeps the dust behind the door, a tricky bit of housekeeping that makes all neat, as far as one can see. He has another name, Robin Goodfellow, an ambiguous propitiatory name for a trickster who can do both mischief and unexpected helpful deeds for people who should be helped. Having put these young lovers to quarreling with one another he uses his talents in mimicry both to stir them up and keep them far enough apart so they can do no hurt. Having set them at odds he makes these odds all even, and no more triangles.

> Yet but three? Come one more,
> Two of both kinds makes up four.

Having gathered them, unknown to one another, on the ground and sleeping, he works his medicinal magic once again.

> I'll apply
> To your eye,
> Gentle lover, remedy.

And that does the job, just as the proverb provides:

> Jack shall have Jill,
> Naught shall go ill:
> The man shall have his mare again, and
> all shall be well.
>
> (III, ii, 437-63)

Having charmed Lysander's eye with the juice of love-in-idleness to send him chasing the wrong girl he has Oberon's remedy, the chaste juice of Dian's bud, to clear the eye, make the boy see the right girl. That is the counter-charm.

These young lovers, for all their bright qualities, are not much for depth or complexity, only young lovers, and that *is* their character. They are easy to confuse with one another. "Thou shalt know the man / By the Athenian garments he hath on," Oberon had instructed Puck (II, i, 263-64), which we may think is not a wonderfully effective method of identification coming from the King of Fairies; but then to his eye there cannot be much essential distinction between one young mortal lover and another; and Puck by dropping the juice in the wrong man's eye makes what might be called a natural mistake, which pleases him. What difference does it make except to make mortal confusion more apparent? Helena has always been understandably insistent on the lack of distinction between her and Hermia. "Through Athens I am thought as fair as she" (I, i, 227), a fact Demetrius will see as soon as his vision is corrected. Helena knows they two have always been indistinguishable, working on one sampler, while sitting on one cushion, warbling one song, both in one key,

> As if our hands, our sides, voices, and minds
> Had been incorporate . . .
> Two lovely berries moulded on one stem . . .
> (III, ii, 203-14)

A reader needs a mnemonic device to keep them straight in his mind. On the stage, where they live, it is plan that one is tall, fair and timid, the other little, dark and fierce, but the point is that such details matter not at all; young men may fall in or out of love with the same details, finding them attractive or repellent from one moment to the next. To be young and in love is all that counts. With not much to choose between them we would not be greatly offended if they switched partners—as the young men do, shortly, several times—but since the pattern of pairing does seem to matter greatly to them we defer to their desires, even if we can see little reason why they can be satisfied only by so specific a solution.

With little difference or depth to begin with there is not much development to expect from them. It is pleasant to see, in the women, that under the pressures of the fairies in the night certain little suppressed qualities do pop out—like the revelation of the spitfire in Hermia, of which there had been a hint in the opening of the play. And then we hear the news that Helena (that less than dependable keeper of a friend's secret plan), for all her sweet-talk of two lovely berries molded on one stem, and for all her pathetic appeal to Hermia's feminine solidarity not to join with men in scorning a poor friend, has known of Hermia's keen and shrewish quality for some time and is now willing to tattle when it may do her own cause some service: "She was a vixen when she went to school" (III, ii, 215-19, 323-25). The young men do change as much as they are able and fulfill whatever potential was there. Each does see finally which young woman is the right young woman for him and that's rather more than they seemed capable of at the start. Their history may make us wonder a bit about future stability but we must accept, on high authority, that this is the end of the change. Back to Athens shall the lovers wend, Oberon assures us, "With a league whose date shall never end," a kingly decree then independently corroborated by the other ruler, who joins them, for in the temple with us, Theseus says, "These couples shall eternally be knit" (III, ii, 372-73; IV, i, 177-78). Of course these authorities, both fairy and human, have had their own problems in love, but that's all over now. Or at least this story is over and if other characters in every time and place will play this story again in their own lives, as they surely will, for these particular creatures we have come to a conclusion.

It seems that the young men have grown up, or so they insist, even if they do not understand how they managed to do that. "I wot not by what power," Demetrius says, in echo of Hermia's early declaration of an unknown strength, "But by some power it is." It is that same power of love: his mistaken love for Hermia, now melted as the snow,

> seems to me now
> As the remembrance of an idle gaud
> Which in my childhood I did dote upon,

and the object and pleasure of his eye is now only Helena (IV, i, 161-68). It is the same declaration of maturity which Lysander had made to Helena, when he abandoned Hermia:

> Things growing are not ripe until their season;
> So I, being young, till now not ripe to reason,

had been led to Helena's eyes (II, ii, 123-24). It is the sort of repetition which should leave us with an amused and healthy skepticism, but again our own vision should be wise enough to recognize and accept the distinction between the middle and the end of a story. Lysander was under the false charm and his words were the false words of the doting young man, Demetrius is under the true counter-charm and his words are the true words of the man in love. The sententious boy Lysander had been pompous in his certainty of reason, the no longer doting Demetrius is modest in his self-knowledge and limited understanding of what power it is, which makes him more credible. And of course we are not dependent only on his word. These are now young lovers who have become, to their capacities, small or large, ready to marry, and to marry under the auspices of those who have overseen their growing. They and their best bride-bed are blessed and they will have babies, not just any chance babies but, as we would expect in this play, perfect babies, promised by those who can make good the guarantee: the issue they create ever shall be fortunate.

> And the blots of nature's hand
> Shall not in their issue stand.
> (V, i, 387-88)

The accidents of love are so happily behind them and, so wonderfully, the accidents of natural gestation and time are suspended for them. That is worth a word more.

Time is peculiar in *A Midsummer Night's Dream*. For one thing, as Dr. Johnson said, "I know not why *Shakespear* calls this play a *Midsummer-Night's Dream,* when he so carefully informs us that it happened on the night preceding *May* day" (his annotation on IV, i, 110). It has been often explained by other annotators but it finally doesn't make much difference.

> Good morrow, friends, Saint Valentine is past;
> Begin these woodbirds but to couple now?
> (IV, i, 136-37)

We are told at the start that the play will end on new moon, and then the almanac says the moon will shine that night. But it really doesn't make much difference. And Shakespeare doesn't seem to have paid much attention to the time-scheme of the action. Theseus says in the first speech of the play that it will be four days and nights until the nuptial hour and Hippolyta repeats that, sensibly telling him not to be so impatient in desire, that the days will quickly turn to night and the nights will quickly dream away the time; she is right, the time goes quickly and is largely dreamed away. His prediction isn't true and neither he nor any of his subjects seems to notice that it cannot be much more than forty-eight hours (with one very long night). But then it really doesn't make much difference. No one can be confused by any of this except any foolish mortal who tries to stop the action to get the timing right. All this in a magnificently crafted, jewelled play. Time is dramatically quite unimportant in *A Midsummer Night's Dream.* We are given an expectation of a tight dra-

matic chronology which indicates tension—Hermia must make her decision and the lovers must work out their fates within four days, the clowns must get their play into production in that same short rehearsal schedule, the fairies must do their work before the night in the wood ends—but we in the audience can all hang loose. Time is unimportant because once we enter the wood, under the moon, in the dream, the complications and the resolution will all be moved instantly, magically. Puck drops the juice of the charm in the eye and the vision is distorted, he applies the antidote, the counter-charm, and the vision is clear. No time is needed in that more than mortal realm (and in fact these fairies don't have to run at the end of the black-browed night). Like everything in this play, changes are perfect, immediate.

We can believe in that magic because we can believe in these fairies. They speak a more than mortal language. But we believe too because it is not a meaningless stage-magician magic, mechanical tricks which seem to violate the order of nature and have no consequence, no revelation. "O strange! We are haunted!" (III, i, 86), but this is magic which makes palpable the reality which we then recognize as true when it is opened before *our* eyes. Bottom is translated for us— "Bless thee, Bottom, bless thee! Thou art translated!" (98)—into the ass's head he has always carried on those shoulders. We see his metaphor; it is a clever turn. As the translator explicates, ". . . those things do best please me / That befall prepost'rously" (III, ii, 32, 120-21), back to front; and, in this instance, it shall be called Bottom's figure because the ass is foremost. But Bottom returns it upon us as well as upon his fellow clowns: "What do you see? You see an ass head of your own, do you?" (III, i, 97). Such simple magical sport with space—the best magicians need little paraphernalia to achieve great effects—changes the vision. What we see has always been there, and we know that, but we have never seen it with such eyes before. There is nothing much to *Gulliver's Travels,* as Dr. Johnson saw: "When once you have thought of big men and little men, it is very easy to do all the rest" (Boswell's *Life,* 24 Mar. 1775), and he is simply right. Quite simply, as we say, once you've read *Gulliver's Travels* and have seen that strange translation of space you will never see human beings on the same scale again. In their magical sport with time the fairies let us see, what we can now recognize in quick-time, or no-time, the common human processes we cannot see so brilliantly with our daily vision by a daily clock. Young lovers fall in and out of love with an unreasonable readiness and frequency, so we are not disbelieving but greet delightedly what is made more apparent here by the fairy spell. Lysander, in the wood, chases the wrong girl, but young men have been known to do that without supernatural intervention; Demetrius was doing it in the first act. One understands too, by way of further sharpening our daily vision, that the magic has entered this play before the fairies. "This man hath bewitched the bosom of my child," Egeus had been complaining as we started; the young man has given her rhymes, he has by moonlight been singing to her with feigning voice verses of feigning love, stolen the impression of her fantasy, her imagination (I, i, 27-32). Egeus hasn't got it all straight but in his stuffy way he is telling us about the sort of thing that goes on in the magical dream. It is also true that the kinds of transformations worked on the mortals in the dream are, at long last, what they have been always longing for. Helena wanted translation before it came upon Bottom. Sickness is catching, she said, and she'd give the world if she could catch Hermia's looks that way, her ear, her eye, her tongue, to make herself as attractive to Demetrius.

> Were the world mine, Demetrius being bated,
> The rest I'd give to be to you translated.
>
> (186-91)

And her wish is granted, they two being already so much alike that a drop in Demetrius' eye makes all the difference.

The sport is taken one step more, because no one is exempt from the magic. It is a funny foolish mortal show Puck is directing and watching:

> Shall we their fond pageant see?
> Lord, what fools these mortals be!
>
> (III, ii, 114-15)

But his role, above the pageant of the laughter, is, even for him, impossible to sustain untouched. At least, as the fairies are themselves dramatic creatures, participants in an action, they have, necessarily by that condition it seems, their own problems, their lovers' quarrels, complications, resolutions, and they too play their roles in the fond pageant. Oberon and Titania are not quite faithful, something willful and petty, tricky and tricked, capable of mistakes in the night. There is evidently some power which handles that show, some "fate" which "o'errules," as Puck says (93), who sees to it that Oberon and Puck slip from that glorious language to an imprecise communication which leads Puck to drop the juice in the wrong eye: some super-Puck who laughs and says, "Lord, what fools these fairies be." All things circle in this play.

All desires are fulfilled and everything works out to a complete harmony and reconcilement of all opposites. Theseus and Hippolyta, the mature lovers, have turned their war to love before the play begins and have set a good example. The young lovers have been sorted out and Theseus ratifies the obviously desirable arrangement he finds. "I beg the law, the law upon his head!" Egeus demands against Lysander, but Theseus is both a lover himself and a more sensible judge and

will not grant that. "Egeus, I will overbear your will" (IV, i, 152, 176). Oberon and Titania have already settled their difference in their way; that is important because the order of nature, the order of human time, had been disturbed by their quarrel—things won't grow up

> and the green corn
> Hath rotted ere his youth attained his beard;

this is a matter of not only unseasonable weather but of the medical problems it brings, contagious fogs, murrain, rheumatic diseases, distemperature (II, i, 88 ff). The kinds of immaturity and sickness which have been giving Demetrius such troubles and which, now "in health come to my natural taste," he recognizes (IV, i, 165-71), have been cured by Puck's remedy; as the now loving amity of the fairies helps make possible a healthful resolution of the human problems. The fairies dance, something they do so well. A dance of this sort celebrates the attainment of desires, the ceremony when all participate harmoniously, all are lovingly alive and active and all is delightfully ordered: there is at once full freedom and full union, to signal the happy solution and the restored or newly shaped kinetic stability. In their double capacity the fairies lead the mortals "about a round" and they dance in "a round" (III, i, 88; II, i, 140). The circle is completed.

And the most discordant sounds harmonize, as even the dispersed company of clowns is reunited and is joyful. Bottom, that perfect clown who has always thought that he can play any and every role, who can create chords that would be impossibly self-contradictory for anyone else, can roar you as gentle as any sucking dove, has been at home among the fairies too because he has "a reasonable good ear in music. Let's have the tongs and the bones" (IV, i, 26-27). Shortly after this request is offered—we are getting a remarkable orchestration—there follows the very different fairy music and the dance that ends the dream. Which in turn is immediately succeeded by the dawn and the hunting horns that will wake the lovers. Theseus is there with his love and his hounds. "My love shall hear the music of my hounds." He wants her to

> mark the musical confusion
> Of hounds and echo in conjunction.

As one who has been with Hercules and Cadmus once, when in a wood of Crete they bayed the bear with hounds of Sparta, she has heard such gallant chiding, when groves, skies, fountains and every region seemed "all one mutual cry":

> I never heard
> So musical a discord, such sweet thunder.

In this friendly rivalry he will not be outdone because his magnificent hounds are bred out of that same kind and "matched in mouth like bells, / Each under each. . . . Judge when you hear" (103-24). It is at this point in the strange composition that he sees the sleeping lovers and is surprised to find the clashing young men in such unity.

> I know you two are rival enemies:
> How comes this gentle concord in the
>   world . . . ?
>
> (139-40)

They can reply only more amazedly, because no one can understand the marvellous harmony of the dream and the wisest is he who hath simply the best wit of any handicraft man in Athens, who knows it hath no bottom.

But in fact not everything has been brought into a concordance, because all this dance and all these wonders are accomplished by the end of Act IV and there is still an act to follow. The clowns haven't yet done their act. They've been looking forward to this performance to complete their happiness and gain their reward—Bottom could not have scaped sixpence a day—and we've been looking forward, too; and some sort of general rejoicing, not for fairies only but for the clowns and for the lovers young and not so young, would be appropriate. The last act certainly is fun and worth the wait and it couldn't very well have been offered before the resolution of the several problems. But that's a pretty long afterpiece, if that's what it is, a bit much for a playwright who has been working with a delicate shaping touch. In that shaping, of course, Pyramus and Thisbe does seem right in the place where it is, because we have begun in Act I in a world of reality, such as reality is in our base line in Duke Theseus' Athens, then we have adjourned to a long middle passage in the world of the fairies, wood within this wood, and now we return to the home reality again; and that arrangement is, like everything in this play, perfectly symmetrical. If anything, we are more real than ever as we leave the fairy cobweb for the "palpable gross," for onion and garlic eaters. But then to what reality are we returning? A very strange reality, it seems, which is a play within the play and, as scripted and presented, the most absurdly unreal thing we've seen, a tragically disastrous parody of the course of true love. No problems get solved here, either by Pyramus and his love or by their personators. This is, in its own effort, less credible than the dream. Which should we believe?

It is a question worth debating and Theseus and Hippolyta talk it over, in two stages; which leads us to think that this marriage of two mature and experienced people, both like and unlike one another, whose acquaintance began in a less understanding dispute, will be a good marriage. The young lovers had been amazed as they came out of the dream, "Half sleep, half waking," "cannot truly say" at first how they came to be where they are. For a moment their eyes hesitate between a vision of the two worlds:

> Methinks I see these things with parted eye,
> When everything seems double . . .
>   Are you sure
> That we are awake? It seems to me
> That yet we sleep, we dream.

But in their youthful bounce it doesn't bother them much or stop them long in thought and, confident that they are now awake, off they go: "And by the way let us recount our dreams. [*Exeunt lovers*]" (IV, i, 143-44, 186-96). But Hippolyta is stopped by the recount: "'Tis strange, my Theseus, that these lovers speak of." Not so Theseus, who doesn't believe the dream at all: "More strange than true. I never may believe / These antic fables, nor these fairy toys." Lovers, madmen, have such seething brains, shaping fantasies, "that apprehend / More than cool reason ever comprehends," imagine more than any sane person can understand. His cool reason knows that "The lunatic, the lover, and the poet / Are of imagination all compact." Theseus is a very sensible man and a good ruler and has given his proofs, and by a life's experience he knows a thing or two about being in love. Hippolyta knows rather less but she has a more open mind on this subject, not certain in skepticism as he is, and not credulously insistent either:

> But all the story of the night told over,
> And all their minds transfigured so together,
> More witnesseth than fancy's images,
> And grows to something of great constancy . . .

If all the lovers had the same dream, a transfiguration of all minds that has a coherence, then there seems to be evidence of a story of life, a story with more meaning than the antic fable of seething brain, or of poet's eye rolling in a frenzy of art, those images of fancy so confidently dismissed by the single-visioned Theseus. She doesn't know what happened—how could she? who could?—but knows that even if she can't understand it something remarkable happened: "But howsoever, strange and admirable." She accepts the possibility of the inexplicable and wonderful, the shared dream of love. Theseus turns off the question: "Here come the lovers, full of joy and mirth," which, though it is not his intention, is as close to an explanation as we are likely to come (V, i, 1-28). To us who have been listening to this little inconclusive lovers' disputation it would appear that if the dream is more than cool reason ever comprehends and it more witnesseth than fancy's images—well, at that point, between reason and fancy, it is useless to argue in oppositions, for discords disappear in love and mirth. In this work we are suspended, perfectly, it seems, in a moment in a place of concordant reason-imagination, real-unreal, life-art. And now here come the clowns, full of life and art.

Theseus wants something more delightful than this dream he can't believe, to wear away the anguish of three hours before the wedding bed. Masques, dances, mirth, "What revels are in hand? Is there no play . . . ?" (V, i, 32-38). There is a choice of old stuff, pseudo-serious stuff, not sorting with a nuptial ceremony, but also on the menu he reads

'A tedious brief scene of young Pyramus
And his love Thisbe; very tragical mirth'—
Merry and tragical? Tedious and brief?
That is hot ice and wondrous strange snow.

Theseus has found another question in harmony. "How shall we find the concord of this discord?" (56-60). That piques his interest, more than he asked for or could have thought possible, this kind of strangeness. He is told that it is a very poor play, really both brief and tedious, really tragical with a death which makes the eyes water, but "more merry tears / The passion of loud laughter never shed." That increases his curiosity. "What are they that do play it?" He is told that they are hard-handed men that work in Athens, men who never labored in their minds till now, and have now toiled to present this play for his wedding. "And we will hear it." He is told it is not for him, it is nothing, nothing in the world, unless he can find sport in their intents, so little ability so stretched with cruel pain to do him service. "I will hear that play." This is an impressive Duke. He knows that "never anything can come amiss / When simpleness and duty tender it . . . take your places, ladies" (61-84). His own lady is not pleased. The Queen of the Amazons is a gracious and feeling lady. We have seen her sensitive, thoughtful response to the dream, better than his confident assurance. She feels for these toiling men; she loves not to see wretchedness overcharged and duty in its service perishing. He honors her feeling but this is something in which he knows more than she. "Why, gentle sweet, you shall see no such thing." But the master of the revels has just said they can do nothing in this kind. "The kinder we"—witty man—"to give them thanks for nothing."

Our sport shall be to take what they
  mistake;
And what poor duty cannot do, noble respect
Takes it in might, not merit.

It is not only these inarticulate simples who mistake, because experienced Theseus has seen great clerks in their premeditated speech, with practiced accent, shiver and look pale, not paying him welcome, "Make periods in the midst of sentences" (as Quince the Prologue will now do). "Trust me," he says, ". . . Love . . . and tonguetied simplicity / In least speak most, to my capacity" (85-105). She should trust him, as a Duke of noble respect who knows how to value "might" and who knows how to watch a play. So it starts.

Those young lovers, Lysander and Demetrius, are witty fellows, very clever in their language, very witty spectators of the foolishness of that play and players they are watching. One might think they should be more thoughtful, more self-conscious at this replay of their own fond pageant. But no, that's all past—Oberon has in kindness erased the memory—for why should happy lovers be obliged to draw solemn lessons from their own conduct and not leave that to other, unseen, spectators? Hippolyta, not very happy with this whole idea of watching such incompetent actors on the stage, can't stand the thing. "This is the silliest stuff that ever I heard." She didn't say that about the dream. Theseus, enjoying himself thoroughly, instructs her in dramatic illusion: "The best in this kind are but shadows; and the worst are no worse, if imagination amend them." He knows how to transfer from his inward nature a human interest and a semblance of truth sufficient to procure for these "shadows of imagination" that willing suspension of disbelief for the moment, which constitutes poetic faith (*Biographia Literaria,* ch. xiv). She is the sensible one now and she won't have any of that: "It must be your imagination then, and not theirs." But he understands how to see shadows of this kind— "If we imagine no worse of them than they of themselves, they may pass for excellent men"—because he is ready to allow for imagination here. "Here come two noble beasts in, a man and a lion" (V, i, 204-10). Theseus disbelieves the fairy toy of the dream but willingly suspends disbelief to enjoy the play; to Hippolyta the play is silly but the dream is something of great constancy. Theseus has one kind of imagination, for a play of very tragical mirth, but he cannot extend that effort to the dream; Hippolyta, who cannot dismiss the dream, lacks the imagination to enjoy the play. For us spectators, needing both kinds of the faculty, because we know what we have witnessed and can deny neither scene, dream and play seem to bear a mutual effect, each gaining credibility for each, discords resolving in concord.

The art of the mechanicals cannot be dismissed. Fairies are poets, in their language and in their dramatic art, as inventors of amusing scenes in which they direct the actors who do not know how wonderfully they are being staged. That art needs an imagination of power; and even within Puck's play about lovers, in their own less knowing imaginations the distracted lovers themselves sometimes think that they are being made to play roles in scenes invented by one another. Clowns are lunatics trying to be poets, and do not have that imagination of power, that imagination which can take the forms of things unknown and turn them to shapes and give to airy nothing a local habitation and a name. Shapes and names give them endless problems. And Bottom fears they will be too real—"you think I come hither as a lion . . . No, I am no such thing; I am a man, as other men are"—or not be real enough—"Look in the almanac—find out moonshine, find out moonshine!" (III, i, 32-34, 40-41). In their chaos this company cannot find out that constancy of a story told by a shaping imagination. But then if we see how the best in this kind does it, the King of Shadows, we cannot think too badly of these less good shadows. We have been hearing and watching Oberon play a scene for well over a hundred lines when he informs us, at the moment when this remarkable confidence suddenly becomes necessary: "I am invisible" (II, i, 186). Yes, we say, we can see that now. It is a mutual endeavor. This shadow teaches us and, as Theseus instructs Hippolyta, our imagination must amend this shadow; we now see him with our eyes (perhaps he draws about him his invisibility robe) and we see with our imaginations, at once. So for all his clownish incompetence as an artist neither we nor anyone can simply look down on Bottom or his imagination. Theseus, the ruler by day, for all the excellence of his kind of imagination, does not have the imagination to see how much he has in common with this sweet Bottom who has been transported; Theseus, like the lovers and no more aware than they, has been watched over by the fairies: but Theseus, like Bottom and still less aware than he, has been loved, in one strange sense or another, by the Queen of the fairies. Bottom had given him and us, his two audiences, fair warning on our vision: "let the audience look to their eyes" (I, ii, 20). Bottom has wit; nay, he can gleek upon occasion. But he won't flaunt it, won't set his wit to so foolish a bird as a cuckoo, and more impressively, won't let the Queen of the fairies, in her unknowing irony, flatter his beauty or his wisdom. Not so, neither, but if he had wit enough to get out of this wood, as he says, he has enough to serve his own turn; and she may croon the fairy blandishment, "Out of this wood do not desire to go," and she may try to feed him with fairy fruit, "with apricots and dewberries, / With purple grapes, green figs and mulberries," but his great desire is to a peck of provender, to munch your good dry oats, or hay, for "Good hay, sweet hay hath no fellow" (III, i, 112-26, 144-45; IV, i, 29-31). He knows the limits of wit. If Bottom's senses and language have been more than ordinarily mixed in a dream, and the eye of man hath not heard and the ear of man hath not seen, and if his tongue is not able to conceive nor his heart to report what his dream was, if he has not the imaginative language to recount it, and if he thinks touchingly that only a ballad by that poet Peter Quince could do the job, he is not such an ass as to go about to expound this dream which, in either of its double senses, has no bottom. He has had an exposition of sleep come upon him. To the lovers all the derision shall seem "a dream and fruitless vision" (III, ii, 370-71), but he has had what no other sees, except for us with whom he shares it. "I have had a most rare vision. I have had a dream, past the wit of man to say what dream it was" (IV, i, 200-09).

The wit of man in the night, in the dream, the shadow, under the moon, has difficulties seeing all that is there and those varied, opposing and changing forces. The night is a time of fear and of love. The moon brings the hours of beauty and of lunacy. Dreams are nightmares, or, in their fulfillment of all desire, everything. Shadows are the least substantial things, ghosts, at a remove, or two removes, from reality, and they are the most substantial, the spirit, the essence, the revelation of the meaning. Shadows, like dreams, may be airy nothing, like dreams may be strange and wonderful. They are the stuff of art, that thing which is least real and most real, taking us to the edge of another world. Puck in his last words invites the audience to meet him there, at the border:

> If we shadows have offended,
> Think but this, and all is mended:
> That you have but slumbered here
> While these visions did appear . . .

He invites us into the dream and the play and we have reason not to trust him wholly; this may be his last and best trick. But he needs us there, half-way, as we need him. The best in this kind are but shadows, we know by now, and need imagination to help mend them.

> Gentles, do not reprehend;
> If you pardon, we will mend.

It is an extraordinarily modest request from one who seems to need offer no apologies to us, who are all in his debt. But he insists on having our friendship and we are ready to respond because he has so much to offer in return.

> Give me your hands, if we be friends,
> And Robin shall restore amends.
>   (V, i, 401-16)

It is all a special experience, in a created world carefully marked off in time by the brief days and nights of confusion and celebration preceding the nuptial hour, indeed by the immediate no-time magic of the fairies, carefully marked off in space by the roundel and fairy song that fence Titania's bower and hold out spotted snakes, thorny hedgehogs, spiders, beetles black and snails (II, ii, 1-30). It is essential that we know such things do live outside the charmed circle, look in upon us here because they are explicitly excluded, and that we know, as Puck tells us, there are ghosts wandering here and there home to churchyards, and damned spirits who go to and from their wormy beds (III, ii, 381-87). Ladies need not fear when lion rough in wildest rage doth roar because he assures all that he is Snug the joiner, and it is understood that he is a very gentle beast, and of a good conscience; but Puck reminds us before he sweeps the dust behind the door that there is another kind of beast and now that hungry lion roars (V, i, 211-19, 349). There are the disfiguring mole, harelip, scar, mark prodigious, those blots of nature's

hand that frighten parents and at other times than now certainly may be upon their children (387-92). We have known from the beginning that in the history of the course of true love not everything has run smoothly at the end, that even if there were sympathy and no other tried to stop the course, war, death or sickness did lay siege to it,

> Making it momentany as a sound,
> Swift as a shadow, short as any dream,
> Brief as the lightning in the collied night,
> That in a spleen unfolds both heaven and
>   earth,
> And, ere a man hath power to say 'Behold!',
> The jaws of darkness do devour it up.
> So quick bright things come to confusion.
>   (I, i, 141-49)

The shadow, the dream, the night, may not be friends, the quickness of time may bring the brightness to confusion and not bring it back. Not all fairies are so helpful and even these we see have given proofs that they too can do harm enough. But if these have the charm to put their mischief upon the sight they are dependably there with the charm that takes off the blindness, opens the eye. They have the language— charm is a song, the carmen that casts the spell—and it is the magic of the language which creates that special circle of beauty, on the bank

>   where the wild thyme blows,
> Where oxlips and the nodding violet grows,

and encloses it completely,

> Quite overcanopied with luscious woodbine,
> With sweet musk-roses and with eglantine.

There sleeps Titania (II, i, 249-53). It is, for that moment, verifiable by the human senses (Bacon, writing of gardens, says the sweetest smell in the air is yielded by the violet, next to that the muskrose, then too sweetbriar, i.e., eglantine, then honeysuckles, i.e. woodbine; and among those few flowers that perfume the air most delightfully, being trodden upon, is the wild thyme). In that created circle and in that way, with the shapes and colors and odors and tastes and motions so specific and of such constancy, the reality of that imagination cannot be denied; and in that way the play never becomes sentimental but a most rare vision of completed aspiration. . . .

Bibliography

The text is the edition by R. A. Foakes, "New Cambridge Shakespeare" (Cambridge, 1984). References are to act, scene and line numbers; where successive quotations in the same paragraph are from the same scene the act and scene numbers are not repeated.

Shaw is quoted from *Shaw on Shakespeare*, ed. Edwin Wilson (New York, 1961), pp. xiii-xiv.

Barber, C. L., *Shakespeare's Festive Comedy* (Princeton, 1972 ed.)

Berry, Ralph, *Shakespeare's Comedies: Explorations in Form* (Princeton, 1972)

Bevington, David, "'But We Are Spirits of Another Sort': The Dark Side of Love in *A Midsummer Night's Dream,*" *Medieval and Renaissance Studies,* VII (1975, published 1978), 80-92

Brown, John Russell, *Shakespeare and His Comedies* (London, 1957)

Calderwood, James L., *Shakespearean Metadrama* (Minneapolis, 1971)

Cope, Jackson I., *The Theater and the Dream: From Metaphor to Form in Renaissance Drama* (Baltimore, 1973)

Dent, R. W., "Imagination in *A Midsummer Night's Dream,*" *Shakespeare Quarterly,* XV, No. 2, (1964), 115-29

Dunn, Allen, "The Indian Boy's Dream . . . Shakespeare's *A Midsummer Night's Dream,*" *Shakespeare Studies,* XX (1988), 15-32

Evans, Bertrand, *Shakespeare's Comedies* (Oxford, 1960)

Fender, Stephen, *Shakespeare: A Midsummer Night's Dream* (London, 1968)

Garber, Marjorie B., *Dream in Shakespeare* (New Haven, 1974)

Girard, René, "Bottom's One-Man Show," *The Current in Criticism,* edd. Clayton Koelb and Virgil Lokke (West Lafayette, 1987)

Huston, J. Dennis, *Shakespeare's Comedies of Play* (New York, 1981)

Kermode, Frank, "The Mature Comedies," in *Early Shakespeare,* "Stratford-Upon-Avon Studies" 3 (1961)

Kott, Jan, *The Bottom Translation* (Evanston, 1987)

Leggatt, Alexander, *Shakespeare's Comedy of Love* (London, 1974)

Nemerov, Howard, "The Marriage of Theseus and Hippolyta," *Kenyon Review,* XVIII (1956), 33-41

Nevo, Ruth, *Comic Transformations in Shakespeare* (London, 1980)

Summers, Joseph H., *Dreams of Love and Power: On Shakespeare's Plays* (Oxford, 1984)

Young, David P., *Something of Great Constancy: The Art of* A Midsummer Night's Dream (New Haven, 1966)

Zimbardo, R. A., "Regeneration and Reconciliation in *A Midsummer Night's Dream," Shakespeare Studies,* VI (1970), 35-50

FURTHER READING

Absher, Tom. "A Midsummer Night's Dream." In *Men and the Goddess: Feminine Archetypes in Western Literature,* pp. 85-96. Rochester, Vt.: Park Street Press, 1990.

> Argues that both *Macbeth* and *A Midsummer Night's Dream* demonstrate methods of contacting the supernatural world and "touching the web of sacred, symbolic reality."

Arthos, John. "The Spirit of the Occasion." In *Shakespeare's Use of Dream and Vision,* pp. 85-110. Totowa, N.J.: Rowman and Littlefield, 1977.

> Explores the theme of change in the play and argues that part of the play's appeal "is the fun in the proposition that humans are as helpless as the creatures in dreams."

Boehrer, Bruce Thomas. "Bestial Buggery in *A Midsummer Night's Dream.*" In *The Production of English Renaissance Culture,* edited by David Lee Miller, Sharon O'Dair, and Harold Weber, pp. 123-50. Ithaca: Cornell University Press, 1994.

> Explores the play's "symbolic coupling of human erotic desire to animal objects" within the historical context of "Elizabethan theatrical decorum."

Calderwood, James L. "*A Midsummer Night's Dream*: A Note on the Text" and "*A Midsummer Night's Dream*: The Stage History and Critical Reception." In *Harvester New Critical Introductions to Shakespeare: A Midsummer Night's Dream,* pp. xiv-xxvi. New York: Harvester Wheatsheaf, 1992.

> Offers a general introduction to the play, commenting on the differences between the quarto and folio editions, the date of composition, the sources from which Shakespeare drew, and the critical reception of the play from the mid-1600s through the twentieth century.

Faber, M. D. "Hermia's Dream: Royal Road to *A Midsummer Night's Dream.*" *Literature and Psychology* 22, No. 4 (1972): 179-90.

> Attempts to get to "essential meaning" of *A Midsummer Night's Dream* by using dream analysis to interpret Hermia's dream.

Gui, Weston A. "Bottom's Dream." *The American Imago* 9, Nos. 3 and 4 (Fall-Winter 1952): 251-305.

> Uses Freudian psychoanalysis to investigate the meaning of the play as a dream, and to uncover the aspects of Shakespeare's life which contributed to the creation of the play.

Heuscher, Julius E. "Theseus and Hippolyta on the Couch." *The American Journal of Psychoanalysis* 49, No. 4 (1989): 319-27.

> Examines the "interlacing psychological worlds" in the play, as well as the play's mythological and ancient Greek sources and themes.

Holland, Norman N. "Hermia's Dream." In *Representing Shakespeare: New Psychoanalytic Essays,* edited by Murray M. Schwartz and Coppélia Kahn, pp. 1-20. Baltimore: The Johns Hopkins University Press, 1980.

> Examines different ways of reading Hermia's dream in *A Midsummer Night's Dream,* and claims that psychoanalytic identity theory "can go beyond the earlier relationships with literature that psychoanalysis made possible."

Langley, T. R. "Shakespeare: Dream and Tempest." *The Cambridge Quarterly* XX, No. 2 (1991): 118-37.

> Compares *A Midsummer Night's Dream* and *The Tempest* within the context of Elizabethan entertainment in general and the masque in particular, a genre to which both plays allude.

Richardson, Brian. "'Time is Out of Joint': Narrative Models and the Temporality of the Drama." *Poetics Today* 8, No. 2 (1987): 299-309.

> Reviews the time schemes of the play, noting that Shakespeare presents two distinct time schemes which are "internally consistent but mutually incompatible," and argues for a new way of understanding such narrative sequences.

Slights, William W. E. "The Changeling in *A Dream.*" *Studies in English Literature 1500-1900* 28, No. 2 (Spring 1988): 259-72.

> Analyzes the role of the changeling boy in the play, stressing that at the play's end, the issue of the boy has been left, like many other aspects of the play, unresolved, and that the unpleasantness of such irresolutions are left to coexist with the marital bliss and the joys of comic theater.

The Tempest

For further information on the critical and stage history of *The Tempest,* see *SC* Volumes 8, 15, and 29.

INTRODUCTION

During the past three decades there has been a dramatic shift in critical commentary on *The Tempest.* Traditionally, critics have viewed the play as Shakespeare's somewhat melancholy farewell to his art. Such interpretations generally presented Prospero as a powerful but benevolent figure who brings about redemption and reconciliation. More recently, however, critics approaching *The Tempest* from the perspective of Marxist, feminist, or new historicist theory have seen it as a paradigm of oppression. They frequently read it as a parable of colonial expansionism in the early modern age, equating Prospero with Europeans who exploited the New World and Caliban with persecuted or enslaved Native Americans.

Throughout this change in critical reception, traditional interpretations of the play have persisted. R. A. Foakes (1971), for example, has examined the complex nature of Prospero's sovereignty of the island, proposing that his harshness toward others reflects the suffering he had earlier received at the hands of Antonio and Alonso. Although Foakes emphasizes the harmonious conclusion of the play and Prospero's restoration as Duke of Milan, he also remarks on the sense of unresolved issues that underlies the final notes of joy and restitution. Writing more than twenty years later, Philip C. McGuire (1994) has also evaluated the play's ending, particularly the significance of Antonio's silence in the final scene, and questions whether everyone who has wronged Prospero is truly repentant. Additionally, McGuire has maintained that despite the unusual degree to which the audiences' perceptions of other characters and the dramatic action is controlled by Prospero, we gradually come to realize that his representation of Caliban is not the only one we should accept.

The ambiguous nature of Caliban continues to interest commentators, all of whom regard him as a central figure in the play. In their book-length treatment of Caliban, Alden T. Vaughan and Virginia Mason Vaughan (1991) have explored the reception of Prospero's slave by actors, directors, critics, and audiences since his conception in the early seventeenth century. They conclude that he has become a cultural figure because of his vivid and enigmatic characterization, maintaining that he is particularly susceptible to variant interpretations as social currents change and different ideologies become dominant. Bryan Crockett (1991) has scrutinized Caliban in terms of the theological controversy over predestination that was current in early seventeenth-century England. He argues that while at first Caliban appears to be a model of bestial depravity, subsequently he emerges as a creature capable of seeking, and receiving, divine grace. William M. Hamlin (1994) similarly has considered the seemingly contradictory portrayal of Caliban. Arguing that Caliban's depiction owes much to Renaissance travel literature, Hamlin proposes that it reflects early ethnographers' ambivalent views of Native Americans as mysterious and alien—yet no less human than their European counterparts.

The relation between life and dreams, and reality and illusion, has also received considerable attention from critics. Marjorie B. Garber (1974) has compared the island setting itself to a dream world, remarking that all who enter its realm find it irrational and shrouded in mystery. As in dreams, she suggests, the island becomes the place where reality is transformed and truth is unveiled. John Arthos (1977) has proposed that *The Tempest* is deeply concerned with the relation between truth and paradox. In the critic's estimation, Prospero comprehends—as no other character in the play does—that human understanding is limited, and that there is a deep and impenetrable gulf between human reason and the unnameable powers that control existence. Richard P. Wheeler (1995) has also discussed the play's presentation of life as a dream. He contrasts Caliban's vision of opulence—unattainable and wholly divorced from reality—with Prospero's decision, once he comes to recognize that he cannot control every situation, to abjure his powers and retreat to a sphere where action is meaningless.

The issue of control—more specifically the question of political dominance—is the focus of many late twentieth-century readings of *The Tempest.* Francis Barker and Peter Hulme (1985), for example, have contended that the play is profoundly concerned with the structure of power relations and with various characters' attempts to subvert or overturn the hierarchy of authority. These critics perceive an implicit colonialist ideology in Prospero's justification of his authority over the island and his having wrested control of it from Caliban. They maintain that although the legitimacy of Prospero's rule is frequently questioned, the play ultimately sanctions his version of events. Michael Payne (1988) has identified a variety of political aspects in the play, including the interplay of magic and politics, the historical circumstances that provided the context for its earliest performances at court, and Shakespeare's modifications of his contemporary sources. Payne describes as "subjective magic" the means by which Prospero learns self-control, and "transitive magic" as the way he manages to influence others.

The present decade has seen a continuing critical preoccupation with the question of dominance and resistance in *The Tempest,* particularly as this may be reflected in the master-slave relationship of Prospero and Caliban. Richard Halpern (1994) has asserted that the play anticipates the merging of New World and Western cultures, the mingling of Native American and European ideologies. In the critic's judgment, *The Tempest* does not favor either colonizer or colonized; instead, it examines the nature of power structures and reveals the violence that sustains utopian projects. Howard Felperin (1995) has also recently analyzed the ideological foundations of the play. Colonial discourse is only one of many historical or political dimensions in *The Tempest,* he argues, noting that references in the play to the New World waver in purpose and content, and pointing out that they are dismissed or denied as quickly as they are raised. Much more significant, Felperin declares, is Shakespeare's representation of history as a recurring nightmare of conquest and tyranny, and his final affirmation of a collective destiny in which differences among people will become insignificant and traditional concepts of authority will be abolished.

OVERVIEWS

R. A. Foakes (essay date 1971)

SOURCE: "Shakespeare's Last Plays: *The Tempest,*" in *Shakespeare: The Dark Comedies to the Last Plays: From Satire to Celebration,* The University Press of Virginia, 1971, pp. 144-72.

[*In the excerpt below, Foakes traces the flow of the dramatic action in* The Tempest, *maintaining that Prospero's return to his rightful place in Milan is the central motivation of the play. Additionally, the critic describes the nature and limitations of Prospero's art, the corresponding visions of temporal order in the play and heavenly order in the masque, and the underlying tone of melancholy at the close.*]

Although *The Tempest* has much in common with *Cymbeline* and *The Winter's Tale,* and has often been interpreted as a kind of 'necessary development' from

them, it is also in many ways a new departure as a play. Thematic resemblances between these plays have been charted, and they have been analysed as different versions of the same basic 'myth';[1] but however they may be linked in these ways, *The Tempest* has its own distinctive structure, sets up its own peculiar pattern of expectations, and demands to be assessed as a unique work of art in its own right. Some of the more obvious peculiarities of this play would seem at first sight to set it apart from the others. Instead of an inscrutable providence manifesting itself from time to time in oracles, miracles, or appearances of gods, this play has in Prospero a controller who exercises through his magic a power like that of heaven. Certain oppositions in it, such as those between beauty and ugliness, or nurture (education) and nature (brutishness) seem so schematically rendered, as in the contrasts between Caliban and Miranda, as to allow an allegorical interpretation.[2] The extensive use of masque and spectacle has also encouraged a treatment of the whole play as based on masque.[3] At the same time, *The Tempest* is the only one among the late plays that observes the neo-classical unities of time and place. All these features in themselves suggest that Shakespeare was moving in a new direction in this play, a view confirmed by an examination of its dramatic shaping.

At the beginning of I.ii, Miranda confirms our impression of what we have witnessed in the opening scene, a shipwreck in which all, boat and crew alike, were lost; she suffered with those she saw suffer, watched the ship 'Dash'd all to pieces' (l. 8), and is convinced the people on it died, 'Poor souls, they perish'd!' (l. 9). She is amazed (l. 14), but accepts what has happened, supposing her father may have raised the storm by his art, but not that he has caused the wreck. In fact she and we quickly learn that he has ordered the shipwreck, but:

> I have with such provision in mine Art
> So safely ordered, that there is no soul—
> No, not so much perdition as an hair
> Betid to any creature in the vessel
> Which thou heard'st cry, which thou saw'st sink.

(I.ii.28)

What we saw happened, and yet did not happen; Prospero's art is so powerful that with his 'provision' or foresight (supposing this word to be a correct emendation of the Folio reading 'compassion'), he can destroy and save simultaneously.[4] He has, through the agency of Ariel, dispersed the crew in groups about the island, and the ship, as we learn when the boatswain returns in V.i. is undamaged. If what he has done on one level is to deceive by a trick or illusion, some vanity of his art, on another level what he has done is real, as it controls the actions of people, and shapes the course of events.

At the same time Prospero's art is limited, and in narrating to Miranda the history of Antonio's usurpation of Milan, and of the way in which she and her father were left to drift at sea in a 'rotten carcass of a butt' (l. 146), Prospero also indicates something of what the nature and limits of his art are. For one thing, his magic powers seem to have been acquired since he and Miranda arrived on Setebos, for he was unable to foresee or prevent Antonio and Sebastian depriving him of his dukedom, and counter their treachery. Moreover, these powers are in some sense a function of the island, and only operate in its vicinity. Their development has to do with the books which Gonzalo provided for Prospero, 'volumes that I prize above my dukedom' (l. 167), and with the latter's 'secret studies' (l. 77) when he was in Milan; their nature perhaps is connected with that neglect of wordly ends for the bettering of his mind Prospero speaks of, with the sense we have of his goodness. Human treachery drove him from Milan, and he was saved, he tells Miranda, 'By Providence divine' (l. 159); now a strange chance has brought his enemies to the island:

> By accident most strange, bountiful Fortune,
> (Now my dear lady) hath mine enemies
> Brought to this shore; and by my prescience
> I find my zenith doth depend upon
> A most auspicious star, whose influence
> If now I court not, but omit, my fortunes
> Will ever after droop.
>
> (I.ii.178)

Fortune, once hostile to him, brought about his fall, but is now his 'dear lady', and he must seize the opportunity she offers. So Prospero's powers are circumscribed, dependent geographically on the island, and operating in relation to providence on the one hand, and fortune on the other.

The zenith or highest point of Prospero's fortunes will in any case be to recover what he has lost, and reinstate himself as:

> the Duke of Milan, and
> A prince of power.
>
> (I.ii.54)

His magical art or power subserves another end, that of regaining his temporal or princely power; and it is with this in mind that he has educated Miranda carefully as a princess (l. 172). Indeed, he has made himself ruler of the strange island, and by his magic art has made Ariel and Caliban his servants, or rather, to use his own word, his slaves. Ariel had been imprisoned within a cloven pine by the witch Sycorax until Prospero released him; he had been 'her servant' and has now become Prospero's, earning his eventual liberty through service. Prospero requires absolute obedience, and no complaint:

> If thóu more murmur'st, I will rend an oak
> And peg thee in his knotty entrails, till
> Thou hast howl'd away twelve winters.
>
> (I.ii.294)

The threatened punishment coincides exactly in nature and length of time with that inflicted on Ariel by Sycorax, which was, as Prospero describes it, 'a torment To lay upon the damn'd' (l. 289). So although Ariel and Prospero respect each other as 'great master' (l. 189), and 'Fine apparition! My quaint Ariel' (l. 317), their relationship is basically that of slave and master. Prospero's other slave, Caliban, serves him and Miranda in the most menial offices, and is despised by Miranda as a 'villain', and by Prospero as a 'poisonous slave' (ll. 309, 319); he is imprisoned in a 'hard rock' (l. 343) by his own and Miranda's account, hates his service and his master and mistress, and for the slightest sign of unwillingness in carrying out commands, he is racked with horrible pains and tortures. Miranda tried to educate him, and taught him language as Prospero had taught her, but the purposes of his brutish nature could only seem vile to her, as he would not take 'any print of goodness' (l. 352); his imprisonment and slavery are apparently punishments for his 'wickedness' in seeking to rape Miranda. The standards Prospero applies are those of Milan, of his own civilization, and Caliban's version of what has happened raises some questions about the validity of those standards on the isle. For Prospero is himself in some sense a usurper, as he has taken the island from Caliban, who in the first place 'educated' him by showing him 'all the qualities o'th'isle' (l. 337), and who now can lament with some reason;

> I am all the subjects that you have,
> Which first was mine own king,
>
> (I.ii.341)

After the shipwreck of the opening scene, Prospero's first exercise of his art is to use Ariel to lure Ferdinand to the presence of Miranda. At the first glance they see one another as 'thing divine' (l. 418) and 'goddess' (l. 421), but know themselves for man and woman too, and duly fall in love, as Prospero desires; how far his art has effected this is not clear, but for them to be in love is to put them 'both in either's powers' (l. 450). Ferdinand has entered half in grief, and weeping the King his father's death, and half in self-congratulation, as now he can say, 'myself am Naples' (l. 434); but here he is in Prospero's kingdom, and in his power, as, like Jupiter 'crossing' Posthumus in *Cymbeline,* Prospero makes Ferdinand suffer:

> thou dost here usurp
> The name thou ow'st not; and hast put thyself
> Upon this island as a spy, to win it
> From me, the lord on't.

Ferdinand   No, as I am a man.
Miranda There's nothing ill can dwell in
   such a temple:
If the ill spirit have so fair a house,
Good things will strive to dwell with't.
Prospero   Follow me.
Speak not you for him: he's a traitor. Come;
I'll manacle thy neck and feet together. . . .

              (I.ii.453)

Prospero imposes on Ferdinand tasks fit for a slave, and, in the same sense that it applied earlier to Caliban, 'imprisons' him; this is designed as a kind of test, or rather, education in self-rule, and the presence of Miranda makes confinement easy; so Ferdinand cries:

      all corners else o'th'earth
Let liberty make use of; space enough
Have I in such a prison.

              (I.ii.491)

At the same time, we witness a display of power by Ferdinand's 'enemy' (l. 466), Prospero, who speaks as if he were King indeed, twice using the word 'traitor', which rings somewhat oddly on the island; it is also in its way an exercise of tyranny, and the 'punishment' Ferdinand has to endure corresponds exactly to that inflicted upon Caliban, who had attempted to violate Miranda. In II.ii Caliban enters carrying wood, and meets Trinculo and Stephano, whose wine makes him drunk, frees him from Prospero's impositions, and enables him to escape to the forbidden parts of the island. Ferdinand in effect takes the place of Caliban, and the following scene (III.i) opens with him 'bearing a log'.

Prospero rules as King, and uses his magic arts to order his kingdom somewhat as if it were still Milan, as when he uses a term like 'traitor'. He has in some sense usurped upon Caliban's island, and imprisoned him; but in another perspective, Prospero himself has seen his own kingdom usurped, and is himself 'imprisoned' on an uncivilized island. Here what Prospero has learned by the necessary exercise of patience and self-rule will emerge in the course of the play, as will the way the harshness he imposes matches the harshness he has suffered. He is also a father carefully arranging an appropriate marriage for his daughter, but delighted, too, to find that she and Ferdinand at once fall in love—delighted and at the same time angry:

Miranda   Sir, have pity;
I'll be his surety.
Prospero   Silence! one word more
Shall make me chide thee, if not hate thee.
   What!
An advocate for an impostor!

              (I.ii.475)

Prospero says he must make their courtship difficult, 'lest too light winning Make the prize light' (l. 451), but they do not know this, and to them he is simply cross-grained and harsh. He becomes temporarily, and in a minor perspective, a father-figure out of conventional romantic comedy, opposing his daughter's wishes, because the fulfilment of her desires will end parental control over her. The lovers are now in the power of each other, and through this gain a kind of freedom, just as Caliban gains a different kind of freedom when drunk. So in III.i, Miranda, watching Ferdinand bearing logs, promises to be his 'servant' (l. 85), even as he accepts the 'bondage' of love to become her 'slave':

The very instant that I saw you, did
My heart fly to your service; there resides,
To make me slave to it; and for your sake
Am I this patient log-man.

              (III.i.64)

Prospero may impose bodily labour on Ferdinand, but the power of love is greater than Prospero's in the sense that it transmutes menial slavery into service to Miranda, and makes Ferdinand's labours into pleasures.

Meanwhile, Alonso, cast up on the island with his little 'court' remains inconsolable in the conviction that his son and heir, Ferdinand, has drowned. The good Gonzalo likewise wrongly assumes that Ferdinand is dead, and, in his attempts to comfort the King, gets his facts wrong about the location of Tunis, and proposes such a self-contradictory idea of a commonwealth that he lays himself open to the mockery of Sebastian and Antonio. In all this he 'talks nothing' (II.i.164) to Alonso to encourage 'merry fooling' (l. 168) and relieve the mood of the King. Gonzalo's image of the ideal commonwealth he would establish if he could colonize the isle and 'were the King on't' (l. 139) may in some sense be a critique of the primitivism of the essay of Montaigne on which it is largely based, but in any case it has an immediate and potent relevance to the action of the play. His ideal commonwealth would have no laws, no magistrates, no contracts, no inheritance, no letters, no labour and no treason or crime:

No occupation; all men idle, all;
And women too, but innocent and pure:
No sovereignty. . . .

              (II.i.148)

It would be a return to a prelapsarian Eden, with Nature bringing forth of itself all necessities, but an Eden filled with his 'innocent people' (l. 158); and yet Gonzalo would be king:

I would with such perfection govern, sir,
T'excel the Golden Age.

              (II.i.161)

A people of such innocence would not need to be governed, but a king might well wish to have a state such as Gonzalo imagines. Gonzalo talked 'nothing', but something at the same time, for the idea of a perfect commonwealth underlies all rule, and the idea of paradisial innocence and the golden age provides a point of reference by which civilization demands to be measured.[5]

Sebastian and Antonio mock Gonzalo, and have no conception of innocence, but can think of his 'subjects' only as idle 'whores and knaves' (l. 160), and when Ariel enters playing the solemn music which, though not heard by them, puts Alonso, Gonzalo and the rest to sleep, at once Antonio's 'strong imagination' (l. 199) works to propose another image of rule. It is just that as Antonio has driven out Prospero and made himself Duke of Milan, so may Sebastian get rid of his brother Alonso and seize the kingdom of Naples. Sebastian sees himself as King for a moment before Ariel comes to wake Gonzalo and prevent murder:

> as thou got'st Milan,
> I'll come by Naples. Draw thy sword: one
> stroke
> Shall free thee from the tribute which thou
> payest;
> And I the King shall love thee.
>
> (II.i.282)

Rule for them lies in the mere possession of power, not in the quality of the man who rules, and in their barbarity they are worse than Stephano and Caliban, whose plot against Prospero is conceived in drink rather than in cold blood. The next scene shows us these characters. Caliban enters with a load of wood and cursing his master and tormentor who sets his spirits on him to plague him 'for every trifle' (l. 8). He has seen no other human beings besides Prospero and Miranda, and it is natural for him to take Trinculo and Stephano for spirits, just as it is natural for them to regard Caliban as 'some monster of the isle' (l. 62). When Trinculo creeps under Caliban's gaberdine to hide from the storm, they make together a four-legged monster with two mouths which becomes very funny as Stephano converses with both voices at once. The re-appearance of Trinculo, pulled forth by Stephano, serves to emphasize how much less of a 'monster' Caliban himself is. Caliban is described in the list of actors given in the Folio text as 'a salvage and deformed slave', and he has links with Indian savages and cannibals, and with the wild man of European folklore, embodied in drama in such a figure as Bremo of *Mucedorus;* he has been well described in terms developing these basic dimensions:[6]

> His origins and character are natural in the sense that they do not partake of grace, civility and art; he is ugly in body, associated with an evil natural magic, and unqualified for rule or nurture. He exists at the simplest level of sensual pain and pleasure, fit for lechery because love is beyond his nature, and a natural slave of demons. He hears music with pleasure, as music can appeal to the beast who lacks reason; and indeed he resembles Aristotle's bestial man.

However, there is more to Caliban as we see him in the action of the play. He not only hears music, but makes it, and his natural medium, it seems, is verse of some distinction, as against the prose of Trinculo and Stephano; also, like the others, he has a sense of the role he might play in the body politic. Prospero is a 'tyrant' (l. 152) to him, and he is glad to change his master, when the new spirits or men he now meets offer him liquor that is not earthly, and through that a vision of freedom. Stephano and Trinculo assume the King is dead, and determine to be rulers of the island, 'we will inherit here' (l. 163), even as Caliban swears allegiance, 'I'll kiss thy foot; I'll swear myself thy subject' (l. 142).

In this posture of humility before the drunken butler Stephano, Caliban appears ridiculous to Trinculo, who cries, 'I shall laugh myself to death at this puppy-headed monster' (l. 144); but however absurd and comic he may be here, Caliban retains a kind of superiority over his companions. He knows the qualities of the isle, and without him they would be lost; he has a poetic response to it, and where Trinculo sees a 'most ridiculous monster' (l. 155), we see Caliban vividly and imaginatively reacting to his natural environment as Trinculo never could, and promising to

> Show thee a jay's nest, and instruct thee how
> To snare the nimble marmoset; I'll bring thee
> To clustering filberts, and sometimes I'll get
> thee
> Young scamels from the rock.
>
> (II.ii.159)

The adjectives 'nimble' and 'clustering' reveal his appreciation of what he has seen. There is something visionary too about Caliban's feeling for freedom, even if he is mistaken in supposing that it will lie in serving Stephano. To him Prospero is the tyrant who robbed him of the island, made use of him, sought to impose his own values and morality on him, and when he rebelled, made him a prisoner and a slave, and any escape from this would be freedom. Prospero taught him language, but Caliban's use of it is his own, and the surprising thing about this is the extent to which Caliban's language matches that of Prospero; Caliban's curses against Prospero are as rich and inventive as Prospero's invective and threats against him in I.ii, and his poetry is every bit as good as that of his master. While, then, we may think of Caliban as in some sense inhuman, and find evidence to support a view of him as almost a beast, as representing the irreducible element of bestiality in human nature,[7] the son of a witch, and, in Prospero's words:

> Thou poisonous slave, got by the devil himself
> Upon thy wicked dam,
>
> (I.ii.319)

it is not merely this Caliban we are involved with in the action. On the stage we see in the one figure both a brute and a human being (played by an actor like other actors, however disguised), who speaks fine and sophisticated verse, itself a product of both nurture, in his command of language, and nature, in the sensibility he reveals. At first when Prospero made much of him, Caliban 'lov'd' the newcomer to the island, and served Prospero by educating him in 'all the qualities o'th'isle' (I.ii.337); so now in offering to do the same for Stephano, Caliban, kissing the foot of the new master, is expressing, in his kind, his 'love', and this new service seems at first to be perfect freedom.

So the presentation of Caliban here has links with the treatment of Ferdinand in the next scene, who gains a freedom in yielding to the bondage of love, and kneels or makes obeisance of some kind in sign of his service to Miranda ('And I thus humble ever', III.i.87). The analogy continues, however, into the next scene (III.ii), where we find Stephano's 'kingdom' in a state of discord, as he quarrels with Trinculo over Caliban:

> Trinculo, keep a good tongue in your head: if you prove a mutineer,—the next tree! The poor monster's my subject, and he shall not suffer indignity.
>
> (III.ii.34)

Here, too, we learn that 'freedom' means to Caliban 'revenge' (l. 51) on Prospero for getting the isle by 'sorcery' from him, as he kneels again to Stephano to present his suit, and begs him to kill the 'tyrant'. Caliban's service to his new master is to offer him the opportunity of braining Prospero, and also to 'give' him that nonpareil of beauty Miranda, whom Caliban had wished to possess for himself; and the vision is irresistible for Stephano, 'I will kill this man: his daughter and I will be king and queen—save our graces!— and Trinculo and thyself shall be viceroys' (l. 102). The mood of this scene is different from that of II.ii, as the brutishness of the plot to kill Prospero emerges, and especially in Caliban's images of the deed;

> with a log
> Batter his skull, or paunch him with a stake,
> Or cut his wezand with thy knife.
>
> (III.ii.84)

Yet Caliban retains a kind of superiority over his companions, even in the fuddle of drink which besets them; he makes the scene comic, and takes a good deal of the

sting out of their scheming; for his aim is freedom, theirs merely to seize power and rule, and he speaks verse which expresses his sense of beauty and of harmony, while their apprehension is bound by prose.

By this point in the play the drift of the action is settled. Prospero himself has happily witnessed the interchange of vows of love between Ferdinand and Miranda. His spirit Ariel has intervened at Prospero's behest as Sebastian and Antonio were about to murder Alonso and Gonzalo, so that we know these are under supervision. Now Ariel intervenes again, but apparently of his own accord, to promote the quarrel between Stephano and Trinculo, and to lead them astray as they follow his music offstage; here he may, in his capacity as fairy, be 'thwarting the unchaste', as fairies were supposed to 'abhor unchastity',[8] and again he is thwarting a plot of murder. Before the final unravelling and reconciliations of Act V, there now follow two scenes (III.iii and IV.i) in which the focus is on elements corresponding to anti-masque and masque. The play has already provided a sense of spectacle, notably in the opening shipwreck scene, in the way Prospero charms Ferdinand, and as Ariel, 'invisible' to other characters, may control or guide their actions. The island, too, is full of music, the sweet and strange airs of Ariel, whose songs and 'solemn music' suggest order in their power to put men to sleep or wake them, to charm or compel them to follow where the music leads; there are also the drunken songs of Stephano and Caliban, whose 'howling' (II.ii.167) sets up by contrast a discord, and yet, as it is music, both mitigates our sense of their brutishness, and represents the contribution they can make to that quality of the island best appreciated by Caliban:

> the isle is full of noises,
> Sounds and sweet airs, that give delight, and hurt not.
> Sometimes a thousand twangling instruments
> Will hum about mine ears; and sometimes voices,
> That, if I then had wak'd after long sleep,
> Will make me sleep again: and then, in dreaming,
> The clouds methought would open, and show riches
> Ready to drop upon me; that, when I wak'd,
> I cried to dream again.
>
> (III.ii.130)

These harmonious sounds of music and voices seem to bring him pleasant dreams and visions, to raise him out of his ordinary existence, even if the scope of his visions is limited to the display of riches about to drop on him.

All this prepares for what in this play is equivalent to a crisis in the action, namely the masque of III.iii to

IV.i. In the first of these scenes, Alonso and his com-panions, with Sebastian and Antonio, weary and frus-trated in their search for Ferdinand, and still supposing him drowned, pause to rest; and Antonio and Sebastian think they have a chance to carry out their plot to mur-der the King and Gonzalo. At this point they see a vi-sion and we see a masque, as, with Prospero placed 'on the top' as a regal spectator, and ultimate creator of what follows, various 'strange shapes' bring in a ban-quet to 'solemn and strange music'. Gonzalo thinks of these as 'people of the island', and in their 'monstrous shape' (1. 31) they perhaps look like cousins of Caliban, but gentle servants, made in the image of what Prospero would have liked Caliban to be. As Alonso plucks up his courage and makes as if to eat, Ariel, as presenter of the masque, enters 'like a Harpy' in thunder and light-ning to clap his monstrous bird's wings upon the table and make it vanish. A harpy as a wind-spirit, and as servant of the Erinyes or avenging Furies is a very ap-propriate figure for Ariel to take at this point; in his speech addressed to Alonso, Sebastian and Antonio, the 'three men of sin' (1. 53), he speaks to them from within the masque, claiming that he and his fellows are 'min-isters of Fate' (1. 61), servants of Destiny, agents of 'The powers' (1. 73). At the same time he speaks to us both as harpy and as Ariel, Prospero's agent, skilfully carrying out his master's instructions, and receiving his congratulations as the business is completed. As the 'shapes' first entered in a dance, so now they return in a dance to carry out the table, and Ariel 'vanishes in thunder'. The men of sin, afflicted with a sense of guilt by the strange vision that demanded of them

> nothing but heart-sorrow
> And a clear life ensuing,
>
> (III.iii.81)

show their affliction in 'desperate' behaviour (1. 104); they had drawn their swords when Ariel appeared as a harpy, but were charmed from using them; now, after the vision ends, they run into strange antics, and rush offstage, Alonso in thoughts of drowning, and Sebastian and Antonio fighting imaginary fiends. So the scene ends in disorder and grotesque actions. The whole may be seen as a kind of elaborate anti-masque, in which the monstrous shapes that vanish with grimaces and mocking actions, the harpy, and the disordered rushing about of the men of sin at the end, constitute a driving out of evil, which is to be followed in IV.i by the masque proper.

The punishment Prospero inflicted on Ferdinand turns out to have been but a trial of his love, a kind of symbolic task; by completing it successfully he proves himself fit to marry Miranda, and 'earns' her. As Prospero showed earlier that he had never relinquished his place as ruler of his state by treating Ferdinand as a 'traitor', so now he gives him his daughter within the framework of full social and religious ceremonies:

> If thou dost break her virgin-knot before
> All sanctimonious ceremonies may
> With full and holy rite be minister'd,
> No sweet aspersion shall the heavens let fall . . .
>
> (IV.i.15)

The emphasis on virginity here is often noted, and it is of course important as relating to the moral discipline of the individual, and to the opposition between Miranda's chastity and Caliban's unrestrained lechery; but what is equally important is Prospero's insistence on 'sanctimo-nious ceremonies', for where is the priest to perform these rites? The normal social, political and religious order of society is assumed in the way Prospero talks. In this context, he bestows on the lovers a vanity of his art in the form of a masque, which, in terms of what a court-masque signifies, has the effect of giving the be-trothal a full social sanction, and announcing it publicly.

In fact the masque does more than this. I do not know of any extant masque of this period that is a betrothal masque, though several wedding masques survive, like those for the marriage of Princess Elizabeth in 1613, or Ben Jonson's masque for Lord Harrington's mar-riage in 1608, or the masque in Beaumont and Fletcher's *The Maid's Tragedy* for the marriage of Amintor and Evadne. The masque in these instances provided a public ceremonious congratulation on the occasion of the union, and although it could, in *The Maid's Trag-edy,* be skilfully distorted to foreshadow the darkness and disaster that were to follow in the action of that play, it could also, and especially in the lofty vein of Ben Jonson's conceptions, go far beyond compliment and decorative splendour. In his most sophisticated masques, the expulsion of evil or darkness is followed by a blaze of virtue and light suggesting something beyond happiness or pleasure, and becoming an em-blem of order and harmony passing into a hint of uni-versal order and harmony. The dances which formed a central feature of the masque could be very important in this, as is shown by the commentary of the presenter Daedalus, the legendary artist and inventor of the laby-rinth of Minos, in *Pleasure Reconciled to Virtue* (1618):

> Then as all actions of mankind
>   Are but a labyrinth or maze,
> So let your dances be entwined,
>   Yet not perplex men unto gaze;
> But measured, and so numerous too,
> As men may read each act you do,
> And when they see the graces meet,
> Admire the wisdom of your feet;
>   For dancing is an exercise
> Not only shows the mover's wit,
>   But maketh the beholder wise,
> As he hath power to rise to it.

The dance exhibits through the 'wisdom' of the danc-ers' feet a pattern in what appears to be a maze, and the beholder who can understand this may be made wise, as he sees an image of order in the intricacies of movement, suggesting that all human actions, though inexplicable and bewildering to us, make a pattern in a larger scheme of order, the cosmic dance, the order of providence. In making Daedalus interpret the dance here in this way, Jonson was exploiting in a sophisticated and complex way a familiar Renaissance analogy, as exemplified in *Orchestra* (?1596), addressed by Sir John Davies to Queen Elizabeth:

> Dancing, bright lady, then began to be,
>   When the first seeds whereof the world did spring,
> The fire, air, earth, and water did agree
>   By love's persuasion, nature's mighty king,
> To leave their first discorded combating,
>   And in a dance such measure to observe,
>   As all the world their motion should preserve.
>
> Since when they still are carried in a round,
>   And changing come one in another's place;
> Yet do they neither mingle nor confound,
>   But every one doth keep the bounded space
> Wherein the dance doth bid it turn or trace.
>   This wondrous miracle did Love devise,
>   For dancing is love's proper exercise.

Dancing as the exercise of love signifies the divine harmony controlling the spheres, the planets in their movements, and all nature. Dancing as 'measure' or order, signifying matrimony, as at the end of so many of Shakespeare's comedies, carries in it hints of a greater harmony or order, that of the heavens.

What Prospero introduces as 'Some vanity of mine Art' (1. 41) would have meant much more than this to audiences at the Globe or Blackfriars. After the grotesque shows and dances of III.iii, ending in the confused rushing about of Alonso, Sebastian and Antonio, there follows now the harmonious masque proper, with Ariel again as presenter, playing, as I take it, the part of Iris. This seems the best interpretation of his phrase at 1. 167, 'when I presented Ceres'; and even without this comment, a link between the Harpy of III.iii and Iris might have been suspected. For, according to Hesiod, Iris was the sister of the Harpies, and as Ariel appeared in III.iii with a woman's face and a bird's wings and talons, or, as Shakespeare phrased a simile in *Pericles:*[9]

> like the harpy,
> Which, to betray, dost with thine angel's face
> Seize with thine eagle's talons,
>
> (IV.iii.46)

so now in Iris the same angelic face is seen, but Ariel is dressed to suggest the goddess of the rainbow. Iris,

messenger of the gods, and, as rainbow, a link between heaven and earth, summons Ceres, presented here as goddess of harvest and of earth, to attend on Juno, queen of heaven, and like Ceres, a mother-goddess. Their business is first to make sure that Venus and Cupid are at a safe distance, so that no wantonness or lust may attend on the proceedings, and then to 'celebrate A contract of true love' (1. 133). The two goddesses, who are shown as sisters (1. 103), join in song to bless Ferdinand and Miranda, and their song is, in effect, a marriage song:

> *Juno* Honour, riches, marriage blessing,
> Long continuance, and increasing,
> Hourly joys be still upon you!
> Juno sings her blessings on you.
> *Ceres* Earth's increase, foison plenty,
> Barns and garners never empty;
> Vines with clust'ring bunches growing;
> Plants with goodly burthen bowing. . . .
> Ceres' blessing so is on you.
>
> (IV.i.106)

This blessing seems to be the 'donation' (1. 85) they bestow on the lovers, a promise of honour, riches, and fruitfulness. So although the young couple have vowed

> that no bed-right shall be paid
> Till Hymen's torch be lighted,
>
> (IV.i.96)

the masque becomes implicitly a marriage-masque, and as such is indeed, as Ferdinand calls it, a 'most majestic vision' (1. 118).

Juno and Ceres then call on Iris to summon a group of 'temperate nymphs' (1. 132) to join with a group of reapers or 'sunburn'd sicklemen' (1. 134) in a graceful dance linking the Naiads of the water, cool and fresh, with the hot harvesters, weary with August; the union of these perhaps symbolizes the state of marriage, and certainly as a harvest dance their performance is more appropriate to a wedding than a betrothal. At this point Prospero interrupts the masque, and the spirits vanish in a 'strange, hollow, and confused noise'; the stage direction calls for him to intervene 'towards the end' of the dance, and 'interrupts' is perhaps the wrong word to describe his action, for the masque is in fact complete. The 'anti-masque' of the monstrous shapes and men of sin in III.iii gives way to a harmonious vision looking forward to prosperity, honour and a blessed life for Ferdinand and Miranda; it offers them congratulation, compliment, and closes with a dance of reapers and nymphs, symbolizing the union of ripeness with temperance in marriage. It is so compelling as a vision that Prospero loses himself in it, and forgets the 'foul conspiracy' of Caliban and his companions, so that the 'confused noise' and discords heard at the end of the masque represent the troubled mind of Prospero, and do not reflect on the masque except to show again that it is in one sense a projection of Prospero's mind or 'art'. On another level we share the lovers' acceptance of it as a splendid vision, harmonious and wise; and we see it also as a real masque enacted by performers on a stage.

It is true that one element of the conventional masque, that final stage in which the masquers 'take out' spectators into the dance and make them participants, is lacking here. Ferdinand and Miranda are kept at a distance from it as onlookers, so that they will see it as a vision acted out by spirits raised by Prospero's art. This is how Prospero himself speaks of it too, notably in his famous speech to Ferdinand:

> Our revels now are ended. These our actors,
> As I foretold you, were all spirits, and
> Are melted into air, into thin air:
> And, like the baseless fabric of this vision,
> The cloud-capp'd towers, the gorgeous
>   palaces,
> The solemn temples, the great globe itself,
> Yea, all which it inherit, shall dissolve,
> And, like this insubstantial pageant faded,
> Leave not a rack behind. We are such stuff
> As dreams are made on; and our little life
> Is rounded with a sleep.
>
> (IV.i.148)

There has been much discussion of this speech as a comment in particular on masques, and in general on human life and the mutability of all things; but if in one perspective life itself appears no more than an 'insubstantial pageant' like the masque, a fleeting vision or dream, in another perspective the pageant is most substantial, and reflects a view of life as rich and significant. For this vision or masque is itself an imaginative achievement of a high order, combining visual spectacle, poetry, music and dance in an art-form which emerges out of centuries of civilization and concern for the flowering of the human spirit. Moreover, the descent of Juno as queen of heaven constitutes a theophany in the play corresponding in some measure with the theophanies in *Cymbeline* (the descent of Jupiter), and in *The Winter's Tale* (the coming to life of the statue-goddess in the figure of Hermione). In this sense, the masque relates to an order outside Prospero, and beyond his control, a heavenly order. The masque belongs in a scheme of social and cosmic order to which Prospero himself subscribes, as is shown by his determination that the wedding of the lovers shall be celebrated with 'full and holy rite', in his ratifying his gift of Miranda to Ferdinand 'afore Heaven' (l. 7), and in his concern throughout to restore himself to his rightful place as Duke of Milan. As vision and performance the masque passes and melts into air, but as theophany and as a masque full of substance seen by the audience, it

contradicts the notion of human insignificance in Prospero's phrase, 'our little life Is rounded with a sleep'.

In his admiration of the vision Prospero has his spirits enact, and of his prospective father-in-law as magician, artist, poet, choreographer and producer, Ferdinand cries:

> Let me live here ever;
> So rare a wonder'd father and a wise
> Makes this place Paradise.
>
> (IV.i.122)

The vision renews the image of Ferdinand and Miranda as first man and first woman, or Adam and Eve figures, recalling her first thought of him as a 'thing divine', and his sense of her as 'goddess' (I.ii.418, 421). Human beings cannot remain for ever in paradise, or in what the masque of Juno and Ceres hints at, the golden world of pastoral; these belong to visions, dreams, poetical 'fancies', to use Prospero's word (l. 122). Ferdinand has already had to endure a temporary loss of 'paradise' in the hard labour of log-bearing, and must return again to the workaday world. So Caliban's vision of Stephano as a 'brave god' (II.ii.109), and Gonzalo's fancy of an ideal commonwealth, dissolve and leave not a rack behind. Yet the visions and dreams are real, if transitory, and work, as by analogy the whole play, Shakespeare's 'vision', does, to open vistas on higher possibilities and orderings of human life. At the same time, they link with the masque-like elements in the play and come to a focus in the great masque of IV.i to insist on the artifice of the incredible fiction which composes the play's action. But paradoxically, this masque, as theophany, in the substance of what it says, and by its social function, both affirms an order in the heavens beyond Prospero's art, and firmly returns us to the social order, as it looks to a future of riches and honour for the young couple, and to the formal celebration of the marriage-rites it, so to speak, assumes in advance. It thus reinforces what is the primary drive in the play, the return of Prospero to his proper place in Milan, as he has been waiting for the day when it would be possible for this most civilized of Shakespeare's characters to recover his role in the civilization to which he belongs.[10]

The confused noise at the end of the masque marks Prospero's recollection of his role as 'king' of the island, and the need to take action against the 'foul conspiracy' of Caliban and his companions; the harmony of the vision or masque gives way to a display of passion by Prospero, whom Miranda has never seen so 'touch'd with anger' (l. 145). The large perspective from which 'our little life' appears no more than a dream is replaced by the immediate view of practical life, with its urgencies, passions, and its important moral and social meanings. Prospero becomes again 'compos'd of harshness', as Ferdinand saw him in III.i, when he puts down the rebellion of Stephano. Caliban discovers what fools his companions are, to be diverted from their plot by the 'trumpery' hung up on show by Ariel; a wardrobe fit for a king becomes more important to them than the kingdom itself, and Caliban's remonstrance is turned aside by Stephano with the threat, 'help to bear this away . . . or I'll turn you out of my kingdom' (l. 249). At this point Prospero and Ariel enter like hunters to set a pack of 'Spirits, in shape of dogs and hounds' upon them, two of them bearing the names 'Fury' and 'Tyrant'. The hounds embody the wrath of Prospero, and something like vindictiveness, as he congratulates himself on having all his 'enemies' at his mercy, and summons goblins to torture Stephano, Trinculo and Caliban, and 'grind their joints With dry convulsions' (l. 257).

Now, at the beginning of Act V, Ariel reports on the King, Alonso, and his followers, and by a nice touch prompts Prospero to mercy:

> Your charm so strongly works 'em
> That if you now beheld them, your affections
> Would become tender.
>
> (V.i.17)

Prospero accepts the hint, and, while admitting to 'fury', the word echoing the name of the hound in the previous scene, he renounces his anger:

> Though with their high wrongs I am struck to
>   th'quick,
> Yet with my nobler reason 'gainst my fury
> Do I take part: the rarer action is
> In virtue than in vengeance.
>
> (V.i.25)

Here 'pardon' would be the obvious word, rather than 'virtue',[11] which, however, is much stronger, as implying his desire to make his conduct conform to moral laws, and indirectly invoking a Christian sanction for his action. The climax has arrived, the moment when Prospero can renounce too his magic, and reclaim his place in society. He has another great speech here, matching in poignancy and resonance his dismissal of the masque, with the lines beginning 'Our revels now are ended'; both speeches express a kind of farewell, and both are moving, with their mood of regret and resignation, nostalgia for pleasures that have passed, and acceptance of what must be. They are, however, very different in kind; the first speech marks the end of a majestic vision which embodies the highest imaginative working of Prospero's magic art, even if it is in one aspect a mere show or 'vanity'; the second speech follows on from the display of another sort of magic, in which Prospero hunts his enemies with spirits in the shape of hounds. It is based on the incantation of the witch Medea in Ovid's *Metamorphoses,* and although it has been argued that 'only those elements which are

consistent with "white" magic are taken over for Prospero',[12] this is to make a dubious, and from the point of view of an audience watching the play, oversubtle distinction. For the speech shows Prospero excited by, and almost boasting about, feats of 'rough magic' such as we have not seen him perform:

> I have bedimm'd
> The noontide sun, call'd forth the mutinous
>   winds,
> And 'twixt the green sea and the azur'd vault
> Set roaring war: to the dread rattling thunder
> Have I given fire, and rifted Jove's stout oak
> With his own bolt; the strong-bas'd
>   promontory
> Have I made shake, and by the spurs pluck'd
>   up
> The pine and cedar: graves at my command
> Have wak'd their sleepers, op'd, and let 'em
>   forth
> By my so potent Art. But this rough magic
> I here abjure. . . .
>
> (V.i.41)

We have seen him create a storm and shipwreck, but only for the special purpose of distributing the boat's crew and passengers about the isle, and we have seen Prospero use his powers to confine, hunt, and torment his 'slaves' and 'enemies'; but here, for the first time, we learn of his delight in using his magic for its own sake, to disturb the natural order, and make discord and destruction in ways traditionally associated with witchcraft. So, for example, his power over the 'mutinous winds', to make them serve him, was commonly attributed to witches, and is made much of in *Macbeth,* where the First Witch proposes to punish a sailor by using winds to toss his boat with tempests, and where Macbeth later tries to compel the Witches to answer him, crying:

> Though you untie the winds, and let them
>   fight
> Against the churches; though the yesty waves
> Confound and swallow navigation up. . . .
>
> (IV.i.52)

His words sufficiently anticipate Prospero's lines to indicate how far the latter moves towards traditional claims for witchcraft in a speech which ends with the most sinister statement of all, that he has brought back the dead from the grave, a feat for which Dr Faustus was well known.

At this point in the play Shakespeare seems to emphasize Prospero's connection with black magic deliberately, as indeed there can have been no graves on the isle for him to open. Prospero has the mantle and staff proper to the magician; he has forced Ariel, in return for a promise of his freedom, to bind himself as his servant for a specific length of time (I.ii.245); and we have seen him in anger use his magic to cruel effect. At the same time, we have the overriding sense of Prospero as a practiser of white magic, and of his major effort to restore order and harmony. This seeming contradiction is resolved in the distinction between magic and the magician; in other words, *The Tempest* does not offer a sharp clash between black magic and white magic, but offers rather a sense of magic as an art at best neutral, and perhaps dubious in its common use, but available to good or bad ends, depending on the user. Prospero is sometimes seen as a neo-Platonic mage, 'whose Art is to achieve supremacy over the natural world by holy magic', and who renounces his 'rough magic' as a stage in his enlightenment and ascension to the 'First Cause', in the phrase of Cornelius Agrippa.[13] In fact, Agrippa, whose book on *Occult Philosophy* provides an apologia for white magic, was popularly known as a black magician, and probably gave his name to Cornelius, one of the advisers of Doctor Faustus in Marlowe's play, in which the hero looks forward to becoming:

> as cunning as Agrippa was,
> Whose shadows made all Europe honour him.
>   (I.i.116)

The allusion is to Agrippa's supposed ability to summon up the dead, a power which Prospero also claims to possess. All magic tends to look like black magic, and *The Tempest* shows Prospero's passionate and difficult endeavour to control his art by controlling himself. The art itself is the same in kind as that practised by the witch Sycorax, a point made effectively early in the play, when Prospero, having told us how he released Ariel from the twelve years' imprisonment in a cloven pine inflicted on him by Sycorax, goes on almost immediately to threaten his 'brave spirit' with a corresponding punishment:

> If thou more murmur'st, I will rend an oak,
> And peg thee in his knotty entrails, till
> Thou hast howl'd away twelve winters.
>   (I.ii.294)

The difference lies in the way the art is used, and Prospero's is higher and more potent than that of Sycorax because the orders he gives to his ministers are proper for a spirit

> too delicate
> To act her earthy and abhorr'd commands.
>   (I.ii.272)

The harmonious vision of the masque, the finest product of Prospero's magic art, ends in a blaze of intense emotion for him, as he recalls Caliban, and is reminded that the ideal, the dream, is no more than a dream, denied by the very existence of brute forces exemplified in this 'born devil' and his murderous plot. Prospero's farewell now to his 'rough magic' ends, by contrast, with the sound of 'heavenly music', as Ariel brings Alonso and his companions into a magic circle. As one ends with a reminder of the need to control Caliban, so the other ends with the return of Ariel, and Prospero recalling his obligation to set free his 'dainty' spirit. Even as Ariel helps Prospero to put on his ducal clothes, and show himself as he 'was sometime Milan' (V.i.85), in the full acceptance of his social role and its obligations, Ariel sings his song of freedom, 'Where the bee sucks, there suck I', and Prospero cries:

> Why, that's my dainty Ariel! I shall miss thee;
> But yet thou shalt have freedom.
>   (V.i.95)

Here Ariel seems to be associated with those fancies Prospero could give rein to on the island, as in the vision of the masque, but which, as ruler of Milan, he must henceforth curb; so Ariel is liberated to live merrily in a world of flowers. Ariel is, of course, more than this, as he is a 'familiar', bound by a pact to serve Prospero in a relationship that has in it elements of black magic. Ariel in this aspect is essentially independent of Prospero and of human beings, as a spirit or fairy, a 'tricksy spirit', at times mischievous, and able to work for good or evil. In bidding farewell to his 'rough magic', Prospero is renouncing a power which has given him pleasure, and which could serve black ends. It is appropriate that this speech, with its mood of regret combined with a sense of willing abjuration, should lead directly into the final resolution of the action, and the recovery for Prospero of his full role in society.

Ariel carries out his last tasks, to bring Alonso and the courtiers into the presence of Prospero, then the crew of the ship, and finally Caliban, Stephano and Trinculo. As Alonso and his companions 'stand charm'd' in a magic circle, Prospero changes his costume, removing his magician's robe:

> I will discase me, and myself present
> As I was sometime Milan
>   (V.i.85)

At this point Prospero assumes royal authority again, as the group on stage suggests a tableau of his court, an image he realizes in dialogue a little later, as the courtiers emerge from their initial 'wonder and amazement', and he welcomes Alonso:

> Welcome, sir;
> This cell's my court: here have I few
>   attendants,
> And subjects none abroad.
>   (V.i.165)

Wonder is to be renewed and strengthened, as more is revealed; first, Alonso experiences another 'vision of the island' (l. 176), his first thought being that he is seeing another illusion, like the 'shapes' of III.iii, when Prospero 'discovers' Ferdinand and Miranda playing chess. It is the more wonderful that this really is his son Alonso sees, and a girl he cannot but think for a moment is a 'goddess' (l. 187), just as Miranda, seeing the group of courtiers for the first time, exclaims 'O wonder!' There is more to come, as the Boatswain and crew enter 'amazedly following' Ariel, and Alonso cries:

> These are not natural events; they strengthen
> From strange to stranger.
>
> (V.i.227)

Finally, Caliban, Stephano and Trinculo are driven in, to modify the image of a brave new world seen by Miranda, and perhaps by Alonso, as both Stephano and Trinculo are reeling in drink, and more bestial than Caliban, who realizes now what a fool he has been 'to take this drunkard for a god, And worship this dull fool!' (l. 296).

It is tempting to take Gonzalo's words as a general comment on this scene, and indeed, as some would have it, on the play:

>   O, rejoice
> Beyond a common joy! and set it down
> With gold on lasting pillars: in one voyage
> Did Claribel her husband find at Tunis,
> And Ferdinand, her brother, found a wife,
> Where he himself was lost, Prospero his
>   dukedom
> In a poor isle, and all of us ourselves
> Where no man was his own.
>
> (V.i.206)

Earlier, in II.i, his sense of the island as 'lush and lusty' (II.i.49) had led him to develop his vision of the ideal commonwealth, a new golden age, on it, even as Sebastian and Antonio mocked him, seeing the island as uninhabitable desert and rotten fen; and now, as then, Gonzalo's sentiments are noble, but his vision a partial one. Not only does Antonio remain silent throughout this scene, as if aloof and unchanged, not sharing in repentance or wonder, but also there is little sign that Sebastian has found himself, while the last episode brings on Stephano and Trinculo lost in drink, and Caliban. Alonso must 'know and own' his drunken servants, even as Prospero accepts responsibility for Caliban:

>   Two of these fellows you
> Must know and own; this thing of darkness I
> Acknowledge mine.
>
> (V.i.274)

Caliban becomes, momentarily, part of Prospero, an emblem of the evil subdued in himself, but also, in a larger sense, is seen, with his drunken companions, to be part of the body politic, and presumably is to return with Prospero to Milan; and however Caliban may hope to 'be wise hereafter, And seek for grace' (l. 294), there seems to be no expectation of a change in him by Prospero, whose last words about him are to call him 'demi-devil' and 'thing of darkness'.

Gonzalo describes well enough what one might call the nominal resolution of the action in accordance with the experience of many of the characters, as they have moved from shipwreck, loss and disharmony, to recovery, joy, and harmony. The drive of Prospero to recover rule in himself and in his dukedom has shaped the play, and is now fulfilled. On a deeper level the ending is less simple and comfortable than Gonzalo's image of it, and underneath the joy and restoration of the last scene, the force of the paradoxes established by the play remains held in suspension. Only by exile from Milan, from civilization, does Prospero learn how to rule, by being somehow refreshed and restored by the new world of a primitive island, on which he may be seen as regaining 'access to sources of vitality and truth'.[14] There, in what may be seen as a desert wilderness or a kind of Arcadia, if one accepts the view of either Sebastian or Gonzalo in II.i, and which in fact contains both, Prospero tames nature by his art, establishes what civilization he can, and learns the uses of power. His contact with Arcadia and the possibility of an ideal commonwealth as envisaged by Gonzalo, his return to nature, only serves to teach him the necessity of rule. The innocent native of the desert Arcadia proves to be the brutish Caliban, in whom man's sensual impulses have free range; and if a return to Arcadia can restore the image of the golden age to the good, but somewhat naïve, old Gonzalo, and growing up there can give Miranda a fresh and golden image of the first men she sees:

> How beauteous mankind is! O brave new
>   world,
> That has such people in't!
>
> (V.i.183)

At the same time it serves to remind Prospero of the beast in man too, that the thing of darkness is his, and only through the struggles to achieve inward rule has he succeeded in establishing outward order. As Caliban discovers that service to Prospero ('I'll be wise hereafter, And seek for grace') is more like freedom than liberty as the subject of Stephano, so Ferdinand and Miranda learn to renounce their freedom in the voluntary bondage of love, a paradox emblematized as Prospero discovers them playing chess, a game at which the sexes meet as equals, and which had been often allegorized in terms of the courtship of two lovers making their moves in turn, and also in terms of life itself, as the chessmen 'stand for the different ranks and occupations of men'.[15] The game in which they may, as Miranda puts it, wrangle 'for a score of kingdoms', is serious as it ends in mate; their love-play bears on their relation to come as husband and wife, and as prince and princess, rulers of men.

At the centre of the play the masque of IV.i serves as a focus for these paradoxes. The masque in a sense realizes as a vision Gonzalo's idea of the golden age, in the image of Ceres and Juno together offering a prospect of perpetual natural plenty, and echoing Spenser's Garden of Adonis:

> Spring come to you at the farthest
> In the very end of harvest!
>
> (IV.i.114)

> There is continuall spring, and harvest there
> Continuall, both meeting at one time. . . .
> (*The Faerie Queene*, III.vi.42)

However, this is not Gonzalo's primitive world of innocence, a sort of Eden where society might begin over again in a new setting of unspoiled nature, but rather the end-product of an age-old civilization, embodied in the highest imaginative reach of Prospero's art.[16] The masque is a court entertainment, of a stylized and highly structured kind, which contains the vision of innocence within a pattern involving tradition, myth, history, and social obligation; the pastoral scene itself is no longer primitive, but cultivated with

> rich leas
> Of wheat, rye, barley, vetches, oats and pease,
> (IV.i.61)

and the whole masque is designed to celebrate a contract of true love in betrothal pointing to marriage. It is the most sophisticated version of pastoral in the late plays, and though only a 'vanity', an 'insubstantial pageant', it is as substantial and 'real' as the 'reality' of the world of Naples and Milan to which the play returns us at the end. It is the vision, like the other wonders and games contrived by art, that gives that social and political world its bearings, enables it to understand the relation between nature and civilization, and illustrates the necessity and nature of rule; and finally, it images the moral and religious sanctions necessary for society.

The marriage of Ferdinand to Miranda, and the return to Milan, will complete all that Prospero aimed to do; the drive that has sustained him is exhausted. His art is no longer necessary, and the emotional power of his farewell to it is bound up with the larger farewell to the island, and, in a sense, to his life. All the years on the island were a preparation for a return to Milan, and for the proper restoration of his daughter to her

place in society, and these things achieved, Prospero has made his masterpiece, and the rest is preparation for death; so he says that in Milan:

> Every third thought shall be my grave.
>
> (V.i.311)

The epilogue wittily continues this image, as he comes to beg the favour of the audience:

> Now I want
> Spirits to enforce, Art to enchant;
> And my ending is despair,
> Unless I be reliev'd by prayer.

His 'ending' is the death of the magician, conventionally dying, like Faustus, in despair, unless his prayers can save him and win the indulgence of the audience. This perhaps confirms that final paradox for Prospero, that the success of his art in completing all his desires is also the completion of his life, in the sense that it leaves him nothing more to live for; which accounts for the sense of melancholy that many people carry away from what is superficially a joyful ending.[17]

Notes

[1] See, for example, G. Wilson Knight, *The Shakespearian Tempest* (1932), and *The Crown of Life* (1947); also D. A. Traversi, *Shakespeare; The Last Phase* (1954), and Frank Kermode's discussion of critical attitudes to the play in his Introduction to the New Arden edition (1958), pp. lxxxiv-lxxxv.

[2] On the question of allegory in relation to the play, see A. D. Nuttall, *Two Concepts of Allegory* (1967). *The Tempest* is also sometimes treated as if it were to be properly regarded less as play than as poem; so Reuben Brower calls it 'a Metaphysical poem of metamorphosis' in his essay, 'The Mirror of Analogy', included in his book, *The Fields of Light* (1951), and reprinted in *Shakespeare; 'The Tempest'*, edited D. J. Palmer (1968), pp. 153-75.

[3] See Enid Welsford's *The Court Masque* (1927), pp. 336-49; the climax of the play for her lay in the discovery of Ferdinand and Miranda playing chess, and she wrote, 'the spirit of *The Tempest* is far nearer to the spirit of masque than is *Comus*' (p. 340).

[4] For other instances of Prospero's ability to foresee what is to happen, see I.ii.180 and II.i.288.

[5] This is elaborated in Leo Marx's brilliant account of the play as 'Shakespeare's American Fable', in *The Machine in the Garden* (1964), pp. 34-72.

[6] Frank Kermode, in his Introduction to *The Tempest*, p. xlii.

[7] See the complex and subtle discussion of Caliban by Kermode, pp. xxiv-xxv and pp. xxxviii-xliii; he sees the extent to which Caliban serves as an 'inverted pastoral hero, against whom civility and the Art which improves Nature may be measured', but still regards him too much in terms of ideas, and not enough in terms of the actor playing the part.

[8] Kermode, *op. cit.*, p. 144. The account he gives of Elizabethan ideas of fairies is based, as he acknowledges, on M. W. Latham's *The Elizabethan Fairies* (1930).

[9] The parallel with *Pericles* is cited in Kermode, *op. cit.*, p. 89n.

[10] Many commentaries on *The Tempest* ignore the masque of Ceres, or regard it as of little consequence. I have come across two accounts of the play which see it as of central importance structurally; one is by R. J. Nelson, *Play Within a Play* (1958), pp. 30-5, who sees the mood of *The Tempest* as shifting 'from the comic to the tragic or something akin to it' after the masque; the other is the fine analysis of the masque and its links with pastoral by Leo Marx in *The Machine in the Garden*, pp. 61-5, to which I am indebted.

[11] A point noted by Kermode, p. 114.

[12] Kermode, *op. cit.*, p. 149.

[13] See Kermode, *op. cit.*, pp. xl-xli.

[14] Leo Marx *op. cit.*, p. 69.

[15] H. J. R. Murray, *A History of Chess* (1913). p. 533; see also pp. 435-7.

[16] Leo Marx, *op. cit.*, p. 62, sees the setting as 'an idealized version of Old England'.

[17] David Grene in *Reality and the Heroic Pattern* (1967) registers especially sharply his feeling that 'a play which is an uninterrupted story of success for its chief actor leaves one with the prevailing sense of melancholy and failure' (p. 100). I do not share his view, but his essay deserves attention as a sensitive reading of the play.

Philip C. McGuire (essay date 1994)

SOURCE: "*The Tempest*: 'Something Rich and Strange'," in *Shakespeare: The Jacobean Plays*, St. Martin's Press, 1994, pp. 175-97.

[*In the following essay, McGuire emphasizes the essentially theatrical nature of* The Tempest, *and suggests possible interpretations of the text—especially of Antonio's silence at the end—that can be represented on stage but might not be apprehended by readers. He also points out unique or distinctive qualities of the work which include the unconventional deception of the audience, concern with the New World, observance of Neoclassical unities of time and place, and a heterogeneous mixture of sources.*]

No Shakespearean play uses music more extensively than *The Tempest,* widely regarded for more than one hundred and fifty years now as the final play Shakespeare wrote singlehandedly even though, as Stephen Orgel notes, there is no way to determine 'chronological priority' between it and *The Winter's Tale* (1987, p. 63). The second of nine songs in *The Tempest* tells of changes being worked upon the body of Ferdinand's father, drowned, he is certain, in the shipwreck he himself has just survived:

> *Full fadom five thy father lies;*
> *Of his bones are coral made;*
> *Those are pearls that were his eyes:*
> *Nothing of him that doth fade,*
> *But doth suffer a sea-change*
> *Into something rich and strange.*
>
> (I.ii.399-404)

The song itself—sung by Ariel—is 'something rich and strange'. On the one hand, it is a lie; Ariel knows that Ferdinand's father is not dead. On the other, it is the play's most compelling articulation of the profoundly transformative process—equivalent to a 'sea-change'—through which characters pass as their sense of the past, their visions of others and of themselves, and their personal and political relationships are radically reshaped.

The song is part of a play that is itself not only 'rich' but also 'strange' in the sense of being different from the other plays called Shakespeare's. That strangeness makes itself felt in various ways, including a decidedly atypical opening moment. Unlike the vast majority of Shakespearean plays, *The Tempest* begins (like *Macbeth*) with a stage effect: '*A tempestuous noise of thunder and lightning heard*'. Audiences take that '*noise*' as evidence of a ferocious storm raging within the fictional realm of the play. That they do is fully consistent with perhaps the most basic of the conventions—the network of assumptions, habits, and practices agreed upon by audience, players, and playwright—without which no theatrical performance can occur: that audiences accept what they know full well to be theatrical illusions as actual events within the world of the play. As audiences continue to look and listen, they behold a ship caught in that storm break apart, exposing all on board to watery deaths.

In the next scene *The Tempest*, taking the kind of risk that *The Winter's Tale*, the Shakespearean play written closest in time to it, delays until the final moments, makes its audiences aware that they have been deceived.

That awareness does not come in a manner—via a soliloquy by Prospero, for example, or a chorus—that preserves their customary privileged position by giving them knowledge withheld from other characters. As they see and hear Prospero comforting Miranda, distraught at the shipwreck she, too, has witnessed, her perspective as a character within the theatrical fiction and theirs as spectators of that fiction converge. Deceived like Miranda by what they have just seen and heard, they become, in effect, Prospero's daughters, learning in tandem with her, as virtual equals, that the tempest has harmed no one. 'The direful spectacle of the wrack,' Prospero says,

> I have with such provision in mine Art
> So safely ordered that there is no soul—
> No not so much perdition as an hair
> Betid to any creature in the vessel
> Which thou heard'st cry, which thou saw'st
>   sink.

> (I.ii.26-32)

Even the ship that broke apart, audiences soon hear Ariel report, is intact, 'safely in harbour', the mariners themselves out of peril and asleep, 'all under hatches stow'd' (I.ii.226, 230).

The storm with which *The Tempest* opens is not the only one in a Shakespearean play. There are storms in *Othello, King Lear,* and *Macbeth,* to name but three. What makes the storm in *The Tempest* 'strange' is that it is the only one controlled by a character within the play. Nor is the shipwreck that the storm (seemingly) causes the only one in a Shakespearean play. Storms destroy ships in *Twelfth Night,* one of Shakespeare's Elizabethan comedies, and in *Pericles* and *The Winter's Tale,* both written closer in time to *The Tempest.* None of those shipwrecks is enacted onstage, however. The (seeming) shipwreck in *The Tempest* is, strangely, the only one that Shakespeare ever calls upon the King's Men to take the theatrical risk of actually staging. Even more strangely, it is also the only one that proves to be an illusion *within* the fictional world of the play.

During the opening two scenes, the illusions of storm and shipwreck generated by playwright and players while performing *The Tempest* merge with those generated by Prospero. Although deprived twelve years earlier of his office as Duke of Milan by his younger brother Antonio and Alonso, the King of Naples, Prospero possesses magical powers that give him control and thus *de facto* authority over all who are on or even near the island, including Antonio and Alonso, that is far greater than that exercised by any other Shakespearean character. Working with and through Ariel, Prospero not only raises a storm but also induces sleep, inflicts pain, compels manual labour, imposes paralysis, and conjures visions that confound as well as enchant. What is most extraordinary about Prospero is the degree to which he exercises authority over not only his fellow characters but also the audiences of *The Tempest.* To an extent unmatched by any other Shakespearean character, he has the power to determine what audiences see and hear, and he is frequently taken as Shakespeare's self-portrait, the character through whom he most directly expresses his own feelings.[1]

The characters who survive what they think is a shipwreck find themselves on an unfamiliar island, in a landscape all the stranger because Prospero's 'art' enables him to determine what they hear and see. *The Tempest* places its audiences in a theatrical situation that is analogously unfamiliar, strange—one in which the convention that enables what audiences know are theatrical illusions to function as signs of actualities within the dramatic fiction is no longer a reliable frame of reference. One measure of the deception generated by the merging of theatrical illusion and Prosperian magic is that were 'the direful spectacle' of the opening scene an actual shipwreck within the dramatic fiction, nothing in the opening scene would be different.

The Tempest is also 'strange' by virtue of being the only Shakespearean play set in a place associated with the New World. The island over which Prospero rules and on which the survivors of what they think is the destruction of the ship carrying them from Tunis to Naples find themselves is situated somewhere in the Mediterranean, yet it is endowed with New World qualities. In fashioning *The Tempest,* Shakespeare drew upon accounts of what happened in 1609 to the *Sea-Adventure,* a ship bearing the governor of Virginia to Jamestown as part of a fleet carrying several hundred colonists. In late July a hurricane off the coast of Virginia separated the *Sea-Adventure* from the rest of the fleet, eventually driving it aground in what Ariel refers to as 'the still-vexed Bermoothes' (I.ii.229). Those on board spent the winter there, then set out again for Jamestown, arriving safely in May of 1610—to the astonishment of their fellow colonists who were certain they had perished. Gonzalo's extended description of the utopian 'commonwealth' he would establish 'Had I plantation of this isle' (II.i.143, 139) comes virtually verbatim from Montaigne's essay 'Of the Cannibals', widely available in England from 1603 on in John Florio's translation. The name Caliban is an anagram of 'cannibals', the term, not yet associated with the eating of human flesh, that Montaigne used for the natives of the New World. Set on and near a Mediterranean island endowed, strangely, with New World qualities, *The Tempest* stands apart as the Shakespearean play that most directly registers, responds to, and thus helps to determine the impact of the project of trans-Atlantic colonisation on which England embarked in the final decades of Elizabeth's reign. During the first decade of James's, which saw the establishment of the Virginia Company in 1606 and the founding of Jamestown in 1607, it pursued that project with renewed vigour.

Caliban challenges Prospero's right to rule the island, basing his claim on inheritance and prior possession. 'This island's mine,' he insists during his first appearance in the play, 'by Sycorax my mother, / Which thou tak'st from me' (I.ii.333-4). 'I am all the subjects that you have,' he tells Prospero, 'Which first was mine own King' (I.ii.343-4). Soon after, Caliban willingly accepts the drunken Stephano as his new master and king and, subsequently chastened by that experience, he tells Prospero as the play closes, 'I'll be wise hereafter, / And seek for grace' (V.i.294-5). Caliban's early words challenging Prospero have acquired a distinctive resonance during the post-Second World War era, which has seen the breakup of the vast empires that Britain, France and other European countries had acquired in Asia, Africa, and the Caribbean. So compelling is that resonance—so expressive of the displaced and oppressed—that it is not uncommon these days for directors and commentators to regard *The Tempest* as an examination of colonialism.

The presence of Caliban also contributes to the strangeness of *The Tempest* in another way—by virtue of his being a character for whom there is no Shakespearean precedent. Moments before audiences first see him, Prospero calls him 'Thou earth' (I.ii.316) and he is, in many respects, the antithesis of Ariel, whom the First Folio describes as an 'airy spirit' in the 'Names of the Actors' provided at the end of the play. Caliban's presence poses a challenge—beyond that found in any other Shakespearean play—to the capacity, of audiences and characters alike, to distinguish between two categories central to all cultures: the human and the non-human. Taking advantage of the process of performance, *The Tempest* poses that challenge in specifically theatrical terms by setting what audiences and characters see on first encountering Caliban against what they hear.

Of the Europeans who think themselves shipwrecked, the first to encounter Caliban is Trinculo, who sees him before hearing him make any sounds. What he sees is so 'strange' that he takes him to be something other than human. 'What have we here?' he asks, eyeing, sniffing, and perhaps even nudging the creature lying silent before him, 'a man or a fish? dead or alive?' (II.ii.24-5). 'A fish,' he concludes, 'A strange fish' (II.ii.25, 27-8). When Trinculo, seeking shelter against the storm that is 'come again', creeps under the creature's 'gaberdine' (II.ii.38-9), the human and what he regards as the inhuman merge, and when Stephano, the second shipwrecked European to encounter Caliban, enters moments later, he sees a four-legged creature. Like Stephano, he takes it to be something non-human, a 'monster of the isle' (II.ii.66). When that 'monster' utters sounds that he recognises as his own language, Stephano finds himself confronting a paradox. 'Where the devil,' he asks, 'should he learn our language?' (II.ii.67-8). For the Elizabethan-Jacobean era, the capacity to speak was the most direct manifestation of

the rationality that sets humankind apart from and above the lower orders of creation, among them the fish. The words coming from Caliban's mouth force Stephano and Trinculo to face the presence of some element of the human within the non-human, in the monstrous and fish-like.

In contrast to Trinculo and Stephano, who see Caliban before they hear him speak, audiences hear Caliban speak before they see him. His first appearance in the play is orchestrated so that audiences find themselves called upon to face the non-human in a being they initially take to be human. When Prospero calls, 'What, ho! slave! Caliban! / Thou earth, thou! speak', audiences hear a voice answer from *'within'*, from offstage or even understage: 'There's wood enough within' (I.ii.315-16). Hearing that voice speaking 'our language', they assume the humanity of the unseen speaker. Prospero then orders Caliban to enter: 'Come forth, I say! . . . Come, thou tortoise! when?' (I.ii.317-18). At that point, a stage direction calls for the entrance of a figure that looks *'like a water-nymph'* (I.ii.318) and proves to be Ariel, not Caliban. The timing of Ariel's entrance not only delays the audience's first sight of Caliban but also provides a contrast with what they behold when they do see him.

The play further delays the audience's first sight of Caliban by having Prospero confer with Ariel: 'Hark in thine ear' (I.ii.320). For readers, the conference lasts no longer than it takes to read 'Hark in thine ear' and move on to Ariel's obedient reply, 'My lord, it shall be done' (I.ii.320). In performance, however, the conference need not be virtually instantaneous, and the longer it lasts, the longer audiences must wait to see the recalcitrant Caliban, whose entrance Prospero, after Ariel's exit, again commands: 'Thou poisonous slave, got by the devil himself / Upon thy wicked dam, come forth!' (I.ii.321-2). This time Caliban obeys, and audiences at last see him. What they see is a character whom the First Folio, in the 'Names of the Actors', describes as 'a salvage [savage] and deformed slave'.

Earlier, the sound of an unseen Caliban speaking 'our language' had prompted them to assume that he is human. Now, his entrance into their field of vision, delayed so as to increase its impact, challenges them to reconcile their sense of what is human with their sight of a figure so non-human in appearance—so 'deformed'—that Trinculo and Stephano, seeing it, take it to be a fish or, to use the term by which they repeatedly address Caliban throughout the play, a 'monster'. Caliban is the Other, the embodiment of that awareness of difference against which, and thus in inescapable relationship to which, one knows one's own identity as an individual and as a member of various social and cultural groupings. To the extent that Caliban's presence prompts audiences to re-conceive and re-work their sense of what is human and extend it to include facets of Caliban, if not Caliban himself, it also prompts them to reconsider their sense of themselves. In so doing, they enter into a complex affiliation with Caliban—involving simultaneous recognition of likeness and difference—akin to that voiced by Prospero, who near the end of *The Tempest* says of Caliban: 'this thing of darkness I / Acknowledge mine' (V.i.275-6). Prospero may be stating that Caliban is his slave or a member of his party rather than Alonso's, but his words also attest to and accept the existence of a bond between them that includes some element of responsibility on his part for what and even who 'this thing of darkness' is. His word for Caliban is 'thing', a term that does not emphasise whatever human qualities Caliban possesses. Prospero explicitly grants freedom to Ariel—'[T]hen to the elements / Be free, and fare thou well' (V.i.317-18)—but Caliban's fate, after he obediently and without delay departs to 'trim' Prospero's cell 'handsomely' (V.i.293), is left disturbingly vague. It is not clear from the playtext whether Caliban goes to Milan with Prospero or remains on the island. Beerbohm Tree's 1904 production responded to that vagueness by showing Caliban, after Prospero's epilogue, alone and gazing mournfully out to sea after the departing ship, towards which he stretches out his arms. In Jonathan Miller's 1988 production at the Old Vic, on the other hand, Caliban found himself facing, after Prospero's withdrawal from the island, not loneliness but the prospect of a new subordination, this time to Ariel, who, having fitted together the parts of the magical staff Prospero had broken, began using it to establish dominance over all who remained on the island.

The wealth flowing into England from the colonies in the New world accelerated the extremely complex process of social change already under way as part of England's movement into the early modern era. On first encountering Caliban, both Trinculo and Stephano see an opportunity to earn riches out of keeping with their social places in the world beyond the island. Calculating Caliban's value as a 'monster' that speaks 'our language', Stephano says, 'If I can recover [cure] him, and keep him tame, and get to Naples with him, he's a present for any emperor that ever trod on neat's-leather' (II.ii.69-72). He does not, however, anticipate making a present of Caliban should he get him back to Naples. Instead, responsive to the financial opportunities of the emerging marketplace economy, he foresees making a profit by selling him, declaring that no price will be too high: 'I will not take too much for him; he shall pay for him that hath him and that soundly' (II.ii.78-80).

Moments before, Trinculo, gazing on Caliban for the first time, had also envisaged the wealth that would be his 'Were I in England now, as once I was, and had but this fish painted, not a holiday-fool there but would give a piece of silver' (II.ii.28-30). 'There,' he adds,

thinking about the fortune he could make, 'would this monster make a man; any strange beast there makes a man' (II.ii.30-1).[2] Stephano's vision of charging admission to see Caliban glances at, and almost parodies, what occurred each time the King's Men performed *The Tempest* at Blackfriars or the Globe: audiences paid to see one of those Men 'make' a 'strange beast' named Caliban by playing him. By (dis)playing Caliban on two of Jacobean London's commercial stages, the King's Men appropriated the practice of bringing natives back to England, thereby tapping into the wealth flowing from the New World and diverting some of it into their own pockets.

Still another way in which *The Tempest* is 'strange' is that it departs from Shakespeare's standard compositional practices. In composing the vast majority of his plays across the full span of his career, he typically worked from, with, and on one, occasionally two, major sources, sometimes preserving, sometimes altering, sometimes even—as in *King Lear* and *The Winter's Tale*—inverting what he found there. In fashioning *The Tempest* for performance by the King's Men, however, Shakespeare abandoned that practice. It is his only Jacobean play—and one of but three[3] among the thirty-seven generally attributed to him—for which no major source has been identified.

For *The Tempest,* Shakespeare, instead of working extensively with one or two sources, combined a farrago of writings, some contemporary, some classical. Elements from accounts of what happened in the New World to those aboard *The Sea-Adventure* co-exist with echoes of Virgil's *Aeneid,* most prominently the discussion of Dido (II.i.73-97). The combination associates the voyage from Tunis to Italy that Alonso and his court are making when the opening storm (seemingly) destroys their ship, with both a specific voyage to the New World in the recent past and the voyage that Aeneas, abandoning Dido in Carthage, undertook at some point in the far-distant epic past. That voyage led to the founding of Rome, with whose first emperor, Caesar Augustus, James was often compared in order to distinguish his style of rule from Elizabeth's.[4] The founding of Rome in turn led to the founding of Britain by Brutus, Aeneas's grandson, and James saw, in the sovereignty he exercised over England, Wales, and Scotland, an opportunity to re-establish Britain's primeval unity. Gonzalo's 'commonwealth' speech (II.i.139-64) comes from Montaigne's 'Of the Cannibals', and, in a borrowing from Ovid's *Metamorphoses* that blurs the distinction between Prospero and Sycorax, 'white' and 'black' magic, Shakespeare lifts from the sorceress Medea's incantation of the powers she commands much of the long speech (V.i.33-57) in which Prospero describes the scope of his 'so potent Art'.

The change in Shakespeare's compositional practices is related to *The Tempest*'s associations with the New

World. One impact of the discovery and colonisation of the New World was a change in the conception and construction of authority in European cultures.[5] In the Middle Ages, authority flowed from the ability of thinkers and writers to make events meaningful by placing them in a context provided by the books that formed the basis for the systems of knowledge by which people of that epoch made sense of their world: the Bible in theology and the writings of Ptolemy in astronomy, Constantine in medicine, Boethius in arithmetic, Cicero in rhetoric, Aristole in dialectic, and the ancient poets in grammar. What could not be explained in terms sanctioned by those authoritative books was not acknowledged as having any reality. The engagement with the New World shattered that conception and construction of authority by bringing Europeans into contact with utterly new systems of realities—peoples, languages, artifacts, laws, customs, plants, animals—of which those books made no mention and which in some cases could not even be named, let alone comprehended, using the terms they provided. To speak about what lay in the New World required making up new words or borrowing words from the natives—required, that is to say, changing what Ferdinand, encountering Miranda for the first time, proprietarily calls 'my language' (I.ii.431) and what Stephano, encountering Caliban for the first time, calls 'our language' (II.ii.68). To English, the language of *The Tempest,* the New World contributed such words as *canoe, hurricane,* and *skunk,* and Caliban's list of the delicacies he will provide for Trinculo and Stephano includes 'young scamels' (II.ii.172), a word whose precise meaning remains unknown to this day.

The gap between what was found in the New World on the one hand and in the authoritative books of the Old World on the other spurred the development of a novel and competing conception of authority based not on the capacity to apply traditional cultural precedents but on the capacity to represent what was new, different, other, 'strange', by assembling, fabricating—from whatever diverse elements are at hand—a framework within which the events presented take on cultural coherence and meaning. The mixture of writings, contemporary as well as classical, upon which *The Tempest* draws is an example of such fabrication, and by endowing a Mediterranean island with New World qualities and placing on it a creature such as Caliban, the King's Men and their playwright claimed for themselves and for the recently emergent institution that was commercial theatre the authority to represent that which was radically new.

. . . . .

The Tempest is also 'strange' because, at least partly in response to the challenge such representation poses, it arises from and incorporates the equivalent of 'a sea-change' in the handling of dramatic place and time

typical of the other plays Shakespeare provided for the Lord Chamberlain's-King's Men over the course of an association that, at the time *The Tempest* was most likely written—late 1610 or early 1611—had lasted more than sixteen years. In 1595, the year after Shakespeare helped to found the Lord Chamberlain's Men and became that company's attached playwright, Sir Philip Sidney's *Defence of Poesy,* written in the early 1580s, was posthumously published. It includes a forceful critique of contemporary plays for 'being faulty both in place and time, the two necessary companions of all corporal actions':

> For where the stage should always represent but one place, and the uttermost time presupposed in it should be, both by Aristotle's precept and common reason, but one day, there is both many days and many places inartificially [i.e., unartfully] imagined.
>
> (1965, p. 134)

By Sidney's standards, every play but one that Shakespeare provided for the Lord Chamberlain's-King's Men from 1594 on is glaringly 'faulty'. The single exception is *The Tempest.* With all action situated on an island and its adjacent waters, it comes close to observing unity of place, and it conforms to the unity of time by concentrating events within a single day, the hours between sometime after two in the afternoon and six in the evening specified in the following exchange:

> PROSPERO: What is the time o'th'day?
> ARIEL: Past the mid season.
> PROSPERO: At least two glasses. The time 'twixt six and now
> Must by us both be spent most preciously.
>
> (I.ii.239-41)

The Tempest comes closer than any other Shakespearean play to observing the strictest form of unity of time, in which the span of time covered during the play corresponds exactly to the length of time needed to perform it.

That 'sea-change' in the treatment of dramatic time and place is all the more 'strange' if one considers the three plays that, like *The Tempest,* are associated with the closing phase of Shakespeare's career and are included with it in the grouping known variously as his 'last' plays, 'late' plays, 'romances', and 'tragicomedies'.[6] None of them shows any concern with conforming to Sidney's dictum that 'the stage should always represent but one place'. Quite the opposite. They disregard it, sometimes flamboyantly. *Pericles* takes place in half a dozen cities along the coast of the eastern Mediterranean Sea; *Cymbeline* places scenes in Italy and various parts of Britain, including Wales; *The Winter's Tale* opens in Sicily, shifts to a succession of sites in Bohemia, and for the final act returns to Sicily.

Sidney also scorns plays that, failing to confine themselves to the events of a single day, are 'liberal' with time:

> For ordinary it is that two young princes fall in love; after many traverses she is got with child, delivered of a fair boy; he is lost, groweth a man, falleth in love, and is ready to get another child, and all this in two hours' space.

(1965, p. 134)

Pericles is 'liberal' in almost exactly that way. Pericles meets Thasia early in the second act, and at the start of the third she dies giving birth to their daughter Marina, who, before the play ends, has grown into a young woman of wondrous beauty and virtue. *The Winter's Tale* is also 'liberal' with time. Perdita, with whom her mother is pregnant at the start of the play, appears onstage as an infant in Act III, and by the beginning of Act IV, she is sixteen years of age and ready for marriage.

In subjecting to 'a sea-change' a dramaturgical practice that had shaped his work for some sixteen years, Shakespeare may have been acting upon the willingness to take 'extraordinary risks' that David Daniell says is common in the 'last works' of 'a very great artist' (1986, p. 119). In addition, there may have been an imitative, perhaps even competitive factor: the desire to match, if not surpass, the example of Ben Jonson's dazzling use of the unities of time and place in *The Alchemist,* which the King's Men performed in 1610. The handling of place and time in *The Tempest* may also be evidence of the lengths to which Shakespeare was willing to go—and capable of going—to help the King's Men cope with the problems. . . that from 1609 on performing at both the Globe and Blackfriars posed. Such factors are not mutually exclusive, and they interact with pressures arising from the concern, unique to *The Tempest,* with the New World. The compositional technique of the play involves weaving together elements from a potpourri of diverse sources rather than—in accord with the traditional conception of authority—applying or adapting one or two sources. As if in compensation for cutting loose from the kind of authority provided by the use of specific sources, Shakespeare, for the only time during his long association with the Lord Chamberlain's-King's Men, shapes a play that conforms to the unity of time and comes close to observing the unity of place. By thus breaking with his own long-established practice, Shakespeare in effect endows *The Tempest* with the authority of Sidney and Aristotle.

The attention to the unities of place and time that makes *The Tempest* 'strange' in the sense of different from every other play Shakespeare wrote during his association with the Lord Chamberlain's-King's Men is the basis for still another kind of strangeness: its similarity to *The Comedy of Errors,* most likely written in 1590, well before the formation of that acting company in 1594. *The Comedy of Errors* is the only other Shakespearean play that is not by Sidney's criteria 'faulty both in place and time'. The similar treatment of dramatic time and place in *The Tempest* and *The Comedy of Errors* establishes a strange symmetry between what has long been regarded as the final play Shakespeare wrote singlehandedly and what is almost certainly his first comedy and possibly even his first play of any kind. 'In the New World,' Stephen Orgel observes, 'Europe could see its own past, itself in embryo' (1987, p. 35). In writing, towards the end of his career, the play of his that most directly engages the Old World's experience of the New, Shakespeare returned, as the symmetry of *The Tempest* and *The Comedy of Errors* shows, to the embryonic phase of his career, delving into that area of his professional past before 1594 that corresponds to what Prospero, summoning Miranda at age fourteen to tell him of her earliest memories, calls 'the dark backward and abysm of time' (I.ii.50).

Fashioned by a process that, at least in part, involves Shakespeare's reaching far back into his professional memory, *The Tempest* is a play that, as Douglas L. Peterson (1973) has emphasised, insists upon the vital importance of remembering. As it repeatedly requires characters to look into their own pasts, the play links remembering with self-knowledge and with the capacity to act effectively in time by making past actions bear upon present conduct. Prospero's revelation to Miranda, during their first appearance onstage, that the storm and shipwreck are illusions generated by his art changes her sense of what has just passed. Through that revelation, the play brings its audiences to revise their sense of their own immediate theatrical past. They reassess not only the 'direful spectacle' they have just witnessed but also the spectatorly convention, based upon past theatrical experiences, in accordance with which they had construed what they saw and heard in the opening scene as actual events within the dramatic fiction. Prospero goes on to ask Miranda—'ignorant of what thou art'—if she can 'remember / A time before we came unto this cell' (I.ii.38-9). As he proceeds to tell her 'what' she is, she also learns who she is and who her father is. In effect, Prospero uses his power to remember in order to change—and in changing, to shape—her sense of her own past and thus of her own identity. Across the centuries since they came into being on the stages of early modern London's commercial theatres, *The Tempest* and other Shakespearean plays have come to serve a similar function. In ways that have only recently begun to receive attention, they are now—and have long been—factors in the process of cultural formation, always under way, by which 'this people or that, this period or that, makes sense of itself, to itself' (Geertz, 1980, p. 167). The 'sense' thus collectively made varies from era to era, people to people, but it is in relationship to the specific 'sense' prevailing at a given historical moment that individuals who share that 'sense' develop and preserve a sense of their distinctive personal identities, a consciousness of who (uniquely) each of them is.

Prospero's ability to tell Miranda about their past rests upon his power to remember, and he associates his brother Antonio's act of usurpation with a failure to remember. Interrupting himself three times, twice breaking off in mid-sentence, to ask if Miranda is listening,[7] Prospero tells of giving Antonio 'The manage of my state', thus irresponsibly relinquishing his ducal duties in order to devote himself to 'secret studies' (I.ii.70, 77). He also tells of how, in the process of 'executing th'outward face of royalty, / With all prerogative', Antonio 'Made such a sinner of his memory . . . he did believe / He was indeed the duke' (I.ii.104-5, 101-3). Acting as Prospero's substitute, Antonio in effect forgets his identity. Prospero goes on to describe the usurping ambition that grows from Antonio's violation of his own memory: 'To have no screen between this part he played / And him he play'd it for, he needs will be / Absolute Milan' (I.ii.107-9). Explicitly theatrical, Prospero's terminology directs attention to how, in performance—but not when read—*The Tempest* itself rests upon and arises from memory, from the ability of actors playing dramatic parts to remember not only the words but also the gestures and movements they have rehearsed.

Later in the same scene, when first Ariel and then Caliban object to the work he calls upon them to perform, Prospero responds by imposing his memory of past events upon theirs. Reminded by Ariel of the freedom he has promised to give him, Prospero insists, over Ariel's repeated objections, that Ariel has failed to remember 'From what a torment I did free thee' and proceeds to 'recount what thou hast been, / Which thou forget'st' (I.ii.251, 262-3). When Caliban objects to the confinement imposed upon him—'here you sty me / In this hard rock, whiles you do keep from me / The rest o'th'island' (I.ii.344-6)—Prospero reminds him of his attempt to rape Miranda.

Prospero uses one of the most spectacular demonstrations of his art—and one of the strangest moments in *The Tempest*—to spur the memories of those responsible for his usurpation: Alonso, Antonio, and Sebastian. To *'Solemn and Strange music'*, as *'Prosper[o] on the top'* looks on, *'several strange Shapes'* bring in a banquet and invite the three men and those with them to eat (III.iii.17). When they approach the food, however, Ariel, attired 'like a Harpy', enters, *'claps his wings upon the table; and, with a quaint device, the banquet vanishes'* (III.iii.52). Ariel then defines for the 'three men of sin' the relationship between their present situation as they understand it—marooned on 'this island, / Where no man doth inhabit'—and their past evil, which makes them ''mongst men . . . most unfit to live' (III.iii.53, 56-8). 'But remember,' he tells them,

> For that's my business to you,—that you three
> From Milan did supplant good Prospero:
> Expos'd unto the sea, which hath requit it,
> Him and his innocent child: for which foul
>   deed
> The powers, delaying, not forgetting, have
> Incens'd the seas and shores, yea, all the
>   creatures,
> Against your peace.
>
> (III.iii.68-75)

The next scene includes another spectacular demonstration of the power of Prospero's art that also involves remembering: the entertainment he provides to celebrate the betrothal of Miranda and Ferdinand.[8] It offers the couple a vision of a world in which, with neither 'Venus or her son' Cupid present, the imperatives of sexual desire—'th'fire in' th'blood' (IV.i.53)—are held in check, to be exercised only within the marital bond. That vision is a reminder to Ferdinand and Miranda of his pledge not to 'break her virgin-knot before / All sanctimonious ceremonies may / With full and holy rite be minister'd' (IV.i.15-17). It is also a foretaste of the blessings that will come if the betrothed couple are 'true' to that pledge instead of indulging in the unrestrained lust that would have peopled the island with Caliban's rape-engendered offspring or Stephano's 'brave brood' (III.ii.103). The entertainment provides a glimpse of a world in which there is no winter—*'Spring come to you at the farthest / In the very end of harvest'* (IV.i.114-15)—and no death.

Prospero calls the entertainment an enactment of 'My present fancies' (IV.i.122), and it takes the form of a Jacobean court masque like those at which the King's Men, as Gentlemen of the Chamber and thus formally members of the royal household, were present and in some of which they may have performed (Orgel, 1987, p. 43). Both the Globe and Blackfriars were commercial theatres, open to anyone, regardless of social rank, who paid the price of admission. In choosing to present Prospero's entertainment as a masque rather than a play-within-a-play, Shakespeare and the King's Men offered all who paid to see *The Tempest* played a representation of, an encounter with, an exclusively royal form of entertainment. Before the masque begins, Prospero instructs Ferdinand and Miranda, its onstage audience, how to behave: 'No tongue! all eyes! be silent' (IV.i.59).[9] Those instructions also function as directions to the play's first audiences on how to conduct themselves while hearing and watching a form of theatricalised entertainment that was 'strange' to the overwhelming majority of them—part of a royal world as far beyond the horizon fixed by their places in Jacobean society as the New World was beyond the western horizon.

The betrothal entertainment occasions the only moment when Prospero's concentration upon his 'project' falters, and that lapse takes the form of a failure to re-member. As Nymphs and Reapers summoned by Iris join *'in a graceful dance'* to *'celebrate / A contract of true love'*, *'Prospero starts suddenly and speaks'*:

> I had forgot that foul conspiracy
> Of the beast Caliban and his confederates
> Against my life: the minute of their plot
> Is almost come.
>
>   (IV.i.138, 132-3, 138, 139-42)

Interrupting the dance, itself an instance of human actions performed in harmony with time, he cuts short the entertainment, abruptly ordering the spirits perform-ing it to depart—'Well done! avoid! / no more'—and *'to a strange, hollow, and confused noise, they heavily vanish'* (IV.i.142-3, 138). Prospero's forgetfulness is a consequence of his absorption with the entertainment, and that absorption with what he himself calls 'some vanity of mine Art' (IV.i.41) briefly repeats the more extended fascination with 'secret studies' that, twelve years before, made him vulnerable to another, and more successful, set of usurpers.

Disturbed and angry—at his own lapse as well as the perfidy of the approaching assassins—Prospero voices, in lines frequently taken as expressing Shakespeare's personal feelings, a despairing, keenly felt sense of the transience and insubstantiality of human structures and human life itself. Like the 'vision' provided for Ferdin-and and Miranda that has abruptly ended, 'The cloud-capp'd towers, the gorgeous palaces, / The solemn temples', even 'the great globe itself' and 'all which it inherit, shall dissolve' (IV.i.152-4) leaving nothing behind. 'We are,' Prospero goes on to tell the betrothed couple, 'such stuff / As dreams are made on; and our little life / Is rounded with a sleep' (IV.i.156-8). His despair is intense, but it is only briefly disabling. After apologising for 'my weakness' and 'my infirmity' (IV.i.159, 160), he sends Ferdinand and Miranda away and, summoning Ariel, prepares to deal with Caliban and his confederates, whom he easily defeats, at least in part because of another lapse of memory. Drawn to the *'glistering aparel'* (IV.i.193) hanging on a line, Stephano and Trinculo, disregarding Caliban's instructions on how to deal with Prospero, fail to 'Remember / First to pos-sess his books . . . Burn but his books' (III.ii.89-90, 93).

Prospero's passage from despair to action demonstrates how, although he is not immune to the temptations that made him vulnerable twelve years before, he is ca-pable now—as he was not then—of the self-conquest required of a ruler. Another such moment occurs when, with all his enemies now at his mercy, he sets 'my nobler reason 'gainst my fury' (V.i.26). Choosing 'the rarer action', which lies 'In virtue [rather] than in ven-geance', he decides to forgive rather than take full revenge on Alonso, Antonio, and Sebastian, with whose 'high wrongs I am struck to th'quick' (V.i.27, 28, 25).

John Gielgud prepares to play Prospero in a London production of The Tempest, *ca. 1935.*

'[T]hey being penitent,' he tells Ariel, 'The sole drift of my purpose doth extend / Not a frown further' (V.i.28-30). Prospero goes on to renounce not only vengeance but also, in what can be regarded as still another act of self-conquest, 'the rough magic' that in Milan made him vulnerable to his enemies and that now on the island gives him nearly total power over them. 'I'll break my staff,' he declares, 'Bury it certain fadoms in the earth, / And deeper than did ever plum-met sound /I'll drown my book' (V.i.54-7).

In fact, however, the playtext never specifies the mo-ment when Prospero executes his pledge to 'break my staff' and 'drown my book' (V.i.54, 57), thereby leav-ing those who perform the play free to determine when Prospero carries out his pledge. Perhaps while Pro-spero is waiting for Ariel to return with his ducal at-tire. Perhaps as Prospero says, 'so, so, so' (V.i.96), after, with Ariel's help, he is newly attired as Duke of Milan. Perhaps at the conclusion of the Epilogue, when Prospero calls upon audiences to set him free. Perhaps not at all.

The playtext also leaves open the issue of whether all who have wronged Prospero 'to th'quick' do in fact come to feel 'penitent' and thus leaves undetermined the related issues of the success of his project and the full efficacy of his art. His political success is beyond doubt. He regains his dukedom, and he succeeds, via the impending marriage of Ferdinand and Miranda, in reconciling the longstanding enmity between Naples and Milan that prompted Alonso to assist Antonio in overthrowing him. That marriage is part of Prospero's design, but it is also one to which the other parties freely assent. Prospero brings Ferdinand and Miranda into one another's presence, but the love they feel for one another comes from their hearts, not his art. He does not, for example, apply to their eyes a love juice like that employed in *A Midsummer Night's Dream*. Alonso, still convinced that Ferdinand is dead, responds to Prospero's revelation that 'I / Have lost my daughter' by spontaneously wishing for the marriage: 'O heavens that they were living both in Naples, / The King and Queen there' (V.i.147-8, 149-50). There is also no doubt that Alonso feels the penitence that Prospero says completes his 'purpose'. Seeing Prospero for the first time in the play, he declares, unprompted, 'Thy dukedom I resign, and do entreat / Thou pardon me my wrongs' (V.i.118-19).

The response of Antonio—Alonso's co-conspirator as well as Prospero's brother—is sharply different, however. He says nothing at all when Prospero tells him:

> For you, most wicked sir, whom to call brother
> Would even infect my mouth, I do forgive
> Thy rankest fault,—all of them; and require
> My dukedom of thee, which perforce, I know,
> Thou must restore.
>
> (V.i.130-4)

For readers the silence that follows those words lasts no longer than it takes for their eyes to move to the next speech, but in performance Antonio's wordlessness begins a silence that can be lengthy or short, depending on how long the actor playing Alonso waits before ending it by calling on Prospero to 'Give us particulars of thy preservation' (V.i.135). Having Alonso be the one who speaks sets Antonio's silence against the voice of the man whose support made it possible for him to usurp Prospero's dukedom. Antonio never assents in words to relinquishing the dukedom, never acknowledges verbally any 'fault', even the 'rankest', and—in contrast to Alonso—never asks Prospero or anyone else to 'pardon me my wrongs'.

In fact, Antonio speaks but once during the final scene, when he says of Caliban, newly entered with Stephano and Trinculo, 'one of them / Is a plain fish, and, no doubt, marketable' (V.i.265-6).[10] Those words help to bring into focus another contrast—between Antonio's silence when Prospero forgives him and Caliban's use of language during the play's final moments. During Caliban's first appearance, Miranda asserts that when

he could 'but gabble like / A thing most brutish', she 'Took pains to make thee speak' and 'endow'd thy purposes / With words that made them known' (I.ii.356-60). Caliban replies, 'You taught me language; and my profit on't / Is, I know how to curse' (I.ii.365-6). During his final moments onstage, however, Caliban, who like Antonio has instigated a conspiracy to unseat Prospero, uses that language to express purposes unlike any he has uttered before. Ordered to trim Prospero's cell, he pledges, 'Ay, that I will; and I'll be wise hereafter, / And seek for grace' (V.i.294-5). His words convey a willingness to obey, a desire to reform, and a sense of penitence that contradict Prospero's characterisation of him as 'A devil, a born devil, on whose nature / Nurture can never stick' and as 'this thing of darkness' (IV.i.188-9; V.i.275). Caliban's final pledge also accentuates the fact that, even when he does speak, Antonio never uses the language at his command to express such sentiments.

Most productions over recent decades have taken Antonio's silence as evidence of his failure or refusal to feel 'penitent'. In John Barton's 1970 production for the Royal Shakespeare Company, for example, Antonio responded to Prospero's words requiring 'my dukedom of thee' by giving him the badge of office, bowing, and then walking away in silence. His wordless actions conveyed grudging acceptance of what, given Prospero's demonstrated powers, was unavoidable, but there was no sign of any penitence or of any resolve to do good in the future. In Clifford Williams's 1978 production, also for the Royal Shakespeare Company, Antonio broke away from Prospero without returning any badge of office or offering even so much as a perfunctory bow, and for the remainder of the play he kept himself apart from those participating in the developing reconciliation between Naples and Milan. Both productions conveyed the sense that Antonio's malevolence has been checked by Prospero's superior powers but not extirpated, defeated but not destroyed or redeemed. He remains, dangerously, what Prospero, shortly before forgiving him, declares him to be: the 'brother mine' who has 'Expell'd remorse and nature' (V.i.75-6).

During 1988 three major English acting companies staged productions of *The Tempest* that, for all their many differences, concurred in presenting Antonios who were resolutely impenitent. In Nicholas Hytner's production for the Royal Shakespeare Company, Prospero struggled to bring himself to kiss Antonio, who, holding himself motionless, was unmoved by and unresponsive to that gesture of fraternal reconciliation. Even after Prospero required 'My dukedom of thee', the Antonio of Peter Hall's production for the National Theatre continued wearing the ducal coronet, and he kept his back to both the audience and to the others onstage. In Jonathan Miller's Old Vic production, Alonso removed a ring from his finger and gave it to Prospero as he told him, 'thy dukedom I resign'. That 'thy' conveyed his abandonment of Antonio, and when Antonio stared in dismayed surprise at him, the king who had been his partner in the conspiracy to unseat Prospero and make Milan subject to Naples turned away. After Prospero expressed forgiveness and required 'My dukedom' from him, Antonio hesitated perceptibly, assessing the realignment of power that had just occurred, then, kneeling, kissed the ring his brother now wore. Rising to his feet following that gesture of submission to his brother's authority and Alonso's, Antonio again looked at his erstwhile partner, who avoided his gaze. As the stage cleared following the Epilogue, Prospero and Antonio were the last to leave, and before passing from view, the two brothers exchanged a long, wary stare.

Those presentations of Antonio's silence are consistent with analysis offered in three editions currently widely used in studying, teaching, and performing *The Tempest*. In his vastly influential Arden edition, first published in 1954 and reprinted as recently as 1988, Frank Kermode calls Antonio 'one of Prospero's failures' because 'as far as can be deduced from the closing passages, in which Antonio is silent, he will not choose the good' (1954, p. lxii). Antonio, Kermode insists, is 'another thing of darkness' that 'Prospero must acknowledge' (1954, p. lxii). In his 1987 New Oxford single-volume edition of *The Tempest*, Stephen Orgel comments, 'It is important to observe that Antonio does not repent here—he is, indeed, not *allowed* to repent' (1987, p. 53). In his most recent edition of *The Complete Works of Shakespeare*, David Bevington concurs, stating, 'Antonio never repents' (1992, p. 1528).

'A world without Antonio,' Kermode observes, 'is a world without freedom; Prospero's shipwreck cannot restore him if he desires not to be restored, to life' (1954, p. lxii). Freedom is a major concern in *The Tempest*. Both Ariel and Caliban call for it during their first appearance. Caliban, drunkenly and mistakenly, exults in it after accepting Stephano as his new master: 'Freedom, high day! high-day, freedom! freedom, high-day, freedom!' (II.ii.186-7). In the last song of this most musical of Shakespearean plays, Ariel, helping Prospero to don his ducal attire, sings in anticipation of it: *'Merrily, merrily shall I live now / Under the blossom that hangs on the bough'* (V.i.93-4). Prospero grants it to him as the play nears its conclusion: 'then to the elements / Be free, and fare thou well' (V.i.317-18). 'Free' is also the final word spoken in the play, and it is Prospero who speaks it. At the end of the Epilogue, speaking as a magician who has renounced his magic and as an actor whose part is ending, Prospero, who no longer exercises the extraordinary control over what audiences see and hear that sets him, strangely, apart from every other Shakespearean character, asks those who have watched the play to grant him freedom: *'As you from crimes would pardon'd be, / Let your indulgence set me free'* (V.i.19-20).

Antonio's freedom flows from his silence. Prospero can 'require' him to return the ducal power he usurped, but he cannot compel him to be sincerely and everlastingly 'penitent'. Antonio's freedom goes beyond that which Kermode, rightly, attributes to him. His situation, as *The Tempest* draws to an end, is not one in which he 'never repents' or is 'not *allowed* to repent'. More accurately, it is one in which the Shakespearean playtext never allows him to *say* that he repents. He is given no words to speak equivalent to Alonso's asking pardon or Caliban's pledging to reform. It is, however, equally true—and equally significant—that Antonio is also not allowed to *say* that he does not repent.[11] He is given no words to speak revealing what he feels and does, nor is any other character. In *The Winter's Tale*, Hermione, newly returned to life, says nothing at all to her husband Leontes, whose groundless jealousy had caused her 'death' sixteen years earlier. Comments by the amazed onlookers make clear, however, that her silence is not a sign of any resentment or ill-will towards Leontes. 'She embraces him,' says one; 'She hangs about his neck,' says another (V.iii.111, 112). In *The Tempest*, by contrast, no one watching as Prospero forgives his brother and reclaims the dukedom offers any equivalent comment clarifying what Antonio does or feels. In the absence of words—Antonio's or anyone else's—indicating what his silence signifies, it is possible that he does not feel penitent. Most recent productions enact that possibility, and editors such as Kermode, Orgel, and Bevington present it as a certainty. In fact, however, Antonio's silence is also fully compatible with another, directly antithetical possibility: he feels penitence so intense that, in contrast to Alonso and Caliban, he has no words to express it.

Robin Phillips's 1976 production at the Stratford (Ontario) Festival enacted that possibility. Antonio sank speechlessly to his knees on hearing Prospero's words to him, and Prospero, in a gesture confirming the forgiveness he voiced, took his kneeling brother's hands in his. In that production, the silent Antonio was a profoundly penitent man. No longer making 'a sinner of his own memory', he was part of an extraordinary process, summarised by Gonzalo, that brings good from evil and from disorientation self-discovery:

> Was Milan thrust from Milan, that his issue
> Should become Kings of Naples? O, rejoice
> Beyond a common joy! and set it down
> With gold on lasting pillars: in one voyage
> Did Claribel her husband find at Tunis,
> And Ferdinand, her brother, found a wife
> Where he himself was lost; Prospero his dukedom
> In a poor isle, and all of us ourselves
> When no man was his own.
>
> (V.i.205-13)

In Phillips's production, the 'all of us' who have found 'ourselves' included Antonio, penitent beyond words.

Such inclusion, however, is contrary to what is becoming an editorial-critical consensus that takes Antonio's silence as evidence of resolute, enduring impenitence that sets him apart from 'all of us'. That consensus is another, highly typical instance of how any era, responding to and seeking confirmation of its own vision(s) of the human condition, tends to focus and thus to narrow the possibilities presented by a Shakespearean playtext. The currently developing consensus reflects a deep, prevailing scepticism about, on the one hand, the capacity of individuals to change and, on the other, the efficacy of authority, particularly governmental authority, in dealing with evil. The irony, in this instance, is that, under the guise of preserving Antonio's freedom, the emerging editorial-critical consensus in fact restricts it, transforming the freedom to be impenitent that his silence allows into a mandate that he must not feel 'penitent'. In so doing, that consensus denies the freedom to be penitent that likewise flows from his silence.

The freedom thus compromised is not Antonio's alone. It is also the freedom of the actors who play him and of those who direct them. In the absence of words specifying what Antonio feels and does when Prospero forgives him and requires the return of the dukedom, responsibility for determining what he feels and does passes to them. More than that, the freedom being compromised is that which the play itself possesses. *The Tempest* is a play that—edited and performed at and for a given moment in history—presents Antonio's malevolence as beyond the scope of Prospero's art, as checked but not transformed by 'rough magic' capable of dimming the noon-time sun and waking the dead. It is also, however, a play that   performed and edited at and for a different moment of history—allows that 'rough magic' to awaken in Antonio a capacity for remorse and for goodness so long dormant that its revival leaves him wordless.

Notes

[1] The tendency to identify Prospero with Shakespeare reached somewhat bizarre fulfilment in Peter Greenaway's 1991 film *Prospero's Books,* which rests on the premise that Prospero himself wrote the play that history knows as *The Tempest.*

[2] Trinculo's words also participate in the play's concern with the relationship between the human and non-human. They can mean, as Terence Hawkes (1985) has noted, that in England the 'any strange beast' is taken to be, passes for, a human being.

[3] The other two are *A Midsummer Night's Dream* and *The Merry Wives of Windsor.*

[4] See Chapter 1 [in *Shakespeare: The Jacobean Plays*] for a fuller discussion of this point.

[5] This paragraph draws upon Donald E. Pease's (1990) essay 'Author'

[6] Chapter 1 [in *Shakespeare: The Jacobean Plays*] discusses why this grouping is problematic.

[7] These interruptions arise less from any inattentiveness on the part of Miranda than from the force of the feelings that the act of narrating, and therefore remembering, the past stirs in Prospero.

[8] *The Tempest* was performed during the festivities before the marriage of James's daughter Elizabeth to the Elector Palatine on 14 February 1613. The first performance on record was at court on 1 November 1611.

[9] The behaviour of onstage audiences during the plays-within-the-play in *A Midsummer Night's Dream* and *Hamlet* suggests that far from being silent during performances, audiences of that time tended to be talkative.

[10] Like Stephano and Trinculo, Antonio first responds to Caliban in terms of the commercial possibilities he offers.

[11] For example, he is given no words like those assigned to him in W. H. Auden's 1945 poem 'The Sea and the Mirror':

> Your all is partial, Prospero;
>   My will is all my own;
> Your need to love shall never know
> Me: I am I, Antonio,
>   By choice myself alone.

Bibliography

Bevington, David (1992) *The Complete Works of Shakespeare,* 4th edn. (New York: Harper Collins).

Daniell, David (1986) 'Shakespeare and the Traditions of Comedy', in *The Cambridge Companion to Shakespeare Studies,* ed. Stanley Wells (Cambridge, New York, Melbourne: Cambridge University Press; reprinted 1987) pp. 101-41.

Geertz, Clifford (1980) 'Blurred Genres: The Refiguration of Social Thought', *The American Scholar,* 49, pp. 165-79.

Kermode, Frank (1954) *The Tempest,* Arden edition (London and New York: Routledge; reprinted 1988).

Orgel, Stephen (1987) *The Tempest,* The Oxford Shakespeare (Oxford and New York: Oxford University Press).

Peterson, Douglas L. (1973) *Time, Tide, and Tempest: A Study of Shakespeare's Romances* (San Marino: The Huntington Library).

Sidney, Philip (1965) *An Apology for Poetry or The Defence of Poesy,* ed. Geoffrey Shepherd (London: Nelson & Sons).

CALIBAN

Bryan Crockett (essay date 1991)

SOURCE: "Calvin and Caliban: Naming the 'Thing of Darkness'," in *The University of Dayton Review,* Vol. 21, No. 1, Spring, 1991, pp. 131-44.

[*In the following essay, Crockett argues that although Caliban initially appears to be emblematic of human corruption, midway through the play he begins to demonstrate a capacity for self-reformation, and at the end of the drama he is truly penitent. Underlying the characterization of Caliban, the critic maintains, is Shakespeare's mockery and rejection of the rigid Calvinist doctrine of predestination.*]

Shakespeare's Caliban has received a strikingly varied body of critical interpretation, from John C. McCloskey's treatment of the character as a "savage clown" and a "Commedia dell'arte buffoon" (345) to Frank Kermode's agreement with Prospero's assessment: Caliban is "a born devil" (xl). More recently, revisionist commentators have stressed a relatively helpless Caliban's victimization at the hands of an imperialistic Prospero.[1] Corona Sharp has gone so far as to read Caliban in a wholly sympathetic light: unjustly despoiled of the ownership of his island and enslaved by an unnecessarily brutal Prospero, Caliban repeatedly exhibits at least equality to his master in morality, intellect, and imagination. So startlingly virtuous is Sharp's Caliban that she finds it necessary to remind her readers that the character is not a noble savage (283, n. 35).

Of course, Caliban has frequently been seen as the antithesis of the noble savage. In fact, it has been suggested that Shakespeare created the monster for the specific purpose of countering the idyllic portrayal of the Native Americans in Montaigne's "Of the Caniballes." While Montaigne's essay is more an indictment of European corruption than a wholehearted endorsement of Native American culture, some of his language does anticipate Rousseau's doctrine of the noble savage:

> . . . what in those nations we see by experience, doth not only exceed all the pictures wherewith licentious Poesie hath proudly imbellished the golden age, but also the conception and desire of Philosophy.
>
> (164)

There is no doubt that Shakespeare was familiar with Florio's translation of Montaigne's essay; numerous echoes in *The Tempest* of Florio's language confirm the fact.[2] As I hope to demonstrate, however, Caliban is more than simply a reaction to Montaigne, just as he is more than a mere buffoon. Certainly he emerges as something other than "a born devil." Moreover, Sharp's sympathetic reading of the character is too heavily colored with the Caliban of Act V, just as other interpretations seem to begin and end with the Caliban of Act I. In my reading Caliban begins as a comic embodiment of the totally depraved man of popular Calvinism and ends as a full human being, effecting the audience's participation in Shakespeare's vision of divine grace.

This is not to say that discussion of the myth of the noble savage is misguided; as a number of recent discussions of *The Tempest* have stressed, the whole debate surrounding European treatment of American Indians was very much in the intellectual forefront of Shakespeare's England.[3] Particularly influential were treatises translated into English in 1583, in which the Spanish missionary Bishop Bartolome de Las Casas, the primary European proponent of a favorable depiction of the Indians, was pitted against his countryman Juan Gines de Sepulveda, who claimed that the Indians were naturally inferior to Europeans and were therefore suited only for slavery. Naturally, the debate was essentially theological: if the Indians were in fact full human beings, then the Europeans' first duty was to bring them Christianity. If not, there were to be no scruples about imperialistic exploitation. The alternatives, then, were baptizing the Indians or enslaving them; almost no one, not even Montaigne, suggested leaving them alone.[4] Fueled by the English explorers' conflicting reports about the character of the Indians, the debate between Las Casas and Sepulveda was a particularly live issue in England in large part because the doctrine of election was also in the forefront of public discussion.

The idea of double predestination—that some have been preordained to election and others to reprobation—was common to all the various shades of Calvinism that had combined to define orthodoxy in the Elizabethan church.[5] By the last years of the sixteenth century, though, this orthodoxy was beginning to be challenged by those who would come to be known as Arminians— those who wanted to find some place for human cooperation in the process of salvation and who warned against attempting to penetrate too deeply into the mysteries of predestination. As Lancelot Andrewes maintained in a late Elizabethan sermon. "we are not curiously to enquire and search out God's secret will touching reprobation or election" (5: 197). On the other side were preachers such as the enormously popular William Perkins, who insisted on the rigid categories of predestination and who seldom missed an opportunity to point out the precise nature of the difference between the true Christian and the reprobate. For Perkins, salvation was something like an exact science; in his treatises and sermons he was fond of listing the identifying characteristics of the elect.[6] Until the death of James and the accession of Charles in 1625, the predestinarians remained in firm control of the Church of England. This meant that those with Arminian leanings, those who saw salvation as linked to human initiative, needed to find a cultural outlet other than the Church for their views.[7] One such cultural institution was the theater.

At the time Shakespeare wrote *The Tempest,* then, the question of human cooperation in the process of salvation was all the more insistent for its ecclesiastical suppression. Jacobean playwrights were far enough removed from the center of the theological controversy that they were permitted to depict characters who worked out their own salvation, as long as the plays did not directly and explicitly challenge the doctrine of predestination.[8] Shakespeare and his contemporaries, then, were in a peculiar position: their culturally marginal status paradoxically allowed them to explore matters central to Renaissance self-understanding. In the case of *The Tempest,* one such concern is the crucial theological problem of reprobation and election. An examination of the naming of two of the play's major characters, Caliban and Prospero, proves fruitful in addressing the matter of Shakespeare's relation to the complex Christianity of his culture.

The wonderful speculation that the name "Caliban" is a consciously derived anagram for "cannibal" is taken for granted by some commentators on *The Tempest.*[9] E. K. Chambers argues for a derivation from "cauliban," a Romany word meaning "blackness" (1: 494). A further conjecture as to the origin of the name, and one that I have not seen advanced, is that Shakespeare may have had in mind a back-handed swipe at Calvin. The similarity of the names "Caliban" and "Calvin" would seem entirely fortuitous were the whole development of Caliban's character not set in the context of the theological debate concerning Calvin's doctrine of predestination.

There is even some chance that early seventeenth-century French pronunciation of the reformer's name would make it sound more like "Calvan" than "Calvin," just as it does in present-day French, and therefore even closer to "Caliban" than it seems to us, but evidence—such as it is—of Jacobean English pronunciation of French names ending in "in" is inconclusive (Dobson 904, Zachrisson 117). In any case, Caliban's actions raise fascinating questions that bear

on the theology of the time, particularly the questions surrounding Calvin's doctrine of election.

Shakespeare's naming of Prospero may well also have its origin in this theological debate. One possibility that I have not seen advanced is that Shakespeare derived the name from Prosper of Aquitaine, a fourth-century Church Father and disciple of Augustine. Prosper's name appears frequently in the discourse of Shakespeare's day; he was among the Fathers widely read and widely quoted throughout the Middle Ages and the Renaissance.[10] Interestingly, Prosper's position regarding his main theological concern—the relation between free will and grace—seems to have shifted somewhat during his literary career from a hard-line late-Augustinian (in retrospect, one might say, "Calvinistic") insistence on predestination to an acknowledgement of the possibility of some human cooperation in the process of salvation.[11] The following, from Prosper's *Grace and Free Will,* is indicative of his earlier position: " . . . it is vain, even impious, to want to make a place for merits existing before grace. . . . " The later Prosper, however, writing *The Call of All Nations,* could be quoted with approval by Richard Hooker, whose *Of the Laws of Ecclesiastical Polity* attempted to remove the exclusivism of predestination from the center of Christian theology:

> The Church every where maketh prayers unto God not only for saints and such as already in Christ are regenerate, but for all infidels and enemies of the Cross of Jesus Christ, for all idolaters, for all that persecute Christ in his followers, for Jews to whose blindness the light of the Gospel doth not yet shine, for heretics and schismatics, who from the unity of faith and charity are estranged.[12]

Although the difference between Prosper's earlier and later positions is perhaps more one of emphasis than of doctrine, the softening of his earlier position is noteworthy in that it is paralleled in *The Tempest* by a similar change on Prospero's part. The nature of Prospero's theological development will be examined below. At this point it is enough to say that there is at least some likelihood that Shakespeare derived Prospero's name from the historical Prosper. (The "o" is even dropped from the end of the character's name three times in the play.)[13] Although we cannot say with certainty that Prosper is among Shakespeare's sources, there can be little doubt that Prosper's concerns are Shakespeare's concerns in *The Tempest;* the language of both Caliban and Prospero is heavily colored with the rhetoric of election and reprobation.

In the whole corpus of Shakespeare's work, the term "election" is usually used in its purely political sense, but at times the playwright puns on the Calvinistic meaning of the term, as in *Cymbeline* when Cloten complains that Imogen has chosen not him but Post-humus as her husband. The Second Lord says in an aside, "If it be a sin to make a true election, she is damned."[14] Shakespeare's humorously ironic treatment of the Calvinistic doctrine of election argues that here as elsewhere in his comedies, there is no reason to suppose that any character—with the apparent exception of Caliban—has been preordained to villainy. Even in the tragedies, where fate often plays a more obvious role than in the comedies, it would be difficult to demonstrate that any character's end had been predestined. Rather, the operative principle in the tragedies seems to be a paradoxical interplay between free will and fate (Grudin). Shakespeare's comedies, even more than his tragedies, appear to assume the operation of free will. The comedies are decidedly not "humors plays," in which every character behaves according to a preconceived, stereotypical pattern. Except for the Caliban of the early part of *The Tempest,* Shakespeare's comic villains appear not to have been preordained to their villainy; they have chosen it. Malvolio in *Twelfth Night* and Angelo in *Measure for Measure,* for example, come across as hypocrites who have chosen their own Puritan rigidity; there is no reason to suppose that they have been locked beside their will into an unalterable reprobation.

Given Calvinism's emphasis on the rigid categories of election and reprobation, it is not difficult to see how a pervasive interest in assurance of election arose among late Tudor and early Stuart Calvinists. Accompanying this emphasis on assurance was an obsessive desire to identify and denounce reprobates. Although the Calvinists of Shakespeare's day saw themselves as following the letter of the *Institutes,* Calvin himself had foreseen the danger of looking for signs of election:

> But what proof have you of your election? When once this thought has taken possession of any individual, it keeps him perpetually miserable, subjects him to dire torment, or throws him into a state of complete stupor. . . . The mind cannot be infected by a more pestilential error than that which disturbs the conscience, and deprives it of peace and tranquillity in regard to God.
>
> (3.24.4)

Elsewhere in the *Institutes,* however, Calvin indicates that a perpetually tranquil conscience is not to be expected in the Christian life:

> When we say that faith must be certain and secure, we certainly speak not of an assurance which is never affected by doubt, nor a security which anxiety never assails, we rather maintain that believers have a perpetual struggle with their own distrust, and are thus far from thinking that their consciences possess a placid quiet, uninterrupted by perturbation.
>
> (3.2.17)

These two statements appear to be contradictory, but each is meant to forestall a different excess: in the first case, an excessive desire for assurance of salvation, and in the second, an excessive desire for an unperturbed conscience. Despite the reformer's warnings, Calvinists in Shakespeare's England were prone to both excesses. The extremely popular preacher Arthur Dent, for example, in a frequently reprinted tract called *The Plaine Mans Path-way to Heaven: Wherein every man may clearly see, whether he shall be saved or damned,* advocated absolute assurance: "For, he, that knoweth not in this life that he shall be saved, shall never be saved after this life."[15] Regarding peace of conscience, William Perkins made his position plain in *A Treatise Tending unto a Declaration whether a man be in the estate of damnation, or in the estate of grace:* "That religion whose precepts are no directions to attaine peace of conscience, leaveth a man still in a damnable case" (396).

It is not surprising that the late Elizabethan and early Jacobean Calvinists departed somewhat from the *Institutes,* for Calvin himself, never one to countenance alternating states of confidence and despair, advocates a simultaneous recognition of depravity and beatitude.[16] Interestingly, it is "to keep pious minds from despair" that he reminds his readers of the persecuted saints: "Though they feel bitterly, they are at the same time filled with spiritual joy; though pressed with anxiety, breathe exhilarated by the consolation of God" (3.2.24). If Calvinists felt themselves incapable of maintaining an awareness of themselves as simultaneously saints and sinners, it was comparatively easy, by emphasizing certain aspects of Calvin's doctrine, to declare themselves saints and look for sinners in the rest of the world. Had Calvin himself not exhorted his followers to do just that?

> . . . comparing their good cause with the evil cause of the wicked, they thence derive confidence of victory, not so much by the commendation of their own righteousness as by the just and deserved condemnation of their adversaries.
>
> (3.14.18)

In fairness to Calvin, it should be mentioned that such language is rare in the *Institutes.* More frequent are reminders of the Augustinian doctrine that all human beings are to be treated as members of the elect since "we know not who belongs to the number of the predestined" (3.23.14). By the late sixteenth century, however, the dualism implicit in Calvin's doctrine of predestination led to a widespread interest in identifying and condemning reprobates (Rozett 41).

Stephen Greenblatt sees this process of condemnation as a part of the self-fashioning peculiar to the Renaissance:

> . . . self-fashioning is achieved in relation to something perceived as alien, strange, or hostile.

This threatening Other—heretic, savage, witch, adulteress, traitor, Anti-Christ—must be discovered or invented in order to be attacked and destroyed.[17]

Greenblatt's idea of self-fashioning in the Renaissance can be seen as the incipient stage of the self-assertion that characterizes the modern age. Hans Blumenberg sees the Calvinistic dualism of election and reprobation as the re-emergence of Gnosticism, which was never fully conquered by the early Church Fathers (135). In Blumenberg's view the modern age has successfully overcome Gnosticism, but the battle was far from over in the early seventeenth century (126). A Gnostic insistence on the pervasive presence of real evil in the phenomenal world, coupled with a new tendency toward self-assertion, demanded that believers learn to identify and condemn their demonic counterparts.

Suitable objects for reproach were often incorporated into worship services such as the rites of public penance at Paul's Cross. These sessions attracted some of the most famous preachers in the land, each of whom on his appointed day would share space on a wooden platform with a penitent. Frequently the audience at Paul's Cross numbered in the thousands, and the sermon lasted for up to two hours. The penitent, dressed in white and holding a taper or a faggot, represented the antithesis of the preacher. This "sinner" would endure the jeers of the crowd as well as blows from the "rod of correction." In vehemently denouncing the sins of the penitent, the members of the audience strengthened their identity with the preacher and the moral order he represented (Rozett 41).

This sort of display's counterpart—and its competition—was of course the stage. Despite their basic animosity toward the theater, many Puritans saw dramatic portrayals of the downfalls of reprobate sinners as serving a useful purpose in edifying the elect (Rozett 72). The English Renaissance stage was thus in one sense an extension of English Protestant thought, adding range and flexibility to the possibilities for dramatic depictions of an essentially dualistic universe. This dualism, combined with the strong tradition of didactic drama derived from the Middle Ages, meant that the Jacobean stage was heavily peopled with characters designed to be hated, reinforcing the audience's identification with these characters' virtuous counterparts.

At first glance Caliban seems to be another character designed to be loathed—another candidate for this sort of education by reverse example. Caliban's depravity is seemingly without limit; the character appears to be a striking dramatic embodiment of Calvin's fallen, unregenerate man. He arrives on stage cursing magnificently:

> As wicked dew as e'er my mother brush'd
> With raven's feather from unwholesome fen

> Drop on you both! a south-west wind blow on ye
> And blister you all o'er!
>
> (1.2.323-26)

Despite his demonic parentage, Caliban seems to serve admirably as an emblem of human depravity. Shakespeare's Caliban is both loathsome and ridiculous; the physical appearance of this "salvage and deformed Slave," this "freckled whelp hag-born," invites derision (1.2.283).

Certainly this Caliban, who can use language masterfully—albeit to curse—is intellectually capable of realizing that the punishment for his outburst will be swift and unpleasant. The question of what drives Caliban to persist in his rebellious behavior despite its obvious futility can be answered in a number of ways. One possibility is that his indomitable desire for freedom leads him to struggle admirably, even heroically, against impossible odds. But such a reading is undercut not only by Shakespeare's humorous portrayal of Caliban but also by Caliban's own refusal to embrace freedom; he is more than willing to serve and even worship the likes of Stephano.

Another possibility is that on a psychoanalytic level, Caliban represents the darker side of Prospero, perhaps the narcissistic willfulness of his childhood.[18] In this reading, Prospero must acknowledge the "other" within in order to attain full maturity.

Such a psychoanalytic reading is compelling in the twentieth century, but of course a Jacobean audience would register the perception differently. In terms of seventeenth-century sensibilities, the simple possibility that presents itself is that the Caliban of the first half of *The Tempest* is a reprobate. There is no reason to suppose that an audience culturally predisposed to denounce reprobates would find any fault in Prospero's response to Caliban's outburst:

> For this, be sure, tonight thou shalt have cramps,
> Side-stitches that shall pen thy breath up. Urchins
> Shall, for that vast of night that they may work,
> All exercise on thee; thou shalt be pinched
> As thick as honeycomb, each pinch more stinging
> Than bees that made 'em.
>
> (1.2.327-32)

Caliban replies that he has been betrayed and unjustly enslaved by Prospero, to whom he has dutifully shown "all the qualities of the isle, / The fresh springs, brine-pits, barren place and fertile" (1.2.339-40). Caliban's next lines combine a curse with a wry comment on the limits of Prospero's authority:

All the charms
Of Sycorax, toads, beetles, bats, light on you!
For I am all the subjects that you have,
Which first was mine own King. . . .

                                        (1.2.341-44)

But any sympathy the audience feels for Caliban is quickly undercut by Prospero's response:

Thou most lying slave,
Whom stripes may move, not kindness! I have
    us'd thee,
Filth as thou art, with human care; and lodg'd
    thee
In mine own cell, till that thou didst seek to
    violate
The honour of my child.

                                        (1.2.346-50)

Especially in terms of seventeenth-century sensibilities, Prospero's punishment of Caliban is necessary and morally justifiable; Prospero has tried compassion, but Caliban has rejected it. Even now Caliban remains unrepentant of the attempted rape:

O ho, O ho! would't had been done!
Thou didst prevent me; I had peopled else
This isle with Calibans.

                                        (1.2.351-53)

Despite Sharp's suggestion that the plurality of Caliban's envisioned offspring is an indication of his desire for honorable marriage, it is safe to assume that a Jacobean audience would find Prospero's treatment of the would-be rapist more humane than the circumstances merited, not less (276). The law against rape in Jacobean England provided for the death penalty (or, if the judge favored leniency, blinding and/or castration [Pollock and Maitland, 2:491]). Miranda reminds Caliban that his punishment has been light; he has "deserved more than a prison" (1.2.304). At this point, the audience has no reason to doubt the validity of Miranda's invective:

Abhorred slave,
Which any print of goodness wilt not take,
Being capable of all ill!

                                        (1.2.353-55)

Later, Prospero calls him,

A devil, a born devil, on whose nature
Nurture can never stick; on whom my pains
Humanely taken, all, all lost, quite lost. . . .

                                        (4.1.188-90)

Apparently, Caliban is a Calvinistic reprobate; his condition appears to be such that he is incapable of receiving grace. The pinches, cramps, and imprison-

ment are necessary not as salutary punishment, not as the means of bringing about repentance, but as the only way of keeping the monster's passions in check. The physicality of the punishment is commensurate with Caliban's excessive bestiality. In Calvinistic terms, Caliban is receiving the punishment befitting a reprobate slave, not a wayward son. Calvin makes a distinction between God's chastisements of "our sins" and his punishments of "the wicked and reprobate." Quoting with approval St. John Chrysostom, Calvin says,

"A son is whipt, and a slave is whipt, but the latter
is punished as a slave for his offence: the former
is chastised as a free-born son, standing in need of
correction." The correction of the latter is designed
to prove and amend him; that of the former is
scourging and punishment.

                                        (3.4.31)

Clearly, Caliban appears to be such a reprobate slave. His congenitally corrupted will leads him to abuse all gifts, including the gift of language. He says to Miranda,

You taught me language, and my profit on't
Is, I know how to curse. The red plague rid
    you
For learning me your language!

                                        (1.2.365-67)

In terms of the popularly perceived Calvinism of Shakespeare's day, Caliban's inability to make good use of the gifts he has received is a clear indication of his status as a reprobate.

A little later in the play Caliban enters, cursing in characteristic fashion:

All the infections that the sun sucks up
From bogs, fens, flats, on Prosper fall, and
    make him
By inch-meal a disease!

                                        (2.2.1-3)

He then neatly encapsulates his predicament: "his spirits hear me, / And yet I needs must curse" (2.2.3-4). This creature who "needs must curse" in spite of the certainty of retribution amounts to a strikingly dramatic embodiment—albeit a humorous one—of the Calvinistic reprobate. It is Caliban's inability to change his condition, despite his knowledge of it, that marks the characterization as distinctly Calvinistic.

Shakespeare's comic treatment of this reprobate continues as Trinculo enters and mistakes him first for a fish and then for an islander stricken by a thunderbolt. Despite the powerful, fish-like smell, Trinculo crawls under Caliban's gaberdine to escape the impending rainstorm. Stephano mistakes the pair for a four-legged, double-headed monster and gives wine to both ends in an attempt to calm the beast. Hereafter the three join in a drunken pact, a hopelessly misguided plot to murder Prospero. All three have become objects of the audience's ridicule, but in Act III the difference between Caliban and the others becomes apparent. When Stephano and Trinculo are terrified by the invisible Ariel's music, Caliban calms them, revealing a heartrending capacity for imagination:

> Be not afeard; the isle is full of noises,
> Sounds and sweet airs, that give delight, and
>   hurt not.
> Sometimes a thousand twangling instruments
> Will hum about mine ears; and sometime
>   voices,
> That, if I then had wak'd after long sleep,
> Will make me sleep again: and then, in
>   dreaming,
> The clouds methought would open, and show
>   riches
> Ready to drop upon me; that, when I wak'd,
> I cried to dream again.
>
> (3.2.132-41)

An element of pathos is added to the audience's perception of Caliban; he can imagine blessings, but even in his dreams he is unable to receive them.

The Caliban who begins to emerge is a being distressingly like the audience members. Like them, he has an acute sense of the gap between life as it is and life as it might be. Although the "riches" of his dreams will eventually have to be given up in favor of a humbler, more human aspiration, his "when I wak'd, / I cried to dream again" is a far cry from his earlier, bestial cursing of his situation. Shakespeare underscores this development by contrasting Caliban's awareness with that of the merely venal aspirations of Stephano and Trinculo. It is Caliban who recognizes the "glistering apparel" brought by Ariel as "trash" and "luggage" (4.1.224, 231). Caliban's aspirations are not yet what they ought to be, but his recognition of the vanity of the "trumpery" is a prelude to his recognition of his own limitations (4.1.186). In short, Caliban has begun to emerge as more than a mere buffoon, more than simply a reply to the proponents of the myth of the noble savage, more even than the reprobate of Calvinism. The audience members, who have been invited to laugh at Caliban, are now challenged to recognize him as essentially human—to recognize something of him in themselves. In the fifth act Caliban finally repents. Shakespeare's rhetorical technique leaves the audience only two alternatives: to reject the Caliban of the second half of the play as inconsistent with the reprobate slave of Act I, or to embrace the character as a fellow human being, one capable of reform.

In the end, Caliban makes just the recognition that the play is designed to effect in the audience. In order for Prospero to embrace full humanity in abjuring his magic, he must come face to face with a part of himself that his magical powers have heretofore kept at a distance. He says of Caliban, "this thing of darkness I / Acknowledge mine" (5.1.275-76). If the members of the audience are still reluctant to make a similar acknowledgement, Shakespeare makes it clear that the "thing of darkness" is in fact capable of regeneration. In his last speech Caliban says, "I'll be wise hereafter and seek for grace" (5.1.294-95).

Shakespeare is certainly doing more here than sacrificing continuity of character to his desire for a happy ending that includes everyone, even Caliban. (Antonio and Sebastian, after all, make no indication that they intend to reform.)[19] Caliban's statement about seeking grace seems out of character only because the audience has been drawn into the popularly perceived Calvinistic notion that some readily identifiable souls are incapable of regeneration. Caliban, the very embodiment of human depravity, is actually a human being capable of receiving grace. The audience's habit of self-identification in opposition to a reprobate has been challenged; if even Caliban can be saved, who can be excluded?

The instrument of Caliban's regeneration is self-knowledge arising from his repentance. He recognizes his own idolatry and the folly he shares with others:

> What a thrice-double ass
> Was I, to take this drunkard for a god,
> And worship this dull fool!
>
> (5.1.295-97)

The members of the audience are invited to a similar sort of recognition of shared human frailty. Shakespeare beautifully incorporates this idea into Prospero's epilogue, which contains much more than the usual request for applause. In his voluntary rejection of all illusion, Prospero has become fully human, fully vulnerable; he has given up his magic and forgiven his enemies. Now even the illusory wall between actor and theatergoer is broken down as Prospero speaks directly to the audience. The perspectives of character and author blend, and the members of the audience, having witnessed the repentance of an apparent reprobate and the humanization of a powerful magician, are invited to participate in Shakespeare's vision of salvation. Like the audience, Prospero and Caliban are now utterly dependent on God's grace. Fortunately, as Prospero points out, it is a grace that is not confined within the rigid categories of Calvinistic predestination, but is readily accessible through prayer,

> Which pierces so, that it assaults
> Mercy itself, and frees all faults.
>
> (Epilogue, 17-18)

Notes

[1] See, e. g., Cartelli, Brown, Siegel, Hulme (1981), Erlich, Leininger, and Greenblatt (1976).

[2] According to Kermode, xxxiv, Montaigne's essay is "the only undisputed source for any part of *The Tempest*." See also Woodhead, 126.

[3] See Skura, Orgel ("Shakespeare and the Cannibals"), Hulme (1986 and 1981), Griffiths, and Barker and Hulme.

[4] In "Of the Canniballes," p. 164, Montaigne says in passing that the inhabitants of the New World are in such a state of purity that "I am sometimes grieved the knowledge of it came no sooner to light, at what time there were men, that better than we could have judged of it."

[5] See, e. g., Calvin, 3.21.5: "All are not created on equal terms, but some are preordained to eternal life, others to eternal damnation."

[6] See, e.g., Perkins's *A Case of Conscience, the Greatest that Ever Was: How a man may know whether he be the childe of God, or no.*

[7] It is instructive that at Cambridge in the mid-1590s, anticipators of Arminianism such as Peter Baro and William Barrett incurred the wrath of the Calvinist authorities for asserting that Christ died for all people and that grace was not irresistible. See Dickens, 426-27.

[8] One factor in the degree of latitude afforded playwrights with Arminian leanings may have been Archbishop Bancroft's readiness to denounce extreme forms of Puritanism. For a treatment of censorship laws see Patterson.

[9] See, e. g., Skura, Hulme (1981), Levin, and Haskins.

[10] See O'Donnell's comment in Prosper, *Grace*, p. 342. Although I have not done an exhaustive study of the frequency with which Prosper's name is mentioned in the discourse of Shakespeare's day, I have happened across a good many references, in all of which Prosper is cited as a familiar and reliable authority. For example, Prosper's name appears frequently in both volumes of the official Elizabethan homilies (which, in theory at least, every English citizen heard regularly), in Hooker, and in the sermons of the popular Elizabethan preacher Thomas Playfere. Particularly instructive is a reference in a 1627 letter from Richard Montague to John Cosin: "I shall not Calvinise it, not yet Arminianise it, but with the Church of England, Augustine and Prosper, go the middle way" (quoted in Collinson, p. 83, n. 71).

[11] See O'Donnell's introduction to Prosper, *Grace,* p. 339.

[12] 5.49.6. P. De Letter, in his introduction to Prosper's *The Call of All Nations,* p. 3, dates the treatise at about the year 450, some twenty years after Prosper's writing *Grace and Free Will.*

[13] "Prosper" is used instead of "Prospero" twice by Caliban (2.2.2 and 2.2.83) and once by Alonso (3.3.99).

[14] In the Arden edition, 1.3.26. Some editors combine the first two scenes, in which case the reference is 1.2.26. Cf. 1.2.68 (or 1.1.138), in which Cymbeline asks his daughter whether she is "past obedience" and "past grace." She turns her father's intended meaning into an ironic comment on theological despair: "Past hope, and in despair, that way past grace."

[15] Quoted in Rozett, p. 43. Dent's tract, first published in 1601, was in its twelfth printing in 1611, when Shakespeare wrote *The Tempest.* By contrast, there was only one new printing of the English edition of Calvin's *Institutes* between 1587 and 1611.

[16] Calvin denounces those "semi-papists" who "give conscience a position between hope and fear, making it alternate, by successive turns, to the one and the other" (3.2.24).

[17] Greenblatt (1980), p. 9. See also Fiedler.

[18] See Skura, pp. 64-66. Cf. Leininger, p. 105, and Holland's Freudian interpretation of Caliban's dream.

[19] In his introduction to the Oxford *Tempest,* Stephen Orgel remarks that it seems odd that Antonio does not repent, that "the demand for repentance has been deflected from Antonio to Alonso," p. 51. It seems to me just as accurate to say that the demand for repentance has been deflected from Antonio to the audience. A few pages later Orgel himself bears out the idea in his discussion of Prospero's epilogue: "The spells are now ours; we have become the enabling factor in the fiction. Our breath, not Ariel's, must send his ship back to Italy, and it is we who must forgive him his faults as a higher power forgives ours," pp. 55-56.

Works Cited

Andrewes, Lancelot. *Sermons.* 5 vols. Oxford: Anglo-Catholic Library, 1875-82.

Barker, Francis and Peter Hulme. "Nymphs and Reapers Heavily Vanish: the Discursive Con-texts of *The Tempest*." *Alternative Shakespeares.* Ed. John Drakakis. London: Methuen, 1985.

Blumenberg, Hans. *The Legitimacy of the Modern Age.* Trans. Robert M. Wallace. Cambridge, Mass.: M.I.T. Press, 1983.

Brown, Paul. "'This Thing of Darkness I Acknowledge Mine': *The Tempest* and the Discourse of Colonialism." *Political Shakespeare: New Essays in Cultural Materialism.* Ithaca: Cornell UP, 1985. 48-71.

Calvin, John. *Institutes of the Christian Religion.* Trans. Henry Beveridge. Grand Rapids: Eerdmans, 1957.

Cartelli, Thomas. "Prospero in Africa: *The Tempest* as Colonialist Text and Pretext." *Shakespeare Reproduced: The Text in History and Ideology.* Eds. Jean Howard and Marion O'Conner. London: Methuen, 1987. 99-115.

Chambers, E. K. *William Shakespeare.* 2 vols. Oxford: Clarendon Press, 1930.

Collinson, Patrick. *The Religion of Protestants: The Church in English Society, 1559-1625.* Oxford: Clarendon Press, 1982.

Dent, Arthur. *The Plaine Mans Path-way to Heaven: Wherein every man may clearly see, whether he shall be saved or damned.* London, 1607.

Dickens, A. G. *The English Reformation.* London: Fontana, 1964.

Dobson, E. J., ed. *English Pronunciation, 1500-1700.* 2nd ed. Oxford: Clarendon Press, 1968.

Erlich, Bruce. "Shakespeare's Colonial Metaphor: On the Social Function of Theatre in *The Tempest.*" Science and Society 41 (1977): 43-65.

Fiedler, Leslie. *The Stranger in Shakespeare.* New York: Stein and Day, 1972.

Greenblatt, Stephen. "Learning to Curse: Aspects of Linguistic Colonialism in the Sixteenth Century." *First Images of America.* Ed. Fredi Chiappelli. 2 vols. Los Angeles: Univ. of California Press, 1976. 2: 561-80.

————. *Renaissance Self-Fashioning from More to Shakespeare.* Chicago: Univ. of Chicago Press, 1980.

Griffiths, Trevor R. "'This Island's mine': Caliban and Colonialism." *Yearbook of English Studies* 13 (1983): 159-80.

Haskins, John E. "Caliban the Bestial Man." *PMLA* 62 (1947): 793-801.

Holland, Norman. "Caliban's Dream." *The Design Within: Psychoanalytic Approaches to Shakespeare.* Ed. M. D. Faber. New York: Science House, 1970. 521-33.

Hooker, Richard. *Of the Laws of Ecclesiastical Polity. The Works of Mr. Richard Hooker.* Ed. John Keble. 3 vols. 7th ed. New York: Burt Franklin, 1888. Rpt. 1970.

Hulme, Peter. *Colonial Encounters: Europe and the Native Caribbean, 1492-1787.* London: Methuen, 1986. 89-134.

————. "Hurricanes in the Caribbees: The Constitution of the Discourse of English Colonialism." *1642: Literature and Power in the Seventeenth Century.* Proceedings of the Essex conference on the Sociology of Literature. Eds. Francis Barker et. al. Colchester: Univ. of Essex, 1981. 55-83.

Kermode, Frank, ed. (See Shakespeare.)

Las Casas, Bartolome de. *The Spanish Colonie. . . .* Trans. M. M. S. London: 1583. Rpt. Amsterdam: Theatrum Orbis Terrarum, 1977.

Leininger, Lorie. "Cracking the Code of *The Tempest.*" *Bucknell Review* 25 (1980): 121-31.

Levin, Harry. "Shakespeare's Nomenclature." *Shakespeare and the Revolution of the Times.* Oxford: Oxford University Press, 1976. 51-77.

McCloskey, John C. "Caliban, Savage Clown." *College English* 1 (1940): 354-59.

Montaigne, Michel de. *The Essayes of Montaigne.* Trans. John Florio. New York: The Modern Library, 1933.

Orgel, Stephen. "Shakespeare and the Cannibals." *Cannibals, Witches, and Divorce: Estranging the Renaissance.* Ed. Marjorie Garber. Baltimore: Johns Hopkins UP, 1987. 40-66.

————. ed. (See Shakespeare.)

Patterson, Annabel. *Censorship and Interpretation: The Conditions of Writing and Reading in Early Modern England.* Madison: Univ. of Wisconsin Press. 1984.

Perkins, William. *The Work of William Perkins.* Appleford: The Sutton Courtenay Press, 1970.

Pollock, Sir Frederick and Frederick William Maitland. *The History of English Law.* 13 vols. 2nd ed. Cambridge: Cambridge UP, 1968.

Prosper of Aquitaine. *The Call of All Nations.* Intro. P. De Letter. Westminster, Maryland: The Newman Press, 1952.

————. *Grace and Free Will.* Trans. J. R. O'Donnell. Vol. 7 in *The Fathers of the Church.* New York: Fathers of the Church. Inc., 1949.

Rozett, Martha Tuck. *The Doctrine of Election and the Emergence of Elizabethan Tragedy.* Princeton: Princeton UP, 1984.

Shakespeare, William. *The Tempest.* Ed. Frank Kermode. The Arden Shakespeare. 6th ed. Cambridge, Mass.: Harvard UP, 1958.

————. *The Tempest.* Ed. Stephen Orgel. Oxford: Clarendon Press, 1987.

Sharp, Corona. "Caliban: The Primitive Man's Evolution." *Shakespeare Studies* 14 (1981): 267-83.

Siegel, Paul N. "Historical Ironies in *The Tempest.*" *Shakespeare Jarhbuch* 119 (1983): 104-11.

Skura, Meredith Anne. "Discourse and the Individual: The Case of Colonialism in *The Tempest.*" *Shakespeare Quarterly* 40 (1989): 42-69.

Woodhead, M. R. "Montaigne and *The Tempest:* An Addendum," *Notes and Queries* (April, 1982): 126.

Zachrisson, Robert Eugen. *Pronunciation of English Vowels, 1400-1700.* Goeteborg, 1913. Rpt. New York: AMS Press, 1971.

Alden T. Vaughan and Virginia Mason Vaughan (essay date 1991)

SOURCE: "Caliban's Debut," in *Shakespeare's Caliban: A Cultural History,* Cambridge University Press, 1991, pp. 3-20.

[*In the excerpt below, the Vaughans discuss Caliban's physical features, his dramatic function, and the ambiguity of his characterization.*]

> Caliban, a salvage and deformed slave.
> *The Tempest* (names of the actors, 1623 Folio)

> Caliban is the core of the play.
>   Frank Kermode (1954).

Caliban. In modern poetry he is a recurring symbol for the victimization of Third World peoples. In the theatre he can be anything the director imagines, from amphibian to punk rocker to black militant. Contemporary film shows him as the id: In *Forbidden Planet* he is Dr. Morbius's (Walter Pidgeon's) destructive impulse, ready to kill rather than be suppressed; in Paul Mazursky's adaptation *Tempest,* he (Raul Julia) is a libidinous Peeping Tom, ogling Miranda from fake foliage and blaring "New York, New York" on his clarinet. Caliban can even play two roles at once: The protagonist in *Mrs. Caliban,* a recent novel by Rachel Ingalls, is a six-foot seven-inch human amphibian of insatiable sexual appetite and simultaneously a fetus; both are figments of the heroine's starved libido.[1] Such bizarre characters, inspired by Shakespeare's Caliban, attest to the monster's integral place in our cultural heritage, a symbol that can be endlessly transformed yet is always recognizable.

Caliban in the late twentieth century is, of course, far removed in both time and interpretation from the character Shakespeare created in 1611. This chapter goes back to the beginning of Caliban's metaphorical odyssey to examine Shakespeare's text in detail, for Caliban as Shakespeare portrayed him (or, rather, as he first appears in print in the Folio edition) sets a necessary background to the discussion that follows.

We have hewed as closely as possible to the printed text, but we caution readers that any understanding of the play inevitably involves judgments about words and contexts that are in themselves interpretive. Similarly, it is a matter of textual interpretation to accept or reject the characters' "accuracy" in reporting "events," as in Prospero's charge that Caliban tried to rape Miranda or that Caliban is the issue of a witch and the devil. On these and other matters, did Shakespeare want us to take Prospero literally? How a reader answers that question largely determines his or her interpretation of Caliban and the broader conception of the play.

I

Records from the early seventeenth century show that *The Tempest* was performed at the court of King James I on 1 November 1611 and was repeated (possibly with alterations) in the winter of 1612-13 at the wedding celebrations for Princess Elizabeth and Frederick, elector of Palatine.[2] There may have been other, unrecorded showings—and revisions—before Shakespeare's death in 1616. No texts survive before 1623. Why John Heminges and Henry Condell placed it first in their Folio edition is open to speculation, as is the text's possible evolution from 1611 to 1623.[3]

The general context in which Shakespeare composed *The Tempest* is less ambiguous. By 1610, James had substantially stabilized his regime; England enjoyed an uneasy peace with her traditional enemies France and Spain, and the religious squabbles within the Anglican church that had marked Elizabeth's later and James's early years had largely subsided. Royal marriages commanded considerable attention, as did England's precarious footholds in North America. It seems likely that Shakespeare was well aware of current news; his contacts were numerous and notable, especially among investors in the Virginia Company of London. Several topical references in *The Tempest*—Indians, a fortuitous shipwreck, Bermuda—attest to the dramatist's awareness of New World events. But other events, both foreign and domestic, may have exerted equal or greater influence, as, no doubt, did literary and theatrical concerns that were the warp and woof of Shakespeare's livelihood.

The Tempest was an appropriate play to stage before Princess Elizabeth and her fiancé. A major plot of the play—the dynastic marriage of a duke's daughter to a king's son—no doubt had topical appeal for a royal audience celebrating an equally political and dynastic marriage. David M. Bergeron argues, in fact, that "James and his family are re-presented in *The Tempest* through the issues of peaceful succession, royal genealogy, interpretation, and the union of the kingdoms."[1] The union of Naples and Milan through Miranda's marriage may have been a projection of James's continuing concern for the peaceful union of his native Scotland with England. It could also suggest the union of Protestant England and Germany embodied in the marriage between Elizabeth and Frederick.

But *The Tempest* seems to have sparked special attention from the author. It was the last drama Shakespeare wrote without a collaborator and may have been the last of his plays staged by the King's Men before he retired to Stratford. Significantly, perhaps, *The Tempest* depicts a magician absorbed in his art, the power to craft illusions, who, at the drama's conclusion, deliberately renounces his gift, drowns his book, and returns to a life of responsibility rather than creativity. Although modern critics resist overt biographical readings of Shakespeare's dramas, *The Tempest* remains implicitly autobiographical. By 1611, Shakespeare, like James, was concerned about the marriage of his daughters and what inheritance he could leave them;[5] Shakespeare died only five years after the probable date of the play's composition. No wonder Prospero's farewell to his art is often taken for the author's retirement declaration.[6]

As a member of the King's Men, Shakespeare crafted a play that had more than topical appeal. To suit the royal palate, he included within his play an elaborate masque of gods and goddesses, similar in many respects to the spectacles designed by Inigo Jones for James and Queen Anne. Shakespeare arranged his play so that it would roughly fit the "unity of time" (four hours) and the "unity of place" (a small island)—classical protocols he never bothered with elsewhere, except in the early and Plautine *Comedy of Errors*. He also focused his plot on issues of royal concern: Conspiracy and possible usurpation must have appealed to the monarch who had escaped annihilation during the Gunpowder Plot of 1605.[7] As a king who styled himself the "father of his people," James surely had some interest in issues of government and authority. The play's supernatural elements may also have intrigued him; in 1597 he had published a treatise on demonology, and throughout his life he remained interested in witchcraft and magic.[8] Duke Prospero, a ruler who lost power by devoting himself to his studies, could have been a surrogate for a king who preferred hunting and collecting rare animals to governing. And Caliban, perhaps, represented (as anti-masque) the unruly forces of English society—rowdies and malcontents who undermined the ideal unity and harmony of James's body politic. That the king saw Shakespeare's drama as a mirror image of his own court and country is unlikely. But the parallels are evident in hindsight and could not have been wholly lost on *The Tempest*'s early audiences.

II

It should be apparent from this brief introduction that Caliban is not the most important character in *The Tempest*, though he is, as most critics and directors make clear, essential. As Frank Kermode observed in his influential introduction to the second Arden edition, "Caliban is the ground of the play."[9] He has a scant 177 lines of text (compare Prospero's 653 lines), and he appears in only five of the nine scenes, yet Caliban is central to *The Tempest*'s plot and structure and to its dialogue. He speaks more words than any character except Prospero, though barely more than Stephano or Ariel. (The exact proportions, meticulously measured by Marvin Spevack, are Prospero 29.309%, Caliban 8.393%, Stephano 8.137%, and Ariel 7.888%, each of the other characters has less than 7.5% of the text's words.[10]) Not that a character's importance can be quantified. Surely Caliban is qualitatively more important to the play's dynamics than anyone but Prospero, regardless of the number of his words. Almost as important as his own lines, of course, are the volume and significance of the words spoken to him or about him; by this measure Caliban is clearly, next to Prospero, *The Tempest*'s predominant character. But our principal concern is Caliban's ambiguity rather than his importance: Of all the characters in *The Tempest*, Caliban is the most enigmatic and the most susceptible to drastic fluctuations in interpretation. He is Shakespeare's changeling.

The Folio edition of 1623 simply describes Caliban in the cast of characters as "a salvage and deformed slave." (The *l* in "salvage" was probably silent, as in "calm."[11]) Each of the operative words illuminates Caliban's character. His savagery, for example, attests to his crudeness and lack of qualities that Englishmen in the early seventeenth century considered essential to human progress.[12] In Shakespeare's day, "savage" meant wild, barbarous, uneducated, undomesticated—in short, *uncivilized* by upper-class European standards.[13] The supposed shortcomings of savage people often were enumerated in long lists of negatives: They had no religion, no written language, no established laws, no hierarchical government, no refined (again, by upper-class European standards) habits of dress, speech, and eating.[14] "Savage" was thus shorthand for someone culturally inferior to the smug observer. Englishmen lavished the label on the Irish and on the American Indians, the ethnic groups most newsworthy in Tudor-Stuart times, and also on a host of other peoples in Africa, Asia, and even Europe. Shakespeare used variants of "savage"—as noun, adjective, or adverb—in a score of plays, without exhibiting any pattern of ethnic or geographic preference. Savagery could exist anywhere, even in England, especially (in the eyes of the upper classes) among vagabonds, gypsies, and "sturdy beggars." Accordingly, "savage" tells us much about Caliban's cultural condition (as perceived by Prospero and Miranda) but nothing about his physical appearance or moral attributes.

Caliban's social condition is clear too. Prospero repeatedly calls him a slave—"Caliban, my slave," "What ho, slave!" "poisonous slave," "most lying slave." Miranda chides the "Abhorred slave," though the line may be Prospero's, in which case only he explicitly labels Caliban a slave.[15] Ariel, too, is called a slave, but, unlike Caliban, he is promised his freedom after a few more hours of servitude. In any event, Caliban himself admits and laments his bondage, complaining to Stephano and Trinculo that he is "subject to a tyrant" (III.ii.40). Most important, Prospero treats him as a slave throughout the play, ordering him about and punishing his indolence or recalcitrance ("If thou neglect'st, or dost unwillingly" [I.ii.367]) with cramps, stitches, and stings. Caliban's slavery begins before the play's action opens and lasts a bit past the final curtain, when he will regain his liberty and his island.[16]

Whereas *The Tempest* is precise about Caliban's slavery, it is annoyingly imprecise about his deformity. Morton Luce's lament is initially tempting: "If all the suggestions as to Caliban's form and feature and endowments that are thrown out in the play are collected, it will be found that the one half renders the other half impossible."[17] Yet when the clues are arranged in some semblance of order and context, Luce's complaint is palpably overstated.

Of principal importance—though misread by Luce and many others—is the Folio's assertion that Caliban has a *human* form, however misshapen. Before Caliban appears on stage, Prospero tells Ariel that when Caliban's mother Sycorax confined Ariel in a cloven pine,

. . . Then was this Island
(Saue for the Son that [s]he did littour heere,
A frekelld whelpe, hag-borne) not honour'd with
A humane shape.
    (TLN 408-11; Orgel ed. I.ii.281-84)[18]

If the final two lines of that passage are wrenched from context, as they have often been, they are easily misinterpreted; they seem to deny rather than affirm

Caliban's human stature.[19] That impression is unintentionally encouraged by the new Arden and Folger Library editions, where the penultimate line of the crucial passage begins a new page, thus visually distorting the syntax. The new Arden and Oxford editions, moreover, substitute dashes for the First Folio's parentheses, which is especially misleading if the last two lines are read independently of their essential precursors.[20] When the passage is read intact, including the First Folio's parentheses, it clearly establishes Caliban as the only human-shaped creature on the island before Prospero and Miranda arrived. Ariel, though necessarily appearing on stage as a human, takes any form Prospero desires.[21]

Any doubt about Caliban's physical humanity is removed, temporarily at least, when Miranda exclaims on her first glimpse of Ferdinand: "This / Is the third man that e'er I saw, the first / That e'er I sigh'd for" (I.ii.445-47); Prospero and Caliban must be the others, for she has already denied any memory of her life before arrival on the island. A few lines later, Prospero indirectly corroborates Miranda when he chides her for unseemly excitement over Ferdinand: "Thou think'st there is no more such shapes as he, / Having seen but him and Caliban" (I.ii.479-80). Because Miranda has surely seen a wide assortment of beasts and fish, these lines strongly suggest that the only "shapes" under consideration are human. (We assume that Prospero has excluded himself. As Miranda's father, he would not suggest himself as a possible object of her amorous affections.) On the other hand, in Act III Miranda implicitly contradicts her earlier testimony. She tells Ferdinand that her own is the only female face she's seen (in a looking glass)

. . . nor have I seen
More than I may call men than you, good friend,
And my dear father. . . .
    (III.i.50-52)

Does she not consider Caliban a man? In the context of her passion for Ferdinand, Caliban is apparently beneath consideration, whatever his biological status.

Adding to the certainty that Caliban is human are the efforts Prospero and Miranda take to educate and civilize him. They have attempted what can be done only to a human; there is no hint that they tried to teach language and astronomy to an animal or a fish. Caliban proved, in their judgment, impervious to nurture, but he did learn their language, and he continues to serve them in wholly human ways. "We cannot miss [i.e., do without] him," Prospero reminds his daughter: "He does make our fire, / Fetch in our wood, and serves in offices / That profit us" (I.ii.311-13). Although Caliban is a "savage" and therefore potentially educable, he is not, in Prospero's or Miranda's eyes, either admirable or an acceptable suitor. But that he is biologically capable of impregnating Miranda, and hence probably human, is clear enough from Prospero's charge that Caliban tried to violate her honor and Caliban's retort that had Prospero not prevented him, "I had peopled else / This isle with Calibans" (I.ii.349-50).

Despite the overwhelming evidence of Caliban's basic physiology, several passages suggest that he is barely—to Prospero, Miranda, and the others (but not necessarily to Shakespeare)—on the human side of the animal kingdom. A partial list of the epithets Prospero flings at Caliban includes "earth," "filth," "hag-seed," "beast," "misshapen knave," and "a bastard one." He is, Prospero insists, "as disproportioned in his manners / As in his shape" (V.i.290-91). Miranda almost matches her father's venom, if the disputed passage in the First Folio is hers, for she calls Caliban "A thing most brutish" and condemns his "vile race" (I.ii.356-57). And in lines that are unquestionably hers, Miranda tells her father that Caliban is "a villain, sir, / I do not love to look on" (I.ii.309-10). Caliban, in sum, earns no laurels from father or daughter, yet on balance they both affirm his human shape, however physically and psychologically distorted he may be.

Trinculo and Stephano, the besotted idlers, are no more flattering and no clearer on Caliban's shape, but they too affirm his humanity. Trinculo initially calls Caliban a "fish," based on his smell: "What have we here—a man or a fish? . . . he smells like a fish; a very ancient and fish-like smell" (II.ii.24-26). Trinculo then sees that the creature is "Legged like a man, and his fins like arms!" (II.ii.32-33). (Trinculo's description of Caliban's upper limbs as "fins like arms" indicates that the presumed [by smell] fish has, in fact, arms, yet Caliban is often portrayed on stage and in illustrations with arms made to look like fins, thus reversing the import of Trinculo's observation.) At this point, Caliban is hiding under a gaberdine, his head and torso not clearly visible. Trinculo examines him further and concludes that "this is no fish, but an islander that hath lately suffered by a thunderbolt" (II.ii.34-35)—in sum, a human inhabitant. Later, Trinculo reverts to aquatic imagery (of which he has almost a monopoly in the play), again probably for olfactory reasons; he labels Caliban "debosh'd Fish" (TLN 1376; "debauched fish" in Orgel, III.ii.26) and "half a fish and half a monster" (III.ii.28-29), but these are epithets rather than descriptions. Trinculo surely categorizes Caliban as human when he tells him and Stephano, " . . . there's but five upon this isle: we are three of them" (III.ii.5).

Two uses of aquatic imagery do not come from Trinculo. Near the end of the play, Antonio calls Caliban "a plain fish" (V.i.266), which could refer to either appearance or odor; the conspirators have recently been chin-deep in a "foul lake" (IV.i.183). More significant—and controversial—is Prospero's "thou tortoise" (I.ii.316). At first glance this might imply a tortoiselike body, but when read in context, and especially in view of the word that follows "tortoise," the epithet unquestionably refers to Caliban's dilatoriness. (In I.ii.315-16, Caliban fails to respond when called; Prospero demands "Come forth, I say; there's other business for thee. / Come, thou tortoise, when?") By Shakespeare's day, an abundance of fables, beginning with Aesop's, and numerous zoological treatises emphasized the tortoise's leisurely pace; the metaphor would have been obvious to a Jacobean audience.[22] Some illustrators and critics have nonetheless avidly seized the tortoise image. In the nineteenth century, for example, one scholar proposed that "Caliban is . . . a kind of tortoise, the paddles expanding in arms and hands, legs and feet." Another commentator saw Caliban as a dwarf in stature, with the legs and forefins of a turtle, and, "if the hardly human face were fashioned after that of a tortoise . . . the eyes would be 'deepset' by nature as well as by drink . . . and he would be 'dim-eyed' and 'beetle-browed,'" his body covered with patches of "loathsome leprosy." More recently and more temperately, two American critics have argued that "'Come, thou tortoise' tended to give a vague approximation of the shape of the deformity."[23] More often, Caliban has been portrayed with fish rather than turtle attributes—scales, fins, and shiny skin—which reflect the critic's or artist's or actor's fixation on offhand epithets rather than the overwhelming evidence of Caliban's essentially human form. By contrast, Frank Kermode insists (correctly, we believe) that Caliban is occasionally called a fish "largely because of his oddity, and there should be no fishiness about his appearance."[24]

"Monster" is Caliban's most frequent sobriquet, but it comes only from Trinculo and Stephano and may therefore be less descriptive than simply pejorative—attempts by a jester and a butler to assert a modicum of superiority over their self-proclaimed "foot-licker." In any event, "monster" appears in the text some forty times, usually with a pejorative adjective: "shallow," "weak," "credulous," "most perfidious and drunken," "puppy-headed," "scurvy," "abominable," "ridiculous," "howling," "ignorant," and "lost." Only "brave," used twice, might be a favorable modifier, and it is almost certainly meant sarcastically. More neutral are "servant-monster," "man-monster," "lieutenant-monster," and "poor monster." To the extent that "monster" implies physical deformity, as it did generally but not exclusively in Shakespeare's time, these abundant reminders strengthen the notion of Caliban as grotesque.[25] They do nothing, however, to specify the deformity. Nor does Alonso's quip that "This is a strange thing as e'er I looked on" (V.i.289). The text tells us that Caliban had long nails to dig pignuts (II.ii.162); otherwise his physical deformities are unspecified.

Other references to Caliban are little help. Several times he is called "mooncalf," suggesting stupidity and an amorphous shape. Pliny's *Natural History,* translated into English in 1601, described a mooncalf as "a lumpe of flesh without shape, without life, ... Howbeit, a kind of moving it hath."[26] Prospero once dubs Caliban "this thing of darkness" (V.i.275), possibly implying a dusky skin, though more likely a faulty character. Similarly, Prospero's "thou earth" (I.ii.314) hints at darkness or dirt or, more likely, baseness of character. Stephano once calls Caliban "cat" (II.ii.70), but the text itself and contemporaneous proverbs clearly link the epithet to alcohol's purported ability to make even a cat speak.[27]

Several times Caliban's parentage—his mother, Prospero tells us, was an Algerian witch, his father the devil—is invoked, as in "demi-devil" and "a born devil"; such lineage may imply a less-than-human shape, for unions with the devil, especially by a witch, often brought forth—according to conventional wisdom—all sorts of grotesque births.[28] The charge of devilish parentage may be Prospero's hyperbole.[29] In light of the other evidence in the text that Caliban is essentially human, the attribution of satanic parentage, if such it was, more likely testifies to Caliban's inherently warped character. And the progeny of a witch and the devil *could* have been human—again, according to conventional wisdom—in fundamental shape, though inwardly and outwardly deformed. As George Steevens observed in his 1793 edition of *The Tempest,* "It is not easy to determine the shape which our author designed to bestow on his monster. That he has hands, legs, etc. we gather from the remarks of Trinculo, and other circumstances in the play. . . . Perhaps Shakespeare himself had no settled ideas concerning the form of *Caliban.*"[30] In any event, the confusion of epithets that abounds in *The Tempest* encourages artists, actors, and readers to see Caliban however they wish. For three centuries they have enthusiastically accepted the invitation.

III

Aside from its specific language, the text also provides clues to Caliban's role, and to some extent his nature, through the structure of the plot. He is a pivotal character who, by means of parallels and contrasts, frequently elucidates the ways one views the other characters. His first appearance, for example, is sandwiched between Prospero's opening interview with Ariel and his first encounter with Ferdinand. Caliban manifests significant similarities with, and differences from, both of these characters—parallels and contrasts highlighted by juxtapositions in the text. Caliban, of course, is unaware of these contrasts and parallels because he never appears on stage with either Ariel or Ferdinand. He presumably does not know of Ferdinand at all, and he may be oblivious to Ariel's existence. He suffers the pinches caused by Ariel, but he assigns such bodily punishments to Prospero's magic. Caliban insists to Stephano that to thwart

Prospero and succeed in their conspiracy, they must begin by stealing the magician's books.

Caliban first crawls from his cave in a scene of exposition that follows the audience's initial view of Ariel. The airy spirit had asked for freedom from Prospero's domination; after reviewing Ariel's history, Prospero threatens his spirit-servant with a return to the cloven pine, then promises freedom as a reward for a bit more service. Ariel, though often in fear of Prospero, gladly agrees. Despite Prospero's irascibility, there clearly is affection between them.

Caliban is in many ways Ariel's opposite, although their situations are somewhat similar. Both were on the island when Prospero and Miranda arrived. Both are now servants. Both are afraid of the magician's powers. But Ariel is a spirit; he enters from above, flies aloft, and can make himself invisible. Caliban is earthy and earth-bound. He crawls from a cave; his deformity may keep him hunched over, close to the ground. And his earthiness—a near-beastiality (Prospero insists) that prevents him from assimilating civility and morality—makes his relationship with Prospero differ sharply from Ariel's. The spirit-servant had originally been imprisoned in a cloven pine because he would not enact Sycorax's "earthy and abhorred commands" (I.ii.273). Nonhuman spirit though he is, Ariel understands right from wrong. Human though he is, Caliban lacks moral perception. He responds chiefly to appetite.

The principles of parallelism and contrast equally govern Caliban's position vis-à-vis Ferdinand, who is introduced directly after Caliban's first appearance. Both men apprehend the music of the isle, yet it affects them differently. Music, "with its sweet air," allays Ferdinand's passion and leads him to Miranda. She assumes at first that Ferdinand is a spirit, but Prospero assures her that "it eats and sleeps and hath such senses / As we have" (I.ii.413-14). Ferdinand's courtship of Miranda is chaste, its purpose honorable marriage. Caliban, who hears the same music, is also attracted to Miranda, but he has no "nurture"—no moral awareness—to allay his passions. He had lodged in Prospero's cell until he tried to rape Miranda, and he wishes his attack had succeeded: "O ho, O ho! Would't had been done!" (I.ii.348).

The parallels between Caliban and Ferdinand are conveyed visually as well as verbally. Caliban enters (in II.ii) with a "burden of wood"; his task is to carry logs for Prospero. That is also Ferdinand's task: In the scene immediately following Caliban's wood-fetching assignment, Ferdinand enters "bearing a log." Unlike Caliban, he delights in his labor because he is inspired by love of Miranda. Thus, both Caliban and Ferdinand are human creatures with appetites who must perform tiresome labor, but whereas the prince is civilized and controls his appetites and even enjoys his work, the mooncalf has no higher aspirations than to overthrow Prospero and is enslaved by his own desires.

Caliban's situation on the island also parallels Miranda's. At a young age both were isolated from their peers and educated by Prospero. Such limited experience makes them vulnerable and naive. Caliban has seen only one woman besides his mother, and she (Miranda) "as far surpasseth Sycorax / As great'st does least" (III.ii.100-01). Because Miranda has seen no men besides her father and Caliban, she assumes that Ferdinand is a spirit, until her father exclaims

> Thou think'st there is no more such shape as he,
> Having seen but him and Caliban. Foolish
>   wench,
> To th' most of men this is a Caliban,
> And they to him are angels.
>
> (I.ii.479-82)

Similarly, Caliban mistakes Stephano and Trinculo for gods; Miranda admires Antonio and Sebastian as part of a "brave new world." Both the beast and the beauty misjudge the basic characters of those they initially admire.

Prospero prides himself on Miranda's education. He boasts that on the island

> Have I, thy schoolmaster, made thee more
>   profit
> Than other princes can that have more time
> For vainer hours, and tutors not so careful.
>
> (I.ii.172-74)

He has not been so successful with Caliban. The monster first learned language: how to name "the bigger light and how the less, / That burn by day and night" (I.ii.335-37). But Caliban would not retain "any print of goodness," Miranda charges, and instead is "capable of all ill!" (I.ii.351-52)

> . . . I pitied thee, [she chides him],
> Took pains to make thee speak, taught thee
>   each hour
> One thing or other. When thou didst not, savage,
> Know thine own meaning, but wouldst gabble
>   like
> A thing most brutish, I endowed thy purposes
> With words that made them known. But thy
>   vile race—
> Though thou didst learn—had that in't which
>   good natures
> Could not abide to be with. . . .
>
> (I.ii.352-59)

For all Miranda's and Prospero's efforts, Caliban remains (to them, at least) "a born devil, on whose nature / Nurture can never stick" (IV.i.188-89). His

bestiality and stubbornness contrast starkly with Miranda's beauty and obedience.

Juxtaposed to Antonio's and Sebastian's brutal plot against Alonso is Caliban's conspiracy to murder Prospero. Stephano's "celestial liquor" is a comic parallel to Prospero's magic. Like Sebastian, Stephano aspires to become a king; both men seek total power through murder. Prospero interrupts their schemes by spectacles: A banquet that suddenly disappears confounds the Italian nobles, while Prospero's rich garments, hanging on a line near the entrance to his cave, distract Stephano and Trinculo—despite Caliban's warnings—into a comic parade of "borrowed robes."

There remains an important contrast, however, between the several conspirators. Alonso, the intended victim of Antonio's most recent scheming, repents his past and reconciles himself to Prospero. Antonio has no lines in the conclusion, and most commentators consider him unrepentant and unlikely to change. Raised with the benefits of "civilization," Antonio knowingly chooses the path of evil. By contrast, Caliban seems to learn from his mistakes, especially his misguided adoration of Stephano and Trinculo. In his final speech he promises that

> I'll be wise hereafter,
> And seek for grace. What a thrice-double ass
> Was I to take this drunkard for a god,
> And worship this dull fool!
>
> (V.i.294-97)

Though Caliban remains "natural" man in contrast to "civilized" Antonio, the monster's desire for grace underlines the civilized world's debasement and, once again, emphasizes Caliban's ultimate humanity.[31]

The play ends soon after this speech. Prospero and the nobles will return to Italy the next morning, their ship and sailors suddenly as good as new. Ariel will be free to soar, and Caliban will reinherit his island. The play's conclusion says nothing about Caliban's fate or how he feels about Prospero's and Miranda's departure. Perhaps this is why so many sequels to *The Tempest* have been written, most of them concerning Caliban's subsequent career. Caliban is a loose end; for centuries readers and playgoers have wanted to tie him up. He captures their fancy, and they, unlike Prospero, are reluctant to abandon him. . . .

Notes

[1] Rachel Ingalls, *Mrs. Caliban* (London: Faber & Faber, 1983).

[2] For the bare facts of *The Tempest*'s early performances, see E. K. Chambers, *William Shakespeare,* Vol. I (Oxford: Clarendon Press, 1930), p. 491.

[3] For a concise printing history of *The Tempest,* see Orgel's edition (Oxford University Press, 1987), pp. 56-62.

[4] David M. Bergeron, *Shakespeare's Romances and the Royal Family* (Lawrence: University of Kansas Press, 1985), p. 181.

[5] Susannah married Dr. John Hall in 1608; Judith married Thomas Quiney in 1616. S[amuel] Schoenbaum, *William Shakespeare: A Compact Documentary Life* (Oxford University Press, 1977), pp. 286-93.

[6] Thomas Campbell, ed., *The Dramatic Works of William Shakspeare, with a Life by Thomas Campbell* (London: Edward Moxon, 1838), pp. lxiii-lxiv. Shakespeare collaborated on two, perhaps three, subsequent plays: *Henry VIII, The Two Noble Kinsmen,* and *Cardenio* (no text survives). *The Tempest,* however, marks the end of his phenomenal productivity and thorough commitment to the stage.

[7] Glynne Wickham suggests that Caliban's plot to murder Prospero may be a direct reference to "the Gunpowder treason." See "Masque and Anti-Masque in 'The Tempest'," in *Essays and Studies 1975,* ed. Robert Ellrodt (London: John Murray, 1975), pp. 1-14, esp. p. 12.

[8] Jacqueline E. M. Latham argues that *The Tempest* was directly influenced by Shakespeare's reading of James's *Daemonologie* and that Caliban's parentage (born of a devil and a witch) would have sparked particular interest in the monarch. See "'The Tempest' and King James's 'Daemonologie'," *Shakespeare Survey,* XXVIII (1975): 117-23.

[9] *The Tempest,* ed. Frank Kermode, "The Arden Shakespeare," 6th ed. (London: Methuen, 1958), p. xxv.

[10] Marvin Spevack, *A Complete and Systematic Concordance to the Works of Shakespeare,* 9 vols. (Hildesheim, Germany: Georg Olms, 1968-80), Vol. I, pp. 36-62. The other characters' percentages, according to Spevack, are Gonzalo 7.221, Miranda 6.242, Antonio 6.167, Ferdinand 6.098, and Trinculo 5.088.

[11] On the pronunciation of "salvage," see Richard Grant White, ed., *The Works of William Shakespeare,* Vol. II (Boston: Little, Brown, 1875), p. 94, which asserts that the word was pronounced both ways in Shakespeare's time because it entered English through both the French *sauvage* and the Italian *salvaggio.* We contend, however, that Shakespeare probably did not pronounce the *l,* because that spelling appears only twice in the canon: in *The Tempest*'s list of characters, which may have been added by the First Folio's editors, and in "salvages and men of Inde" ("savages" in Orgel's edition [II.ii.57]); the only other use of the word in *The Tempest* omits the *l* (I.ii.354). The more than forty other uses (including the variants "savagely," "savageness," and "savagery") in more than twenty other Shakespearean plays do not include *l.* See Marvin Spevack, *The Harvard Concordance to Shakespeare* (Cambridge, Mass.: Harvard University Press, 1973), pp. 1081, 1083; and Horace Howard Furness, comp., *Notes on Studies of The Tempest. Minutes of the Shakspere Society of Philadelphia for 1864-65* (Philadelphia: The Shakspere Society, 1866), p. 33. See also Helge Kökeritz, *Shakespeare's Pronunciation* (New Haven, Ct.: Yale University Press, 1953), pp. 310-11.

[12] In the text of the play, Caliban is called "savage" only once—by an angry Miranda (I.ii.354). But the inclusion of the word in the cast of characters suggests (unless it was inserted by the Folio's editors) that it was central to Shakespeare's conception of Caliban.

[13] The *Oxford English Dictionary (OED)* lists thirteen definitions of "civility." Among those that were current in the sixteenth century are (1) "connected with citizenship, and civil polity"; (6) "Good polity . . . social order, as distinct from anarchy and disorder"; (10) "The state of being civilized; freedom from barbarity"; (11) "Polite or liberal education; training in the 'humanities', good breeding; culture, refinement"; and (12) "Behaviour proper to the intercourse of civilized people; ordinary courtesy."

[14] Among the many modern studies of early English notions of savagery, see Margaret T. Hodgen, *Early Anthropology in the Sixteenth and Seventeenth Centuries* (Philadelphia: University of Pennsylvania Press, 1964), esp. ch. 9; and Bernard Sheehan, *Savagism and Civility: Indians and Englishmen in Colonial Virginia* (Cambridge University Press, 1980), ch. 1-3. For an example from Shakespeare's day, see [Thomas Palmer], *An Essay of the Meanes how to Make our Trauailes, into Forraine Countries the More Profitable and Honourable* (London: Printed for Mathew Lownes, 1606), esp. pp. 60-68.

[15] For a summary of the debate over the proper assignment of the "abhorred slave" speech, see *The Tempest,* ed. Horace Howard Furness, "A New Variorum Edition of Shakespeare," Vol. IX (1892; repr. New York: American Scholar Publications, 1966), pp. 73-74; Furness, *Notes on Studies of The Tempest,* pp. 18-19; *The Tempest,* ed. Orgel, p. 17.

[16] Caliban's age is never mentioned in the text; his behavior implies young adulthood. Clues in the text suggest that he is approximately 24 years old: Prospero and Miranda have been on the island for 12 years, and Caliban was about age 12 when they arrived. See *The Tempest,* ed. Morton Luce (the first Arden edition) (London: Methuen, 1901), p. xxxiv; *The Tempest,* ed. Orgel, p. 28 (n. 1).

[17] *The Tempest,* ed. Luce, p. xxxv.

[18] Lines from the 1623 Folio are taken from *The Norton Facsimile of the First Folio of Shakespeare,* ed. Charlton Hinman (New York: Norton, 1968). Nicholas Rowe's edition (London: Jacob Tonson, 1709) was the first to emend the Folio's "he" to "she."

[19] *Shakespeare's Comedy, The Tempest, as Arranged for the Stage by Herbert Beerbohm Tree* (London: J. Miles, 1904), pp. x-xi, presented one of the early arguments for Caliban's human shape. Some commentators follow suit, but many, including some of the most prominent scholars, continue to misread the passage. *The Oxford Companion to English Literature,* ed. Margaret Drabble (London: Guild Publishing, 1985), p. 159, asserts that Caliban "is only semi-human," a fairly frequent assumption of literary critics and stage directors.

[20] *The Tempest,* ed. Kermode (Arden edition), p. 28; *The Tempest,* ed. Louis B. Wright, (Folger edition) (New York: Washington Square Press, 1961), p. 16; *The Tempest,* ed. Orgel (Oxford edition), p. 116.

[21] As Stephen Orgel points out (Oxford edition, p. 27), Ariel appears in the text as a male and yet is assigned essentially "female" tasks.

[22] See, for example, John Leo [Leo Africanus], *A Geographical History of Africa,* trans. John Pory (London: George Bishop, 1600), p. 951; and Edward Topsell, *The Historie of Serpents* (London: Printed for William Jaggard, 1608), p. 282r.

[23] Joseph Hunter, *A Disquisition on the Scene, Origin, Date, Etc. of Shakespeare's Tempest* (London: Printed by L. Whittingham, 1839), p. 123; Brinsley Nicholson, "Shakespeare Illustrated by Massinger," *Notes and Queries,* 4th ser., I (1868): 289-91; Barry Gaines and Michael Lofaro, "What Did Caliban Look Like?" *Mississippi Folklore Register,* X (1976): 175-86. All three works implicitly or explicitly misread the lines about Caliban's human shape. Gaines and Lofaro further contend (p. 178) that "tortoise" did not imply slowness until the late seventeenth century, and hence Prospero must have referred to Caliban's appearance. They base that judgment on the *OED,* in which the earliest citation of *one* meaning of the word is 1670, yet overlook a 1589 usage ("Venus standeth on the Tortoys, as shewing that Loue creepeth on by degrees") that clearly equates the animal with dilatoriness. Aesop's *Fables* was first published in English in 1485; more than a dozen editions followed before 1611.

[24] *The Tempest,* ed. Kermode, p. 62. Cf. Willard Farnham, for example, who insists that Caliban's body "is part primitive man and part crude fish": *The Shakespearean Grotesque* (Oxford: Clarendon Press, 1971), p. 166. . . .

[25] The *OED*'s basic definitions all stress abnormality, usually (but not always) manifested in outsized proportions.

[26] Caius Plinius Secundus, *The Historie of the World,* trans. Philemon Holland (London: A. Islip, 1601), p. 163.

[27] See Kermode's note, *The Tempest,* p. 65.

[28] Gaines and Lofaro, "What Did Caliban Look Like?" pp. 179-88.

[29] *The Tempest,* ed. Orgel, p. 25.

[30] *The Plays of William Shakspeare,* 4th ed., 15 vols., Vol. III, ed. George Steevens and Samuel Johnson (London: Printed for T. Longman, 1793), p. 158.

[31] Deborah Willis's "Shakespeare's *Tempest* and the Discourse of Colonialism," *Studies in English Literature,* XXIX (1989): 277-89, argues that "the play's true threatening 'other' is not Caliban, but Antonio" (p. 280).

William M. Hamlin (essay date 1994)

SOURCE: "Men of Inde: Renaissance Ethnography and *The Tempest,*" in *Shakespeare Studies: An Annual Gathering of Research, Criticism, and Reviews,* Vol. XXII, 1994, pp. 15-44.

[*In the following excerpt, Hamlin explores the relationship between Shakespeare's characterization of Caliban and Renaissance voyagers' narratives that depict Native Americans as fully human yet significantly different from Europeans. Just as with the ambiguous portrait of Caliban, the critic suggests, these accounts acknowledge basic affinities with New World natives even as they insist on their otherness.*]

Throughout *The Tempest* an air of ambiguity surrounds Caliban. His name—almost certainly an anagram of "cannibal"—appears in the First Folio's cast list among the play's human characters (as opposed to its spirits) and above those of Trinculo and Stephano, but he is described there as "a salvage and deformed slave."[33] And when Prospero first mentions him to Ariel in act 1, it is difficult to decide whether the bestial or the human plays a greater role in his constitution:

> Then was this island
> (Save for the son that [she] did litter here,
> A freckled whelp, hag-born), not honor'd with
> A human shape.
>
> (1.2.281-84)

Although Peter Hulme cites these lines as proof of Prospero's "grudging admittance of Caliban's humanity" and rails against those who seize upon the last six words as "'evidence' of Caliban's lack of human shape,"[34] I think rather that a sense of uncertainty is exquisitely balanced here, that "litter," "whelp," "hag-born" and the parenthetical exception play off against "son" and the main clause in such a way as to reveal Prospero's own deep confusion about Caliban's status. I will argue later that *The Tempest* moves gradually—almost inexorably—toward affirming Caliban as a man, but I believe that in the play's earlier scenes his status is deliberately mystified. However, unlike many colonialist readers, who interpret this mystification as Prospero's ruse to justify usurpation, I think its presence is due primarily to the genuine uncertainty regarding the human status of cultural aliens that emerges as a pervasive motif in the early modern period. Again and again in the travel literature, ethnographic description reveals a deep-seated ambivalence toward ethnic otherness and perceived savagery, and while this ambivalence is undoubtedly exploited at times by conquerors and colonists, its initial presence does not appear to be a necessary function of the European will to power.

Take, for example, Richard Johnson's 1609 description of the natives of Virginia near the colony at Jamestown:

> [The region] is inhabited with wild and savage people that live and lie up and downe in troupes like heards of Deere in a Forrest: they have no law but nature, their apparell skinnes of beasts, but most goe naked, . . . they are generally very loving and gentle, and do entertaine and relieve our people with great kindnesse; they are easy to be brought to good, and would fayne embrace a better condition.[35]

Here we see a people likened to "heards of Deere" and alleged to have "no law but nature," yet we also hear that they are capable of "great kindnesse" and—like Caliban when he claims that he will "be wise hereafter, / And seek for grace" (5.1.295-96)—desire to "embrace a better condition." Similarly, in the writings of Captain John Smith we encounter such seemingly contradictory portrayals of the Chesapeake Algonquians as that, on the one hand, they are "sterne Barbarians,"

Stephano, Ariel, and Trinculo with Jack Hawkins as Caliban in a 1940 production of The Tempest.

"fiends," "inconstant Salvages," and "naked Divels," and that, on the other, they "have amongst them such government, as that their Magistrates for good commanding, and their people for due subjection, and obeying, excell many places that would be counted very civill."[36] It is as if the authors of these passages can relinquish neither their wonder at the seemingly "natural" or "bestial" condition of American natives nor their ever-recurring recognition—or suspicion, at any rate—that these people, like Europeans, possess genuine forms of "civility." And while such a comment as Johnson's that the Virginians "would fayne embrace a better condition" may certainly be read within the frame of colonial discourse as a projection of the colonists' desire for defensible hegemony, it also may reflect a more concrete kind of observation—perhaps of the sort we see in Thomas Harriot when he tells us that despite the coastal Algonquians' clear exhibition of spiritual culture, "they were not so sure grounded, nor gave such credite to their traditions and stories, but through conversing with us they were brought into great doubts of their owne, and no small admiration of ours."[37]

Critics who have touched, however perfunctorily, upon the presentation of Caliban as in some way indebted to New World ethnography have tended either to trace a speculative genealogy through specific travel accounts or to allude somewhat unassuredly to the sort of ambivalence reflected in the above quotations. The former inclination has been present at least since the time of Edmund Malone—who claimed in 1821 that Caliban was Shakespeare's version of a Patagonian—and perhaps reached its apogee in Leslie Fiedler's pronouncement that "Caliban seems to have been created, on his historical side, by a fusion in Shakespeare's imagination of Columbus's first New World savages with Montaigne's Brazilians, Somers's native Bermudans, and those Patagonian 'giants' encountered by Pigafetta during his trip around the world with Magellan, strange creatures whose chief god was called, like Caliban's mother's, 'Setebos'."[38] The latter tendency, however, while relatively common, has provoked few interesting observations beyond the rather obvious generality that Caliban's portrayal relies upon a conflation of contradictory descriptions and evaluations of cultural otherness—particularly American otherness. Geoffrey Bullough, for example, writes that "the ambiguity of travelers' opinions about the American natives affects Shakespeare's handling of Caliban," and Peter Hulme goes so far as to say that "Caliban, as a compromise formation, can exist only within discourse: he is fundamentally and essentially beyond the bounds of representation."[39] But few critics have, to my knowledge, explored the ambiguity or the "compromise formation" of Caliban at any length. Many seem inclined, after acknowledging ambivalence, to settle upon rather reductive conclusions; a representative example is the claim that "By every account in the play, Caliban is

something less than a man. . . . He is an American savage, clearly humanoid though not fully human."[40]

Two commentators, however, have come close to focusing on the sort of ambivalence to which I want to draw attention. In stressing the distinction between the European views that, on the one hand, "Indian language was deficient or non-existent" and that, on the other, "there was no serious language barrier," Stephen Greenblatt anticipates Tzvetan Todorov's useful schematization of European perceptions of native Americans as either acknowledging *difference* and concluding *inferiority,* or acknowledging *equality* and concluding *identity.*[41] Greenblatt writes, for instance, that the tensions of this dichotomy "either push the Indians toward utter difference—and thus silence—or toward utter likeness—and thus the collapse of their own, unique identity."[42] And in a slightly different vein, Richard Marienstras has observed that Caliban possesses a "dubious ontological status"; he "can be seen as a complete and irreducible contradiction or, alternatively, as having two positive but separate natures, each stemming from a different scale of values."[43] What Greenblatt and Marienstras do not do, however, is point toward a middle range of perception that either acknowledges *difference* without immediately concluding *inferiority* or acknowledges *equality* without positing *identity.* Yet we see views within this range expressed implicitly, for example, by various early writers in their recognition and description of distinctly different tribes and social groups among native American peoples:

Alvar Núñez Cabeza de Vaca (1542): The inhabitants of all this region [Malhado] go naked. The women alone have any part of their persons covered, and it is with a wool that grows on trees. The damsels dress themselves in deerskin. The people are generous to each other of what they possess. They have no chief. All that are of a lineage keep together. They speak two languages; those of one are called Capoques, those of the other, Han. They have a custom when they meet, or from time to time when they visit, of remaining half an hour before they speak, weeping; and, this over, he that is visited first rises and gives the other all he has, which is received, and after a little while he carries it away, and often goes without saying a word. They have other strange customs; but I have told the principal of them, and the most remarkable, that I may pass on and further relate what befel us.

Jean de Léry (1578): Although like other Brazilians [the Ouetaca] go entirely naked, nonetheless, contrary to the most ordinary custom of the men of that country (who, as I have already said and will later expand upon, shave the front of their head and clip their locks in the back), these wear their hair long, hanging down to the buttocks. . . . The Margaia, Cara-ia, or Tupinamba (which are the names of the three neighboring nations), or one of the other savages of that country, without trusting or approaching the Ouetaca, shows him from afar what he has—a pruning-hook, a knife, a comb, a mirror, or some other kind of wares brought over for trade—and indicates by a sign if he wants to exchange it for something else.

José de Acosta (1589): It is a popular error to treat the affairs of the Indies as if they were those of some farm or mean village and to think that, because the Indies are all called by a single name, they are therefore of one nature and kind. . . . The nations of Indians are innumerable, and each of them has its own distinct rites and customs and needs to be taught in a different way. I am not properly qualified to handle the problem, since a great many peoples are unknown to me, while even if I knew them well it would be an immense task to discuss them all one by one. I have therefore thought it proper to speak primarily of the Peruvians in this work.

William Strachey (1612): [T]hus it may appear how they are a people who have their several divisions, provinces, and princes, to live in and to command over, and do differ likewise (as amongst Christians) both in stature, language, and condition; some being great people, as the Susquehannas, some very little, as the Wicocomocos; some speaking likewise more articulate and plain, and some more inward and hollow, as is before remembered; some courteous and more civil, others cruel and bloody; Powhatan having large territories and many petty kings under him, as some have fewer.

John Smith (1624): Upon the head of the Powhatans are the Monacans, whose chiefe habitation is at Rasauweak, unto whom the Mowhemenchughes, the Massinnacacks, the Monahassanughs, the Monasickapanoughs, and other nations pay tributes. Upon the head of the river of Toppahanock is a people called Mannahoacks. To these are contributers the Tauxanias, the Shackaconias, the Ontponeas, the Tegninateos, the Whomkenteaes, the Stegarakes, the Hassinnungaes, and divers others, all confederates with the Monacans, though many different in language, and be very barbarous, living for the most part of wild beasts and fruits. Beyond the mountaines from whence is the head of the river Patawomeke, the Salvages report inhabit their most motall enemies, the Massawomekes, upon a great salt water, which by all likelihood is either some part of Canada, some great lake, or some inlet of some sea that falleth into the South sea.[44]

To the extent that these descriptions register plurality and allow a varied yet specific cultural inheritance to the native groups introduced they represent anti-*tabula rasa* views and thus stand in opposition to such bald and overarching characterizations as Samuel Purchas's that American natives are "bad people, having little of Humanitie but shape, ignorant of Civilitie, of Arts, of Religion; more brutish then the beasts they hunt, more wild and unmanly then that unmanned wild countrey,

which they range rather then inhabite."[45] Yet to the extent that they point explicitly to differences among these natives—and implicitly to differences between them and Europeans—they resist both the easy conclusion of inferiority and the more insidious one of identity. In short, they fall outside the polarizing rubric suggested by Greenblatt and Todorov. Rather than countering claims that native Americans are subhuman *tabulas rasas* by wholly assimilating them into Europeanness, these descriptions—and others like them—allow the natives their difference and in fact stress their cultural diversity. Thus they provide a more subtle contrast than that proposed by Greenblatt, a contrast more relevant, I think, to *The Tempest.* If we can admit that early modern ethnography allows for an ambivalence not solely between the binary opposites of subhumanity and virtual identity, but also among the range that includes subhumanity, identity, and cultural—but fully human—difference, we can sharpen our account of the way this ambivalence sheds light on the characterization of Caliban.

An interesting way of producing this account lies in situating Caliban within an ethnographic context and then contrasting him with another curiously ambiguous character from English Renaissance drama: the "wild man" Bremo in the anonymous and highly popular play *Mucedorus.*[46] Caliban has been connected to Bremo before, notably by Frank Kermode in his eclectic genealogy of Caliban's character; but while Kermode points to Bremo's conventionality as a wodewose or salvage man, he does not dwell on the association with Caliban.[47] Yet there is much of interest to focus on, particularly given an ethnographic contextualization.

Like the Wild Man in Book Four of *The Faerie Queene,* Bremo lives in a cave in the woods (7.7, 17.94), carries a club (7.5, 21, 29), and is lustful and cannibalistic (11.16-19, 11.21, 11.25-30, 15.59-60); but unlike Spenser's Wild Man (or, for that matter, the Salvage Man of Book Six), Bremo possesses language and demonstrates an ability to relent and to recognize changes within himself (11.38-54, 15.105). Moreover, he is represented as having the capacity to fall in love (11.37-55, 15.1-55), though exactly what this love means to him remains unclear.[48] Finally, like Caliban, he is poetic, particularly in the description of his immediate surroundings (15.23-55): he knows the forest's oaks, quail, partridges, blackbirds, larks, thrushes, nightingales, springs, violets, cowslips, marigolds, and deer, and if his catalogue strikes us as more conventional and symbolic than realistic, it nonetheless suggests a genuine love of place. Bremo seems, therefore, a rather more attractive character than the standard wodewose or *homo ferus,* and certainly less violent and lecherous than the type described as common in the late sixteenth century by R. H. Goldsmith.[49] Yet Bremo is duped and then brutally killed onstage by Mucedorus late in the play (17.35-67), and nothing in the response of Amadine or Mucedorus to the murder invites us to regard it as anything more consequential than the slaughter of an offending beast. Bremo is dismissed as a "tyrant" and "wicked wight" (17.68,74); that he has grown progressively more sympathetic and dies in the act of providing instruction to Mucedorus (17.51-67) is utterly forgotten. The play seems to tell us that a wild man, regradless of his apparent capacity for improvement or potential for civility, is subhuman and may be killed without remorse or consequence.

Contrast this with Caliban's portrayal in *The Tempest*. Like Bremo, who is called a "cruel cutthroat" and a "bloody butcher" (17.6,27), Caliban serves as the target of many dubious allegations: Prospero terms him a "demi-devil" (5.1.272) and a "poisonous slave, got by the devil himself / Upon thy wicked dam" (1.2.319-20); Miranda reviles him as an "Abhorred slave, / Which any print of goodness wilt not take, / Being capable of all ill!" (1.2.351-53). Yet much more than *Mucedorus*, *The Tempest* offers forms of resistance to these allegations, both in the speeches of Caliban and in the words and actions of other characters. For every suggestion that Caliban is not fully human, a counter-suggestion emerges that he *is;* Miranda's dual attitude (1.2.445-46; 3.1.50-52) becomes emblematic of this tendency. Moreover, in opposition to the view that Caliban is devoid of goodness, we have the uncontested claim of Caliban himself that his initial relationship with Prospero was thoroughly reciprocal:

> When thou cam'st first,
> Thou strok'st me and made much of me, wouldst give me
> Water with berries in't, and teach me how
> To name the bigger light, and how the less,
> That burn by day and night; and then I lov'd thee
> And show'd thee all the qualities o' th' isle,
> The fresh springs, brine pits, barren place and fertile.
> Curs'd be I that did so!
>
> (1.2.332-39)[50]

Caliban goes on to point out that he is now Prospero's subject, when earlier he was "mine own king" (1.2.342), and of course Prospero responds to this implied charge of usurpation by making the counter-accusation that Caliban attempted to rape Miranda and thus deserves his subjugation. But if, as Stephen Orgel has suggested, Caliban's unrepentant attitude toward this attempted rape may be partly explained by the fact that "free love in the New World is regularly treated [in Renaissance travel narratives] not as an instance of the lust of savages, but of their edenic innocence,"[51] Prospero's allegation that Caliban is a "slave / Whom stripes may move, not kindness!" (1.2.344-45) loses much of its persuasiveness. Indeed, the problems of subordination and rebellion highlighted by the Prospero/Caliban re-

lationship may be usefully contrasted with the relative absence of such problems in the Prospero/Ariel interdependence; Ariel's nearly perfect modelling of subservience and service ultimately rewarded may be possible precisely because Ariel, quite explicitly, is *not* human. Such behavior, and such social relations, are far more problematic for Caliban.

Many Renaissance descriptions of New World natives have been adduced as sources or models of the subhuman or near-human element of Caliban's characterization, among them Peter Martyr's depiction of "certeyne wyld men" in Española who "neuer . . . wyll by any meanes becoome tame. . . . [and] are withowte any certaine language" and Robert Fabian's portrayal of three Eskimos who "spake such speach that no man could understand them, and in their demeanour like to bruite beastes."[52] But far fewer descriptions have been produced in support of another side of this characterization: Caliban as fully human, though radically different. Giovanni Verrazzano's observation that the native peoples of Florida "did not desire cloth of silke or of golde, much lesse of any other sort, neither cared they for things made of steele and yron" is perhaps typical of these descriptions in that it serves as an analogue of a specific incident in *The Tempest:* Caliban's rejection of the "glistering apparel" so attractive to Stephano and Trinculo (4.1.222-54).[53] But there are other anti-*tabula rasa* ethnographic views available in the Renaissance, views less likely to be seen as pertinent to *The Tempest* because broader in scope and not as easily associated with particular passages in the play. And I refer not only to the comparatively well-known writings of Las Casas and Montaigne. Jean de Léry, for instance, emphasizes the social harmony of the Tupinamba even as he exposes the conceptual limitations attendant upon his own religious bias: "As for the civil order of our savages, it is an incredible thing—a thing that cannot be said without shame to those who have both divine and human laws—how a people guided solely by their nature, even corrupted as it is, can live and deal with each other in such peace and tranquility."[54] José de Acosta describes the Incas' indigenous form of literacy: "Unbelievable as it may seem, the Peruvians made up for their lack of letters with so much ingenuity that they were able to record stories, lives, laws, and even the passage of time and numerical calculations by means of certain signs and aids to the memory which they had devised and which they call *quipos*. Our people with their letters are commonly unable to match the skill of the Peruvians with these devices. I am not at all certain that our written numerals make counting or dividing more accurate than their signs do."[55] Alexander Whitaker writes that the inhabitants of Virginia are "lustie, strong, and very nimble: they are a very understanding generation, quicke of apprehension, suddaine in their dispatches, subtile in their dealings, exquisite in their inventions, and industrious in their labour. . . . there is a civill government amongst them which they strictly observe"; William Strachey characterizes the elaborate dressing and ornamentation of a Virginian queen as "ceremonies which I did little look for, carrying so much presentment of civility"; and Thomas Harriot, in a passage to which I will return, avers of the Algonquians, "Some religion they have alreadie, which although it be farre from the trueth, yet being as it is, there is hope it may be the sooner and easier reformed. They beleeve that there are many Gods."[56] It is true that Léry's and Whitaker's remarks, like those of Las Casas, emanate from a Christian essentialist perspective; this emerges explicitly in Whitaker's opinion that "One God created us, they have reasonable soules and intellectuall faculties as well as wee; we all have *Adam* for our common parent: yea, by nature the condition of us both is all one, the servants of sinne and slaves of the divell."[57] It is true as well that Acosta's "Unbelievable as it may seem" and Harriot's "farre from the trueth" disclose the strongly ethnocentric tendencies of these early ethnographic accounts. But some degree of subjective assimilationism is inevitable in any description of a cultural other; the above quotations—and others like them—are remarkable in the degree to which they avoid the easy conclusion of *identity* and insist upon a measure of *difference*. And if, as I believe, such views as these played a role in the evolution of Caliban's character, it is not hard to understand why Caliban seems far less "unaccommodated" than *Mucedorus*'s Bremo. Even Bremo's portrayal reveals certain suggestions of contemporary ethnographic influence, but by and large his conventionality as a wodewose preempts the possibility of any lasting ambivalence in his character: like Doctor Chanca's New World natives, whose "bestiality is greater than that of any beast upon the face of the earth," Bremo is essentially less than fully human; like them, easy to kill without remorse.[58] But Caliban, whose depiction relies heavily on Renaissance ethnography— and particularly on the ambivalences I have stressed between the other as subhuman, identical, and human but different—is thereby rendered far less easy to dismiss. If he is a "salvage" man, his savagery is nonetheless treated by Shakespeare with more tolerance and more respect for its potential or concealed civility than is Bremo's by his anonymous creator.

A final word about *Mucedorus*. The play's *Dramatis Personae* not only lists the characters but provides instructions for the doubling (and tripling) of parts; thus, for example, Bremo is to be played by the same actor who plays Tremelio and Envy.[59] I find this intriguing for several reasons. Tremelio is a would-be assassin, a captain persuaded by the jealous Segasto to kill Mucedorus (6.62-82); in fact, precisely the opposite occurs, Mucedorus killing *him* in self-defense, calling him a "Vile coward" (6.81). And Envy, a figure who appears only in the induction and epilogue, is constantly reviled by his allegorical counterpart, Comedy, as, among other things, a "monster" (Ind. 16), an

"ugly fiend" (Ind. 75), a "hellhound" (Epi. 24), a "Nefarious hag" (Epi. 26), and a "bloody cur, nursed up with tiger's sap" (Ind. 35). In short, the trio of Bremo, Tremelio, and Envy—all playable by the same actor—represents something like a principle of monstrosity or unnaturalness, and these characters' purpose in the play is perhaps indirectly suggested by Comedy's urgent wish that Envy "mix not death 'mongst pleasing comedies" (Ind. 50). In fact, death *is* present in *Mucedorus,* and the play becomes more a tragicomedy than a simple comedy treating "naught else but pleasure and delight" (Ind. 51). In spite of the play's happy ending, Envy insists to Comedy, "yet canst thou not conquer me" (Epi. 12) and threatens that in the future he will overthow her by the following strategem:

> From my study will I hoist a wretch,
> A lean and hungry neger cannibal,
> Whose jaws swell to his eyes with chawing malice;
> And him I'll make a poet.
>
> (Epi. 34-37)

This implies that if an outcast or "native monster" (Epi. 20) of the sort Envy describes had the linguistic command of a poet, he would represent a true threat to Comedy's complacence; he would have the power of subversion. And while Comedy dismisses this threat as nonsense and easily manages to subdue Envy by the epilogue's end, the description of a poetic "neger cannibal" nonetheless has a strangely prophetic ring for readers familiar with *The Tempest.* In spite of Caliban's alleged aphasia at the initial contact with Prospero, he learns language—learns it astonishingly well—and this acquisition, perhaps more than any other trait, marks his humanity and signals his potential dangerousness to the intruding Europeans. Envy's threat, with its suggestion that characters like Bremo and the "neger cannibal" are necessary to the workings of comedy even as they endanger its survival and structural integrity, prefigures in a peculiar way Prospero's elusive remark about Caliban: "this thing of darkness I / Acknowledge mine" (5.1.275-76). Comedy cannot thrive without the dangerous potency of Envy: *Mucedorus* needs Bremo and Tremelio just as *The Tempest* needs Alonso, Antonio, and Sebastian—and just as Prospero needs Caliban.

One of *The Tempest*'s most explicit mystifications of Caliban's status lies in Stephano's reference to him as "My man-monster" (3.2.12). Clearly, such a phrase would be less appropriate with respect either to Bremo, notwithstanding his command of language, or to *The Faerie Queene*'s Salvage Man, in spite of his aphasia; but for Caliban—especially at this point in the play— it seems a perfect designation, emblematic of the pervasive ambivalence regarding his condition which the play has created. Stephano utters it early in the second of four scenes in which he and Trinculo appear with

Caliban. In the first of these scenes, Trinculo makes the thoroughly ambiguous remark—after coming upon Caliban wrapped in a gaberdine—that in England "would this monster make a man; any strange beast there makes a man" (2.2.30-31); Stephano seconds this ambiguity by alluding to "salvages and men of Inde" (2.2.58) and marvelling that the composite Caliban/Trinculo is "some monster of the isle with four legs, . . . Where the devil should he learn our language?" (2.2.65-67). Interestingly, however, this uncertainty regarding Caliban is mirrored by Caliban's own uncertainty regarding the Neapolitans—especially Stephano. And it is in this pair of corresponding and reinforcing ambivalences that we begin to see perhaps the greatest value of locating *The Tempest* within an ethnographic context.

Prompted by his drinking of Stephano's sack—itself an action resonant with contemporary New World associations—Caliban exclaims to himself, "These be fine things, and if they be not sprites. / That's a brave god, and bears celestial liquor. / I will kneel to him" (2.2.116-18). This is followed by such exclamations as "Hast thou not dropp'd from heaven? . . . I do adore thee. . . . I prithee, be my god. . . . Thou wondrous man" (2.2.137-64). Like *The Faerie Queene*'s Artegall when he meets Britomart—or the satyrs in their encounter with Una—Caliban "makes religion" of his wonder.[60] It is true that he swears allegiance to Stephano, and true also that this willing subordination is often interpreted as proof of his natural slavishness[61]; but Shakespeare makes it clear that Caliban takes Stephano for a "brave god" (2.2.117) *before* he promises to be his "true subject" (2.2.125). Thus, notwithstanding the comic mode of the scene or its status as subplot in the play's larger design, Caliban does not necessarily reveal an abject propensity to be a slave. Stephen Greenblatt has written, in a discussion of the *Diario,* that Columbus occasionally demonstrates a recognition of "reverse wonderment" among the native Americans he encounters in the Caribbean[62]; I would argue that Caliban's behavior here suggests a literary transformation of that wonderment. His subservience, initially, is not that of man-monster to man, but of man-monster to man-god; and while it is in some respects comic, it merits far more than ridicule.[63] We must not forget, for example, that Caliban possesses a concept of divinity of godhead: his references to his "dam's" god, Setebos, make this clear (1.2.373, 5.1.261). And since it is virtually beyond dispute that Shakespeare takes "Setebos" from Antonio Pigafetta's account of Magellan's voyage, it bears noting that in an adjacent passage Pigafetta describes the reaction of a Patagonian native confronted by Europeans: "When he sawe the capitayne with certeyne of his coompany abowte hym, he was greatly amased and made signes holdynge vppe his hande to heauen, signifyinge therby that owre men came from thense."[64] Indeed, the motif of native Americans regarding Europeans as gods appears frequently

in the voyagers' accounts.[65] And while this representation, due to its utter one-sidedness, is clearly unreliable as a descriptive characterization, its implicit reliance upon the idea that idolatry can evolve into "true" religion suggests that at its core lies the accurate perception, among European observers, that the native inhabitants of America practiced forms of devotion that could only be categorized as "religious." Thomas Harriot, in a passage quoted earlier, expresses this best:

> Some religion they have alreadie, which although it be farre from the trueth, yet being as it is, there is hope it may be the easier and sooner reformed.[66]

The Europeans' very theory of evangelization—or, at any rate, their most successful theory—relied in part upon the premise that what they deemed idolatry was in fact a conclusive indication of humanity and a positive step toward Christian conversion. The ability to confuse men for gods, as Caliban does, is thus a confirmation of the views expressed in the anti-*tabula rasa* descriptions quoted above. When American natives are represented as overestimating the status of Europeans, they are simultaneously—if indirectly—represented as fully human in status and as possessing cultural forms of their own. They are not blank pages, not unaccommodated.

The emphasis which Shakespeare gives to the ambivalences I have discussed both highlights the play's debt to voyagers' accounts and propels it toward its romantic conclusion. Stephano cannot decide whether Caliban is monster or man; Caliban, equally, cannot decide whether Stephano is man or god. And, as if in sympathy with these uncertainties, Miranda wonders whether Ferdinand is human or divine (1.2.410-20), and neither Ferdinand nor Alonso can initially decide whether Miranda is a maid or a goddess (1.2.422-29, 5.1.185-88).[67] Gradually, however, the uncertainties are resolved, the multiple possibilities collapsed. Prospero assures Miranda that Ferdinand "eats, and sleeps, and hath such senses / As we have" (1.2.413-14); Miranda describes herself to Ferdinand as "No wonder, sir, / But certainly a maid" (1.2.427-28); Ferdinand tells his father that Miranda "is mortal" (5.1.188); and Caliban curses himself for his error: "What a thrice-double ass / Was I to take this drunkard for a god, / And worship this dull fool!" (5.1.296-98). And while no explicit recognition surfaces in Stephano or Trinculo that Caliban is human, there remains the far more significant remark by Prospero that "this thing of darkness I / Acknowledge mine" (5.1.275-76). As Stephen Greenblatt has pointed out, Prospero "may intend these words only as a declaration of ownership, but it is difficult not to hear in them some deeper recognition of affinity, some half-conscious acknowledgment of guilt."[68] Affinity and guilt indeed; many years ago, assuming the persona of Caliban and addressing a composite Prospero/Shakespeare, W. H. Auden characterized this recognition as follows:

Striding up to Him in fury, you glare into His unblinking eyes and stop dead, transfixed with horror at seeing reflected there, not what you had always expected to see, a conquerer smiling at a conquerer, both promising mountains and marvels, but a gibbering fist-clenched creature with which you are all too unfamiliar, for this is the first time indeed that you have met the only subject that you have, who is not a dream amenable to magic but the all too solid flesh you must acknowledge as your own; at last you have come face to face with me, and are appalled to learn how far I am from being, in any sense, your dish; how completely lacking in that poise and calm and all-forgiving because all-understanding good nature which to the critical eye is so wonderfully and domestically present on every page of your published inventions.[69]

Prospero's acknowledgment may imply that Caliban is what he—Prospero—can become, or what he has *in futurum videre* within himself, or what his nurture may, in the end, amount to; in any of these cases, his remark hints at the same interpenetration of the conventionally savage and the civil suggested by the portrayal of *The Faerie Queene*'s Salvage Man. Perhaps Prospero is also implicitly admitting that Caliban possesses a perceptive subjectivity and thus stands in a dialogic relationship with him. At all events, this acknowledgment—coming as it does from the character who, more than anyone else, has been responsible for the mystification of Caliban's status—goes far toward finally drawing Caliban within the bounds of humanity.

Throughout *The Tempest* we look at Caliban much in the way that Renaissance explorers must have looked at New World natives. In some ways he seems bestial; but in others—among them his intimate knowledge of the isle, his initial nurturing of Prospero and Miranda, his later resentment of Prospero's rule, his capacity for forming warm attachments, his vulnerability, and his dreamy, reflective poetry—he seems entirely human. Above all, there is his decision, late in the play, to "be wise hereafter, / And seek for grace" (5.1.295-96).[70] Perhaps this means that he will seek Christian prevenient grace—the divine favor of God—or perhaps the pardon or indulgence of Prospero.[71] But in this particular instance, the word "grace" need not necessarily refer either to divine dispensation or human forgiveness; it *could* be being used in the alternative sense of "virtue," as it is twice elsewhere in the play (3.1.45, 5.1.70) and in such other instances as Donne's famous lines about "man, this world's vice-emperor, in whom / All faculties, all graces are at home" or the moment in *Macbeth* when Malcolm speaks of "The King-becoming graces" and mentions, among other traits, "justice," "temp'rance," "lowliness," "Devotion," and "patience" (4.3.91-94).[72] Caliban, in vowing to "seek for grace," may very well be vowing not submission (and thus containment by the dominant culture) but rather an independent project of self-betterment; the virtue he

may be seeking is that of proper judgement, so that in the future he will not again make his past mistake of confusing humans and gods. In any case, though Shakespeare never explicitly resolves the matter of Caliban's status, he suggests—to the extent that he gradually allows the play's other uncertainties about character identity to dissolve into thin air—that Caliban, like Ferdinand, Miranda, and Stephano, is a fully human being. And this suggestion is reinforced by *The Tempest*'s thorough contradiction of Prospero's allegation that Caliban is ineducable, "a born devil, on whose nature / Nurture can never stick" (4.1.188-89); the same could be said, after all, of Antonio and Sebastian, neither of whom—unlike Caliban—show any sign of repentance for their conspiracy, though both have had the advantage of more refined and extended nurture. One might even argue that Caliban, in his initial and fully reciprocal relationship with Prospero, exhibits a nurture that, far from failing to "stick" to his nature, lies at is very essence.

Placing *The Tempest* within an ethnographic context goes far toward explaining why Caliban cannot be discarded in the way that Bremo is, for example, in *Mucedorus*. Caliban is not merely a "wild man," a sinister, shadowy figure derived from European folklore and medieval tradition; he remains far more complex and distinct, and though his portrayal certainly reveals bestial elements, it is also vivified by an acknowledgment of the existence of culturally alien humans across the ocean. Like the ambivalences of New World ethnography, the ambivalences of *The Tempest* gradually move toward human inclusiveness. And this levelling tendency, which shows the failings of aristocrats as well as the virtues of an alleged "demi-devil," bears a resemblance both to movements in other late plays of Shakespeare and to the ideals of what might be referred to as "Montaignesque pastoral"—a more radical pastoral than that typical of Spenser, more informed by the speculative and critical spirit that characterizes the *Essais*. As the whoreson and the Bedlam beggar must be acknowledged in *King Lear* (1.1.24, 3.4.28-180) and the strange Tupinamba in Montaigne's "Des Cannibales," so, too, must Caliban.

Notes

I wish to express my gratitude to Joanne Altieri, David Bevington, and Charles Frey for reading and carefully responding to earlier drafts of this essay. I have learned much from their acuity and generosity. . . .

[33] As Meredith Anne Skura points out, these words appear in the Folio's "Names of the Actors"; Shakespeare may or may not have written them ("Discourse and the Individual: The Case of Colonialism in *The Tempest*," *Shakespeare Quarterly* 40.1 (Spring 1989): 48).

³⁴ Peter Hulme, *Colonial Encounters* (London: Methuen, 1986), 114.

³⁵ *Nova Brittania* (London: 1609), in *Tracts and Other Papers, Relating Principally to the Origin, Settlement, and Progress of the Colonies in North America,* ed. Peter Force, 4 vols. (New York: Peter Smith, 1947), 1 (6): 11.

³⁶ *The Generall Historie of Virginia* (London, 1624), in *The Complete Works of Captain John Smith,* ed. Philip L. Barbour (Chapel Hill: University of North Carolina Press, 1986) 2: 152, 183, 189, 198, 125-26.

³⁷ *A briefe and true report of the new found land of Virginia* (London, 1588), in *Virginia Voyages from Hakluyt,* ed. David B. Quinn and Alison M. Quinn (London: Oxford University Press, 1973), 70.

³⁸ Edmund Malone, *The Plays and Poems of William Shakespeare,* 21 vols. (London, 1821) 15: 11-14; Leslie Fiedler, *The Stranger in Shakespeare* (New York: Stein Day, 1972), 233. Sidney Lee also points to the varied ethnographic roots of Caliban, including the Guianans described by Ralegh, but he curbs his enthusiasm enough to recollect—unlike Fiedler—that there were no "native Bermudans" ("The American Indian in Elizabethan England," in *Elizabethan and Other Essays,* ed. F. S. Boas [London: Oxford University Press, 1929], 263-301).

³⁹ Bullough, *Narrative and Dramatic Sources of Shakespeare* (London: Routledge & Kegan Paul, 1975) 8: 257; Hulme, *Colonial Encounters,* 108. See also Robert Ralston Cawley, who argues that Caliban is not a mélange of types but a representation of the changing attitudes toward native Americans held by the colonists ("Shakespere's Use of the Voyagers in *The Tempest,*" *PMLA* 41 [1926]: 719n); Sister Corona Sharp, who writes that Caliban's character "took shape under the influence of conflicting opinions held on the American Indians during Shakespeare's lifetime" ("Caliban: The Primitive Man's Evolution," *Shakespeare Studies* 14 [1981]: 267); and Karen Flagstad, who adds that "the savage Caliban conflates contradictory stereotypes" ("'Making this Place Paradise': Prospero and the Problem of Caliban in *The Tempest,*" *Shakespeare Studies* 18 [1986]: 221).

⁴⁰ Bernard W. Sheehan, *Savagism and Civility: Indians and Englishmen in Colonial Virginia* (Cambridge: Cambridge University Press, 1980), 85, 87.

⁴¹ Greenblatt, "Learning to Curse: Aspects of Linguistic Colonialism in the Sixteenth Century," in *First Images of America,* ed. Fredi Chiappelli, 2 vols. (Berkeley: University of California Press, 1976), 2: 574; Todorov, *The Conquest of America* (New York: Harper & Row, 1984), 42-43.

⁴² Greenblatt, "Learning to Curse," 575.

⁴³ *New Perspectives on the Shakespearean World* (Cambridge: Cambridge University Press, 1985), 169-70. I disagree with Marienstras, however, when he asserts that Caliban's uncertain status "gives the reader a feeling of instability that remains with him through to the end of the play" (170).

⁴⁴ Cabeza de Vaca, *Relation of Nuñez Cabeza de Vaca,* trans. Buckingham Smith (New York, 1871; Ann Arbor: University Microfilms, 1966), 82; Léry, *History of a Voyage to the Land of Brazil,* trans. Janet Whatley (Berkeley: University of California Press, 1990), 29; Acosta, *How to procure the salvation of the Indians,* excerpted in John Howland Rowe, "Ethnography and Ethnology in the Sixteenth Century," *Kroeber Anthropological Society Papers* 30 (1964): 16; Strachey, *Historie of Travell into Virginia Britannia,* excerpted in *The Elizabethans' America: A Collection of Early Reports by Englishmen on the New World,* ed. Louis B. Wright [Cambridge, Mass: Harvard University Press, 1965], 215; Smith, *Generall Historie,* in *The Complete Works of Captain John Smith,* ed. Philip L. Barbour (Chapel Hill: University of North Carolina Press, 1986), 2: 119.

⁴⁵ "Virginias Verger," in *Hakluytus Posthumous, or Purchas His Pilgrimes* (London: 1625), 20 vols (Glasgow: J. MacLehose & Sons, 1905-7) 19: 231.

⁴⁶ All quotations from *Mucedorus* (London, 1598) are drawn from *Drama of the English Renaissance,* ed. Russell A. Fraser and Norman Rabkin, 2 vols. (New York: Macmillan, 1976), 1: 463-80. *Mucedorus* was published in seventeen separate editions between 1598 and 1658. It was performed by the King's Men in 1610 "before the King's majesty at Whitehall on Shrove-Sunday night" (Fraser and Rabkin, 463); thus Shakespeare probably knew the play, and may have acted in it.

⁴⁷ Introduction to the Arden *Tempest* (London: Methuen, 1954), xxxviii-ix. Norman Rabkin writes that "Bremo the wild man is something of a forerunner of Caliban, suggesting the interest of an age of exploration in the phenomenon of natural man while ensuring that the play remains fairy tale" (Introduction to *Mucedorus,* 463).

⁴⁸ Bremo's encounter with Amadine in scene 11 reveals obvious similarities to the conventional motif of the wild man's transformation to civility in the presence of a beautiful and virtuous woman. But this particular encounter is presented, I think, as a more sentimental and less thoroughly transforming experience.

⁴⁹ Goldsmith, "The Wild Man on the English Stage," *Modern Language Review* 53 (1958): 481-91.

50 This speech, with its indication of Caliban's intelligence and appreciation of Prospero's gifts, echoes numerous accounts of New World natives, among them James Rosier's 1605 description of Indians along the New England coast: "They seemed all very civil and merry, showing tokens of much thankfulness for those things we gave them. We found them then (as after) a people of exceeding good invention, quick understanding, and ready capacity" (*A True Relation of the Most Properous Voyage Made This Present Year 1605 by Captain George Weymouth*, excerpted in *The Elizabethans' America*, 149). On Weymouth's voyage, see Sidney Lee, "The American Indian in Elizabethan England," 282.

51 Orgel, introduction to the Oxford *Tempest* (Oxford: Oxford University Press, 1987), 34. Sister Corona Sharp takes this view even further in calling the attempted rape "Caliban's failure in European sexual ethics" ("Caliban: The Primitive Man's Evolution," 273). And Paul Brown asserts that Caliban's "inability to discern a concept of private, bounded property concerning his own dominions is reinterpreted as a desire to violate the chaste virgin, who epitomizes courtly property" ("'This thing of darkness I acknowledge mine': *The Tempest* and the discourse of colonialism," *Political Shakespeare*, ed. Jonathan Dollimore and Alan Sinfield (Ithaca: Cornell University Press), 62). See also Orgel's "Shakespeare and the Cannibals," in *Cannibals, Witches, and Divorce*, ed. Marjorie Garber (Baltimore: Johns Hopkins University Press, 1987), 55.

52 Martyr, *The Decades of the new worlde or west India* (London: 1555; Ann Arbor: University of Michigan Microfilms, 1966), decade 3, bk. 8, p. 134; Fabian, in Richard Hakluyt, *Principal Navigations, Voyages, Traffiques and Discoveries of the English Nation* (London: 1598-1600; New York: AMS Press, 1965), 7: 155. The three Eskimos Fabian describes were brought by Sebastian Cabot to England from the North American Arctic in 1502 and presented to Henry VII. See Sidney Lee, "The American Indian in Elizabethan England," 270.

53 "The relation of John de Verrazzano a Florentine, of the land by him discovered in the name of his Majestie. Written in Diepe the eight of July 1524," in Hakluyt, *Principal Navigations* 8: 433.

54 Léry, *History of a Voyage*, 158.

55 Acosta, *How to procure the salvation of the Indians*, 17.

56 Whitaker, *Good Newes from Virginia* (London: 1613; New York: Scholars' Facsimiles and Reprints, 1936), 26-27; Strachey, *Historie of Travel into Virginia Britannia* (London: 1612), excerpted in *The Elizabethans' America* (New York: Harper, 1959), 212; Harriot, *A briefe and true report* (London: 1588), in *Virginia Voyages*, 68.

57 Whitaker, *Good Newes from Virginia*, 24.

58 Diego Alvarez Chanca, a Spanish surgeon, accompanied Columbus on his second voyage to the West Indies (1493-96) and wrote about the natives in his "Letter addressed to the Chapter of Seville" (*Four Voyages to the New World: Letters and Selected Documents*, trans. and ed. R. H. Major [Gloucester, Mass.: Peter Smith, 1978], 66).

59 Alan C. Dessen discusses this role-doubling as "a means to call attention to structural or thematic analogies" in "Conceptual Casting in the Age of Shakespeare: Evidence from *Mucedorus*," *Shakespeare Quarterly* 43 no. 1(Spring 1992): 67-70.

60 *The Faerie Queene*, ed. Thomas P. Roche, Jr. (New Haven: Yale University Press, 1981), 4.6.22 and 1.6.7-19.

61 Richard Marienstras, for example, writes that Caliban "rushes into servitude even when striving for freedom" (*New Perspectives on the Shakespearean World* (Cambridge: Cambridge University Press, 1985), 175).

62 Stephen Greenblatt, *Marvelous Possessions* (Chicago: University of Chicago Press, 1991), 77.

63 For a fascinating and sustained example of native Americans confronting Europeans whom they cannot, at first, satisfactorily categorize, see Diego Durán, *The Aztecs: The Indies of New Spain* (New York: Orion, 1964), esp. chap. 69-74. Durán claims, for instance, that Moteczoma and his ministers plotted various strategies of resistance to Cortés and the other conquistadors even while alluding to them as immortal beings: "'I do not know' [said Moteczoma] 'what measures to take to prevent these gods from reaching the city or seeing my face. Perhaps the best solution will be the following: let there be gathered enchanters, sorcerers, sleep-makers and those who know how to command snakes, scorpions and spiders, and let them be sent to enchant the Spaniards. Let them be put to sleep, let them be shown visions, let the little beasts bite them so that they die.' . . . 'O powerful lord' [responded Tlillancalqui] 'your decision seems good to me, but if they are gods who will be able to harm them? However, nothing will be lost in the attempt'" (276).

64 Martyr, *Decades*, 219.

65 Drake's men found that the Miwok natives of California "supposed us to be gods, and would not be perswaded to the contrary" (Richard Hakluyt, "The famous voyage of Sir Francis Drake into the South sea," *Principal Navigations* 11: 119). And Thomas Harriot writes of the Indians near the Roanoke Colony, "some people could not tel whether to thinke us gods or men" (*A briefe and true report of the new found-*

land of Virginia [London: 1588], in *Virginia Voyages from Hakluyt,* ed. David B. Quinn and Alison M. Quinn [London: Oxford University Press, 1973], 73). See also Robert Cawley, *The Voyagers and Elizabethan Drama* (Boston: MLA, 1938), 385-88. In one of the classic English fictions dealing with the encounter of European and native American, Daniel Defoe exploits this motif in portraying the relationship between Crusoe and the "savage" Friday: "I believe, if I would have let him, he would have worshipped me and my gun" (*The Life and Adventures of Robinson Crusoe,* ed. Angus Ross [Harmondsworth: Penguin, 1965], 214).

[66] Harriot, *A briefe and true report,* 68.

[67] On connections between Miranda and the American native Pocahontas, see Morton Luce's Arden edition of *The Tempest* (London: 1902) 169-70; Geoffrey Bullough's *Narrative and Dramatic Sources* 8: 241; and Jeffrey Knapp, *An Empire Nowhere,* 240-41.

[68] Stephen Greenblatt, *Shakespearean Negotiations,* 157: *The Circulation of Social Energy in Renaissance England* (Berkeley: University of California Press, 1988), See also Skura, "Discourse," 66; Knapp, *An Empire Nowhere,* 239; and Lynda E. Boose, "The Father and the Bride in Shakespeare," *PMLA* 97.3 (1982): 341. When Ferdinand speaks to Prospero of "our worser genius" as a force that can potentially "melt . . . honor into lust" (4.1.27-28), he perhaps anticipates Prospero's "thing of darkness" speech inasmuch as he suggests that a principle of wildness or savagery lies within all humans.

[69] "The Sea and the Mirror," in *The Collected Poetry of W. H. Auden* (New York: Random House, 1945), 387-88.

[70] In claiming that he will "be wise hereafter, / And seek for grace" (5.1.295-96), Caliban is almost certainly *not* speaking ironically; the tone of self-annoyance in which he castigates himself for taking the drunkard Stephano for a god and worshipping the "dull fool" Trinculo (5.1.297-98) seems strongly to preclude this.

[71] On prevenient grace, see article 10 of the Church of England's thirty-nine articles (1571): "The condition of man after the fall of Adam is such, that he cannot turn and prepare himself, by his own natural strength and good works, to faith and calling upon God: Wherefore we have no power to do good works pleasant and acceptable to God, without the grace of God preventing us, that we may have a good will, and working with us, when we have that good will" (from Thomas Rogers, *The Faith, Doctrine, and Religion, Professed and Protected in the Realm of England . . . Expressed in 39 Articles* [Cambridge, 1607; rpt. New York: Johnson Reprint Corporation, 1968], 103). If Caliban is capable of seeking prevenient grace, the presumption is strong that he is fully human.

[72] Donne, "An Anatomy of the World: The First Anniversary" (ll. 161-62) in *John Donne: The Complete English Poems,* ed. A. J. Smith (Harmondsworth: Penguin, 1973), 274. See also *As You Like It,* 3.2.11 and 3.2.17, and *Hamlet,* 4.7.21. The *OED* defines this meaning of "grace" as "In persons: Virtue; an individual virtue; sense of duty or propriety" (2.13b).

DREAMS

Marjorie B. Garber (essay date 1974)

SOURCE: "The Truth of Your Own Seeming: Romance and the Uses of Dream," in *Dream in Shakespeare: From Metaphor to Metamorphosis,* Yale University Press, 1974, pp. 186-214.

[*In the excerpt below, Garber reads* The Tempest *as Shakespeare's most complete dramatic treatment of the dream world as a representation of human imagination and creativity. As in his previous plays, she argues, the dream world here is a timeless and transcendent state of mind in which illusion and reality are momentarily reconciled, and through which the dreamer achieves self-understanding.*]

The Winter's Tale is fundamentally a play of metamorphosis in which the stage of "becoming" is central to the action. Time and change, "things dying" and "things new born," underlie each of its essential symbols and processes; the space of sixteen years between the third and fourth acts, a violation of the "unities" which Shakespeare deliberately elects to make, is indicative of a tendency to render credible the most improbable events through a mature integration of poetry and action. With *The Tempest,* which immediately succeeds it in chronology, Shakespeare's attention turns to yet another way of treating the same major themes. Where *The Winter's Tale* was designedly cyclical, analogous patterns repeating themselves as redemption and reconciliation emerged from the union of the temporal and eternal, in *The Tempest* events are even more directly transcendent. Essentially, things happen in *The Winter's Tale* against a background of their having happened before and with the possibility that they may happen again; in *The Tempest,* the most remarkable of all Shakespeare's dream worlds, things happen on the island *in order* that they need never happen again. Our attention is drawn from the first to the moment of revelation and discovery, the dream that unveils truths and self-truths. At the very close of the play, Gonzalo puts this redemptive discovery into words which once more recall Berowne:

> in one voyage
> Did Claribel her husband find at Tunis,
> And Ferdinand her brother found a wife

Where he himself was lost; Prospero his
  dukedom
In a poor isle, *and all of us ourselves*
When no man was his own.

> [V.i.208-13]

The theme of losing and finding here attains its ultimate expression, the journey to the enchanted isle which
is the dream world, the conversion of loss into new
and transcendent awareness. For *The Tempest* is a play
which takes the dream state for its subject, deliberately
and directly exploring the poles of sleeping and waking, vision and reality, art and the human condition.

Both the spatial and the temporal worlds of the play
are tightly circumscribed, as compactly constructed as
The Winter's Tale was deliberately broad. In his first
interview with Ariel, Prospero stipulates that they have
only four hours to do their work, and Ariel confirms
the success of this design at the beginning of the denouement (V.i.4). The entire action takes place on
Prospero's island, although behind it we can see the
political world of Milan, from which the travelers have
come and to which they will return, and beyond even
that the limitless scope of Tunis and "the great globe
itself." Prospero's island is both subjective and objective, a state of mind as well as a location; his neglect
of political affairs in Milan, as he explains to Miranda,
came about because he inclined instead to the private
study of the "liberal Arts."

Those being all my study,
The government I cast upon my brother
And to my state grew stranger, being
  transported
And rapt in secret studies.

> [I.ii.74-77]

The dream world of the island is simultaneously the
world of these "secret studies," which Prospero will
not abjure until the play's close. From the examples of
Richard III and *Antony and Cleopatra* we know that
such neglect of political responsibility is dangerous:
the experience of the island is therefore redemptive for
him as well, persuading him to "discase" himself and
appear "as [he] was sometime Milan." (V.i.85-86). But
within the dream work of the play itself he stands apart,
as the stage direction fittingly says "at a distance,
unseen," the final and greatest of Shakespeare's poet
and stage-manager figures, whose world is the creative
world of the imagination.

The play begins with the tempest of its title, which
resembles in symbolic purpose the similar storms of
Pericles and *The Winter's Tale*. The uproar of the storm
and the anguished cries of the mariners are in deliberate contrast to the calm of the island, and are significantly associated with the strife and confusion of the
external Milan world, dominated by usurpation and

greed. The characters of the Milanese company—the
surly, cynical Sebastian, the arrogant Antonio, the good-
hearted but abstracted Gonzalo—are all for a moment
adumbrated against the background of crisis and fear.
The scene is itself a nightmare of sorts, a dark scene cut
through with thunder and lightning, the symbolic equivalent of the more psychologically conceived opening scene
of *Othello*. With Gonzalo's despairing cry for "an acre
of barren ground, long heath, broom, furze, anything"
(I.i.64-65), the scene rapidly shifts to the island itself, a
lush and romantic haven in marked contrast to the harshness of this description. We are immediately transported
into a world of dream and dreams, as unlike the assumptions and expectations of the new arrivals as is Gonzalo's
word picture from fact.

Prospero and his daughter Miranda have watched the
storm from the island; and Miranda, whose name implies that she is both "wondered at" and "wondering,"
begs him to intervene:

If by your art, my dearest father, you have
Put the wild waters in this roar, allay them.

> [I.ii.1-2]

Were she "any god of power" (10), she says, she would
have acted to save the "brave vessel" (6) and its crew.
"Brave" is a word which recurs frequently in her language; it is later used to describe both Ferdinand and
the "brave new world" of men she has discovered, and
it carries, always, an innocent hope which is very like
the Shakespearean "grace." As the storm abates, Prospero reassures her that no harm has been done to the
passengers, and in what is really a long, broken monologue, narrates for her the story of their arrival on the
island. Significantly, he first lays aside the magic robe
in which he has been dressed, saying "Lie there, my
art" (I.ii.25), in the first of what will be many direct
associations of his magical powers with the related
transforming power of poetry. The robe is a costume,
and thus an agent of willed metamorphosis. Throughout the play there will occur similar garment images,
all having to do with illusion, transformation, or self-
deception: the "sustaining garments" of the ship's survivors (I.ii.218), the "glistering apparel" which seduces
Stephano and Trinculo (IV.i.SD), and the costume of
Prospero as "sometime Milan" (V.i.86). Disguise is
thus from the first integrated into the radical symbolism of the play, supporting an allegorizing tendency
which is yet not sufficient to disturb the delicate balance of the play's poetry.

Prospero prefaces his tale by asking if Miranda remembers her life before they came to the island. "'Tis
far off," she replies,

And rather like a dream than an assurance
That my remembrance warrants.

> [I.ii.44-46]

This is the first explicit reference to dream in the play. Miranda, whose only reality is the world of the island, significantly refers to life beyond it as "like a dream," while all those who come from without will find the island itself dreamlike and inexplicable. The "dark backward and abysm of time" (50) to which Prospero alludes is a temporal frame, like the spatial frame of the Tunis-world, against which the figural and timeless present action is performed; the phrase is both specific and symbolic. He now proceeds with his narrative, pausing every few moments to make sure she is attending: his role is now that of storyteller, and he is anxious to properly affect his audience. His description of the usurper Antonio is a diagram of self-delusion:

> like one
> Who having into truth—by telling of it—
> Made such a sinner of his memory
> To credit his own lie, he did believe
> He was indeed the duke.
>
> [99-103]

This is the pattern of falsehood to self, self-disguise, which the play will seek to unravel; the exchange of "lie" and "truth" is a familiar one, and the characteristic task of the dream world will be to restore "truth" to its proper place. There is another familiar pattern in the account of the expulsion of Prospero and the infant Miranda from Milan; the tempest in which they are set adrift, though it is mentioned after the present storm, temporally foreshadows it, again in a mythic or figural manner. Gonzalo's bounty, in placing upon the ship "rich garments, linens, stuffs and necessaries" (164), recalls the launching of the richly laden coffin of Thaisa or the cloth and gold which accompanied the infant Perdita. The recapitulated narrative of the "dark backward and abysm of time" is thus deliberately evocative and echoic, a collection of symbolic actions as well as a tale of past events. We might say that this kind of multiple referent, at once factual and mythic, is metaphorically in the imperfect tense, the tense of recurrent action, as opposed to the simple past. It is a mode which will be frequently used in *The Tempest,* as it has been to a certain extent in *The Winter's Tale,* and it makes the luminous dream of the narrow four-hour span expand to fill up all of time.

Having finished his tale, Prospero now induces Miranda to drowsiness, a drowsiness which has in part been abetted by the rhythmic periodicity of his narrative:

> Thou art inclined to sleep. 'Tis a good
>   dullness,
> And give it way. I know thou canst not
>   choose.
>
> [I.ii.185-86]

The readiness with which Miranda falls asleep is a sign of virtue, as has been true in other plays we have examined. Her sleep here is coterminous with the arrival of Ariel, the dominant spirit of the play's dream world, and she is therefore to be associated with innocence rather than with art. For Ariel's nature, which is central to the play as a whole, is supremely that of art and the imagination; he is at once the agent, the instrument, and the substance of transformation.

In the course of the play Ariel undergoes a number of metamorphoses: during the tempest he is himself the fire in the riggings of the ship, which, in a lovely transference of epithet, is said to have "flamed amazement" (198); at the end of his conversation with Prospero he is told to make himself "like a nymph o' the sea" (302), recalling and extending into the supernatural Florizel's image of natural metamorphosis, "When you do dance, I wish you / A wave o' th' sea" (*WT* IV.iv.140-41); through much of the play he is invisible to all except Prospero, thus approximating the condition of the air to which he is so closely related; and in the climactic speech of the play, the remarkable address to the "three men of sin" (III.iii.53ff.) he appears as a harpy, and calls himself and his fellows "ministers of Fate" (III.iii.61). But somatic transformation is rather the beginning than the end of his powers. As we have mentioned above, it is difficult to avoid looking at *The Tempest* in partly allegorical terms, associating Prospero with mankind and the poet, Ariel with the imagination, and Caliban with the body and with natural or instinctive man. Plainly these are only beginnings, and approximate ones, but it seems clear that Ariel's association with the imaginative part of man is a very close one; he anticipates the thoughts of others, and his language is "poetic" in the most extended sense of that term. It is Ariel who both plays and sings throughout the play, and his songs are themselves transformations in little. His music, which can be as light as a pipe or as common as a tabor, is the accompaniment of the acts of "magic" or vision which recur throughout the play, and which are the operative dreams within the dream world. He is at once an elemental spirit, compact of water, air, and fire, an English fairy of the type of Puck, and the embodiment of poetry as a transforming power; of all the quicksilver characters we have discussed, he is the most consummate. Yet his bondage to Prospero is enforced though good-tempered, and his progress to freedom first necessitates imprisonment by the chthonic natural forces of Sycorax. His definition, like his appearance, must elude us, for he is a mood and a quality; and like dream itself he appears and sings only in moments of transcendence which shed light on more ordinary experience. Here in his first appearance we learn of his part in the tempest and of the effect the experience has had upon the travelers:

> *Prospero:*   My brave spirit!
> Who was so firm, so constant, that this coil
> Would not infect his reason?

Ariel: Not a soul
But felt a fever of the mad and played
Some tricks of desperation.

[I.ii.206-10]

Once again, the rejection of "reason" appears as a necessary prelude to the dream experience. The "madness" which seizes the voyagers is not unlike the much more psychologically determined madness of Hamlet or Lear, a first essential step into subjectivity which is likewise basic to dream. The mariners, we may notice, are excluded from this translation; when they awaken in the first act at Ariel's bidding, they serve as the ground of common experience, the frame within which the action and reconciliation have occurred. Ariel reports that he has left them asleep "'with a charm join'd to their suffer'd labor" (231), their ship safely in harbor. The noble passengers have made their way to shore, and Ariel describes their condition in terms of clothing imagery:

On their sustaining garments not a blemish,
But fresher than before.

[I.ii.218-19]

The transforming power of the island is already at work upon them, freshening their external as it will their internal selves.

Ariel's truest language, however, is song, and it is through song that he is able to cross the boundary between the internal and the external, the thought and the heard; his music throughout, but most particularly the two haunting songs sung to Ferdinand, approach the condition which T. S. Eliot has described as

            music heard so deeply
That it is not heard at all, but you are the
    music
While the music lasts.

["The Dry Salvages," V]

This is the dream state again, the intrusion of the fictive and the irrational into the known. We have discussed these two songs elsewhere, and here need only emphasize the extraordinary multiplicity of meaning and thematic relevance contained in so simple and controlled a form. The first song, "Come unto these yellow sands," is an invitation to reconciliation, in which the storm image ("the wild waves") refers simultaneously to the physical tempest and the spiritual turmoil within. The phrase "sweet sprites bear / The burthen" carries the primary sense of "sing the refrain," as indeed they do in the voices of dog and cock, the night watch and the morning of reawakening and rebirth. But "burthen" also retains its nonmusical meaning of "responsibility" or "obligation," and it is to some degree true that the responsibility of carrying out the reconciliation is entrusted by Prospero to Ariel and his

attendant spirits. The first song is thus a song of hope, and Ferdinand associates it with "some god o' th' island" (392). "This music," he says,

        crept by me upon the waters,
    Allaying both their fury and my passion
    With its sweet air.

[394-96]

This "allaying" is the beginning of the fulfillment of the song's prophecy, the "wild waves whist"; "sweet air" is at the same time "music" and "atmosphere," a rich ambiguity which *The Tempest* will continue to develop. Both interpretations, and most especially the blending of the two, suggest the elusive condition of Ariel.

The remarkable beauty and relevance of the second song have been discussed at some length at the beginning of this chapter [not excerpted here]: the themes of transformation, transmutation into art, and the concept of the "sea change" are articulated, and the effect is such that Ferdinand concludes

    This is no mortal business, nor no sound
    That the earth owes.

[409-10]

The imputation of divinity or divine inspiration is important to all of the romances, but most particularly to *The Tempest;* later in the same scene Ferdinand will exclaim at the sight of Miranda

        Most sure the goddess
    On whom these airs attend!

[424-25]

and Miranda, seeing the "brave form" of Ferdinand, is moved to call him "a spirit" (414) but finds herself refuted by Prospero: "No, wench; it eats and sleeps and hath such senses / As we have, such" (415-16). Caliban's encounter with Stephano and Trinculo leads to a parodic conception of the drunken butler as a "brave" god, and in the final reconciliation scene Alonso asks of Miranda

    Is she the goddess that hath severed us
    And brought us thus together?

[V.i.187-88]

We may be reminded of Hamlet's observation, though it is cast in a different key:

            What a piece of work is a
    man, how noble in reason, how infinite in faculties,
    in form and moving how express and admirable, in
    action how like an angel, in apprehension how like
    a god: the beauty of the world, the paragon of animals;
    and yet to me, what is this quintessence of dust?

[*Ham.* II.ii.311-16]

The illusion of godhead and the subsequent acknowledgment of mortality are equally valuable and important; the island's occupants are the more wonderful for their human condition. For the pattern of *The Tempest,* as of *The Winter's Tale,* is to take man through dream to a renewed appreciation of his mortal state, bringing him through dream to a transfigured reality.

This sharpening of experience is part of Prospero's purpose in affecting to discourage the attraction of the lovers; echoing the god Jupiter in *Cymbeline,* he fears "lest too light winning / Make the prize light" (I.ii.454-55). Moreover, Ferdinand's response to this pretended sternness is, fittingly, a willing acknowledgment of the strong subjective power of dream:

> My spirits, as in a dream, are all bound up.
> My father's loss, the weakness which I feel,
> The wrack of all my friends, nor this man's
>   threats
> To whom I am subdued, are but light to me,
> Might I but through my prison once a day
> Behold this maid. All corners else o' th'earth
> Let liberty make use of. Space enough
> Have I in such a prison.
>
> [I.ii.490-97]

It is interesting that heightened emotional experience converts itself for Ferdinand, as it does for the play as a whole, into spatial terms. Like the lover of [Richard] Lovelace's Althea, he paradoxically finds liberty in bondage, just as his fellows will find enlightenment in privation. It is the theme of Gonzalo's summation again: "Ferdinand, her brother, found a wife / Where he himself was lost"; "and all of us ourselves, / When no man was his own."

The arrival of the shipwreck victims has a similarly paradoxical effect upon Prospero's island. Before their advent it is tranquil, harmonious, virtually uninhabited—a dream in the sense of an idyll, atemporal and ruled by magic. With the intrusion of political and personal strife in the persons of the voyagers, this dream world is disrupted and replaced by internal dream episodes, levels of conscious and subconscious discovery which will lead to a greater and more far-reaching synthesis. Hints of this are sharply adumbrated in the conversation of the survivors at the beginning of the second act, as the wordy Gonzalo, aided by Adrian, tallies the charms of the island:

> *Adrian:* The air breathes upon us here most
>   sweetly.
> *Sebastian:* As if it had lungs, and rotten ones.
> *Antonio:* Or as 'twere perfumed by a fen.
> *Gonzalo:* Here is everything advantageous to
>   life.
> *Antonio:* True, save means to live.
> *Sebastian:* Of that there's none, or little.

> *Gonzalo:* How lush and lusty the grass looks!
>   How green!
> *Antonio:* The ground indeed is tawny.
> *Sebastian:* With an eye of green in 't.
> *Antonio:* He misses not much.
> *Sebastian:* No; he doth but mistake the truth
>   totally.
>
> [II.i.49-60]

This stichomythic dialogue is a demonstration of the subjectivity of the dream state, which is essential to transformation. Gonzalo and Adrian see the island as a fertile and aromatic paradise; its fertility is thematically significant and is substantiated by the words "lush and lusty," which are hotly contested by the others. Sebastian's jest about the air possessing "lungs," since Adrian has poetically said that it "breathes," demonstrates a literalism of spirit which is opposed to imagination. Truth on the island is clearly subjective, as protean as the denizens of dream themselves, and the allegation that it is Gonzalo who is mistaken is usefully countered by a remark he himself makes to Sebastian earlier in the scene: "you have spoken truer than you purposed" (21-22). We have frequently come upon this circumstance in the world of dream, the partial truth of the speaker superseded by the greater truth communicated to the audience, and an acknowledgment of it this early in the play hints at a willingness on the part of the speaker to accept the irrational and the inexplicable. But Gonzalo, though more amiable than the others, is nonetheless in need of the transfiguring power of the dream world. His vision of the island as an innocent Arcady is reminiscent of Polixenes' vision of eternal innocence and suffers from the same misconception about the necessity of time and change:

> I' th' commonwealth I would by contraries
> Execute all things. For no kind of traffic
> Would I admit; no name of magistrate;
> Letters should not be known; riches, poverty,
> And use of service, none; contract, succession,
> Bourn, bound of land, tilth, vineyard, none;
> No use of metal, corn, or wine, or oil;
> No occupation; all men idle, all;
> And women too, but innocent and pure:
> No sovereignty.
>
> All things in common nature should produce
> Without sweat or endeavor. Treason, felony,
> Sword, pike, knife, gun, or need of any engine
> Would I not have; but nature should bring forth,
> Of it own kind, all foison, all abundance,
> To feed my innocent people.
>
> [II.i.152-61; 164-69]

The determining element here is timelessness, a disregard of the processes of natural growth and experience which are necessary for redemption. Gonzalo's vision is a dream of sorts, but a delusory one, and the truth it reveals is a misconception on its speaker's part. The need for a radical transformation of this attitude is symbolically demonstrated during the next episode by Ariel, the embodiment of subconscious action, who must forcibly awaken the sleeping Gonzalo with song in order to warn him of the plot against the king.

The entrance of Ariel at this point in the action, as Gonzalo quibbles on the sign word "nothing" (181-83), produces the third literal "sleep" of the play, following those of Miranda and the mariners. Though visible to the audience, he is unseen by the courtiers, and the "solemn music" he plays is likewise apparently below the level of consciousness, for it is not remarked. Sleep here, as ever in Shakespeare, is a mark of spiritual innocence; it comes instantly to all but those who are guilty of past misdeeds or contemplating present ones. Gonzalo finds himself "very heavy" (193) and sleeps at once, as do all but Alonso, Antonio, and Sebastian. Alonso, whose guilt (in arranging with Antonio for tribute from Milan) is at least partially balanced by his sorrow at the supposed loss of his son, is the next to succumb:

> What, all so soon asleep? I wish mine eyes
> Would, with themselves, shut up my thoughts.
>   I find
> They are inclined to do so.
>
> [II.i.195-97]

He is preparing, by a consideration of his own state, for the moment of redemption which will transform him finally from guilt to grace.

Antonio and Sebastian remain awake, and are indeed both amazed and slightly contemptuous of the slumber of their fellows:

> *Sebastian:* What a strange drowsiness
>   possesses them!
> *Antonio:* It is the quality o' th' climate.
> *Sebastian:*   Why
> Doth it not then our eyelids sink? I find not
> Myself dispos'd to sleep.
> *Antonio:*   Nor I: my spirits are nimble.
> They fell together all, as by consent.
> They dropped as by a thunderstroke.
>
> [203-08]

Here again they "speak truer than they have purposed"; the climate does induce the slumber of the courtiers, but out of its dream function rather than for merely meteorological reasons. Antonio's assertion of "nimble" spirits seems to imply that sleep is weakness, and the apolcalyptic note in the lines which follow suggests a subconscious awareness of supernatural powers at work and a derogation of their objects. But though both remain awake, there is a decided difference in the tone of their conversation. For Sebastian the period that

follows is itself like a dream: "it is a sleepy language," he says, "and thou speak'st / Out of thy sleep" (215-16). Antonio's attempt to persuade him to kill the king and inherit the crown is couched in images of the dream world; in a passage which bears a strong resemblance to the witches' scene in *Macbeth* (I.iii),[13] he begins with a seductive image phrased like a vision:

> My strong imagination sees a crown
> Dropping upon thy head.
>
> [212-13]

This is the malignant imagination of the conscious mind, Iago's sphere, the dream enforced and thrust upon the latent ambition of Sebastian.

> *Sebastian:*   What? Art thou waking?
> *Antonio:* Do you not hear me speak?
> *Sebastian:*   I do; and surely
> It is a sleepy language, and thou speak'st
> Out of thy sleep. What is it thou didst say?
> This is a strange repose, to be asleep
> With eyes wide open; standing, speaking,
>   moving
> And yet so fast asleep.
> *Antonio:*   Noble Sebastian,
> Thou let'st thy fortune sleep—die, rather;
>   wink'st
> Whiles thou art waking.
> *Sebastian:*   Thou dost snore distinctly;
> There's meaning in thy snores.
>
> [213-22]

Sebastian is yet again speaking truer than he has purposed; the "strange repose" he speaks of is indeed much more like dream as we have observed it than like waking. Antonio, sensing his advantage, pursues the metaphor with more directness; in a reference to the distant Claribel, the rightful heir after Alonso and Ferdinand, he apostrophizes

>   "Keep in Tunis,
> And let Sebastian wake!" Say this were death
> That now hath seized them, why, they were no
>   worse
> Than now they are. There be that can rule
>   Naples
> As well as he that sleeps; lords than can
>   prate
> As amply and unnecessarily
> As this Gonzalo; I myself could make
> A chough of as deep chat. O, that you bore
> The mind that I do! What a sleep were this
> For your advancement!
>
> [263-72]

And Sebastian's reponse is itself like an awakening, deliberate, halting, with a note of the dazed and the tentative:

Antonio: Do you understand me?
Sebastian: Methinks I do.
Antonio: And how does your content
Tender your own good fortune?
Sebastian: I remember
You did supplant your brother Prospero.

[272-75]

The startling effect of this last is itself an indication of the vestiges of dream; its apparent irrelevancy speaks to the subject covertly behind Antonio's remarks, rather than to the less significant remarks themselves. The effect of this entire episode is not unlike the "jealousy" passages at the beginning of *The Winter's Tale.* We are here presented with the dangers of dream, although dream is related in this case to ambition rather than to sexual jealousy, to *Macbeth* rather than to *Othello.* But the creative and benevolent actions of Ariel are deliberately counterpointed by incidences of irrational destructiveness. When, swords drawn, they are frustrated in their attempt at assassination by the watchful machinations of Ariel, they produce a fictive account of their intentions which fittingly mirrors the truth: they have heard, they say, a "hollow burst of bellowing / Like bulls, or rather lions" (315-16). The implications of "hollow" and the created and "untrue" image of discordant sound are symbolic translations of the dream scene which has gone before. Gonzalo, by contrast, has heard "a humming, / And a strange one" (321-22), the harmonious and almost undetectable dream actions of Ariel in defense of the king. The two realms, symbolic and dramatic, are fused in Gonzalo's pious hope for Ferdinand: "Heavens keep him from these beasts!" (328). And with this note the scene shifts to the literal beasts of the play, Caliban and the drunken butler and jester, whose seriocomic conspiracy is a symbolic counterpart of the sophisticated political plots of the courtiers.

The nature of Caliban, like that of Ariel, is a crux for the play as a whole. He is the only true native of the island, the son of "the foul witch Sycorax, who with age and envy / Was grown into a hoop" (I.ii.258-59), an earth magician of black and chthonic sorceries who is the unredeemed counterpart of Prospero and his theurgic arts. Prospero has supplanted Sycorax, taking over the rule and management of the island, but he has retained Caliban in bondage to serve him. This retention has a dual significance in light of our association of the island with the dream world. Prospero keeps Caliban because he is necessary to life:

But, as 'tis,
We cannot miss him. He does make our fire,
Fetch in our wood, and serves in offices
That profit us.

[I.ii.312-15]

Yet he also keeps him because he cannot let him go: "this thing of darkness," he says at the close, "I ac-

knowledge mine" (V.i.275-76). Caliban is, like Ariel, a denizen of the dream world of the irrational, but his is the dark side of dream. His attempt on Miranda, his foulness of language, his desire to usurp the power of the island are all manifestations of an impulse toward destruction which is centered in the subconscious mind. Like Prospero, we must have Caliban if we are to have Ariel; further, we must keep Caliban, even when, as we must, we let Ariel go.

The dramatic world which surrounds Caliban is an effective analogue to this spiritual condition. The comic scene in which he is discovered by Stephano and Trinculo has many of the aspects of dream or nightmare: Stephano, fearing devils, observes a strange shape and takes it for a monster, when actually it is the combined form of Caliban and Trinculo half-hidden beneath a cloak. Moreover, the "monster" inexplicably speaks the language of the Neapolitans, further startling Stephano with its incongruities. This is a visible enactment of metamorphosis, the "monster of the isle, with four legs" (II.ii.65-66) turning into a pair of people, one of whom is himself seen as a "monster." In the momentary union of Caliban and Trinculo there is a direct manifestation of the aspect of the dream work described by Freud as "condensation": Trinculo, a man with many of the malign qualities which Caliban symbolizes, is conflated with Caliban, the metaphorical embodiment of those qualities. Stephano's mistake, in thinking the two to be one, and "monstrous," is presented as a symbolic truth.

But just as we were able to perceive something of the quicksilver nature of Ariel through his language, we may also profit from a study of the language of Caliban. We know from Caliban himself that his speech is something with which he has been endowed by Prospero:

You taught me language, and my profit on't
Is, I know how to curse.

[I.ii.365-66]

Even the medium of language, then, can be misshapen and transformed. But often in this play Caliban's language seems to contain, not coarseness, but a strange and transforming lyricism. His naïve vision of the early days on the island recalls the omnipresent time theme, presenting a brief glimpse of lost innocence:

When thou cam'st first,
Thou strok'st me and made much of me; wouldst give me
Water with berries in 't; and teach me how
To name the bigger light, and how the less,
That burn by day and night, and then I loved thee
And showed thee all the qualities o' th' isle,
The fresh springs, brine pits, barren place and fertile.

[334-40]

Just as Miranda, familiar only with the island world, finds wonder in the shape of man, so Caliban, the island's sole native inhabitant, sees a paradise in the teachings of civilization; the enchantment of transformation, wrought by the island upon its recent visitors, is produced in them by the visit itself.

The most striking instance of Caliban's transforming use of language, however, is his enchanting address to his fellow conspirators on the subject of music:

> Be not afeard; the isle is full of noises,
> Sounds and sweet airs that give delight and
>   hurt not.
> Sometimes a thousand twangling
>   instruments
> Will hum about mine ears; and sometime
>   voices
> That, if I then had waked after long sleep,
> Will make me sleep again; and then, in
>   dreaming,
> The clouds methought would open and show
>   riches
> Ready to drop upon me, that, when I waked,
> I cried to dream again.
>
> [III.ii.138-46]

His pleasure in music is itself musical. The dream he here describes is a recurrent one, the only such dream which we have encountered with the exception of Lady Macbeth's. And while Lady Macbeth's dream was a recapitulation of past action in the world of fact, Caliban's dream is clearly a fantasy or wish fulfillment. Music, which we have seen to be the sign and instrument of transfiguration, lulls him to sleep; and he dreams of riches dropping from heaven, a dream so seductive that he "cries" to dream again. It is in part an enlightenment dream, a dream of missed or only partially realized opportunity; the "hum" of voices like Ariel's intimates to him, though only in the actual state of dream, the transcendent possibilities of the world they inhabit. The aspect of recurrence is a particularly interesting one, since in psychoanalytic theory recurrent dreams are considered regressions to an anxiety of childhood; such a dream, says Freud, "was first dreamt in childhood and then constantly reappears from time to time during adult sleep."[14] Caliban is conceived as a character uniquely child and man at once, as the wonderful simplicity and purity of his diction in this dream passage bears witness: the sheer imitative enjoyment of "twangling," the concern for those things that "hurt not," the readiness with which he "cries," both vocally and, perhaps, through tears. As a childlike figure he is more than ever indissolubly bound to Prospero in a compact which neither can escape. Shakespeare's intuitive understanding of the dream process is once more demonstrated in a dream form which precisely mirrors the thematic and symbolic identity of the dreamer.

In a wider sense the conspirators' scene has a dream form of its own. The existence of two bands of conspirators, the "high" (Antonio, Sebastian, Alonso) and the "low" (Stephano, Trinculo, Caliban) is similar to the process of "doubling" in the dream work, where more than one image is called up by the mind to express a certain idea or theme. Ariel's incidental appearances in the scene enhance the dream feeling as well: the echo incident, in which, while invisible, he intermittently "gives the lie" to the conspirators, causes them to turn upon one another in confusion; later, when Stephano and Trinculo begin to sing a song to the wrong tune, he corrects them by playing the tune accurately on a tabor and pipe, prompting them to call him—with the usual dimension of hidden meaning—"the picture of Nobody" (130). But the designs of the low conspirators, though too uncompromising to be comic, are only antecedent to the pivotal scene which exposes and confronts the nobles with their greater iniquity. In this scene Ariel plays a critical role, and through the agency of metamorphosis the subconscious world of dream becomes again vivid and visible upon the stage.

The dumb show of the "several strange Shapes" which precedes the appearance of Ariel is accompanied by "solemn music" of the kind that recurs throughout the play. The king and his company are astonished at their "excellent dumb discourse" (III.iii.39), but when the shapes vanish, the royal party abandons speculation:

> *Francisco:* They vanished strangely.
> *Sebastian:*   No matter, since
> They have left their viands behind; for we
>   have stomachs.
>
> [40-41]

Before they are able to reach the banquet, however, it disappears in thunder and lightning and is replaced by the vision of Ariel as a harpy. Structurally the harpy's sudden appearance is a refinement of the descents of Diana and Jupiter in *Pericles* and *Cymbeline*: here it is not an external deity appearing for the first time, but rather a significant metamorphosis of a familiar and central character which precipitates the sudden access of self-knowledge. Ariel's successive transformations have reflected both Prospero's and Shakespeare's purposes; from the invisible singer of subconscious thoughts he has become a visible and frightening judgmental figure who allies himself with destiny. When he addresses the "three men of sin" (Antonio, Sebastian, and Alonso), he descants upon the theme of retribution as a stern prelude to the play's ultimate objective, reconciliation.

> You are three men of sin, whom destiny—
> That hath to instrument this lower world
> And what is in't—the never-surfeited sea
> Hath caused to belch up you and on this
>   island,

Where man doth not inhabit, you 'mongst men
Being most unfit to live. I have made you
  mad;
And even with suchlike valor men hang and
  drown
Their proper selves.

[III.iii.53-60]

Madness as a preface to renewed vision is the culminating image of a series of thematic summations: the
world, and most particularly the familiar symbol of the
cleansing and devouring sea, is a purposeful "instrument" of their arrival; the island, heretofore regarded
as fair, is seen as the proper isolation of the less-than-
human, as well as the found haven of the exemplary.
"I and my fellows / Are ministers of Fate" (60-61);
thus the natural and the supernatural are joined in an
overwhelming search for redemption.

The appearance of the harpy is yet another dream within
the larger dream of *The Tempest* itself, directed by the
unseen stage-manager figure of Prospero and invisible
except to those to whom it has relevance. Like Macbeth's guests at the banquet, Gonzalo is baffled by
behavior of the others: "Why stand you," he asks, "in
this strange stare?" (III.iii.94-95). Those who do hear
are caught in a solemn "ecstasy" (108), "all knit up /
In their distractions" (89-90)—they are in the dream
state, attentive only to the vision of conscience. Their
interpretation of the event includes yet another factor
of the dream work, "secondary revision," which tries
to make waking sense out of the irrational and inexplicable happenings of the moment of dream. Thus
Alonso attributes the message to some concatenation
of natural forces;

Methought the billows spoke and told me of
  it;
The winds did sing it to me; and the thunder,
That deep and dreadful organ pipe,
  pronounc'd
The name of Prosper; it did bass my trespass.

[96-99]

Ariel is indeed a spirit of wind and water; in Alonso's
rationalizing view, it is these externals only which
remain in the conscious mind. But the process of awakening has begun; the "ecstasy" to which Gonzalo refers is the liberating madness of dream, a madness
which will, in Alonso's case at least, lead to self-knowledge. For Sebastian and Antonio the vision provokes
anger rather than sadness, moral blindness rather than
acceptance. Unlike Alonso they adhere stubbornly to
the objective state of consciousness, and so the harmony of nature, even in reproach, is a radical awareness denied them.

This harmonious relationship of human life to the natural world and the round of the seasons is the subject of

the scene which follows, the performance of the masque
and the contract between the lovers. The dialogue which
begins this scene is reminiscent of the conversation
between Florizel and the old shepherd in *The Winter's
Tale*. Again the father and the young lover recount the
praises of the beloved:

> *Prospero:*   O Ferdinand,
> Do not smile at me that I boast her off,
> For thou shalt find she will outstrip all praise
> And make it halt behind her.
> *Ferdinand:*   I do believe it
> Against an oracle.
>
> [IV.i.8-12]

The image of the oracle takes the rhetorical place of
"that/ Which he not dreams of" in *The Winter's Tale*—
the meaning in both is that the beloved's quality is
such that it surpasses the ability of the supernatural
world to define it, a superlative mode which recalls in
turn Cleopatra's "past the size of dreaming." Both are
"nature's piece 'gainst fancy, / Condemning shadows
quite," and thus they move toward the reconciliation of
the illusory and the real which is part of the play's
purpose.

The masque itself reinforces a number of themes we
have associated with dream and its transforming power:
the structural unit of the play-within-a-play and the
recurrent images of metamorphosis and transformation.
The mention of the myth of Proserpina functions as a
reminder both of natural fertility and of the danger of
unlawful love. Fundamentally, however, the role of the
masque is secondary to that of the play which surrounds it; Ferdinand's remarks before and after the
performance carry more weight than the performance
itself. Thus he engages Prospero in a significant dialogue after the marriage song of Juno:

> *Ferdinand:* This is a most majestic vision,
>   and Harmonious charmingly. May I be bold
>   To think these spirits?
> *Prospero:*   Spirits, which by mine art
> I have from their confines called to enact
> My present fancies.
> *Ferdinand:*   Let me live here ever!
> So rare a wond'red father and a wise
> Makes this place Paradise.
>
> [IV.i.118-24]

"Vision" and "harmonious" substantiate the symbolic
integrity of the masque as it relates to the ongoing
action. The enactment of "present fancies," on the other
hand, is a note of warning, which is soon to be validated by Prospero's remembrance of Caliban and the
conspirators. And Ferdinand's plea for eternity on the
island makes clear the fact that a further transformation is required. Eternity in the dream world, as we
have before discovered, is an illusory concept, one

which fails to take into account the imperatives of the human condition. Ferdinand will have to acknowledge the serpent in the paradisal garden, or, in Leontes' figure, the spider in the cup, in order that his renewed awareness may be fused with purpose in the Milan world to which he must return. It is to this end that the "harmonious" masque is disrupted by Prospero's sudden memory of treason. His exclamation, "the minute of their plot / Is almost come" (141-42), touches again on the time theme, bringing the precision of specific time to interrupt and terminate the dream of eternity. The celebrated speech with which he ends the episode is yet another such reminder of mortality:

> Our revels now are ended. These our actors,
> As I foretold you, were all spirits and
> Are melted into air, into thin air;
> And, like the baseless fabric of this vision,
> The cloud-capped towers, the gorgeous palaces,
> The solemn temples, the great globe itself,
> Yea, all which it inherit, shall dissolve,
> And, like this insubstantial pageant faded,
> Leave not a rack behind. We are such stuff
> As dreams are made on, and our little life
> Is rounded with a sleep.
>
> [IV.i.148-58]

The reflexive quality of the image has already been noted: the actors upon the stage are spirits playing actors who in turn play gods and nymphs. So too the physical world is at once illusory and real; the two framing phrases, "like the baseless fabric of this vision," and "like this insubstantial pageant faded," reinforce one another and contain between them three lines which, though fictive and "poetic" in tone, are descriptions of that which is real. Prospero's tone is at once regretful and proud, a glorification of man and an acknowledgment of his radical limitations. With the phrase "our little life / Is rounded with a sleep," he recapitulates in language the structural organization of the play, in which sleep becomes the boundary between one kind of life and another. This calm resolution—that "we are such stuff / As dreams are made on"—is curiously reminiscent of Hamlet's tortured imaginings, though it differs wholly in tone:

> To die, to sleep—
> No more—and by a sleep to say we end
> The heartache, and the thousand natural
>   shocks
> That flesh is heir to! 'Tis a consummation
> Devoutly to be wished. To die, to sleep—
> To sleep—perchance to dream.
>
> [*Ham.* III.i.60-65]

Again, as in the transmutation of the skull image from Clarence's dream [in *Richard III*] to Ariel's second song, the vision presented by *The Tempest* is purified of passion, sublime in its acceptance of the real. For Prospero's whole great speech is in fact an exploration of the relationship between the dream world and the world we know as real, in which the analogy is finally resolved into identity, and metaphor becomes metamorphosis. His speech suggests on the level of language what *The Tempest* in its entirety will accomplish in dramatic terms: the merging of the worlds of dream and reality in the creative mind of man.

As has happened so many times, a rhetorical evocation of the dream world passes into a vision of that world itself; Ariel in his "shape invisible" (IV.i.185) reveals the bewitched Caliban and his confederates. Having lured them with music, he now tempts them with "glistering apparel," which continues the prevailing clothing imagery and introduces the question of the fictive and the real. Stephano and Trinculo, more "montrous" than the "monster" himself, are captivated by the display; Caliban, fruitlessly insisting "it is but trash" (224) pleads without success that they perform the murder first, or else

> We shall lose our time
> And all be turned to barnacles, or to apes
> With foreheads villainous low.
>
> [247-49]

Once again the time theme is closely linked with metamorphosis; even the choice of "barnacles" alludes to the widely held notion that the sea animal transformed itself into a barnacle goose. With the entry of "divers spirits" shaped like dogs and hounds, the nightmare quality of the scene is completed, balancing the idyll of the masque with an equally persuasive vision of the dangerous and passionate irrational.

Reconciliation and revelation, the deciphering of dream, are the tasks which remain to Prospero; having created a world of illusion, in which each man perceives in the dream state truths he does not know in the external world, he now prepares to restore them to "reason" transfigured by self-knowledge. Significantly, this final turn in the pattern of the play is prefaced by a change in Prospero himself: "The rarer action," he confirms, "is / In virtue than in vengeance" (V.i.27-28), love and grace taking the place of anger and revenge. This is in itself a returning to the real world of men, an accommodation toward grace which takes note of human frailty. Dispatching Ariel for the "spell-stopped" courtiers, he sounds once more the tonic note of new reality found through illusion:

> My charms I'll break, their senses I'll restore,
> And they shall be themselves.
>
> [V.i.31-32]

Like Gonzalo's later echo, "all of us ourselves / When no man was his own," this declaration asserts at once the primacy of dream as an agency of transformation and the necessity of a return to "senses," to "them-

Margaret Leighton as Ariel and Ralph Richardson as Prospero in a 1952 Stratford-upon-Avon production of The Tempest.

selves," as participants in the ongoing round of time. His abdication of his art ("but this rough magic I here abjure") is accompanied by yet another evocation of metamorphosis, an address to the spirits of the island which closely follows *Golding's Ovid* (33 ff.).[15]

But these spirits, like the spirits of a *A Midsummer Night's Dream,* are part of the special dream world they inhabit, and cannot function in the full daylight world of reality. Music, ever the harbinger of transformation, accompanies the entrance of the courtiers; and Prospero's description of the lifting of the spell recalls Oberon's "spirits of another sort," transforming citizens of the dawn:

> the charm dissolves apace;
> And as the morning steals upon the night,
> Melting the darkness, so their rising senses
> Begin to chase the ignorant fumes that mantle
> Their clearer reason.
>
> [64-68]

Here too imagination and the dream world give way in the half-light of morning to "clearer reason," both clearer than the "fumes" which cloud them and clearer than before their transformation. The image of the "rising senses," like the sun rising through morning mist, is an image of awakening and of new birth, binding the idea of transcendence once more to the round of nature. From this point there begin the series of awakenings which will culminate in reconciliation. Prospero "discases" himself and appears to the courtiers "as I was sometime Milan" (86), fusing the idea of identity with that of locality in a usage which, though common, nonetheless echoes a major symbolic theme. With conscious double meaning, he discusses the "loss" he shares with the grieving Alonso, who has not yet learned that his son is alive:

> *Prospero:* I Have lost my daughter.
> *Alonso:*   A daughter?
> O heavens, that they were living both in Naples,
> The king and queen there! That they were, I wish
> Myself were mudded in that oozy bed
> Where my son lies. When did you lose your daughter?
> *Prospero:* In this last tempest.
>   [V.i.147-53]

The subsequent "discovery" of Ferdinand and Miranda playing chess is yet another naturalized rebirth, like the awakening of Hermione in *The Winter's Tale.* Miranda underscores the sense of renewal in her delighted exclamation, "O brave new world / That has such people in't! (183-84), which is immediately undercut by Prospero's customary warning note of realism, "'Tis new to thee" (184); Alonso's expressed fear lest "this prove / A vision of the island" (175-76) becomes yet another proof of the identity of the visionary and the real. The master and boatswain of the ship now appear, reporting that their ship is "tight and yare and bravely rigged as when / We first put out to sea" (223-24); and the boatswain recounts the mariners' dream:

> If I did think, sir, I were well awake,
> I'd strive to tell you. We were dead of sleep
> And (how we know not) all clapped under hatches;
> Where, but even now, with strange and several noises
> Of roaring, shrieking, howling, jingling chains,
> And moe diversity of sounds, all horrible,
> We were awak'd; straightway at liberty;
> Where we, in all our trim, freshly beheld
> Our royal, good, and gallant ship, our master
> Cap'ring to eye her. On a trice, so please you,
> Even in a dream, were we divided from them
> And were brought moping hither.
>
> [229-40]

Like so many others, they, too, have had the experience and missed the meaning. Finally, the trio of low conspirators is driven in by Ariel, and their treacheries exposed. Caliban withdraws after anatomizing his own fictive transmutation:

> What a thrice-double ass
> Was I to take this drunkard for a god
> And worship this dull fool!
>
> [296-98]

Yet Prospero's great phrase of acceptance, "this thing of darkness I / Acknowledge mine" (275-76) advises us that Caliban's withdrawal is only temporary and that his anarchic energies, though they can be restrained, can never be wholly forgotten. By contrast Ariel and the whole sphere of the creative imagination which he represents are by necessity released from service; the utility of the dream world has been to regenerate the company, and that transformation accomplished, the worlds of art and nature once more diverge. Their intersection has been momentary but transcendent.

In the superb octasyllabic couplets of the Epilogue, Prospero once again expresses the identity of reality and vision, the transforming uses of the world of dream:

> Now my charms are all o'erthrown,
> And what strength I have's mine own,
> Which is most faint. Now 'tis true
> I must be here confined by you,
> Or sent to Naples. . . .
> . . . Now I want
> Spirits to enforce, art to enchant;
> And my ending is despair
> Unless I be relieved by prayer.
>
> [1-5, 13-16]

The speaker is a magician bereft of his magic; he is also, manifestly, an actor who has finished with his part. In the traditional appeal to the audience for applause, there is implicit the deeper appeal of Paulina's admonition: "It is required / you do awake your faith." The life of the play is the condition of the dream state, that subjective state in which reason gives place to imagination. Its existence is momentary and yet for all time, as the play itself exists in time and beyond it. The poet in this moment speaks through his character, asserting the identity of art and dream. His affirmation here, and in the last plays as a whole, is an acknowledgment of the central role of the creative imagination, the vital transforming power of the world of dream in the life of man.

Notes

[13] For other echoes of *Macbeth* in this play, see G. Wilson Knight, "The Shakespearian Superman," in *The Crown of Life* (London: Oxford University Press, 1947), pp. 212-13.

[14] Sigmund Freud, *The Interpretation of Dreams,* trans. and ed. James Strachey (Standard Edition, London: The Hogarth Press and the Institution of Psycho-analysis, 1953; rpt., New York, 1965), pp. 222-23.

[15] Ovid *Met.* VII.197-209.

John Arthos (essay date 1977)

SOURCE: "Dream, Vision, Prayer: *The Tempest*," in *Shakespeare's Use of Dream and Vision,* Rowman and Littlefield, 1977, pp. 173-202.

[*In the following essay, Arthos examines the metaphysical and spiritual principles implicit in the dramatic action of* The Tempest. *He looks closely at aspects of the play that compare life to a dream in which the dreamer is powerless and uncomprehending, and concludes that of all the characters only Prospero accepts the reality that freedom is an illusion and that the mysterious forces which redeem humankind are ineffable.*]

From the first, watching the spectacular storm and the crazed behavior of those aboard the ship, we are not moved as we might expect to be by drama in which the representation is so vivid. There is a great 'noise' that should be drowning every voice, yet as the sailors and passengers curse and pray and even jest their words come through as it were unweakened, and there is as much of the ridiculous as the desperate in what we hear. Then, when the storm subsides and we join the two who have watched it from the shore, going over with them all that has been happening, we learn how little there was indeed to fear. The cracks of sulfurous roar, Jove's lightnings, Neptune's boldness were no more harmful than the St. Elmo's fire that was not even that but the guise Ariel had taken to bring it all about. And in the words that tell the real enough distress of those who thought God was punishing them we come to recognize the act of a power moved as much by concern as anger.

Brought into the quiet where Prospero and Miranda are watching, we are hardly surprised to hear music, whether from the air or earth, leading a young prince out of the sea to before the feet of these two.

> Come unto these yellow sands,
>   And then take hands.
> Curtsied when you have and kissed,
>   The wild waves whist,
> Foot it featly here and there;
>   And, sweet sprites, the burden bear.
>
> (I.ii. 375-80)

We have learned of powers effecting wonders at sea, at the same time lightening fear and gracing the terrible, and now there are signs of what might be still others, loving and gentle and humorous. A young fellow rescued from the very heart of a tempest finds his spirits suddenly rapt with beauty.

> Where should this music be? I' th' air or th' earth?
> It sounds no more; and sure it waits upon
> Some god o' th' island. Sitting on a bank,
> Weeping again the King my father's wrack,
> This music crept by me upon the waters,
> Allaying both their fury and my passion
> With its sweet air.
>
> (I. ii. 387-93)

It is not Ferdinand's bemusement that suggests divinity at work in this disembodied music so much as the words with which Ariel embodies it. In their simplest sense they are wonderful enough—bearing an invitation and promising an unthought of satisfaction, blessing a betrothal more kindly than even the magnificent songs ending *Love's Labour's Lost*. But the words are also prophetic, and it is in this character that they are the strangest for they speak as if present and past and future were in a single moment, leading Ferdinand on step by step while telling of something that is yet to happen as by one who has already seen it come to pass. The words seem to belong outside time.

To add to what Prospero tells us about Ariel we are being led to think of him as someone like a sorcerer's medium who knows more than anyone possibly could unless consciousness inhabited the very nature of things and took a voice. But the most provocative indications that Ariel has commerce with another, mysterious realm of being are in the song he next addressed to Ferdinand:

> Full fathom five thy father lies,
>   Of his bones are coral made,
> Those are pearls that were his eyes,
>   Nothing of him that doth fade
> But doth suffer a sea change
> Into something rich and strange.
>   Sea-nymphs hourly ring his knell.
>
> (I. ii. 396-402)

This is mockery—Ferdinand's father is alive, still walking the earth. No one rings his knell, least of all the nymphs that never were. And Ariel himself, 'beginning it', ringing the bells, is enjoying this playful way of leading Ferdinand on, persuading him he is surviving and is his father's heir, and that in a little while he will be making Miranda his queen, death leading to this joy too. Ariel is taking delight in the idea, in the fancy and fun, in the deceit, and in the happiness he foresees for the young prince. He is also celebrating a most wonderful power and act, imagining transfigurations in which a body and a skeleton by the grace of the all-sustaining sea have become jewels and marvel-

lous sea-growths. Besides the mockery and the fun, besides the fancifulness and the factuality—that in the course of nature death distributes its mortal objects among the other forms of the world—there is the astonishing clarity of his perception. In the mere naming of eyes and pearls and bones and coral he endows them with such beauty and strangeness as we would not have known the objects of sense possess. It is this clarity Milton responded to so directly in picturing the jewel-paved streams of Paradise, water and stone becoming turkis-blue and emerald-green and azure, the lucidity all things own when honored rightly. All is seen by such a light as Ariel says will be his forever after he has left Prospero's service—

> Where the bee sucks, there suck I,
> In a cowslip's bell I lie,
> There I couch when owls do cry,
> On the bat's back I do fly
> After summer merrily.
> Merrily, merrily shall I live now,
> Under the blossom that hangs on the bough.
>
> (V. i. 88-94)

As Prospero prepares to give over his last responsibilities, thinking of his grave, he imagines a time when all else will have disappeared in a rounding sleep. His sense of things now is the opposite to the burden of Ariel's song that death is the means of transformation into the rich and strange, and in that 'nothing' he speaks of in the dead, that nothing that will fade, we also read, endless, ceaseless change. It is Prospero who is speaking at the end, and we may think the play is concluding in pressing his assertion of the vanity of all things even though his words are not unambiguous.

But the irony in his conclusion is sharp enough, as it also is in the epilogue, to keep us from forgetting the continuing existence Ariel was planning, an almost impish defiance of any constraining power whatever—

> Merrily, merrily shall I live now,
> Under the blossom that hangs on the bow.

Earth's increase, revels, marriages and christenings may all be done with, now and forever, when the globe is gone, but from the time of that first sight of Ariel's work and his first singing we are kept mindful of an illimitable spirit, a capacity whose limits are unknown. His strange knowledge, the resonance of his words, his power not only over the forms of matter but in penetrating minds, all seem to say he could do what he would—we cannot perceive what limits there would be for him beyond that vague contract with Prospero. And when Prospero with his gloriously beautiful words allows us to think there might be an end to all that humans have ever known he but re-invokes our wonder at what we have come to think is unconstrained. Ariel is no more to be bound, as unconstrained now as that power that transfigured a dead man, quick with what freedom makes possible, a power never to be a party to obliteration.

It is not only with the flowers of summer, or when freed from a curse, no longer subject to the pinchings of a master or the harassment of Caliban and the imps of the earth that Ariel, a delicate spirit, will joy in his liberty. He is assured he will be everywhere always, partaking of existence in every form nature and time and understanding take.

Prospero has used Ariel to perform miracles, to introduce dreams and madness into men's fancies, to chastise, to condemn, to guide, and Ariel has of himself conceived and devised what he needed in managing these most difficult matters. And like the songs he ornaments his work with, all he does pays as full respect to the way things are as it does to the playing of the imagination. He will be as free and immaculate as light and will thereby honor thought and being as much as nature.

As the drama moves towards its end, and the Milanese and Neapolitans prepare to return to the mainland, Caliban is being left behind to whatever his lonely future, and Ariel has disappeared. But nothing leads us to think he is vanishing into any such darkness as Prospero prophesies for humans. He has simply been let go, to exist as he knows existence—wherever it is, however to be thought of, it is inseparable from light.

A magician avenged himself and arranged a decent future for his daughter. Approaching the end of his life he began to prepare for it. He looked back upon it all as the evanescent thing it was, as all earthly life, full of illusion, passing traceless from all knowledge.

His own labors had been finally successful, partly fortuitously, partly through real spiritual insight and the power that had been lent to him, provisionally as it were. He had pursued justice, and executed it upon the wicked and the shameless, he was returning Milan and Naples to order and the promise of a decent future. The usual uncertainties were to be anticipated but meanwhile he had been just and merciful. And even though in the course of his precarious and difficult undertaking he had brought forward the most sustained and searching reasonings to support his faith in a God of justice and mercy, he knew well enough he had accomplished no more than any proper magistrate would have. And so it is that I think we are to take his valedictory as one might take anyone's—an affirmation that he has done as well as he could, it was not good enough, he has not effected what divinity itself would have, and with his own passing all may foresee their own.

But his language remains pretentious, it is full of the metaphysical affirmations he and much of his enterprise had depended on. So we must accept his declaration as much as ever as by his lights, and not identify it as the burden of the play—he is a bilked old man who succeeded in settling a claim and thinks he has earned a rest.

He may of course have been as capable of divine intimations as anyone, as his author, and his author may not too ironically for a moment or two allow himself to be brought forward in Prospero's words as someone whose life was also writ on water. But there is also the author who more obviously introduces himself in the Epilogue as someone not identical with Prospero, offering a belief to take the place of Prospero's philosophy. This figure suggests that the end of life may be another life. Prospero may have believed, until he was disabused, that for faithful and perfect service salvation was to be his reward. But the words of the epilogue say something else—the soul devoted to thought, to the service of philosophy and justice, is still imprisoned, and the freedom that is eternal life thought itself cannot earn. Prospero has done well, the dream of efficacious power was rightly enchanting, but it was a dream, the idea that he could do God's work. The suggestion has been denied that virtue would take him beyond the sphery chime. If he is to wake it will be through God's free act.

> But how is it
> That this lives in thy mind? What seest thou else
> In the dark backward and abysm of time?
> (I. ii. 48-50)

> We are such stuff
> As dreams are made on, and our little life
> Is rounded with a sleep.
> (IV. i. 156-8)

The words 'dark backward and abysm of time' and 'rounded with a sleep' invite speculation upon realms of being 'outside' that the senses and even thought know. The very word 'outside' is paradoxical, since it signifies normally what is accessible to experience. Yet the language and matter of the play themselves compel us not only to treat with paradox but to accept what the paradox is founded on, the notion of a realm of unchanging being, the only basis that can be suggested as contrast to the world of change and time, a realm of the changeless and timeless. 'Certainly through Prospero's speech on the vanishing of the globe Shakespeare is not affirming that we last forever, but rather the exact reverse. Yet the nature of the denial is metaphysical in its assumption of pathos. It only makes sense in the context of immortal longings.'[1] Leaving aside whether it is Shakespeare or Prospero who is thought to be affirming this, the question persists—in this conception, in these dim figurings of 'abysm' and 'darkness' and 'roundness' is there a power the poetry and the play sustain deriving from an assured metaphysics?

The subject and the question were with Shakespeare from the beginning. They took a charming form in the humor of the Princess of France when she repelled the too importunate pleas of the suitors, deferring an answer, this being

> A time . . . too short
> To make a world-without end bargain in.
> (*Love's Labour's Lost,* V. ii. 774-5)

In the Sonnets, as Mr. J. W. Lever so well rehearsed it, human love has truly deific power:

> '. . . the co-existence of beauty and corruption, of truth and mutability, and the universal tyranny of Time, which were the issue of Shakespearean drama, became in the sonnets the issue of personal integrity; and through the prepotency of human love, on a plane customarily reserved for divine grace, a poetic resolution was affirmed for the antinomies of life.'[2]

Something very close to the wonder in the conception underlying these images in *The Tempest* is at the heart of the magnificence of *Antony and Cleopatra:*

> O sun,
> Burn the great sphere thou mov'st in, darkling
>   stand
> The varying shore o' th' world!
> (IV. xv. 9-11)

'The darkening shore, the determining centre of the world dissolved, the obliteration of all that gives distinction and difference, so that the moon must look in vain for anything to invest with mystery, abundance surfacing from the containing medium—all this poetry has for its basic idea, not a particular bounding line, but in widest conceivable terms the border between the formed and the formless, that alien region with which a great part of the poetry of the last plays occupies itself.'[3]

In Sonnet LX we read what we may take to be almost an outline of the conclusion Prospero has been led to:

> Nativity once in the main of light,
> Crawls to maturity, wherewith being crowned,
> Crooked eclipses gainst his glory fight,
> And Time that gave, doth now his gift
>   confound.

The question arises—in such words as these, are we being presented with metaphysics proposed responsibly, or are these merely playful figurings, useful simply for teasing thought? And then, since we meet with the same suggestions again and again in the poems and plays, in an almost infinite sounding, even sometimes developed into arguments, is there some constancy in the repetitions that would indicate a fixed disposition and cast of mind if not belief of the author's? Or are

these ideas that go to the heart of Platonic and Christian philosophy being allowed to dissolve in ambiguity? Professor Nuttall thinks that in *The Tempest* scepticism took on a new life:

> 'It is as if a second wave of scepticism has passed over the poet. It is quite different from the coprologous indignation of *Troilus and Cressida.* He no longer, for the sake of one transgression, denies the authenticity of love itself. But a reservation as to the truth-value of the assertions love provokes seems to have reappeared. Time, the old grey destroyer of the Sonnets, was not, after all, put down by love. After the enthusiastic reaffirmation of the later Sonnets and the first three Romances, a sadder and more complex reaction has set in, slightly ironical perhaps, but not at all cynical. The world has not been wholly redeemed by love; look at it. The subjective vision of the lover may transcend objective facts, but it does not obliterate them. The lover has one level, the hater another; perhaps there are a thousand more such levels, each as unreal as the rest.'[4]

It is clear that throughout *The Tempest* we meet with many indications that the ultimate triumph of good is far from certain, for no more than in the tragedies is there any scanting of the power of evil and of death. Yet I do not think the ending effect is simply ironic or sceptical, or that the prayer of the epilogue is but the recognition of defeat in the face of the conclusion that all we love is doomed. Nor does Professor Nuttall think this is the conclusion we must certainly draw. The wonder suffusing the entire work is so powerful we must be sure we have made all the discriminations we can before unresolved doubt is accepted as the final suggestion the play is making.

For one thing, we must discover if anywhere in the play, or elsewhere in Shakespeare's writings, there are matters that not only bring us to a still closer comprehension of what we would judge to be not merely metaphysical speculations but religious commitments; if here and there arguments are so resolved that *il gran rifiuto* should seem inconceivable. Do the poetry and drama, through images and symbols, ever develop meanings that the arguments do not include? In short, are there conceptions evidently so religious that contradiction would leave them unaffected?

The 'dark backward and abysm of time' is paradoxically an image of space in which we are led to negate the idea of duration. The bottomless pit of the abyss, or else the formlessness of chaos, suggests endlessness in the other sense: our imagination, our memory, our sight, looking back to that dimly sensed time before thought came to life and light lost itself in the notion of endless space. And as the images of space and duration become confused we are compelled to try to conceive at once of nothingness and of the timeless, and of how there could be such a thing as coming-into-being—out of 'the jaws of darkness'.

'Rounded with a sleep' presents us also with opposites. The globe and all that inhabited it having vanished, life and consciousness are said to end. Yet that which we can only know as waking is said to be in sleep, and we are bound to infer, such sleep out of which waking has taken its life. Consciousness is ended as a circle ends, and that completion which is ending one thing is continuing that very thing; the annhilation of what we have taken to be life is yet the continuance of a sort of life. We vanish and yet sleep.

The reasoning underlying these paradoxes opposes on the one hand duration to timelessness and space to nothingness, and on the other, being to non-being. This reasoning is, I think charmed with the notion of perfect being *(ens perfectissimum),* the reality underlying all change.[5]

But it is not the abstractions of thought, or the appeal of metaphysics that are finally holding us through these words of Prospero's but rather the sense they establish of persons searching the abyss, or waking from sleep, images of particular persons taking the form of life. Miranda, of course, and Prospero, or ourselves, what it is that gives particularity to persons treating with each other and with reality. What holds us above all and will not let go is the sense that such words are saying as much as can be said of being born into the world of sight and touch and breath. We are drawn to wonder not at truths about Being but about the survival or disappearance of individuals, and, as some of the key devices of the play will make clear, about the nature of our own coming into being and passing away. The metaphysical substance is here but it is not without reference to the concern for individuals peculiar to religion.

Mr. D. G. James had this in mind when he wrote of what it was that Miranda remembered when her father appealed to her:

'Canst thou remember
A time before we came unto this cell? . . .
Of anything the image tell me that
Hath kept with thy remembrance.
(I. ii. 38-9, 43-4)

We see the mind fetching out of its past some fragment of our infant dream—"of anything the image tell me"—stumbling in the vast darkness of what lies behind us, in the immeasurable depths which lie beneath us; a sense of the incalculable immensity out of which our lives appear and with which they are continuous, which we know, but cannot contain, within ourselves. (We think of the second of those last chapters of St. Augustine's *Confessions* which M. Gilson has called the *Paradiso* of the *Confessions,* and the words: "Great

is this force of memory . . . a large and boundless chamber. Who ever sounded the bottom thereof? Yet is this a power of mine, and belongs unto nature; nor do I myself comprehend all that I am.") Out of this vast darkness, Miranda brings the image of herself, royally attended.'[6]

Mr. James has taken the paradoxes—'immeasurable', 'incalculable', and yet to be known—and thinks it right to equate Prospero's notion of the abysm of consciousness and Miranda's summoning of her first remembrances with Augustine's *abyssum humanae conscientiae (Confessions,* X, 2), carrying forward what else the play has suggested of the Platonic metaphysics into Augustine's Neo-Platonizing and Christianity. I think we may agree that much in the play supports him in this although the dialogue itself may be thought to stop short. What gives his paraphrase the authority it does obtain is all that in the play is likening life to a dream. The subject is not only the relation of images coming out of the memory to the truth of things, or the likenesses of memory to the kind of thought that is called dreaming, it is also all that the play in telling of dreams and of truth, of illusions and reality, is treating with the authority by which an individual judges himself to be dreaming.

Prospero is to speak of life as a pageant, which signifies somewhat dimly but clearly enough a patterned procession of humans across time and space. The substance of the notion was his at the beginning when he was explaining to Miranda how those returning from the wedding in Tunis had come into his power. The moon, the tides, the plans of many persons, the coming of age of his daughter, all as it were conjoined.

By accident most strange, bountiful Fortune
. . . hath mine enemies
Brought to this shore.
(I. ii. 178-80)

What in his later perspective is a pageant is to those caught up in it a troubled sleep, a driven motion whose direction they cannot know. Prospero will also say that life in the pageant is an insubstantial stuff, that most if not all of the actors are dully sensitive, their reason muddy where it should be clear. (V. i. 82). Even 'things certain' (V. i. 125) they disbelieve. Yet knowing neither themselves nor what is driving them they are all too sure of suffering and confusion, of sorrow and loss, of hate, of crime, of being strangely manipulated.

All torment, trouble, wonder, and amazement
Inhabits here.
(V. i. 104-5)

Prospero can look upon the pageant and the dream as if detached from it, although he concludes he is not, but the others never gain his wisdom. They are told of truth and the work of Providence, they did what they could to master confusion, but all they ever came to know was that they were powerless before mysterious impulses, some learned they were being brought to judgment, and even to a beginning knowledge of themselves. (V. i. 212-213). All sensed the intrusion of mysterious forces.

As Ferdinand, Alonso, Gonzalo searched for clues to their predicaments we see in their uncertainty just such obscurity as faced Miranda. Confronting experience they cannot account for or comprehend, their memory itself confused, even what is before their eyes is 'rather like a dream than an assurance.' (I. ii. 45) Alonso, when told Prospero is his brother, hardly dares acknowledge what he might be expected to know if he knew anything:

> Whe'r thou be'st he or no,
> Or some enchanted trifle to abuse me,
> As late I have been, I not know. Thy pulse
> Beats as of flesh and blood; and, since I saw
>   thee,
> Th'affliction of my mind amends, with which,
> I fear, a madness held me. This must crave
> (An if this be at all) a most strange story.
>   (V. i. 111-17)

But it is of course Caliban's confusion as he recalls the celestial music that seemed to him the very rain of grace, when if ever it was truth, not a dream, that held him, causing him to pray to dream again. It is this that says most plainly of all how far everyone but Prospero is from what he will call understanding. Prospero's assurance, and, at the end, his serenity rest on his acceptance of the paradox, that we know change for what it is from knowing of changelessness. Miranda probably rests in wonder—which may be a deeper understanding still, and Ferdinand may learn to. The others must take on trust that what they do become assured of is for their good. They must believe it is right that they should become themselves again, but they will have no inkling of how it all began or ends, where it ends, or how the parts they played became theirs even though they themselves had chosen them like Plato's souls in choosing good or evil.

The strange necessities that brought these dim images into Miranda's remembrance were at work in what one after another took to be his dreaming. It was these same necessities in their apparent incoherence that Prospero solicited with his magic. We sense them in what we learn of the origins of Caliban, in the purposes of his terrible parent, in Ariel's history. There is an indication of the same strangeness in Prospero's likening the whole earthly existence to a pageant, a procession whose commencement is as undefined as its conclusion, though its existence and its passing are evidence of indeflectible compulsions. What all attempt to do is to take these strange stirrings to be life—their

remembrances of the past that is the prologue, their existence which seems no existence, their annhilation which they do not succeed in imagining. So it is, I think, that we may not take Prospero's wonderful summing up of his conclusions as the play's, for what he says is but another dimly recognized shape taking form out of the abysses in his understanding, and the light by which we are to perceive this is not to take form until the epilogue. Other words of Augustine in the passage Mr. James pointed to apply as well to Prospero as to the others—'the mind is too narrow to contain itself entirely.' (X, 8).

In speaking of the end as a rounded sleep Prospero is in one sense using words to point to what may not be possible even to conceive of. In another sense he is applying to death a characterization one after another in the play was applying to his present life. Paradox, absurdity—whatever—the words signify limitation and constraint, the loss of consciousness, of the power to act, of freedom. Many in the play had been led to think their waking life not unlike this, and their acting as their inaction like somnolence. On occasion a charm transfixed them, but even without a charm there were occasions when they felt the helplessness men know in dreams. And in likening what they continued to think of as their waking state to this they felt they had lost possession of themselves, the dream no longer evanescent but, rather, all there was. However lightly sketched much in the play is, the import of this fear, and desire, was developed to the limit, to the conclusion Prospero drew. Powerlessness, confinement, the loss of consciousness. If there was illusion in all this it would have been chiefly in the thought that freedom had been wholly taken from the living. On the other hand, the fundamental irony of *The Tempest* is in precisely this, that it is not an illusion.

Sometimes one or another had an intimation of another existence entirely, apparently not transient but enduring, through hearing celestial music, or through a vision, or in the sight of what appeared to be gods. Sometimes circumstance, sometimes a succession of events seemed to testify to the reality of fortune and destiny and providence. But unless it was Ariel, no one was to rest for long in the assurance of anything other than bondage. Until at the end they were returned to themselves—as Gonzalo said, 'no man was his own.' (V. i. 213). Prospero alone entertained the thought of lasting non-existence—when his understanding had gone as far as it could he found a paradox to account for the time when he, too, would no longer be his own. Each thought of his confinement differently, and the conditions were indeed different, but on one matter all agreed, no challenge would disturb the rule of what was fated.

Long before the audience supposes anything like this to be the burden of the play we are presented with a number of indications, apparently trivial in themselves, that are preparing for it. As the storm rages the boatswain curses the passengers who are getting in his way. Gonzalo reproves such insolence, offering the old joke that the rascal is clearly destined not to drown but to be hanged. Fate, if not society, he is suggesting, has ways of correcting license. There are other such instances of insubordination. We are reminded of the worst by Prospero's presence on the island, expelled from Milan by his brother. One reference after another establishes the very action of the play within a history of rebelliousness—Ariel had been locked into a pine tree because he would not comply with all that Sycorax required; Sycorax had been driven from Argier for outrages; her god, Setebos, would have been the most incorrigible of all—Caliban but inherited his and his dam's disposition. Never content they were all seeking to break free from the conditions life had set for them.

As such indications were multiplied we are bound to notice a certain consistency in the fortunes of the visitors to the island as they continue in the ways of insubordination and rebellion. Conspirators, having been successful in bringing down a duke, set out to kill a king. Confounded once, they set to again, they become desperate when they are thwarted this time, and imagine it is a legion of devils they must hereafter fight against. Seeking to free themselves from the limitations imposed by another's sovereignty they end in the prison of hysteria. Caliban and his new friends enjoy a wonderful exhiliration in their drunkenness, they think the island is to be theirs almost for the asking, and yet they end by being hounded as never before, and are returned to the same galling servitude.

There had been irony in Antonio's 'What's past is prologue', suggesting that the dispossession of Prospero was but an act in a drama leading to the removal of the King of Naples, a drama already written. He spells it out, this is destined—

> And, by that destiny, to perform an act
> Whereof what's past is prologue, what to
>   come,
> In yours and my discharge.

(II. i. 245-7)

The nature of that destiny may not be what he supposes—Ariel saw it differently: destiny caused the sea to belch Antonio and his companions upon the island, caused them to go mad, even arranged for their perdition. Ambition in truth was everlastingly promising rewards for those who would overthrow authority in seeking more and more scope, and it appeared that it was in the nature of things for such attempts to lead but to other restraints. Such ambitions were misconceived, the world was inhospitable, and every success bore within itself the requirement of its own frustration.

What was true for the noble conspirators was also true for the others, each undertaking was self-defeating: Caliban's rebellions led to more scourging. Moreover, had he succeeded, Miranda ravished would have no more been won than Milan conquered was possessed. The ambitions of the good and the just were conceived in deeper respect for the ways of nature and destiny, but these too would fall short and discover their limits. Whatever promises love and the service of justice made, or seemed to make, the way of the world was still unfathomable, there was much no one could give direction to. Ferdinand and Miranda understood that in some sense they were discovering freedom in devotion, but for them, too, there was the long future with its mysteries that Juno and Ceres were to celebrate. Not only death but time itself would see to it that Prospero should put down his task. Ariel alone was assured of complete emancipation, but through means no human could even know of.

Who it is Prospero serves may not be named. It is certainly not a person, and not love, if that could be thought of as a power in nature or as a goddess. He can reasonably enough refer what happens to fortune and providence, even as if they were deities, yet we shall not find him using such words as those on the ship who pray when they see death coming near; or such as Ariel spoke in reminding the wicked of the need for contrition and satisfaction, words that point unmistakably to the traditional observances of Christians and even to sacramental doctrine. He hardly ever allows himself such language as Ferdinand, that all the devils have left Hell in order to people the storm; nor is he ever to suppose, as the young prince does, that he has come into the presence of a deity. Prospero, of course, has summoned up spirits who take the form of Juno and Ceres—(Ariel represented Iris)—and in making it clear these are not the goddesses themselves he but continues his consistent reticence. He has proof enough of the reality of spirits, of the hierarchy of demons, of the terms on which spirit and matter treat with each other according to the complex of emanations in which all eventually derives from a single source. This everlasting, divine power he continually consults and obeys, and within the limits of his understanding he is able to conspire with it in effecting good. But whatever he himself brings about is only what force could have effected—transformations of mind and the growth of love he may encourage, but that is all, these proceed according to other necessities.

Prospero also knows how limited his understanding is. He may speak of the thoughts of others as 'muddy' (V. i. 82) and even promise their ultimate enlightenment, but he can only dimly apprehend his own future. His reason has in every respect informed him that there are abysses reason will never sound. No god—Eros or Chronos or any—will for him ever take form out of the abyss of being, no object will through the power of love inspire in him such promises as Ferdinand and Miranda treasure.

It was left to Ariel to delineate and celebrate all that Prospero holds in honor even if he himself is imprecise—the idea of a transcendent power that is also immanent, that shows the means of redemption and indeed authorizes them, that transforms the dead, that is assured of the existence of perfect freedom. But even Ariel does not give this power a name.

The idea that there might be something more to human existence than conforming to the obligation of command and service, to law in whatever form, was first put forward in the loveliest of senses when Ferdinand knew himself enthralled to Miranda. Being goddess-like she drew his entire devotion, and so he took joy in the menial tasks Prospero set for him in order that he might not think he had gained this wonder too easily:

> There be some sports are painful, and their
>   labour
> Delight in them sets off; some kinds of
>   baseness
> Are nobly undergone, and most poor matters
> Point to rich ends. This my mean task
> Would be as heavy to me as odious, but
> The mistress which I serve quickens what's
>   dead
> And makes my labors pleasures.
>
> (III. i. 1-7)

The piling of logs—'this wooden slavery' (III. i. 62)—thousands of them—becomes a patient nothing done in her service. It becomes a game, and more, a means of gaining heaven's favor—

> The very instant that I saw you, did
> My heart fly to your service; there resides,
> To make me slave to it.
>
> (64-6)

And Miranda, supposing the worst—that she will not become his bride—swears she will become his servant. (85). The two of them never tire of playing upon the idea of servitude—and so, finally, Ferdinand proposes marriage,

> with a heart as willing
> As bondage e'er of freedom.
>
> (88-9)

The language has made the meaning all but explicit—love transforms subjection into the enjoyment of power that ambition was always seeking—possession, union, exultation. Constraints cease to be known as constraints when content promises to follow upon content. All the

insubordinate motions that looked towards power mistook their ends as they mistook their means. Instead of honoring what they would possess, they treated it with dishonor, seeking mere domination—reducing Miranda to an object, kingship to tyranny, loyalty to manipulation. Ambition, ever restless, never satisfied, was its own confinement. Even dedication to the work of justice could but set the stage for the correction of wrong since the unregenerate were free to remain so. Love, however, endowed humans with the conviction of power extending limitlessly, even though much of what was to come would be unforeseen. In the ceremony blessing the betrothal of Ferdinand and Miranda, Juno and Ceres tell them that such affection as theirs nature itself blesses. Nature, bringing offspring, causing the earth to flourish, forwards what divinity blesses, what love has indeed prophesied. Those who love well are being told their faith is sound whatever is to happen in the course of time.

This sense of being moved about despite themselves is in part the recognition that particular efforts fail in their intent and have disappointing consequences. In part, also, it follows from the recognition that forces the characters are more or less ignorant of are intruding in their affairs. Prospero himself acknowledges the activity of powers he may be aware of only intermittently but that he must believe are ever-present—the bountiful fortune that has brought the ship to the island when he is able to make the most of the opportunity to effect his purposes; the fortune, also, that takes on the attributes of providence. There is the sense of an even more instantly directing power in the consciousness of what time brings about—the education of Miranda, the maturing of Ferdinand, the period allotted for Ariel's service and the fixing of the time for his emancipation. As impressive a witness of the power of time as anything else is in our notice of the vision Caliban has had of a celestial life, for in this we believe there to be inherent the suggestion of a fulfilment possibly yet to come. There is above all the ceremony of the goddesses, Juno and Ceres, looking towards the fruition of nature through the years.

The sense of time passing and in its passing bringing to birth is pressed upon us insistently, in innumerable circumstances, and just as in Prospero's soliciting of Miranda's memories and the sense his words there give of the womb of time, so the plotters against his life express the same all-encompassing meaning—'What's past is prologue' (II. i. 257). Even as it were in incidental remarks the pervasiveness of the idea is made known to us, as when Antonio speaks to his accomplice, suggesting the murder of the sleeping king—

> O, that you bore
> The mind that I do! What a sleep were this
> For your advancement!
>
> (II. i. 259-61)

In whatever circumstances, and with whatever empha-sis or reference, this sense of powers and of powerless-ness is but the extension into philosophy and supersti-tion and religiousness of the theme struck in the first scene of subordination and insubordination, of the cost of responsibility, of the vexation of the ruled, of the desire for emancipation. Almost everyone is chafing at the bit—Prospero with his impatience, Alonso with his grief, Antonio and Sebastian like the boatswain and the drunken butler and Caliban himself in their self-willed ambitions. The desire for emancipation is con-ceived of not as freedom from the demands of power, but from the demands of authority. The slaves will become slave-owners, the lieutenants kings. Antonio's words fit them all—all except Ariel—

> My brother's servants
> Were then my fellows, now they are my men.
> (II. i. 266-7)

Subject to the circumscriptions of existence, life and the dream as the images of fatality, in another dimen-sion are images of the misery of the ruled—of servants and children and ministers, of all subordinates, of the dissatisfaction inherent in mortal life. As of Prospero himself before his expulsion—

> Which first was mine own king.
> (I. ii. 342)

Even in humor Prospero returns to the theme, teasingly rebuking Miranda—

> What, I say,
> My foot my tutor?
> (I. ii. 468-9)

In the dream all are stupefied, in society all are goaded. Which is to say, for all that thoughts are free (III. ii. 118), for all—with spirits bound up—that minds may hold fast to visions or to truths or to justice or to enmity and hatred and rebelliousness, all in nature is confinement.

The world of master and subject, of nature and hus-bandman, the only world we do know, can be nothing else than one in which men accommodate themselves to each other and to the universe either in strife or in co-operation. It is folly to dream to escape to some state in which rulers are accountable to no one or any thing. The thirst for power can no more be freed from the con-straints of power than the creatures of dreams may es-cape dreaming. The point is extended, and the question becomes from every viewpoint, is liberty an illusion?

The play begins in violence and with the threat of catastrophe, it ends in stillness, in happy and decent prospects, calm seas and auspicious gales. After the spectacular beginning there was an elaborate, even a drawn-out setting of the scene, renewing what the audience as well as Miranda need to know. We were then shown newcomers to the island devising conspira-cies almost immediately, and we witness marvellous, even miraculous happenings. We were initially im-pressed with hints of what Prospero was planning to do, particularly as we learned of his extraordinary powers, but as the scenes succeed each other it is not this that focuses our interest so much as a series of encounters—Ferdinand meeting Miranda; the reuniting of the passengers from the foundered ship; Caliban's joining up with Stephano and Trinculo. We become interested in what these meetings are leading to, what enterprises are under way and how they may affect each other, and largely independently of our concern for Prospero's ultimate success.

Some of the encounters had been arranged, others had come about by chance. Sometimes they seem to have been the work neither of humans or spirits but of in-visible influences that suggest the manipulations of fortune or destiny or providence. But in their succes-sion there is so little to be thought of as a plot, the entanglements are so little constraining, that we see that in this play the imitation of the action is as Aristotle conceived of it—an imitation of the energy in life that moves towards fulfilments, or, when perverted, towards frustration. And so when Ferdinand comes upon Mir-anda, when Antonio and Sebastian and Alonso are reunited, when the clown and the drunken butler join up with the monster, we are but lightly held by such a knitting of interests that constitute a plot, and we are more held by what we see to be at work in the lives of those before us. By the growth of love in Ferdinand and Miranda ('It works'—I. ii. 493); by the energy and inventiveness of malice as well as by the limitations that show themselves to be inherent in evil (Prospero's foes hysterically pursuing legions of fiends); by the words of Ariel that for a moment we may take to be those of an avenging angel ('You are three men of sin.' III. iii. 53). Prospero, of course, has a plan he has plotted, and much comes about as he wishes, but there is so much more that is at work that we are prevented from identifying what he is devising as either the plot or the action of the drama. We are more held in dis-covering how love and the directions of nature con-spire, how dreams may claim authority, how character as well as magic perform charms ('They are both in either's pow'rs'—I. ii. 450) and, above all, we are held by our developing sense of something not to be de-fined that may be giving direction to all this.

In the various meetings now one now another moves to advance his purpose. Prospero sets Ferdinand tasks that will teach him to value what he hopes to gain, Antonio and Sebastian grab at the chance to murder Alonso and Gonzalo. Successes and failures alike require other undertakings, and the actions in their various stages are as it were punctuated either by apparitions or an account of what might be at their root, as when Ariel sings fancifully of the death of Ferdinand's father, and when Caliban remembers a vision. The apparitions themselves—a banquet appearing and vanishing, evocations of harpies and hounds, goddesses performing a ritual—cap as it were this or that incident with a symbolic reference that attests to the moral and spiritual issues that have arisen in the course of the action. In their sum they attest to still something else, to the continuous presence of the powers ultimately responsible for the existence of what is appearing before us, being themselves translations of the events of the play into expressions of another order of existence. They illuminate the nature of the action of the play, what it is that is giving the lives of the characters their directions, what makes of it all, in Prospero's term, a pageant.

Prospero instigated several of the ghostly appearances and, knowing we may suppose, their import, but what is said by the figures in the apparitions would seem to have gone beyond what he could have conceived. Ariel, most especially, carrying out his orders, speaks as from someone within the vision, addressing sinners as if possessing divine authority, while Prospero can at most, and from the outside, approve. And what Juno and Ceres do in blessing is beyond what even a magician could hope to perform. Then, too, these marvellous sights, accompanied so often as they must have been by music from unseen instruments—as it was when Ariel with her singing led Ferdinand to Prospero and Miranda—would seem to have taken form in another world. By that very suggestion the import they bear would seem to possess something of the character of the chorus in ancient drama, not submerged in the circumstances of the drama's action but granted the special power that belongs to truth itself—comprehending, judicial, serene.

In addition to their spectacular nature many of these marvels hold us with the sense of the same mysterious and fascinating power of so many of the images of the play, the same strangeness that stirs us in Prospero's words asking Miranda to search her memory, and in what goes so far beyond the commonplace when he recalls the infant's smile that encouraged him when the two were adrift—

> O, a cherubin
> Thou wast that did preserve me! Thou didst
>   smile,
> Infusèd with a fortitude from heaven,
> When I have decked the sea with drops full
>   salt,
> Under my burden groaned; which raised in
>   me
> An undergoing stomach, to bear up
> Against what should ensue.
>   (I. ii. 152-8)

But nothing, probably, speaks more for the importance of this power in defining the interest that holds us in the unfolding of the action than Ariel's song to Ferdinand telling what has happened to the dead.

The words begin in tolling, 'Full fathom five,' and then out of the fearful beat there arises a strange beauty. We are struck with the preposterousness of so swift a change of bones and eyes to among the loveliest of sea-growths. But in the startling we recognize too the truth of what we have always known, that in death as in life there are continuous transformations, all is to be wondered at, all changes being preposterous, always to be expected and always surprising. And in these lines there is the promise of the most astonishing marvel of all, that the man himself will take another form, and not merely his bones and eyes. With such apparent guilelessness promised such beauty, such marvels, led into still more expectation, and especially of the strange, the words inevitably strike us with the suggestion of a mystery in what is being done, in the course of things, and in what it all is to end in. In what might have been simply a beautiful mocking song, some celebration of something like the jewel-paved streams of Paradise, we are held by the sense of power at work, transforming and transfiguring the remnants of a man and the man himself.

Nothing is more important to the marrying of the marvellous and the natural than what the production of the play would owe to spectacle and music. The storm scene with its great 'noise' is succeeded by the sight of a young prince rescued from the sea and led to safety by music that enraptures him. Music and singing interrupted a murder—to Gonzalo asleep it was a strange humming, to the murderers the sound of an earthquake and the roaring of lions. Solemn and strange music, then thunder and lightning, then soft music and dancing shapes accompany the magical appearance and disappearance of a banquet. The most glorious effects would have supported the enactment of the ceremony in which the images of Juno and Ceres blessed the betrothal of Ferdinand and Miranda.

I believe it is agreed that in no other play of Shakespeare's is music so vital to the conception although of course we do not have enough to help us re-create the original productions. It is, I think, a misconception—or at least, the argument is unsatisfactory—that speaks of *The Tempest* as a form developing out of masque into opera, but this I think we may say, that spectacle and music are as integral to the conception of the work as are the representation of persons and the movement of verse and meanings. And the marvels we behold together with music that would have been worthy of the songs would give the finally lasting impress to the metaphysical and religious postulates that underly the action. Mr. J. H. Long could not have worked out all that would finally substantiate his judgment but I think we must generally agree with his idea of the play as a sustained musical movement ending in rhythmic and harmonic resolution.[7]

The notion of a single, completed movement led Prospero to liken the existences of humans and of the world to a pageant, but Shakespeare's perspective of the form of the play is not precisely this. Prospero had acted in bringing certain matters to a conclusion, and in laying down his task he is preparing for death. He has hopes for those who are succeeding him and for those who are yet to come, but his own perspective is that of one whose power is now gone and whose life shortly will be. It is his work and life that is vanishing. Much has been as he planned, and he has looked upon all that has happened as one apart from it. Ariel, by contrast, time and time again speaks as from within the very processes of things, as at the source of the power Prospero has solicited and depended on. The form of the play is established in relating the realm in which Ariel has his being to that of Prospero. It is accordingly not defined as a journey or a procession that is over with but as a celebration of what is and what is to come. The climax of the play is in the ceremonial in which images of goddesses bless the future.

Prospero in arranging to right wrongs and provide for Miranda and in coping with his unwilling minister and servant and those who plot against him submitted himself to an order in things he had learned something of. His magic, his solicitation of memory, and his prescience all attest to his respect for a special hierarchy of demonic powers that he had come to understand at least partly. But he was equally respectful of powers he made no claim to fathom—fortune, the ways of time, destiny, providence. He deferred to all these, indeed he honored them, and he used enough of the language of orthodox Christian doctrine to make it certain he had no interest in going beyond the prerogatives of humans. He could only solicit, not govern. He did not even claim the authority of a priest, blessing, pardoning. He was far from being the intermediary of grace. At most he prays:

> Fair encounter
> Of two most rare affections! Heavens rain
>   grace
> On that which breeds between 'em!
>
> (III. i. 74-6)

The ways of fortune and destiny he knew were beyond his comprehension, and that he must work with them— it was through these his enemies were brought within his power, and it was through destiny and providence that this should be at a time when there could be a betrothal for his daughter. He knows himself to be subject to the laws that put spirits to the service of men as well as to something he cannot define that he yet recognizes to be at work in the ways in which time brings things to pass. His effectiveness depends upon

obedience, his doing right depends on it, his freedom is in choosing to obey the right. And then he must resign his power, leave to nature and fortune and destiny the future of those he has so cared for. He had fostered the union, he had, so to speak, offered to the gods. Now he would depart, the task never to be finished by him, he returning to that death in which fish might feed upon his flesh, and his bones, too, might become coral, all that was certain would be that he would be ending in the fated ways of all things, lifeless, powerless.

In a certain obvious respect Prospero acted to obtain what King Lear dreamed of, the consolation that redeems suffering, and his conception of what the gods wanted led him to act out the vision suffering engendered. The authority of the idea of blessedness in *Lear* is in the power of the representation of human suffering and how in such as the king it is instrumental in purification and in ennoblement. But in *The Tempest* all that is in the abyss of the past, and Prospero is not among the sainted, as Lear madly imagined he might be, he is alive and sane and burdened. He cannot afford the illusion of believing he and another Cordelia might pass eternity in God's kind nursery, he must merely make the best of things.

If one wishes to call this motive love, and to agree that here as in so many of the sonnets and in *King Lear* Shakespeare is allowing it such power as the gods possess, yet one must say that the governing conception of *The Tempest* is not in the celebration of love as such, whatever its authority, but of what has brought life into being and consigned it to the care of humans. What governs the play, I think, is the conception of being that Shakespeare earlier sounded in *The Phœnix and Turtle*. For such a conception the idea of love which perhaps inevitably carries with it a personal and human character is too limiting.[8]

Notes

[1] A. D. Nuttall, *Two Concepts of Allegory, A Study of Shakespeare's The Tempest and the Logic of Allegorical Expression,* London, 1967, p. 147.

[2] *The Elizabethan Love Sonnet,* London, 1956, p. 276.

Professor Nuttall, in the most adept philosophical treatment we so far have of *The Tempest,* has taken up the meanings that Mr. Lever has analyzed so finely and extended them: 'The concept of extended duration at last gives way to the frankly metaphysical concept of eternity when the two strands of the Sonnets—the intricate love story and the horror of mutability—are joined in the third remedy, love. It was not the poet's verses that should free his friend from the tyranny of time, but rather his love. Love itself (the now-familiar locution is forced upon us) is timeless and invulnerable.' (*Two Concepts of Allegory,* p. 122).

In *The Tempest* itself, with its insistent suggestions of the metaphysical, Mr. Nuttall continues, 'Love *is* conceived as a supernatural force, and any number of protestations of metaphor and apologetic inverted commas cannot do away with the fact that a sort of deification, and therefore *a fortiori* reification has taken place. Whether these concepts should be allowed to be meaningful, or whether they should be permitted only a "merely aesthetic" force (and that presumably spurious) I do not know. The unassertive candour of Shakespeare's imagination has left the question open.' (p. 160).

We have long understood that it is not only in *The Tempest* we must come to terms with what Shakespeare is doing with the suggestions of supernatural power and benevolence. Sooner or later we arrive at whatever conclusions we judge proper when it is proposed that Shakespeare is depending upon Christian faith. For my part I believe that the effects of the poetry itself—this communication of the quality I have spoken of as stillness and serenity—should initially be referred to that state the ancients spoke of as close to the divine. This is a character I think we must allow such expression in Shakespeare whether or not we are drawn to other conclusions as well. On this matter we may be grateful for the summary M. Ragnar Holte provides: 'Si l'on cherche à condenser en une formule générale ce que signifie εὐδαιμονία pour un Grec, on peut dire—nous laissons ici de côté les sens affaiblis, secondaires—qu'il désigne un idéal de vie amenant les hommes aussi près de la vie des dieux qu'ils peuvent en avoir le désir sans pour autant se rendre coupables de démesure, ὕβρις. . . . L'εὐδαιμονία est l'état de l'homme où l'élément divin n'est ni affaibli ni étouffé, mais se trouve au contraire actualisé avec son maximum de plénitude et de force, les autres puissances vitales étant soit déracinées soit soumises à sa direction. Cet état est toujours conçu comme dépendant de la vertu, ἀρεγή, surtout de la plus haute des vertus, la sagesse, φοφία, ou comme s'identifiant avec elle.' (*Béatitude et Sagesse, Saint Augustin et le problème de la fin de l'homme dans la philosophie ancienne,* Paris, 1962, pp. 14-15.

[3] John Armstrong, *The Paradise Myth,* London, 1969, p. 46.

[4] *Two Concepts of Allegory,* pp. 156-7.

[5] The Aristotelean sense here agrees in important respects with the Platonic: ' "To be" anything, in the world of natural processes, means "to be something that comes into being and passes away", something that is subject to change. In this sense, anything that is, any *ousia,* is anything that is what it is as the result of a process, a *kinesis.*' (J. H. Randall, *Aristotle,* New York, 1960, p. 111).

This is the argument of the *Metaphysics,* and here as well as in *On Philosophy* Werner Jaeger believes that

Aristotle carries on the Platonic notion that the best *(ariston)* and the purest reality *(ousia)* coincide. (*Aristotle,* Oxford, 1948, p. 222).

In *The Tempest* Shakespeare does not of course introduce either the terms or the arguments that would point us towards certain refinements of speculation, nor does he, as Marston and Jonson on occasion do, supply footnotes in reference. Nor, however carefully articulated we judge the reasoning of *The Phœnix and Turtle* or any other work to be, may we refer to that for precise corroboration when any number of modifications would be possible from moment to moment. One is merely required to refer to what in traditional thought is coherent with conceptions developed in the particular work.

[6] *The Dream of Prospero,* Oxford, 1967, p. 39.

[7] *Shakespeare's Use of Music: The Final Comedies,* Gainesville, 1961, p. 96: 'Let us consider the play as some great plagal cadence whose passing chords are resolved by the soul-satisfying completeness and finality of the tonic chord.'

[8] The integrity of this composition is such one is bound to relate the political and ethical matters that arise in representing the claims of liberty and subordination to the more general matters that come to mind in reflecting upon Prospero's abjuring of power and upon the temper with which the play ends. This calls for still other perspectives one is obliged to take account of in any effort at a summary.

It is of course impossible to identify the state of mind the play leads to in its conclusion with any other than the author's own resolution of the issues that arose in handling his material. But where so much has to do with obedience and with the recognition of divine powers it would be remiss to exclude from any summary estimate the consideration of a certain Christian perspective upon such matters. I have already cited words of M. Ragnar Holte in characterizing the serenity within the grasp of the ancients to help us in assessing not only Prospero's quietness at the end, but elsewhere, such as Hamlet's also, when he speaks of the felicity he credits Horatio with, and Horatio's state, also, in commending the soul of his friend to the care of angels. The traditional Christian view may offer even more light in helping us reflect upon the conclusion of *The Tempest,* particularly as we keep in mind that this is looking towards the celebration of a marriage with all that that implies. In exploring such a perspective, M. Holte's further observations can be of great help: ' . . . les deux traits de l'amour, la joie et la subordination, ne peuvent entrer en conflit, si l'homme se conduit bien. Ils forment un tout, fondé sus la structure ontologique de la charité (conçue selon le couple *participatio-imago*). Cette unité est déjà exprimée dans la notion *Deo propter seipsum frui,* laquelle signifie un don du sujet à un objet situé en dehors de lui. Sans doute le moi ne cesse jamais d'être sujet de l'amour—comment cela serait-il possible?—et jamais non plus l'amour ne peut oublier qu'il s'adresse à celui dont il attend tout bien—sinon il se rendrait coupable d'un péché grave d'ingratitude. . . .

'Nous comprenons maintenant comment Augustin peut identifier le désir de la béatitude avec la recherche de Dieu. Dieu est *beata vita,* il y a plaisir et joie à l'aimer: Dieu est volonté, l'aimer c'est lui obéir. Si cette unité est fondée philosophiquement sur la structure onto-logique de la charité, elle a en même temps son fonde-ment dans la théologie chrétienne de la création. L'homme est créé, pour vivre dans la béatitude, soumis à la volonté de Dieu. Augustin marque particulièrement qu'il n'est pas destiné à une béatitude exempte de soumission. Un degré aussi parfait de béatitude n'appartient qu'à celui qui possède son être et sa béatitude en soi, *per se,* à savoir Dieu lui-même. Les "notions" que possède l'homme même déchu, constitu-ent des exhortations à realiser sa vocation, qui lui est donnée dans sa création même. Mais l'homme dans l'état déchu ne prend point plaisir à la volonté de Dieu, il est au contraire dominé par le désir d'être son propre maître *(superbia).* Alors qu'il était créé pour la béatitude sous la souveraineté de Dieu, voilà qu'il ne cherche plus que le plaisir à l'exclusion de la soumission. Mais Dieu ne lui permet pas d'y réussir. En effet même lorsqu'il se tourne vers les choses sensibles pour en jouir avec un amour qui vise à la *fruitio propter seipsam rei,* cet amour le pousse à une subordination qui va à l'encontre de ses intentions. Il devient l'esclave du sensible, il perd la maitrîse de soi-même. En prenant un être autre de Dieu pour objet de *fruitio,* il a transgressé *l'ordo.* Suivant une logique inexorable, la sanction se trouve déjà dans la struc-ture ontologique de cet amour faux, laquelle est semblable à celle de l'amour vrai. *Frui* comporte dans les deux cas un abandon de soi et une soumission; mais, si la subordination à Dieu est liberté et béatitude, la subordination au sensible est au contraire esclavage, avilissement profond et malheur.' (*Béatitude et Sagesse,* pp. 230-1).

'L'immutabilité ne désigne pas pour Augustin un état statique, mort, mais au contraire un état de plénitude ontologique et de force, source d'une activité dyna-mique qui, lois d'ébranler la consistance propre de l'être, met en mouvement une existence ontologique-ment inférieure. *Constantia* est une notion relative, qui n'est pas réservée à Dieu seul. L'âme aussi possede une certaine 'consistance' par comparaison avec le corps, laquelle croît si l'âme acquiert la *virtus* pro-prement dit, la vertu.' (pp. 233-4).

It has been observed that 'essentialism' rather than 'existentialism' provides the base for Shakespeare's conceptions, and in the Scholastic sense, being imply-ing essence. (G. C. Herndl, *The High Design,* Lexing-ton, 1970, pp. 50-1).

Richard P. Wheeler (essay date 1995)

SOURCE: "Fantasy and History in *The Tempest,*" in *The Tempest,* edited by Nigel Wood, Open University Press, 1995, pp. 127-64.

[*In the excerpt below, Wheeler focuses on Prospero's aggressive dominance of others and on Caliban's pas-sive dream of sensual opulence. From a psychoana-lytic perspective, the critic calls attention to the simi-larities between this pair and others in the Shake-spearean canon—Bottom and Oberon, Richard II and Bolingbroke, Falstaff and Henry V—who represent the opposition of narcissistic eloquence and theatrical control.*]

The story Prospero tells Miranda about their past, whatever its claim to historical veracity, contains a simple and important truth at the heart of his post-Milan life. Once when he gave his brother his trust he lost his inherited political power; now that he has found another source of power he will trust no one. Prospero's power over the action of *The Tempest* is unparalleled in Shakespeare's drama—control by physical coercion over the worker Caliban; control by contractual agree-ment backed by physical threat over Ariel; control through Ariel over the men who took away his duke-dom and over all the other visitors Prospero brings to his island; control over every condition of his daughter's courtship by and marriage to Ferdinand.

As Prospero tells of Antonio's treachery, a rather star-tling metaphor stands out. Antonio transformed the loyalties of the Milanese subjects, turning their hearts where he pleased, creating a situation in which, Pro-spero says, 'now he was/The ivy which had hid my princely trunk,/And sucked my verdure out on't' (I.ii.85-7). Antonio was the parasitical ivy wrapped around and sucking the living substance out of Prospero the ducal tree.

Perhaps the vine/tree metaphor seems startling here because it links two brothers in a figure often gendered female and male. In benign forms, the vine is a grape-vine associated with fruitfulness and nurture. An ap-parent biblical source—'Thy wife shall be as a fruitful vine by the sides of thy house' (Psalms 128: 3)—links wife/vine/fruitfulness, though without situating the hus-band as tree. In proverbial uses, vine and the tree unite in harmony: 'The Vine and Elme, converse well to-gether', or 'As we may see of the Vine, who imbraceth the Elme, ioying and reioycing much at his presence' (Tilley 1950, V: 61). In Ovid, the female vine and the male tree are joined to mutual benefit in a story used in an attempt to seduce Pomona, a garden-tending nymph who has spurned many suitors. Pointing to an elm supporting vines loaded with grapes, the satyr Vertumnus (disguised as an old woman promoting his own cause) observes that if the vine did not grow round it the beautiful tree would be barren of fruit, and that if 'the vyne which ronnes upon the Elme had nat/The tree too leane untoo, it should uppon the ground ly flat' (Ovid 1961: 183). Here form, strength and uprightness gendered male and fruitfulness gendered female combine in an image of two joined in one to mutual benefit and to the benefit of others. In Prospero's image, the male ivy hides the male tree and drains its strength to the detriment of a dukedom thus bent 'To most ignoble stooping' (I.ii.116).

Shakespeare uses the vine/tree metaphor in two earlier comedies in which magic is a preoccupation. In *Comedy of Errors,* benign and parasitical forms indicate alternative fates for the man Adriana thinks is her husband.

> Thou art an elm, my husband, I a vine,
> Whose weakness, married to thy stronger state,
> Makes me with thy strength to communicate.
> If aught possess thee from me, it is dross,
> Usurping ivy, briar, or idle moss,
> Who, all for want of pruning, with intrusion
> Infect thy sap, and live on thy confusion.
>
> (II.ii.165-72)

Adriana, as a vine who shares in and is strengthened by her husband's strength, does not offer her own fruitfulness in the metaphor, but neither does her sharing of the husband's strength diminish its source. She is pleading her need, flatteringly, not her bounty. The invasive ivy (or briar or moss) alternative—the other woman Adriana suspects—is parasitical growth out of control, which contaminates the man/tree's strength and thrives on the destruction resulting from her 'intrusion'. The ivy/sap/intrusion link here closely parallels the ivy/verdure/extrusion link in *The Tempest;* the breakdown of the parallel—female ivy that invasively corrupts the manly substance rather than sucks it out— adds to the interest. 'Usurping ivy' certainly would seem to connect with the usurpation of Prospero's place and power by his ivy-like brother. But the female ivy Adriana refers to suggests a sexual threat to her husband. Is there any relation here to Prospero's metaphorical rendering of his brother's past crime?

Titania speaks the most eloquent and moving instance of the ivy/tree metaphor in *A Midsummer Night's Dream:*

> Sleep thou, and I will wind thee in my arms.
>
> . . . . .
>
> So doth the woodbine the sweet honeysuckle
> Gently entwist; the female ivy so

> Enrings the barky fingers of the elm.
> O, how I love thee! How I dote on thee!
>
> (IV.i.37-42)

Here what is expressed is not the woman's bounty nor her need but her satisfaction. Enchanted Titania finds the fulfilment of her desire in her embrace of ass-headed Bottom.

Although Bottom is powerless to escape Titania's attentions—'Out of this wood do not desire to go:/Thou shalt remain here, whether thou wilt or no' (III.i.126-7)—her power over him hardly seems to be the contaminating power Adriana imagines for 'usurping ivy', much less the eviscerating power Prospero claims his brother exercised over him. And as the object of her desire, Bottom does not seem to figure male strength either as complemented or diminished by female ivy. As with an infant, Bottom's dependence creates a situation in which he seems to be magically empowered; he will come to experience omnipotence of mind, a magical responsiveness of the world to wish, defined for him by Titania's bounty:

> I'll give three fairies to attend on thee,
> And they shall fetch thee jewels from the deep,
> And sing, while thou on presséd flowers dost sleep;
> And I will purge thy mortal grossness so
> That thou shalt like an airy spirit go.
>
> (III.i.131-5)

For Bottom the demands of maintaining a masculine identity in opposition to the otherness of female sexuality—the demands that structure Oberon's world—are suspended. Without ever ceasing to be 'bully Bottom', the centre of his experience is 'translated' back into the realm of infantile at-oneness with comfort, pleasure, fantasy, and conflict-free sensuality. The sight of the sleeping pair appears pitiful and hateful to Oberon, but Bottom awakens to recall 'a most rare vision', a 'dream, past the wit of man to say what dream it was', indeed, a dream that 'shall be called "Bottom's Dream", because it hath no bottom' (IV.i.200-9).

Bottom's dream can point us back to *The Tempest,* but not directly to Prospero's curious use of the ivy/elm figure. Titania promises to purge Bottom's 'mortal grossness', letting him 'like an airy spirit go', but the figure in *The Tempest* who recalls Bottom's experience is not the airy spirit Ariel but the unpurged monster Caliban. As with Bottom, Caliban's monstrousness is clearly connected to sexuality and taboo. But whereas Bottom is for a brief time transported into a magical realm defined in part by a temporary suspension of taboo, for Caliban, a past, failed effort to break taboo has radically and permanently altered the world he inhabits. Bottom, ass-headed only for the night he spends in Titania's arms, regains his non-monster status as soon as Oberon reclaims his sexual partner. Caliban's irredeemable monstrousness, 'Which any print of goodness wilt not take' (I.ii.351), is represented most vividly by his early effort to rape Miranda. Bottom's night of pleasure is licensed by Oberon, who uses the occasion to recover his status as Titania's lover. Caliban has failed to overcome the taboo on Miranda's sexuality enforced by her father, who is also subject to it.

Caliban's account of his island's magical bounty, however, provides a curious parallel to the enchanting presence Bottom recalls. 'Be not afeard', Caliban comforts the frightened Stephano and Trinculo:

> the isle is full of noises,
> Sounds, and sweet airs, that give delight and hurt not.
> Sometimes a thousand twangling instruments
> Will hum about mine ears; and sometime voices,
> That, if I then had waked after long sleep,
> Will make me sleep again, and then in dreaming
> The clouds methought would open and show riches
> Ready to drop upon me, that when I waked
> I cried to dream again.
>
> (III.ii.133-41)

Caliban, too, has had a most rare vision, one of sublime, passive fulfilment—though with Caliban it seems to be fulfilment always just out of reach, something lost to the new order Prospero has brought to the island, particularly since the failed rape of Miranda. Bottom awakens to recall, as if in a dream, a world in which wish and reality corresponded, where one's complete dependence on the other was experienced as magical omnipotence. His emergence from this dreamlike world is experienced as a gain—it has given him something he can bring into the world he re-enters upon awakening, his characteristic zest for life renewed and enriched. For Caliban, by contrast, the sounds and sweet airs, the twangling instruments, the lulling voices, the riches poised to drop from the clouds of his dream, all are experienced as utterly alien to his everyday life of subjection.

The pleasures Caliban knows through a dreamlike rapport with the island's mysterious musical and sensual abundance have no place in his present reality. Something of the tenderness of the experience he describes to Stephano and Trinculo seems to have had a place in social reality in the distant past of his earliest relationship to Prospero:

> When thou cam'st first,
> Thou strok'st me and made much of me; wouldst give me

> Water with berries in't, and teach me how
> To name the bigger light and how the less,
> That burn by day and night; and then I loved thee,
> And showed thee all the qualities o'th' isle,
> The fresh springs, brine pits, barren place and fertile
>
> (I.ii.332-8)

Something of this readiness for adoring submission emerges again in Caliban's response to Stephano and the fantasy he brings of a future released from subjection to Prospero. But in his ongoing reality, there is no place for the responsiveness he brings to the island's bounty, or which that bounty elicits in him. Bottom wakes to bring a sense of dreamlike wonder back into his world, but Caliban cries to dream again.

I have moved from Prospero's ivy/elm metaphor describing his brother's treachery to Titania's use of that metaphor to describe her embrace of Bottom, then moved from Bottom's recollection of that embrace as a dream back to *The Tempest* and Caliban's experience of dreamlike riches. But whereas the two moments from *A Midsummer Night's Dream* provide two vantage points on the same blissful encounter, the two instances from *The Tempest* are quite remote from one another: Prospero tensely reconstructing the past treachery of his brother; Caliban, his slave, poignantly describing the near escape into dreamlike bliss the island can provide for him with its music. Can the connections to and within *A Midsummer Night's Dream* I have been trying to make illuminate the relationship between these two moments in *The Tempest?*

The psychological connection that has presented itself so far sees Bottom's account of his dream and Caliban's of his dreamlike relation to the island's musical abundance as fantasies deriving from early infantile relations to a nurturing Other, relations that provide the field upon which later fantasies are articulated. The early nurturing environment, if it is sufficient to ensure the infant's survival, will countenance the emergence of polarized fantasies of omnipotence and of total helplessness; of fusion with a benign, nurturant world and of annihilation by a hostile, rejecting world; of good objects and of bad objects located indeterminately inside and outside of a subjectivity still establishing its boundaries; of being loved unconditionally, and returning it in bliss, and of being hated without limit, and of returning that in rage. Introjection and projection—taking bits of the world in and making them parts of one's experience of one's person and taking parts of one's person and casting them into a world of not-self—are dominant psychic mechanisms, shaping a sense of one's person along the coordinates of need, satisfaction/frustration, pleasure/unpleasure, security/distress, bliss/rage.

Bottom's and Caliban's lyrical dreamlike riches share a base in the sensual and nurturant qualities of this level of psychic experience. Prospero's image of the ivy that hid his princely trunk and sucked out his vital spirit suggests a base in the negative register of early infantile experience. If we look just at the action components of the metaphor—the ivy embraces the elm, hiding it, and sucks the verdure from it—the connections come into focus. Holding and sucking, the principal actions conveyed in Prospero's metaphor, are basic to the formative beginnings of an individual. D.W. Winnicott gives the name 'holding phase' to the very earliest stage of infantile existence: the physical experience of being held is central to and prototypical for the infant's relations to an environment that attends to all its needs (Winnicott 1965, 44-50). Freud calls 'sucking at his mother's breast, or at substitutes for it', the 'child's first and most vital activity' (Freud 1953-74, VII: 181). In the action of sucking, sexual pleasure originates and is split off from need satisfaction: when the sucking that seeks to satisfy the infant's hunger produces pleasurable sensations desirable in their own right, 'the need for repeating the sexual satisfaction now becomes detached from the need for taking nourishment' (Freud 1953-74, VII: 182). With the activity of sucking, the infant is initiated into human sexuality. As it negotiates experience within what Winnicott calls the 'holding environment', the infant 'comes to have an inside and an outside, and a body-scheme' (Winnicott 1965, 45).[2]

Psychic manoeuvres that characterize fantasies and dreams account for the transformations necessary to get from the infantile situation to Prospero's metaphor. Whereas the holding environment locates the infant in a world in which the subject can begin to know itself through the attention the world returns, Prospero speaks of the ivy that 'hid' him (or at least hid that part of him designated by 'princely trunk') from the world. The holding is malevolent rather than facilitating—a withholding. Its action is generated by projection and reversal: the sucking fundamental to the infant's hold on life becomes the action of the ivy that 'sucked my verdure out'. Angry, destructive feelings, associated with frustrations of sucking and feeding, are projected into a fantasied attack by the other.

In Prospero's metaphor for Antonio's ill-doing, two kinds of threat coalesce, mingling two kinds of relation (brother to brother, infant to mother) and two kinds of past (the fictionalized recollection from what the play ascribes to Prospero's young manhood and an infantile past lent to Prospero by his creator). That we can think about the maternal threat being submerged in the sibling threat seems richly suggestive in thinking about this play in which the role of women is so generally suppressed or restricted and in which the only strongly evoked maternal presence is the dead but sinister Sycorax, Caliban's mother and Prospero's predecessor. But now it is less important to pursue a subordinating structure than to note that the two threats point to a single infantile prototype: a male child for whom an apparently exclusive claim on the love of his mother is disrupted, not by a father, but by the arrival of a younger brother and by what appears to be the withdrawal of the mother's attention away from him into her preoccupation with the newborn son. Not surprisingly, Shakespeare's drama never represents this situation directly—that is, in the experience of very young children. But the basic structure—a male's love for a female is disrupted by a second male—is pervasive and powerful.

Oberon is in a situation like this when Titania's devotion to the Indian boy disrupts his sexual bond to her. Oberon disposes of his problem by passing on his situation to the Indian boy, whose claim on Titania's love is displaced by Bottom's, who can then be displaced by Oberon. The task is easy enough for Oberon, supernaturally secure in his own exotic manhood, and with a strong prior sexual bond to Titania to renew. The disruption of Prospero's bond to Miranda by the appearance of a young suitor is of a different sort. *The Tempest* must dramatize, not the comic renewal of a sexual bond that has been interrupted, but a father's relinquishing to another, younger man, the daughter upon whom his life has been centred ever since his exile to the island, and whose entry into adult sexuality must be her exit from his world.

As with *King Lear,* the jealous intensity of a father's investment in his daughter shapes the bond the younger man will interrupt. Like Lear, Prospero has gone to elaborate lengths to control the conditions of the marriage. Lear, however, tries to use the ritual division of his kingdom to ensure that Cordelia will go on loving her father all, even after her dynastic marriage to another man about to be ritualistically chosen by him; her refusal to cooperate in his plan sets in motion the play's tragic action. Prospero arranges to bring Ferdinand to his island as his chosen husband for Miranda, and he oversees a courtship between them that follows exactly his plan for it; their complicity and his willingness or capacity to make a gift of his daughter to the younger man make possible the play's comic outcome. But what enables Prospero to do what Lear could not? Or, what enables Shakespeare to move from the destructive exploration of Lear's love for Cordelia to the comic outcome of Prospero's love for Miranda?

There are certainly signs that Prospero is not wholly free of what drives Lear to act so tyrannically at the prospect of giving up Cordelia. Though he assures the play's audience that he could not be more pleased to welcome Ferdinand into the family, Prospero renders the young man powerless, threatens him with violence, mocks him in his apparent loss of a father, enslaves and imprisons him, and finally, when making a gift of his daughter, puts a curse on their relationship should they have sex before he binds them in marriage. And Shakespeare seems to want to make things as easy as possible for Prospero, on this count at least: Ferdinand is clearly a right-thinking young man, susceptible to the pieties Prospero enforces, chaste and worshipful in his love for Miranda, and appropriately awed by her magician father. But if one assumes the action of *The Tempest* opens on to the destructive potentiality realized in *King Lear,* it is not yet clear how these measures can protect the movement towards marriage from comparable violence.

Caliban's function as a nasty double to Ferdinand provides one way of defusing the anxieties in the marital situation: it lets Prospero disown and repudiate his own incestuous longing for Miranda and lets him expend his rage against a potential usurper on a vilified embodiment of brute sexuality. I think even more important, however, are the ways in which the play provides multiple situations shaped by the structure that organizes the comic movement toward marriage. Usurpation, of course, is everywhere in *The Tempest:* Antonio's past treachery when he stole Milan from Prospero; Caliban's conviction that Prospero has robbed him of an island properly his by inheritance from his mother; Prospero's charge that Ferdinand usurps his father's place as king of Naples; the plot to kill Alonso and make Sebastian king of Naples; the plot to murder Prospero, which would give Stephano both the island and Miranda. The two I want to focus on, and which I think are most crucial to the action, concern Prospero's charges against his brother and Caliban's experience of losing the island's bounty—Prospero's ivy/elm metaphor and Caliban's 'cried to dream again' situation.

Although Prospero condenses fantasies of maternal threat and sibling threat into a single metaphor, the action of the play for the most part separates them out again—into Antonio's treachery, which points back especially to the extensive sibling violence of the very early histories, and into the evil legacy of Sycorax, the mother as powerful witch and Satan's partner in sex, heir to Joan de Pucelle, Queen Margaret, and Lady Macbeth. Here separation serves a double function of isolation: by keeping the threat posed by Antonio's betrayal separate from that posed by Sycorax's legacy of malevolent female power and debased sexuality, and by keeping both separate from the romance of Ferdinand and Miranda, it protects the marriage plot from the explosive violence engendered by the actions of *Othello* or *Antony and Cleopatra* or *The Winter's Tale,* where brothers or friends come to be seen as usurping enemies and beloved women are repudiated as whores.

I think, however, that the play's most complex, cruel and tender development of a pervasive Shakespearian structure of usurpation and betrayal is in the presentation of Caliban. Caliban's experience of betrayal closely parallels Prospero's story of an inherited claim usurped by someone he trusted and treated generously: 'This island's mine by Sycorax my mother,/Which thou tak'st from me' (I.ii.331-2). Caliban's relation to the island's bounty has been interrupted by the usurper Prospero. But Caliban's story of his past introduces a period between Prospero's arrival and Caliban's effort to rape Miranda in which the intruder Prospero has been the object of his love. In this interim period, the fantasy of maternal bounty is located in the relationship to the intruder, who stroked Caliban, made much of him, taught him how to read and how to name his world. Indeed, Caliban's story of trust and reciprocity recalls the infantile roots common to his situation and Prospero's more directly than anything Prospero says.

The generosity of Caliban's initial response to Prospero dramatizes a procedure, which Anna Freud called altruistic surrender, that compensates with exaggerated tenderness for resentment toward a rival for parental love; the subject seeks his own fulfilment in his service to another; the usurper is embraced and adored (Freud 1966: 123-34). Altruistic surrender is built deeply into the extravagant generosity and adoration that Shakespeare the poet lavishes on the fair friend of the Sonnets, and into the poet's inclination towards extreme and sometimes almost savage self-effacement when that seems the only way to sustain his love. Caliban keeps the impulse towards adoration and generosity alive in *The Tempest,* not only through his recollection of his once worshipful regard for Prospero, but in his readiness to bring adoration and allegiance to Stephano: 'Hast thou not dropped from heaven?' 'I do adore thee.' 'I'll kiss thy foot. I'll swear myself thy subject' (II.ii.131, 134, 146). But where the Sonnets poet debases himself to celebrate the glory of the friend, 'Myself corrupting, salving thy amiss' (Sonnet 35, l. 7), the play debases Caliban, makes a monster of him.

On this island where Prospero subordinates everything to his power, and trusts no one, attitudes of trust and worshipful regard are given extensive thematic development. Gonzalo's fantasy of a sovereignless utopia on the island assumes that trust can replace power as society's basic mode of relating. Ferdinand believes Miranda must be the goddess the island's spirits attend, and he quickly devotes himself to a worshipful love for the sake of which he is happy enough to endure enslavement and imprisonment by Prospero. Miranda thinks Ferdinand must be 'A thing divine' (I.ii.419); at the end, she sees her famous 'brave new world' in the tarnished old order Prospero has reconstituted on the island. In these instances, Prospero's hard-nosed distrust is played against forms of sentimentality or *naïveté* that manage to ennoble, even while identifying the limits of, the characters who express them. Prospero's relationship to the debased Caliban is more complex. Caliban's pathetic tendency to enslave himself in the service of self-liberation is played against

Prospero's wise but tough mastery. But Caliban's openness to, and need for, trust, joy and self-surrender can be set against Prospero's willed estrangement from that part of a human life brought into existence through the nurture of a trusted Other. Slave Caliban dreams about riches ready to drop upon him; master Prospero dreams about an 'insubstantial pageant faded' (IV.i.155), a world that recedes into dreamlike emptiness, and about death. Caliban embodies not only the lust and crude violence, but also the access to trust and spontaneity Prospero has repudiated in himself.

Having waded far enough into the troubled waters of authorial allegory to identify Caliban partially with the impulse toward adoration and subjection in the *Sonnets,* I find it tempting to situate Caliban's powerful lyricism against the aggressive theatricality by which Prospero manipulates the action of the play as if it were his play to write. I believe it makes sense to think of the astonishing, distancing control Shakespeare achieves through the drama as crucial to protecting his temperament from the potentiality for adoring self-surrender that many of the sonnets embody. Prospero uses his magic art to manifest that kind of dramatic control from within his position as character/on-stage director; he controls Caliban, and distances himself from him, with particular brutality.

I think, however, the play makes this distinction only to collapse it in the end. If Prospero in some fashion represents Shakespeare's power as dramatist, Caliban represents an impulse as basic to his theatrical art as Prospero's executive power. Where Prospero accomplishes sharply defined social and political purposes in the drama he stages through his magic, Caliban seeks his fulfilment in showing his world to others and sharing it with them. 'I loved thee,/And showed thee all the qualities o'th' isle' (I.ii.336-7), he reminds Prospero. 'I'll show thee every fertile inch o'th' island', he assures Stephano: 'I'll show thee the best springs'; 'Show thee a jay's nest'; 'Wilt thou go with me?' (II.ii.142, 154, 163, 166). Caliban, in short, seeks himself in the pleasure he gives others; gives fundamentally by showing and surrendering to others the world he has a special claim to; and takes pleasure for himself in a kind of worshipful abjection that accompanies the giving: 'I'll kiss thy foot' (II.ii.146). It is an impulse built into Shakespeare's relation to the theatre. As the character Prospero dissolves into the actor who speaks the Epilogue, begging forgiveness and indulgence, it is the impulse that needs to find its recognition and reward in the audience's applause, 'or else my project fails,/ Which was to please' (Epilogue, V.i.330-1).

W.B. Yeats once described his 'fancy that there is some one myth for every man, which, if we but knew it, would make us understand all he did and thought' ('At Stratford-on-Avon', in Yeats 1961: 107). Yeats's notion is an extreme version of the sameness and differ-

ence issues raised in the first section of this essay: it makes everything each of us does into a variant or elaboration of a core theme. Indeed, Norman Holland has put Yeats's formulation to very interesting psychoanalytic use in developing his own claim that a core identity or identity theme, developed in an infant's early relations to a maternal provider, acts as a kind of master key to any individual's thought and behaviour.[3] I do not wish to make a claim for the comprehensive interpretative power of a single myth or theme in the manner of either Yeats or Holland. But I think that Yeats's formulation of a unifying myth that controls variation in Shakespeare points to a pattern that links up suggestively with patterns I have been discussing in moving from *A Midsummer Night's Dream* to *The Tempest.*

Yeats (1961: 107) wrote: 'Shakespeare's myth, it may be, describes a wise man who was blind from very wisdom, and an empty man who thrust him from his place, and saw all that could be seen from very emptiness.' Yeats sees this myth being worked out in the succession of Hamlet, 'who saw too great issues everywhere to play the trivial game of life', by the soldier Fortinbras. But his chief instance, in this essay prompted by his having just viewed six of the English history plays acted 'in their right order' (Yeats 1961: 97), is 'in the story of Richard II, that unripened Hamlet, and of Henry V, that ripened Fortinbras'. Yeats's clear sympathies are with the otherworldly Richard II, whom he situates on one side of this opposition, and not with the all-too-worldly figure who occupies the pragmatic side:

> instead of that lyricism which rose out of Richard's mind like the jet of a fountain to fall again where it had risen, instead of that fantasy too enfolded in its own sincerity to make any thought the hour had need of, Shakespeare has given [Henry V] a resounding rhetoric that moves men as a leading article does today.
>
> (Yeats 1961: 108)

Yeats's curious celebration of Richard the poet-king as 'lovable and full of capricious fancy' (Yeats 1961: 105) but blinded by an excess of wisdom, along with his strong distaste for Henry V as a heartless and ultimately inconsequential politician, sentimentalizes the English history plays. It also introduces an evaluatory register into the myth Yeats associates with Shakespeare that greatly diminishes its interpretative power. If we pull that evaluative register out, the opposition between Richard and Henry V looks rather like the opposition between Caliban's lyricism and Prospero's aggressive theatricality, mentioned earlier.

I do not wish to claim that Caliban is a 'wise man who was blind from very wisdom'—although a powerful trend within criticism of *The Tempest* has long been occupied with a recognition that there is something in

Caliban's way of relating to the world that is both precious and incompatible with the sort of order Prospero brings to the island, variants of the mix of attitudes built into the Renaissance notion of the noble savage.[4] Nor do I wish to argue exactly that Prospero, who 'thrust [Caliban] from his place' on the island, is 'an empty man, and saw all that could be seen from very emptiness'. I do, however, find Yeats's use of the idea of emptiness here quite resonant, especially so since he makes it central to Shakespeare's own vantage point on human life: 'He meditated as Solomon, not as Bentham meditated, upon blind ambitions, untoward accidents, and capricious passions, and the world was almost as empty in his eyes as it must be in the eyes of God' (Yeats 1961: 106-7).

To formulate his Shakespearian myth in terms of an opposition between Richard II and Henry V, Yeats, of course, elides two crucial figures. Richard II is not thrust from his position by Henry V, but by Henry Bullingbrook, who thus becomes Henry IV. In order for his son Hal to become Henry V, the figure who must be thrust aside is Falstaff. If the figures missing from Yeats's account are restored, this opposition is worked out doubly in the movement from *Richard II* to *Henry V:* Richard II/Bullingbrook-Henry IV and Falstaff/Prince Hal-Henry V. In both cases, the dominating figure is the one with the superior power to manipulate history theatrically. Richard II is, of course, theatrical to the point of histrionics, but it is Bullingbrook who has the controlling theatrical imagination, who uses theatricality, not for expressive, but for political purposes. And although nobody loves play-acting more than Falstaff, it is Prince Hal who uses theatre for effective political purposes, who makes Falstaff an actor in the political scenario he orchestrates throughout both parts of *Henry IV* to validate his power when he becomes King Henry V.

Both Richard II and Falstaff, like Caliban, are subdued by superior masters of theatre. Do they have anything else in common? I think what they share is a psychological heritage I tried to associate with Bottom and Caliban, a psychological rootedness in themes characteristic of very early phases of infantile development. These connections can be clarified by returning briefly to Bottom and Caliban.

Bottom, too, wants to be an actor; he, too, is manipulated by a man of superior theatrical power when Oberon casts him in the role of Titania's beloved; he, too, will be thrust from his place in Titania's arms after he has served the theatrical effect Oberon seeks by making the Queen of Fairies fall in love with an ass. Bottom's extraordinary good fortune is to inhabit an unusually benign version of this situation. It is as if Bottom recovers in Titania's doting, nurturant love a symbolic replication of the infantile past that would account for the buoyant narcissism of his grown-up

character, whereas Caliban can know those nurturant riches only in the longing created by their failure to survive the realm of dream. Bottom's ready self-love is complemented and completed in Titania's adoration of him; Caliban's need to know himself through his surrender of self to a worshipped other who will accept his service reflects his situation in a world where he can only know his place through the hatred and contempt of others. Only in Bottom's hunger for play-acting do we get any hint of the neediness that will drive Caliban to seek recognition through a new and adored master in Stephano. But if bully Bottom is ultimately empowered by his experience, others who share his slot in the opposition I am tracing are not.

Bottom's robust egotism is completed through his inadvertent stumbling into the magical world of Titania; Richard's grandiose but brittle egotism is grounded on a magical identification of his person with a mystical conception of kingly omnipotence. It is an identification in which even Richard can never quite believe, except in so far as he can play the role of omnipotent king before an audience eager to validate his illusion. Because he has no identity apart from this identification, he seeks out those who will sustain his illusion with flattery. When the inevitable crisis approaches, he swings wildly back and forth between assertions of himself as the invulnerable because 'anointed king' (*Richard II*, III.ii.55) and approaches to what finally is completed in his knowledge of himself as 'nothing' (V.v.38) when the grandiose illusion has been shattered by Bullingbrook. What reaches from one extreme to the other is Richard's language, which he uses for purposes quite different from those of any other character in *Richard II*. The 'lyricism' that Yeats associates with Richard springs from his use of language, not to negotiate a world, but to constitute a self, alternatively through illusions of omnipotence and through a kind of masochistic cherishing of every nuance of his psychic distress.

Richard's necessary failure to merge with an ideal of kingly omnipotence engages the same level of psychic development as is invoked by the happy fantasy Bottom enacts in *A Midsummer Night's Dream*. Bottom's rough and ready narcissism rests on a deep trust of self and world that enables him both to inhabit the seeming omnipotence of his position within Titania's dreamworld and to sustain himself when the dream is over. Richard's inability to know himself apart from his identification with his dream of kingly omnipotence represents a failure to carry a securely internalized sense of trust into and through the individuation process.

'I have long dreamt of such a kind of man', says the newly crowned Henry V to Falstaff, 'So surfeit-swelled, so old and so profane,/But being awaked, I do despise my dream' (*2 Henry IV*, V.v.45-7). But the prince has been dreaming with his eyes open, always shaping the dream to his own shrewdly conceived and theatrically executed political purpose. That is what he does best. It is Falstaff who has been blinded to reality by his own dream of the prince as king and himself as the king's beloved favourite. Like Caliban, who welcomed the exiled Prospero to his world and 'showed [him] all the qualities o'th' isle' (*Tempest* I.ii.337), Falstaff has welcomed the self-exiled prince to his tavern world and shared it with him. 'When thou cam'st first,/Thou strok'st me and made much of me', Caliban reminds Prospero, 'and then I loved thee' (I.ii.332-3, 336). The wonderfully childlike situation evoked here by Caliban's recollection of Prospero's arrival on the island could hardly be more different from the sophisticated and sometimes rather savage give and take that has long marked the curious bond of Falstaff and Hal. But different as their relationship has been, Hal has, in his own way, made much of Falstaff as well, and Falstaff has, in his own way, responded with love: 'My king, my Jove, I speak to thee, my heart' (*2 Henry IV*, V.v.42).

Like Richard and Falstaff, Caliban plays a part in a script controlled by another, but he brings to that part a spontaneous expressiveness he shares with no one else in *The Tempest*. Characters who open themselves most fully to those inner dimensions of psychic experience often speak the most widely and vividly expressive poetry in the plays, the poetry that conveys the texture of joy or agony, of rage or bliss, of a self fulfilled or left desolate. They also make themselves vulnerable to those who distance themselves from, or carefully mediate their relationship to, the force of such inner impulses.

Such a distancing process is exactly what Prospero narrates to Miranda as his past history at the opening of *The Tempest*. For him it is a movement from trust through betrayed trust to the assertion of power and control. Prospero, overthrown by his brother when he was himself lost in his imaginative engagement with magic, 'transported/And rapt in secret studies' (I.ii.76-7), his library a 'dukedom large enough' (I.ii.110), has made himself over as a figure of power. His power is that of a dramatist who has waited for years for those characters to arrive whom he needs to act his script.

One Shakespearian genealogy for Prospero would emerge from the theatrical manipulators of those figures I have tried to link to the lyrical impulse manifest in Caliban: Oberon in *A Midsummer Night's Dream*, Bullingbrook and Henry V in the history plays. It would be a group that emphasizes, whether for good or for ill, the effective integration of psychic components in selves geared towards accommodation of, and action taken to, shape social reality. Instead I would like to look briefly at a group of speeches, spread out over a wide range of Shakespeare's work, including a speech by Prospero, in which the immediacy of social accommodation and mastery recede behind the trope of life

as a dream, or as theatre, or as both. In these speeches, theatricality does not represent manipulative mastery and dream does not represent longing or desire.

'All the world's a stage', says Jaques in *As You Like It*, 'And all the men and women merely players' (II.vii.139-40). 'Thou hast nor youth, nor age', Duke Vincentio counsels Claudio in *Measure for Measure*, 'But as it were an after-dinner's sleep/Dreaming on both' (III.i.32-4). 'Life's but a walking shadow', Macbeth says to no one in particular, 'a poor player/That struts and frets his hour upon the stage,/And then is heard no more' (V.v.24-6). Prospero explains to Ferdinand, after the wedding masque is interrupted by his recollection of Caliban's conspiracy:

> Our revels now are ended.
>   These our actors,
> As I foretold you, were all spirits, and
> Are melted into air, into thin air,
> And, like the baseless fabric of this vision,
> The cloud-capped towers, the gorgeous palaces,
> The solemn temples, the great globe itself,
> Yea, all which it inherit, shall dissolve,
> And, like this insubstantial pageant faded,
> Leave not a rack behind. We are such stuff
> As dreams are made on, and our little life
> Is rounded with a sleep.
>
>   (IV.i.148-58)

These speeches do not demonstrate theatrical control over an action, but something of how the world looks from the vantage point of Shakespearian drama when it is fully theatricalized. Each is spoken by a character who has rigorously distanced himself in one way or another from direct engagement in human intimacy and from direct responsiveness to powerful inner feelings. Of course, each of these speeches plays a complex dramatic function in the action to which it belongs. What is important to note here, however, is that all these very different characters, in their very different dramatic situations—in a comedy, a problem comedy, a tragedy and a romance—are making the same kind of point: they see life as merely theatre, as no more substantial than a dream.

Jaques, the melancholy satirist who covets the fool's role; Duke Vincentio, the disguised ruler who has stepped out of his political role and is playing at being priest; the murderous tyrant Macbeth, who has cut all close ties to the living and has 'almost forgot the taste of fears' (V.v.9); and Prospero, who has just married off his daughter—all become, in these speeches, poets of desolation. These are not versions of the 'empty man' Yeats believed Fortinbras and Henry V to be, but their haunting expressions of a fundamental emptiness in human life recalls Yeats's claim that 'the world was almost as empty in [Shakespeare's] eyes as it must be in the eyes of God' ('At Stratford-on-Avon', in Yeats 1961: 107).

The emptiness evoked in Jaques's summary of the seven ages of man lies at the centre of his melancholy; it reflects the distance imposed between himself and the world by his satiric spirit. Duke Vincentio's 'absolute for death' speech expresses the emptiness of a character whose most compelling motive for action is to distance himself from what makes the other characters of *Measure for Measure* human, vulnerable, and flawed. Macbeth's 'walking shadow' is split off from the futile hysterics of his engagement with the enemy; the remote and hollow theatricality of his meditative voice and the desperate violence of his actions present themselves as the double legacy of the disintegration of his merger with Lady Macbeth.

What about Prospero? What can account for the sudden retreat from the immediacy of action in this character who has controlled, with astonishing precision, the minute-by-minute activities of every other notable character in the play?

Prospero's great speech emerges from the only moment in the play when he is not actively controlling the lives of all the other characters in it. He speaks it when he has been startled to realize that, having allowed himself to become absorbed in the wedding masque, he has forgotten to attend to 'that foul conspiracy/Of the beast Caliban and his confederates/Against his life' (IV.i.139-41). He offers the speech to Ferdinand, who with Miranda has been startled by his agitation, as reassurance:

FERDINAND This is strange. Your father's in some passion
　That works him strongly.
MIRANDA 　　　　　　　　Never till this day
　Saw I him touched with anger, so distempered.
PROSPERO You do look, my son, in a moved sort,
　As if you were dismayed. Be cheerful, sir;
　Our revels now are ended. . . .
　　　　　　　　　　　(IV.i.143-8)

After he has brought his vision of life as the stuff dreams are made on to completion, Prospero himself comments on his 'distempered' state:

　　　　Sir, I am vexed.
Bear with my weakness, my old brain is troubled.
Be not disturbed with my infirmity.

Gently and humbly, he offers Miranda and Ferdinand the use of his cell for rest:

　If you be pleased, retire into my cell,
　And there repose.

But he still feels the aftermath of his strange agitation:

　　　　　A turn or two I'll walk
To still my beating mind.
　　　　　　　　　　　(IV.i.158-63)

This lingering distractedness that completes Prospero's speech presents yet a new voice. He has himself demanded rapt attentiveness of Miranda and Ferdinand at the beginning of the masque: 'No tongue! All eyes! Be silent!' (IV.i.59). The only other interruption of the masque comes when Ferdinand questions him about the nature of the actors: 'May I be bold/To think these spirits?' (IV.i.119-20). Prospero explains: 'Spirits, which by mine art/I have from their confines called to enact/My present fancies' (IV.i.120-2). After Ferdinand rejoices at the paradisal prospect of spending his life where 'So rare a wondered father' (IV.i.123) resides, Prospero again calls for silent attentiveness, this time with just a touch of anxiety that something could go wrong:

　　　　　　　　Sweet, now, silence!
Juno and Ceres whisper seriously.
There's something else to do. Hush, and be mute,
Or else our spell is marred.
　　　　　　　　　　　(IV.i.124-27)

Then, within the masque, Iris summons 'temperate nymphs . . . to celebrate/A contract of true love' and 'sunburned sickle-men' to join them 'in a graceful dance' (IV.i.132-3; 134; 138 s.d.). A particularly elaborate stage direction describes what happens then:

Enter certain Reapers, properly habited. They join with the nymphs in a graceful dance, towards the end whereof Prospero starts suddenly and speaks, after which, to a strange hollow and confused noise, they heavily vanish.

What precipitates the rapid decay of the dance is Prospero's sudden recollection: 'I had forgot that foul conspiracy/Of the beast Caliban . . .' (IV.i.139-40). When Miranda and Ferdinand are alarmed by Prospero's agitation, he tries to calm them with the eloquent nihilism of 'Our revels now are ended'. Then immediately we hear this master of energy and execution sounding old, out of control, weak and infirm—'vexed' and 'troubled'.

Critics have understandably found it difficult to understand either why Prospero should be so agitated by the thought of Caliban and company,[5] since Ariel clearly has those pathetic conspirators under firm control, or exactly why the serene nihilism of this speech should be designed to bring cheer to the newly-wed couple. But perhaps the nature of the recollection that has broken Prospero's absorption in the masque is less significant than the uniqueness of Prospero's discovery that he has indeed been so absorbed, that for the first time in the play he has forgotten to attend to his

Ferninand and Miranda in a Leigh's company production of The Tempest *at the Court Theatre in London.*

plans. Or perhaps Caliban springs to mind here for some other reason than the danger he and his fellows pose to Prospero's life. And perhaps the purposes the speech accomplishes for its speaker are more prominent than its intended effect on Prospero's immediate audience.

The interrupted masque culminates the marriage plot, which drives the overall action of the play. Miranda has arrived at sexual maturity on an island in which the only two-legged males are her father and Caliban. Neither is an appropriate mate. Caliban has earlier posed a sexual threat to Miranda. As Prospero puts it: 'thou didst seek to violate/The honour of my child' (I.ii.347-8). Caliban is hardly repentant about this thwarted transgression:

> O ho, O ho! Would't had been done!
> Thou didst prevent me—I had peopled else
> This isle with Calibans.
>
> (I.ii.349-51)

In his hopeful new servitude, Caliban concedes Miranda to Stephano: 'she will become thy bed, I warrant,/And

bring thee forth brave brood' (III.ii.102-3). But Caliban remains powerfully associated in Prospero's mind with the sexual threat to Miranda. This threat has defined the social structure of the island ever since it was made. Expelled from Prospero's cell and 'confined into this rock' (I.ii.360), Caliban's enslavement dates from and perpetually punishes his aborted rape of Miranda.

Prospero replaces Caliban, a 'thing most brutish' who tried to rape Miranda, with Ferdinand, a 'thing divine' (I.ii.356, 419) who sees Miranda as the goddess of the island. Caliban's degraded sexuality gives way to the idealized and idealizing Ferdinand, all by Prospero's careful design. The psychoanalytic allegory that is being worked out here looks something like this: Prospero's repressed sexual desire for his daughter is purged by his projection of it on to the loathsome Caliban; Ferdinand, ritualistically identified with Caliban by being temporarily imprisoned and enslaved as Prospero's log-carrier, is both punished in advance for the sexuality he brings to Miranda and ritualistically purged of the identification with Caliban's degraded sexuality when he has, with appropriate humility, 'strangely stood the test' (IV.i.7); Prospero maintains his control over Miranda's sexuality with his management of the steps leading to a marriage in which he gives her to the young suitor.[6]

The processes of control by splitting off and projection at work here are characteristic of Prospero, and they are turned towards what is, for him, the central issue in the play and in his life—the sexual maturation of Miranda and the impossible situation this creates for the two of them on the island. But these defensive processes cannot simply erase the deep connections that underlie them, nor can they undo what the passage of time has done to bring Miranda into young womanhood. Prospero sees the circumstances that allow him to bring the Italian ship to the island as depending on an 'accident most strange', 'bountiful Fortune' and a 'most auspicious star' (I.ii.178, 182). But the deeper necessity for the events of the play is Miranda's maturation. Prospero dramatizes the urgencies of this most time-conscious play in terms of his astrological art, but the clock that ultimately drives the play is a natural one, the biological clock in Miranda's body. And if Ferdinand is going to be the solution to the problem, he must, for all the idealizing that is going on, be a sexual solution; he must enact a desire that corresponds to the repressed desire in Prospero, earlier played out in degraded form in Caliban's attempt to rape Miranda.

Prior to the masque, Prospero is still struggling to control the conflicts deriving from his recognition of the need to marry Miranda to an appropriate mate and his repressed desire to keep his daughter for himself. He controls entirely the circumstances of the marriage, offering Miranda as 'a third of mine own life', 'my rich gift', 'my gift', 'my daughter', possessing her in his language even while making her Ferdinand's 'own acquisition/Worthily purchased' (IV.i.3, 8, 13-14). Should Ferdinand 'break her virgin-knot' (IV.i.15) prior to the ceremony Prospero has arranged, however, the marriage will be destroyed by the father's curse:

> barren hate,
> Sour-eyed disdain, and discord shall bestrew
> The union of your bed with weeds so loathly
> That you shall hate it both.
>
> (IV.i.19-22)

Ferdinand provides the appropriate reassurance that nothing can convert 'Mine honour into lust' (IV.i.28), and, when warned again a few moments later about 'th' fire i' th' blood', insists that 'The white cold virgin snow upon my heart/Abates the ardour of my liver' (IV.i.53, 55-6).

The marriage masque is itself constructed to dramatize an idealized image of marriage as a perfect harmony that somehow elides the sexual dimension.[7] The famous exclusion of Venus and Cupid from the ceremony explicitly averts 'Some wanton charm' (IV.i.95), but the effect is to exclude sexuality altogether, which can only, in Prospero's controlling imagination, be imaged as degraded.

What is presented, in Ferdinand's language, as 'a most majestic vision, and/Harmonious charmingly', does, as Prospero says, 'enact/My present fancies' (IV.i.118-19, 121-2). This majestic vision, however, expresses only part of Prospero's present fancies, the idealized part, whereby he can keep at a distance the repressed desires for Miranda that form the unconscious dimension of his fancies. When the 'graceful dance' of the reapers and nymphs is violently interrupted, when Prospero 'starts suddenly and speaks' about 'that foul conspiracy/Of the beast Caliban and his confederates/Against my life' (IV.i.139-41), and the dancers, 'to a strange hollow and confused noise, . . . heavily vanish' (IV.i.138 s.d.), what is dramatized is the disruptive convergence of what Prospero has worked so hard to keep separate. Prospero's sudden memory of Caliban's plot against his life represents the intrusion of Prospero's own repressed desires into the idealizing process of the marriage masque.

The masque itself provides the verbal cue for Prospero's response. After 'certain nymphs' have entered, Iris calls forth their dancing partners, rustic field-workers:

> You sunburned sickle-men, of August weary,
> Come hither from the furrow and be merry;
> Make holiday; your rye-straw hats put on,
> And these fresh nymphs encounter every one
> In country footing.
>
> (IV.i.134-8)

Iris calls for a rustic dance, described as 'graceful' in the subsequent stage direction. But the language calling for that action provides the link to the underside of Prospero's imagination: 'encounter . . . /In country footing' gives us a remarkably dense, redundant, sexual pun, recalling some of the most famous punning moments in Shakespeare.

One is Hamlet's bawdy exchange with Ophelia prior to the play within the play about 'country matters' (III.ii.108). In Partridge's (1968:87) reckoning, 'country matters' here means 'matters concerned with cu*t; the first pronouncing-element of *country* is coun'. 'Coun', or 'count', of course, is given its most notorious independent exercise in *Henry V*, with the English lesson Princess Katherine gets from Alice her gentlewoman:

> KATHERINE Comment appelez-vous les pieds et
> la robe?
> ALICE *De foot,* madame, et *de cown.*

KATHERINE *De foot* et *de cown?* O Seigneur
Dieu! Ils sont les mots de son mauvais,
corruptible, gros, et impudique, et non pour
les dames d'honneur d'user. . . . Foh! *De
foot* et *de cown!*

(*Henry V,* III.iv.44-51)

Here 'foot' for French 'foutre'—'to copulate with'
(Partridge 1968: 108)—is added to the pun on 'count'.

As it is, indeed, in *The Tempest.* For all the effort to
dissociate sexuality from the marriage masque, Iris's
instructions to the reapers—'these fresh nymphs en-
counter every one/In *country foot*ing'—release into the
masque the debased sexuality associated with Prospero's repressed desire, and with Caliban. Caliban here
represents the return of the repressed for Prospero, and
the intractable permanence of the repressed as well, its
resistance to the demands of civilized morality:

A devil, a born devil, on whose nature
Nurture can never stick; on whom my pains,
Humanely taken, all, all lost, quite lost.

(IV.i.188-90)

'The minute of their plot/Is almost come' (IV.i.141-2),
Prospero says in his distraction. What I am trying to
argue is that the intrusion of the Caliban plot to murder Prospero into the dance that culminates the marriage masque of Ferdinand and Miranda makes a kind
of deep psychological sense. It is not, I believe, the
threat to Prospero's life that is at issue here, but the
threat to his psychic equilibrium posed by his repressed
incestuous desires. In surrendering himself to the progress of the masque, in letting himself become absorbed into a process that does 'enact/My present fancies', Prospero loses conscious control over the direction in which his 'fancies' lead him. The '*country foot*-
ing' of the reapers and the nymphs comes to represent
for him the repressed sexual dimension of his longing
for his daughter, and the violent dissolution of the dance
breaks the hold of the masque turned to nightmare.
Prospero's understanding of the interruption as his
sudden memory of Caliban's plot both disguises the
threat and identifies it, since it is Caliban as a representation of his own repressed sexuality that figures
unconsciously into the memory.

The exquisite poetry of 'Our revels now are ended'
expresses Prospero's full recoil from his dangerous absorption in his 'present fancies'. The masque has drawn
him into a process that, for the first time in the play,
eludes his control, draws him into a closeness with deeply
repressed dimensions of himself—not only his desire
for Miranda but his very capacity to give himself over
to an experience that follows a logic deeper than his
conscious manipulations. The psychological result, as
he recovers himself, and before he turns to the business
of resuming control over the action, is a movement in

the opposite direction from control. After the marriage
masque has drawn him too deeply into its symbolic
action, Prospero retreats to a vantage point where nobody is in control and where it does not much matter.

Prospero's lyrical vision of the world as 'insubstantial
pageant' in some respects recalls Caliban's account of
his dream of imminent riches that are all but his, but
that waking deprives him of. 'I am full of pleasure'
(III.ii.114), Caliban says, when he thinks all will work
out with Stephano. It is a momentary perception, ill
grounded, but its expression catches the whole orientation of Caliban's character. This orientation is most
fully expressed in his account of the 'Sounds, and sweet
airs, that give delight and hurt not' (III.ii.135), of the
clouds he thinks will 'open and show riches/Ready to
drop upon me' (III.ii.139-40)—the experience to which
he gives himself in his dreams, and for which, upon
awakening, he cries to dream again.

My notion here is that Prospero's marriage masque
captures him in something of the same way that Caliban
is captured by his dream of imminent but elusive riches.
It is the closest this power-dominated man comes to a
point where it would make sense for him to say, with
Caliban, 'I am full of pleasure'. In his absorption in
the masque, which represents his 'present fancies', that
pleasure proves to be disruptive. Suddenly vulnerable
to a threat from within himself, Prospero for the first
time finds himself in a situation where he cannot address his crisis by magically manipulating the external
world. He cannot act on, cannot even acknowledge directly, the sexual component of his need for Miranda—
though he will, later, in a famous and problematic statement, say of Caliban: 'this thing of darkness I/Acknowl-
edge mine' (IV.i.275-6). And he cannot stop the socially inflected but ultimately natural clock that has
brought Miranda to sexual maturation and that demands
that he surrender her to another. In short, Prospero, the
master manipulator, the nearly omnipotent controller of
the action of this play, finds himself in a position beyond the limits of his control, a position of helplessness
before his own need and before developments in his
world that will not yield to his magic.

Prospero's immediate response is not to cry to dream
again. Nor is it to reassert the sort of control that has
been crucial to his life on the island. Instead, Prospero
retreats to a vantage point from which neither the nature of his feelings nor the control he exercises over
his world matters. Where Caliban, in his dream, envisions a world heavy with riches ready to drop upon
him, Prospero envisions a receding world, of no more
substance or consequence than 'this insubstantial pageant faded', dissolving, without a trace, into nothingness. His life, those of his daughter, her suitor, the
usurping visitors to the island on whom he still seems
to plan vengeance—a little world of people about whom
Prospero has made the finest distinctions, ranging from

his precious daughter to his pernicious brother, from the venerable Gonzalo to the despised Caliban—all are simply 'such stuff/As dreams are made on'. Their lives, all lives, add up to a 'little life/ . . . rounded with a sleep' (IV.i.155-8).

When Prospero the master of magical power confronts his own helplessness in the face of a situation beyond the limits of his control, he retreats to a vantage point in which action no longer matters, where the precise distinctions and discriminations and the minute-by-minute timing that have characterized his relation to the world are dissolved in the blank emptiness of eternity. On the one hand, this vision of all of life as an insubstantial pageant faded is the extreme form of theatricality as a defence, Prospero's version of Macbeth's poor player who struts and frets his hour upon the stage, and then is heard no more. But the tone or feeling of the speech could hardly be more different from that of Macbeth's. Prospero describes an emptiness as radical as Macbeth's, an emptiness that suggests Yeats's notion of Shakespeare meditating on a world 'almost as empty in his eyes as it must be in the eyes of God'. But Prospero's speech conveys something very different from the embittered desolation of Macbeth. It is offered to comfort Miranda and Ferdinand; and it seems to bring comfort to Prospero, to break the agitation of his thought of Caliban.

Part of Prospero's comfort, of course, derives simply from the distancing this vantage point provides, the relief of watching his inner conflict and the vexations of managing his world recede into oblivion. But the comfort provided seems to be more richly textured than the comfort of the world's absence. And Prospero's speech, unlike Macbeth's, seems shielded from the perception of life's emptiness as a source of despair, or of terror.

It is harder to point to what there is in the language of this speech that accounts for this more positive sense of comfort and reassurance. But I think important keys are in the lines that bring Prospero's vision of the world's emptiness to a culmination:

> We are such stuff
> As dreams are made on, and our little life
> Is rounded with a sleep.

It seems to me that there may be some sense in which 'stuff' brings as much substantiality to 'dreams' as 'dreams' brings ephemerality to 'stuff'. There is, moreover, a kind of gentleness about this utterance, a tenderness even, quite uncharacteristic of Prospero elsewhere in the play. But I think more important is what happens in the last clause.

The plain sense of the passage is that human lives emerge out of a dark, sleeplike void and pass back into

it at death and that these brief lives are of small matter in this everlasting movement from nothing to nothing. But 'our' in 'our little life' seems to play against the sense of dispossession that the speech has turned on. The word 'little' does not suggest paltriness or insignificance here so much as the vulnerability of tininess. I associate 'little life' here with infancy, a little living person. The phrase 'little life . . . / . . . rounded with a sleep' seems to present a kind of holding, almost a caressing image, the little life held by the sleep, or held in ways that facilitate sleep, protecting it from the hurly-burly of the larger world. And 'rounded' here seems to me to convey something of the same tenderness that we can find in this account from *A Midsummer Night's Dream:* 'For she his hairy temples then had rounded/With coronet of fresh and fragrant flowers' (IV.i.48-9), describing Titania's tender and protective dotage over Bottom.

In short, the speech has submerged within it the tender infant-mother paradigm I earlier associated with Bottom's fulfilment through Titania. In this phase of Shakespeare's development, I think it suggests a point of connection to the two romances from which it most differs: to the promise for renewed life associated with Marina's infancy in *Pericles* and Perdita's in *The Winter's Tale.* Within *The Tempest,* it points back to the nostalgic evocations of Miranda's infancy, both to her distant memory, 'rather like a dream than an assurance/That my remembrance warrants' (I.ii.45-6), of being attended by feminine presences in Milan, and to Prospero's memory of the courage he gathered from Miranda's infantile presence on the 'rotten carcase of a butt' (I.ii.146) that brought them to the island in their exile: 'O, a cherubin/ Thou wast that did preserve me' (I.ii.152-3).

Within the play, it also reaches out to Caliban's dream of maternal riches about to drop upon him. If Caliban's sexuality unconsciously represents to Prospero his repressed incestuous longing for Miranda, Caliban's psychological orientation toward a nurturant, giving world represents for Prospero a comparably repressed wish to turn oneself over in trust to a world understood as the heritage of the infantile world of oneness with maternal bounty. Foregoing this wish has defined Prospero's post-Milan world of magic, power, mastery. Obliquely, but poignantly, following his recognition of his helplessness before his own desires and developments in his world, and in the course of an imaginative vision of universal emptiness, Prospero touches base with that wish. It is, I think, an important moment for him, one that contributes crucially to the gestures that culminate his role in the play: his surrender of his magical power, his foregoing of his plan for vengence, his final, formal release of Miranda to Ferdinand, his acknowledgement of Caliban, and his readiness to prepare himself for death in Milan, 'where/Every third thought should be my grave' (V.i.310-11) and where his own little life will be rounded with a sleep.

Notes

[2] Drive-centred theories and object-relations theories of psychoanalysis have their respective points of departure in this situation—the emergence of infantile sexuality within the nurturant environment that provides both the first objects of desire and the object relation in which the infant's primary sense of being in the world is anchored.

[3] See Holland's chapter on the poet H.D., called 'A Maker's Mind', in Holland (1973: 5-59).

[4] Recent readings of the play as either a complicit celebration of or a subversive indictment of the colonialist enterprise complicate and extend that trend. When Caliban complains to Prospero that his 'profit' from learning the Europeans' language is 'I know how to curse' (I.ii. 362-63), Greenblatt (1990: 25) writes: 'Ugly, rude, savage, Caliban nevertheless achieves for an instant an absolute if intolerably bitter moral victory.' For Paul Brown, even the dream that seems to give Caliban something he 'may use to resist, if only in dream, the repressive reality which hails him as villain', is ultimately the expression of desire generated by and within colonialism: 'the colonialist project's investment in the processes of euphemisation of what are really powerful relations here has produced a utopian moment where powerlessness represents *a desire for powerlessness*' (' "This thing of darkness I acknowledge mine": *The Tempest* and the discourse of colonialism', in Dollimore and Sinfield (1985: 65, 66).

[5] Skura (1989: 60-5), however, points tellingly to several situations in Shakespeare's earlier drama that provide parallels to this moment when the exiled, manipulative, paternalistic duke erupts in anger in response to a figure who embodies qualities he has repudiated in himself: Antonio to Shylock in *The Merchant of Venice;* Duke Senior to Jaques in his satiric mood ('thou thyself hast been a libertine') in *As You Like It;* Duke Vincentio to Lucio in *Measure for Measure;* the newly crowned Henry V to Falstaff in *2 Henry IV.*

[6] The psychoanalytic components of this narrative have been distributed variously in different psychoanalytic accounts, but they have been in place since 'Otto Rank [in *Das Inzest-Motiv in Dichtung und Sage* (1912)] set out the basic insight' (Holland, 1966: 269).

[7] Prospero's pageant presents a mythic utopian vision which Skura (1989: 68) compares to Gonzalo's 'more socialized' utopia and to Caliban's dream: all three 'recreate a union with a bounteous Mother Nature. And like every child's utopia, each is a fragile creation, easily destroyed by the rage and violence that constitute its defining alternative a dystopia of murderous vengeance; the interruption of Prospero's pageant is only the last in a series of such interruptions.'

References

Unless otherwise indicated, place of publication is London.

Dollimore, Jonathan and Sinfield, Alan (eds) (1985) *Political Shakespeare: New Essays in Cultural Materialism.* Manchester.

Freud, Sigmund (1953-74) *The Standard Edition of the Complete Psychological Works,* ed. J. Strachey, 24 vols.

Greenblatt, Stephen (1990) *Learning to Curse: Essays in Early Modern Culture.* New York.

Holland, Norman (1966) *Psychoanalysis and Shakespeare.* New York.

Holland, Norman (1973) *Poems in Persons: An Introduction to the Psychoanalysis of Literature.* New York.

Ovid (1961) *Shakespeare's Ovid, Being Arthur Golding's Translation of the Metamorphoses,* ed. W.H.D. Rouse.

Skura, Meredith Anne (1989) 'Discourse and the individual: the case of colonialism in *The Tempest'*, *Shakespeare Quarterly,* 40: 42-69.

Tilley, M.P. (1950) *A Dictionary of Proverbs in England in the Sixteenth and Seventeenth Centuries.* Ann Arbor, MI.

Winnicott, D.W. (1965) *The Maturational Processes and the Facilitating Environment.*

Yeats, W.B. (1961) *Essays and Introductions.*

POLITICS AND IDEOLOGY

Michael Payne (essay date 1988)

SOURCE: "Magic and Politics in *The Tempest,*" in *Shakespeare and the Triple Play: From Study to Stage to Classroom,* edited by Sidney Homan, Bucknell University Press, 1988, pp. 43-57.

[*In the following essay, Payne takes a pluralistic approach to* The Tempest, *discussing its political dimensions with reference to its depiction of Prospero's magic. In the critic's judgment, Prospero uses his magic to bring others to self-knowledge and to rectify his own original error in choosing the magical world over the political.*]

Recent critical interpretation of *The Tempest,* perhaps more than that of any other of Shakespeare's plays, has become thoroughly polarized. Those who have concentrated their attention on Prospero's magic and the traditions it reflects have, with rare exception, seen the play as the crowning glory of Shakespeare's achievement and Prospero as a character who grows in power and moral stature to a height unmatched by any other of the playwright's creations. This view of the play has come to be strongly supported by a series of studies emanating from the Warburg Institute that have reconstructed the traditions of natural and spiritual magic, which Shakespeare carefully draws upon. These interwoven traditions extend from Ficino's complex network of Neoplatonism, hermeticism, and occult philosophy—whose goal is the attainment of knowledge and wisdom—through the more pragmatic teachings of Agrippa and Paracelsus—who would give the magician not only the power to attract but also to control good and evil spirits—on to the tradition's fulfillment in Bruno and Dee—who establish the tradition firmly in England just before its precipitous decline.[1]

Confidently asserting the magician's power to transcend the earth for the sake of "far other worlds and other seas," Bruno expands on the idea of man's ability to ascend in thought to a state almost divine that Pico mentions in a famous passage in his *Oration on the Dignity of Man:* "It will be within your power to rise, through your own choice, to the superior orders of divine life." John Dee encourages the occult philosopher to take a further step. In his *Preface to Euclid* he instructs the magical polymath to return from heaven to the world of nature and to practice his occult art there:

> Thus can the mathematical mind deal speculatively in his own art and by good means mount above the clouds and stars; . . . he can [then] by order descend, to frame natural things to wonderful uses; and when he list, retire home into his own center and there prepare more means to ascend or descend by; and all to the glory of God and our honest delectation in earth.[2]

When Prospero is considered in light of this magical history, it is not surprising that he is seen either as Shakespeare's recapitulation of occult tradition or more specifically as the reenactment on the stage of John Dee's career.[3] Prospero confesses to having neglected worldly ends in Milan for the improvement of his mind (1.2.89-90)[4] and appears in the course of the play to follow Dee's directive "to frame natural things to wonderful uses." His motive for creating the tempest is not revenge but primarily the attempt to regenerate his former enemies; thus, he declares,

> Though with their high wrongs I am struck to
>   th' quick,
> Yet with my nobler reason 'gainst my fury

> Do I take part: the rarer action is
> In virtue than in vengeance: they being
>   penitent,
> The sole drift of my purpose doth extend
> Not a frown further.
>
>   (5.1.25-30)

The storm is not only a means of bringing those who wronged Prospero to the island, but also an occasion for the display of his extensive magical powers, which give him command of both the worlds of nature and of spirits. It is, however, only retrospectively that the audience is informed, along with Miranda, of Prospero's beneficent control over the tempest. Throughout most of the play we mainly witness his ability to command spirits, while the other characters are restricted to seeing displays of Prospero's artistic or dramatic virtuosity. Indeed, as an ultimate indication of his self-confidence and artistic control, Prospero conceals his magical and artistic powers. Finally, with those powers at their height, he gives them up entirely in order to resume his common humanity and to allow others the freedom to "be themselves" (5.1.32), which includes his brother's freedom to reject regeneration.

In explicit opposition to this affirmative view of Prospero is a rapidly growing body of revolutionary, polemical commentary that condemns not only Prospero but also the play and Shakespeare himself for promoting a self-deceptive psychology of colonization. Although this view of *The Tempest* has a complex history that reaches back at least as far as Renan's *Caliban* (1878), the case against Prospero has been most powerfully made in two important studies published in 1985.[5] Paul Brown's essay in *Political Shakespeare: New Essays in Cultural Materialism* goes beyond earlier polemical studies in arguing that the play does not simply reflect colonialist practices but is itself "an intervention in an ambivalent and often contradictory discourse" promoting a colonialist political psychology. *The Tempest*'s "powerful and pleasurable narrative" tries but fails, in Brown's view, to harmonize or transcend the irreconcilable internal contradictions of colonialist discourse.[6] Francis Barker and Peter Hulme, in an essay in *Alternative Shakespeares,* develop a similar argument. They believe that Shakespeare today is made to participate in the construction of a false English past "which is picturesque, familiar and untroubled." But in *The Tempest* the usual opposition between the autotelic text and its historically problematic context actually invades the text of the play itself. This invasion can now be properly understood, they argue, because of the displacement of the old critical paradigm of liberal humanism by the poststructuralist emphasis on intertextuality. An important consequence of such an emphasis, they conclude, is to see the play as two irreconcilable dramas that undermine or deconstruct each other. Prospero's play is preoccupied with his attempts to legitimate his power by securing recognition of his claim to Milan; in Caliban's play Prospero suppresses a reenactment of the original usurpation of his kingdom when he puts down Caliban's mutiny, which allows him (in the words of Barker and Hulme) "to annul the memory of his failure to prevent his expulsion from the dukedom."[7] Both of these essays find the play—and by extension Shakespeare himself—guilty of being controlled by a political unconscious that awaits, not criticism, but a critique powerful enough to make the play's latent politics fully manifest. The essays claim to offer such a critique of the play and its use by generations of critics and performers, who have, perhaps unwittingly, promoted liberal humanism and Western imperialism by accepting *The Tempest*'s politics without question.[8]

The evidence offered to support such a negative view of the play includes Prospero's need, in scene 2, to establish his own version of the past, which no one (least of all Miranda) is able to question. Furthermore, his usurpation of the native authority of Caliban; his need to make both Caliban and Ariel his slaves; his suppression of the matriarchal magical order of Caliban's mother Sycorax; his dualistic categorization of others as virgins or rapists, friends or foes; his insisting on regulating his daughter's sexuality; his division of the shipwrecked travelers into two clear groups of aristocrats and plebians—all lend considerable support to a polemical deconstruction of the play in an effort to expose its place in a Shakespearean hegemony.

Rather than being necessarily exclusive of each other, the two views of the play I have summarized—the one emphasizing the tradition of magic and Prospero's personal growth and the other emphasizing politics and Caliban's enslavement—not only need but also require each other. To suggest, however, the complementarity of magic and politics is to confess resistance to recent attempts to displace a liberal, humanistic tradition of history. The editor of *Alternative Shakespeares* warns his readers that "'historical' and, in certain cases, historicist, accounts of Shakespearean texts, pluralist in emphasis and liberal in their capacity to assimilate revisionist, or even radical, challenges, have become a staple of Shakespeare criticism."[9] To this, one may respond simply that Shakespeare himself may be the model for such pluralistic assimilation, especially in the all-encompassing ecumenicism of the dramatic romances.[10]

Magic and politics are linked throughout *The Tempest.* In the narrative past Prospero neglected politics for magic. In the dramatic present he uses magic as a means to achieve specific political ends. The reclaiming of his dukedom, establishing a line of succession through Miranda and Ferdinand, creating amity between Milan and Naples, controlling the conspiracies against Alonso and himself, regenerating his enemies in preparation for the return to Italy, and restoring Caliban to authority over the island are all political accomplishments of

his magical art. In the future, to which the Epilogue points, Prospero will lack the authority he has drawn from magic; yet in choosing vulnerable weakness, he displays his greatest strength and highest art. By the end of the play he has made a complete transition from what D. P. Walker has called transitive magic, used to manipulate others, to subjective magic, directed inward to the control of himself.[11] In aesthetic terms this is an achievement of an artistic style of such subtlety and refinement that it hides itself, transferring power from playwright, director, and actor to the audience. In religious terms it is the attainment of the state of grace, a willing suspension of presumed self-sufficiency that makes one receptive to an act of mercy. Prospero combines in his Epilogue the religious, aesthetic, political, and magical significance of his chosen weakness:

> Now my charms are all o'erthrown,
> And what strength I have's mine own,
> Which is most faint: now, 'tis true,
> I must be here confin'd by you,
> Or sent to Naples. Let me not,
> Since I have my dukedom got,
> And pardon'd the deceiver, dwell
> In this bare island by your spell.
>   . . . Now I want
> Spirits to enforce, Art to enchant;
> And my ending is despair,
> Unless I be reliev'd by prayer,
> Which pierces so, that it assaults
> Mercy itself, and frees all faults. . . .
>   (Epil. 1-8, 13-18)

Prospero's salvation requires the audience's mercy that is made possible by a full imaginative identification with his desire for freedom and absolution.

The complementary relationship between magic and politics is diffused throughout the action of the play. It shapes the characterization of Prospero, whose control over the action is greater than that of any of Shakespeare's other creations, and it determines an important part of the audience's perspective on the play. The action of the play may be thought of as consisting of three tempests, each one manifest in a different form. The first is the visual spectacle of the storm itself that occupies the first scene and is the most dazzling display of Prospero's magical powers. In his account of how he brought about the storm at Prospero's command, Ariel suggests that what he did was to play upon the visual perceptions of the voyagers, enflaming their imaginations:

> I flam'd amazement: sometime I'd divide,
> And burn in many places; on the topmast,
> The yards and boresprit, would I flame
>   distinctly,
> Then meet and join. Jove's lightnings, the
>   precursors

O'th' dreadful thunder-claps, more momentary
And sight-outrunning were not: the fire and
    cracks
Of sulphurous roaring the most mighty
    Neptune
Seem to besiege, and make his bold waves
    tremble,
Yea, his dread trident shake. . . . Not a soul
But felt a fever of the mad, and play'd
Some tricks of desperation. All but mariners
Plung'd in the foaming brine, and quit the
    vessel,
Then all afire with me.

                            (1.2.198-206, 208-12)

Ariel concludes his account by insisting that the effect of their ordeal by water and fire was to make the voyagers fresher than before, as Prospero had specifically commanded:

                            Not a hair perish'd;
On their sustaining garments not a blemish,
But fresher than before: and, as thou bad'st
    me.

                            (1.2.217-19)

These words reinforce Prospero's earlier assurances to Miranda and firmly establish his intent to regenerate and restore his former enemies rather than avenge himself upon them.

Immediately following the visual spectacle of the storm but preceeding Ariel's account of his role in creating it is Prospero's narrative of the tempestuous series of events occurring before the play begins—his neglect of his responsibilities as Duke of Milan, his entrusting the dukedom to his brother Antonio, and his own banishment following Antonio's usurpation—all caused by Prospero's apparently selfish absorption in the inactive and purely bookish delights of "the liberal Arts" and "secret studies" (1.2.73, 77). Rather than condemning Prospero's attraction to magic, the play emphasizes his error in choosing between the political world and the magical, an error that he has had twelve years to contemplate and now the opportunity to rectify. Thus, Shakespeare would seem to be supporting Dee's advocacy of the active use of magic by a sage who may have first mounted "above the clouds and stars" in pursuit of spiritual truth but who at last retires "home into his own center," applying his knowledge to the affairs of the world.

Following the spectacular tempest of the play's first scene and Prospero's narrative of his stormy past in scene two, the dramatic action of the play itself unfolds, joining the consequences of Prospero's past with his new redemptive purpose. The main action includes Prospero's bringing his tutelage of Miranda to an end by preparing her to return to Italy with a new husband, Ferdinand. Just as he gives his daughter her freedom, so also does Prospero end his control over the lives of Ariel and Caliban. In the midst of these affairs he also attempts to regenerate the usurpers of his dukedom by allowing them the freedom to reenact their crimes against him in the plot to supplant Alonso. In restraining his power over Miranda, Ariel, Caliban, and the voyagers, Prospero exhibits his own self-regenerative control that is also a manifestation of the highest refinement of the art he practices. His abjuration of magic is no second abdication. Rather it is a confident expression of Prospero's self-realization, of his belief in the powers of freedom and self-determination, and of his artistic style that conceals itself by encouraging the recreative participation of his audience, first the several audiences of the masques within the play and then the larger audience of *The Tempest* to whom Prospero finally—in the Epilogue—entrusts himself. This main action may be seen as moving through a complete revolution: from Prospero's self-indulgence in the magical arts with its political cost, to his using art for the purpose of regenerating himself and others; from the bondage of Miranda, Ariel, and Caliban, to their liberation to "be themselves"; from Prospero's "neglecting worldly ends," to his abjuring "rough magic" and reassuming a common humanity.

In bringing Prospero's tempestuous past to bear on the present action of the play, Shakespeare simultaneously divides up the characters into significant groups and arranges those groups and the individuals within them in a hierarchy of discrepant awarenesses, further strengthening the link between magic and politics. The principal division initially lies between those who are on the island from the beginning of the play—Prospero, Ariel, Miranda, and Caliban—and those who are shipwrecked there by the storm. The second group is further subdivided into three: Ferdinand; the royal party (Alonso, Gonzalo, Antonio, and Sebastian); and the clowns Stephano and Trinculo. Although the manipulations or "practices" of one character upon another leading to different degrees of knowledge is a basic ingredient in Shakespeare's dramatic art, *The Tempest* is unique in placing Prospero on a pinnacle of awareness that allows him to tower, however briefly, even over the audience.[12] Beneath him, from Miranda to Stephano and Trinculo, the characters occupy different positions of varying ironic limitation in a pattern that is recapitulated even within the royal party, as Antonio and Sebastian scheme to overthrow Alonso in an act of treachery that would parallel the original usurpation of Prospero's dukedom. As though to undermine any static sense of hierarchy in these groupings, having once established them, Shakespeare meshes the islanders with the shipwrecked voyagers, bringing Ferdinand and Miranda together, Ariel into a position of control over the royal party, and Caliban into contact with the clowns, while Prospero interacts with them all. The continuum from Prospero to the clowns represents a range of regenerative possibility, from Prospero's radical reorientation to the world and his power over it to Antonio's final, stubborn silence and the clowns' punishment. Prospero's magical power, conducted through his agent Ariel, controls all of these groups and maintains the advantage for the islanders. Even Caliban finally rises above the mindless scheming of the clowns.

The minidramas set within each of these groups are essentially political. The meeting of Ferdinand and Miranda establishes the order of rightful succession in Milan, as well as the union of two Italian states; and in terms of sexual politics it insures the equality of husband and wife, as the chess game with its accompanying wit combat between the lovers suggests. Sebastian's and Antonio's intrigue recapitulates the political treachery of Shakespeare's tragedies: brother conspires against brother and against rightful heirs in a manner that shatters the utopian illusions of Gonzalo. Thinking themselves masterless men, Stephano and Trinculo would replace the only authority they believe remains and substitute their own debauched tyranny for it. Despite all these acts of rebellion (even Miranda believes she is defying her father in loving Ferdinand), none of these characters finally realizes how much Prospero's magic controls them. Instead, they see an effacement of his magic in the four entertainments that he produces for their enlightenment. For the court party the disappearing banquet (3.3.18 ff.) exposes the appetite for illusory power; for Miranda and Ferdinand the wedding masque (4.1.60 ff.) captures their prospect for harmonious love and fruitful marriage that has the potential of renewing their soon to be united kingdoms; for Stephano and Trinculo their being hunted and hounded (4.1.255) is a means of singling them out for punishment because of their incapacity for regeneration, or what Henri Bergson would have called their mechanical inelasticity; and for Alonso and the royal party the scene of Ferdinand and Miranda at chess (5.1.172) is both an occasion for reunion of father and son and a forecast of a greater union to come of Prospero's and Alonso's states.

All of these internal dramas contribute to the triumph of Prospero's "rarer action" that ultimately manifests itself rather "in virtue than in vengeance" (5.1.27-28) and that makes possible through his art the restoration of all of the characters to their own true selves, as well as the restoration of the play's several political worlds. Alonso facilitates the return of Prospero's dukedom, Prospero provides for the union of their dynasties, the rebellions against both of them are exposed, and Caliban regains his island kingdom. Prospero's magic, thus, provides the world of the play with the security and pleasurable resolution of the romantic comedies, which typically move from a state of bondage to an old law or a dark past to a new and liberated society based on love, "natural perspective," and the promise of new life. The shipwrecked voyagers, on the other hand, bring

to the island all the dangers of violence, evil, death, and lost identity that permeate the tragedies. In Prospero, Shakespeare creates a protagonist who has grown and developed out of a past marked by many of the same losses suffered by Lear—indeed, Bradley notes how *The Tempest* in effect continues Lear's story[13]— yet Prospero is also complete from the beginning of the play, as his unusual autobiographical narrative in the second scene reveals.

In defining Prospero's character, Shakespeare further develops in this play a dramatic psychology that conceives of the self as consisting of a repertoire of external, socially interactive roles, which clothe or encase a vulnerable inner core of being. The recurring metaphor for this psychology throughout Shakespeare's works equates the roles with the parts an actor plays—these are further called "spirits" in Prospero's revels speech (4.1.149)—and the inner being is equated with the actor's true personality, which is what remains of Prospero after he ceases to play the magician's part. Each role is a means of relating to others and can be terminated at will. The core of being is given at birth, like Antonio's "evil nature," but it can change and develop through experience or be hidden by the roles one plays.

Prospero's roles as father and teacher that have occupied him for the past twelve years are brought to an end in the course of the play. Indeed, Prospero implies that there is a logic of self-effacement in both roles: the father invites his child to assert her own will as a necessary consequence of her maturing independence that he has fostered, and the teacher's authority must finally give way to the student's need to test what she has learned against her experience of the world. As magician, on the other hand, Prospero's achievements have been absolute and cosmic in scope, as he recalls in his speech on abjuring magic. Addressing the daemons who have assisted him, he recalls,

> I have bedimm'd
> The noontide sun, call'd forth the mutinous winds,
> And 'twixt the green sea and the azur'd vault
> Set roaring war: to the dread rattling thunder
> Have I given fire, and rifted Jove's stout oak
> With his own bolt; the strong-bas'd promontory
> Have I made shake, and by the spurs pluck'd up
> The pine and cedar: graves at my command
> Have wak'd their sleepers, op'd, and let 'em forth
> By my so potent Art.
>
> (5.1.33-50)

Indeed as he looks back on his magical career, Prospero claims as achievements the very powers Marlowe's Faustus longed to possess:

                    Emperors and kings
Are but obey'd in their several provinces:
Nor can they raise the wind, or rend the
    clouds:
But his dominion that exceeds in this,
Stretcheth as far as doth the mind of man.
A sound magician is a mighty god.
                    (*Doctor Faustus,* II. 85-90)

Unlike Faustus, however, Prospero serves a moral purpose with his magic. He uses it to bring others to a full realization of themselves by first working "upon their senses" (5.1.53) until "their understanding / Begins to swell," flooding their "foul and muddy" minds with reason (79-82).

Although his final rejection of magical power forms the dramatic climax of the play, Prospero acts principally as a magician in all that we see him do. His fatherly care of Miranda and his instruction of her and Caliban are in the past, while the resumption of his political role is projected into the future. Indeed it would seem that whereas magic costs Faustus his soul, it is the means by which Prospero regains his and restores those who come under his influence. According to the familiar distinction, Faustus practices goetic magic, calling up evil spirits and commercing with the devil, while Prospero practices theurgic magic, commanding planetary spirits in order to turn loss into restoration. Despite Gonzalo's irrepressible enthusiasm, which has inspired the stage convention of depicting him as a complete fool, he does see clearly the dominant pattern of loss and restoration that extends from Prospero's exile and the marriage of Alonso's daughter Claribel to the concluding action of *The Tempest:*

Was Milan thrust from Milan, that his issue
Should become Kings of Naples? O, rejoice
Beyond a common joy! and set it down
With gold on lasting pillars: in one voyage
Did Claribel her husband find at Tunis,
And Ferdinand, her brother, found a wife
Where he himself was lost, Prospero his
    dukedom
In a poor isle, and all of us ourselves
When no man was his own.
                    (5.1.205-13)

Gonzalo does not see Prospero's magical agency creating this pattern because Prospero presents himself to the royal party not as the magician he has been but as Duke of Milan. Immediately after breaking his staff and drowning his book, Prospero directs Ariel to attire him in his princely garb:

Fetch me the hat and rapier in my cell:
I will discase me, and myself present
As I was sometime Milan.
                    (5.1.84-86)

The audience alone has witnessed the full extent of Prospero's power.

This unique role of the audience in the play makes the circumstances of *The Tempest*'s earliest performances especially significant, adding as well another political dimension to the play. The Revels Accounts list the presentation of *The Tempest* at Court by Shakespeare's company in 1611, which is its first recorded performance. In the winter of 1612-13 it was played again as part of the Court entertainments between the betrothal and marriage of the Elector to Princess Elizabeth, both of whom are specifically mentioned in the record of payment to the King's Men. It is not surprising, therefore, that *The Tempest* abounds in themes and details that mirror concerns and interests of the royal family: the politics of succession, the desire to unify two kingdoms, interest in New World exploration, the study of magic and demonology, the rights of kingship, the theatrical role of the monarch, even Prince Henry's fascination with ships are all reflected in the play and can easily be imagined to have been a powerful part of the royal audience's apparent pleasure at its first performance. Alonso's situation throughout much of *The Tempest* parallels James's when he saw the play for a second time in 1613.[14] Just as Alonso's daughter Claribel is married to the sovereign of faraway Tunis and his son Ferdinand presumed by him to be drowned, so within four months had James's son Prince Henry died of typhoid and his daughter Elizabeth become the "Winter Queen" of Bohemia. Such parallels create an almost irresistible temptation to resort to various forms of topical reductionism or historical determinism in interpreting the play. Recent studies of Shakespearean mimesis by Jonathan Goldberg, Howard Felperin, and David Bergeron, however, have emphasized the ways in which Shakespeare mediates by "re-presentation" all of the sources that can now be identified.[15] In re-presenting the traditions of magic, the interests of the royal family, and his identifiable written sources, it is Shakespeare's transubstantiation of those sources rather than his duplication of them that is most important for an understanding of his art.

In his re-presentation of the traditions of magic, Shakespeare gives Prospero a sense of his magical power that is close to John Dee's; but unlike Dee, Prospero chooses art, theater, and specifically the masque as the means of exercising that power. In reflecting the contemporary political preoccupations of the Jacobean Court, Shakespeare embodies those topical concerns more specifically in the Alonso subplot than in his account of Prospero, thus invoking those concerns but not allowing them to dominate the play. Despite *The Tempest*'s thematic preoccupations with politics and Prospero's manifesting his magic in the creation of masques, Shakespeare specifically avoids using the masque to flatter James's illusions of imperial power.[16] Instead, either Ariel or Prospero offer sufficient commentary on each of the masques to transform them into moral allegories. Shakespeare's transformation of his written sources is an even more telling instance of his art of re-presentation. Unlike the sources for most of his other plays, those for *The Tempest* do not provide Shakespeare with a narrative. The Bermuda pamphlets and Montaigne's essay "Of Cannibals" instead offer points of view on the contact between Europe and the New World, which Shakespeare weaves into his depiction of the relationship between Caliban and Prospero.

Samuel Purchas's travel books, though they contain the first published version of William Strachey's *True Repertory of the Wrack,* which was written and privately circulated in 1610, carefully surround the reporting of new facts about foreign exploration with accounts of classical voyages and an apology for colonization based on religious and moral ideas. Drake, for example, is typologized as a Christian Moses who brings the law to savages. Montaigne, on the other hand, argues that the New World is a place of natural virtue, free of the corruption of civilization. In the Indians, he writes, "are the true and most profitable vertues, and naturall properties most lively and vigorous, which in these we have bastardized, applying them to the pleasure of our corrupted taste."[17] The authors of the Bermuda pamphlets generally maintain the high moral tone of those, like Purchas, who rationalized colonization; but when Strachey and Jourdain describe the islands and the life they found there, the point of view they adopt, based on personal experience, approaches Montaigne's naturalism. Strachey confronts the issue directly:

> . . . I hope to deliver the world from a foule and generall errour: it being counted of most, that they can be no habitation for Men, but rather given over to Devils and wicked Spirits; whereas indeed wee find them now by experience, to be as habitable and commodius as most Countries of the same climate and situation. . . . Men ought not to deny every thing which is not subject to their owne sense. . . . [18]

When he created Caliban, Shakespeare had available to him these three views of natural man; that he was wild and immoral, in need of the virtuous instruction and saving grace of Christianity; that he exhibited natural virtues and enviable vitality that civilized man is ready to corrupt; and that he is like other men and can be understood by anyone who takes the trouble to cut through propaganda and see native life for oneself.[19]

Rather than choosing to follow one of his sources and to reject the others, Shakespeare blends in Caliban all three views of natural man, combining in effect Strachey and Montaigne. Caliban recalls that when Prospero first came to the island, the relationship between them was one of affection, mutual care, and love:

> When thou cam'st first,
> Thou strok'st me, and made much of me;
>   wouldst give me
> Water with berries in 't; and teach me how
> To name the bigger light, and how the less,
> That burn by day and night: and then I lov'd
>   thee,
> And show'd thee all the qualities o' th' isle,
> The fresh springs, brine-pits, barren place and
>   fertile.
>
> (1.2.334-40)

That initial relationship, like that of father and child, was shattered by Caliban's attempt to violate Miranda, which Caliban recalls in terms of Montaignean biological growth—"Thou didst prevent me; I had peopled else / This isle with Calibans" (1.2.352-55)—but which Prospero and Miranda understandably consider in moral terms:

> Abhorred slave,
> Which any print of goodness wilt not take,
> Being capable of all ill!
>
> (1.2.353-55)

Throughout the play, however, Caliban identifies himself with the minute details of natural life on the island. He offers to take Stephano and Trinculo where crabs grow, to dig them pig-nuts, to show them a jay's nest, to instruct them in snaring the marmoset, and to provide them with filberts and sea birds (2.2.166-72). This aspect of Caliban reflects the humane interest among some sixteenth- and seventeenth-century explorers in careful observation of life in the New World that led to the level of achievement in ethnographic art found in John White's drawings of American Indians.[20] These drawings pose a sharp contrast to the physical deformity of Caliban, which is apparently the result of his unnatural birth from the union of the devil and a witch (1.2.321). Finally, however, Caliban is redeemed. His being duped by Stephano and Trinculo not only makes him willing to return to Prospero's service but also leads him to wisdom and the desire for grace (5.1.294-95). In this repentance Caliban rises in moral stature above Antonio. In exchange for the final act of service to Prospero in preparing his cell to receive the royal party, Caliban can look forward to the pardon and freedom he desires. Caliban's life, thus, recapitulates the view of natural man to be found in Shakespeare's sources: Strachey denies that the Bermudas are "given over to Devils and wicked Spirits," which Shakespeare identifies with the birth of Caliban and the worship of his mother's god Setebos (1.2.375). From the time of Prospero's arrival on the island until the end of the play, Caliban is the natural historian of the island, intimately acquainted as he is with its flora and fauna. By the end of the play he moves into the moral and theological order that Prospero himself has commanded since his exile. In Caliban, Prospero's magic and the politics of the play come fully together: his theurgic art of self-realization is defined in contrast to the goetic practices of Caliban's mother Sycorax, and his commitment to the freedom of self-determination arising out of service leads him simultaneously to abjure that magic and to allow others to be themselves.

The polarization of recent critical commentary on the play was anticipated by Oscar Wilde in the Preface to *The Picture of Dorian Gray:*

> The nineteenth century dislike of Realism is
> the rage of Caliban seeing his own face in a
> glass.
>
> The nineteenth century dislike of Romanticism
> is the rage of Caliban not seeing his own
> face in a glass.[21]

The Tempest, like all of Shakespeare's works, invites us to see his art as reflecting both his time and our own—"the very shape and body of the time, his form and pressure," as Hamlet calls it. It invites us as well to see our own image reflected back to us. A dislike of either Shakespeare's realism or his romanticism, Wilde suggests, turns us into raging Calibans, unredeemed by the art of Prospero and Shakespeare.

Notes

[1] The best recent study of this tradition is Barbara Howard Traister, *Heavenly Necromancers: The Magician in English Renaissance Drama* (Columbia: University of Missouri Press, 1984), pp. 1-32.

[2] "Preface to Euclid," sig. Ciii^v. Bruno's views are conveniently available in *Giordano Bruno: His Life and Thought,* ed. and trans. Dorothea Woley Singer (New York: Abelard-Schulman, 1950), esp. p. 249. The passage from Pico appears in *Renaissance Philosophy I: The Italian Philosophers,* ed. and trans. Arturo B. Fallico and Herman Shapiro (New York: Modern Library, 1967), p. 144.

[3] This is the view of Frances Yates in *Shakespeare's Last Plays: A New Approach* (London: Routledge and Kegan Paul, 1975) and *The Occult Philosophy in the Elizabethan Age* (London: Routledge and Kegan Paul, 1979). For a comprehensive study of Dee's life and thought, see Peter French, *The World of an Elizabethan Magus* (London: Routledge and Kegan Paul, 1972).

[4] Quotations from *The Tempest* are from the Arden edition, ed. Frank Kermode (London: Methuen, 1962).

[5] The earlier studies are summarized by Philip Mason in *Prospero's Magic* (London: Oxford University Press, 1962), pp. 75-97.

[6] Paul Brown, "'This thing of darkness I acknowledge mine': *The Tempest* and the Discourse of Colonialism," in Jonathan Dollimore and Alan Sinfield, eds., *Political Shakespeare: New Essays in Cultural Materialism* (Ithaca: Cornell University Press, 1985), p. 48.

[7] Francis Barker and Peter Hulme, "Nymphs and Reapers Heavily Vanish: The Discursive Con-texts of *The Tempest,"* in John Drakakis, ed., *Alternative Shakespeares* (London: Methuen, 1985), p. 201.

[8] Terry Eagleton, *William Shakespeare* (Oxford: Basil Blackwell, 1986), pp. 90-96, and Terence Hawkes, *That Shakespeherian Rag* (London: Methuen, 1986), pp. 1-25, 51-71, develop a similar argument. Eagleton and Hawkes stress Shakespeare's identification with "the retiring magus" to the point of seeing them both as capitalists who inhumanly create unemployment by the policy of land enclosure (Hawkes) or as practitioners of "oppressive patriarchalism" and a "colonialism which signals the imminent victory of the exploitative, 'inorganic' mercantile bourgeoise" (Eagleton). Eagleton's earlier study of *The Tempest* sees Prospero as a positive and sympathetic figure (*Shakespeare and Society* [New York: Schocken Books, 1967], p. 168).

[9] Barker and Hulme, "Nymphs and Reapers," p. 17.

[10] Cf. Northrop Frye, *The Secular Scripture: A Study of the Structure of Romance* (Cambridge: Harvard University Press, 1976), p. 53.

[11] *Spiritual and Demonic Magic from Ficino to Campanella* (London: The Warburg Institute, 1958), pp. 82-83.

[12] Bertrand Evans, *Shakespeare's Comedies* (Oxford: The Clarendon Press, 1960), p. 332.

[13] A. C. Bradley, *Shakespearean Tragedy* (London: Macmillan, 1905), pp. 328-330.

[14] For a detailed discussion of the parallels, see David M. Bergeron, *Shakespeare's Romances and the Royal Family* (Lawrence: University Press of Kansas, 1985), pp. 182-87.

[15] Jonathan Goldberg, *James I and the Politics of Literature: Jonson, Shakespeare, Donne and Their Contemporaries* (Baltimore: Johns Hopkins University Press, 1983); Howard Felperin, *Shakespearean Representation: Mimesis and Modernity in Elizabethan Tragedy* (Princeton: Princeton University Press, 1977); David Bergeron, *Shakespeare's Romances and the Royal Family.*

[16] See Stephen Orgel, *The Illusion of Power: Political Theatre in the English Renaissance* (Berkeley: University of California Press, 1975).

[17] Florio translation, reprinted in *The Tempest,* ed. Kermode, p. xxxv.

[18] Reprinted in ibid., p. 137.

[19] For an excellent history of the wild man, see Hayden White, "The Forms of Wildness: Archaeology of an Idea," in Edward Dudley and Maximillian Novak, eds. *The Wild Man Within: An Image in Western Thought from the Renaissance to Romanticism* (Pittsburgh: Pittsburgh University Press, 1972), esp. pp. 20-21. White slights the third view, however.

[20] See Paul Hulton, *America 1585: The Complete Drawings of John White* (London: British Museum Publications, 1984), esp.p. 9.

[21] *Complete Works of Oscar Wilde* (London: Collins, 1966), p. 17.

Richard Halpern (essay date 1990)

SOURCE: "'The Picture of Nobody': White Cannibalism in *The Tempest,*" in *The Production of English Renaissance Culture,* edited by David Lee Miller, Sharon O'Dair and Harold Weber, Cornell University Press, 1994, pp. 262-92.

[*In the excerpt below, originally presented in 1990 at the Seventeenth Alabama Symposium in English and American Literature, Halpern examines cross-cultural elements in* The Tempest *and the way in which the Western myth of the Golden Age intersects with New World accounts of an American arcadia. Concluding a wide-ranging discussion of Gonzalo's commonwealth, colonialism, and modern as well as Renaissance political concepts, the critic asserts that the play expresses skepticism about utopian attempts that deny the significance of cultural and racial fusion.*]

> Tupi or not Tupi, that is the question.
> —Oswald de Andrade, *Manifesto Antropófago*

In his 1971 essay "Caliban," the Cuban critic Roberto Fernández Retamar writes: "A European journalist, and moreover a leftist, asked me a few days ago, 'Does a Latin-American culture exist?' . . . The question . . . could also be expressed another way: 'Do you exist?' For to question our culture is to question our very existence, our human reality itself, and thus to be willing to take a stand in favor of our irremediable colonial condition, since it suggests that we would be but a distorted echo of what occurs elsewhere. This elsewhere is of course the metropolis, the colonizing centers."[1] For a critic writing in a revolutionary country just ninety miles from a hostile superpower, questions of cultural and human non-existence are more than merely theoretical. Yet for Retamar, they cannot be

reduced to the crude but real possibility of actual annihilation, either. To destroy Latin American culture one need only reduce it to the status of an imitation, simulation, or—as he puts it—"distorted echo" *(eco desfigurado)* of the metropolitan culture. Retamar's phrase is both resonant and precise. In Ovid, the mythological Echo is indeed disfigured by her unrequited love for Narcissus: she wrinkles, ages, wastes away to skin and bone before decorporealizing entirely into pure, disembodied voice.[2] Latin America as "disfigured echo" is not only condemned by the dominating metropolis to mere repetition, it is also drained of strength and vitality by a vampire-like extraction of cultural and material wealth. The metropolis itself, according to the logic of this figure, plays the role of Narcissus, caught in a self-enclosed, specular enjoyment of its own cultural productions, and unable to read in the post-colonial world anything more than another, inferior image of itself.[3]

Retamar's response to this paralyzing double bind is the figure of the mestizo, of what José Marti called "our *mestizo* America" (p. 4). The racially mixed figure of the mestizo, compounded of Native American, African, and European blood, represents a culture that chooses miscegenation over imitation; instead of simply repeating *or* rejecting the metropolitan culture, it assimilates, depurifies, and transforms it by mixing it with non-European strains. As employed by Retamar, the notion of a mestizo culture has clear affinities with certain themes of post-structuralist thought: it denies unique or delimited points of origin, it replaces a monological conception of cultural discourse with a dialogical or indeed disseminative one, and it problematizes boundaries and deconstructs binary oppositions, including that of center and periphery.[4] For having once applied the notion of *mestizaje* ("mixedness" or "mestizoization") to Latin American culture, Retamar then insists that "the thesis that every man *[sic]* and even every culture is *mestizo* could easily be defended" (p. 4).[5] Mestizoization is thus not a derivative or peripheralized or parasitic state but the inescapable condition of culture as such, including metropolitan culture.

But unlike some of its post-structuralist cousins, *mestizaje* is not an abstractly textual or discursive concept. It is founded, rather, on the image of the racially mixed body, and insists on this materiality. To borrow Retamar's distinction, it represents human as well as cultural existence. Unlike the emaciated and ultimately disembodied figure of Echo, the mestizo is a corporeal as well as a cultural presence.[6] At the same time, *mestizaje* also invokes a history. For if the figure of the mestizo celebrates cultural mixedness in the present, it also recalls that this mixedness arose from a colonial situation, and that it was originally the product of violence, domination, and desire. *Mestizaje* is, in a sense, a Nietzschean revaluation of the past, a transformation of defeat through the cultural will to power of the colonized.

In taking Shakespeare's Caliban as the literary symbol for American mestizo culture, Retamar joins a tradition of Caribbean, Latin American, and African writers who have adapted or appropriated *The Tempest* in an effort either to represent the colonial situation or develop a counter-discourse to it.[7] A colonial reading of the play has long been available in the Anglo-American critical tradition as well, at least in the latent form of an awareness of Shakespeare's use of reports from the New World, his informal affiliations with the Virginia Company, and so forth.[8] However, it is only in the past decade or so that colonialism has established itself as a dominant, if not *the* dominant code for interpreting *The Tempest.*[9] Colonialist discourse is typically buttoned onto the play primarily through allegory: the master-slave dialectic between Prospero as colonizing subject and Caliban as colonized.[10] Generally it is assumed that Prospero occupies a hegemonic position not only on his island but also in the play's ideological field; *The Tempest,* in other words, somehow endorses or mystifies colonial domination. It is also frequently noted, however, that Caliban manages at least to question if not undermine the colonizer's assumptions of superiority, in part through political argument (such as Caliban's claim that the island was originally and rightfully *his*) and in part through a poetic side to his nature which remains invisible to Prospero.[11]

Such readings have tended to "Americanize" the play, or at least Caliban, by identifying him with the natives described in colonial reports. Leslie Fiedler epitomizes this Americanist reading, arguing that by the end of *The Tempest,* "the whole history of imperialist America has been prophetically revealed to us in brief parable: from the initial act of expropriation through the Indian wars to the setting up of reservations, and from the beginnings of black slavery to the first revolts and evasions."[12] Even if we hesitate in the face of so closely detailed a prophecy, we ought nevertheless to admit that the play manages in some respects to anticipate later developments, and thereby gains much of its cultural force and pertinence. I myself argue that the play's significance is largely American and anticipatory, and to do so I explore paths blazed by both Retamar and Fiedler. More precisely, I want to examine the ways in which the play both advances and erases the mestizoization of Western culture.

I

I begin by shifting attention away from the Prospero-Caliban axis in the play and toward a possibly unexpected focus: the humanist councillor Gonzalo. Gonzalo, that kind and idealistic if somewhat befuddled character, is generally taken to provide a kind of counterpoint both to the machiavellian plotting of Sebastian and Antonio and to the colonialist domination represented by Prospero. Best remembered, perhaps, for the ideal commonwealth he depicts in II.i., Gonzalo seems to embody an ineffectual utopianism which nevertheless offers a moral contrast to the power politics of the play. In fact, however, Gonzalo's real function is to shift the play's colonialist politics into another mode.

This he does most strikingly when he imagines (or tries to imagine) his ideal commonwealth, accompanied by Antonio's and Sebastian's cynical commentary:

> *Gonzalo.* Had I plantation of this isle, my
>   lord—
> *Antonio.* He'd sow't with nettle seed.
> *Sebastian.* Or docks, or mallows.
> *Gonzalo.* And were the king on't, what would
>   I do?
> *Sebastian.* 'Scape being drunk for want of wine.
> *Gonzalo.* I' th' commonwealth I would by
>   contraries
> Execute all things. For no kind of traffic
> Would I admit; no name of magistrate;
> Letters should not be known; riches, poverty,
> And use of service, none; contract, succession,
> Bourn, bound of land, tilth, vineyard, none;
> No use of metal, corn, or wine, or oil;
> No occupation; all men idle, all;
> And women too, but innocent and pure;
> No sovereignty.
> *Sebastian.* Yet he would be king on't.
> *Antonio.* The latter end of his commonwealth
>   forgets the beginning.
> *Gonzalo.* All things in common nature should
>   produce
> Without sweat or endeavor. Treason, felony,
> Sword, pike, knife, gun, or need of any engine
> Would I not have; but nature should bring
>   forth,
> Of it own kind, all foison, all abundance,
> To feed my innocent people.
> *Sebastian.* No marrying 'mong his subjects?
> *Antonio.* None, man, all idle—whores and
>   knaves.
> *Gonzalo.* I would with such perfection govern,
>   sir,
> T'excel the Golden Age.[13]

When he speculates on getting "plantation" of the isle, Gonzalo expresses the only positive *desire* for colonial dominion in the play. Even Prospero is a colonialist *malgré lui,* and he and the other Italians desert their island at the first opportunity. (Unlike the English or Spanish, Italians in general would not be coded for Shakespeare's audience as fanatical colonizers of the New World.) Only Gonzalo exhibits anything like a colonialist imagination in the play, though an apparently benign and utopian one.

Gonzalo's ideal commonwealth, as has long been recognized, paraphrases a passage in John Florio's English translation of Montaigne's essay *On Cannibals;*

indeed, it borrows with such fidelity that little attention has been paid to the small but significant changes that Gonzalo rings on his source. The passage from Montaigne offers an idyllic or Golden Age description of the life of the Tupi Indians of Brazil as reported in various colonial accounts. Shakespeare's audience might not have recognized the specific borrowing from Montaigne, but such Golden Age descriptions of the New World had become a kind of setpiece in colonial writings from Columbus, Vespucci, and Peter Martyr on, and hence would have been instantly recognizable as a genre.

Gonzalo's first significant alteration comes in the word "plantation," which unambiguously signifies an exclusively European colony. Hence the "innocent and pure" subjects of Gonzalo's imagined polity are not Montaigne's Indians but white Europeans, who now somehow occupy an American Indian arcadia. Yet they don't do that either, owing to Gonzalo's second alteration. For while Montaigne's passage at least purported to be a description of a real culture in the New World (and I will take up this issue of accuracy later), Gonzalo's commonwealth makes no such claim. Though recognizably derived from New World accounts, then, this ideal commonwealth appears to be peopled by Europeans and modeled on Ovidian and Virgilian descriptions of the Golden Age. All explicit reference to the New World vanishes, though an implicit and ghostly reference still inheres in the arcadian genre itself.

By substituting Europeans for American Indians in his utopian polity, Gonzalo reproduces a recently current strain of English colonialist discourse. Idyllic, Golden Age descriptions of the New World and its native inhabitants were disseminated by propagandists for the Virginia Company in order to lure Englishwomen and men to America by suggesting that they might appropriate and enjoy the arcadian landscape now peopled by friendly Indians.[14] *Eastward Ho* (1605), by Jonson, Marston, and Chapman, parodies such propaganda in ways suggestive for Shakespeare's play:

> *Seagull.* Come, boys, Virginia longs till we share the rest of her maidenhead.
>
> *Spendall.* Why, is she inhabited already with any English?
>
> *Sea.* A whole country of English is there, man, bred of those that were left there in '79. They have married with the Indians, and make 'em bring forth as beautiful faces as any we have in England; and therefore the Indians are so in love with 'em, that all the treasure they have, they lay at their feet.
>
> *Scapethrift.* But is there such treasure there, captain, as I have heard?
>
> *Sea.* I tell thee, gold is more plentiful there than copper is with us; and for as much red copper as I can bring, I'll have thrice the

weight in gold. Why, man, all their dripping pans and their chamber pots are pure gold; and all the chains, with which they chain up their streets, are massy gold; all the prisoners they take are fettered within gold; and for rubies and diamonds, they go forth on holidays and gather 'em by the seashore, to hang on their children's coats, and stick in their caps, as commonly as our children wear saffron-gilt brooches, and groats with holes in 'em.

> *Scape.* And is it a pleasant country withal?
>
> *Sea.* As ever the sun shined on, temperate and full of all sorts of excellent viands: wild boar is as common there as our tamest bacon is here; venison, as mutton. And then you shall live freely there; without sergeants, or courtiers, or lawyers, or intelligencers—only a few industrious Scots, perhaps, who, indeed, are dispersed over the face of the whole earth.[15]

This exchange has a clarifying effect on Gonzalo's ideal common-wealth, cynically literalizing a number of features that Gonzalo invokes only implicitly and idealistically. In *Eastward Ho* the "Golden Age" becomes actual gold, and the Indians are described as willing sexual partners, in an all-too-obvious attempt to lure potential colonists. By merging his white plantation with an Indian arcadia, Gonzalo also (if only latently) performs or acts out the desires produced by colonialist advertisement. Of course, this dream of expropriation and substitution had already turned sour by the time *The Tempest* was written. The winter of 1609-10 had caused widespread starvation in the Jamestown Colony followed by a breakdown in social order and the imposition of strict martial law: the most recent colonial reports would thus have suggested the very opposite of Gonzalo's arcadian vision.[16]

Such topical resonances, which render Gonzalo's commonwealth "utopian" in a bad sense, also point to more fundamental contradictions within the ideology and reality of New World colonization. As is well known, early English settlers found themselves embarrassingly dependent on the technologies of native populations for their own survival—a theme of intermittent interest in *The Tempest*.[17] Appropriation of Native American lands was thus impossible without some *imitation* of their culture, even if this was limited to piecemeal borrowings stripped from any cultural context.[18] Native social, political, and cultural life elicited official reactions ranging from guarded admiration to outright contempt, and even the most openminded colonists never suggested that native culture should serve as a model for Christian Europeans.[19] Nevertheless, this culture and social structure were felt to possess a dangerous appeal. Well into the eighteenth century, colonial officials and others inveighed against so-called "white Indians"—that is, Europeans who either fled to indigenous tribes in order to escape the harsh conditions of life in the colonies, or, having been captured by natives and integrated into their social world, refused to return to their families and friends when released. Cotton Mather denounced the "*Criolian* Degeneracy" which afflicted English youth when they were "permitted to run wild in our Woods."[20] To many colonists, Native American life offered a higher degree of both liberty and social cohesion than did the authoritarian government of the colonies. By inserting European subjects directly into a description of an Indian arcadia, then, Gonzalo's ideal commonwealth might be said to invoke the perilously utopian allure associated with the colonial imitation of native culture, and the subsequent mixing or "Criolian degeneracy" which this could entail. More explicitly, *Eastward Ho* raises the tempting prospect of cultural and physical miscegenation, but then masters it by insisting on the genetic dominance of European blood. ("They have married with the Indians, and make 'em bring forth as beautiful faces as any we have in England.")[21]

I think, however, that the relation of Gonzalo's commonwealth to the colonial project is more mediated than this, and that its primary focus is on the assimilation of New World culture by European, and specifically humanist, thought. While it borrows its descriptive detail from Montaigne, Gonzalo's ideal commonwealth also alludes in a more general way to Thomas More's *Utopia.*[22] More, of course, sets his utopia in the New World, and colonial reports on native culture inspire the *Utopia* to some degree, though the extent of this influence has been the subject of longstanding debate. In *Eastward Ho,* Seagull borrows More's famous golden chamberpots and chains and relocates these among the Indians of Virginia, suggesting that for early modern audiences, at least, *Utopia* was strongly associated with the indigenous cultures of the New World. Hence Shakespeare's double allusion to Montaigne and More unmistakably draws attention to New World influences on the humanist imagination, and particularly on its utopian, political strain.

It does so, however, only to stage the disappearance or rather the repression of this influence. For in describing his ideal polity, Gonzalo, unlike More or Montaigne, avoids any direct allusion to the New World; his only explicit point of reference is the classical Golden Age, which installs him in a conservative and restrictively humanist genealogy. Gonzalo's utopian project appropriates colonial descriptions of the New World but effaces or occults this influence by reinscribing it within a closed and Eurocentric textual economy. When Antonio cynically remarks that "the latter end of his commonwealth forgets the beginning," he refers to Gonzalo's inconsistency in handling the problem of sovereignty or kingship, yet his words apply as well to the cultural genesis of Gonzalo's vision. This commonwealth actively "forgets" its non-Western beginnings.

Gonzalo's erasure of non-Western influences is completed when he populates his ideal commonwealth with Europeans rather than Native Americans, thereby removing the bodily as well as the cultural presence of those indigenous subjects. Consuming or erasing the racial body covers up all remaining traces of non-Western origin: Gonzalo's commonwealth is now peopled by Europeans and apparently created by the Western philosophical imagination drawing on the classical tradition. This double process of erasure is what I have chosen to call white cannibalism: Gonzalo in effect consumes the body of the racial other in order to appropriate its cultural force. In this respect he becomes a counterpart to Caliban, the anagrammatical cannibal—a connection I pursue later.

Gonzalo and his imaginary commonwealth do not counter colonialist domination in *The Tempest,* then, but rather transpose it to a cultural plane. Gonzalo usurps the Indian utopia in thought, just as Prospero usurps Caliban's isle in fact.[23] Yet it may seem strange to invest Gonzalo with such dire, or even coherent, intentions. Indeed, the erasure of cultural origins I have just outlined might well be ascribed not to imperialist design but to mere forgetfulness, a frequent attribute of the comic *senex* or old man figure. Antonio even mocks Gonzalo by calling him "this lord of weak remembrance" (II.i.236),[24] and there may be an additional irony in the fact that Gonzalo is a forgetful *humanist,* given that humanism is generally associated with the restoration of cultural and historical memory. Yet it is truer to say that Renaissance humanism inaugurated a dialectic of memory and forgetting which is here embodied in Gonzalo. Erasmus's writings on rhetorical copia, for instance, recommended "digesting" classical authors in order to produce new, distinct, and individual styles. As a strategy of appropriation through the consumption or erasure of textual origins,[25] copia converts forgetfulness from a lapse or weakness into a mechanism of stylistic sovereignty and a means of mastering cultural authority. Erasmian stylistics and its cannibalistic metaphors provide a suggestive analogue to Gonzalo's white cannibalism, and they suggest that Gonzalo's gaps in memory can be read not only as a sign of individual weakness but as a characteristic strategy of Renaissance humanism. Gonzalo is indeed a "lord of weak remembrance" in that his forgetfulness is a *source* of sovereignty, guarding the cultural coherence of humanism from the shock of non-Western influence.

A telling, indeed paradigmatic, example of Gonzalo's active forgetfulness occurs in the famous "widow Dido" exchange of II.i, shortly before the utopian reverie:

> *Gonzalo.* Methinks our garments are now as
>   fresh as when we put them on first in Afric,
>   at the marriage of the King's fair daughter
>   Claribel to the King of Tunis.

Sebastian. 'Twas a sweet marriage, and we
  prosper well in our return.

Adrian. Tunis was never graced before with
  such a paragon to their queen.

Gonzalo. Not since widow Dido's time.

Antonio. Widow? A pox o' that! How came
  that "widow" in? Widow Dido!

Sebastian. What if he had said "widower
  Aeneas" too?

Good Lord, how ill you take it!

Adrian. "Widow Dido," said you? You make
  me study of that. She was of Carthage, not
  of Tunis.

Gonzalo. This Tunis, sir, was Carthage.

Adrian. Carthage?

Gonzalo. I assure you, Carthage.

Antonio. His word is more than the miraculous
  harp.

Sebastian. He hath raised the wall and houses
  too.

Antonio. What impossible matter will he make
  easy next?

(II.i.71-93)

The topic of conversation is the marriage of Alonso's daughter Claribel to the King of Tunis: significantly, a mixed or miscegenating marriage of white European and black African. Gonzalo's muddled pedantry, which confuses Tunis with the ancient city of Carthage, leads to the exchange about "widow Dido." Yet Gonzalo's apparently random dithering is hardly unmotivated. By recalling Aeneas's romance with Dido, the non-African queen of African Carthage, Gonzalo both evokes and denies the miscegenous marriage of Claribel.[26] Further, by confusing Tunis with Virgil's fictionalized vision of Carthage, he transforms a real African city into a spot in the literary geography of *The Aeneid,* thus supplanting the material existence of a non-European society with a founding text of the Western tradition and, not incidentally, the great epic of Roman imperialism. Consuming both the cultural presence of Tunis and its material or bodily existence, Gonzalo's forgetfulness performs an act of white cannibalism. *Tunis delenda est* is the ideological maxim here, and Tunis is in fact deleted by being reinscribed within a humanist textual tradition. All of this prepares for a more important and culturally central act: the textual purgation of Gonzalo's utopian commonwealth.

Within Renaissance humanism, the genre of the utopia served as a privileged medium for both the importation and the neutralization of political ideas from the New World. At the level of content, Thomas More's *Utopia* is clearly influenced by colonial reports describing communal ownership of property, social equality, and the absence of kingship and marked class differences within some Native American cultures. The New World provides both the content and a hypothetical vantage point for criticizing the dominant social order of late-

feudal Europe. Yet this political and geographical exteriority is then abstracted from any specific locale or origin. As a place that is pointedly "nowhere" the utopia posits an inadequacy in all extant cultural systems— Western and non-Western—and is fully at home in none of them. More's Utopia does not, for the most part, legitimate itself by reinscribing New World practices within a humanist genealogy. Instead, it appeals on the one hand to the supposedly self-evident rationality of its social logic and, on the other, to the purely empirical or pragmatic claim that it really exists and works, though not within a known cultural geography.[27] The utopian genre thus aspires to autonomy and self-legitimation. Thomas More's *Utopia* is set in motion when King Utopus separates it from the mainland, a gesture which we may read as the text's desire to cut all lines of cultural influence. But it is precisely because the utopia claims to legitimate itself that it can borrow features from non-European cultures without seriously decentering the West's sense of cultural self-sufficiency. It is not New World culture but utopian culture that indicts the West, and this indictment is so global as to seem to come from nowhere in particular. Precisely because it is autolegitimating, the utopia can be a seemingly innocuous medium for the covert or semi-covert importation of non-Western influences into Western political discourse.

Gonzalo's ideal commonwealth doubly effaces its references to the New World. On the one hand it reinscribes them within a humanist genealogy. Yet insofar as it invokes the generic codes of the utopia, it denies all lines of origin by posing as an autonomous act of philosophical speculation. To the degree that Gonzalo's commonwealth *is* a utopia, it does not suffice to say that its subjects are "Europeans." Rather, they are the abstract subjects of political philosophy, without racial or cultural characteristics: genuinely "white" subjects in the sense that they are blanks inserted in, or rather produced by, a scheme of political reason. Gonzalo's replacement of Native American subjects with Europeans is, in this sense, only the first step toward a more complete disembodiment. As utopia, Gonzalo's commonwealth is genuinely "the picture of Nobody."[28]

But Gonzalo's scheme is afflicted by a slippage of genre. It clearly begins as utopia: by dubbing his vision a commonwealth, and by claiming to "execute all things" by himself, Gonzalo seems to invoke the utopian interest in planned, formal institutions. Yet his description passes almost immediately into a neighboring but rather different genre: the pastoral arcadia, which is characterized rather by a lack of formal institutions.[29] Gonzalo's citizens are not the purposefully, even obsessively productive inhabitants of a fully rationalized polity but rather the idle denizens of the Golden Age. The end of Gonzalo's commonwealth forgets its generic beginnings as well. But this slippage of literary genre revives all the questions of cultural origin that the utopia works to suppress. For while the Golden Age was a recognizably classical or Western topos, it had also become inescapably associated with colonial reports from the New World. Whereas Thomas More had incorporated New World arcadia into a humanist utopia, Gonzalo reverses this genetic order, and by so doing he reveals the obscure anatomy of Western utopian discourse.[30]

One of the assumptions of this essay is that European colonialism extracted not only gold, raw materials, and slave labor from the New World, but forms of political, social, and cultural knowledge as well. It might be objected, however, that arcadian descriptions of New World culture reflected only the values, desires, and nostalgias of the colonists themselves. Hence what appears to be cultural expropriation or transfer may in fact be only ideological projection and feedback. Indeed, this latter view has become widely dominant among historians of New World colonization and settlement.[31]

Colonial reports from the New World were, to be sure, marked by factual and ideological distortion, often massive. Yet they were rarely mere hallucinations. Karen Ordahl Kupperman has persuasively argued that the more outlandish and ethnocentric visions of the New World were almost exclusively produced by writers who had never been there, and that settlers who regularly interacted with North American Indians often achieved a fairly sophisticated understanding of their culture.[32] William Brandon, meanwhile, maintains that even the so-called Golden Age reports produced by the earliest explorers were not without *some* factual basis. Brandon points out that other non-Western cultures, in Africa or Asia, did not provoke comparisons to the Golden Age, and that a number of New World cultures did in fact possess certain features that at least roughly corresponded to this western myth, common possession of property being one of the most important. Furthermore, while the myth of the Golden Age was imposed on American cultures from without, and interpreted their structures selectively and ethnocentrically, the process of influence was actually more mutual and dialogical than it might seem. For while the classical Golden Age generally depicted an arcadian existence under the rule of a good king, the New World Golden Age generally emphasized political liberty and masterlessness. Thus observation of American Indian culture had a reciprocal influence on the imported model of the Golden Age. Brandon goes on to argue that the conception of political liberty entered Western political discourse largely by means of colonial reports from the Americas.[33] The image of the New World as Golden Age is, clearly, neither a pure European projection nor an accurate description of native societies. It is, rather, a mestizoized formation that enabled a number of cultural and ideological operations, many of them contradictory: operations of advertisement and colonial propaganda, the reinscription of native societies as pre-cultural rather than cultural, and, I would insist, the appropriation of native socio-cultural practices by the West.

Critics of cultural imperialism tend to emphasize the *imposition* of Western cultural norms and practices onto non-Western societies, and to view this as concomitant with political and economic dominion. Yet by depicting non-Western cultures as being too fragile, ineffectual, or inconsequential to exert a counterinfluence on the metropoles, a merely monological or one-way theory of cultural imperialism may actually feed the West's characteristic illusions of cultural self-sufficiency. Moreover, by understanding cultural dominion only as the imposition of Western forms, it may elide very real and equally serious acts of cultural appropriation by the West.[34] In *The Tempest,* Gonzalo's ideal commonwealth is the conduit for both appropriating Native American social structures into humanist utopian thought and denying this influence by consuming the body of the racial other. Yet the physical presence, at least, of the repressed other endures in the person of Caliban. If Gonzalo's commonwealth both enacts and erases the mestizoization of Western culture, Caliban is the very embodiment of the mestizo: his mother is an Algerian witch, and he himself exhibits traits of both the American Indian and the European wild man. Again, if Gonzalo's commonwealth is a disembodied social order, Caliban seems at times to be pure body removed from any social order.

One ideological effect of applying the myth of the Golden Age to New World cultures was, as I have said, to reinscribe them as *pre-political,* arcadian existences, and thus to view American Indians themselves as, at best, noble savages. Shakespeare's Caliban, an isolated being lacking any cultural context, is precisely the pre-political, pre-cultural being produced by arcadian myth. An anomic racial body, a bundle of ungovernable drives, Caliban is the ideological precipitate or residue that remains once Gonzalo's commonwealth has abstracted the cultural forms of Native American life.[35]

To speak of Caliban as "pure body" may seem unjust. He is not, after all, some grunting, heaving piece of nature but a complex and articulate character. Though his drunkenness and attempted rape signify bodily intemperance, he is not in the end defined by these things. Only to Prospero and Miranda does he appear an ineducable savage whose "vile race" both lacks and positively resists culture. By reducing him to a bearer of firewood, Prospero actually *makes* Caliban into a merely corporeal being, a "natural slave." Gonzalo and Prospero thus cooperate in "processing" the non-European subject. One absconds with his culture, and the other reduces him to bodily labor. Together they create a savagism that they then treat as an antecedent to culture rather than its product. "Pure body," in other words, is not some irreducible substratum but a kind of dramatic role—partly foisted onto Caliban, partly present as an innate disposition, partly adopted as a mode of defense.

When he first spots Trinculo, for example, Caliban deems him a tormenting spirit sent by Prospero, and he pretends to be a corpse in order to avoid further punishment. Trinculo's speculations on the seemingly dead body are instructive:

> What have we here? A man or a fish? Dead or alive? A fish! He smells like a fish; a very ancient and fishlike smell; a kind of not of the newest Poor John. A strange fish! Were I in England now, as once I was, and had but this fish painted, not a holiday fool there but would give a piece of silver. There would this monster make a man; any strange beast there makes a man. When they will not give a doit to relieve a lame beggar, they will lay out ten to see a dead Indian.

> (II.ii.25-34)

Miming death, Caliban has become pure body. In Trinculo's eyes (and nose) he is not mestizo but amphibian, a mixture of species rather than of race,[36] tending toward brute corporeality. Trinculo's plan to exhibit Caliban in England alludes to the importation and exhibition of American Indians which began during the reign of Henry VII and had become regular policy under King James.[37]

While Trinculo's is a more popular form of spectacle than Shakespeare's courtly play, it adumbrates Caliban's place within a larger system of colonialist representation which included *The Tempest*. The English beheld American Indians only as isolated specimens, removed from their native lands and cultures and reinserted into a discontinuous, carnivalesque series of curios and wonders.[38] "The Indian," a detached spectacle, is produced by abstracting indigenous subjects from sociocultural collectives and repositioning them within something akin to natural history.[39] As "wonder," Caliban is interchangeable with a great fish; reduced to visual object, to pure body, he is of equal interest alive or dead. When Trinculo speaks of "painting" this fish, he means reproducing it on a sign to be hung outside of a booth at a fair; Gonzalo's picture of Nobody finds its counterpart and completion, then, in Trinculo's picture of mere body, likewise founded both on the erasure of cultural origin and on the death of the represented subject.[40] Disembodied utopia and lifeless body are dialectical products of one system of colonial representation.

"When they will not give a doit to relieve a lame beggar, they will lay out ten to see a dead Indian," remarks Trinculo. Since relieving beggars is a prime motive of More's *Utopia,* Trinculo implicitly designates England both as the negation of Utopia (as More himself had done) and, in the same breath, as the negation of the Indian. The visitors to Trinculo's booth are the descendents of More's idealized petty-producing class, now fully commercialized and hostile to the vagrant population from which, in More's day, they had recently been sundered by the process of primitive accumulation.[41] No longer the potential citizens of a utopian polity, they renounce any imaginary "fusion" with New World models of a communist society, preferring instead to be regaled with the spectacle of the (dead) Indian body.

Yet if Caliban measures the historical deterioration of More's utopian ideal, he also opens up the space of a counter-utopia. Interestingly, this effort centers on a non-act, or at least an uncompleted one: the reported attempt to rape Miranda. Confronted by Prospero, Caliban is less than remorseful: "Oh ho!, Oh ho! Wouldn't had been done! / Thou didst prevent me; I had peopled else / This isle with Calibans" (I.ii.349-51). His evident pride in this attempted rape is perhaps the play's most difficult moment for those readers, including myself, who elsewhere find Caliban to be an appealing or at least a sympathetic character. Here, for one moment, he seems to correspond exactly with the sickest fantasies of colonialist and racist ideology; as Leslie Fiedler puts it, he is "the first nonwhite rapist in white man's literature."[42] Reduced entirely to a racial being, to the impure, mestizoized body which is extruded by Gonzalo's disembodying utopia, Caliban nevertheless becomes Gonzalo's double as well. For in wishing to "people the isle with Calibans," he, like Gonzalo, produces an imaginary society. Indeed, Caliban here makes the play's first and only allusion, however indirect, to the idea of a non-European collectivity—the very thing that inspired Gonzalo's commonwealth in the first place before disappearing from view.

In glimpsing the "original" of Gonzalo's stolen commonwealth, however, we do not attain to a more genuine or appealing utopia. On the contrary, Caliban's imagined polity is locked into symmetry with Gonzalo's only to be rejected in its turn. By locating utopia precisely in the context of rape, Shakespeare suggests that the way to utopia is always lined with violence—that this path is cut, as it were, in the hide of the other, no matter who does the cutting. Instead of liberating himself, Caliban merely extends the chain of oppression, displacing violence onto new victims as his sole means of revenge.

My reading of Gonzalo's ideal commonwealth may wrongly have been taken to imply that *The Tempest* is a covertly anti-colonial play. It does contain an anti-colonial strain, and this strain does deftly ensnare Gonzalo, but only so that none of the play's characters, no matter how apparently inoffensive or gentle, may escape being implicated in the exercise of power. The critique of Gonzalo's commonwealth does not work on behalf of some more authentic utopian ideal, then, or even on behalf of the colonized as victims, but as part of a rigorously anti-utopian current which swamps both Caliban and Gonzalo. *The Tempest* does not "side" with either colonizer or colonized, but cynically undercuts both in the name of a shared but fallen human nature. The play's political shrewdness, which devastatingly reveals the subtlest folds of power, ultimately serves a game which admits of no solidarities. In *The Tempest,* as in Shakespeare's plays generally, critique is radically disjoined from utopia.

Although apparently evenhanded, Shakespeare's skepticism purveys an ultimately conservative message: yes, the way of the world is a violent one, but utopian projectors only multiply the violence they pretend to oppose. In this particular case, however, such rueful and apparently hard-headed moralizing is rather artfully contrived, for despite their own fantasies it was the colonizers themselves who, in their relations with the colonized, held a virtual monopoly on rape and sexual violence. Readers who find themselves casuistically tallying Caliban's sexual assault against the prior wrongs done to him, or who try to "revalue" this assault in light of the anti-colonial utopia it projects, are caught in a false historical premise, one which builds specious symmetries for conservative ends. Retamar's choice of a rapist as anti-colonial hero not only betrays a striking indifference to matters of gender, but falls into an ideological trap set by *The Tempest.*

Caliban's ideal commonwealth mirrors Gonzalo's not only in its reliance on violence but, ironically, in its apparent attempt to expunge the racial other. Just as Gonzalo requires the New World arcadia to construct his own polity, but then represses this dependency by claiming sole authorship himself, so Caliban's imagined *socius* can be embodied only through the reproductive agency of Miranda, but Caliban then denies his dependency on her by claiming that he would people the isle with Calibans—that is, with racial clones of himself. Yet if this symmetry bars all paths to utopia, it nevertheless admits of some internal difference, because Caliban is *already* a mixed or mestizoized being. The fictive children of Miranda and Caliban would be "Calibans" in the sense that they would further the process of mestizoization which is Caliban's legacy. Unlike Gonzalo, then, Caliban does not try to totalize division by eliminating the racial other; he dismantles division through a disseminative, though violent, practice. (Again, we may contrast Seagull's fantasy in *Eastward Ho!* of mixed couplings producing white children.) As a mestizoized space, Caliban's polity seems to possess a genuinely utopian content—a content which is not neutralized but rather blocked, because its only visible means of access is Miranda's rape.

In mirroring one another, Gonzalo and Caliban are both drawn into the other's field. It is only as read against

Alec Clunes as Caliban, Patrick Wymark as Stephano, and Clive Revill as Trinculo in a 1957 Stratford-upon-Avon production of The Tempest.

Gonzalo's ideal commonwealth that Caliban's rape can even hint at a utopian end; conversely, that rape manifests the otherwise latent violence behind Gonzalo's commonwealth. If *The Tempest* does not seem to "prefer" either Gonzalo's or Caliban's brand of violence, it nevertheless allows some distinctions to be drawn between them. For Caliban's violence is at least explicit and thus allows us to take its measure; no reader of the play needs to be reminded of the assault on Miranda. Gonzalo's more symbolic violence, however, conceals itself by annihilating or consuming its victims. While colonial violence is generally quite visible both in the real world and in *The Tempest* (via Prospero), Gonzalo's case suggests that such violence becomes latent, if ever, not when its modalities are gentle but when its effects are total, and no one remains to report it.

Strikingly similar issues of annihilation and cultural memory are raised in an historical context by Bruce E. Johansen's controversial book, *Forgotten Founders: How the American Indian Helped Shape Democracy.* Johansen's thesis is that Iroquoian principles of government, as set down in their constitution, "The Great Law of Peace," had a significant influence on such figures as Benjamin Franklin and Thomas Jefferson when they formulated the principles of American government.[43] According to Johansen, the conceptual armature of both the Declaration of Independence and—more indirectly—the Constitution of the United States were significantly informed by Iroquoian example. No explicit reference to native models survives in these documents, however, and historical memory of any possible contribution tended to disappear with the Iroquois themselves, who were nearly exterminated by their erstwhile allies the English after the successful conclusion of war against the French.

The title of Johansen's book—*Forgotten Founders*—clearly bears on issues central to this essay. In fact, as construed by Johansen, the United States Constitution bears a notable resemblance to Gonzalo's ideal commonwealth in *The Tempest*. Both are utopian documents modeled on (mediated) reports of Native American societies—demonstrably and systematically in Gonzalo's case, possibly and inferentially in the case of the Constitution. Yet both utopias are intended for habitation by Europeans. Both repress their mestizoized origins by erasing all traces of native influence. And both complete this erasure by consuming or destroying the body of the racial other—metaphorically in Gonzalo's case, all too literally in the case of America. Johansen's book constructs North American history as a disturbingly real enactment of the white cannibalism implicit in Gonzalo's ideal commonwealth.

Setting Retamar against Johansen, we may suggest that while Caliban's mestizoized counter-utopia takes historical root in the Latin American culture of José Marti, Gonzalo's ideal commonwealth affixes itself farther north. More generally, we ought to distinguish between North and South American "models" when discussing the topic of colonialism in *The Tempest*. The South American model often retains the bodies of indigenous occupants in order to employ them as slave labor. This model is represented historically by Spain's use of native labor in its American mines, and, in *The Tempest*, by Prospero's enslavement of Caliban. The North American model, by contrast, expropriates not the labor power but the socio-cultural forms of indigenous peoples. And having done so it then consumes their bodily existence in an act of white cannibalism. The result in literature is Gonzalo's ideal commonwealth; the result in history is the United States, the picture of nobody.

Notes

This essay has benefited enormously from discussion, critique, and editorial queries following its presentation at the Seventeenth Alabama Symposium on English and American Literature. I especially thank Francis Barker, Margaret Ferguson, Christopher Kendrick, and the editors of this volume.

[1] Roberto Fernández Retamar, *Caliban and Other Essays*, trans. Edward Baker (Minneapolis: University of Minnesota Press, 1990), p. 3. Subsequent references are to this edition. Retamar's essay originally appeared in *Casa de las Américas* 68 (1971): 124-51.

My epigraph, from Oswald de Andrade's *Manifesto Antropófago*, is taken from Emir Rodríguez Monegal, "The Metamorphoses of Caliban," *Diacritics* 7 (1977): 82. In the Brazil of the 1920s, de Andrade's *Movimento Antropófago* or Cannibal Movement "advocated the creation of a genuine national culture through the consumption and critical reelaboration of both national and foreign influences. Imported cultural influences were to be devoured, digested, and reworked in terms of local conditions." The Brazilian modernists dated their Cannibal Manifesto "the year the Bishop Sardinha was swallowed," thus commemorating the date on which Brazilian Indians had devoured a Portuguese bishop (*Brazilian Cinema*, ed. Randal Johnson and Robert Stam [London: Associated University Presses, 1982], pp. 81-83).

[2] Ovid, *Metamorphoses*, trans. Frank Justus Miller (Cambridge: Harvard University Press, 1936), 3:393-401.

[3] In Raul Ruiz's film *On Top of the Whale*, a Dutch anthropologist studies two Patagonian Indians kept on the estate of a man appropriately named "Narcisso." In the house of Don Narciso, the dichotomy between Western subject and indigenous object of knowledge breaks down into a complex array of doublings and self-deceptions.

[4] When Emir Rodríguez Monegal accuses Retamar of "aping the French intellectuals" ("The Metamorphoses of Caliban," p. 82), he means francophones such as O. Mannoni, Franz Fanon, and Aimé Césaire rather than the French poststructuralists. Nevertheless his expression is a striking one, evoking both imitative Echo and the bestial qualities of Caliban.

[5] In "Against the Black Legend" (*Caliban*, pp. 56-73), Retamar develops the theme that Spanish culture is a mestizoized formation of Christian, Moorish, Islamic, and Jewish influences. Under Retamar's gaze, the image of Europe as unified oppressor disintegrates into that of multiple and competing traditions: elite and popular, "central" and "peripheral," and so forth.

[6] As employed by Retamar, it also invokes a specifically *male* presence. The implicit opposition of Echo and Caliban clearly genders the resistance to cultural dependency in a troublingly masculinist way. It would be unfair, surely, to place sole blame for this on Retamar; colonialism had already been gendered, both literally and figuratively, for centuries. Yet it is also true that some male contemporaries of Retamar's, such as

the filmmaker Tomas Guttiérez Alea, later came to give more serious thought to the sexual politics of post-revolutionary culture in Cuba. See Alea's *Up to a Certain Point* (1984).

[7] Rob Nixon, "Caribbean and African Appropriations of *The Tempest,*" in *Politics and Poetic Value,* ed. Robert von Hallberg (Chicago: University of Chicago Press, 1987), pp. 185-206.

[8] On Shakespeare and the Virginia Company, see Charles Mills Gayley, *Shakespeare and the Founders of Liberty in America* (New York: Macmillan, 1917); according to Frank Kermode, Shakespeare's use of colonial reports and pamphlets was first noted by Malone in 1808 (Kermode, Introduction to *The Tempest* [London: Methuen, 1954], p. xxvi).

[9] Deborah Willis, "Shakespeare's *Tempest* and the Discourse of Colonialism," *Studies in English Literature* 29 (1989): 277-89. Willis both traces the ubiquity of colonial readings and devotes considerable polemical energy to arguing that *The Tempest might* be about something other than (or rather, something in addition to) colonialism.

[10] Two important examples are Paul Brown, "'This thing of darkness I acknowledge mine': *The Tempest* and the Discourse of Colonialism," in *Political Shakespeare: New Essays in Cultural Materialism,* ed. Jonathan Dollimore and Alan Sinfield (Ithaca: Cornell University Press, 1985), pp. 48-71; and Francis Barker and Peter Hulme, "Nymphs and Reapers Heavily Vanish: The Discursive Con-texts of *The Tempest,*" in *Alternative Shakespeares,* ed. John Drakakis (London and New York: Methuen, 1985), pp. 191-205.

[11] See, for example, Stephen J. Greenblatt, "Learning to Curse: Aspects of Linguistic Colonialism in the Sixteenth Century," in *First Images of America: The Impact of the New World on the Old,* ed. Fredi Chiappelli, 2 vols. (Berkeley: University of California Press, 1976), 2:561-80: "Ugly, rude, savage, Caliban nevertheless achieves for an instant an absolute, if intolerably bitter, moral victory" (p. 570). Compare Stephen Orgel, "Shakespeare and the Cannibals," in *Cannibals, Witches, and Divorce: Estranging the Renaissance,* ed. Marjorie Garber (Baltimore: Johns Hopkins University Press, 1987), p. 54; and Willis, p. 284.

[12] Leslie A. Fiedler, *The Stranger in Shakespeare* (New York: Stein and Day, 1972), p. 238. See also Alden T. Vaughan, "Shakespeare's Indian: The Americanization of Caliban," *Shakespeare Quarterly* 39 (1988): 137-53.

[13] William Shakespeare, *The Tempest,* ed. Robert Langbaum (New York: New American Library, 1964), II.i.148-73. Subsequent references are to this edition.
[14] Karen Ordahl Kupperman, *Settling with the Indians:*

The Meeting of English and Indian Cultures in America, 1580-1640 (Totowa, N.J.: Rowman and Littlefield, 1980), pp. 34, 40-41; William Brandon, *New Worlds for Old: Reports from the New World and Their Effect on the Development of Social Thought in Europe, 1500-1800* (Athens: Ohio University Press, 1986), pp. 66-87.

[15] George Chapman, Ben Jonson, John Marston, *Eastward Ho,* ed. R. W. Van Fosser, The Revels Plays (Baltimore: Johns Hopkins University Press, 1979), III.iii.15-46.

[16] See Stephen Greenblatt, "Martial Law in the Land of Cockaigne," *Shakespearean Negotiations: The Circulation of Social Energy in Renaissance England* (Berkeley: University of California Press, 1988), pp. 129-63. Gonzalo's knowledge of the New World is quite pointedly outmoded; his Golden Age reports, along with his monstrous visions of "mountaineers / Dewlapped like bulls, whose throats had hanging at 'em / Wallets of flesh" and "men / Whose heads stood in their breasts" (III.iii.44-47) derive in the main from medieval and early Renaissance travel literature. Likewise the very figure of the humanist councillor and utopian projector is somewhat archaic. Gonzalo represents a brand of humanism whose time had clearly passed when *The Tempest* was written.

[17] Caliban, of course, reminds Prospero that he showed him "all the qualities o' th' isle" (I.ii.337) and later promises to teach Stephano and Trinculo how to fend for themselves (II.ii.155-80). In his song celebrating freedom from Prospero, Caliban exclaims "No more dams I'll make for fish" (II.ii.188), a line Sidney Lee describes as "a vivid and penetrating illustration of a peculiar English experience in Virginia" ("The American Indian in Elizabethan England," in *Elizabethan and Other Essays,* ed. Frederick S. Boas [Oxford: Clarendon Press, 1929], p. 297). Early Virginian settlers were heavily dependent for their food on natives' fish-dams whose construction and operation they could never master themselves. The settlers were thus in a constant state of anxiety lest they alienate the natives and provoke them to destroy the dams. Writes Lee: "The gloomy anticipation of the failure of the dam through native disaffection came true in those early days, and was a chief cause of the disastrous termination of the sixteenth-century efforts to found an English colony in Virginia. The narratives of the later Virginian explorers, Captain John Smith and William Strachey, whose energies were engaged in the foundation of Jamestown, bear similar testimony to the indispensible service rendered by the natives' fish-dams to the English colonists. Caliban's threat to make 'no more dams for fish' consequently exposed Prospero to a very real and a familiar peril" (pp. 298-99).

[18] James Axtell, "The Indian Impact on English Colonial Culture," in *The European and the Indian: Essays*

in the Ethnohistory of Colonial North America (Oxford: Oxford University Press, 1981), pp. 272-315.

[19] See Axtell, "The Indian Impact," and Kupperman, *Settling with the Indians,* pp. 141-58.

[20] Quoted in Axtell, "The Indian Impact," p. 160. See also Axtell, "The White Indians of Colonial America," in *European and Indian,* pp. 168-206.

[21] In his dedicatory epistle to King Charles, George Sandys introduces his translation of Ovid by invoking the issue of cultural miscegenation: "It needeth more then a single denization, being a double Stranger: Sprung from the Stocke of the ancient Romanes; but bred in the New-World, of the rudeness whereof it cannot but participate; especially having Warres and Tumults to bring it to light in stead of the Muses." George Sandys, *Ovid's Metamorphosis Englished, Mythologized, and Represented in Figures,* ed. Karl K. Hulley and Stanley T. Vandersall (Lincoln: University of Nebraska Press, 1970), p. 3.

[22] As both humanist councillor and philosophical traveler Gonzalo combines the roles played by More and his fictional character Raphael Hythlodaeus; his egalitarian, communist utopia bears a generic though clearly imperfect resemblance to Thomas More's fictive polity. See Arthur J. Slavin, "The American Principle from More to Locke," in Chiappelli, *First Images of America,* 1:147-48.

[23] Prospero eagerly adopts a specular relation to Gonzalo: "Holy Gonzalo, honorable man, / Mine eyes, ev'n sociable to the show of thine, / Fall fellowly drops" (V.i.62-64). The two old men do indeed mirror each other, for better and for worse.

[24] Antonio's remark may possibly refer to Francisco, not Gonzalo. The Variorum Edition records differing views (pp. 113-114) but ultimately endorses Gonzalo as the referent of Antonio's remark, as does Stephen Orgel in the Oxford edition. Orgel thinks Antonio refers to Gonzalo's confusion while describing his ideal commonwealth.

[25] See Terence Cave, *The Cornucopian Text: Problems of Writing in the French Renaissance* (Oxford: Clarendon Press, 1979), pp. 45, 182.

[26] For a more extended discussion of the importance of Virgil for this scene, see Orgel, "Cannibals," pp. 58-64.

[27] James Holstun, *A Rational Millennium: Puritan Utopias of Seventeenth-Century England and America* (New York: Oxford University Press, 1987), pp. 63-64, discusses the importance of empirical claims for utopian fiction, as does Slavin, "American Principle," p. 144.

[28] In III.iii., Trinculo, Stephano, and Caliban hear Ariel invisibly playing a tune on a tabor and pipe. Trinculo remarks, "This is the tune of our catch, played by the picture of Nobody" (III.iii.131-32). The phrase refers to an anonymous, early seventeenth-century play titled *No-body and Some-body,* and to the sign of its printer, John Trundle, which depicted a man composed of head and limbs but without a trunk. In the play itself, the characters Nobody and Somebody are employed as satirical devices to depict the displacement or denial of social responsibilities. For instance:

> Come twentie poore men to his gate at once,
> *Nobody* gives them mony, meate and drinke,
> If they be naked, clothes, then come poore
> 　　souldiers,
> Sick, maymd, and shot, from any forraine
> 　　warres,
> *Nobody* takes them in, provides them harbor.

(*Nobody and Somebody* [Glasgow: privately reprinted, 1877], sig. B4r). Likewise, when Somebody orders his men to oppress the poor and widows, rack rents, raise prices, and so forth, he tells them to blame it on Nobody. The displacement of social and moral agency carried out by this simple device is relevant to *The Tempest* in general and to Gonzalo's ideal commonwealth in particular.

[29] Holstun, *A Rational Millennium,* p. 67.

[30] James Holstun's fine discussion of arcadia and utopia in *A Rational Millennium* (pp. 67-77) is crucial to my argument here. Holstun is surely correct in arguing that arcadia and utopia are antithetical in principle, and that "Utopia is the violent civil negation of pastoral arcadia" (p. 74). I nevertheless want to suggest that, in More's case at least, this negation is never fully carried out, that the genre of the *Utopia* remains irreducibly mixed, and that this mixture is both medium and sign of the work's mestizoized status. To this extent I disagree with Holstun's insistence that the early modern utopia is *entirely* produced by Western processes of rationalization and technological domination.

[31] See Henri Baudet, *Paradise on Earth: Some Thoughts on European Images of Non-European Man,* trans. Elizabeth Wentholt (New Haven: Yale University Press, 1965), pp. 26-27; Robert F. Berkhofer, Jr., *The White Man's Indian: Images of the American Indian from Columbus to the Present* (New York: Knopf, 1978).

[32] See Kupperman, *Settling with the Indians,* p. 106 and passim. John Howland Rowe, "The Renaissance Foundations of Anthropology," *American Anthropologist* 67 (1965): 1-20, argues that even Peter Martyr, who did not visit the New World himself, relates "ethnographic information [which] is relatively abundant and is presented in a notably objective fashion" (p.

13). Rowe adds that "no one who makes a general survey of the literature bearing on historical ethnography which has come down to us from 16th century Europe can fail to be struck by the fact that it provides better and more detailed information on New World Cultures than on those of the other parts of the world which the Europeans were exploring at the same time" (p. 14).

33 Brandon, *New Worlds,* pp. ix, 21, 23, 38, 60, 151. As Karen Kupperman points out in *Settling with the Indians* (pp. 49-50, 143-44), English colonists interpreted the chieftainship of North American tribes as analogous to European monarchy. The imperial structures of the great mesoamerican cultures were also evident to explorers and colonists. Reports of South American, and especially Brazilian, peoples seem more often to have mentioned the absence of kings (see, for example, Brandon, p. 38). The Golden Age theme of masterlessness is, in any case, raised by Caliban, who complains to Prospero that "I am all the subjects that you have, / Which first was mine own king" (I.ii.341-42).

34 By "appropriation" I do not mean the mere fact of cultural borrowing, or even the transformation of foreign cultural practices that inevitably accompanies importation into another socio-cultural system. I mean a mode of appropriation which entails the erasure of origins. At the same time, it is abundantly clear that abstract constructions such as "the West" and "the New World" are only provisionally useful for purposes of analysis. To assume that New World influences were evenly absorbed by some unified entity called "the West" is as naïve as assuming that New World gold was equally distributed among all the citizens of Spain. (Needless to say, the "New World" is an equally artificial construct.) Differences in national and class cultures, theological outlook, and so forth obviously determined both the extent and mode of cultural appropriation. Historically, the New World clearly played a significant role in anti-monarchical and anti-aristocratic thought. It was assimilated more visibly into bourgeois-democratic than into popular-radical discourse, and for fairly obvious reasons it was more apparent in, say, eighteenth-century France than in seventeenth-century England, where it had little visible influence on radical sectarian literature during the revolutionary era. A more materialist version of this essay would insist on specifying the social conditions under which New World reports were, or were not, included in political or literary discourse. My remarks here are limited to humanist and certain post-humanist assimilations of colonial reports.

35 Elsewhere I have argued that More's *Utopia* effects a similar split between a "proto-Hobbesian 'natural man'" and an abstractly rational polity (Richard Halpern, *The Poetics of Primitive Accumulation: English*

Renaissance Culture and the Genealogy of Capital [Ithaca: Cornell University Press, 1991], pp. 150-51). In More's case, I maintained, this was entirely a symptom of commodity fetishism: "the reified impulse is the necessary and dialectical mirror image of the reified commodity" (p. 151). The present essay offers another, supplementary explanation of the same phenomenon, this time rooted in the dynamics of colonialism. My earlier reading must be included among the more or less "Eurocentric" readings of the *Utopia,* for which this essay may serve in part as corrective.

36 At III.ii.30-31, Trinculo describes Caliban as "half a fish and half a monster."

37 The natives, it was thought, would learn the virtues of Christian, civilized life and report on the kind treatment they had received when they returned to America. Conversely, it was hoped that they would inspire interest in the New World among the English, thus promoting colonization (Lee, *The American Indian,* pp. 268-69, 282-83). Exhibiting Native Americans as popular curiosities was also profitable in its own right, as Trinculo grasps. While a number of these American "guests" died of disease, cold, or the hardships of travel, this did not much reduce their exhibition-value—if Trinculo is to be believed.

38 J. H. Elliott, *The Old World and the New 1492-1650* (Cambridge: Cambridge University Press, 1970), pp. 30-32. On *Wunderkämmer,* see also Steven Mullaney, "Strange Things, Gross Terms, Curious Customs: The Rehearsal of Cultures in the Late Renaissance," in *Representing the English Renaissance,* ed. Stephen Greenblatt (Berkeley: University of California Press, 1988), pp. 65-68.

39 John White's watercolor paintings of American Indians, turned into engravings by the Dutchman Theodore De Bry, illustrate the fusion of early American ethnography with natural history. White was sent along with Thomas Harriot to depict unknown and possibly profitable resources in the New World, and his Indian portraits are therefore interspersed with paintings of herbs, plants, and animals. In White's portraits the isolated Indian is at once a natural object and a potential commodity.

40 Lee, *The American Indian,* p. 275, lists more than one instance of American Indians who were imported to England, had their portraits painted by distinguished or fashionable artists, and subsequently died before they could return home.

41 On More's *Utopia* and the petty producing class, see Christopher Kendrick, "More's *Utopia* and Uneven Development," *boundary* 2 13 (1985): 233-66. On primitive accumulation, see Halpern, *The Poetics of Primitive Accumulation,* pp. 61-75.

[42] Fiedler, *The Stranger in Shakespeare,* p. 234.

[43] Bruce E. Johansen, *Forgotten Founders: How the American Indian Helped Shape Democracy* (Boston: Harvard Common Press, 1982). On the Indians' use of wampum as a system of writing, see pp. 29-31.

FURTHER READING

Adamson, David. "Authority and Illusion: The Power of Prospero's Book." *Comitatus* 20 (1989): 9-19.

> Discusses the connection between learning and magic in *The Tempest,* and suggests that Prospero's book is both an image of power and a symbol of the fictitious nature of authority.

Barker, Francis and Peter Hulme. "Nymphs and Reapers Heavily Vanish: The Discursive Con-Texts of *The Tempest.*" In *Alternative Shakespeare,* edited by John Drakakis, pp. 191-205. London: Methuen, 1985.

> Examines the diverse forms of colonialist discourse in that are inherent in *The Tempest*, as well as the conflicting accounts of usurpation in the play.

Bennett, Susan. "The Post-Colonial Body?: Thinking through *The Tempest.*" In *Performing Nostalgia: Shifting Shakespeare and the Contemporary Past,* pp. 119-50. London: Routledge, 1996.

> Analyzes the complex history of *The Tempest* as it has been revised, rewritten, and performed in terms of anti-colonialism, post-colonialism, neo-colonialism, and pre-colonial nostalgia.

Bloom, Harold, ed. *William Shakespeare's "The Tempest."* New York: Chelsea House, 1988, 171 p.

> A collection of late twentieth-century essays on *The Tempest,* reprinted from various books and periodicals. The assembled writings deal with many aspects of the play, including the characters of Prospero and Caliban, the theme of time, the comic and tragic elements in the play, and political / ideological issues.

———., ed. *Caliban.* New York: Chelsea House, 1992, 262 p.

> A casebook of critical extracts and essays, from the seventeenth century to the 1990s, that evaluate the characterization and function of Caliban.

Bourgy, Victor. "On Caliban's Nature." *Cahiers Élisabéthains* 43 (April 1993): 35-42.

> Argues that Caliban symbolizes the natural or instinctive condition of man. Bourgy acknowledges the difficulty of analyzing Caliban as a dramatic character but asserts that he represents the core of meaning in *The Tempest.*

Campbell, Heather. "Bringing Forth Wonders: Temporal and Divine Power in *The Tempest.*" In *The Witness of Times,* edited by Katherine Z. Keller and Gerald J. Schiffhorst, pp. 69-89. Pittsburgh: Duquesne University Press, 1993.

> Maintains that while *The Tempest* ostensibly promotes the values of absolutist monarchy, it ultimately depicts a power structure that is unstable, repressive, and only superficially effective. Campbell also analyzes the play's treatment of gender relations, the masque as a statement of triumphal authority and the subplot as a parodic antimasque, and the nature of Prospero's rule.

Chaudhuri, Sukanta. "Men, Monsters and Fairies: From *A Midsummer Night's Dream* to *The Tempest.*" *Yearly Review* 4 (December 1990): 26-42.

> Compares the illusory nature of the dramatic worlds in these two plays arguing that *The Tempest* provides a penetrating critique of the notion of moral hierarchy, subversively depicting a moral order in which everyone is capable of both good and evil actions.

Felperin, Howard. "Political Criticism at the Crossroads: The Utopian Historicism of *The Tempest.*" In *The Tempest,* edited by Nigel Wood, pp. 29-31. Buckingham: Open University Press, 1995.

> Examines the broad historical vision of collective destiny embedded in the political unconscious of *The Tempest.*

Ferguson, Ian. "Contradictory Natures: The Function of Prospero, His Agent and His Slave in *The Tempest.*" *Unisa English Studies* XXVIII, No. 2 (September 1990): 1-9.

> Explores Prospero as an enigmatic character, Caliban as violent and anarchic yet imbued with a unique perception of the island's beauty, and Ariel as capable of inspiring terror as well as delight.

Griffiths, Trevor R. "Caliban on the Stage." *Yearbook of English Studies* 13 (1983): 59-80.

> Describes the most significant portrayals of Caliban on the English stage from the 1890s to 1980.

Hantman, Jeffrey L. "Caliban's Own Voice: American Indian Views of the Other in Colonial Virginia." *New Literary History* 23, No. 1 (Winter 1992): 69-81.

> Examines the character of Caliban in relation to colonial narratives circulating in London around the time *The Tempest* was written.

Hunt, John S. "Prospero's Empty Grasp." *Shakespeare Studies* XXII (1994): 277-313.

> Focuses on the ambiguous nature of Prospero's imperious authority and his emotional isolation from others. The play demonstrates the hollowness of mortal attempts at divine self-sufficiency, Hunt argues, and dramatizes the dependence of even the most powerful men on other human beings for spiritual fulfillment.

Hunt, Maurice. "*The Tempest.*" In *Shakespeare's Romance of the Word,* pp. 109-40. Lewisburg: Bucknell University Press, 1990.

Appraises the connection in *The Tempest* between the characters' self-knowledge and their linguistic ability. Hunt looks closely at the methodology of Prospero's instruction of Miranda, Caliban's alternating eloquence and curses, the educative function of the harpy's banquet, and Ariel's use of similes to show Prospero the vanity that shapes his desire for revenge.

Kahn, Coppélia. "The Providential Tempest and the Shakespearean Family." In *Man's Estate: Masculine Identity in Shakespeare,* pp. 193-225. Berkeley: University of California Press, 1981.

Offers a psychoanalytic interpretation of Prospero and his relationship to his family.

Kinney, Arthur F. "Revisiting *The Tempest.*" *Modern Philology* 93, No. 2 (November 1995): 161-77.

Reads *The Tempest* as a cultural document that records ideas and values of English Renaissance culture while simultaneously questioning them.

McNamara, Kevin R. "Golden Worlds at Court: *The Tempest* and Its Masque." *Shakespeare Studies* XIX (1987): 183-202.

Links the subversion of traditional masque conventions in *The Tempest* with the sense of tragic experience in the play. From McNamara's perspective, the abrupt ending of the betrothal masque in IV.i signifies Prospero's recognition of the limitations of his art and the emptiness of his vision of a newly created world in which good invariably triumphs over evil.

Mebane, John S. "Magic as Love and Faith: Shakespeare's *The Tempest.*" In *Renaissance Magic and the Return of the Golden Age,* pp. 174-99. Lincoln: University of Nebraska Press, 1989.

Asserts that Prospero is a benevolent magician whose art serves as a means by which the will of God may be achieved. In keeping with Renaissance occult philosophy, Mebane contends, Shakespeare depicts Prospero as having attained his magical powers through mastery of his physical passions and the cultivation of his spiritual nature.

Mirsky, Mark Jay. "What Prospero Knows." In *The Absent Shakespeare,* pp. 125-39. Rutherford, N.J.: Fairleigh Dickinson University Press, 1994.

A pessimistic reading of *The Tempest* that views it as a drama of deep sexual anxiety. Mirsky alludes to the themes of time, death, and control in the play but focuses on what he regards as Prospero's repressed desire for Miranda.

Novy, Marianne. "Transformed Images of Manhood in the Romances." In *Love's Argument: Gender Relations in Shakespeare,* pp. 164-87. Chapel Hill: University of North Carolina Press, 1984.

In the concluding pages of this chapter, Novy briefly discusses the significance of family ties and relations in *The Tempest.*

Palmer, D. J., ed. *Shakespeare: The Tempest.* London: Macmillan, 1968, 212 p.

A compilation of representative commentary on the play. The selections include adaptations and extracts from pre-twentieth-century authors and critics as well as the texts of recent studies.

Porter, David. "His Master's Voice: The Politics of Narragenitive Desire in *The Tempest.*" *Comitatus* 24 (1993): 33-44.

Asserts that Prospero suffers from severe sexual anxiety, stemming from a fear of betrayal. To compensate for this, Porter maintains, Prospero seeks to create and control the narrative of his own story, and to rewrite the histories of his daughter, his slaves, and the usurpers.

Slights, William W. E. "'His Art Doth Give the Fashion': Generic Fashions and Fashioning in *The Tempest.*" *Forum* XXX, No. 1 (Winter 1989): 20-32.

Discerns a pattern of generic reference in *The Tempest* that serves as a mode of instruction to reform the state and its rulers. Slights identifies a technique of allusion to a variety of literary genres that is designed to emphasize the disparate kinds of learning necessary for cultural survival and coherence.

Solomon, Julie Robin. "Going Places: Absolutism and Movement in Shakespeare's *The Tempest.*" *Renaissance Drama* n.s. XXII (1991): 3-45.

Reads *The Tempest* as Shakespeare's sophisticated dramatic refinement of early modern conceptions of political authority. From Solomon's perspective, the play's indirect representation of the contest between royal prerogatives and commercial-class rights is embodied in Prospero's rejuvenation of absolute monarchy—first through empirical awareness of facts and conditions, and then by successful exploitation of these circumstances.

Stephens, Charles. "Shakespeare." In *Shakespeare's Island: Essays on Creativity,* pp. 6-31. Edinburgh: Polygon, 1994.

Speculates about *The Tempest* in terms of sixteenth-century historical analogues, concluding that Prospero eventually comes to terms with various threats—divine, natural, and human—and uses his creativity to reconcile, at least for a brief period, seemingly irreconcilable forces.

Takaki, Ronald. "*The Tempest* in the Wilderness: The Racialization of Savagery." *Journal of American History* 79, No. 3 (December 1992): 892-912.

Views the attitudes of other characters in *The Tempest* toward Caliban as prefiguring the demonizing of Native Americans by English settlers.

Thompson, Ann. "'Miranda, Where's Your Sister?':
Reading Shakespeare's *The Tempest.*" In *Feminist
Criticism: Theory and Practice,* edited by Susan Sellers,
pp. 45-55. New York: Harvester Wheatsheaf, 1991.

    Contends that *The Tempest* apparently denies the
importance of female characters yet simultaneously
ascribes immense power to female chastity and
fertility; the critic asks—and leaves unanswered—the
question of whether a feminist approach to the play
must inevitably result in a negative reading.

Vaughan, Alden T. "Shakespeare's Indian: The
Amcricanization of Caliban." *Shakespeare Quarterly* 39,
No. 2 (Summer 1988): 137-53.

    Examines the origins and development of
interpretations of *The Tempest* as a paradigm of New
World colonialism and of Caliban as a symbolic Native
American.

The Winter's Tale

For further information on the critical and stage history of *The Winter's Tale*, see *SC*, Volumes 7, 15, and 36.

INTRODUCTION

In 1672, John Dryden considered *The Winter's Tale*, along with *Measure for Measure* and *Love's Labour's Lost*, to be "grounded on impossibilities, or at least, so meanly written, that the Comedy neither caus'd your mirth, nor the serious part your concernment." Such an opinion typifies the history of ambivalence toward *The Winter's Tale*. Since its first performance critics have been perplexed by the play's disparate elements. Among other things, *The Winter's Tale* offends against classical standards of dramatic unity and genre, mixing tragedy and comedy and leaving a sixteen-year lapse in the action. Additionally, it presents the audience with an incredible plot, which includes the sudden restoration of Hermione after her long absence, and the survival of Perdita and her eventual union with the son of her father's former best friend. It also engages in historical and geographical confusion, giving landlocked Bohemia a coastline and bringing together an ancient Greek oracle with the Emperor of Russia, among others.

Although *The Winter's Tale* has generally confounded its audience, recently a number of critics have tried to discover meaning in the play's disorder, particularly by analyzing Shakespeare's use of dreams. Scholars such as Marjorie B. Garber (1974) and Julie Burton (1988) provide the groundwork for such a discussion by examining Shakespeare's source materials, including the literature of ancient Greece and Rome (particularly Ovid) and traditional English folklore. Insight into the operations of dream work in the play has provided critics new avenues of interpretation. For example, while those working against a Christian background have found little reason for Leontes' outbursts, recent explorations, particularly by Garber, have contended that Leontes subconsciously substitutes his dreaming for reality in an effort to vent his latent propensity for sexual jealousy. Kay Stockholder (1987) claims that Leontes isolates himself through his dreaming in order to idealize his surroundings and rescue himself from his destructive passions. She cites Leontes' redemption and his incredible reunion with Hermione to be a dream-like resolution. For Ruth Nevo (1987), the play's dreaming instructs Leontes and the audience that regret is not enough to regenerate the past unless it is infused with a transcendence of this isolation. The

return of Hermione is brought about paradoxically by both overcoming the self-involvement of dreaming and accepting the possibility of dream-like metamorphoses: "It is required / You do awake your faith" (*The Winter's Tale*, Act 5, Scene 3).

Reinforcing the centrality of dreaming to the play's narrative is Shakespeare's use of time. According to critics such as Stanton B. Garner, Jr. (1989), dramatic tensions arise from the nostalgic recollections of the past coming into conflict with an imaginary network of present events. In this interpretation, Leontes' jealousy is jarring primarily because of its coming into conflict with the idyllic picture of his childhood friendship with Polixenes. Leontes' reunion with Hermione marks the overcoming of loss by the overcoming of time. According to Garner, "the harsh line between past and present blurs, shading the memorial presence of the statue into the living presence of Hermione." For Nevo, the severance of the play by a sixteen-year gap in time provides a structure of duplications in which events of the first part are repeated in the second part, when jealousy and fear of usurpation are reenacted—with Polixenes for Leontes, Florizel for Polixenes, and Perdita for Hermione. Humanity's tragic folly is iterated in the later events of the play, marking a shift in emphasis in Shakespeare's late romances. As David Bevington (1988) notes, although the return to an idyllic countryside is reminiscent of Shakespeare's comedies, in *The Winter's Tale* "the restoration is at once more urgently needed and more miraculous than in the 'festive' world of early comedy." So, while the structure and characterization of *The Winter's Tale* have historically troubled its audience, recent critical approaches have appealed to Shakespeare's use of dreams and manipulation of time in an effort to understand the actions of Leontes, to analyze the dramatic tensions, and to relate the play's tragic and comic elements.

OVERVIEWS

David Bevington (essay date 1988)

SOURCE: An introduction to *The Winter's Tale*, in *William Shakespeare: The Late Romances, Pericles, Cymbeline, The Winter's Tale and The Tempest*, written and edited by David Bevington, Bantam Books, 1988, pp. 335-39.

[*In this essay, Bevington relates* The Winter's Tale *to Shakespeare's late romances in an effort to highlight its tragic elements, particularly Leontes' jealousy.*]

The Winter's Tale (c. 1610-1611), with its almost symmetrical division into two halves of bleak tragedy and comic romance, illustrates perhaps more clearly than any other Shakespearean play the genre of tragicomedy. To be sure, all the late romances feature journeys of separation, apparent deaths, and tearful reconciliations. Marina and Thaisa in *Pericles,* Imogen in *Cymbeline,* and Ferdinand in *The Tempest,* all supposed irrecoverably lost, are brought back to life by apparently miraculous devices. Of the four late romances, however, *The Winter's Tale* uses the most formal structure to evoke the antithesis of tragedy and romance. It is sharply divided into contrasting halves by a gap of sixteen years. The tragic first half takes place almost entirely in Sicilia, whereas the action of the second half is limited for the most part to Bohemia. At the court of Sicilia we see tyrannical jealousy producing a spiritual climate of "winter / In storm perpetual"; in Bohemia we witness a pastoral landscape and a sheep-shearing evoking "the sweet o' the year," "When daffodils begin to peer" (3.2.212-213; 4.3.1-3). Paradoxically, the contrast between the two halves is intensified by parallels between the two: both begin with Camillo onstage and proceed to scenes of confrontation and jealousy in which, ironically, the innocent cause of jealousy in the first half, Polixenes, becomes the jealous tyrant of the second half. This mirroring reminds us of the cyclical nature of time and the hope it brings of renewal as we move from tragedy to romantic comedy.

Although this motif of a renewing journey from jaded court to idealized countryside reminds us of *As You Like It* and other early comedies, we sense in the late romances and especially in *The Winter's Tale* a new preoccupation with humanity's tragic folly. The vision of human depravity is world-weary and pessimistic, as though infected by the gloomy spirit of the great tragedies. And because humanity is so bent on destroying itself, the restoration is at once more urgently needed and more miraculous than in the "festive" world of early comedy. Renewal is mythically associated with the seasonal cycle from winter to summer.

King Leontes's tragedy seems at first irreversible and terrifying, like that of Shakespeare's greatest tragic protagonists. He suffers from irrational jealousy, as does Othello, and attempts to destroy the person on whom all his happiness depends. Unlike Othello, however, Leontes needs no diabolical tempter such as Iago to poison his mind against Queen Hermione. Leontes is undone by his own fantasies. No differences in race or age can explain Leontes's fears of estrangement from Hermione. She is not imprudent in her conduct, like her counterpart in Robert Greene's *Pandosto* (1588), the prose romance from which Shakespeare drew his narrative. Although Hermione is graciously fond of Leontes's dear friend Polixenes and urges him to stay longer in Sicilia, she does so only with a hospitable warmth demanded by the occasion and encouraged by her husband. In every way, then, Shakespeare strips away from Leontes the motive and the occasion for plausible doubting of his wife. All observers in the Sicilian court are incredulous and shocked at the King's accusations. Even so, Leontes is neither an unsympathetic nor an unbelievable character. Like Othello, Leontes cherishes his wife and perceives with a horrifying intensity what a fearful cost he must pay for his suspicions. Not only his marriage, but his lifelong friendship with Polixenes, his sense of pride in his children, and his enjoyment of his subjects' warm regard, all must be sacrificed to a single overwhelming compulsion.

Whatever may be the psychological cause of this obsession, it manifests itself as a revulsion against all sexual behavior. Like mad Lear, Leontes imagines lechery to be the unavoidable fact of the cosmos and of the human condition, the lowest common denominator to which all persons (including Hermione) must stoop. He is persuaded that "It is a bawdy planet," in which cuckolded man has "his pond fished by his next neighbor, by / Sir Smile, his neighbor" (1.2.195-201). Leontes's tortured soliloquies are laden with sexual images, of unattended "gates" letting in and out the enemy "With bag and baggage," and of a "dagger" that must be "muzzled / Lest it should bite its master" (ll. 197, 206, 156-157). As in *King Lear,* order is inverted to disorder, sanity to madness, legitimacy to illegitimacy. Sexual misconduct is emblematic of a universal malaise: "Why, then the world and all that's in 't is nothing, / The covering sky is nothing, Bohemia nothing, / My wife is nothing" (ll. 292-294). Other characters too see the trial of Hermione as a testing of humanity's worth: if Hermione proves false, Antigonus promises, he will treat his own wife as a stable horse and will "geld" his three daughters (2.1.148). Prevailing images are of spiders, venom, infection, sterility, and the "dungy earth" (l. 158).

Cosmic order is never really challenged, however. Leontes's fantasies of universal disorder are chimerical. His wife is in fact chaste, Polixenes true, and the King's courtiers loyal. Camillo refuses to carry out Leontes's order to murder Polixenes, not only because he knows murder to be wrong but because history offers not one example of a man "that had struck anointed kings / And flourished after" (1.2.357-358). The cosmos of this play is one in which crimes are invariably and swiftly punished. The Delphic oracle vindicates Hermione and gives Leontes stern warning. When Leontes persists in his madness, his son Mamillius's death follows as an immediate consequence. As Leontes at once perceives, "Apollo's angry, and the heavens themselves / Do strike at my injustice" (3.2.146-147). Leontes paradoxically welcomes the lengthy contrition he must undergo, for it confirms a pattern in the universe of just cause and effect. Although as tragic protagonist he has discovered the truth about Hermione moments too late, and so must pay richly for his error, Leontes has at least recovered faith in Hermione's transcendent goodness. His nightmare now over, he accepts and embraces suffering as a necessary atonement.

The transition to romance is therefore anticipated to an extent by the play's first half, even though the tone of the last two acts is strikingly different. The old Shepherd signals a momentous change when he speaks to his son of a cataclysmic storm and a ravenous bear set in opposition to the miraculous discovery of a child: "Now bless thyself. Thou mett'st with things dying, I with things newborn" (3.3.110-111). Time comes onstage as Chorus, like Gower in *Pericles,* to remind us of the conscious artifice of the dramatist. He can "o'erthrow law" and carry us over sixteen years as if we had merely dreamed out the interim (4.1). Shakespeare flaunts the improbability of his story by giving Bohemia a seacoast (much to the distress of Ben Jonson), and by employing animals onstage in a fanciful way (*"Exit, pursued by a bear";* 3.3.57 s.d.). The narrative uses many typical devices of romance: a babe abandoned to the elements, a princess brought up by shepherds, a prince disguised as a swain, a sea voyage, and a recognition scene. Love is threatened not by the internal psychic obstacle of jealousy, but by the external obstacles of parental opposition and a seeming disparity of social rank between the lovers. Comedy easily finds solutions for such difficulties by the unraveling of illusion. This comic world also properly includes clownish shepherds, coy shepherdesses, and Autolycus, the roguish peddler, whose songs help set the mood of jollity and whose machinations contribute in an unforeseen manner to the working out of the love plot. Autolycus is in many ways the presiding genius of the play's second half, as dominant a character as Leontes in the first half and one whose delightful function is to do good "against my will" (5.2.125). In this paradox of knavery converted surprisingly to benign ends, we see how the comic providence of Shakespeare's tragicomic world makes use of the most implausible and outrageous happenings in pursuit of its own inscrutable design.

The conventional romantic ending is infused, however, with a sadness and a mystery that take the play well beyond what is usual in comedy. Mamillius and Antigonus are really dead, and that irredeemable fact is not forgotten in the play's final happy moments. Conversely, in Shakespeare's most notable departure from his source, Greene's *Pandosto,* Hermione is brought back to life. All observers regard this event, and the rediscovery of Perdita, as grossly implausible, "so like an old tale that the verity of it is in strong suspicion"

(5.2.29-30). The play's very title, *The Winter's Tale,* reinforces this sense of naive improbability. Why does Shakespeare stress this riddling paradox of an unbelievable reality, and why does he deliberately mislead his audience into believing that Hermione has in fact died (3.3.15-45), using a kind of theatrical trickery found in no other Shakespearean play? The answer may well be that, in Paulina's words, we must awake our faith, accepting a narrative of death and return to life that cannot ultimately be comprehended by reason. On the rational level we are told that Hermione has been kept in hiding for sixteen years, in order to bring Leontes's contrition to fulfillment. Such an explanation seems psychologically incomprehensible, however, for it casts both Hermione and her keeper Paulina in the role of sadistic punishers of the King. Instead we are drawn toward an emblematic interpretation, bearing in mind that it is more an evocative hint than a complete truth. Throughout the play, Hermione has been repeatedly associated with "Grace" and with the goddess Proserpina, whose return from the underworld, after "Three crabbèd months had soured themselves to death" (1.2.102), signals the coming of spring. Perdita, also associated with Proserpina (4.4.116), is welcomed by her father "As is the spring to th' earth" (5.1.152). The emphasis on the bond of father and daughter (rather than father and son), so characteristic of Shakespeare's late plays and especially his romances, goes importantly beyond the patriarchalism of Shakespeare's earlier plays in its exploration of family relationships. Paulina has a similarly emblematic role, that of Conscience, patiently guiding the King to a divinely appointed renewal of his joy. Paulina speaks of herself as an artist figure, like Prospero in *The Tempest,* performing wonders of illusion, though she rejects the assistance of wicked powers. These emblematic hints do not rob the story of its human drama, but they do lend a transcendent significance to Leontes's bittersweet story of sinful error, affliction, and an unexpected second happiness.

T. G. Bishop (essay date 1996)

SOURCE: "*The Winter's Tale*; or, Filling Up the Graves," in *Shakespeare and the Theatre of Wonder,* Cambridge University Press, 1996, pp. 125-75.

[*In the following essay, Bishop provides an overview of* The Winter's Tale, *focusing on the characterization, the sources of Leontes' paranoia, and the mythological and narrative patterns that structure the play.*]

O what venerable creatures did the agèd seem!
Immortal Cherubims! And the young men glittering
and sparkling Angels, and maids strange seraphic
pieces of life and beauty! I knew not that they were
born or should die; but all things abided eternally.

Thomas Traherne

Gib Deine Hand, Du schön und zart Gebild!
Bin Freund und komme nicht zu strafen.
Sei guten Muts, ich bin nicht wild.
Sollst sanft in meinen Armen schlafen!
                    Der Tod und das Mädchen

Dum stupet et medio gaudet fallique veretur,
rursus amans rursusque manu sua vota retractat;
corpus erat: saliunt temptatae pollice venae.
                                            Ovid

Shakespeare seems to have been the first English dramatist to give his plays "poetic" titles, by which I mean
not high-flown ones, but ones that stand in a complex
figurative relation to the plays they name. Earlier dramatists offered proverbial titles such as *Enough is as
Good as a Feast* or *Like Will to Like*, but this is not
quite the same thing. The practice begins as early as *The
Comedy of Errors* and *Love's Labours Lost* and reaches
a kind of climax with *Twelfth Night or What You Will.*
Given this attentiveness to the resonance of title, we
ought especially to pay attention when one of the plays
makes a point of citing its title during the action. It does
not happen very often, but when it does it orients us
strongly on where the playwright himself sees the network of complex interrelations having one of its primary interpretive nodes. This is especially true of his
comedies, for which there is a less neutrally designating
set of title conventions than for, say, *The Life of Henry
the Fift* or *The Tragedy of Julius Caesar* (though that
"of" teases). At one point in the middle of his career,
Shakespeare seems deliberately to have set out to mock
or wrong-foot this very kind of attention with apparent
throwaway titles like *As You Like It* and *Much Ado
about Nothing. All's Well that Ends Well* looks like the
same sort of gesture, except that the phrase then appears
twice in increasingly rocky straits on the very lips of the
heroine (IV.iv.35, V.i.25) and makes us pay attention.

In both *The Winter's Tale* and *The Tempest*, as if in this
they were a pair, this underlining gesture is not merely
a secret citation for our ears alone, but a reference to an
act or occasion of story-telling itself, with an even higher
degree of self-consciousness. Of Prospero we might
expect such a metadramatic gambit, since he is at once
magician and theatre-manager. He speaks his line to
Ariel, almost to himself, looking back on his master-
plot as its final suite of gestures is about to unfold:

PROSPERO Now does my project gather to a
    head:
My charms crack not: my spirits obey, and Time
Goes upright with his carriage: how's the day?
ARIEL On the sixth hour, at which time, my
    Lord,
You said our work should cease.
PROSPERO   I did say so,
When first I rais'd "The Tempest."

                                        (V.i.3-6)

This punctuation is tendentious, of course, but I think
it matches what audiences hear, and the line points
them to an enhanced awareness of the closing movement of the whole play.[1]

In *The Winter's Tale,* on the other hand, the title-allu-
sion has little of this deliberate affirmative to it. A
small boy makes it, without even quite "getting it right,"
so that we may even work a bit harder to notice. Why
would such a gesture of self-consciousness be given to
a minor character in a scene that looks like an introduction or prologue to the main event of the act?[2] Or
is Mamillius closer to the center of the play than he
appears? What sorts of things do we learn about him
in his two short scenes that might justify the dignity of
having him allude to the play's title in this canny way?
We know, or we may already feel, that he is to be
sacrificed. Insofar as his name associates him with his
mother, we may wonder whether he can escape his
father's blind wrath against her.[3] And though Leontes
apparently decides that the child is after all his, solicitude for his son's welfare does not include actually
bringing him with him in subsequent scenes: he is as
effectively banished from the King's company as his
mother is, more so in fact. Whether he cries on being
haled from her we do not know, but we are reasonably
sure he grieves terribly later on. Even Leontes proclaims this much, though he glosses it as shame at his
mother's behavior—or on her behalf.

But what do we see that might help us understand why
his small story bears the weight of the whole play? By
his own criteria, his is a "winter's tale"—brief and
clouded, haunted by haunted figures. His two appearances revolve first around his father, then his mother.
"Revolve" as there is a prominent element of oscillation in the boy's movement in each case: he moves
away (is pushed away in fact) and returns. This pattern
of separation and recovery in relation to both parents
is important for defining him as a dramatic figure. The
stakes, it will appear, are high both for him and the
play in understanding the tentative alternations between
identification, detachment, and resistance that these
stage movements come to map.[4]

It is in the scene with his mother, more set off from its
surroundings than that with his father, that the play
marks him for its own. Stanley Cavell has drawn attention to Leontes' discovery of the boy whispering to his
mother, and read it as another scene of suspicion to
add to his burgeoning fear and rage at the insidious
knowledges of him he sees proliferating around him.[5]
For Cavell the moment focuses Leontes' secret wish—
secret perhaps even from himself—to make away with
Mamillius, and through and with him all generation.
But the odd thing about Cavell's attention to this scene
is that it seems in some ways to repeat Leontes' own
gesture by banishing Mamillius himself from real consideration. For we see more of the scene than Leontes,

and we know that Mamillius is *not* whispering a secret about him—or at least, not the secret he most fears and desires. What then is he doing with his "sad tale . . . of sprites and goblins"? Cavell speaks of the moment between mother and son as "a result of mutually seductive gestures," which is acute, but there are many kinds of seduction. What are the elements of this one that it should issue in this story?

I

The scene begins with Hermione pushing Mamillius—his mother's boy—away, in exasperation at something he has been doing, as if she were afraid he is about to exhaust her patience: "Take the boy to you; he so troubles me, / 'Tis past enduring." She speaks over his head, into an adult world that converts her command into a gamesome and seductive entreaty: "Come, my gracious lord, / Shall I be your playfellow?" But Mamillius knows enough to know what is going on, if not enough to respond with urbanity: "No, I'll none of you. . . . You'll kiss me hard and speak to me as if / I were a baby still." If he has been irritating his mother, perhaps the rub has been mutual: he is trying to grow away from a defenseless dependency he considers past. Making his own play for power, he tries to set his antagonist against her companion ("I love you better"), who is indulgent ("And why so, my lord?"). And now Mamillius has a chance to strut his discriminating knowledge of female beauty. Contrary to Polixenes' claims in the previous scene for the lambkin innocence of boyhood, this boy has a keen eye for sexual attractiveness and an interest in seeing how he can exploit what he sees. He even claims to have his lore from his own observation ("I learn'd it out of women's faces"), and he knows and perhaps resents it when his precocity is made fun of ("Nay, that's a mock"). The playfulnesses of this exchange are clear enough, yet they are not the same for boy and women, and the delicate psychological observation of the small scene rests in these differences. Though he relaxes into their indulgent teasing, even uses it to shine in, Mamillius has more to lose, and he finds in the end that their power to hurt is more real than he had hoped when they put before him the image of his strutted independence unpleasantly taken at its word, and begin to speak, again almost over his head, of "women's matters":

[1.] LADY   Hark ye,
The Queen your mother rounds apace; we shall
Present our services to a fine new prince
One of these days, and then you'ld wanton with us,
If we would have you.
2. LADY   She is spread of late
Into a goodly bulk. Good time encounter her!
                                 (II.i.15-20)

Hermione interrupts the pair at this point with a rebuke, as though she knows the conversation is heading into deeper waters. She readmits the boy to her, offering reassurance of her continued presence and love, as though this were also a pledge for the future: "Come, sir, now / I am for *you* again."[6] The expedient she hits on for letting him show his authority over her is that of story-telling, a move that allows mother and son to collaborate in a mutual dependence where he is active and controlling but still needs her consent and scope for his showcase. The two negotiate and Mamillius plays once more at refusal and aggression, a gambit Hermione is willing, even eager, to accommodate:

HERMIONE   Pray you sit by us,
And tell's a tale.
MAMILLIUS Merry or sad, shall't be?
HERMIONE   As merry as you will.
MAMILLIUS A sad tale's best for winter. I have one
Of sprites and goblins.
HERMIONE   Let's have that, good sir.
Come on, sit down, come on, and do your best
To fright me with your sprites; you're pow'rful at it.
MAMILLIUS There was a man—
HERMIONE   Nay, come sit down; then on.
MAMILLIUS Dwelt by a churchyard. I will tell it softly,
Yond crickets shall not hear it.
HERMIONE   Come on then.
And giv't me in mine ear.
       Enter Leontes, Antigonus, Lords
                                 (II.i.22-32)

This is deft stuff. We watch Mamillius and his mother together shaping the stakes and prospect of his frightening her. No doubt she will exclaim with fear at suitable intervals, giving him the delicious pleasure of mastering at once her and his aggressive impulse against her, since he will know of course that she is not "really" frightened. The "winter's tale" proves a narrative device to stage and explore the psychic strain of their coming separation, alike feared and desired by both. It maps and cycles anxiety into story, just as the spatial movement away from and towards Hermione maps more complex separations ahead of the threat of his displacement—a threat contained in his own maturation, but also threateningly hastened by her insistent "goodly bulk." The story about ghosts itself ghosts much that cannot be directly faced. These are indeed "mutually seductive gestures," but they are carefully hedged by a definite agression also acknowledged sidelong by both.

What must Mamillius make then of his father's terrible irruption into this scene? It is sometimes asserted that Leontes in some sense "is" the man who "dwelt by a churchyard." For Mamillius, however, the "winter's tale" does not so much continue as spin wildly out of his control and into some weirdly hyper-literal realm, as though he had all along been casting a spell without knowing it. There could hardly be a worse nightmare than the sudden appearance of this dark phantasm of accusation in the person of his father. At some level, this is profoundly *not* what Mamillius had in mind, yet it may seem to him as if his own desires have somehow called forth this vengeful demon in the shape of his father: just how much of Leontes' appalling musings may we think of the boy garnering in the previous scene? As long as there is a medium for managing and so dispelling such forebodings, Mamillius can play secure. But now he must watch his own deeper half-promptings realized in the father who both demands and banishes him, at once fulfillment and retribution for his daring against his mother:

> LEONTES   Give me the boy. I am glad you
> did not nurse him.
> Though he does bear some signs of me, yet
> you
> Have too much blood in him.
> HERMIONE   What is this? Sport?
> LEONTES   Bear the boy hence, he shall not
> come about her.
> Away with him! and let her sport herself
> With that she's big with, for 'tis Polixenes
> Has made thee swell thus.
>
> (II.i.56-62)

To Mamillius, this exchange must be both horrifying and deeply inscrutable. To hear that he "bears some signs of" this Leontes comes too close to what he has been imagining himself: recall his earlier claim to his father "I am like you, they say"—but would he want to be like *this* father? To be forced from his mother's side in this manner, leaving her to "sport" with the new child, is also too much like the way the scene began ("and then you'ld wanton with us, / If we would have you") and carries a darker undercurrent mixing childish and adult sexuality in Leontes' bitter reference to Hermione's "sport." Have his entwined desire for and rejection of independence begotten such a monstrosity as this between them? What relations obtain between the boy's desire against his mother and his desire for her? Is his mother now to suffer for what he has thought and felt, and at the hands of this dark cartoon of himself grown-up?[7]

Such considerations cast a terrible light on what we hear of the boy's decline through the rest of the play. It is important that Leontes' claim on him does not extend to more than enquiring after him, as far as we know. Mamillius is sequestered from both his parents, and Leontes' cry "Away with him" is only the first of many such cries to follow, cries that seek apparently to banish the whole world and leave him in the company only of his own fantasies ("Away with her, to prison";

"Away with that audacious lady"; "My child? Away with't"). Cavell's suggestion that Leontes' rage is against Mamillius as well as Hermione, in spite of his apparent solicitude, seems only too accurate, and although this may be because of the "too much blood in him" of which he speaks, it seems also to speak of a more pervasive aggression, one we find turning even on himself—sleepless, restive, and thought-fretted as he becomes.

Mamillius, then, awakes from a world whose nightmares he controls to one where they are alive, where they strut and glower and spit accusations. His response to what he has done is to sicken, neurotically as we may suppose from Leontes' description, though we need not accept Leontes' specific diagnosis:

> LEONTES How does the boy?
> SERVANT   He took good rest tonight;
> 'Tis hop'd his sickness is discharg'd.
> LEONTES To see his nobleness,
> Conceiving the dishonour of his mother!
> He straight declin'd, droop'd, took it deeply,
> Fasten'd and fix'd the shame on't in himself,
> Threw off his spirit, his appetite, his sleep,
> And downright languish'd.
>
> (II.iii.10-17)

Cavell on these lines is worth quoting directly: "this sounds more like something Leontes himself has done, and so suggests an identification Leontes has projected between himself and his son. The lines at the same time project an identification with his wife, to the extent to which one permits 'conceiving' in that occurrence to carry on the play's ideas of pregnancy."[8] But may this not also be something Mamillius has done? If Leontes' interpretation of Mamillius' condition is suspect, his description of it need not be. Though "the boy," as he calls his son, has perhaps not "conceived" Hermione's dishonor (and both their notions of "conception" must be important here), he may regard her slander and punishment as in some way his doing, in which case his "fixing" of "the shame on't in himself" would be an attempt to undo what his momentary aggression has so rashly and magically done. This would be acute child psychology certainly, and would explain and complete a strange circle of identifications among the members of this apparently doomed family. Mamillius is trapped between identifications with father and mother. Too like his father in his violence and sleepless languishing, he is now willing himself to take his mother's place in conceiving and drooping. It is indeed a noble gesture, but not quite of the kind Leontes imagines. By it Mamillius attempts to take his mother's part as the object of his father's sexual violence, and to perform this part partly to deny his part in his father (and his father's part in him). Bastardizing himself is, in a sense, the price of redeeming his mother. In effect, he will kill himself for being like his father by becoming like his mother, taking her place to pay for both his own and his father's violence.[9] "With mere conceit and fear / Of the Queen's speed" he races his mother to a death he now identifies as the outcome (and perhaps the engine) of male desire. In this heroic resolution he is all too successful.

There is a sense of Mamillius as having "seen the spider" through these brief glimpses, but the spider in this case is a sexual intimation for which he has inadequate preparation and no expressive recourse save this of his fatal sickening. The question of his mimetic "conception" of his mother's dishonor is shadowed, and perhaps interpreted, by the fact of his own "conception" by her at an earlier time through an act of "sport" not unlike aggression.[10] Paulina's language in describing the etiology of the Prince's decline touches directly on this point, since it sees Leontes' current slanderous rage to "sully the purity and whiteness of my sheets" (his own phrase at I.ii.326-7) as intimately but obscurely connected to the Prince's secret "conception" of the act that created him:

> PAULINA Nor is't directly laid to thee, the death
> Of the young Prince, whose honourable thoughts,
> Thoughts high for one so tender, cleft the heart
> That could conceive a gross and foolish sire
> Blemish'd his gracious dam.
>
> (III.ii.194-8)

Paulina here clearly indicates she regards the boy's death as induced by a "high" revenge enacted on himself for having a "heart" base enough to "conceive" of his mother's staining by his "gross" father. Some part of a divided Mamillius has made itself a party to that imagined or real act of pollution, while another part has determined to wipe it out as far as he can—by wiping out at once both the cause (his heart) and the effect (himself). Leontes, more ruthless or more selfish, has meanwhile chosen to attack what he calls, with his typical obscure clarity, "the cause . . . part o' the cause" (II.iii.3). But children often confuse cause and effect like this. D. W. Winnicott has spoken of the imaginative paradox of the "transitional object" in a way that deeply illuminates Mamillius' predicament:

> it can be said that it is a matter of agreement between us and the baby that we will never ask the question: 'Did you conceive of this or was it presented to you from without?' The important point is that no decision on this point is expected. The question is not to be formulated.[11]

For Mamillius the imaginative object has spun horribly out of his control, and fused itself with dark images of "conception" that point fearfully to him. The threat to his mother precipitates the need to formulate and decide the question of "conception" as a matter of urgency through suggesting that some magical potency in his own tentative aggressions has re-created the world as a nightmare. Has he produced his father's accusation or not? If he has, he must punish himself; if he has not, he must protect his mother. Further underlying this traumatic complex of ambivalences lies a terrible but obscure intimation of sexual generation—the very act that produced him, that he has somehow now repeated—as intimately involved with violence, staining, and mortality. Rather than consent to his inevitable part in that nest of spiders, Mamillius revenges himself on mortality by depriving it of its prize in him.

II

These conjectures on the relation between the Prince and his parents may seem somewhat overdeveloped, but they follow strictly what we see or are told, and they have the advantage that they do not rely on Leontes' surely confused sense of "the cause" to explain what happens to the boy. The obscurity of the connections Mamillius makes is registered by the play both lexically and dramatically, in their withdrawal deep within the texture of his lines, and of his character itself from the action. Where Leontes "stages" his suspicions, for Mamillius the process of violent desire goes on "behind the scenes." The play shows us a complex triangle of identifications in which both males deeply, and perhaps similarly, mistake the nature of their relations with Hermione and with each other. We need therefore now to look at the play's own dreadful "primal scene" of Leontes' suspicions, a scene in which Mamillius is also an intrusive—and, I believe—catalytic, presence.

It has been argued recently that Leontes' resentment and paranoia spring from his suspicion of female generativity in general, and his dependence on Hermione's in particular. His violence has been linked thence to the general history of patriarchy and its simultaneous use and devaluation of childbirth as "the woman's part." There is much truth in this view, yet it also seems to me insufficiently precise to account for just what happens in this case, where, for all the mystery of their genesis, there is a clear and precise notation of "events." One serious problem to be faced by the diagnosis of misogynist suspicion of women as the root cause though it is certainly the route Leontes' rhetoric takes once mobilized is that it is touched off not by femaleness in general (as it is in, say, Iago) or even with birth *per se,* but specifically with the birth of a *second* child. If it was merely a matter of suspicion of female sexuality in general, one would have expected it to have broken out with Hermione's first pregnancy, her first evidence of "openness" to male penetration, or even earlier, as it apparently does with Othello, around the initial moment of marital consummation.[12]

But this is not what happens. Instead the crisis precipitates only when mediated through the presence not only of Polixenes but of Mamillius, the latter a genuinely new element in the familial equation. It is worth recalling that the boy is first mentioned in the opening scene, in what seems otherwise a rather awkward transition, immediately after Archidamus has said of the two kings' love: "I think there is not in the world either malice or matter to alter it."[13] And though Leontes comes upon or is seized by his suspicion unprompted by any explicit thought of his boy, its efflorescence is curiously interleaved with another scene in which the child moves towards and away from his parent, alternately embraced and dismissed by him.

Yet if the actual genesis of Leontes' suspicions unfolds independent of Mamillius (though the boy is on stage and presumably doing something, perhaps playing, while his elders talk), the question of the sort of sexual consciousness boyhood has is very much in the air. It is discussed at some length between Polixenes and Hermione (does Hermione have her son in mind? are he and Leontes playing together?), and its nature is explored in images of a pastoral mutuality elsewhere reserved in Shakespeare for girlhood.[14] What Polixenes recalls, or fantasizes, with especial plangency is a lack of any sense either of development and change or of sin, specifically of sexual sinnings associated with the appearance of women on the scene as occasions or, more strongly, instigators of (male) desire. The highlighting enjambment at "chang'd" is very relevant here, as though when we revise its meaning from "altered" to "exchanged" we, with Polixenes, avoid a thought of mutability:

HERMIONE   Come, I'll question you
Of my lord's tricks and yours when you were
    boys.[15]
You were pretty lordings then?
POLIXENES   We were, fair queen,
Two lads that thought there was no more
    behind
But such a day tomorrow as today,
And to be boy eternal.
HERMIONE   Was not my lord
The verier wag o' th' two?
POLIXENES We were as twinn'd lambs that did
    frisk i' th' sun,
And bleat the one at th'other. What we
    chang'd
Was innocence for innocence; we knew not
The doctrine of ill-doing, nor dream'd
That any did.
                                (I.ii.60-71)

If we suppose for the sake of argument that Polixenes and Hermione are here watching Leontes and Mamillius at play, the scene before them becomes doubled by an imagined scene which peculiarly charges it with a nostalgic pathos springing from the necessity of whatever was "chang'd" in adult development. A heretofore perfect economy between equals then suffered an imbalance, coincident both with the perception of time as mortality and with "the doctrine of ill-doing." Polixenes seems here peculiarly to repeat a moment in the past where, like Mamillius in a later scene, he had to decide whether the "stronger blood" of sexual excitement that bears within it the intuitions of both mortality and punishment has come to him from within or without. Hermione points out the implication despite Polixenes' delicate attempt to turn it aside by framing her as "most sacred":

                    Had we pursued that life
And our weak spirits ne'er been higher rear'd
With stronger blood, we should have answer'd
    heaven
Boldly, "Not guilty"; the imposition clear'd,
Hereditary ours.
HERMIONE   By this we gather
You have tripp'd since.
POLIXENES   O my most sacred lady,
Temptations have since then been born to's: for
In those unfledg'd days was my wife a girl;
Your precious self had then not cross'd the
    eyes
Of my young playfellow.
HERMIONE   Grace to boot!
Of this make no conclusion, lest you say
Your queen and I are devils.
                                (I.ii.72-83)

Polixenes' way of putting it—of temptation's having been "born to's"—both points to the particular issue at stake and neatly sidesteps the need to decide precisely where the origins were of this "conception" for him and Leontes.[16] His description of Hermione "crossing the eyes" of "my young playfellow"—which sounds rather like Leontes on Mamillius—likewise conceals inside a more neutral phrase a (remembered?) resentment or taunt or sense of damage at her hands. After seeing Hermione, Leontes' vision became faulty, even as his desire fledged.

The later scene between Hermione and Mamillius, from this point of view, explicitly responds to Polixenes' vision of male childhood as insulated innocence, and with it we can be precise about the latter's sentimentality. Sexual knowledge is continually in development, mediated and modulated through play and fantasy and in constant contact with other emotions such as anger and fear. It is not a catastrophic creation from some female "nothing." But the question that needs answering here is: does Leontes too think this is what happened to him? There is some evidence that he does, at some level—though this thought itself may, as we shall see, screen a deeper self-knowledge he wishes *not* to call to account.[17]

If we continue to imagine Leontes as coming into the scene from playing with Mamillius (hence as himself in contact with boyhood, even as Polixenes describes it), we can see at once the relevance of what Polixenes says about "eye-crossing" to what Leontes now finds before him. Indeed Leontes' testing and accusing of the world from here on frequently appeal to the arrant and visible truth of his fantasies to any "head-piece extraordinary." Though the "lower messes" are still "purblind" (as once both he and all were "Blind with the pin and web"), now *he* has "eyes / To see" all that's "beneath the sky" (I.ii.310, 180). His fierce accusation that Camillo is one who "Canst with thine eyes at once see good and evil" (I.ii.303) sounds not unlike resentment at having had his own eyes "cross'd" by his wife. And when he later confronts Hermione, he has the half-indulgent rage of an enlightened demystifier before his former illusion, redeeming himself by helping others on to the cure:

> You, my lords,
> Look on her, mark her well; be but about
> To say she is a goodly lady, and
> The justice of your hearts will thereto add
> 'Tis pity she's not honest—honourable.
> Praise her but for this her without-door form
> (Which on my faith deserves high speech) and
>   straight
> The shrug, the hum or ha (these petty brands
> That calumny doth use—O I am out—
> That mercy does, for calumny will sear
> Virtue itself), these shrugs, these hums and
>   ha's,
> When you have said she's goodly, come
>   between
> Ere you can say she's honest: but be't known
> (From him that has most cause to grieve it
>   should be)
> She's an adultress.
>
> (II.i.64-78)

There is a remarkable anticipation here of the eventual image of Hermione's fate at Leontes' hands. With a brutal connoisseurish swagger, Leontes gives his men a tour of his wife as though she were some object of aesthetic pleasure and moral inspection he had unveiled for them, to delight and to instruct. The "aesthetic" distance he thus achieves measures the extent to which he must defend himself from the possibility of responding to her as a human presence. She is as it were an exemplary picture, a monitory emblem labelled "feminine fraud." Only a fool would take her for the real thing. The play here imagines Leontes' aesthetics as a defense against his psychology, against a deeper commitment or a more carnal knowledge. And as usual, wrapped up in his fulminations, Leontes lets a truth slip "out" which he must either ignore or repudiate. Here the neatly chiastic form of the passage—his calumny coming between him and his wife—telegraphs

the "insideness" of this truth to Leontes, around which he buttresses the more extravagantly his theatrical, aestheticizing gestures. Now at last, with a colder vision, Leontes thinks he can recognize the truth of Polixenes' charge that Hermione "cross'd his eyes."

Polixenes' low but distinct note of suspicion against Hermione is also picked up and amplified into the theatrical in Leontes' own recollection of his courtship as a time when "Three crabbed months had soured themselves to death, / Ere I could make thee open thy white hand, / And clap thyself my love" (I.ii.102-4). Sexual longing and the intimation of mortality, a sense of being closed out, a sense Leontes has of forcing Hermione, and also a strange and alienating theatrical dependency—as if he were on a stage awaiting Hermione's applause—all intertwine here. (The last sense prefigures Hermione's scene with Mamillius, where she provides an audience for his performance.) As Leontes watches Hermione now give that same hand to Polixenes, much that was allayed by her speaking then is stirred up again.

If Leontes' experience of childhood and the springing of desire has been as Polixenes describes it, then the relevance of Mamillius to the scene as a potential double of a young Leontes is immediately clear. Leontes himself admits this much, and we need not assume he is fabricating; indeed, *his* sense that he is so hides the deeper truth of a man who keeps his variant self-knowledges precariously concealed from one another:

> Looking on the lines
> Of my boy's face, methoughts I did recoil
> Twenty-three years, and saw myself
>   unbreech'd
> In my green velvet coat, my dagger muzzled,
> Lest it should bite its master, and so prove
> (As ornament oft does) too dangerous.
> How like (methought) I then was to this
>   kernel,
> This squash, this gentleman. Mine honest
>   friend,
> Will you take eggs for money?
> MAMILLIUS No, my lord, I'll fight.
> LEONTES   You will? Why, happy man be's
>   dole!
>
> (I.ii.153-63)

Leontes' identification with his son is quite explicit here, even if the instant of recognition makes him (uncomfortably) "recoil." The figure of "myself unbreech'd" (incidentally revealing Leontes to be younger than we often think: under thirty—Hamlet's age), "unbreech'd"—either "not yet breech'd" or "with breeches removed"—and with his power to hurt in restraint or underdeveloped, is both a regression and an inversion of the adult, revealing by contraries how Leontes now thinks of himself.[18] Particularly worth considering is the dagger: it seems, like a dog, to have a life of its own. In its adult form it is presumably unmuzzled and ready to bite, and its clearly phallic resonance suggests again that sexual maturity and damage go together, though an adult ought to be in control of both. But against whom is it now turned? The fear of the child's dagger biting "its master" might suggest that sexual maturity and desire threaten as much a self-wounding as an aggression directed against others, say against women. Deeper yet, the two potential woundings may be understood as one. Does the perception of desire as a wounding of others or of the self come first? The vision of rape or the vision of castration: can one say which is prior, or do they emerge simultaneously and without hope of disentanglement? Antigonus, a genial chauvinist, later takes his potency and patrimony alike to depend on Hermione's faith. If she is, as Don John would put it, "any man's Hero," then all bloodlines are as good as scrambled, and men might as well castrate themselves ("I had rather glib myself") and find some other means of grasping at the future than generation ("I'll geld 'em all; fourteen they shall not see / To bring false generations"). But Antigonus, with all his huffing and puffing, does not really see what's at stake for Leontes here. What kind of mastery does Leontes imagine himself to have achieved over his own violence, and what relation does that imagined violence have to the reproductive potency that both dagger and son shadow?[19]

Desire and violence are thus very intimately linked. When Hermione "cross'd the eyes" of Leontes, the harmlessness of his muzzled dagger was converted into danger, and it at once bit or breached its master. The "mutually seductive gestures" of the scene between Hermione and Mamillius also gloss the remembered scene of courtship.[20] Leontes' desire to wound Hermione, which she provokes and which is (a response to) his sexual desire, wounds him also by its inhuman aggression, so much against the tenor of a would-be idealization ("O my most sacred lady"). Desire's intimation of mortality and its revelation of himself as an aggressive and stained and staining figure are all alike laid at her door. His resentment and fear of his own violence is (inadequately) cloaked in the intuition of her crime—of her having (yet again) "cross'd his eyes." In response to Winnicott's "question not to be asked" Leontes wishes to reply that his "conception" has come from outside, from her. It was and is all her fault. Hence his central assertion throughout the following scenes, the one intuition that he *must* uphold, is: "It was not *I* who impregnated her." The rest follows from that. ("Yet it was someone *like* me—who better than my brother? Yes, it must have been he: look at him now—disgusting.") It is an implicit rejection of the universe of generation and mortality as one to which Leontes is necessarily bound through his desire.[21] Leontes thinks to stand away from the world of generation and regard it as an object of contemplation, of lessons,

even perhaps of beauty, but as fundamentally remote from him. Hence his intense frustration in Act II at his inability to find the "peace" which ought to come with his sequestration.

Such considerations can help us find our way through one of the most deeply obscure passages in Shakespeare, during the course of which Leontes tries to unfold to himself (or fold up in himself) his sense of what is happening to him:

> Can thy dam?—may't be?—
> Affection! Thy intention stabs the centre!
> Thou dost make possible things not so held,
> Communicat'st with dreams (how can this be?),
> With what's unreal thou co-active art,
> And fellow'st nothing. Then 'tis very credent
> Thou may'st conjoin with something, and thou
>   dost
> (And that beyond commission) and I find it
> (And that to the infection of my brains,
> And hardening of my brows).
>
> (I.ii.137-46)

The dark stuttering that gives way to a hectic rhythm here suggests a deep disturbance that moves many ways at once. Leontes seems to be talking at once about perception, imagination, and sexual desire, uncertain where to locate or how to feel any of them: each bleeds over into the next. "Affection!" is a cry that refuses to settle even into clear rhetoric: is it noun? verb? apostrophe? diagnosis? accusation? Is it her emotion or his? Whose center does it stab, even supposing it *is* the referent of the following pronoun? It is at least the cry of itself as it wounds Leontes, as through Leontes it wounds Hermione with its/his unmuzzled dagger. "Thy intention" is equally difficult: as though an emotion could have one—and if it can, there is a sense of Leontes as possessed by some force with its own inscrutable, perhaps malevolent, designs. Is this perhaps a "tenting in" that stabs at some wound in the—heart? genitals? Some such quasi-etymology seems implied. But which way are affection and intention moving: towards or away from Leontes? "Affection" is somehow transformed into "infection," combated as an invader.

Any commentary on these lines threatens to reproduce their own turbulent movement, as the critic's imagination becomes "co-active" and joins in the act of reading Leontes' sense of being pushed around by obscure implicating forces. The same applies to the spectator, for whom the actor's expression and movement may both clarify and complicate.[22] What the lines uncover or create or "fellow"—in a manner at once poetic and sexual—is an indeterminate and alarming hermeneutic plasticity which mimes a vertigo within or surrounding Leontes, where ambivalent cross-currents of attraction and repulsion coincide. All we can really count on is Leontes' sense that he has come across (but does he "find" or create it?) something that causes "infection" and "hardening"—terms that suggest at once groin and head, in a play that inquires how these two sites of knowledge are related. The very non-specificity of Leontes' first suspicious remark becomes important here: "Too hot, too hot! / To mingle friendship far is mingling bloods" (I.ii.108-9). Though the coldness of his irony bespeaks adult control and self-observation, this is rather vague as the opening gambit of a specific jealousy. It sounds more like a horror at sexuality in general as contamination or overheating than at adultery in particular: the horror and disgust a child might express at discovering the truth (which so often seems like a bad joke) about its sexual origins. Just who is it that is (or was) "too hot"? And when? He and Hermione have just recalled their courtship and the "clapping" that concluded it. Only slowly does the particular accusation Leontes wants emerge, and it might as easily be a displacement resisting his own implication in acts of "mingling bloods," either as producer or as product. The play undertakes a curious "layering" of occasions from its beginning, insistently citing the kings' boyhood, their courtships, their progeny, and introducing an immediate image of the latter in Mamillius. The associative plasticity of Shakespeare's rhetoric at such moments invites us to see how many of these "stages" are caught up and addressed through the ongoing work of Leontes' fantasy.

Leontes' attitude to Mamillius throughout this "primal scene" of suspicion oscillates, not surprisingly, between identification and rejection: he hugs him ("Sweet villain! / Most dear'st! my collop!") and he spurns him ("Go play, boy, play."). His search of his son's face for signs of himself works not only in the obvious way to test and confirm paternity, but more deeply to evoke self-recognition ("yet were it true / To say this boy were like me")—and he finds himself there, not only in the nose which "they say . . . is a copy out of mine," but also in the "smutch" on the nose: the boy is sullied, as he has been (but when?), sinking both suddenly and gradually "Inch thick, knee-deep, o'er head and ears." He treats his son with a kind of indulgent contempt, as if embarrassed at his own affection: the boy is a "kernel," a "squash," but also "mine honest friend" who will show how his manly spirit is being "higher rear'd" by offering to "fight," perhaps to fight him.[23] Yet he is no sooner alone with him than he sends him away in disdain, as though the thought of any relationship were greatly to his distaste. Marking this ambivalence is his use of the word "honest" ("Go play, Mamillius, thou'rt an honest man," I.ii.211), which has the ring at once of Iago on Cassio and, more oddly, of Othello on Iago. That Leontes is his own Iago is a commonplace, but it comes as more of a shock to hear him making his son one too.

Leontes' search for connection to his son thus gives him both less and more than he desires: less in that it

does not seem satisfactorily to still the doubts and intimations that prompted it in the first place, more in that it revives in him thoughts and modes of thought long thought overcome or put aside—thoughts that re-emerge from the strange amalgam of childhood, friendship, rivalry, and courtship that the scene anneals. This "complex" of thought and feeling is further glossed—from a developmental perspective—by the subsequent scene between Mamillius and his mother, where a broadly similar moment of tension is about to be allayed or managed by the introduction of "a winter's tale"—a tale not only *for* winter but also *of* winter, that winter of the heart in which aggression defeats, or worse unmasks, love.

III

The centrality of Mamillius to the unfolding of *The Winter's Tale* will now be clear. But the connection of his childish "play" to Shakespeare's own has still not been fully explored. Play is what we see him doing, and what most explicitly links him to his parents in Leontes' savagely punning formulation: "Go play, boy, play. Thy mother plays, and I / Play too" (I.ii.187-8). Childish recreation, female sexuality, and male self-consciousness are yoked together in this triad, and allude in turn to the Shakespearean stage that represents them all. Before we reach the metadramatic proper, however, and the relation of Leontes' theatre of cruelty to Shakespeare's, we need first to face the question of Mamillius' play as child's play. Again, it is the emergence of Mamillius' play-story as the name also for Shakespeare's play-story (augmented into *the* winter's tale) that we are looking to explain.

There is no doubt that Shakespeare's play is interested from the outset in the question of "development," that is, as an aspect of time, and that the task of "development"—as we now speak of "childhood development"—is especially focused in Mamillius. Shakespeare seems as aware as any modern psychologist of the implications of "play" in this sense. Leontes also knows, though he uses the knowledge dismissively, that what children characteristically do, and must do as part of the business of becoming adults, is "play." But the concern with time and what it requires also goes deeper. It is the opening subject of the play. In the first scene, Archidamus and Camillo trace both the occasion of their speech and its urgent sense of economic and social indebtednesses to an earlier time when the recent difficult and attornied negotiations now perhaps becoming a burden—were part of a simpler structure. The large register of economic language in the play noted by Cavell—all the talk of debt, payment, gift, redress, revenge, just desert, and so forth—emerges from a need to confront and reconcile differences that emerge developmentally as gaps, branches, partings, and "vasts."[24] What one party owes to another—that is, the difference between them and what to do about it (and among others what to do or say about *sexual* difference)—is an almost ubiquitous concern. Difference is the topic of the opening remark of the play, and its implications as debt are disputed in a courtly manner between Archidamus and Camillo throughout the first scene:

> ARCHIDAMUS If you shall chance, Camillo, to visit Bohemia on the like occasion whereon my services are now on foot, you shall see (as I have said) great difference betwixt our Bohemia and your Sicilia.
>
> CAMILLO I think, this coming summer, the King of Sicilia means to pay Bohemia the visitation which he justly owes him.
>
> ARCHIDAMUS Wherein our entertainment shall shame us: we will be justified in our loves; for indeed—
>
> CAMILLO Beseech you—
>
> ARCHIDAMUS Verily, I speak it in the freedom of my knowledge: we cannot with such magnificence—in so rare—I know not what to say—We will give you sleepy drinks, that your senses (unintelligent of our insufficience) may, though they cannot praise us, as little accuse us.
>
> CAMILLO You pay a great deal too dear for what's given freely.
>
> (I.i.1-18)

Archidamus' sense of "difference" between their two countries here concerns less their societies or landscapes than their resources for discharging the great debt of hospitality. Insofar as the kings take their names from their countries, this also suggests a network of obligation between the friends (one also expressed by Polixenes at the opening of the next scene). Camillo's denial of the obligation does not relieve Archidamus of his sense of an invidious and unbridgeable "difference" which will only be overcome by some subterfuge—whether "sleepy drinks" or "cross'd eyes." Camillo in reply begins himself to chafe, and denies the need to feel any burden of "insufficiency" by explaining the essential unity of the two kings from childhood friendship, a unity which has maintained its perfectly equilibrated economy of love almost by miracle. Within such a relationship there cannot be any question of a difference that can "count," of any "too much." Yet the strain of this mutual unity appears in a sense of the gigantic effort now expended to sustain it:

> CAMILLO Sicilia cannot show himself overkind to Bohemia. They were trained together in their childhoods; and there rooted betwixt them then such an affection, which cannot choose but branch now. Since their more mature dignities and royal necessities made separation of their society, their encounters (though not personal) have been royally attorney'd with interchange of gifts, letters, loving embassies, that they have seem'd to

be together, though absent; shook hands, as over a vast; and embrac'd, as it were, from the ends of oppos'd winds. The heavens continue their loves!

(I.i.21-32)

Camillo's concluding prayer almost suggests that something more than human will be required to maintain this stance. An immense quantity of material and social energy is being expended to "fill up" (as Polixenes will say) and hence in some sense to deny what is to all others a very palpable sundering. The flaw, as Camillo expresses it, lies in the inevitable changes of "development," of young trees "trained" together (are there two or one?), their roots intermixed but growing only to "branch." This suggests that development itself—the organic processes of life—necessitates the unraveling of primary unities into difference and separation, and that this unraveling can be traumatic, and hence generate resistance. Like Hegel's bud that contains in dialectic both the stem and the flower, time here is the engine of an unfolding that both flourishes and severs—two senses in which "affection" may "branch." Leontes and Polixenes strain ever more energetically to preserve a superseded version of their relation. And perhaps the strain is beginning to tell. It is precisely at this point that Archidamus first refers to Mamillius.

If the language of debt, gap, gulf, vast—and also "part"—emerges from this concern with ineluctable development and the management of its transforming consequences, the young Prince's task in relation to his parents—his play that is an attempt to cope with change within himself and his family—once more becomes a central focus of the tale. Change, ambivalence, the presence of contrary states of being or feeling in developmental dialectic with one another: how are these to be accommodated, processed, and represented by and to the ongoing self that mediates them? Mamillius' "sad tale . . . for winter" is, we saw, an attempt to do just this, and the play takes it appropriately as a model for its own processes of adjustment and symbolization. If we understand the child's play of the ghost story to be a way of responding to his developing ambivalences at once about his parents and about his feelings towards them, Shakespeare's play will also be understood as a tale told to mediate a complex ambivalence, to respond to a developmental pressure by acting on it symbolically through the control and disposition of the energies of narrative. But what ambivalence and pressure are at issue?

The answer is surely that they are, at least in part, Leontes' sexual paranoia and hysteria, and this returns us to the relation between Mamillius as "player" and Leontes' remark that "thy mother plays and I / Play too, but so disgraced a part, whose issue / Will hiss me to my grave" (I.i.187-9). If we understand Leontes not only to be speaking of "a part" that he "plays" here in some diabolical theatre (to that implication we will return), but also to be engaged in "play" like that of Mamillius in thus rubbing the quat of his desire into a wound of delusive jealousy, what do we imply that he is doing? Precisely that his jealousy is a narrative structure with its own logic and progress under his control which covers, manages, and substitutes for something else. Leontes almost admits this very connection between his imaginings and those of child's play in a moment of outraged self-justification:

> No; if I mistake
> In those foundations which I build upon,
> The centre is not big enough to bear
> A schoolboy's top. Away with her to prison!
>   (II.i.100-3)

The "centre" here seems moreover to refer back obscurely to that earlier "centre" stabbed by affection at the heart of his dark feeling. Both Leontes' jealousy and Shakespeare's play provide an "intermediate area"— and they provide it in response to the same fundamental fact or fantasy: male terror at the nature and implications of sexual desire.

Leontes' behavior invites us to see him as an hysteric terrified of his own capacity and wish to inflict the aggressive pain of his sexuality on the female. So terrified in fact that, "deciding" such an inhuman (as he sees it) impulse can hardly come from himself, he "prefers" to arrange it or act it out as a fantastic scenario of *her* guilt and his justice.[25] Leontes gives himself a sleepy drink to avoid knowledge of his own "insufficience"—hence the link between his spider-poisoned cup and Archidamus' joke.[26] This allows him the vicarious and secret pleasure of acting on his aggression even while denying it, in fact while outwardly justifying it as Hermione's fault even against his own more secret "knowledge" of the untruth of this charge. Hence Leontes' extraordinary and quite uncanny tendency all through these early acts to speak directly about his situation and yet not hear himself. Over and over again, in breathtaking acts of "unsight," he shouts out the truth: "Your actions are my dreams. / You had a bastard by Polixenes, / And I but dream'd it" (III.ii.82-4).[27]

His bitter but exquisite announcement that "I play too" is therefore in part an acknowledgment of the constructing and manipulating aspect of his suspicion, of its aspects at once active and passive, exactly corresponding to his deep doubts about his sexuality— whether it is more properly "his" or something that "comes upon" him from outside, from Hermione. This split in the origin of his desire for "play" explains the sudden and overwhelming irruption of a theatrical consciousness into Leontes' world and language at just this point. As desire is both "his" and "not his," so also Leontes sees himself as both ruler and instru-

ment, both on stage and remote manipulator/observer of the spectacle, at once (anti-)hero and playwright.

Leontes casts himself as either villain or dupe (or both) with "so disgraced a part / Whose issue will hiss me to my grave"—fatherhood becomes a demeaning, secondary role. His theatricalized consciousness even begins to bleed male suspicion out into the audience in an attempt to infect others in its own defense. The effect on an audience can be very disturbing indeed, the more so as it is difficult to shrug off:

> There have been
> (Or I am much deceiv'd) cuckolds ere now,
> And many a man there is (even at this
>   present,
> Now, while I speak this) holds his wife by th'
>   arm,
> That little thinks she has been sluic'd in's
>   absence,
> And his pond fish'd by his next neighbour.
>   (I.ii.190-5)

This is equal parts disgust at female sexuality and comfort—even exultation—at the community of sufferers. The "it" to which the speech insistently returns is also presumably Leontes' way of referring to, without explicitly examining, the surging source of this kind of thought in a sort of primal "itness" at once of perception and feeling, his and not his. Metatheatricality is just one way of showing Leontes as half-aware of, intervening in, several levels of manipulation from this point on.

As playwright and supervisor, Leontes can assign roles himself, can arrange events to fit his fancy. This is a way to "solidify" perception by giving it at last reliable and external objects, everting it from the darker and more terrible contemplation of his own self-division: it distances comfortingly into a stance of spectation, erects a boundary between the play and audience along which a judicial and policing action can be staged. Yet that same staging must at the same time go unacknowledged, lest the spectator discover himself all along as the secret author of the piece, and therefore as implicated in its fantastic elaboration. Leontes continues to speak of himself at once as plotter and plotted against: "There is a plot against my life, my crown; / All's true that is mistrusted" (II.i.47-8) but "I am angling now, / Though you perceive me not how I give line" (I.ii.180-1) and

> the harlot king
> Is quite beyond mine arm, out of the blank
> And level of my brain, plot-proof; but she
> I can hook to me—say that she were gone. . . .
>   (II.iii.4-7)

Leontes creates spectacles of Hermione ("You, my lords, / Look on her, mark her well") to keep her at arms' length, yet at the same time to control her, "hook her" to him in a terrible parody of an embrace. The trial he stages, as he says, to "openly / Proceed in justice" against one "too much belov'd" is a theatrical fiction already plotted out by him, "devis'd / And play'd to take spectators" (III.ii.36-7) as Hermione knowingly phrases it. The "flatness" of her misery, which she wishes her father could behold "with eyes of pity, not revenge" (III.ii.120-3), is the flatness of cardboard characters devised by an amateur and melodramatic imagination. And in the end the king's own sense of being trapped in a play not of his making, of being a foolish and infuriating theatrical spectacle, is part and parcel of his suspicion of his own fantasy: the only way to cast out his doubt is to make of it a finished device he can then stand aside from. Again, the impulse towards the aesthetic, towards the perception of a definite "shape" for judgment, defends against the inchoate threat of the psychological, with its implication of implication. Reading defends against being read. "Play out the play," cries Leontes, "I have much to say in the behalf of that Leontes!"

Leontes' imaginings are therefore a "theatre of cruelty" not only in that they are cruel, but also in Artaud's sense that that same cruelty is intended to be cathartic in some way—to purge passions and representations Leontes can neither disown nor acknowledge. Leontes himself speaks of prosecuting Hermione "to the guilt or the purgation" (III.ii.7), but it might as well have suited his purpose to say "the guilt *and* the purgation" since enforcing the one will accomplish, for him, the other. The courtroom drama is one devised to cover and deflect a deeper scenario of intertwined violence and desire which he cannot accept either as "his own or not his own." Unable to intuit the desire without the violence, he wishes to expropriate both. Yet this is not only or wholly a vicious strategy if we accept that an important reason why Leontes cannot accept his desire is that he finds its implications of violence towards its object at some level morally and humanly repulsive. Leontes' paranoia is scarcely an advance over Mamillius' suicide, yet it is rooted in the same impulse to refuse violence. Perhaps this sense that Leontes has the right problem but the wrong solution goes some way to explaining why the play in the end wants to recover him.[28] He has seen the spider all right—but the appropriate thing to do is to find the antidote, not smash the goblet.

IV

That versions of theatre seem to multiply in the middle acts of the play is only one way of drawing our attention to the stakes *for* theatre once Leontes has begun his pageant of calumny. *The Winter's Tale* incorporates a kind of "career in review" of the manifold dramatic modes in which Shakespeare has worked over the years. In the present case, our revulsion at the "Leontine" dramaturgy of paranoia and scandal threat-

ens to turn itself backwards upon Shakespearean tragedy and expose it as no more than a vast and incomparably more sophisticated (but not therefore less impugnable) version of the same thing. *Hamlet, Othello, King Lear, Macbeth, Coriolanus*—all those delirious plays of female-blaming parade themselves, unwittingly indicted by Leontes' own desperately compensatory rage. Is *this* what has been at stake through those works, *The Winter's Tale* prompts us to ask? What fantasy were those plays all along managing and concealing that this play seeks at last to expose, confront, and, if possible, undo? Is the choice of Mamillius' "winter's tale" as the title of this play merely a way of denying the more apposite simulacrum in Leontes' forensic melodrama?[29] That Shakespeare should represent man's sexual impulses as a source of hysterical terror and self-alienation to men themselves is one thing. That he should go on to see this terror as hysterically refused and converted into an animus against generation in general and women in particular, and then link this gesture to the modes of his own poetic and dramatic work, suggests great depth of self-reflection.

But Leontes' theatre is not the only one made available to us, and does not exhaust the range of Shakespeare's theatrical fictions. Alternative theatres or versions of theatre multiply throughout *The Winter's Tale,* according to the developmental principle of dialectical "branching" announced by Camillo: no one theatre will serve all consciousnesses or states of mind.[30] Even as Leontes speeds on in his theatre of blame towards an inevitable appointment with the death he must refuse to acknowledge in his own desires, his messengers, Cleomenes and Dion, tell us of another spectacle and voice, and another, if rarer, auditorium. Themselves "theorists" of a certain kind of knowledge, they are also "theatrists" of certainty in knowledge—a certainty guaranteed for us by the impact they record as audience of its impress on them.[31] If Shakespeare cannot have us meet the gods directly (as he tried in *Pericles* and *Cymbeline*), he can at least suggest what an audience who felt they had might be moved to say:

> DION   . . . O, the sacrifice!
> How ceremonious, solemn, and unearthly
> It was i' th' off'ring!
> CLEOMENES   But of all, the burst
> And the ear-deaf'ning voice o' th' oracle,
> Kin to Jove's thunder, so surpris'd my sense,
> That I was nothing.
>
>   (III.i.6-11)

Much of the thematic vocabulary of wonder sketched out in Chapter One appears here: the appeals to eye and ear as distinct portals of perception, the sense of imminent damage which goes hand in hand with a rush to knowledge, the apocalyptic thrust, the ambush by a superior force, all play their part in sketching in the image of a "theatre of total conversion" in which selves and their knowledges are battered and reconstituted by a divine afflatus to which they willingly accede. Yet for us this remains an echo only, an ideal perhaps of a kind of drama never to be for us, since a modern stage at least could not present it without a self-consciousness that would inevitably at some point keep us at a distance. The play's presentation of such an experience through Cleomenes and Dion offers us a limit case at once of an absolute knowledge and an absolute theatre—a theatre whose powers of skepticism have been abolished by *force majeure,* and which has therefore abolished itself as theatre. This is what principally we take to guarantee that what Apollo says—with unusual clarity for an oracle—is a truth beyond the theatre of its saying.[32]

Along with the Apollonian (anti-)theatre of absolute knowledge there is also the gelid theatre of remorse that emerges under Paulina's direction after Hermione's death. This theatre refuses all impulse of development: it remains stuck in a rocky and willed wilderness of abjection whose very unflinching severity is a punitive allegory of the stoniness of heart that brought it into being. It is also a futile performance since it cannot win the attention of the very audience it seeks:

> PAULINA   . . . therefore betake thee
> To nothing but despair. A thousand knees,
> Ten thousand years together, naked, fasting,
> Upon a barren mountain, and still winter
> In storm perpetual, could not move the gods
> To look that way thou wert.
>
>   (III.ii.209-14)

This is a ghost-theatre, the permanent ossification of remorse into the posture forecast for it by Mamillius in the story of the churchyard man. Yet by being here lived instead of told, it cannot be escaped: it is a prison lacking a principle of release, of dénouement. Since the proper audience (the gods? Hermione?) is never present, it cannot fulfill itself, cannot be forgiven. It is damned to perpetual repetition: "Once a day I'll visit / The chapel where they lie, and tears shed there / Shall be my recreation" (III.ii.238-40), where the latter is also "re-creation." There is no other principle of development but this one of obsessive commemoration: any other gesture, as we are informed in Act V, is horribly shadowed by the repetitive vengefulness of its own sense of self-wrong in wronging others:

> LEONTES   Whilest I remember
> Her and her virtues, I cannot forget
> My blemishes in them, and so still think of
> The wrong I did myself; which was so much
> That heirless it hath made my kingdom, and
> Destroy'd the sweet'st companion that e'er
>   man
> Bred his hopes out of.
>
>   (V.i.6-12)

There is no way out of such a structure. It must repeat in an older, colder key that same conjugation of Hermione's virtue and breeding, between which came Leontes' "blemishes" that killed her. Were it not for what Paulina knows in secret, she and Leontes would torment each other forever with images of Hermione's "sainted spirit," conjuring it to "Again possess her corpse, and on this stage / (Where we offenders now) appear soul-vexed" (V.i.57-9). Marriage in such a theatre is still and always linked to murder.[33] What now holds Leontes is only a moralized abreaction from his earlier contradictory intuitions about desire—this has not gone beyond them, it merely seeks to pay their price.

V

I have attempted to locate the origins of theatricality in the first half of *The Winter's Tale* in the difficult meditations of the self on its desires and in its attempts to shape responses to its intuitions about the meaning of those desires. *The Winter's Tale* is hardly exceptional among Shakespeare's plays in focusing attention on how human life copes with time and the changes it forces. Yet it does insist with unusual strength on the psychic difficulty of change, on the potential disasters that can occur. By this late stage in his career, Shakespeare's dramatic language has become an instrument subtle and searching enough to register not only the surface gestures of a character, but also the secret affections or intentions that inform those gestures. The imagination has become a layered thing, often obscure to itself, inventing its purposes moment by moment at several levels. Characters at times hardly hear what they say, so deeply can they become self-enchanted. In order to read such a language, it is sometimes necessary to extrapolate or extend an obscure inkling into an entire line of thought. In doing so, I have been employing a mode of discussion familiar to modern psychoanalysis, but I have preferred not to use the more technical vocabulary and, in particular, the shaping fantasies of that mode of interpretation. This is because it seems to me these modern fictions conceal at least as much about the pattern of Shakespearean psychology as they reveal. It is by no means certain that the mythological narratives that recent depth psychology has constructed will correspond to the inner mythography of a Shakespearean fiction. For that to be the case, one would have to posit either a universal structure not only of feeling but also of mythic transcription of that feeling, or a specific inheritance in psychoanalysis from Shakespeare (perhaps the most likely), or some common source for both.[34] That Shakespeare was a writer interested in the life and permutations of deeper fantasy, and in the possibility of curative action where fantasy was distorting personality, we have no reason to doubt. But the more pressing question for a full account of Shakespeare's psychology is the one not asked by most modern psychoanalytic critics: what are the particular mythological or narrative patterns subtending Shakespearean dramatic fictions, on which the fictions themselves are built and which they reflect? From what experience of the persistence of fantasies or fictional structures in the imagination did Shakespeare himself develop, without the benefit of modern psychology, his particular sense of their "layering," their struggle for expression, and their potential for change?

In the readings of *The Comedy of Errors* and *Pericles,* I attempted to demonstrate the workings of a dynamic of self-recognition in Shakespeare's drama, by which the poetic underpinnings of the plays are eventually brought to light and transformed. It is a curious fact about these structures that a surface influence or indebtedness often conceals a deeper one which emerges only during the course of the action. Thus the elaborately Plautine surface action of *Errors* converts itself eventually into a Biblical-Ovidian amalgam that shapes an early version of a peculiarly Shakespearean poetics I have called "incarnational." And in *Pericles,* an elaborately acknowledged indebtedness to Gower also overlies and eventually cedes to an awareness of underlying Ovidian myths—in particular those of Niobe and Narcissus. *The Winter's Tale* represents Shakespeare's fullest working-out of this pattern, and in it at last the presence of latent narrative substructures shaping action beneath acknowledged schemata is not only the method of the action but also one of its subjects. Mamillius' small tale already points us in this direction insofar as it shows surface narrative as an occasion for confronting and controlling less easily acknowledged kinds of feeling and knowing. So we are returned once more to Shakespeare's choice of title: at the level of the Shakespearean imagination what foundational myth is being confronted and metamorphosed anew by the action of dramatic composition?

Jonathan Bate's recent work on the complex relations between Shakespeare and Ovid notes of the opening act of *The Winter's Tale* that it "does not contain a single mythological reference. Everything seems to come from within Leontes' brittle psyche, nothing from the gods."[35] In fact the whole of the early part of the play having to do with Leontes is devoid of mythological or mythographic reference until very late, as though the king's "brittle psyche" had swept all clear. Yet this very brittleness and surface absence may point to a mastering myth within: there is no one so keen not to acknowledge the presence of a myth as he who is its captive. Following a suggestion variously put forward by both Stanley Cavell and Ruth Nevo, that Shakespeare's composition often moves, in Nevo's phrase, "backwards through a retrospective succession of partial recognition scenes," we should expect the relevant latency to emerge into view later in the play.[36] Bate's work points to one possible answer in his study of Perdita, the figure the play positions most forcefully opposite the dark king who governs its secret and in-

terior undertale, and who will be eventually the corrective to his terrors. Perdita's chief mythological association in the play, as she herself announces, is with Proserpina. What Leontes throughout the opening action may be both resisting and, by the very hysterical intensity of his resistance, confirming, is the intuition of male desire as capture by death, couched in the archaic tale of the rape of Ceres' daughter.[37]

E. A. J. Honigmann proposed some time ago that Ovid's tale and Golding's translation of it in particular provide a "secondary source" for the play, and showed how traces of Golding have worked themselves back into the play in several places.[38] It is possible to go further than these verbal traces, however, if one connects the tale of Proserpina's abduction by the King of Death, a terrible figure for all his imperial dignity, with Leontes' own dark intuition of the damage lurking in sexuality. There is some evidence that the myth (with that of Narcissus, one of Shakespeare's deepest purchases from Ovid) pervades the whole play, often in unexpected places. Leontes himself directly echoes Golding's Jove in calling his child a "collop" of himself, and the whole Ovidian episode provides a mythic background for the nomination of "winter" as the mode of the play's opening, as well as for its location in Sicily, where the rape took place.[39] As far back as *A Midsummer Night's Dream,* the passage in which Ceres curses the ground of Sicily and strips it of fertility had haunted Shakespeare's imagination.[40] Now that act of abomination, and the violence of male desire that underlay it and whose inner deathliness it responds to, returns as the deeper inkling of Leontes' fantasy, and turns the play he heads from a tale "for" or "about" winter into *"The" Winter's Tale,* the tale of Winter in its mythic origin, its sexual meaning, and its psychological inflection.

In Ovid's tale, initiation into sexual life for Proserpina is the rush into a darkness never to be thrown off, a snatching by and into the embrace of a frozen shadow. Dis' sexual desire is male sexual voraciousness *as death,* deriving from and inflicting death. In Ovid, its violence is figured in the blow of the "sceptrum regale" that opens a passage for Dis through the lacerated earth into the underworld.[41] This may be the original blow that "stabs the center." In resisting the image of himself as Dis, Leontes resists all involvement in the sexual. Leontes will be Jove, judging from a distance, putting it all in order, righting the wrong his brother Dis/Polixenes has done. Paulina calls on him at last, like Ceres to Jove, to "Look down / And see what death is doing" (III.ii.148-9), to pretend no longer to the immortality of the Olympian master, but to acknowledge himself at last as the very figure of Death, the bringer of death to his wife and child. Terribly, Leontes awakes and finds it true. The "man who dwelt by a churchyard" was the man who saw himself as Dis. For him sexual desire and death have secretly shared a certain hardness, which is also that of win-ter—*rigor mortis* and *rigor sexualis* have been coactive.

Other aspects of the play seem likewise to root in Ovid's tale. What happens to Hermione, deprived of her children by death and abduction, is given in what happened to Ceres when she heard at last where Proserpina had been taken: "Hir mother stoode as stark as stone, when she these newes did heare, / And long she was like one that in another world had beene" (632-3). Goddesses recover more quickly than humans, and it takes Ceres much less than sixteen years to put aside "hir great amazednesse" (634). But when she does, her announcement is strikingly similar to the one with which Paulina undoes Hermione's stony captivity: "Behold our daughter whome I sought so long is found at last" (643).[42]

Even the fearful and silly bear may be an Ovidian/ Leontine bear, a final emblematic product of the angry, wintry world. If he is hungry (as the Clown suggests) it may be because he has just endured—and woken from—his winter sleep. There is a strange verbal anticipation in some of Leontes' remarks that seems to conjure up the bear before his time, lurking especially within the more violent of his outbursts: "Bear the boy hence" (II.i.59); "the centre is not big enough to bear / A schoolboy's top" (II.i.102-3); "It is but weakness / To bear the matter thus" (II.iii.2-3) or "and that thou bear it / To some remote and desert place" (II.iii.175-6). This last puts the burden of bearishness on Antigonus immediately in advance of his fatal encounter.[43]

So much for the underworld of Leontes' fantasy. But a "winter's tale" is also a story told *against* the apparent devastation that surrounds: it wants to shield us from the storm of aggression, to make it bearable, to explain, protect, and deliver us from winter's intimation of universal death. Shakespeare's play, that is, may also be a tale *against* male sexual violence, not merely opposing it, but attempting to recognize and incorporate it into a larger pattern in order to rewrite or control it, as the tale by the fire offers to deliver us from the regime that howls outside of and for our death. Shakespeare's drama would then speak of Leontes' enchantment by the vision of death only eventually to cure both him and itself of captivity to that vision, a captivity once embraced as tragedy. In enacting the undoing of Leontes' fantasies, the play also works through its own relation both to Shakespearean tragedy and, even deeper, to Ovidian fictions of metamorphosis. The bear is the emblem and commencement of a general unloosing both of narrative stringency and of tragic emotion insofar as its appearance must always be, for the audience, a moment of intense self-consciousness coupled with laughter—a laughter that, as Andrew Gurr has pointed out, looses the audience by its very staginess from too literal-minded and, following Barthes, "hysterical" a bondage to tragic fiction. Gurr comments that the bear "exploits [the] base level,

the hysterical reaction, and then pushes the level of audience response higher up the scale by the blatant challenge to credulity which the bear offers," and Nevill Coghill calls the bear, in its staginess "a kind of hinge . . . passing from tears to laughter."[44]

In the task of "unbinding" that the second half of the play undertakes. Perdita is the crucial figure. Where the disguised Florizel hints at a repetition of the pattern of metamorphosis and sexual betrayal, Perdita counters with a wish to go back to the play's primal deep moment of disaster and undo it, to recoup Proserpina's flowers at the very moment of their loss and by so doing bring what was dead back to life. This will be her function at the level of the family story also: she is a general solvent of overgrown rigidities.

VI

From the moment of her appearance. Perdita exhibits a profound suspicion of the various designs and theatricalities thrust upon her. Her response to Florizel's opening accolade to her "unusual weeds" that "to each part of you / Does give a life" (IV.i.1-2) is that these are "extremes" in which she has been "pranked up." In part these fears are inflected socially and address the distance between aristocrat and shepherdess, yet at the same time social distance also figures an anxiety about female vulnerability to male predation, also felt as a discrepancy in power. Perdita's response to Florizel's citation of Olympian precedents for his love, even with his added promise that "my desires / Run not before mine honor, nor my lusts / Burn hotter than my faith" (IV.iv.33-5), is distinctly skeptical:

> PERDITA   O but, sir,
> Your resolution cannot hold when 'tis
> Oppos'd (as it must be) by th' power of the
>   King.
> One of these two must be necessities,
> Which then will speak, that you must change
>   this purpose,
> Or I my life.
>   (IV.iv.35-40)

The last lines here may as easily intimate that the change will be in Perdita's life as a virgin as in her life as shepherdess, or that Florizel's changed "purpose" will be his protestation of honor. Florizel himself picks up the latter hint when he calls these "forc'd thoughts."

The scene of the presentation of flowers that follows has been commented on many times, but it is important to note that during its course Perdita at last refers directly to the myth of Proserpina I believe underpins so much of the play. Its open citation occurs here because now at last the implications of the myth are being directly confronted and resisted. Despite her doubts about the intentions inside male theatrical fictions such as

Florizel's, Perdita publicly declares herself committed
to active sexual expression, and to Florizel. Of all
Shakespeare's young women, save perhaps Juliet, she
is the most open in welcoming the biological life of
the sexual body. But in order to assert this rightness of
sexuality, she must somehow confront and defeat the
pervasive connection between desire and death which
has so far dominated the play.

For even as the play celebrates Perdita in the scene, it
also hedges its account of her beauty with a male death-
gaze whose implications we should by now be alive to.
Perhaps jogged by her clearly expressed desire to have
Florizel "breed by" her, together with her citation of
the marigold "that goes to bed wi' th' sun, / And with
him rises weeping" (IV.iv.105-6), Camillo's response
to Perdita's beauty has wintry undertones that she
quickly pinpoints and laughs away:

> CAMILLO I should leave grazing, were I of your
>   flock,
> And only live by gazing.
> PERDITA   Out, alas!
> You'ld be so lean, that blasts of January
> Would blow you through and through.
>
>   (IV.iv.109-12)

Within Camillo's image of himself as "gazing" we may
descry Leontes' use of the aesthetic stance as a way of
resisting human connection. Though Camillo himself
does not see it, his way of putting it "freezes" both
himself and Perdita into the postures of statuary. Perdita
follows up the implications for sexual life of such an
idolatry in order to undo them. She at once turns to
Florizel and her companion shepherdesses "that wear
upon your virgin branches yet / Your maidenheads
growing," and it is to apprehend and gloss the moment of defloration that the thought of Proserpina's
flowers springs up. The lines are famous, but for that
reason often skimmed. For instance, the metrical pause
at the first "daffadil" may well be a way to mark the
difficulty of negotiating imaginatively the very moment of abduction and winter. The mythographic profusion, the sexual personality and reach with which
the flowers are conjured from this hiatus is remarkable, and indexes the intensity of Perdita's wish to
exercise imaginative control over the choice and meaning of sexual surrender:

>   O Proserpina,
> For the flow'rs now, that, frighted, thou let'st
>   fall
> From Dis's waggon! daffadils,
> That come before the swallow dares, and take
> The winds of March with beauty; violets, dim,
> But sweeter than the lids of Juno's eyes,
> Or Cytherea's breath; pale primeroses,
> That die unmarried, ere they can behold
> Bright Phoebus in his strength (a malady

> Most incident to maids); bold oxlips, and
> The crown imperial; lilies of all kinds
> (The flow'r-de-luce being one). O, these I
>   lack,
> To make you garlands of, and my sweet friend,
> To strew him o'er and o'er!
>
>   (IV.iv.116-29)

Lively enjambments, especially of the sexually-charged
"take" and of "behold," give the passage great energy.
The lines are infused with metamorphic and creative
power, growing out of their population by images of
reproductive potency. Jonathan Bate comments elo-
quently of them that:

> the undertow of allusion to the classical gods forces
> us to read this speech mythologically as well as
> naturally. Flowers here have a metamorphic power—
> daffodils can charm the wild winds of March and
> yellow fritillaries can signify royalty. . . . And the
> language itself is metamorphic: "O, these I lack"
> comes as a shock because in the mind's eye the
> flowers have been present. . . . Something similar
> happens with the apostrophe to Proserpina: Perdita is
> saying that she is not like Proserpina, because she
> lacks the flowers, but in realizing the flowers
> linguistically she becomes Proserpina. She has picked
> up what her predecessor dropped when whisked away
> by Dis.[45]

Yet this is not quite so: Perdita becomes not Proserpina,
but the maiden for whom Proserpina's story stands as
a warning—to whom it has *not* happened. The flowers
emblematize what must not be allowed to happen, what
Perdita's strong imaginative response to the energies,
even dangers, of sexuality will war against in the name
of life. It is Florizel, like Leontes before him, who sees
himself as "taken" into death by the profusion of flower-
language, who associates it not with reproduction but
with elegy: "What? like a corse?" Perdita insists that
Florizel's desire will *not* become the portal of death
("icta viam tellus in Tartara"), but will remain forever
the body of his life, the "sceptrum regale" "not to be
buried / But quick and in mine arms." Its only rigor
will be hers willingly to enjoy: "a bank for love to lie
and play on," its death one to be played out "o'er and
o'er" in the dying and rising of sexual love. And suddenly she seems to have overcome Dis, to have the
very flowers she wished for: "Come, take your flow'rs."

Imaginative energy intercoupled with sexual longing
have carried Perdita herself into a strangely metamorphic ambience, which she now registers with some
hesitation as a version of the very theatricality over
which she had earlier hesitated: "Methinks I play as I
have seen them do / In Whitsun pastorals. Sure this
robe of mine / Does change my disposition" (IV.iv.133-
5). Sexual inventiveness, it seems, creates out of its
own—human—energy a correspondent impulse into
fiction and theatre. The insight, over which Perdita is

in doubt, answers more surely than anything so far the rather stiff conversation on "art and nature" with Polixenes that has preceded. Sexuality spins itself a metamorphic theatricality that rushes to keep up with, express, and render for consciousness the developmental urgencies of generative process and time. Perdita's local myth of the flowers of life thus not only provides a dialectical outgrowth of her own and Polixenes' positions from the earlier dialogue on "art" and "nature," it also answers very carefully across the waste of Leontes' tragic nightmare to Mamillius' abortive allegory of his frostbitten desires.

That the moment of Perdita's triumph is full of poetic release for Shakespeare also is suggested by the extraordinary hymn to Perdita that he now finds for Florizel. It has been little noticed how the rhythm of her conjuration is sustained and answered by the drive of his. The interchange is surely motivated by the energies unleashed through Perdita's exorcism of the covering figure of sexual death. Unchained from that dark intimation, Florizel sees Perdita as the miraculously human site of a kind of endlessly mobile self-reproduction he can only apprehend as the charging of each separate moment with the force and sweetness of the whole motion—and vice versa. Perdita seen so is a force never expended and ever renewing, that resists the freezing even of aesthetic celebration. His is a strange outburst, synthesizing a kind of stop-action perception with the sense of a fluid energy and continuity, whose best formula is the abstract and motionless motion of a wave, and whose achieved rhetorical image a chiasmus wrapped around an oxymoron and prolonged into a pun, all instances of a complex tension between motion and rest at once syntactic, semantic, and lexical. It is infinitely stronger than the "grazing/gazing" gambit of old Camillo it recalls, and we can measure in that difference the transformative work done by Perdita's refiguration of desire in between. It is the crowning moment of the scene, and will be answered itself in turn in the final animation of Hermione's statue, also a greatly stilled and moving moment:

FLORIZEL   What you do
Still betters what is done. When you speak,
    sweet
I'ld have you do it ever; when you sing,
I'ld have you buy and sell so; so give alms;
Pray so; and for the ord'ring your affairs,
To sing them too. When you dance, I wish
    you
A wave o' th' sea, that you might ever do
Nothing but that; move still, still so,
And own no other function. Each your doing
(So singular in each particular)
Crowns what you are doing in the present
    deeds,
That all your acts are queens.
                    (IV.iv.135-46)

Aesthetic perception here is in constant dialectic with the vitality of the world. Florizel experiences both a desire to arrest Perdita's movement for contemplation and a counter-desire to give himself over to that movement in its unexpectedness. His formalizing impulse is constantly deferred by the worldward orientation of his love and desire. We are close here to the heart of what *The Winter's Tale* wants to make of the relation between sexuality and fiction as aspects and motives of human activity. The fictions that humans create are energetic responses to the complex and ever-metamorphic motions of desire within them. They take their shifting life in turn from the constant and developing transformations of consciousness in dialectic with what comes to it—both from within and from without. Camillo's opening principle of dialectical "branching" becomes a description of how the production of fiction must answer the needs it is called upon to translate and manage into representation. The slight rhetorical stiffness of the "carnation" dialogue on art and nature that precedes these passages represents the same issue seen more abstractly as a question of the ethics of control. The carefully positioned ironies of dramatic situation between Perdita and Polixenes, so well explored by Rosalie Colie, work in part to frame our detachment from the exchange as a recognizable "topos" or debate.[46] Perdita is suspicious of just this kind of formalizing impulse imposed on the natural object, while Polixenes' sophistical chop-logic seeks to defend the prerogatives of planned intervention. But the central issue as the play has developed it is a slightly different one, less a matter of control than of decorum or correspondence: of what "kind" is the knack that fits a fiction to the need it answers, and how can we defend ourselves and others—as Leontes could not—against our generation of fictions that destroy or deform our needs into postures of sorrow or fatality, that "crush the sides o' th' earth together, / And mar the seeds within." The Bohemian pastoral shapes an answer to this only in the impassioned exchange of mutual fictions of desire between Perdita and Florizel.

VII

Seen in this light, Leontes' jealousy and the deep Ovidian generation of *The Winter's Tale* are intimately related to each other, and both to the small moment with which we began—in which a little boy gropes for a story whose purposes he hardly knows. The connection runs through their common practice of seeing the dynamic mediation of self and world performed via an imaginative structure, a story or fantasy which puts inner and outer fields of perception in touch with each other, sometimes benignly or even in such a way as to rectify or assuage discomfort, but sometimes in disastrous misprision. As Winnicott puts it: "the task of reality-acceptance is never completed, . . . no human being is free from the strain of relating inner and outer reality, and . . . relief from the strain is provided by an intermediate area of experience which is not challenged (arts, religion, etc.)."[47] The case of an aberrant or dangerous fantasy of the kind that Leontes develops, the idea of which runs all through Shakespeare's work, is also described by Winnicott and again related to other modes of imaginative elaboration which we associate with artistic activity:

> Should an adult make claims on us for our acceptance of the objectivity of his subjective phenomena we discern or diagnose madness. If however, the adult can manage to enjoy the personal intermediate area without making claims, then we can acknowledge our own corresponding intermediate areas, and are pleased to find a degree of overlapping, that is to say common experience between members of a group in art or religion or philosophy.[48]

The ease of movement from private to public fantasies here, and the sense of interconnection between danger and necessity in the functioning of the imagination to connect self and world, touch Shakespearean matters closely. In moments like the exchange of mutual imaginative visions between Florizel and Perdita, we see this process vividly at work as a spontaneous upwelling of imaginative apprehensions that feed at once and deeply on the needs of the self and its perceptions of the needs of the other. Florizel needs to be assured that his desire is not death-dealing, Perdita that her transformations are not self-betraying.

Janet Adelman suggests that the pastoral of Bohemia—and Perdita, its dramatic center—are a version of Winnicott's "object that survives" its destruction by the child, therefore the proof to the child's imagination of a universe outside the self that is not subject to the regime of death at the hands of the subject's aggression.[49] This complex of perceptions, I have argued, appears in the play as a doubt about the human value of sexual expression rather than as a problem in infant development *per se,* though it could no doubt be argued that the former is a translated reprise of the latter. For the play, the rural environs of Bohemia are indeed a place of survival. Leontes casts Perdita forth, as he imagines, to "some remote and desert place" (II.iii.176) only to have her return intact from the plenitude of Bohemia—a plenitude as much of fictions as of flowers. In Bohemian pastoral, the abundance of theatrical forms in apposition—songs, dances, masquing, roguery, gods, and satyrs all mixed up—the very length of the scene itself, witness a resiliency and productivity of pleasure that Leontes' absolute regime has shrunk and truncated. Even when the Leontine violence returns in the fearful images of what Polixenes will have done to those who oppose him, Camillo as playwright and Autolycus as survival's ready rogue (for whom "the red blood raigns[50] in the winter's pale") have their ways of outflanking and skewering that severity into a kind of comic impotence. From this point of view the infamous Bohemian "sea-coast" is neither a blunder nor a thumbing of the nose, but an insistence on the transgressive prerogative of the imagination in answering the needs of survival.

From this perspective too, the question of Autolycus' relation to the rest of the play becomes clear: he presents at once the necessary freedom of story to range where it will in order to find its always-variable rightness ("And when I wander here and there / I then do go most right," IV.iii.17-18), and the transgressive or resistive impulse resident within that freedom. He is a rogue always cheered by audiences because they see in him a spirit of their own energetic resistance to darker necessities, a resistance innately part of the impulse to play: Autolycus catches us grinning because in the theatre we are (or wish to be) his counterparts in imaginative ranging. His adoption—or theft—from Ovid is itself openly admitted in his name: poets take what they need and as they must.[51] The prerogatives of fiction are subject to no law except that they must answer the needs that generate them. In Autolycus, as in Perdita though in different registers, we encounter a constant self-revision figuring a Shakespearean account of the temporality of fictions. The business of fiction-making is a never-ending one, endlessly and dialectically entwined with both itself and the need from which it springs to touch and open the world. Inside Shakespeare's play lie the husks of those fictions he has himself consumed or been fertilized by, sedimented in varying layers of acknowledgment and power: Greene, Peele, Ovid. As the occasion of playing transforms, so the medium and content of the play must also develop, in part out of its own history. *The Winter's Tale,* long observed to thematize seasonal transformation and renewal, also proffers that cycle of loss and recovery as the way of its own imaginative genealogy. It is necessary to learn to imagine the absoluteness of neither life nor death in order to enter such a landscape. These are hard lessons, not learned in Leontes, who precipitates out of Polixenes' fantasy of absolute boyhood life a terrible and reactionary image of absolute death, of "nothing."

The openness with which Shakespeare acknowledges his own poetic genealogy through the play is of a piece with his whole understanding of the dynamics of composition as a version of the general dynamics of human life in time. Though the Ovidian fictions that lie inside *The Winter's Tale*—Proserpina, Arachne, Niobe, Autolycus, even Pygmalion—all unfold in *Metamorphoses* as directly or indirectly associated with challenges to the authority of the gods, Shakespeare's own writing in the end does not display such challenge and competition.[52] Harold Bloom has remarked (*Anxiety of Influence,* p. 11) on what he calls Shakespeare's extraordinary ability to "swallow his precursors whole." But perhaps "eating" is less apposite here than "breeding by." It appears from *The Winter's Tale* that his assur-

Claire Jullien as Perdita and Graham Abbey as Florizel in a 1998 Stratford Festival production of The Winter's Tale.

ance, so unlike that of Marlowe or Jonson, springs ultimately from an understanding of human fictions as always in need of transformation, an understanding that absorbs the lessons of metamorphosis and generation not only at the level of bodies, but also at that of fictions.[53] Time has already stripped putative precursors of the necessity they had—from age to age, from reading to reading, they are not what they are. Hence Shakespeare's recurrent insistence, as also in *Pericles,* on the audience's active role in absorbing and recirculating fictions. And hence also perhaps his apparent, and to some puzzling, unconcern about publication, again so unlike Jonson, since his own "works" must in their turn be changed to answer the world they have in part transformed by their participation in it.

The climactic scene of the play's attention to the life of fictions is the final one of Hermione's statue. By now many strands of the play have gathered to make "the statuesque" a topic that combines a number of issues. It is for that reason principally that our consideration of wonder in *The Winter's Tale,* which must

inevitably take the final scene as its central meditation, has had first to traverse the entire play. For whatever energies are released, caught up, opened, or conducted by the ceremonious and ecstatic rhythms of this scene, they have been led there carefully over the long haul. Though the scene celebrates and affirms, as commentators have pointed out, the vivifying and wish-fulfilling powers of theatre, there is a sense in which it also tells us of how at some point the theatre must be given up or relinquished. Through this feeling of "letting go" of theatre, a feeling linked to the other kinds of letting go the scene does—of mourning, of recrimination, of fear—the final moments of *The Winter's Tale* resemble nothing so much as the scene of relinquishment that concludes *The Tempest.*[54] In both plays Shakespeare points to a need to move beyond theatre towards some more direct recognition which will have no need of shadows, even if the latter have been the very media by which the imagination has arrived where it is. The theatre emerges at the end of the play as a homeopathic remedy for itself—but as fantasy and purgation negate one another, so both must accordingly be given up as theatricality, and the world inhabited once more unfantasied—for the time being.[55]

VIII

The sense of undoing, of release, is almost overwhelming in the final scene of *The Winter's Tale*. Imagined most fully in the "depetrification" of the statue, it is also explicitly a verbal process sustained throughout, like saying a spell backwards. There is scarcely a line that does not deliberately tag a counterpart somewhere back in the first part of the play. Cordial for cordial, issue for issue, kiss for kiss, stain for stain, grace for grace, wooing for wooing, warmth for heat: each echo arises to its invocation as a kind of "underword," a ghost word to be laid and replaced by the strength of the scene to which it is summoned. The decision to confront the image of Hermione, and then the further attempt to recover Hermione herself from her being of stone, is a corollary of this process insofar as it reaches "underneath" the structure of likelihoods put in place by the play to the deeper rootedness of its sorrow and rupture, in order to effect an answering repair. At the same time, the scene shapes a gesture of almost direct acknowledgment to the Ovidian material that subtends so much of the earlier action, setting its Ovidian pretexts against one another, so that the myth of Pygmalion's misogyny and its overcoming is made to confront and resolve that of Proserpina's rape, the latter itself a tale of how life and time were split into antithetical halves by an abduction into an underworld realm. As a version of Shakespearean theatre and its vivifying powers, the scene also complements and negates its own internal competitors: Leontes' tragic theatre of calumny, the Bohemian pastoral of the self and its liberties, even the trumpery animal-act of the bear.[56]

This is in short a scene that risks more than perhaps any other in Shakespeare's works: no other play brings the pressure of an entire structure to bear on its conclusion in quite this way. That it succeeds so well with most critics and audiences only makes it the more difficult to account for—since it seems willfully to violate all accepted canons of construction.[57] But then the necessity of risking excess is part of the scene's point also; in this too Shakespeare has a Blake-like energy. The scene has always had powerful and moving encomiasts, but each approach to it enters a risky defile and must carefully work through the turbulent dynamics of a peculiar Scylla and Charybdis: between a credulity that believes too much and a resistance that hardens too fast.

It is in just such a "between" as this that the peculiar and overwhelming effect of the scene develops: within the ambit of powerful transactions between words now and their counterparts then, between the statue and the living body (of both actor and character), between the present fiction and its pressing analogues, between stage and audience. The risk the critic runs is that of the characters—Leontes or Hermione in particular—of negotiating the transition between impression and expression, between silence and speech, between stone and flesh, improperly. The scene is one of general trial and to venture onto its ground is dangerous. Paulina knows this very well, and how failure to negotiate this exchange may rebound disastrously on all. Hence her protestations, her stern protocols and caveats, which must be ours too in approaching the articulation of our wonder at what the scene stirs in us.

Let me begin with a remark of Leonard Barkin's that "Leontes and Hermione are not independent organisms but a pair of Shakespearean twins, two halves of a single system. The husband treats the wife lovelessly, and she becomes a stony lady."[58] This sense of the couple as entwined, even in separation, we might take to be part of the point of having their "keeper" named Paulina, pointing us back to Shakespeare's Pauline sense of marriage as a "making one flesh"—or one stone. There is indeed a deep interdependence between the imperviousness of Leontes earlier in the play and the present immobility of Hermione's statue. But we should consider carefully the multiple resonances of this mutual stoniness. Barkin points to Hermione's petrification as an image of Leontes' coldness (Cavell would say, of his skepticism), and so it is; but it is also possible to see it as a defensive manoeuver in response, and therefore at once an effect or image of what Leontes does and a reply to it. Leontes certainly sees the stone as a moralization of his cruel error, and hence as an image of the connection of their fates: "does not the stone rebuke me / For being more stone than it?" (V.iii.37-8). But for Hermione, the advantage of stone lies in its safety from attack, its impenetrability: within it she can survive, as it were, in hibernation. Hers is the gesture of Galatea discovering—at some later date—the misogyny and distrust of (female) sexuality which led Pygmalion to carve and love her in the first place.[59]

There is a further thought within this dialectical circuit: what if stone were also the fate Leontes had himself imagined to protect Hermione from the brutality and hardness of his desire for her (here we are close to Cavell's discussion of *Othello*)—even perhaps to return that hardness in some way upon him, as the statue is now "piercing to my soul"? If Pygmalion's desire, even as it turned Galatea into a living woman, had turned his love of her to a brutal and implacable hardness, he might have wished to spare her that. Here we glimpse once more Shakespeare's churchyard horror-story of heterosexual desire: that it should make men hard even as it softens women.[60] This would make of Leontes' own venture towards stone in the same scene at once a quest for Hermione's presence and experience and a homeopathic repetition of his own desire, scanning and testing it for residual blockishness and blindness (we recall the danger lurking still in his first response to Perdita, even as a simulacrum of Hermione). His impulses to kiss the statue and to become like the statue would then be counterparts in the scene's tracing of various modes of his relation to the thought of Hermione in him.

Another way of putting this would be to note that the scene undoes the making of Hermione into an object of cool aesthetic interest that we saw characterized one stage of Leontes' relation to her. Indeed it proceeds carefully backwards from the stance of the aesthete with his evaluative and technical gaze through the collapse or absorption of that distance into the more dynamic and interactive relations of the psychological, and finally the erotic. The scene insists with a fair degree of literalness on the absorption of Leontes—and to a lesser extent those around him—towards the mode of being of the statue, their sharing its stillness as a precondition of its coming to share their life. Perdita is observed "standing like stone with thee" and declares she could "stand by, a looker-on" for twenty years; Leontes' sense of the statue's life turns him to the thought of his own death ("Would I were dead but that methinks already—"); when Paulina offers to awake the image, Leontes declares "No foot shall stir," they must "all stand still," and when she moves he must "Start not" and must be told, like her, when to move and to "present your hand." The ideas of her (potential) motion and their lack of it are intertwined throughout. Only by creating a world of stilled lives can the statue be tempted to share any life.

This gradual, painful approach worked out between Leontes and the statue is not without risk. Kenneth Gross has best described what is at stake in the play's recalling other images of return (and, I would add, of artifice):

such images are like ghosts that the play must both conjure and exorcize before any further enchantment or disenchantment of the statue is possible. . . . The general fantasy of return is shared by many spectators; but Shakespeare allows us at least the thought that Leontes with Hermione could all too easily become like Lear with Cordelia, torn at the end of his tragedy between the deluded knowledge of his daughter's being restored to life and the absolute certainty that she is a corpse.[61]

Other ghost fates threaten as well, and not only for Leontes: other tales of animated idols press to mind, and may lie behind Paulina's apprehensions about how her conjuration may be understood, if things should go badly.[62] Paulina's image of Leontes "marring" the stone lips and "staining" his own suggests a range of partial and improper relations between feeling and representation, lover and object, reader and text. They cannot simply meet: they must first exchange properties, even become metaphors for one another: mutual desire and mutual attentiveness are alike required.[63] What does it

mean to read an aesthetic object as more than just an occasion for the exercise of one's skill or force in interpretation? What does it mean to respond to a person with fully engaged human attention? What, above all, is the relation between these two questions? (And what is it about our needs as humans that we must ask it?) Paulina's answer is "It is requir'd / You do awake your faith." But faith in *what* she does not say.

Likewise deliberately evoked is a correspondence between the statue's artifice and Leontes' frozen ceremonial of grief, that "theatre of remorse" we observed before as the ash of tragedy. The similarity is made plain by Camillo:

> PAULINA   O, patience!
> The statue is but newly fix'd; the colour's
> Not dry.
> CAMILLO My lord, your sorrow was too sore
>   laid on,
> Which sixteen winters cannot blow away,
> So many summers dry.
>
>   (V.iii.14-22)

Camillo has perhaps noticed Leontes weeping here, but the odd image of him as painted picked up from Paulina's lines (as if his grief were make-up) also recalls Perdita's earlier objections against "painting" as falsification—even if augmenting a genuine impulse. This brings up the question once more of what fiction or form of representation can best match itself to or answer feeling. Camillo complains, albeit gently, that Leontes, in overdoing it, has only continued to damage himself, but it is enough here that Leontes' wet tears match the statue's undried color to indicate the way the two are approaching one another, mutual images or representations of artifice as a refuge from the pain of change as well as mutual figures of death in life. Art and desire front life and death in a complex dialectic of mutual combination in which each serves as the precondition of its antithesis. The structure has an inevitable temporal dynamic—a necessarily developmental impetus of binding and loosing. Each modifies the others and what one kills, its contrary vivifies.

One way to get at the way this complex motion works is to consider a key pair of terms that run through the scene: "mock" and "like." These seem chosen specifically to suggest at once modes of representation and moods of feeling, and to provide a subtle network of relations between these. Through them the scene exposes and works through the connection of perception and emotion as explicitly as it can, a connection that goes back at least as far as the problem of Leontes' "crossed eyes" and his imagined trip-wire spider, and that underlies his increasingly hysterical attempts to straitjacket complex ambivalences in the paranoid theatricality of conspiracy theory. Consider the moment of unveiling the statue:

PAULINA   As she liv'd peerless,
So her dead likeness, I do well believe,
Excels what ever yet you look'd upon,
Or hand of man hath done; therefore I keep it
Lovely, apart. But here it is; prepare
To see the life as lively mock'd as ever
Still sleep mock'd death. Behold, and say 'tis
    well.

Hermione like a statue.
I like your silence, it the more shows off
Your wonder; but yet speak.

(V.iii.46 51)[64]

There is an insistent jingle here among "likeness," "look'd," "lovely," "life," "lively," and "like" which links what is "like" to what "likes" according to an ancient and true etymological connection that Shakespeare seems here to be dramatizing. Hermione's "likeness" will revive in Leontes his "liking"—not just his remorse—which in turn will lead on to her "life." A true likeness, one made as here "to the life" is, as Aristotle said of theatrical spectacle, "psychagogic": it attracts the soul. The silent response, the intensity of attention turned to the statue by its viewers, are things Paulina "likes."

And yet bracketed inside this intercourse of likeness with liking is a counterpun in which life is "mock'd": imitated, yet also made fun of as sleep makes fun of or plays games with death (Paulina knows the statue can be awakened). The specific simile here insists on the one hand that aesthetic or mimetic "mocking" of this kind is as much a heightening of "life" as it is a gaming; one might even go further and say a gaming *in order to* heighten. But it also insists on a power to humiliate or damage the living that resides in artifice (recall Hermione's sense of her trial as a "mock-trial"). Leontes will reinforce this sense of vulnerability or victimization at the hands of the statue twice, and both times the "mockery" is keyed to the statue's ability to challenge ordinary notions of what constitutes "liveliness" and what sort of emotion ought to be directed towards works of art: "The fixure of her eye has motion in't, / As we are mock'd with art" and at last, desperately, "Let no man mock me, / For I will kiss her" (V.iii.67-8; 79-80). With Paulina's warning reply that what Leontes proposes is only a mistaken parody of the contact he seeks (like Pygmalion bedding his ivory), the scene reaches a momentary stalemate. Paulina will allow no further approach, Leontes will not let the curtain fall but stands, as his daughter says, for ever "a looker-on."

Each of these postures of response, we may feel, even this risking of indecorum and humiliation, must be passed through as stages of Leontes' "trial by mockery" before the statue can be invoked to life, according to the crucial condition "If you can behold it." Hermione's return takes place on a middle ground "be-

tween" stone and flesh onto which Leontes in particular ventures in love and danger. And the scene compares this transaction between man and stone to the complex mediations of all our forms of address to fictional objects: the emotional investment we make in them, their mode of being through that investment for us, our mode of being through their challenge to us, the claims we make on them and on each other through them, and so forth.

Yet the moment of Hermione's revival remains extraordinary by any measure. Nevill Coghill has drawn attention to the length of the scene as a way of confirming for us her actual stoniness through her lack of motion, so that an audience may be "reconvinced against hope that she is a statue." This strategy is the play's own version of the deferral of Leontes' desire. Coghill demonstrates the point by reprinting the Folio text of the passage, remarking that "only at the end of the long, pausing entreaty, when the suspense of her motionlessness has been continued until it must seem unendurable, is Hermione allowed to move":[65]

PAULINA   Musick; awake her: Strike:
'Tis time: descend: be Stone no more:
    approach:
Strike all that looke vpon with meruaile: Come:
Ile fill your Graue vp: stirre: nay, come away:
Bequeath to Death your numnesse: (For from
    him,
Deare Life redeemes you) you perceiue she
    stirres. . . .

The insistent and repetitive character of the lines is well caught by the look of the Folio text. Apart from "'Tis time"—a kind of declarative command—only one utterance before Hermione's stirring is not an imperative. Each seems to punch itself into being against a resistance, a resistance registered in the strange sense of violence and blockage in the lines, as if Paulina's call had somehow to bore through or chisel away layers of deafness to reach its target ear. "Strike," she cries as though directing a blow at the statue, and an echo rebounds off it into her invitation to deliver a return blow that will "Strike all that looke vpon with meruaile," as if the statue should revenge on "the lookers-on" all the trauma of its awakening through their wonder at it. Yet Paulina's very insistence that "'Tis time" overgoes itself, to suggest that it is in the end up to the statue to approach them rather than to be summoned. The spectators invite, would relish, would take pleasure in, nothing so much as suffering the statue's marvelous blow if it only meant their dream of life and motion had come true. Paulina's imperatives are those of entreaty, even prayer; her cry of "Come" is a version of the ancient hymn: "Veni, creator spiritus."

These lines, in their complex mixture of exultation, power, fear, and vulnerability, crystallize from the scene as a whole the typically turbulent metaphoric energy of "wonder" that is the focus of this study. All the elements of wonder reappear here, and much more vividly realized than with Cleomenes and Dion: the sense of inhabiting a borderline "between" knowledge and emotion, of a fearful power both in and beyond the spectator, an acute self-consciousness of the medium of representation which reinforces rather than drains the expectation of enlightenment. Even the recurrent sense of spectral doubles as pressing onto the scene of wonder appears, not only in the twinning of Leontes and Hermione, but also in Paulina's odd phrasing of her warning to Leontes not to "shun her / Until you see her die again, for then / You kill her double" (V.iii.105-7).[66] And as we have already seen, there is a programmatic exploration throughout of ways in which Leontes and Hermione are alike. Longinus spoke of the strange sense of readers "producing what they had only heard." Here that very sense is taken by the play to correspond to and "justify" the general desire that Hermione's recovery be real. What Paulina calls their (and our) "faith" will produce its object "if you can behold it." It is not enough here to speak of "the power of theatre" or of "art": the impact of the scene grows also from the power of a collective desire for its success which stems from its audience. It answers a general need to test what fiction can be called upon to do in the way of reparative and sustaining work for us; to justify at last, despite the pathos of his own failure, Mamillius' sense that what was needed to deliver himself and his mother safely to one another was some fiction, if only the right one could be found. The dangers of that search, its delicacies, are recalled here through Paulina's sense of her perils, of her responsibility. The one sentence in her invocation which is *not* a command must be construed as in part an offer, in case of disaster, to go down to death herself in Hermione's place: "I'll fill your grave up." This beautifully resonant line suggests that Hermione's may have been somehow an open grave all these years—or one just reopened, at great risk. The gap of the gaping grave is now to be closed, its image of sundering to be not merely denied, like that of Polixenes and Leontes with which we began ("Time as long again / Would be fill'd up . . ."), but repaired. In a dialectical reversal, Hermione will die to death, bequeathing him the very "numnesse" that belongs to him. So that the fatal shadow of Dis can at last depart.

It is therefore appropriate that the play's image for the consummation of this repair, and I think its most moving moment (at any rate the one that angles for *my* eyes) should be a slow, hesitant, astonished clasping of hands closing the gap between two bodies through their organs of most developed, most typically human feeling. And again, according to the scene's therapy of repetitive reversal, recalling that very moment of Leontes' hostility for being made a spectacle before a Hermione who would not "open thy white hand and clap thyself my love." The play deliberately draws attention to this in Paulina's urging that "When she was young you woo'd her; now, in age, / Is she become the suitor." The Folio does not give a question mark here, and this seems to me right. On stage the moment is electrifying: its element of the startling breaks forth through Leontes, our surrogate in touching the impossible, in that expressive "O," as if he had been given a shock: "O, she's warm!" The claims of imagination to deliver the world we wish, and sustain us, if anything can, from death are now specifically ratified by his proclamation: "If this be magic, let it be an art / Lawful as eating."

Yet, as long as we are in the presence of someone called Paulina, we ought to be at least careful of claims about what may and may not be eaten. For though eating *per se* is lawful, this does not imply that all eating is lawful, or even appropriate at all times. In Jacobean England, some kinds of eating were expressly forbidden. Meat in Lent, for instance, was unlawful without special dispensation (as for pregnancy). And so was theatre. Moreover, even if lawful, it is not always a good idea to eat just anything: some things are positively dangerous as foods, and some are dangerous for some people at some times. Proserpina, for instance, might have done better not to have eaten seven pomegranate seeds in the halls of Dis. And though bears may eat people when hungry, people mostly do not—unless they are really bears in disguise, or have names like Tereus and Tamora. Paulina instructs those on stage that they should their "exultation / Partake to every one" as though it were a food like the feast that ends many another comedy. But if fiction is to be our food, we should be discriminating about it, and only eat what is good for us, what is lawful, what sustains. But how shall we know it?

The answer is that we cannot, but that certain signs can make us confident and "awake our faith." One of these is the presence of a certain kind of intuitional and self-conscious surprise at a pertinence beyond the moment, a sudden waiving of the barriers to self-knowledge, what I have been describing throughout this study as an experience of "wonder." In speaking of his psychiatric work with children, Winnicott tells of the "scribble game"—an improvisation in which child and physician alternate making and interpreting scribbles on paper. Sometimes the game would yield out of its own insouciant dynamics of mutual play a moment of enlightenment, of which Winnicott remarks that "the significant moment is that at which *the child surprises himself [or] herself*. It is not the moment of my clever interpretation that is significant."[67] The emphasis on surprise here seems to me close to the use in Shakespearean drama of wonder as "the significant moment" at which the whole fiction aims through its various divagations, the precipitation out of an experience of play of a moment that addresses the world directly, not only in terms of knowledge about it but in ways that release emotion at once towards it and towards the self in it. Winnicott's surprised children come upon themselves and their stories unexpectedly, excitedly, in the scribble game. Audiences of Hermione's recovery, on stage and off, come upon themselves, though less unexpectedly, in the act of wishing her fervently back into life—and this tells them something about themselves, about their own desires, and about the uses of fictions in recognizing, enacting, and understanding those desires. This is so even for those in the audience who might *not* wish in this way, who might need, for whatever reason, to resist such a wish, to imagine some other theatre.

These considerations illuminate both why the imagination that needs to find itself in the world among other imaginations should turn to the thought of theatre to screen itself, and why that same thought of theatre must eventually be given up in its turn. As the figure of Father Time explicitly shows with his hour-glass, time is always at once both a flowing and a turning. The Time who says "I turn my glass," and presumably does so, visually embodies both. He even suggests that the flowing might itself prove a turning insofar as the sands of his glass flow back on themselves. His whole speech speaks of a process that, while it moves always forward, both "makes and unfolds error" (as if error were at times a folded thing), and can both create and "slide O'er" a "wide gap." The theatre is implicated in this "branching" process, even in the moment of its self-recognition, since Time will "make stale / The glistering of this present, as my tale / Now seems to it" (IV.i.13-15). Through the set of deep puns on "depart, parting, departure, apart, party to, partner, and, of course, bearing a part" noted by Cavell, the question of coping with Time's partitioning (and parturitioning) flow is linked to the finding of a form of play in response.[68] And this link allows us once more to see that the source of Leontes' theatrical self-awareness in Act I was of a piece with his implication in Time's flow through his growth into desire and with his resistance against the world of generation that spoke of his emasculating mortality. Against Leontes' theatre of "one self king," the play eventually ripostes another of collective desire *for* vulnerability after all, for risking the wounds alike of wonder and of love. Truth may be the daughter of Time, but her other parent is Imagination, and their marriage is that of Blake's Prolific and Devourer.

Shakespeare's elaboration of wonder as a "between" state that precipitates recognitions, that marries Time and Imagination, necessarily includes—even begins with—the actors who inhabit and enliven the play's "parts" and who actively adjust the fit between self and role moment by moment in the theatre to answer the flow of "live" performance with a new inflection here, a more sudden movement there. As actors are the ones who take on and interact most deeply with the theatrical fiction, so the final scene is, as has been often noted, charged with the heady self-consciousness of an explicitly "actorly" task: what is the actress playing Hermione doing? Playing a statue? Playing Hermione playing a statue? How long can she hold the pose without breathing, etc? Our skepticism and our pleasure at the pretenses of the theatrical meet each other in pursuing this kind of question, and the result is a tremendous influx of self-conscious excitement, so that we feel our very attentiveness to the scene, even our sense of being "mock'd," becoming part of the developing action.[69] Kenneth Gross comments: "That the closing scene allows us neither self-evident faith in magic nor the quiet comforts of disenchanted irony is where its real difficulty lies. Finally, the enchantment . . . is in the willfulness of the fiction of disenchantment, the fantasy of the relinquishment of fantasy."[70] The fine balance of that formulation itself reproduces the sense of being "caught between" that the scene so carefully fosters. Bate remarks of the final scene that "It is not enough to say of the statue scene that nowhere does Shakespeare's art substitute more brilliantly for myth, nowhere is there more powerful testimony to the creative, even redemptive, power of drama, nowhere is there a creative coup more *wonder*ful. For it must also be said that the redemption is only partial, it is neither a reversal of time nor a transcendence into eternity" (pp. 238-9). It seems to me, however, that the wonder so finely caught in the first sentence draws its power precisely from the point made in the second: not its war against time, but its awareness of the temporal in the imaginative, its finely balanced sense of their balance. Fervencies of self aside, it calls on us to see the aspect of surrender inside that imaginative demythologizing Bate calls "the distinctively Shakespearian *species humanitatis.*"

The ancient metaphor of the human being as an actor and life as a stage here touches a new elaboration: the making and unmaking, the composition and decomposition of the self in its fictions becomes a process of continual dialectical pulsion and response, like the actor making his performance—not in slavish obedience to the script, but in interpretive and immediate tension with it. The theatre which was a screen for Leontes' darknesses is removed to reveal another theatre. Each in its turn must be acknowledged, and given up. But if we must give up the theatre, we do so only for an interval, before its return.

As our own excitement becomes the "subject" of the final scene, even as it prepares to end itself and leave us to ourselves, so the space "between" stage and audience becomes the site of the scene's imaginative activity, in which the whole community may "participate." No doubt this sort of thing is occurring all the time in the theatre: where else is the action at any time if not between us? But we are not always made so deliberately conscious of the stakes of our "investment" in this way. When Hermione prays: "You gods, look down / And from your sacred vials pour your graces /

Upon my daughter's head!" (V.iii.121-3, beautifully undoing as she does so Paulina's agonized cry to Leontes to "Look down / And see what death is doing") there is a sense in which the theatre audience are at once co-petitioners and the powers to whom the petition is being addressed. The audience contemplates the action from within and without, and stands beside older fictions invoked as gods around their latest offspring to offer it, as much as precursors can, deliberate blessing.[71] This self-conscious invocation of the audience as parties to the outcome is also presumably one point of the return, at the play's end, of the theatrical language first introduced in Leontes' fear of and resistance to the world of generation. Through Leontes' last lines, the actor seems to speak to his fellows of a get-together in the green room, with jokes about dropped cues and missing props, and how good Autolycus was tonight, and how the bear tripped up on his way offstage:

> LEONTES   Good Paulina,
> Lead us from hence, where we may leisurely
> Each one demand, and answer to his part
> Perform'd in this wide gap of time, since first
> We were dissever'd. Hastily lead away.
>   (V.iii.151-5)

If these last lines call upon both cast and audience to "answer to," and hence to move away from, this theatre, as though to stay in it too long might risk repetrification, the lines also insist there must be an "answer" to this theatre somewhere else, that it must take in turn a "part" in some other life. As in *Pericles,* the work of the theatre does not stop at the stage door. It prolongs itself and finds its proper answer in some future turning of Time's glass. And we should note that even inside this imagined off-stage fellowship another, more truly final scene shapes itself, where each hearer will more strictly "answer to his part" as Polixenes once saw himself answering "heaven / Boldly, 'Not guilty'." The eschatological impulse that becomes explicit at the end of *The Tempest* is also present in *The Winter's Tale,* if hidden for now behind the image of our fellowship. The gap between the two marks an interval at once of play, of reflection, and of reflection on play, since what we will be called to answer to will be the kind of part we have played—not only in our lives but in the fictions that fed, and fed on, those lives. Leontes' "wide gap of time" extends back through the two hours' traffic, the sixteen years, and all our lifetimes of "branching," to our collective distance from an ancient sundering and an all-but-forgotten Paradise where "first" we were "Not guilty." Yet though that gap admonishes, it also invites. Between this end and The End the work of poetry must go on unfolding its metamorphic task. Though fiction quails in the final analysis, in today's green room and street and by tomorrow's hearth there is still room for it to branch and bud. Hence even in foreshadowing the end of fiction, the play concedes

that that end is not yet, and that the question of how this fiction has answered its part arises for us as a question about the life, death, and afterlife of fictions in the world of generation.

It is not therefore surprising to find that this scene is at once one of Shakespeare's most powerful and characteristic and at the same time one of the most saturated with the presence of other fictions, especially Ovidian ones. Just as the fantasy generating Leontes' nightmare theatre of jealousy is both repeated and overcome, so also a secret register of alternative fictions at the level of composition bodies itself forth as an open allusiveness of acknowledgment and transfiguration. In part the scene's sense of being released from constriction registers the way it both realizes and undoes its indebtedness to earlier fantasies of mortality and animation, demonstrating their corrosive power as motivating fantasies in Leontes, then forcing them to the surface and repealing them. Shakespeare transmutes the myths of both Proserpina and Galatea by confounding and contaminating them into something new. In the recurrent search for the antidote to a fiction that has become petrified and petrifies, Shakespeare looks not to a counterfiction that "confronts" but one that "answers to" and so includes its occasion. The dynamics of psychological and poetic process are analogous to each other rather than recourses from each other, and neither is properly prior. Critics have often marveled at Shakespeare's invention of a newly resonant or "deep" psychological complexity in representing character. *The Winter's Tale* makes clear that that invention and the poetic question of *inventio* are intimately linked, that is that the framing of psychological complexity goes hand in hand with a complex response to the fact of "sources and analogues" as the sites of poetic invention.[72] There is therefore no question of a final, workable distinction between art and life. Where Ovid declares Pygmalion's artistry in creating Galatea one in which "ars adeo latet arte sua"—a formulation that became a Renaissance touchstone—Shakespeare's scene of vivification insists on deliberately displaying its intimate investment in and by works of art.

The dialectic of creative absorption and conversion has important implications for a Shakespearean conception of "tradition." I argued earlier that Shakespeare was essentially conservative in artistic practice insofar as he looked to preserve and adapt from what came to him whatever could continue to serve the needs of the present. This is a specifically "dynamic" conservatism, one that insists on recognizing the Mutabilitie (as Spenser would put it) of social and psychological structures. For such a view, tradition lives and does its sustaining work most of all in the vortex of its rupture and reassembly, in the struggle at once to retain what we have known and loved and to fit it to what we know and love now. In such fires tradition burns—to re-emerge as the phoenix, or as the turtle, or in some yet unknown shape of darkness or glory. It is not a Homeric or, more to the point, Miltonic battle of giant forms in a celestial and apocalyptic eyrie. The energy of its self-overcoming is Ovidian. Tradition is like wax before the fire, waiting for the thumb to turn and mold it again.

It follows further, and last, that we should not be surprised to find Shakespeare's work unfurling a similar relation of adaptation and inclusive correction to itself. *The Winter's Tale* seems, almost alone of Shakespeare's works, to be able in the end to affirm the image of a sexually vigorous and assertive woman, both in Perdita's explicit longing for Florizel and in the final scene's emphasis on Hermione's longing for her daughter. Indeed, the tale of the play is in part that of its own desire to rescue and affirm that image from behind the screen of an anger that repeats the gestures of tragedy. The play's ability to face and face down some of the fantasy substructures that have informed Shakespearean drama itself is one of its most remarkable and moving powers. Though Shakespearean wonder arises throughout his work in the context of imagined sexual generation, of the reproduction of the world (likewise the task of drama), after *The Comedy of Errors* the maternal figure who most literally embodies and enacts such regeneration is largely withheld.[73] Adelman relates this impulse to withhold the maternal figure, to keep her locked in an Abbey, an Ephesian Temple or a "remov'd house" until the play's dénouement, to a fear of the overwhelming image of a "suffocating mother." I want here rather to extend the argument to include the dramatic occasion. What implications does the appearance of this figure have for the relations, on the one hand, between the play and the "matrix" of earlier fictions from which it springs, and, on the other, between the play and the attendant audience towards which it is directed? To return to the image of mothers and generation at the end of these plays points to an entire complex of ideas about the source and direction of imaginative energy.

I noted earlier that Shakespeare's final scenes find in themselves both the ease and the fragility of a "right" language for desire's success in the world as love. The restless metaphoric energy of Shakespeare's dramatic language is both heightened and, for a moment, stilled into a silence full of the energy of contact. In the final scene of *The Winter's Tale,* this contact is at once erotic as between characters, theatrical as between play and audience, poetic as when a metaphor finds or makes its world, and what we might call "metapoetic" as when a fiction joins hands with its fellows. The image of the mother registers origin and connection in more ways than that of developmental psychology. It emerges as Shakespeare's most charged image for the discovery of the world, that world that desire touches with a confidence that expresses the faith of an imagining self as it, we might say, "matriculates" into it. It is through the search for this contact that the notion of

"incarnation" becomes so important for Shakespeare. Through "incarnation" conceptions are made acts, desires are made bodies, and scripts are made actors. Because the regimes of the imagination and of the bodily world are alike metamorphic and complex, the work of making them touch is difficult. The recovery of contact acknowledges the mutual turbulences, even while subliming them.

But we must not give in to the temptation to identify the world into which we matriculate as at once and only material and maternal. Such an identification has an ancient history, but one finally refused by Shakespeare, if not by other parts of his culture.[74] The world has its materiality, of course, but it also is composed of the residue of past words, images, and fictions, just as the imagination that meets it has "taken in" impressions we call "objects." The process is a mutual conception. To label this side "self" and the other side "mother" is to refuse to acknowledge their interfusion in a "between" space that is both and neither. As Hermione's revival shows, it is the shared "between" ground that must be ventured onto in order for the petrified world to become a presence to and of the human.

What Shakespeare offers in the last scene of *The Winter's Tale* is not the "unearthly" revelation, the "burst / And th'ear-deaf'ning voice of the oracle" that Cleomenes and Dion experience at the theatre of Apollo. Shakespeare's theatre of wonder speaks to a mortality renewed in its sense of the rightness and the vivid earthwardness of its language and desires. Language and desire meet the world not in the form of a pronouncement (a scroll or a pair of tablets) but as a human body, vulnerable and marked in time. In Shakespearean wonder, one hears not so much the great voice calling (as in Milton) as the human tongue speaking. The strenuous and fatal energies of challenge and competition are converted into aspects of a continuing, fecund dialectic of life and death, art and desire.

Notes

[1] I note also that the 1623 Folio gives the phrase as "rais'd the Tempest" (*The First Folio of Shakespeare,* ed. Charlton Hinman, p. 34), though it is not unusual to find nouns capitalized like this. My sense that we are close to allegorical and metadramatic talk here is also reinforced by what seems a hidden picture of a human in the passage—one with a "head," "charm," and "spirits" who "goes upright." The famous Oedipal riddle may also be somewhere close by: though it is late in the day, human time still has his two legs and all his charming faculties. In particular this suggests Prospero as designer of the entire enterprise. (Caliban, of course, slouches under his many burdens.)

[2] Other title-allusions are, as with Prospero, given to major or principal characters: Helena in *All's Well,* the

Duke in *Measure for Measure* (V.i.411). More remote cases are Rosalind in the epilogue to *As You Like It,* the Princess in *LLL* (V.ii.520), Don Pedro in *Much Ado* (II.iii.57) and Hortensio at the very end of *Shrew.*

3 "Mamillius" has no precise meaning (perhaps that is part of the boy's problem), but suggests at once mother, breast, and littleness, as though he were a kind of diminutive or (more strongly) dependent of his mother's body. For an interpretation that makes this relation the central issue of the play, see Janet Adelman, *Suffocating Mothers: Fantasies of Maternal Origin in Shakespeare's Plays* (New York: Routledge, 1992), pp. 220-38. I read Adelman's account of the play after mine was already drafted, but note several points of similarity between us, especially a shared sense that the work of D. W. Winnicott has much to say to it.

4 Freud's description of the game of "fort-da" he watched his grandson play with a toy he interpreted as representing the child's mother is relevant here. See *Beyond the Pleasure Principle,* in James Strachey, ed. and trans., *Standard Edition of the* [. . .] *Works of Sigmund Freud,* 24 vols. (London: Hogarth Press, 1955), vol. XVIII, pp. 14-17. Even more so is D. W. Winnicott's discussion of "transitional phenomena" and the developmental process of "illusion-disillusion" throughout his *Playing and Reality* (New York: Basic Books, 1971).

5 Stanley Cavell, *Disowning Knowledge in Six Plays of Shakespeare* (Cambridge University Press, 1987), pp. 194-5.

6 My emphasis, but the meter supports it.

7 At the same time, the very literality and solidity of the Leontes who now enters, with his own history and agenda, marks a crucial difference in representational strategy between the Shakespearean mode and that of the allegory that seems imminent yet avoided here. Consider how our reading of the scene would differ if it were to take place in *The Faerie Queene.* In Shakespeare, an allegorical relation is registered yet overgone by a preference for "personation" or what I have been calling "incarnational" translation. Yet though this difference is crucial for the definition of Shakespearean representation, the play as a whole remains aware of Spenser in a spectral, perhaps sponsoring way. Other contacts include the baby-and-bear conjunction in III.iii, so teasingly reminiscent of *Faerie Queene* VI.iv, and the location of the final scene in a Spenserian chapel/gallery where a statue comes to life and invokes the gods (cf. Britomart's dream in Isis Church in *F. Q. V,* yet there the image is not living flesh). Such resemblances suggest a deeper relation between the epic and the dramatic poet than is usually claimed. The most extensive exploration remains W. B. C. Watkins, *Shakespeare and Spenser* (Princeton University Press, 1950).

8 Cavell, *Disowning Knowledge,* p. 194.

9 Oscar Wilde's wry homoerotic joke that a man's tragedy is that he does not become like his mother is queerly apposite here. At this point we should also reveal that a dying Camillo confessed that Mamillius did not die at all, but was transported to the sea-coast of Denmark, where he was adopted as the King's son and re-christened "Hamlet" after him. A scrambled echo of his former name remained nonetheless, and he later had a recurrence of the "old tale": Leontes returned in a dream disguised as the Danish King's ghost to make the same old accusations about his "brother." Mamillius/Hamlet thereupon himself became the man who dwelt by a churchyard and finally accomplished the protracted self-murder he had forgotten how to seek, while using on the "harlot king" Camillo's old poison-cup, which had made the voyage with him in his childhood bundle.

10 Freud's concept of the "primal scene" of parental copulation might be invoked here, though my reading does not depend on it. Freud's sense of the child as perceiving an act of violence performed by the father brings the two models into particularly close alignment. Freud's interest in this fantasy first appears in *The Interpretation of Dreams* (Standard Edition, vols. IV and V, 1905), though it is not until the "Wolf Man" case study (1918) that the term "primal scene" is specifically applied. The theatrical resonance of the idea of a "scene" is especially relevant to my argument later—note that Freud did not insist that the "scene" should actually have been witnessed, but rather thought it could be compiled phantasmatically through hints and inferences. See also J. Laplanche and J-B. Pontalis, *The Language of Psychoanalysis,* trans. D. Nicholson-Smith (New York: Norton, 1973) under "Primal Phantasies" pp. 331-3 and "Primal Scene" pp. 335-6.

11 Winnicott, *Playing and Reality,* p. 12. The whole of Winnicott's conception of the transitional nature of "play" is acutely relevant to Shakespeare's dramatic fable, insofar as both are concerned with the vicissitudes and dangers of growth and "development," whose deformation in the play deeply illuminates the relation between sexuality, fantasy, and dramatic mimesis.

12 On *Othello* from this perspective, see both Cavell, *Disowning Knowledge,* Ch. 3 and Peter Stallybrass, "Patriarchal territories; the body enclosed," in Margaret W. Ferguson, Maureen Quilligan and Nancy Vickers, eds., *Rewriting the Renaissance* (Chicago: University of Chicago Press, 1986), pp. 123-42.

13 This apparent change of subject that may hide a clue to the real direction of the play may be compared with the similar moment in the opening scene of *King Lear,* where Kent responds "Is not this your son, my lord?" to Gloucester's remark of Albany and Cornwall that "curiosity in neither can make choice of either's moi'ty"

(I.i.6 8). The "curiosity of nations," as Edmund calls it, in choosing their proper heirs will be precisely the source of Gloucester's problem.

[14] Between Hermia and Helena in *Midsummer Night's Dream* for instance, or Rosalind and Celia in *As You Like It,* and perhaps Marina and Philoten in *Pericles.*

[15] This line might be stressed " . . . when *you* were boys" to emphasize the child's presence.

[16] One might compare here Angelo's fudging of the similar issue of whether he or Isabella is to blame for his desires when he speaks of "the strong and swelling evil / Of my conception" (II.iv.1-7; this just after we have seen the pregnant Juliet catechized by the Duke in prison). The tactic is still unfortunately familiar in contemporary legal proceedings on rape and sexual assault.

[17] "Screen". here should be understood in the senses both of concealing ("screen from view") and revealing ("screen a film"). Compare Freud's concept of a "screen memory."

[18] This linking of clothing with wounding rather recalls the discovery of Duncan's body in *Macbeth* (both the embroidered corpse and the grooms' daggers "unmannerly breeched with gore"), and suggests there may be a further pun on Leontes the boy as "unbreeched"— that is not yet wounded with that master-biting dagger.

[19] We might also consider whether the identification of father and son here (and the connection of this scene with II.i) suggests that within the adult's discovery of his wife and friend as secret adulterers lies a dim and difficult memory of discovering his own parents as partners in a sexual "crime" that also excluded him. This might well have been Freud's reading, but the play is not quite explicit about it. Of course, Leontes is not quite explicit about his mental processes either.

[20] Cavell (*Disowning Knowledge,* pp. 190-1) sees a similar strategy of "deferred representation" as shaping the final scenes of several of Shakespeare's plays, among them *The Winter's Tale.*

[21] Here we may note an important *difference* between Leontes' jealousy and that of Othello. Where Othello's torments generate a heightened sense of the sexual appeal of Desdemona, most horribly played out in the "brothel" scene, in Leontes there is no such sense of any residual attraction to his wife. Yet as though a powerful feeling of "heat" were being fiercely imagined somewhere, his thoughts seem to run a great deal on the literal fire with which he will consume Hermione and the bastard child.

[22] Stephen Orgel has recently discussed this passage and its difficulties under the heading of "The poetics of incomprehensibility," *Shakespeare Quarterly* 42:4 (1991), 431-8. Orgel's warnings on the dangers of forcing meanings on the passage or others like it in the play are salutary. I would note however that the fact that this sort of speaking is very frequent in *The Winter's Tale* is something about which a critic might legitimately frame questions: why would a play deliberately, as it seems, cultivate obscurity as an aspect of its texture? What is the dramatic function of this sense of sense as veiled or layered in too much possibility?

[23] Leontes' references to Mamillius as a "kernel" and a "squash" continue the submerged sexuality of his line of thought, especially the latter, aptly glossed in G. B. Harrison's edition (London: Penguin, 1947, p. 131) as a "peapod before the peas have swelled." Cf. Bottom's joke to Peaseblossom: "Commend me to Mistress Squash, your mother, and to Master Peascod [cf. Codpiece] your father" (*MND* IV.i.186-7).

[24] On the economic register of the play, in addition to Cavell, see Michael Bristol, "In search of the bear: spatiotemporal form and the heterogeneity of economies in *The Winter's Tale,*" *Shakespeare Quarterly* 42:2 (1991), 145-67.

[25] These verbs must remain in quotation marks to indicate that they are not quite mental acts, but nor are they quite "unconscious." They are rather "overlooked" or "ignored." But perhaps the latter is a closer characterization of what is often called "unconscious" thought.

[26] The link goes right through the crossed eyes again, since Leontes has now "seen the spider." Hence too the more ghastly pun on the "cordial" poisoncup he wishes to have Polixenes given that will give him "a lasting wink," as if in parodic revenge for his duplicitous carnality. Note that the word "cordial" returns when Leontes looks upon the statue: "For this affliction has a taste as sweet / As any cordial comfort" (V.iii.75-6).

[27] A similar point is made by Ruth Nevo, *Shakespeare's Other Language* (New York: Methuen, 1987), p. 115.

[28] That this be not thought merely a sentimentality, I note that the reason Hermione is restored to Leontes is *not* because of his long repentance, but because he was persuaded not to have Perdita "consumed with fire" in Act II. This persuasion in turn seems to stem from Leontes' desperate need to refuse the image of himself as a man of violence, the same need that lies together with violence at the heart of his intuition about desire.

[29] Recent feminist criticism has described Shakespearean drama, and especially the tragedies, as produced by just such a paradigm of scandal and blame, generated out of male anxiety. See, among others, Madelon Gohlke, "'I wooed thee with my sword': Shakespeare's tragic paradigms" in Murray Schwartz and Coppelia Kahn, eds.,

Representing Shakespeare (Baltimore: Johns Hopkins University Press, 1980), pp. 170-87; Coppelia Kahn, *Man's Estate: Masculine Identity in Shakespeare* (Berkeley: University of California Press, 1981); Adelman, Janet, *Suffocating Mothers: Fantasies of Maternal Origin in Shakespeare's Plays* (New York: Routledge, 1992). *The Winter's Tale* is at one level an acknowledgment of the strength of this critique, yet also frames an attempt to look further, to how the knot might be loosed.

[30] On the proliferation of theatres and the defiance of orderly generic expectations by the play, see esp. Rosalie Colie's account in *Shakespeare's Living Art* (Princeton University Press, 1974), pp. 265-83.

[31] On the etymology of "theorist" alluded to here, see Chapter One above. It is always possible to cast doubt on such reports, as Howard Felperin has recently attempted to do. Casting doubt is one of the things theatre is for, but also a thing represented here in Leontes himself as autist and skeptic. It seems truer to say that the play here reads the critic than vice versa. But this is a danger we all run. See Felperin, "The deconstruction of presence in *The Winter's Tale*" in *The Uses of the Canon* (Oxford University Press, 1990), Ch. 1.

[32] It is worth pondering the choice of Apollo as the play's sponsoring deity (that Shakespeare followed Greene in this is neither here nor there: he *chose* to do so where he need not have). The choice is justified in particular by the play's concern to show Leontes as involved with questions of poetic composition through his deliberate "scripting" of Hermione's infidelity. The change made to Greene in having Leontes deny the truth of the oracle not only heightens the dramatic moment through the blasphemy, but frames a concealed instance of an "agon" of the poets, in which Leontes plays Marsyas to Apollo's oracle. Leontes attempts to outscript the god by calling the divine plot "mere falsehood"—a piece of business, a red herring. As usual, Apollo is quick to punish challenges not only to his divinity, but to his poetic pre-eminence. The god knows an overweening rival when he sees one. The punishment of child-deprivation might even be compared to that of Niobe, who boasted she had excelled Apollo's mother in fecundity—she ended up, of course, frozen and petrified in grief.

[33] The link between this play and *Hamlet* appears again in the curious echo of Paulina's proposing to appear as Hermione's ghost, to "shriek, that even your ears / Should rift to hear me, and the words that follow'd / Should be 'Remember mine.'" (V.i.65-7). The combination of second marriage, mourning, and murder is presumably part of the trigger here, but the connections go deeper, as I have already suggested.

[34] As a result of its dependence on recent myth, psychoanalytic criticism of *The Winter's Tale* has for the most part been forced to import sooner or later into its reading a symbolic transcription of Shakespearean psychological tokens into Freudian or post-Freudian ones. A particular popular instance has been Leontes' "spider in the cup." Some recent critics have translated this into a fearful fantasy of the overwhelming pre-Oedipal mother poisoning the maternal milk, while others have preferred to see the ravenously sexual Oedipal mother of a later stage of development. The basic insight here—developmental ambivalence towards the residues of infantile dependence—is hardly a modern instance, but these particular translations have a decidedly arbitrary feel. The play is, I would argue, deliberately occluding the spider from transcription, and that blockage is what needs to be noted the more so as Leontes *thinks* he is expounding an image for the acquisition of (infected) knowledge. For this reason, such readings cannot help feeling to me distinctly partial at this point: insofar as they do not explore the contours of a particularly Shakespearean psychic mythology, they can read the historical dimension of Shakespeare's work only imperfectly, and cannot incorporate the question of his theatre and its self-awareness into the psychological dynamic. For my part, it seems to me more likely that the spider is Arachne—who competed with Athena for pre-eminence by weaving a tapestry of divine rapes. Arachne's tapestry figures via *Pandosto* in Florizel's later catalogue of divine metamorphoses (IV.iv.25-31). See esp, the citations gathered in Adelman, *Suffocating Mothers,* p. 354, n. 54.

[35] Jonathan Bate, *Shakespeare and Ovid* (Oxford University Press, 1993), p. 222.

[36] Nevo, *Shakespeare's Other Language,* p. 41. For Cavell, see above, n. 20.

[37] See Bate, *Shakespeare and Ovid,* pp. 230-3. Bate is, of course, not the only commentator to identify the story of Proserpina as relevant to the play: see the next note.

[38] See Honigmann, "Secondary sources of *The Winter's Tale*," in *Philological Quarterly* [hereafter, *PQ*] 34 (1955), 27-38. Ovid is only one of three proposed "sources," and the pervasiveness of traces of Golding especially is not followed out in the brief note. Honigmann is following up a suggestion originally made by W. F. C. Wigston in 1884. Honigmann's complaint that work up until the time of writing "failed to bring the Proserpine-myth into the discussion" no longer applies, as the Ceres Proserpina story has become a regular discussion point. See esp. Carol Thomas Neely, "Women and issue in *The Winter's Tale,*" *PQ* 57 (1978), 181-94 (revised in *Broken Nuptials in Shakespeare's Plays,* New Haven: Yale University Press, 1985, pp. 198-9); Adelman, *Suffocating Mothers,* p. 360. The tale is now usually cited in discussing the mother-daughter axis of the play, without inquiring into

its image of male sexuality or the role of that image in the play, or indeed of the deeper aspects of an Ovidian "source" generally. Yet if one is dealing with questions of "issue" or "origin," it seems important to ask where and how the question of "poetic source" obtrudes.

[39] Honigmann ("Secondary sources," p. 37) was the first to suggest the connection between the Sicily of Ceres' curse and the location of Shakespeare's play. It explains Shakespeare's otherwise puzzling reversal of the locales from Greene. Bate incorrectly (*Shakespeare and Ovid,* p. 232n) attributes the word "collop" to Golding's Ceres. That this echo is not a coincidence is suggested by the fact that both Leontes and Jove are asserting their part in their offspring against a challenge: Ceres has just begged that Jove "have not lesser care / Of hir (I pray) bicause that I hir in my bodie bare." But for Leontes, the challenge comes from himself, and may turn on precisely such questions as lie within Ceres' entreaty. See Golding's translation printed as *Shakespeare's Ovid,* ed. W. H. D. Rouse (Carbondale: Southern Illinois University Press, 1961), p. 114, ll. 641-2.

[40] Following out this suggestion, we might re-envision Oberon as a kind of middle figure between Dis and Leontes—a dark and jealous spirit who wishes to capture and manage female sexual expression. Like Leontes, Oberon wishes to wrest a boy from his spouse, and occupies himself creating images of the monstrosity of her desire ("ounce or cat or bear / pard or boar with bristled hair"). We might also recall Oberon's epithet "King of shadows" (*MND* III.ii.347), which closely translates Ovid's "rex . . . silentum" (V.356), and his ancient kinship with Alberich and the Nibelungen tribe of earth-dwellers. Ceres' curse in Golding is also worth scanning with Titania's account of the recent weather in mind (*MND* II.i.88ff.):

But bitterly above the rest she banned Sicilie,
In which the mention of her losse she plainly
    did espie.
And therefore there with cruell hand the
    earing ploughes she brake,
And man and beast that tilde the ground to
    death in anger strake.
She marrde the seede, and eke forbade the
    fieldes to yeelde their frute.
The plenteousnesse of that same Ile of which
    there went such brute
Through all the world, lay dead: the corn was
    killed in the blade:
Now too much drought, now too much wet
    did make it for to fade.
The stars and blasting winds did hurt, the
    hungry foules did eat
The corn in grounde: the Tines and Briars did
    overgrow the Wheate,

And other wicked weedes the corne
    continually annoy,
Which neyther tylth nor toyle of man was able
    to destroy.
    (*Shakespeare's Ovid,* ed. Rouse, p. 113)

[41] The relevant lines in Ovid follow the vain attempt of the pool-nymph Cyane to invoke the proper course of courtship and to stop Dis. They are among the more horrible pictures of rape in classical literature:

haud ultra tenuit Saturnius iram
terribilesque hortatus equos in gurgitis ima
contortumque valido sceptrum regale lacerto
condidit, icta viam tellus in Tartara fecit
et pronos currus medio cratere recepit.
    (*Metam.* V.420-4)

Latin citations of Ovid are from the edition of William S. Anderson (Leipzig: Teubner, 1977). Golding translates these lines (ll. 525-8) as:

His hastie wrath Saturnus sonne no lenger
    then could stay.
But chearing up his dreadfull Steedes did
    smight his royall mace
With violence in the bottom of the Poole in
    that same place.
The ground streight yeelded to his stroke and
    made him way to Hell,
And downe the open gap both horse and
    Chariot headlong fell.

[42] Likewise the Paulina who takes the newborn girl to Leontes *in loco matris,* insisting that "We do not know / How he may soften at the sight o' th' child" may recall Golding's Ceres, who avows to Jove: "I hither come if no regard may of the mother be, / Yet let the child hir father move." The episode is not in Greene.

More remotely, the image of Hermione in Antigonus' dream (III.ii), where her eyes become "two spouts," resembles in wateriness the fate of Cyane, the nymph who attempts to prevent Dis from abducting Proserpina, and whose grief at her failure and his abuse of "her fountaines priviledge" causes her to dissolve "so that nothing now remained whereupon / Ye might take hold, to water all consumed was anon" (ll. 542-3). In Ovid, Cyane seems to stand for the deep, inarticulate grief alike of mother and daughter at the violence of the rape, as Cyane directly witnesses the blow of Dis' "royall mace." Martin Mueller argues for the additional presence of some version of the Alcestis myth in the play's final scene ("Hermione's wrinkles, or, Ovid transformed: an essay on *The Winter's Tale,*" *Comparative Drama* 5:3 [1971], 226-39). Though a narrative of descent into death and return is covered both in the Proserpina myth and in the Orphic frame of the Pygmalion story in Ovid, the (non-Ovidian) Alcestis tale may also be relevant.

[43] The Old Shepherd later calls authority "a stubborn bear" (IV.iv.802). For the bear as an Ovidian beast, see also Bate, *Shakespeare and Ovid,* pp. 224-7. The inchoate shape of bear-cubs made them especially apt as metamorphs, of course. I note also that the title pages of the first three editions of Golding's Ovid (*STC* 18956, 57, and 58, dated respectively 1567, 1575, and 1584) all sport the emblem of a bear muzzled, chained down and leaning on a dead tree stump. Shakespeare had already associated bearishness with the violence of a man's desires, both to himself and others, in the Count Orsino ("Bearlet") of *Twelfth Night,* who begins the play speaking of himself as hunted (though as "an hart" not a bear) and ends it threatening to kill others out of frustration. Bear-baiting also figures several times in the play, and an Ovidian context is provided by Orsino-as-Actaeon, and perhaps Malvolio-as-Narcissus "practicing behavior to his own shadow." Bristol, "In search of the bear," has more information on bears and bear-lore.

[44] Andrew Gurr, "The bear, the statue and hysteria in *The Winter's Tale,*" *Shakespeare Quarterly* 34 (1983), 420-5 at p. 424; Nevill Coghill, "Six points of stage-craft in *The Winter's Tale,*" *Shakespeare Survey* 11 (1958), 31-41 at p. 35. Barthes' "hysterical" reader who takes the text as literal truth is the lowest in a hierarchy to be found in *Le Plaisir du texte* (Paris: Editions Tel Quel, 1973), pp. 99-100. Gurr does not connect the bear and its moment of hysterical "resolution" with the character of Leontes and the tragic theatre of transferred blame which has dominated the preceding acts. It remains also to consider whether taking the stage action for "true" at some level is entirely so primitive a response as Gurr (and Barthes) seem inclined to claim. This is an issue which will be addressed most fully in the closing scene of the play.

[45] Bate, *Shakespeare and Ovid,* pp. 231-2.

[46] Colie, *Living Art,* pp. 274-7.

[47] Winnicott, *Playing and Reality,* p. 13.

[48] Ibid., p. 14.

[49] Adelman, *Suffocating Mothers,* pp. 231-2 and 358-60.

[50] This is the Folio spelling which suggests "reigns in," "reins in," and "rains in" all at once.

[51] The question of "thievery" that emerges with Autolycus also connects with the insistent economic language of the play. On Autolycus' Ovidian roots, see Bate, *Shakespeare and Ovid,* pp. 228-9.

[52] The sequence of stories involving Proserpina, Niobe, and Arachne is told in Ovid's Books V and VI, in a framework set of "mortals competing with gods." The set begins with the Pierides' challenge to the Muses, against whom Calliope sings the tale of Proserpina, which victory prompts Minerva to think of Arachne's challenge, whose unhappy destiny fails to instruct her friend Niobe, whose fate in turn reminds her townsmen of that of Marsyas, the final and most disastrous example. Not only is Autolycus born in the competition between Mercury and Apollo to impregnate Chione, his mother, but she in turn is killed for boasting against Diana of her motherhood (*Metam.* Book XI). Pygmalion's decision to sculpt a bride stems from his disgust at the whoredom of the Propoetides, their punishment for refusing to acknowledge Venus (Book X). On the latter, see also Leonard Barkan, "Living sculptures: Ovid, Michelangelo, and *The Winter's Tale,*" *ELH* 48 (1981), 639-67, esp. p. 644.

[53] Barkan ("Living sculptures") suggests that an element of competition emerges not at the level of authors or authority, but at that of artistic media through the tradition of the *paragone* or contest among the arts, which Shakespeare incorporates into the end of the play when he compares the incredible narrations of the Gentlemen in V.ii against first the silence of sculpture in Hermione's statue and finally the "living statues" of the theatre when she descends. Barkan points out (p. 663) that "the ultimate destination of the *paragone* . . . is the rivalry of art and life." Even here, however, competition evaporates into the more complex dialectic of what Barkan calls (p. 664) "the mutual triumph of art and nature." But at this point the competitive language of "triumph" begins to get in the way and might be abandoned in favor of some other relation, such as the complementary or the dialectical.

[54] See also the remarks on this point of Mueller, "Hermione's wrinkles," 236-7.

[55] Here once again, Cavell's account of the return of Hermione as the recovery of "the ordinary" against the forces of both cynical skepticism and excessive enchantment is pertinent. I have also found the discussions of "the statuesque" by Barkan ("Living statues") and especially by Kenneth Gross illuminating and suggestive. See Gross, "Moving statues, talking statues" in *Raritan* 9:2 (1989), 1-25 and expanded in *The Dream of the Moving Statue* (Ithaca: Cornell University Press, 1992).

[56] On the statue scene and the bear scene as counterparts in self-consciousness, see Gurr, "The bear, the statue and hysteria." This time, however, the challenge offered to the audience is precisely to credit and embrace what Gurr identifies as an "hysterical" reaction: that the action is literally taking place—an actor is no longer pretending to be a statue—and that the faith and pleasure in that trick legitimately stand for deeper repairs of trust and enlivenings of story. At this level,

the play insists on the reality of its theatricality as a force of truth-telling, and opposes its therapeutic "hysteria" of "faith" to the pathological and misplaced hysteria of Leontes' skepticism.

[57] See the brief citations given by Barkan, "Living sculptures," p. 664, n.1 and the editorial strictures cited by Coghill, "Six points," *passim.*

[58] Barkan, *The Gods Made Flesh* (New Haven: Yale University Press, 1986), p. 284. See also Cavell's remarks on the couple's relation, on how "For her to return to him is for him to recognize his relation to her; in particular to recognize what his denial of her has done to her, hence to him. So Leontes recognizes the fate of stone to be the consequence of his particular scepticism" (*Disowning Knowledge,* p. 125). But I wonder whether Hermione's part in the transaction must be as passive as this suggests. What does Leontes' attack mean for her, and how is stone *her* response to it?

[59] Bate's claim that the tale of the Propoetides is "not relevant" to the scene (*Shakespeare and Ovid,* p. 234) seems to me wrong-headed. That prehistory of misogynist disgust forms a close parallel, which Shakespeare transforms by fusion with the Dis abduction story. Both the fate of the Propoetides and that of Proserpina, incidentally, stem in Ovid from a parallel refusal to acknowledge Venus: "Pallada nonne vides iaculatricemque Dianam / abscessisse mihi? Cereris quoque filia virgo, / si patiemur, erit" (V.375-7).

[60] Shakespeare had first represented such an antithesis and interrelation in *The Rape of Lucrece,* where Tarquin's desire and Lucrece's vulnerability are explicitly linked (though the poem does not suggest any softening of desire in her): "His ear her prayers admits, but his heart granteth / No penetrable entrance to her plaining: / Tears harden lust, though marble wear with raining" (558-60); cf. Lucrece's lament: "For men have marble, women waxen minds, / And therefore are they form'd as marble will" (1240-41), where "they" refers to both men and women, linked by the shaping of a hardened "will" at once noun and verb, mental act and physical implement. Mentation migrates and hardens into the erection itself, and becomes insensible.

[61] Gross, "Moving statues," p. 17.

[62] In the case of *Lear* it is those around him that Lear accuses of having been turned into "men of stones" by the deadness they confront, as if it exposes or creates a deadness in them. Apart from the "monumental alabaster" that Othello makes of Desdemona, there are also Viola's spectral self who "sat like Patience on a monument" and the "marble-breasted tyrant" Olivia, the Mariana who warrants her truth by offering herself as a "marble monument" in its guarantee (V.i.230-3),

the Marina who looks "like Patience gazing on kings' graves," and, in her own monument, the Cleopatra who declares herself "marble-constant" (V.ii.240). Some of these return to life and some do not, but all are images of the survival of female will in its chosen posture beyond the power of onlookers to get at it. That Coriolanus of the crystalline will who advances on Rome like a revenging robot is another, more alarming image of the animate idol. See Barkan, "Living statues," p. 665 n. 2 and Honigmann, "Secondary sources." Gross, *The Dream of the Moving Statue,* discusses the larger issues in detail. The *topos* of animation survives into modern fiction of course—my own favorite instance of how *not* to wake a statue occurs in C. S. Lewis's *The Magician's Nephew.*

[63] I have in mind here W. H. Auden's description of love as an "intensity of attention" which seems to me highly relevant to this scene. It may be worth noting that another forum for such intense attention is that of the inquisitor, which Leontes has already adopted in default of love. Paulina's deliberate "slowing down" of Leontes' desire here, forcing it to attend to the right moment, may be a counterspell to the terrible haste of Dis in the Ovidian story, a hotness of libidinal sight which was nevertheless blind in every other way to its object: "paene simul visa est dilectaque raptaque Diti: / usque adeo est properatus amor" (V.395-6).

[64] I have given here the Folio readings of "Louely" and the stage direction. Most modern editors expand the latter and emend the former to "Lonely." Either reading is possible: one emphasizes the power of the statue's "likeness" to stir love—a key thread of the scene; the other prefigures the discovery of life and emotion in the statue itself, since it makes little sense to speak of a statue as *per se* "lonely."

[65] Coghill, "Six points," p. 40. Coghill also notes that this passage is "the most heavily punctuated passage I have found in the Folio," which points to the way it makes visually clear its interest in (the difficulty of) getting from one moment to the next, an interest we should compare to Florizel's encomium of Perdita discussed above. (The lines are V.iii.98-103 in Riverside.)

[66] This strange sense of alternative or "ghost" figures of other versions of the play being present at its end is found in other final scenes of wonder in Shakespeare. In particular there is the darkening pressure exerted by that "other" and happier Claudio and Hero at the end of *Much Ado about Nothing* in Hero's words upon her unveiling: "And when I liv'd, I was your other wife, / And when you lov'd, you were my other husband" (V.iv.60-1). When the Friar counsels all to "let wonder seem familiar" (l. 70), we may wonder how much his words point to the unexorcised, "familiar" ghosts of a less shadowed matrimony.

[67] Winnicott, *Playing and Reality,* p. 51, emphasis in original. For particular, often very moving, examples of these sessions, see also Winnicott, *Therapeutic Consultations in Childhood* (New York: Basic Books, 1971).

[68] Cavell, *Disowning Knowledge,* p. 200. He continues: "That last phrase, saying that parts are being born, itself suggests the level at which theater . . . is being investigated in this play; hence suggests why theater is for Shakespeare an *endless* subject of study; and we are notified that no formulation of the ideas of participation and parturition in this play will be complete that fails to account for their connection with theatrical parts[.]"

[69] There is a comparable moment of metadramatic fun at the end of *Henry IV, Part One* when (the actor playing) Falstaff makes fun of (the actor playing) Hotspur for obeying the rules about being dead on stage. An audience's recurrent, and enjoyable, cynicism about "dead" actors ("I can see him breathing!") is thereby incorporated into the play's gaming with itself, just as here. Rosalie Colie's remarks on "tragicomedy" as a genre of various "mixings" and of the "between" are also relevant here (*Living Art,* pp. 278-83).

[70] "Moving statues," p. 20.

[71] A similar double movement out to the immediate audience and up to the gods as a second ring of spectators is explored by Harry Levin for the Player's Speech in *Hamlet* in his *The Question of Hamlet* (New York: Oxford University Press, 1959), pp. 139-64.

[72] As so often, William Empson anticipates this way of putting it in his reflections on the importance to *Hamlet* of the existence of a previous hit play on the same subject. See Empson, *Essays on Shakespeare,* ed. David B. Pirie (Cambridge University Press, 1986), Ch. 3.

[73] A partial but powerful exception to this is the persistent association of Titania with motherhood (and with the mortality that so frequently attends it), so that the scenes with Bottom take on a peculiar blithe confidence and indulgence, with Bottom in part "his Majesty the Baby" in delicious and beguiling fantasy. Only from without, and from the perspective of aristocratic disdain, are these scenes called disgusting. Within them they have an amplitude of mutual enchantment untouched by anxiety that has come to be an index of the Shakespearean dramatic imagination itself. That Oberon regards this with vengeful loathing is important, but not conclusive.

[74] Adelman bases her identification of "fantasies of maternal origin" in part on a review of early modern views of childbirth and nursing that saw "matter" as "Mater." See Adelman, *Suffocating Mothers,* pp. 1-10

and 239-45. And though Shakespeare consistently identified this aspect of the world, what I am calling its "matriculation" of us, as female, there seems no essential or inherent need for that function in fact to be performed only by females.

Stephen Orgel (essay date 1996)

SOURCE: "Pastoral" and "Nature and Art," in *The Winter's Tale,* edited by Stephen Orgel, Oxford at the Clarendon Press, 1996, pp. 37-47.

[*In this excerpt, Orgel explores the importance of Bohemia to Shakespeare's development of pastoral elements, as well as the play's treatment of the relationship between nature and art.*]

Pastoral

To anyone familiar with the tremendous variety and vitality of Renaissance pastoral (as of its Virgilian and Theocritean models), the modern division of the mode into idyllic and realistic visions, the critical dichotomy of 'soft' and 'hard', will seem absurdly reductive. Indeed, the play that established tragicomedy as a serious genre in the Renaissance was itself a pastoral, Guarini's *Il Pastor Fido* (1590, first translated into English anonymously in 1602); and for most of the dramatists of Shakespeare's age, pastoral was the mode in which tragedy and comedy became inseparable. The lives of shepherds, Renaissance pastoral assumes, exhibit within a small compass all the elements of human life—that is why it is worth attending to: not because it is an escapist fantasy about the golden age, but because of its moral and emotional capaciousness.

In *The Winter's Tale* the tragicomic aspects of the mode are epitomized at once in those two touchstones of theatrical perversity, the shipwreck on the seacoast of Bohemia and the bear that devours Antigonus. The bear, indeed, has been shown by Louise Clubb to constitute, in itself, a tragicomic topos in sixteenth-century continental drama, a generic commonplace.[1] As for the Bohemian seacoast, which Shakespeare found in *Pandosto* and retained, it is not an error, but one of the elements stamping the play as a moral fable—like the title itself, it removes the action from the world of literal geographical space as it is removed from historical time.[2] Despite the fact that Shakespeare plays are not notable for geographical accuracy, the setting has provoked several centuries of complaint and specious explanation. In 1619, Jonson told Drummond of Hawthornden that 'Shakespeare in a play brought in a number of men saying they had suffered shipwreck in Bohemia, where there is no sea near by some 100 miles'.[3] Hanmer resolved the problem by declaring the Folio's compositor to be at fault and changing Bohemia to Bithynia. No subsequent editor followed his lead, though both Garrick, for his version of the play, *Florizel and Perdita,* and Charles Kean for his famous production at the Princess's Theatre in 1856, set the pastoral scenes in Bithynia. . . .[4] But Furness observed that since Jonson complained about the play's geography four years before the Folio was printed, the error must have been Shakespeare's. Several critics (one as recently as 1955) have argued that since for brief periods in the thirteenth and early sixteenth centuries Bohemia was part of the Austrian empire, it therefore did have a seacoast—this is rather like arguing that since the 1536 Act of Union Wales has been on the North Sea. But most commentators have been content to explain the error away as Pafford and Schanzer do, by observing that it is simply adopted from Greene. However, if there is a problem, this merely shifts it from Shakespeare to Greene.

It is, of course, entirely possible that both writers found Bohemia a pleasantly euphonious name (by early 1610 it had the additional merit of its staunch and embattled Protestantism) and considered the facts of geography irrelevant to the fairy-tale world of the story. But the seacoast of Bohemia seems also to have had a special resonance in Jacobean England. The *Variorum* cites three instances in which references to the Bohemian coast are used to characterize a particularly foolish or ignorant speaker; S. L. Bethell argues on the basis of these that the setting was an old joke, analogous in modern times to references to the Swiss Navy or Wigan Pier, and suggests that if W. S. Gilbert 'presented us with an admiral in the Swiss navy', this would be a good indication to a Savoy audience of 'the degree of reality to be attributed to his plot'.[5] If this is correct, the setting of the pastoral scenes would then be, like Shakespeare's title, an alienating device, and an index to both tone and genre.

In any case, the relevance of seacoasts to Bohemia in the Renaissance imagination is in fact demonstrable: Wenceslaus IV, King of Bohemia (1361-1419), took as his *impresa* a storm-tossed ship, with the motto *Tempestati Parendum* ('stormy weather must be prepared for') . . . . I am not suggesting that Greene and Shakespeare were familiar with the ancient King of Bohemia's *impresa,* but rather that the ruler of this landlocked country found a ship in a storm an appropriate emblem of his condition for moral and ethical reasons, not geographical ones.

Antigonus' vision of Hermione and his encounter with the bear make it clear that pastoral is no more a golden world than the Sicilian court is. It is violent and dangerous, nature at its wildest; it exhibits, moreover, from the outset the same problems of knowledge, judgement and interpretation as the world Antigonus has left. And if faith is required for Leontes' ultimate salvation, it provides no help in Antigonus' case, merely misleading him and demonstrating his naïvety. His belief in a providential universe convinces him that since fate has brought him to Bohemia, Perdita must be Polixenes' child; and despite his earlier adamant assertion of Hermione's innocence, he interprets his vision of her 'In pure white robes, / Like very sanctity' (3.3.21-2) to imply her death, and if her death, her guilt as well. He arrives at this conviction not passionately or maliciously, but through reason and faith (under the circumstances, his return to Sicily would scarcely be auspicious). And the bear assures us that nature in this play is no kinder than civilization.

Antigonus' death is another of the play's unrestored losses. He is the faithful servant to an irrational and vindictive master. He has been criticized for obeying Leontes, but however barbarous the King's orders may be, the alternative to obeying them is to see Perdita burnt. He commits himself and the infant to the protection of Providence—naïvely, no doubt, but that is the point. Paulina essentially writes him off as soon as he leaves (see 3.2.228-9), and when, at the play's end, Camillo is offered as a replacement, there is no question of her remaining true to her husband's memory: he is, in the play's terms, a total loss. But the fatal bear is also the pivot on which the play turns from tragic to comic, the index to a radical change not of subject but of tone.[6] 'Though authority be a stubborn bear,' says the Clown late in Act 4, 'yet he is oft led by the nose with gold' (4.4.795-6): by this time there are even ways of dealing with the savagery of authority and bears. Antigonus' death, as the Clown recounts it, becomes a black comedy; the abandoned infant, as the shepherd takes it up, is assumed to be the offspring of 'some stair-work, some trunk-work, some behind-door work' (3.3.71-2)—to be, in fact, exactly what Leontes had claimed—but this is now no impediment to pity, charity, love. Bohemia, as the play develops, is hardly an ideal world, except perhaps for disguised princes and con-men looking for easy marks; but it offers a set of alternatives to the dramatic issues of Sicily, a way of rethinking and re-enacting them.

The most striking of these, in terms of dramaturgy, is the introduction of a narrator, Time personified, as Chorus to Act 4—the tale begun by Mamillius and interrupted by the drama of Leontes now becomes the play. Criticism has on the whole been unhappy with this; Hazlitt considered it (along with Antigonus on the coast of Bohemia) one of the play's 'slips or blemishes';[7] Quiller-Couch used it as a prime example of the play's 'flagrant specimens of inferior artistry',[8] and Dover Wilson rescued Shakespeare from it by declaring it the work of a collaborator.

The presentation of a narrator had been, in *Pericles,* a consciously archaizing device, reviving moral Gower to supply the authority for Shakespeare's only morality play. The expedient had been popular but artistically dubious, according to Ben Jonson, who saw the play exactly as Shakespeare intended, but in the worst way—not as a drama but as 'a mouldy tale, . . . stale / As the shrive's crust, and nasty as his fish'.[9] In *The Winter's Tale,* Time's narration expresses quite a different kind of moral authority. The speech is unnecessary for the purposes of conveying information; everything we learn from Time is repeated at once in the ensuing dialogue between Camillo and Polixenes. But the move from action to narration is another pivot, turning the drama we have experienced with such immediacy into a tale with a teller who both claims control over the apparently free play of the characters and offers a disturbingly amoral overview:

> I that please some, try all; both joy and terror
> Of good and bad, that makes and unfolds
>   error . . .

Through the operation of Time both good and bad experience both joy and terror; some are pleased, all are tried; both error and its painful revelation are Time's responsibility. *Veritas filia temporis,* 'Truth', the aphorism says, 'is the daughter of Time'; but this has ceased to be a comforting commonplace—the only truth revealed is, ironically, 'error'. Nor do human institutions, such as the orderly operation of what we normally understand as time (or, as Capell shrewdly suggested, such as the dramatic unities)[10] constrain this figure, for

>   it is in my power
> To o'erthrow law, and in one self-born hour
> To plant and o'erwhelm custom.

Like the Chorus in *Henry V* impugning the power of the stage, reducing the theatre's representations to its physical limitations, Time returns *The Winter's Tale* to its source, a narrative which declares itself, in its subtitle, *The Triumph of Time.* The difference, however, is that we have become Time's creatures too.[11]

Nature and Art

Theocritus wrote his idylls from the Alexandrian court for an audience of powerful, educated and sophisticated readers; pastoral is, in its inception, embedded in the courtly. The mode had always been available as a way of talking about that other world of ambition, privilege and power. For George Puttenham, in 1589, its primary character was indirection, 'under the veil of homely persons and in rude speeches to insinuate and glance at greater matters, and such as perchance had not been safe to have been disclosed in any other sort'.[12] Alexander Barclay, in the first English eclogues, published in 1515, explains that through his shepherds he delineates 'the miseries of courtiers and courts of all princes in general'.[13] The involvement of court with pastoral was not, moreover, a poetic fiction in Shakespeare's England. Keeping sheep was big business, enclosures had been an increasingly serious economic

and political issue for almost a century, and the impulse of pastoral poetry to represent the world of shepherds as pretty and harmless has a political dimension that is quite invisible to us. The idyllic pastoral is predicated on the satiric pastoral—Barclay's shepherds, like Spenser's in *The Shepheardes Calender,* are as likely to curse their masters as to celebrate their country pleasures. The double edge of the mode is evident in the double vision of Rosalind and Celia, fresh from court, overhearing the shepherd Silvius elegantly complaining about love, and then receiving a straightforward lesson from his colleague Corin in the hard economics of the pastoral life.[14]

The presence of aristocrats in the rustic world, therefore, is of the essence of pastoral. It is also, however, a threat to it, and is sometimes positively destructive: the effects of Florizel's and Polixenes' presence at the sheep-shearing are, in their way, entirely conventional. When, in Book VI of *The Faerie Queene,* the knight of Courtesy enters the pastoral world in pursuit of the Blatant Beast, he finds the traditional *otium* and love in the person of Pastorella, but he also abandons his knightly quest, intrudes upon and disrupts a dance of rustic deities, and drives away the Graces, the source not only of poetry but of the Courtesy he himself embodies. The classic model for the destructive intrusion of royalty into pastoral is invoked by Perdita herself: the appearance of Dis, King of the Underworld, to carry Proserpina off from the Sicilian field of Enna as she gathers the flowers Perdita catalogues.

Perdita's catalogue has a long history relating to love and death. In Theocritus, the lovesick Polyphemus offers Galatea lilies and poppies, flowers respectively of winter and summer; Adonis' bier is strewn with garlands and blossoms in Bion's elegy, and Moschus calls on roses, anemones, hyacinths, and 'flowers in sad clusters' to mourn for the dead Bion.[15] Virgil, elaborating Polyphemus' offer, has the shepherd Corydon tempt the disdainful youth Alexis with flowers in profusion, precisely enumerated:

>   for you the nymphs
> bring—look!—baskets of lilies; a fair naiad
> gathers pale wallflowers and the buds of
>   poppies,
> and blends narcissus and the fragrant dill,
> then interweaves with cassia and sweet herbs
> soft hyacinth and yellow marigold . . . [16]

Renaissance examples abounded (see the note on 4.4.104-27), but for English poetry, Shakespeare's catalogue established the norms of the topos, both in its elaboration and detail, and in its extraordinary expressive range.

'O Proserpina, / For the flowers now that frighted thou letst fall / From Dis's wagon . . .': the ensuing list depicts the natural world as engaged in a cosmic love affair, and thereby evokes a nature that is no longer Virgilian but Ovidian. Indeed, the association of the flower catalogue with the rape of Proserpina derives from Ovid. In the *Metamorphoses,* she is gathering only 'violets or white lilies' (5.392), but in the *Fasti,* the list is extensive: her companions picked marigolds, violets, poppies, hyacinth, amaranth, thyme, rosemary, sweet clover, roses, and *'sine nomine flores'*—'nameless flowers', more flowers than can be catalogued; she herself picked crocuses and white lilies (4.435-42). Why is the rape of Proserpina being invoked in the middle of a country sheep-shearing festival? It acknowledges, to begin with, the dangerous aspects of pastoral love affairs, and thereby serves as another version of Polixenes' Edenic myth; but it also reverses it: in this case the interloper is male, the innocence destroyed female. The mythological association of flowers with rape, indeed, is already implicit in the scene in the very persona Florizel has devised for Perdita: he has costumed her as Flora, goddess of flowers (4.4.2-3, 9-10). The costume does more than reflect his name; Flora, according to Ovid, was at first the simple nymph Chloris, beloved of Zephyrus, the west wind. He pursued her, she fled, but he seized her and raped her, and then to make amends filled the earth with flowers and gave her dominion over them—*'arbitrium tu, dea, floris habe'.*[17] Florizel several times denies that his intentions are anything but honourable; but in the allusive structure of the play, the rape has already been committed twice. Florizel himself, indeed, cites three additional examples as precedents for his own behaviour:

> The gods themselves,
> Humbling their deities to love, have taken
> The shapes of beasts upon them. Jupiter
> Became a bull and bellowed; the green
>   Neptune
> A ram and bleated; and the fire-robed god,
> Golden Apollo, a poor humble swain,
> As I seem now.
>
>   (4.4.25-31)

The scene invokes myths in which male sexuality is characteristically disguised, violent, compulsive, often bestial, but also an essential part of nature; and through it—through acts of sexual violence against women—the world is filled with flowers and poetry.[18]

The Proserpina story is also a story about time, refining and redefining both the terms of Time's chorus and the very concept of a winter's tale. It is a myth that explains the cycle of seasons: the abduction of Ceres' daughter, like the loss of innocence in Eden, is responsible for the fact that winter exists at all, that the 'perpetual spring and harvest' of Spenser's Garden of Adonis, or the eternal round of growing and reaping that Ceres promises Ferdinand and Miranda, can be no more than a poetic fiction.[19] But the cycle also includes a time of restoration and reconciliation, with

the annual return of Proserpina to her home in Sicily. If Shakespeare took the Proserpina story as an underlying fable for the play, rather than as a mere local allusion, it would explain why he switched the locations he found in *Pandosto,* so that Perdita's return, as 'Welcome hither, / As is the spring to th'earth' (5.1.150-1), would be to Sicily, not to Bohemia, and would thus be true to the myth.[20]

Nature, as Perdita presides over it, excludes 'the fairest flowers o'th' season . . . carnations and streaked gillyvors, / Which some call nature's bastards'; as cultivated flowers, they do not grow naturally in her garden, 'and I care not / To get slips of them' (4.4.81-5). The term 'bastard' was used for hybrids; it also meant 'counterfeit', a sense which colours the botanical usage (ironically, the child who is prejudicially called 'natural' provides the prejudicial epithet for the art that usurps nature). In her resolute resistance to bastards, Perdita doubtless shows herself to be her father's daughter, but her brief debate with Polixenes on the uses of art extends beyond the play and is informed by topoi reaching back to antiquity. Kermode in his introduction to the Arden *Tempest* gives an excellent overview of the matter, citing parallel passages from Florio's Montaigne and Puttenham's *Arte of English Poesie* expressing Perdita's and Polixenes' positions respectively, and observes that the latter commonplace can be found as far back as Democritus.[21] Polixenes' view, that the hybridizer's art is learned from nature and acts as its agent to improve it, is countered by Perdita's, that anything that interferes with nature will necessarily corrupt it. The 'bastard' flower, she implies, is thus correctly characterized, an index to our own corruption as it is the creation of our illicit pleasure. This, in fact, constitutes her ultimate moral position: her objection to the 'art' is not to its practice (she agrees that 'the art itself is nature') but to the impulse motivating it, which is to produce a more attractive flower,

> No more than, were I painted, I would wish
> This youth should say 'twere well, and only
>   therefore
> Desire to breed by me.
>
>   (4.4.101-3)

The ironies inhabiting this brief exchange are obvious: the invocation of the art that mimics nature, Giulio Romano's lifelike sculpture, is essential to the play's resolution, the embodiment of restoration, forgiveness, grace; and marrying 'A gentler scion to the wildest stock' (l. 93) is precisely what Florizel proposes in marrying Perdita, and what Polixenes adamantly forbids. But the ironies are, in human terms, rather less telling than criticism has found them; our opinions, even philosophical ones, are not invariably consistent—if this is a failing, it is a very ordinary one—and what we believe to be right for flowers we need not necessarily believe to be right for our children. It is the violence of Polixenes' response to his son's rustic fiancée that is surprising, not its failure to coincide with his botanical observations.

Notes

[1] 'The Tragicomic Bear', *Comparative Literature Studies,* 9 (1972), 17-30. Other particularly useful discussions of the bear are Dale B. J. Randall, ' "This is the Chase": or the Further Pursuit of Shakespeare's Bear', *Shakespeare Jahrbuch,* 121 (1985), pp. 89-95, which calls attention to Horace's complaint, in *Epistles* II.1.185-6, against audiences who 'call in the middle of a play for a bear or for boxers'; Dennis Biggins's '"Exit Pursued by a Beare": A Problem in *The Winter's Tale',* ShQ 13 (1962), pp. 3 ff.; and Michael Bristol's 'In Search of the Bear', *ShQ* 42 (1991), pp. 145-67, which places the bear in the context of both Renaissance folklore and seasonal economics. Daryl Palmer relates the bear to Hermione's invocation of her imperial Russian father, pointing out that the Russian emperor best known to Shakespeare's age was Ivan IV ('the Terrible', d. 1584), who murdered his son and, according to Purchas, amused himself 'with letting bears loose in throngs of people': 'Jacobean Muscovites: Winter, Tyranny and Knowledge in *The Winter's Tale',* ShQ 46 (1995), 323-39.

[2] In *Pandosto* the kingdoms are reversed; Pandosto is King of Bohemia and Egistus King of Sicilia. But Bohemia still has a seacoast: Egistus 'provided a navy of ships and sailed into Bohemia to visit his old friend and companion' (see Appendix B, p. 235). For a speculation on the reason for the reversal, see below, pp. 45-6.

[3] *Conversations with Drummond,* in *Ben Jonson,* ed. Herford and Simpson, vol. ii, ll. 208-10.

[4] For the printed version of *Florizel and Perdita,* Garrick returned the play to Bohemia.

[5] *The Winter's Tale: A Study,* pp. 32-5.

[6] Nevill Coghill calls the bear 'a dramaturgical hinge, a moment of planned structural antithesis', 'Six Points of Stage-craft in *The Winter's Tale',* Sh. Survey, 11 (1958), p. 35.

[7] *The Characters of Shakespeare's Plays* (1817), in A. R. Waller, ed., *Collected Works* (1902), i. 324.

[8] New Shakespeare *Winter's Tale,* pp. xxv, 159.

[9] 'On *The New Inn:* Ode. To Himself', 21-3.

[10] Cited in the *Variorum,* p. 156.

[11] The best discussion of time in the play is Inga-Stina Ewbank's 'The Triumph of Time in *The Winter's Tale',* REL 5 (1964), pp. 83-100.

[12] *The Arte of English Poesie* (1589), i. 18; the text is modernized.

[13] Beatrice White, ed., *Eclogues of Alexander Barclay* (1928), p. 1.

[14] *As You Like It* 2.4. The pioneering discussion of the relation between pastoral and the Elizabethan wool industry is Louis Adrian Montrose's 'Eliza, Queene of the shepheardes', *ELR* 10 (1980), 153-82.

[15] Theocritus, *Idyll* 11, 56-7; Bion, *Idyll* 1, *Lament for Adonis,* 75-6; Moschus, *Idyll* 3, *Lament for Bion,* 5-7

[16] Eclogue 2, 45-50; the translation is by the editor, and appears in *Poetry* 116 (1970), 353-5.

[17] *Fasti,* 5.212

[18] Paul Alpers sees Florizel's pastoral guise, and more specifically his Ovidian allusions, as an antidote to the destructive hyperbole of the opening scenes, a redemptive and liberating mode of idealization: 'After the anguish of Leontes' Sicily, where fantasies of bestial sex and the wearing of horns poison the imagination . . . Florizel . . . provides an alternative to a courtly habit of hyperbolic asseveration that is implicated in the tragedy of the first three acts' (*What Is Pastoral?,* forthcoming).

[19] See *Faerie Queene* 3.6.42; *Tempest* 4.1.114-15.

[20] E. A. J. Honigmann calls attention to the play's Ovidian background, and includes a similar speculation on the reversal of the locations, in 'Secondary Source of *The Winter's Tale',* Philological Quarterly, 34.4 (1955), pp. 27-38.

[21] *The Tempest* (1954), pp. xxxv-xxxvi; Pafford argues that the importance of the debate has been greatly overstated, but nevertheless gives extensive quotations from the sources cited by Kermode. Both discussions are indebted to Harold S. Wilson, 'Nature and Art in *The Winter's Tale',* Shakespeare Association Bulletin, 18 (1943), pp. 114-20. See the note on 4.4.87-103.

CHARACTERIZATION

Barbara A. Mowat (essay date 1991)

SOURCE: "Rogues, Shepherds, and the Counterfeit Distressed: Texts and Infracontexts of *The Winter's Tale* 4.3," in *Shakespeare Studies: An Annual Gathering of Research, Criticism, and Reviews,* Vol. XXII, 1994, pp. 58-76.

[*In the essay that follows, originally presented at the Shakespeare Association of America in 1991, Mowat explores act four, scene three of* The Winter's Tale—*where Autolycus is introduced—as a dramatic moment in which the surface context and its "infracontexts" create a number of tensions that establish Autolycus as a rogue character.*]

As I look at a particular intertextual moment in *The Winter's Tale* (the scene in which we meet Autolycus), I begin by assuming that the first printing of the play in the 1623 Shakespeare First Folio is a "text"—that is, dialogue initially crafted as a script for performance but nevertheless preserved for us as printed symbols, inked pages. I also assume that this moment of Autolycus's appearance came into existence within a field of printed texts to which it was contextually related. By describing and thus delimiting the moment's context as "printed," I do not deny it other contexts; rather, I argue that among the many contexts—social, cultural, variously semiotic—implicated in Shakespeare's text, one of the more significant is that massive field of discourse that issued from printing houses.

Not that the boundary between printed discourse and surrounding discourses is fixed or impermeable. Indeed, as we trace the interweavings of printed texts within Shakespeare's *Winter's Tale,* we trace at the same time the social and moral worlds represented in those texts, and we hear the debates in which the texts engaged. There is merit, though, in focussing attention as unwaveringly as possible on printed discursive systems. Such careful focussing forces us to acknowledge the constructedness of even supposed eye-witness accounts and heightens our awareness of the ideological freight carried by both the most fanciful of mythological tales and the most laconic of statutes and chronicles.

The word *text* in my title, then, refers primarily to the Folio words that preserve and transmit *The Winter's Tale* 4.3 and secondarily to printed discourse in general. The word *infracontext* I borrow from Claes Schaar, whose work in intertextual theory I find particularly helpful vis-à-vis Shakespeare.[1] Schaar suggests that the works of certain poets can best be described as vertical context systems; in these works, within and beneath, as it were, the surface context are embedded infracontexts that "constitute a matrix, a bed or mould which serves as the base for the surface context" and which, when recognized, expand and stratify meaning. The surface context functions as signal, sometimes in an overt or covert allusion, sometimes as a mere reminiscence or faint echo. Once the reader or listener recognizes the infracontexts and "recognition turns to understanding, the signal . . . and [the] infracontexts coalesce"; in some cases, the surface context is, in effect, annotated by the infracontext; in other cases, the meaning of the surface context is expanded

through a vaguer merging as the infracontexts "rub off" on the surface context. Schaar's construct is a variant of familiar intertextual models from Bakhtin through Kristeva to Riffaterre.[2] It differs from other intertextual models in that it bases itself "on distinctive, mostly verbal similarities between surface and infracontexts" and in that it focusses on a given intertextual moment as "a closely connected semantic whole, a functional entity" whose meaning is expanded and enriched by its infracontexts.

In these pages I argue that *The Winter's Tale* 4.3 is a dramatic moment in which the surface context and its infracontexts create a wonderfully complex contextual universe, one that, like so much of Shakespeare's work, constitutes a special variant of Schaar's vertical context system. Beneath the moment's surface context are distinct sets of infracontexts, some of which supplement and intensify each other, while others set up sharply contrasting associations and patterns. These conflicting infracontexts generate intensely complex meanings as, to quote Schaar, "irreconcilable worlds and value systems are pitted against each other."[3]

The Winter's Tale as a whole is, of course, an interesting intertextual transformation of Robert Greene's *Pandosto.* Woven into and transforming Greene's story of jealousy, attempted incest, and suicide are Ovidian, Apuleian, and Euripidean incidents and motifs that lift the play out of Greene's sordid and prosaic pages and into an almost mythic world of metamorphoses: of shepherdesses into princesses, of raging tyrants into repentant fathers, of statues into living women. Act 4, scene 3, has no parallel in *Pandosto.* It opens with the entrance of a new character who introduces himself to the audience as a thief and explains how he got the name Autolycus. A second character, the son of the Old Shepherd, enters, trying to calculate the money that this year's shearing will bring in; unable to do it "without counters," he abandons the effort and instead begins to read aloud his shopping list for the coming sheepshearing festival: sugar, currants, rice, saffron, mace, nutmegs, ginger, "four pound of prunes, and as many of raisins o' the sun."[4] Autolycus, to lure this "prize" into his trap, lies down and cries out for help, claiming that he has been robbed and beaten. As the shepherd charitably lifts him up, offering him money and offering to take him to shelter, Autolycus cleans out the shepherd's purse. They part, the shepherd going, he thinks, to buy spices for the feast, and Autolycus making plans to attend the festival himself, where, he says, he will turn the shearers into sheep for his own fleecing.

The signals in this scene that have alerted previous scholars to two of the scene's infracontexts are Autolycus's name and the general configuration of the trick he plays on his victim. "My father named me Autolycus," he tells us, "who, being, as I am, littered under

A party scene in Sicilia from the Stratford Festival's 1986 prodution of The Winter's Tale.

Mercury, was likewise a snapper-up of unconsidered trifles." This single sentence compresses several Greek-mythological pieces of text (most of them reprised in Ovid's *Metamorphoses*) that tell the story of the master thief Autolycus, son of the god Mercury. While Shakespeare's Autolycus is "littered under Mercury" in the sense, one presumes, that he was born when the planet Mercury was in the ascendant, his namesake was actually sired by the god Mercury, inheriting from his father the magic power to transform stolen booty into new, unrecognizable forms. As Ovid writes (in Golding's 1567 translation), the maiden Chyone

> . . . bare by *Mercurye*
> A sonne that hight *Awtolychus,* who provde a
> wyly pye
> And such a fellow as in theft and filching had
> no peere.
> He was his fathers owne sonne right; he could
> mennes eyes so bleere
> As for to make the black things whyght, and
> whyght thinges black appeere.[5]

Shakespeare's Autolycus does his namesake proud. He, too, is "a wyly pye" who "in theft and filching" has no peer. His link to Mercury—the trickster god, god of thieves, lord of roads, known primarily for his "subtle cunning"[6]—gives Shakespeare's Autolycus a quasi-mythological status, casting a kind of glamor on his thieving. One finds a parallel glamorizing of the thief in the second infracontext that has been cited by scholars, a story in Robert Greene's *Second Part of Conny-Catching,* one of five such books written by Greene in 1591-92 that describe con men (or, as he calls them, conny-catchers); Greene's announced purpose is to display the evil doings of conny-catchers and alert honest citizens to their tricks. Among Greene's tales of clever crooks versus innocent gulls is that of a wary farmer unknowingly stalked by conny-catchers. As he walks the inner regions of St. Paul's, the farmer refuses to take his hand off his "well lined purse." The hero/villain of this tale is a master deceiver—"one of the crue," writes Greene, "that for his skill might haue bene Doctorat in his misterie."[7] Having tried a series of ploys to get the wealthy farmer to remove his hand from his purse, the thief disguises himself as a gentle-man and falls down as if ill at the farmer's feet, begging the farmer to help him; as the farmer "stept to him, helde him in his armes, rubd him & chaft him," the farmer's purse is neatly removed. This tale, "A kinde conceit of a Foist performed in Paules," is generally accepted as underlying the Autolycus gulling-incident.[8]

The tale of the wary farmer and the clever pickpocket is a London story, set in the middle aisle of St. Paul's. *The Winter's Tale* sets its parallel incident in the coun-try and has its con man fall down beside what, within the fiction of the play, is a country road. This seem-ingly minor shift in the story's location begins the process of bringing into play sharply conflicting infra-contexts. As I have already suggested, the mythologi-cal context and the conny-catching context, though they take us into radically different discourses, do not them-selves markedly differ in the stance taken toward Auto-lycus the thief. Both contexts convey a more-than-sneak-ing admiration for the trickster. It is not such a long step from Ovidian commentary on the subtle cunning of Mercury, god of thieves, and on his son Autolycus as a "wyly pye," to Greene's statement that his pick-pocket "for his skill might haue bene Doctorat in his misterie." However, when Greene's young gentleman is taken from London and put in rags and made to cry out for help from beside a roadway, a signal is given that opens another, immensely complicating set of infracontexts in which Autolycus is far from glamor-ized. When, in his seeming distress, the ragged Auto-lycus is succored by a stranger passing along the road, what is replayed is the familiar story of the Good Samaritan[9]—except that in Shakespeare's version of the story, the part of the man set upon by thieves, stripped, beaten and left by the side of the road, is enacted by Autolycus, the thief, and the charitable Samaritan is presented as a gullible fool taken in by outward signs of victimization and suffering.

This complicated dramatic moment represents with remarkable economy the essence of a century-long struggle among and within texts as to how individuals and states should respond to those in distress. In the biblical text, Jesus tells the story of the Good Samari-tan to illustrate what is meant by "loving one's neigh-bor." Loving one's neighbor means aiding anyone in distress.[10] But, beginning in texts in the late fifteenth century, one finds the question posed again and again: how can one know whether apparent distress is genu-ine? In Brandt's *Ship of Fools,* in "Cocke Lorelles Bote," and in the *Liber Vagatorum*—all published around 1500 and all drawing, to a greater or lesser extent, on an advisory issued by the Senate of Basel around 1475[11]—we read about healthy "beggars who sit at the church doors . . . with sore and broken legs . . . [tying] a leg up or besmear[ing] an arm with salves . . . and all the while as little ails him as other men"; we read about beggars who pretend to suffer from

epilepsy, falling down "with a piece of soap in their mouths, whereby the foam rises as big as a fist"; we read about beggars who apply corrosives to their skin or who leave their clothes at the hostelry

> and sit down against the churches naked, and shiver terribly before the people that they may think they are suffering from great cold. They prick themselves with nettle-seed and other things, whereby they are made to shake. Some say they have been robbed by wicked men; some that they have lain ill and for this reason were compelled to sell their clothes. Some say they have been stolen from them; but all this is only that people should give them more clothes, [which] they sell . . . and spend a whoring and gambling.[12]

When the *Liber Vagatorum*—from which the above quotations are taken—went into its nineteenth printing in 1528, it included a preface by Martin Luther, who wrote that "the . . . true meaning of the book . . . is . . . that princes, lords, counsellors of state, and every-body should be prudent, and cautious in dealing with beggars, and learn that, whereas people [who] will not give and help honest paupers and needy neighbors, as ordained by God, . . . give . . . ten times as much to Vagabonds. . . . I have myself of late years been cheated and befooled by such tramps and liars more than I wish to confess."[13]

The theme of the evil perpetrated by what I call "the counterfeit distressed" continues throughout the cen-tury. In Robert Copland's *Hye way to the Spyttell house,* written in the 1530s, the truly poor and infirm are shown as left to die in the cold while those merely pretending to be poor and sick receive charity:

> Some beggarly churls . . .
> . . . walk to each market and fair
> And to all places where folk do repair,
> By day on stilts or stooping on crutches
> And so dissimule as false loitering flowches,
> With bloody clouts all about their leg,
> And plasters on their skin when they go beg.
> Some counterfeit lepry, and other some
> Put soap in their mouth to make it scum,
> And fall down as Saint Cornelys' evil.
> These deceits they use worse than any devil;
> And when they be in their own company,
> They be as whole as either you or I.[14]

The tricks purportedly used by healthy beggars to prey upon the pity of charitable individuals appear in text after text as warnings to gullible Christians: from the *Liber Vagatorum* and the *Ship of Fools* to Copland, from Copland to Awdeley (in 1561) and thence to Harman (in 1567), and from Harman verbatim into Dekker's 1608 *Bellman of London.*[15] Nor does it stop there: Robert Burton, who, in his copy of the *Bellman of London,* traces Dekker's liftings from Harman, includes in his 1621 *Anatomy of Melancholy* a discussion of beggars who "counterfeit severall diseases, . . . dismember, make themselves blind, lame, to haue a more plausible cause to beg, and lose their limmes to recover their present wants."[16]

But it was not only individuals who were represented as concerned about how to be charitable but not gullible. English statutes, annals, and chronicles beginning in the second half of the sixteenth century represent the state as aware of the need to distinguish the distressed from the counterfeit distressed so that those who genuinely need help can be relieved. Earlier in the century, English statutes and royal proclamations attack vagabonds and sturdy beggars (i.e., beggars who are healthy enough to work) not on the grounds that they fraudulently receive aid that rightfully belongs to the legitimately distressed but rather because, as a statute passed in 1547 put it, "Idlenes and vagabundry is the mother and roote of all theftes Robberyes and all evill actes and other mischiefe."[17] Although the 1547 statute does not address the question of how the state should take care of the truly distressed when the realm is purportedly filled with "a multitude of people given to" idleness and begging, chronicles represent the state as becoming aware of this issue by mid-century.

For example, in Grafton's 1569 *Chronicle* (from which it was picked up by later chroniclers) we read that in 1553, the last year of Edward VI's reign, Bishop Ridley preached a sermon on poverty and the urgent need for charity that so moved the king that he had Ridley set up a council to find a solution to the problem of how to relieve the needy. The council began its work by classifying the poor into three major categories and recommended that two of the three (those legitimately in need) should receive charity, and that those in the third category, "the thriftless poor" (i.e., "the riotous that consumeth all," "the vagabond that will abide in no place," and "the idle person, as the strumpet and other"), should be sent to workhouses.[18]

A statute passed in the fifth year of Elizabeth's reign suggests that Edward's plan did not solve the state's problem. "To thintent," it begins, "that idell and loytering persons and valiant [i.e., healthy] Beggers may be avoyded, and thimpotent, feble, and lame, which are the Poore in very dede, should bee hereafter relieved and well provided for: Bee it enacted . . ."—and the statute goes on to order that the truly distressed should be taken care of by local governments while the healthy unemployed poor should be publicly whipped and put to work.[19] Statutes from the fourteenth and thirty-ninth years of Elizabeth's reign and from the first and seventh years of James I's reign make clear that the state's response to the truly distressed and to the counterfeit distressed were represented as a problem throughout the period, up to the very year in which *The Winter's Tale* was probably written.[20]

When Autolycus pretends to be in need of aid, then, and when he caps that pretense by robbing the man who ministers to him, he incarnates a figure presented in a host of texts as an evil disrupter of the commonwealth. Autolycus himself calls attention to this ominous infracontext of pamphlets, statutes, and chronicles when, in his dialogue with the shepherd, he labels his current knavish profession as that of "rogue." Pretending to describe the thief who robbed him, Autolycus says: "I knew [Autolycus] once a servant of the Prince. . . . He hath been since an ape-bearer, then a process-server . . . , and, having flown over many knavish professions, he settled only in rogue." "A rogue," of course, is what Autolycus is called in the Folio dramatis personae list. Shakespeare had used this word in earlier plays in some of its looser senses, but in *The Winter's Tale* 4.3 it seems technical, as if it were the name of a "knavish profession."

The word did, in fact, have such a specific, legal meaning. The word *rogue* entered the English language—in print, at least—in 1561, with John Awdeley's *Fraternity of Vagabonds*.[21] There, *rogue* is the name given a particular kind of vagabond, a beggar who uses as his excuse for being on the road the tale that he is seeking a kinsman. Thomas Harman, who, in 1567, expanded Awdeley's small book into the more substantial *A caueat or warening for common cursetors vulgarely called Vagabones,* gives a much fuller character sketch:

> A Roge is neither so stoute or hardy as the vpright man. Many of them will go fayntly and look piteously when they see [or] meete any person, hauing a kercher, as white as my shooes, tyed about their head, with a short staffe in their hand, haltinge, although they nede not, requiring almes of such as they meete, or to what house they shal com. But you may easely perceiue by their colour that thei cary both health and hipocrisie about them, wherby they get gaine, when others want that cannot fayne and dissemble. Others therebee that walke sturdely about the countrey, and faineth to seke a brother or kinsman of his, dwelling within som part of the shire. . . . These also wyll pick and steale. . . . [22]

Harman's *Caueat* puts the rogue primarily among the counterfeit distressed, one of the twenty-three kinds of vagabonds and beggars Harman claims to have himself met.

The word *rogue* spread quickly after Harman's very popular book was published in 1567.[23] As the word spread and was taken up into legal terminology, it lost much of the meaning that Awdeley and Harman had given it and became a more general term used to name the healthy unemployed poor. Most significantly, in the statute against vagabonds passed and published in 1572 (14 Eliz. c.5), a rogue is legally defined as a healthy person who has neither land, nor master, nor a legitimate trade or source of income. In that same statute, the phrase "Beggars, Vagabonds, and Idle Persons"—a phrase that had appeared with slight variations in comparable statutes back to the time of Richard II[24]—now becomes, for the first time, "Rogues, Vagabonds, and sturdy Beggars," and thus it appears in every statute for punishment of the unemployed poor throughout the reign of Elizabeth and into the reign of King James. From the 1572 statute the word *rogue* passed immediately into Stow's 1573 *Summarye of the Chronicles* and from there directly into Holinshed's 1577 *Chronicles*—and even into the *Chronicles'* index.[25]

We learn from the statutes and the chronicles that, for the crime of having neither land nor master nor legitimate source of income, the rogue received various punishments: from 1572 to 1597, he or she was stripped to the waist, whipped until bloody, and had a hole burned through the gristle of the right ear; from 1597 to 1604, he or she was merely whipped until bloody, then sent back to his or her place of birth and put to work. In 1604, in James's first parliament, the 1597 statute was declared ineffective

> for that the said Rogues hauinge no marke upon them . . . may . . . retire themselves into some other parts of this Realme where they are not knowne, and soe escape the due punishmente . . . : For remedie whereof be it ordained and enacted, That such Rogues . . . shall . . . be branded in the lefte Shoulder with an hot burning Iron . . . , with a greate Romane R upon the Iron, . . . [so] that the letter R be seene and remaine for a perpetuall marke upon such Rogue during his or her life.[26]

The fierceness of attack—both physical and rhetorical—on the unemployed destitute is usually linked in the chronicles, statutes, and pamphlets to the biblical injunction against idleness. God had ordered man to labor; anyone who did not labor did not deserve to live. As Sir John Cheke wrote in 1549, people think of drones, caterpillars, and vermin as noisome beasts in the commonwealth. But what, he asks, is an idle person?

> A sucker of honie, a spoyler of corne, a destroyer of fruite, Naye a waster of money, a spoyler of vittaile, a sucker of bloud, a breker of orders, a seeker of brekes, a queller of life, a basiliske of the commune wealthe, whiche by companie and syght doth poyson the whole contrey and staineth honeste mindes with the infection of his venime, and so draweth the commune wealthe to deathe and destruction.[27]

According to Cheke (and to many others writing throughout the century), unemployed persons simply hated work,

leauing labour, which they like not, and following idlenes, which they should not. For euery man is easely and naturally brought, from labor to ease, . . . from diligence to slouthfulness. . . . [V]aliaunte beggers play in tounes, and yet complaine of neede, whose [beggar's] staffe if it be once hoat in their hande, or sluggishnes bred in their bosome, thei wil neuer be allured to labour againe, contenting them selues better with idle beggary, then with honest and profitable labour.[28]

William Harrison's "Description of England," printed as an introduction to Holinished's 1577 and 1587 *Chronicles,* includes a section entitled "Of Provision Made for the Poor."[29] Echoing the commonplace that many are idle because they hate to work—they "straie and wander about, as creatures abhorring all labour and euerie honest exercise," he writes—Harrison lashes out at the unemployed poor with a vigor comparable to Cheke's:

> [the idle] are all theeues and caterpillers in the commonwealth and by the word of God not permitted to eat, sith they do but licke the sweat from the true laborers browes & bereue the godlie poore of that which is due unto them . . . , consuming the charitie of well disposed people . . . after a most wicked & detestable maner.[30]

But Harrison, in describing the numbers of rogues and beggars in the commonwealth, asks a question of the situation that places Autolycus and his shepherd victim in a different light. Noting that "[i]dle beggers are such either through other mens occasion, or through their owne default," he writes that,

> By other mens occasion (as one waie for example) when some couetous man . . . espieng a further commoditie in their commons, holds, and tenures, doth find such meanes as thereby to wipe manie out of their occupiengs and turne the same unto his priuate gaines.

In the margin of Harrison's text appears this statement: "A thing often seene." The text then continues: "Hereupon it followeth, that . . . the greater part [of those so dispossessed] commonlie hauing nothinge to staie vpon . . . do either prooue idle beggers, or else continue starke theeues till the gallows do eat them vp." The marginal comment on this sentence reads: "At whose hands shall the bloud of these men be required?"[31]

This small questioning of who is to blame for the numbers of unemployed poor who haunt the English streets and countryside summons up a host of texts that present the story of the vagrant from quite a different perspective than that shown in the statutes against vagabonds or in the moralizings by Harman and Cheke and all the others who attack the idle poor. The other side of the story, as Harrison so briefly suggests, is that many are unemployed because their lands or jobs have been taken away from them, a point that is made in statutes "for the maintenance of husbandrie and till-age" throughout the century and in numerous pamphlets and tracts that plead to various English monarchs on behalf of the dispossessed.[32] Nowhere is this side of the story told more poignantly than in More's *Utopia*. There the point is made that England is overrun by thieves, not because thieves enjoy stealing (as one of the characters in *Utopia* claims) but because people have lost their livings: serving men out of work, returned soldiers, evicted farm laborers thrown out of work when farms are sold—these are the men and women frantic for food and driven to begging and stealing: "they that be thus destytute of seruice, other [i.e., either] starue for honger, or manfullye playe the theaues. For what wolde yow haue them to do?" Hythloday asks.[33] "I pray you," he goes on to ask, "what other thing do you [Englishmen do, but] . . . make [people into] theues and then punish them?" That which sets England apart from other nations, Hythloday says, is the way English sheep are responsible for such problems. These supposedly peaceful animals "consume, destroy, and deuoure hole fieldes, howses, and cities." Noblemen, gentlemen, and abbots, he explains, "leaue no grounde for tyllage, [but] enclose all in pastures: they throw downe houses; they plucke downe townes, and leaue nothing stondynge." One greedy sheep owner may

> inclose many thousand acres of grounde together . . . [while] the husbandmen be . . . compelled to sell all; by one meanes . . . or by other, . . . by howke or crooke they must nedes departe awaye, pore, sylie [i.e., simple], wretched soules, men, women, husbandes, wyves, fatherles chyldren, widdowes, woful mothers, with their yonge babes. . . . Awaye they trudge . . . out of their . . . howses, fyndying no places to rest in. . . . And when they haue wanderynge about sone spent [all that they have], what can they then els do but steale, . . . or else go about beggyng? And yet then also they be caste in prison as vagaboundes, because they go aboute and worke not: whom no man will set a worke, though they neuer so willingly offer them selfes thereto.[34]

This yet darker side of vagrant life in England, with its textually familiar picture of wealthy, covetous men who buy up land for pasturage and in the process dispossess thousands of people, shadows the scene in *The Winter's Tale* at which we are looking, a meeting between a rogue and a wealthy owner of sheep. Their vocations can hardly be seen as coincidental: it is not alone in More's *Utopia* that the sheep owner is blamed for the plight of vagrants and thieves.[35] Nor can it be a coincidence that the shepherd enters calculating the amount of money that will come in from this year's shearing—more than £140, a goodly sum at that time—and that he then lists the expensive delicacies that he is off to buy. In the previous scene, we were told that

this shepherd and his father had "beyond the imagination of [their] neighbors . . . grown into an unspeakable estate" (4.2.39-40). We know that the money that purchased that estate was the money found with the baby Perdita sixteen years before (3.3.116-20), but the shepherd's calculation of the money coming in this year merely from the wool of fifteen hundred of their sheep tells us that, as More and others make clear—and as is wonderfully exemplified by the fortunes of the sheep-raising family of Spencers (by 1610 having achieved a baronetcy and the reputation of having the most money of any family in England[36])—the wealth from their sheep-herding estate will bring in annually more and more wealth. In contrast, Autolycus's downward descent from serving man of the prince to the profession of rogue echoes the progress catalogued by More and many others describing the background of England's thieves. Autolycus is thus reminiscent of one of More's wretched souls who steal because "what would you have them do?"

But here the struggle between infracontexts becomes intense. Autolycus may incarnate the unemployed vagrant, a figure represented as either scandalously evil or truly pitiable. But Autolycus is given songs and dialogue that signal contexts in which he is neither evil nor pitiable. Like the vagabond poets of the twelfth and thirteenth centuries, he claims to love his life of wandering: he enters singing songs that echo both the well-known medieval "Confessions of a Vagabond," in which the wandering life is celebrated, as well as goliardic rejoicings in spring and in casual sexual encounters.[37] This lyric infracontext immensely complicates the emotive and ideological stance of the scene. Further, Autolycus's catalog of the history of his progress from one knavish profession to another signals yet another complicating infracontext, that of sixteenth-century picaresque tales that recount the adventures of the antihero who moves from profession to profession, celebrating himself and being celebrated by others for his quick wit and ability to survive.[38]

The vagabond songs and the dialogue's picaresque tonality supplement and intensify the infracontexts mentioned at the outset—the mythological texts that make Autolycus a trickster in the likeness of Mercury and the conny-catching tales that point up his cleverness vis-à-vis the foolish gull. One set of infracontexts, then, makes of the dramatic moment a variously nuanced celebration of the cunning of the trickster. Another set makes the moment instead an enactment of frightening social conflicts. When Claes Schaar briefly discusses this kind of complicated variant of his vertical context system, he notes that, in texts like this, "complex significance is very clearly to the fore" and "meaning is movable, shifting radically as different infracontexts are brought into focus." "The semantic result," he writes, is "quite different as we 'tilt' the text one way or the other."[39] In *The Winter's Tale* 4.3, if we tilt the text toward Autolycus the trickster, the moment becomes resonant with the mythology of the trickster archetype, and Autolycus can be seen as a stand-in for the artist himself, endowed with Mercury's gifts of eloquence and illusion-making, a kind of earlier-day Felix Krull.[40] If we tilt the text toward Autolycus the rogue, mentally branding his left shoulder with a great Roman R, the moment speaks more of social and economic struggle, of counterfeiting, of acting, if you will, as Autolycus first licks the sweat off the true laborer's brow and then exits to change his costume for his next actorly role.

Over the centuries, *The Winter's Tale* 4.3 has been read primarily as tilted toward the trickster infracontexts, and Autolycus has been seen as a great comic creation, a figure in which to delight. In 1611, the tilt—at least for Simon Forman—was instead toward Autolycus the rogue. As Forman wrote, after having seen the play at the Globe:

> Remember also the Rog that cam in all tottered like coll pixci. and howe he feyned him sicke & to haue bin Robbed of all that he had and howe he cosoned the por man of all his money. . . . beware of trustinge feined beggars or fawninge fellouss.[41]

Forman's use of the terms "rog," "feyned him sicke" and "feined beggars" foregrounds the moment's economic and social infracontexts; his reference to the play's wealthy shepherd as "the por man" and his warning to "beware of trustinge . . . fawninge fellouss" place Forman himself on the side of those who, like Martin Luther, felt threatened by such impostors. Forman's description of Autolycus as coming in "all tottered [i.e., tattered] like coll pixci" suggests that Forman had picked up (from the costuming, it would seem) an infracontext with links to the mythological (a coll-pixie was a mischievous supernatural being that lured people astray, into pixie paths and bogs),[42] but, for Forman, even the mythological infracontext tilts the meaning of Autolycus toward the ominous.

Today, the word *rogue* has lost its darker pejorative resonance, shepherds are no longer viewed as a primary enemy of the downtrodden, and one suspects that few readers or auditors pick up the allusion to Autolycus's namesake. For today's audience, these contexts, then, are mostly "absent structures," to borrow Umberto Eco's phrase, infracontexts that "remain inaudible like . . . voice[s] out of earshot."[43] As with so many moments in Shakespeare, though, once the voices are heard, the moment becomes tantalizing in its complexity. Thus, although Shakespeare turned printed texts not directly into other printed texts but into air, into scripts for the ephemeral breath of the stage, I would add his name to those of such poets as Dante, Milton, and Eliot, artists whose poetic effects are "powerful and dynamic [in part because they are] based . . . on

. . . complex meanings emerging along vertical axes."[44] To read Shakespeare intertextually, as I've tried to show, is to recover those complex meanings, to recognize "powerful and dynamic" poetic *and* dramatic effects, and to exchange the amusing surface context of *The Winter's Tale* 4.3 for a supercharged contextual world.

Notes

An earlier version of this paper was presented at the annual meeting of the Shakespeare Association of America in Vancouver, March 1991. I am grateful to the Newberry and the Huntington Libraries for research support.

[1] Claes Schaar, *The Full Voic'd Quire Below. Vertical Context Systems in* Paradise Lost. Lund Studies in English 60 (Lund: CWK Gleerup, 1982), 11-33.

[2] See, e.g., Mikhail Bakhtin, *The Dialogic Imagination,* trans. C. Emerson and M. Holquist (Austin: University of Texas Press, 1981); Julia Kristeva, "Word, Dialogue, and Novel," trans. Alice Jardine, Thomas Gora and Léon S. Roudiez, in *The Kristeva Reader,* ed. Toril Moi (New York: Columbia University Press, 1986), 34-61, and *Revolution in Poetic Language,* trans. Margaret Waller (New York: Columbia University Press, 1984), 13-17, 57-61; and Michael Riffaterre, "Syllepsis," *Critical Inquiry,* 6 (1980). For helpful discussions of intertextuality, see John Frow, "Intertextuality," *Marxism and Literary History* (Cambridge, Mass: Harvard University Press, 1986), 125-69, and Louise Schleiner, "Latinized Greek Drama in Shakespeare's Writing of *Hamlet,*" *Shakespeare Quarterly* 41 (1990): 29-48, esp. 45-48.

[3] Schaar, *The Full Voic'd Quire Below,* 24.

[4] All quotations from *The Winter's Tale* are from *The Complete Works of Shakespeare,* ed. David Bevington (New York: Harpercollins, 1992).

[5] *The xv. Bookes of P. Ouidius Naso, entytuled Metamorphosis, translated oute of Latin into English meeter* by Arthur Golding (London: Willyam Seres, 1567), bk. 11, ll. 359-63. Lewis Theobald, in his edition of *The Winter's Tale,* writes that "The Allusion is, unquestionably, to this Passage in Ovid. . . . The true *Autolycus* was the Son of Mercury; our fictitious one, born under his Planet; the first a Copy of his Father; the other, suppos'd to derive his Qualities from natal Predominance." *The Works of Shakespeare,* 1733, 3:116, n. 23.

[6] Walter F. Otto, "Hermes," in *The Homeric Gods,* trans. Moses Hadas (London: Thomas and Hudson, 1979; orig. pub. 1954), 104-24, esp. 104. Otto notes that Hermes (i.e., Mercury) "distinguished his son Autolycus among all men in the accomplishments of

thieving and perjury," citing *Iliad* 10.267 and *Odyssey* 19.395 (p. 104; see also p. 108). See also Robert Graves, *The Greek Myths,* 2 vols. (Pelican Books), 1:65, 216-19, and passim.

[7] Robert Greene, *The Second Part of Conny-Catching, 1592,* in The Bodley Head Quartos, ed. G. B. Harrison (London: John Lane, The Bodley Head, 1923), 40-42, esp. 41.

[8] Sir Arthur Quiller-Couch, in his introduction to the New Cambridge *Winter's Tale,* 1931, seems to have been the first scholar to note the parallel: "let anyone turn to Greene's *Second Part of Conny-catching* (1592), he will find the trick played by Autolycus on the Clown so exactly described as to leave no doubt that poor Greene was again drawn upon." Kenneth Muir, in *The Sources of Shakespeare's Plays* (1977), writes that "Autolycus . . . might have stepped out of one of the pamphlets of Harman, Greene, or Dekker, exposing the iniquities of the criminal underworld. Several of his tricks do in fact come from Greene's coney-catching pamphlets," one of which "describes . . . Autolycus' . . . robbing of the shepherd's son" (275-76).

[9] The parable is found in The Gospel of Saint Luke 10.25-37. This parable, according to the 1539 *Book of Common Prayer,* was to be read in church each thirteenth Sunday after Trinity.

[10] Jesus tells "a certain expounder of the law" (Geneva translation) that, in order to inherit eternal life, he must "love thy Lord God with all thine heart . . . , & thy neighbour as thy self." When the lawyer "said unto Iesus, Who is then my neighbour? . . . Iesus answered, and said, A certeine man went down from Ierusalem to Ierico, and fell among theues, and they robbed him of his rayment, and wounded him, & departed, leauyng him halfe dead." "A certeine Priest" and then "a Leuite" pass by the wounded man while "a certeine Samaritan . . . had compassion on him and went to him, & bounde vp his woundes, and powred in oyle and wine, and put him on his owne beast, and brought him to an ynne, and made prouision for him. And on the morowe when he departed, he toke out two pence [marginal note: which was about 9 pence of sterling money], and gaue them to the hoste, and said unto him, Take care of him, and whatsoeuer thou spendest more, when I come againe, I wil recompense thee." Jesus then asks the lawyer, "Which now of these thre, thinkest thou, was neighbour vnto him that fell among the theues?" "And he said, He that shewed mercy on him. Then said Iesus unto him: Go, and do thou lykewyse." In the Geneva Bible (from which this is quoted) the marginal gloss on Jesus's final sentence reads: "Helpe him that hath nede of thee although thou knowe him not."

[11] Sebastian Brandt, *Narrenschiff,* 1494 (trans. Alexander Barclay as *Shyp of folys* [London: Pynson, 1509]);

"Cocke Lorelles Bote" (London: Wynkyn de Worde, 1510? [reprinted in *Ancient Poetical Tracts of the Sixteenth Century,* ed. E. F. Rimbault [London: for the Percy Society, 1843]); *Liber Vagatorum der betler orden* (Augsburg: Joh. Froschauer, ca. 1509; reprinted eighteen times before being issued in 1528 under the title *Von der falschen Betler Bueberey.* It is this 1528 edition that is translated as *The Book of Vagabonds and Beggars with a Vocabulary of Their Language and a Preface by Martin Luther,* ed. D. B. Thomas [London: Penguin Press, 1932]).

The relationship among these books is not clear, in part because it has been impossible to determine when "Cocke Lorelles Bote" and *Liber Vagatorum* were first printed. All are dependent, directly or indirectly, on the advisory about beggars and vagrants issued by the Senate of Basel sometime in the fifteenth century. This advisory was transcribed, probably in 1475, by Johannes Knebel, then chaplain of the Cathedral of Basel. Because Brandt published *Narrenschiff* in 1494 when he was living in Basel, and because many details in *Narrenschiff* come from the advisory, D. B. Thomas has surmised that Knebel drew Brandt's attention to the advisory (*The Book of Vagabonds,* 11). "Cocke Lorelles Bote" seems to have been inspired either by *Narrenschiff* or *Shyp of folys.* The *Liber Vagatorum* depends on the Basel advisory for both substance and form; much of it is taken verbatim from the advisory, which is available to us in volume 1 of Heinrich Schreiber's *Taschenbuch für Geschichte und Alterthum in Suddeutschland* (Freiburg, 1839), 330-43.

[12] Thomas, ed., *The Book of Vagabonds,* 75-77, 89, 103-5.

[13] Ibid., 63-65.

[14] Robert Copland, *The hye way to the Spyttell house* (London: R. Copland, 1536?, reprinted in A. V. Judges, *The Elizabethan Underworld* [London: George Routledge & Sons, 1930), 1-25, esp. 7. Copland draws on both *Shyp of folys* and "Cocke Lorelles Bote," but he gives much more space to describing beggars and vagrants than do these earlier works.

[15] John Awdeley, *The Fraternitye of Vacabondes. As wel of ruflyng Vacabondes, as of beggerly, of women as of men, of Gyrles as of Boyes, with their proper names and qualities. With a description of the crafty company of Cousoners and Shifters. Whereunto also is adioyned the .xxv. Orders of Knaves, otherwyse called a Quartern of Knaues. Confirmed for euer by Cocke Lorell.* (London: 1575; reprinted in *Awdeley's Fraternitye of Vacabondes, . . . ,* ed. Edward Viles and F. J. Furnival [London: published for the Early English Text Society, 1869; rpt. 1975]). Furnival and Viles argue persuasively that this book was first published in 1561 (i-iv). Thomas Harman, *A caueat or warening for com-*

mon cursetors vulgarely called Vagabones (1567; Harman refers to this earliest extant copy as "the second edition"), ed. Viles and Furnivall, 19-91; Thomas Dekker, *The belman of London bringing to light the most notorious villanies now practised in the kingdome* (N. Okes for N. Butter, 1608).

[16] Robert Burton, *The Anatomy of Melancholy,* pt. 1, sec. 2, memb. 4, subs. 6 (Oxford: J. Lichfield and J. Short, 1621), 202-11, esp. 209.

[17] "1 Edw. VI.c.3. "An Acte for the Punishment of Vagabondes and for the Relief of the poore and impotent Persons." *Statutes of the Realm . . . from Original Records and Authentic Manuscripts,* 9 vols. (1801-1822), vol. 4, pt. 1, p. 5. This particular statute, sometimes called the "slavery act," set as punishment for any unemployed person who refused to work that he or she be declared a vagabond, branded on the chest with a burning iron in the shape of the letter V, and made a slave for two years; the statute was soon repealed on the grounds that the punishment was so severe that few would enforce it—though as A. L. Beier notes, "the first proposal of the 'Considerations delivered to the Parliament' of 1559 was the revival of the slavery act of 1547 against vagrants." "Vagrants and the Social Order in Elizabethan England," *Past and Present,* 64 (1974): 3-29, esp. 27.

[18] Richard Grafton, *A Chronicle at large . . . of the affayres of Englande . . .* (London: 1569). Two volumes in one. 2:1320-22.

[19] 5 Eliz. c. 3 "An Acte for the Releif of the Poore," *Statutes of the Realm,* vol. 4, pt. 1, p. 411.

[20] 14 Eliz. c. 5 "An Acte for the Punishement of Vacabondes, and for Releif of the Poore and Impotent"; 39 Eliz. c. 3, "An Acte for the Releife of the Poore"; c. 4, "An Acte for the punyshment of Rogues, Vagabonds, and Sturdy Beggars"; 1 Jac. I. c. 7, "An Acte for the Continuance and Explanation of the Statute . . . intituled An Acte for Punishmente of Rogues, Vagabonds, and Sturdie Beggars [39 Eliz. c. 4]"; 7 Jac. I. c. 4, "An Acte for the due execucion of divers Lawes and Statutes heretofore made against Rogues, Vagabonds, and sturdy Beggars and other lewde and idle persons." (*Statutes of the Realm,* vol. 4, pt. 1, pp. 590-98; vol. 4, pt. 2, pp. 896-99; vol. 4, pt. 2, pp. 899-902; vol. 4, pt. 2, pp. 1024-25; vol. 4, pt. 2, p. 1159.) The parliament that passed 7 Jac. I. c. 4 was held in 1609-10. *The Winter's Tale* is thought to have been written in 1610 or early 1611; Simon Forman saw a performance of it on 15 May 1611 at the Globe.

[21] For Awdeley and Harman, see note 15.

[22] Viles and Furnival, *Fraternitye of Vacabondes,* 36-37.

[23] For the argument that Harman's lost original version and the (expanded) earliest extant version were both published in 1567, see F. J. Furnival, preface to Viles and Furnival, *Fraternitye of Vacabondes,* iv.

[24] See, e.g., 12 Ric. II, c. 7-10, "Punishment of wandering beggers," *Statutes of the Realm,* vol. 2, p. 58.

[25] John Stow includes in his account of the year 1572 the following summary of that year's Parliament:

> "In this Parliamente, for so much as the whole Realme of England was excedinglye pestered with Roges, vagaboundes & sturdye beggers . . . it was enacted that all persons above the age of 14 yeares, being taken begging, vagrant, & wandring misorderly, should be apprehended, whipped, and burnt through the gristle of the right eare, with a hot Iron of one inche compasse. . . ."

In the margin appear the words "Roges burnt through the eare." (*A summarye of the Chronicles of Englande from the first comminge of the Brute into this Land, unto this present year of Christ, 1573* [London: Thomas Marshe, 1573], fol. 430.)

Holinshed's 1577 *Chronicles* (fol. 1862) reproduces this passage verbatim, and lists in the index [sig. K4v, 1st column, 13th entry] "Roges appoynted to be burnt through the eare. 1862.2". Raphael Holinshed, *The laste volume of the Chronicles of England, Scotlande, and Ireland* (London: 1577.) The passage appears in *The Third volume of Chronicles . . . first compiled by Raphael Holinshed . . . now newlie . . . augmented and continued . . . to the yeare 1586* (London: 1587), 1228. The 1587 index adds as an entry the word "Vagabonds" and cross-references "Roges" and "Vagabonds."

[26] 1 Jac. I c.7. *Statutes of the Realm,* vol. 4, pt. 2, p. 1025.

[27] *The hurt of Sedition, how grieueous it is to a Commune welth* (1549), sig. E5v. This work was included as an "Admonition" from Sir John Cheke in Holinshed's 1577 *Chronicles,* 1688-89 [1689 is incorrectly numbered 1869], and in Holinshed's 1587 *Chronicles,* 1042-55.

[28] Cheke, sigs. E4v-E5.

[29] Harrison's *Description* appears as "An Historicall Description of the Islande of Britayne, with a briefe rehearsall of the nature and qualities of the people of Englande . . ." in Raphael Holinshed, *The firste volume of the Chronicles of England, Scotlande, and Irelande. . . .* (London: 1577), fols. 1-125; the section on the poor appears as bk. 3, chap. 5, fols. 106 v-107 r. The *Description* appears as "An Historicall description of the Iland of Britaine . . . Comprehended in three bookes," in Holinshed, *The first and second vol-*

umes of Chronicles . . . London: 1587, 1:1-250; the section on the poor appears as bk. 2, chap. 10, pp. 182-30.

[30] Holinshed, *The first and second volumes of Chronicles* . . . London: 1587, 1:183.

[31] Ibid.

[32] See, e.g., Simon Fish, *A Supplication for the Beggers* (ca. 1529) and *A Supplication of the Poore Commons* (1546), in *Four Supplications,* ed. J. M. Cowper, pp. 1-18, 59-92. See also Robert Crowley who, in 1550, addressed the wealthy as follows:

> If you charge them wyth disobedience, you were firste disobedient. For without a law to beare you, yea contrarie to the law which forbiddeth al maner of oppression & extortion, & that more is contrarie to conscience . . . ye enclosed from the pore their due commones, leavied greater fines then heretofore have been leavied, put them from the liberties . . . that they held by custome, & reised theire rentes. . . . if you had loved your contrei, would you not have prevented the great destruction that chanced by the reason of your unsaciable desire? . . . How you have obeyed the lawes in rakeing together of fermes, purchaising and prollynge for benefices. . . . (*The Way to Wealth, wherein is plainly taught a most present Remedy for Sedicion,* in J. M. Cowper, ed., *The Select Works of Robert Crowley* [Early English Text Society, extra series, 15, 1872; rpt. Kraus Reprint, 1975], 130-50, esp. 144-45.)

Crowley again, in his *An information and Peticion agaynst the oppressours of the pore Commons of this Realme,* writes to the wealthy:

> Beholde, you engrossers of fermes and teynements, beholde, I say, the terible threatnynges of God, whose wrath you can not escape. The voyce of the pore (whom you haue with money thruste out of house and whome) is well accepted in the eares of the Lord. . . . Knowe then that he hath not cauled you to the welthe and glorie of this worlde, but hath charged you wyth the greate and rude multitude. And if any of them perishe thorowe your defaute, know then for certentye, that the bloode of them shall be required at your handes. If the impotent creatures perish for lacke of necessaries, you are the murderers, for you have theyr enheritaunce and do minister vnto them. If the sturdy fall to stealeyng, robbyng, & reueynge, then are you the causers thereof, for you dygge in, enclose, and wytholde from the earth out of whych they should dygge and plowe theyr lyueynge. (J. M. Cowper, ed., *Select Works of Robert Crowley,* 151-76, esp. 161-64.)

[33] *A fruteful and pleasant worke . . . called Utopia . . . by Syr Thomas More.* trans. Raphe Robynson (London: Abraham Vele, 1551), sig. C4v.

[34] Ibid., sigs. C6v-C8.

[35] See, eg., *Certayne causes gathered together wherein is shewed together the decaye of England, only by the great multitude of shepe, to the utter decay of houshold keping. . . .* (1550-53), a petition addressed to Edward VI's council:

> We saye, as reason doeth leade us, that shepe & shepemasters doeth cause skantyte of corne [;] . . . where tillage was wont to be, nowe is it stored with greate vmberment of shepe. . . . [As people are thrown off the land,] whether shall then they go? foorth from shyre to shyre, and to be scathered thus abrode, within the Kynges maiestyes Realme, where it shall please Almighty God; and for lack of maisters, by compulsion dryuen, some of them to begge, and some to steale.

> . . . thre hundred thousand persons were wont to have meate, drinke, and rayment, uprysing and down lying, paying skot and lot to God & to the Kyng. And now they haue nothynge, but goeth about in England from dore to dore, and axe theyr almose for Goddes sake. And because they will not begge, some of them doeth steale, and then they be hanged, and thus the Realm doeth decay. . . .

Four Supplications, (Early English Text Society, extra series, 13, 1871; rpt. Kraus Reprint, 1981), ed. J. Meadows Cowper, 95-102, esp. 95-98, 101-2.

[36] Mary E. Finch, "Spencer of Althorp," in *The Wealth of Five Northamptonshire Families. 1540-1640* (Oxford: Printed for the Northamptonshire Record Society, 1956), 38-65.

[37] See, e.g., the following stanza of the most popular of all the goliardic lyrics, the "Vagabond's Confession," by the "Archipoeta" in *Vagabond Verse: Secular Latin Poems of the Middle Ages,* trans. Edwin W. Zeydel (Detroit: Wayne State University Press, 61):

> Down the highway broad I walk,
>   Like a youth in mind,
>   Implicate myself in vice,
>   Virtue stays behind,
>   Avid for the world's delight
>   More than for salvation,
>   Dead in soul, I care but for
>   Body's exultation.

[38] See, e.g., *The Pleasaunt historie of Lozarillo de Tormes,* trans. D. Rouland (London: A. Jeffes, 1586); Henry Chettle, *Piers Plainnes seauen yeres Prentiship* (London: J. Danter, 1595); Nicholas Breton, *A Merrie Dialogue betwixt the Taker and the Mistaker* (London: James Shaw, 1603; published in 1635 as *A Mad World My Masters*); Thomas Nashe, *The Unfortunate Trav-*

eler (T. Scarlet for C. Burby, 1594). See also Robert Alter, *Rogue's Progress. Studies in the Picaresque Novel* (Cambridge, Mass.: Harvard University Press, 1964).

[39] Schaar, *The Full-Voic'd Quire Below,* 27.

[40] For Mercury as god of eloquence, see Walter F. Otto, *The Homeric Gods* (note 6, above); for Thomas Mann's Felix Krull as the trickster/artist, see Donald Nelson, *Portrait of the Artist as Hermes. A Study of Myth and Psychology in Thomas Mann's* Felix Krull (University of North Carolina Press, 1971), and Alter, *Rogue's Progress,* 126-29.

[41] This record of the performance of *The Winter's Tale* at the Globe on 15 May 1611 is found in Forman's manuscript *The Bocke of Plaies and Notes thereof per formans for Common Pollicie.* The record is printed by J. N. P. Pafford in his Arden edition of *The Winter's Tale,* xxi-xxii.

[42] Pafford notes that "*coll pixci* (i.e., Colle- or Colt-pixie)" is "a hobgoblin, particularly in the form of a ragged (tattered) colt which leads horses astray into bogs, etc." (xxi). In *Nimphidia: The Court of Fayrie,* (published in *Battaile of Agincourt,* 1627, 117-34), Michael Drayton conflates the "colt-pixie" with Hobgoblin or Puck:

> This Puck seemes but a dreaming dolt,
> Stil walking like a ragged Colt,
> And oft out of a Bush doth bolt,
>   Of purpose to deceive us.
> And leading us makes us to stray,
> Long Winters nights out of the way,
> And when we stick in mire and clay,
>   Hob doth with laughter leave us.
> (Stanza xxxvii)

[43] Umberto Eco, *La Struttura Assente* (Milan, 1968; cited by Schaar, 17); Schaar, 17.

[44] Schaar, 24.

DREAMS

Ruth Nevo (essay date 1987)

SOURCE: "Delusions and Dreams: *The Winter's Tale,*" in *Shakespeare's Other Language,* Methuen, 1987, pp. 95-129.

[*In the following essay, Nevo contends that, while the traditional dramatic unities are flouted in* The Winter's Tale, *fantasy shapes the drama's two interrelated plots* around a pair of dreams, "*where one represents a terror inelectably realized and the other a restitutive wish-fulfillment.*"]

> Death, as we all know, is not something to be looked at in the face.
>
> (J.-B. Pontalis)

In *The Winter's Tale* the once mandatory dramatic "unities"—time, place, action and motivation tumble to the ground like a house of cards. Constructed out of two antithetical parts, in two different geographical locations, it is halved in the centre by a "wide gap of time" and propelled into action by an unmotivated outburst of ruinous rage. Among other notorious oddities, such as the bear-infested but nonexistent sea-coast of Bohemia, there is a memorable rogue who accompanies the second half of the play in a way which has defeated most attempts at interpretation.[1] These are no longer regarded as preposterous, as lapses, crudities or absurdities.[2] *The Winter's Tale* is safely ensconced among the masterpieces. Yet perplexities and uneasinesses remain.

Let me make a bold foray into the thicket of *The Winter's Tale.* If I were asked to formulate in one short sentence the gist of what *The Winter's Tale* is "about" I would say the following: In *The Winter's Tale* a child is lost, and a lost child is found: between these extremities *The Winter's Tale* runs its course. And I would add that the deeply embedded inner tale is Mamillius', a "sad tale" of "sprites and goblins" and of "a man" who "dwelt by a churchyard" (II.i.25-30), which has only a beginning, and is for Hermione's ear alone.

My attempt in the following pages is to reconstruct the fantasy which, I believe, animates and unifies the play, from which it derives its power to move us, and which determines and shapes its manifest drama. The fantasy has its roots in the deepest, most archaic, and most painful of our human experiences; yet, at the same time its expression by means of formal invention and mimetic verisimilitude, its orchestration of manifold means of dramatic representation and of dramatic utterance is particularly elaborate and rich. I believe that a rereading of *The Winter's Tale* receptive to the resonances of deep-level fantasy can take us beyond the traditional explanatory themes which are invoked as organizers and arbiters of meaning—the seasons of great creating nature, for instance, or the miracles of a benign providence—to uncover the sources of the play's emotional power. It can also take us beyond (or at least put into brackets) the orthodox psychoanalytic explications of Leontes' sudden onset of delusional jealousy.

In its own time the play was a masterpiece in a new and popular mode. The particular version of pastoral called *tragicomoedia* (or, as it was sometimes called, *comitragoedia*) had become over the two decades preceding the composition of *The Winter's Tale*, one of the central projects in the Renaissance literary itinerary. It had bred, among other taxonomic peculiarities, a Latin closet drama of 1612-14 by Mario Bettini subtitled *Hilarotragoedia Satyropastoralis* which, besides out-Heroding Polonius, offered a smorgasbord of situations, character types, figures, topoi, and devices from the Renaissance repertory. It also developed a legitimate hybrid genre called *commedia grave* which was a conjunction of features from Cinthio's *tragedia de lieto fin* and from Arcadian comedy.[3] Its declared intent was the mingling of hornpipes and funerals which Sidney had found so objectionable. Thus the compounding, conflating and juxtaposing of incompatible plots had become fashionable in late sixteenth-century Italy, intent upon a mannerist subversion of neoclassical rules, and an aesthetic of paradox and indeterminacy. That Shakespeare's art was affected by such trends is not in question. One recalls, among other anachronisms—English Whitsun pastoral rubbing shoulders with Greek oracles, for instance—the odd presence of Guilio Romano, Raphael's mannerist successor, at the court of Leontes, or at least within reach of Paulina's commission. As Rosalie Colie reminds us, "*The Winter's Tale* is an astonishingly *timely* play, seen against continental preoccupations" (1974, 265). That there is a craftsman's pride in the violence with which the two halves of the play are split apart, and the cunning with which they are spliced together, as if the controlling structures of tragedy and comedy were pitted against each other and locked in mortal combat, is perhaps indicated by the third gentleman's description of Paulina in the scene of reunions: "But O! the noble combat that 'twixt joy and sorrow was fought in Paulina! She had one eye declin'd for the loss of her husband, another elevated that the oracle was fulfill'd" (V.ii.72-6). *The Winter's Tale*, with its twinning of genres and generations, its gap (or compression) of time, its triumphantly double resolution and its bogus miracle is a contemporary *tour de force*. Pauline thus described, is a bizarre emblem of the play's duality, possibly a covert plea for the audience's admiration.

How are we to respond to this hybrid form? Are we merely to applaud a triumph of conscious virtuosity? We cannot easily say whether the tragedy is embedded in the comedy or vice versa. Is Leontes' destructive aberration a wintry episode in an ongoing unending story of growth and renewal? Or is the family good fortune a happy contingency in an ongoing unending Schopenhauerian story of loss and grief? Which of these *is* the *The Winter's Tale?* "A sad tale's best for winter" (II.i.25) Mamillius tells his mother and, since he is one of the play's two casualties, his view has a certain cogency; but does he point to part or whole? *The Winter's Tale*, fissured by its oppositions of time, place, tempo, mood, style, mode and genre is bound by innumerable linkages and mirrorings; yet in it tragedy will not absorb or synthesize comedy, nor comedy tragedy.

The gentleman who reports on the joyful reunion between Leontes and Polixenes makes this very point, and is unable to read the signs: "There was speech in their dumbness, language in their very gesture; they look'd as they had heard of a world ransom'd, or one destroy'd" (V.ii.13-15).

The two halves of *The Winter's Tale* present us with a tragic structure powerfully compressed, and a recognizably familiar New Comedy in the pastoral mode which defers, but finally extends and deepens the anagnorisis. The final Act enacts a double resolution: the conflicts of both plots are defused by one and the same recognition—the discovery of the foundling Perdita—an admirable instance of the "well-tied knot" to which the writers of tragicomedy aspired, and a wish-fulfillment of the most tormenting of all human desires—to undo irreversible error.

The second part of the play, then, redeems the first, but it is also obsessively repetitive of the first, as if it were haunted by the same ghosts and goblins. New life is born in the first part and cast out to sea; new young love is born in the second, and cast out to sea, and in each case by "wintry" passions, Leontes' and Polixenes', doubles in their tyrannical ferocity as they were in their boyhood twinship. Antigonus saves an unacknowledged daughter from her father in the first part, Camillo an unrecognized son from his father in the second. The second part replays, reiterates the first in manifold ways. The triangle of the first part—Leontes, Hermione, Polixenes—is twice realigned, with intermingled variations, in the second: Leontes accuses his wife of relations with his old friend, and comes between them; or, if you will, the old friend comes between the couple. The old friend accuses his son of relations with Leontes' daughter, and comes between them; or, if you will, Hermione's daughter comes between father and son. Finally Leontes, momentarily tempted to come between his own daughter and the friend's son, sanctions their union. As James Edward Siemon puts it:

> Each of the two halves of the play has a wrathful king; innocent victims; a princess slandered; a servant who serves his master's highest interests by betraying him; a kingdom without an heir or threatened with the loss of its heir; a voyage over a stormy sea; a providential revelation . . . each part has at its center two men and a woman: two "brothers" and a queen of Sicilia; father and son and a princess of Sicilia. There can be little doubt that the second part of the play represents a conscious variation on the themes and plot motives of the first. (1974, 13)

How do we respond to these obsessive doublings? The recurrences bind the contrasting structures, but they bind with a difference—as the suturing of a wound draws attention to the wound. They suggest the unstable asymmetry of a triad struggling, again and again, to right itself. The grip over our minds exerted by *The Winter's Tale* is beyond the cunning of connoisseurship or virtuosity. The play is not only a *tour de force* in contemporary dramaturgy; it is a *tour de force* in the theatre of reverie, which, . . . is the mode of Shakespearean romance. There is therefore another kind of cunning which I would wish to invoke in an account of *The Winter's Tale:* that of the most cunning of interpreters, and of his subject matter.

In his "Revision of the Theory of Dreams," collected in *New Introductory Lectures,* Freud writes:

> Franz Alexander (1925) has shown in a study on pairs of dreams that it not infrequently happens that two dreams in one night share the carrying-out of the dream's task by producing a wish-fulfilment in two stages if they are taken together, though each dream separately would not effect that result. Suppose, for instance, that the dream-wish had as its content some illicit action in regard to a particular person. Then in the first dream the person will appear undisguised, but the action will be only timidly hinted at. The second dream will behave differently. The action will be named without disguise, but the person will either be made unrecognizable or replaced by someone indifferent. This, you will admit, gives one an impression of actual cunning. Another and similar relation between the two members of a pair of dreams is found where one represents a punishment and the other the sinful wish-fulfilment. It amounts to this: "if one accepts the punishment for it, one can go on to allow oneself the forbidden thing." (1933, 56)

These remarks are extremely suggestive, though cast in terms too minatory and judgemental to be quite applicable to the eudaemonic ends of Shakespearean comedy. Freud's hypothetical case of a pair of dreams does not exactly fit the carriage of fantasy in Shakespeare's pair of interrelated plots, but his comment suggests a structural model with which to go to work. With *The Winter's Tale* in mind one would add a sentence to his: "Another and similar relation between two members of a pair of dreams is found where one represents a terror ineluctably realized and the other a restitutive wish-fulfillment." This, I shall argue, helps us to chart the trajectory of fantasy in *The Winter's Tale* and enables us to account for and respond to its particular force.

The text obtrudes its contradictory double nature from the very beginning. The prologue scene imparts preliminary information about the two kings' friendship, but the exchange of courtesies between Camillo and Archidamus is riddled by ambiguities—a palimpsest whose ulterior meanings subvert or nullify the decorous overt intention. "If you shall chance, Camillo, to visit Bohemia, on the like occasion whereon my services are now on foot, you shall see (as I have said) great difference betwixt our Bohemia and your Sicilia"

(I.i.1-4); "We will give you sleepy drinks, that your senses (unintelligent of our insufficience) may, though they cannot praise us, as little accuse us" (13-16); "You pay a great deal too dear for what's given freely" (17-18); Sicilia and Bohemia "were train'd together in their childhoods; and there rooted betwixt them then such an affection, which cannot choose but branch now" (22-4). Benignly horticultural, the branch—metaphor for flourishing growth—is itself also a metaphor for parting and division; and the image, rebuslike, conceals (or does not conceal) the ubiquitous Elizabethan cuckold's horns. The euphuistic description of the two kings' friendship contains its own antithesis: "they have seem'd to be together, though absent; shook hands, as over a vast; and embrac'd as it were from the ends of oppos'd winds" (29-33). It is totally reversible, indeterminately an affirmation of their togetherness when apart, or their estrangement even when together. These double, or treble, entendres in which the two possibilities, the idyllic and the catastrophic, coexist reflect the larger structure of the play and of Leontes' dilemma. The rhetoric of courtesy slyly rehearses it seems, the entire ensuing drama.

In the grand opening scene too, Polixenes' "Nine changes of the wat'ry star" (I.ii.1) refers ostensibly to the duration of his absence from Bohemia. But the presence on stage of Leontes' pregnant queen ineluctably fills, so to speak, the semantic space, and magnetizes, or sexualizes, in consequence the entire subsequent text: "Without a burthen," "filled up," "standing in rich place," "what may chance/Or breed," "to tire your royalty" (to weary you? to wear your robes? to prey upon you?). If the unconscious is structured like a language, in Lacan's famous apothegm, this language certainly seems to be structured like an unconscious, in which the benign and the threatening are held in contradictory suspension. What are we to make of this unruly text which seems to be constructing its own counterplot in defiance of any narrative logic? For on the face of it, in the prologue the courtiers are merely exchanging prefatory courtesies. In Act I, scene ii Polixenes is politely refusing his friend's pressing hospitality. Equivocation in the dialogue with Leontes must surely undermine the speaker's own purpose, for Polixenes would be unlikely to be interested in insinuating into his host's mind suspicions of a liaison with the latter's wife, should there have been any such. Does Leontes hear what we hear? Does he hear what we are not supposed, as it were, to hear? Or are we privy to a communication neither of the protagonists hear?

William H. Matchett provides an ingenious answer:

> The language, no less than Hermione, is pregnant. Hermione, we are by now convinced, is accustomed to using more warmth with Polixenes. It is true that we must later discover that we were wrong, that this was all innocent, but Shakespeare's dramatic

method here is first to mislead *us* in order to hasten the process of misleading Leontes. He has in fact misled us twice; first in scene i by preparing us for innocent friendship and now in scene ii by presenting an image of guilt where there is in fact innocence. (1969, 96, and passim)

Matchett fails to explain, however, why it is the manifest meaning, the "innocent" meaning that is operative in the prologue scene whereas in scene ii he claims priority for the innuendo—the "guilty" meaning. By line 77 Polixenes' "Temptations have since been born to's," ostensibly an elegiac lament for the passing of childhood innocence, *we* hear, Matchett is persuaded, "a sophisticated understatement shared with Hermione and the audience behind Leontes' back" (97), and by this time "we would be wondering when Leontes will face what is going on." Similarly, Hermione's

> Th'offenses we have made you do we'll
>   answer,
> If you first sinn'd with us
>
> (I.ii.83-4)

is not, according to Matchett, to be read as a confidant disavowal but, with the accent upon "first," as a sly confession. Shakespeare's "masterful manipulation," in Matchett's reading, causes us to become suspicious long before Leontes does. We should feel, he says, not that Leontes is too rapidly jealous, but that he has been very slow about it. And the point? If we ourselves have been led to mistake innocence for guilt, how can we entirely blame Leontes?

M. Mahood, who preceded Matchett in the study of the ambiguities, disagrees:

> It is possible, of course, to read long-standing suspicion into all Leontes' speeches to Polixenes and Hermione, from the first appearance of the three characters. But this impairs the dramatic contrast between the happiness and harmony of the three characters when Polixenes has agreed to stay, and Leontes' subsequent outburst of passion ("Too hot, too hot"). . . . a sudden outburst of normally suppressed feelings, which struggle for their release in savage wordplay." ((1957) 1971, 348)

However, she, intent upon evidence of a wise Shakespearean tolerance of inexplicable human frailty, does not explain why there should have been such an outburst. Both these astute Empsonians construe univocally, in terms of their differing interpretative purposes, the entire string of comments with which Leontes punctuates his wife's persuasion of Polixenes, although at any point in the series ("Tongue-tied, our Queen? (27), "Well said, Hermione" (33), "Is he won yet?" (86), and "At my request he would not./Hermione, my dearest, thou never spok'st/To better purpose" (87-9)) either a

generous and gracious innocence or a dissimulated but tormenting suspicion might be what is signified.

Let us attempt to relocate Leontes within the linguistic web of this scene. The undertones in Polixenes' "nine changes" speech cannot, with any dramatic feasibility, incriminate Polixenes, but they can be heard by Leontes with certain triggering effects. The mere reference to the number nine, Freud noted, "whatever its connection, directs our attention to the phantasy of pregnancy" ("A Seventeenth Century Demonological Neurosis" (1923) SE.XIX,93). This is a useful reminder, for if we read the resonances of the "nine months" speech as pointing towards Leontes' fantasy rather than as incriminating Polixenes, we then are enabled to perceive that a certain anxiety attends the fact, in itself, of his wife's condition. Polixenes has left his throne without a burden, he says. For Leontes "burden" may well evoke the thought of that with which his own throne is "filled up." In the ambivalence of "to tire your royalty," the hint of succession is subverted by the simultaneous hint of usurpation. If Leontes is reading himself in Polixenes' text, then "like a cipher standing in rich place" (I.ii.6-7) succinctly suggests the nothingness, the emptiness of exclusion from a once experienced plenitude. Our third ear, moreover, catches a disturbing note in both Hermione's exchanges with her husband. It is not perhaps Hermione's most felicitious move to offer to allow Leontes to overstay as long as a whole month in Bohemia should the occasion arise, and with the assurance: "yet, good deed, Leontes,/I love thee not a jar o'th'clock behind/What lady she her lord" (42-4). Any lady? Whatever lady you care to mention? It is an oddly noncommittal claim, surely, but worse is to follow:

> What? have I twice said well? When was't
>   before? . . .
> But once before I spoke to th'purpose? when?
> Nay, let me hav't; I long.
>
> (89-101)

This is spoken jestingly, of course, but it is not unknown for jests to be used to camouflage resentments. Neither Leontes' description of the "three crabbed months" which soured themselves to death before Hermione's "I am yours forever" was uttered, nor his pointed reference to his dagger, muzzled "Lest it should bite its master, and so prove,/[As ornament] oft does, too dangerous" (157-8) do much to mitigate the impression we might receive of a couple in considerable marital stress, if not positive crisis.

It is in this context that Polixenes describes a nostalgic fantasy of perfect unity, when he and Leontes were as "twinn'd lambs, that did frisk i'th'sun,/And bleat the one at th'other" exchanging "innocence for innocence" (67-9).[4] The yearning is for the timeless—"Two lads that thought . . . to be boy eternal" (63-65)—and, significantly, the speechless: for a moment, known in infancy and long since lost, of undifferentiated oneness with another being. Hermione, jesting, provokes the insertion into the scene of the mutations, the depradations, of time—"By this we gather/You have tripp'd since" (75-6). Polixenes' reply is fervent:

> O my most sacred lady,
> Temptations have since then been born to's: for
> In those unfledg'd days was my wife a girl;
> Your precious self had then not cross'd the
>   eyes
> Of my young playfellow
>
>   (76-9)

hers is flippant:

> Grace to boot!
> Of this make no conclusion, lest you say
> Your queen and I are devils. Yet go on,
> Th'offenses we have made you do we'll
>   answer,
> If you first sinn'd with us.
>
>   (80-4)

and Leontes' entire string of comments, as we have seen, is opaquely ambiguous until his explicit. "Too hot, too hot!" (108):

> I have *tremor cordis* on me; my heart dances,
> But not for joy; not joy. This entertainment
> May a free face put on, derive a liberty
> From heartiness, from bounty, fertile bosom,
> And well become the agent; 't may, I grant.
> But to be paddling palms and pinching fingers,
> As now they are, and making practic'd smiles
> As in a looking glass; and then to sigh, as
>   'twere
> The mort o'th'deer—O, that is entertainment
> My bosom likes not, nor my brows.
>   Mamillius,
> Art thou my boy? . . .
>   How now, you wanton calf,
> Art thou my calf?
>
>   (110-20, 126)

Leontes' torment is felt and uttered first as a problem of doubt, of what he can know, be sure of, in respect of his wife's fidelity, and subsequently as conviction of her sexual betrayal, but the question of adultery, we are enabled to perceive, is a mask, or a defence against a breach in his certainty which lies far deeper, in infantile fears of isolation, separation and abandonment. Leontes has been (visibly) separated, isolated, by the *tête-à-tête* between Hermione and Polixenes, especially by the intimacies of the twinned lambs exchange; but he has already been separated or isolated by Hermione's new intimacy with her unborn child. That it is by the archaic rage of a sibling rivalry for an undivided mother

that he is overthrown is perhaps confirmed later by the ferocious violence with which he would consign the babe (and its mother) to the flames, in Act II, scene iii, would see it "commit[ted] to the fire" (96); "I'll ha'thee burned" (114); "Better burn it now" (156).

It is the ancient loss, I believe the play tells us, that lies at the root of Leontes' seizure. There is, we are told, in every delusion a grain of truth. Hermione does betray Leontes, with her children, and it is the repetition of that maternal betrayal which is displaced upon the supposed adulterers, doubly determined figures in the primal drama. If we take a cue from psychoanalytic theory it is in such primal drama that all tragedy is rooted, and from its unassuaged pain that theatre-going draws its appeal. Leontes himself sets up the structure of a fantasied primal scene, in which he is the excluded third, spying, watching, testing, angling—"I am angling now,/ Though you perceive me not how I give line. . . . How she holds up the neb, the bill to him!" (I.ii.180-3)—trapping Hermione in a double bind: "How thou lov'st us, show in our brother's welcome" (174). If she is cold she will appear an uncompliant and disobedient wife; if warm, a self-betraying adulteress; she cannot win, nor does he wish her to win, for beneath the available postures of patriarchal male jealousy ("Should all despair/That have revolted wives, the tenth of mankind/Would hang themselves" (188-200) and "Go play, boy, play. Thy mother plays, and I/Play too, but so disgrac'd a part, whose issue/Will hiss me to my grave; contempt and clamor/Will be my knell" (187-9)) lies the threat that is the greater because it is unknown. "Gone already" (185) on the face of it refers to the speed with which Hermione and Polixenes vanish together into the garden, but its resonance surely comes from an absence long ago experienced.

Ostensibly Leontes' questioning of Mamillius' likeness to himself expresses a worry about his paternity of the boy, but if this were really so, surely the answer would not be so insistently affirmative. What does he seek as he gazes into the face of his son, his "sweet villain," flesh of his flesh? It is a "copy" of his own—they are "almost as like as eggs" (note the image of symbiotic enclosure and totality) though it is false women who say so (122-36, passim). It is the paternity, after all, of the second child, not of Mamillius, that has been, if it has, placed in doubt. It is that imminent interloper who has reawakened the archaic loss, the archaic grief and rage, has made Leontes, at this moment, a replaced, or supplanted child, reliving the anguish of the mother's betrayal.

Dissimulating his agitation Leontes avows the "folly" of his "tenderness" for Mamillius:

>   Looking on the lines
> Of my boy's face, methoughts I did recoil
> Twenty-three years, and saw myself unbreech'd,

In my green velvet coat . . .
How like (methought) I then was to this
 kernel,
This squash, this gentleman. Mine honest
 friend,
Will you take eggs for money?

                              (153-61)

We recall "We are almost as like as eggs" a few
moments before, so that it is possible to interpret the
question as a pained recognition of the illusoriness (as
against the reality of money) of the unity-in-identity, the
existential certainty that he had longed to find, if not in
the mother, then at least in the mirror of his son's "wel-
kin eye" (136). Then he turns to Polixenes with a question for his "brother": "Are you so fond of your young
prince as we/Do seem to be of ours?" (163-4); and receives the expected tenderly affectionate reply:

              If at home, sir,
He's all my exercise, my mirth, my matter;
Now my sworn friend, and then mine enemy;
My parasite, my soldier, statesman, all.
He makes a July's day short as December,
And with his varying childness, cures in me
Thoughts that would thick my blood.

                              (165-71)

It is worth pausing a moment over that reply. Why
would one wish a long summer day to be as short as
a winter one? On the face of it Polixenes is describing
childish games—he is a father who enjoys playing
cowboys and Indians or cops and robbers with his young
son—but can we ignore the subversive connotations of
"enemy," of "parasite," above all of the strange inversion of July and December? The game itself acts out
subliminal hostilities. Thoughts that would thick the
blood are indeed soothed, stilled, by the charm of a
child but the child is also a threat, a supplanter, a
usurper. The face that is his own will one day efface
his own. Leontes hears what we hear and replies, "So
stands this squire officed with me" (172-3). The strange
double message of Polixenes reflects, then, an emotion
shared by these two twinned figures, and enables us to
take a further step in the understanding of Leontes.

Leontes' passionate cleaving to the boy is rooted in
identification—they are both ousted rivals for the
mother's love—but it is also traversed by the deeper,
unrecognized source of dread. He sees himself in Mamillius: the child in himself, his double (154-5), but he
also sees his successor, and his death. Later, we recall,
he cannot bear Paulina's insistence upon the new-born
baby's resemblance to himself.

It becomes of the greatest interest to follow the course
of Leontes' struggle against the upsurge of a turbu-
lence which threatens to overthrow him, his half-aware
struggle to maintain a foothold in reality:

                    Come, sir page . . .
Most dear'st, my collop! Can thy dam?—
 may't be?
Affection! thy intention stabs the centre.
Thou dost make possible things not so held
Communicat'st with dreams (how can this
 be?),
With what's unreal thou co-active art,
And fellow'st nothing. Then 'tis very credent
Thou mayst co-join with something, and thou
 dost
(And that beyond commission), and I find it
(And that to the infection of my brains
And hard'ning of my brows).

                              (135-46)

This speech has been much commented upon. I think
we can best understand it as exhibiting the moment of
the switch-over in Leontes' thinking from the rational
procedures of reality testing to the autistic, associa-
tional imagery of the primary processes, the imagery
produced by the self's inner needs and dreads.[5] It is his
last bulwark. Henceforth ratiocination itself will be
flooded by fantasy, saturated by an influx of representations welling up from the depths of the mind, eluding
all attempts at repression. If "affection" is glossed, as
it often is, to refer to Hermione's alleged aberrant
passion, which stabs to the very center of Leontes' (or
the world's) being, the rest of the speech becomes
extremely obscure;[6] but suppose we read it as a re-
arguard action, so to speak, half in sight, half in blindness, of a mind on the very brink of a self-induced,
defensive delusion? "Affection" then is his own jealousy, which, seeking confirmation in reality has found,
"communicat[ing] with dreams . . . with what's unreal," only that which feeds its flames. What if these
intuitions do indeed stab the center, the bull's eye?
The acknowledged power of fantasy to find a bush a
bear now presents itself as doubly forceful confirmation of its divinatory powers when the bush really is a
bear! Caught in these toils this Shakespearean snowman
experiences the

   intricate evasions of as,
 In things seen and unseen, created from
  nothingness . . .
 The heavens, the hells, the worlds, the longed
  for lands[7]

and totally embraces the fiction which protects him,
with the possessive masculine postures available to him
in his society, from the deeper vulnerability, the unrecognized source of dread. Hence, in the flood of ob-
scene images which follows, birth and copulation, entry
and exit are scarcely to be distinguished.

                    Gone already!
Inch-thick, knee-deep, o'er head and ears a
 forked one! . . .

And many a man there is (even at this present,
Now, while I speak this) holds his wife by
  th'arm,
That little thinks she has been sluic'd in's
  absence,
And his pond fish'd by his next neighbor—by
Sir Smile, his neighbor. Nay, there's comfort
  in't,
Whiles other men have gates, and those gates
  open'd,
As mine, against their will. . . .
                              Be it concluded,
No barricado for a belly. Know't,
It will let in and out the enemy,
With bag and baggage.

                              (I.ii.185-206, passim)

Earlier, in the exchange with Mamillius on the need to be "neat" the threat of the primary process image-language of dream is still under control, though the pressure of its metaphors to subsume reality is formidably great:

                              Come, captain,
We must be neat; not neat, but cleanly, captain:
And yet the steer, the heifer, and the calf
Are all call'd neat.—Still virginalling
Upon his palm? How now, you wanton calf,
Art thou my calf? . . .
Thou want'st a rough pash and the shoots that
  I have
To be full like me

                              (122-9)

Now his world is a bestiary: "How she holds up the neb! the bill to him!" (183). Now Leontes is entirely at the mercy of his fantasy, as if the whole lexis is alive with pointing fingers, or with poisoned arrows. Every world of Camillo in the dialogue between them at once inflames his imagination and provides proof positive for his conviction: "You had much ado to make his anchor hold/When you cast out it still came home" (213-14); "Satisfy/Th'entreaties of your mistress? *Satisfy?*/Let that suffice" (233-5; my italics). Hermione is a "hobbyhorse . . . rank as any flax-wench" (276-7); were her liver as infected as her life, "she would not live/The running of one glass" (304-6). In his persuasion of Camillo fantasy positively parades itself, ostentatiously, as reality-testing, but reality is no longer separable from image:

                              Is whispering nothing?
Is leaning cheek to cheek? is meeting noses?
Kissing with inside lip? stopping the career
Of laughter with a sigh . . .
                              horsing foot on foot?
Skulking in corners? wishing clocks more
  swift?
Hours, minutes? noon, midnight? and all eyes

Blind with the pin and web but theirs . . .
                              Is this nothing?
Why then the world and all that's in't is
  nothing,
The covering sky is nothing, Bohemia nothing,
My wife is nothing, nor nothing have these
  nothings,
If this be nothing.

                              (284-95)[8]

Rhetorically, the figure he employs is an apodiosis, the indignant rejection of an argument as impertinent or absurdly false (Lanham, 1968, 13), but the ratiocinative appeal to items of evidence virtually conjures an act of intercourse into being. The body imagery, progressing from cheeks, noses, inside lip, horsing foot on foot, to the metaphorically sexual pin and web, and the "covering" sky, exacerbates an inflamed imagination, verbally creates the coupling that he imagines watching, that we imagine watching with him.

This "everything" with which Leontes now fills his dreadfully experienced nothingness (we recall "a cipher standing in rich place" (6-7)) denudes and impoverishes him, diminishes his very being—he is a "pinch'd thing" (51)—while it fills him with a sexual revulsion which the rhetoric of rational argumentation, again, to Camillo, ignites, rather than defuses. The metaphor of a soiled name collapses into the literality of a soiled bed, repulsive, loathsome:

Dost think I am so muddy, so unsettled,
To appoint myself in this vexation, sully
The purity and whiteness of my sheets
(Which to preserve is sleep, which being
  spotted
Is goads, thorns, nettles, tails of wasps)

                              (325-30)

Antigonus, whose rhetoric of denial echoes and aggravates his master's—if Hermione is "honor-flawed" he will "geld" his daughters (II.i.145, 147)—is rebuked for lacking just such enflamed—enlightened!—"seeing" as "communicat'st with dreams, with what's unreal": "You smell this business with a sense as cold/As is a dead man's nose; but I do see't, and feel't" (151-2). Leontes has seen the spider in the cup, and "cracks his gorge, his sides,/With violent hefts" (44-5), vomiting what he drinks.

What the play has exhibited is the process of self-entrapment whereby a deeply confused, insecure and unhappy man enmeshes himself in the web that he spins to defend himself from thoughts that lie too deep for knowledge. The force and vividness with which primary process imagery invades the mind and speech of Leontes make him an astonishingly realistic, individualized figure. We can be lured into reacting to "him" as not merely realistic, but virtually real. Yet he is a fabrication, an epiphenomenon of the text. "What does Leontes want?" we ask, inducting ourselves into an invented mind as we simultaneously watch the manner of its invention. "What does Leontes want?" is thus, strictly speaking, a rhetorical question. What Leontes, or any textual personage wants is what we ourselves could conceivably want were our world constructed out of the same set of displaced signifiers. What Leontes wants is what we discover to be comfortable, as we adjust empathetic introspection to the text's evocations, its figures, its twists and turns, its insistences, its peculiarities, with a meaningful scheme of things. Clues to that meaningful scheme of things we find wherever we can—in the language that we share with the Shakespearean personae, in the language that we no longer share with the Shakespearean personae, but that has to be reexplicated, in the language of symbols which is a remarkably tenacious subdivision of the shared language.

Spider venom, folklore informs us, is effective only if seen when the cup is drained. Leontes' metaphor for the curse of knowledge comes from this source. Spiders, psychoanalytic lore informs us, unconsciously symbolize devouring mother imagos;[9] but in whose unconscious? Leontes'? Shakespeare's? The reader's? The fact that just that metaphor occurs at this point is surely interesting, and I offer it as a test case for the usefulness of the portmanteau notion of a textual unconscious, which, in terms of the Lacanian ellipse, includes the circuit from author to reader via the fictional persona who is no more than a synechdoche—a part standing for the whole of the textual transaction.

Our understanding of the fixation which will give Leontes no peace until it has compelled him to its own recognition is further advanced in the next phase of the play. Act II opens with Hermione, nearing her time and understandably bothered by her lively young son. "Take the boy to you; he so troubles me, Tis past enduring," she says (II.i.1). Her ladies, and the precocious Mamillius, who, we note, doesn't want to be treated "as if I were a baby still" (5), amuse themselves happily enough with reciprocal teasing, but there has been a rejection; and whatever wounded feelings we may impute to Mamillius can hardly be said to be mollified by the first lady's deliberate provocation "we shall/Present our services to a fine new prince/One of these days," says the First Lady, "and then you'll wanton with us, If we would have you" (16-19). The episode ends with renewed intimacy, out of earshot of the "cricket" ladies, between Mamillius and his mother, now recovered. A momentary maternal rejection, a provocation to sibling jealousy, a child's game effort to master fear with a story—this utterly ordinary little nursery scene has effectively reminded us of the griefs and losses that haunt the minds of children like the very sprites and goblins in Mamillius' tale; and it throws a melancholy light upon Leontes' breakdown.

What Leontes sees is the intimate communion of mother and son, Hermione and the boy with the mother-like name, from which he in his isolation is excluded, as he believed he was at the beginning, as Mamillius has just been. There is certainly no sport in his savage "Give me the boy. I am glad you did not nurse him . . . Away with him! and let her sport herself/With that she's big with" (56-9, passim). Leontes is now a man driven by an unassuagable rage, defended only by the revengeful jealousy to which he clings, which he will not relinquish and from which he will not emerge until he has cast out his new-born infant to well-nigh certain destruction, received the news of Mamillius' death and, in effect, hounded Hermione to hers.

It is the news of Mamillius' death that brings him to his senses, releases him from the grip of the fantasy which the sexual jealousy masks. The key to that deepest level fantasy is to be found in Leontes' reiterated "nothing" in the speech quoted above. What the speech contends is that the evidence of Hermione's infidelity is so palpable as to be impossible to ignore. Its rhetorical form is the setting out of an impossible postulate: if whispering, etc. is nothing, then nothing is anything; but the ulterior meaning of these frenetically iterated "nothings" is best understood as a rhetorical barricade against the admission of that which "has already been experienced"—I take the phrase from D.W. Winnicott's account of the "fear of breakdown" (1974, 104). "There are moments," he writes, "when a patient needs to be told that the breakdown, a fear of which destroys his or her life, *has always already been*." It is something the ego is unable to encompass because it is unthinkable: "a fear of the original agony which caused the defence . . . a fact that is carried round hidden away in the unconscious." Leontes' sense of nothingness, of emptiness, of annihilation is exactly that state which "cannot be remembered except by being experienced for the first time now." What we cannot remember we are forced to repeat, as we know. The death of the child who is Leontes', who is Leontes, following the abandonment of the other child that he feared, is thus the terror, the unthinkable agony, which is experienced "for the first time now."

Winnicott's insight illuminates to perfection the plight of Leontes, the backward drift which the tragic part of *The Winter's Tale* articulates. The nightmare of the child's death realizes the terror of a child's death which has already been, which has always already been, for Leontes as for Everyman. It is because that dread resonates with our own most primal terrors that we yield with such pleasure to the counterfantasy of the pastoral in Act IV, the transition to which, however, must first engage our attention.

The central scene of Act III, and of the play, is the great scene of the trial in which Leontes arraigns his Queen in a travesty of the justice he invokes. The scene shows Leontes totally isolated, and imprisoned, in his wounded narcissism. She is dignified, noble, abused as wife, as mother, as daughter ("The Emperor of Russia was my father. O, that he were alive, and here beholding/His daughter's trial" (III.ii.119-20)) by this unleashed male aggression. He is omnipotent, punitive, persecutory; she defenceless, deprived of her children, dragged from her prison childbed. "Sir," she says,

> You speak a language that I understand not.
> My life stands in the level of your dreams,
> Which I'll lay down.
>
> (80-2)

One of the remarkable features of *The Winter's Tale* is the degree of unaware awareness with which its characters are endowed. We have already heard Leontes struggling, half-knowingly, with his own conflicting modes of cognition. Now his scathingly scornful reply, ironically affirming what it denies, causes one to shudder at the identity of rhetorical denial with its unconscious counterpart:

> Your actions are my dreams.
> You had a bastard by Polixenes,
> And I but dreamt it.
>
> (82-4)

In terms of formal tragedy the scene enacts both reversal and recognition. Its action is the inevitable issues of choices already made—the culmination of error—and results in the ironically irreversible fatality which marks the midpoints of Shakespeare's tragic structures. Hermione, blameless, is condemned, but the oracle justifies her. The oracle is read but its message defied. Mamillius' death—immediate nemesis—is announced, Hermione collapses and to the now heartstruck Leontes is brought the news of her death. Leontes is led away to his sorrows, but we do not witness his terrible remorse. The play, as we know, will swerve away from tragic closure into the luxury of a dream of undoing, but the passage from nightmare to dream is mediated by another death.

Since *Measure for Measure* Shakespeare has bettered his instruction in the art of tragi-comic conjunction. In *Measure for Measure* the genre shift occurs abruptly, at the height of the crisis of Act III, with an unprecedented change of style, diction and mode. In *The Winter's Tale,* Act III, the Act which at once opens the breach between its two localities and bridges them, *obtrudes* its intermediary function, achieving a remarkable chiastic interlocking, both formal and symbolic. Act III consists of three scenes symmetrically divided to form a triptych. The two flanking scenes suggest the two antagonistic drives which tragicomedy commingles, each representing a landscape of the mind appropriate to the two opposed halves of the play. For Cleomenes and Dion on their way back from the oracle the climate

is "delicate, the air most sweet,/Fertile the isle" (III.i.1-2); the sacrifice was "ceremonious, solemn, and unearthly" (7), their journey "rare, pleasant, speedy" (14). This scenic symbolism suggests the landscape of a mind whole and at peace. In extreme contrast with the benign and sensuous serenity of this *locus amoenus,* a maternal body, is the "savage clamor" (III.iii.56) of the Bohemian coast where Antigonus lands with his charge. Scene iii recounts the fate of the "poor souls" aboard Antigonus' ship, and of Antigonus himself, against a seascape ruinous, disintegrated and chaotic: "I am not to say it is a sea, for it is now the sky; betwixt the firmament and it you cannot thrust a bodkin's point. . . . how it chafes, how it rages . . . now the ship boring the moon with her mainmast, and anon swallow'd with yeast and froth, as you'd thrust a cork into a hogshead. And then for the land-service, to see how the bear tore out his shoulder bone, how he cried to me for help . . . how the sea flap-dragon'd it . . . how the poor souls roar'd, and the sea mock'd them; and how the poor gentleman roar'd, and the bear mock'd him, both roaring louder than the sea or weather. . . . I have not wink'd since I saw these sights. The men are not yet cold under water, nor the bear half din'd on the gentleman" (87-106, passim). The clown's imagery grotesquely mingles pity and terror, records dismemberment with a cannibalistic detachment, condenses orgasm and death-throe. Where the temperate climate of Cleomenes evokes a longed-for restitution still to come, this chaotic seascape figures the breakdown already undergone.

The ambassadors to the oracle in scene i, certain of Hermione's innocence, anticipated rescue and remedy, yet catastrophe occurred; the Bohemian shepherd who rescues the abandoned babe has no doubt about ill-doing: "Though I am not bookish, yet I can read waiting-gentlewoman in the scape. This has been some stair-work, some trunk-work, some behind-door-work," he says (72, 73), yet he is the agent of deliverance. The babe is rescued and the treasure found, to the haunting rhythm of the shepherd's "thou met'st with things dying, I with things new-born" (113-14), as the play moves into its remedial phase, accompanied by the pitiful and pitying figure of Hermione in Antigonus' strange vision.

Antigonus' gruesome death and his vision have puzzled many commentators. "Shakespeare's solution," says Tillyard, referring to the problem of transition from the tragic to the pastoral, "is to drive the tortured world of Leontes and Hermione to a ridiculous extreme in Antigonus' vision. In so doing he really puts an end to it" ((1938), in Kermode (1938, 78)). There is nothing ridiculous, I submit, in Antigonus' powerful soliloquy as he deposits the babe on the Bohemian shore. It is a premonition of his own death he will never see his wife again—and the account of an hallucination. It records an experience truly uncanny:

I have heard (but not believed) the spirits
    o'th'dead
May walk again. If such thing be, thy mother
Appear'd to me last night; for ne'er was dream
So like a waking. To me comes a creature,
Sometimes her head on one side, some
    another—
I never saw a vessel of like sorrow,
So fill'd, and so becoming
                    (III.iii.16-22)

Antigonus himself is in doubt about the status of his vision, uncertain whether he has dreamed a dream or seen a ghost. He settles, with somewhat anachronist Protestant scepticism, for the ghost theory—"for this once, yea superstitiously" (40)—he believes that "this was so, and no slumber" (39). We may recognize hallucination (for which there was as yet no word available in Shakespeare's vocabulary)[10] but what, we must ask, is its function in the drama.

In accordance with the principles of splitting and replication in dramatic (and dream) representation when psychic burdens become too heavy to be borne, Antigonus, I suggest, is a part of the Leontes persona. Counterpart to Paulina, who is an externalized conscience to Leontes throughout, he is the latter's destructive, ambivalent will in the abandonment of the babe. He has already echoed Leontes' violent, reflex misogyny (he would "geld" his daughters should Hermione prove false, we recall). The oscillation in his view of women as either ideal or animal represents the ferocious need of the frail masculine ego for a feminine ideal which will defend it against Oedipal anxieties. He has born the brunt of Leontes' projective accusation regarding his emasculated dependency upon his "Dame Partlet." The apparition he experiences is an angelic suffering figure, who was nevertheless, he is persuaded, guilty, and therefore justly punished. Leontes' secret sharer, he thus reflects the violent psychic split which was his master's; and suffers his retributory death as scapegoat for the latter's guilt. If his vision represents, in already fading retrospect, the precedent split in Leontes, Antigonus' behavior prefigures the reparative renewal of tenderness, of compassion—"Blossom, speed thee well" (III.iii.46) which will take the place of the flaying self-punishment Leontes embraces at the end of the trial scene. A similar transition is adumbrated by Paulina when, following her

                O thou tyrant . . .
            A thousand knees,
Ten thousand years together, naked, fasting,
Upon a barren mountain, and still winter
In storm perpetual, could not move the gods
To look that way thou wert
                    (III.ii.207-14)

she is moved to pity him.

In both the tragic Shakespearean form and the comic, the penultimate Act plays with remedy. In tragedy possible remedies (like the return of Cordelia in *Lear*) are, so to speak, offered, only to be snatched away, terribly, by the onward momentum of the consequences of previous fatal errors. In comedy remedy, the absent identity, or person, or information required to solve the errors and conflicts which in the play's center come to an impasse is found, or begins to be found. In *The Winter's Tale* this is indeed the case, except that disaster, for Leontes, has already happened, and that this "remedy," the finding and eventual recovery of Perdita, is given an entire expanded, separate comic plot of its own, which, however, reproduces, as it were, compulsively, the plot which fathers it.

The play's structure of duplications allows for complex reevaluations, as samenesses and differences are simultaneously taken in. As has been pointed out, the second part reiterates the first. It repeats the story of rupturing, envious jealousy, of fear of usurpation, with Polixenes doubling for Leontes, Florizel for his father Polixenes, and Perdita for her mother Hermione. Polixenes' disavowal of his previous approval of the marriage of "a gentler scion to the wildest stock" (IV.iv.93) when his own posterity is at issue is as violent as the flare-up in Leontes of a possessive and dispossessed rage. Polixenes' ferocity is partly conventional—expected in a New Comedy *senex*—as is Florizel's unfilial indifference: "One being dead," he says, "I shall have more than you can dream of yet" (387-8); and in reply to the question whether he has a father, and whether his father knows of his betrothal, his cavalier reply is: "I have; but what of him? . . . He neither does, nor shall" (392-3). Partly, at least, the generational conflict serves as a recurrence and confirmation of the usurpation theme in the first part of the play.

Yet, as indeed the play informed us in its first lines: "If you shall chance, Camillo, to visit Bohemia, on the like occasion whereon my services are now on foot, you shall see (as I have said) great difference betwixt our Bohemia and your Sicilia" (I.i.1-4). *The Winter's Tale* realizes its dream of a second chance in Bohemia, through its second generation, as well as its second genre. New life means new possibilities, new comprehensions, new solutions. In Bohemia, the generational conflict is acted out overtly, in its own terms and without dissimulation. The desires of the young lovers in Bohemia are not undermined by the grip of archaic fears, by the drift back into the claustral recesses of the mind: "I was not much afeard," says Perdita, despite the dire threats of Polixenes,

                  for once or twice
I was about to speak, and tell him plainly
The self-same sun that shines upon his court
Hides not his visage from our cottage, but
Looks on alike.
                    (IV.iv.443-6)

Wayne Best as Leontes, Kate Trotter as Hermione, and Juan Chioran as Polixenes in a 1998 Stratford Festival production of The Winter's Tale.

And Florizel is "but sorry, not afeard" (463) as he renounces "succession" to be "heir to [his] affection" (480-1).

The green world in *The Winter's Tale* is a return, not of an unreconstructed childhood but to a childhood—a fantasied (benign) childhood, where fathers are good shepherds, and children unthreatened, and therefore unafraid—restitutive, rather than exorcist in its emotional effect. The sprites and goblins of Mamillius' sad tale have been exorcized, violently, in the first part of the play. In the wide gap of time, off stage, expiation is undergone by the absent Leontes, mourning his losses. What the play's dreaming tells us is that expiation, self-condemnation, is not enough. If consciousness is not irradiated by a knowledge of what could constitute a transcendence both of isolation and of fusion, a harmony of needs, mutual recognition, freely expressed desire, no reparation, or rehabilitation, or renewal will take place. It is this possibility of a different outcome that the pastoral fantasy of Florizel and Perdita, most eudaemonic of Shake-speare's green worlds, opens up. Nobody, perhaps, puts it better than the shepherd:

> He says he loves my daughter.
> I think so too; for never gaz'd the moon
> Upon the water as he'll stand and read
> As 'twere my daughter's eyes.
>
> (171-4)

What Perdita says with flowers undoes courtly duplicity without foregoing courtesy, as she tactfully adjusts her floral offerings to her guests, or rather to the age her guests would like to think they belong to, while nevertheless stubbornly maintaining her position regarding gillyvors. The flowers mesh into a Renaissance debate about art and nature (read: culture and heredity) which is relevant to the question of a Queen of curds and cream, but they are richly symbolic in other ways too. They mediate the passage from winter to spring by themselves moving, so to speak, backwards through the seasons: Perdita begins with the offering of rosemary and rue which last through the winter, attempts to mollify Polixenes' response to the gift of wintry flowers with an emphasis on the present autumn season, "not yet on summer's death, nor on the birth/Of trembling winter" (80-1), negotiates the gillyvors hurdle triumphantly with the lavender, mint, savory, marjoram and marigold "of middle summer" (107) and only then turns to Florizel with the famous lyrical invocation of the flowers of the spring, and of Persephone. Perdita's mythopoeia conjugates erotic awakening with seasonal rebirth, moving from the virgin branches, Proserpina's fallen flowers, the daffodils that take the winds of March with beauty, the dim, sweet eyelids of Juno, Cytherea's breath, the pathos of primroses "that die unmarried ere they can behold/ Bright Phoebus in his strength," to the frankly phallic "bold oxslips" and "crown imperial" (118-26) and the final routing of Thanatos:

> No, like a bank for Love to lie and play on;
> Not like a corse; or if, not to be buried,
> But quick and in my arms.
>
> (130-2)

The separate Perdita story is a chapter in the Greek romance narrative of long-lost children, family vicissitudes and family reunions, but it is also a recognizable Terentian comedy with all the formulaic constituents: a foundling, a casket to provide identification when required, a high-born lover in disguise on account of parental disapproval, the fortunate disclosure not only of a desirable identity for the girl, but positively of her own lost parents, and the restoration of amity both within and between the families concerned. It even has a tricky servant to negotiate the errors, mishaps, and mistaken identities of the comic plot in which young lovers outwit or evade parental disapproval. But has it?

Autolycus has been Florizel's servant, we learn, but is no longer, though we are not told why he is "out of service" (IV.iii.14). He is now in business on his own but nevertheless it is he who exchanges clothes with Florizel so that his may provide the prince with a further disguise for his escape with Perdita from the wrath of Polixenes. Later, removing another piece of disguise, his peddlar's beard, for the purpose, he becomes ambassador from Perdita's shepherd father to Polixenes to whom the bundle is to be shown, thus proving the shepherd adoptive father only and so saving him from retribution for his adopted daughter's fatal charms. This is a con, however, and instead of conducting the shepherd-with-bundle to Polixenes' court, he conducts him to his former master's escape ship, wondering, reprobate that he is, how it is that Fortune insists upon tempting him into "honesty" do what he will. (IV.iv.831). These machinations of Autolycus in fact delay the discovery of the bundle's contents, so that the secret remains undiscovered until the shepherd carries his fardel to Polixenes himself (now also in Sicilia), and is catapulted into the status of "gentleman born" (V.ii.127) as a reward. It turns out, therefore, that Autolycus, who prides himself upon the possession of an open ear, a quick eye, a nimble hand and a good rogue's nose for the smelling out of opportunities for advancement has allowed himself to be deprived of an obvious bonus. Ebullient as ever, he resigns himself to the set-back: "But 'tis all one to me; for had I been the finder-out of this secret, it would not have relish'd among my other discredits" (V.ii.121). In the role of tricky servant, it seems, Autolycus does not shine, but he has other resources for making a living, learned partly from the distinguished company of sharp-witted vagabonds who were beginning to populate the literature of the picaresque, and partly from his Ovidian genealogy. Ovidian Autolycus (in Golding's translation "a wyly pye" without peer for filching and theft) was, it will be recalled, the son of no other than Mercury/Hermes.

Hermes, hardly out of his cradle, was already stealing the oxen of Apollo, who was appeased however, by the child's skill at the lyre (which he invented by stretching strings across a tortoise shell). Messenger, herald, conductor of souls between the worlds of the living and the dead, protector of travelers, whose signposts and landmarks were named for him, worshipped by shepherds in his native Arcadia, god of trading, good luck and gambling, of divination (he invented sign-systems), of eloquence, cunning and fraud; and of dream.

Shakespeare's cony-catching rogue (his only lowlife foolish-wise clown with a Greek name), a reembodiment of this versatile god, is a wonderful composite of the mercurial and the picaresque, of failure and recovery. Born under the appropriate star, "litter'd under Mercury" as he puts it (IV.iii.25), he is a snapper-up of unconsidered trifles, a singer of lowlife catches about daffodils and doxies, in which the "red blood reigns in (reins in? rains in?) the winter's pale" (4); a titillator of preposterous fancies about usurers' wives brought to bed of twenty money-bags at once (263). Never at a loss, he has been ape-bearer, process-server, puppeteer, impersonator, gambler, whoremaster; he pinches sheets hanging out to dry (and anything else that comes in handy); he peddles tawdry trinkets and bawdy broadsheet ballads with such hypnotic success that all "senses stuck in ears: you might have pinched a placket, it was senseless; 'twas nothing to geld a codpiece of a purse" (IV.iv.610-11); and the last we see of him bodes ill for his latest patron, or victim—his old acquaintance the shepherd, newly come into a fortune. He, "having flown over many knavish professions . . . settled only in rogue" (IV.iii.98-100), but his *coup de théâtre* in *The Winter's Tale* is to con the clown by enacting the part of his own victim, in order to rob him of the money for the raisins and currants, prunes, pear-pies, rice, nutmeg and ginger for the feast.

Trickster, cutpurse, masquerader, shape-changer—what do we make of this strangely *gratuitous,* outlaw character, so apt for his part, yet without, it would seem, a part?

We know that he pleases us; that he marks the transition from winter to spring and from dire consequences for actions to lucky improvizations and escapes. He provides what is desired, reputable or disreputable, markets fancies, images, caters to and exemplifies the instinctual and uninhibited appetites. What he feels like doing he does, with the cunning of disguise and dissimulation and a total disregard for regulatory conscience. So we see in him a pleasure principle, laxity and relaxation, and welcome his conduct of us from the repressive world of Sicilian punishments to the compensatory wish-fulfillment of Bohemia. Yet he is a thief. What is a thief doing in Shangri-La? Possibly he is there for the same reason as is Polixenes' rage. In the dream they are harmless and judgment is suspended, but their presence reminds us that harmless surfaces conceal explosive depths.

Critics, reading the play and read by it, have recorded contradictory responses in interesting ways. He is a harbinger of spring, says Northrop Frye, "imaginary cuckoo where Leontes is imaginary cuckold" ((1963) 1971, 333). Traversi, more sentimental, finds in him an "affirmation of the warm, living 'blood' of youth against the jealousy and care-laden envy of age"; his song represents the "tender, reborn heart of the year"; his vitality saves the play from abstraction (1965, 136-7). For Tillyard, on the other hand, he is delinquent but "prophylactic," "his delinquencies keep the earthly paradise sufficiently earthly" ((1938) in Kermode, 1938, 84). For Lawlor too, he "offsets any unrealities of pastoral" ((1962) in Palmer, 1971, 300). One might add that the ballads he purveys to the village girls are not without a certain polyphonic relation to the fancies Leontes has entertained. One tells of a monstrous birth, how "a usurer's wife was brought to bed of twenty money-bags at a burden"; another of a fish-woman "turned into a cold fish for she would not exchange flesh with one that loved her" (IV.iv.263, 279). Most comprehensive perhaps is Joan Hartwig's formulation: "Autolycus absorbs some of the disordering aspects of Leontes' disturbed imagination. . . . contain[s] disorder through comic inconsequence" (1978, 101). In sum: Autolycus is a figure of libido, unruly, lawless and volatile, uninhibited, cunning, subversive. Harmless, even benign sometimes, however reluctantly, he offers a semilegitimized illicit enjoyment; but there is a self, and a wolf also, in his name.

He is a pervasive presence in the wishful Bohemian scenes, but he is demoted in Sicily, where he must seek preferment under the patronage of the new "true gentlemen" clowns (V.ii.162). Act V deserts the pastoral fantasy to return to the world. There Leontes' restoration is figured, not by dream, but by the art of drama.

The statue scene is the culminating moment of the play. It is carefully prepared for by a cumulative series of encounters, all but the first reported, in order, I suggest, not to detract from the climax, but also to establish the latter's peculiar difference.

A mode of transference takes place in these encounters. The old traumas are reactivated, lived through again, the old wrongs done "stir afresh" within Leontes (V.i.148-9): the death of Hermione. "She I kill'd? I did so; but thou strik'st me/Sorely, to say I did. It is as bitter/Upon thy tongue as in my thought" (16-9); the childhood twinship:

> Were I but twenty-one,
> Your father's image is so hit in you,
> (His very air) that I should call you brother,
> As I did him, and speak of something wildly
> By us performed before
>
> (126-30)

the loss of his children: "O! alas/I lost a couple that 'twixt heaven and earth/Might thus have stood, begetting wonder" (131-3); the threat to a "gracious couple" through betrayal.

The old desires too. Leontes' instant attraction to Perdita (in the source story resulting in actual incest), which requires Paulina's stern monitoring to deflect, is touching because of the daughter's resemblance to her mother, but it is again threatening. If then Leontes desired a lost mother, and now desires, though unknowingly, his daughter, he is not yet out of the wood. Yet, remembering Autolycus, are we not to see that this piecing together of a dismembered whole—a family, a mind—depends upon the resurgence of desire which is itself beneficent. The reunions are not merely a return of the oppressive past, a nostalgia. The children are as "welcome hither, as is the spring to th'earth" (151-2):

> What might I have been,
> Might I a son and daughter now have look'd
>   on,
> Such goodly things as you!
>
> (176-8)

These recognition scenes are as yet partial. Leontes first recognizes Polixenes' son in the encounter with the young lovers; then Perdita's identity is discovered in the meeting between all three and Polixenes. This second scene *narrates* the finding of the King's daughter with all the oratorical art the third gentleman can muster:

> Sorrow wept to take leave of them, for their joy waded in tears. . . . Our king, being ready to leap out of himself for joy of his found daughter, as if that joy

were now become a loss, cries, 'O, thy mother, thy mother!'; then asks Bohemia forgiveness, then embraces his son-in-law; then again worries he his daughter with clipping her. Now he thanks the old shepherd. . . .   I never heard of such another encounter, which lames report to follow it, and undoes description to do it (V.ii.45-62, passim)

and the whole series is parodied by the counterpoint drollery of the clown's version of these wondrously moving events:

For the King's son took me by the hand and call'd me brother; and then the two kings call'd my father brother; and then the Prince, my brother, and the Princess, my sister, call'd my father father; and so we wept; and there was the first gentlemanlike tears that ever we shed. (140-5)

Only then is the culmination of these reunions brought about in the final scene. Shakespeare's self-reflexive art in the earlier comedies had constantly called attention to itself by means of metadramatic comment and epilogue: we recall Theseus' "The best in this kind are but shadows," and Puck's riposte, "If we shadows have offended." Now we are offered a *tour de force* in the kind, under the sign of Paulina's wildly anachronistic "rare Italian master," and the *trompe-l'oeil* of illusionist art.

Guilio Romano, "who, had he himself eternity and could put breath into his work, would beguile Nature of her custom, so perfectly he is her ape" (92-100) is the creator of Hermione's "statue," the instrument of Paulina's bogus miracle, and, artist as con-man, the *genius loci* of the play's closing phase, as Autolycus was of its wishful dream.

Guilio Romano was a famous mannerist artist of the sixteenth century. In Vasari's *Lives* his Latin epitaph is as follows: "Jupiter saw sculptured and painted statues breathe and earthly buildings made equal to those in heaven by the skill of Giulio Romano" (see Schanzer, 1969, 230). There are good reasons, therefore, for Paulina's (or Shakespeare's) choice, though the entire reference to Romano, has been found pointless. "We do not need his kind of art," says Northrop Frye, "when we have the real Hermione . . . neither he nor the kind of realism he represents seems to be very central to the play itself" (1963; 113). But, I submit, it is central. Because the bogus miracle is a mask for the remedial therapy of Paulina.

The magical effect is made possible by the concealment from the audience of the fact that Hermione is alive. Such concealment is rare in Shakespeare, and its effect is to pull the audience perforce into the experience, making it "real" in a distinctive way: we really see what Leontes sees. The point I am making is that it is a mirror-image of Romano's illusionist skill. Rom-

ano's craft made statues so real-seeming that they seemed real persons. Paulina has made a real person so statuesque as to seem a statue. There is of course, no miracle at all. Hermione, never dead, is not resurrected, but what we are shown—Leontes' transport of mingled anguish and joy at its lifelikeness, and then its descent from the pedestal—feels as miraculous, and mysterious, as a return from death or as a birth. We are truly deluded, momentarily, with Leontes. Leontes anticipated a frozen image from the past—"not so much wrinkled, nothing/So aged as this seems" (V.iii.28-9)—with which, perhaps, to prolong and memorialize his stony remorse, to perpetuate nostalgia. This moment creates an illusion of resurrection for Hermione, for Leontes, which is a true *coup de théâtre,* a triumph of the illusionist's art. But the fictive resurrection of Hermione effects a real resurrection in Leontes. Fantasy is transformed into reality as the lost is found. The enchanting moment carries us beyond illusion or deception. It is an embodiment of return—the always unimaginable, the always imagined desire.

When Hermione steps down from the pedestal she is not only a wifely, but a maternal presence. Though she embraces him first, her first words are for her daughter. She is the agent of his rebirth, of his enfranchisement from the sprites and goblins that haunted him when he was death-possessed, seeing only the skull beneath the skin. It is surely not fortuitous, but a wheel come full circle, when Leontes remembers her "as tender/As infancy" (26-7) and has recourse to an image of primal need, of primal containment and content to express the fullness of his joy "If this be magic, let it be an art/Lawful as eating" (110-1). It is an odd simile, taken at face value. Yet how powerfully resonant it becomes when it can be seen in the chain of signifiers which allow us to reconstruct the untold story of *The Winter's Tale.* Consider the primal oral fantasies which erupted in the tragic phase of the play: the spider-poisoned cup which made Leontes "crack his gorge . . . with violent hefts" (II.i.44-5); the "bespiced" cup which will give his enemy "a lasting wink" (I.ii.316-17); Hermione's provocative "cram's with praise, and make's/As fat as tame things" (I.ii.91-2). Voracious bears and devouring seas accompany the catastrophe. In Bohemia Perdita is "queen of curds and cream" (IV.iv.160), Autolycus steals the money for the festive delicacies which the clown evocatively enumerates, and in his grotesque ballad the usurer's wife "longs to eat adders' heads and toads carbonadoed" (264). Now at last, in Leontes' "lawful as eating," is hunger legitimized, and, no longer signifying a fantasy of incorporation, but a real communion, stilled; family likeness can speak of regeneration, not usurpation, and the existence of others, separate from the shadow play of one's own mind, be acknowledged.

The sprites and goblins are dispersed, but they haunt still, as does, surely, the ghost of Mamillius. The image of gap (Old Norse yawn; a hole or opening made by breaking or parting; a breach) with which *The Winter's Tale* would end the text of its temporal narrative evades closure, evoking not only the fierce disruptions we have witnessed, but beyond these the painful trauma of birth itself, with its continuing, ineluctable, besetting anxieties:[11]

> Good Paulina,
> Lead us from hence, where we may leisurely
> Each one demand and answer to his part
> Performed in this wide gap of time since first
> We were dissevered.
>
> (V.iii.151)

Notes

[1] For confusion about his role see Lee Sheridan Cox, "The role of Autolycus in *The Winter's Tale,*" *Studies in English Literature,* 9 (1969) 287, and passim.

[2] Nevill Coghill, "Six Points of Stage-Craft in *The Winter's Tale,*" *Sh.Survey* (1958) introduced his defence of the play with the statement: "It is a critical commonplace that *The Winter's Tale* is an ill-made play: its very editors deride it" (31). How far the balance had been redressed by 1978 may be judged by Charles Frey's judgement in "Tragic Structure in The Winter's Tale": "*The Winter's Tale* carries its often painful but always instructive burden extremely well" (Kay and Jacobs, 1978, 124).

[3] See Louise George Clubb, "Shakespeare's Comedy and Late Cinquecento Mixed Genres" in *Shakespearean Comedy,* ed. M. Charney (New York, New York Literary Forum, 1980).

[4] Psychoanalytically minded critics have pounced upon the "twinned lambs" speech as upon a treasure trove for explication. J.I.M. Stewart, *Character and Motive in Shakespeare* (1948) was the first to find a displaced return of repressed homosexuality in Leontes' obsessional outburst, and W.H. Auden ("The Alienated City," *Encounter,* 1961) was convinced that "Leontes is a classic case of paranoid sexual jealousy due to repressed homosexual feelings" (11). Stephen Reid, *"The Winter's Tale"* (*American Imago* 27 (1970)) and Murray Schwartz, "Leontes' Jealousy in *The Winter's Tale*" (*American Imago* 30 (1973)) and *"The Winter's Tale*: Loss and Transformation" (*American Imago* 32 (1975)), proceed from Freud's formula for defensive projection ("I do not love him. She does") to further analytical variations on the theme of delusional jealousy. These critics provide a clinical diagnosis for a sudden seizure like Leontes'; what they do not do is to provide an entry into the play. They lead out of the drama, not into it. Their phantasmagoric choreography of Kleinean projections and introjections is unlikely to be available to readers and audiences, even those most closely at-

tuned to the vagaries of primary process; and they produce a distinct impression of overkill. There is a danger in overexplication; the danger, as J-B. Pontalis aptly puts it in a corrective essay, "of strangling the eloquence of oneiric life" ("Dream as an Object," *Int. Rev. of Psychoanalysis,* 1974, 1).

[5] For a useful account of the two principles of mental functioning see Pinchas Noy (1979), 185 and passim. See also Robert Rogers (1978). Carol Thomas Neely, "*The Winter's Tale*: The Triumph of Speech," *Studies in English Literature,* 15 (1975) gives an account of the speech in terms of the rationalistic language of euphuism and the "indeterminate" language of passion.

[6] See the Arden edn, (London, Methuen, 1963) for extended commentary on the speech. Older commentary extends to three pages (27-30) in the Variorum.

[7] Wallace Stevens, "An Ordinary Evening in New Haven," xxviii, *The Palm at the End of the Mind* (New York, Vintage, 1972), 349.

[8] David Willbern, "Shakespeare's Nothing" (Schwartz and Kahn, 1980) gives an illuminating exposition of the imagery of Shakespeare's "dialectic of nothing and all" (252). See also Antoinette Dauber, "This Great Gap of Time," *Hebrew University Studies in Literature and the Arts,* 11, 2 (1983) for an excellent reading of the play along similar lines.

[9] See Freud, "Revision of Dream Theory," *New Introductory Lectures* (1933) 53.

[10] OED gives 1604 for the first usage of the term; the sense was "to deceive or blind." The word occurs nowhere in Shakespeare.

[11] I am much indebted to discussion with Stanley Cavell for insight into this manifestation of the textual unconscious.

Kay Stockholder (essay date 1987)

SOURCE: "From Matter to Magic: *The Winter's Tale,*" in *Dream Works: Lovers and Families in Shakespeare's Plays,* University of Toronto Press, 1987, pp. 184-96.

[*In the essay that follows, Stockholder considers the sexual conflict of* The Winter's Tale *to be resolved by dream-visions.*]

In *Macbeth* Shakespeare expressed the psychic and sexual dynamic of a mature and fully heterosexual relationship through public action that expressed metaphorically the protagonist's private state. In that play Macbeth associates the sexual centre of his mature relationship with a vision of evil and corruption that destroys the relationship and the harmony of the familial state that contains it.

The Winter's Tale more directly than *Macbeth* explicitly concerns itself with family relations and with distorted sexual passions that warp them. In this play, however, the consequent political disorder does not overshadow the family relations. As though in compensation for this greater directness, like the earlier romances it is more emotionally distant. The whole play is not permeated by the force of the protagonist's fantasy; rather the course of Leontes' passion for the most part is sketched rather than fully elaborated, so that we, like the figures with which he populates his world, observe him from a distance. And while his compulsive passions shape the lives of the other characters, they do not permeate the language of those characters with multiplying ironies that radiate from a dark centre. Leontes isolates himself in the dark world of his mind, and keeps others as observers outside his orbit rather than drawing them into it, as do Othello or Macbeth. As dreamer, therefore, Leontes has isolated his own figure as a strategy to preserve idealized surroundings that can rescue him from the passions to which he gives licence.

Within that safety Leontes boldly defines himself as king, husband, and father. In Hermione he has generated a stronger version of the good woman than have other protagonists. He allows her to be mother as well as wife, endows her with adult dignity and articulateness rather than virginal virtues, and he refrains from generating an Iago on whom to project his self-hatred and self-blame. At the same time, remote from himself initially, he generates an alternate self-image, clothed in nostalgia, of a presexual innocence that suggests the conflict shortly to become overt. Camillo and Archidamus surround the early affection between Leontes and Polixenes with idyllic romance that is opposed to and invulnerable to any 'matter or malice' of the present. Archidamus links that golden past with the present by juxtaposing it to Leontes' son, Mamillius, when after confirming the abiding love between Leontes and Polixenes he adds, 'You have an unspeakable comfort of your young prince Mamillius' (I.i.34-5). The configuration suggests that Polixenes represents Leontes' effort to retreat from mature sexuality into nostalgia for a simpler past, an attempt that later, ironically, revives the infantile roots of the sexual conflict it was intended to suppress.[1]

The erotic colouring of the two kings' early relationship appears when Archidamus describes how through the years they have exchanged gifts, sent 'loving embassies,' and 'though absent; shook hands, as over a vast; and embraced, as it were, from the ends of opposed winds' (I.i.28-32). Polixenes adds a sensuous note in saying, 'We were as twinn'd lambs that did frisk i' th' sun, / And bleat the one at th' other' (I.ii.67-8). Leontes clothes his homoerotic impulses in the vision of childhood purity, and opposes that prelapsarian purity to the world of women. He equates heterosexuality with the Fall, and by implication with all consequent evil and corruption, when Polixenes says that had they remained in their childhood world they 'should have answer'd heaven / Boldly "not guilty," the imposition clear'd / Hereditary ours' (I.ii.69-74). To Hermione's surmise that they must have 'tripped since,' he responds by associating prelapsarian innocence with ignorance of women, particularly of wives, when he says 'In those unfledg'd days was my wife a girl; / Your precious self had then not cross'd the eyes / Of my young play-fellow' (I.ii.78-80). Hermione's objection spells out the implication: 'Of this make no conclusion, lest you say / Your queen and I are devils' (I.ii.81-2), especially since even as she says those words Leontes is already in the process of transforming her into a devil. Leontes sees even sexuality legitimized within marriage as the source of sin and corruption in contrast to a vaguely erotic male childhood companionship.[2]

Leontes compensates for his hidden association of women with evil by idealizing Hermione. This psychological strategy makes him like a person whose marriage appears to others ideal, but whose perfect-seeming wife makes him feel rebuked for his unacknowledged dark imagination of women, isolated, unloved, and empty within the image of familial bliss. Leontes expresses such dissatisfaction in calling into his present, 'over a vast,' feelings that he associates with past happiness, only to find, once he materializes Polixenes, that he has opened the hornets' nest from which his feeling of emptiness and nostalgia was designed to protect him.

The relation between the sexual conflict hidden in Leontes' nostalgia and his mature sexuality appears in the strained urgency with which he persuades his friend to stay, and Polixenes' equally unexplained urgency to depart. It appears as well in the fusion of Polixenes' visit with the onset of Leontes' jealousy. When Leontes ignores Polixenes' protest that to hinder his return home 'were (in your love) a whip to me' (I.ii.25), he seems jealous of his friend's obligations that take him away; at the same time his desire to be rid of him appears in Polixenes' determination to leave. The lack of naturalistic explanation for the urgency of either figure emphasizes the psychological significance for Leontes of his almost equal desires to keep Polixenes, and the associated idyllic childhood, present, and to avoid the revival of infantile conflicts hidden beneath and expressed in the nostalgic aura. Though not explicitly sexual, the intense love between the two men, placed in the past but carried to the present by association with Mamillius, functions as an alternative to Leontes' relationship to Hermione.

In Hermione's successful petition Leontes expresses his desire to keep Polixenes at hand, while he handles the implicit dangers by imagining the two together. Leontes' unease with his wife's sexuality appears when he casts himself in the role of a rejected lover while his wife flirts with his friend. Leontes says that she has for the second time 'said well,' the first time being when 'three crabbed months had sour'd themselves to death, / Ere I could make thee open thy white hand / And clap thyself my love' (I.ii.102-4). When Hermione gives that white hand to Polixenes and engages him in talk of their past, Leontes achieves the configuration from which can emerge all in his emotional life that violates his self-image. The intensity acquires the quality of a dream within a dream, as Leontes observes their retreating figures and murmurs 'too hot, too hot.'

During the trial scene Hermione says, 'You speak a language that I understand not: / My life stands in the level of your dreams, / Which I'll lay down' (III.ii.80-2). A distanced level of Leontes' awareness, externalized in the plot, maintains an innocent Hermione, while most of his consciousness succumbs to the explosion of feeling expressed in his sudden jealousy. Like Othello, he maintains the split image of the woman, the good and the bad, in two levels of consciousness rather than in two figures. In the plot configuration he keeps Hermione ideally innocent, while his own figure is overwhelmed by a vision of women as besmirched and betraying. Though less naturalistic, this event is comparable to the decisive psychic moments of other plays. The content of Leontes' experience is most like Othello's, but the quality of it is like Macbeth's, except that Macbeth experiences an altered state of consciousness, whereas Leontes denies, even while he betrays knowledge of, his state of mind when he says, 'Your actions are my dreams. / You had a bastard by Polixenes, / And I but dream'd it!' (III.ii.82-4). In another very convoluted passage, Leontes reflects on the relationship between dream and reality, seeming in the process to attribute greater reality to dream:

Affection! thy intention stabs the centre:
Thou dost make possible things not so held,
Communicat'st with dreams;—how can this be?—
With what's unreal thou coactive art,
And fellow'st nothing: then, 'tis very credent
Thou may'st co-join with something; and thou dost,
(And that beyond commission) and I find it,
(And that to the infection of my brains
And hard'ning of my brows).

                                        (I.ii.138-46)

Whether Leontes refers to Hermione's dream of affection, which then finds a real object, or to his own affection for her that has generated his dream of her infidelity, the passage indicates a brief moment of

struggle before he detaches himself from his sense of ordinary reality and allows his compulsive passion to overwhelm his consciousness.

Leontes has been flirting on the edges of his inner dream from the moment he asked Hermione to persuade Polixenes to stay, as though wanting an opportunity to bring to the surface, to 'co-join with something' what his unknown passions were already generating. Before committing himself totally to his compulsions he, like Othello, makes one effort to keep his dream from becoming nightmare: 'This entertainment / May a free face put on, derive a liberty / From heartiness, from bounty, fertile bosom, / And well become the agent: 't may, I grant'(I.ii.111-114). Like Macbeth, he foresees the loss entailed in satisfying his darker desires when he counters Camillo's efforts to dissuade him by opposing to uncommon desires an inadequate common sense. Leontes thinks he could not be so 'muddy' as to sully

The purity and whiteness of my sheets,
(Which to preserve is sleep, which being spotted
Is goads, thorns, nettles, tails of wasps)
Give scandal to the blood o' th' prince, my son,
(Who I do think is mine and love as mine)
Without ripe moving to't?

                                        (I.ii.321-32)

Leontes cannot forgo his new image of Hermione for two reasons. First, even though he says that Hermione's actions are his dreams, he cannot conceive how he might desire what he fears. Second, the image of a sullied Hermione and betraying friend frees him from the painful contrast between himself and a radiant Hermione. His fantasy allows him to externalize in her the self-hatred that previously festered inside him. Hermione must be guilty, because if she is not, then he is.

Having substituted Polixenes for his own figure, Leontes vents his image of sexuality in language like Iago's when he sees Polixenes and Hermione 'paddling palms and pinching fingers,' and reflects that there is many a man 'That little thinks she has been sluiced in's absence / And his pond fished by his next neighbor' (I.ii.192-5). Women, as false 'as o'er-dy'd blacks, as wind, as waters' bring disease—'were my wife's liver / Infected as her life' (I.ii.304-5)—that both infects men's sexuality and turns them into objects of ridicule.

While Lear expressed the process of his diseased imagination by casting himself in progressively more infantile roles, Leontes in a more detached way undergoes a similar process signified by his changing views of his own children. His already established identification with Mamillius becomes firmer when he sees him, and by implication himself, as a product of the foul adult sexuality he imagines between Hermione and Polixenes. As he and his son talk of childhood innocence, Leontes seeks detachment from the image of himself as child when, with pretended playfulness, he questions his paternity, asking Mamillius, 'Art thou my boy?' and observing that he has 'smutch'd [his] nose.' As Lear uses the smells of hell to describe women's gentitals when he says 'there is the sulphurous pit: burning, scalding, stench, consumption,' so Leontes sees in the dirt on his son's nose traces of sexuality needful for conception. It brings to his mind images of bestiality, which he translates into images of cuckoldry by concentrating on horned animals, 'the steer, the heifer and the calf,' when he punningly tells Mamillius that he must be 'neat.' While he sees Hermione 'still virginalling / Upon his palm!' Mamillius, as a 'wanton calf,' becomes a metaphor for and sign of Leontes' belief that his wanton wife has given him cuckold's horns. The previously innocent-seeming animal imagery that described himself and Polixenes as 'twinn'd lambs that did frisk i' th' sun' now clearly is tarnished by sexuality, and he attempts to repudiate this now disturbing image by breaking his identification with the child, discounting the physical resemblance that, he says, women affirm.

Leontes' retreat from and advance towards his son reproduce the ambivalent movements he made towards Polixenes. Each time he draws Mamillius to him, the proximity intensifies his repulsion and turns his endearments into rejections. He calls Mamillius 'sweet villain! / Most dear'st! my collop!' then reflects, 'Can thy dam?' The image of Hermione as a 'dam' joins Hermione and his son, both male and female sexuality, within animal-like lowness. But being identified with his son, Leontes expresses his own sexuality in his images of Mamillius, and gives the lie to the prelapsarian innocence he had wanted as an alternative to mature heterosexuality. This process becomes clearer when he explains his distraction to Hermione by saying that 'this kernel, this squash, this gentleman' reminded him of himself as a child 'unbreech'd, / In my green velvet coat; my dagger muzzled / Lest it should bite its master, and so prove, / As ornaments oft do, too dangerous' (I.ii.155-8). In the process of repudiating it, he deepens his identification with his son within a recollection of childhood that has changed colour. The muzzled dagger suggests the erotically violent passions that were hidden in the idyllic memories, which now, having been unmuzzled, are biting their master. He makes a last effort to keep the image of childhood innocence uncontaminated when he says 'Give me this boy: / I am glad you did not nurse him: / Though he does bear some signs of me, yet you / Have too much blood in him' (II.i.55-7). But he is unsuccessful, and at his command Mamillius disappears and, unlike his sister, is not resurrected, suggesting that Leontes decisively has repressed the homosexuality he associates with his childhood.[3]

Like Lear, he moves from an image of himself as a boy to one of himself as an infant, when Paulina brings his baby daughter, whom he with less obvious ambivalence but also less finality, obliterates. Enraged at the child for representing her mother's unreliable sexuality, he enacts Lady Macbeth's image when he says, 'The bastard brains with these my proper hands / Shall I dash out. Go, take it to the fire' (II.iii.139-40). Along with the child, he repudiates his wife's sexuality, which generates children, and himself as a trusting infant at a maternal breast.

But eliminating with these figures his childlike feelings from his consciousness increases rather than diminishes their power to colour his perception of his entire world. Within the overriding safety of his fairy-tale world in which an ideally good Hermione is empowered to punish and cancel the consequences of his attemped crimes, he indulges what now becomes a fully paranoid vision that justifies his rage. Seeing all his court in a conspiracy of silent mockery, he associates Polixenes' and Hermione's supposed sexual betrayal with political conspiracy. He enters a self-enclosed and self-confirming system which uses all contrary evidence as grist for its mill.

The distance between Leontes' passion and the idealized world kept present by other figures appears in the unique way in which this play's most powerful image lacks resonance elsewhere in this text, but in other plays epitomizes both male and female sexuality with betrayal, cruelty, cannibalism, and death. Leontes, caught in his paranoid vortex and reflecting on the pain he incurs from his 'true opinion,' says,

> There may be in the cup
> A spider steep'd, and one may drink, depart,
> And yet partake no venom, (for his knowledge
> Is not infected); but if one present
> Th' abhorr'd ingredient to his eye, make known
> How he hath drunk, he cracks his gorge, his sides,
> With violent hefts. I have drunk, and seen the spider.
>
>   (II.i.36-45)

The spider in the cup is an image of the way in which Leontes' conception of sexuality poisons his imagination of social and creature pleasures. The immediate context associates the spider with Hermione's supposed infidelity, and by extension to her sexuality, which Leontes has already described in images of disease and bestiality. He now adds to these an image of women, like spiders, deceitfully luring men into beautiful-seeming nets, like the snare from which Antony momentarily escapes, in order to poison and devour them. But the implicit net image is also suitable for Leontes' entanglement in his paranoid fantasy spun out of his own imagination. He both places himself outside of the image, and implies a secret recognition of his own complicity by attributing to his own knowledge the power to render the spider poisonous. He experiences with sharply focused intensity the nausea that has been suggested by previous images. If one sees Leontes' experience of the spider in relation to the nausea Hamlet felt before he directed Yorick's skull into 'my lady's chamber,' then Leontes confronts in the spider an image of the snare-producing womb that transforms men to insects and becomes their tomb as they are devoured.[4]

While on one level of consciousness Leontes allows his imagination full licence to project itself onto the figures with which he populates his world, on another level, as said before, he keeps at a distance from himself a reversed image in which a good world can release him from his evil impulses. This split consciousness is expressed most dramatically in the trial scene. His own figure expresses his impregnable fantasy system and the impossibility of a solution to the polarity in which it has entangled him, while in the other figures he clings to a vision of a world that will save him from himself. Both sides of his desire, and the self-confirming mechanism of his fantasy, appear in his deafness to Hermione's clarion assertion of her innocence. When the oracle most uncharacteristically and unambiguously affirms Hermione's guiltlessness he says, 'There is no truth at all i' th' Oracle; / The sessions shall proceed: this is mere falsehood' (III.ii.140-1). It is as though Leontes says of himself that even if the gods themselves should speak, which they never do, their intervention could not release him from the snare of his passions. As was the case with Macbeth, only by being enacted can the power of those passions be depleted. Therefore it is not the oracle but news of Mamillius' and Hermione's deaths that dissipate his compulsive desires. Having obliterated from consciousness both child and adult versions of male and female figures, he experiences himself as awakening from dreamlike compulsions. He defines himself now as in isolation and remorse, but on the periphery of his consciousness he has already set in motion the figures who, by punishing him, will revoke the seemingly irrevocable consequences of his action to provide a dream of a love consummated otherwise than in death.[5]

However, the process by which Leontes tries to persuade himself of the reality of fairy-tales reveals the same network of fears and desires from which he seeks rescue. Leontes' split consciousness generates two worlds. In Sicilia he replaces Hermione with Paulina, to whom he in his own figure becomes a submissive and punished child. In the overtly fairy-tale realm of Bohemia Perdita replaces Hermione as idealized female. There, the storm that destroys the ship and drowns the men, and the bear that devours Antigonus are the displaced and removed remnants of Leontes' rage and jealous passion. Like Lear's, his storm, which wears

itself out on Bohemia's shores, functions as an externalized image of his inner upheaval, and the bear, humorous in the stage direction, retains its force when the clown relates how it devours Antigonus' shoulder bone and is about to consume the rest of him.[6] The bear is a distanced image of Leontes' fears, but also frees Paulina of a husband so that she can become a quasi-maternal figure for him.

In opposition to those forces represented by the storm and the bear, Leontes generates and excludes his own contaminating figure from a quasi-magical world in which a providentially benign nature and beneficent coincidence cancel ordinary causality amid elements of realism that remain oddly juxtaposed to images of the transcendently improbable. In this way Leontes refuses to admit the impossibility of the event he needs to effect his cure. Signs of his uneasy attempt to join the fairy-tale vision, in which impediments to love are external to the lovers, to a probable world appear in several ways, but are first notable in Autolycus, whose single plot function, one that could have been accomplished in other ways, is to expedite the process which proves Perdita's true parentage. Dramatically, however, his comic debasement of the otherwise golden world prevents a full polarization of Sicilia and Bohemia that would completely divorce from each other the realms of tragic consequence and comic resolution. Autolycus' presence in Bohemia asserts the possibility of lives being brought to redeeming resolution through accidental and unlikely but real instruments. Autolycus himself comments on the irony of his having unwittingly brought about the reconciliation between children and parents, when only the thought of profit can console him for the loss of his trickster pleasures. He is a kind of Puck without a master, or one whose master is concealed in the force of benign accident that, when it assumes the lineaments of Prospero, will turn him into Ariel. As well, as the comic rogue, Autolycus further links the pastoral Bohemia to the more probable Sicilia, which contains in Paulina another quasi-trickster figure.

The other element in Bohemia by which Leontes reveals his disbelief in the restoration he generates appears in the logical problems that are involved in the portrayal of Polixenes' anger at Florizel for wanting to marry a peasant girl, an episode that echoes his own anger at Hermione. The incompatability of probable causality with idealized fantasy appears when Polixenes, despite previously having observed of Perdita that 'nothing she does or seems / But smacks of something greater than herself, / Too noble for this place' (IV.iv.157-9), threatens Perdita with death and Florizel with disinheritance should they persist in their love. Though Perdita's beauty, which makes her the 'queen of curds and cream' (IV.iv.161), and her charming boldness in asserting that 'The selfsame sun that shines upon his court / Hides not his visage from our cottage' (IV.iv.475-6), cast Polixenes in an unsympathetic light, the social appropriateness of his anger is confirmed by Florizel's secrecy. He is illogically blamed for his unavoidable ignorance that Perdita is an appropriate choice for his son.

This disparity of levels produces a false analogy that shows Leontes' dream of restoration to be at cross-purposes to his own unacknowledged conception of reality. Our knowledge that Polixenes' anger is inappropriate to the 'true' circumstances creates a parallel between him and Leontes, for both figures discern evil where there is none. The overt point of the parallel is that true value or virtue is hidden beneath appearances, its perception requiring, as Paulina tells Leontes, an awakening of faith. The implied argument is that as Leontes should have known Hermione's worth, so Polixenes should have known Perdita's. But Leontes undermines the argument, for as we have seen, he gives himself no excuse to suspect Hermione other than the normal flirtatiousness of men and women. But he gives Polixenes good reason to object to his son's behaviour and so deviously expresses his unbelief in the resolution he generates through the distanced images of himself and of Hermione in the figures of Florizel and Perdita.

In this way the play indulges the romantic fantasy that true love can transcend all social obstacles and heal all spiritual wounds, while at the same time guaranteeing that this particular true love violates no social propriety. The romantic vision of an ideally loving couple as the source of transcendent spiritual value gains an easy, not to say false, victory over an illusory opposition in the magical world of Bohemia. Polixenes' socially justified outrage is made to seem inappropriate to the magical spirit that can save baby princesses on the seashore.

While Leontes tries to realize in distant Bohemia his idealized images of lovers free from destructive emotions, in Sicilia he submits himself to the punitive parental figure he has generated in Paulina.[7] His unease appears in the discrepancy between her depiction as a comic shrew, by which he restrains the frightening dimensions associated with similarly powerful female figures in other plays, and the gravity of the context. This mixed tone surrounding Paulina's portrayal is significant in relation to Hermione. Having allowed within his horizon a powerful woman, Leontes has tried to disperse her power over him by thinking her sullied, and to obliterate her maternal force by depriving her of children. He then avoids the love-death paradigm by collapsing into a passive and childlike submission to an alternate and semi-comic maternal figure, taming in the comically tinged Paulina the more awesome dimensions he has attributed to Hermione, and replacing in his own person the child-figures he has eliminated. Within the protected magical aura at the periphery of his consciousness represented by Bohemia, he allows himself, on condition of thinking it punishment, the passive gratification of becoming a version of Lear. In

Paulina's not-so-kind nursery he finds a comic compromise between those nurseries that Cordelia and Goneril and Regan might provide on which to lay his head.[8]

Under the guise of submission to the process of spiritual regeneration, Leontes satisfies his desire for maternal nurturing. That nurturing, however, retains sexual overtones, and thereby betrays his association of sexuality with incest, because of the concealed identification of the now maternal Paulina with Hermione, and it acquires masochistic dimensions from being placed in a context that fuses it with punishment. Paulina's identification with Hermione appears most strongly in relation to the punitive force of both figures. In order to keep Leontes in constant self-castigation, Paulina accuses him of Hermione's murder while reminding him of her unparalleled virtues. With painful pleasure he co-operates by acknowledging his guilt and adding, 'but thou strik'st me / Sorely, to say I did: it is as bitter / Upon thy tongue as in my thought. Now, good now, / Say so but seldom' (V.i.17-20). Paulina's figure merges with an image of Hermione as a punishing ghost when, after having timidly suggested that he might remarry, Leontes agrees with Paulina that if he married 'one worse, / And better us'd,' Hermione's offended ghost 'would incense me / To murder her I married' (V.i.61-2). The new wife and the ghostly Hermione become a single image that punishes him by reinforcing his guilt. With his guilt comes his rage, so that he kills again in a cycle of guilt that increases through his efforts to deny it, just as he intensified the image of himself as a child by trying to destroy it. Paulina both identifies herself with the ghostly Hermione and emphasizes her punitive fury when she says that if she were the ghost, she would 'bid you mark / Her eye, and tell me for what dull part in't / You chose her: then I'd shriek, that even your ears / Should rift to hear me; and the words that follow'd / Should be, "Remember mine"' (V.i.63-7). Understandably, Leontes capitulates: 'I'll have no wife, Paulina.'

Having eliminated the homosexual alternative with Mamillius' death, Leontes has left only two versions of the same image—a vision of himself in a childlike celibacy that conceals frightening masochistic impulses, and one of mature sexuality in which women become avenging mothers. To escape these and to retrieve his identity as husband and father, he defines Paulina's maternal power as magically restorative, and calls on the machinery he has kept all along in the wings.

In Paulina he fuses the maternal punitive power, shades of the bad mother, with the beneficent good mother as she stage-manages the return of the lost. When Paulina makes Leontes promise not to remarry until 'Your first queen's again in breath,' Perdita is about to reappear in fulfilment of the oracles' prediction that 'the king shall live without an heir, if that which is lost be not found' (III.ii.134-6). Though we do not as yet know that Hermione will also reappear, the seeming impossibility of her doing so is brought into relationship with the violation of probability already coming to pass in Perdita's reappearance. The images of Perdita and Hermione begin to merge with each other, and both become associated with a semi-magical quality associated with Paulina. A more mature version of Rosalind, Paulina has mysterious power both to spirit Hermione away for sixteen years and orchestrate her resurrection along with Perdita's. Like her person, Paulina's strategies hover between an inadequately explained naturalistic realm and an incomplete magical one.

Within this uneasy union of naturalistic emotions and magical resolution Leontes clothes the complex incestuous feelings for mothers and daughters in the aura of spiritual redemption. As said earlier, Leontes associates Perdita with the passive and vulnerable self that he rejected in the process of recoiling from the image of woman as mother. At the cost of their sexuality, Lear and Pericles tried to purify their image of the young female by separating her from the fearsome maternal image and from themselves. Leontes reveals the fundamental identity of mother and daughter images in the way the images of Perdita and Hermione overlie each other. Both the interdependence and coincidental timing of their return and verbal associations identify them. The third gentleman tells how Leontes said 'O, thy mother, thy mother!' when he looks on his daughter, and of how 'the majesty of the creature in resemblance of the mother, the affection of nobleness which nature shows above her breeding, and many other evidences proclaim her with all certainty, to be the king's daughter' (V.ii.35-41). To reclaim the daughter is to reclaim the mother, but since Leontes envisions a sexual reunion with the woman as wife, the incestuous basis of his feelings for his daughter are revealed in the identification of the two, which emphasizes Hermione's maternal function.[9] Though Leontes consciously feels that his having submitted to punishment has freed him from the destructive desires that caused him to lose Hermione and Perdita, both the punishment and the restoration show, in greater concealment and in different tones, the same configurations that they were designed to obliterate. Only fairy-tale and magical forms can represent his restoration because there is nothing in the imagery to suggest an inner transformation of his desires, which alone would eliminate his need for both punitive and restorative mothers.

The concluding episodes of *The Winter's Tale* replace the tortured sexuality of the first part with an ideological fairy-tale. Leontes is reunited with Hermione, Florizel and Perdita become the magically ideal heterosexual pair whose flawless but unexplored love will reunite the two divided kingdoms, and by implication the division in Leontes' soul. The suggestion of sexual masochism involved in Leontes' submission to Paulina is replaced by a more or less Christian ideology, for

Hermione's 'resurrection' implies that if one accepts one's guilt and embraces punishment, suffering will not only change one's psychic and emotional structure but will also obliterate the consequences of evil. The play recognizes the dream-vision quality of its resolution, but it turns that recognition into another kind of ideology. The comparisons between the stage action and old tales, which increase in frequency as the play draws to its close, suggest that old tales—by implication the play itself—carry into life an ideology of redemption that can compensate for life's failures. Also, the self-reflexive references to the action, particularly in connection with Hermione's revival, as being like that in a play imply that the work of art can come to life and obliterate the distinction between dream-vision and reality. There is a curious double motion. On the one hand the end of the play shows life becoming art—an old tale, a play, a statue—and in so doing obscures the unresolved conflicts depicted on a naturalistic plane. But on the other hand, as though uneasy at that evasion, the play attemps also to assert that art, the statue, can re-enter the realm of life to become flesh.[10]

Shakespeare abandoned that attempt in *The Tempest*. At the same time as he reversed the power relation between man and woman, giving Paulina's magical power to a more than paternal Prospero, he also gave up the effort to envision an unambiguously good and powerful female, and moved fully into the magical realm, abandoning naturalistic causality. However, in *The Tempest* the structure and detail of the fairy-tale resolution still betray both the problems that require such strenuous control and its human cost.

Notes

[1] Coppélia Kahn in 'The Providential Tempest and the Shakespearean Family,' *Representing Shakespeare,* ed Murray M. Schwartz and Coppélia Kahn (Baltimore: Johns Hopkins University Press, 1981), 217-63, says rightly that the homosexuality implied between Leontes and Polixenes expresses Leontes' unwillingness to trust his manhood to women and sexuality, and accounts for his jealousy (233).

[2] Stephen Reid in *'The Winter's Tale,'* *American Imago* 27 (1970) 262-77, sees homosexual attachment and Oedipal guilt underlying Leontes' jealousy, the guilt overlying the homosexuality and thereby lending to it the aura of innocence (277).

[3] In a related comment Murray M. Schwartz in *'The Winter's Tale:* Loss and Transformation,' *American Imago* 32 (1975) 145-99, states that Shakespeare here makes psychic reality a dramatic fact (156).

[4] In 'Leontes' Jealousy in *The Winter's Tale,'* *American Imago* 30 (1973) 250-73, Murray M. Schwartz sees

the spider expressing Leontes' primary fear of maternal engulfment. One gets a more precise sense of the emotions involved, however, by surveying earlier contexts in which the spider appears. In *2 Henry VI* York, who will become Richard III, says 'My brain more busy than the laboring spider / Weaves tedious snares to trap mine enemies' (III.i.339-40). That first image resembles the last one in *Henry VIII,* when Wolsey is described as attaining his success by creating deceiving illusions 'spider-like, / Out of his self-drawing web' (I.i.62-3). In both of these images the spider suggests snares of deceit, drawn from the inward being of one who by means of these snares appears virtuous to others. The Duke in *Measure for Measure* makes Angelo's plot to seduce Isabella an example of how one may use idle spiders' strings to draw others into evil and distort their views of reality.

Women's duplicity is added to these images of male deceit by the spider image in *The Merchant of Venice;* Bassanio says of Portia's portrait that 'the painter plays the spider, and hath woven / A golden mesh to entrap the hearts of men' (III.ii.122-4). Though Portia overtly functions positively, the description of woman's beauty as that which entraps man, turning him into a gnat, suggests the darker ranges that also subtly attach to her character as she weaves a web around Shylock. That female association with the spider's power to entrap and devour is also connected with cruelty, when the Bastard in *King John* says that should Hubert consent to the child's murder in the ensuing despair, 'the smallest thread / That ever spider twisted from her womb / Will serve to strangle thee' (IV.iii.126-9). Women's sexual and generative powers here become the spider-like snares of deceit that, like Cleopatra's, are both drawn from and are designed to draw men back into the horrible womb that creates them. *A Midsummer Night's Dream* links the spider to creeping things that destroy the beauty of Titania's bower, and *Richard II* associates spiders with toads and with poison, wishing his enemies inflicted with 'spiders that suck up thy venom, / And heavy-gaited toads, lie in their way' (III.ii.14-15).

The association of spiders with other obnoxious insects, as well as with poison, pervades *Richard III.* Anne wishes her husband's murderer more wretched things than she can wish to 'adders, spiders, toads, / Or any creeping venom'd thing that lives!' (I.ii.19-20), and the image acquires more force when Margaret, calling Richard a 'poisonous bunchbacked toad,' asks Elizabeth why 'strew'st thou sugar on that bottled spider? / Whose deadly web ensnareth thee about?' (I.iii.246,242-3). These images are used specifically in connection with Richard's sexual seduction of women into embracing his spider self in order to get revenge for his misshapen body by making them love him. That combination of images to describe a foul sexuality also appears in *Cymbeline* when Guiderius tells Cloten that

'Toad, or Adder, Spider' (IV.ii.90) are less disgusting names than his own. These images bring the spider into the range of Othello's foul cistern in which toads 'knot and gender,' and also suggest the various disgusting toads, blindworms, snakes, and other horrors with which the witches fill their cauldron to entrap Macbeth. They also recall the poisonous asp from Nilus' slime that is both Cleopatra's power to poison Antony's hours, and the baby that lulls her asleep.

When all these associations are taken into account the spider in Leontes' cup can be seen to embody Leontes' fear of woman's sexual charms, which will expose and punish his foul sexuality by reducing him to an insect, and will by devouring him incorporate him into her interior foulness.

[5] Roger Stilling in *Love and Death in Renaissance Tragedy* (Baton Rouge: University of Louisiana Press, 1976) sees Leontes re-enacting the death of love occasioned by the misogyny of Hamlet and of Othello, but redeemed by Perdita and Florizel, who are reborn versions of Romeo and Juliet. He argues that in the earlier works the romantic view, and in the later works the anti-romantic view, lead to death.

[6] Schwartz, in 'The Winter's Tale: Loss and Transformation,' says that the play is about fear, represented by the bear (156), and desire for maternal power (158).

[7] R.E. Gajdusek in 'Death, Incest, and the Triple Bond in the Later Plays of Shakespeare,' *American Imago,* 31 (1974) 109-58, argues that Paulina as a hag-cummagician uses rites of renewal and restoration to save Leontes from the living death of incestuous desires (152). In ' "O My Most Sacred Lady": Female Metaphor in *The Winter's Tale,*' *English Literary Renaissance* 5 (1975) 375-95, Patricia Southard Gourlay says that Paulina functions as a female magus, anticipating Prospero in reawakening a lost ideal (394).

[8] Charles Frey in *Shakespeare's Vast Romance: A Study of* The Winter's Tale (Columbia: University of Missouri Press, 1980) also sees Leontes as a contracted rendering of the issues involved in Hamlet's and Lear's dark vision of sexuality (79).

[9] This argument for the incestuous implication of the reunion scene harmonizes with the play's source, Robert Greene's *Pandosto,* in which the father kills himself after falling in love with his unrecognized daughter. It may have been that the incest motif in the source generates the play, but is itself replaced by the final uneasy merger of naturalistic and magical plotting, and by the penumbra of transcendent value that surrounds Perdita and Hermione.

[10] In 'The Winter's Tale, *Othello* and *Troilus and Cressida:* Narcissism and Sexual Betrayal,' *American*

Imago 36 (Spring 1979) 80-93, Joan M. Byles finds Leontes too emotionally thin to be dramatically related to the miraculous restoration (92).

TIME

Marjorie B. Garber (essay date 1974)

SOURCE: "The Truth of Your Own Seeming: Romance and the Uses of Dream," in *Dream in Shakespeare: From Metaphor to Metamorphosis,* Yale University Press, 1974, pp. 163-86.

[*In the following excerpt, Garber examines the importance of time in* The Winter's Tale, *especially with regard to dreams and the metamorphoses concomitant with seasonal changes.*]

The Winter's Tale, . . . centers much of its attention on problems of timelessness and time. Metamorphosis is everywhere in its plot and imagery. The large structural units of the play are the four seasons of the year: winter in the opening "jealousy" scene at Leontes' court; spring with the finding of the child in Bohemia; summer in the great pastoral scene of the sheepshearing; and autumn or harvest in the return to Sicilia and the restoration of the king's wife and child, assuring order and fertility. This cyclical movement is occasionally cut, or halted, by moments of the sort we have been calling timeless, when the world of dream and the irrational intersects with the ongoing world which surrounds it. We are now purposely using "dream" in a double sense, for the entire world of *The Winter's Tale* is indeed a dream world as we have described it, and the fundamental element of dream, metamorphosis or transformation, will continue to inform it throughout. The other kind of dream is frequently accompanied by an artifact—a tale, play, or statue. This is the redemptive element, the moment beyond time, often attended by music, which suggests that the cyclical action may not after all have to repeat itself endlessly. T. S. Eliot, writing of these moments of the "intersection of the timeless with time," calls them "only hints and guesses," and so they are in *The Winter's Tale.* But it may be that the play is suggesting that hints and guesses are all that man is given, that always underneath these startling moments of transcendence and insight there must be cycle and change, metamorphosis, life and death. Just as the young Mamilius dies and is not revived, so mortality, the moment of Hamlet in the graveyard, is ultimately the radical condition of man.

The metamorphosis of seasonal change in the play is, of course, matched by appropriate human actions in each season. Contained within this broad structure, however, there are many little cycles; and these too are

enlightening on the question of metamorphosis and dream. For example, in the opening moments of the play, Polixenes, recalling his childhood with Leontes, describes them as

> Two lads that thought there was no more
> behind
> But such a day tomorrow as today,
> And to be boy eternal.
>
> [I.ii.63-65]

Had they remained in that state, he suggests, they would have avoided the taint of original sin. He is thus evoking a kind of golden age, an almost Wordsworthian innocence which is simultaneously Christian and pagan. But in longing to be "boy eternal" he is protesting against the very cycle which gives life, against the necessity of experience before eternity. The "Ode: Intimations of Immortality from Recollections of Early Childhood," is perhaps the best commentary on his wish; the children on the shore in Wordsworth's poem are very like the "boy eternal," but the "sober colouring" of mortality is essential to Polixenes, to Shakespeare, and to any permanency which is to come out of *The Winter's Tale.* Just as in the Intimations Ode the man of imagination succeeds the child of nature, so in *The Winter's Tale* the essential experiences of nature and time alone produce imagination and art. The critical turning point at which Wordsworth praises

> Those obstinate questionings
> Of sense and outward things,
> Fallings from us, vanishings

is very like Paulina's crucial call to "awake your faith." Geoffrey Hartman writes that

> the strength which [the child's] imagination exhibits in going out of itself and blending with a lesser nature is the source of all future strength: it is for Wordsworth *the* act of regeneration. . . . The mature man . . . bases his faith in self-transcendence on the ease or unconsciousness with which the apocalyptic imagination turned in childhood toward life. Then the crisis was to go from self-love (unconscious) to love of nature, and now it is to go from self-love (conscious) to love of man.[9]

A very similar psychological process seems to be animating the transcendent activity of dream in the romances.

Polixenes' assertion is therefore a clue to lack of self-knowledge, manifested in a resistance to the normal flow of the seasons. His deficiency is at the outset much less evident than Leontes', although they are actually very similar figures, because much of the first act is occupied by Leontes' internal monologue of jealous suspicion. And the substance of Leontes' remarks testifies to a limited understanding of dream which is also an aversion to change:

> Affection! Thy intention stabs the center.
> Thou dost make possible things not so held,
> Communicat'st with dreams—how can this
>   be?—
> With what's unreal thou coactive art,
> And fellow'st nothing. Then 'tis very credent
> Thou mayst co-join with something, and thou
>   dost,
> And that beyond commission, and I find it,
> And that to the infection of my brains,
> And hardening of my brows.

>   [I.ii.138-46]

According to this reasoning "affection," or passionate emotion, since it is known to ally itself with dreams and "what's unreal," is even more likely to be provoked by a real stimulus, such as sexual infidelity. The logic is extremely dubious, itself affected by "affection." Once more Shakespeare shows remarkable insight into the operations of the dream work, for Leontes' problem is precisely that he has subconsciously displaced and substituted the fictive for the real in order to give vent to a latent "affection," a propensity for sexual jealousy. As a synonym for dream he uses the significant "nothing," which anticipates his Tourneurian interrogation of Camillo:

>   Is whispering nothing?
> Is leaning cheek to cheek? Is meeting noses?
> Kissing with inside lip? . . .
>   . . . Is this nothing?
> Why then the world and all that's in't is
>   nothing,
> The covering sky is nothing, Bohemia nothing,
> My wife is nothing, nor nothing have these
>   nothings,
> If this be nothing.

>   [I.ii.284-86; 292-96]

The manifest irony here is of course that these things *are* nothing in the sense of Leontes' question—they do not exist and are therefore not evidence of suspicious conduct between Hermione and Polixenes. As always, however, "nothing" is a richly ambiguous word, and here particularly so, since Leontes himself has equated it with dream, and since it so clearly draws attention to itself in the lines just quoted. All the grievances he catalogues are indeed Leontes' dreams and delusions, though he means to assert the contrary. What is more interesting, however, is the reading of the last four lines we produce if we answer the preceding question ("Is this nothing?") with its proper answer, yes. Then, following Leontes' logic, "the world," "the covering sky," "Bohemia," and his wife are all nothing, dreams, as well. But what are these elements but the primary components of the drama itself—the fictive world, the

stage, the scene, the characters? In its way Leontes' hyperbole is an anticipation of Prospero's great speech at the close of the masque in *The Tempest:*

>   like the baseless fabric of this vision,
> The cloud-capped towers, the gorgeous palaces,
> The solemn temples, the great globe itself,
> Yea, all which it inherit, shall dissolve,
> And, like this insubstantial pageant faded,
> Leave not a rack behind.

>   [*Tmp.* IV.i.151-56]

With consummate skill the poet suggests an underlying sense of reflexivity, even in Leontes' most self-delusive moments. Leontes himself is, so to speak, confounded by his own logic. From the first he confuses reality and illusion in the court world of Sicilia, and his illusion is nightmare, malign fiction: "I have drunk, and seen the spider" (II.i.45). In the trial scene in act III his dialogue with Hermione further bares his confusion, which is not a transcendent reversal but rather an error of fact.

> *Hermione:*　　　　　　　　　Sir,
> You speak a language that I understand not.
> My life stands in the level of your dreams,
> Which I'll lay down.
> *Leontes:*　　　　Your actions are my dreams.
> You had a bastard by Polixenes,
> And I but dreamed it.

>   [III.ii.77-82]

Again he speaks truth in the guise of irony; he *has* "but dreamed it." Hermione asserts that her life is totally at the mercy of his delusions. His reply, that her actions "are his dreams," has been true in many dream situations in past plays but is wholly untrue here. One of the many effects of this symmetrical and devastating exchange is to warn us about the negative power of dreams, a facet hinted at in *A Midsummer Night's Dream.* The world of dream possesses the power it does because its creative energy produces poetry and art. But the essence of dream is the irrational, and the irrational contains the seeds of danger and destruction. Leontes' progression from this point to the awakened faith of the unveiling scene is in part a progress from bad dream to good, from daemonic nightmare to creative imagination. Here is metamorphosis of yet another kind, coupled with a serious and sober appraisal of the doctrine of dream.

The immediate effect of these unwholesome "dreams" upon Leontes is to produce sleeplessness, a malady which is by now familiar to us from the cases of Macbeth and Richard III. Leontes' delusory daydreams have crowded out the possibility of normal sleeping dreams; and he, like Macbeth, is forced to live in a waking world governed by his own fictions. Leontes himself is aware of this, though characteristically he disregards facts for impressions;

Dost think I am so muddy, so unsettled,
To appoint myself in this vexation? Sully
The purity and whiteness of my sheets—
Which to preserve is sleep; which being
   spotted,
Is goads, thorns, nettles, tails of wasps—

[I.ii.326-30]

"Goads, thorns, nettles"—Leontes uses these words as metaphors for a psychological state. His world is all "in the mind." When the same images appear in *The Tempest,* they will be part of an externalized dream world, the "Toothed briers, sharp furzes, pricking goss, and thorns" (*Tmp.* IV.i.180) with which Ariel abuses the shins of Stephano, Trinculo, and Caliban. But Leontes is the fabricator of his own delusions and the cause of his own inability to sleep. Paulina acknowledges this fact in her reply to the servant who tries to keep her from entering the court with the newborn Perdita:

I come to bring him sleep. 'Tis such as you
That creep like shadows by him, and do sigh
At each his needless heavings—such as you
Nourish the cause of his awaking.

[II.iii.33-36]

Again we have the verbal contrast between "his awaking," which is a barren state, and the awakened faith at the close of the play. Leontes' state of mind is frozen and sterile, and he denies evidence of his own fertility, the child who is "the whole matter / And copy of the father" (II.iii.98-99). Images of physical dream, sleeping and waking, are thus early integrated into the larger pattern of change and growth.

The seasonal metaphor of reawakening has as its counterpart in the plot the "death" and resurrection of Hermione. It is the knowledgeable Paulina, again, who suggests the possibility of such a revival as early as the third act. Like all her most significant utterances, however, this one is slightly gnomic, because it is deliberately phrased as a condition contrary to fact.

                    if you can bring
Tincture or luster in her lip, her eye,
Heat outwardly or breath within, I'll serve you
As I would do the gods.

[III.ii.202-05]

There is some possibility that when Shakespeare wrote this scene and the one that follows, Antigonus's dream, he had not yet conceived the idea of reviving Hermione. It is difficult to think, however, that he would have let this passage stand, after altering the play's ending, if it conflicted with his dramatic or symbolic purposes. The net effect of Paulina's avowal, in any case, is to put into the minds of the audience the very possibility she denies. The scene thus becomes a dramatic anticipation of the denouement, an emphatic statement of

the impossibility and irrationality of something which will turn out to be true. It is the pattern of dream in little again, a cycle within the cycle.

We have discussed the large structure of metamorphosis in terms of time. That structure can also be analyzed spatially, in the geographical fluctuation from Sicilia to Bohemia and back again. Sicilia here is initially the "real" world of the court, Bohemia and its inhabitants the dream world and its spirits; and the return to Sicilia brings with it a faith in dream by which what was previously impossible, Hermione's regeneration, becomes possible and true. Again and again in this play large movements of this sort are anticipated by smaller ones, and thus in the lyric "window" passage at the opening of the third act we catch a glimpse of redemption. Cleomenes and Dion have been sent by Leontes to the oracle of Apollo, which Shakespeare mistakenly places on the isle of Delos. The mistake serves him well, however; Delphi, the actual site of the oracle, is inland, while Delos, an island, provides opportunity for a symbolic sea journey and itself becomes proleptic to the Bohemian dream world of the main plot. Cleomenes' report of the island is indicative:

The climate's delicate, the air most sweet,
Fertile the isle, the temple much surpassing
The common praise it bears.

[III.i.1-3]

It might almost be a description of Prospero's isle. We may especially take note of the emphasis on fertility, associating that trait with poetic inspiration (Apollo) and again anticipating the pastoral abundance of the Bohemia scenes. This short scene functions like a metaphor in the play as a whole; the two messengers are for a moment in that state of "grace" which is so central to the language of *The Winter's Tale.* When Cleomenes says the oracle "so surprised [his] sense / That I was nothing" (III.i.10-11), we see the other side of the question of "nothingness," a transcendent subjectivity which leads to insight. The breathing space is short-lived, however; Leontes denies the oracle, the deaths of Mamilius and Hermione are reported, and Perdita is doomed to exile. At this point the scene shifts to Bohemia, a tempest, and a dream.

Antigonus's dream vision of the dead Hermione is the only literal dream in the play, and like the dream visions of Pericles and Posthumus this one lacks the real energy and imagination of Shakespeare's maturest writing. Its tone is discursive and its images somewhat underdeveloped, hints of symbols rather than symbols themselves. Antigonus makes a number of observations about dream and the dream state of a kind which have become wholly familiar to us by now: "ne'er was dream / So like waking"; "I . . . thought / This was so, and not slumber"; "Dreams are toys; / Yet for this once, yea superstitiously, / I will be squared by this. I do believe . . ." (III.iii.14-45). He defines himself as a person who ordinarily scoffs at dreams, implying that there is something unusual about this particular dream which sets it apart. In outline the dream itself is an old-style monitory dream, the return of a spirit from the dead to warn the living: the figure of Hermione, "in pure white robes / Like very sanctity" (21-22), requests him to take Perdita to the shores of Bohemia and informs him that he will never see his wife again. This last circumstance, one of the two irreversible tragedies of the play (the death of Mamilius is the other), is partially responsible for a sense of sobriety that obtains even at the play's close, when Paulina points out that all are revived and reunited but he. Yet there is internal justification for Antigonus's death more than for Mamilius's: when he says of the infant Perdita "this being indeed the issue / Of King Polixenes" (42-43), he demonstrates his own lack of faith. The apparent fact of Hermione's death in the dream is at first more puzzling, since she is later demonstrated to be alive. Yet in a metaphorical sense she is properly imaged as dead, since in the imaginative worlds of poetry and dream "death" is a failure of belief, another instance of unawakened faith. What is most interesting, however, is the language of imagery with which he chooses to describe her, in a long passage relatively devoid of images. "Her eyes," he says, "became two spouts" as she began to speak. The picture calls to mind the figure of Niobe from the *Metamorphoses* of Ovid (VI.146ff.), who turns into a fountain and weeps for the loss of her children. Like the "pure white robes / Like very sanctity" this is in part an allegorizing tendency, but it is also a hint of transformation. When Perdita, at the close of the passage, is addressed as "Blossom," the covert growth and transformation imagery is once more supported.

If the dream of Antigonus is in some ways the least successful symbolic incident in the play, it is followed by what might be called the most successful: the unexpected entry of the bear and the extraordinarily rich and vivid dialogue between the shepherd and the clown. Greene's *Pandosto*, the direct source of *The Winter's Tale,* makes no mention of the bear who pursues Antigonus and is later so placidly described by the clown. But the bear is an important symbol for the play as a whole; though it exemplifies the wild and irrational character of the land of Bohemia, it seems unanticipated by anything in the previous action. Yet in folklore the bear is one of the most common symbols of immortality and resurrection, because of its habit of winter hibernation.[10] Adherents of the cult of the Thracian Salmaxis, the bear-god, believed that the bear first feasted, then slept in an underground chamber as though dead, returning to the world of the living with the spring thaw. The bear was thus the symbol of a cult of immortality, his own cycle coinciding with the pattern of the *sacre du printemps,* the spring resurrection festival. The related legend of Kallisto, the Great Bear,

includes the fact that the bear child, her son Arkas, the ancestor of the Arcadians, was sacrificed at a feast of the clan. Mimetically in his memory a human child was annually offered at the shrine of Zeus Lykaios, in a gesture not unlike the abandonment of Perdita. It is also interesting to note that the house of Odysseus was traditionally associated with the bear, and that the heroes Melikertes ("honey-cutter"), Sisyphos, and Autolykos are closely related to one another and to Odysseus.[11] Autolykos, the maternal grandfather of Odysseus, is the father of Sisyphos; and Sisyphos, the Master Thief of Greek folktale, is the hero of a story about the outwitting of death which takes the same general pattern (apparent death, descent to Hades, release and revival) as the bear cult and the fertility myths. The episode of the bear is thus symbolically related to the appearance of Autolycus at the same time that it reinforces the cyclical framework of regeneration with which we have been concerned.

With the exit of the bear there arrive onstage the shepherd and the clown, the native inhabitants of Bohemia, possessed of much of the uncalculated insight we have come to expect from the denizens of a dream world. A great deal of what they say in this pivotal scene has an arresting simplicity, a vividness of image which strikes the ear. The old shepherd's first remark is a recapitulation of the hibernation motif:

> I would there were no age between ten and three-and-twenty, or that youth would sleep out the rest; for there is nothing in the between but getting wenches with child, wronging the ancientry, stealing, fighting.
>
> [III.iii.58-62]

The tone of this, as of many of the shepherd's observations, is detached, removed from the difficult human passions which trouble the other characters. His son's account of the destruction of the ship and the death of Antigonus has the same curious and striking fictive distance; it is much more like the telling of a dream than was Antigonus's tale:

> O, the most piteous cry of the poor souls! Sometimes to see'em, and not to see'em; now the ship boring the moon with her mainmast, and anon swallowed with yeast and froth, as you'd thrust a cork into a hogshead. And then for the land-service, to see how the bear tore out his shoulder bone, how he cried to me for help, and said his name was Antigonus, a nobleman! But to make an end of the ship, to see how the sea flapdragoned it; but first, how the poor souls roared, and the sea mocked them; and how the poor gentleman roared, and the bear mocked him, both roaring louder than the sea or weather.
>
> [III.iii.88-99]

The immediacy of images, the lack of logical development, and the way in which no background is supplied for events narrated are all characteristics of the process of dream. The clown's world is indeed one in which dream enters the waking consciousness, as the world of Bohemia is illustrative of that consciousness. And just when we are caught by the haunting power of his prose, Shakespeare has the same clown break the spell, saying without transition "the men are not yet cold under water, nor the bear half dined on the gentlemen; he's at it now" (102-03). The spurious elegance of "dined," together with the sudden insistence of "now," removes the previous narration some distance from the quality of fable, without investing it with human horror. The shepherd and the clown are observers for us; they translate us into the realm of Bohemia, by talking of tragedy as if it were romance—as, indeed, Shakespeare is to do in *The Winter's Tale* as a whole. It is at this point, ascribing the development to "fairies" in whom he most fittingly believes, that the old shepherd makes his crucial observation: "thou met'st with things dying, I with things new born" (110-11). Again such a stark and pivotal assessment of the play's purposes, in which myth for a moment rises to the surface of language, is placed at the midpoint of the action. From this moment *The Winter's Tale* moves toward renewal and redemption. The pattern of natural metamorphosis is again affirmed.

We touched briefly upon Antigonus's evocation of Niobe in the vision of Hermione with eyes which "became two spouts." Specific uses of Ovid's *Metamorphoses,* whether allusively, as here, or more directly, as in the tale of Tereus in *Cymbeline,* are highly significant in the larger context of metamorphosis and the dream world. In the great pastoral scene we now approach (IV.iv.), the internal pattern of seasonal growth and decay is once more recapitulated. In its opening lines Florizel describes Perdita as "no shepherdess but Flora, / Peering in April's front" (IV.iv.2-3). Flora is described in Ovid (*Fasti* V.231 ff.) as possessing a magical flower which, given to Juno, makes her pregnant; later in the scene Perdita will herself enact this role, giving flowers to the assemblage at the sheepshearing and both directly and symbolically encouraging fertility and fruition. "April's front" is of course an image of the shyness of early spring flowers; it is succeeded in act IV, scene iv, by the full blossoming of summer: "the year growing ancient, / Not yet on summer's death, nor on the birth / Of trembling winter" (79-81). This is a literal description of the time in which the sheepshearing is taking place, but it is also a figurative way of expressing the temper of the moment of flower-giving. With the announcement of the love of Perdita and Doricles and the plighting of troth, the idea of maturation and harvest is introduced, and this in turn quickly gives way to a new repressive and authoritarian regime with the unmasking of the irate Polixenes. Within this framework the idea of metamor-

phosis is continuously suggested. Florizel, explaining the appropriateness of his disguise as a shepherd and hers as a queen, cites Ovid for a precedent,

> The gods themselves,
> Humbling their deities to love, have taken
> The shapes of beasts upon them. Jupiter
> Became a bull and bellowed; the green Neptune
> A ram, and bleated; and the fire-robed god,
> Golden Apollo, a poor humble swain,
> As I seem now. Their transformations
> Were never for a piece of beauty rarer,
> Nor in a way so chaste, since my desires
> Run not before mine honor, nor my lusts
> Burn hotter than my faith.
>
> [IV.iv.25-34]

Florizel's classical examples, characteristically, have both a local and a broader significance; they are not randomly chosen. Jupiter the king, Neptune the sea-god, and Apollo the poet and giver of inspiration are the three gods regnant in the play as a whole. The same relevance characterizes Perdita's later invocation of Proserpina:

> O Proserpina,
> For the flow'rs now, that, frighted, thou let'st fall
> From Dis's wagon!
>
> [116-18]

The story of Proserpina and Ceres is of course the pattern of the story of Perdita and Hermione, the cycle of death and rebirth. These small grace notes from the mythological past add dimension and timelessness to the play as it proceeds. So naturally are they introduced into the action that they do not jar or obtrude, yet their presence in itself contributes to the quality of myth or fable the poet has carefully been developing. Each such moment is yet another "window," opening on the inexhaustible past on which the present action draws.

The espousal of the process of metamorphosis by Perdita and Florizel is closely related to the problem of disguise, which in turn is part of the larger problem of illusion and reality. Florizel is a prince disguised as a shepherd; Perdita is a princess who thinks she is a shepherdess disguised as a queen. Thus unmaskings in Perdita's case are really maskings of a sort, since they reveal a partial truth and hide a full one. Even the sheepshearing itself is a symbol of the shedding of disguise. Given this complexity of fact, the uses of the concept of dream in the pastoral scene acquire an additional significance. For example, early in the scene the old shepherd speaks with pride to Polixenes about his daughter's virtues. "If young Doricles / Do light upon her," he says,

she shall bring him that
Which he not dreams of.

[IV.iv.179-80]

The context of this observation is praise of her dancing, and by "that / Which he not dreams of" the shepherd refers overtly to her personal graces and accomplishments. Yet there is a covert meaning to his words
as well, since he knows of the gold left by her side as
an infant, and the "bearing-cloth for a squire's child"
(III.iii.112-13) in which she was wrapped. His phrase
is thus also an aside to himself, a reminder that he
knows more than the others about the true situation.
And the audience, of course, knows more still; for them
"that / Which he not dreams of" encompasses as well
the fact of her royal birth and the expectation that this
will affect the relationship between Leontes and Polixenes. Similarly, later in the same scene, the shepherd
and Florizel discuss the question of the marriage portion, and the shepherd, thinking of the gold, announces
to the assemblage:

I give my daughter to him, and will make
Her portion equal his.

[388-89]

Florizel, believing her a shepherdess and knowing the
truth of his own condition, replies in words very like
the shepherd's:

O, that must be
I' th' virtue of your daughter. One being dead,
I shall have more than you can dream of yet,
Enough then for your wonder.

[389-92]

"Dream" in both these cases is used to mean "imagine." But in each case the speaker's point is that what
his audience "dreams of" (or "not dreams of," which
carries an even further implication of impossibility)
will in fact turn out to be true. This is the reversal of
categories yet again, its application complicated and
enriched here by the concrete fact of disguise and the
entire atmosphere of dream.

Perdita herself has throughout the scene been particularly conscious of the fictive aspect of her role and her
disguise. She has continual recourse to the play metaphor, which brings together the themes of change (role
playing, metamorphosis) and timelessness (transmutation into art). "Methinks," she says,

I play as I have seen them do
In Whitsun pastorals; sure this robe of mine
Does change my disposition.

[133-35]

She herself makes the implicity equation between the
play and the dream, as fictive constructs which—from

her point of view—perpetrate illusion. Thus when
Polixenes finally reveals his identity, Perdita speaks to
Florizel in·the metaphor of dream:

Will't please you, sir, be gone?
I told you what would come of this. Beseech you,
Of your own state take care: this dream of
   mine
Being now awake, I'll queen it no inch farther
But milk my ewes, and weep.

[IV.iv.449-53]

Here is the same reversal yet again. The "dream" of
being a queen is more true than the apparent "reality"
of being a shepherdess. Further, it is from this point,
and the subsequent flight of the lovers, that there is
precipitated the true awakening or unmasking. Florizel
unconsciously emphasizes the exchange that has taken
place between the true and the fictive by a reply to the
cautious Camillo which recalls the language of Theseus's speech on imagination. "Be advised," says Camillo, and Florizel responds

I am, and by my fancy; if my reason
Will thereto be obedient, I have reason;
If not, my senses better pleased with madness,
Do bid it welcome.

[485-88]

A variation on the theme of "we lose our oaths to find
ourselves," his reply is a sign that he has accepted the
world of dream. When Camillo advises Perdita to disguise herself for flight, urging her to

disliken
The truth of your own seeming

[655-56]

the vocabularies of seeming and being, disguise and
revelation are once more joined in an act of transformation. Yet at the same time the note of reflexivity,
the out-of-time recognition of the play as an artifact, is
struck again. Camillo assures Florizel that "it shall be
so my care / To have you royally appointed, as if / The
scene you play were mine" (594-96), and Perdita's reply
to his suggestion about disguise is

I see the play so lies
That I must bear a part.

[658-59]

The play metaphor, thus integrated into the ongoing
action, is a hint of what will come. If the process is
metamorphosis and transformation, the product is art.
With the appearance of Autolycus in the fourth act, the
two realms are fused in a single character.

Of all the agents and objects of metamorphosis in *The
Winter's Tale,* Autolycus is the master. He belongs to

the category of quicksilver characters which also in-cludes Puck and Ariel. To a certain extent he *is* trans-formation itself and not merely a practitioner of it. His lightning facility with disguise and his almost aesthetic pleasure in gulling others with a pretended identity places him thematically near the center of the play, though his dramatic role of poet-observer precludes true participation in the society of the play's world. When we first meet him, alone, he is himself, a thief by choice and an enjoyer of the goods of the world. Under our gaze he rapidly transforms himself into a "robbed man" who robs the clown, a peddler of bal-lads and furbelows at the sheepshearing, and a "court-ier" purportedly in the service of King Polixenes. In a way he is like the fox and ape of Spenser's *Mother Hubberd's Tale,* satirizing the pretensions of society by pretending to have those pretensions. But his fictive and symbolic role is clearly even more complex than this. He is the play's artist and poet and thus its master of imagination and manipulator of dream. When he enters the house of the shepherd in his guise as peddler, an impressed servant reports his prowess to the company:

> Why,
> he sings 'em over, as they were gods or
>   goddesses;
> you would think a smock were a she-angel, he
>   so
> chants to the sleevehand, and the work about
>   the
> square on't.
>
> [IV.iv.207-11]

The servant's report, the more believable for its naïveté, is essentially an account of transformation. The image is amusing to the audience, especially because we are familiar with the "peddler's" other activities, but plainly the audience that Autolycus has set out to please is already under his spell. Moreover, Autolycus is a seller and singer of music; his entrance in the fourth act is the first appearance of music in the play. In all he sings six songs and snatches of two others; calling himself a "snapper-up of unconsidered trifles" (IV.iii.26), he makes of those trifles, whether song or costume, another version of Wallace Stevens's "fictive cover-ing." His first song, "When daffodils begin to peer" (IV.iii.1-12) is a song of the seasons and the passions, which rejoices in the arrival of spring and summer, making yet another small cycle within the larger one; and the witty image of melting snow as sheets pulled off hedges seems to suggest that Autolycus himself is in a way responsible for the coming of the spring. Two of the subsequent songs, sung in his guise as peddler, are about the peddler's wares, considered as fictions or affectations, "masks for faces and for noses" (IV.iv.222). Language is designedly his medium, and he is a dream figure of the most direct sort, assuming whatever guise his situation and companions demand; at the close of the fourth act, encountering the terrified shepherd and

his son, he articulates their basest fears and inner thoughts. Like other quicksilver figures of the Shake-spearean dream world, he finds himself ultimately outside the charmed circle of resolution, and is not included in the summing-up.

Autolycus's language is the language of metamorpho-sis by reason of his command of craft. By contrast, the clown, the old shepherd's son, is for *The Winter's Tale* a figure parallel to the *Hamlet* gravedigger, the *Macbeth* porter, or the clown in *Antony and Cleopatra.* His malapropisms carry multiple meanings, the more effec-tive for his total unawareness of them. Thus after the offstage recognition scene at Leontes' court (V.ii.) he confronts Autolycus (still in his role of courtier) with his new position: "See you these clothes?" he crows,

> Say you see them not
> and think me still no gentleman born; you
> were best say these robes are not gentlemen
> born. Give me the lie, do; and try whether I
> am now a gentleman born.
>
> [V.ii.132-36]

To which Autolycus amusedly replies, "I know you are now, sir, a gentleman born" (137-38). Clothing and high birth are here images deliberately related to an absolute belief in transformation. The episode is a comic diminution of an idea which has been of the utmost seriousness throughout. Perhaps the best example, how-ever, is the clown's venture into the special world of music, as reported to us by Autolycus. "No hearing, no feeling, but my sir's song, and admiring the nothing of it" (IV.iv.615-16). "My sir" is of course the clown; and "nothing" is simultaneously "poor quality," "fic-tiveness," and "noting," or singing.[12] To Autolycus this is merely an opportunity to cut purses; the sense that the rustics are spellbound, however, is important to the play's major themes, here once more presented in comic re-duction. Music in all its forms has a particular signifi-cance in *The Winter's Tale,* and the clown's attempt to emulate Autolycus, like the dances of shepherds and satyrs at the feast, is positioned in part to prepare us for the very different music of the final scene.

The great accomplishment of this scene is its reconcili-ation of the fictive and the real, the metaphoric and the literal. The reawakening of Hermione is a transcendent event, made possible by "faith" and art, but it is at the same time carefully made explicable in natural terms. Hermione is not dead; her rebirth is subjective, in the minds of the onlookers, and not objective or magical. This "naturalizing" of the supernatural is startling in its effect; once again it is the "art that Nature makes" which leads to new insight, and the world of dream which demonstrates its primacy over the merely "real." There is an interesting anticipation of this moment earlier in the act, during the discussion between Paulina and Leontes on the subject of remarriage. It is useless for him to remarry, she contends; the oracle has plainly said that he will have no heir "till his lost child be found" (V.i.40). Moreover, no woman could match the dead queen. Leontes concurs, and in doing so he creates a rhetorical ghost, a fictive shade of Hermione:

> One worse,
> And better used, would make her sainted
>   spirit
> Again possess her corpse, and on this stage,
> Where we offenders now appear, soul-vexed,
> And begin, "Why to me?"
>
> [56-59]

The spirit here is entirely subjective, a figure of speech, and yet in his imagination it walks and speaks. Paulina, quick to catch his mood, reinforces the image with embellishments of her own:

> Were I the ghost that walked, I'd bid you
>   mark
> Her eye, and tell me for what dull part in 't
> You chose her; then I'd shriek, that even your
>   ears
> Should rift to hear me, and the words that
>   followed
> Should be, "Remember mine."
>
> [63-67]

The resemblance to the ghost in *Hamlet* is striking. Revenge for a moment hovers in their air and then is put aside in favor of grace. Relenting of her sternness, Paulina now begins to blend the fictive ghost with the real one, the mental image with the living statue. If Leontes must marry again, she says,

> she shall not be so young
> As was your former, but she shall be such
> As walked your first queen's ghost, it should
>   take joy
> To see her in your arms.
>
> [78-81]

The double meaning here is perceptible only to Paulina; neither Leontes nor the audience know that Hermione is still alive. At this point the arrival of Perdita and Florizel is announced, and Leontes greets them "Welcome hither, / As is the spring to th' earth!" (V.i.151-52). The underlying natural cycle again reinforces the larger pattern of regeneration.

The actual "resurrection" of Hermione takes place, significantly, in a part of Paulina's house variously described as a "chapel" and a "gallery." The contents of the gallery are works of art, artifacts of the sort we have described as being removed from the round of time. The statue of Hermione, however, is insistently linked with time and life, even while it partakes of the stillness of eternity: "Prepare," says Paulina,

> To see the life as lively mocked, as ever
> Still sleep mocked death
>
> [V.iii.19-20]

reminding us of Juliet and Imogen, and later Leontes, "transported" (69), will exclaim "we are mocked with art" (68). Just as Perdita was a princess who thought she was a shepherdess masquerading as a queen, so the "statue" of Hermione is a living woman who is thought to be a statue but described as looking "alive." These are dream equivalences too, the subjective dream state rendering the onlookers unable to distinguish between art and life. Even the visible contribution of "great creating Nature," the wrinkles on Hermione's face, are described by Paulina as evidence of the "carver's excellence" (30), showing her as she would be if she were still alive. The process of reawakening is deliberately a slow one, as Leontes begins to become aware of reality; "no longer shall you gaze on't," says Paulina, "lest your fancy / May think anon it moves" (60-61), yet in fact his fancy is once again more accurate than reason. The final breaking of the boundary, the flowing together of dream and reality, is preceded by Paulina's crucial pronouncement:

> It is required
> You do awake your faith.
>
> [94-95]

The sleeping-waking metaphor is no accident here, but rather the culmination of a figure which has been highly significant throughout; faith is to be awakened by an acceptance of the possibility of dream. And once the faith is awakened, so too is the "statue":

> Music, awake her: strike.
> 'Tis time; descend; be stone no more;
>   approach;
> Strike all that look upon with marvel;
>   come;
> I'll fill your grave up.
>
> [98-101]

Music is the sign of metamorphosis and redemption, the union of the myths of Proserpina and Galatea. Time and timelessness, the art object and the process of mortal growth and change, are brought together for a moment in a symbol of regeneration.

It is important that the condition of art is here transitional, rather than terminal and eternal; Hermione returns to life, returns moreover with the wrinkles of time upon her and the final emphasis is on mortality. Even in the last glad moments of reconciliation we are reminded of the death of Antigonus. For in *The Winter's Tale* Shakespeare has measured art and nature, the dream world and the real world, and resolved them into the "art that Nature makes." The stage of art is essential to the play's resolution: the play itself contains a number of internal artifacts—the "winter's tale" itself, the songs of Autolycus, the play-within-a-play in the pastoral scene. But fundamentally the play moves through art to life again, the statue descends and becomes flesh. Without the transcendent insight of the dream state this movement could not have occurred, but just as the return to Sicilia is necessary, so too is the return to mortality. The very perfection of the re-animated statue as a symbol is its blending of the two states into one. In the "winter" section of the play the boy Mamilius, asked for a tale, replied

> A sad tale's best for winter; I have one
> Of sprites and goblins.
>
> [II.i.25-26]

"Sprites and goblins"—the traditional denizens of dream, the spirits of *A Midsummer Night's Dream.* By the time of the last scene Paulina will declare

> that she is living,
> Were it but told you, should be hooted at
> Like an old tale; but it appears she lives.
>
> [V.iii.115-17]

The "sprites and goblins" have been replaced by kings and shepherds, the tale, though it seems fictive, is real. The imperative word of the last scene is "awake," and the progress through dream to a renewed and heightened reality, the symbolic fulfillment of dream, is achieved through a coming together of symbols which express and contain it.

Notes

[9] *Wordsworth's Poetry 1787-1814* (New Haven: Yale University Press, 1964), p. 277.

[10] Rhys Carpenter, *Folk Tale, Fiction, and Saga in the Homeric Epics* (Berkeley: University of California Press, 1946), pp. 112-56.

[11] H. J. Rose, *A Handbook of Greek Mythology* (New York: E. P. Dutton, 1959), p. 294.

[12] The quibble on *noting* is suggested by J. Dover Wilson in the New Cambridge edition of *The Winter's Tale* (ed. Arthur Quiller-Couch and J. Dover Wilson [London: Cambridge University Press, 1931]), who compares *Much Ado About Nothing* II.iii.56: "Note notes, forsooth, and nothing."

Stanton B. Garner, Jr. (essay date 1989)

SOURCE: "'Grace and Remembrance': *The Winter's Tale*," in *The Absent Voice: Narrative Comprehension in the Theater,* University of Illinois Press, 1989, pp. 80-99.

[*In the essay that follows, Garner considers the dramatic tension of* The Winter's Tale *as a conflict between the present and time, as a place of innocence versus a realm of regret and longing.*]

Literally as well as figuratively, Time stands at the center of *The Winter's Tale,* giving strikingly emblematic stage life to a theme that had occupied Shakespeare's imagination since the sonnets and the earliest plays, through the often turbulent drama of the playwright's middle years, and into the romances, those strangely fabulous works that play variations on what came before. The confusions of Syracuse and Illyria sort themselves out in the movements of time; Richard of Gloucester and Macbeth draw back to seize time's promise; an aging poet reminds his younger friend, still in time's graces, of time's quiet ravages: "That time of year thou mayst in me behold / When yellow leaves, or none, or few, do hang."[1] Though time constitutes an organizing motif in Shakespeare's nondramatic work, as this last example suggests, its presence is actionally more central to the world of the plays, where characters must confront dramatic time as it unfolds in the present and where actors must navigate through the temporal movement of performance. In drama, as we have seen, time is a theme by necessity, for in the medium of performance it stands as a structuring component of stage activity, and of the dramatic action that this activity bodies forth. In the sonnets, time makes its appearance through reflection, with the virtual atemporality characteristic of meditation and address; its movements and their consequences are presented within linguistic parameters, manifested through a poetic utterance that, textually fixed, itself eludes time. In the plays, time intrudes itself experientially, through the unmediated temporality of performance: moments happen in the theater and within the play, establishing time as a felt reality for characters and audience alike. Time lies at the heart of Shakespeare's dramatic interests, in large part, because of its centrality to the theater for which he wrote.

The Winter's Tale—with its memories fond and bitter, its plans and prophecies, its tales and ballads, and its striking leap of sixteen years—explores the experience of temporality with a prominence and self-consciousness unusual even for Shakespeare. As Inga-Stina Ewbank notes, "while in *The Winter's Tale* time has largely disappeared from the verbal imagery, it is all the more intensely present as a controlling and shaping figure behind the dramatic structure and technique."[2] In keeping with the other pairs that serve to organize this dramatic diptych—Sicilia and Bohemia, youth and age, Nature and Art, rosemary and rue—*The Winter's Tale* presents human engagement with time in terms of a duality edging into paradox. On one hand, humanity lives in the present, a moment so complete in its immediacy that it seems to escape time entirely. This experience of the Now, and its apparent eternity, infuses Polixenes' description of the childhood innocence that he and Leontes shared:

> We were, fair queen,
> Two lads that thought there was no more
>   behind
> But such a day to-morrow as to-day,
> And to be boy eternal.
>
>   (I.ii.62-65)

His lines undermine the very idea of time, for the word *today,* charged with the force of the "eternal," subsumes *behind* and *tomorrow* in such a way that temporal distinctions blend and dissolve. Past and future warp into the seemingly boundless expanse of the present, and sequence unravels into a moment of Wordsworthian innocence, experienced as a condition outside Time's hourglass.

For all its apparent timelessness, however, this Edenic state is a memory, telescoped into what Prospero calls "the dark backward and abysm of time" (*The Tempest,* I.ii.50) in part by the very tense through which it is articulated. The stage presence of Leontes and Polixenes, both adults, constitutes a visual reminder of temporality, in which the present is barely an instant, collapsed into recollection by inexorable change. As Time boasts,

> I witness to
> The times that brought them in; so shall I do
> To th' freshest things now reigning, and make
>   stale
> The glistering of this present, as my tale
> Now seems to it.
>
>   (IV.i.11-15)

These words recall the temporal world of the sonnets, where existence is subject to the ironies of mutability as it plays its movement from "glistering" to "staleness"—a world where "every thing that grows / Holds in perfection but a little moment."[3] From this vantage point, time confronts humanity with the inevitability of consequence, since action, in the temporal realm, always has outcomes, foreseen or unforeseen: "I, that please some, try all, both joy and terror / Of good and bad, that makes and unfolds error" (IV.i.1-2). The contrast is pronounced: if the present in *The Winter's Tale* is the realm of an almost prelapsarian joy, time is the province of memory and anticipation, nostalgia and longing, regret and foreboding. It is, in short, the province of narrative, public and private, that cognitive and social domain where the images of events assume a fixed relationship with each other.

That presence and temporality rule this play, halved as it is by its dramatic caesura between III.iii and IV.ii, comes as no surprise, for Shakespeare's dramaturgical break forces characters and audience alike to come to terms with time's changes and consequences. But the sixteen-year gap signaled by Time's appearance is only one of many instances in which temporal change dramatically and ironically counterpoints the present. Down to the level of individual lines, like those fondly spoken by Polixenes, the play displays a temporal intricacy rivaled, perhaps, only by Shakespeare's other romances. As a number of critics have noted, Shakespearean drama is characterized, as a rule, by relatively little antecedent action[4]: unlike the drama of Kyd or Tourneur, its action falls largely within a present that moves forward to its culmination. But the past bears on the present of *The Winter's Tale* through a number of subtler inclusions: the childhood of the two kings; the courtship of Hermione; the Old Shepherd's wife; the man who "Dwelt by a churchyard," frozen in Mamillius' "sad tale" (II.i.25-32); numerous moments of story and remembrance. This layering of past on present and present on past becomes more pronounced as the very stage moment in which the characters move is set against the broader passage of years, and as these years in turn verge upon an ever-emerging present. As *The Winter's Tale* progresses, in other words, it acquires—like *Pericles, Cymbeline,* and *The Tempest*—a temporal double vision tonally reminiscent of the opening lines of a fourth-century Chinese poem: "Swiftly the years, beyond recall. / Solemn the stillness of this fair morning."[5]

For the play's characters, double vision of this kind eventually bridges the gap between memory and the present, between the frozen image of the past and the often robust vitality of the moment. For the play's audience, such multiple perspective constitutes the experiential matrix against which the play's action unfolds. Like the characters, though at an aesthetic remove, the audience is faced during performance with a dramatic world subject to the laws of temporal relationship, and with a stage present that is actual, changing, always somewhat outside the structures of time created to enclose it. *The Winter's Tale,* then, Shakespeare's most explicit treatment of time, counterpoints the twin experiences of temporality and presence, not only in its dramatic action, but also in its narrative and theatrical effects. As elsewhere in his plays, Shakespeare grounds thematic issues within theatrical experience, and makes performance fundamental to dramatic meaning through the audience's cognitive engagement. In relation to both characters and audience, *The Winter's Tale* displays a profound concern with perception and its consequences, and with the personal and social challenges posed by temporality in life and in the theater. In this chapter, we will trace Shakespeare's broader dramaturgical balancing in *The Winter's Tale* of time's outlines with a dramatic and theatrical present that can never be fully "staled." In so doing, we will see that this strange but powerful Shakespearean play, like *Everyman* and *Mankind,* forges clear experiential links between the dramatic action on stage and the stage's "action" on its audience.[6]

Brian Bedford as Leontes, Rod Beattie and Peter Hutt as Lords, James McGee as an Attendant, Gregory Wanless as a Lord, and Martha Henry as Paulina in the Stratford Festival's 1978 production of The Winter's Tale.

When Time exits from the middle of *The Winter's Tale,* he leaves a world disrupted by his passage. For the play's characters, time's impact is concentrated in "that wide gap" (IV.i.7) between the dramatic present and the events of the first three acts, a temporal fissure during which, as Time informs us, Leontes has continued to mourn "Th' effects of his fond jealousies" (1. 18) and Perdita and Florizel have grown up. This span, though, bears differently upon the various characters. Those who have lived through it, the members of the now older generation, have hardened themselves against time by maintaining a sharp remembrance of its losses, a remembrance that they are nonetheless powerless to erase. Camillo misses Sicilia and still feels bonds of loyalty to Leontes, whose "sorrows" remain so tangible that Camillo calls them "feeling" (IV.ii.7-8). Polixenes, too, lives in memory, burdened with a past that refuses to fade:

> Of that fatal country Sicilia, prithee speak no more,
> whose very naming punishes me with the
> remembrance of that penitent (as thou call'st him)

and reconcil'd king, my brother, whose loss of his most precious queen and children are even now to be afresh lamented. (ll. 20-25)

Focused through trauma's inward gaze, time only underscores the memory of what has been lost, and in its irrevocability the past seems more real than the present that has taken its place.

Polixenes, however, has more recent concerns to temper his bitterness: shifting from friend to father, he urges Camillo to accompany him on a mission to discover the cause of his son's disappearance from court. The scene likewise shifts, and before the two arrive at the Shepherd's cottage the stage is given to Perdita and Florizel, who demonstrate a markedly different relationship to time. Neither is burdened by the events at Sicilia, and both show an attitude toward their more immediate pasts less rigorous than that of their elders. Perdita says nothing of her early years as a shepherdess, and Florizel hides the signs of his past by donning rustic clothes. In response to Perdita's concern over his father's disapproval of their match, he modulates between the languages of present and future and affirms a love outside such threat:

> To this I am most constant,
> Though destiny say no. Be merry, gentle!
> Strangle such thoughts as these with any thing
> That you behold the while. Your guests are
>   coming:
> Lift up your countenance, as it were the day
> Of celebration of that nuptial, which
> We two have sworn shall come.
>
> (IV.iv.45-51)

Both are characterized by this forward-gazing anticipation, conceiving of the future as a never-ending continuation of the present, with "such a day tomorrow as to-day." In their innocence, free of time's psychic damages, they dwell on this present and on the sounds, objects, and gestures that constitute it. Florizel's description inscribes Perdita within the moment:

> Each your doing
> (So singular in each particular)
> Crowns what you are doing in the present
>   deeds,
> That all your acts are queens.
>
> (ll. 143-46)

Perdita, more the realist, nevertheless allows hope to "strangle such thoughts." "O Lady Fortune," she exclaims, "Stand you auspicious!" (ll. 51-52).

When Polixenes and Camillo enter disguised, then, and the sheep-shearing scene gets under way, the stage contains a mixture of attitudes toward time and its relationship to the present. On one hand, it offers the lovers, with their sense of the immediate and their vision of possibility; on the other, the king and counselor, aged by time and scarred by its memories, their awareness of consequence a potential threat to Perdita and Florizel. By this point in the play, though, the audience has had its own experience of dramatic time shifted and modulated, through the play's broader dramaturgical rhythms. Theatrical versions of immediacy and temporality are counterpointed throughout the play's development, often in sharp juxtaposition, as we can see if we review the audience's comprehension of dramatic time in the first three acts. There is, for instance, the play's beginning, in which the stage image of friendship between Polixenes and Leontes, the present's version of the past's innocence, is abruptly dispelled by the King's distorted jealousy. William H. Matchett points out sexual ambiguities in the lines between Polixenes and Hermione and claims that the audience is made to feel suspicious,[7] but these ambiguities are subliminal and largely recollected, if at all, in light of Leontes' misinterpretation of them. More pronounced is the audience's awareness of their "timeless" friend-

ship, of which Archidamus has said "I think there is not in the world either malice or matter to alter it" (I.i.33-34) and of which Polixenes has described the childhood origins. The initial stage interaction between the characters does little to dispel these accounts: gracefulness and compliment characterize the scene's beginning, and the "gestural dialogue between hands" that Charles Frey discerns throughout the play here expresses bond and affection.[8] When Leontes' *"tremor cordis"* does appear, it constitutes an intrusion of dissonance into the scene's easiness, and the stage present becomes abruptly shadowed by the threat of disturbance: "I am angling now, / Though you perceive me not how I give line" (I.ii.180-81). The words *angling* and *line* are revealing, for it is the essence of Leontes' jealousy to form imaginary connections between people and between incidents, quickly generating a web of misperception and suspicion that includes even Mamillius and Camillo. As Leontes begins to act on these misperceptions, consequences multiply with rigorous inevitability, and the stage present becomes increasingly pressured by a network of events, imaginary as well as real.

One of the most remarkable features of the developing Sicilia sequence (I.i through III.ii) is its narrative tightness and autonomy; omitting Perdita's survival, it could stand by itself, brief but complete. Its incidents are relentlessly forward-moving and continuous. For one thing, the narrative line of Leontes' jealousy and its effects is, to an extent unusual even in Shakespearean tragedy, unrelieved by breaks. Hermione's exchange with Mamillius constitutes only thirty-two lines, and the scene in which Cleomines and Dion describe their visit to Delphos is shorter still (twenty-two lines). Far from serving as self-contained interruptions, both are themselves interrupted, and devoured, by the omnivorous main action: the former by Leontes' entrance, the latter by a reminder of the proclamations against Hermione. For another thing, incidents and details are introduced and linked with a high degree of narrative continuity. Shakespeare changed the source material of *Pandosto* to increase the "probability" of the story's incidents,[9] and he did so, in part, by tightening its plot connections: whereas Greene's young prince Garinter dies suddenly, for instance, Shakespeare's Mamillius sickens and dies specifically out of grief concerning his mother's predicament. This tight sense of antecedents and consequences focuses audience attention even more closely on the unfolding narrative sequence, on dramatic time in its actual and potential outlines.

The sequence concludes with a pronounced note of closure, heightened by the rapidity with which its final events take place. The oracle's tersely declarative pronouncements reveal the truth concerning the preceding actions, a truth the audience and all the characters save Leontes have known. Entering with news of Hermione's death, Paulina condemns his folly by outlining the consequences of his misconceived actions on Polixenes, Camillo, his abandoned daughter, Mamillius, and Hermione: "O, think what they have done, / And then run mad indeed—stark mad!" (III.ii.182-83). Her speech (ll. 175-214) rings with summary force, and—together with Leontes' heartbroken resolve to bury his wife and son in a single grave, to display an account of "the causes of their death" (l. 237), and to visit it every day for the rest of his life—it gives the sequence of the Sicilian first half what J. H. P. Pafford has called "a Miltonic close fitting for the end of a tragedy."[10]

"The King shall live without an heir, if that which is lost be not found" (III.ii.134-36). A strand remains incomplete—an opening, as it were, in the closed sequence of action and its consequence that the audience has followed for over two acts. With Antigonus' entrance in III.iii, the narrative sequence continues. But the audience's temporal comprehension of *The Winter's Tale's* events and its orientation toward the stage and its actions shift in two important ways. First, attention no longer centers on the inevitable triumph of truth and the stripping away of a central character's delusion. Throughout the Sicilian sequence, the audience has indeed enjoyed an Olympian distance upon Leontes' jealousy, secure in its awareness of the actual state of events. The audience, in other words, stands in the position of superior awareness that Bertrand Evans considers one of the characteristic dramatic principles of Shakespearean drama;[11] and although its awareness is far from complete, the audience's understanding of temporal outlines is more closely aligned to that of Time than to that of the action's participants. Once the truth is revealed, though, subsequent actions become open-ended: although the oracle's pronouncement suggests further resolution, this final clause is cast as a riddle and contains no details about how the resolution might be achieved. Uncertainty, therefore, replaces inevitability; the outcome of events becomes less determinate, less subject to rigorously constrained consequence. Ironic awareness is replaced by uncertainty, and the audience, like Perdita, is left in the wilderness—a wilderness, in this case, of the stage and its unpredictability.

Second, the coherent narrative of the first part is replaced by a remarkable sequence of incidents, each of which is characterized by striking immediacy, and all of which stand in sharp juxtaposition to each other. Immediacy is achieved partly through a dazzling array of "theatrical" effects: effects of sound, movement, and spectacle that display the stage at its most physical. Such effects are strikingly absent from the Sicilian sequence of the play's first half: although the earlier sequence is characterized, as Daniel Seltzer points out, by numerous examples of "intimate stage business" between characters,[12] there is nothing to compare with the storm effects (suggested by the text), the famous bear, the sound of hunting horns, or the archaic staginess of Time's entrance. The immediacy of the sequence's

incidents is heightened by their almost Brechtian juxtaposition: the mixture of tones and effects gives each a kind of discontinuous autonomy on stage, and this sudden, unprepared-for variety, following the vastly more streamlined narrative of the first half, forces abrupt, disorienting shifts in audience response.

Matchett observes that this sequence wrenches us "from our response to the plot and the action to a wider perspective. . . . Challenging our awareness, it opens us to fresh experience."[13] He discusses this shift in terms of the art/nature opposition, but his observations apply still more valuably to the basic level of audience attention that this sequence engages. On this level, the sense of "fresh experience" is a result of elements that draw attention away from broader temporal outlines and heighten the autonomy of individual stage moments, much as the storm scenes do to the dramatic world of *King Lear*. Such "fresh experience" in Shakespearean (as in all) drama is that experience uniquely available in the theater: of a stage present existing in its own right, intruding itself into the very "tales" that dramatists make it tell. When Time stands forward to signal the leap of years, in other words, he addresses an audience that is already undergoing its own experiential leap, from prescience and irony to uncertainty and surprise, in the face of a stage turned strange and new.

As with the graceful present of the play's first scene, this scenic presence is diverted and distanced. The couplets of Time's soliloquy telescope the seacoast sequence into the past and return the audience to the play's main narrative line. But this line, with its rigid chain of consequence, has been weakened by the appearance of incidents and stage elements outside its projected outcomes, and the theatrical moment in all its presence and autonomy looms large in time's subsequent developments. Indeed, the stage is now set for the sheep-shearing scene, one of the longest scenes of heightened stage presence in all of Shakespeare. This scene is introduced three times—by Time, by Polixenes and Camillo, and by Autolycus—and each introduction contributes a nonnarrative "timelessness" to its action. The first two are usually viewed as connective scenes, linking past and present, and indeed (as we have seen) each does include references to the play's first half. Oddly, though, these references are less conjunctive than disjunctive: Time's reference to Leontes, after all, is offered to take "leave" of him (IV.i.17), and Polixenes finally urges Camillo to "lay aside / the thoughts of Sicilia" (IV.ii.51-52). Both scenes look ahead to Florizel and Perdita, and both do so, in part, by distancing the play's first half. As a result, the sheep-shearing scene bears few reminders of the Sicilian past, and even the Bohemian past is rendered less consequential to the festival present: Shakespeare omits the marriage plans that Greene's Egistus made for his son Dorastus and has Polixenes visit the Shepherd's cottage as much from curiosity as from suspicion.

The third introduction to the sheep-shearing scene also introduces one of its main participants. Despite the number of critical attempts to integrate Autolycus into the play's thematic structure,[14] this stage rogue continues to baffle the play's readers (while delighting its spectators). He is introduced later (IV.iii) than probably any other pivotal Shakespearean character, yet he plays no part in the play's concluding scene. He becomes almost a *genius* of the pastoral festivities, yet he was once a member of Florizel's retinue, a detail introduced so casually (between stanzas of a song) that it risks being missed. But if we put aside attempts to incorporate Autolycus into the play's thematic framework and concentrate, instead, on his stage presence, his dramatic function within the play (and within the sheep-shearing scene in particular) becomes clearer. In a play that counterpoints modes of time and presence, Autolycus represents life (and drama) at their most theatrically immediately.

Speaking to the Clown in a self-dramatizing third-person, Autolycus characterizes himself as a figure of Protean identity:

> I know this man well; he hath been since an ape-bearer, then a process-server, a bailiff, then he compass'd a motion of the Prodigal Son, and married a tinker's wife within a mile where my land and living lies; and, having flown over many knavish professions, he settled only in rogue. Some call him Autolycus. (IV.iii.94-100)

On stage, he displays a similar fluidity of roles, moving between them with an improvisational randomness that suggests his opportunism and delight in mischief. Like the mischief figures of morality drama, he plays upon the moment, and the impulsiveness of his actions makes them strikingly self-contained. His major contribution to the main plot (discovering the Old Shepherd's secret and deciding to act on it) originates largely out of whim: "Though I am not naturally honest, I am so sometimes by chance" (IV.iv.712-13). Moreover, like Nowadays, New-Guise, and Nought, his incessant acting and tumbling prose are charged with a vibrant self-assertiveness that draws attention away from more serious matters and toward himself. His wonder at the rustics' response to his ballads—"No hearing, no feeling, but my sir's song, and admiring the nothing of it" (IV.iv.612-13)—captures much of the distracting effect of his stage presence as a whole. Like the wares he hawks, Autolycus himself is largely an "unconsider'd trifle" (IV.iii.26), "inconsequential" in the strictest sense, a carefully placed dramaturgical tangent to his world's fixed sequence.

His appearance before and during the sheep-shearing scene, then, contributes to its self-contained immediacy: along with the Shepherd's dance that precedes him and the "Saltiers" who succeed him, his presence during the scene—with his "ribbons of all colors i' th' rainbow" (ll. 204-5), songs and ballads, and other antics—constitute some of the play's most frenetic stage activity. Even before Autolycus' entrance as ballad-monger, this scene has drawn characters and audience alike into an experience of atemporality. Among the characters, the past is suspended almost by consent: as we have seen, Polixenes and Camillo suspend memories of Sicilia, and Perdita and Florizel "strangle" thoughts of his superior rank. Time and its effects (as well as its threat) remain present during the scene, especially in the disguised visitors, but the emphasis is on the moment, and even age is brought within its domain. Matching Florizel's "timeless" admiration, Camillo tells Perdita: "I should leave grazing, were I of your flock, / And only live by gazing" (ll. 109-10). Polixenes, too, participates in the festival atmosphere to an extent not generally acknowledged in discussions of the scene; his famous debate with Perdita concerning the "streak'd gillyvors," for all its potential allusion to Perdita's station and its implications, is largely playful, a quality more evident in the theater than in the text, and one that tends to undercut threat. Moreover, when later in the scene the Clown remarks that "My father and the gentlemen are in sad talk" (l. 310), Polixenes is "refreshed" enough by the entertainment to request the Saltiers. It would be a mistake to claim that Polixenes "forgets" his mission, even temporarily, but it would also be a mistake to neglect the extent to which even he surrenders to his disguise and submits to the scene and its diversions. Both visitors could, with truth, join Perdita in her confession: "Methinks I play as I have seen them do / In Whitsun pastorals. Sure this robe of mine / Does change my disposition" (ll. 133-35).

The audience, too, is offered a "fresh experience" of the stage present, one that tends to subsume awareness of time and its consequences. Francis Berry claims that the audience, remembering the play's first half, "frames" the sheep-shearing scene and modifies its response to the lovers in light of their parents' experience.[15] But pictorial metaphors such as this are misleading, since the theater is a temporal as well as a spatial medium: earlier moments are rapidly distanced in performance, and memory often requires explicit reminders if it is to "frame" the stage present with what has already occurred. Such reminders are few, and the audience's awareness of threat is subordinated, in large part, to the scene's compelling immediacy, an immediacy heightened by the innocent love of Perdita and Florizel, by Autolycus' antics, and by a gracefulness of gesture finding its natural culmination in dance. The audience never completely abandons its apprehensive detachment from the lovers, but we must not underestimate how much the stage draws all who watch into its easiness.

With the exit of the dancing Saltiers, however, and Polixenes' interruption of the festivities, the audience is abruptly returned to an awareness of consequence and the claims that time exerts on the present. If Leontes' earlier attack of jealousy is painful because of the idyllic picture we have been given of his childhood friendship with Polixenes, the latter's remark to Camillo—"'Tis time to part them" (l. 344)—is even more chilling, because we have been given an extended stage version of such carefreeness. Like Prospero's truncation of *The Tempest*'s wedding masque, Polixenes' subsequent explosion completes the disillusionment for the audience and for Perdita and Florizel, returning the former to its awareness of consequence as it returns the latter to the realities of their disparate stations. Perdita tells Florizel:

> Beseech you
> Of your own state take care. This dream of
>   mine
> Being now awake, I'll queen it no inch
>   farther,
> But milk my ewes, and weep.
>
> (ll. 447-50)

Just as Time makes "stale" the "glistering" present, so Polixenes' rage makes the festival timelessness seem itself a dream.

When Camillo persuades the lovers to sail to Sicilia, the audience returns one last time to the play's broader narrative outline, resuming a more privileged distance concerning events. Freed from the tragic irony of the first part, the audience now enjoys the perspective of comic irony. With the secret of Perdita's birthright secure, the audience watches the characters, each of whom lacks at least one piece of information, move toward a reconciliation with romance inevitability. All converge on Sicilia: Florizel with Perdita, Polixenes with Camillo, Autolycus with the rustics and their secret. Audience attention centers on the logic of events, which unfolds with a neatness both providential and artistic; time, "that makes and unfolds errors," begins to right the situation, and the audience is allowed the omniscience to appreciate its workings. Anticipation runs high, looking forward to a reconciliation that will redeem the present from the apparent irrevocability of the past, awaiting the wonder on the part of the characters when the apparently miraculous is disclosed.

It is a measure of the dramaturgical complexity of *The Winter's Tale* that these expectations are at once fulfilled, unfulfilled, and more than fulfilled. On one hand, the Gentlemen who report the reunion between Leontes and Perdita underscore the miracle of the encounter, calling it "so like an old tale, that the verity of it is in strong suspicion" (V.ii.28-29). On the other hand, despite Nevill Coghill's attempt to defend the effectiveness of these messenger speeches,[16] if there is any clear *scène à faire* in the play, the disclosure of Perdita's identity is it—since, in fulfilling the oracle's prophecy, it gives Leontes an heir, Florizel a wife, and Perdita a royal family. The reunion effects a reconciliation between age and youth, past and present, Sicilia and Bohemia. Such a scene the audience expects to see; ironically, the messenger scene is disappointing precisely because *The Winter's Tale* is not a tale but a play, and a play's most powerful moments are its stage moments. The very quality of the reunion that "lames report to follow it, and undoes description to do it" (ll. 57-58) is that quality of immediacy the stage provides. We want the scene to be represented as dramatic present, not deflected into a narrative past.[17]

The usual justification for the messenger scene is that the reunion is described to lend focus to the final scene, but this explanation underestimates both the disappointment of the former and the theatrical coup of the latter. For the audience, there is no play beyond this reunion; at least this is what the earlier scenes have indicated. The oracle's only prophecy concerns the lost child, as does Time's anticipation of the play's second half:

> What of her ensues
> I list not prophesy; but let Time's news
> Be known when 'tis brought forth. A
>   shepherd's daughter
> And what to her adheres, which follows after,
> Is th' argument of Time.
>
> (IV.i.25-29)

In terms of the audience's expectations since the shipwreck, Perdita's return represents the projected end of the narrative movement, and the audience has anticipated it as final. To extend the play beyond this promised conclusion is to press stage action, once again, beyond the apparent confines of plot.

We have been studying *The Winter's Tale* in terms of two interrelating perceptions: that of time, evidenced through its effects of change and consequence, and that of the moment, experienced as something seemingly beyond these effects. We have explored, too, how the play represents a complex dramaturgical manipulation of temporality as it is experienced within performance: drawing attention away from narrative outlines into the stage present, distancing the present by the perceived intrusion of time and its effects. In the play's own vocabulary, occasioned by Perdita's gift of "rosemary and rue" to the disguised king and counsellor, we have been exploring the interacting rhythms of something like "grace and remembrance" (IV.iv.74-76) and the ways in which Shakespeare builds these rhythms into the play's dramaturgy and stagecraft. The statue scene, justly praised as one of the culminations of Shakespeare's art, represents the play's crowning interpenetration of these two realms of temporal experience.

As in *The Tempest,* the final reunion of this play is orchestrated by a master of ceremonies in command of the secrets behind external events. When Paulina reappears with Leontes at the beginning of the fifth act, however, she does so, not as a provider of second chances, but as a spokesperson for memory at its most fixed, keeping fresh the remembrance of an apparently irretrievable past and feeding its hold on the present with almost unpleasant insistence. Cleomines appeals to Leontes to "Do as the heavens have done, forget your evil, / With them, forgive yourself" (V.i.5-6), and Dion urges him to consider his heirless kingdom; but Paulina, who "hast the memory of Hermione . . . in honor" (ll. 50-51), pressures his conscience with the claims of the past:[18]

> Were I the ghost that walk'd, I'ld bid you
>   mark
> Her eye, and tell me for what dull part in't
> You chose her; then I'ld shriek, that even
>   your ears
> Should rift to hear me, and the words that
>   follow'd
> Should be "Remember mine."
>
>   (ll. 63-67)

To the servant's praise of Perdita's beauty, Paulina laments:

>   O Hermione,
> As every present time doth boast itself
> Above a better gone, so must thy grave
> Give way to what's seen now!
>
>   (ll. 95-98)

Her lines deny the possibility that loss can ever be replaced, or that the present can in any way heal the past. At the same time, unknown to Leontes and to the audience, these lines are half-truths, since the play's conclusion will dramatize a transcendence of memory and a better "present" that will fill time's grave. In their paradoxical truths and untruths, Paulina's lines anticipate the transformation of time that structures the statue scene itself: a transformation from the realm of memory, associated with lifelessness and sepulchral coldness, to the more vibrant present of "what's seen now."

This transformation, when it occurs, is seamless in its movement from one temporal vision to the other. Leontes' initial response to the statue's unveiling is an acute "remembrance," directed toward a past so cunningly recreated in stone that its image is resurrected, with equal vividness, in memory: "O, thus she stood, / Even with such life of majesty (warm life, / As now it coldly stands), when first I woo'd her!" (V.iii.34-36). The statue, in other words, confronts Leontes with the past and with his responsibility for its loss, while paradoxically bringing it so vividly into the present that this loss seems to vanish. As he continues to gaze, the harsh line between past and present blurs, shading the

memorial presence of the statue into the living presence of Hermione. In a word that reverberates throughout the scene, time's apparent irrevocability is "mocked" by a reappearance that seemingly occurs outside time's laws, and memory is both dissolved and brought to life in the face of the present's revelation. With this dramatic stroke, Shakespeare moves beyond Aristotle, whose third form of *anagnorisis* bears striking resemblance to the statue scene: "The third kind of recognition is through memory: we see one thing and recall another, as a character in the *Cyprians* of Dicaeogenes saw the picture and wept, or the recognition scene in the lay of Alcinous, where Odysseus listens to the bard and weeps at his memories, and this leads to the recognition" (*Poetics,* XVI).[19] As Aristotle's examples make clear, art serves a function much like memory, giving form to the flux of experience, and in Aristotle's moments of recognition it points to the life from which it has been abstracted. Recognition in *The Winter's Tale,* by contrast, moves beyond memory into the miraculous: it occurs when what is seen actually becomes what is recalled, through a transformation that merges past and present, image and life, narrative and a moment beyond its predictions.

Paulina commands the statue to "Strike all that look upon with marvel" (l. 100), and the final accomplishment of Shakespeare's stagecraft in *The Winter's Tale* lies in the audience's inclusion in the striking marvel of this scene. The stage reconciliation that the audience was denied in V.iii takes place, but the disclosure that makes it possible, Hermione's survival, comes as a revelation for the audience as well as for the characters. The earlier image of Hermione falling to the stage floor, Paulina's confirmation of her death, Leontes' plans to bury her, and Antigonus' ghost-like dream apparition (recalling "visitors from the dead" elsewhere in Shakespeare), all establish the Queen's death as a dramatic reality for the audience, breaking sharply with Shakespeare's usual practice (in plays such as *Twelfth Night* and *Pericles*) of making his audience confidants to all secrets and partners to all contrivance. Much more in the manner of Beaumont and Fletcher, Shakespeare withholds a narrative detail, the revelation of which transforms both the outcome of the play and the significance of what has preceded it. That the play hinges on such a deception is, by now, a commonplace in criticism of *The Winter's Tale*. But, like many Shakespearean commonplaces, its full implications for audience response remain imperfectly understood, even though dramaturgical decisions invariably adjust the audience's relationship with the developing stage action. Most obviously, the audience is forced into a collective experience that mirrors that of the stage characters, chiefly Leontes, whose discovery constitutes the scene's principle focus. Like Leontes, the audience is initially forced into its own moment of remembrance. It matters little at what point the audience realizes that Hermione is alive; when the statue shows signs of life, the audience scans its memories, recalling the play's earlier scenes, trying to find the connections that could justify a development so beyond expectation. Hermione explains to Perdita that she remained in hiding to await the fulfillment of the oracle's prophecy, but this detail, like all others in the closing scene, is subsumed in the moment itself, luminous in its freedom from anticipation. In place of the ironic superiority over characters usually enjoyed during such dramatic reconciliations, Shakespeare creates a theatrical experience for which, as we noted earlier, the critical lexicon lacks descriptive terminology, an experience that constitutes the opposite of irony, for in this instant, as the statue becomes that which it has commemorated, the present is vastly more than we thought: fuller and richer, freed from irony's frameworks.

By setting the statue scene outside the audience's comprehension of plot and time, and by making the stage action, literally, beyond the anticipation that has sought to contain it, Shakespeare allows the stage itself, one last time, to assume a heightened autonomy. As in the sheep-shearing scene, attention is directed toward individual objects, movements, and gestures, carefully orchestrated by dramatic speech highlighting the particular.[20] Polixenes' "The very life seems warm upon her lip" and Leontes' "The fixure of her eye has motion in't" (ll. 66-67) recall, in their specificity, Autolycus' ribbons, the "flow'rs of winter," and (most tellingly) Florizel's admiration of Perdita's movements:

> When you do dance, I wish you
> A wave o' th' sea, that you might ever do
> Nothing but that; move still, still so,
> And own no other function.
>   (IV.iv.140-43)

Ewbank writes of this scene: "Speeches are short, the diction plain, the language almost bare of imagery: as if Shakespeare is anxious not to distract attention from the significance of action and movement. . . . An unusual number of speeches are devoted just to underlining the emotions and postures of people on stage, as in Paulina's words to Leontes: 'I like your silence, it the more shows off / Your wonder' [ll. 21-22]."[21] This shift of emphasis away from language and toward gesture is heightened by the audience's own attention on the actress playing Hermione, as it watches for signs of breathing and movement, trying to detect the gesture that will reveal whether or not Hermione lives. The final discovery of *The Winter's Tale*, then, lies in a surrender to the moment; and for the audience, this involves a surrender to the stage moment, in which the most riveting activity is pure gesture outlined, almost pictorially, within the stillness of performance, and to which the most appropriate response is rapt attention and "wonder." With the accompanying music, movement and gesture acquire balletic expressiveness.

It is easy to see why the play's conclusion has tempted critics toward Christian interpretations of the play, especially in light of Paulina's reference to redemption from death and her pronouncement that "It is requir'd / You do awake your faith" (ll. 94-95), and in light of the word *grace,* which recurs throughout the play like a musical motif.[22] Though strictly Christian frameworks are hard to attach to the play as a whole, the final scene is indeed charged with an almost religious sense of grace as something freely given, beyond desert. Hermione's reappearance provides characters and audience with a development beyond the apparent consequence of events as the play has suggested them, with "the experience of restoration after total loss."[23] In this sense, the scene is beyond time, or at least beyond time as it has constituted a reality in the minds of characters and audience. If time participates in the play's denouement, it is less the stock figure of the play's middle than a force of mystery, always outside comprehension's hold, revealing itself in the miracles of the present. For the audience, grace is born in the "wink of an eye" (V.ii.110), when the stage action severs itself from rigorous connection with the "dramatic time" that has ruled for much of the play.

In the midst of its transformations, however, such grace is never completely free of remembrance. The first four acts have presented grace in terms of freshness, innocence, and gracefulness of gesture and bearing: Hermione has been called "a gracious innocent soul" (II.iii.29), and Perdita was described by Time as "now grown in grace / Equal with wond'ring" (IV.i.24-25). This grace, like the youth of Polixenes and Leontes, is timeless because it has not yet been subjected to the laws of change and consequence. The "grace" of the final scene, however, is richer because more dearly bought, and the passage of time from which it emerges leaves traces to spark remembrance. For one thing, the scene contains reminders of irreversible change. Hermione has grown old: "Hermione was not so much wrinkled, nothing / So aged as this seems" (ll. 28-29). And while Perdita has found a mother, she has also acquired a history, which, like Prospero's narration to Miranda in Act I of *The Tempest,* marks her emergence into a world that contains, among other things, time and its changes. Also apparent are reminders of consequences not redeemed by the present. Paulina recalls the dead Antigonus with moving regret, and Leontes' decree that she should marry Camillo does not fully dispel this awareness of "wither'd" loss (l. 133). Similarly, the scene lacks Mamillius, who actually was buried. Although he is never explicitly mentioned in the final scene, he has been mourned as recently as V.i, and his absence leaves the reunited family vaguely incomplete. While Florizel serves as a replacement for Mamillius, he also stands as a reminder of his loss.

The play's conclusion, in other words, resolves the plot with its image of a world ransomed from time, but it nevertheless remains marked by the memory of what time has destroyed. The paradox of temporal experience resolves itself into a duality of perception, a double vision in which time and actuality infuse and qualify each other, a balance of faculties appropriate to a world of coexistent loss and gain. The play has shown that time's effects are inescapable, since action, for all the world's miracles, does have consequences. One cannot escape the reality of change in a sublunary world ruled by mutability's "staling" hand. Festivity must end: Perdita and Florizel enter the cycle of the generations, and Autolycus, after his appearance in the penultimate scene, simply vanishes. Nonetheless, through Shakespeare's manipulation of the stage and its narrative possibilities, the audience feels the rigor of temporality open, again and again, into a stage presence always slightly beyond time's changes and consequences. Sicilia gives way to the wilderness of Bohemia; Polixenes, despite his age and station, succumbs in part both to the festival's liveliness and Perdita's charm. Most of all, in the play's final stroke, the audience discovers that, when it tries to predict time's outlines and outcomes, it risks amazement—that the present can mock not only consequence, but comprehension as well.

Notes

[1] Sonnet 73, ll. 1-2.

[2] Inga-Stina Ewbank, "The Triumph of Time in 'The Winter's Tale,'" *Review of English Literature,* vol. 5, no. 2 (April, 1964), p. 84.

[3] Sonnet 15, ll. 1-2.

[4] "It was Shakespeare's usual practice, histories apart, to bring the whole action of his plays within the frame of the picture, leaving little or nothing to narrative exposition" William Archer, *Play-Making: A Manual of Craftsmanship* [New York: Dodd, Mead, and Co., 1912] p. 98).

[5] T'ao Ch'ien (A.D. 365-427). Arthur Waley, trans., *A Hundred and Seventy Chinese Poems* (New York: Alfred A. Knopf, 1919; popular ed. 1923), p. 116; quoted (with slight inaccuracy) and discussed in William Empson, *Seven Types of Ambiguity* (London: Chatto and Windus, 1930), pp. 30-32. This thematic duality of the temporal and the atemporal no doubt drew upon the opposition present in the Elizabethan/Jacobean conception of temporality, in which time was viewed both as an unchanging realm of universal abstraction and as the more familiar realm of contingency and temporal change. Bernard Beckerman terms these two notions of time *iconic* and *historic,* and suggests that the development of Tudor drama saw a general movement from the former conception of time to the latter; see "Historic and Iconic Time in Late Tudor Drama," in

Shakespeare: Man of the Theater, ed. Kenneth Muir, Jay L. Halio, and D. J. Palmer (Newark: University of Delaware Press, 1983), pp. 47-54. While the thematic celebration of unchanging ideals may have been relatively muted by the reign of James, *The Winter's Tale* demonstrates that the theatrical manifestation of iconic time in the stage's immediacy was being explored with unabated dramatic interest.

[6] Investigating this connection brings us into the company of those critics who have approached this play's dramaturgy and stagecraft: Nevill Coghill, "Six Points of Stage-Craft in *The Winter's Tale,*" *Shakespeare Survey,* 11 (1958), pp. 31-41; William H. Matchett, "Some Dramatic Techniques in 'The Winter's Tale,'" *Shakespeare Survey,* 22 (1969), pp. 93-107; Barbara A. Mowat, *The Dramaturgy of Shakespeare's Romances* (1976); and Charles Frey, *Shakespeare's Vast Romance: A Study of The Winter's Tale* (Columbia: University of Missouri Press, 1980). *The Winter's Tale* has made itself available to some of the finest "theatrical" readings in Shakespearean criticism, perhaps because (as we have long sensed) its dramatic effects depend more than any other play on its realization in performance. The statue scene alone has been an important school for such readings.

[7] Matchett, "Some Dramatic Techniques," pp. 94-98. Shakespeare, after all, makes the relationship between Hermione and Polixenes much less "ambiguous" than Greene did in *Pandosto,* where Bellaria, "willing to shew how unfainedly she loved her husband, by his friends entertainment, used him likewise so familiarly, that her countenance bewrayed how her mind was affected towards him: oftentimes comming her selfe into his bedchamber, to see that nothing shuld be amisse to mislike him." James Winny, ed., *The Descent of Euphues: Three Elizabethan Romance Stories* (Cambridge: Cambridge University Press, 1957), p. 69. For ways in which this question has been addressed in productions of *The Winter's Tale,* see Dennis Bartholomeusz, *The Winter's Tale in Performance in England and America, 1611-1976* (Cambridge: Cambridge University Press, 1982), esp. pp. 229-32.

[8] Frey, *Shakespeare's Vast Romance,* pp. 134-38.

[9] See Stanley Wells, "Shakespeare and Romance," in *Later Shakespeare,* Stratford-upon-Avon Studies 8 (London: Edward Arnold, 1966), pp. 66-67, and J. H. P. Pafford, ed., *The Winter's Tale,* The Arden Shakespeare (London: Methuen, 1963), pp. lxiii-lxvii.

[10] Ibid., p. lv. Though Mowat disputes the claim of critics such as E. M. W. Tillyard that Acts I through III constitute the equivalent of Shakespearean tragedy (*The Dramaturgy of Shakespeare's Romances,* pp. 5-21), it is nonetheless striking how dramaturgically similar this concluding scene is to the tragedies and how many

devices it borrows from them: the stage configuration of assembled characters grouped around a locus of suffering, commemoration of the tragic events in the form of narrative, the ironic counterpointing of knowledge and loss.

[11] Evans, *Shakespeare's Comedies* (1960) and *Shakespeare's Tragic Practice* (Oxford: Oxford University Press, 1979).

[12] Daniel Seltzer, "The Staging of the Last Plays," in *Later Shakespeare,* pp. 137-38.

[13] Matchett, "Some Dramatic Techniques," p. 101.

[14] One of the most extensive thematic studies of Autolycus' role within the play is Lee Sheridan Cox, "The Role of Autolycus in *The Winter's Tale,*" *Studies in English Literature,* 9 (1969), pp. 283-301.

[15] Francis Berry, "Word and Picture in the Final Plays," in *Later Shakespeare,* pp. 93-94.

[16] Coghill, "Six Points of Stage-Craft," pp. 38-39. "In practice this scene is among the most gripping and memorable in the play" (p. 39).

[17] To a much lesser extent, the reunions between Leontes and Polixenes and between Leontes and Camillo are also "obligatory," and these too are merely reported. The Messenger speeches do contribute something important to the play's conclusion, in part through their narrative activity. The Messengers present the offstage events in the terms of story and fable—"like an old tale" (V.ii.28); "like an old tale still" (l. 61)—contributing to the almost formal narrativity of the play's final scenes. But the scene itself underscores the limits of such narrativity, for the burden of these reports is to suggest how fully the offstage reconciliations *exceed* the bounds of story—"Such a deal of wonder is broken out within this hour that ballad-makers cannot be able to express it" (ll. 23-25); "I never heard of such another encounter, which lames report to follow it, and undoes decription to do it" (ll. 56-58)—and to make the conventions of narrative feel inadequate to the "wonder" recounted and (unknown to the audience) soon to be staged. Marjorie Garber discusses the messenger scene in terms of the "inexpressibility topos"; see "'The Rest is Silence': Ineffability and the 'Unscene' in Shakespeare's Plays," in *Ineffability: Naming the Unnamable from Dante to Beckett,* ed. Peter S. Hawkins and Anne Howland Schotter (New York: AMS Press, 1984), pp. 47-48.

[18] In this role, she anticipates Ariel, who likewise scourges memory in his "ministers of Fate" speech to Alonso, Antonio, and Sebastian: "But remember / (For that's my business to you) that you three / From Milan did supplant good Prospero, / Expos'd unto the sea

(which hath requit it) / Him, and his innocent child" (*The Tempest,* III.iii.68-72).

[19] Aristotle, *On Poetry and Style,* trans. G. M. A. Grube (Indianapolis: Bobbs-Merrill, 1958), p. 33. For Grube's "Antinous," I have substituted the more familiar "Alcinous." See *Aristotle's Poetics,* p. 28.

[20] For a discussion of the ways in which Shakespeare uses specific notations in the text to control the theatrical realization of the statue scene, see Jörg Hasler, "Romance in the Theater: The Stagecraft of the 'Statue Scene' in *The Winter's Tale,*" in *Shakespeare: Man of the Theater,* pp. 203-11.

[21] Ewbank, "The Triumph of Time," p. 97. On the importance of gesture within Shakespearean drama, see David Bevington, *Action is Eloquence: Shakespeare's Language of Gesture* (Cambridge, Mass.: Harvard University Press, 1984), esp. pp. 67-98.

[22] See S. L. Bethell, *The Winter's Tale: A Study* (London: Staples Press, [1947]), and Roy Battenhouse, "Theme and Structure in 'The Winter's Tale,'" *Shakespeare Survey,* 33 (1980), pp. 123-38.

[23] Matchett, "Some Dramatic Techniques," p. 106.

FURTHER READING

Adams, Robert M. "*The Winter's Tale.*" In *Shakespeare: The Four Romances*, pp. 90-122. New York: W. W. Norton & Company, 1989.

> Compares *The Winter's Tale* with Robert Greene's *Pandosto*, the prose romance thought to be Shakespeare's source for the play.

Bristol, Michael D. "Social Time in *The Winter's Tale.*" In *Big-time Shakespeare*, pp. 147-74. London: Routledge, 1996.

> Claims that spatio-temporal discontinuities shape the social relationships in the play.

Burton, Julie. "Folktale, Romance and Shakespeare." In *Studies in Medieval English Romances: Some New Approaches*, edited by Derek Brewer, pp. 176-97. Cambridge: D. S. Brewer, 1988.

> Positions *The Winter's Tale* in the history of Middle English romances according to its manipulation of the pattern of traditional folktale types, most notably the separation of family members and their eventual reunion.

Cohen, Derek. "Patriarchy and Jealousy in *Othello* and *The Winter's Tale.*" *Modern Language Quarterly* 48, No. 3 (September 1987): 207-23.

Contends that, in both *Othello* and *The Winter's Tale*, "the examples of Othello and Leontes demonstrate that in a patriarchy the fidelity of wives is the major prop and condition of social order."

Girard, René. "The Crime and Conversion of Leontes in *The Winter's Tale*." *Religion and Literature* 22, Nos. 2-3 (Summer-Autumn 1990): 193-219.

Against a religious background, views Leontes' conversion as an overcoming of "mimetic desire."

Hardman, C. B. "Shakespeare's *Winter's Tale* and the Stuart Golden Age." *The Review of English Studies* XLV, No. 178 (May 1994): 221-29.

Contends that *The Winter's Tale* contains "a consistent series of allusions which function as a reinforcement of the tragicomic structure: the harmonious conclusion to potentially tragic events may be seen as analogous to the promised restoration of the [Jacobean] Golden Age."

Hunt, Maurice. "*The Winter's Tale*." In *Shakespeare's Romance of the Word*, pp. 74-108. Lewisburg: Bucknell University Press, 1990.

Claims that the play dramatizes the breakdown in the communicative power of language.

Overton, Bill. "Part Two: Appraisal." In *The Winter's Tale*, pp. 55-85. Basingstoke: Macmillan, 1989.

Places the play in its historical context in an effort to appreciate the meaning of several frequently misunderstood scenes, including the theatricality of Leontes' jealousy and the dramatic function of Autolycus.

Sanders, Wilbur. "The Hypothesis of Hope (Act 5)." In *The Winter's Tale*, by William Shakespeare, pp. 101-114. Brighton, Sussex: The Harvester Press, 1987.

Argues that a tragic background looms over the comic elements of *The Winter's Tale*.

Sokol, B. J. "The Statue's Tale: Metaphoric Art." In *Art and Illusion in* The Winter's Tale, pp. 55-84. Manchester: Manchester University Press, 1994.

Examines Hermione's statue against Shakespeare's possible source materials in an effort to illuminate his psychological topography.

Spriet, Pierre. "*The Winter's Tale* or the Staging of an Absence." In *The Show Within: Dramatic and Other Insets. English Renaissance Drama (1550-1642)*, edited by François Laroque, pp. 253-66. Montpellier: Publications de Université Paul-Valéry, 1992.

Deconstructs the claims of many modern interpreters of *The Winter's Tale* in an effort to expose their ideological assumptions and contrast them with those of Shakespeare's contemporaries.

Tylus, Jane. "'Put yourself under his shroud, / The universal landlord': Shakespeare and Resistance to Authorship." In *Writing and Vulnerability in the Late Renaissance*, pp. 144-73. Stanford: Stanford University Press, 1993.

Explores *The Winter's Tale* in order to reconstruct Shakespeare's attitude toward James' monarchy; Tylus interprets the play to be "a carefully crafted challenge to the cultural poetics of the Jacobean court."

Ward, David. "Affection, Intention, and Dreams in *The Winter's Tale*." *The Modern Language Review* 82, Part 3 (July 1987): 545-54.

Examines a puzzling passage in act one, scene two of *The Winter's Tale*, interpreting it as a reflection of multiple levels of consciousness and self-deception.

Watterson, William Collins. "Shakespeare's Confidence Man." *The Sewanee Review* CI, No. 4 (Fall 1993): 536-48.

Discusses the character of Autolycus, concluding that "Autolycus's unrepentant egotism [is] an avatar of Shakespeare's creative self."

Guide to *Shakespearean Criticism* Series

VOLUMES 1-10	Provides an historical overview of the critical response to each Shakespearean work. Includes criticism from the seventeenth century to the present.
VOLUMES 11, 12, 14, 15, 17, 18, 20, 21, 23, 24, 26	Examines the performance history of Shakespeare's plays on the stage and screen through eyewitness reviews and retrospective evaluations of individual productions. Also provides comparisons of major interpretations and discusses staging issues.
VOLUMES 27, 29-31, 33-36, 38-41, 43-45	Focuses on criticism published after 1960. Each volume is ordered around a theme, such as politics, religion, or sexuality, with a topic entry that introduces the volume and several entries devoted to individual works.
Yearbooks: **VOLUMES 13, 16, 19, 22, 25, 28, 32, 37, 42**	Compiled annually beginning in 1989. Includes the most noteworthy essays of the year published on Shakespeare as recommended by an international advisory board of distinguished Shakespearean scholars.

Cumulative Character Index

The Cumulative Character Index identifies the principal characters of discussion in the criticism of each play and non-dramatic poem. The characters are arranged alphabetically. Page references indicate the beginning page number of each essay containing substantial commentary on that character.

Character Index

Character Index

Cumulative Critic Index

Critic Index

Critic Index

Critic Index

Hatton, Joseph
The Merchant of Venice **12**: 31

Hawkes, Terence
Love's Labour's Lost **2**: 359
Richard II **6**: 374

Hawkins, C. Halford
Julius Caesar **17**: 289

Hawkins, F. W.
King John **24**: 179
Macbeth **20**: 92
Richard II **24**: 267
Romeo and Juliet **11**: 397

Hawkins, Harriet
Antony and Cleopatra **25**: 257
Othello **25**: 257
Romeo and Juliet **25**: 257

Hawkins, Sherman H.
Henry IV, 1 and 2 **39**: 100

Hawkins, William
Cymbeline **4**: 19

Hayes, Richard
Much Ado about Nothing **18**: 166

Hayles, Nancy K.
Appearance vs. Reality (topic entry) **34**: 5
As You Like It **5**: 146
Cymbeline **4**: 162

Hayman, Ronald
Hamlet **21**: 183
Julius Caesar **17**: 357
King Lear **11**: 67
A Midsummer Night's Dream **12**: 254
Othello **11**: 295
Romeo and Juliet **11**: 474

Hays, Janice
Much Ado about Nothing **8**: 111

Hazlitt, William
All's Well That Ends Well **7**: 9
Antony and Cleopatra **6**: 25
As You Like It **5**: 24
The Comedy of Errors **1**: 14
Coriolanus **9**: 15; **17**: 129
Cymbeline **4**: 22
Hamlet **1**: 96; **21**: 30, 41
Henry IV, 1 and 2 **1**: 312
Henry V **5**: 193
Henry VI, 1, 2, and 3 **3**: 25
Henry VIII **2**: 23
Julius Caesar **17**: 273
King John **9**: 219; **24**: 174
King Lear **2**: 108; **11**: 12, 16
Love's Labour's Lost **2**: 303
Macbeth **3**: 185; **20**: 58, 59, 86
Measure for Measure **2**: 396
The Merchant of Venice **4**: 195; **12**: 9, 10, 11
The Merry Wives of Windsor **5**: 337
A Midsummer Night's Dream **3**: 364; **12**: 152
Much Ado about Nothing **8**: 13

Othello **4**: 402; **11**: 191, 195, 196, 197, 198
Pericles **2**: 544
The Rape of Lucrece **10**: 65
Richard II **6**: 258; **24**: 267
Richard III **8**: 161, **14**: 376, 377, 380
Romeo and Juliet **5**: 421; **11**: 393, 395
Sonnets **10**: 160
The Taming of the Shrew **9**: 320
The Tempest **8**: 297
Timon of Athens **1**: 460
Titus Andronicus **4**: 617
Troilus and Cressida **3**: 540
Twelfth Night **1**: 544
The Two Gentlemen of Verona **6**: 439
Venus and Adonis **10**: 415
The Winter's Tale **7**: 384

Heath, Benjamin
The Tempest **8**: 292
Titus Andronicus **4**: 614

Hecht, Anthony
Sonnets **37**: 346

Hecht, Anthony B.
The Tempest **25**: 357

Heffernan, Carol F.
The Taming of the Shrew **31**: 345

Heilbrun, Carolyn G.
Hamlet **44**: 237

Heilman, Robert
Politics and Power (topic entry) **30**: 22

Heilman, Robert Bechtold
Antony and Cleopatra **6**: 175
Henry IV, 1 and 2 **1**: 380
King Lear **2**: 191
Macbeth **3**: 312, 314; **29**: 139; **44**: 306
Othello **4**: 508, 530
Richard III **8**: 239
The Taming of the Shrew **9**: 386

Heine, Heinrich
The Merchant of Venice **4**: 200
Richard III **8**: 164
Troilus and Cressida **3**: 542

Heinemann, Margot
King Lear **22**: 227

Helgerson, Richard
Henry VI, 1, 2, and 3 **22**: 156

Helms, Lorraine
Gender Identity (topic entry) **40**: 27
Shakespeare's Representation of Women (topic entry) **31**: 68
Troilus and Cressida **43**: 357

Hemingway, Samuel B.
Henry IV, 1 and 2 **1**: 401; **14**: 159
A Midsummer Night's Dream **3**: 396

Henneman, John Bell
Henry VI, 1, 2, and 3 **3**: 46

Henze, Richard
The Comedy of Errors **1**: 57
Julius Caesar **30**: 321
The Taming of the Shrew **9**: 398
Twelfth Night **34**: 287

Heraud, J. A.
Antony and Cleopatra **6**: 37
Othello **4**: 421
Sonnets **10**: 191

Herbert, T. Walter
A Midsummer Night's Dream **3**: 447

Herford, C. H.
Antony and Cleopatra **6**: 76
The Phoenix and Turtle **10**: 16

Herring, Robert
Cymbeline **15**: 46
Henry VIII **24**: 105

Hethmon, Robert H.
Measure for Measure **23**: 407

Hewes, Henry
Antony and Cleopatra **17**: 43
Hamlet **21**: 232, 239, 288
King John **24**: 210
King Lear **11**: 72, 89, 103
The Merchant of Venice **12**: 54, 62, 71, 79
A Midsummer Night's Dream **12**: 240
Much Ado about Nothing **18**: 173
Othello **11**: 314
The Taming of the Shrew **12**: 365
Timon of Athens **20**: 456
Troilus and Cressida **18**: 337
Twelfth Night **26**: 247

Hewison, Robert
Coriolanus **17**: 208
A Midsummer Night's Dream **12**: 274
Twelfth Night **26**: 316

Heyse, Paul
Antony and Cleopatra **6**: 38

Hibbard, George R.
Antony and Cleopatra **27**: 105
Love's Labour's Lost **23**: 233
Othello **4**: 569
The Taming of the Shrew **9**: 375

Hic et Ubique
See also Steevens, George; Collier, Jeremy; Longinus, and Lorenzo
Hamlet **1**: 87
Twelfth Night **1**: 542

Hieatt, A. Kent
Cymbeline **13**: 401

Hieatt, Charles W.
The Winter's Tale **36**: 374

Higgins, John
Antony and Cleopatra **17**: 65

Coriolanus **17**: 190
The Merry Wives of Windsor **18**: 42
The Taming of the Shrew **12**: 386
The Two Gentlemen of Verona **12**: 490

Hignett, Sean
Richard III **14**: 473

Hill, Aaron
Hamlet **1**: 76; **21**: 377

Hill, Errol G.
The Tempest **15**: 322

Hill, R. F.
Richard II **6**: 347
Romeo and Juliet **5**: 492

Hill, Sir John
Antony and Cleopatra **6**: 21
Romeo and Juliet **11**: 494

Hill, William
Henry V **14**: 174

Hillebrand, Harold Newcomb
Richard II **24**: 272

Hillman, David
Troilus and Cressida **42**: 66

Hillman, Richard
Hamlet **44**: 219
Henry IV, 1 and 2 **19**: 170
Henry V **19**: 170
Measure for Measure **22**: 302
Richard II **19**: 170
The Tempest **8**: 464; **22**: 302
The Two Noble Kinsmen **19**: 394; **41**: 301
The Winter's Tale **22**: 302

Hinely, Jan Lawson
The Merry Wives of Windsor **5**: 397
A Midsummer Night's Dream **45**: 107

Hinman, Chariton
Timon of Athens **1**: 518

Hirsch, Foster
Richard III **14**: 447

Hirsh, James
Othello **19**: 276

Hirst, David L.
The Tempest **15**: 327

Hirvela, David P.
King John **24**: 241

Hobday, C. H.
Henry V **30**: 159
The Two Noble Kinsmen **41**: 317

Hobson, Harold
Antony and Cleopatra **17**: 33
Henry IV, 1 and 2 **14**: 54, 84
Henry V **14**: 281

Critic Index

Critic Index

Critic Index

Critic Index

Cumulative Topic Index

The Cumulative Topic Index identifies the principal topics of discussion in the criticism of each play and non-dramatic poem. The topics are arranged alphabetically. Page references indicate the beginning page number of each essay containing substantial commentary on that topic. A parenthetical reference after a topic indicates that the topic is extensively discussed in that volume.

433

Topic Index

Topic Index

Topic Index

Cumulative Topic Index, by Play

The Cumulative Topic Index, by Play identifies the principal topics of discussion in the criticism of each play and non-dramatic poem. The topics are arranged alphabetically by play. Page references indicate the beginning page number of each essay containing substantial commentary on that topic. A parenthetical reference after a play indicates which volumes discuss the play extensively.

Topic Index, by Play

religious, mythic, or spiritual content **2:** 559, 561, 565, 570, 580, 584, 588; **22;** 315; **25:** 365

riddle motif **22:** 315; **36:** 205, 214

Shakespeare's other romances, relation to **2:** 547, 549, 551, 559, 564, 570, 571, 584, 585; **15:** 139; **16:** 391, 399; **36:** 226, 257

spectacle **42:** 359

sources **2:** 538, 568, 572, 575; **25:** 365; **36:** 198, 205

staging issues **16:** 399

suffering **2:** 546, 573, 578, 579; **25:** 365; **36:** 279

textual revisions **15:** 129, 130, 132, 134, 135, 136, 138, 152, 155, 167, 181; **16:** 399; **25:** 365

The Phoenix and Turtle (Volumes 10, 38)

allegorical elements **10:** 7, 8, 9, 16, 17, 48; **38:** 334, 378

art and nature **10:** 7, 42

authenticity **10:** 7, 8, 16

autobiographical elements **10:** 14, 18, 42, 48

bird imagery **10:** 21, 27; **38:** 329, 350, 367

Christian elements **10:** 21, 24, 31; **38:** 326

complex or enigmatic nature **10:** 7, 14, 35, 42; **38:** 326, 357

consciously philosophical **10:** 7, 21, 24, 31, 48; **38:** 342, 378

constancy and faithfulness **10:** 18, 20, 21, 48; **38:** 329

Court of Love **10:** 9, 24, 50

Donne, John, compared with **10:** 20, 31, 35, 37, 40

satiric elements **10:** 8, 16, 17, 27, 35, 40, 45, 48

love **10:** 31, 37, 40, 50; **38:** 342, 345, 367

as metaphysical poem **10:** 7, 8, 9, 20, 31, 35, 37, 40, 45, 50

Neoplatonism **10:** 7, 9, 21, 24, 40, 45, 50; **38:** 345, 350, 367

as "pure" poetry **10:** 14, 31, 35; **38:** 329

Scholasticism **10:** 21, 24, 31

Shakespeare's dramas, compared with **10:** 9, 14, 17, 18, 20, 27, 37, 40, 42, 48; **38:** 342

sources **10:** 7, 9, 18, 24, 45; **38:** 326, 334, 350, 367

structure **10:** 27, 31, 37, 45, 50; **38:** 342, 345, 357

style **10:** 8, 20, 24, 27, 31, 35, 45, 50; **38:** 334, 345, 357

The Rape of Lucrece (Volumes 10, 33, 43)

allegorical elements **10:** 89, 93

Brutus **10:** 96, 106, 109, 116, 121, 125, 128, 135

Christian elements **10:** 77, 80, 89, 96, 98, 109

Collatine **10:** 98, 131; **43:** 102

Elizabethan culture, relation to **33:** 195; **43:** 77

irony or paradox **10:** 93, 98, 128

language and imagery **10:** 64, 65, 66, 71, 78, 80, 89, 93, 116, 109, 125, 131; **22:** 289, 294; **25:** 305; **32:** 321; **33:** 144, 155, 179, 200; **43:** 102, 113, 141

Lucrece

chastity **33:** 131, 138; **43:** 92

as example of Renaissance *virtù* **22:** 289; **43:** 148

heroic **10:** 84, 93, 109, 121, 128

patriarchal woman, model of **10:** 109, 131; **33:** 169, 200

self-responsibility **10:** 89, 96, 98, 106, 125; **33:** 195; **43:** 85, 92, 158

unrealistic **10:** 64, 65, 66, 121

verbose **10:** 64, 81, 116; **25:** 305; **33:** 169

as victim **22:** 294; **25:** 305; **32:** 321; **33:** 131, 195; **43:** 102, 158

male/female relationships **10:** 109, 121, 131; **22:** 289; **25:** 305; **43:** 113, 141

narrative strategies **22:** 294

Roman history, relation to **10:** 84, 89, 93, 96, 98, 109, 116, 125, 135; **22:** 289; **25:** 305; **33:** 155, 190

Shakespeare's dramas, compared with **10:** 63, 64, 65, 66, 68, 71, 73, 74, 78, 80, 81, 84, 98, 116, 121, 125; **43:** 92

sources **10:** 63, 64, 65, 66, 68, 74, 77, 78, 89, 98, 109, 121, 125; **25:** 305; **33:** 155, 190; **43:** 77, 92, 148,

structure **10:** 84, 89, 93, 98, 135; **22:** 294; **25:** 305; **43:** 102, 141

style **10:** 64, 65, 66, 68, 69, 70, 71, 73, 74, 77, 78, 81, 84, 98, 116, 131, 135; **43:** 113, 158

Tarquin **10:** 80, 93, 98, 116, 125; **22:** 294; **25:** 305; **32:** 321; **33:** 190; **43:** 102

tragic elements **10:** 78, 80, 81, 84, 98, 109; **43:** 85, 148

the Troy passage **10:** 74, 89, 98, 116, 121, 128; **22:** 289; **32:** 321; **33:** 144, 179; **43:** 77, 85

Venus and Adonis, compared with **10:** 63, 66, 68, 69, 70, 73, 81; **22:** 294; **43:** 148

violence **43:** 148, 158

Richard II (Volumes 6, 24, 39)

abdication scene (Act IV, scene i) **6:** 270, 307, 317, 327, 354, 359, 381, 393, 409; **13:** 172; **19:** 151; **24:** 274, 414

acting and dissimulation **6:** 264, 267, 307, 310, 315, 368, 393, 409; **24:** 339, 345, 346, 349, 352, 356

allegorical elements **6:** 264, 283, 323, 385

audience perception **24:** 414, 423; **39:** 295

Bolingbroke

comic elements **28:** 134

guilt **24:** 423; **39:** 279

language and imagery **6:** 310, 315, 331, 347, 374, 381, 397; **32:** 189

as Machiavellian figure **6:** 305, 307, 315, 331, 347, 388, 393, 397; **24:** 428

as politician **6:** 255, 263, 264, 272, 277, 294, 364, 368, 391; **24:** 330, 333, 405, 414, 423, 428; **39:** 256

Richard, compared with **6:** 307, 315, 347, 374, 391, 393, 409; **24:** 346, 349, 351, 352, 356, 395, 419, 423, 428

his silence **24:** 423

structure, compared with **39:** 235

usurpation of crown, nature of **6:** 255, 272, 289, 307, 310, 347, 354, 359, 381, 385, 393; **13:** 172; **24:** 322, 356, 383, 419; **28:** 178

Bolingbroke and Richard as opposites **24:** 423

Bolingbroke-Mowbray dispute **22:** 137

carnival elements **19:** 151; **39:** 273

censorship **24:** 260, 261, 262, 263, 386; **42:** 120

ceremonies, rites, and rituals, importance of **6:**

270, 294, 315, 368, 381, 397, 409, 414; **24:** 274, 356, 411, 414, 419

comic elements **24:** 262, 263, 395; **39:** 243

contractual and economic relations **13:** 213

costumes **24:** 274, 278, 291, 304, 325, 356, 364, 423

deposition scene (Act III, scene iii) **24:** 298, 395, 423; **42:** 120

Elizabethan attitudes, influence of **6:** 287, 292, 294, 305, 321, 327, 364, 402, 414; **13:** 494; **24:** 325; **28:** 188; **39:** 273; **42:** 120

Essex Rebellion, relation to **6:** 249, 250; **24:** 356

family honor, structure, and inheritance **6:** 338, 368, 388, 397, 414; **39:** 263, 279

fate **6:** 289, 294, 304, 352, 354, 385

garden scene (Act III, scene iv) **6:** 264, 283, 323, 385; **24:** 307, 356, 414

Gaunt **6:** 255, 287, 374, 388, 402, 414; **24:** 274, 322, 325, 414, 423; **39:** 263, 279

gender issues **25:** 89; **39:** 295

historical sources, compared with **6:** 252, 279, 343; **28:** 134; **39:** 235

irony **6:** 270, 307, 364, 368, 391; **24:** 383; **28:** 188

King of Misrule **19:** 151; **39:** 273

kingship **6:** 263, 264, 272, 277, 289, 294, 327, 354, 364, 381, 388, 391, 402, 409, 414; **19:** 151, 209; **24:** 260, 289, 291, 322, 325, 333, 339, 345, 346, 349, 351, 352, 356, 395, 408, 419, 428; **28:** 134; **39:** 235, 243, 256, 273, 279, 289; **42:** 175

language and imagery **6:** 252, 282, 283, 294, 298, 315, 323, 331, 347, 368, 374, 381, 385, 397, 409; **13:** 213, 494; **24:** 269, 270, 298, 301, 304, 315, 325, 329, 333, 339, 356, 364, 395, 405, 408, 411, 414, 419; **28:** 134, 188; **39:** 243, 273, 289, 295; **42:** 175

Marlowe's works, compared with **19:** 233; **24:** 307, 336; **42:** 175

medievalism and chivalry, presentation of **6:** 258, 277, 294, 327, 338, 388, 397, 414; **24:** 274, 278, 279, 280, 283; **39:** 256

mercantilism and feudalism **13:** 213

mirror scene (Act IV, scene i) **6:** 317, 327, 374, 381, 393, 409; **24:** 267, 356, 408, 414, 419, 423; **28:** 134, 178; **39:** 295

negative assessments **6:** 250, 252, 253, 255, 282, 307, 317, 343, 359

Northumberland **24:** 423

Richard

artistic temperament **6:** 264, 267, 270, 272, 277, 292, 294, 298, 315, 331, 334, 347, 368, 374, 393, 409; **24:** 298, 301, 304, 315, 322, 390, 405, 408, 411, 414, 419; **39:** 289

Bolingbroke, compared with **24:** 346, 349, 351, 352, 356, 419; **39:** 256

characterization **6:** 250, 252, 253, 254, 255, 258, 262, 263, 267, 270, 272, 282, 283, 304, 343, 347, 364, 368; **24:** 262, 263, 267, 269, 270, 271, 272, 273, 274, 278, 280, 315, 322, 325, 330, 333, 390, 395, 402, 405, 423; **28:** 134; **39:** 279, 289

dangerous aspects **24:** 405

delusion **6:** 267, 298, 334, 368, 409; **24:** 329, 336, 405

homosexuality **24:** 405

kingship **6:** 253, 254, 263, 272, 327, 331,

Topic Index, by Play

Topic Index, by Play

Topic Index, by Play

ISBN 0-7876-2421-7

90000

9 780787 624217